ROTHMANS RUGBY UNI YEARBOOK 1997-98

**Editors: Mick Cleary
and John Griffiths**

ROTHMANS

HEADLINE

Copyright © 1997 Rothmans Publications Ltd

The right of Mick Cleary and John Griffiths to be identified as the authors of the Work has been asserted by them in accordance with the Copyright, Designs and Patents Act 1988.

First published in 1997
by HEADLINE BOOK PUBLISHING

Cover photographs.
Front: Jeremy Guscott (Bath and England) kicks ahead during the second Lions Test against South Africa at Durban on 28 June 1997.
Back: Jason Leonard (Harlequins and England) in action against France at Twickenham on 1 March 1997.

All photographs by Colorsport unless otherwise credited.

10 9 8 7 6 5 4 3 2 1

All rights reserved. No part of this publication may be reproduced, stored in a retrieval system, or transmitted, in any form or by any means without the prior written permission of the publisher, nor be otherwise circulated in any form of binding or cover other than that in which it is published and without a similar condition being imposed on the subsequent purchaser.

ISBN 0 7472 7732 X

Copy-editing by Andrew Kinsman, First Rank Publishing, Brighton

Typeset by Letterpart Limited, Reigate, Surrey

Printed and bound in Great Britain by
Mackays of Chatham plc, Chatham, Kent

HEADLINE BOOK PUBLISHING
A division of Hodder Headline PLC
338 Euston Road
London NW1 3BH

CONTENTS

ABBREVIATIONS USED IN THIS YEARBOOK

International Teams

A – Australia; Arg – Argentina; AW – Anglo-Welsh; B – British Forces and Home Unions teams; Bb – Barbarians; BI – British Isles teams; C – Canada; Cv – New Zealand Cavaliers; Cz – Czechoslovakia; E – England; F – France; Fj – Fiji; I – Ireland; It – Italy; Iv – Ivory Coast; J – Japan; K – New Zealand Services; M – Maoris; NAm – North America; Nm – Namibia; NZ – New Zealand; NZA – New Zealand Army; P – President's XV; Po – Poland; Pt – Portugal; R – Romania; Ru – Russia; S – Scotland; SA – South Africa; SAm – South America; SK – South Korea; Sp – Spain; Tg – Tonga; US – United States; W – Wales; Wld – World Invitation XV; WS – Western Samoa; Z – Zimbabwe.

Other abbreviations used in the international listings

(R) – Replacement; (t) – temporary replacement; [ ] – Rugby World Cup appearances.

NB: When a series has taken place, figures are used to denote the particular matches in which players have featured. Thus NZ 1,3, would indicate that a player has appeared in the First and Third Tests of the relevant series against New Zealand.

Irish Clubs

CIYMS – Church of Ireland Young Men's Society; KCH – King's College Hospital; NIFC – North of Ireland Football Club.

French Clubs

ASF – Association Sportive Française; BEC – Bordeaux Etudiants Club; CASG – Club Athlétique des Sports Generaux; PUC – Paris Université Club; RCF – Racing Club de France; SB – Stade Bordelais; SBUC – Stade Bordelais Université; SCUF – Sporting Club Universitaire de France; SF – Stade Français; SOE – Stade Olympien des Etudiants; TOEC – Toulouse Olympique Employés Club.

South African Provinces

Bor – Border; Bol – Boland; EP – Eastern Province; GW – Griqualand West; N – Natal; NT – Northern Transvaal; OFS – Orange Free State; R – Rhodesia; SET – South-East Transvaal; SWA – South-West Africa; SWD – South-West Districts; Tvl – Transvaal; WP – Western Province; WT – Western Transvaal; Z–R – Zimbabwe–Rhodesia.

Australian States

ACT – Australian Capital Territory; NSW – New South Wales; Q – Queensland; V – Victoria; WA – Western Australia.

EDITORIAL PREFACE

In British and Irish Rugby Union circles 1997 will go down as the Year of the Lion, and the exploits of the team managed by Fran Cotton, coached by Ian McGeechan and captained by Martin Johnson are duly given extensive coverage in this the 26th edition of the Yearbook. Although the class of '97 narrowly failed to make a clean sweep of the Test series with the South Africans, the Lions, we felt, thoroughly deserved a clean sweep of the annual Rothmans Awards. The tourists take the Team of the Year award, Scott Gibbs, for his aggressive defence in the Tests, is the Player of the Year, and the senior management team are the recipients of the Personality of the Year award.

Elsewhere on the international front Rugby Union made great advances. The inaugural Tri-Nations series was a big success in the southern hemisphere and full details of that competition are now presented alongside the long established Five Nations Championship review.

The proliferation of international matches has been at the expense of the international tour. In the new era it seems that Test sides are more likely to jet in for three or four Tests spread over three weeks rather than undertake the ten or twelve match tour, including club and provincial matches, that had been the staple of international rugby since the 1960's.

We have therefore thought carefully about our tour coverage and, for the moment, have decided to trim details to the bare minimum. In trying to squeeze the proverbial quart into a pint pot, we have restricted details to teams and results only. We have removed the extensive tour section so that instead readers will now find Wales's visit to Australia, for example, in the Welsh section of the Yearbook. Likewise, Australia's European tour last autumn is included in the Australian section, and so on.

The statistics sections have also been overhauled. Our comprehensive records for all of the major international nations are now expanded to include the leading five entries in each category. Moreover, full career records of all players capped between 1 May 1996 and **30 April 1997**, the usual deadline on our statistics, are presented. For the first time, too, we have included a section on the game in Italy which we hope to expand as the *azzurri* stake their claim for inclusion in an expanded version of the Five Nations Championship.

The 1996-97 season was the first of the professional era for European club rugby and the Yearbook has been redesigned to give in depth coverage of the progress made by the major clubs in the Home Unions. There are fuller club reviews to illuminate the

John Bentley celebrates the Lions' victory over South Africa in the second Test.

essential statistics of the League seasons, while the European Cup feature is expanded to include the English clubs' first venture into the competition.

It is with considerable regret that we note our final change. For the past 15 years, this Yearbook has benefited from the expert guidance of Caroline North as its house editor. Owing to other commitments, Caroline has had to pass on the baton to Andrew Kinsman who with calm efficiency has overseen the publication of this edition.

At the same time as extending our warm thanks to Caroline, thanks are also due to our increasing web of correspondents and statisticians who keep us informed of events worldwide. Like the Lions, their approach has been highly professional and they have achieved high standards.

Mick Cleary
John Griffiths

ROTHMANS AWARDS 1996-97

Player of the Year: Scott Gibbs (Swansea, Wales and the British Lions)

When Scott Gibbs left Swansea to join St Helens Rugby League club in a £150,000 deal in 1994 it was assumed that he would never be seen in a union shirt again. Then the game changed and attitudes changed. Even those who had voiced their anger at the manner of his initial departure welcomed Gibbs back in the summer of 1996 in a £250,000 deal part-subsidised by the Welsh Rugby Union.

He was a massive influence on the Welsh resurgence in the early part of the Five Nations Championship; his partnership with Allan Bateman in the Welsh midfield helping to rip great holes in the Scottish defence at Murrayfield. Gibbs's selection for the Lions was a formality. Not only was he in great shape, but his presence also gave Ian McGeechan the opportunity to reassemble the Lions centre pairing of 1993. On that tour Gibbs had nudged England captain Will Carling out of the Test reckoning to team up with Jeremy Guscott. The same was to happen on the 1997 Lions tour, Gibbs and Guscott winning the Test places in a very competitive field.

Gibbs's strong, full-frontal charges were the perfect foil to the angled, floating runs of Guscott outside or the shimmying breaks of Gregor Townsend inside. South African defences were never at ease with Gibbs around. They knew what to expect but they simply couldn't handle it. Gibbs had bulked up during his time in League and now tops the scales at 15st 10lbs. He makes every last ounce count. Gibbs put a large dent in South African manhood when he flattened the supposedly impregnable Os du Randt, the Springbok loosehead, in the course of one of his typical barrel-chested surges upfield. Gibbs was indestructible save for one scare in an early tour game against Border when he was stretchered from the field with a serious-looking ankle injury. Gibbs recovered only to then have to serve a one-match ban for a punch thrown against Northern Transvaal. He still made it to the Test team, testimony not just to his obvious physical assets but also to the subtlety of his passing and his all-round reading of the game.

Gibbs made his debut for Wales against England in 1991, aged 19. He joined Swansea from Neath that same year and changed codes in 1994, joining St Helens. During his time at St Helens he helped them to the Super League title in 1996 and to the final of the Challenge Cup the same year, before re-joining Swansea for £250,000. He has won 27 caps for Wales and five for the British Lions.

Scott Gibbs tries to evade a tackle from No 8 and Springbok captain Gary Teichmann.

Team of the Year: The British Lions

No one gave them much of a chance. The bookmakers had them out at almost double figures for the series, damning odds for a two-horse race. The Springboks had swept all before them on their autumn tour, finishing off in style in Cardiff by hammering Wales. The British and Irish players had also all been involved in the most arduous season of their careers. All were fatigued and many were still carrying niggles or deeper-rooted injuries. Factor into the equation also the fact the Springboks had only ever twice lost a series, at home – to Willie John McBride's 1974 Lions and to the All Blacks of 1996 – and you can appreciate the enormity of the task.

But if few had faith in them then the Lions at least had faith in themselves. This was one of the most united, harmonious and dedicated parties ever to leave these shores. There was not one sign of a crack in the facade throughout the entire two months. On any tour that is some achievement. On a Lions tour, where egos and national rivalries are prone to erupt at any moment, it is a considerable feat. This collective purpose shone through at telling moments, notably in the last 10-15 minutes of nearly every game on tour. The Lions invariably finished the stronger side, not because their fitness levels were necessarily higher, but because they were committed to each other and to the Lions badge itself. They ran and supported to the very last second because they dared not let their mates down.

The Lions defence was also a gripping illustration of character at work. All the planning in the world will come to nothing if the players do not haul themselves off the floor that half-second quicker so as to be in place to make the next tackle. Time and again on the tour the Lions were in position, at no time more significantly than in the second and decisive Test. The Springboks had all the play on that theatrical Durban evening; but the Lions had the spirit and resolve to match and eventually overhaul them.

The manner of the Lions victories in the provincial matches also firmly put British and Irish rugby back on the map. They played with a verve, style and intelligence not seen in domestic circles for a very long time. There were impressive wins over Free State, Natal and Mpumalanga when the play flowed and tries were scored all over the field. The Lions scored 56 tries in their 13 matches with John Bentley and Tony Underwood top try-scorers with seven apiece.

The forwards also came through strongly. After early problems in the scrum the Lions pack finished in credit in the Tests. Props Tom Smith of Scotland and Ireland's Paul Wallace were surprise choices but ones which were fully vindicated. So too Ireland's Jeremy Davidson at lock. The goal-kicking of Neil Jenkins, playing in the unfamiliar position of full-back, was invaluable. Jenkins scored 110 points in all on tour, one fewer than Newcastle's Tim Stimpson who had an excellent campaign too.

But to highlight individuals is to undermine the greatest strength of these Lions – their simple, honest pride in being together and playing for one another on an historic adventure.

The British Lions 1997. L-R, back row: Allan Bateman, Mark Regan, Rob Howley, Neil Jenkins, Barrie Williams, Paul Grayson, Nick Beal, Tim Stimpson, John Bentley, Tom Smith, Gregor Townsend, Paul Wallace, Neil Back, Austin Healey, Andy Keast (Technical Coaching Assistant); L-R, middle row: Stan Bagshaw (Baggage Master), Alan Tait, Keith Wood, Eric Miller, Scott Quinnell, Will Greenwood, Jeremy Davidson, Simon Shaw, Doddie Weir, Tim Rodber, Lawrence Dallaglio, Richard Hill, Graham Rowntree, Matt Dawson, Dave McLean (Fitness Advisor), Bob Burrows (Media Liaison Officer), Richard Węgrzyk (Masseur); L-R, front row: Samantha Peters (Administrative Assistant), Dr James Robson (Medical Officer) Jason Leonard, David Young, Ieuan Evans, Mark Davies (Physiotherapist), Fran Cotton (Team Manager), Martin Johnson, Ian McGeechan (Head Coach), Jim Telfer (Assistant Coach), Jeremy Guscott, Rob Wainwright, Tony Underwood, Scott Gibbs, David Alred (Kicking Coach).

Personality of the Year: The British Lions management – Fran Cotton, Ian McGeechan and Jim Telfer

The planning began a year before they left home to take on the supposedly invincible Springboks. First came the appointment of Fran Cotton as manager. Cotton had been there before and done it as a player on the 1974 British Lions tour. He had travelled again six years later only to return early through illness. His experience and sense of resolution in any arena, be it business or sport, were to be key qualities. Cotton wasted no time in bringing on board two of the most respected coaches in the game, Ian McGeechan and Jim Telfer.

This was to be McGeechan's third tour as Lions coach. He was also supremely successful as a player, winning eight Lions caps as a centre in 1974 and 1977. In 1989 he had coached the Lions to victory in Australia and only narrowly missed out on beating New Zealand with the Lions in 1993. He had worked alongside Jim Telfer with Scotland, the pair taking their country to a Grand Slam against the odds in 1990. The alliance was to prove every bit as effective in a Lions context.

The Lions was to be the first fully professional tour. The term 'professional' means far more than merely accepting money for services rendered. These Lions proved to be model professionals in every sense. McGeechan spent two weeks in South Africa in the summer of 1996 watching the All Blacks win there for the first time ever. On the basis of that McGeechan worked out the playing philosophy for the Lions. The 1997 Lions style would be to play expansively and dynamically, with variety but with power too. The entire selection was based on this premise, hence the inclusion of a strong Rugby League contingent and the emphasis on mobility among the forwards. McGeechan also advocated a 35-man squad, thus allowing the specialist positions of hooker and scrum-half a rest from bench duties.

The management were also adamant that there was to be no divide in the camp. Everyone was put on the same pay scale, £10,000 basic and £7,500 if the Test series was won. The ethos extended to everything the Lions did. There was no split between midweek and Saturday teams if only because competition for places was so fierce, a sure sign that the original selection was right. The front-line management had great support themselves from their own back-up staff – Andy Keast as technical advisor, Dave Alred, kicking coach, Dave McLean, fitness advisor, James Robson, doctor, Mark Davies, physio, Richard Wegrzyk, masseur, Stan Bagshaw, baggage master, Bob Burrows, media liaison officer and Sam Peters, administrative assistant.

The British Lions victory in the series was a triumph of management in every sense.

11

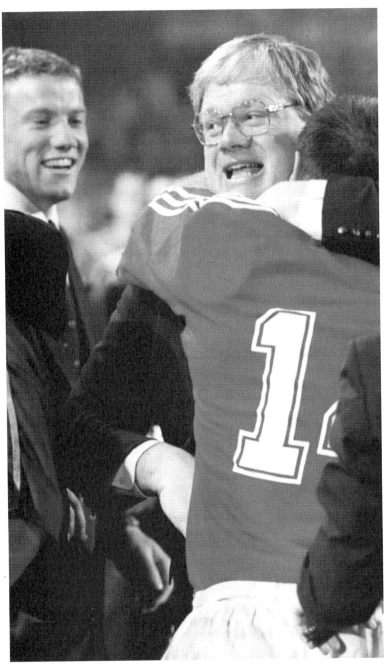

British Lions manager Fran Cotton celebrates the second Test triumph with Alan Tait.

TURBULENT RIDE ON RUGBY'S MONIED ROLLER-COASTER

REVIEW OF THE 1996-97 SEASON
Mick Cleary

There were two different approaches to this season, the first fully tooled-up, no-holds-barred run at professionalism. There were those who sank to their knees clutching their head and beating their breasts at the woes to come. And there were those who rushed out to greet the new dawn with whoops of delight at the promise, excitement and joy on offer. That's right – the game was at a crossroads, the pessimists converging from one way clinging to their half-empty bottles, the optimists coming from the other direction proudly displaying their half-full containers.

It was the latter who were proved right. Of course there were teething problems; several clubs felt the cold draught of financial reality whistling through their corridors as they struggled to drag revenue and expenditure together. Yes, there were many bust-ups along the way. The suspicion must now be that Frank Warren only became involved in rugby, through Bedford, so that he could eventually get his hands on the rights to the longest running scrap in the fight game, the Hallett-Brittle battle, with occasional tag interventions from Fran Cotton. It was all tiresome in the extreme. And yes, there were, too, a few corpses slumped along the wayside by the season's end, casualties of the relentless drive for success and, with it, cash for the coffers. John Hall of Bath and Dick Best of Harlequins were the big name stiffs in rugby's morgue, Tony Russ (Leicester), Paul Turner (Sale), Barrie Corless (Moseley), Murray Kidd (Ireland), Andre Markgraaff (South Africa), Peter Williams (Orrell) and Mark Ring (West Hartlepool) were others who, for differing reasons, moved out of their managerial or coaching seats.

But to hell with the bad news. There was so much to admire in the first 12 months of open rugby that it would be churlish to dwell solely on the negative aspects, not that that has prevented some Jeremiahs from predicting chaos and destruction still for the fledgling professional game. Money galvanised everyone and everything. The players were fitter and faster; the game quicker and more skilful as a result. In a nutshell that is why 1996-97 should be declared a resounding success. The standard of club rugby was three times better than it has ever been. So too on the brilliantly successful Lions tour.

The obligation to entertain a crowd who have paid to see professionals perform was cited as the motivation for the more fluid and more fluent rugby player, but the whole issue is far more complex than instructing players to go out and chuck a ball about as often as possibly they can, so as to satisfy public demand. If that really were the demand of the public then they might as well go and watch performing seals of Billy Smart and his troop. Rugby satisfies different needs in different types. It is too simplistic to state that there is guaranteed pleasure to be had from pass after pass, try after try. If there is no defence, no thumping tackles, no fiery resistance in the pack, no grasping, mauling mayhem to stem the tide, then there is no satisfaction to be had at all. One of the best club games of the season was Leicester's 18-12 victory over Wasps towards the end of the season. There were no tries scored on the night, but the spectacle was gripping, full of tension, drama, skill, character, ingenuity and creativity. Of course if the evening had been topped off with a few tries then fine. The key thing was that there didn't *have* to be tries for it to be immensely enjoyable.

Over the course of the season a host of club matches in all the home countries delighted the spectators, entertaining them because all the elements of Rugby Union were on show. The beauty of the sport lies in its variety and complexity; reduce these elements and you reduce the sport. We need fearsome forward confrontation and tactical guessing games between the playmakers. Yes, we rose to salute the Super-12 games where the ball was fizzing about the field; but the players weren't doing this just because they wanted to offer a few cheap, easy thrills. They were doing it because it was the most effective way of winning rugby matches. Entertainment, or the game being easier on the eye, was a by-product of this. The whole concept of Super-12 is based on encouraging positive play. The TV executives had a say in nudging the administrators to this end, and while, so far, the arrangement has been successful, rugby has to be aware that it is walking along a dangerous path hand-in-hand with whom – a maiden or a monster? How long before television suggests that those boring scrums should be done away with; or those time-consuming line-outs trimmed and anaesthetised still further?

The line-out laws need careful monitoring, as this phase of play is in danger of being emasculated. With lifting now legitimised it is nigh on impossible to win the opposition ball. As long as you've got a couple of forklift trucks either side of your (so-called) jumper to hoist him aloft and fix him somewhere in the clouds above until the ball reaches him, then your possession is guaranteed. Of course this is exactly what the lawmakers intended as it deters sides from kicking the ball off the park in the first place; so the rationale has merit but the process is unsatisfying.

At the moment the balance has slipped just the other side of acceptability. Jumping, catching and timing skills ought to be important, so too the attributes of the genuine athletic line-out jumper. Instead it matters not a damn that your man may be taller, more agile or better co-ordinated. The other lot will invariably win the ball if it is their throw. I had expected the second-row unions to be up in arms about all this, working on a collective industrial protest. But no. A couple of beers with that great All Black, Ian Jones, when he was passing through London cleared that one up. Jones loves it simply because of the continuity it generates.

A guarded eye would not go amiss however. The Super-12, with its bonus point system (an extra point for more than four tries scored and another for finishing within seven points of the winner), four points for an outright win and two for a draw produced some outrageous scorelines. How long before the system makes its way north? It seems a better, more equitable system than the one used in Wales. With a new sponsor on board for the English League, now might be the time for a change. After ten years Courage have withdrawn to be replaced by Allied Dunbar, who have invested £7.5 million, all of which will go to the top 24 clubs. From this season the top tier of clubs will be playing in the Allied Dunbar Premiership.

Courage were good sponsors in their time. Much as their heads must have dropped time and again in the closing months as yet another RFU spat became public, Courage kept out of it. Pilkington, too, have shown great ethical largesse towards the union. They too kept diplomatically shtoom even though their showpiece Cup final was railroaded two years in succession. At the time of going to press it's unclear just what the ramifications of yet another volatile AGM might be. There had been several calls from the Brittle wing, most vociferously expressed by Lions manager, Fran Cotton, for RFU secretary and chief executive-elect Tony Hallett to resign. This faction claim that Hallett knowingly misled the members over important matters of the union's deal with BSkyB, a contract which comes into effect from this season.

The charges principally concern the influence of Sky on the competitions themselves, the issue of pay-per-view and whether Hallett kept the membership properly informed at the preceding year's AGM. It is said that Hallett knew of the decision to expel England from the Five Nations on the very day of the 1996 AGM. It seems to me a complete and utter irrelevance as to whether he knew formally or not. The prospect of expulsion was absolutely real and had been trailed for many weeks. If the Celts had decided to expel England then it was *their* responsibility to announce it formally through the usual public channels. That is the designated procedure in all things and the only guaranteed way to ensure that the RFU membership knew. For all Hallett knew, any informal message to that effect – which he denies having received anyway – might well have been yet more brinkmanship on the part of the Celts.

The release of a letter from BSkyB's solicitors in May 1997 provided a definitive rebuttal to the claim that the RFU would have no veto over pay-per-view. The letter states quite clearly that they do have such a caveat, although the formal contract has yet to be absolutely finalised on other points. Again it does not seem to me to matter whether the veto clause was in the Heads of Agreement or not. It is now there and there the matter should end.

In the course of the year all these issues were raised at full RFU committee meetings (which comprise 63 democratically elected members), RFU executive meetings and another specially convened SGM in March. If that is not democracy at work then I do not know what is. There is right and wrong on both sides in all this. What the Brittle faction do not seem to appreciate is the untold damage they are doing to the reputation of the game at large by pursuing their agenda to the bitter end. If their case had never been heard then fair enough. But it has and they should back off.

As we went to press last year there was to be no Five Nations championship. News that a compromise had been reached to save the tournament came in dramatic fashion. RFU treasurer Colin Herridge interrupted the launch of the 1996-97 *Rothmans Rugby Union Yearbook* clutching a piece of paper with the official confirmation. The deal probably cost the RFU in the region of £20 million, monies which would now be put into the collective pot over five years. It was also agreed that there would never again be unilateral negotiations on the part of England to broker their own TV deal. The RFU's five-year £87.5 million deal with BSkyB stands. It took the Celtic countries several more months before they came up with their own deals for broadcast rights to rugby in their territories. The BBC signed a £40 million deal to broadcast international rugby in Wales, Scotland and Ireland. There are also other arrangements signed in each of the countries with Wales, for example, agreeing a four-year deal with HTV Wales and S4C for League and Cup rugby. The rights to the European Cup went to BSkyB. Overall the division of spoils among the broadcasters is more complex than it has ever been, all of which meant that the BBC's *Rugby Special* came to an end after 31 years on the airwaves. It would be a great pity if that were to happen. The sport needs all the marketing it can get. Even Sky accept that it is in everyone's interests if there is a mixed package of satellite and terrestrial television.

BSkyB would seem to have the draw cards in the deals made. Certainly the European Cup was the club highlight of last season. It was a mystery why ITV pulled out of their £5 million a year contract, which had two years to run. They claimed they were unhappy with the scheduling, being promised things which were not delivered; and the administrators did seem in a muddle on many matters. Originally there was to be no quarter-final stage. It was then brought in, almost surreptitiously. As this season approaches there is still argument over representation, with England and France demanding a bigger share of places. The French and English teams did hold the whip hand, particularly in the Conference where France supplied seven of the quarter-finalists, England the other through Northampton. In the Cup itself there were titanic battles everywhere. Leicester won a fiery game at Pau, Munster demolished Wasps on a rain-lashed day, only for Wasps to run riot against the reigning champions, Toulouse, a week later. Pontypridd saw off Bath at home and Cardiff worked their way through their group and in a marvellous quarter-final defeated Bath 22-19. But all the way through everyone feared going to Brive. They may have been unheralded coming in, but tales soon spread like wildfire of their partisan support, of great passionate nights down in the middle of France. Brive were on the march. Leicester, on a frozen January afternoon, performed heroics to get their semi-final played and then rewarded their supporters and helpers by hammering Toulouse. Brive did a similar demolition job on Cardiff. The final took place at the national stadium in Cardiff and everyone expected Leicester to set the pace. We couldn't have been more wrong. Brive were out of this world. Viars, Lamaison, Carrat, Kacala – these are just a few of the names which will live with us after witnessing Brive's triumph.

The Five Nations was engaging, even if many of the scorelines were disturbingly lop-sided. England rattled up record scores against the Celts and seemed set for a Grand Slam. They comfortably led France after an hour's play at Twickenham but fell apart to let France through 23-20. France's Grand Slam, their fifth ever and their first in ten years, was confirmed against Scotland a fortnight later. England had had a mixed build-up, beating Italy but losing to the New Zealand Barbarians and struggling to beat Argentina, 20-18. However there was enough promise in their brief flurries against Ireland, Scotland and Wales to suggest that they are finally bedding down. Even Jack Rowell seemed to be getting the hang of tactical substitutions – one of the season's innovations – by the end of the campaign. Thank goodness, or we would have seen little at all of Jeremy Guscott, scandalously omitted from the starting line-up. The reason lay in the captaincy. After much speculation and delay Phil de Glanville was appointed captain to succeed Will Carling. Politics had once again interfered, the long-running RFU-EPRUC dispute persuading Jack Rowell to hold back from nominating his new man. The players themselves had boycotted an early England session as a gesture of solidarity to their clubs. Only prop Robin Hardwick from Coventry turned up. It was not until January that the RFU and the clubs announced agreement, with the formation of the England Rugby Partnership. England made decent

Jonathan Davies in action in his last Test match, against England at Cardiff Arms Park.

strides through the season, so too France who had looked forlorn after their series defeat against South Africa in the autumn. The Springboks beat all-comers, so too Australia who defeated Italy, Wales, Scotland and Ireland on their travels, becoming the first Australian side to return from Britain with an unblemished record.

There is great concern that the Celts are being left behind and rumours abounded that England might quit on their own terms and play a world series against the southern hemisphere and France. It would be folly to do so at this stage. The sport in these parts needs the Five Nations. It provides pleasure and it provides profile. But, and it's a sorrowful but, what if the results were to continue in this vein for the next three years? Would spectators get the same enjoyment from seeing their team concede 40 points and more to England year in, year out? It is in everyone's interest to stimulate and nurture the game throughout Britain and Ireland, and to this end there are strenuous efforts being made to keep players in their respective home leagues. The Irish union announced a sliding scale of payments ranging from £70,000 downwards, while the SRU have contracted over 60 players to make up their districts sides which will once again represent them in Europe. The WRU, amid much acrimony, has cut its First Division from 12 to eight clubs to try and improve competition standards.

Wales welcomed back their prodigal sons – Allan Bateman, Scott Gibbs, David Young and, after a salary wrangle, Scott Quinnell. These players had a sizeable impact on what was a reasonable season for the Welsh, three of them combining vividly at Murray-field to produce a stunning try. Arwel Thomas was re-born; Colin Charvis was a great find; Jonathan Davies too had his emotional return to the fold; but the outstanding player was once again Robert Howley who scored a memorable try against England. Wales bid farewell to the Arms Park to make way for the £114 million millennium stadium, and will play its major home internationals at Wembley this season. Pontypridd were much-acclaimed winners of the League, Cardiff of the Cup.

Ireland had an Irish sort of season – great despair quickly turning to huge momentary elation before a quiet, stoical gloom descended again. Murray Kidd was sacked as coach after home defeats to Italy and Western Samoa and was replaced by Brian Ashton, the respected former Bath coach. Ashton galvanised his men immediately, with a heartening show against France and victory again in Cardiff, only for the roof to fall in against England. In the end 35 players were used for Ireland's seven matches. Back to square one. Shannon ruled the roost on the club front, winning their third successive title, while Munster took the Inter-Provincial title.

Scottish rugby had a difficult year. There was heated debate about the best way forward – club or district. The SRU opted for district rugby. It will be a testing time. Their three representatives in the European Cup won only one out of 12 matches. On the international front life was, as ever, a struggle, not without merit on occasions but far from straightforward. It must be worrying too that Murrayfield was not filled for the visit of the Australians. Italy were beaten – just – but Wales, France and England all had the upper hand. Gregor Townsend was disappointing simply because too many expectations were heaped upon him, while Kenny Logan continued the talent drain south when he signed for Wasps in mid-season. Melrose were the undisputed championship club, carrying all before them: League, Cup and their own coveted sevens title.

The champion club in England was Wasps, whose whole-hearted virtues did them proud. Lawrence Dallaglio was an inspirational captain, Rob Smith, Roger Uttley and Nigel Melville a shrewd, thoughtful and supportive management team. It looked as if the title might elude them when they lost that crucial League game at Leicester. However an injury time conversion by Gareth Rees, one of the players of the season, earned them a point against Bath a few days later and, more importantly, kept body and soul together. Leicester then fell apart and Wasps romped away to only their second ever title. In the end Leicester made it into Europe only by the skin of their teeth, drawing at Sale on the last Saturday after being 20-3 down. The Cup final between the same two teams a week later was a huge disappointment, Leicester winning 9-3. Richmond won the Second Division title with Newcastle just tucked in behind.

Va'aiga Tuigamala became the first £1 million player when he signed a five-year deal with Newcastle. The foreign legion increased with the arrival of South Africans, Francois Pienaar and Joel Stransky, and Frenchmen, Thierry Lacroix, Laurent Cabannes and Laurent Benezech. The shrewdest overseas signings were almost unnoticed but were probably the most significant. John Mitchell and Simon Mannix arrived from New Zealand and added steel to Sale's natural exuberance.

Lest we forget how trivial all this is, Ian Tucker, a talented centre threequarter from Sydney, died after sustaining injuries when playing for Oxford University against Saracens. Other great friends were lost during the season, notably Wilf Wooller and the immortal Clem Thomas. Days across the Severn Bridge just won't be the same without them. The rugby world was shocked, too, when the young Kiwi sensation, Jonah Lomu, revealed in January that he was suffering from a serious kidney infection and might never play again. We wish him well.

Those two old sluggers of the front-row, Brian Moore and Graham Dawe departed from the rugby scene. Will Carling also announced that he was retiring from international rugby.

The canvas changes daily. These are exciting times.

LIONS SET NEW STANDARDS

THE BRITISH LIONS TOUR TO SOUTH AFRICA 1997

They arrived unfavoured and unknown; but by the end of the tour they had demonstrated to a sceptical public both at home and abroad that British rugby was not all flat, dull, predictable and one-dimensional. They became only the third side to win a series in South Africa following in the wake of the 1974 Lions and the All Blacks of 1996. The 1997 Lions took the provinces by storm, playing from the very first minute of the first game against Eastern Province with style, verve and precision. There were some troughs along the way, notably against Northern Transvaal, the only provincial defeat on tour, but these were no more than minor dips when compared to the glorious highs of victories over the likes of Gauteng, Natal and, in particular, the Free State.

The spirit of the party was first-rate. The management team of Fran Cotton, Ian McGeechan and Jim Telfer did a superb job in fostering a harmonious squad, one committed to each other and to the cause itself. There was little discernible difference between the midweek and Saturday sides; an ideal situation when trying to keep the whole group together and focused. Indeed the Test team had never played together before they took the field at Newlands for the first Test.

There were several surprises in that first selection, notably in the pack where props Tom Smith of Scotland and Paul Wallace of Ireland came through superbly. Jeremy Davidson of Ireland also found favour with the selectors ahead of England's Simon Shaw. Eric Miller, also of Ireland, was desperately unlucky to miss a starting Test line-up, having to withdraw with 'flu after being selected for the First Test. Behind the scrum Allan Bateman was unfortunate to miss out on a centre spot. McGeechan publicly stated that he would have been very happy to have come into the Test with any one of about five other candidates.

Six players had to return home injured – Doddie Weir, Paul Grayson, Scott Quinnell, Robert Howley, Ieuan Evans and Will Greenwood. Their replacements were Nigel Redman, Mike Catt, Tony Diprose, Kyran Bracken and, briefly, Tony Stanger who came off the Scotland tour to South Africa to play against Northern Free State. By the time of the final Test there were six other Lions players unavailable for selection through injury, making this one of the most attritional tours ever.

The cruciate ligament injury to Doddie Weir came in the Mpumalanga game when his leg was brutally stamped on by their lock, Marius Bosman. The Lions called for Bosman to be banned.

The local union only fined him R10,000 (£1,250) instead. Bosman ought to have been suspended for at least a year, so savage and cowardly was the act.

The Rugby League returnees came through well – Scott Gibbs, Allan Bateman, Alan Tait and John Bentley all winning Test places. Neil Back was another who came back from the wilderness to stake his claim for further international honours. His support play and tackling were a feature of every game in which he played. In a completely different vein, the goal-kicking of Neil Jenkins, so assured, so composed, was a vital ingredient in the Lions success; at no time more tellingly than in the second Test. Jenkins kicked 15 points; the South Africans missed 15 points of kicks. The decision to bring a specialist kicking coach, Dave Alred, paid off with Newcastle full-back, Tim Stimpson, also having a field day in the midweek team.

The 1997 Lions will go down in history as one of the most committed, disciplined and close-knit parties of all time. They were great ambassadors for British and Irish rugby on and off the field.

THE TOURING PARTY

Manager FE Cotton   **Coach** IR McGeechan   **Assistant Coach** JW Telfer
Technical Coaching Assistant A Keast   **Captain** MO Johnson

FULL-BACKS

N R Jenkins (Pontypridd & Wales)
T R G Stimpson (Newcastle & England)

THREEQUARTERS

T Underwood (Newcastle & England)
N D Beal (Northampton & England)
J Bentley (Newcastle & England)
I C Evans (Llanelli & Wales)
AG Bateman (Richmond & Wales)
IS Gibbs (Swansea & Wales)
J C Guscott (Bath & England)
A V Tait (Newcastle & Scotland)
W J H Greenwood (Leicester)
*AG Stanger (Hawick & Scotland)

HALF-BACKS:

P J Grayson (Northampton & England)
G P J Townsend (Northampton & Scotland)
M J S Dawson (Northampton & England)
A S Healey (Leicester & England)
R Howley (Cardiff & Wales)
*M J Catt (Bath & England)
*K P P Bracken (Saracens & England)

FORWARDS

J Leonard (Harlequins & England)
D Young (Cardiff & Wales)
G C Rowntree (Leicester & England)
T J Smith (Watsonians & Scotland)
P S Wallace (Saracens & Ireland)
M P Regan (Bristol & England)
K G M Wood (Harlequins & Ireland)
B Williams (Richmond)
S D Shaw (Bristol & England)
M O Johnson (Leicester & England)
J W Davidson (London Irish & Ireland)
G W Weir (Newcastle & Scotland)
R A Hill (Saracens & England)
R I Wainwright (Watsonians & Scotland)
L B N Dallaglio (Wasps & England)
E R P Miller (Leicester & England)
T A K Rodber (Northampton & England)
L S Quinnell (Richmond & Wales)
*N C Redman (Bath & England)
*A J Diprose (Saracens & England)

Replacement during tour

TOUR RECORD
All matches Played 13 Won 11 Drawn 0 Lost 2 Points for 480 Against 278
International matches Played 3 Won 2 Lost 1 Points for 59 Against 66

SCORING RECORD
All matches   **International matches**
For: 56T 40C 38PG 2DG 480 Pts   For: 3T 1C 13PG 1DG 59 Pts
Against: 32T 20C 26PG 0DG 278 Pts   Against: 9T 3C 5PG 0DG 66 Pts

MATCH DETAILS

1997	OPPONENTS	VENUE	RESULT
24 May	Eastern Province XV	Port Elizabeth	W 39-11
28 May	Border	East London	W 18-14
31 May	Western Province	Cape Town	W 38-21
4 June	Mpumalanga	Witbank	W 64-14
7 June	Northern Transvaal	Pretoria	L 30-35
11 June	Gauteng Lions	Johannesburg	W 20-14
14 June	Natal	Durban	W 42-12
17 June	Emerging Springboks	Wellington	W 51-22
21 June	SOUTH AFRICA	Cape Town	W 25-16
24 June	Free State	Bloemfontein	W 52-30
28 June	SOUTH AFRICA	Durban	W 18-15
1 July	Northern Free State	Welkom	W 67-39
5 July	SOUTH AFRICA	Johannesburg	L 16-35

MATCH 1   24 May, Boet Erasmus Stadium, Port Elizabeth

Eastern Province Invitational XV 11 (2PG 1T)   **British Lions 39** (4G 2PG 1T)
Eastern Province Invitational XV: JTJ van Rensburg; D Keyser, R van Jaarsveld, HP le Roux, H Pedro; K Ford, C Alcock; D Saayman, GJ Kirsten *(capt)*, W Enslin; JJ Wiese, A du Preez; M Webber, J Greeff, SJ Scott-Young *Replacements* W Lessing for Enslin (38 mins); M van der Merwe for Webber (44 mins); R Fourie for Ford (42 mins)
Scorers *Try:* Keyser   *Penalty Goals:* van Rensburg (2)
British Lions: Jenkins; Evans, Guscott, Greenwood, Beal; Townsend, Howley; Smith, Wood, Leonard *(capt)*; Weir, Shaw; Dallaglio, Quinnell, Hill *Replacements* Underwood for Evans (67 mins); Williams for Wood (67 mins); Davidson for Shaw (77 mins)
Scorers *Tries:* Guscott (2), Weir, Underwood, Greenwood *Conversions:* Jenkins (4)   *Penalty Goals:* Jenkins (2)
Referee A Turner (Western Province)

MATCH 2   28 May, Basil Kenyon Stadium, East London

Border 14 (3PG 1T)   **British Lions 18** (1PG 3T)
Border: RG Bennett; K Hilton-Green, G Hetcher, K Malotana, A Claassen; G Miller, J Bradbrook; H Kok, R van Zyl *(capt)*, D du Preez; S Botha, J Gehring; M Swart, A Fox, A Botha *Replacements* D Maidza for Molotana (42 mins); D Coetzer for A Botha (79 mins)
Scorers *Try:* Claassen   *Penalty Goals:* Miller (3)
British Lions: Stimpson; Bentley, Bateman, Gibbs, Underwood; Grayson, Healey; Rowntree, Regan, Young; Weir, Davidson; Wainwright *(capt)*, Miller, Back *Replacements* Tait for Gibbs (45 mins); Dawson for Healey (54 mins); Wallace for Young (68 mins)

Scorers *Tries:* Bentley, Regan, Wainwright   *Penalty Goal:* Stimpson
Referee A Burger (Transvaal)

MATCH 3   31 May, Newlands, Cape Town

Western Province 21 (3G)   **British Lions 38** (3G 4PG 1T)
Western Province: J Swart; JT Small, R Fleck, DJ Muir *(capt)*, S Berridge;
P Montgomery, S Hatley; GL Pagel, A Paterson, KS Andrews; FJ Van Heerden,
L Louw; RA Brink, AD Aitken, C Krige *Replacements* L Koen for Muir (temp
57-60 mins); A van der Linde for Pagel (60 mins); B Skinstad for Krige (64 mins)
Scorers *Tries:* Muir (2), Brink   *Conversions:* Montgomery (3)
British Lions: Stimpson; Evans, Tait, Guscott, Bentley; Townsend, Howley;
Rowntree, Williams, Leonard; Johnson *(capt)*, Shaw; Dallaglio, Rodber, Hill
Replacements Quinnell for Rodber (62 mins); Greenwood for Tait (72 mins)
Scorers *Tries:* Bentley (2), Tait, Evans   *Conversions:* Stimpson (3)
Penalty Goals: Stimpson (4)
Referee A Schoonwinkel (Free State)

MATCH 4   3 June, Johann van Riebeeck Stadium, Witbank

Mpumalanga *(ex SE Transvaal)* **14** (2G)   **British Lions 64** (7G 3T)
Mpumalanga: E Gericke; J Visagie, R Potgieter, G Gendall, P Nel; R van As,
D van Zyl; H Swart, H Kemp, A Botha; M Bosman, E van den Berg; F Rossouw,
T Oosthuizen *(capt)*, P Joubert *Replacements* J Buekes for Oosthuizen (71 mins);
A van Rooyen for Nel (77 mins)
Scorers *Tries:* Joubert (2)   *Conversions:* van As (2)
British Lions: Beal; Evans, Bateman, Greenwood, Underwood; Jenkins, Dawson;
Smith, Wood, Wallace; Weir, Davidson; Wainwright, Rodber *(capt)*, Back
Replacements Regan for Wood (52 mins); Shaw for Weir (67 mins); Young for
Wallace (74 mins)
Scorers *Tries:* Wainwright (3), Underwood (2), Evans (2), Dawson, Jenkins, Beal
Conversions: Jenkins (7)
Referee C Spannenberg (Western Province)

MATCH 5   7 June, Loftus Versfeld, Pretoria

Northern Transvaal 35 (3G 1T 3PG)   **British Lions 30** (3G 3PG)
Northern Transvaal: G Bouwer; W Lourens, J Schutte, D van Schalkwyk,
C Steyn; R de Marigny, C Breytenbach; L Campher, H Tromp, P Boer;
D Grobbelaar, D Badenhorst; N van der Walt, A Richter *(capt)*, S Bekker
Replacements G Esterhuizen for Lourens (33 mins); G Laufs for Grobbelaar (38
mins); J Brooks for Tromp (40 mins); R Schroeder for Badenhorst (65 mins);
J Taljaard for Boer (71 mins)
Scorers *Tries:* Van Schalkwyk (2), Steyn, Richter   *Conversions:* Steyn (3)
Penalty Goals: Steyn (3)
British Lions: Stimpson; Bentley, Guscott, Tait, Underwood, Townsend, Howley;
Rowntree, Regan, Leonard; Johnson *(capt)*, Shaw; Dallaglio, Quinnell, Miller
Replacements Gibbs for Bentley (59 mins); Young for Leonard (74 mins)
Scorers *Tries:* Guscott (2), Townsend   *Conversions:* Stimpson (3)
Penalty Goals: Stimpson (3)
Referee A Watson (Eastern Province)

MATCH 6   11 June, Ellis Park, Johannesburg

Gauteng Lions *(ex Transvaal)* **14** (3PG 1T)   **British Lions 20** (2G 2PG)
Gauteng Lions: D du Toit; JW Gillingham, J van der Walt, HP le Roux,

P Hendriks; L van Rensburg, JP Roux; RD Grau, C le C Rossouw, K van
Greuning; JJ Wiese *(capt)*, B Thorne; A Vos, W Brosnihan, P Krause
Replacements J Dalton for Rossouw (52 mins); IS deV Swart for Grau (60 mins)
Scorers *Try:* Vos *Penalty Goals:* du Toit (3)
British Lions: Beal; Bentley, Guscott, Greenwood, Underwood; Catt, Healey;
Smith, Williams, Wallace; Redman, Davidson, Wainwright, Rodber *(capt)*, Back
Replacement Jenkins for Underwood (57 mins)
Scorers *Tries:* Healey, Bentley *Conversions:* Jenkins (2) *Penalty Goals:* Catt,
Jenkins
Referee WTS Henning (Northern Transvaal)

MATCH 7   14 June, King's Park, Durban

Natal 12 (4PG)   **British Lions 42** (3G 6PG 1DG)
Natal: GE Lawless; S Payne, JRD Thomson, PG Muller, J Joubert; H Scriba,
RJ du Preez; A-H le Roux, J Allan, R Kempson; GN Wegner, J Slade;
W van Heerden, D Kriese, W Fyvie *(capt)* *Replacements* R Strudwick for van
Heerden (temp 6-10 mins and 29 mins); J Smit for A-H le Roux (67 mins)
Scorer *Penalty Goals:* Lawless (4)
British Lions: Jenkins; Evans, Bateman, Gibbs, Tait; Townsend, Howley; Smith,
Wood, Young, Johnson *(capt)*, Shaw; Dallaglio, Miller, Hill *Replacements* Dawson
for Howley (12 mins); Wainwright for Johnson (temp 25-33 mins); Catt for
Bateman (66 mins); Leonard for Smith (67 mins)
Scorers *Tries:* Townsend, Catt, Dallaglio *Conversions:* Jenkins (3)
Penalty Goals: Jenkins (6) *Dropped Goal:* Townsend
Referee J Meuwessen (Eastern Province)

MATCH 8   17 June, Boland Stadium, Wellington

Emerging Springboks 22 (2G 1PG 1T)   **British Lions 51** (6G 3PG)
Emerging Springboks: MJ Smith (Griqualand West); D Kayser (Eastern
Province), P Montgomery (Western Province), McN Hendriks (Boland); P Treu
(SW Districts); L van Rensburg (Gauteng Lions), J Adlam (North West);
R Kempson (Natal), D Santon (Boland)*(capt)*, N du Toit (Boland); B Els,
R Opperman (both Free State); W Brosnihan (Gauteng Lions), J Coetzee (Free
State), P Smit (Griqualand West) *Replacements* K Myburgh (Griqualand West) for
Adlam (11 mins); M Goosen (Boland) for van Rensberg (22 mins); K Malotana
(Border) for Smith (65 mins); L Campher (Northern Transvaal) for Kempson (68
mins)
Scorers *Tries:* Brosnihan, Goosen, Treu *Conversions:* Smith,
Montgomery *Penalty Goal:* Smith
British Lions: Stimpson; Beal, Bateman, Greenwood, Bentley; Catt, Healey;
Rowntree, Regan, Leonard *(capt)*; Redman, Davidson; Wainwright, Diprose, Back
Scorers *Tries:* Beal (3), Rowntree, Stimpson, Catt *Conversions:* Stimpson (6)
Penalty Goals: Stimpson (3)
Referee I Rogers (Natal)

MATCH 9   21 June, Newlands, Cape Town   1st Test
SOUTH AFRICA 16 (2PG 2T)   BRITISH ISLES 25 (5PG 2T)

No side that has lost a first Test has ever gone on to win a series in
South Africa. As the shattered Springboks left the field at Newlands the
weight of history bore down on their slumped shoulders. They had

taken the game to the Lions in the early stages but had been unable to subdue their opponents, leaving the Lions the scope to bounce back off the ropes to score two tries in the last seven minutes through Dawson and Tait.

Dawson's try was a magnificent piece of opportunism. He broke from a scrum on the South African 22 but appeared hemmed in by the touchline. Instead he dummied, shaped to pass, checked and then dummied again to leave the likes of Teichmann, Joubert and van der Westhuizen looking inside for the pass which never came. It was a touch of genius, one which emphatically swung the game the Lions way. On the stroke of full-time Scott Gibbs drove hard into the Springbok 22. The ball was recycled, and Rodber threw a long pass for Jenkins to put Tait in at the corner.

Jenkins had kept the Lions in the hunt up to that point with five penalty goals, three in the first half and two after the interval. Lubbe kicked a penalty in the third minute for South Africa. In the 21st minute Os du Randt hammered over from a line-out drive for a try. Four minutes into the second half Teichmann broke through Gibbs's tackle to send Russell Bennett, a half-time replacement for Lubbe, in at the corner. These were the only breaches in a magnificent defensive performance by the Lions.

SOUTH AFRICA: AJ Joubert (Natal); JT Small (Western Province), E Lubbe (Griqualand West), JC Mulder (Gauteng Lions), AH Snyman (Northern Transvaal); HW Honiball (Natal), JH van der Westhuizen (Northern Transvaal); JP du Randt (Free State), AE Drotské (Free State), AC Garvey (Natal); J J Strydom (Gauteng Lions). MG Andrews (Natal); RJ Kruger (Northern Transvaal), GH Teichmann (Natal) *(capt)*, AG Venter (Free State)
Replacement RG Bennett (Border) for Lubbe (40 mins)
Scorers *Tries:* du Randt, Bennett   *Penalty Goals:* Lubbe, Honiball
BRITISH ISLES: Jenkins; Evans, Guscott, Gibbs, Tait; Townsend, Dawson; Smith, Wood, Wallace; Johnson *(capt)*, Davidson; Dallaglio, Rodber, Hill
Replacement Leonard for Smith (79 mins)
Scorers *Tries:* Dawson, Tait   *Penalty Goals:* Jenkins (5)
Referee CJ Hawke (New Zealand)

MATCH 10   24 June, Free State Stadium Bloemfontein

Free State 30 (3G 3PG)   **British Lions 52** (4G 3PG 3T)
Free State: MJ Smith; JF van Wyk, HL Muller *(capt)*, B Venter, S Brink; J H de Beer, S Fourie; D Groenewald, C Marais, W Meyer; RJ Oppermann, BWW Els; C van Rensburg, J Coetzee, J Erasmus *Replacements* H Jacobs for Fourie (40 mins); D Heymans for Meyer (60 mins)
Scorers *Tries:* Brink (2), de Beer   *Conversions:* de Beer (3)
Penalty Goals: de Beer (3)
British Lions: Stimpson; Bentley, Bateman, Greenwood, Underwood; Catt, Healey; Rowntree, Williams, Young; Redman *(capt)*, Shaw; Wainwright, Miller, Back *Replacements* Leonard for Rowntree (temp 16-20 and from 73 mins); Jenkins for Greenwood (40 mins)
Scorers *Tries:* Bentley (3), Stimpson, Bateman, Jenkins, Underwood
Conversions: Stimpson (4)   *Penalty Goals:* Stimpson (3)
Referee J Kaplan (Natal)

MATCH 11   28 June, King's Park, Durban   2nd Test

SOUTH AFRICA 15 (3T) BRITISH ISLES 18 (5PG 1DG)

This was one of the most improbable victories in Test history. The Springboks had so much of the game, so much possession and so many positions; yet could not finish off the Lions. South Africa scored three tries to nil but were hopelessly inadequate when it came to goal-kicking. They missed 15 points in all and went through three goal-kickers. In contrast the Lions kept calling up Neil Jenkins to knock the ball between the posts.

Jenkins was faultless. His first success in the 16th minute came after the Lions had been under ferocious pressure. They then managed to sneak their way into the South African half where Jenkins struck a penalty from 45 metres. That set the tone for rest of the game. If Test rugby is about the taking of every slender opportunity then the Lions were the perfect embodiment of the theory. Jenkins kicked goals on the half hour, and in the 46th, 65th and 74th minutes. That last penalty brought the Lions level at 15-15.

It was time for one last dash for glory. Hooker Keith Wood kicked out of defence and set off on a pounding chase. Montgomery fumbled and had to shepherd the ball into touch. From the line-out the Lions

Jeremy Guscott scores the winning dropped goal in the second Test between the British Lions and South Africa.

drove, Townsend tried a shimmying dart for the line, the ball came back to Guscott who coolly dropped the goal.

South Africa, who fielded two new caps in the backline, Montgomery and Rossouw, scored their first try in the 35th minute when van der Westhuizen thrust his way over from short-range. Just seconds after the restart Montgomery scored the second try after Tait had made a hash of coming out of defence, his flip pass only finding Honiball who put his centre over. The third try in the 54th minute came from another Lions error, John Bentley allowing Andre Joubert to hand him off and run in from the 22 to the try-line.

The Lions were patient and resilient in the face of the Springbok onslaught and it won them the day.

SOUTH AFRICA: AJ Joubert (Natal); AH Snyman (Northern Transvaal), P Montgomery (Western Province), D van Schalkwyk (Northern Transvaal), PWG Rossouw (Western Province); HW Honiball (Natal), JH van der Westhuizen (Northern Transvaal); JP du Randt (Free State), AE Drotské (Free State), AC Garvey (Natal); JJ Strydom (Gauteng Lions), MG Andrews (Natal); RJ Kruger (Northern Transvaal), GH Teichmann (Natal) *(capt)*, AG Venter (Free State) *Replacements* FJ van Heerden (Western Province) for Teichmann (temp 3-5 mins) and Kruger (50 mins); DF Theron (Griqualand West) for Garvey (67 mins)
Scorers *Tries:* van der Westhuizen, Montgomery, Joubert
BRITISH ISLES: Jenkins; Bentley, Guscott, Gibbs, Tait; Townsend, Dawson; Smith, Wood, Wallace; Johnson *(capt)*, Davidson; Dallaglio, Rodber, Hill *Replacements* Back for Hill (57 mins); Healey for Tait (76 mins); Miller for Rodber (77 mins)
Scorers *Penalty Goals:* Jenkins (5)   *Dropped Goal:* Guscott
Referee D Mene (France)

MATCH 12   1 July, Noord-wes Stadium, Welkom

Northern Free State 39 (4G 2PG 1T)   **British Lions 67** (7G 1PG 3T)
Northern Free State: M Ehrentraut; R Harmse, A van Buuren, T de Beer, W Nagel; E Herbert, J Jerling *(capt)*; K Appelgryn, O Wagener, B Nel; K Heydenrich, S Nieuwenhuysen; H Kershaw, M Venter, E Delport *Replacements* J Burrows for Ehrentraut (66 mins); A Michau for Delport (75 mins)
Scorers *Tries:* Pen try, Ehrentraut, Wagener, van Buuren, Herbert *Conversions:* Herbert (4)   *Penalty Goals:* Herbert (2)
British Lions: Stimpson; Stanger, Beal, Bateman, Underwood; Catt, Bracken; Leonard *(capt)*, Regan, Young; Redman, Shaw; Wainwright, Diprose, Back *Replacements* Rowntree for Leonard (41 mins); Healey for Bracken (52 mins)
Scorers *Tries:* Underwood (3), Shaw (2), Stimpson (2), Back, Bracken, Regan *Conversions:* Stimpson (7)   *Penalty Goal:* Stimpson
Referee D de Villiers (Western Province)

MATCH 13   5 July, Ellis Park, Johannesburg   3rd Test
SOUTH AFRICA 35 (3G 3PG 1T)   BRITISH ISLES 16 (1G 3PG)

It was a game too far for the British Lions. They were spent in body and drained emotionally after winning the series the week before. Even so they gave a rousing display, finally playing the sort of expansive rugby which was the hallmark of all their provincial games. However, they could not manage to attain the same levels of concentration and self-discipline, giving away too many penalties and making too many errors at crucial stages. The Springboks, stung by the fear of conceding their first ever series whitewash on home soil, played with more authority and nerve behind the scrum, scoring four tries, two of them in the last six minutes to give a favourable spin to the scoreboard.

The cast-list for both sides was radically different. South Africa made six changes, selecting two new caps, Erasmus on the flank and de Beer at fly-half. The Lions made four changes originally, three enforced and Back being preferred to Hill, and one more on the morning of the match when Rodber withdrew with 'flu, to be replaced by Wainwright.

South Africa made a good start, de Beer kicking two goals and converted Montgomery's try to give them a 13-0 lead after 16 minutes. Jenkins then bailed out the Lions yet again, slotting three penalties to make it 13-9 at half-time. Jeremy Guscott, suffering from a broken bone in his arm, was replaced at half-time by Allan Bateman. Van der Westhuizen slipped Dawson's tackle to score in the 47th minute, de Beer converting and adding a penalty 15 minutes later. The Lions rallied with Dawson squirming over from short-range in the 65th minute to close the scores to 23-16. It was not to be, Snyman and Rossouw crossing in the closing stages to save face for South Africa.

SOUTH AFRICA: R G Bennett (Border); AH Snyman (Northern Transvaal), P Montgomery (Western Province), D van Schalkwyk (Northern Transvaal), PWG Rossouw (Western Province); JH de Beer (Free State), JH van der Westhuizen (Northern Transvaal); JP du Randt (Free State), J Dalton (Gauteng Lions), DF Theron (Griqualand West); JJ Strydom (Gauteng Lions), K Otto (Northern Transvaal); AG Venter (Free State), GH Teichmann (Natal) *(capt)*, J C Erasmus (Free State) *Replacements* HW Honiball (Natal) for Montgomery (53 mins); AC Garvey (Natal) for du Randt (63 mins); AE Drotské (Free State) for Dalton (69 mins), J Swart (Western Province) for de Beer (71 mins); FJ van Heerden (Western Province) for Teichmann (73 mins); W Swanepoel (Free State) for van der Westhuizen (81 mins)
Scorers *Tries:* van der Westhuizen, Montgomery, Snyman, Rossouw *Conversions:* de Beer (2), Honiball *Penalty Goals:* de Beer (3)
BRITISH ISLES: Jenkins; Bentley, Guscott, Gibbs, Underwood; Catt, Dawson; Smith, Regan, Wallace; Johnson *(capt)*, Davidson; Wainwright, Dallaglio, Back *Replacements* Stimpson for Underwood (30 mins); Bateman for Guscott (40 mins); Healey for Dawson (82 mins)
Scorers *Try:* Dawson *Conversion:* Jenkins *Penalty Goals:* Jenkins (3)
Referee WJ Erickson (Australia)

Tim Stimpson (111) and Neil Jenkins (110) were the leading points scorers on the tour; John Bentley and Tony Underwood (seven each) the leading try scorers

POKER GAME ENDS UP TRUMPS

THE INTERNATIONAL CHAMPIONSHIP 1997

Was it worth all that haggling, all those bluffs, counter-bluffs and dangerous games of poker? The Celts had taken such umbrage at the RFU's covert satellite television deal that for many long, fretful months through 1996 there was to be no championship. Finally, common sense got the better of ego and slighted pride and England, at no small financial cost, were readmitted. Were they grateful? Not if you judge solely by the scoreboard. They drove the Celts into the ground, rattling up various record scores against each of them, finished unbeaten by Home Union teams for the third season in a row – the first time they have achieved such a feat – and won a record 20th Triple Crown. Yet it was France who took the ultimate honour and glory. They won the Grand Slam for only the fifth time, finishing with 129 points (12 fewer than England) and 14 tries, both French records.

Meanwhile, it was a woeful return for the other three home nations, which triggered the rumour mill at the season's end. British Lions manager Fran Cotton claimed that a powerful lobby within the RFU was plotting to cut loose from the Five Nations and form an alliance with France to play the southern hemisphere countries instead in an annual five-way championship. This would be an absolute disaster if it ever came to pass. So much sheer pleasure was derived from this particular tournament, both in the watching and in what the French call the *troisième mi-temps* – the third half – that to dismantle the competition would be to do a massive disservice to spectators, those simple souls who are so easily overlooked when TV companies start talking multi-million pound deals. If you take the spectator out of the equation, then pretty soon you have no spectator and no game. The 1997 Five Nations proved, once again, a wonderful marketing tool for the game, drawing uncommitted thousands to the sport for the first time. And if they happened to sample the delights of a Dublin or Edinburgh weekend in the process, then it certainly would not be for the last time.

Rugby is still too small a sport globally to risk pensioning off some of its senior citizens to amuse each other along with Italy, Romania and the like. Of course it's a grave concern that Ireland, Scotland and Wales should be so overwhelmed, and yes, there is a serious need for all the home countries to liaise about the best way forward. But let's rejoice that there was some majestic rugby along this pot-holed way.

Mind you, you had to be careful not to blink or you would have missed much of it. England scored many of their record 141 points in the tournament – 23 more than their previous best, achieved in 1992 – in short, sudden bursts. They began in disjointed fashion against Scotland and laboured again for an hour in Dublin, but then hit their stride magnificently. They continued against France in similar purposeful mood, playing their best rugby of the championship as they built a 20–6 lead during an hour's play. But fatally, they left the door ajar, and France barged in to plunder the goodies by 23–20. France may well rail against Anglo-Saxon bias, but nevertheless there was an overpowering sense of England losing the match rather than of France winning it. Saracens openside Richard Hill was a conspicuous new arrival; so, too, was Newcastle full-back Tim Stimpson. Why, oh why, though did we see only glimpses of Jeremy Guscott, the genius shackled to the bench for most of the championship?

France were battered by adversity. Their injury list was enormous. In rising above it all, they defined themselves as a side with great potential for the 1999 World Cup. They paraded some unknown stars – Lamaison, Venditti, Magne – reinvigorated a couple of others, Sadourny and Benazzi, and reinvented one old bruiser in Olivier Merle. The new management triumvirate of Jean-Claude Skrela, Pierre Villepreux and Jo Maso was a great success.

Ireland's new coaching guru, former Bath man Brian Ashton, did not have it so easy. He began well, but then saw his charges disintegrate completely. Ashton, appointed just ten days before the championship began, was granted a six-year contract just before the end of the tournament. He'll need every last day to turn Ireland's fortunes around. Lock Jeremy Davidson and Leicester No 8 Eric Miller were the lone stars.

Wales had the makings of a stylish campaign. The return of their Rugby League contingent, Scott Quinnell, David Young, Scott Gibbs and Allan Bateman, brought steel and drive into the team. But the euphoria of their astonishing victory at Murrayfield evaporated quickly in Cardiff with the defeat by Ireland, whom they have not managed to beat at home since 1983. A good performance in Paris was then undermined by injuries, which deprived them of a fifth of that team for the visit by England. Wales still need more power in the tight five, but, with Charvis settling into the back row and the impish Arwel Thomas at fly-half, there is a silver lining.

Scotland, who joined Ireland in the doghouse, will have to sift through the ashes of their season more carefully to find equal comfort. The rehabilitation of their Rugby League exile Alan Tait was good to see; so was the form of Doddie Weir and Craig Chalmers and the emergence of prop Tom Smith. Townsend, though, was disappointing, and clearly burdened by the expectations heaped upon him.

A Celtic revival is imperative, for England and France are a distant speck on the horizon at the moment.

FINAL TABLE

	P	W	D	L	F	A	Pts
France	4	4	0	0	129	77	8
England	4	3	0	1	141	55	6
Wales	4	1	0	3	94	106	2
Scotland	4	1	0	3	90	132	2
Ireland	4	1	0	3	57	141	2

The points tally for the season was 511, a new Five Nations record. The previous high, 363, was established six years ago.

The points comprised 53 tries (the previous post-war record try tally was 41 in 1980, the last time the tournament yielded more than 50 tries was in 1924, and the all-time record, 55, was set in 1911), 39 conversions, 52 penalty goals and 4 dropped goals.

The leading individual scorers were: 52 – Paul Grayson (England); 42 – Rowen Shepherd (Scotland), Christophe Lamaison (France); 36 – Neil Jenkins (Wales). David Venditti and Laurent Leflamand (four each for France); Ieuan Evans, Tony Underwood and Alan Tait (three each) were the season's top try-scorers.

French captian Abdelatif Benazzi supported by Marc Dalmaso, Hugues Miorin and Didier Casadei during the France-Scotland match in which the French clinched the Grand Slam.

18 January 1997, Murrayfield
SCOTLAND 19 (1G 3PG 1DG)   WALES 34 (4G 2PG)

It came like a bolt from a clear blue sky. In the 52nd minute, Wales, trailing 16–10, suddenly hit Scotland with three tries in six minutes, the fastest hat-trick in Five Nations history, to turn the match on its head. Scotland had already been rocked by some thunderclap Welsh tackling, particularly in midfield, but appeared to have weathered the worst. Their illusions were shattered by a Welsh revival prompted by the mercurial Arwel Thomas, the shrewd, muscular interventions of Gibbs and Bateman and the towering presence of Scott Quinnell.

By the end of a dramatic afternoon Wales had equalled their highest away score in the Five Nations. Neil Jenkins scored 19 points to equal the Welsh individual record for a Five Nations match. He also hoisted his points total for Five Nations games to 174, overtaking Paul Thorburn to establish a new Welsh record, and became only the fifth player to pass 500 points in Test rugby.

The first half had seen two well-crafted tries from each side: in the 27th minute, Wainwright initiated a move on one side of the pitch with a typical straight-backed drive which, several phases later, ended with Scott Hastings cantering over. The Welsh try eight minutes later was just as impressive, the product of fine work by the Rugby League returnees, Bateman, Gibbs and, finally, Scott Quinnell.

The triple-whammy began with a try by Jenkins, followed by Thomas latching on to a bouncing ball and skipping gleefully 40 metres to the posts. Then Ieuan Evans spirited the ball from under the noses of the dithering Shepherd and Armstrong. Scotland slumped and Wales rejoiced.

SCOTLAND: R J S Shepherd (Melrose); A G Stanger (Hawick), S Hastings (Watsonians), G P J Townsend (Northampton), K M Logan (Stirling County); C M Chalmers (Melrose), G Armstrong (Newcastle); D I W Hilton (Bath), D G Ellis (Currie), M J Stewart (Northampton), G W Weir (Newcastle), A I Reed (Wasps), P Walton (Newcastle), R I Wainwright (Watsonians) *(capt)*, M I Wallace (GHK) *Replacements* D S Munro (GHK) for Reed (55 mins); D A Stark (Melrose) for Chalmers (77 mins)
Scorers *Try:* Hastings *Conversion:* Shepherd *Penalty Goals:* Shepherd (3) *Dropped Goal:* Chalmers
WALES: N R Jenkins (Pontypridd); I C Evans (Llanelli), A G Bateman (Richmond), I S Gibbs (Swansea), G Thomas (Bridgend); A C Thomas (Swansea), R Howley (Cardiff); C D Loader (Swansea), J M Humphreys (Cardiff) *(capt)*, D Young (Cardiff), G O Llewellyn (Harlequins), M Rowley (Pontypridd), S M Williams (Neath), L S Quinnell (Richmond), C Charvis (Swansea) *Replacements* J C Quinnell (Richmond) for Rowley (66 mins); R G Jones (Cardiff) for Charvis (75 mins); J Davies (Cardiff) for Gibbs (79 mins)
Scorers *Tries:* S Quinnell, Jenkins, A Thomas, Evans *Conversions:* Jenkins (4) *Penalty Goals:* Jenkins (2)
Referee H A Smith (Ireland)

18 January 1997, Lansdowne Road
IRELAND 15 (5PG) FRANCE 32 (3G 2PG 1T)

The Lansdowne Road faithful have been here many times before. The pain, though, does not become any easier to bear. The Irish storm which swirled about the French blew out after an hour's play, and France took full advantage of the late lull. They ran up 20 points in the last quarter to post their highest away score in a Five Nations match and their 13th win in a row against Ireland. Brive winger David Venditti scored a hat-trick, only the fourth time the feat has been achieved by a Frenchman in the championship.

Irish hopes tend to swing from the wildly optimistic to the wildly pessimistic. Their thoughts ought to have been tinged with gloom after hapless showings against Western Samoa and Italy, but there was a bounce in their step due to the surprise appointment of Lancastrian, Brian Ashton, as coach. It was hoped that Ashton, well respected in the game, might do a Jack Charlton for them. France had not been in the best fettle themselves. They had lost the pre-Christmas Test series against the Springboks by 2–0, failing to score a single try.

The first half was marked by several flare-ups: Ireland were intent on giving the opposition a warm welcome. The assault stung the French into retaliation and Merle and Pelous were yellow-carded. Ireland had passion but not enough guile in their game. There were a couple of neat breaks from Bell and Topping to admire, but the only points-scoring came from the boot of Elwood.

France scored their first try in the sixth minute, when Galthié slipped over after a powerful forward rumble. Venditti scored his first in the 32nd minute, outstripping Topping. His second came in the 61st minute on the back of more forward pressure, and he rounded off proceedings in injury time.

IRELAND: C M P O'Shea (London Irish); J A Topping (Ballymena), J C Bell (Northampton), M J Field (Malone), D J Crotty (Cork Const); E P Elwood (Lansdowne), N A Hogan (Terenure Coll); N J Popplewell (Newcastle), K G M Wood (Harlequins) (*capt*), P S Wallace (Saracens), P S Johns (Saracens), J W Davidson (London Irish), D S Corkery (Bristol), E R P Miller (Leicester), W D McBride (Malone) *Replacements* A T H Clarke (Northampton) for Wood (38 mins); K P McQuilkin (Lansdowne) for Field (temp & 47 mins); P Flavin (Blackrock Coll) for Popplewell (85 mins)
Scorer *Penalty Goals:* Elwood (5)
FRANCE: J-L Sadourny (Colomiers); E Ntamack (Toulouse), S Glas (Bourgoin), T Castaignède (Toulouse), D Venditti (Brive); A Penaud (Brive), F Galthié (Colomiers); C Califano (Toulouse), M Dal Maso (Agen), F Tournaire (Narbonne), O Merle (Montferrand), H Miorin (Toulouse), A Benazzi (Agen) (*capt*), F Pelous (Dax), P Benetton (Agen) *Replacements* P Carbonneau (Brive) for Galthié (43 mins); R Castel (Béziers) for Miorin (62 mins); J-L Jordana (Toulouse) for Califano (temp)
Scorers *Tries:* Venditti (3), Galthié *Conversions:* Castaignède (3) *Penalty Goals:* Castaignède (2)
Referee A Watson (South Africa)

1 February 1997, Twickenham
ENGLAND 41 (3G 5PG 1T)   SCOTLAND 13 (1G 2PG)

The kilted ones traipsed dejectedly from Twickenham, having seen the heart ripped out of their side in a few astonishing moments for the second match in succession. Scotland were buried by a three-try blitz within five minutes. There were only 13 minutes remaining of what had been a stodgy, error-strewn match when England cut loose and went on to finish with their highest-ever score in a Five Nations game – and this in a fixture renowned for its tightness and caution. England had not scored a Calcutta Cup try for four years, but by the end they had inflicted Scotland's worst defeat since the tournament began in 1910 and set a new record for the series, winning their eighth consecutive match against the auld enemy.

It was the first game of England's campaign and it took them a fair old time to dust down the cobwebs. When they did, however, they looked polished, inventive and assured, finally playing the sort of integrated, expansive game they had so often talked about but had invariably failed to deliver. Even though they spent an hour fretting and stuttering, there were a few names exempt from criticism, notably that of Will Carling. His play bristled with purpose and menace. He was rewarded with his first try against Scotland in 11 games, the second of England's three-try burst. Their first of the match, in the 15th minute, was controversial: New Zealand referee Paddy O'Brien awarded a penalty try for persistent infringement. Rob Wainwright had been a fingertip away from a try for Scotland just moments earlier, and Eriksson did get over in the 24th minute after Logan corkscrewed through a dozy defence. Gomarsall started the rout for England in the 67th minute after a deft pass from Johnson. Carling took a Rodber lobbed pass and De Glanville provided the captain's encore after smart work by Grayson. It was a deluge in the midst of a drought.

ENGLAND: T R G Stimpson (Newcastle); J M Sleightholme (Bath), W D C Carling (Harlequins), P R de Glanville (Bath) (*capt*), T Underwood (Newcastle); P J Grayson (Northampton), A C T Gomarsall (Wasps); G C Rowntree (Leicester), M P Regan (Bristol), J Leonard (Harlequins), M O Johnson (Leicester), S D Shaw (Bristol), L B N Dallaglio (Wasps), T A K Rodber (Northampton & Army), R A Hill (Saracens)
Scorers *Tries:* pen try, Carling, Gomarsall, de Glanville *Conversions:* Grayson (3) *Penalty Goals:* Grayson (5)
SCOTLAND: R J S Shepherd (Melrose); D A Stark (Melrose), A G Stanger (Hawick), B R S Eriksson (London Scottish), K M Logan (Stirling County); G P Townsend (Northampton), B W Redpath (Melrose); T J Smith (Watsonians), D G Ellis (Currie), M J Stewart (Northampton), G W Weir (Newcastle), A I Reed (Wasps), P Walton (Newcastle), R I Wainwright (Watsonians & Army) (*capt*), I R Smith (Gloucester) *Replacement* S Hastings (Watsonians) for Eriksson (70 mins)
Scorers *Try:* Eriksson *Conversion:* Shepherd *Penalty Goals:* Shepherd (2)
Referee P D O'Brien (New Zealand)

1 February 1997, Cardiff Arms Park
WALES 25 (2G 2PG 1T)   IRELAND 26 (1G 3PG 2T)

Such hope, such dejection. The long-suffering Welsh fans once again saw the light snuffed out on their promised new dawn. After the wild joy of Murrayfield they were brought back down to earth by a careless performance which was long on spirit but short on control. Ireland, buoyed by the increasing input of their new coach, Brian Ashton, scored three first-half tries and then hung on as Wales strove to work their way back into contention. Wales failed – just.

So Ireland extended their unbeaten sequence in Cardiff to seven matches, dating back to 1983. No other nation has ever achieved such a run in the Welsh capital. The score was also their highest ever on Welsh soil. But they went about creating history the hard way, allowing Wales to cross their try-line within 33 seconds. Ieuan Evans' try, which came after Arwel Thomas cleverly switched the kick-off and Charvis, Gibbs and Howley all piled in before the ball was spun across to Evans, was the fastest ever by a Welshman in internationals.

Ireland took the setback in their stride. Elwood nudged them back into contention with a straightforward penalty goal in the fourth minute. His next contribution was far less orthodox: a steepling Garryowen in the tenth minute which rebounded off the goalpost padding. Bell took advantage of Jenkins' confusion to plunge over. Then the Ireland pack, in which Davidson and Johns were prominent, gradually seized the upper hand, enabling them to establish a 20–10 lead at the interval.

An arcing run by Arwel Thomas released the flying Evans for his second try in the 45th minute. The goal-kickers, Elwood and Jenkins, kept plugging away to keep the scoreboard busy. Then, with just four minutes remaining, Scott Quinnell touched down from a driving maul. But it was too little, too late.

WALES: N R Jenkins (Pontypridd); I C Evans (Llanelli), G Thomas (Bridgend), I S Gibbs (Swansea), D R James (Bridgend); A C Thomas (Swansea), R Howley (Cardiff); C D Loader (Swansea), J M Humphreys (Cardiff) *(capt)*, D Young (Cardiff), G O Llewellyn (Harlequins), M Rowley (Pontypridd), S M Williams (Neath), L S Quinnell (Richmond), C L Charvis (Swansea) *Replacements* J C Quinnell (Richmond) for Rowley (62 mins); K P Jones (Ebbw Vale) for Charvis (68 mins)
Scorers *Tries:* Evans (2), S Quinnell *Conversions:* Jenkins (2) *Penalty Goals:* Jenkins (2)
IRELAND: J E Staples (Harlequins) *(capt)*; D Hickie (St Mary's Coll), J C Bell (Northampton), M J Field (Malone), D J Crotty (Cork Const); E P Elwood (Lansdowne), N A Hogan (Terenure Coll); N J Popplewell (Newcastle), R P Nesdale (Newcastle), P S Wallace (Saracens), P S Johns (Saracens), J W Davidson (London Irish), D S Corkery (Bristol), E R P Miller (Leicester), W D McBride (Malone) *Replacement* G M Fulcher (London Irish) for Johns (73 mins)
Scorers *Tries:* Bell, Miller, Hickie *Conversion:* Elwood *Penalty Goals:* Elwood (3)
Referee W J Erickson (Australia)

15 February 1997, Lansdowne Road
IRELAND 6 (2PG)   **ENGLAND 46** (2G 4PG 4T)
The Irish supporters poured into Lansdowne Road in a mood of optimism; they poured out of Lansdowne Road a couple of hours later with dark thoughts – Guinness; and lots of it. They had invested their hope in the burgeoning form of their forwards, particularly the youthful zest of Miller and Davidson, and in the canny influence of Brian Ashton as he came face to face with his old Bath colleague Jack Rowell.

There was nothing wrong with the logic of such thinking: Irish spirits had risen after the Cardiff victory, while England were not firing on all cylinders. Ten of their team were at Ireland's national stadium for the first time. But those who were clutching their rosary beads as they made their confident predictions had due cause first to invoke divine intervention and then to curse it as Irish hopes were shredded by injuries to Miller (11th minute) and Elwood, who eventually gave way in the 25th.

Once again in this tournament a bolt from the blue completely demolished the opposition as England notched up 29 points in the last 16 minutes, including four tries in the final eight minutes. Ireland crumbled to their heaviest-ever championship defeat and their second-worst to anyone. England's winning margin was the biggest ever by any team in a Five Nations match, while for the second game running, their score was their highest in the championship. They also became the first country to score 40-plus points in successive matches.

It was the late arrival of Healey and Guscott which added pace, bite and imagination to the England attack. The English back row was dominant, and by the end Ireland had collapsed completely. Tony Underwood blazed across the turf, scoring two tries, as did Jon Sleightholme, whose 18th-minute score owed much to Field's missed touch. The England winger finished brilliantly, fixing Topping with a lovely feint. Gomarsall began the final surge in the 63rd minute, waltzing round unmolested from a short scrum. Sleightholme got his second try in the 73rd minute after good work by Hill and Dallaglio, and Healey put Hill over two minutes later. Then came Underwood's double, Guscott carving the space for the first and half the England team handling for the second. It was a great Dublin day for the English.

IRELAND: J E Staples (Harlequins) (*capt*); D A Hickie (St Mary's Coll), J C Bell (Northampton), M J Field (Malone), J A Topping (Ballymena); E P Elwood (Lansdowne), N A Hogan (Terenure Coll); N J Popplewell (Newcastle), R P Nesdale (Newcastle), P S Wallace (Saracens), P S Johns (Saracens), J W Davidson (London Irish), D S Corkery (Bristol), E R P Miller (Leicester), W D McBride (Malone) *Replacements* A G Foley (Shannon) for Miller (11 mins);

D G Humphreys (London Irish) for Elwood (25 mins); B T O'Meara (Cork Const) for Hogan (65 mins)
Scorer *Penalty Goals:* Elwood (2)
ENGLAND: T R G Stimpson (Newcastle); J M Sleightholme (Bath), W D C Carling (Harlequins), P R de Glanville (Bath) *(capt)*, T Underwood (Newcastle); P J Grayson (Northampton), A C T Gomarsall (Wasps); G C Rowntree (Leicester), M P Regan (Bristol), J Leonard (Harlequins), M O Johnson (Leicester), S D Shaw (Bristol), L B N Dallaglio (Wasps), T A K Rodber (Northampton & Army), R A Hill (Saracens)
Replacements A S Healey (Leicester) for Gomarsall (72 mins); J C Guscott (Bath) for Carling (76 mins)
Scorers *Tries:* Sleightholme (2), Underwood (2), Gomarsall, Hill
Conversions: Grayson (2) *Penalty Goals:* Grayson (4)
Referee C J Hawke (New Zealand)

15 February 1997, Parc des Princes
FRANCE 27 (2G 1PG 2T) WALES 22 (2G 1PG 1T)

It had been 22 years since Wales last won in Paris, and this time only four of the side – Evans, Gibbs, Jenkins and Gareth Llewellyn, who became the second most-capped Welshman of all time, had played at the Parc des Princes before. France, too, were handicapped by a lengthy injury list which deprived them of the likes of Saint-André, Ntamack, Castaignède, Roumat and Benetton. It was time for a change, thought the Welsh. Fate thought otherwise.

Yet Wales were the absolute equal for much of this enthralling encounter. They played with adventure, thought and edge, which must have been a great comfort to coach Kevin Bowring in his quest to produce quality winning rugby. The elusive victory might even have been his had it not been for yet another infuriating stroke of misfortune for full-back Neil Jenkins. Against Ireland a padded post had been his undoing. Here it was the freak bounce of a ball which unstitched the makeshift full-back. Aucagne's dropped goal bounced back from the in-goal area to elude Jenkins and gift a second try, France's fourth, to Leflamand.

There were many mistakes from both sides, failings which added to, rather than detracted from, the entertainment value. The Welsh pack had the measure of their opponents, and Llewellyn dominated the line-out: France scarcely won a ball in the second half. The back row featured strongly and the intelligent, incisive running of Bateman was again a joy to behold.

France were away from the traps quickly, Merle rumbling over within three minutes. Wales were not overawed however: they took the game to France, spurred by the strong running of Howley. It was no surprise when Gareth Thomas forced his way over in the 15th minute. Aucagne replaced Dourthe, who dislocated a shoulder, before a chip by Glas resulted in a try for Leflamand in the 36th minute. The French hooker, Dal Maso, was in thundering form, his storming drive creating a try for Venditti two minutes later. It was 20-10 at half-time.

Bateman's try nine minutes after the restart narrowed the gap, but then came Jenkins' moment of woe. Wales drew some consolation from Howley's try in the 68th minute, the best of an absorbing afternoon.

FRANCE: J-L Sadourny (Colomiers); L Leflamand (Bourgoin), R Dourthe (Dax), S Glas (Bourgoin), D Venditti (Brive); C Lamaison (Brive), P Carbonneau (Brive); C Califano (Toulouse), M Dal Maso (Agen), J-L Jordana (Toulouse), O Merle (Montferrand), H Miorin (Toulouse), A Benazzi (Agen) (*capt*), F Pelous (Dax), R Castel (Béziers) *Replacements* D Aucagne (Pau) for Dourthe (22 mins); O Magne (Dax) for Miorin (53 mins)
Scorers *Tries:* Leflamand (2), Merle, Venditti   *Conversions:* Dourthe, Aucagne *Penalty Goal:* Aucagne
WALES: N R Jenkins (Pontypridd); I C Evans (Llanelli), A G Bateman (Richmond), I S Gibbs (Swansea), G Thomas (Bridgend); A C Thomas (Swansea), R Howley (Cardiff); C D Loader (Swansea), J M Humphreys (Cardiff) (*capt*), D Young (Cardiff), G O Llewellyn (Harlequins), M Rowley (Pontypridd), S M Williams (Neath), L S Quinnell (Richmond), C L Charvis (Swansea) *Replacement* J Davies (Cardiff) for Evans (52 mins)
Scorers *Tries:* G Thomas, Bateman, Howley   *Conversions:* Jenkins (2) *Penalty Goal:* Jenkins
Referee P Marshall (Australia)

1 March 1997, Murrayfield
SCOTLAND 38 (5G 1PG)   IRELAND 10 (1G 1PG)

If Ireland coach Brian Ashton thought he had a difficult task ahead of him when he took up the job, then he was left in no doubt about it by the end of the championship. Ireland were firmly in contention at 7-7 at the interval, but in the second half they were obliterated. In that period Scotland scored four tries, virtually unopposed, to notch up their highest score in a championship game. The margin of victory equalled their tournament record (31-3) set against France 85 years ago. Ireland have not beaten Scotland since 1988.

Scotland rediscovered a crucial aspect of their game – their appetite. They punched the blind side with venom, led by some thundering charges from Wainwright, Walton and the mobile prop Tom Smith. They also had the game's most influential player in Craig Chalmers, restored to Scotland's colours after the Twickenham debacle. The fly-half had battled through some turbulent form and a personal tragedy: his father, Bryan, a major figure at Melrose, had died three weeks earlier. Doddie Weir put himself in contention for the Lions slot with a commanding performance.

There was another name to conjure with in this spirited tartan revival – that of Alan Tait, the 32-year-old Newcastle centre who became the first former Scotland cap to return to international Rugby Union from Rugby League. Tait, impressive in the tackle and shrewd in attack, scored Scotland's opening try in the 32nd minute, courtesy of a sublime dummy by Chalmers.

Once again Ireland suffered through injury. Midway through the first half they lost captain Jim Staples, who carved out Ireland's try with a magnificent break from deep and a chip ahead to set up Hickie. In the process he ripped a hamstring.

Walton prised open the floodgates for Scotland, powering off a scrum in the 57th minute. Weir followed suit ten minutes later. The backs got in on the second-half action when Townsend completed a sweeping movement in the 77th minute. Tony Stanger rounded it all off on the stroke of full time. Rowen Shepherd converted all five of Scotland's tries to set a new series record.

SCOTLAND: R J S Shepherd (Melrose); A G Stanger (Hawick), A V Tait (Newcastle), G P J Townsend (Northampton), K M Logan (Stirling County); C M Chalmers (Melrose), B W Redpath (Melrose); T J Smith (Watsonians), D G Ellis (Currie), M J Stewart (Northampton), G W Weir (Newcastle), A I Reed (Wasps), R I Wainwright (Watsonians & Army) *(capt)*, P Walton (Newcastle), I R Smith (Gloucester)
Scorers *Tries:* Tait, Townsend, Weir, Walton, Stanger *Conversions:* Shepherd (5) *Penalty Goal:* Shepherd
IRELAND: J E Staples (Harlequins) *(capt)*; D A Hickie (St Mary's Coll), M J Field (Malone), K P McQuilkin (Lansdowne), J C Bell (Northampton); D G Humphreys (London Irish), B T O'Meara (Cork Const); P Flavin (Blackrock Coll), R P Nesdale (Newcastle), P S Wallace (Saracens), P S Johns (Saracens), J W Davidson (London Irish), D S Corkery (Bristol), B M Cronin (Garryowen), W D McBride (Malone) *Replacements* C M P O'Shea (London Irish) for Staples (25 mins); P A Burke (Bristol) for McQuilkin (65 mins); S C McIvor (Garryowen) for O'Meara (67 mins)
Scorers *Try:* Hickie *Conversion:* Humphreys *Penalty Goal:* Humphreys
Referee G Simmonds (Wales)

1 March 1997, Twickenham
ENGLAND 20 (4PG 1DG 1T)   FRANCE 23 (2G 2PG 1DG)

England were 20-6 ahead after an hour, and playing so well. Their game was etched through with class, conviction and authority. There was simply no way back for France, who had laboured in the early stages. So much for the theory. In fact the enduring capacity of sport to defy logic once more came into play as France heaved back the boulder and rose from the dead. It was not that France were irresistible and forceful, more that England just rolled over meekly. In 475 internationals since 1871, they had never before lost a Test after holding a 14-point lead.

Moreover, this most unlikely of victories was France's first win at Twickenham for ten years and their highest score at the ground in 22. Where there had been doubt and hesitation, suddenly there was certainty and menace. Olivier Merle and his mates, who had been tetchy and ineffective, began to chisel out territory, and the French

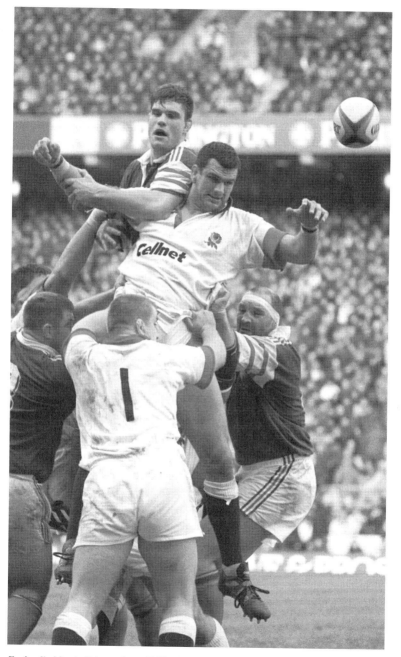

England's Martin Johnson beats Fabien Pelous in the line-out during the England-France encounter in the Five Nations Championship.

threequarters used it to best advantage, scoring two tries within eight minutes. Then, with five minutes left, Christophe Lamaison knocked over the penalty goal which sent French supporters into ecstasy. Lamaison collected 18 points – a full house of a try, conversions, penalties and a dropped goal – to pass Guy Laporte's French record of 17 points in the fixture, set in 1986.

England had begun so well. Finally they played the rugby they aspired to. The forwards gave them drive, the half-backs direction and variety. Rodber was a storming presence, so too his back-row lieutenants, Dallaglio and Hill. It was Dallaglio who scored the game's best try just before half-time, the blindside flanker striding majestically to the line from 35 metres. That took England to 14-6. Grayson's dropped goal and penalty within 11 minutes of the restart then extended the lead.

Then came the French *coup de grâce* as Gomarsall and Grayson lost their bearings. A neat Lamaison chip behind the English defence in the 61st minute caught Underwood on the hop, allowing Leflamand to nip in and score. Eight minutes later a sustained attack ended with Penaud setting up Lamaison who skipped over. The death knell was ringing loudly.

ENGLAND: T R G Stimpson (Newcastle); J M Sleightholme (Bath), W D C Carling (Harlequins), P R de Glanville (Bath) (*capt*), T Underwood (Newcastle); P J Grayson (Northampton), A C T Gomarsall (Wasps); G C Rowntree (Leicester), M P Regan (Bristol), J Leonard (Harlequins), M O Johnson (Leicester), S D Shaw (Bristol), L B N Dallaglio (Wasps), T A K Rodber (Northampton & Army), R A Hill (Saracens)
Scorers *Try:* Dallaglio   *Penalty Goals:* Grayson (4)   *Dropped Goal:* Grayson
FRANCE: J-L Sadourny (Colomiers); L Leflamand (Bourgoin), C Lamaison (Brive), S Glas (Bourgoin), D Venditti (Brive); A Penaud (Brive), P Carbonneau (Brive); C Califano (Toulouse), M Dal Maso (Agen), F Tournaire (Narbonne), O Merle (Montferrand), H Miorin (Toulouse), A Benazzi (Agen) (*capt*), F Pelous (Dax), O Magne (Dax) *Replacements* R Castel (Béziers) for Miorin (48 mins); M de Rougemont (Toulon) for Benazzi (65 mins)
Scorers *Tries:* Leflamand, Lamaison   *Conversions:* Lamaison (2)
Penalty Goals: Lamaison (2)   *Dropped Goal:* Lamaison
Referee J M Fleming (Scotland)

15 March 1997, Parc des Princes
FRANCE 47 (3G 6PG 1DG 1T)   SCOTLAND 20 (2G 2PG)

It was a day of emotion, nostalgia, beauty and style; party-time in Paris. The French were bent on signing off at the Parc des Princes, their home for 24 years, with a flourish; and they did. In their 50th Five Nations match played at the stadium, they rattled up their highest ever championship score to complete their fifth Grand Slam, the first time they have ever secured it at home. Christophe Lamaison equalled the Five Nations record for most points in a match – 24, a record he shares with Rob Andrew and Sebastien Viars.

As ever, bare statistics only tell a small part of the story. France had suffered badly from injuries. And yet, rather than burdening them, adversity lifted and inspired them. They made errors along the way but it all came together here, and quite gloriously too.

The French gave signs of their intent by running over a photographer as they roared out of the tunnel. Just seconds later Scotland had to figure how to stem a seemingly irresistible white-shirted tide, led by the imperious figure of Abdelatif Benazzi. They did well to keep France at bay in the opening stages. Referee Ed Morrison was lenient in not awarding a penalty try when Townsend pulled Benazzi back as he steamed on to a pass, but Benazzi righted the scales of justice in the 25th minute, blasting through Shepherd and over the try-line after Leflamand and Merle had made inroads. Shepherd at least got Scotland on the scoresheet with two penalties to leave them at 16-6 after half an hour. But it was one-way traffic. Leflamand slipped in at the corner in the 31st minute, set up by Sadourny's break and Magne's clever link play. Then Sadourny dropped a goal in the 39th minute.

There was then a brief Scottish revival with Tait bundling over for two tries within 15 minutes, the first on the stroke of half-time. Chalmers was flattened by a reckless tackle by Lamaison, an offence for which he was cited, but this was the only blot on a great day for the French. All the replacements were ushered on to enjoy the romp. Tournaire scored in the 68th minute before the *pièce de résistance* in the 74th minute, Magne rounding off a magnificent length-of-the-field movement. It was a champagne moment.

FRANCE: J-L Sadourny (Colomiers); L Leflamand (Bourgoin), C Lamaison (Brive), S Glas (Bourgoin), D Venditti (Brive); D Aucagne (Pau), G Accoceberry (Bègles-Bordeaux); D Casadei (Brive), M Dal Maso (Agen), F Tournaire (Narbonne), O Merle (Montferrand), H Miorin (Toulouse), A Benazzi (Agen) (*capt*), F Pelous (Dax), O Magne (Dax) *Replacements* R Castel (Béziers) for Miorin (55 mins); M de Rougemont (Toulon) for Dal Maso (73 mins); J-L Jordana (Toulouse) for Tournaire (75 mins); P Bondouy (Narbonne) for Venditti (75 mins); P Carbonneau (Brive) for Accoceberry (75 mins); U Mola (Dax) for Leflamand (75 mins)
Scorers *Tries:* Benazzi, Leflamand, Magne, Tournaire *Conversions:* Lamaison (3) *Penalty Goals:* Lamaison (6) *Dropped Goal:* Sadourny
SCOTLAND: R J S Shepherd (Melrose); A G Stanger (Hawick), A V Tait (Newcastle), G P J Townsend (Northampton), K M Logan (Stirling County); C M Chalmers (Melrose), B W Redpath (Melrose); T J Smith (Watsonians), D G Ellis (Currie), M J Stewart (Northampton), G W Weir (Newcastle), A I Reed (Wasps), R I Wainwright (Watsonians & Army) (*capt*), P Walton (Newcastle), I R Smith (Gloucester) *Replacements* D F Cronin (Wasps) for Walton (20 mins); D W Hodge (Watsonians) for Chalmers (54 mins); I C Glasgow (Heriot's FP) for Tait (74 mins)
Scorers *Tries:* Tait (2) *Conversions:* Shepherd (2) *Penalty Goal:* Shepherd (2)
Referee E F Morrison (England)

15 March 1997, Cardiff Arms Park
WALES 13 (1G 2PG)   ENGLAND 34 (4G 2PG)

On an afternoon dedicated to farewells it was the unscripted arrival of an old favourite which made the headlines. Jeremy Guscott upstaged everything: the last match at the stadium itself, and the last outings for Jonathan Davies, Rob Andrew and Will Carling.

Guscott came on for the injured Jon Sleightholme at half-time. At that stage of an uneven, fitful match England led by just 6–3. Guscott transformed the scoreboard and the mood. He brought colour and excitement to a drab canvas. First he made a beautiful contribution to Stimpson's try eight minutes after the interval, holding the defence with his swaying balanced run like a snake charmer toying with his pet. Then he did the same again for England's third try, fixing Thomas and then gliding past Williams before slipping the ball away to Hill from the midst of a massed tackle with the ease of a pickpocket filching a wallet away to his mates. Between these scores Underwood raced clear from 55 metres. England's fourth try came from a tap penalty near half-way, Healey passing to Catt who cut through gloriously before feeding de Glanville.

By this stage Wales were ravaged in body and spirit. They were without five front-line players, notably Gibbs, Ieuan Evans and Charvis, and lost Neil Jenkins within six minutes of the start with a fractured arm. Howley and Bateman were left trying valiantly to kick-start those around them. Davies was given one last trot when Arwel Thomas withdrew injured. It was rearguard action, the arch creator forced into the role of chief defender. Howley, with a twinkling run scored Wales's try in the dying seconds. It was no consolation.

WALES: N R Jenkins (Pontypridd); S D Hill (Cardiff), A G Bateman (Richmond), N G Davies (Llanelli), G Thomas (Bridgend); J Davies (Cardiff), R Howley (Cardiff); C D Loader (Swansea), J M Humphreys (Cardiff) *(capt)*, D Young (Cardiff), G O Llewellyn (Harlequins), M J Voyle (Llanelli), S M Williams (Neath), L S Quinnell (Richmond), K P Jones (Ebbw Vale) *Replacement* W T Proctor (Llanelli) for Jenkins (15 mins); S C John (Llanelli) for Loader (22 mins); D L M McIntosh (Pontypridd) for Jones (64 mins); J C Quinnell (Richmond) for Voyle (69 mins)
Scorers *Try:* Howley   *Conversion:* J Davies   *Penalty Goals:* J Davies (2)
ENGLAND: T R G Stimpson (Newcastle); J M Sleightholme (Bath), W D C Carling (Harlequins), P R de Glanville (Bath) *(capt)*, T Underwood (Newcastle); M J Catt (Bath), A S Healey (Leicester); G C Rowntree (Leicester), M P Regan (Bristol), J Leonard (Harlequins, M O Johnson (Leicester, S D Shaw (Bristol), B B Clarke (Richmond), T A K Rodber (Northampton & Army), R A Hill (Saracens) *Replacements* P B T Greening (Gloucester) for Regan (40 mins); J C Guscott (Bath) for Sleightholme (40 mins); C M A Sheasby (Wasps) for Clarke (69 mins); C R Andrew (Newcastle) for Catt (72 mins); D J Garforth (Leicester) for Rowntree (77 mins)
Scorers *Tries:* Stimpson, Underwood, Hill, de Glanville   *Conversions:* Catt (4) *Penalty Goals:* Catt (2).
Referee J Dumé (France)

ALL BLACKS REDRAW RUGBY MAP

THE TRI-NATIONS SERIES 1996

The inaugural Tri-Nations tournament was contrived, commercially-driven, highly-pressurised, lacking in tradition; yet brilliantly successful. The concept, in which the three sides play each other home and away, was derived from the negotiations with NewsCorp television executives prior to and during the 1995 World Cup. The £360 million, ten-year deal between the three southern hemisphere countries was eventually signed and announced on the eve of the World Cup final. If there were any doubts that it may have all been agreed in haste, that the detail was not clearly enough worked out and that the load on the players may prove to be too great, then they were all blown away by the sheer dynamism and quality of this first tournament, won so emphatically by New Zealand.

In fact so convincing and exhilarating was the play of the All Blacks that the rest of the world sat up and took notice. More than anything else the style, pace and imagination of their game revolutionised attitudes across the rugby map. The bonus point system devised for this competition (one bonus point for scoring four or more tries, one for team losing by fewer than or equal to seven points) also encouraged open play.

In recent years the southern hemisphere nations have considered the Five Nations to be a second-rate competition. The simple retort used to be that it was envy talking; that all these countries would give their right arm for a tournament which generated such interest and revenue. Now there can be no more talk even of jealousy. The southern hemisphere countries have their own little competition. And rather good it looks too.

FINAL TABLE

	P	W	D	L	F	A	Bonus	Pts
New Zealand	4	4	0	0	119	60	1	17
South Africa	4	1	0	3	70	84	2	6
Australia	4	1	0	3	71	116	2	6

(Four points are awarded for a win; two for a draw. One bonus point is awarded to a team scoring four or more tries in a match and one bonus point awarded to a team losing by less than or equal to seven points.)

6 July, Athletic Park, Wellington
NEW ZEALAND 43 (2G 3PG 4T)   AUSTRALIA 6 (2PG)

The conditions were atrocious; the rugby sublime. This will rank as one of the great Test match performances of all time. The rain lashed Wellington, turning the Athletic Park pitch into a greasy swamp. And yet the All Blacks produced some of the most controlled, skilful, technically accomplished rugby ever played. The display exposed the myth peddled in the northern hemisphere that it is impossible to play rugby in such conditions for what it is – an excuse for inadequacies.

New Zealand began at a gallop, barely making a mistake at all in the opening 20 minutes. They scored three tries in that period and led 15-3. Australia could but hang on for grim death. In the end New Zealand ran in six tries and posted their highest score and biggest winning margin ever against Australia, even though it was their first Wellington success against the Wallabies since 1978. This was also the biggest score Australia have conceded against anyone. Andrew Mehrtens reached 200 points in only his 12th Test to beat Grant Fox's world record.

NEW ZEALAND; C M Cullen (Manawatu); J W Wilson (Otago), F E Bunce (North Harbour), W K Little (North Harbour), J T Lomu (Counties); A P Mehrtens (Canterbury), J W Marshall (Canterbury); C W Dowd (Auckland), S B T Fitzpatrick (Auckland) (*capt*), O M Brown (Auckland), I D Jones (North Harbour), R M Brooke (Auckland), M N Jones (Auckland), Z V Brooke (Auckland), J A Kronfeld (Otago) *Replacements* N J Hewitt (Southland) for Fitzpatrick (74 mins); E J Rush (North Harbour) for Cullen (temp)
Scorers *Tries:* M Jones, Cullen, Marshall, Z Brooke, Wilson, Lomu *Conversions:* Mehrtens (2) *Penalty Goals:* Mehrtens (3)
AUSTRALIA: M Burke (NSW); B N Tune (Queensland), J W Roff (ACT), T J Horan (Queensland), D I Campese (NSW); S Bowen (NSW), S J Payne (NSW); R L L Harry (NSW), M A Foley (Queensland), D J Crowley (Queensland), G J Morgan (Queensland), J A Eales (Queensland) (*capt*), O Finegan (ACT), M C Brial (NSW), D J Wilson (Queensland)
Scorer *Penalty Goals:* Burke (2)
Referee E F Morrison (England)

13 July, Sydney Football Stadium
AUSTRALIA 21 (1G 3PG 1T)　SOUTH AFRICA 16 (1G 3PG)

No one fancied Australia after their mauling the week before, least of all their own countrymen. The Wallabies, who made four changes, took the criticism on the chin and gave the best possible reply in the best possible place – victory out on the field. It was the character of the side, exemplified in the unremitting tackling, which won the day here. No 8 Michael Brial, and full-back, Matthew Burke, got through a huge amount of work in defence. The Springboks were profligate in running penalties they should have kicked and even their stars, van der Westhuizen and Joubert, had poor games.

Australia's crucial try, scored by Horan, which gave them a 19-9 lead 25 minutes into the second half, came after an attempted counterattack by Joubert was halted. Roff's earlier try followed good work by Manu and Howard. Some respectability was brought to the scoreline by Hendriks's try, crafted by Joubert. The defeat ended the longest run of South African victories in Test history, 15 on the trot (including the World Cup in 1995), which began against Argentina in 1994.

AUSTRALIA: M Burke (NSW); D I Campese (NSW), J W Roff (ACT), T J Horan (Queensland), B N Tune (Queensland); P W Howard (ACT), G M Gregan (ACT); D J Crowley (Queensland), M A Foley (Queensland), A Heath (NSW), G J Morgan (Queensland), J A Eales (Queensland) (*capt*), D T Manu (NSW), M C Brial (NSW), D J Wilson (Queensland) *Replacements* R L L Harry (NSW) for Crowley (temp); O Finegan (ACT) for Manu (temp)
Scorers *Tries:* Roff, Horan   *Conversion:* Burke   *Penalty Goals:* Burke (3)
SOUTH AFRICA: A J Joubert (Natal); J T Small (Natal), J C Mulder (Transvaal), B Venter (Free State), P Hendriks (Transvaal); H W Honiball (Natal), J H van der Westhuizen (Northern Transvaal); J P du Randt (Free State), J Allan (Natal), M H Hurter (Northern Transvaal), J Ackermann (Northern Transvaal), M G Andrews (Natal), J F Pienaar (Transvaal) (*capt*), G H Teichmann (Natal), R J Kruger (Northern Transvaal) *Replacements* J P Roux (Transvaal) for van der Westhuizen (79 mins); A E Drotské (Free State) for Pienaar (82 mins)
Scorers *Try:* Hendriks   *Conversion:* Honiball   *Penalty Goals:* Honiball (2), Joubert
Referee A J Spreadbury (England)

20 July, Lancaster Park, Christchurch
NEW ZEALAND 15 (5PG)   SOUTH AFRICA 11 (2PG 1T)

The game was a fall from grace after the high standard of the opening two encounters. Only Mehrtens's fifth successful penalty kick of the afternoon in the last minute pulled the All Blacks clear at the end of a fractious contest. Referee, Ray Megson, had a difficult afternoon. Many felt that Springbok hooker, John Allan, was lucky to stay on the field after being penalised for head-butting in the first scrum. It was not all the referee's fault, of course. Both sides were intent on spoiling. The All Blacks struggled to launch their running game because their front five were under such pressure. Once again they failed to score a try against South Africa, who have now gone 320 minutes since they last conceded a try against the All Blacks. Joubert's try was a rare moment of beauty. It came after a neat switch by Stransky and a powerful charge by second-row, Andrews.

NEW ZEALAND: C M Cullen (Manawatu); J W Wilson (Otago), F E Bunce (North Harbour), W K Little (North Harbour), J T Lomu (Counties); A P Mehrtens (Canterbury), J W Marshall (Canterbury); C W Dowd (Auckland), S B T Fitzpatrick (Auckland) (*capt*), O M Brown (Auckland), I D Jones (North Harbour), R M Brooke (Auckland), M N Jones (Auckland), Z V Brooke (Auckland), J A Kronfeld (Otago) *Replacement* E J Rush (North Harbour) for Wilson (73 mins)
Scorer *Penalty Goals:* Mehrtens (5)
SOUTH AFRICA: A J Joubert (Natal); J T Small (Natal), J C Mulder (Transvaal), B Venter (Free State), P Hendriks (Transvaal); J T Stransky (Western Province), J P Roux (Transvaal); J P du Randt (Free State), J Allan (Natal),

M H Hurter (Northern Transvaal), J Ackermann (Northern Transvaal)
M G Andrews (Natal), J F Pienaar (Transvaal) (*capt*), G H Teichmann (Natal),
R J Kruger (Northern Transvaal)
Replacement J Swart (Western Province) for Joubert (53 mins)
Scorers *Try:* Joubert   *Penalty Goals:* Stransky (2)
Referee R J Megson (Scotland)

27 July, Suncorp Stadium, Brisbane
AUSTRALIA 25 (5PG 2T)   NEW ZEALAND 32 (2G 6PG)

There will be many Australians wondering for ever more just how
they managed to lose this Test. Australia seemed as if they would
gain ample revenge for their Wellington defeat as they dominated
the first hour of this match, which doubled as a Bledisloe Cup Test.
Instead the All Blacks rattled up 23 points in the final 20 minutes to
steal an unlikely victory and, in so doing, win the Tri-Nations
series.

It was a stormy encounter. Wallaby No 8 Michael Brial was
fortunate not to be dismissed after raining down blows on Frank
Bunce. Andrew Mehrtens had a good afternoon with the boot for
the All Blacks, missing only one attempt at goal, landing six
penalties and a conversion in all. Gregan scored Australia's first try
in the 12th minute before full-back, Matt Burke, crowned a
wonderful display with a quite staggering try just before half-time.
He beat five defenders as he weaved his way over the line from 80
metres.

Australia led 22-9 going into the final quarter, but gradually New
Zealand edged their way back. With only 64 seconds left the scores
stood at 25-25. Then Christian Cullen ran off Mehrtens, was
checked, but got the ball away to Bunce who picked up and scored.
Burke finished with 20 points, the highest individual contribution
by a Wallaby in a Test against New Zealand. It was no consolation
at all.

AUSTRALIA: M Burke (NSW); B N Tune (Queensland), J W Roff (ACT),
R C Tombs (NSW), D I Campese (NSW); P W Howard (ACT), G M Gregan
(ACT); R L L Harry (NSW), M A Foley (Queensland), A Heath (NSW),
G J Morgan (Queensland), J A Eales (Queensland) (*capt*), D T Manu (NSW),
M C Brial (NSW), D J Wilson (Queensland) *Replacement* T B Gavin (NSW) for
Morgan (23 mins)
Scorers *Tries:* Gregan, Burke   *Penalty Goals:* Burke (5)
NEW ZEALAND: C M Cullen (Manawatu); J W Wilson (Otago), F E Bunce
(North Harbour), W K Little (North Harbour), J T Lomu (Counties);
A P Mehrtens (Canterbury), J W Marshall (Canterbury); C W Dowd (Auckland),
S B T Fitzpatrick (Auckland) (*capt*), O M Brown (Auckland), I D Jones (North
Harbour), R M Brooke (Auckland), M N Jones (Auckland), Z V Brooke
(Auckland), J A Kronfeld (Otago)
Scorers *Tries:* Marshall, Bunce   *Conversions:* Mehrtens (2)
Penalty Goals: Mehrtens (6)
Referee J M Fleming (Scotland)

3 August, Free State Stadium, Bloemfontein
SOUTH AFRICA 25 (1G 6PG) AUSTRALIA 19 (1G 4PG)

There was only one man South Africa had to thank for this victory, fly-half Joel Stransky who scored all their points to set a new record for the most individual points by a player in a South Africa-Australia match. It was reminiscent of his performance in the opening match of the 1995 World Cup when he set the previous record with 22 points.

Victory took the Springbok run of home victories to 13. After kicking two early penalties Stransky, who had been under pressure for his place, then scored his sixth try in 18 internationals midway through the first half. Wing Justin Swart made the initial dent and Stransky was on hand to finish it off. He then converted from the touchline. Two further penalties gave his side a commanding 16-3 lead at the interval.

Wallaby skipper John Eales took over the goal-kicking duties from the injured Matt Burke and landed four goals from four attempts. Australia trailed by 16 points with 14 minutes remaining but came right back into it with a try by Ben Tune.

SOUTH AFRICA: J T Small (Natal); J Swart (Western Province), J C Mulder (Transvaal), B Venter (Free State), P Hendriks (Transvaal); J T Stransky (Western Province), J P Roux (Transvaal); J P du Randt (Free State), J Allan (Natal), I S Swart (Transvaal), J Ackermann (Northern Transvaal), M G Andrews (Natal), J F Pienaar (Transvaal) *(capt)*, G H Teichmann (Natal), R J Kruger (Northern Transvaal) *Replacements* J J Strydom (Transvaal) for Ackermann (36 mins); D F Theron (Griqualand West) for Swart (40 mins); J H van der Westhuizen (Northern Transvaal) for Roux (59 mins)
Scorers *Try:* Stransky *Conversion:* Stransky *Penalty Goals:* Stransky (6)
AUSTRALIA: M Burke (NSW); D I Campese (NSW), D J Herbert (Queensland), P W Howard (ACT), B N Tune (Queensland); S Bowen (NSW), G M Gregan (ACT); D J Crowley (Queensland), M A Foley (Queensland), A Heath (NSW), J Welborn (NSW), J A Eales (Queensland) *(capt)*, M C Brial (NSW), T B Gavin (NSW) D J Wilson (Queensland) *Replacement* J W Roff (ACT) for Burke (40 mins)
Scorers *Try:* Tune *Conversion:* Eales *Penalty Goals:* Burke, Eales (3)
Referee B W Stirling (Ireland)

10 August, Newlands, Cape Town
SOUTH AFRICA 18 (1G 2PG 1T) NEW ZEALAND 29 (2G 5PG)

The All Blacks are making a habit of late surges, pulling this game out of the fire by scoring 23 points in the final 22 minutes. They made up a 12-point deficit and set a new points record in the process for games between these two great rivals. (The record was subsequently bettered in the following Test series.) Andrew Mehrtens set a new All Black points total (19) for a match between the two countries.

It was a bruising match. Francois Pienaar and Os du Randt were both stretchered off. After an early exchange of penalties, Springbok centre Japie Mulder set up the opening try with a scything run. After the ball was recycled Mulder was able to run in unopposed. Stransky converted and then added another penalty. Atherton then took a line-out for du Randt to burrow through and score.

The All Blacks clawed their way back and only formidable South African defence kept them at bay. Mehrtens knocked over the penalties to put his side to within six points with 10 minutes left. Then Cullen opened the defence for Osborne to score before Craig Dowd rounded off a forward drive with a touchdown.

SOUTH AFRICA: J T Small (Natal); P Hendriks (Transvaal), J C Mulder (Transvaal), H P le Roux (Transvaal), J Swart (Western Province); J T Stransky (Western Province), J H van der Westhuizen (Northern Transvaal); J P du Randt (Free State), J Allan (Natal), M H Hurter (Northern Transvaal), S Atherton (Natal), M G Andrews (Natal), J F Pienaar (Transvaal) *(capt)*, G H Teichmann (Natal), R J Kruger (Northern Transvaal) *Replacements* J J Strydom (Transvaal) for Pienaar (53 mins); D F Theron (Griqualand West) for du Randt (78 mins)
Scorers *Tries:* Mulder, du Randt *Conversion:* Stransky *Penalty Goals:* Stransky (2)
NEW ZEALAND: C M Cullen (Manawatu); J W Wilson (Otago), F E Bunce (North Harbour), W K Little (North Harbour), G M Osborne (North Harbour); A P Mehrtens (Canterbury), J W Marshall (Canterbury); C W Dowd (Auckland), S B T Fitzpatrick (Auckland) *(capt)*, O M Brown (Auckland), I D Jones (North Harbour), R M Brooke (Auckland), M N Jones (Auckland), Z V Brooke (Auckland), J A Kronfeld (Otago) *Replacements* A I Ieremia (Wellington) for Little (41 mins); A F Blowers (Auckland) for Kronfeld (65 mins)
Scorers *Tries:* Osborne, Dowd *Conversions:* Mehrtens (2)
Penalty Goals: Mehrtens (5)
Referee D T M McHugh (Ireland)

New Zealand's Justin Marshall makes a break in the South Africa v New Zealand Tri-Nations match, Newlands, Cape Town.

NEW PUMAS SWEEP CLEAN

THE PAN-AM SERIES 1996

Rugby supremacy in the American continents rests with Argentina, winners of the Pan-American Tournament staged in Ontario, Canada, in mid-September 1996. Without experienced campaigners Diego Cuesta Silva, Martin Teran, Sebastian Salvat and front-rowers Federico Mendez and Patricio Noriega, the Argentinian management had to blood more than a dozen new caps in its bid to retain the Pan-Am title won in Buenos Aires 18 months earlier. Nevertheless the new-look Pumas adapted quickly to the rigours of international rugby and won all three of their matches.

The United States Eagles joined the competition for the first time. Like the Pumas and Canadians, they have suffered the consequences of the game's new professional era. Only a handful of the seven Americans and ten Canadians who had signed professional contracts overseas were able to make the tournament. The Eagles captain, Dan Lyle of Bath, managed to join his squad, but a knee injury prevented him from taking part in the matches.

The Uruguayans, very much the outsiders, nevertheless made a positive contribution to the tournament. Easily the smallest playing nation among the participants, they modelled their tactics on those of their Argentinian neighbours. The Teros possessed a sturdy front row – their experienced prop Marcelo Calandra is closing on 30 caps – and mauled as effectively as the much-vaunted packs they met in the competition.

The Pan-Am tournament ran on the double-header round-robin system and tournament favourites Canada and Argentina were tested in the first round. The United States led Argentina 20-19 and were level at 26-26 until Gonzalo Quesada popped over a late penalty to give the Pumas a narrow win. On the same afternoon, Uruguay opened the scoring against Canada and unsettled their hosts with a tremendous second-half rally. Canada led by only 21-18 before a Bob Ross penalty stretched their winning lead to six points. 'Full marks to them, they knew what to do,' commented Canada's relieved coach, Pat Parfrey, of Uruguay at the end of the game.

As expected, Canada and Argentina won their midweek matches, leaving the tournament's organisers with the battle of the continents, or South v North, for the Brahma Cup on the final Saturday of the competition. Argentina started strongly and rattled up a comfortable 18-9, half-time lead. Then the Canadians, cheered on by 4,500 partisan spectators, finally began to play their best rugby of the week. The Canuck forwards started to clear all before them, paving the way for a recovery which tied the scores at 21-21 as play entered the final quarter.

Alas for Canada, their energy had been completely spent during their comeback. The young Pumas were quick to exploit the host's decline and thereafter ran the ball wide at every opportunity. Subsequent tries by Octavio Bartolucci (two) and Rolando Martin took Argentina to their highest-ever score against Canada and past the 35 points scored by Hugo Porta's side in Buenos Aires in 1981. Moreover, it was Argentina's first away win against the Canadians, and gave immense encouragement to a Puma squad facing upcoming Tests against South Africa and England.

ARGENTINA Captain L Arbizu **Referee** S Borsani

Full-backs: S E Mesón (San Isidro Club), D Giannantonio (Tala Club, Córdoba) *Threequarters:* F Soler (Tala Club, Córdoba), J Légora (Tablada Club), T Solari (Hindú Club), O Bartolucci (Atlético, Rosario), E Simone (Liceo Naval), J Orengo (Atlético, Rosario) *Half-backs:* G Quesada (Hindú Club), L Arbizu (Belgrano Athletic), L Lobrauco (Atlético, Rosario), G F Camardón (Alumni), C O Barrea (Córdoba Athletic) *Forwards:* R D Grau (Liceode Mendoza), O Hasan Jalil (Natación y Gimnasia), G Rivero (Urú Curé), M Scelzo (Banco Hipotecario), F Werner (Club Atlético San Isidro), M Ledesma (Curupaytí), M Palou (Jockey Club, Rosario), R N Pérez (Duendes), J E Simes (Tala Club, Córdoba), P L Sporleder (Curupaytí), R Travaglini (Club Atlético San Isidro), R A Martin (San Isidro Club), C I Fernandez Lobbe (Liceo Naval), P J Camerlinckx (Regatas de Bella Vista)

CANADA Captain A J Charron **Referee** I Hyde Lay

Full-backs: D S Stewart (U of British Columbia OB), J Haley (U of British Columbia) *Threequarters:* W Stanley (U of British Columbia), C Smith (Meralomas), D Nichols (Wanderers, Ontario), S T Lytton (Meralomas), S D Gray (Kats) *Half-backs:* S Bryan (Balmy Beach), R P Ross (James Bay), J Penaluna (U of Victoria), M O'Regan (U of Victoria), R Card (Oak Bay Castaways) *Forwards:* B Mosychuk (Abbotsford), D W Penney (Swilers & Oxford U), R G A Snow (Dogs & Newport), K Wirachowski (Velox Valhallians), M E Cardinal (James Bay), S Hendry (Balmy Beach), M Felix (Cowichan), T Healy (James Bay), B McCarthy (Ajax Wanderers), J R Hutchinson (U of British Columbia OB), C D Michaluk (Vancouver Rowing Club), C Meyers (Cole Harbour), A J Charron (Ottawa Irish), M Schmid (Abbotsford)

UNITED STATES Captain D Lyle **Referee** J MacLemore

Full-backs: M Sika (Rhinos) *Threequarters:* R Lockrem (Denver Barbarians), J Grobler (Kansas City Blues), V Anitoni (Yankees), M Dabuvaya (OMBAC), E Schram (OMBAC), M Scharrenberg (Golden Gate) *Half-backs:* M Alexander (Denver Barbarians), K Schuman (Pennsylvania State U), K Dalzell (U of California), A Bachelet (Old Blues) *Forwards:* T Kluempers (Kansas City Blues), R Lehner (Old Blues), L Gross (Cincinnati Wolfhounds & Harlequins), W Leversee (OMBAC), A Parker (Gentlemen of Aspen), R Randell (Old Blues), D Hodges (OMBAC), D Lyle (OMBAC & Bath), J Wilkerson (Belmont 〔 〕re),

R Tardits (Life Coll, Marietta), P Vogl (Chicago Lions), J Walker (Gentlemen of Aspen), R Lumkong (OMBAC)

URUGUAY Captain D Ormaechea **Referee** G Lopez

Full-backs; D Aguirre (Carrasco Polo) *Threequarters:* M Ferrés (Carrasco Polo), P Costabile (Carrasco Polo), A Cardozo (OB), P Vecino (Carrasco Polo), F Paullier (Old Christians), M Reyes (OB), A Luongo (Carrasco Polo) *Half-backs:* S Silva (OB), M Mendaro (Carrasco Polo), F Sciarra (Carrasco Polo) *Forwards:* M Calandra (Montevideo CC), R Sánchez (Carrasco Polo), G Storace (Old Christians), J Machado (Carrasco Polo), P Lemoine (Montevideo CC), A Suárez (Montevideo CC), P Acerenza (Carrasco Polo), J C Bado (OB), A P de Leon (Carrasco Polo), M Lame (Carrasco Polo), A Dabo (Carrasco Polo), M Panizza (Carrasco Polo), M Mosca (Los Cuervos), D Ormaechea (Carrasco Polo)

MATCH 1 14 September, Twin Elms Rugby Park, Nepean

ARGENTINA 29 (1G 4PG 2T) **UNITED STATES 26** (2G 4PG)
ARGENTINA: Mesón; Camardón, Simone, Arbizu (*capt*), Bartolucci; Quesada, Lobrauco; Werner, Grau, Scelzo, Palou, Pérez, Travaglini, Camerlinckx, Fernández Lobbe *Replacements* Légora for Camardón; Simes for Fernández Lobbe; Rivero for Scelzo
Scorers *Tries:* Travaglini, Bartolucci, Simone *Conversion:* Mesón
Penalty Goals: Mesón (2), Quesada (2)
UNITED STATES: Sika; Anitoni, Grobler, Scharrenberg, Schram; Alexander, Bachelet; Lippert (*capt*), Billups, Lehner, Leversee, Parker, Randell, Lumkong, Tardits *Replacement* Walker for Randell
Scorers *Tries:* Lumkong, Bachelet *Conversions:* Alexander (2)
Penalty Goals: Alexander (4)
Referee I Hyde Lay (Canada) *replaced by* G Lopez (Uruguay)

MATCH 2 14 September, Twin Elms Rugby Park, Nepean

CANADA 24 (1G 4PG 1T) **URUGUAY 18** (1G 1PG 1DG 1T)
CANADA: Haley; Smith, Stewart, Bryan, Nichols; Ross, Card; Wirachowski, Hendry, Mosychuk, Healy, Felix, Charron (*capt*), Schmid, Hutchinson *Replacement* Penaluna for Stewart
Scorers *Tries:* Wirachowski, Penaluna *Conversion:* Ross *Penalty Goals:* Ross (4)
URUGUAY: Aguirre; Ferrés, Luongo, Paullier, Costabile; Mendaro, Sciarra; Calandra, Suárez, Lemoine, Acerenza, Lame, Panizza, Ormaechea (*capt*), de Leon *Replacements* Machado for Calandra; Bado for Acerenza; Dabo for Panizza; Silva for Mendaro
Scorers *Tries:* Calandra (2) *Conversion:* Aguirre *Penalty Goal:* Aguirre
Dropped Goal: Silva
Referee S Borsani (Argentina)

MATCH 3 18 September, Mohawk Sports Park, Hamilton

CANADA 23 (2G 3PG) **UNITED STATES 18** (6PG)
CANADA: Stewart; Smith, Gray, Bryan, Lytton; Ross, Card; Wirachowski, Hendry, Penney, Healy, Felix, Charron (*capt*), Schmid, Hutchinson *Replacement* McCarthy for Healy
Scorers *Tries:* Smith (2) *Conversions:* Ross (2) *Penalty Goals:* Ross (3)

UNITED STATES: Sika; Anitoni, Grobler, Scharrenberg, Lockrem; Alexander, Bachelet; Lippert (*capt*), Billups, Lehner, Gross, Parker, Randell, Lumkong, Wilkerson
Scorers *Penalty Goals:* Alexander (6)
Referee G Lopez (Uruguay)

MATCH 4 18 September, Mohawk Sports Park, Hamilton

ARGENTINA 54 (7G 1T) **URUGUAY 20** (2G 2PG)
ARGENTINA: Giannantonio; Légora, Orengo, Arbizu (*capt*), Solari; Quesada, Barrea; Grau, Ledesma, Hasan Jalil, Palou, Sporleder, Martin, Camerlinckx, Pérez *Replacements* Camardón for Arbizu; Travaglini for Camerlinckx; Rivero for Grau
Scorers *Tries:* Giannantonio (2), Martin, Hasan Jalil, Camardón, Orengo, Barrea, Quesada *Conversions:* Quesada (7)
URUGUAY: Aguirre; Ferrés, Vecino, Paullier, Cardozo; Silva, Sciarra; Sánchez, Suárez, Storace, Acerenza, Bado, Panizza, Ormaechea (*capt*), Mosca *Replacements* Luongo for Sciarra; Lemoine for Storace; Reyes for Panizza
Scorers *Tries:* Mosca, Ormaechea *Conversions:* Silva (2) *Penalty Goals:* Silva, Sciarra
Referee J McLemore (United States)

MATCH 5 21 September, Fletcher's Field, Markham, Toronto

UNITED STATES 27 (1G 5PG 1T) **URUGUAY 13** (1PG 2T)
UNITED STATES: Sika; Anitoni, Grobler, Scharrenberg, Lockrem; Alexander, Dalzell; Lippert (*capt*), Billups, Rissone, Gross, Parker, Walker, Lumkong, Wilkerson *Replacement* Hodges for Lumkong
Scorers *Tries* Anitoni, Walker *Conversion:* Alexander *Penalty Goals:* Alexander (5)
URUGUAY: Aguirre; Ferrés, Vecino, Luongo, Costabile; Mendaro, Sciarra; Calandra, Suárez, Lemoine, Acerenza, Bado, Panizza, Ormaechea (*capt*), Lame *Replacements* Reyes for Ferrés; Machado for Suárez
Scorers *Tries:* Calandra, Mendaro *Penalty Goal:* Sciarra
Referee I Hyde Lay (Canada)

MATCH 6 21 September, Fletcher's field, Markham, Toronto

CANADA 21 (1G 3PG 1T) **ARGENTINA 41** (2G 4PG 3T)
CANADA: Stewart; Smith, Gray, Bryan, Lytton; Ross, Card; Wirachowski, Hendry, Penney, Healy, McCarthy, Charron (*capt*), Schmid, Hutchinson
Scorers *Tries:* Wirachowski, Hendry *Conversion:* Ross *Penalty Goals:* Ross (3)
ARGENTINA: Mesón; Solari, Camardón, Arbizu (*capt*), Bartolucci; Quesada, Barrea; Grau, Ledesma, Hasan Jalil, Simes, Sporleder, Martin, Camerlinckx, Pérez *Replacement* Travaglini for Simes
Scorers *Tries:* Bartolucci (2), Solari (2), Martin *Conversions:* Quesada (2) *Penalty Goals:* Quesada (4)
Referee J McLemore (United States)

Final Table

	P	W	D	L	F	A	Pts
Argentina	3	3	0	0	124	67	12
Canada	3	2	0	1	68	77	8
United States	3	1	0	2	71	65	6
Uruguay	3	0	0	3	51	105	1

Four points awarded for a win, two for a draw and one for losing by 7 points or less

WORLD CUP SEVENS

21-23 March 1997, Hong Kong
Final: Fiji 24 (2G 2T)   **South Africa 21** (3G)

The rest of the world may ponder and fiddle, unsure of the role that
sevens has to play in modern professional rugby. But in one
country, and for one man in particular, there is no doubt at all. For
Fiji, and for their captain, Waisale Serevi, there is only one version
of rugby that counts and there is only one country in the world in
which it is pre-eminent. The romantics wanted to see Fiji ruling
their sevens kingdom once again. For once the romantics got their
way. 'The last time we won the Hong Kong Sevens there was a
national holiday,' said an emotional Serevi. 'Maybe this time there
will be at least two national holidays. We were stronger physically,
mentally and spiritually than anyone else.' And so they were. The
Springboks mounted a stirring campaign to become world champions of both games. They had brought a mix of experienced
internationals, led by Joost van der Westhuizen, and relative newcomers such as Stephen Brink. South Africa were eager, committed
and accomplished. They demolished the All Blacks, 31-7, in the
semi-final and raced to a 14-0 lead in the final itself, knocking Fiji
out of their stride with their relentless pressure defence and
swooping opportunist attack. Andre Venter, the Free State flanker
who had had such an outstanding winter at XVs, showed that he
was a dab hand at the shorter game in scoring both tries.

Fiji though had been this way before. They know that tries can be
scored in a trice in sevens. Sure enough, guided by the masterful,
artful and inventive touch of Serevi, they mounted their charge.
Marika Vunibaka and Luke Erenavula levelled the scores before
Lemeki Koroi turned the stiletto with two tries in two minutes.
Brink crowned a fine tournament with a consolation try for the
Springboks, his ninth of the competition.

Fiji were worthy champions. They won their seven matches 49-5
on tries, scoring 323 points in the process: Serevi garnering 117 of
them. Their superiority was overwhelming. Vunibaka, a giant of a
man, was their new star. He is unemployed and earns just £10 a day
expenses from the Fijian Rugby Union. Vunibaka finished as the top
try scorer in the tournament with 12 tries, including four in four
minutes against Western Samoa in the semi-final. It was the intent
and spirit of the Fijians which carried them so far. Their desire to
show themselves the undisputed masters was all too evident. They
even bared their souls to the capacity 45,000 crowds which once
more turned this event into the world's biggest rugby party. Across
their shirts they inscribed a biblical message which read: 'Phil 4; 13.'

A reference to the Epistle to the Philippians, chapter 4, verse 13. 'I can do everything through Him who gives me strength.'

Serevi, who guarded his jersey at the whistle as the Springboks sought to exchange them said: 'I wrote the message on the shirts as a constant reminder for the whole team.'

Fiji had been untroubled on their route through to the final, a more extended path than normal as the organisers stretched the event to three days to satisfy the commercial demands of sponsors and television. The format did not meet with universal approval. Not only did it sap the players' energy; it also meant that several teams finished up playing the same opposition on Day Two after the initial groups had been redrawn. England, for example, played Canada on both days on their way to qualifying for Sunday's quarter-finals. The seeding was determined according to who scored the most points in their group, which, as several sides won both opening games, meant that the secondary criteria of most tries scored was invoked.

England, winners of the inaugural World Cup at Murrayfield four years before, made a disappointing defence of their title. Although they won their four pool matches (Zimbabwe, Canada [twice] and Cook Islands) they lacked real authority. Captain Lawrence Dallaglio had pulled out on the eve of departure suffering from the virus which caused him to miss the Wales-England international in Cardiff. He was replaced by Saracens openside, Richard Hill. The England squad contained five of those who had won at Murrayfield (Rodber, Sheasby, Scully, Adebayo and Beal) and were managed by the 1993 captain, Andrew Harriman. Healey, Catt, Sleightholme and Back made up the rest of the squad.

England's lack of preparation showed against Western Samoa who went through to the semi-finals, 21-5. England captain, Tim Rodber, was angered by his side's showing. 'I'm furious,' he said. 'We simply did not perform and you would have to ask why. Out of those involved there were a few who didn't fire. There's nowhere to hide. That was a game we should have won.'

Wales almost got the better of the Samoans on the first day, a try in the last five seconds robbing them of victory. However, they could only draw 12-12 with Namibia as a result of which they were consigned to a second day grouping with Fiji, who beat them 35-0. Wales then lost 26-12 to Tonga in the Plate quarter-final.

Scotland had a bright opening day sharing a 19-19 draw with Australia. James Craig, son of former Celtic footballer Jim, scored two tries as Scotland opened up a 19-5 lead. It took David Campese's appearance from the bench to rescue the Wallaby cause. Scotland tailed away somewhat on the second day, losing 31-19 to Australia. Although they made it through to the semi-final of the Plate, beating Romania 43-19 in the quarter-final, they were then

Waisale Serevi (Fiji) is tackled by Joost van der Westhuizen (South Africa) in the final of the World Cup Sevens in Hong Kong.

taken apart 43-7 by the hosts, the multi-national Hong Kong side, in the semi-finals. Scottish coach Andrew Kerr was not amused by the cosmopolitan make-up of the opposition. 'It may be acceptable in a Mickey Mouse tournament, but not a World Cup,' he said.

Ireland fared the worst of the home countries. They lost both opening matches, 31-22 to Argentina and 38-5 to South Africa. The second day was just as miserable with defeats by South Africa again, 34-7, and Hong Kong, 26-5. In the Bowl Ireland beat Portugal 33-5 in the quarter-final, but slipped to a 24-22 semi-final defeat by Japan.

Tournament organisers insisted that the annual Hong Kong Sevens would proceed even though the colony was to be handed over to China and the two long-standing sponsors had withdrawn.

RESULTS

Day One
Poor A: England 33, Canada 12; Zimbabwe 42, Canada 7; England 26, Zimbabwe 7 **Pool B:** Australia 19, Scotland 19; Romania 14, Scotland 26; Australia 38, Romania 7 **Pool C:** New Zealand 47, Japan 14; Tonga 35, Japan 7; New Zealand 21, Tonga 7 **Pool D:** Fiji 59, Portugal 0; Hong Kong 33, Portugal 12; Fiji 45, Hong Kong 0 **Pool E:** France 35, USA 5; S Korea 7, USA 33; France 38, S Korea 5 **Pool F:** Spain 26, Morocco 5; Cook Islands 31, Morocco 17; Spain 31, Cook Islands 12 **Pool G:** S Africa 38, Ireland 5; Ireland 22, Argentina 31; S Africa 45, Argentina 7 **Pool H:** W Samoa 48, Namibia 5; Wales 12, Namibia 12; Wales 24, W Samoa 26

Day Two
Pool A: Fiji 35, Wales 0; Wales 40, Namibia 5; Fiji 66, Namibia 0 **Pool B:** S Africa 29, Hong Kong 6; Hong Kong 26, Ireland 5; S Africa 34, Ireland 7 **Pool C:** W Samoa 28, Argentina 12; Argentina 33, Morocco 7; W Samoa 42, Morocco 0 **Pool D:** France 40, USA 0; Romania 17, USA 12; France 26, Romania 0 **Pool E:** New Zealand 31, Tonga 5; Tonga 35, Japan 26; New Zealand 47, Japan 0 **Pool F:** England 29, Cook Islands 10; Cook Islands 5, Canada 0; England 30 Canada 7 **Pool G:** Spain 19, Zimbabwe 12; S Korea 21, Zimbabwe 10; Spain 12, S Korea 12 **Pool H:** Australia 31, Scotland 19; Scotland 28, Portugal 7; Australia 26, Portugal 7

Bowl
Quarter-finals: Ireland 33, Portugal 5; Japan 24, Namibia 22; USA 24, Canada 21; Zimbabwe 12, Morocco 19 **Semi-finals:** Ireland 22, Japan 24; USA 24, Morocco 0 **Final:** Japan 28, USA 40

Plate
Quarter-finals: Spain 0, Cook Islands 36; Wales 12, Tonga 26; Argentina 5, Hong Kong 26; Scotland 43, Romania 19 **Semi-finals:** Scotland 7, Hong Kong 43; Cook Islands 10, Tonga 43 **Final:** Hong Kong 19, Tonga 40

Melrose Cup
Quarter-finals: Fiji 56, S Korea 0; England 5, Western Samoa 21; South Africa 19, France 14; New Zealand 38, Australia 12 **Semi-finals:** Fiji 38, Western Samoa 14; South Africa 31, New Zealand 7

Final
Fiji 24 (2G 2T)   **South Africa 21** (3G)
Fiji: M Vunibaka, L Erenavula, M Bari, W Serevi; L Koroi, A Naituyaga, J Tuikabe
Scorers *Tries:* Koroi (2), Erenavula, Vunibaka *Conversions:* Serevi (2)
South Africa: J Olivier, S Brink, A Snyman, J van der Westhuizen; A Venter, P Rossouw, B Skinstad
Scorers *Tries:* Venter (2), Brink *Conversions:* Brink (3)
Referee S Lander (England)

OTHER INTERNATIONAL MATCHES 1996-97

2 July 1996, Loftus Versfeld, Pretoria
SOUTH AFRICA 43 (3G 4PG 2T) FIJI 18 (1G 2PG 1T)

SOUTH AFRICA: A J Joubert (Natal); J T Small (Natal), J C Mulder (Transvaal), H P le Roux (Transvaal), J Swart (Western Province); H W Honiball (Natal), J H van der Westhuizen (Northern Transvaal); J P du Randt (Free State), J Allan (Natal), M H Hurter (Northern Transvaal), M G Andrews (Natal), J N Ackermann (Northern Transvaal), J F Pienaar (Transvaal) *(capt)*, G H Teichmann (Natal), R J Kruger (Northern Transvaal)
Replacements D van Schalkwyk (Western Province) for Joubert (50 mins); J T Stransky (Western Province) for le Roux (78 mins)
Scorers *Tries:* Joubert, Mulder, Andrews, van Schalkwyk, pen try
Conversions: Honiball (2), Joubert *Penalty Goals:* Honiball (2), Joubert (2)
FIJI: F Rayasi (King Country); A Tuilevu (Nadroga), L Little (North Harbour), S Sorovaki (Wellington), W Serevi (Sanyo, Japan); N Little (Waikato), J Raulini (Queensland); J Veitayaki (King Country) *(capt)*, G Smith (Waikato), E Naituivau (Queensland), E Katalau(Poverty Bay), M Black, T Tamanivalu (Queensland), D Rouse (Nadi), I Tawake (Nadroga) *Replacement* A Uluinayau (Auckland) for L Little (21 mins)
Scorers *Tries:* Raulini, Veitayaki *Conversion:* N Little *Penalty Goals:* N Little (2)
Referee J Meuwesen (Namibia)

24 August 1996, Cardiff Arms Park
WALES 31 (3G 2T) BARBARIANS 10 (2T)

WALES: W T Proctor (Llanelli); I C Evans (Llanelli), L B Davies (Cardiff), N G Davies (Llanelli), G Thomas (Bridgend); N R Jenkins (Pontypridd), R Howley (Cardiff); C D Loader (Swansea), J M Humphreys (Cardiff) *(capt)*, J D Davies (Neath), G O Llewellyn (Harlequins), D Jones (Cardiff), K P Jones (Ebbw Vale), S M Williams (Neath), M E Williams (Pontypridd)
Replacements P Arnold (Swansea) for D Jones (67 mins); W J L Thomas (Cardiff) for N G Davies (73 mins); P John (Pontypridd) for Howley (temp 47–53 mins)
Scorers *Tries:* N Davies (2), Proctor, Humphreys, Howley *Conversions:* Jenkins (3)
BARBARIANS: D Arrieta (Biarritz); A Bose (Mana), R Dourthe (Dax), S Glas (Bourgoin), N Walker (Cardiff); P W Howard (Queensland), A Pichot (San Isidro); A G J Watt (Currie), J A Hay (Hawick), R G A Snow (Newfoundland Dogs), R J McCall (Queensland), D Sims (Gloucester), M Gusuna (Mana), A R B Pene (Kaneka) *(capt)*, D S Corkery (Bristol) *Replacement* R G Collins (Pontypridd) for Gusuna (29 mins)
Scorers *Tries:* Pene, Corkery
Referee J M Fleming (Scotland)

25 September 1996, Cardiff Arms Park
WALES 33 (3G 4PG) FRANCE 40 (4G 4PG)

WALES: W T Proctor (Llanelli); I C Evans (Llanelli), L B Davies (Cardiff), N G Davies (Llanelli) *(capt)*, G Thomas (Bridgend); N R Jenkins (Pontypridd), R Howley (Cardiff); C D Loader (Swansea), B Williams (Neath), J D Davies (Neath), M J Voyle (Llanelli), G O Llewellyn (Harlequins), K P Jones (Ebbw Vale), S M Williams (Neath), M E Williams (Pontypridd) *Replacements* S D Hill (Cardiff) for N G Davies (14 mins); A C Thomas (Swansea) for Evans (19 mins)

Scorers *Tries:* B Williams, Evans, G Thomas   *Conversions:* Jenkins (3)
Penalty Goals: Jenkins (4)
FRANCE: J-L Sadourny (Colomiers); E Ntamack (Toulouse), R Dourthe (Dax),
S Glas (Bourgoin), P Saint-André (Montferrand) *(capt)*; A Penaud (Brive),
P Carbonneau (Brive); F Tournaire (Narbonne), M de Rougemont (Toulon),
J-L Jordana (Toulouse), O Merle (Montferrand), F Pelous (Dax), P Benetton
(Agen), A Benazzi (Agen), R Castel (Béziers)   *Replacements* D Berty (Toulouse)
for Saint-André (33 mins); T Lièvremont (Perpignan) for Benetton (40 mins);
G Accoceberry (Bègles-Bordeaux) for Carbonneau (67 mins)
Scorers *Tries:* Glas (2), Sadourny, Benazzi   *Conversions:* Dourthe (4)
Penalty Goals: Dourthe (4)
Referee G Gadjovich (Canada)

5 October 1996, Olympic Stadium, Rome
ITALY 22 (1G 5PG) WALES 31 (2G 4PG 1T)

ITALY: M Ravazzolo (Calvisano); P Vaccari (Calvisano), S Bordon (Rovigo),
I Francescato (Treviso), L Manteri (Treviso); D Dominguez (Milan), A Troncon
(Treviso); Massimo Cuttitta (Milan) *(capt)*, C Orlandi (Milan), F Properzi-Curti
(Milan), P-P Pedroni (Milan), D Scaglia (Treviso), A Sgorlon (Treviso),
C Checchinato (Treviso), O Arancio (Milan)   *Replacements* J A Pertile (Rome) for
Vaccari (69 mins); R Rampazzo (Padova) for Checchinato (72 mins); A Castellani
(Treviso) for Properzi-Curti (80 mins)
Scorers *Try:* Francescato   *Conversion:* Dominguez   *Penalty Goals:* Dominguez (5)
WALES: W T Proctor (Llanelli); S D Hill (Cardiff), G Thomas (Bridgend),
I S Gibbs (Swansea), D R James (Bridgend); N R Jenkins (Pontypridd), R Howley
(Cardiff); C D Loader (Swansea), J M Humphreys (Cardiff) *(capt)*, J D Davies
(Neath), G O Llewellyn (Harlequins), D Jones (Cardiff), H T Taylor (Cardiff),
S M Williams (Neath), K P Jones (Ebbw Vale)   *Replacements* L B Davies for
Proctor (50 mins); M E Williams (Pontypridd) for K P Jones (temp 17-19 mins)
Scorers *Tries:* G Thomas (2), James   *Conversions:* Jenkins (2)
Penalty Goals: Jenkins (4)
Referee C Spannenberg (South Africa)

*Kingsley Jones (Wales) making a typically aggressive break during the Italy-Wales
international at the Olympic Stadium, Rome.*

12 November, Lansdowne Road
IRELAND 25 (1G 6PG) WESTERN SAMOA 40 (3G 3PG 2T)

IRELAND: S J P Mason (Richmond); R M Wallace (Saracens), R A J Henderson (London Irish), J C Bell (Northampton), J A Topping (Ballymena); D G Humphreys (London Irish), N A Hogan (Terenure College) *(capt)*; H D Hurley (Moseley), A T H Clarke (Northampton), P S Wallace (Saracens), M J Galwey (Shannon), J W Davidson (London Irish), D S Corkery (Bristol), P S Johns (Saracens), W D McBride (Malone) *Replacement* V C P Costello (London Irish) for McBride (72 mins)
Scorers *Try:* P Wallace *Conversion:* Mason *Penalty Goals:* Mason (6)
WESTERN SAMOA: H V Patu (Vaiala); A So'oalo (Marist St Joseph), G E Leaupepe (Counties), T M Vaega (Te Atatu), V L Tuigamala (Wasps); E Va'a (Wellington RL), J Filemu (Wellington); B P Reidy (Marist St Patrick), T Leiasamaivao (Wellington), A Le'uu (Vaimoso), P L Leavasa (Hawke's Bay), M L Birtwistle (Suburbs), S Ta'ala (Wellington), I Feaunati (Marist St Patrick), P R Lam (Canterbury) *(capt)* *Replacement* P J Paramore (Bedford) for Leavasa (58 mins)
Scorers *Tries:* Vaega (2), So'oalo, Leaupepe, Patu *Conversions:* Va'a (3) *Penalty Goals:* Va'a (3)
Referee S Borsani (Argentina)

23 November, Twickenham
ENGLAND 54 (5G 3PG 2T) ITALY 21 (3G)

ENGLAND: T R G Stimpson (Newcastle); J M Sleightholme (Bath), W D C Carling (Harlequins), P R de Glanville (Bath) *(capt)*, A A Adebayo (Bath); M J Catt (Bath), A C T Gomarsall (Wasps); G C Rowntree (Leicester), M P Regan (Bristol), J Leonard (Harlequins), M O Johnson (Leicester), S D Shaw (Bristol), T A K Rodber (Northampton & Army), C M A Sheasby (Wasps), L B N Dallaglio (Wasps) *Replacements* R J K Hardwick (Coventry) for Leonard (71 mins); P B T Greening (Gloucester) for Regan (76 mins); K P P Bracken (Saracens) for Gomarsall (79 mins)
Scorers *Tries:* Gomarsall (2), Sleightholme, Johnson, Dallaglio, Rodber, Sheasby *Conversions:* Catt (5) *Penalty Goals:* Catt (3)
ITALY: J A Pertile (Rome); P Vaccari (Calvisano), S Bordon (Rovigo), I Francescato (Treviso), L Manteri (Treviso); D Dominguez (Milan), A Troncon (Treviso); Massimo Cuttitta (Milan), C Orlandi (Milan), F Properzi-Curti (Milan), W Cristofoletto (Treviso), C Checchinato (Treviso), M Giovanelli (PUC) *(capt)*, O Arancio (Milan), C Covi (Padova) *Replacements* A Sgorlon (Treviso) for Covi (56 mins); A Barattin (Tarvisium) for Checchinato (80 mins); G-L Guidi for Troncon (temp 32–35 mins)
Scorers *Tries:* Vaccari, Troncon, Arancio *Conversions:* Dominguez (3)
Referee P Deluca (Argentina)

14 December, Murrayfield
SCOTLAND 29 (3G 1PG 1T) ITALY 22 (1G 4PG 1DG)

SCOTLAND: R J S Shepherd (Melrose); A G Stanger (Hawick), S Hastings (Watsonians), G P J Townsend (Northampton) *(capt)*, K M Logan (Stirling County); C M Chalmers (Melrose), B W Redpath (Melrose); D I W Hilton (Bath), K D McKenzie (Stirling County), M J Stewart (Northampton), D F Cronin (Wasps), A I Reed (Wasps), M I Wallace (Glasgow High/Kelvinside), E W Peters (Bath), I R Smith (Gloucester) *Replacements* D A Stark (Melrose) for Shepherd (42 mins); G W Weir (Newcastle) for Cronin (53 mins)

Scorers *Tries:* Logan (2), Stanger, Stark   *Conversions:* Chalmers (3)
Penalty Goals: Shepherd
ITALY: J A Pertile (Rome); N Mazzucato (Padova), P Vaccari (Calvisano),
I Francescato (Treviso), Marcello Cuttitta (Milan); D Dominguez (Milan),
A Troncon (Treviso); Massimo Cuttitta (Milan), C Orlandi (Milan), A Castellani
(Treviso), G Croci (Milan), W Cristofoletto (Treviso), M Giovanelli (PUC) *(capt)*,
O Arancio (Milan), A Sgorlon (Treviso)   *Replacements* A Moscardi (Treviso) for
Orlandi (40 mins); L Manteri (Treviso) for Mazzucato (65 mins)
Scorers *Try:* pen try   *Conversion:* Dominguez   *Penalty Goals:* Dominguez (4)
Dropped Goal: Dominguez
Referee D Gillet (France)

4 January, Lansdowne Road
IRELAND 29 (8PG 1T) ITALY 37 (4G 3PG)

IRELAND: C M P O'Shea (London Irish); J A Topping (Ballymena), J C Bell
(Northampton), M C McCall (Dungannon), D J Crotty (Cork Constitution);
P A Burke (Bristol), S C McIvor (Garryowen); N J Popplewell (Newcastle),
K G M Wood (Harlequins) *(capt)*, P S Wallace (Saracens), G M Fulcher (London
Irish), J W Davidson (London Irish), D S Corkery (Bristol), A G Foley
(Shannon), E R P Miller (Leicester)   *Replacements* W D McBride (Malone) for
Miller (33 mins); P S Johns (Saracens) for Fulcher (66 mins)
Scorers *Try:* Bell   *Penalty Goals:* Burke (8)
ITALY: J A Pertile (Rome); P Vaccari (Calvisano), S Bordon (Rovigo), A Stoica
(Milan), Marcello Cuttitta (Milan); D Dominguez (Milan), A Troncon (Treviso);
Massimo Cuttitta (Milan) *(capt)*, C Orlandi (Milan), F Properzi-Curti (Milan),
G Croci (Milan), W Cristofoletto (Treviso), A Sgorlon (Treviso), O Arancio
(Milan), J M Gardner (Treviso)   *Replacements* N Mazzucato (Padova) for Marc
Cuttitta (43 mins); C Checchinato (Treviso) for Cristofoletto (65 mins)
Scorers *Tries:* Vaccari (2), Mass Cuttitta, Dominguez   *Conversions:* Dominguez (4)
Penalty Goals: Dominguez (3)
Referee R G Davies (Wales)

22 March, Stade Lesdiguières, Grenoble
FRANCE 32 (3G 2PG 1T) ITALY 40 (4G 4PG)

FRANCE: J-L Sadourny (Colomiers); S Ougier (Toulouse), Y Delaigue (Toulon),
P Bondouy (Narbonne), P Saint-André (Montferrand); D Aucagne (Pau),
G Accoceberry (Bègles-Bordeaux); M de Rougemont (Toulon), M Dal Maso
(Agen), F Tournaire (Narbonne), O Merle (Montferrand), H Miorin (Toulouse),
P Benetton (Agen), F Pelous (Dax) *(capt)*, A Costes (Montferrand)
Replacements S Betsen (Biarritz) for Costes (59 mins); R Ibanez (Dax) for Dal
Maso (75 mins)
Scorers *Tries:* Bondouy (2), Sadourny, pen try   *Conversions:* Aucagne (3)
Penalty Goals: Aucagne (2)
ITALY: J A Pertile (Rome); P Vaccari (Calvisano), S Bordon (Rovigo),
I Francescato (Treviso), Marcello Cuttitta (Milan); D Dominguez (Milan),
A Troncon (Treviso); Massimo Cuttitta (Milan), C Orlandi (Milan),
F Properzi-Curti (Milan), G Croci (Milan), W Cristofoletto (Treviso),
M Giovanelli (PUC) *(capt)*, J M Gardner (Treviso), A Sgorlon (Treviso)
Replacements F Mazzariol (Treviso) for Francescato (25 mins); G-L Guidi
(Livorno) for Troncon (temp 39–41 mins)
Scorers *Tries:* Francescato, Gardner, Croci, Vaccari   *Conversions:* Dominguez (4)
Penalty Goals: Dominguez (4)
Referee D T M McHugh (Ireland)

A INTERNATIONALS 1996-97

13 November 1996, Donnybrook
Ireland A 28 (2G 1T 3PG)   **South Africa A 25** (2G 1T 2PG)

Ireland A: D Crotty (Garryowen); C O'Shea (London Irish), B Walsh (Cork Con), M McCall (Dungannon), N Woods (London Irish); E Elwood (Lansdowne), B O'Meara (Cork Con.); P Flavin (Blackrock), K Wood (Harlequins) (*capt*), A McKeen (Lansdowne), M O'Kelly (London Irish), S Leahy (Lansdowne), A Foley (Shannon), E Miller (Leicester), B Cronin (Garryowen) *Replacement* C McEntee (Lansdowne) for O'Kelly (65 mins)
Scorers *Tries:* O'Shea (2), Miller   *Conversions:* Elwood (2)
Penalty Goals: Elwood (3)
South Africa A: D du Toit (N Transvaal); T Linee (W Province), J van der Walt (Transvaal), E Lubbe (Griqualand West), J Joubert (Natal); L Koen (W Province), C Lotter (Boland); R Kempson (Natal), N Drotske (Free State) (*capt*), W Meyer (Boland), R Opperman (Free State), B Els (Free State), J Coetzee (Boland), R Erasmus (Free State), C Krige (W Province) *Replacement* G Scholtz (W Province) for Lotter (30 mins)
Scorers *Tries:* Koen, du Toit, Scholtz   *Conversions:* Koen (2)
Penalty Goals: Koen (2)
Referee C Muir (Scotland)

10 December 1996, Northampton
England A 22 (1G 5PG)   **Argentina 17** (1G 2T)

England A: I Hunter (Northampton); S Hackney (Leicester), W Greenwood (Leicester), A Blyth (Newcastle), D Luger (Harlequins); P Grayson (Northampton), M Dawson (Northampton); K Yates (Bath), R Kellam (London Irish), J Mallett (Bath), G Archer (Newcastle), D Sims (Gloucester), W Davison (Harlequins), R Hill (Saracens), A Diprose (Saracens) (*capt*) *Replacements* N Walshe (Harlequins) for Dawson (19 mins), J Ewens (Bath) for Blyth (30 mins), G French (Bath) for Kellam (57 mins), P Sampson (Wasps) for Hunter (79 mins)
Scorers *Try:* Hackney   *Conversion:* Grayson   *Penalty Goals:* Grayson (5)
Argentina: D Giannantonio; T Solari, G Camardon, L Arbizu (*capt*), F Soler; J Cilley, C Barrea; M Reggiardo, M Ledesma, O Hasan-Jalil, J Simes, G Llanes, R Martin, R Perez, C Viel
Scorers *Tries:* Hasan-Jalil, Soler, pen try   *Conversion:* Cilley
Referee J Kaplan (S Africa)

11 December 1996, Kingsholm, Gloucester
England A 20 (2G 2PG)   **South Africa A 35** (2G 3T 2PG)

England A: C Catling (Gloucester); B Johnson (Newbury), J Baxendell (Sale), N Greenstock (Wasps), S Bromley (Harlequins); M Mapletoft (Gloucester), A Healey (Leicester); M Volland (Northampton), S Mitchell (Wasps), N Webber (Moseley), D Grewcock (Coventry), R Fidler (Gloucester), G Allison (Harlequins), R Jenkins (Harlequins), S Ojomoh (Bath) (*capt*) *Replacement* P Sampson (Wasps) for Catling (78 mins)
Scorers *Tries:* Bromley, Healey   *Conversions:* Mapletoft (2)
Penalty Goals: Mapletoft (2)
South Africa A: D du Toit (N Transvaal); M Hendriks (Boland), J Joubert (Natal), E Lubbe (Griqualand West), M Goosen (Boland); L Koen (W Province), G Scholtz (W Province); O le Roux (Natal), N Drotske (Free State) (*capt*), W Mayer (E Province), R Opperman (Free State), H Louw (W Province), C Krige (W Province), P Smit (Griqualand West), R Erasmus (Free State) *Replacement* J Coetzee (Boland) for Krige (20-22 mins)
Scorers *Tries:* Krige (2), Goosen, Hendriks, Erasmus   *Conversions:* Koen (2)
Penalty Goals: Koen (2)
Referee D McHugh (Ireland)

63

13 December 1996, Gateshead
England A 22 (2G 1T 1PG)   Queensland 25 (1G 5PG 1DG)

England A: J Mallinder (Sale); D Luger (Harlequins), W Greenwood (Leicester), J Ewens (Bath), J Fallon (Richmond); R Liley (Leicester), N Walshe (Harlequins); K Yates (Bath), R Cockerill (Leicester), D Garforth (Leicester), C Murphy (West Hartlepool), D Sims (Gloucester), D Davison (Harlequins), R Hill (Saracens), A Diprose (Saracens) (*capt*) *Replacements* A Healey (Leicester) for Walshe (41 mins), S Ojomoh (Bath) for Davison (49 mins), P Mensah (Harlequins) for Ewens (55 mins), M Perry (Bath) for Mallinder (64 mins)
Scorers *Tries:* Mallinder, Luger,Mensah   *Conversions:* Liley (2)   *Penalty Goal:* Liley
Queensland: T Mandrusiak; D McInally, R Constable, N Grey, T Boston; E Flatley, B Free; G Panoho, C Knapp, P Clohessy, B Cockbain, R Johnson, M Cockbain, N Murray (*capt*), M Gabey
Scorers *Try:* McInally   *Conversion:* Mandrusiak   *Penalty Goals:* Mandrusiak (5)
Dropped Goal: Mandrusiak
Referee K McCartney (Scotland)

17 January 1997, Goldenacre
Scotland A 56 (6G 1T 3PG)   Wales A 11 (1T 2PG)

Scotland A: D Lee (Watsonians); J Craig (West of Scotland), A Tait (Newcastle), P Rouse (Dundee HSFP), C Glasgow (Heriot's); S Welsh (Hawick), A Nicol (Bath); G Graham (Newcastle), G Bulloch (West of Scotland), P Wright (Melrose), S Campbell (Melrose), S Grimes (Watsonians), E Peters (Bath), C Hogg (Melrose) (*capt*), S Holmes (London Scottish) *Replacements* S Lang (Heriot's) for Craig (70 mins), J Manson (Stirling Co) for Graham (72 mins), C Mather (Watsonians) for Peters (76 mins)
Scorers *Tries:* Craig (3), Glasgow, Grimes, Peters, Lang   *Conversions:* Welsh (6)
Penalty Goals: Welsh (3)
Wales A: J Thomas (Cardiff); G Evans (Llanelli), L Davies (Cardiff), N Davies (Llanelli) (*capt*), D James (Bridgend); L Jarvis (Cardiff), A Moore (Richmond); N Eynon (Pontypridd), R McBryde (Llanelli), S John (Llanelli), V Cooper (Llanelli), P Arnold (Swansea), A Gibbs (Llanelli), C Wyatt (Llanelli), N Thomas (Bath) *Replacement* B Hayward (Ebbw Vale) for Jarvis (72 mins)
Scorers *Try:* Cooper   *Penalty Goals:* Jarvis (2)
Referee A Watson (Ireland)

17 January 1997, Donnybrook
Ireland A 23 (2G 3PG)   France A 44 (4G 2T 2PG)

Ireland A: C Clarke (Terenure); D Hickie (St Mary's), B Carey (Blackrock), K Keane (Garryowen), R Wallace (Saracens); A McGowan (Blackrock), B O'Meara (Cork Con.); H Hurley (Moseley), M McDermott (Lansdowne), A McKeen (Lansdowne), M Galwey (Shannon) (*capt*), B Cusack (Bath), A Foley (Shannon), E Halvey (Shannon), B Cronin (Garryowen) *Replacement* A Reddan (Lansdowne) for Carey (14 mins)
Scorers *Tries:* Wallace, Clarke   *Conversions:* McGowan (2)   *Penalty Goals:* McGowan (3)
France A: N Brusque (Pau); P Bernat-Salles (Pau), E Artiguste (Castres), O Campan (Agen), U Mola (Dax); D Aucagne (Pau), J Cazalbou (Toulouse) (*capt*); L Toussaint (Castres), O Azam (Montferrand), P Triep-Capdeville (Pau), C Gaston (Castres), T Cleda (Pau), O Magne (Dax), A Chazalet (Bourgoin), P Raschi (Bourgoin)
Scorers *Tries:* Chazalet, Artiguste, Cleda, Mola, Bernat-Salles, Cazalbou
Conversions: Aucagne (4)   *Penalty Goals:* Aucagne (2)
Referee C White (England)

31 January 1997, Sardis Road, Pontypridd
Emerging Wales 34 (3G 2T 1PG)   Ireland A 14 (2G)

Emerging Wales: M Back (Swansea); S Hill (Cardiff), L Davies (Cardiff), D Davies (Llanelli) (*capt*), G Evans (Llanelli); S Conner (Newport), A Moore (Richmond); A Lewis

(Cardiff), B Williams (Neath), J Davies (Neath), V Cooper (Llanelli), P Arnold (Swansea), A Gibbs (Llanelli), N Thomas (Bath), D McIntosh (Pontypridd)
Scorers *Tries:* Arnold (2), Cooper, Davies, Gibbs   *Conversions:* Conner (3)
Penalty Goal: Conner
Ireland A: C O'Shea (London Irish); J Cunningham (Dublin Univ), A Reddan (Lansdowne), K Keane (Garryowen), N Woods (London Irish); N Malone (Leicester), B O'Meara (Cork Con.); H Hurley (Moseley), M McDermott (Lansdowne), G Walsh (Northampton), M Galwey (Shannon) (*capt*), B Cusack (Bath), E Halvey (Shannon), K Dawson (London Irish), A Foley (Shannon)
Scorers *Tries:* Halvey, Woods   *Conversions:* Keane (2)
Referee T Spreadbury (England)

31 January 1997, Stoop Memorial Ground
England A 52 (3G 5T 2PG)   Scotland A 17 (1G 2T)

England A: N Beal (Northampton); A Adebayo (Bath), W Greenwood (Leicester) (*capt*), N Greenstock (Wasps), D Luger (Harlequins); A King (Wasps), K Bracken (Saracens); K Yates (Bath), R Cockerill (Leicester), J Mallett (Bath), G Archer (Newcastle), D Sims (Gloucester), C Sheasby (Wasps), A Diprose (Saracens), N Back (Leicester)
Replacements J Mallinder (Sale) for Luger (50 mins), G Allison (Harlequins) for Sheasby (temp 56-66 mins)
Scorers *Tries:* Greenwood, Bracken (2), Beal, Luger, Diprose, Adebayo, Sheasby
Conversions: King (3)   *Penalty Goals:* King (2)
Scotland A: D Lee (Watsonians); C Glasgow (Heriot's), P Rouse (Dundee HSFP), D Hodge (Watsonians), J Craig (West of Scotland); S Welsh (Hawick), A Nicol (Bath); J Manson (Stirling Co), G Bulloch (West of Scotland), P Wright (Melrose), S Campbell (Melrose), S Grimes (Watsonians), E Peters (Bath), M Wallace (GHK), C Hogg (Melrose) (*capt*)
Replacements I Fairley (Kelso) for Nicol (60 mins), S Ferguson (Peebles) for Wright (temp 5-9 mins)
Scorers *Tries:* Lee (2), Peters   *Conversion:* Welsh
Referee C Hawke (New Zealand)

31 January 1997, Bristol
England A 15 (3T)   Otago 42 (4G 1T 3PG)

England A: C Catling (Gloucester); D Rees (Sale), P Mensah (Harlequins), M Allen (Northampton), H Thorneycroft (Northampton); M Mapletoft (Gloucester), S Benton (Gloucester); M Volland (Northampton), D West (Leicester), V Ubogu (Bath), R Fidler (Gloucester), J Fowler (Sale), M Corry (Bristol), R Jenkins (Harlequins), S Ojomoh (Bath) (*capt*) *Replacement* R Liley (Leicester) for Catling (74 mins)
Scorers *Tries:* Mapletoft, Thorneycroft, Allen
Otago: M Carrington; B Laney, R Ropati, M Colling, M Bari; S Culhane, S Forster (*capt*); C Hoeft, A Tiatia, K Meeuws, T Hami, J Blaikie, L Falaniko, K Vanisi, I Maka
Replacement R Parkinson for Ropati (38 mins)
Scorers *Tries:* Maka, Vanisi, Laney, Carrington, Parkinson
Conversions: Culhane (4)   *Penalty Goals:* Culhane (3)
Referee P Bolland (Wales)

14 February 1997, Donnybrook
Ireland A 30 (2G 2T 2PG)   England A 44 (4G 2T 2PG)

Ireland A: C O'Shea (London Irish) (*capt*); D Crotty (Garryowen), K McQuilkin (Lansdowne), K Keane (Garryowen), N Woods (London Irish); P Burke (Bristol), S McIvor (Garryowen); H Hurley (Moseley), M McDermott (Lansdowne), G Walsh (Northampton), S Jameson (St Mary's), B Cusack (Bath), S Duncan (Malone), B Cronin (Garryowen), K Dawson (London Irish) *Replacements* N Malone (Leicester) for Burke (19 mins), A McKeen (Lansdowne) for Walsh (76 mins), M Lynch (Young Munster) for Keane (76 mins)
Scorers *Tries:* Keane, O'Shea, Walsh, Malone   *Conversions:* Burke (2)
Penalty Goals: Keane (2)
England A: N Beal (Northampton); D Luger (Harlequins), N Greenstock (Wasps), W Greenwood (Leicester) (*capt*), A Adebayo (Bath); M Mapletoft (Gloucester), S Benton

(Gloucester); R Hardwick (Coventry), D West (Leicester), J Mallet (Bath), G Archer (Newcastle), J Fowler (Sale), M Corry (Bristol), A Diprose (Saracens), N Back (Leicester) *Replacement* S Ojomoh (Bath) for Corry (61 mins)
Scorers *Tries:* Adebayo, Diprose, Benton, Greenstock, Back, Mapletoft   *Conversions:* Mapletoft (4)   *Penalty Goals:* Mapletoft (2)
Referee P Adams (Wales)

14 February 1977, Perigeux
France A 41 (5G 2PG)   Emerging Wales 6 (2PG)

France A: S Ougier (Toulouse); U Mola (Dax), E Artiguste (Castres), P Bondouy (Narbonne), D Berty (Toulouse); B Bellot (Perpignan), J Cazalbou (Toulouse) (*capt*); D Casadei (Brive), R Ibanez (Dax), O Sourgens (Begles), O Brouzet (Begles), J-P Versailles (Montferrand), S Betsen (Biarritz), S Dispagne (Toulouse), A Costes (Montferrand) *Replacement* F Ribeyrolles (Montferrand) for Bondouy
Scorers *Tries:* Ribeyrolles, Cazalbou, Ougier, Bellot, Betsen   *Conversions:* Bellot (5) *Penalty Goals:* Bellot (2)
Emerging Wales: W Proctor (Llanelli); S Hill (Cardiff), J Lewis (Pontypridd), N Davies (Llanelli) (*capt*), D James (Bridgend); A Williams (Swansea), A Moore (Richmond); S John (Llanelli), B Williams (Neath), J Davies (Neath), V Cooper (Llanelli), M Voyle (Llanelli), A Gibbs (Llanelli), C Wyatt (Llanelli), N Thomas (Bath) *Replacements* D Llewellyn (Ebbw Vale) for Moore; S Moore (Swansea) for Cooper
Scorer *Penalty Goals:* Williams (2)
Referee S Piercey (RFU)

28 February 1997, Leicester
England A 25 (2G 1T 2PG)   France A 34 (2G 1T 4PG 1DG)

England A: J Mallinder (Sale); H Thorneycroft (Northampton), N Greenstock (Wasps), W Greenwood (Leicester) (*capt*), J Naylor (Orrell); A King (Wasps), K Bracken (Saracens); K Yates (Bath), R Cockerill (Leicester), R Hardwick (Coventry), G Archer (Newcastle), D Sims (Gloucester), C Sheasby (Wasps), A Diprose (Saracens), N Back (Leicester) *Replacements* M Mapletoft (Gloucester) for King (64 mins), M Corry (Bristol) for Sheasby (70 mins)
Scorers *Tries:* Mallinder (2), Greenwood   *Conversions:* King, Mapletoft *Penalty Goals:* King (2)
France A: S Ougier (Toulouse); P Bernat-Salles (Pau), P Bondouy (Narbonne), E Artiguste (Castres), S Viars (Brive); B Bellot (Perpignan), J Cazalbou (Toulouse) (*capt*); D Casadei (Brive), R Ibanez (Dax), O Sourgens (Begles), G Ross (Brive), O Brouzet (Begles), S Betsen (Biarritz), A Costes (Montferrand), T Lievremont (Perpignan) *Replacements* G Bouic (Agen) for Viars (32 mins), F Heyer (Montferrand) for Sourgens (64 mins)
Scorers *Tries:* Viars, Costes, Bondouy   *Conversions:* Bellot (2) *Penalty Goals:* Bellot (4)   *Dropped Goal:* Bellot
Referee A Lewis (Ireland)

28 February 1997, Myreside
Scotland A 33 (4G 1T)   Ireland A 34 (3G 2T 1PG)

Scotland A: D Lee (Watsonians); J Craig (West of Scotland), C Murray (Hawick), R Eriksson (London Scottish), J Kerr (Watsonians); A Donaldson (Currie), G Burns (Watsonians); P Wright (Melrose), G Bulloch (West of Scotland), S Ferguson (Peebles), S Murray (Bedford), S Grimes (Watsonians), S Reid (Boroughmuir), C Hogg (Melrose) (*capt*), S Holmes (London Scottish)
Scorers *Tries:* C Murray (2), Eriksson (2), Kerr   *Conversions:* Donaldson (4)
Ireland A: C Clarke (Terenure); D Crotty (Garryowen), B Carey (Blackrock), M Lynch (Young Munster), N Woods (London Irish); R Governey (Lansdowne), N Hogan (Terenure); H Hurley (Moseley), M McDermott (Lansdowne) (*capt*), A McKeen (Lansdowne), S Jamieson (St Mary's), B Cusack (Bath), E Halvey (Shannon), A Foley (Shannon), K Dawson (London Irish)
Scorers *Tries:* Woods (2), Hogan, Clarke, Halvey   *Conversions:* Lynch (3) *Penalty Goal:* Lynch
Referee N Whitehouse (Wales)

14 March 1997, Rodez
France A 23 (2G 3PG)   Scotland A 9 (3PG)

France A: S Ougier (Toulouse); S Viars (Brive), E Artiguste (Castres), F Ribeyrolles (Montferrand), W Olombel (Beziers); B Bellot (Perpignan), L Balue (Beziers); C Soulette (Beziers), R Ibanez (Dax), O Sourgens (Begles), O Brouzet (Begles), J-P Versailles (Montferrand), A Costes (Montferrand), S Dispagne (Toulouse), S Betsen (Biarritz) *Replacements* L Mazas (Biarritz) for Ribeyrolles (26 mins), J Cazalbou (Toulouse) for Balue (54 mins), O Azam (Montferrand) for Soulette (58 mins), R Crespy (Brive) for Sourgens (70 mins)
Scorers *Tries:* Viars, Artiguste   *Conversions:* Bellot (2)   *Penalty Goals:* Bellot (3)
Scotland A: D Lee (Watsonians); D Stark (Melrose), C Murray (Hawick), R Eriksson (London Scottish), J Kerr (Watsonians); A Donaldson (Currie), G Burns (Watsonians); M Browne (Melrose), G Bulloch (West of Scotland), S Ferguson (Peebles), S Murray (Bedford), S Grimes (Watsonians), C Mather (Watsonians), C Hogg (Melrose) (*capt*), S Holmes (London Scottish) *Replacements* S Nichol (Melrose) for Eriksson (31 mins), S Reid (Boroughmuir) for Mather (59 mins), J Manson (Stirling Co.) for Browne (61 mins)
Scorer *Penalty Goals:* Donaldson (3)
Referee A Rowden (England)

24 May 1997, Bucharest
Romania A 33 (4G 1T) Wales A 42 (4G 3PG 1T)

Romania A: V Maftei (Dinamo); L Colceriu (Steaua), G Solomie (Timisoara Univ), M Dumitru (Farul), V Brici (Farul); N Nichitean (Cluj Univ) (*capt*), V Flutur (Cluj Univ); L Costea (Steaua), M Radoi (Dinamo), N Dragos (Steaua), V Nedelcu (Dinamo), T Brinza (RCF), F Corodeanu (Steaua), A Girbu (Farul), E Septar (Farul) *Replacements* C Gheoghe (Grivita) for Dragos (35 mins); C Stan (Dinamo) for Costea (60 mins); C Dragnea (Petrosani Univ) for Flutur (70 mins)
Scorers *Tries:* Radoi (2), Nichitean, Brici, Maftei   *Conversions:* Nichitean (4)
Wales A: M Back (Swansea); G Wyatt (Pontypridd), N Boobyer (Llanelli), J Lewis (Pontypridd), R Shorney (UWIC); A Thomas (Swansea), P John (Pontypridd) (*capt*); C Loader (Swansea), G Jenkins (Swansea), L Mustoe (Cardiff), S Moore (Swansea), M Voyle (Llanelli), M Lloyd (Pontypridd), S Williams (Neath), R Appleyard (Swansea) *Replacements* N Watkins (Neath) for Moore (temp 37-40 mins & 66 mins); I Buckett (Swansea) for Loader (65 mins); R McBryde for Appleyard (temp 56-58 mins); L Jarvis (Cardiff) for Thomas (78 mins)
Scorers *Tries:* John, Back, Watkins, Thomas, Appleyard   *Conversions:* Thomas (3), Jarvis   *Penalty Goals:* Thomas (3)
Referee G Sciova (Italy)

A AND STATE TOURS TO BRITAIN 1996–97

SOUTH AFRICA 'A' TO BRITAIN 1996

Match 1 – 1 November v **Cambridge University** won 57-11
Match 2 – 4 November v **Bedford** won 41-27
Match 3 – 8 November v **Scotland A** lost 19-32
Match 4 – 12 November v **Ireland A** lost 25-28
Match 5 – 16 November v **Oxford University** won 49-12
Match 6 – 20 November v **South Western Counties** won 62-20
Match 7 – 23 November v **London Counties** won 43-17
Match 8 – 27 November v **Northern Counties** won 29-13
Match 9 – 1 December v **Midland Counties** won 62-7
Match 10 – 9 December v **Cardiff** won 40-7
Match 11 – 11 December v **England A** won 35-20
Match 12 – 14 December v **Emerging Wales** won 42-26

QUEENSLAND TO BRITAIN 1996

Match 1 – 13 November v **Cambridge University** lost 20-27
Match 2 – 17 November v **Michael Lynagh XV** won 28-5
Match 3 – 20 November v **Northern Counties** won 27-18
Match 4 – 24 November v **Midland Counties** won 29-25
Match 5 – 28 November v **South West** won 30-9
Match 6 – 1 December v **London Division** won 64-16
Match 7 – 4 December v **Pontypridd** won 28-19
Match 8 – 10 December v **Scotland Development XV** won 63-31
Match 9 – 13 December v **England A** won 25-22

OTAGO TO ENGLAND & SCOTLAND 1997

Match 1 – 18 January v **Cambridge University** won 47-23
Match 2 – 26 January v **London Irish** won 82-14
Match 3 – 28 January v **Scottish Development XV** won 44-19
Match 4 – 31 January v **England 'A' XV** won 42-15
Match 5 – 4 February v **Bath** won 31-18
Match 6 – 11 February v **Northampton-Leicester XV** won 37-8
Match 7 – 13 February v **Richmond** won 70-0

AUCKLAND TO EUROPE 1997

Match 1 – 13 February, **Bristol** won 62-21
Match 2 – 18 February v **Harlequins** won 33-29
Match 3 – 22 February v **Brive** won 47-11

LEICESTER STUNNED BY BRIVE ENCOUNTER

HEINEKEN EUROPEAN CUP 1996-97

You wonder now why it took so long a' coming. The European Cup, in only its second year, is such a wonderful competition, such a stimulating incentive for all clubs, such a gripping spectacle for fans and a wonderful marketing platform for the game itself, that it's difficult to work out why we didn't think of it before. Rather like the round ball game, it was hard work winning over the sceptics and breaking into traditional, entrenched fixture lists. The tournament is here not only to stay but also to grow. How ITV must rue their decision to pull the plug on their three-year deal to televise the competition just days before it all began. They had (quite rightly) become frustrated, if not angry, that the organisers had not kept them fully briefed about the scheduling of games. Just days after ITV withdrew from their £15 million commitment it was announced that there was, after all, to be a quarter-final stage, one of ITV's original requests.

The League was enhanced last season by the arrival of English and Scottish sides. This year will see the format altered to allow for home and away matches in the pool stages. The competition has brought off a remarkable coup. After decades of stubbornness it has forced the Five Nations committee men to sit down and work out an integrated calendar, serving the best interests of everyone.

It was not just the overwhelming nature of the final itself which brought this about, a game which drew praise from all corners of the rugby map. Even those cynics down below the equator, who have been basking in the success and pre-eminence of their Super-12 competition, acknowledged the relevance and quality of the entire European tournament. How long now before we see a play-off between the winners of both competitions. The Brive-Auckland match staged in February (won so emphatically, 47-11, in France by Auckland) was an ad-hoc, last-minute arrangement, designed more to fine-tune Auckland's Super-12 preparations than as a championship in itself. To have real significance the match has to have a genuine context.

That Brive should lose so heavily, particularly on home turf, was astonishing to those who witnessed not only their splendid demolition of Leicester in the final but also the zeal with which they defended their home record during the course of the competition. They beat Neath and Harlequins in pool matches, the latter match crowned by a staggering length-of-the-field try by Sebastien Carrat, a score which prompted an orgy of celebration among their passionate supporters. The Welsh then tried to storm the Limousin fortress. First Llanelli (35-14) in the quarter-final and then Cardiff (26-13) in the semi-final failed. Welsh captain, Jonathan Humphreys was sent off in that match for a second yellow card offence. Brive also won away at Caledonia (32-30) and Ulster (17–6).

Leicester also came through undefeated, the highlight of their campaign being victories at Pau (19-14) in Pool B, then a glorious unravelling of Toulouse's colours in the semi-final at a snowbound Welford Road by 37-11. Leicester, after a sluggish start to their domestic season, were in powerful form by the time the European Cup got under way. Under the masterly guidance of new coach, Bob Dwyer, they were rarely troubled on their way to the final, accounting for Leinster, Scottish Borders and Llanelli in the group games and Harlequins in the quarter-final.

The Scottish had more cause for disappointment with their showing. There had been much internal wrangling over who should represent them in their first year. The district lobby won. The leading clubs will reckon that they could hardly have fared any worse than the one win from 12 matches achieved by Edinburgh, Caledonia and Scottish Borders, the latter scoring Scotland's only victory with a 24-16 win over Llanelli.

The Irish proved more troublesome opposition, Munster producing one of the shock scorelines of the early stages, beating Wasps 49-22. That Wasps were to bounce back the following week to smash the reigning European champions Toulouse, 77-17, illustrates the quality and dramatic capacity of the competition. We thought it also told us everything we needed to know about the fragility of French teams away from home. Brive shot that little myth to pieces in the final.

The tournament threw up matches of great intensity, skill and commitment. Pontypridd's 19-6 defeat of Bath on a wet October day at Sardis Road was an epic; so too Cardiff's 22-19 quarter-final triumph over Bath. The west country club's two months of woe, which eventually saw coach Brian Ashton and manager John Hall leave the club, almost dated from that day.

The tournament broke all records. Television audiences totalled 35 million; 18 countries took the final live with another 68 showing recorded action. No wonder they were queuing up for a slice of the action. Almost 350,000 went through the turnstiles for the 47 matches, which produced 275 tries at an average of 5.85 a match. Sebastien Carrat for Brive was easily the tournament's leading try-scorer with ten tries, followed by Cardiff's Robert Howley and Ugo Mola of Dax with six apiece.

FINAL
25 January 1997, Cardiff Arms Park
Brive 28 (1G 3T 1PG 1DG) **Leicester 9** (3PG)

This was defeat on a monumental scale. England's finest at the time were utterly routed by a Brive side which was fast, powerful, passionate and durable throughout. The unthinkable unfolded before 35,000 disbelieving eyes. The actual attendance was just over 41,000, some 6,000 of whom were Frenchmen. They knew what their men could offer. The rest of us watched stunned and then enthralled as the mighty men of Leicester were reduced to pygmies. Even Martin Johnson, so often the colossus of the line-out, looked shrivelled. Leicester won only one clean line-out in the entire second-half.

Brive out-muscled, out-fought and out-thought Leicester. Their back row of van der Linden, Duboisset and Kacala, the giant from Gdansk, was outstanding. Their powerful charges triggered many an attack. It was all Leicester could do to hang on to their bootlaces as they surged past. Leicester's tackling was decidedly flimsy on occasions, but even so you sensed that the sheer, breathtaking style and power of the Brive game would have found a way through.

And yet for all their early dominance, Brive could not put the points on the board. Indeed when Leicester's John Liley kicked his third penalty goal in the 54th minute it seemed for a few seconds as if the Tigers were about to get away with one of the biggest acts of larceny in the history of the sport. Justice arrived swiftly on the spot, right wing Gerald Fabre blasting his way over for a try almost from the restart. The floodgates were open. Wing Sebastien Carrat purred through for two tries to add to Viars's try in the fourth minute. The scoreline could easily have registered an even more humiliating margin of victory for, in all, nine kicks at goal were missed by Brive.

It was not a day for carping about mistakes. The Brive support was boisterous and colourful; their players responded in like fashion. Those who witnessed the carnival knew they had seen rugby's future.

Brive: S Viars; G Fabre, C Lamaison, D Venditti, S Carrat; A Penaud (*capt*), P Carbonneau; D Casadei, L Travers, R Crespy, E Allegret, G Ross, L van der Linden, F Duboisset, G Kacala *Replacements* R Paillat for Penaud (70 mins); E Bouti for Casadei (72 mins); A Recs for Ross (67 mins), Y Domi for van der Linden (79 mins); T Labrousse for Duboisset (49 mins)
Scorers *Tries:* S Carrat (2), S Viars, G Fabre *Conversion:* C Lamaison
Penalty Goal: C Lamaison *Dropped Goal:* C Lamison
Leicester: J Liley; S Hackney, W Greenwood, S Potter, R Underwood; R Liley, A Healey; G Rowntree, R Cockerill, D Garforth, M Johnson, M Poole, J Wells, D Richards (*capt*), N Back *Replacements* L Lloyd for Underwood (74 mins); P Freshwater for Garforth (temp 17-22 mins); E Miller for Richards (67 mins)
Scorer *Penalty Goals:* J Liley (3)
Referee Derek Bevan (Wales)

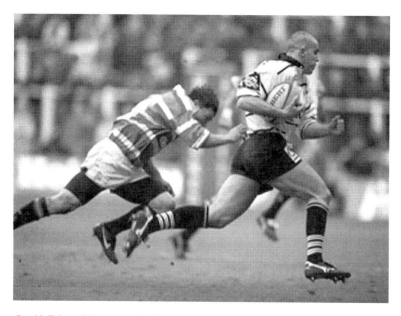

Gerald Fabre (Brive) outstrips Rory Underwood on his way to scoring a try in the Heineken Cup final against Leicester at Cardiff Arms Park.

SEMI-FINALS
4 January 1997, Welford Road
Leicester 37 (3G 2T 2PG)   Toulouse 11 (1T 2PG)

Leicester's most difficult task on the day eventually proved to be getting the game on in the first place. Up until the morning of the match itself there were grave doubts that the snow-covered, icy pitch would be fit for play. Leicester hired a hot air balloon-type covering, but even so the consensus on Friday evening was that the game would not go ahead. A slight thaw on Saturday morning and sterling work through the night meant that the pitch was perfectly playable. Whether all this ate into the morale of the French players we shall never know. Whatever it was Toulouse, defending their European crown, were a desperate disappointment. Leicester were raring to go; Toulouse were not.

Leicester set the pace from the very first minute. Their forwards had the whip hand, Johnson and Poole dominating the line-out. Given the perfect platform, the Leicester backs made full use of the opportunity. They had the best possible link man to help continuity in Neil Back. The Tigers openside had an outstanding game. He scored one try in the 19th minute, taking an inside pass from Will Greenwood, and was instrumental in sustaining so many Leicester attacks. Healey was at his opportunistic best for his try. Steve Hackney glided in for his try, Garforth hammered over from short range, and the forwards had their reward with a penalty try, awarded for a collapsed scrum. Toulouse showed only rare glimpses of what they could offer, notably in their consolation score when Marfaing rounded off a flowing move.

Leicester: J Liley; S Hackney, S Potter, W Greenwood, L Lloyd; R Liley, A Healey; G Rowntree, R Cockerill, D Garforth, M Johnson, M Poole, J Wells, N Back, D Richards (*capt*) *Replacement* R Underwood for Hackney (74 mins)
Scorers *Tries:* N Back, S Hackney, D Garforth, pen try, A Healey
Conversions: J Liley (3) *Penalty Goal:* J Liley (2)
Toulouse: S Ougier; E Ntamack (*capt*), M Marfaing, T Castaignede, D Berty; C Deylaud, J Cazalbou; C Califano, P Soula, J-L Jordana, H Miorin, F Belot, D Lacroix, R Sonnes, S Dispagne *Replacements* P Lassere for Soula (73 mins); H Manent for Sonnes (56 mins)
Scorers *Try:* M Marfaing *Penalty Goals:* C Deylaud (2)
Referee J Fleming (Scotland)

5 January 1997, Parc Municipal des Sports, Brive
Brive 26 (2G 4PG) Cardiff 13 (1G 2PG)

Central France resembled central Siberia on the morning of the match, but the energy sparked by hundreds of volunteers who cleared 200 tons of snow from the pitch ensured that the atmosphere by kick-off was red hot. There are few more passionate crowds anywhere in the world than that of Brive. The sheer, sustained volume inspires one side and intimidates the other.

The team itself fits perfectly into the backdrop. They play with a hunger and intensity at home which is difficult to resist. Cardiff did their best to stem the tide, but it became a hopeless cause in the 53rd minute when they lost their hooker and Welsh captain, Jonathan Humphreys. Humphreys, who had been booked in the first half, was given a second yellow card for obstruction as Brive tried to take a quick tap penalty near the Cardiff line. Strangely, although Humphreys was dismissed by Irish referee Brian Stirling, a penalty try was not awarded.

Cardiff were already trailing 16-6 at that point. Lamaison kicked three of his seven penalty attempts in the first half while Jonathan Davies replied with a short range effort. Early in the second half David Venditti skated past three defenders on his way to the try-line. Immediately after Humphreys's sending-off Duboisset scored from a scrum. Although Cardiff were awarded a penalty try after Brive infringed four times in succession on their own line, it was a minor consolation for the Welsh.

Brive: S Viars; G Fabre, C Lamaison, D Venditti, S Carrat, A Penaud (*capt*), P Carbonneau, D Casadei, L Travers, R Crespy, E Allegret, G Ross, L van der Linden, G Kacala, F Duboisset *Replacements* C Heymans for Carrat (64 mins); S Bonnet for Carbonneau (74 mins); E Bouti for Casadei (61 mins); T Rees for Allegret (58 mins); Y Domi for van der Linden (77 mins)
Scorers *Tries:* D Venditti, F Duboisset *Conversions:* C Lamaison (2)
Penalty Goals: C Lamaison (4)
Cardiff: J Thomas; S Hill, M Hall, L Davies, N Walker; J Davies, R Howley; A Lewis, J Humphreys, L Mustoe, J Wakeford, D Jones, H Taylor (*capt*), G Jones, E Lewis *Replacement* P Young for D Jones (53 mins)
Scorers *Try:* Pen try *Conversion:* J Davies *Penalty Goals:* J Davies (2)
Referee B Stirling (Ireland)

QUARTER-FINALS
16 November 1996, Cardiff
Cardiff 22 (1G 5PG) **Bath 19** (1G 4PG)

This game was a titanic tussle with only a penalty goal dividing the teams at the final whistle. Bath even had a chance to tie the scores in the last minute, but opted to tap a penalty awarded 45 metres from goal. Proven goal-kicker Jon Callard had been left on the bench; Rugby League's Henry Paul controversially getting the nod. Even so Bath should have shot for goal. Bath had only pulled that close through a last-minute try by Nathan Thomas. Howley and Jonathan Davies gave Cardiff direction and poise at half-back. Nigel Walker scored a wonderful try for Cardiff just before the hour, cutting in off his left foot.

Cardiff: J Thomas; N Walker, M Hall, L Davies, S Hill; J Davies, R Howley; A Lewis, J Humphreys, D Young, J Wakeford, D Jones, M Bennett, J Ringer, H Taylor *(capt)* *Replacements* L Jarvis for Thomas (62 mins); O Williams for Bennett (13 mins)
Scorers *Try:* Walker *Conversion:* J Davies *Penalty Goals:* J Davies (3), Jarvis (2)
Bath: J Robinson; H Paul, P de Glanville *(capt)*, J Guscott, A Adebayo; M Catt, A Nicol; D Hilton, G French, V Ubogu, M Haag, N Redman, N Thomas, E Peters, S Ojomoh *Replacements* I Sanders for Nicol (3 mins)
Scorers *Try:* Thomas *Conversion:* Catt *Penalty Goals:* Catt (4)
Referee G Black (Ireland)

16 November 1996, Welford Road
Leicester 23 (2G 3PG) **Harlequins 13** (2T 1PG)

Leicester gave thanks to the old dame, Lady Luck, after they escaped unscathed from this quarter-final. The London side had dominated the first half to such an extent that it seemed only a matter of working out how many they would win by. Instead Harlequins spurned two gilt-edged chances which came their way and then gifted Leicester a score through a moment of folly from Laurent Cabannes. By the end it was business as usual with the Leicester pack back in control.

Harlequins made an electric start, Carling's flat pass to Staples setting up the position for Luger to eventually score. Just after half-time Staples was again prominently involved as this time Carling scored. Gary Connolly missed an easy overlap and then O'Leary and Staples fluffed a promising opening. Then came Cabannes's faux pas, the Frenchman fatally dithering in his own 22. He did scramble the ball away, but Leicester came back, Cockerill being driven over the try-line. Rob Liley started slotting goals and then rounded off the day by scampering in under the Harlequins posts.

Leicester: J Liley; S Hackney, W Greenwood, S Potter, L Lloyd; R Liley, A Healey; G Rowntree, R Cockerill, D Garforth, M Johnson, M Poole, J Wells, D Richards *(capt)* N A Back *Replacements* R Underwood for Lloyd (63 mins); R Field for Poole (55 mins); E Miller for Back (33 mins)
Scorers *Tries:* Cockerill, R Liley *Conversions:* R Liley (2) *Penalty Goals:* R Liley (3)
Harlequins: J Staples; D O'Leary, G Connolly, W Carling, D Luger; P Challinor,

H Harries; J Leonard (*capt*), K Wood, L Benezech, Gareth Llelwllyn, Glyn
Llewellyn, R Jenkins, L Cabannes, B Davison
Scorers *Tries:* Luger, Carling *Penalty Goal:* Challinor
Referee C Thomas (Wales)

16 November, Dax
Dax 18 (1G 1T 2PG) Toulouse 26 (2G 4PG)

Dax knew that they had to take the game to their illustrious opponents
if they were to have any chance at all. They were as good as their word
as they stormed to a 15-3 lead within the opening half hour through
two tries by winger Ugo Mola. Toulouse needed to draw on their vast
experience to find a semblance of composure. Gradually, against a
raucous backdrop, their forwards won control. They were awarded a
penalty try just before half-time as the Dax pack was forced into
ignominious retreat. In the second half Marfaing finished off a Toulouse passage of play which began in their own 22.

Dax: R Dourthe; U Mola, P Giordani, F Tauzin, P Labeyrie; J-F Dubois,
N Morlacs; O Gouaillard, R Ibanez, D Laperne, P Berau, O Roumat (*capt*),
R Berek, O Magne, F Pelous *Replacements* F Duberger for Mola (44 mins);
W Rebeyrotte for Gouaillard (63 mins); T Rechou for Ibanez (72 mins);
F Dupleichs for Beraud (51 mins)
Scorers *Tries:* Mola (2) *Conversion:* Dourthe *Penalty Goals:* Dourthe (2)
Toulouse: S Ougier; E Ntamack (*capt*), M Marfaing, T Castaignede, D Berty;
C Deylaud, J Cazalbou; P Califano, P Soula, J-L Jordana, H Miorin, F Belot,
D Lacroix, S Dispagne, R Sonnes *Replacement* H Manent for Sonnes (48 mins)
Scorers *Tries:* Pen try, Marfaing *Conversions:* Deylaud, Castaignede
Penalty Goals: Deylaud (2), Castaignede (2)
Referee P Thomas (France)

17 November, Brive
Brive 35 (2G 7PG) Llanelli 14 (2G)

Llanelli may have matched their opponents in try-scoring, but in every
other department they were comprehensively outplayed. The Brive
forwards were in irrepressible mood and it was no surprise when their
No 8 Thierry Labrousse powered over from a scrum under the posts. If
it hadn't been for the sublime finishing of Ieuan Evans, Llanelli would
have been mightily embarrassed. His first try came after a break and
kick-through by Wayne Proctor, the second from a sharp-eyed bit of
play following a tap penalty. Venditti's try was fortunate in that there
appeared to be a knock-on, but not even Welshmen were complaining
about the justice of the final result.

Brive: S Viars; G Fabre, C Lamaison, D Venditti, S Carrat; A Penaud (*capt*),
P Carbonneau; D Casadei, L Travers, R Crespy, E Alegret, T Rees, Y Domi,
G Kacala, T Labrousse *Replacements* C Heymans for Penaud (78 mins); E Bouti
for Travers (56 mins); A Boudi for Crespy (76 mins); F Duboisset for Domi (32
mins)
Scorers *Tries:* Labrousse, Venditti *Conversions:* Lamaison (2)
Penalty Goals: Lamaison (7)

Llanelli: W Proctor; I Evans (*capt*), M Wintle, N Boobyer, G Evans; F Botica, R Moon; R Jones, R McBryde, S John, S Ford, V Cooper, M Perego, I Jones, C Wyatt *Replacements* P Morris for Perego (41 mins)
Scorers *Tries:* I Evans (2)   *Conversions:* Botica (2)
Referee B Campsall (England)

KNOCK-OUT STAGE

Pool A

	P	W	D	L	F	A	Pts
Dax	4	3	0	1	141	69	6
Bath	4	3	0	1	136	88	6
Pontypridd	4	3	0	1	97	60	6
Benetton Treviso	4	1	0	3	106	135	2
Edinburgh	4	0	0	4	71	199	0

Pontypridd 28, Treviso 22; Bath 55, Edinburgh 26; Edinburgh 10, Pontypridd 32; Treviso 14, Dax 34; Pontypridd 19, Bath 6; Dax 69, Edinburgh 12; Bath 25, Dax 16; Edinburgh 23, Treviso 43; Pontypridd 18, Dax 22; Treviso 27, Bath 50

Pool B

	P	W	D	L	F	A	Pts
Leicester	4	4	0	0	114	43	8
Llanelli	4	2	0	2	97	81	4
Leinster	4	2	0	2	86	109	4
Pau	4	1	0	3	137	103	2
Scottish Borders	4	1	0	3	80	178	2

Pau 85, Scottish Borders 28; Llanelli 34, Leinster 17; Scottish Borders 24, Llanelli 16; Llanelli 31, Pau 15; Leicester 43, Scottish Borders 3; Leinster 10, Leicester 27; Pau 14, Leicester 19; Scottish Borders 25, Leinster 34; Leinster 25, Pau 23; Leicester 25, Llanelli 16

Pool C

	P	W	D	L	F	A	Pts
Brive	4	4	0	0	106	65	8
NEC Harlequins	4	3	0	1	131	95	6
Neath	4	2	0	2	83	109	4
Ulster	4	1	0	3	75	87	2
Caledonia	4	0	0	4	117	156	0

Brive 34, Neath 19; Caledonia 34, Ulster 41; Neath 27, Caledonia 18; Ulster 15, Harlequins 21; Harlequins 44, Neath 22; Caledonia 30, Brive 32; Brive 23, Harlequins 10; Neath 15, Ulster 13; Ulster 6, Brive 17; Harlequins 56, Caledonia 35

Pool D

	P	W	D	L	F	A	Pts
Cardiff	4	3	0	1	135	97	6
Toulouse	4	3	0	1	157	142	6
Wasps	4	2	0	2	156	115	4
Munster	4	2	0	2	109	135	4
Milan	4	0	0	4	73	141	0

Munster 25, Milan 5; Wasps 24, Cardiff 26; Cardiff 48, Munster 18; Milan 26, Toulouse 44; Munster 49, Wasps 22; Toulouse 36, Cardiff 20; Wasps 77, Toulouse 17; Cardiff 41, Milan 19; Toulouse 60, Munster 19; Milan 23, Wasps 33

HEINEKEN EUROPEAN CONFERENCE 1996-97

26 January 1997, Stade de la Mediterranee, Béziers
Bourgoin 18 (5PG 1DG) **Castres 9** (3PG)

Bourgoin won the all-French final for the European Conference title in a battle of the boots in front of 10,000 spectators at the Stade de la Mediterranee, Beziers. These two fierce rivals could not conjure up a try between them, despite Bourgoin having scored 30 tries and Castres 33 in their seven matches en route to the final.

Centre Alexandre Peclier, who had already contributed 104 points in Bourgoin's march to the final, was the first to make an impression on the scoreboard with an eighth minute penalty. Later in the first half he added another and then wrapped up the match with a last-minute drop goal. The rest of the damage was done by Patrice Favre, who came on as replacement fly half for Gilles Cassagne in the 47th minute and turned the game in Bourgoin's favour with three penalty goals.

Underdogs Castres never gave up, and twice drew level in the first half with penalties from Sebastien Paillat and Cyril Savy, but all they could manage after half-time was a Savy penalty as Bourgoin took command.

Bourgoin: N Geany; L Leflamand, A Peclier, S Glas, L Belligoi; G Cassagne, D Mazille; P Vessiller, J-P Sanchez, L Gomez, J Daude, M Cecillion (*capt*), A Chazalet, P Raschi, M Malafosse *Replacements* P Favre for Cassagne (47 mins) D Morgan for Gomez (48 mins) F Nibelle for Daude (58 mins) J-F Martin-Cullet for Sanchez (72 mins)
Scorers *Penalty Goals:* A Peclier (2), P Favre (3) *Dropped Goal:* A Peclier
Castres: C Savy; C Lucquiaud, J-M Auc, E Artiguste, P Garrigues; S Paillat, F Seguier (*capt*); L Toussaint, C Bataut, T Lafforgue, C Gaston, J-F Gourragne, B Dalla-Riva, N Hallinger, L Loppy *Replacements* M Reggiardo for Lafforgue (58 mins) S Vile for Paillat (66 mins)
Scorers *Penalty Goals:* S Paillat, C Savy (2)
Referee Patrick Robin (France)

Quarter-finals
Bourgoin 17 Montferrand 15
Narbonne 23 Northampton 22
Castres 23 Toulon 15
Agen 20 Begles 15 (aet)

Semi-finals
Bourgoin 29 Narbonne 6
Castres 23 Agen 9

Final
Bourgoin 18 Castres 9

BLUES LIVE UP TO BILLING

THE SUPER-12 SERIES 1997

The Super-12 competition has been lauded in most parts of the globe. Only in the UK do some see potentially dangerous flaws in the free-rolling extravaganza that the Super-12 has become. There perceptive critics have raised doubts about the slavish devotion to continuity which the Super-12 administrators seem keen to promote at all costs. Finally even the International Board themselves have recognised that the balance had tilted too far in favour of the side in possession. At a conference hosted in Cape Town during the British Lions first Test with South Africa the delegates announced that they would be addressing the issue. 'We must restore the balance more in favour of the defender and more against the ball-carrier,' said Lee Smith, the game development officer for the International Board.

The remark was clearly directed at the Super-12. There have been some astonishing scores, notably the 75-43 scoreline which Natal and Otago managed to produce in Durban. There is no doubt that the rugby played has an enormous amount to commend it. However, the ease of scores, which is nothing to do with airy-fairy tackling but which is simply induced by the interpretation of the laws, does the traditions of the game a disservice.

On the field Auckland Blues reigned supreme, their only blemish on a mighty campaign being a 40-40 against Northern Transvaal in baking conditions in Pretoria. The Blues then went on to win in scorching Bloemfontein against Free State. 'I don't think I could have asked for anything more than what the players achieved on this trip,' said Auckland coach Graham Henry. Small wonder that Buck Shelford should say after Auckland's triumph in the final: 'Auckland are the best team in the world outside Test rugby.'

FINAL
31 May, Auckland

Auckland Blues 23 (2G 3PG)   **ACT Brumbies 7** (1G)

The Auckland Blues came into the competition as favourites and they lived up to their billing. This was a disappointing final, though, in that so much of the build-up had been stylish and creative. However, two factors contributed to a more intense, attritional final. The first was the weather, the heavens opening above Eden Park to make the pitch extremely wet and handling difficult. The second factor was the power of the opposition pack, the Brumbies matching their vaunted opponents in every phase. At one scrum Auckland tighthead Olo Brown was popped out only for the Aucklander to return the insult to ACT's

Argentinian-born loosehead, Patricio Noriega, at the very next scrum.
   Auckland, in the end, had too much class and composure, not to
mention the succour of home advantage, for their Australian opponents. They scored two tries to one and at one stage just after half-time
looked as if they might streak clear, but the Brumbies, driven forward
by Gregan, came back to finish strongly. The Auckland loose trio of
Zinzan Brooke, Michael Jones and Mark Carter were in imperious
form, hounding the ACT half-backs and midfield and forcing many
turnovers. The key tactical switch came in the second half. 'I told them
to keep the ball in front of the forwards at half-time and that is what
worked,' said Auckland coach, Graham Henry.
   The opening was tense and close. It took 28 minutes for the first
score to arrive. Zinzan Brooke drove into the ACT 22 from a line-out
and was halted just short of the line. Craig Dowd picked up and
ploughed over although ACT players claimed that their fly-half, David
Knox, had got a hand under the ball. Cashmore converted and then
scored a penalty just before half-time.
   Just after the interval Cashmore kicked two more penalties to extend
Auckland's lead to 16-0. ACT were forced to play catch-up rugby. In
the end it succeeded only in catching up with them. Trying to force the
play from their own half, a Knox pass was intercepted by Michael Jones
who trotted in under the posts. Cashmore converted to make it 23-0.
Joe Roff scored a consolation try for the Brumbies.

Auckland Blues: A R Cashmore; J Vidiri, E Clarke, L Stensness, B P Lima;
C J Spencer, O F J Tonu'u; C W Dowd, S B T Fitzpatrick, O M Brown,
R M Brooke, L Lafaiali'i, M N Jones, Z V Brooke (*capt*), M P Carter
Replacements D G Mika for Jones (temp 11-15 mins); C C Riechelmann for
Lafaiali'i (60 mins); D G Mika for Z Brooke (75 mins)
Scorers *Tries:* Dowd, Jones *Conversions:* Cashmore (2)
Penalty Goals: Cashmore (3)
ACT Brumbies: S Larkham; M Hardy, J Holbeck, P W Howard, J W Roff;
D J Knox, G M Gregan; E P Noriega, M Caputo, E J A McKenzie, J Langford,
D Giffin, O Finegan, T Coker, B J Robinson (*capt*) *Replacements* G Logan for
Howard (temp 28-50 mins); I Fenukitau for Finegan (53 mins); R Kafer for
Gregan (75 mins)
Scorers *Try:* Roff *Conversion:* Roff
Referee W T S Henning (South Africa)

SEMI-FINALS
24 May, Auckland
Auckland Blues 55 (6G 1PG 2T) **Natal Sharks 36** (3G 3T)

Auckland Blues: A R Cashmore; J Vidiri, E Clarke, L Stensness, B P Lima;
C J Spencer, O F J Tonu'u; C W Dowd, S B T Fitzpatrick, O M Brown,
R M Brooke, L Lafaiali'i, M N Jones, Z V Brooke (*capt*), M P Carter
Replacements D G Mika for Z Brooke (48 mins); P Thomson for Brown (70 mins);
C C Riechelmann for Lafaiali'i (70 mins); J Stanley for Vidiri (71 mins);
A T Roose for Fitzpatrick (78 mins); M Scott for Tonu'u (78 mins)
Scorers *Tries:* Vidiri (2), Clarke (2), Z Brooke, Carter, Spencer, Cashmore
Conversions: Cashmore (6) *Penalty Goal:* Cashmore

Natal Sharks: A J Joubert; S Payne, J R D Thomson, P G Muller, J Joubert;
H W Honiball, K B Putt; R Kempson, J Allan, A C Garvey, J Slade,
W Boardman, W van Heerden, G H Teichmann (*capt*), W Fyvie
Replacements D Kriese for van Heerden (30 mins); R Strudwick for Boardman (55
mins); A-H Le Roux for Kempson (60); E Stewart for J Joubert (73 mins)
Scorers *Tries:* Payne (2), J Joubert (2), Honiball, Stewart   *Conversions:* Honiball (3)
Referee W J Erickson (Australia)

24 May, Canberra
ACT Brumbies 33 (1G 2PG 4T)   **Wellington Hurricanes 20** (2G 2PG)

ACT Brumbies: S Larkham; M Hardy, J Holbeck, P W Howard, J W Roff;
D J Knox, G M Gregan; E P Noriega, M Caputo, E J A McKenzie, J Langford,
D Giffin, O Finegan, T Coker, B J Robinson (*capt*) *Replacements* I Fenukitau for
Coker (17 mins); J Harrison for Giffin (74 mins)
Scorers *Tries:* Holbeck (2), Hardy, Roff, Gregan   *Conversion:* Knox
Penalty Goals: Knox (2)
Wellington Hurricanes: C M Cullen; T J F Umaga, R M Ranby,
J D O'Halloran, R Q Randle; S J Bachop, J P Preston; M R Allen (*capt*),
N J Hewitt, P H Coffin, M G Russell, M S B Cooksley, K Barrett, F I Tiatia,
M Leslie *Replacements* F Maka for Leslie (10 mins); D A G Waller for Russell (64
mins); V B Cavubati for Coffin (22 mins)
Scorers *Tries:* Cullen (2)   *Conversions:* Preston (2)   *Penalty Goals:* Preston (2)
Referee A Watson (South Africa)

ROUND-ROBIN SUMMARY

28 Feb	Wellington 18, Waikato 23	(*Palmerston North*)
1 Mar	Queensland 19, ACT 24	(*Brisbane*)
1 Mar	N Transvaal 40, Auckland 40	(*Pretoria*)
2 Mar	Free State 20, Gauteng 24	(*Bloemfontein*)
7 Mar	Canterbury 19, Wellington 17	(*Christchurch*)
7 Mar	Free State 15, Auckland 24	(*Bloemfontein*)
8 Mar	NSW 26, Waikato 33	(*Sydney*)
8 Mar	N Transvaal 14, Queensland 3	(*Pretoria*)
8 Mar	Natal 75, Otago 43	(*Durban*)
9 Mar	Gauteng 44, ACT 36	(*Johannesburg*)
14 Mar	Gauteng 47, Otago 29	(*Johannesburg*)
14 Mar	NSW 25, Canterbury 8	(*Sydney*)
15 Mar	Waikato 16, Auckland 26	(*Albany*)
15 Mar	Free State 35, Queensland 24	(*Bloemfontein*)
16 Mar	Natal 35, ACT 26	(*Durban*)
16 Mar	Wellington 64, N Transvaal 32	(*New Plymouth*)
22 Mar	Otago 27, N Transvaal 7	(*Dunedin*)
22 Mar	Gauteng 36, NSW 27	(*Johannesburg*)
22 Mar	Waikato 31, Queensland 16	(*Hamilton*)
22 Mar	ACT 49, Canterbury 29	(*Canberra*)
22 Mar	Free State 45, Natal 40	(*Bloemfontein*)
28 Mar	ACT 38, N Transvaal 19	(*Canberra*)
29 Mar	Canterbury 24, Waikato 15	(*Timaru*)
29 Mar	Natal 28, NSW 23	(*Durban*)
29 Mar	Gauteng 35, Wellington 37	(*Johannesburg*)
30 Mar	Otago 18, Free State 49	(*Invercargill*)
31 Mar	Auckland 49, Queensland 26	(*Auckland*)
4 Apr	Auckland 29, Canterbury 28	(*Pukekohe*)
4 Apr	ACT 50, Free State 23	(*Canberra*)
4 Apr	Natal 29, Wellington 24	(*Durban*)

5 Apr	Queensland 37, Otago 24	*(Brisbane)*
6 Apr	NSW 43, N Transvaal 29	*(Sydney)*
11 Apr	Waikato 15, Natal 33	*(Albany)*
12 Apr	Auckland 41, ACT 29	*(Pukekohe)*
12 Apr	Otago 37, Canterbury 29	*(Dunedin)*
12 Apr	NSW 36, Free State 11	*(Sydney)*
12 Apr	Gauteng 16, N Transvaal 16	*(Johannesburg)*
12 Apr	Queensland 29, Wellington 47	*(Brisbane)*
18 Apr	Otago 9, ACT 15	*(Invercargill)*
19 Apr	NSW 16, Queensland 26	*(Sydney)*
19 Apr	Auckland 63, Gauteng 22	*(Auckland)*
19 Apr	N Transvaal 34, Waikato 27	*(Pretoria)*
19 Apr	Canterbury 26, Natal 26	*(Christchurch)*
20 Apr	Wellington 59, Free State 30	*(Wellington)*
25 Apr	Canterbury 23, Gauteng 0	*(Christchurch)*
26 Apr	ACT 56, NSW 9	*(Canberra)*
26 Apr	Wellington 60, Otago 34	*(Wellington)*
26 Apr	Free State 27, Waikato 13	*(Bloemfontein)*
27 Apr	Auckland 39, Natal 17	*(Auckland)*
2 May	Wellington 19, NSW 3	*(Napier)*
3 May	N Transvaal 23, Canterbury 22	*(Pretoria)*
3 May	Otago 28, Auckland 45	*(Dunedin)*
3 May	Queensland 40, Natal 3	*(Brisbane)*
3 May	Waikato 47, Gauteng 9	*(Hamilton)*
9 May	Otago 16, NSW 27	*(Dunedin)*
9 May	ACT 48, Waikato 34	*(Canberra)*
10 May	Free State 11, Canterbury 16	*(Bloemfontein)*
10 May	Auckland 45, Wellington 42	*(Auckland)*
10 May	Queensland 40, Gauteng 27	*(Brisbane)*
11 May	Natal 27, N Transvaal 27	*(Durban)*
16 May	Waikato 18, Otago 34	*(Taupo)*
16 May	N Transvaal 23, Free State 35	*(Pretoria)*
17 May	NSW 20, Auckland 34	*(Sydney)*
17 May	Canterbury 48, Queensland 3	*(Christchurch)*
17 May	Gauteng 42, Natal 8	*(Johannesburg)*
18 May	Wellington 29, ACT 35	*(Wellington)*

FINAL TABLE

	P	W	D	L	F	A	Bonus	Pts
Auckland Blues	11	10	1	0	435	283	8	50
ACT Brumbies	11	8	0	3	406	291	9	41
Wellington Hurricanes	11	6	0	5	416	314	10	34
Natal Sharks	11	5	2	4	321	350	6	30
Gauteng Lions	11	5	1	5	302	346	6	28
Canterbury Crusaders	11	5	1	5	272	235	4	26
Free State Cheetahs	11	5	0	6	301	327	5	25
Northern Transvaal Blue Bulls	11	3	3	5	264	342	4	22
New South Wales Waratahs	11	4	0	7	255	296	4	20
Queensland Reds .	11	4	0	7	263	318	4	20
Waikato Chiefs	11	4	0	7	272	295	3	19
Otago Highlanders	11	3	0	8	299	409	5	17

Leading points scorers in round-robin: 170 – G Lawless (Natal Sharks); 150 – M Burke (NSW Waratahs); 143-J Preston (Wellington Hurricanes)
Leading try-scorers in round-robin: 13 – J Roff (ACT Brumbies); 12 – T Umaga (Wellington Hurricanes); 9 – C Cullen (Wellington Hurricanes)

JOURNEY INTO THE DARK SHEDS LIGHT

THE 1996-97 SEASON IN ENGLAND

Did anyone know quite what the new season held in store for them? As the season swung into view in late August, no-one could have crossed their hearts and given a positive answer to this question. At that point England were not even in the Five Nations Championship, so Jack Rowell could have had little definite idea as to what he was planning towards. He had no captain either and, for as long as the seemingly interminable EPRUC-RFU dispute dragged on, he would not announce Will Carling's successor. In the end, after much speculation, it was early November before Phil de Glanville was announced as the man to lead England into a new campaign.

The months before had been full of acrimony and speculation. On August 29th the leading clubs under the EPRUC banner announced that they were going to split from the RFU six weeks hence unless more money and delegated power were put their way. On September 4th, as a gesture of solidarity, the entire England squad bar one, a barrel-chested prop from Coventry by the name of Robin Hardwick, boycotted a full training session. It was a very public, unprecedented show of support for the clubs, whom the players regarded as their essential and primary paymasters.

The following day the outlook in another part of the kingdom took a seismic shift for the better. Last year's official launch for *Rothmans Rugby Union Yearbook* was dramatically interrupted by RFU treasurer Colin Herridge with news that the Five Nations Championship was back together. At a secret meeting in Bristol the previous day (in fact the same day as the gathering only broke up in the wee small hours), representatives from all the countries agreed a compromise deal whereby England were allowed back into the tournament in return for a large slice of England's BSkyB money being put back into the collective pot. A formula was to be drawn up to precisely calibrate England's contribution, which was believed to be of the order of £25 million over five years. England also agreed never to negotiate separately again after their current satellite contract runs out in June 2002.

Peace, or at least a truce of some sorts, was thereby declared in the EPRUC-RFU dispute, so freeing the hands of Jack Rowell to get on with the only thing the vast majority of supporters cared about – playing rugby. There had been a lot of speculation as to who would follow Carling into the captaincy hot seat. The front-runners were Lawrence Dallaglio, Phil de Glanville, Jason Leonard and Tim Rodber. Dallaglio and Leonard were the bookmakers'

The England team which beat Scotland at Twickenham. L-R, back row: B B Clarke (replacement), W D C Carling, R A Hill, T R G Stimpson, S D Shaw, M O Johnson, T A K Rodber, L B N Dallaglio, G C Rowntree, J Leonard, D J Garforth (replacement) ; front row: P B T Greening (replacement), M P Regan, T Underwood, P J Grayson, A C T Gomarsall, P R de Glanville (capt), J Rowell (coach), J M Sleightholme, J C Guscott (replacement), A S Healey (replacement), M J Catt (replacement).

favourites, but at a Hollywoodesque press conference it was de Glanville, 28, who marched through the doors to a flash of light and blast of music.

The immediate consequence for Rowell of appointing the man he had first come across at Bath in 1990 fresh out of Oxford University, was that he had to work out the centre conundrum in the England midfield. This issue was to plague Rowell throughout the year, and draw criticism from most quarters. He opted to retain Carling alongside his new captain for the first match against Italy on November 23 to the exclusion of Jeremy Guscott. Guscott was to flit in and out of the side all season, either as a tactical substitute or, with de Glanville injured for the Argentina match, as a stop-gap replacement. But as Sod's law would have it, Guscott was in the best form of his life. His tantalising, short-lived but devastatingly effective interventions left a nation gasping for more. Carling, too, was in good nick, making it very difficult to drop him after his initial selection. However the pairing of such similar players in the midfield never came off.

Rowell grasped the nettle fully elsewhere in a year of change for the side. Rowell blooded five new caps in the opening match of the campaign against Italy, where Tim Stimpson (Newcastle, fullback), Adedayo Adebayo (Bath, wing), Andy Gomarsall (Wasps, scrum-half), Simon Shaw (Bristol, lock) and Chris Sheasby (Wasps, No 8) all took the field. By the season's end new boys Richard Hill (Saracens, openside) and Austin Healey (Leicester, scrum-half) had also elbowed their way to the top of the pile.

The three pre-Christmas matches were a useful bedding-down time for a side in obvious transition. With so many new faces and a new leader to boot, it was perhaps unrealistic to expect England to hit a groove immediately. However the management were far too eager to latch on to these mitigating circumstances as excuses for several sub-standard phases in the three matches. Italy were comfortably dispatched on the scoreboard, 54-21, although the Italians played the entire match without any sort of a line-out. England won 79% of possession from this phase, a return they are unlikely to see again. But England, even though they scored seven tries, were never truly fluent.

The New Zealand Barbarians provided a much sterner test and came through 34-19. It did England little good to point out that they had held the whip hand for the early part of the match, leading 19-13 at one point. When it came to the crunch the Kiwis simply turned on the pressure, stretching clear in the final stages with alarming and decisive ease. The manner in which Carlos Spencer, the young uncapped stand-off, ripped England apart after he came on as substitute in the 60th minute, suggested that there is still a gulf between the best the southern hemisphere can offer and our own young talent. Jack Rowell will also have appreciated the benefit of tactical substitutes, an option he had yet to invoke.

There were three enforced changes for the Argentina match, Guscott coming in for the injured Adebayo on the wing before moving inside as a late replacement for de Glanville. Tony Underwood then stepped into the breach. Nick Beal won his cap in place of Stimpson, the Newcastle full-back, who was suffering from concussion. There were many England supporters wishing for a bout of amnesia after this performance. It took a late try by Jason Leonard to spare the Twickenham blushes. Mike Catt had one of his worst ever days in an England shirt, but the blame was not entirely his. The decision-making of several players was pitiful. Rowell had wanted to use these games as a springboard for the Five Nations and beyond. It would be a long haul yet.

Others thought so too. On the eve of the Five Nations stories circulated that Rowell was about to be sacked. Despite official denials, there was little doubt that Rowell's position had been discussed at secret meetings. Three months down the line and Rowell could finally allow himself a proper smile of satisfaction. There was still work to be done, but at last there were real glimpses of development.

His England team had been rudely deflected from their Grand Slam route to glory by a French team showing unusual Anglo-Saxon traits of fortitude and patience. France came to Twickenham with hope but not real expectation. They had not won at Twickenham in ten years. So when, after an hour's play, the French fans looked to the scoreboard and saw that England led 20-6, their hearts and minds would have told them to expect the worst. It didn't happen. France came thundering back into the game to take victory and to all intents and purposes the Five Nations Championship and Grand Slam into the bargain.

England had a perplexing championship. They shattered nearly every record in the book, rattling up huge scores against Scotland, Ireland and Wales; scoring more points than any team in the history of the Five Nations. And yet they still struggled for long passages of play. Their points invariably came bunched together and in a late charge. Mike Catt was eased out from fly-half and Paul Grayson restored, while Richard Hill helped produce a much better balanced back-row. Gomarsall ran into one blind alley too many and Austin Healey seized his opportunity. The anxiety which is never far from Jack Rowell's manner was illustrated in the bizarre decision to recall Rob Andrew to the colours for the Welsh match. Andrew duly came off the bench for one final appearance.

This game was also to prove the 72nd and last international appearance of Will Carling. In 59 matches as England captain Carling led England to 46 victories, including three Grand Slams. At the season's end one of his lieutenants, Brian Moore, who had helped Richmond to the Second Division title, also retired. Carling, though, intends to carry on for his club, Harlequins.

The club season was fiercely contested at every level. The professional era, for all the problems it had caused off the field, had nothing but a beneficial effect on it. Every club realised that the only way to prosper was by playing bright, expansive rugby. There were a host of high-profile foreign newcomers to welcome – Michael Lynagh, Philippe Sella, Francois Pienaar, Thierry Lacroix, Laurent Cabannes and Joel Stransky among others – as well as many names to spot in unfamiliar colours as the transfer merry-go-round swung into action. The race for the First Division title went all the way into the final month. Wasps, brilliantly led by Lawrence Dallaglio, held their nerve and their bodies together to take only their second ever championship on the penultimate Saturday. Leicester, fancied for a double after beating Wasps in early April, completely disintegrated thereafter losing four out of five League matches. They only hung on to fourth place by the skin of their teeth. A scrambled 20-20 draw at Sale on the last Saturday, having trailed 20-3 at one point, gave them the necessary point to stay ahead of Sale in the table and thus obtain entry to Europe.

The Pilkington Cup between the same two sides was a massive disappointment. It seemed as if all the energy and sparkle had been drained from the teams by the previous week's meeting. Either that or the sides lacked ambition and nerve when under pressure. This has been a failing of Leicester in the past and certainly one that coach Bob Dwyer will want to address most urgently. The 9-3 win may have put silverware in the trophy cabinet, but it did absolutely nothing to win friends outside of a ten-mile radius of Leicester.

Bath, after their mid-season trauma, finished in good fettle in second place. Harlequins were third, a reasonable enough showing although there were signs of outright unrest at the club as the season closed. Orrell and West Hartlepool were relegated.

The play-offs were a torment in their own right, dreamt up by cruel administrators who jibbed at trimming the League in size to ten clubs and came up with this formula instead. It would have been a major upset if either Bristol or London Irish had succumbed over two legs to Bedford and Coventry. First Division tenth spot was playing Second Division fourth and eleventh playing third. Bristol duly beat Bedford 39-23 on aggregate, London Irish seeing off Coventry 42-23.

As expected the big spenders, Richmond and Newcastle, bought their way into the First Division, while the have-nots, Nottingham and Rugby, fell further down the ladder, slipping into the Third Division. High-flying, financially well-endowed Worcester and Newbury continued their rise through the ranks, winning the respective titles in League Four North and South. Money was doing all the talking in this first fully-fledged professional season.

WASPS TAKE COURAGE WITH THEIR CONVICTIONS

THE COURAGE LEAGUES 1996-97

There were several farewells to be made at the end of this dramatic season. To Courage, admirable sponsors over the last decade; to Orrell who have been with them all the way in the top flight of the Leagues; to Nottingham and Rugby lower down, whose battle against the monied elite was a doomed cause. One of the great individual face-offs of the last ten years also came to an end when those battling hookers, Graham Dawe of Bath and Brian Moore, once of Harlequins, latterly of Richmond, announced their retirements.

But it was a time of welcome too. To a new sponsor, Allied Dunbar. To new champions, Wasps, who broke the Bath-Leicester duopoly in convincing style, winning only their second ever title by six points. They held firm while all around wilted at some stage or other, notably Leicester. The Tigers beat Wasps 18-12 in what had appeared to be a decisive result at the beginning of April, but the Leicester challenge then completely collapsed. They lost 32-30 in a wonderful, if frantic, game at Gloucester and thereafter could barely string two passes together let alone muster a decent performance. Bath gained absolute revenge for their Cup defeat with a 47-9 win over them at the Rec, confirmation, if any were needed, that Leicester were out on their feet. Their European and Pilkington Cup commitments, combined with bad weather postponements, meant they had to play seven games in 22 days. It was beyond them.

Bath had their hiccup in mid-winter. While all around fretted, Wasps showed their mettle. Lawrence Dallaglio was a magnificent captain. Wasps traded shrewdly in the transfer market, Rob Henderson and Kenny Logan were judicious mid-season acquisitions; Gareth Rees was a pillar of reliability. His last-second conversion against Bath in the championship run-in was a crucial motivating moment.

The League campaign was theatrical. There were four European places on offer and the alarming prospect of the play-offs for those at the bottom end. Bristol and London Irish were the unlucky two, although Northampton must have had a few anxious moments over the closing matches. The Saints, Second Division champions the year before, underachieved in finishing ninth. Bristol and London Irish prevailed over Bedford and Coventry in the play-offs.

The Second Division belonged to the big spenders. Richmond and Newcastle took the honours at a canter, Newcastle busting through the 1,000 point barrier to finish with an average of 57 points a match. Bedford and Coventry have their sights firmly set on promotion next season. Bedford played delightful rugby in beating Newcastle 34-28 in the closing weeks.

The Third Division was keenly fought at the top, particularly between Leeds and Exeter for the second promotion slot. The latter eventually prevailed, condemning big-spending Leeds to another season in League 3. Newbury and Worcester, both with money to spend, romped through their respective Fourth Divisions, Newbury finishing with an unblemished record. They're on their way.

Wasps celebrate winning the Courage League Division 1 title.

THE COURAGE LEAGUES 1996-97

NATIONAL DIVISION

National 1

	P	W	D	L	F	A	Pts
Wasps	22	18	1	3	685	406	37
Bath	22	15	1	6	863	411	31
NEC Harlequins	22	15	0	7	755	416	30
Leicester	22	14	1	7	600	395	29
Sale	22	13	2	7	603	525	28
Saracens	22	12	1	9	568	459	25
Gloucester	22	11	1	10	476	589	23
Northampton	22	10	0	12	515	477	20
Bristol	22	8	1	13	432	625	17
London Irish	22	6	0	16	502	747	12
W Hartlepool	22	3	0	19	382	795	6
Orrell	22	3	0	19	350	886	6

National 2

	P	W	D	L	F	A	Pts
Richmond	22	19	2	1	986	410	40
Newcastle	22	19	1	2	1255	346	39
Coventry	22	16	1	5	738	394	33
Bedford	22	15	0	7	720	482	30
London Scottish	22	11	0	11	549	568	22
Wakefield	22	11	0	11	504	557	22
Rotherham	22	10	0	12	525	661	20
Moseley	22	9	0	13	492	741	18
Waterloo	22	8	0	14	506	661	16
Blackheath	22	7	0	15	412	641	14
Rugby Lions	22	3	0	19	317	1060	6
Nottingham	22	2	0	20	344	827	4

National 3

	P	W	D	L	F	A	Pts
Exeter	30	25	0	5	923	443	50
Fylde	30	24	1	5	813	439	49
Leeds	30	24	0	6	1209	432	48
Morley	30	22	0	8	928	570	44
Harrogate	30	18	0	12	832	599	36
Reading	30	17	1	12	869	631	35
Wharfedale	30	17	0	13	710	635	34
Rosslyn Park	30	17	0	13	630	620	34
Otley	30	13	0	17	720	766	26
Lydney	30	13	0	17	668	766	26
London Welsh	30	12	0	18	632	777	24
Liverpool St H	30	9	0	21	665	827	18
Walsall	30	8	0	22	640	980	16
Havant	30	8	0	22	580	954	16
Redruth	30	8	0	22	565	1116	16
Clifton	30	4	0	26	518	1347	8

National 4 North

	P	W	D	L	F	A	Pts
Worcester	26	23	3	0	833	378	49
B'ham S'hull	26	19	0	7	746	391	38
Preston Grass	26	17	2	7	568	394	36
Manchester	26	16	1	9	763	514	33
Sandal	26	15	1	10	618	572	31
Stourbridge	26	14	1	11	704	579	29
Winnington Park	26	14	1	11	641	565	29
Sheffield	26	12	2	12	496	451	26
Kendal	26	11	1	14	541	451	23
Aspatria	26	10	1	15	616	713	21
Lichfield	26	10	0	16	544	713	20
Nuneaton	26	8	1	17	457	670	17
Hereford	26	4	0	22	287	970	8
Stoke on Trent	26	2	0	24	391	854	4

National 4 South

	P	W	D	L	F	A	Pts
Newbury	25	25	0	0	1170	295	52
Henley	26	19	2	5	754	477	40
Barking	26	16	1	9	740	496	33
Camberley	26	15	2	9	688	513	32
Cheltenham	26	15	2	9	559	420	32
Plymouth Albion	26	13	3	10	709	591	29
Met Police	26	14	1	11	659	558	29
Weston-s-Mare	26	12	0	14	503	501	24
Tabard	26	10	3	13	511	557	23
North Walsham	26	10	1	15	426	604	21
Berry Hill	26	10	0	16	425	643	20
High Wycombe	26	8	1	17	560	707	17
Charlton Park	26	3	1	22	351	1140	7
Askeans	25	2	1	22	340	893	5

LONDON DIVISION

London 1

	P	W	D	L	F	A	Pts
Esher	13	12	0	1	458	171	22
Norwich	13	9	1	3	267	181	19
Ruislip	13	8	0	5	235	207	16
Harlow	13	7	1	5	405	311	15
Basingstoke	13	7	1	5	237	246	15
Staines	13	7	0	6	345	289	14
G'ford & God	13	7	0	6	321	279	14
Sutton & Epsom	13	6	0	7	288	225	12
Wimbleton	13	6	0	7	286	235	12
Old Colfeians	12	7	0	5	258	347	12
Sudbury	12	5	1	6	204	232	9
O Mid-Whitgift	13	3	0	10	170	321	6
Southend	13	3	0	10	197	413	6
Thurrock	13	1	0	12	179	393	2

London 2 North

	P	W	D	L	F	A	Pts
Cheshunt	11	9	1	1	319	152	19
Bishop's Stortford	11	8	0	3	336	159	16
R'ford & Gidea Pk	11	8	0	3	275	216	16
Cambridge	11	7	0	4	267	203	14
Ipswich	11	6	0	5	290	252	12
Old Albanians	11	6	0	5	257	254	12
Old Verulamians	11	5	0	6	185	261	10
Finchley	11	4	0	7	200	253	8
Colchester	11	4	1	6	185	252	7
Brentwood	11	3	0	8	151	227	6
Woodford	11	3	0	8	220	310	6
Ealing	11	2	0	9	180	326	4

London 2 South

	P	W	D	L	F	A	Pts
Thanet Wands	12	11	0	1	392	172	22
Gravesend	12	10	0	2	380	158	20
Beckenham	12	9	0	3	312	201	18
Westcombe Park	12	7	0	5	414	228	14
Horsham	12	7	0	5	283	238	14
Old Blues	12	7	0	5	298	265	14
O Wimbledonians	12	6	0	6	253	233	12
Old Juddian	12	7	0	5	238	236	12
Old Guildfordians	12	4	0	8	235	289	8
Dorking	12	4	0	8	224	281	8
S'ham-Croydon	12	3	0	9	142	498	6
Old Reigatian	12	2	0	10	198	308	2
Brockleians	12	1	0	11	152	414	2

London 3 North-East

	P	W	D	L	F	A	Pts
Diss	12	10	1	1	378	131	21
Chingford	12	10	1	1	334	157	21
Braintree	11	9	1	1	263	198	19
Canvey Island	12	6	1	5	238	306	13
Lowestoft & Yar	12	5	1	6	205	216	11
Woodbridge	12	5	0	7	252	245	10
Bury St Edmunds	12	6	0	6	247	258	10
Maldon	12	5	0	7	217	289	10
Eton Manor	11	4	1	6	222	249	9
West Norfolk	12	4	2	6	218	232	8
Chelmsford	12	4	0	8	177	233	6
Rochford	12	4	0	8	212	291	4
Old Edwardians	12	1	0	11	132	290	2

London 3 North-West

	P	W	D	L	F	A	Pts
O M Taylors	12	10	1	1	415	202	21
Welwyn	12	10	1	1	323	146	21

	P	W	D	L	F	A	Pts
Barnet	12	9	0	3	415	134	18
Hertford	12	9	0	3	305	153	18
Grasshoppers	12	7	1	4	275	198	15
Old Gaytonians	12	5	3	4	267	267	13
Letchworth	12	6	0	6	287	312	12
Hampstead	12	5	1	6	346	280	11
Old Millhillians	12	5	1	6	226	223	11
Lensbury	12	3	0	9	289	337	6
Fullerians	12	3	0	9	210	315	6
Kingsburians	12	1	0	11	103	555	2
Haringey	12	1	0	11	147	491	2

London 3 South-East

	P	W	D	L	F	A	Pts
Lewes	12	11	0	1	301	182	22
Sevenoaks	12	10	0	2	506	146	20
Haywards Heath	12	10	0	2	475	126	20
Maidstone	12	9	0	3	273	141	18
Worthing	12	6	0	6	326	257	12
Canterbury	12	6	0	6	245	235	12
Park House	12	6	0	6	285	302	12
Tunbridge Wells	12	6	0	6	243	323	12
Sidcup	12	5	0	7	237	323	10
Chichester	12	4	0	8	154	246	6
Bognor	12	3	0	9	174	362	4
Old Beccehamian	12	1	0	11	167	325	2
Brighton	12	1	0	11	124	542	2

London 3 South-West

	P	W	D	L	F	A	Pts
Winchester	12	10	0	2	344	133	20
Warlingham	12	9	1	2	330	168	19
Portsmouth	12	9	1	2	351	205	19
Gosport	12	9	0	3	328	183	18
Alton	12	8	0	4	263	218	16
Old Alleynian	12	7	0	5	296	233	14
Jersey	12	6	0	6	322	235	12
Old Emanuel	12	6	0	6	252	296	12
Old Whitgiftians	12	4	2	6	188	286	10
Purley	12	3	0	9	246	345	6
Old Walcountians	12	2	1	9	158	369	5
Guy's Hospital	12	2	0	10	221	348	2
Barnes	12	0	1	11	126	406	1

Eastern Counties 1

	P	W	D	L	F	A	Pts
Basildon	12	12	0	0	395	125	24
Campion	12	10	0	2	359	127	20
Upminster	12	9	0	3	233	211	18
Holt	12	8	0	4	258	238	16
Wymondham	12	7	0	5	332	190	14
Newmarket	12	7	0	5	204	183	14
Shelford	12	6	0	6	310	218	12
Cantabrigian	12	5	0	7	263	244	10
Ilford Wanderers	12	5	0	7	197	235	10
Ely	12	4	0	8	208	301	8
Wanstead	12	3	0	9	181	351	6
Harwich & D'ct	12	1	0	11	154	394	2
Saffron Walden	12	1	0	11	118	395	0

Eastern Counties 2

	P	W	D	L	F	A	Pts
Hadleigh	12	12	0	0	724	74	24
Bancroft	12	10	0	2	345	176	20
Felixstowe	12	9	0	3	297	114	18
Westcliff	12	8	0	4	287	202	16
Old Cooperians	12	8	0	4	194	160	16
Thetford	12	7	0	5	361	225	12
Loughton	12	6	0	6	255	260	12
Met Pol Chigwell	12	4	1	7	203	285	9
Old Palmerians	12	4	0	8	127	247	8
Fakenham	12	4	0	8	147	394	8
Thames	12	2	1	9	102	348	5
Southwold	12	2	0	10	180	433	4
Ravens	12	1	0	11	117	421	2

Eastern Counties 3

	P	W	D	L	F	A	Pts
S Woodham F	11	11	0	0	336	84	22
Mersea Island	11	9	0	2	272	125	18
Crusaders	11	8	0	3	279	112	16
Billericay	11	8	0	3	283	141	16
Beccles	11	8	0	3	266	174	16
Broadland	11	5	0	6	212	215	8
Ipswich YM	11	4	0	7	186	192	8
East London	11	3	0	8	177	221	6
Stowmarket	11	2	0	9	102	290	4
Lak'ham Hewett	11	2	0	9	106	304	4
Thurston	11	2	0	9	115	431	4
Wisbech	11	4	0	7	126	171	2

Eastern Counties 4

	P	W	D	L	F	A	Pts
March	9	9	0	0	343	67	18
Burnham-on-C	9	8	0	1	345	101	16
Haverhill	9	6	0	3	143	107	12
Ongar	9	5	0	4	209	185	10
Sawston	9	5	0	4	132	128	10
Stanford	9	4	0	5	162	185	8
Brightlingsea	9	3	0	6	168	184	6
Norwich Union	9	3	0	6	96	267	6
Witham	9	2	0	7	184	261	2
Clacton	9	0	0	9	53	350	0

Eastern Counties 5

	P	W	D	L	F	A	Pts
Millwall Albion	8	7	0	1	282	84	14
Swaffham	8	6	0	2	196	145	12
May & Baker	8	5	1	2	264	110	11
Rayleigh	8	5	1	2	141	142	11
Fairbairn-Chig	8	5	0	3	120	100	10
Dagenham	8	3	1	4	173	138	5
Mistley	8	1	1	6	172	305	3
RAF Lakenheath	7	1	0	6	161	169	2
Orwell	7	0	0	7	62	378	0

Hampshire 1

	P	W	D	L	F	A	Pts
Esso	12	11	0	1	285	152	22
Southampton	12	10	0	2	503	179	20
Farnborough	12	11	0	1	399	99	20
US Portsmouth	12	9	0	3	367	163	18

	P	W	D	L	F	A	Pts
Millbrook	12	9	0	3	362	176	18
Andover	12	6	0	6	358	186	12
Isle of Wight	12	5	0	7	221	311	10
Eastleigh	12	4	0	8	126	292	8
Guernsey	12	4	0	8	246	445	8
Petersfield	12	3	0	9	306	313	6
Tottonians	12	3	0	9	262	272	6
Ventnor	12	3	0	9	187	467	6
Fordingbridge	12	0	0	12	57	624	-4

Hampshire 2

	P	W	D	L	F	A	Pts
Overton	14	11	1	2	473	132	23
New Milton	14	11	1	2	442	203	21
Trojans	14	10	0	4	381	176	20
Romsey	14	8	3	3	294	236	19
S'down & Shank	14	6	1	7	268	287	11
Fareham Heathens	14	5	0	9	262	397	10
Nomads	14	2	0	12	105	400	4
Alresford	14	0	0	14	103	497	-2

Hampshire 3

	P	W	D	L	F	A	Pts
Southampton I	12	11	1	0	555	146	23
A C Delco	12	9	0	3	380	174	18
Hamble	12	8	0	4	335	134	16
Waterlooville	12	7	0	5	320	224	14
Fleet	11	3	1	7	191	279	7
Ellingham	11	1	0	10	86	563	2
Kingsclere	12	1	0	11	92	439	0

Herts/Middlesex 1

	P	W	D	L	F	A	Pts
Harpenden	12	11	0	1	388	128	22
St Albans	12	9	0	3	374	181	18
O Meadonians	12	9	0	3	271	156	18
Tring	12	8	0	4	267	199	16
Old Elizabethians	12	9	0	3	233	193	16
Hackney	12	6	0	6	282	233	12
Uxbridge	12	6	0	6	204	159	12
Mill Hill	12	6	0	6	202	235	12
Hemel Hempstead	12	6	0	6	254	173	8
St Mary's Hosp	12	4	0	8	264	272	8
Old Hamptonians	12	2	0	10	199	312	4
Hendon	12	2	0	10	136	335	4
Centaurs	12	0	0	12	122	620	-2

Herts/Middlesex 2

	P	W	D	L	F	A	Pts
Harrow	12	12	0	0	394	130	24
Upper Clapton	12	9	1	2	265	159	19
Twickenham	12	9	0	3	287	172	18
Wembley	12	8	0	4	258	181	16
Old Paulines	12	7	1	4	212	233	15
HAC	12	6	0	6	270	282	12
L New Zealand	12	4	2	6	168	216	10
Enfield Ignatians	12	4	1	7	230	227	9
Civil Service	12	4	1	7	170	183	9
Old Haberdashers	12	3	3	6	170	218	9
Stevenage Town	12	1	3	8	159	259	5
Datchworth	12	2	1	9	133	274	5
Old Actonians	12	2	1	9	118	300	5

Herts/Middlesex 3

	P	W	D	L	F	A	Pts
London Nigerians	11	11	0	0	595	163	22
UCS Old Boys	11	9	1	1	330	132	19
Old Abbotsonians	11	9	1	1	313	119	19
Hitchin	11	6	0	5	212	224	12
London French	11	5	0	6	244	307	10
London Exiles	11	5	0	6	171	265	10
Roxeth Man OB	11	4	0	7	117	236	8
Barclays Bank	11	5	0	6	264	218	6
Antlers	11	4	0	7	218	277	6
Bank of England	11	3	0	8	209	334	6
Watford	11	3	0	8	113	318	6
Sudbury Court	11	1	0	10	99	292	2

Herts/Middlesex 4

	P	W	D	L	F	A	Pts
Feltham	11	11	0	0	397	109	22
London Cornish	11	10	0	1	372	119	18
Old Ashmoleans	11	7	0	4	299	308	14
Royston	11	6	1	4	175	125	13
H'smith & Ful	11	7	0	4	277	113	10
Southgate	10	5	0	5	162	188	10
Old Isleworthians	11	4	1	6	182	194	9
Old Grammarians	11	4	0	7	201	230	8
Old Standfordians	11	4	1	6	155	214	7
Pinner & Gram	11	1	0	10	82	276	2
Hayes	11	0	0	11	50	568	-2
Royal Hospitals	10	4	1	5	296	204	-11

Herts/Middlesex 5 North

	P	W	D	L	F	A	Pts
Millfield Old Boys	6	6	0	0	222	93	12
St Nicholas O B	6	5	0	1	225	46	10
Cuffley	6	4	0	2	117	140	8
Old Tottonians	6	2	0	4	129	134	4
Old Streetonians	6	2	0	4	122	153	2
QE II Hospital	6	1	0	5	54	168	2
Hatfield	6	1	0	5	36	171	2

Herts/Middlesex 5 South

	P	W	D	L	F	A	Pts
Northolt	5	5	0	0	311	6	10
GWR	7	5	0	2	136	105	10
Quintin	7	3	2	2	92	106	8
Orleans FP	7	3	1	3	106	148	7
British Airways	7	4	0	3	58	111	6
Osterley	6	1	1	4	46	202	3
Meadhurst	6	1	1	4	73	115	1
Middlesex Hosp	5	0	1	4	64	93	-7

Kent 1

	P	W	D	L	F	A	Pts
Cranbrook	11	10	1	0	277	153	21
Medway	11	9	0	2	198	111	18
Sheppey	11	7	1	3	306	229	15
Old Dunstonians	11	7	0	4	302	216	14
Gillingham Anch	11	7	1	3	263	154	13
Dartfordians	11	6	0	5	214	229	12
Betteshanger	11	5	1	5	258	164	11
O Shootershillians	11	4	1	6	178	253	9
Ashford	11	4	0	7	139	175	8

	P	W	D	L	F	A	Pts
Bromley	11	2	0	9	130	294	4
Met Police, Hayes	11	1	1	9	131	288	3
Dover	11	1	0	10	190	320	2

Kent 2

	P	W	D	L	F	A	Pts
Folkestone	12	11	0	1	527	123	22
Whitstable	12	9	1	2	254	86	19
Showdown CW	12	8	0	4	202	142	16
Deal	12	7	1	4	269	191	15
Nat West Bank	12	7	1	4	250	186	15
Sittingbourne	12	6	2	4	220	120	14
Lordswood	12	7	1	4	241	185	13
Tonbridge	12	6	0	6	319	196	12
Aylesford	12	3	2	7	97	239	8
O Gravesendians	12	4	0	8	185	350	8
O Williamsonians	12	3	0	9	158	302	6
Old Elthamians	12	3	0	9	147	304	6
Greenwich Acad	12	0	0	12	70	515	-4

Kent 3

	P	W	D	L	F	A	Pts
Midland Bank	9	9	0	0	332	105	16
New Ash Green	9	7	0	2	200	79	14
Bexley	9	6	0	3	171	128	12
Vigo	9	5	0	4	181	118	10
Edenbridge	9	4	1	4	122	130	9
STC Footscray	9	2	1	6	94	225	5
Citizens	9	3	0	6	81	137	4
Orpington	9	2	0	7	114	227	4
Old Olavians	9	2	0	7	78	205	4
Canterbury Exiles	9	4	0	5	161	180	-22

Kent 4

	P	W	D	L	F	A	Pts
Darenth Valley	8	6	0	2	225	91	12
Greenwich	8	6	0	2	173	94	12
Faversham	8	6	0	2	146	53	10
Meopham	8	2	0	6	59	183	4
Westerham	8	0	0	8	75	257	0

Surrey 1

	P	W	D	L	F	A	Pts
Old Reedonians	12	10	0	2	418	138	20
Effingham	12	9	0	3	265	113	18
Univ Vandals	12	9	0	3	294	195	18
Cranleigh	12	9	1	2	234	132	17
Chobham	12	7	0	5	282	219	14
Chipstead	12	7	0	5	236	207	12
Woking	12	6	0	6	231	203	12
Old Caterhamians	12	4	0	8	209	248	8
Old Cranleighans	12	4	0	8	166	262	8
KCS Old Boys	12	4	0	8	185	319	8
Batt Ironsides	12	3	0	9	152	300	6
John Fisher OB	12	2	1	9	127	275	5
Kingston	12	3	0	9	139	327	4

Surrey 2

	P	W	D	L	F	A	Pts
Raynes Park	12	12	0	0	440	109	24
Wandsworthians	12	9	1	2	323	160	19
Farnham	12	9	0	3	335	159	18

	P	W	D	L	F	A	Pts
Merton	12	8	1	3	227	154	17
Old Rutlishians	12	6	2	4	290	221	14
Old Haileyburians	12	6	1	5	336	216	13
London Media	12	6	0	6	319	291	12
Cobham	12	5	0	7	257	227	10
Old Tiffinians	12	4	0	8	219	301	8
Law Society	12	4	0	8	225	439	8
Shirley Wanderers	12	3	1	8	197	225	7
Old Freemans	12	3	0	9	162	399	6
Old Suttonians	12	0	0	12	107	536	0

Surrey 3

	P	W	D	L	F	A	Pts
Old Wellingtonian	10	9	0	1	316	75	18
Reigate & Redhill	10	8	1	1	282	133	17
Mitcham	10	7	0	3	167	94	12
Kings Coll Hosp	10	6	0	4	230	183	12
Lightwater	10	5	1	4	199	155	11
Croydon	10	5	0	5	125	230	10
Worth Old Boys	10	4	0	6	222	202	8
London Fire Brig	10	3	0	7	166	236	6
Old Bevonians	10	2	0	8	151	275	4
Egham	10	2	0	8	110	334	4
Bec Old Boys	10	3	0	7	136	187	2

Surrey 4

	P	W	D	L	F	A	Pts
Haslemere	7	6	0	1	212	101	12
Old Johnians	7	6	0	1	139	87	10
St Georges Hosp	7	4	0	3	124	15	8
Racal-Decca	7	4	0	3	92	144	8
Surrey University	7	3	0	4	136	138	6
Economicals	7	3	0	4	85	104	6
Surrey Police	7	1	0	6	103	156	2
Oxted	7	1	0	6	41	187	2

Sussex 1

	P	W	D	L	F	A	Pts
H'field & Wald	12	12	0	0	428	102	24
Uckfield	12	10	0	2	401	117	20
East Grinstead	12	9	0	3	409	113	18
Crawley	12	8	1	3	357	151	17
Eastbourne	12	8	1	3	289	132	17
Hove	12	7	0	5	242	173	14
Ditchling	12	7	0	5	194	245	14
Hastings & Bex	12	3	2	7	256	254	8
Crowborough	12	3	1	8	168	254	7
Old Brightonians	12	3	1	8	158	438	7
Seaford	12	3	0	9	215	298	4
Pulborough	12	2	0	10	110	392	4
Burgess Hill	12	0	0	12	121	679	0

Sussex 2

	P	W	D	L	F	A	Pts
BA Wingspan	12	10	1	1	297	78	21
S All Horsham	12	9	0	3	223	103	18
Newick	12	8	1	3	174	99	17
St Francis	11	5	0	6	215	112	10
Hellingly	12	5	0	7	187	222	10
Sussex Police	11	3	0	8	101	232	6
Plumpton	12	0	0	12	57	408	0

Sussex 3

	P	W	D	L	F	A	Pts
Shoreham	10	10	0	0	292	51	20
Rye	10	5	2	3	143	113	12
Midhurst	10	5	1	4	130	179	11
Robertsbridge	10	4	0	6	189	145	8
Barns Green	10	2	1	7	132	203	5
Arun	10	2	0	8	89	284	4

MIDLANDS DIVISION

Midlands 1

	P	W	D	L	F	A	Pts
Hinckley	16	14	0	2	601	178	28
Burton	16	13	1	2	457	173	27
Belgrave	16	12	1	3	371	244	25
Scunthorpe	16	12	0	4	345	253	24
Broad Street	16	11	0	5	434	230	22
Whitchurch	16	9	1	6	435	304	19
Syston	16	9	0	7	253	253	18
Camp Hill	16	7	1	8	323	339	15
Wolverhampton	16	7	1	8	287	394	15
Leighton Buzzard	16	7	1	8	285	407	15
Westleigh	16	5	3	8	307	283	13
Derby	16	5	3	8	319	412	13
Barkers Butts	16	6	0	10	329	441	12
Mansfield	16	5	1	10	238	323	11
Stafford	16	4	0	12	282	520	8
Leamington	16	2	0	14	268	556	4
Stockwood Park	16	1	1	14	198	512	3

Midlands 2

	P	W	D	L	F	A	Pts
Banbury	17	13	2	2	511	231	28
Kenilworth	17	14	0	3	442	283	28
Old Laurentians	17	13	1	3	406	177	27
Kettering	17	13	1	3	457	234	27
Luctonians	17	12	2	3	426	168	26
Dudley	17	13	0	4	434	212	24
Bedford Athletic	17	11	1	5	362	206	23
Bromsgrove	17	10	0	7	271	293	20
Ampthill	17	9	0	8	348	310	18
Sutton Coldfield	17	7	1	9	344	413	15
Newport	17	6	1	10	261	353	13
Towcestrians	17	7	0	10	286	283	12
Paviors	17	4	2	11	286	442	10
Huntingdon	17	5	0	12	255	506	10
Keresley	17	4	0	13	218	352	6
Long Buckby	17	3	0	14	269	550	6
Matlock	17	3	0	14	257	555	6
Bedworth	17	0	1	16	185	450	1

Midlands East 1

	P	W	D	L	F	A	Pts
Moderns	16	14	0	2	425	152	28
O Northampton	16	13	0	3	370	208	26
Wellingborough	16	10	1	5	379	269	21
Lutterworth	16	9	2	5	388	245	20
Lincoln	16	10	0	6	367	226	20
Stewarts & Lloyds	16	9	0	7	293	255	18
Ilkeston	16	9	0	7	222	241	18
Newark	16	8	0	8	255	264	16
Peterborough	16	7	1	8	266	310	15
Stoneygate	16	8	0	8	296	247	14
Coalville	16	5	3	8	206	253	13
Ashbourne	16	6	1	9	227	275	13
Spalding	16	5	2	9	230	301	12
Vipers	16	5	3	8	170	219	11
Amber Valley	16	5	1	10	222	419	11
Biggleswade	16	3	1	12	163	362	7
Northampton Boys Bri	16	2	1	13	213	446	5

Midlands East 2

	P	W	D	L	F	A	Pts
Northampton Mens Own	16	15	0	1	594	220	30
Northampton OS	16	14	0	2	614	162	28
South Leicester	16	14	0	2	400	236	28
Dunstablians	16	12	0	4	433	268	24
West Bridgford	16	11	1	4	340	183	23
Loughborough	16	9	0	7	373	343	18
Nottingham Cas	16	8	1	7	285	246	17
Long Eaton	16	7	2	7	307	312	16
Kibworth	16	8	0	8	232	382	16
Stamford	16	7	1	8	320	356	15
Oadby Wyggest	16	6	1	9	347	256	13
Grimsby	16	6	1	9	296	344	13
Kesteven	16	5	0	11	167	260	10
Bedford Queens	16	4	1	11	173	300	9
Mellish	16	4	0	12	180	369	8
East Retford	16	2	0	14	212	437	4
Chesterfield	16	0	0	16	141	740	0

East Midlands/Leics 1

	P	W	D	L	F	A	Pts
Luton	15	15	0	0	609	183	30
Oakham	15	14	0	1	651	126	28
Market Bosworth	15	11	1	3	685	189	23
Bedford Swifts	15	11	1	3	426	183	23
Rushden & High	15	9	0	6	326	295	18
Daventry	15	9	0	6	258	248	18
Old Bosworthians	15	8	1	6	325	233	17
Bugbrooke	15	7	1	7	331	394	15
Colworth House	15	7	1	7	271	377	15
Aylestone St J	15	5	1	9	211	290	11
Brackley	15	5	1	9	252	418	11
St Neots	15	5	0	10	204	452	10
Melton Mowbray	15	5	1	9	244	257	9
St Ives	15	3	0	12	160	574	6
Wellingb'gh OG	15	1	0	14	172	467	2
Old Ashbeians	15	1	0	14	144	583	2

East Midlands

	P	W	D	L	F	A	Pts
Deepings	9	8	0	1	263	31	16
Northampton Cas	9	8	0	1	291	80	16
Oundle	9	7	0	2	311	76	14
Thorney	9	5	0	4	201	174	10
Vauxhall Motors	9	5	0	4	162	173	10
Corby	9	4	1	4	175	135	9
Kempston	9	4	0	5	175	177	8
Northampton H	9	2	1	6	260	225	5
Westwood	9	1	0	8	114	318	2
Biddenham	9	0	0	9	58	621	0

Leics 1

	P	W	D	L	F	A	Pts
Loughb'gh Stu	10	9	0	1	377	75	18
Wigston	10	7	0	3	445	119	14
Old Newtonians	10	6	1	3	270	130	13
New Parks	10	5	1	4	206	159	9
West Leicester	10	2	0	8	96	459	4
Aylestonians	10	0	0	10	57	509	0

Leics 2

	P	W	D	L	F	A	Pts
Burbage	8	7	0	1	282	72	12
Braunstone Town	8	6	0	2	195	118	6
Aylestone Athletic	8	4	1	3	150	135	5
Cosby	8	2	1	5	116	210	5
Shepshed	8	0	0	8	33	241	0

Notts, Lincs & Derby 1

	P	W	D	L	F	A	Pts
Buxton	16	14	1	1	433	153	29
Dronfield	16	12	2	2	305	131	26
Ashfield Swans	16	11	1	4	316	199	21
Glossop	16	9	2	5	291	159	20
Southwell	16	9	2	5	343	216	20
Bakewell Mann	16	9	1	6	421	249	19
Keyworth	16	9	1	6	293	305	19
All Spartans	16	10	0	6	286	212	18
Castle Donington	16	7	1	8	197	252	15
Melbourne	16	8	0	8	274	212	14
Leesbrook	16	6	1	9	233	274	13
Mkt Ras & Louth	16	7	0	9	303	280	12
Worksop	16	8	1	7	206	267	11
Sleaford	16	3	1	12	134	289	7
Boston	16	4	0	12	188	298	6
North Kesteven	16	2	0	14	131	482	4
East Leake	16	1	0	15	142	518	2

Notts, Lincs & Derby 2

	P	W	D	L	F	A	Pts
Boots Athletic	13	13	0	0	276	107	26
Stamford College	13	12	0	1	374	156	24
Cotgrave	13	9	0	4	245	125	18
Belper	13	9	0	4	219	140	16
Nottinghamians	13	8	0	5	227	177	16
Rolls Royce	13	5	1	7	213	232	11
Barton & District	13	6	0	7	198	139	10
Nottingh'shire C	13	5	0	7	183	255	10
Meden Vale	13	5	0	8	192	234	8
Bourne	13	5	0	8	191	316	8
Ollerton	13	3	1	9	127	287	7
Yarborough Bees	13	3	0	10	174	313	6
Cleethorpes	13	4	1	8	290	274	3
Univ of Derby	13	1	1	11	134	288	-3

Notts, Lincs & Derby 3

	P	W	D	L	F	A	Pts
Hope Valley	12	11	1	0	499	53	23
Gainsborough	12	8	3	1	199	159	19
Skegness	12	7	1	4	364	160	15
Tupton	12	4	2	6	164	211	10
Bingham	12	5	0	7	148	233	10
Whitwell	12	2	0	10	94	430	4
Bilsthorpe	12	1	1	10	102	324	3

Midlands West 1

	P	W	D	L	F	A	Pts
Longton	16	13	1	2	579	176	27
Malverns	16	12	0	4	425	198	24
Old Coventrians	16	12	0	4	381	274	24
Ludlow	16	10	1	5	258	211	21
Aston O Edward	16	10	0	6	494	326	20
Selly Oak	16	10	1	5	382	292	19
Old Halesonians	16	9	0	7	444	387	18
Stratford-U-Avon	16	9	0	7	258	300	18
Willenhall	16	8	1	7	316	257	17
Kings Norton	16	8	0	8	231	239	16
Newbold	16	7	0	9	272	213	14
Nuneaton O Edw	16	7	0	9	262	441	14
O Leamingt	16	5	2	9	289	361	12
Leek	16	4	2	10	243	333	10
Tamworth	16	4	2	10	163	331	10
Stoke Old Boys	16	2	0	14	189	555	4
Dixonians	16	1	0	15	144	436	2

Midlands West 2

	P	W	D	L	F	A	Pts
Telford	16	12	1	3	456	207	25
Woodrush	16	12	0	4	387	208	24
Edwardians	16	12	0	4	348	174	24
Shrewsbury	16	12	0	4	343	184	24
Southam	16	12	0	4	336	186	24
Old Yardleians	16	11	0	5	391	214	22
Pershore	16	10	1	5	381	281	21
Erdington	16	9	0	7	319	273	18
Evesham	16	9	0	7	344	310	16
Coventry Sar	16	6	1	9	276	375	13
Warley	16	7	0	9	323	319	12
Old Griffinians	16	6	0	10	333	399	12
GPT Coventry	16	5	0	11	199	383	10
Manor Park	16	4	1	11	278	382	7
Rugby St And	16	4	0	12	189	362	2
Newcastle (Staffs)	16	1	0	15	162	393	2
Trinity Guild	16	2	0	14	182	597	2

North Midlands 1

	P	W	D	L	F	A	Pts
B'gham C Off	16	16	0	0	520	136	32
Kidderminster	16	14	0	2	493	181	28
Bridgnorth	16	12	0	4	467	176	24
Redditch	16	12	0	4	396	179	24
Tenbury	16	12	0	4	409	235	24
Bromyard	16	11	0	5	290	222	22
Droitwich	16	10	0	6	409	297	20
Veseyans	16	9	0	7	315	262	18
Old Saltleians	16	8	0	8	304	250	16
Old Centrals	16	6	1	9	268	390	13
Kynoch	16	5	0	11	194	274	10
Upton-on-Severn	16	5	0	11	215	317	10
B'gham Welsh	16	5	0	11	216	417	10
Birmingham C S	16	5	0	11	218	458	10
Five Ways O Ed	16	2	1	13	208	343	5
Ross-on-Wye	16	2	0	14	160	443	4
Wulfrun	16	1	0	15	147	649	2

North Midlands 2

	P	W	D	L	F	A	Pts
Ledbury	11	10	1	0	335	73	21
Bishops Castle	11	7	2	2	268	75	16
Oswestry	11	7	1	3	279	169	15
Harborne	11	7	0	4	246	188	14
Stourport	11	4	2	5	200	163	10
Bourneville	11	5	0	6	212	220	10
Witton	11	4	2	5	164	203	10
Yardley & District	11	5	1	5	236	147	9
Cleobury Mort	11	4	1	6	145	206	9
Birchfield	11	6	0	5	226	154	6
Market Drayton	11	2	0	9	82	237	4
Bredon Star	11	0	0	11	90	648	-2

Staffs/Warwicks 1

	P	W	D	L	F	A	Pts
Berkswell & Bal	14	13	1	0	308	100	27
Spartans	14	12	0	2	357	138	24
Alcester	14	9	2	3	266	191	20
Earlsdon	14	8	2	4	250	174	16
Old Wheatleyans	14	8	0	6	329	283	16
Silhillians	14	7	2	5	280	250	16
Trentham	14	8	0	6	215	167	14
Dunlop	14	6	1	7	216	137	13
Handsworth	14	6	1	7	222	208	11
Pinley	14	5	1	8	191	178	11
Shipston Stour	14	5	0	9	177	271	8
GEC St Leonards	14	3	0	11	163	313	6
Coventry Welsh	14	4	0	10	230	286	4
Coventrins	14	3	0	11	100	378	4
Atherstone	14	3	0	11	180	410	2

Staffordshire

	P	W	D	L	F	A	Pts
Burntwood	16	14	1	1	482	165	29
Wednesbury	16	12	1	3	366	149	25
Wheaton Aston	16	11	0	5	372	266	22
Linley	16	8	1	7	293	271	17
Rubery Owen	16	8	0	8	328	295	16
Uttoxeter	16	8	0	8	279	370	16
Rugeley	16	5	0	11	190	284	10
Cannock	16	2	1	13	171	496	5
Bloxwich	16	2	0	14	208	393	4

Warwickshire

	P	W	D	L	F	A	Pts
Claverdon	16	14	1	1	403	112	29
Ford	16	12	2	2	469	110	26
Standard	16	12	0	4	502	181	24
Harbury	16	10	1	5	389	166	21
Old Warwickians	16	8	0	8	286	235	16
Shottery	16	6	1	9	201	458	11
Rugby Welsh	16	4	1	11	149	336	9
Coventry Tech	16	2	0	14	150	410	2
Warwick	16	1	0	15	79	620	-2

NORTH DIVISION

North 1

	P	W	D	L	F	A	Pts
Sedgley Park	21	16	1	4	632	384	33
Tynedale	21	14	1	6	546	311	29
New Brighton	21	14	1	6	484	381	29
Stockton	21	12	2	7	482	391	26
Wigton	21	12	1	8	467	331	25
Macclesfield	22	10	1	11	308	484	21
Bridlington	21	10	0	11	400	416	20
Widnes	21	10	0	11	340	431	20
Hull Ionians	22	7	2	13	359	456	16
W Pk Bramhope	21	6	1	14	312	450	13
Broughton Park	22	6	0	16	358	425	12
Bradford & Bing	22	6	0	16	312	540	12

North 2

	P	W	D	L	F	A	Pts
Doncaster	21	21	0	0	663	253	42
Middlesbrough	21	18	0	3	685	280	36
Blaydon	22	14	0	8	479	382	28
Huddersfield	20	13	1	6	436	322	27
Alnwick	21	11	1	9	535	422	23
Northern	22	10	1	11	455	506	21
Driffield	21	10	1	10	410	470	21
Lymm	22	9	1	12	407	548	19
Vale of Lune	22	7	0	15	404	478	14
Halifax	22	6	0	16	366	509	12
York	22	4	1	17	357	504	9
Durham City	22	3	0	19	350	873	6

North-East 1

	P	W	D	L	F	A	Pts
Morpeth	18	13	2	3	435	237	28
Old Crossleyans	18	13	2	3	388	213	28
Percy Park	18	12	1	5	397	307	25
Old Brodleians	18	8	2	8	458	401	18
Pontefract	18	9	0	9	345	358	18
Horden	18	7	1	10	371	412	15
Wheatley Hills	18	7	1	10	335	391	15
Gateshead Fell	18	6	2	10	287	328	14
Hartlepool Rovers	18	5	0	13	278	484	10
Keighley	18	4	1	13	218	381	9

North-East 2

	P	W	D	L	F	A	Pts
Beverley	18	15	0	3	504	253	30
Goole	18	14	0	4	401	217	28
Ashington	18	11	1	6	489	360	23
Westoe	18	10	1	7	386	316	21
Cleckheaton	18	10	0	8	381	309	20
D'ton Mow PA	18	9	1	8	417	330	19
Roundhegians	18	7	0	11	313	383	14
North Ribblesdale	18	6	1	11	339	489	13
Selby	18	4	0	14	281	396	8
Redcar	18	2	0	16	181	639	4

North-East 3

	P	W	D	L	F	A	Pts
Darlington	18	16	0	2	702	274	32
Hull	18	14	0	4	452	229	28
Ripon	18	13	0	5	333	237	26
Sunderland	18	9	0	9	404	380	18
Pocklington	18	8	0	10	330	282	14
Thornesians	18	7	0	11	297	356	14
Whitby	18	8	0	10	245	368	14
Bramley	18	6	0	12	281	368	12
Whitley Bay Rock	18	5	0	13	241	468	10
Blyth	18	4	0	14	282	605	8

Yorkshire 1

	P	W	D	L	F	A	Pts
Yarnbury	18	16	1	1	597	185	33
Ilkley	18	12	2	4	387	206	26
Bradford Salem	18	10	2	6	316	291	22
Malton & North	18	10	0	8	423	279	20
Northallerton	18	10	0	8	443	315	20
Wath	18	8	3	7	387	348	19
Leodiensians	18	8	2	8	359	340	18
Old Otliensians	18	5	0	13	273	335	8
Moortown	18	4	1	13	301	466	5
Wibsey	18	1	1	16	136	857	3

Yorkshire 2

	P	W	D	L	F	A	Pts
Castleford	18	16	0	2	485	234	32
Dinnington	18	12	1	5	544	249	25
Barnsley	18	10	0	8	352	268	20
Hullensians	18	10	0	8	300	267	20
Scarborough	18	10	0	8	297	288	20
Halifax Vandals	18	8	2	8	247	297	18
Sheffield Oaks	18	6	3	9	236	211	15
Sheffield Tigers	18	7	0	11	295	387	14
Old Modernians	18	7	0	11	278	441	14
Phoenix Park	18	1	0	17	196	588	2

Yorkshire 3

	P	W	D	L	F	A	Pts
H'field YMCA	16	15	0	1	714	87	30
West Leeds	16	13	0	3	607	191	26
Stocksbridge	16	10	0	6	300	257	20
Hemsworth	16	10	0	6	330	353	20
Wetherby	16	8	2	6	339	324	18
Hessle	16	4	2	10	218	397	10
Aireborough	16	4	2	10	216	429	10
Skipton	16	4	0	12	187	483	8
Hornsea	16	1	0	15	142	532	2

Yorkshire 4

	P	W	D	L	F	A	Pts
York RI	16	14	0	2	396	187	28
Leeds Corinth	16	10	1	5	279	175	21
Stanley Rodillians	16	9	0	7	310	193	18
O Rishworthians	16	9	0	7	290	205	18
Knottingley	16	8	0	8	271	269	16
Heath	16	8	1	7	224	223	15
Baildon	16	7	0	9	233	265	14
Mosborough	16	3	0	13	183	371	6
Knaresborough	16	3	0	13	159	457	6

Yorkshire 5

	P	W	D	L	F	A	Pts
Marist	14	13	0	1	415	127	26
Edlington & Wick	14	12	0	2	324	117	24
Burley	14	8	0	6	268	164	16
Garforth	14	7	0	7	202	187	14
Ossett	14	6	0	8	243	252	12
Rowntrees	14	6	0	8	245	231	10
BP Chemicals	14	4	0	10	171	224	8
Danum Phoenix	14	0	0	14	83	649	-4

Yorkshire 6

	P	W	D	L	F	A	Pts
Adwick Le Street	12	8	1	3	234	116	17
Da La Salle	12	8	0	4	191	122	16
New Earswick	11	7	0	4	158	226	14
Rawmarsh	11	7	0	4	235	144	12
Withernsea	12	5	1	6	200	167	9
Leeds M & D	12	4	0	8	203	166	6
Menwith Hill Q	12	1	0	11	86	366	2

Durham & Northumb 1

	P	W	D	L	F	A	Pts
W Hartlepool	18	18	0	0	643	175	36
Ryton	18	16	0	2	587	228	32
Acklam	18	11	0	7	428	255	22
North Shields	17	11	0	6	365	227	22
Medicals	18	8	0	10	308	345	16
Bishop Auckland	18	9	0	9	308	430	16
Winlaton Vulcans	18	7	0	11	307	317	14
Novocastrians	18	4	0	14	254	365	8
Guisborough	17	3	0	14	165	560	6
Hartlepool	18	2	0	16	176	639	4

Durham & Northumb 2

	P	W	D	L	F	A	Pts
Consett	18	15	2	1	545	178	32
North Durham	18	13	2	3	455	218	28
Barnard Castle	18	13	1	4	509	197	27
Ponteland	18	10	0	8	340	207	20
Chester-Le-Street	18	8	1	9	305	272	17
Seaton Carew	18	8	0	10	310	317	16
S Tyneside Coll	18	8	0	10	297	380	16
Wallsend	18	7	0	11	205	432	14
Darlington RA	18	3	0	15	115	424	6
Wensleydale	18	2	0	16	146	602	4

Durham & Northumb 3

	P	W	D	L	F	A	Pts
Billingham	14	14	0	0	647	160	28
Seghill	14	11	0	3	362	128	22
Richmondshire	14	8	1	5	308	226	17
Seaham	14	8	1	5	282	216	17
Houghton	14	6	0	8	204	363	12
Sedgefield	14	4	0	10	192	339	8
Hartlepool BBOB	14	3	0	11	153	382	6
Wearside	14	1	0	13	139	473	2

Durham & Northumb 4

	P	W	D	L	F	A	Pts
Gosforth	12	12	0	0	721	36	24
Hartlepool Ath	12	9	0	3	206	197	18

	P	W	D	L	F	A	Pts
Jarrovians	12	7	0	5	221	234	14
Washington	12	6	0	6	120	272	12
Durham Const	12	4	0	8	136	329	8
Newton Aycliffe	12	3	0	9	162	322	6
Prudhoe Hospital	12	1	0	11	86	262	2

North-West 1

	P	W	D	L	F	A	Pts
Blackburn	18	14	0	4	410	205	28
W Pk St Helens	18	11	1	6	340	311	23
Aspull	18	11	0	7	323	300	22
Chester	18	10	1	7	425	332	21
Penrith	18	10	0	8	342	343	20
V'bonds (I of M)	18	9	1	8	386	381	19
Birkenhead Park	18	8	2	8	332	324	18
Oldershaw	18	6	0	12	345	403	12
Wilmslow	18	5	0	13	285	433	10
Netherhall	18	3	1	14	291	447	7

North-West 2

	P	W	D	L	F	A	Pts
Old Aldwinians	18	15	0	3	401	167	30
Ashton on Mersey	18	13	0	5	423	236	26
Egremont	18	12	1	5	332	223	25
Leigh	18	10	0	8	337	383	20
Northwich	18	9	0	9	275	380	18
Kirkby Lonsdale	18	8	1	9	376	330	17
Carlisle	18	8	0	10	311	290	16
Old Salians	18	6	0	12	227	346	12
Fleetwood	18	5	0	13	259	388	8
Sandbach	18	3	0	15	240	438	6

North-West 3

	P	W	D	L	F	A	Pts
Merseyside Police	18	14	0	4	400	172	28
Caldy	18	13	0	5	460	215	26
Workington	18	11	0	7	330	274	22
Rossendale	18	9	2	7	267	208	20
Stockport	18	9	2	7	304	325	20
Windermere	18	8	1	9	329	377	17
Cockermouth	18	8	1	9	188	251	17
Wigan	18	6	1	11	299	335	13
Calder Vale	18	6	0	12	258	343	12
Ruskin Park	18	2	1	15	201	536	5

S Lancs/Cheshire 1

	P	W	D	L	F	A	Pts
Altrincham K	18	18	0	0	567	162	36
Wirral	18	15	0	3	537	243	30
Warrington	18	13	0	5	418	221	26
St Edwards OB	18	10	1	7	348	352	21
South Liverpool	17	7	1	9	354	296	15
Eagle	18	7	1	10	317	334	15
Old Anselmians	18	6	0	12	282	436	12
Newton-Le-Will	17	5	0	12	280	431	10
Birchfield	18	4	1	13	244	461	9
Old Parkonians	18	2	0	16	182	593	4

South Lancs/Cheshire 2

	P	W	D	L	F	A	Pts
Southport	18	16	1	1	671	156	33
Crewe & Nant	18	16	0	2	638	191	32

	P	W	D	L	F	A	Pts
Wallasey	18	10	1	7	305	249	21
Dukinfield	18	9	1	8	415	309	17
Bowdon	18	8	1	9	302	391	15
Congleton	18	9	0	9	342	350	14
Didsbury TOC H	18	7	0	11	289	458	14
Sefton	18	6	0	12	241	450	12
Hoylake	18	4	0	14	233	637	8
Port Sunlight	18	3	0	15	190	435	2

S Lancs/Cheshire 3

	P	W	D	L	F	A	Pts
Marple	14	11	2	1	382	153	22
St Marys OB	14	9	0	5	343	145	18
Prenton	14	10	2	2	307	119	18
Douglas (I of M)	14	7	2	5	295	199	16
Helsby	14	5	1	8	261	217	11
Liverpool Coll	14	5	1	8	158	302	9
Mossley Hill	14	2	1	11	115	415	5
Vulcan	14	2	1	11	140	452	3

S Lancs/Cheshire 4

	P	W	D	L	F	A	Pts
Shell Stanlow	8	6	0	2	267	95	12
Halton	8	6	0	2	199	120	12
Moore	8	5	0	3	178	163	10
Hightown	8	2	0	6	88	222	4
Holmes Chapel	8	1	0	7	68	200	2

N Lancs/Cumbria

	P	W	D	L	F	A	Pts
St Benedicts	18	17	0	1	493	173	34
Rochdale	18	14	0	4	546	196	28
Vickers	18	13	0	5	538	218	26
Trafford MV	18	10	0	8	390	305	20
Tyldesley	17	8	1	8	385	327	17
Ashton-u-Lyne	18	8	0	10	338	276	16
Ormskirk	18	7	0	11	248	452	14
Keswick	18	6	1	11	266	460	13
Upper Eden	18	4	0	14	268	489	8
Ambleside	17	1	0	16	190	766	2

North Lancs 1

	P	W	D	L	F	A	Pts
Blackpool	18	17	0	1	613	172	34
Broughton	18	14	0	4	407	222	28
De La Salle	17	14	0	3	362	232	26
Bolton	17	11	0	6	445	276	22
Thornton Clev	18	8	0	10	279	330	16
Bury	18	8	0	10	340	412	16
Littleborough	18	4	2	12	237	371	10
Old Bedians	18	6	0	12	206	327	8
Heaton Moor	18	3	1	14	227	445	7
Colne & Nelson	18	2	1	15	194	523	5

North Lancs 2

	P	W	D	L	F	A	Pts
Oldham	14	14	0	0	605	96	28
Eccles	14	12	0	2	412	125	24
Chorley	14	7	0	7	288	257	12
Culcheth	14	5	1	8	194	298	11
Clitheroe	14	6	0	8	250	273	10
N Manchester	14	6	0	8	181	313	10

Burnage	14	5	1	8	231	257	9
Lostock	14	0	0	14	85	627	0

Cumbria

	P	W	D	L	F	A	Pts
Furness	14	13	0	1	625	100	26
Whitehaven	14	11	0	3	457	207	22
Moresby	14	9	1	4	303	137	19
Millom	14	6	1	7	213	315	13
Carnforth	14	5	0	9	176	337	10
Creighton	13	4	2	7	153	273	8
Silloth	14	3	0	11	205	410	2
Green Garth	13	2	0	11	130	483	0

SOUTH-WEST DIVISION

South-West 1

	P	W	D	L	F	A	Pts
Bridgwater	22	18	0	4	794	318	36
Launceton	22	18	0	4	752	324	36
Maidenhead	22	16	1	5	648	285	33
Barnstaple	22	14	0	8	487	403	28
Gloucester OB	22	13	0	9	518	360	26
Torquay	22	10	0	11	364	354	21
Matson	22	10	0	12	355	362	20
Stroud	22	10	0	12	465	499	20
St Ives	22	8	0	14	313	725	16
Salisbury	22	7	0	15	394	686	14
Brixham	22	6	0	16	382	640	12
Camborne	22	1	0	21	253	769	0

South-West 2 East

	P	W	D	L	F	A	Pts
Bracknell	22	22	0	0	868	201	44
Swanage	21	16	0	5	628	321	32
Aylesbury	22	11	1	10	432	401	23
Dorchester	22	11	0	11	414	366	22
A'sham & Chilt	20	11	0	9	340	312	22
Marlow	22	10	1	11	432	444	21
Oxford	22	10	0	12	476	538	20
Chinnor	22	10	0	12	386	474	20
Sherborne	20	10	0	10	353	513	20
Bournemouth	22	7	0	15	369	497	14
Chippenham	22	6	0	16	381	587	12
Swindon	21	4	0	17	256	681	8

South-West 2 West

	P	W	D	L	F	A	Pts
Penzance	21	18	0	3	636	244	36
Spartans	21	15	0	6	528	265	30
Cinderford	22	15	0	7	481	373	30
Old Patesians	22	13	0	9	447	341	26
Dings Crusaders	22	12	2	8	470	415	26
Penryn	22	11	0	11	462	443	22
Clevedon	22	11	0	11	451	440	22
Tiverton	22	10	1	11	430	530	21
Taunton	22	8	3	11	444	511	19
Gordon League	22	8	2	12	420	520	18
Devonport Serv	22	4	0	18	332	602	8
Combe Down	22	2	0	20	198	615	4

Western Counties North

	P	W	D	L	F	A	Pts
Keynsham	15	14	1	0	584	180	29
St Mary's OB	15	13	1	1	514	140	27
Hornets	15	13	1	1	432	145	27
Cleve	15	10	1	4	396	231	21
Cheltenham N	15	10	0	5	364	261	20
Cirencester	15	8	2	5	340	343	18
Old Redcliffians	15	8	0	7	261	248	16
O Culverhaysians	15	7	1	7	337	383	15
Drybrook	15	6	1	8	311	420	13
Oldfield Old Boys	15	5	0	10	257	386	10
Thornbury	15	5	0	10	254	395	10
North Bristol	15	4	1	10	224	317	9
Whitehall	15	4	1	10	234	336	7
Bristol Harlequins	15	3	0	12	211	405	6
Avonmouth	15	3	0	12	195	429	6
Chard	15	2	0	13	187	482	2

Western Counties West

	P	W	D	L	F	A	Pts
Okehampton	20	16	1	3	461	279	33
St Austell	20	15	0	5	531	288	30
Wellington	20	13	1	6	421	252	27
Paignton	20	11	1	8	365	329	23
Hayle	20	9	1	10	327	376	19
Bideford	20	9	0	11	350	348	18
Sidmouth	20	10	0	10	334	395	18
Ivybridge	20	9	0	11	332	381	16
Old Plymothian	20	7	0	13	260	361	14
Crediton	20	7	0	13	437	404	12
Saltash	20	2	0	18	217	622	4

Southern Counties North

	P	W	D	L	F	A	Pts
Stow-on-Wold	18	17	0	1	722	120	34
Bicester	18	16	0	2	612	273	32
Olney	18	10	0	8	444	272	20
Buckingham	18	8	1	9	368	352	17
Oxf'd Quins	18	9	0	9	439	424	16
Witney	18	8	0	10	334	453	16
Bletchley	18	8	0	10	277	448	16
Slough	18	7	1	10	335	422	15
Milton Keynes	18	5	0	13	304	452	10
Grove	18	1	0	17	144	763	0

Southern Counties South

	P	W	D	L	F	A	Pts
Abbey	18	18	0	0	703	154	36
Wimborne	18	16	0	2	608	165	32
Wootton Bassett	18	12	1	5	367	270	23
Devizes	18	9	1	8	365	280	19
North Dorset	18	6	1	11	355	495	13
Blandford	18	5	3	10	232	375	13
Marlborough	18	6	0	12	254	520	12
Windsor	18	8	1	9	369	474	11
Corsham	18	3	1	14	251	442	7
Redingensians	18	3	0	15	205	534	6

Cornwall & Devon

	P	W	D	L	F	A	Pts
Kingsbridge	14	13	0	1	340	108	26
South Molton	13	10	0	3	295	137	20
Teignmouth	13	8	0	5	260	169	16
Exmouth	14	8	1	5	255	242	15
Bude	14	7	0	7	254	179	14
Honiton	14	4	1	9	220	339	9
Truro	14	2	0	12	151	347	2
Plymouth C S	14	2	0	12	113	367	2

Cornwall 1

	P	W	D	L	F	A	Pts
Falmouth	18	17	0	1	596	175	34
Newquay	18	17	0	1	527	121	34
Helston	18	9	2	7	477	290	20
Perranporth	18	9	0	9	324	285	18
Illogan Park	18	8	0	10	285	308	16
St Just	18	8	0	10	288	377	16
Liskeard-Looe	18	8	2	8	259	376	16
St Agnes	18	7	0	11	360	440	12
Stithians	18	5	0	13	207	408	10
Redruth Albany	18	0	0	18	97	640	0

Cornwall 2

	P	W	D	L	F	A	Pts
Bodmin	10	9	1	0	431	57	19
Wadebridge	10	8	1	1	326	42	17
St Day	10	5	0	5	153	173	10
Camborne S o M	10	4	0	6	146	191	6
Roseland	10	3	0	7	98	236	6
Lankelly Fowey	10	0	0	10	56	511	0

Devon 1

	P	W	D	L	F	A	Pts
Withycombe	18	18	0	0	567	162	36
Newton Abbot	18	15	0	3	557	211	30
Tavistock	18	11	0	7	382	416	22
Topsham	18	9	1	8	412	404	19
Old Technicians	18	8	1	9	337	322	17
Old Public Oaks	18	8	0	10	371	288	16
Torrington	18	7	1	10	335	462	15
Exeter Saracens	18	5	0	13	260	517	10
Totnes	18	4	1	13	291	484	9
Tamar Saracens	18	3	0	15	186	432	6

Devon 2

	P	W	D	L	F	A	Pts
Ilfracombe	18	18	0	0	923	45	36
Dartmouth	18	12	0	6	570	296	24
Plymouth A	18	11	0	7	323	293	22
Prince Rock	18	11	1	6	272	254	21
North Tawton	18	9	0	9	296	317	18
Salcombe	18	8	0	10	266	410	16
Bovey Tracey	18	6	3	9	310	440	15
Cullompton	18	8	1	9	215	407	13
Plymstock	18	4	1	13	208	438	9
St Columba	18	0	0	18	84	567	0

Devon 3

	P	W	D	L	F	A	Pts
Wessex	14	14	0	0	993	52	28
Harjons	14	12	0	2	963	157	24
Devonport HSOB	14	10	0	4	368	184	20
Buckfastleigh	14	8	0	6	289	372	16
Woodland Fort	14	4	1	9	174	556	9
Plympton-Vict	14	4	0	10	164	482	8
Axminster	14	2	1	11	186	613	5
Plymouth YMCA	14	1	0	13	121	842	-4

Glos & Somerset

	P	W	D	L	F	A	Pts
Coney Hill	15	15	0	0	704	122	30
Old Richians	15	11	0	4	461	227	22
Walcot Old Boys	15	10	0	5	380	257	20
Barton Hill	15	10	0	5	308	214	20
Gordano	15	10	0	5	363	288	20
St Bernad'ttes OB	15	10	0	5	299	256	20
Longlevens	15	10	0	5	280	268	20
Brockworth	15	8	0	7	318	330	16
Bream	15	6	0	9	203	235	12
Yatton	15	6	0	9	265	311	12
Mids'er Norton	15	6	0	9	335	401	12
Frampton Cott	15	6	0	9	246	413	12
Tor	15	5	0	10	213	354	10
Wiveliscombe	15	3	0	12	247	420	6
Old Sulians	15	3	0	12	177	376	6
Old Cryptians	15	1	0	14	218	545	2

Gloucester 1

	P	W	D	L	F	A	Pts
Bristol Saracens	12	11	0	1	326	87	22
Old Centralians	12	11	0	1	325	147	22
Painswick	12	7	1	4	224	185	15
Ashley Down OB	12	7	1	4	182	148	15
Old Bristolians	12	6	1	5	330	262	13
Tredworth	12	6	1	5	188	181	13
Hucclecote OB	12	5	3	4	148	150	13
Cheltenham C S	12	5	2	5	197	198	12
Cainsbross	12	4	2	6	164	234	10
Bristol Tel	12	4	0	8	166	312	8
Chelt'm Saracens	12	3	1	8	108	219	7
Bishopston	12	2	1	9	182	250	5
Widden Old Boys	12	0	1	11	86	253	1

Gloucester 2

	P	W	D	L	F	A	Pts
Southmead	12	11	0	1	340	115	22
Chosen Hill F P	12	10	1	1	325	126	21
W'bury on Severn	12	10	0	2	316	127	20
Chipping Sod	12	9	0	3	350	123	18
Cotham Park	12	8	0	4	234	178	16
Smiths (Ind)	12	5	2	5	260	243	12
Tewkesbury	12	5	1	6	164	222	11
Aretians	12	5	1	6	211	295	11
Tetbury	12	4	1	7	197	190	9
Old Colstonians	12	4	0	8	232	294	8
Kingswood	12	3	0	9	176	307	6
Gloucester C S	12	1	0	11	120	493	2
St Brendans O B	12	0	0	12	143	355	0

Gloucester 3

	P	W	D	L	F	A	Pts
Dursley	8	8	0	0	230	54	16
Old Elizabethians	8	6	0	2	179	64	12
Bristol 'Planes	8	6	0	2	119	91	12
Minchinhampton	8	5	0	3	215	64	10
Pilning	8	4	0	4	67	69	8
Gl'ster A ll Blues	8	3	0	5	89	114	6
Dowty	8	3	0	5	72	165	6
Newent	8	1	0	7	56	218	2
Wotton-u-Edge	8	0	0	8	58	246	0

Somerset 1

	P	W	D	L	F	A	Pts
Wells	18	17	1	0	606	172	35
Frome	18	15	0	3	599	206	30
Minehead Barb	18	10	2	6	390	214	22
North Petherton	18	9	1	8	371	261	19
Chew Valley	18	8	2	8	298	279	18
Imperial	18	9	1	8	329	299	17
Stothert & Pitt	18	8	1	9	285	446	17
Avonvale	18	6	1	11	242	415	13
N'sea & Backwell	18	3	0	15	223	560	4
Crewkerne	18	0	1	17	144	635	-1

Somerset 2

	P	W	D	L	F	A	Pts
Winscombe	16	15	0	1	536	144	30
Blaydon	16	13	0	3	456	185	26
Avon	16	12	0	4	522	210	24
Cheddar Valley	16	8	0	8	201	295	16
Broad Plain	16	6	1	9	260	359	13
Castle Cary	16	7	0	9	261	319	12
Old Ashtonians	16	5	1	10	235	334	11
Bath Saracens	16	5	0	11	268	335	10
Bath O Edward-ians	16	0	0	16	110	668	-2

Somerset 3

	P	W	D	L	F	A	Pts
British Gas	10	10	0	0	362	45	20
Burnham on Sea	10	7	0	3	206	85	12
Morganians	10	5	0	5	97	148	10
Wincanton	10	5	0	5	139	299	8
Martock	10	3	0	7	283	257	4
Aller	10	0	0	10	24	277	0

Berks, Dorset & Wilts 1

	P	W	D	L	F	A	Pts
Weymouth	18	16	1	1	513	174	33
Westbury	18	13	0	5	350	215	26
Melksham	18	12	1	5	399	241	25
Calne	18	11	1	6	324	243	21
Aldermaston	18	11	0	7	292	264	20
Trowbridge	18	6	1	11	341	269	13
Bridport	18	6	0	12	203	301	12
Thatcham	18	6	0	12	239	344	12
Lytchett Minster	18	6	0	12	195	416	12
Supermarine	18	1	0	17	102	491	2

Berks, Dorset & Wilts 2

	P	W	D	L	F	A	Pts
Tadley	14	13	1	0	448	95	27
Ivel Barbarians	14	10	2	2	552	139	22
Colerne	14	9	0	5	257	315	18
Swindon College	14	7	1	6	303	256	15
Oakmedians	14	7	1	6	242	397	15
Portcastrians	14	4	0	10	210	242	8
Berkshire Shire H	14	1	1	12	194	397	3
Pewsey Vale	14	2	0	12	144	509	2

Berks, Dorset & Wilts 3

	P	W	D	L	F	A	Pts
Minety	12	10	0	1	246	77	22
Christchurch	12	9	1	2	314	101	19
Hungerford	12	7	0	5	171	110	14
Warminster	12	5	2	5	188	188	10
Bournemouth U	12	3	1	8	273	254	7
Puddletown	12	3	0	9	139	311	6
Poole	12	2	0	10	108	398	4

Bucks/Oxon

	P	W	D	L	F	A	Pts
Chipping Norton	12	11	0	1	362	64	22
Beaconsfield	12	10	0	2	547	127	20
Cholsey	12	10	0	2	416	97	20
Phoenix	12	10	0	2	265	101	18
Drifters	12	7	0	5	289	204	14
Littlemore	12	7	0	5	218	153	14
Wheatley	12	7	0	5	249	208	14
Pennanians	12	6	0	6	212	251	12
Chesham	12	4	0	8	208	252	8
Abingdon	12	3	0	9	79	370	4
Gosford A Blacks	12	2	0	10	85	374	2
Hanwell	12	1	0	11	126	416	2
Didcot	12	0	0	12	501	439	0

TIGERS' WHIMPER IS GOOD ENOUGH

PILKINGTON CUP 1996-97

10 May 1997, Twickenham
Leicester 9 (3PG) **Sale 3** (1PG)

The teams were weary; the game was dreary. After such a long arduous season, particularly for these two sides who had crammed a campaign's worth of activity into the final few weeks, it was perhaps no surprise that the end-of-season jamboree should have been such a dull, flat, fractured, frustrating affair. In theory it was easy to feel sympathy for the players who reached this stage spent in both body and mind. Both sets of players had been put through the physical and emotional mill the week before when Leicester scrambled their way back into a crucial League match, coming from 20-3 behind to earn the draw and the point which took them into Europe.

But in spite of the mitigating circumstances, it was still troubling that the final should have been such a let-down. It was as if we had spun the clock back 18 months to a time when every club side in the land was locked into the old ways of bump and grind. Such attritional, defensive, percentage rugby has been exposed as inadequate for the modern era first by the southern hemisphere sides and latterly by most British teams.

But where there had been colour and variety throughout the season, here there was monochrome activity and widespread monotony. Little was attempted and even less was achieved. Even the flag-waving, drunken putative streaker who tried to lurch on to the pitch in the second half had his clothes on. Small wonder that even the players themselves were a mite embarrassed by the poor spectacle. 'It wasn't much of a game to play in and I'm sure it wasn't great to watch,' said Leicester and Lions skipper Martin Johnson afterwards.

His club coach, Bob Dwyer, who had done so much to broaden Leicester's horizons over the preceding nine months, was not quite as honest. 'I figure people have to get their entertainment out of the players' efforts,' said Dwyer rather cryptically. 'If that was not good enough for the crowd then the 125,000 who wanted tickets but could not get them could come.'

Dwyer knew he was taking false refuge in specious argument. For the neutral there was no defence for the way the game was played. It was stilted, limited and tedious. Leicester followers, of course, are far from neutral. After a season which had promised so much and which threatened to deliver so little, they will have been delighted in seeing the silverware on parade in their colours, their fifth Cup success in ten final appearances. They cheered too when that great Leicester icon, Dean Richards, lumbered on to the pitch as a 67th minute replacement for another loyal servant, John Wells. Johnson ushered Richards up to the steps in front of him to collect the trophy as a gesture to what will surely be Deano's last appearance at Twickenham.

Dean Richards (right) and John Wells hold aloft the Pilkington Cup after Leicester's victory over Sale.

Leicester were intent on slowing the game down in order to make use of their superior forward power and to neutralise the threat from Sale's dangerous back three, Mallinder, Rees and Beim. Sale were deprived of the injured Vyvyan and Fowler in the pack, and missed the duo's poundage and craft. Well as Baldwin battled they could not match Leicester in the line-out.

It was Sale's first ever appearance in the final. It was, in all probability, Dewi Morris's last. The battling former England scrum-half, aged 33, had steered Sale to great success during the season, but even he could do little to break the Leicester stranglehold. Their best openings came in the 24th minute, when Mannix broke only for the move to eventually flounder when Beim threw a poor pass to Rees, and again on the stroke of half-time, when

Hadley raced clear. In the final stages too they pressed hard, Beim cutting round from his wing. Mannix came close to improving his lone 40th minute penalty goal when he struck the crossbar in the with a penalty shot and then hit the post with a dropped goal.

Neither goal-kicker had their sights accurately set. Stransky was successful with only three kicks from the seven attempts. These successes in the 13th, 38th and 49th minutes were enough to see off the spirited if limited Sale challenge. Stransky was responsible for the game's only real class movement when, with a dummy show of the ball in the 34th minute, he turned defence into scintillating attack. Such moments were very few and very far between.

Leicester: N Malone; C Joiner, W Greenwood, S Potter, L Lloyd; J Stransky, A Healey; G Rowntree, R Cockerill, D Garforth, M Johnson (*capt*), M Poole, J Wells, E Miller, N Back *Replacements* D Richards for Wells (67 mins); A Kardooni for Healey (71 mins)
Scorer *Penalty Goals:* Stransky (3)
Sale: J Mallinder (*capt*); D Rees, J Baxendell, A Hadley, T Beim; S Mannix, D Morris; P Winstanley, S Diamond, A Smith, D Erskine, D Baldwin, N Ashurst, J Mitchell, D O'Grady
Scorer *Penalty Goal:* Mannix
Referee B Campsall (RFU)

The do-or-die nature of Cup competition almost did for the much admired but unexpected finalists, Sale. They trailed Second Division Richmond for long periods of their fifth round tie. The Londoners had travelled north with an expensive, multi-talented, multi-national squad, one which was sweeping all before it in the Second Division but which was an untried quantity against higher opposition. They might well have come through against Sale if only one of their stars, Brian Moore, had kept his boots to himself. With his side leading and in control the former England hooker piled in at a ruck, treading on several prostrate Sale backs. Moore claimed he was rucking, the referee adjudged it to be stamping. Off went Moore and the tables turned, Rees crossing for the decisive try which gave Sale a 34-30 victory. They had no such problems in the sixth round, demolishing their northern neighbours, Orrell, by 57-0. The quarter-final was a stiff test but they also came impressively through that, beating Northampton at Franklins Gardens, 22-9, thanks to tries from Morris and O'Grady. Their 26-16 semi-final victory over Harlequins was an exceptional performance, one not accurately reflected in the scoreline. Harlequins, who had beaten Saracens 28-21 in the quarter-final, were comprehensively outplayed. O'Grady, Mallinder and Beim were Sale's try-scorers.

Leicester had a much closer call in their semi-final at Gloucester, before coming through 26-13. The difference between these two evenly matched teams was the reliability and vision of Joel Stransky.

The South African fly-half scored 21 points through five penalty goals and two critical late dropped goals. Gloucester felt that they had not had the rub of the green with refereeing decisions. The only consolation for the Kingsholm faithful was that their team scored the best try of the day, Craig Emmerson weaving 40 metres before handing on to Chris Catling. Gloucester had beaten Wakefield (25-21), Bristol (18-12) and Leeds (55-20) en route to the semi-final.

Leicester travelled to wind-lashed Newcastle in the quarter-final and were cool and controlled as they came through a testing contest, 18-8. Newcastle were abrasive, too abrasive, their indiscipline costing them position and crucial points as Stransky exacted retribution. It was Leicester's win at Bath in the sixth round which was the highlight of the entire competition. Their 39-28 victory was staggering by any standards. The implications were enormous, Bath parting company with their director of rugby, John Hall, just three days later. Leicester were full of wit, pace and imagination, inspired by a glorious performance in the centre by Will Greenwood, one which more than any other earned him his Lions spot. Greenwood scored two tries with Potter, Back and Hackney trotting over for the others.

The format for the competiton is unlikely to change. What must change though is the division of monies and the qualification procedure for Europe. The finalists shared only £80,000, less than four per cent of the takings at the final. There is also no place in Europe for the winners, an anomaly which was brought home in this particular season when the finalists, Sale and Leicester, both admitted that their crucial League game the week before had been of far more importance than the Cup final.

RESULTS

First round

Barking 18, Barnstaple 31; Birmingham & Solihull 37, Old Halesonians 8; Bishop's Stortford 30, Bicester 9; Bradford & Bingley 13, Aspatria 26; Bridgwater & Albion 22, Newbury 46; Bridlington 23, Nuneaton 16; Camberley 24, Plymouth Albion 24; Camp Hill 17, Wigton 35; Charlton Park 11, Askeans 28; Derby 12, Blaydon 13; Esher 20, Ruislip 3; Gosport & Fareham 12, Weston Super Mare 19; Haywards Heath 31, Beckenham 10; Henley 84, Westcombe Park 10; Launceston 25, Cheltenham 37; Lichfield 19, Winnington Park 21; Longton 16, Sheffield 26; Manchester 37, Scunthorpe 10; Marlow 0, Norwich 6; Metropolitan Police 47, Sutton & Epsom 18; New Brighton 29, Hereford 13; North Walsham 17, Gloucester Old Boys 18; Preston Grasshoppers 28, Stoke 10; Southend 24, High Wycombe 41; Staines 27, Gloucester Spartans 20; Stourbridge 17, Kendal 28; Sutton Caulfield 15, Sandal 22; Swanage & Wareham 41, Berry Hill 8; Tabard 19, Bracknell 30; Westleigh 19, Tynedale 20; Widnes 30, Ampthill 17; Worcester 59, Vale of Lune 8

Second round

Askeans 18, Swanage & Wareham 21; Barnstaple 27, Plymouth Albion 14; Bishop's Stortford 22, Metropolitan Police 22; Bridlington 15, Blaydon 7; Cheltenham 30, Worcester 22; Gloucester Old Boys 13, Newbury 26; Haywards Heath 24, Bracknell 58; Manchester 19, Wigton 31; New Brighton 12, Preston Grasshoppers 24; Norwich 12, Esher 38; Sandal 16, Tynedale 9; Sheffield 29, Kendal 31; Staines 20, Henley 31; Weston Super Mare 23, High Wycombe 6; Widnes 19, Birmingham & Solihull 9; Winnington Park 19, Aspatria 46

Third round

Bridlington 22, Wigton 30; Cheltenham 23, Henley 19; Esher 26, Bracknell 15; Exeter 32, Barnstaple 3; Leeds 96, Redruth 6; Liverpool St Helens 30, Walsall 20; London Welsh 11, Reading 16; Morley 30, Aspatria 26; Newbury 58, Clifton 12; Otley 34, Wharfedale 27; Preston Grasshoppers 24, Fylde 12; Rosslyn Park 27, Havant 15; Sandal 20, Kendal 32; Swanage & Wareham 9, Lydney 26; Weston Super Mare 23, Bishop's Stortford 11; Widnes 12, Harrogate 7

Fourth round

Cheltenham 29, Wester Super Mare 10; Leeds 39, Morley 11; Liverpool St Helens 18, Preston Grasshoppers 28; Wigton 16, Otley 11; Exeter 12, Kendal 18; Reading 50, Widnes 3; Rosslyn Park 30, Esher 3; Lydney 15, Newbury 28

Fifth round

Bath 33, London Irish 0; Coventry 79, Kendal 17; Gloucester 55, Leeds 20; Harlequins 47, Cheltenham 11; Leicester 26, Newbury 21; Moseley 49, Wigton 6; Nottingham 11, London Scottish 25; Orrell 34, Bedford 31; Preston Grasshoppers 11, Northampton 40; Reading 3, Saracens 41; Rotherham 41, Rosslyn Park 26; Sale 34, Richmond 30; Wakefield 22, Waterloo 17; Wasps 84, Rugby 8; Bristol 60, Blackheath 17; Newcastle 51, Hartlepool 10

Sixth round

Gloucester 18, Bristol 12; London Scottish 15, Newcastle 39; Northampton 26, Coventry 17; Orrell 0, Sale 57; Rotherham 23, Harlequins 42; Wakefield 24, Moseley 14; Saracens 21, Wasps 17; Bath 28, Leicester 39

Quarter-finals

Newcastle 8, Leicester 18; Wakefield 21, Gloucester 25; Northampton 9, Sale 22; Harlequins 28, Saracens 21

Semi-finals

Sale 26, Harlequins 16; Gloucester 13, Leicester 26

Previous finals (*all at Twickenham*)
1972 Gloucester 17, Moseley 6
1973 Coventry 27, Bristol 15

1974 Coventry 26, London Scottish 6
1975 Bedford 28, Rosslyn Park 12
1976 Gosforth 23, Rosslyn Park 14
1977 Gosforth 27, Waterloo 11
1978 Gloucester 6, Leicester 3
1979 Leicester 15, Moseley 12
1980 Leicester 21, London Irish 9
1981 Leicester 22, Gosforth 15
1982 Gloucester 12, Moseley 12
     (*title shared*)
1983 Bristol 28, Leicester 22
1984 Bath 10, Bristol 9
1985 Bath 24, London Welsh 15
1986 Bath 25, Wasps 17
1987 Bath 19, Wasps 12
1988 Harlequins 28, Bristol 22
1989 Bath 10, Leicester 6
1990 Bath 48, Gloucester 6
1991 Harlequins 25, Northampton 13
     (*aet*)
1992 Bath 15, Harlequins 12 (*aet*)
1993 Leicester 23, Harlequins 16
1994 Bath 21, Leicester 9
1995 Bath 36, Wasps 16
1996 Bath 16, Leicester 15

COUNTY CUP WINNERS 1996-97

Berkshire	**Bracknell**
Buckinghamshire	**Marlow**
Cheshire	**New Brighton**
Cornwall	**Launceston**
Cumbria	**Aspatria**
Devon	**Exeter**
Dorset/Wilts	**Swanage & Wareham**
Durham	**Blaydon**
Eastern Counties	**Norwich**
East Midlands	**Ampthill**
Gloucestershire	**Gloucester OB/ Berry Hill**
Hampshire	**Havant**
Hertfordshire	**Bishop's Stortford**
Kent	**Blackheath**
Lancashire	**Liverpool St Helens**
Leicestershire	**West Leigh**
Middlesex	**Staines**
North Midlands	**Worcester**
Northumberland	**Tynedale**
Notts, Lincs & Derbys	**Derby**
Oxfordshire	**Bicester**
Somerset	**Bridgwater & Albion**
Staffordshire	**Stoke-on-Trent**
Surrey	**Esher**
Sussex	**Haywards Heath**
Warwickshire	**Sutton Coldfield**
Yorkshire	**Morley**

ARGENTINA TO ENGLAND 1996

THE TOURING PARTY
Manager F Conde **Head Coach** J L Imhoff
Assistant Manager J M Rolandi **Technical Advisor** A Wyllie
Backs Coach H Mendez **Captain** L Arbizu

FULL-BACKS
E H Jurado (Rosario Central)
D Giannantonio (Tala)

THREEQUARTERS
T Solari (Hindu)
F Soler (Tala)
G F Camardon (Alumi)
D L Albanese (San Isidro)
O Bartolucci (Rosario Athletic)
F L Garcia (Alumni)
E Simone (Liceo Naval)
L Arbizu (Belgrano Athletic)

HALF-BACKS
J L Cilley (San Isidro)
G Quesada (Hindu)
C O Barrea (Cordoba Athletic)
N Fernandez-Miranda (Hindu)

FORWARDS
M Reggiardo (Castres, France)
M Scelzo (Banco Hipotecario)
R Grau (Liceo)
O Hasan Jalil (Natacion y Gimnasia)
M Ledesma (Curupayti)
C Promanzio (Duendes)
G A Llanes (La Plata)
J E Simes (Tala)
P J Camerlinckx (Regatas Bella Vista)
C I Fernandez-Lobbe (Liceo Naval)
P L Sporleder (Curupayti)
R A Martin (San Isidro)
R N Perez (Duendes)
R Travaglini (San Isidro)
C Viel (Newman)
G Garcia-Orsetti (Duendes)
P Bouza (Duendes)

TOUR RECORD
All matches Played 7 Won 5 Lost 2 Points for 329 Against 125
International matches Played 1 Lost 1 Points for 18 Against 20

SCORING DETAILS

All Matches					International matches				
For:	47T	32C	10PG	329 Pts	For	–	–	6PG	18 Pts
Against:	11T	8C	18PG	125 Pts	Against	1T	–	5PG	20 Pts

MATCH DETAILS

1996	OPPONENTS	VENUE	RESULT
20 Nov	London & South East	Twickenham	W 63-20
24 Nov	South Western Division	Redruth	W 25-17
27 Nov	Midlands Division	Northampton	W 90-24
1 Dec	Northern Division	Huddersfield	W 64-16
4 Dec	Combined Services	Plymouth	W 52-6
10 Dec	England A	Northampton	L 17-22
14 Dec	ENGLAND	Twickenham	L 18-20

MATCH 1 20 November, Twickenham

London & South East 20 (2G 2PG) **Argentina XV 63** (7G 3PG 1T)
London & South East: H Rushin (Havant); A Pinnock (Havant), S Boydell (Havant), J Alexander (Esher), P Futter (Rosslyn Park); C Raymond (London Welsh), D Jones (Havant); D Rees (Havant), N Killick (Haywards Heath), J Davies (Esher) (*capt*); I Campbell-Lamerton (Rosslyn Park), J Fowler (Sale); P Brady (Esher), C Brierley (Orrell), M Reeve (Havant) *Replacements* N Oldham

(Havant) for Brady (47 mins), A Tucker (London Welsh) for Killick (58 mins), B Pearce (Havant) for Brierley (64 mins), R Ashworth (Havant) for Rushin (64 mins), D Ruffelle (Rosslyn Park) for Campbell-Lamerton (64 mins), J Cameron (Havant) for Rees (70 mins), J Coulson (Wasps) for Jones (75 mins)
Scorers *Tries:* Rushin, Alexander *Conversions:* Raymond (2)
Penalty Goals: Raymond (2)
Argentina XV: Giannantonio; Solari, Garcia, Arbizu (*capt*), Bartolucci; Quesada, Barrea; Grau, Promanzio, Scelzo; Simes, Llanes; Travaglini, Bouza, Viel
Replacements Jurado for Giannantonio (48 mins), Cilley for Arbizu (60 mins), Hasan for Grau (68 mins), Fernandez-Miranda for Bartolucci (76 mins), Fernandez-Lobbe for Llanes (77 mins)
Scorers *Tries:* Bartolucci (2), Travaglini, Bouza (3), Jurado, Solari
Conversions: Quesada (7) *Penalty Goals:* Quesada (3)
Referee G Simmonds (Wales)

MATCH 2   24 November, Redruth

South West Division 17 (1G 2T) **Argentina XV 25** (1G 1PG 3T)
South West Division: P Belshaw (Reading); B Johnson (Newbury), A Turner (Exeter), N Osman (Newbury), T Holloway (Newbury); A Green (Exeter), U Davies (Lydney); P Gutteridge (Reading), J Dickin (Rugby Lions), N Collins (Newbury); R Baxter (Exeter) (*capt*), D Pratt (Reading); N Southern (Exeter), R Armstrong (Plymouth), R Hutchinson (Exeter) *Replacements* D Barrett (Reading) for Belshaw (62 mins), A Knox (Lydney) for Southern (62 mins), C Davies (Newbury) for Hutchinson (62 mins)
Scorers *Tries:* Southern, Davies, pen try *Conversion:* Green
Argentina XV: Soler; Solari, Simone, Garcia, Albanese; Cilley, Fernandez-Miranda; Hasan, Promanzio, Scelzo; Perez, Simes; Garcia, Camerlinckx (*capt*), Fernandez-Lobbe *Replacement* Ledesma for Promanzio (67 mins)
Scorers *Tries:* Simone, Albanese, Solari, Promanzio *Conversion:* Cilley
Penalty Goal: Cilley
Referee A Rowden (Berkshire)

MATCH 3   27 November, Sixfields, Northampton

Midlands Division 24 (3G 1PG) **Argentina XV 90** (10G 4T)
Midlands Division: W Kilford (Coventry); A McAdam (Coventry), R Robinson (Coventry), S Glover (Rugby Lions), A Smallwood (Coventry); J Harris (Coventry), T Dawson (Coventry); M Freer (Nottingham), D Addleton (Coventry), L Mansell (Bedford); D Grewcock (Coventry), S Smith (Rugby Lions); L Croft (Coventry), J Horrobin (Coventry), D Eves (Coventry) (*capt*)
Replacement W Bullock (Gloucester) for Mansell (65 mins)
Scorers *Tries:* Kilford (2) Horrobin *Conversions:* Harris (3) *Penalty Goal:* Harris
Argentina XV: Giannantonio; Bartolucci, Simone, Arbizu (*capt*), Albanese; Quesada, Barrea; Reggiardo, Promanzio, Grau; Llanes, Sporleder; Travaglini, Bouza, Camerlinckx *Replacements* Hasan for Grau (65 mins), Fernandez-Lobbe for Sporleder (75 mins)
Scorers *Tries:* Bouza, Llanes, Promanzio (2), Simone (4), Giannantonio (3), Grau, Bartolucci, Albanese *Conversions:* Quesada (10)
Referee G Morandin (Italy)

MATCH 4   1 December, McAlpine Stadium, Huddersfield

Northern Division 16 (1G 3PG) **Argentina XV 64** (7G 3T)
Northern Division: P Massey (Wakefield); G Monaghan (Waterloo), D Elliott (Rotherham), S Burnhill (Rotherham), R Thompson (Wakefield); J Stabler (West

Hartlepool), S Cook (Orrell); M Worsley (Orrell), T Garnett (Wakefield), S Turner (Orrell); P Rees (Orrell), P Stewart (Wakefield); P Angelsea (Orrell), J Dudley (Rotherham), P Manley (Wakefield) *(capt)* *Replacements* C Lee (West Hartlepool) for Elliott (38 mins), D Scully (Wakefield) for Cook (60 mins), A Ludiman (Harrogate) for Stewart (60 mins), A Handley (Waterloo) for Stabler (60 mins), R Latham (Wakefield) for Worsley (70 min), A Moffatt (Orrell) for Garnett (75 mins)
Scorers *Try:* Monaghan   *Conversion:* Stabler   *Penalty Goals:* Stabler (3)
Argentina XV: Giannantonio; Soler, Simone, Arbizu *(capt)*, Solari; Cilley, Fernandez-Miranda; Hasan, Ledesma, Reggiardo; Llanes, Fernandez-Lobbe; Garcia, Bouza, Viel *Replacements* Perez for Garcia (11 mins), Grau for Fernandez-Lobbe (39 mins)
Scorers *Tries:* Viel, Bouza (2), Soler (2), Simone, Giannantonio, Solari (2), Grau   *Conversions:* Cilley (7)
Referee D Mene (France)

MATCH 5   4 December, Recory Field, Devonport, Plymouth

Combined Services 6 (2PG)   **Argentina XV 52** (6G 2T)
Combined Services: R Abernethy; B Johnson, D Sibson, H Graham, S Brown; P Knowles, S Pinder; N Bartlett, J Brammer *(capt)*, B Williams; D Dahinten, A Newsham; L Denham, R Armstrong, S Boote *Replacements* I Morgan for Graham (temp 12-14 mins), J Stewart for Williams (66 mins), P Taylor for Denham (66 mins)
Scorer *Penalty Goals:* Knowles (2)
Argentina XV: Jurado; Albanese, Garcia, Arbizu *(capt)*, Soler; Quesada, Fernandez-Miranda; Grau; Promanzio, Scelzo; Simes, Llanes; Martin, Bouza, Camerlinckx *Replacements* Travaglini for Camerlinckx (40 mins), Bartolucci for Soler (57 mins), Reggiardo for Grau (68 mins)
Scorers *Tries:* Soler, Simes, Bouza, Garcia, Albanese, Arbizu, Martin, Promanzio   *Conversions:* Quesada (6)
Referee R Davies (Swansea)

MATCH 6   10 December, Franklins Gardens, Northampton

England A 22 (1G 5PG)   **Argentina XV 17** (1G 2T)
England A: I Hunter (Northampton); S Hackney (Leicester), W Greenwood (Leicester), A Blyth (Newcastle), D Luger (Harlequins); P Grayson (Northampton), M Dawson (Northampton); K Yates (Bath), R Kellam (London Irish), J Mallett (Bath); G Archer (Newcastle), D Sims (Gloucester); W Davison (Harlequins), A Diprose (Saracens) *(capt)*, R Hill (Saracens)
Replacements N Walshe (Harlequins) for Dawson (19 mins), J Ewens (Bath) for Blyth (30 mins), G French (Bath) for Kellam (57 mins), P Sampson (Wasps) for Hunter (79 mins)
Scorers *Try:* Hackney   *Conversion:* Grayson   *Penalty Goals:* Grayson (5)
Argentina XV: Giannantonio; Solari, Camardon, Arbizu *(capt)*, Soler; Cilley, Barrea; Reggiardo, Ledesma, Hasan; Simes, Llanes; Martin, Perez, Viel
Scorers *Tries:* Hasan, Soler, pen try   *Conversion:* Cilley
Referee J Kaplan (South Africa)

MATCH 7   14 December, Twickenham   Test Match
ENGLAND 20 (5PG 1T)   ARGENTINA 18 (6PG)

ENGLAND: N D Beal (Northampton); J M Sleightholme (Bath), W D C Carling (Harlequins), J C Guscott (Bath), T Underwood (Newcastle); M J Catt (Bath),

A C T Gomarsall (Wasps); G C Rowntree (Leicester), M P Regan (Bristol), J Leonard (Harlequins) (*capt*); M O Johnson (Leicester), S D Shaw (Bristol); T A K Rodber (Northampton & Army), C M A Sheasby (Wasps), L B N Dallaglio (Wasps) *Replacement* B B Clarke (Richmond) for Sheasby (56 mins)
Scorers *Try:* Leonard   *Penalty Goals:* Catt (5)
ARGENTINA: Jurado; Camardon, Simone, Arbizu (*capt*), Albanese; Quesada, Fernandez-Miranda; Grau, Promanzio, Reggiardo; Sporleder, Llanes; Martin, Bouza, Camerlinckx
Scorer *Penalty Goals:* Quesada (6)
Referee W T S Henning (South Africa)

Jeremy Guscott (England) fends off the challenge of Diego Albanese in the England-Argentina international at Twickenham.

ENGLISH INTERNATIONAL PLAYERS
(*up to 30 April 1997*)

Note: Years given for Five Nations' matches are for second half of season; eg 1972 means season 1971-72. Years for all other matches refer to the actual year of the match. When a series has taken place, figures have been used to denote the particular matches in which players have featured. Thus 1984 *SA 2* indicates that a player appeared in the second Test of the series.

Aarvold, C D (Cambridge U, W Hartlepool, Headingley, Blackheath) 1928 *A, W, I, F, S,* 1929 *W, I, F,* 1931 *W, S, F,* 1932 *SA, W, I, S,* 1933 *W*
Ackford, P J (Harlequins) 1988 *A,* 1989 *S, I, F, W, R, Fj,* 1990 *I, F, W, S, Arg 3,* 1991 *W, S, I, F, A, [NZ, It, F, S, A]*
Adams, A A (London Hospital) 1910 *F*
Adams, F R (Richmond) 1875 *I, S,* 1876 *S,* 1877 *I,* 1878 *S,* 1879 *S, I*
Adebayo, A A (Bath) 1996, *It*
Adey, G J (Leicester) 1976 *I, F*
Adkins, S J (Coventry) 1950 *I, F, S,* 1953 *W, I, F, S*
Agar, A E (Harlequins) 1952 *SA, W, S, I, F,* 1953 *W, I*
Alcock, A (Guy's Hospital) 1906 *SA*
Alderson, F H R (Hartlepool R) 1891 *W, I, S,* 1892 *W, S,* 1893 *W*
Alexander, H (Richmond) 1900 *I, S,* 1901 *W, I, S,* 1902 *W, I*
Alexander, W (Northern) 1927 *F*
Allison, D F (Coventry) 1956 *W, I, S, F,* 1957 *W,* 1958 *W, S*
Allport, A (Blackheath) 1892 *W,* 1893 *I,* 1894 *W, I, S*
Anderson, S (Rockcliff) 1899 *I*
Anderson, W F (Orrell) 1973 *NZ 1*
Anderton, C (Manchester FW) 1889 *M*
Andrew, C R (Cambridge U, Nottingham, Wasps, Toulouse, Newcastle) 1985 *R, F, S, I, W,* 1986 *W, S, I, F,* 1987 *I, F, W, [J (R), US],* 1988 *S, I* 1,2, *A* 1,2, *Fj, A,* 1989 *S, I, F, W, R, Fj,* 1990 *I, F, W, S, Arg 3,* 1991 *W, S, I, F, Fj, A, [NZ, It, US, F, S, A],* 1992 *S, I, F, W, C, SA,* 1993 *F, W, NZ,* 1994 *S, I, F, W, SA* 1,2, *R, C,* 1995 *I, F, W, S, [Arg, It, A, NZ, F],* 1997 *W(R)*
Archer, G S (Bristol, Army) 1996 *S, I*
Archer, H (Bridgwater A) 1909 *W, F, I*
Armstrong, R (Northern) 1925 *W*
Arthur, T G (Wasps) 1966 *W, I*
Ashby, R C (Wasps) 1966 *I, F,* 1967 *A*
Ashcroft, A (Waterloo) 1956 *W, I, S, F,* 1957 *W, I, F, S,* 1958 *W, A, I, F, S,* 1959 *I, F, S*
Ashcroft, A H (Birkenhead Park) 1909 *A*
Ashford, W (Richmond) 1897 *W, I,* 1898 *S, W*
Ashworth, A (Oldham) 1892 *I*
Askew, J G (Cambridge U) 1930 *W, I, F*
Aslett, A R (Richmond) 1926 *W, I, F, S,* 1929 *S, F*
Assinder, E W (O Edwardians) 1909 *A, W*
Aston, R L (Blackheath) 1890 *S, I*
Auty, J R (Headingley) 1935 *S*

Back, N A (Leicester) 1994 *S, I,* 1995 *[Arg (t), It, WS]*
Bailey, M D (Cambridge U, Wasps) 1984 *SA* 1,2, 1987 *[US],* 1989 *Fj,* 1990 *I, F, S* (R)
Bainbridge, S (Gosforth, Fylde) 1982 *F, W,* 1983 *F, W, S, I, NZ,* 1984 *S, I, F, W,* 1985 *NZ* 1,2, 1987 *F, W, S, [J, US]*
Baker, D G S (OMTs) 1955 *W, I, F, S*
Baker, E M (Moseley) 1895 *W, I, S,* 1896 *W, I, S,* 1897 *W*
Baker, H C (Clifton) 1887 *W*
Bance, J F (Bedford) 1954 *S*
Barley, B (Wakefield) 1984 *I, F, W, A,* 1988 *A* 1,2, *Fj*
Barnes, S (Bristol, Bath) 1984 *A,* 1985 *R* (R), *NZ* 1,2, 1986 *S* (R), *F* (R), 1987 *I* (R), 1988 *Fj,* 1993 *S, I*
Barr, R J (Leicester) 1932 *SA, W, I*
Barrett, E I M (Lennox) 1903 *S*
Barrington, T J M (Bristol) 1931 *W, I*
Barrington-Ward, L E (Edinburgh U) 1910 *W, I, F, S*
Barron, J H (Bingley) 1896 *S,* 1897 *W, I*
Bartlett, J T (Waterloo) 1951 *W*
Bartlett, R M (Harlequins) 1957 *W, I, F, S,* 1958 *I, F, S*
Barton, J (Coventry) 1967 *I, F, W,* 1972 *F*
Batchelor, T B (Oxford U) 1907 *F*
Bates, S M (Wasps) 1989 *R*
Bateson, A H (Otley) 1930 *W, I, F, S*
Bateson, H D (Liverpool) 1879 *I*

Batson, T (Blackheath) 1872 *S,* 1874 *S,* 1875 *I*
Batten, J M (Cambridge U) 1874 *S*
Baume, J L (Northern) 1950 *S*
Baxter, J (Birkenhead Park) 1900 *W, I, S*
Bayfield, M C (Northampton) 1991 *Fj, A,* 1992 *S, I, F, W, C, SA,* 1993 *F, W, S, I,* 1994 *S, I, SA* 1,2, *R, C,* 1995 *I, F, W, S, [Arg, It, A, NZ, F],* SA, WS, 1996 *F, W*
Bazley, R C (Waterloo) 1952 *I, F,* 1953 *W, I, F, S,* 1955 *W, I, F, S*
Beal, N D (Northampton) 1996 *Arg*
Beaumont, W B (Fylde) 1975 *I, A* 1(R),2, 1976 *A, W, S, I, F,* 1977 *S, I, F, W,* 1978 *F, W, S, I, NZ,* 1979 *S, I, F, W, NZ,* 1980 *I, F, W, S,* 1981 *W, S, I, F, Arg* 1,2, 1982 *A, S*
Bedford, H (Morley) 1889 *M,* 1890 *S, I*
Bedford, L L (Headingley) 1931 *W, I*
Beer, I D S (Harlequins) 1955 *F, S*
Beese, M C (Liverpool) 1972 *W, I, F*
Bell, F J (Northern) 1900 *W*
Bell, H (New Brighton) 1884 *I*
Bell, J L (Darlington) 1878 *I*
Bell, P J (Blackheath) 1968 *W, I, F, S*
Bell, R W (Northern) 1900 *W, I, S*
Bendon, G J (Wasps) 1959 *W, I, F, S*
Bennett, N O (St Mary's Hospital, Waterloo) 1947 *W, S, F,* 1948 *A, W, I, S*
Bennett, W N (Bedford, London Welsh) 1975 *S, A1,* 1976 *S* (R), 1979 *S, I, F, W*
Bennetts, B B (Penzance) 1909 *A, W*
Bentley, J (Sale) 1988 *I* 2, *A* 1
Bentley, J E (Gipsies) 1871 *S,* 1872 *S*
Berridge, M J (Northampton) 1949 *W, I*
Berry, H (Gloucester) 1910 *W, I, F, S*
Berry, J (Tyldesley) 1891 *W, I, S*
Berry, J T W (Leicester) 1939 *W, I, S*
Beswick, E (Swinton) 1882 *I, S*
Biggs, J M (UCH) 1878 *S,* 1879 *I*
Birkett, J G G (Harlequins) 1906 *S, F, SA,* 1907 *F, W, S,* 1908 *F, W,I, S,* 1910 *W, I, S,* 1911 *W, F, I, S,* 1912 *W, I, S, F*
Birkett L (Clapham R) 1875 *S,* 1877 *I, S*
Birkett, R H (Clapham R) 1871 *S,* 1875 *S,* 1876 *S,* 1877 *I*
Bishop, C C (Blackheath) 1927 *F*
Black, B H (Blackheath) 1930 *W, I, F, S,* 1931 *W, I, S, F,* 1932 *S,* 1933 *W*
Blacklock, J H (Aspatria) 1898 *I,* 1899 *I*
Blakeway, P J (Gloucester) 1980 *I, F, W, S,* 1981 *W, S, I, F,* 1982 *I, F, W,* 1984 *I, F, W, SA* 1, 1985 *R, F, S, I*
Blakiston, A F (Northampton) 1920 *S,* 1921 *W, I, S, F,* 1922 *W,* 1923 *S, F,* 1924 *W, I, F, S,* 1925 *NZ, W, I, S, F*
Blatherwick, T (Manchester) 1878 *I*
Body, J A (Gipsies) 1872 *S,* 1873 *S*
Bolton, C A (United Services) 1909 *F*
Bolton, R (Harlequins) 1933 *W,* 1936 *S,* 1937 *S,* 1938 *W, I*
Bolton, W N (Blackheath) 1882 *I, S,* 1883 *W, I, S,* 1884 *W, I, S,* 1885 *I,* 1887 *I, S*
Bonaventura, M S (Blackheath) 1931 *W*
Bond, A M (Sale) 1978 *NZ,* 1979 *S, I, NZ,* 1980 *I,* 1982 *I*
Bonham-Carter, E (Oxford U) 1891 *S*
Bonsor, F (Bradford) 1886 *W, I, S,* 1887 *W, S,* 1889 *M*
Boobbyer, B (Rosslyn Park) 1950 *W, I, F, S,* 1951 *W, F,* 1952 *S, I, F*
Booth, L A (Headingley) 1933 *W, I, S,* 1934 *S,* 1935 *W, I, S*
Botting, I J (Oxford U) 1950 *W, I*
Boughton, H J (Gloucester) 1935 *W, I, S*
Boyle, C W (Oxford U) 1873 *S*
Boyle, S B (Gloucester) 1983 *W, S, I*
Boylen, F (Hartlepool R) 1908 *F, W, I, S*
Bracken, K P P (Bristol, Saracens) 1993 *NZ,* 1994 *S, I, C,* 1995 *I, F, W, S, [It, WS (t)],* SA, 1996 *It* (R)
Bradby, M S (United Services) 1922 *I, F*
Bradley, R (W Hartlepool) 1903 *W*

Bradshaw, H (Bramley) 1892 *S*, 1893 *W, I, S*, 1894 *W, I, S*
Brain, S E (Coventry) 1984 *SA* 2, *A* (R), 1985 *R, F, S, I, W, NZ* 1,2, 1986 *W, S, I, F*
Braithwaite, J (Leicester) 1905 *NZ*
Braithwaite-Exley, B (Headingley) 1949 *W*
Brettargh, A T (Liverpool OB) 1900 *W*, 1903 *I, S*, 1904 *W, I, S*, 1905 *I, S*
Brewer, J (Gipsies) 1876 *I*
Briggs, A (Bradford) 1892 *W, I, S*
Brinn, A (Gloucester) 1972 *W, I, S*
Broadley, T (Bingley) 1893 *W, S*, 1894 *W, I, S*, 1896 *S*
Bromet, W E (Richmond) 1891 *W, I*, 1892 *W, I, S*, 1893 *W, I, S*, 1895 *W, I, S*, 1896 *I*
Brook, P W P (Harlequins) 1930 *S*, 1931 *F*, 1936 *S*
Brooke, T J (Richmond) 1968 *F, S*
Brooks, F G (Bedford) 1906 *SA*
Brooks, M J (Oxford U) 1874 *S*
Brophy, T J (Liverpool) 1964 *I, F, S*, 1965 *W, I*, 1966 *W, I, F*
Brough, J W (Silloth) 1925 *NZ, W*
Brougham, H (Harlequins) 1912 *W, I, S, F*
Brown, A A (Exeter) 1938 *S*
Brown, L G (Oxford U, Blackheath) 1911 *W, F, I, S*, 1913 *SA, W, F, I, S*, 1914 *W, I, S, F*, 1921 *W, I, S, F*, 1922 *W*
Brown, T W (Bristol) 1928 *S*, 1929 *W, I, S, F*, 1932 *S*, 1933 *W, I, S*
Brunton, J (N Durham) 1914 *W, I, S*
Brutton, E B (Cambridge U) 1886 *S*
Bryden, C C (Clapham R) 1876 *I*, 1877 *S*
Bryden, H A (Clapham R) 1874 *S*
Buckingham, R A (Leicester) 1927 *F*
Bucknall, A L (Richmond) 1969 *SA*, 1970 *I, W, S, F*, 1971 *W, I, F, S* (2[1C])
Buckton, J R D (Saracens) 1988 *A* (R), 1990 *Arg* 1,2
Budd, A (Blackheath) 1878 *I*, 1879 *S, I*, 1881 *W, S*
Budworth, R T D (Blackheath) 1890 *W*, 1891 *W, S*
Bull, A G (Northampton) 1914 *W*
Bullough, E (Wigan) 1892 *W, I, S*
Bulpitt, M P (Blackheath) 1970 *S*
Bulteel, A J (Manchester) 1876 *I*
Bunting, W L (Moseley) 1897 *I, S*, 1898 *I, S, W*, 1899 *S*, 1900 *S*, 1901 *I, S*
Burland, D W (Bristol) 1931 *W, I, F*, 1932 *I, S*, 1933 *W, I, S*
Burns, B H (Blackheath) 1871 *S*
Burton, G W (Blackheath) 1879 *S, I*, 1880 *S*, 1881 *I, W, S*
Burton, H C (Richmond) 1926 *W*
Burton, M A (Gloucester) 1972 *W, I, F, S, SA*, 1974 *F, W*, 1975 *S, A* 1,2, 1976 *A, W, S, I, F*, 1978 *F, W*
Bush, J A (Clifton) 1872 *S*, 1873 *S*, 1875 *S*, 1876 *I, S*
Butcher, C J S (Harlequins) 1984 *SA* 1,2, *A*
Butcher, W V (Streatham) 1903 *S*, 1904 *W, I, S*, 1905 *W, I, S*
Butler, A G (Harlequins) 1937 *W, I*
Butler, P E (Gloucester) 1975 *A* 1, 1976 *F*
Butterfield, J (Northampton) 1953 *F, S*, 1954 *W, NZ, I, S, F*, 1955 *W, I, F, S*, 1956 *W, I, S, F*, 1957 *W, I, F, S*, 1958 *W, A, I, F, S*, 1959 *W, I, F, S*
Byrne, F A (Moseley) 1897 *W*
Byrne, J F (Moseley) 1894 *W, I, S*, 1895 *W, I*, 1896 *I*, 1897 *W, I, S*, 1898 *I, S, W*, 1899 *I*

Cain, J J (Waterloo) 1950 *W*
Callard, J E B (Bath) 1993 *NZ*, 1994 *S, I*, 1995 [*WS*], *SA*
Campbell, D A (Cambridge U) 1937 *W, I*
Candler, P L (St Bart's Hospital) 1935 *W*, 1936 *NZ, W, I, S*, 1937 *W, I, S*, 1938 *W, S*
Cannell, L B (Oxford U, St Mary's Hospital) 1948 *F*, 1949 *W, I, F, S*, 1950 *W, I, F, S*, 1952 *SA, W*, 1953 *W, I, F*, 1956 *I, S, F*, 1957 *W, I*
Caplan, D W N (Headingley) 1978 *S, I*
Cardus, R M (Roundhay) 1979 *F, W*
Carey, G M (Blackheath) 1895 *W, I, S*, 1896 *W, I*
Carleton, J (Orrell) 1979 *NZ*, 1980 *I, F, W, S*, 1981 *W, S, I, F, Arg* 1,2, 1982 *A, S, I, F, W*, 1983 *F, W, S, I, NZ*, 1984 *S, I, F, W, A*
Carling, W D C (Durham U, Harlequins) 1988 *F, W, S, I* 1,2, *A2, Fj, A*, 1989 *S, I, F, W, Fj*, 1990 *I, F, W, S, Arg* 1,2,3, 1991 *W, S, I, F, Fj, A, [NZ, It, US, F, S, A]*, 1992 *S, I, F, W, C, SA*, 1993 *F, W, S, I*, 1994 *S, I, F, W, SA* 1,2, *R, C*, 1995 *I, F, W, S, [Arg, WS, A, NZ, F]*, *SA, WS*, 1996 *F, W, S, I, It, Arg*, 1997 *S, I, F, W*
Carpenter, A D (Gloucester) 1932 *SA*
Carr, R S L (Manchester) 1939 *W, I, S*

Cartwright, V H (Nottingham) 1903 *W, I, S*, 1904 *W, S*, 1905 *W, I, S, NZ*, 1906 *W, I, S, F, SA*
Catcheside, H C (Percy Park) 1924 *W, I, F, S*, 1926 *W, I*, 1927 *I, S*
Catt, M J (Bath) 1994 *W* (R), *C* (R), 1995 *I, F, W, S*, [*Arg, It, WS, A, NZ, F*], *SA, WS*, 1996 *F, W, S, I, It, Arg*, 1997 *W*
Cattell, R H B (Blackheath) 1895 *W, I, S*, 1896 *W, I, S*, 1900 *W*
Cave, J W (Richmond) 1889 *M*
Cave, W T C (Blackheath) 1905 *W*
Challis, R (Bristol) 1957 *I, F, S*
Chambers, E L (Bedford) 1908 *F*, 1910 *W, I*
Chantrill, B S (Bristol) 1924 *W, I, F, S*
Chapman, C E (Cambridge U) 1884 *W*
Chapman, F E (Hartlepool) 1910 *W, I, F, S*, 1912 *W*, 1914 *W, I*
Cheesman, W I (OMTs) 1913 *SA, W, F, I*
Cheston, E C (Richmond) 1873 *S*, 1874 *S*, 1875 *I, S*, 1876 *S*
Chilcott, G J (Bath) 1984 *A*, 1986 *I, F*, 1987 *F* (R), *W*, [*J, US, W* (R)], 1988 *J* 2 (R), *Fj*, 1989 *I* (R), *F, W, R*
Christopherson, P (Blackheath) 1891 *W, S*
Clark, C W H (Liverpool) 1876 *I*
Clarke, A J (Coventry) 1935 *W, I, S*, 1936 *NZ, W, I*
Clarke, B B (Bath, Richmond) 1992 *SA*, 1993 *F, W, S, I, NZ*, 1994 *S, F, W, SA* 1,2, *R, C*, 1995 *I, F, W, S*, [*Arg, It, A, NZ, F*], *SA, WS*, 1996 *F, W, S, I, Arg* (R), 1997 *W*
Clarke, S J S (Cambridge U, Blackheath) 1963 *W, I, F, S, NZ* 1,2, *A*, 1964 *NZ, W, I*, 1965 *I, F, S*
Clayton, J H (Liverpool) 1871 *S*
Clements, J W (O Cranleighans) 1959 *I, F, S*
Cleveland, C R (Blackheath) 1887 *W, S*
Clibborn, W G (Richmond) 1886 *W, I, S*, 1887 *W, I, S*
Clough, F J (Cambridge U, Orrell) 1986 *I, F*, 1987 [*J* (R), *US*]
Coates, C H (Yorkshire) 1880 *S*, 1881 *S*, 1882 *S*
Coates, V H M (Bath) 1913 *SA, W, F, I, S*
Cobby, W (Hull) 1900 *W*
Cockerham, A (Bradford Olicana) 1900 *W*
Colclough, M J (Angoulême, Wasps, Swansea) 1978 *S, I*, 1979 *NZ*, 1980 *F, W, S*, 1981 *W, S, I, F*, 1982 *A, S, I, F, W*, 1983 *F, NZ*, 1984 *S, I, F, W*, 1986 *W, S, I, F*
Coley, E (Northampton) 1929 *F*, 1932 *W*
Collins, P J (Camborne) 1952 *S, I, F*
Collins, W E (O Cheltonians) 1874 *S*, 1875 *I, S*, 1876 *I, S*
Considine, S G U (Bath) 1925 *F*
Conway, G S (Cambridge U, Rugby, Manchester) 1920 *F, I, S*, 1921 *F*, 1922 *W, I, F, S*, 1923 *W, I, S, F*, 1924 *W, I, F, S*, 1925 *W, I*, 1927 *W*
Cook, J G (Bedford) 1937 *S*
Cook, P W (Richmond) 1965 *I, F*
Cooke, D A (Harlequins) 1976 *W, S, I, F*
Cooke, D H (Harlequins) 1981 *W, S, I, F*, 1984 *I*, 1985 *R, F, S, I, W, NZ* 1,2
Cooke, P (Richmond) 1939 *W, I*
Coop, T (Leigh) 1892 *S*
Cooper, J G (Moseley) 1909 *A, W*
Cooper, M J (Moseley) 1973 *F, S, NZ* 2 (R), 1975 *F, W*, 1976 *A, W*, 1977 *S, I, F, W*
Coopper, S F (Blackheath) 1900 *W*, 1902 *W, I*, 1905 *W, I, S*, 1907 *W*
Corbett, L J (Bristol) 1921 *F*, 1923 *W, I*, 1924 *W, I, F, S*, 1925 *NZ, W, I, S, F*, 1927 *W, I, S, F*
Corless, B J (Coventry, Moseley) 1976 *A, I* (R), 1977 *S, I, F, W*, 1978 *F, W, S, I*
Cotton, F E (Loughborough Colls, Coventry, Sale) 1971 *S* (2[1C]), *P*, 1973 *W, I, F, S, NZ* 2, *A*, 1974 *S, I*, 1975 *I, F, W*, 1976 *A, W, S, I, F*, 1977 *S, I, F, W*, 1978 *S, I*, 1979 *NZ*, 1980 *I, F, W, S*, 1981 *W*
Coulman, M J (Moseley) 1967 *A, I, F, S, W*, 1968 *W, I, F, S*
Coulson, T J (Coventry) 1927 *W*, 1928 *A, W*
Court, E D (Blackheath) 1885 *W*
Coverdale, H (Blackheath) 1910 *F*, 1912 *I, F*, 1920 *W*
Cove-Smith, R (OMTs) 1921 *S, F*, 1922 *I, F, S*, 1923 *W, I, S, F*, 1924 *W, I, S, F*, 1925 *W, I, S, F*, 1927 *W, I, S, F*, 1928 *A, W, I, F, S*, 1929 *W, I*
Cowling, R J (Leicester) 1977 *S, I, F, W*, 1978 *F, NZ*, 1979 *S, I*
Cowman, A R (Loughborough Colls, Coventry) 1971 *S* (2[1C]), *P*, 1973 *W, I*
Cox, N S (Sunderland) 1901 *S*
Cranmer, P (Richmond, Moseley) 1934 *W, I, S*, 1935 *W, I, S*, 1936 *NZ, W, I, S*, 1937 *W, I, S*, 1938 *W, I, S*

Will Carling (right) and Tony Underwood celebrate the fourth England try in the Calcutta Cup match.

Creed, R N (Coventry) 1971 *P*
Cridlan, A G (Blackheath) 1935 *W, I, S*
Crompton, C A (Blackheath) 1871 *S*
Crosse, C W (Oxford U) 1874 *S*, 1875 *I*
Cumberlege, B S (Blackheath) 1920 *W, I, S*, 1921 *W, I, S, F*, 1922 *W*
Cumming, D C (Blackheath) 1925 *S, F*
Cunliffe, F L (RMA) 1874 *S*
Currey, F I (Marlborough N) 1872 *S*
Currie, J D (Oxford U, Harlequins, Bristol) 1956 *W, I, S, F*, 1957 *W, I, F, S*, 1958 *W, A, I, F, S*, 1959 *W, I, F, S*, 1960 *W, I, F, S*, 1961 *SA*, 1962 *W, I, F*
Cusani, D A (Orrell) 1987 *I*
Cusworth, L (Leicester) 1979 *NZ*, 1982 *F, W*, 1983 *F, W, NZ*, 1984 *S, I, F, W*, 1988 *F, W*

D'Aguilar, F B G (Royal Engineers) 1872 *S*
Dallaglio, L B N (Wasps) 1995 *SA* (R), *WS*, 1996 *F, W, S, I, It, Arg*, 1997 *S, I, F*
Dalton, T J (Coventry) 1969 *S*(R)
Danby, T (Harlequins) 1949 *W*
Daniell, J (Richmond) 1899 *W*, 1900 *I, S*, 1902 *I, S*, 1904 *I, S*
Darby, A J L (Birkenhead Park) 1899 *I*
Davenport, A (Ravenscourt Park) 1871 *S*
Davey, J (Redruth) 1908 *S*, 1909 *W*
Davey, R F (Teignmouth) 1931 *W*
Davidson, Jas (Aspatria) 1897 *S*, 1898 *S, W*, 1899 *I, S*
Davidson, Jos (Aspatria) 1899 *W, S*
Davies, G H (Cambridge U, Coventry, Wasps) 1981 *S, I, F, Arg* 1,2, 1982 *A, S, I*, 1983 *F, W, S*, 1984 *S, I*, 1985 *R* (R), *NZ* 1,2, 1986 *W, S, I, F*
Davies, P H (Sale) 1927 *I*
Davies, V G (Harlequins) 1922 *W*, 1925 *NZ*
Davies, W J A (United Services, RN) 1913 *SA, W, F, I, S*, 1914 *I, S, F*, 1920 *F, I, S*, 1921 *W, I, S, F*, 1922 *I, F, S*, 1923 *W, I, S, F*
Davies, W P C (Harlequins) 1953 *S*, 1954 *NZ, I*, 1955 *W, I, F, S*, 1956 *W*, 1957 *F, S*, 1958 *W*
Davis, A M (Torquay Ath, Harlequins) 1963 *W, I, S, NZ* 1,2, 1964 *NZ, W, I, F, S*, 1966 *W*, 1967 *A*, 1969 *SA*, 1970 *I, W, S*
Dawe, R G R (Bath) 1987 *I, F, W, [US]*, 1995 *[WS]*
Dawson, E F (RIEC) 1878 *I*
Dawson, M J S (Northampton) 1995 *WS*, 1996 *F, W, S, I*
Day, H L V (Leicester) 1920 *W*, 1922 *W, F*, 1926 *S*
Dean, G J (Harlequins) 1931 *I*
Dee, J M (Hartlepool R) 1962 *S*, 1963 *NZ* 1
Devitt, Sir T G (Blackheath) 1926 *I, F*, 1928 *A, W*
Dewhurst, J H (Richmond) 1887 *W, I, S*, 1890 *W*
De Glanville, P R (Bath) 1992 *SA* (R), 1993 *W* (R), *NZ*, 1994 *S, I, F, W, SA* 1,2, *C* (R), 1995 *[Arg* (R), *It, WS]*, *SA* (R), 1996 *W* (R), *I* (R), *It*, 1997 *S, I, F, W*
De Winton, R F C (Marlborough N) 1893 *W*
Dibble, R (Bridgwater A) 1906 *S, F, SA*, 1908 *F, W, I, S*, 1909 *A, W, F, I, S*, 1910 *S*, 1911 *W, F, S*, 1912 *W, I, S*
Dicks, J (Northampton) 1934 *W, I, S*, 1935 *W, I, S*, 1936 *S*, 1937 *I*
Dillon, E W (Blackheath) 1904 *W, I, S*, 1905 *W*
Dingle, A J (Hartlepool R) 1913 *I*, 1914 *S, F*
Dixon, P J (Harlequins, Gosforth) 1971 *P*, 1972 *W, I, F, S*, 1973 *I, F, S*, 1974 *S, I, F, W*, 1975 *I, F*, 1976 *F, I, F, W*, 1978 *F, S, I, NZ*
Dobbs, G E B (Devonport A) 1906 *W, I*
Doble, S A (Moseley) 1972 *SA*, 1973 *NZ* 1, *W*
Dobson, D D (Newton Abbot) 1902 *W, I, S*, 1903 *W, I, S*
Dobson, T H (Bradford) 1895 *S*
Dodge, P W (Leicester) 1978 *W, S, I, NZ*, 1979 *S, I, F, W*, 1980 *W, S*, 1981 *W, S, I, F, Arg* 1,2, 1982 *A, S, F, W*, 1983 *F, W, S, I, NZ*, 1985 *R, F, S, I, W, NZ* 1,2
Donnelly, M P (Oxford U) 1947 *I*
Dooley, W A (Preston Grasshoppers, Fylde) 1985 *R, F, S, I, W, NZ* 2 (R), 1986 *W, S, I, F*, 1987 *F, W, [A, US, W]*, 1988 *F, W, S, I* 1,2, *A* 1,2, *Fj, A,* 1989 *S, I, F, W, R, Fj,* 1990 *I, F, W, S, Arg* 1,2,3, 1991 *W, S, I, F, [NZ, US, F, S, A],* 1992 *S, I, F, W, C, SA,* 1993 *W, S, I*
Dovey, B A (Rosslyn Park) 1963 *W, I*
Down, P J (Bristol) 1909 *A*
Dowson, A O (Moseley) 1899 *S*
Drake-Lee, N J (Cambridge U, Leicester) 1963 *W, I, F, S,* 1964 *NZ, W, I,* 1965 *W*
Duckett, H (Bradford) 1893 *I, S*
Duckham, D J (Coventry) 1969 *I, F, S, W, SA,* 1970 *I, W, S, F,* 1971 *W, I, F, S (2[1C]), P,* 1972 *W, I, F, S,* 1973 *NZ*

1, *W, I, F, S, NZ* 2, *A,* 1974 *S, I, F, W,* 1975 *I, F, W,* 1976 *A, W, S*
Dudgeon, H W (Richmond) 1897 *S,* 1898 *I, S, W,* 1899 *W, I, S*
Dugdale, J M (Ravenscourt Park) 1871 *S*
Dun, A F (Wasps) 1984 *W*
Duncan, R F H (Guy's Hospital) 1922 *I, F, S*
Dunkley, P E (Harlequins) 1931 *I, S,* 1936 *NZ, W, I, S*
Duthie, J (W Hartlepool) 1903 *W*
Dyson, J W (Huddersfield) 1890 *S,* 1892 *S,* 1893 *I, S*

Ebdon, P J (Wellington) 1897 *W, I*
Eddison, J H (Headingley) 1912 *W, I, S, F*
Edgar, C S (Birkenhead Park) 1901 *S*
Edwards, R (Newport) 1921 *W, I, S, F,* 1922 *W, F,* 1923 *W,* 1924 *W, F, S,* 1925 *NZ*
Egerton, D W (Bath) 1988 *I* 2, *A* 1, *Fj* (R), *A,* 1989 *Fj,* 1990 *I, Arg* 2 (R)
Elliot, C H (Sunderland) 1886 *W*
Elliot, E W (Sunderland) 1901 *W, I, S,* 1904 *W*
Elliot, W (United Services, RN) 1932 *I, S,* 1933 *W, I, S,* 1934 *W, I*
Elliott, A E (St Thomas's Hospital) 1894 *S*
Ellis, J (Wakefield) 1939 *S*
Ellis, S S (Queen's House) 1880 *I*
Emmott, C (Bradford) 1892 *W*
Enthoven, H J (Richmond) 1878 *I*
Estcourt, N S D (Blackheath) 1955 *S*
Evans, B J (Leicester) 1988 *A* 2, *Fj*
Evans, E (Sale) 1948 *A,* 1950 *W,* 1951 *I, F, S,* 1952 *SA, W, S, I, F,* 1953 *I, F, S,* 1954 *W, NZ, I, F,* 1956 *W, I, S, F,* 1957 *W, I, F, S,* 1958 *W, A, I, F, S*
Evans, G W (Coventry) 1972 *S,* 1973 *W (R), F, S, NZ* 2, 1974 *S, I, F, W*
Evans, N L (RNEC) 1932 *W, I, S,* 1933 *W, I*
Evanson, A M (Richmond) 1883 *W, I, S,* 1884 *S*
Evanson, W A D (Richmond) 1875 *S,* 1877 *S,* 1878 *S,* 1879 *S, I*
Evershed, F (Blackheath) 1889 *M,* 1890 *W, S, I,* 1892 *W, I, S,* 1893 *W, I, S*
Eyres, W C T (Richmond) 1927 *I*

Fagan, A R St L (Richmond) 1887 *I*
Fairbrother, K E (Coventry) 1969 *I, F, S, W, SA,* 1970 *I, W, S, F,* 1971 *W, I, F*
Faithfull, C K T (Harlequins) 1924 *I,* 1926 *F, S*
Fallas, H (Wakefield T) 1884 *I*
Fegan, J H C (Blackheath) 1895 *W, I, S*
Fernandes, C W L (Leeds) 1881 *I, W, S*
Fidler, J H (Gloucester) 1981 *Arg* 1,2, 1984 *SA* 1,2
Field, E (Middlesex W) 1893 *W, I*
Fielding, K J (Moseley, Loughborough Colls) 1969 *I, F, S, SA,* 1970 *I, F,* 1972 *W, I, F, S*
Finch, R T (Cambridge U) 1880 *S*
Finlan, J F (Moseley) 1967 *I, F, S, W, NZ,* 1968 *W, I,* 1969 *I, F, S, W,* 1970 *F,* 1973 *NZ* 1
Finlinson, H W (Blackheath) 1895 *W, I, S*
Finney, S (RIE Coll) 1872 *S,* 1873 *S*
Firth, F (Halifax) 1894 *W, I, S*
Fletcher, N C (OMTs) 1901 *W, I, S,* 1903 *S*
Fletcher, T (Seaton) 1897 *W*
Fletcher, W R B (Marlborough N) 1873 *S,* 1875 *S*
Fookes, E F (Sowerby Bridge) 1896 *W, I, S,* 1897 *W, I, S,* 1898 *I, W,* 1899 *I, S*
Ford, P J (Gloucester) 1964 *W, I, F, S*
Forrest, J W (United Services, RN) 1930 *W, I, F, S,* 1931 *W, I, S, F,* 1934 *I, S*
Forrest, R (Wellington) 1899 *W,* 1900 *S,* 1902 *I, S,* 1903 *I, S*
Foulds, R T (Waterloo) 1929 *W, I*
Fowler, F D (Manchester) 1878 *S,* 1879 *S*
Fowler, H (Oxford U) 1878 *S,* 1881 *W, S*
Fowler, R H (Leeds) 1877 *I*
Fox, F H (Wellington) 1890 *W, S*
Francis, T E S (Cambridge U) 1926 *W, I, F, S*
Frankcom, G P (Cambridge U, Bedford) 1965 *W, I, F, S*
Fraser, E C (Blackheath) 1875 *I*
Fraser, G (Richmond) 1902 *W, I, S,* 1903 *W, I*
Freakes, H D (Oxford U) 1938 *W,* 1939 *W, I*
Freeman, H (Marlborough N) 1872 *S,* 1873 *S,* 1874 *S*
French, R J (St Helens) 1961 *W, I, F, S*
Fry, H A (Liverpool) 1934 *W, I, S*
Fry, T W (Queen's House) 1880 *I, S,* 1881 *W*
Fuller, H G (Cambridge U) 1882 *I, S,* 1883 *W, I, S,* 1884 *W*

Gadney, B C (Leicester, Headingley) 1932 *I, S,* 1933 *I, S,* 1934 *W, I, S,* 1935 *S,* 1936 *NZ, W, I, S,* 1937 *S,* 1938 *W*
Gamlin, H T (Blackheath) 1899 *W, S,* 1900 *W, I, S,* 1901 *S,* 1902 *W, I, S,* 1903 *W, I, S,* 1904 *W, I, S*
Gardner, E R (Devonport Services) 1921 *W, I, S,* 1922 *W, I, F,* 1923 *W, I, S, F*
Gardner, H P (Richmond) 1878 *I*
Garforth, D J (Leicester) 1997 *W* (R)
Garnett, H W T (Bradford) 1877 *S*
Gavins, M N (Leicester) 1961 *W*
Gay, D J (Bath) 1968 *W, I, F, S*
Gent, D R (Gloucester) 1905 *NZ,* 1906 *W, I,* 1910 *W, I*
Genth, J S M (Manchester) 1874 *S,* 1875 *S*
George, J T (Falmouth) 1947 *S, F,* 1949 *I*
Gerrard, R A (Bath) 1932 *SA, W, I, S,* 1933 *W, I, S,* 1934 *W, I, S,* 1936 *NZ, W, I, S*
Gibbs, G A (Bristol) 1947 *F,* 1948 *I*
Gibbs, J C (Harlequins) 1925 *NZ, W,* 1926 *F,* 1927 *W, I, S, F*
Gibbs, N (Harlequins) 1954 *S, F*
Giblin, L F (Blackheath) 1896 *W, I,* 1897 *S*
Gibson, A S (Manchester) 1871 *S*
Gibson, C O P (Northern) 1901 *W*
Gibson, G R (Northern) 1899 *W,* 1901 *S*
Gibson, T A (Northern) 1905 *W, S*
Gilbert, F G (Devonport Services) 1923 *W, I*
Gilbert, R (Devonport A) 1908 *W, I, S*
Giles, J L (Coventry) 1935 *W, I,* 1937 *W, I,* 1938 *I, S*
Gittings, W J (Coventry) 1967 *NZ*
Glover, P B (Bath) 1967 *A,* 1971 *F, P*
Godfray, R E (Richmond) 1905 *NZ*
Godwin, H O (Coventry) 1959 *F, S,* 1963 *S, NZ* 1,2, *A,* 1964 *NZ, I, F, S,* 1967 *NZ*
Gomarsall, A C T (Wasps) 1996 *It, Arg,* 1997 *S, I, F*
Gordon-Smith, G W (Blackheath) 1900 *W, I, S*
Gotley, A L H (Oxford U) 1910 *F, S,* 1911 *W, F, I, S*
Graham, D (Aspatria) 1901 *W*
Graham, H J (Wimbledon H) 1875 *I, S,* 1876 *I, S*
Graham, J D G (Wimbledon H) 1876 *I*
Gray, A (Otley) 1947 *W, I, S*
Grayson, P J (Northampton) 1995 *WS,* 1996 *F, W, S, I,* 1997 *S, I, F*
Green, J (Skipton) 1905 *I,* 1906 *S, F, SA,* 1907 *F, W, I, S*
Green, J F (West Kent) 1871 *S*
Greening, P B T (Gloucester) 1996 *It* (R), 1997 *W* (R)
Greenwell, J H (Rockcliff) 1893 *W, I*
Greenwood, J E (Cambridge U, Leicester) 1912 *F,* 1913 *SA, W, F, I, S,* 1914 *W, S, F,* 1920 *W, F, I, S*
Greenwood, J R H (Waterloo) 1966 *I, F, S,* 1967 *A,* 1969 *I*
Greg, W (Manchester) 1876 *I, S*
Gregory, G G (Bristol) 1931 *I, S, F,* 1932 *SA, W, I, S,* 1933 *W, I, S,* 1934 *W, I, S*
Gregory, J A (Blackheath) 1949 *W*
Grylls, W M (Redruth) 1905 *I*
Guest, R H (Waterloo) 1939 *W, I, S,* 1947 *W, I, S, F,* 1948 *A, W, I, S,* 1949 *F, S*
Guillemard, A G (West Kent) 1871 *S,* 1872 *S*
Gummer, C H A (Plymouth A) 1929 *F*
Gunner, C R (Marlborough N) 1876 *I*
Gurdon, C (Richmond) 1880 *I, S,* 1881 *I, W, S,* 1882 *I, S,* 1883 *S,* 1884 *W, S,* 1885 *I,* 1886 *W, I, S*
Gurdon, E T (Richmond) 1878 *S,* 1879 *I,* 1880 *S,* 1881 *I, W, S,* 1882 *S,* 1883 *W, I, S,* 1884 *W, I, S,* 1885 *W, I,* 1886 *S*
Guscott, J C (Bath) 1989 *R, Fj,* 1990 *I, F, W, S, Arg* 3, 1991 *W, S, I, F, Fj, A.* [*NZ, It, F, S, A*], 1992 *S, I, F, W, C, SA,* 1993 *F, W, S, I,* 1994 *R, C,* 1995 *I, F, W, S,* [*Arg, It, A, NZ, F*], *SA, WS,* 1996 *F, W, S, I, Arg,* 1997 *I* (R), *W* (R)

Haigh, L (Manchester) 1910 *W, I, S,* 1911 *W, F, I, S*
Hale, P M (Moseley) 1969 *SA,* 1970 *I, W*
Hall, C (Gloucester) 1901 *I, S*
Hall, J (N Durham) 1894 *W, I, S*
Hall, J P (Bath) 1984 *S* (R), *I, F, SA* 1,2, *A,* 1985 *R, F, S, I, W, NZ* 1,2, 1986 *W, S,* 1987 *I, F, W, S,* 1990 *Arg* 3, 1994 *S*
Hall, N M (Richmond) 1947 *W, I, S, F,* 1949 *W, I,* 1952 *SA, W, S, I, F,* 1953 *W, I, F, S,* 1955 *W, I*
Halliday, S J (Bath, Harlequins) 1986 *W, S,* 1987 *S,* 1988 *S, I* 1,2, *A* 1, *A,* 1989 *S, I, F, W, R, Fj* (R), 1990 *W, S,* 1991 [*US, S, A*], 1992 *S, I, F, W*
Hamersley, A St G (Marlborough N) 1871 *S,* 1872 *S,* 1873 *S,* 1874 *S*
Hamilton-Hill, E A (Harlequins) 1936 *NZ, W, I*
Hamilton-Wickes, R H (Cambridge U) 1924 *W,* 1925 *NZ, W, I, S, F,* 1926 *W, I, S,* 1927 *W*

Hammett, E D G (Newport) 1920 *W, F, S,* 1921 *W, I, S, F,* 1922 *W*
Hammond, C E L (Harlequins) 1905 *S, NZ,* 1906 *W, I, S, F,* 1908 *W, I*
Hancock, A W (Northampton) 1965 *F, S,* 1966 *F*
Hancock, G E (Birkenhead Park) 1939 *W, I, S*
Hancock, J H (Newport) 1955 *W, I*
Hancock, P F (Blackheath) 1886 *W, I,* 1890 *W*
Hancock, P S (Richmond) 1904 *W, I, S*
Handford, F G (Manchester) 1909 *W, F, I, S*
Hands, R H M (Blackheath) 1910 *F, S*
Hanley, J (Plymouth A) 1927 *W, S, F,* 1928 *W, I, F, S*
Hannaford, R C (Bristol) 1971 *W, I, F*
Hanvey, R J (Aspatria) 1926 *W, I, F, S*
Harding, E H (Devonport Services) 1931 *I*
Harding, R M (Bristol) 1985 *R, F, S,* 1987 *S,* [*A, J, W*], 1988 *I* 1 (R),2, *A* 1,2, *Fj*
Harding, V S J (Saracens) 1961 *F, S,* 1962 *W, I, F, S*
Hardwick, P F (Percy Park) 1902 *I, S,* 1903 *W, I, S,* 1904 *W, I, S*
Hardwick, R J K (Coventry) 1996 *It* (R)
Hardy, E M P (Blackheath) 1951 *I, F, S*
Hare, W H (Nottingham, Leicester) 1974 *W,* 1978 *F, NZ,* 1979 *NZ,* 1980 *I, F, W, S,* 1981 *W, S, Arg* 1,2, 1982 *F, W,* 1983 *F, W, S, I, NZ,* 1984 *S, I, F, W, SA* 1,2
Harper, C H (Exeter) 1899 *W*
Harriman, A T (Harlequins) 1988 *A*
Harris, S W (Blackheath) 1920 *I, S*
Harris, T W (Northampton) 1929 *S,* 1932 *I*
Harrison, A C (Hartlepool R) 1931 *I, S*
Harrison, A L (United Services, RN) 1914 *I, F*
Harrison, G (Hull) 1877 *I, S,* 1879 *S, I,* 1880 *S,* 1885 *W, I*
Harrison, H C (United Services, RN) 1909 *S,* 1914 *I, S, F*
Harrison, M E (Wakefield) 1985 *NZ* 1,2, 1986 *S, I, F,* 1987 *I, F, W, S,* [*A, J, US, W*], 1988 *F, W*
Hartley, B C (Blackheath) 1901 *S,* 1902 *S*
Haslett, L W (Birkenhead Park) 1926 *I, F*
Hastings, G W D (Gloucester) 1955 *W, I, F, S,* 1957 *W, I, F, S,* 1958 *W, A, I, F, S*
Havelock, H (Hartlepool R) 1908 *F, W, I*
Hawcridge, J J (Bradford) 1885 *W, I*
Hayward, L W (Cheltenham) 1910 *I*
Hazell, D St G (Leicester) 1955 *W, I, F, S*
Healey, A S (Leicester) 1997 *I* (R), *W*
Hearn, R D (Bedford) 1966 *F, S,* 1967 *I, F, S, W*
Heath, A H (Oxford U) 1876 *S*
Heaton, J (Waterloo) 1935 *W, I, S,* 1939 *W, I, S,* 1947 *I, S, F*
Henderson, A P (Edinburgh Wands) 1947 *W, I, S, F,* 1948 *I, S, F,* 1949 *W, I*
Henderson, R S F (Blackheath) 1883 *W, S,* 1884 *W, S,* 1885 *W*
Heppell, W G (Devonport A) 1903 *I*
Herbert, A J (Wasps) 1958 *F, S,* 1959 *W, I, F, S*
Hesford, R (Bristol) 1981 *S* (R), 1982 *A, S, F* (R), 1983 *F* (R), 1985 *R, F, S, I, W*
Heslop, N J (Orrell) 1990 *Arg* 1,2,3, 1991 *W, S, I, F,* [*US, F*], 1992 *W* (R)
Hetherington, J G G (Northampton) 1958 *A, I,* 1959 *W, I, F, S*
Hewitt, E N (Coventry) 1951 *W, I, F*
Hewitt, W W (Queen's House) 1881 *I, W, S,* 1882 *I*
Hickson, J L (Bradford) 1887 *W, I, S,* 1890 *W, S, I*
Higgins, R (Liverpool) 1954 *W, NZ, I, S,* 1955 *W, I, F, S,* 1957 *W, I, F, S,* 1959 *W*
Hignell, A J (Cambridge U, Bristol) 1975 *A* 2, 1976 *A, W, S, I,* 1977 *S, I, F, W,* 1978 *W,* 1979 *S, I, F*
Hill, B A (Blackheath) 1903 *I, S,* 1904 *W, I,* 1905 *W, NZ,* 1906 *SA,* 1907 *F, W*
Hill, R A (Saracens) 1997 *S, I, F, W*
Hill, R J (Bath) 1984 *SA* 1,2, 1985 *I* (R), *NZ* 2 (R), 1986 *F* (R), 1987 *I, F, W,* [*US*], 1989 *Fj,* 1990 *I, F, W, S, Arg* 1,2,3, 1991 *W, S, I, F, Fj, A,* [*NZ, It, US, F, S, A*]
Hillard, R J (Oxford U) 1925 *NZ*
Hiller, R (Harlequins) 1968 *W, I, F, S,* 1969 *I, F, S, W, SA,* 1970 *I, W, S,* 1971 *I, F, S* (2[1C]), *P,* 1972 *W, I*
Hind, A E (Leicester) 1905 *NZ,* 1906 *W*
Hind, G R (Blackheath) 1910 *S,* 1911 *I*
Hobbs, R F A (Blackheath) 1899 *S,* 1903 *W*
Hobbs, R G S (Richmond) 1932 *SA, W, I, S*
Hodges, H A (Nottingham) 1906 *W, I*
Hodgkinson, S D (Nottingham) 1989 *R, Fj,* 1990 *I, F, W, S, Arg* 1,2,3, 1991 *W, S, I, F,* [*US*]

Hodgson, J McD (Northern) 1932 *SA, W, I, S,* 1934 *W, I,* 1936 *I*
Hodgson, S A M (Durham City) 1960 *W, I, F, S,* 1961 *SA, W,* 1962 *W, I, F, S,* 1964 *W*
Hofmeyr, M B (Oxford U) 1950 *W, F, S*
Hogarth, T B (Hartlepool R) 1906 *F*
Holford, G (Gloucester) 1920 *W, F*
Holland, D (Devonport A) 1912 *W, I, S*
Holliday, T E (Aspatria) 1923 *S, F,* 1925 *I, S, F,* 1926 *F, S*
Holmes, C B (Manchester) 1947 *S,* 1948 *I, F*
Holmes, E (Manningham) 1890 *S, I*
Holmes, W A (Nuneaton) 1950 *W, I, F, S,* 1951 *W, I, F, S,* 1952 *SA, S, I, F,* 1953 *W, I, F, S*
Holmes, W B (Cambridge U) 1949 *W, I, F, S*
Hook, W G (Gloucester) 1951 *S,* 1952 *SA, W*
Hooper, C A (Middlesex W) 1894 *W, I, S*
Hopley, D P (Wasps) 1995 *[WS (R)], SA, WS*
Hopley, F J V (Blackheath) 1907 *F, W,* 1908 *I*
Hordern, P C (Gloucester) 1931 *I, S, F,* 1934 *W*
Horley, C H (Swinton) 1885 *I*
Hornby, A N (Manchester) 1877 *I, S,* 1878 *S, I,* 1880 *I,* 1881 *I, S,* 1882 *I, S*
Horrocks-Taylor, J P (Cambridge U, Leicester, Middlesbrough) 1958 *W, A,* 1961 *S,* 1962 *S,* 1963 *NZ 1,2, A,* 1964 *NZ, W*
Horsfall, E L (Harlequins) 1949 *W*
Horton, A L (Blackheath) 1965 *W, I, F, S,* 1966 *F, S,* 1967 *NZ*
Horton, J P (Bath) 1978 *W, S, I, NZ,* 1980 *I, F, W, S,* 1981 *W,* 1983 *S, I,* 1984 *SA 1,2*
Horton, N E (Moseley, Toulouse) 1969 *I, F, S, W,* 1971 *I, F, S,* 1974 *S,* 1975 *W,* 1977 *S, I, F, W,* 1978 *F, W,* 1979 *S, I, F, W,* 1980 *I*
Hosen, R W (Bristol, Northampton) 1963 *NZ 1,2, A,* 1964 *F, S,* 1967 *A, I, F, S, W*
Hosking, G R d'A (Devonport Services) 1949 *W, I, F, S,* 1950 *W*
Houghton, S (Runcorn) 1892 *I,* 1896 *W*
Howard, P D (O Millhillians) 1930 *W, I, F, S,* 1931 *W, I, S, F*
Hubbard, G C (Blackheath) 1892 *W, I*
Hubbard, J C (Harlequins) 1930 *S*
Hudson, A (Gloucester) 1906 *W, I, F,* 1908 *F, W, I, S,* 1910 *F*
Hughes, G E (Barrow) 1896 *S*
Hull, P A (Bristol, RAF) 1994 *SA 1,2, R, C*
Hulme, F C (Birkenhead Park) 1903 *W, I,* 1905 *W, I*
Hunt, J T (Manchester) 1882 *I, S,* 1884 *W*
Hunt, R (Manchester) 1880 *I,* 1881 *W, S,* 1882 *I*
Hunt, W H (Manchester) 1876 *S,* 1877 *I, S,* 1878 *I*
Hunter, I (Northampton) 1992 *C,* 1993 *F, W,* 1994 *F, W,* 1995 *[WS, F]*
Huntsman, R P (Headingley) 1985 *NZ 1,2*
Hurst, A C B (Wasps) 1962 *S*
Huskisson, T F (OMTs) 1937 *W, I, S,* 1938 *W, I,* 1939 *W, I, S*
Hutchinson, F (Headingley) 1909 *F, I, S*
Hutchinson, J E (Durham City) 1906 *I*
Hutchinson, W C (RIE Coll) 1876 *S,* 1877 *I*
Hutchinson, W H H (Hull) 1875 *I,* 1876 *I*
Huth, H (Huddersfield) 1879 *S*
Hyde, J P (Northampton) 1950 *F, S*
Hynes, W B (United Services, RN) 1912 *F*

Ibbitson, E D (Headingley) 1909 *W, F, I, S*
Imrie, H M (Durham City) 1906 *NZ,* 1907 *I*
Inglis, R E (Blackheath) 1886 *W, I, S*
Irvin, S H (Devonport A) 1905 *W*
Isherwood, F W (Ravenscourt Park) 1872 *S*

Jackett, E J (Leicester, Falmouth) 1905 *NZ,* 1906 *W, I, S, F, SA,* 1907 *W, I, S,* 1909 *W, F, I, S*
Jackson, A H (Blackheath) 1878 *I,* 1880 *I*
Jackson, B S (Broughton Park) 1970 *S (R), F*
Jackson, P B (Coventry) 1956 *W, I, F,* 1957 *W, I, F, S,* 1958 *W, A, F, S,* 1959 *W, I, F, S,* 1961 *S,* 1963 *W, I, F, S*
Jackson, W J (Halifax) 1894 *S*
Jacob, F (Cambridge U) 1897 *W, I, S,* 1898 *I, S, W,* 1899 *W, I*
Jacob, H P (Blackheath) 1924 *W, I, F, S,* 1930 *F*
Jacob, P G (Blackheath) 1898 *I*
Jacobs, C R (Northampton) 1956 *W, I, S, F,* 1957 *W, I, F, S,* 1958 *W, A, I, F, S,* 1960 *W, I, F, S,* 1961 *SA, W, I, F, S,* 1963 *NZ 1,2, A,* 1964 *W, I, F, S*

Jago, R A (Devonport A) 1906 *W, I, SA,* 1907 *W, I*
Janion, J P A G (Bedford) 1971 *W, I, F, S (2[1C]), P,* 1972 *W, S, SA,* 1973 *A,* 1975 *A 1,2*
Jarman, J W (Bristol) 1900 *W*
Jeavons, N C (Moseley) 1981 *S, I, F, Arg 1,2,* 1982 *A, S, I, F, W,* 1983 *F, W, S, I*
Jeeps, R E G (Northampton) 1956 *W,* 1957 *W, I, F, S,* 1958 *W, A, I, F, S,* 1959 *I,* 1960 *W, I, F, S,* 1961 *SA, W, I, F, S,* 1962 *W, I, F, S*
Jeffery, G L (Blackheath) 1886 *W, I, S,* 1887 *W, I, S*
Jennins, C R (Waterloo) 1967 *A, I, F*
Jewitt, J (Hartlepool R) 1902 *W*
Johns, W A (Gloucester) 1909 *W, F, I, S,* 1910 *W, I, F*
Johnson, M O (Leicester) 1993 *F, NZ,* 1994 *S, I, F, W, R, C,* 1995 *I, F, W, S, [Arg, It, WS, A, NZ, F], SA, WS,* 1996 *F, W, S, I, It, Arg,* 1997 *S, I, F, W*
Johnston, W R (Bristol) 1910 *W, I, S,* 1912 *W, I, S, F,* 1913 *SA, W, F, I, S,* 1914 *W, I, S, F*
Jones, F P (New Brighton) 1893 *S*
Jones, H A (Barnstaple) 1950 *W, I, F*
Jorden, A M (Cambridge U, Blackheath, Bedford) 1970 *F,* 1973 *I, F, S,* 1974 *F,* 1975 *W, S*
Jowett, D (Heckmondwike) 1889 *M,* 1890 *S, I,* 1891 *W, I, S*
Judd, P E (Coventry) 1962 *W, I, F, S,* 1963 *S, NZ 1,2, A,* 1964 *NZ,* 1965 *I, F, S,* 1966 *W, I, F, S,* 1967 *A, I, F, S, W, NZ*

Kayll, H E (Sunderland) 1878 *S*
Keeling, J H (Guy's Hospital) 1948 *A, W*
Keen, B W (Newcastle U) 1968 *W, I, F, S*
Keeton, G H (Leicester) 1904 *W, I, S*
Kelly, G A (Bedford) 1947 *W, I, S,* 1948 *W*
Kelly, T S (London Devonians) 1906 *W, I, S, F, SA,* 1907 *F, W, I, S,* 1908 *F, I, S*
Kemble, A T (Liverpool) 1885 *W, I,* 1887 *I*
Kemp, D T (Blackheath) 1935 *W*
Kemp, T A (Richmond) 1937 *W, I,* 1939 *S,* 1948 *A, W*
Kendall, P D (Birkenhead Park) 1901 *S,* 1902 *W,* 1903 *S*
Kendall-Carpenter, J MacG K (Oxford U, Bath) 1949 *I, F, S,* 1950 *W, I, F, S,* 1951 *I, F, S,* 1952 *SA, W, S, I, F,* 1953 *W, I, F, S,* 1954 *W, NZ, I, F*
Kendrew, D A (Leicester) 1930 *W, I,* 1933 *I, S,* 1934 *S,* 1935 *W, I,* 1936 *NZ, W, I*
Kennedy, R D (Camborne S of M) 1949 *I, F, S*
Kent, C P (Rosslyn Park) 1977 *S, I, F, W,* 1978 *F (R)*
Kent, T (Salford) 1891 *W, I, S,* 1892 *W, I, S*
Kershaw, C A (United Services, RN) 1920 *W, F, I, S,* 1921 *W, I, S, F,* 1922 *W, I, F, S,* 1923 *W, I, S, F*
Kewley, E (Liverpool) 1874 *S,* 1875 *S,* 1876 *I, S,* 1877 *I, S,* 1878 *S*
Kewney, A L (Leicester) 1906 *W, I, S, F,* 1909 *A, W, F, I, S,* 1911 *W, F, I, S,* 1912 *I, S,* 1913 *SA*
Key, A (O Cranleighans) 1930 *I,* 1933 *W*
Keyworth, M (Swansea) 1976 *A, W, S, I*
Kilner, B (Wakefield T) 1880 *I*
Kindersley, R S (Exeter) 1883 *W,* 1884 *S,* 1885 *W*
King, I (Harrogate) 1954 *W, NZ, I*
King, J A (Headingley) 1911 *W, F, I, S,* 1912 *W, I, S, F,* 1913 *SA, W, F, I, S*
King, Q E M A (Army) 1921 *S*
Kingston, P (Gloucester) 1975 *A 1,2,* 1979 *I, F, W*
Kitching, A E (Blackheath) 1913 *I*
Kittermaster, H J (Harlequins) 1925 *NZ, W, I,* 1926 *W, I, F, S*
Knight, F (Plymouth) 1909 *A*
Knight, P M (Bristol) 1972 *F, S, SA*
Knowles, E (Millom) 1896 *S,* 1897 *S*
Knowles, T C (Birkenhead Park) 1931 *S*
Krige, J A (Guy's Hospital) 1920 *W*

Labuschagne, N A (Harlequins, Guy's Hospital) 1953 *W,* 1955 *W, I, F, S*
Lagden, R O (Richmond) 1911 *S*
Laird, H C C (Harlequins) 1927 *W, I, S,* 1928 *A, W, I, F, S,* 1929 *W, I*
Lambert, D (Harlequins) 1907 *F,* 1908 *F, W, S,* 1911 *W, F, I*
Lampkowski, M S (Headingley) 1976 *A, W, S, I*
Lapage, W N (United Services, RN) 1908 *F, W, I, S*
Larter, P J (Northampton, RAF) 1967 *A, NZ,* 1968 *W, I, F, S,* 1969 *I, F, S, W, SA,* 1970 *I, W, F, S,* 1971 *W, I, F, S (2[1C]), P,* 1972 *SA,* 1973 *NZ 1, W*
Law, A F (Richmond) 1877 *S*

Law, D E (Birkenhead Park) 1927 *I*
Lawrence, Hon H A (Richmond) 1873 *S*, 1874 *S*, 1875 *I*, *S*
Lawrie, P W (Leicester) 1910 *S*, 1911 *S*
Lawson, R G (Workington) 1925 *I*
Lawson, T M (Workington) 1928 *A*, *W*
Leadbetter, M M (Broughton Park) 1970 *F*
Leadbetter, V H (Edinburgh Wands) 1954 *S*, *F*
Leake, W R M (Harlequins) 1891 *W*, *I*, *S*
Leather, G (Liverpool) 1907 *I*
Lee, F H (Marlborough N) 1876 *S*, 1877 *I*
Lee, H (Blackheath) 1907 *F*
Le Fleming, J (Blackheath) 1887 *W*
Leonard, J (Saracens, Harlequins) 1990 *Arg* 1,2,3, 1991 *W, S, I, F, Fj, A, [NZ, It, US, F, S, A]*, 1992 *S, I, F, W, C, SA*, 1993 *F, W, S, I, NZ*, 1994 *S, I, F, W, SA* 1,2, *R, C*, 1995 *I, F, W, S, [Arg, It, A, NZ, F], SA, WS*, 1996 *F, W, S, I, It, Arg*, 1997 *S, I, F, W*
Leslie-Jones, F A (Richmond) 1895 *W, I*
Lewis, A O (Bath) 1952 *SA, W, S, I, F*, 1953 *W, I, F, S*, 1954 *F*
Leyland, R (Waterloo) 1935 *W, I, S*
Linnett, M S (Moseley) 1989 *Fj*
Livesay, R O'H (Blackheath) 1898 *W*, 1899 *W*
Lloyd, R H (Harlequins) 1967 *NZ*, 1968 *W, I, F, S*
Locke, H M (Birkenhead Park) 1923 *S, F*, 1924 *W, F, S*, 1925 *W, I, S, F*, 1927 *W, I, S*
Lockwood, R E (Heckmondwike) 1887 *W, I, S*, 1889 *M*, 1891 *W, I, S*, 1892 *W, I, S*, 1893 *W, I*, 1894 *W, I*
Login, S H M (RN Coll) 1876 *I*
Lohden, F C (Blackheath) 1893 *W*
Longland, R J (Northampton) 1932 *S*, 1933 *W, S*, 1934 *W, I, S*, 1935 *W, I, S*, 1936 *NZ, W, I, S*, 1937 *W, I, S*, 1938 *W, I, S*
Lowe, C N (Cambridge U, Blackheath) 1913 *SA, W, F, I, S*, 1914 *W, I, S, F*, 1920 *W, F, I, S*, 1921 *W, I, S, F*, 1922 *W, I, F, S*, 1923 *W, I, S, F*
Lowrie, F (Wakefield T) 1889 *M*, 1890 *W*
Lowry, W M (Birkenhead Park) 1920 *F*
Lozowski, R A P (Wasps) 1984 *A*
Luddington, W G E (Devonport Services) 1923 *W, I, S, F*, 1924 *W, I, F, S*, 1925 *W, I, S, F*, 1926 *W*
Luscombe, F (Gipsies) 1872 *S*, 1873 *S*, 1875 *I, S*, 1876 *I, S*
Luscombe, J H (Gipsies) 1871 *S*
Luxmoore, A F C C (Richmond) 1900 *S*, 1901 *W*
Luya, H F (Waterloo, Headingley) 1948 *W, I, S, F*, 1949 *W*
Lyon, A (Liverpool) 1871 *S*
Lyon, G H d'O (United Services, RN) 1908 *S*, 1909 *A*

McCanlis, M A (Gloucester) 1931 *W, I*
McFadyean, C W (Moseley) 1966 *I, F, S*, 1967 *A, I, F, S, W, NZ*, 1968 *W, I*
MacIlwaine, A H (United Services, Hull & E Riding) 1912 *W, I, S, F*, 1920 *I*
Mackie, O G (Wakefield T, Cambridge U) 1897 *S*, 1898 *I, S*, 1875 *I*
Mackinlay, J E H (St George's Hospital) 1872 *S*, 1873 *S*, 1875 *I*
MacLaren, W (Manchester) 1871 *S*
MacLennan, R R F (OMTs) 1925 *I, S, F*
McLeod, N F (RIE Coll) 1879 *S, I*
Madge, R J P (Exeter) 1948 *A, W, I, S*
Malir, F W S (Otley) 1930 *W, I, S*
Mallett, J A (Bath) 1995 *[WS (R)]*
Mangles, R H (Richmond) 1897 *W, I*
Manley, D C (Exeter) 1963 *W, I, F, S*
Mann, W E (United Services, Army) 1911 *W, F, I*
Mantell, N D (Rosslyn Park) 1975 *A* 1
Markendale, E T (Manchester R) 1880 *I*
Marques, R W D (Cambridge U, Harlequins) 1956 *W, I, S, F*, 1957 *W, I, F, S*, 1958 *W, A, I, F, S*, 1959 *W, I, F, S*, 1960 *W, I, F, S*, 1961 *SA, W*
Marquis, J C (Birkenhead Park) 1900 *I, S*
Marriott, C J B (Blackheath) 1884 *W, I, S*, 1886 *W, I, S*, 1887 *I*
Marriott, E E (Manchester) 1876 *I*
Marriott, V R (Harlequins) 1963 *NZ* 1,2, *A*, 1964 *NZ*
Marsden, G H (Morley) 1900 *W, I, S*
Marsh, H (RIE Coll) 1873 *S*
Marsh, J (Swinton) 1892 *I*
Marshall, H (Blackheath) 1893 *W*
Marshall, M W (Blackheath) 1873 *S*, 1874 *S*, 1875 *I, S*, 1876 *I, S*, 1877 *S*, 1878 *S, I*
Marshall, R M (Oxford U) 1938 *I, S*, 1939 *W, I, S*
Martin, C R (Bath) 1985 *F, S, I, W*

Martin, N O (Harlequins) 1972 *F* (R)
Martindale, S A (Kendal) 1929 *F*
Massey, E J (Leicester) 1925 *W, I, S*
Mathias, J L (Bristol) 1905 *W, I, S, NZ*
Matters, J C (RNE Coll) 1899 *S*
Matthews, J R C (Harlequins) 1949 *F, S*, 1950 *I, F, S*, 1952 *SA, W, S, I, F*
Maud, P (Blackheath) 1893 *W, I*
Maxwell, A W (New Brighton, Headingley) 1975 *A* 1, 1976 *A, W, S, I, F*, 1978 *F*
Maxwell-Hyslop, J E (Oxford U) 1922 *I, F, S*
Maynard, A F (Cambridge U) 1914 *W, I, S*
Meikle, G W C (Waterloo) 1934 *W, I, S*
Meikle, S S C (Waterloo) 1929 *S*
Mellish, F W (Blackheath) 1920 *W, F, I, S*, 1921 *W, I*
Melville, N D (Wasps) 1984 *A*, 1985 *I, W, NZ* 1,2, 1986 *W, S, I, F*, 1988 *F, W, S, I* 1
Merriam, L P B (Blackheath) 1920 *W, F*
Michell, A T (Oxford U) 1875 *I, S*, 1876 *I*
Middleton, B B (Birkenhead Park) 1882 *I*, 1883 *I*
Middleton, J A (Richmond) 1922 *S*
Miles, J H (Leicester) 1903 *W*
Millett, H (Richmond) 1920 *F*
Mills, F W (Marlborough N) 1872 *S*, 1873 *S*
Mills, S G F (Gloucester) 1981 *Arg* 1,2, 1983 *W*, 1984 *SA* 1, *A*
Mills, W A (Devonport A) 1906 *W, I, S, F, SA*, 1907 *F, W, I, S*, 1908 *F, W*
Milman, D L K (Bedford) 1937 *W*, 1938 *W, I, S*
Milton, C H (Camborne S of M) 1906 *I*
Milton, J G (Camborne S of M) 1904 *W, I, S*, 1905 *S*, 1907 *I*
Milton, W H (Marlborough N) 1874 *S*, 1875 *I*
Mitchell, F (Blackheath) 1895 *W, S, I*, 1896 *W, I, S*
Mitchell, W G (Richmond) 1890 *W, S, I*, 1891 *W, I, S*, 1893 *S*
Mobbs, E R (Northampton) 1909 *A, W, F, I, S*, 1910 *I, F*
Moberley, W O (Ravenscourt Park) 1872 *S*
Moore, B C (Nottingham, Harlequins) 1987 *S, [A, J, W]*, 1988 *F, W, S, I* 1,2, *A* 1, 2, *Fj, A*, 1989 *S, I, F, W, R, Fj*, 1990 *I, F, W, S, Arg* 1,2, 1991 *W, S, I, F, Fj, A, [NZ, It, F, S, A]*, 1992 *S, I, F, W, SA*, 1993 *F, W, S, I, NZ*, 1994 *S, I, F, W, SA* 1,2, *R, C*, 1995 *I, F, W, S, [Arg, It, WS* (R), *A, NZ, F]*
Moore, E J (Blackheath) 1883 *I, S*
Moore, N J N H (Bristol) 1904 *W, I, S*
Moore, P B C (Blackheath) 1951 *W*
Moore, W K T (Leicester) 1947 *W, I*, 1949 *F, S*, 1950 *I, F, S*
Mordell, R J (Rosslyn Park) 1978 *W*
Morfitt, S (W Hartlepool) 1894 *W, I, S*, 1896 *W, I, S*
Morgan, J R (Hawick) 1920 *W*
Morgan, W G D (Medicals, Newcastle) 1960 *W, I, F, S*, 1961 *SA, W, I, F, S*
Morley, A J (Bristol) 1972 *SA*, 1973 *NZ* 1, *W, I*, 1975 *S, A* 1,2
Morris, A D W (United Services, RN) 1909 *A, W, F*
Morris, C D (Liverpool St Helens, Orrell) 1988 *A*, 1989 *S, I, F, W*, 1992 *S, I, F, W, C, SA*, 1993 *F, W, S, I*, 1994 *F, W, SA* 1,2, *R*, 1995 *S* (t), *[Arg, WS, A, NZ, F]*
Morrison, P H (Cambridge U) 1890 *W, S, I*, 1891 *I*
Morse, S (Marlborough N) 1873 *S*, 1874 *S*, 1875 *S*
Mortimer, W (Marlborough N) 1899 *W*
Morton, H J S (Blackheath) 1909 *I, S*, 1910 *W, I*
Moss, F (Broughton) 1885 *W, I*, 1886 *W*
Mullins, A R (Harlequins) 1989 *Fj*
Mycock, J (Sale) 1947 *W, I, S, F*, 1948 *A*
Myers, E (Bradford) 1920 *I, S*, 1921 *W, I*, 1922 *W, I, F, S*, 1923 *W, I, S, F*, 1924 *W, I, F, S*, 1925 *S, F*
Myers, H (Keighley) 1898 *I*

Nanson, W M B (Carlisle) 1907 *F, W*
Nash, E H (Richmond) 1875 *I*
Neale, B A (Rosslyn Park) 1951 *I, F, S*
Neale, M E (Blackheath) 1912 *F*
Neame, S (O Cheltonians) 1879 *S, I*, 1880 *I, S*
Neary, A (Broughton Park) 1971 *W, I, F, S* (2[1C]), *P*, 1972 *W, I, F, S, SA*, 1973 *NZ* 1, *W, I, F, S, NZ* 2, *A*, 1974 *S, I, F, W*, 1975 *I, F, W, S, A* 1, 1976 *A, W, S, I, F*, 1977 *I*, 1978 *F* (R), 1979 *S, I, F, W, NZ*, 1980 *I, F, W, S*
Nelmes, B G (Cardiff) 1975 *A* 1,2, 1978 *W, S, I, NZ*
Newbold, C J (Blackheath) 1904 *W, I, S*, 1905 *W, I, S*
Newman, S C (Oxford U) 1947 *F*, 1948 *A, W*
Newton, A W (Blackheath) 1907 *S*

Newton, P A (Blackheath) 1882 *S*
Newton-Thompson, J O (Oxford U) 1947 *S, F*
Nichol, W (Brighouse R) 1892 *W, S*
Nicholas, P L (Exeter) 1902 *W*
Nicholson, B E (Harlequins) 1938 *W, I*
Nicholson, E S (Leicester) 1935 *W, I, S*, 1936 *NZ, W*
Nicholson, E T (Birkenhead Park) 1900 *W, I*
Nicholson, T (Rockcliff) 1893 *I*
Ninnes, B F (Coventry) 1971 *W*
Norman, D J (Leicester) 1932 *SA, W*
North, E H G (Blackheath) 1891 *W, I, S*
Northmore, S (Millom) 1897 *I*
Novak, M J (Harlequins) 1970 *W, S, F*
Novis, A L (Blackheath) 1929 *S, F*, 1930 *W, I, F*, 1933 *I, S*

Oakeley, F E (United Services, RN) 1913 *S*, 1914 *I, S, F*
Oakes, R F (Hartlepool R) 1897 *W, I, S*, 1898 *I, S, W*, 1899 *W, S*
Oakley, L F L (Bedford) 1951 *W*
Obolensky, A (Oxford U) 1936 *NZ, W, I, S*
Ojomoh, S O (Bath) 1994 *I, F, SA* 1 (R), 2, *R*, 1995 *S* (R), [*Arg, WS, A* (t), *F*], 1996 *F*
Old, A G B (Middlesbrough, Leicester, Sheffield) 1972 *W, I, F, S, SA*, 1973 *NZ* 2, *A*, 1974 *S, I, F, W*, 1975 *I, A* 2, 1976 *S, I*, 1978 *F*
Oldham, W L (Coventry) 1908 *S*, 1909 *A*
Olver, C J (Northampton) 1990 *Arg* 3, 1991 [*US*], 1992 *C*
O'Neill, A (Teignmouth, Torquay A) 1901 *W, I, S*
Openshaw, W E (Manchester) 1879 *I*
Orwin, J (Gloucester, RAF, Bedford) 1985 *R, F, S, I, W, NZ* 1,2, 1988 *F, W, S, I* 1,2, *A* 1,2
Osborne, R R (Manchester) 1871 *S*
Osborne, S H (Oxford U) 1905 *S*
Oti, C (Cambridge U, Nottingham, Wasps) 1988 *S, I* 1, 1989 *S, I, F, W, R*, 1990 *Arg* 1,2, 1991 *Fj, A*, [*NZ, It*]
Oughtred, B (Hartlepool R) 1901 *S*, 1902 *W, I, S*, 1903 *W, I*
Owen, J E (Coventry) 1963 *W, I, F, S, A*, 1964 *NZ*, 1965 *W, I, F, S*, 1966 *I, F, S*, 1967 *NZ*
Owen-Smith, H G O (St Mary's Hospital) 1934 *W, I, S*, 1936 *NZ, W, I, S*, 1937 *W, I, S*

Page, J J (Bedford, Northampton) 1971 *W, I, F, S*, 1975 *S*
Pallant, J N (Notts) 1967 *I, F, S*
Palmer, A C (London Hospital) 1909 *I, S*
Palmer, F H (Richmond) 1905 *W*
Palmer, G V (Richmond) 1928 *I, F, S*
Pargetter, T A (Coventry) 1962 *S*, 1963 *F, NZ* 1
Parker, G W (Gloucester) 1938 *I, S*
Parker, Hon S (Liverpool) 1874 *S*, 1875 *S*
Parsons, E I (RAF) 1939 *S*
Parsons, M J (Northampton) 1968 *W, I, F, S*
Patterson, W M (Sale) 1961 *SA, S*
Pattisson, R M (Blackheath) 1883 *I, S*
Paul, J E (RIE Coll) 1875 *S*
Payne, A T (Bristol) 1935 *I, S*
Payne, C M (Harlequins) 1964 *I, F, S*, 1965 *I, F, S*, 1966 *W, I, F, S*
Payne, J H (Broughton) 1882 *S*, 1883 *W, I, S*, 1884 *I*, 1885 *W, I*
Pearce, G S (Northampton) 1979 *S, I, F, W*, 1981 *Arg* 1,2, 1982 *A, S*, 1983 *F, W, S, I, NZ*, 1984 *SA* 2, *A*, 1985 *R, F, S, I, W, NZ* 1,2, 1986 *W, S, I, F*, 1987 *I, F, W, S*, [*A, US, W*], 1988 *Fj*, 1991 [*US*]
Pears, D (Harlequins) 1990 *Arg* 1,2, 1992 *F* (R), 1994 *F*
Pearson, A W (Blackheath) 1875 *I, S*, 1876 *I, S*, 1877 *S*, 1878 *S, I*
Peart, T G A H (Hartlepool R) 1964 *F, S*
Pease, F E (Hartlepool R) 1887 *I*
Penny, S H (Leicester) 1909 *A*
Penny, W J (United Hospitals) 1878 *I*, 1879 *S, I*
Percival, L J (Rugby) 1891 *I*, 1892 *I*, 1893 *S*
Periton, H G (Waterloo) 1925 *W*, 1926 *W, I, F, S*, 1927 *W, I, S, F*, 1928 *A, I, F, S*, 1929 *W, I, S, F*, 1930 *W, I, F, S*
Perrott, E S (O Cheltonians) 1875 *I*
Perry, D G (Bedford) 1963 *F, S, NZ* 1,2, *A*, 1964 *NZ, W, I*, 1965 *F, W, S*, 1966 *W, I, F*
Perry, S V (Cambridge U, Waterloo) 1947 *W, I*, 1948 *A, W, I, S, F*
Peters, J (Plymouth) 1906 *S, F*, 1907 *I, S*, 1908 *W*
Phillips, C (Birkenhead Park) 1880 *S*, 1881 *I, S*
Phillips, M S (Fylde) 1958 *A, I, F, S*, 1959 *W, I, F, S*,

1960 *W, I, F, S*, 1961 *W*, 1963 *W, I, F, S, NZ* 1,2, *A*, 1964 *NZ, W, I, F, S*
Pickering, A S (Harrogate) 1907 *I*
Pickering, R D A (Bradford) 1967 *I, F, S, W*, 1968 *F, S*
Pickles, R C W (Bristol) 1922 *I, F*
Pierce, R (Liverpool) 1898 *I*, 1903 *S*
Pilkington, W N (Cambridge U) 1898 *S*
Pillman, C H (Blackheath) 1910 *W, I, F, S*, 1911 *W, F, I, S*, 1912 *W, F*, 1913 *SA, W, F, I, S*, 1914 *W, I, S*
Pillman, R L (Blackheath) 1914 *F*
Pinch, J (Lancaster) 1896 *W, I*, 1897 *S*
Pinching, W W (Guy's Hospital) 1872 *S*
Pitman, I J (Oxford U) 1922 *S*
Plummer, K C (Bristol) 1969 *W*, 1976 *S, I, F*
Poole, F O (Oxford U) 1895 *W, I, S*
Poole, R W (Hartlepool R) 1896 *S*
Pope, E B (Blackheath) 1931 *W, S, F*
Portus, G V (Blackheath) 1908 *F, I*
Poulton, R W (later Poulton Palmer) (Oxford U, Harlequins, Liverpool) 1909 *F, I, S*, 1910 *W*, 1911 *S*, 1912 *W, I, S*, 1913 *SA, W, F, I, S*, 1914 *W, I, S, F*
Powell, D L (Northampton) 1966 *W, I*, 1969 *I, F, S, W*, 1971 *W, I, F, S* (2[1C])
Pratten, W E (Blackheath) 1927 *S, F*
Preece, I (Coventry) 1948 *I, S, F*, 1949 *F, S*, 1950 *W, I, F, S*, 1951 *W, I, F*
Preece, P S (Coventry) 1972 *SA*, 1973 *NZ* 1, *W, I, F, S, NZ* 2, 1975 *I, F, W, A* 2, 1976 *W* (R)
Preedy, M (Gloucester) 1984 *SA* 1
Prentice, F D (Leicester) 1928 *I, F, S*
Prescott, R E (Harlequins) 1937 *W, I*, 1938 *I*, 1939 *W, I, S*
Preston, N J (Richmond) 1979 *NZ*, 1980 *I, F*
Price, H L (Harlequins) 1922 *I, S*, 1923 *W, I*
Price, J (Coventry) 1961 *I*
Price, P L A (RIE Coll) 1877 *I, S*, 1878 *S*
Price, T W (Cheltenham) 1948 *S, F*, 1949 *W, I, F, S*
Probyn, J A (Wasps, Askeans) 1988 *F, W, S, I* 1,2, *A* 1, 2, *A*, 1989 *S, I, R* (R), 1990 *I, F, W, S, Arg* 1,2,3, 1991 *W, S, I, F, Fj, A*, [*NZ, It, F, S, A*], 1992 *S, I, F, W*, 1993 *F, W, S, I*
Prout, D H (Northampton) 1968 *W, I*
Pullin, J V (Bristol) 1966 *W*, 1968 *W, I, F, S*, 1969 *I, F, S, W, SA*, 1970 *I, W, S, F*, 1971 *W, I, F, S* (2[1C]), *P*, 1972 *W, I, F, S, SA*, 1973 *NZ* 1, *W, I, F, S, NZ* 2, *A*, 1974 *S, I, F, W*, 1975 *I, W* (R), *S, A* 1,2, 1976 *F*
Purdy, S J (Rugby) 1962 *S*
Pyke, J (St Helens Recreation) 1892 *W*
Pym, J A (Blackheath) 1912 *W, I, S, F*

Quinn, J P (New Brighton) 1954 *W, NZ, I, S, F*

Rafter, M (Bristol) 1977 *S, F, W*, 1978 *F, W, S, I, NZ*, 1979 *S, I, F, W, NZ*, 1980 *W*(R), 1981 *W, Arg* 1,2
Ralston, C W (Richmond) 1971 *S* (C), *P*, 1972 *W, I, F, S, SA*, 1973 *NZ* 1, *W, I, F, S, NZ* 2, *A*, 1974 *S, I, F, W*, 1975 *I, F, W, S*
Ramsden, H E (Bingley) 1898 *W, S*
Ranson, J M (Rosslyn Park) 1963 *NZ* 1,2, *A*, 1964 *W, I, F, S*
Raphael, J E (OMTs) 1902 *W, I, S*, 1905 *W, S, NZ*, 1906 *W, S, F*
Ravenscroft, J (Birkenhead Park) 1881 *I*
Rawlinson, W C W (Blackheath) 1876 *S*
Redfern, S (Leicester) 1984 *I* (R)
Redman, N C (Bath) 1984 *A*, 1986 *S* (R), 1987 *I, S*, [*A, J, W*], 1988 *Fj*, 1990 *Arg* 1,2, 1991 *Fj*, [*It, US*], 1993 *NZ*, 1994 *F, W, SA* 1,2
Redmond, G F (Cambridge U) 1970 *F*
Redwood, B W (Bristol) 1968 *W, I*
Rees, G W (Nottingham) 1984 *SA* 2 (R), *A*, 1986 *I, F*, 1987 *F, W, S*, [*A, J, US, W*], 1988 *S* (R), *I* 1,2, *A* 1,2, *A*, 1989 *W* (R), *R* (R), *Fj* (R), 1990 *Arg* 3 (R), 1991 *Fj*, [*US*]
Reeve, J S R (Harlequins) 1929 *F*, 1930 *W, I, F, S*, 1931 *W, I, S*
Regan, M (Liverpool) 1953 *W, I, F, S*, 1954 *W, NZ, I, S, F*, 1956 *I, S, F*
Regan, M P (Bristol) 1995 *SA, WS*, 1996 *F, W, S, I, It, Arg*, 1997 *S, I, F, W*
Rendall, P A G (Wasps, Askeans) 1984 *W, SA* 2, 1986 *W, S*, 1987 *I, F, S*, [*A, J, W*], 1988 *F, W, S, I* 1,2, *A* 1,2, *A*, 1989 *S, I, F, W, R*, 1990 *I, F, W, S*, 1991 [*It* (R)]
Rew, H (Blackheath) 1929 *S, F*, 1930 *F, S*, 1931 *W, S, F*, 1934 *W, I, S*
Reynolds, F J (O Cranleighans) 1937 *S*, 1938 *I, S*
Reynolds, S (Richmond) 1900 *W, I, S*, 1901 *I*

117

Smith, M J K (Oxford U) 1956 *W*
Smith, S J (Sale) 1973 *I, F, S, A,* 1974 *I, F,* 1975 *W* (R), 1976 *F,* 1977 *F* (R), 1979 *NZ,* 1980 *I, F, W, S,* 1981 *W, S, I, F, Arg* 1,2, 1982 *A, S, I, F, W,* 1983 *F, W, S*
Smith, S R (Richmond) 1959 *W, F, S,* 1964 *F, S*
Smith, S T (Wasps) 1985 *R, F, S, I, W, NZ* 1,2, 1986 *W, S*
Smith, T H (Northampton) 1951 *W*
Soane, F (Bath) 1893 *S,* 1894 *W, I, S*
Sobey, W H (O Millhilians) 1930 *W, F, S,* 1932 *SA, W*
Solomon, B (Redruth) 1910 *W*
Sparks, R H W (Plymouth A) 1928 *I, F, S,* 1929 *W, I, S,* 1931 *I, S, F*
Speed, H (Castleford) 1894 *W, I, S,* 1896 *S*
Spence, F W (Birkenhead Park) 1890 *I*
Spencer, J (Harlequins) 1966 *W*
Spencer, J S (Cambridge U, Headingley) 1969 *I, F, S, W, SA,* 1970 *I, W, S, F,* 1971 *W, I, S* (2[1C]), *P*
Spong, R S (O Millhilians) 1929 *F,* 1930 *W, I, F, S,* 1931 *F,* 1932 *SA, W*
Spooner, R H (Liverpool) 1903 *W*
Springman, H H (Liverpool) 1879 *S,* 1887 *S*
Spurling, A (Blackheath) 1882 *I*
Spurling, N (Blackheath) 1886 *I, S,* 1887 *W*
Squires, P J (Harrogate) 1973 *F, S, NZ* 2, *A,* 1974 *S, I, F, W,* 1975 *I, F, W, S, A* 1,2, 1976 *A, W,* 1977 *S, I, F, W,* 1978 *F, W, S, I, NZ,* 1979 *S, I, F, W*
Stafford, R C (Bedford) 1912 *W, I, S, F*
Stafford, W F H (RE) 1874 *S*
Stanbury, E (Plymouth A) 1926 *W, I, S,* 1927 *W, I, S, F,* 1928 *A, W, I, F, S,* 1929 *W, I, S, F*
Standing, G (Blackheath) 1883 *W, I*
Stanger-Leathes, C F (Northern) 1905 *I*
Stark, K J (O Alleynians) 1927 *W, I, S, F,* 1928 *A, W, I, F, S*
Starks, A (Castleford) 1896 *W, I*
Starmer-Smith, N C (Harlequins) 1969 *SA,* 1970 *I, W, S, F,* 1971 *S* (C), *P*
Start, S P (United Services, RN) 1907 *S*
Steeds, J H (Saracens) 1949 *F, S,* 1950 *I, F, S*
Steele-Bodger, M R (Cambridge U) 1947 *W, I, S, F,* 1948 *A, W, I, S, F*
Steinthal, F E (Ilkley) 1913 *W, F*
Stevens, C B (Penzance-Newlyn, Harlequins) 1969 *SA,* 1970 *I, W, S,* 1971 *P,* 1972 *W, I, F, S, SA,* 1973 *NZ* 1, *W, I, F, S, NZ* 2, *A,* 1974 *S, I, F, W,* 1975 *I, F, W, S*
Still, E R (Oxford U, Ravenscourt P) 1873 *S*
Stimpson, T R G (Newcastle) 1996 *It,* 1997 *S, I, F, W*
Stirling, R V (Leicester, RAF, Wasps) 1951 *W, I, F, S,* 1952 *SA, W, S, I, F,* 1953 *W, I, F, S,* 1954 *W, NZ, I, S, F*
Stoddart, A E (Blackheath) 1885 *W, I,* 1886 *W, I, S,* 1889 *M,* 1890 *W, I,* 1893 *W, S*
Stoddart, W B (Liverpool) 1897 *W, I, S*
Stokes, F (Blackheath) 1871 *S,* 1872 *S,* 1873 *S*
Stokes, L (Blackheath) 1875 *I,* 1876 *S,* 1877 *I, S,* 1878 *S,* 1879 *S, I,* 1880 *I, S,* 1881 *I, W, S*
Stone, F le S (Blackheath) 1914 *F*
Stoop, A D (Harlequins) 1905 *S,* 1906 *S, F, SA,* 1907 *F, W,* 1910 *W, I, S,* 1911 *W, F, I, S,* 1912 *W, S*
Stoop, F M (Harlequins) 1910 *S,* 1911 *F, I,* 1913 *SA*
Stout, F M (Richmond) 1897 *W, I,* 1898 *I, S, W,* 1899 *I, S,* 1903 *S,* 1904 *W, I, S*
Stout, P W (Richmond) 1898 *S, W,* 1899 *W, I, S*
Stringer, N C (Wasps) 1982 *A* (R), 1983 *NZ* (R), 1984 *SA* 1 (R), *A,* 1985 *R*
Strong, E L (Oxford U) 1884 *W, I, S*
Summerscales, G E (Durham City) 1905 *NZ*
Sutcliffe, J W (Heckmondwike) 1889 *M*
Swarbrick, D W (Oxford U) 1947 *W, I, F,* 1948 *A, W,* 1949 *I*
Swayne, D H (Oxford U) 1931 *W*
Swayne, J W R (Bridgwater) 1929 *W*
Swift, A H (Swansea) 1981 *Arg* 1,2, 1983 *F, W, S,* 1984 *SA* 2
Syddall, J P (Waterloo) 1982 *I,* 1984 *A*
Sykes, A R V (Blackheath) 1914 *F*
Sykes, F D (Northampton) 1955 *F, S,* 1963 *NZ* 2, *A*
Sykes, P W (Wasps) 1948 *F,* 1952 *S, I, F,* 1953 *W, I, F*
Syrett, R E (Wasps) 1958 *W, A, I, F,* 1960 *W, I, F, S,* 1962 *W, I, F*

Tallent, J A (Cambridge U, Blackheath) 1931 *S, F,* 1932 *SA, W,* 1935 *I*
Tanner, C C (Cambridge U, Gloucester) 1930 *S,* 1932 *SA, W, I, S*
Tarr, F N (Leicester) 1909 *A, W, F,* 1913 *S*

Tatham, W M (Oxford U) 1882 *S,* 1883 *W, I, S,* 1884 *W, I, S*
Taylor, A S (Blackheath) 1883 *W, I,* 1886 *W, I*
Taylor, E W (Rockcliff) 1892 *I,* 1893 *I,* 1894 *W, I, S,* 1895 *W, I, S,* 1896 *W, I,* 1897 *W, I, S,* 1899 *I*
Taylor, F (Leicester) 1920 *F, I*
Taylor, F M (Leicester) 1914 *W*
Taylor, H H (Blackheath) 1879 *S,* 1880 *S,* 1881 *I, W,* 1882 *S*
Taylor, J T (W Hartlepool) 1897 *I,* 1899 *I,* 1900 *I,* 1901 *W, I,* 1902 *W, I, S,* 1903 *W, I,* 1905 *S*
Taylor, P J (Northampton) 1955 *W, I,* 1962 *W, I, F, S*
Taylor, R B (Northampton) 1966 *W,* 1967 *I, F, S, W, NZ,* 1969 *F, S, W, SA,* 1970 *I, W, S, F,* 1971 *S* (2[1C])
Taylor, W J (Blackheath) 1928 *A, W, I, F, S*
Teague, M C (Gloucester, Moseley) 1985 *F* (R), *NZ* 1, 2, 1989 *S, I, F, W, R,* 1990 *F, W, S,* 1991 *W, S, I, F, Fj, A,* [*NZ, It, F, S, A*], 1992 *SA,* 1993 *F, W, S, I*
Teden, D E (Richmond) 1939 *W, I, S*
Teggin, A (Broughton R) 1884 *I,* 1885 *W,* 1886 *I, S,* 1887 *I, S*
Tetley, T S (Bradford) 1876 *S*
Thomas, C (Barnstaple) 1895 *W, I, S,* 1899 *I*
Thompson, P H (Headingley, Waterloo) 1956 *W, I, S, F,* 1957 *W, I, S, F, W, A, I, F, S,* 1959 *W, I, F, S*
Thomson, G T (Halifax) 1878 *S,* 1882 *I, S,* 1883 *W, I, S,* 1884 *I, S,* 1885 *I*
Thomson, W B (Blackheath) 1892 *W,* 1895 *W, I, S*
Thorne, J D (Bristol) 1963 *W, I, F*
Tindall, V R (Liverpool) 1951 *W, I, F, S*
Tobin, F (Liverpool) 1871 *S*
Todd, A F (Blackheath) 1900 *I, S*
Todd, R (Manchester) 1877 *S*
Toft, H B (Waterloo) 1936 *S,* 1937 *W, I, S,* 1938 *W, I, S,* 1939 *W, I, S*
Toothill, J T (Bradford) 1890 *S, I,* 1891 *W, I,* 1892 *W, I, S,* 1893 *W, I, S,* 1894 *W, I*
Tosswill, L R (Exeter) 1902 *W, I, S*
Touzel, C J C (Liverpool) 1877 *I, S*
Towell, A C (Bedford) 1948 *F,* 1951 *S*
Travers, B H (Harlequins) 1947 *W, I,* 1948 *A, W,* 1949 *F, S*
Treadwell, W T (Wasps) 1966 *I, F, S*
Trick, D M (Bath) 1983 *I,* 1984 *SA* 1
Tristram, H B (Oxford U) 1883 *S,* 1884 *W, S,* 1885 *W,* 1887 *S*
Troop, C L (Aldershot S) 1933 *I, S*
Tucker, J S (Bristol) 1922 *W,* 1925 *NZ, W, I, S, F,* 1926 *W, I, F, S,* 1927 *W, I, S, F,* 1928 *A, W, I, F, S,* 1929 *W, I, F,* 1930 *W, I, F, S,* 1931 *W*
Tucker, W E (Blackheath) 1894 *W, I,* 1895 *W, I, S*
Tucker, W E (Blackheath) 1926 *I,* 1930 *W, I*
Turner, D P (Richmond) 1871 *S,* 1872 *S,* 1873 *S,* 1874 *S,* 1875 *I, S*
Turner, E B (St George's Hospital) 1876 *I,* 1877 *I,* 1878 *I*
Turner, G R (St George's Hospital) 1876 *S*
Turner, H J C (Manchester) 1871 *S*
Turner, M F (Blackheath) 1948 *S, F*
Turquand-Young, D (Richmond) 1928 *A, W,* 1929 *I, S, F*
Twynam, H T (Richmond) 1879 *I,* 1880 *I,* 1881 *W,* 1882 *I,* 1883 *I,* 1884 *W, I, S*

Ubogu, V E (Bath) 1992 *C, SA,* 1993 *NZ,* 1994 *S, I, F, W, SA* 1,2, *R, C,* 1995 *I, F, W, S,* [*Arg, WS, A, NZ, F*], *SA*
Underwood, A M (Exeter) 1962 *W, I, F, S,* 1964 *I*
Underwood, R (Leicester, RAF) 1984 *I, F, W, A,* 1985 *R, F, S, I, W,* 1986 *W, I, F,* 1987 *I, F, W, S,* [*A, J, W*], 1988 *F, W, S, I* 1,2, *A* 1,2, *Fj, A,* 1989 *S, I, F, W, R, Fj,* 1990 *I, F, W, S, Arg* 3, 1991 *W, S, I, F, Fj, A,* [*NZ, It, US, F, S, A*], 1992 *S, I, F, W, SA,* 1993 *F, W, S, I, NZ,* 1994 *S, I, F, W, SA* 1,2, *R, C,* 1995 *I, F, W, S,* [*Arg, It, WS, A, NZ, F*], *SA, WS,* 1996 *F, W, S, I*
Underwood, T (Leicester, Newcastle) 1992 *C, SA,* 1993 *S, I, NZ,* 1994 *S, I, W, SA* 1,2, *R, C,* 1995 *I, F, W, S,* [*Arg, It, A, NZ*], 1996 *Arg,* 1997 *S, I, F, W*
Unwin, E J (Rosslyn Park, Army) 1937 *S,* 1938 *W, I, S*
Unwin, G T (Blackheath) 1898 *S*
Uren, R (Waterloo) 1948 *I, S, F,* 1950 *I*
Uttley, R M (Gosforth) 1973 *I, F, S, NZ* 2, *A,* 1974 *I, F, W,* 1975 *F, W, S, A* 1,2, 1977 *S, I, F, W,* 1978 *NZ* 1979 *S,* 1980 *I, F, W, S*

Valentine J (Swinton) 1890 *W,* 1896 *W, I, S*
Vanderspar, C H R (Richmond) 1873 *S*
Van Ryneveld, C B (Oxford U) 1949 *W, I, F, S*

119

ENGLISH INTERNATIONAL RECORDS
(up to 30 April 1997)

MATCH RECORDS

MOST CONSECUTIVE TEST WINS

10 1882 *W*, 1883 *I*, *S*, 1884 *W*, *I*, *S*, 1885 *W*, *I*, 1886 *W*, *I*
10 1994 *R*, *C*, 1995 *I*, *F*, *W*, *S*, *Arg*, *It*, *WS*, *A*

MOST CONSECUTIVE TESTS WITHOUT DEFEAT

P	W	D	Period
12	10	2	1882–87
11	10	1	1922–24
10	6	4	1878–82
10	10	0	1994–95

MOST POINTS IN A MATCH
by the team

Pts	Opp	Venue	Year
60	J	Sydney	1987
60	C	Twickenham	1994
58	R	Bucharest	1989
58	Fj	Twickenham	1989
54	R	Twickenham	1994
54	It	Twickenham	1996

by a player

30 by C R Andrew v Canada at Twickenham 1994
27 by C R Andrew v South Africa at Pretoria 1994
24 by J M Webb v Italy at Twickenham 1991
24 by C R Andrew v Romania at Twickenham 1994
24 by C R Andrew v Scotland at Twickenham 1995
24 by C R Andrew v Argentina at Durban 1995

MOST TRIES IN A MATCH
by the team

T	Opp	Venue	Year
13	W	Blackheath	1881
10	J	Sydney	1987
10	Fj	Twickenham	1989
9	F	Paris	1906
9	F	Richmond	1907
9	F	Paris	1914
9	R	Bucharest	1989

by a player

5 by D Lambert v France at Richmond 1907
5 by R Underwood v Fiji at Twickenham 1989
4 by G W Burton v Wales at Blackheath 1881
4 by A Hudson v France at Paris 1906
4 by R W Poulton v France at Paris 1914
4 by C Oti v Romania at Bucharest 1989

MOST CONVERSIONS IN A MATCH
by the team

C	Opp	Venue	Year
8	R	Bucharest	1989
7	W	Blackheath	1881
7	J	Sydney	1987
7	Arg	Twickenham	1990

by a player

8 by S D Hodgkinson v Romania at Bucharest 1989
7 by J M Webb v Japan at Sydney 1987
7 by S D Hodgkinson v Argentina at Twickenham 1990

MOST PENALTY GOALS IN A MATCH
by the team

P	Opp	Venue	Year
7	W	Cardiff	1991
7	S	Twickenham	1995
6	W	Twickenham	1986
6	C	Twickenham	1994
6	Arg	Durban	1995
6	S	Murrayfield	1996
6	I	Twickenham	1996

by a player

7 by S D Hodgkinson v Wales at Cardiff 1991
7 by C R Andrew v Scotland at Twickenham 1995
6 by C R Andrew v Wales at Twickenham 1986
6 by C R Andrew v Canada at Twickenham 1994
6 by C R Andrew v Argentina at Durban 1995
6 by P J Grayson v Scotland at Murrayfield 1996
6 by P J Grayson v Ireland at Twickenham 1996

MOST DROPPED GOALS IN A MATCH

by the team

D	Opp	Venue	Year
2	I	Twickenham	1970
2	F	Paris	1978
2	F	Paris	1980
2	R	Twickenham	1985
2	Fj	Suva	1991
2	Arg	Durban	1995
2	F	Paris	1996

by a player

2 by R Hiller v Ireland at
Twickenham   1970
2 by A G B Old v France at Paris   1978
2 by J P Horton v France at Paris   1980
2 by C R Andrew v Romania at
Twickenham   1985
2 by C R Andrew v Fiji at Suva   1991
2 by C R Andrew v Argentina at
Durban   1995
2 by P J Grayson v France at Paris 1996

CAREER RECORDS

MOST CAPPED PLAYERS

Caps	Player	Career
85	R Underwood	1984–96
72	W D C Carling	1988–97
71	C R Andrew	1985–97
64	B C Moore	1987–95
58	P J Winterbottom	1982–93
55	W A Dooley	1985–93
55	J Leonard	1990–97
48	D Richards	1986–96
48	J C Guscott	1989–97
43	A Neary	1971–80

MOST CONSECUTIVE TESTS

Tests	Player	Span
44	W D C Carling	1989–95
40	J Leonard	1990–95
36	J V Pullin	1968–75
33	W B Beaumont	1975–82
30	R Underwood	1992–96

MOST TESTS AS CAPTAIN

Tests	Captain	Span
59	W D C Carling	1988–96
21	W B Beaumont	1978–82
13	W W Wakefield	1924–26
13	N M Hall	1949–55
13	R E G Jeeps	1960–62
13	J V Pullin	1972–75

MOST TESTS IN INDIVIDUAL POSITIONS

Full-back J M Webb	33	1987–93
Wing R Underwood	85	1984–96
Centre W D C Carling	72	1988–97
Fly-half C R Andrew	70	1985–97
Scrum-half R J Hill	29	1984–91
Prop J Leonard	55	1990–97
Hooker B C Moore	63*	1987–95
Lock W A Dooley	55	1985–93
Flanker P J Winterbottom	58	1982–93
No 8 D Richards	47*	1986–96

* excludes an appearance as a temporary replacement

MOST POINTS IN TESTS

Pts	Player	Tests	Career
396	C R Andrew	71	1985–97
296	J M Webb	33	1987–93
240	W H Hare	25	1974–84
210	R Underwood	85	1984–96
203	S D Hodgkinson	14	1989–91

MOST TRIES IN TESTS

Tries	Player	Tests	Career
49	R Underwood	85	1984–96
18	C N Lowe	25	1913–23
18	J C Guscott	48	1989–97
13	T Underwood	25	1992–97
12	W D C Carling	72	1988–97

MOST CONVERSIONS IN TESTS

Cons	Player	Tests	Career
41	J M Webb	33	1987–93
35	S D Hodgkinson	14	1989–91
33	C R Andrew	71	1985–97
17	L Stokes	12	1875–81
14	W H Hare	25	1974–84

MOST PENALTY GOALS IN TESTS

Pens	Player	Tests	Career
86	C R Andrew	71	1985–97
67	W H Hare	25	1974–84
66	J M Webb	33	1987–93
43	S D Hodgkinson	14	1989–91
35	P J Grayson	8	1995–97

MOST DROPPED GOALS IN TESTS

Drops	Player	Tests	Career
21	C R Andrew	71	1985–97
4	J P Horton	13	1978–84
4	P J Grayson	8	1995–97

INTERNATIONAL CHAMPIONSHIP RECORDS

Record	Detail		Set
Most points in season	141	in four matches	1997
Most tries in season	20	in four matches	1914
Highest score	46	46–6 v Ireland	1997
Biggest win	40	46–6 v Ireland	1997
Highest score conceded	37	12–37 v France	1972
Biggest defeat	27	6–33 v Scotland	1986
Most appearances	50	R Underwood	1984–96
Most points in matches	185	C R Andrew	1985–97
Most points in season	67	J M Webb	1992
Most points in match	24	C R Andrew	v Scotland, 1995
Most tries in matches	18	C N Lowe	1913–23
	18	R Underwood	1984–96
Most tries in season	8	C N Lowe	1914
Most tries in match	4	R W Poulton	v France, 1914
Most cons in matches	14	J M Webb	1988–93
Most cons in season	11	J M Webb	1992
Most cons in match	6	J E Greenwood	v France, 1914
	6	G W Parker	v Ireland, 1938
Most pens in matches	50	W H Hare	1974–84
Most pens in season	18	S D Hodgkinson	1991
Most pens in match	7	S D Hodgkinson	v Wales, 1991
	7	C R Andrew	v Scotland, 1995
Most drops in matches	9	C R Andrew	1985–97
Most drops in season	3	P J Grayson	1996
Most drops in match	2	R Hiller	v Ireland, 1970
	2	A G B Old	v France, 1978
	2	J P Horton	v France, 1980
	2	P J Grayson	v France, 1996

MAJOR TOUR RECORDS

Record	Detail	Year	Place
Most individual points	58 by C R Andrew	1994	South Africa
Most points in match	36 by W N Bennett	1975 v W Australia	Perth
Most tries in match	4 by A J Morley	1975 v W Australia	Perth
	4 by P S Preece	1975 v NSW	Sydney

MISCELLANEOUS RECORDS

Record	Holder	Detail
Longest Test career	G S Pearce	14 seasons, 1978–79 to 1991–92
Youngest Test cap	H C C Laird	18 yrs 134 days in 1927
Oldest Test cap	F Gilbert	38 yrs in 1923

ENGLAND INTERNATIONAL CAREER RECORDS (*up to 30 April 1997*)

Player	Debut	Caps since last season	Caps	T	C	PG	DG	Pts
T R G Simpson	1996 v It	1996 *It*, 1997 *S, I F,W*	5	1	0	0	0	5
N D Beal	1996 v Arg	1996 *Arg*	1	0	0	0	0	0
J E B Callard	1993 v NZ		5	0	3	21	0	69
A A Adebayo	1996 v It	1996 *It*	1	0	0	0	0	0
J M Sleightholme	1996 v F	1996 *It, Arg*, 1997 *S, I, F, W*	10	4	0	0	0	20
T Underwood	1992 v C	1996 *Arg*, 1997 *S, I, F, W*	25	13	0	0	0	65
W D C Carling	1988 v F	1996 *It, Arg*, 1997 *S, I, F, W*	72	12	0	0	0	54
P R de Glanville	1992 v SA	1996 *It*, 1997 *S, I, F, W*	21	3	0	0	0	15
J C Guscott	1989 v R	1996 *Arg*, 1997 *I* (R), *W* (R)	48	18	0	0	2	83
M J Catt	1994 v W	1996 *It, Arg*, 1997 *W*	21	2	9	10	1	61
P J Grayson	1995 v WS	1997 *S, I, F*	8	0	8	35	4	133
C R Andrew	1985 v R	1997 *W* (R)	71	2	33	86	21	396
M J S Dawson	1995 v WS		5	0	0	0	0	0
A C T Gomarsall	1996 v It	1996 *It, Arg*, 1997 *S, I, F*	5	4	0	0	0	20
A Healey	1997 v I	1997 *I* (R), *W*	2	0	0	0	0	0
K P P Bracken	1993 v NZ	1996 *It* (R)	12	1	0	0	0	5
M P Regan	1995 v SA	1996 *It, Arg*, 1997 *S, I, F, W*	12	0	0	0	0	0
P B T Greening	1996 v It	1996 *It* (R), 1997 *W* (R)	2	0	0	0	0	0
D J Garforth	1997 v W	1997 *W* (R)	1	0	0	0	0	0
J Leonard	1990 v Arg	1996 *It, Arg*, 1997 *S, I, F, W*	55	1	0	0	0	5
R J K Hardwick	1996 v It	1996 *It* (R)	1	0	0	0	0	0
J A Mallett	1995 v WS		1	0	0	0	0	0
G C Rowntree	1995 v S	1996 *It, Arg*, 1997 *S, I, F, W*	14	0	0	0	0	0
G S Archer	1996 v S		2	0	0	0	0	0
M O Johnson	1993 v F	1996 *It, Arg*, 1997 *S, I, F, W*	30	1	0	0	0	5
S D Shaw	1996 v It	1996 *It, Arg*, 1997 *S, I, F, W*	6	0	0	0	0	0
R J West	1995 v WS		1	0	0	0	0	0
R A Hill	1997 v S	1997 *S, I, F, W*	4	2	0	0	0	10

S O Ojomoh	1994 v I		11	0	0	0	0	0
L B N Dallaglio	1995 v SA	1996 *It, Arg*, 1997 *S, I, F*	11	3	0	0	0	15
T A K Rodber	1992 v S	1996 *It, Arg*, 1997 *S, I, F, W*	31	3	0	0	0	15
N A Back	1994 v S		5	1	0	0	0	5
B B Clarke	1992 v SA	1996 *Arg* (R), 1997 *W*	30	2	0	0	0	10
C M A Sheasby	1996 v It	1996 *It, Arg*, 1997 *W* (R)	3	1	0	0	0	5

Lawrence Dallaglio races away from Abdelatif Benazzi to score a try for England against France at Twickenham.

ENGLISH CLUBS 1996-97

Bath

Year of formation 1865
Ground Recreation Ground, London Road, Bath Tel: Bath (01225) 465328
Colours Blue, white and black
Captain 1996-97 P R de Glanville
Courage Leagues 1996-97 Div 1 2nd   **Pilkington Cup 1996-97** Lost 28-39 to Leicester
(6th round)

It was a year of turmoil and anxiety for the double champions in their first season
without a major trophy since 1988. How long ago those sweet days of May 1996 must
have seemed by the middle of the following winter. The club which had prided itself
on its togetherness, feisty spirit and unsatiable appetite for success was falling apart.
Much respected coach Brian Ashton left in January; director of rugby and club
stalwart, John Hall, was sacked a month later. The most professional club of all in the
amateur era was showing itself to be pitifully amateurish in the professional age.

The short-term Rugby League recruits, Jason Robinson and Henry Paul, never
quite made the grade, Paul in particular. The £2.5 million investment of greetings
card millionaire, Andrew Brownsword, was palpably not working. Chains of command were never properly worked out and the players responded in like fashion to
the confusion all around them. Their normal instinct for the kill deserted them. In
the League they should have seen off Leicester at Welford Road but allowed them a
late rally and a 28-25 victory. Wasps, the eventual champions, should also have been
put away. They too got away with the spoils, this time at the Rec, 40-36.

Bath's season of torment was best illustrated by their showing in the respective
Cup competitions. Their European campaign came to an end in the quarter-final at
Cardiff, 22-19. That match showed the real strain in the Hall-Ashton relationship
with disagreement over selection. The Pilkington Cup was a disaster. Bath were not
only beaten at home by Leicester in the sixth round, they were humiliated, 39-28,
their heaviest defeat in a decade. Hall's acrimonious departure followed three days
later. Clive Woodward and Andy Robinson formed the new coaching panel, backed
up by Nigel Redman. Former Bath winger, Tony Swift took over as chief executive.
The club's rollicking finish to the season with new Argentinian recruits, Federico
Mendez and German Llanes, finally bedded down, only served to illustrate what
might have been.

League Record 1996-97

Date	Venue	Opponents	Result	Scorers
31 Aug	A	Orrell	56-13	*T:* Catt, Geoghegan, Haag, Horne, Nicol, Webster *C:* Callard 4 *P:* Callard 5 *D:* Catt
7 Sept	A	Leicester	25-28	*T:* Catt, Guscott, Nicol *C:* Callard 2 *P:* Callard 2
14 Sept	H	Wasps	36-40	*T:* Catt, J Robinson, Nicol, pen try *C:* Callard 2 *P:* Callard 4
21 Sept	A	Gloucester	45-29	*T:* Adebayo 2, Catt, Callard, Ojomoh, Nicol, J Robinson *C:* Callard 2 *P:* Callard 2
28 Sept	H	West Hartlepool	46-10	*T:* Sleightholme 2, A Robinson, Adams, Adebayo, de Glanville *C:* Callard 5 *P:* Callard 2
5 Oct	A	London Irish	56-31	*T:* Adebayo 3, J Robinson 2, Callard, Guscott, Redman, Webster *C:* Callard 4 *P:* Callard
29 Oct	H	Bristol	76-7	*T:* Guscott 2, Paul 2, Adebayo, Catt, A Robinson, Cusack, Harrison, Hilton, Sleightholme *C:* Catt 4, Harrison 2 *P:* Catt 2 *D:* Catt

9 Nov	A	Northampton	6-9	*P:* Callard 2
7 Dec	H	Harlequins	35-20	*T:* Guscott 2, Adebayo, Thomas *C:* Callard 3 *P:* Callard 3
4 Jan	H	Saracens	35-33	*T:* Guscott, Méndez, Webster, pen try *C:* Callard 3 *P:* Callard 3
11 Jan	A	Harlequins	6-22	*P:* Callard 2
19 Jan	H	Northampton	52-14	*T:* Sleightholme 3, Catt, Lyle, Méndez *C:* Callard 5 *P:* Callard 4
22 Feb	A	Bristol	18-13	*T:* Guscott, Redman *C:* Callard *P:* Callard 2
8 Mar	H	London Irish	46-3	*T:* Sleightholme 3, Lyle 2, A Robinson, Mallett, Yates *C:* Callard 3
27 Mar	A	West Hartlepool	24-16	*T:* Haag, Adebayo, Catt *C:* Callard 3 *P:* Callard
2 Apr	A	Sale	5-11	*T:* Webster
6 Apr	A	Wasps	25-25	*T:* Guscott 2, Adebayo *C:* Callard, Catt *P:* Catt 2
12 Apr	H	Leicester	47-9	*T:* Adebayo 2, Perry 2, Lyle, Méndez *C:* Callard 2, Catt 2 *P:* Catt 3
19 Apr	H	Orrell	40-14	*T:* Peters 2, Adebayo, Ojomoh,Callard, Méndez *C:* Callard, Catt 4
26 Apr	H	Sale	84-7	*T:* Catt 2, Guscott 2, Méndez 2, Lyle, Llanes, Adebayo, Perry, Sleightholme, Webster *C:* Catt 8, Callard 4
30 Apr	H	Gloucester	71-21	*T:* Nicol 3, Perry 2, Sleightholme 2, Adebayo, Thomas, Callard, Lyle *C:* Callard 3, Catt 5
3 May	A	Saracens	29-36	*T:* Adebayo, Méndez, Peters, Yates *C:* Callard 3 *P:* Callard

Bedford

Year of formation 1886
Ground Goldington Road, Bedford Tel: Bedford (01234) 347511
Colours Oxford and Cambridge blue
Captain 1996-97 P Turner
Courage Leagues 1996-97 Div 2 4th; Lost Division 1/2 play-off with Bristol, 23-39 on aggregate   **Pilkington Cup 1996-97** Lost 31-34 to Orrell (5th round)

They had slumbered for too long. Once a force in the land, Bedford had languished in recent years until Frank Warren's Sports Network group pumped in the money and some star names once again put unfashionable Bedford on the map. Sale's Paul Turner led the way as player-coach, with former England manager Geoff Cooke alongside to guide. Cooke became the full-time chief executive at the end of the season. One or two acquisitions may have been long in the tooth but their experience was to prove invaluable. Jeff Probyn, Martin Offiah, Norm Hadley, Rudolf Straueli and Junior Paramore helped mount a persuasive challenge for promotion. A 34-28 victory over Newcastle raised hopes but Bedford had given away too many games in the first part of the season to clinch a promotion spot this time. The play-offs, during which they ran Bristol close, suggested they might set the pace next year.

League Record 1996-97

Date	Venue	Opponents	Result	Scorers
7 Sept	H	Nottingham	41-23	*T:* pen tries 2, Crossland, Oliver, Whetstone *C:* Rayer 5 *P:* Rayer 2
14 Sept	A	Blackheath	3-11	*P:* Rayer
21 Sept	H	Richmond	17-44	*T:* Farr, Rayer, Whetstone *C:* Rayer
29 Sept	A	Rugby	34-6	*T:* Pechey 2, Crossland, Hewitt, Paramore *C:* Rayer 3 *P:* Rayer

5 Oct	H	Wakefield	25-19	*T:* Hyde, Mansell, Rayer *C:* Rayer 2 *P:* Rayer 2
12 Oct	A	Waterloo	34-11	*T:* McCurrie 2, Brown, Murray, Upex *C:* Rayer 3 *P:* Rayer
19 Oct	H	Rotherham	44-30	*T:* Offiah, Paramore, Rayer, Probyn, White, Simons *C:* Rayer 4 *P:* Rayer 2
26 Oct	A	Newcastle	12-49	*T:* Rayer, Whetstone *C:* Rayer
3 Nov	H	Moseley	64-9	*T:* Offiah 2, Hewitt, Hyde, Turner, Pechey, Rennell, Upex, Whetstone, Winters *C:* Rayer 7
9 Nov	A	London Scottish	27-26	*T:* Hewitt, Pechey, Whetstone *C:* Rayer 3 *P:* Rayer 2
16 Nov	H	Coventry	30-23	*T:* Paramore, Pechey, Whetstone *C:* Rayer 3 *P:* Rayer 3
28 Dec	A	Nottingham	36-13	*T:* Probyn 2, Brown, Oliver, Skingsley, Stone *C:* Rayer 3
18 Jan	H	Rugby	57-6	*T:* Brown 2, Marshall 2, Hewitt, Murray, Paramore, Pfluger, Whetstone *C:* Rayer 6
25 Jan	A	Richmond	33-34	*T:* Pfluger 2, Rayer 2, Oliver *C:* Rayer *P:* Rayer 2
8 Feb	A	Wakefield	29-17	*T:* Paramore 2, McCurrie, Murray *C:* Rayer 3 *P:* Rayer
22 Feb	H	Blackheath	72-18	*T:* Offiah 2, Paramore 2, Edwards, Murray, Oliver, Turner, Platford, Probyn, Webster *C:* Rayer 7 *P:* Rayer
8 Mar	H	Waterloo	38-6	*T:* Allen, Edwards, Offiah, Whetstone, pen try *C:* Rayer 5 *P:* Rayer
22 Mar	A	Rotherham	32-11	*T:* Pfluger 2, Offiah, Whetstone *C:* Rayer 3 *P:* Rayer 2
5 Apr	H	Newcastle	34-28	*T:* Boyd, Edwards, Hewitt, Offiah, Whetstone *C:* Rayer 3 *P:* Rayer
12 Apr	A	Moseley	34-40	*T:* Offiah, Paramore, Rayer, Stone, Whetstone *C:* Rayer 2, Turner *P:* Rayer
19 Apr	H	London Scottish	14-28	*T:* Offiah, Whetstone *C:* Rayer 2
26 Apr	A	Coventry	10-30	*T:* Pfluger, Platford
Play-Offs				
7 May	H	Bristol	11-20	*T:* Probyn *P:* Rayer 2
11 May	A	Bristol	12-19	*T:* Matchett, Probyn *C:* Rayer

Blackheath

Year of formation 1858
Ground Rectory Field, Charlton Road, Blackheath, London SE3 Tel: 0181 858 1578
Colours Red and black
Captain 1996-97 J A Gallagher
Courage Leagues 1996-97 Div 2 10th   **Pilkington Cup 1996-97** Lost 17-60 to Bristol (5th round)

There was much discontent at the Rectory Field in the course of a long, traumatic season. The Club, as they are fondly known, were anything but harmonious for long stretches with several players upset by contractual wrangles. This lack of cohesion off the field was reflected on it in several disparate performances. There was never a real danger of relegation for the simple reason that Nottingham and Rugby were some way adrift of the rest. Blackheath, though, with only seven wins from 22 matches, will know that they can ill afford such inconsistency next season in a more competitive division. Their lack of finance will seriously concern those at the club.

League Record 1996-97

Date	Venue	Opponents	Result	Scorers
7 Sept	H	Rotherham	44-5	T: Hoare 3, Friday, Hanslip C: Braithwaite 5 P: Braithwaite 3
14 Sept	H	Bedford	11-3	T: Braithwaite P: Braithwaite D: Braithwaite
21 Sept	A	Newcastle	0-61	
29 Sept	H	Moseley	28-3	T: Friday, Hanslip, Walton C: Braithwaite 2 P: Braithwaite 3
5 Oct	A	London Scottish	31-23	T: Hanslip 2, Fitzgerald C: Braithwaite 2 P: Braithwaite 4
12 Oct	H	Coventry	10-16	T: Friday C: Braithwaite P: Braithwaite
19 Oct	A	Nottingham	22-12	T: Hanslip C: Gallagher P: Gallagher 4 D: Park
26 Oct	H	Richmond	21-40	T: Hanslip, Park C: Gallagher P: Gallagher 3
3 Nov	H	Rugby	24-33	T: Gallagher 2, Park C: Gallagher 3 P: Gallagher
9 Nov	A	Waterloo	10-16	T: Griffiths C: Gallagher P: Gallagher
16 Nov	H	Wakefield	13-17	T: Hanslip C: Howard P: Howard 2
28 Dec	A	Rotherham	11-39	T: Taylor P: Howard 2
18 Jan	A	Moseley	18-21	T: Ekoku, Harris C: Braithwaite P: Braithwaite 2
8 Feb	H	London Scottish	13-19	T: Shortland C: Howard P: Howard 2
22 Feb	A	Bedford	18-72	T: Hanslip, Smith C: Braithwaite P: Braithwaite 2
8 Mar	A	Coventry	10-74	T: Gallagher C: Braithwaite P: Braithwaite
22 Mar	H	Nottingham	24-0	T: Griffiths, Shadbolt C: Braithwaite P: Braithwaite 2 D: Braithwaite 2
5 Apr	A	Richmond	24-29	T: Braithwaite, Gallagher, Wilkins C: Braithwaite 3 P: Braithwaite
12 Apr	A	Rugby	32-24	T: Fitzgerald, Gallagher, Russell, Wilkins C: Braithwaite 3 P: Braithwaite 2
16 Apr	H	Newcastle	10-72	T: Ridgway C: Braithwaite P: Braithwaite
19 Apr	H	Waterloo	27-48	T: M Griffiths 3, Howard C: Braithwaite 2 P: Braithwaite
26 Apr	A	Wakefield	11-14	T: Fitzgerald P: Howard 2

Bristol

Year of formation 1888
Ground Memorial Ground, Filton Avenue, Horfield, Bristol Tel: Bristol (0117) 951448
Colours Navy blue and white
Captain 1996-97 M J Corry
Courage Leagues 1996-97 Div 1 9th; won Division 1 / 2 play-off with Bedford, 39-23 on aggregate   **Pilkington Cup 1996-97** Lost 12-18 to Gloucester (6th round)

There has been a shadow over this part of the west country for too long. Yet again, for all the problems along the road at near neighbours, Bath and Gloucester, it was Bristol who were in the shade of this famous part of the rugby map. They have the infrastructure and potential to be a force but lack the inner will and belief to make it happen. Bristol, in a bid to raise money, became a private limited company in April 1996. It was not enough to keep hold of star names, second row Simon Shaw and Mark Regan who went to Wasps and Bath respectively. There was new blood swirling through the Memorial Ground with Robert Jones, Paul Burke, David Corkery all significant arrivals. England A blindside, Martin Corry, led as ever from the front but even so Bristol were tied to the bottom of the table throughout the year. The low point was a thumping 76-7 defeat at Bath. New director of coaching, former Welsh coach, Alan Davies, could do little to halt the slide.

Bristol were given a chance to fight for their life in the play-offs; and took full advantage, although they were made to fight all the way by Bedford. In the end it was Bristol's greater fire power up front and experience of pressure situations that saw them through. They won the first match at Bedford, 20-11, and the return 19-12.

League Record 1996-97

Date	Venue	Opponents	Result	Scorers
31 Aug	A	London Irish	28-27	*T:* Jones, Tiueti, Waters *C:* Burke 2 *P:* Burke 3
7 Sept	H	Orrell	38-10	*T:* Hull 2, Breeze, pen try *C:* Burke 3 *P:* Burke 4
14 Sept	A	Northampton	21-29	*T:* Corry, Corkery *C:* Burke *P:* Burke 3
21 Sept	H	Harlequins	24-35	*T:* Breeze, Corry, Corkery, Shaw *C:* Tainton 2
28 Sept	A	Sale	33-31	*T:* Tiueti 2, Burke, Regan *C:* Burke 2 *P:* Burke 3
5 Oct	H	Saracens	11-21	*T:* Tiueti *P:* Burke 2
29 Oct	A	Bath	7-76	*T:* Hull *C:* Burke
7 Dec	A	Wasps	13-15	*T:* Corkery, Hull *P:* Burke
18 Dec	H	Leicester	12-38	*T:* Smith, Tiueti *C:* Burke
4 Jan	A	West Hartlepool	8-19	*T:* Jones *P:* Tainton
11 Jan	H	Wasps	18-41	*T:* Burke, Denney *C:* Burke *P:* Burke 2
18 Jan	A	Leicester	19-53	*T:* Filali *C:* Tainton *P:* Tainton 3, Hull
18 Feb	H	Gloucester	18-13	*P:* Burke 6
22 Feb	H	Bath	13-18	*T:* Short *C:* Burke *P:* Burke 2
9 Mar	A	Saracens	15-33	*T:* Maggs, Rollitt *C:* Burke *P:* Burke
22 Mar	H	Sale	34-24	*T:* Tiueti 2, Eagle, Lewsey *C:* Burke 4 *P:* Burke 2
5 Apr	H	Northampton	20-11	*T:* Rollitt, Waters *C:* Burke 2 *P:* Burke 2
12 Apr	A	Orrell	28-27	*T:* Tiueti 2, Corry *C:* Burke 2 *P:* Burke 3
15 Apr	A	Harlequins	6-29	*P:* Burke 2
19 Apr	H	London Irish	26-38	*T:* Breeze, Corkery, Hull, Jones *C:* Burke 3
26 Apr	A	Gloucester	20-20	*T:* Lewsey, Maggs *C:* Burke 2 *P:* Burke 2
4 May	H	West Hartlepool	20-17	*T:* Martin, Temperley, Tiueti *C:* Burke *P:* Tainton
Play-Offs				
7 May	A	Bedford	20-11	*T:* Jones, Breeze *C:* Burke 2 *P:* Burke 2
11 May	H	Bedford	19-12	*T:* Corry, Maggs *P:* Burke 3

Coventry

Year of formation 1874
Ground Coundon Road, Coventry Tel: Coventry (01203) 591274
Colours Navy blue and white
Captain 1996-97 R J K Hardwick
Courage Leagues 1996-97 Div 2 3rd; Lost Division 1 / 2 play off with London Irish, 23-42 on aggregate   **Pilkington Cup 1996-97** Lost 17-26 to Northampton (6th round)

They were fed up with making excuses. The power in the land in the early seventies, Coventry were determined to stop whingeing about the evils of professionalism and get out there and do something for a change. The recruitment of former Bristol captain, Derek Eves, was a masterstroke. Not only did Eves manage to attract talent to the club – old team-mates Alan Sharp and Andy Blackmore – his direction and energy injected vitality and a sense of purpose into a sleeping giant. Prop Robin Hardwick proved a notable captain and was rewarded with his England squad call-up. The crowds returned as Coventry mounted their charge to the play-offs, 5,000 or more turning out in the later stages of the campaign. Coventry finished third and beat London Irish, 16-14, in the first play-off match. Although they were soundly beaten in the return, they will have been heartened by their showing. A sharper cutting edge behind the scrum is required for next season.

League Record 1996-97

Date	Venue	Opponents	Result	Scorers
7 Sept	H	Richmond	16-16	*T:* Dawson *C:* Harris *P:* Harris 3
14 Sept	A	Rugby	61-3	*T:* Hardwick 2, Robinson 2, Smallwood 2, Gallagher, Kilford, Patten *C:* Gallagher 5 *P:* Harris 2
21 Sept	H	Wakefield	24-25	*T:* Horrobin, Kilford *C:* Gallagher *P:* Gallagher 2 *D:* Harris 2
28 Sept	A	Waterloo	36-17	*T:* Eves, Kilford, McAdam, Smallwood *C:* Harris 2 *P:* Harris 4
5 Oct	H	Nottingham	102-22	*T:* McAdam 4, Eves 3, Harris 2, Crofts, Curtis, Gallagher, Lydster, Reayer *C:* Harris 13 *P:* Harris 2
12 Oct	A	Blackheath	16-10	*T:* Crane *C:* Harris *P:* Harris 3
19 Oct	H	London Scottish	66-6	*T:* McAdam 3, Dawson, Grewcock, Harris, Kilford, Smallwood, pen try *C:* Harris 6 *P:* Harris 3
26 Oct	A	Rotherham	42-11	*T:* McAdam 2, Smallwood 2, Crane, Gallagher, Patten *C:* Harris 2 *P:* Harris
3 Nov	H	Newcastle	19-18	*T:* Kilford, Smallwood *P:* Harris 2 *D:* Harris
9 Nov	A	Moseley	35-19	*T:* Crane, Crofts, Dawson, Smallwood, pen try *C:* Brown 2 *P:* Brown 2
16 Nov	A	Bedford	23-30	*T:* Dawson, Patten *C:* Harris 2 *P:* Harris 3
28 Dec	A	Richmond	10-39	*T:* Smallwood *C:* Harris *D:* Harris
18 Jan	H	Waterloo	28-16	*T:* Harris, McAdam, Patten, Smallwood *C:* Harris *P:* Harris 2
8 Feb	A	Nottingham	29-0	*T:* Eves, Minshull, Patten, Robinson, Smallwood *C:* Harris 2
23 Feb	H	Rugby	24-10	*T:* Grewcock 2, Hardwick, McAdam *C:* Harris 2
8 Mar	H	Blackheath	74-10	*T:* Horrobin 3, Patten 2, Smallwood 2, Addleton, Blackmore, Dawson, Gallagher, Harvey *C:* Harris 7
22 Mar	A	London Scottish	14-13	*T:* Smallwood *P:* Harris 2 *D:* Gallagher
5 Apr	H	Rotherham	21-15	*T:* Addleton, Smallwood *C:* Harris *P:* Harris 3
12 Apr	A	Newcastle	17-49	*T:* McAdam, Smallwood *C:* Harris 2 *P:* Harris
19 Apr	H	Moseley	33-18	*T:* Eves, McAdam, Patten *C:* Harris 3 *P:* Harris 3 *D:* Gallagher
26 Apr	H	Bedford	30-10	*T:* McAdam 2, Robinson 2 *C:* Harris 2 *P:* Harris 2
3 May	A	Wakefield	18-37	*T:* Curtis, Irwin *C:* Brown *P:* Brown 2
Play-Offs				
7 May	H	London Irish	16-14	*T:* Minshull *C:* Harris *P:* Harris *D:* Harris 2
11 May	A	London Irish	7-28	*T:* Robinson *C:* Harris

Gloucester

Year of formation 1873
Ground Kingsholm, Kingsholm Road, Gloucester Tel: Gloucester (01452) 381087
Colours Cherry and white
Captain 1996-97 D Sims
Courage Leagues 1996-97 Div 1 7th   **Pilkington Cup 1996-97** Lost 13-26 to Leicester (semi-final)

They did not begin as they went on. Gloucester's opening gambit in the league was to field a reserve side against Harlequins on the basis that they had little chance of winning and should protect the morale and fitness of their first-choice players. It was a desperately flawed notion as coach Richard Hill admitted after their 75-19 humiliation. Things could only get better and they did – eventually. Gloucester were anchored to the bottom, winless after their first five matches. Then the tide, under the astute prompting of Hill, began to turn. Victory after victory was rattled up and the Gloucester surge up the table began. Their finest moment was perhaps their dramatic 32-30 midweek win over Leicester in April, a result which torpedoed the Tigers' season and catapulted Gloucester to an unlikely position on the fringe of the race for Europe. The victory was also some consolation for the 26-13 defeat to Leicester in the semi-final of the Pilkington Cup.

Gloucester forged a tremendous team spirit under the understated yet decisive leadership of second-row Dave Sims. The shrewd influence of half-backs, Scott Benton and Mark Mapletoft, was also significant. Gloucester, for all the strength derived from its powerful local identity (the pack were invariably all Gloucester-born), realised that they needed outside talent if they were ever to thrive. The £150,000 signing of former French captain and winger, Philippe Saint-Andre, in April was the first indication that the club had broader horizons. The announcement of motor-racing's Tom Walkinshaw as the club's backer shortly afterwards confirmed the trend. A life-long supporter, Walkinghsaw invested £2.5 million. Other signings are in the pipeline. These are big steps for the most closely-knit and partisan of rugby strongholds. The hope is that they can do justice to that passionate backing. The fear is that the potent mix of local ingredients may have been diluted. Time will tell.

League Record 1996-97

Date	Venue	Opponents	Result	Scorers
31 Aug	A	Harlequins	19-75	*T:* Lloyd, Mulraine, Osborne *C:* Osborne 2
7 Sept	H	Sale	12-16	*P:* Mapletoft 4
14 Sept	A	Saracens	11-41	*T:* Lloyd *P:* Mapletoft 2
21 Sept	H	Bath	29-45	*T:* Deacon, Greening, Sims *C:* Mapletoft *P:* Mapletoft 4
28 Sept	A	Leicester	14-32	*T:* Anderson *P:* Mapletoft 3
6 Oct	H	Wasps	28-23	*T:* Catling, Saverimutto *P:* Mapletoft 6
9 Nov	A	West Hartlepool	23-14	*T:* Lumsden, Mapletoft *C:* Mapletoft 2 *P:* Mapletoft 3
16 Nov	A	Orrell	49-3	*T:* Saverimutto 2, Benton, Lumsden, Peters, Windo *C:* Mapletoft 5 *P:* Mapletoft 3
7 Dec	H	London Irish	29-19	*T:* Benton, Roberts *C:* Mapletoft 2 *P:* Mapletoft 4 *D:* Mapletoft
11 Jan	A	London Irish	21-20	*T:* Fidler, Glanville *C:* Mapletoft *P:* Mapletoft 2 *D:* Mapletoft
18 Jan	H	West Hartlepool	37-10	*T:* Lloyd 3, Mapletoft, Windo *C:* Mapletoft 3 *P:* Mapletoft *D:* Mapletoft
8 Feb	H	Orrell	30-0	*T:* Mapletoft 2, Lloyd, Peters *C:* Mapletoft 2 *P:* Mapletoft 2
18 Feb	A	Bristol	13-18	*T:* Glanville *C:* Mapletoft *P:* Mapletoft *D:* Catling
4 Mar	H	Northampton	19-6	*T:* Benton *C:* Mapletoft *P:* Mapletoft 4
9 Mar	A	Wasps	10-36	*T:* Catling *C:* Mapletoft *P:* Mapletoft
5 Apr	H	Saracens	9-6	*P:* Mapletoft *D:* Mapletoft 2
8 Apr	H	Leicester	32-30	*T:* Greening, Lumsden *C:* Mapletoft 2 *P:* Mapletoft 6
12 Apr	A	Sale	12-52	*T:* Mapletoft, Lumsden *C:* Mapletoft
19 Apr	H	Harlequins	11-27	*T:* Benton *P:* Mapletoft 2
26 Apr	H	Bristol	20-20	*T:* Carter, Lloyd *C:* Mapletoft 2 *P:* Mapletoft 2

30 Apr	A	Bath	21-71	*T:* Deacon, Mapletoft, Saverimutto
				P: Mapletoft 2
3 May	A	Northampton	27-25	*T:* Catling, Lumsden *C:* Mapletoft
				P: Mapletoft 5

NEC Harlequins

Year of formation 1866
Ground Stoop Memorial Ground, Craneford Way, Twickenham, Middlesex
Tel: 0181 892 0822
Colours Light blue, magenta, chocolate, French grey, black and light green
Captain 1996-97 J Leonard
Courage Leagues 1996-97 Div 1 3rd   **Pilkington Cup 1996-97** Lost 16-26 to Sale
(semi-final)

The name itself tells you all you need to know about how things have changed at the home of England's most distinguished, most recognisable, if not always most loved, club. The official prefixing of their sponsor to their club name illustrated only too clearly that their committee was not prepared to stand back and let professionalism sink the last bastion of the leisured classes. The 'Quins, with probably the richest membership list in the country, were hellbent on trading in their own right in the new market. The NEC sponsorship is worth £1.5 million over three years, and Riverside plc bought up 40% of Harlequin FC Ltd to complete a very lucrative financial package for the club. The Stoop Ground, also used in the late season by London Broncos Rugby League, underwent redevelopment, and a new 5,000 seater stand opened early in the year to increase capacity to 9,500. Dick Best, director of rugby, was not slow to use the resources to bring top names to the Stoop. Two Rugby League players, Gary Connolly and Robbie Paul, made a reasonable impression before departing back north in the New Year. Three Frenchmen, Laurent Cabannes, Laurent Benezech and then Thierry Lacroix arrived, as did the Welsh brothers, Glyn and Gareth Llewellyn. Two Americans, lock Luke Gross and hooker Tom Billups also made their mark towards the end of the campaign.

The most significant close-season signing was Irish hooker Keith Wood. His dynamic play galvanised the whole 'Quins game. They sat unbeaten at the top of the table until Sale finally lowered their colours. An injury to Wood in Ireland's first Five Nations match deprived 'Quins of a potent asset, a loss which coincided with a slump in their form. At one point their European place was very much in jeopardy but a late rally, and a vital 13-12 win at Leicester (revenge for their 23-13 reversal in the quarter-finals of the Heineken Cup) on the penultimate Saturday, eased their worries. They went down badly in the Pilkington Cup, losing tamely 26-16 at Sale in the semi-finals. Their season ended in acrimony with reports of a rift between Best and his players, and notably former England captain, Will Carling. Best was the loser, being unceremoniously sacked.

League Record 1996-97

Date	Venue	Opponents	Result	Scorers
31 Aug	H	Gloucester	75-19	*T:* O'Leary 4, Benezech, Bromley, Cabannes, Mensah, Snow, Staples, pen try *C:* Carling 7 *P:* Carling 2
7 Sept	A	West Hartlepool	41-21	*T:* Challinor 2, Luger 2, Mensah, Walshe *C:* Carling 4 *P:* Carling
14 Sept	H	London Irish	66-7	*T:* Corcoran 3, Jenkins 2, Staples 2, Wood 2, O'Leary, Connolly *C:* Carling 3, Corcoran *P:* Corcoran
21 Sept	A	Bristol	35-24	*T:* Connolly, O'Leary, Staples, Wood, pen try *C:* Carling 4, Corcoran

28 Sept	A	Northampton	20-15	T: Carling, Harries, Staples C: Carling
				P: Carling
5 Oct	H	Orrell	89-18	T: Harries 3, Bromley 2, Connolly 2, Paul 2,
				Benezech, Carling, Davison, Watson, pen try
				C: Carling 8 P: Carling
30 Oct	A	Sale	13-24	T: Connolly, Walshe P: Corcoran
7 Dec	A	Bath	20-35	T: Challinor, Harries C: Challinor 2
				P: Challinor 2
28 Dec	H	Leicester	18-34	T: Harries 2 C: Challinor P: Challinor,
				Pilgrim
5 Jan	A	Wasps	19-17	T: Connolly C: Lacroix P: Lacroix 4
11 Jan	H	Bath	22-6	T: Staples C: Lacroix P: Lacroix 4
				D: Lacroix
19 Jan	A	Saracens	20-28	T: Harries, O'Leary C: Lacroix 2 P: Lacroix 2
8 Feb	H	Sale	30-31	T: G O Llewellyn, Harries C: Lacroix
				P: Lacroix 6
8 Mar	A	Orrell	56-20	T: Chapman 3, O'Leary 2, Davison, Lacroix,
				Mensah C: Lacroix 5 P: Lacroix 2
22 Mar	H	West Hartlepool	48-10	T: Walshe 3, Corcoran 2, Keyter, O'Leary
				C: Lacroix 5 P: Lacroix
5 Apr	A	London Irish	19-20	T: Chapman C: Lacroix P: Lacroix 3
				D: Lacroix
9 Apr	H	Saracens	27-0	T: Mensah, O'Leary, Staples C: Lacroix 3
				P: Lacroix 2
15 Apr	H	Bristol	29-6	T: Wood 2, O'Leary C: Lacroix P: Lacroix 3
				D: Lacroix
19 Apr	A	Gloucester	27-11	T: Lacroix, O'Leary, Williams C: Lacroix 3
				P: Lacroix 2
26 Apr	A	Leicester	13-12	T: O'Leary C: Lacroix P: Lacroix 2
30 Apr	H	Northampton	36-16	T: Mensah 2, Mullins, O'Leary, Wood
				C: Lacroix 4 P: Lacroix
3 May	H	Wasps	22-42	T: Allison, Cabannes, Keyter C: Corcoran,
				Lacroix P: Lacroix

Leicester

Year of formation 1880
Ground Welford Road, Leicester Tel: Leicester (0116) 2540276 or 2541607
Colours Scarlet, green and white
Captain 1996-97 D Richards
Courage Leagues 1996-97 Div 1 4th   **Pilkington Cup 1996-97** *Winners* – beat Sale 9-3
(final)

The Double had escaped them by the narrowest of margins the year before. This time they were leaving nothing to chance. In came former Australian coach, Bob Dwyer, out went old habits. The Tigers had become too set in their ways. And why not? Their tactics were successful – up to a point. As long as the ball was kept close they had no equals. Their heavyweight, talented pack, with Dean Richards at the core, was a match for any. But as Bath showed when edging them out of both Cup and League the previous season, such a strategy would rarely win them the tight games. And so Dwyer went to work.

Leicester were beaten on the opening Saturday by Saracens, a sobering lesson according to Dwyer. By the time the year turned, however, Leicester were transformed. The arrival of Springbok fly-half, Joel Stransky, was the final piece of the jigsaw. Will Greenwood was confirming his reputation as the best uncapped centre in the land; Austin Healey his as the new scrum-half on the block. No reputations were sacred. Rory Underwood was dropped for 19-year-old student, Leon Lloyd. Deano too made way for the young Irishman, Eric Miller. The European Cup final thumping by Brive was a setback but Leicester pulled together immediately to hammer Bath in the Pilkington Cup. Into April and a crucial 18-12 win over Wasps seemed to set them fair for a Double. But their legs gave way and they won only one of their final six matches in the run-up to the Pilkington Cup final. They came through that only by reverting to old type – limited, safe and forward-based. Having only just scraped into Europe by dint of a dramatic 20-20 draw on the last Saturday at Sale, Leicester were desperate for a return, any return, on the season. Bob Dwyer still has work to do.

League Record 1996-97

Date	Venue	Opponents	Result	Scorers
31 Aug	A	Saracens	23-25	*T:* J Liley, Underwood *C:* J Liley 2 *P:* J Liley 3
7 Sept	H	Bath	28-25	*T:* pen try *C:* J Liley *P:* J Liley 7
14 Sept	A	Orrell	29-12	*T:* Greenwood, Hackney, Potter *C:* J Liley *P:* J Liley 4
22 Sept	A	Wasps	7-14	*T:* pen try *C:* J Liley
28 Sept	H	Gloucester	32-14	*T:* Cockerill, Hackney, Underwood, pen try *C:* J Liley 3 *P:* J Liley 2
5 Oct	A	West Hartlepool	30-19	*T:* Drake-Lee, Greenwood, pen try *C:* J Liley 3 *P:* J Liley 3
30 Oct	H	London Irish	46-13	*T:* R Liley 2, Austin, Kardooni, pen try, W Johnson *C:* R Liley 5 *P:* R Liley 2
8 Dec	H	Northampton	23-9	*T:* Back, Potter *C:* R Liley, J Liley *P:* J Liley 2, R Liley
18 Dec	A	Bristol	38-12	*T:* Potter 2, Hackney, R Liley *C:* J Liley 3 *P:* J Liley 4
28 Dec	A	Harlequins	34-18	*T:* Underwood 2, Greenwood, J Liley *C:* J Liley *P:* J Liley 4
11 Jan	A	Northampton	19-22	*T:* Back 2 *P:* J Liley 3
18 Jan	H	Bristol	53-19	*T:* Greenwood, Healey, Lloyd, pen try Stransky, Underwood, *C:* J Liley 4 *P:* J Liley 5
4 Mar	H	Sale	25-9	*T:* pen try *C:* Stransky *P:* Stransky 6
8 Mar	H	West Hartlepool	48-3	*T:* Austin, Garforth, Greenwood, Healey, Jones, Stransky *C:* Stransky 3 *P:* Stransky 4
2 Apr	H	Wasps	18-12	*P:* Stransky 6
5 Apr	H	Orrell	36-14	*T:* Malone 2, Hackney, Joiner, Poole, Underwood *C:* J Liley 3
8 Apr	A	Gloucester	30-32	*T:* Joiner, Kardooni, J Liley, Underwood *C:* Stransky 2 *P:* Stransky 2
12 Apr	A	Bath	9-47	*P:* Stransky 3
16 Apr	A	London Irish	18-25	*T:* Fletcher, Poole *C:* R Liley *P:* R Liley 2
19 Apr	H	Saracens	22-18	*T:* pen try *C:* J Liley *P:* J Liley 5
26 Apr	H	Harlequins	12-13	*P:* J Liley 2, Stransky 2
3 May	A	Sale	20-20	*T:* Potter, pen try *C:* Stransky 2 *P:* Stransky 2

London Irish

Year of formation 1898
Ground The Avenue, Sunbury-on-Thames, Middlesex Tel: Sunbury (01932) 783034
Colours Emerald green and white
Captain 1996-97 G F Halpin
Courage Leagues 1996-97 Div 1 10th; Won Division 1 / 2 play off against Coventry, 42-23 on aggregate   **Pilkington Cup 1996-97** Lost 0-33 to Bath (5th round)

In the wake of professionalism the Exiles underwent some serious soul-searching. They had a close season crisis of identity when coach Clive Woodward, the man who had brought them to the First Division, objected to what he saw as restrictive clauses in the club's constitution about non-Irish members. Woodward was appeased, but not for long, eventually leaving the club in mid-season to be replaced by former Irish lock forward, Willie Anderson. The famous Anderson passion finally seeped into the bones of his players. The team had languished at the lower end of the table for much of the campaign. Although they could point to the slender margin of defeats against Bristol (27-28), Gloucester (20-21) and Wasps (20-22) as evidence of their potential, they did concede over 50 points to both Bath and Harlequins. Then the revival began. The Exiles had a terribly cramped finale, having to fit seven matches into the final three weeks, but they came through with flying colours. The residue of a decent side was always there with the arrival at Sunbury of locks Gabriel Fulcher and Jeremy Davidson (who was rewarded for a fine season with a place in the Lions squad), Victor Costello and, outside, Niall Woods. The simple aim of the Irish at the season's end was to avoid the automatic relegation spots which they managed with some ease. The play-offs were a chance to buy a lifeline; and the Irish seized it. Although they ceded two points in the first match at Coventry, going down 16-14 in injury time, they were quickly out of the traps four days later. They led 28-0 shortly after half-time and ran out comfortable winners, 28-7, for an aggregate 42-23. Skipper Gary Halpin admitted that they needed to buy to survive. 'If we don't get five new players we'll go straight back down,' said Halpin.

League Record 1996-97

Date	Venue	Opponents	Result	Scorers
31 Aug	H	Bristol	27-28	*T:* Woods 2, Henderson *P:* Humphreys 3, Henderson
7 Sept	H	Northampton	34-21	*T:* Costello, Davidson, Woods *C:* Humphreys 2 *P:* Humphreys 4 *D:* Humphreys
14 Sept	A	Harlequins	7-66	*T:* Flood *C:* Humphreys
21 Sept	H	Sale	19-25	*T:* Halpin *C:* Humphreys *P:* Humphreys 3 *D:* Humphreys
28 Sept	H	Saracens	23-37	*T:* Woods, pen try *C:* Humphreys 2 *P:* Humphreys 3
5 Oct	H	Bath	31-56	*T:* O'Shea 2, Briers, Woods *C:* Humphreys 4 *P:* Humphreys
30 Oct	A	Leicester	13-46	*T:* Henderson *C:* Humphreys *P:* Humphreys 2
16 Nov	H	Wasps	20-22	*T:* Bishop *P:* Humphreys 4 *D:* Humphreys
7 Dec	A	Gloucester	19-29	*T:* Henderson 2 *P:* Humphreys 3
28 Dec	H	West Hartlepool	52-41	*T:* Walsh 2, Bishop, Davidson, O'Shea, Henderson *C:* Humphreys 5 *P:* Humphreys 4
11 Jan	H	Gloucester	20-21	*T:* O'Shea *P:* Humphreys 5
22 Feb	A	Orrell	27-32	*T:* O'Shea 2, Humphreys, O'Connell *C:* Humphreys 2 *P:* Humphreys
8 Mar	A	Bath	3-46	*P:* Humphreys
26 Mar	A	Wasps	18-31	*T:* Flood, Fulcher *C:* O'Shea *P:* O'Shea 2
5 Apr	H	Harlequins	20-19	*T:* O'Shea, Walsh *C:* Humphreys 2 *P:* Humphreys 2
12 Apr	A	Northampton	21-31	*T:* Dawson, Hennessy *C:* O'Shea *P:* Humphreys 2, O'Shea
16 Apr	H	Leicester	25-18	*T:* Bishop, Burrows, Fulcher, O'Connell *C:* O'Shea *P:* O'Shea
19 Apr	A	Bristol	38-26	*T:* Humphreys 2, Hennessy, Spicer, Fulcher, Woods *C:* O'Shea *P:* Humphreys 2
23 Apr	A	Sale	25-41	*T:* Yeabsley 2, Hennessy, O'Shea *C:* Woods *P:* Woods
26 Apr	A	West Hartlepool	33-18	*T:* Humphreys, O'Connell, Redmond, Richards, Woods *C:* Woods *P:* Woods 2
30 Apr	A	Saracens	0-45	
3 May	H	Orrell	27-48	*T:* Allen, Dougan, Ewington, Walsh *C:* Ure 2 *P:* Ure

Play-Offs

7 May	A	Coventry	14-16	*T:* Woods *P:* Humphreys 3
11 May	H	Coventry	28-7	*T:* Halpin, Woods, Humphreys
				C: Humphreys 2 *P:* Humphreys 3

London Scottish

Year of formation 1878
Ground Richmond Athletic Ground, Kew Foot Road, Richmond, Surrey Tel: 0181 332 2473
Colours Blue jersey with red lion crest
Captain 1996-97 S D Holmes
Courage Leagues 1996-97 Div 2 5th **Pilkington Cup 1996-97** Lost 15-39 to Newcastle (6th round)

As the season swung into view London Scottish were without doubt the poor relations of the Athletic Ground, suffering in the shadow of the affluent Richmond. Although they tried hard to match the millions of Ashley Levett and did well to entice former player, Tony Tiarks, to part with half a million pounds, it was only as the season drew to a close that the club finally managed to put the whole deal into place. Even though they had begun the season well, and even led the table for a few glorious weeks, they did not have enough strength in depth once injuries took their toll. Their lack of sustained class throughout the side also showed when they faced tougher opposition. A 37-18 defeat by their co-tenants, Richmond, in March illustrated the divide. On the plus side John Steele and Simon Holmes did a creditable job as coach and captain, while Scotland A full-back, Derek Lee, was a great purchase in mid-season, a sure sign that London Scottish will mean business next time.

League Record 1996-97

Date	Venue	Opponents	Result	Scorers
7 Sept	H	Rugby	43-7	*T:* Furley, Griffiths, Hunter, Holmes *C:* Steele 4 *P:* Steele 5
14 Sept	A	Wakefield	30-27	*T:* Tarbuck 2, Hamilton *C:* Steele 3 *P:* Steele 3
21 Sept	H	Waterloo	42-30	*T:* Duthie 2, Eriksson, Smith, Steele *C:* Steele 4 *P:* Steele 3
28 Sept	A	Nottingham	26-12	*T:* Duthie, Eriksson *C:* Steele 2 *P:* Steele 3 *D:* Steele
5 Oct	H	Blackheath	23-31	*T:* Tarbuck, Watson *C:* Steele 2 *P:* Steele 3
12 Oct	A	Richmond	13-54	*T:* Millard *C:* Steele *P:* Steele 2
19 Oct	A	Coventry	6-66	*P:* Stent 2
26 Oct	H	Moseley	42-10	*T:* Wichary 3, Tarbuck 2, Duthie *C:* Steele 3 *P:* Steele 2
3 Nov	A	Rotherham	18-28	*T:* Robinson, Turner *C:* Steele *P:* Steele 2
9 Nov	H	Bedford	26-27	*T:* Rayner, Steele *C:* Steele 2 *P:* Steele 4
16 Nov	H	Newcastle	12-28	*T:* Jankovich, Watson *C:* Steele
18 Jan	H	Nottingham	33-10	*T:* Steele, Thompson, Jankovich *C:* Steele 3 *P:* Steele 4
8 Feb	A	Blackheath	19-13	*T:* Robinson, Holmes *P:* Stent *D:* Stent, Eriksson
8 Mar	H	Richmond	18-37	*T:* Tarbuck 2 *C:* Steele *P:* Steele *D:* Steele
22 Mar	H	Coventry	13-14	*T:* Hunter *C:* Stent *P:* Stent 2
29 Mar	A	Rugby	45-16	*T:* Steele 2, Eriksson, Robinson, Sly *C:* Steele 4 *P:* Steele 4
31 Mar	H	Wakefield	34-3	*T:* Holmes, Hunter, Smith *C:* Steele 2 *P:* Steele 5
5 Apr	A	Moseley	16-44	*T:* Smith, Millard *P:* Steele *D:* Steele

137

12 Apr	H	Rotherham	25-3	*T:* Johnson, Millard, Milligan *C:* Steele 2
				P: Steele 2
19 Apr	A	Bedford	28-14	*T:* E Jackson, Milligan, Tarbuck *C:* Steele 2
				P: Steele 2 *D:* Steele
26 Apr	A	Newcastle	20-71	*T:* Hunter, Lee, Stent *C:* Lee *P:* Lee
3 May	A	Waterloo	17-23	*T:* Burnell, McKenzie *C:* Steele 2 *P:* Steele

Moseley

Year of formation 1873
Ground The Reddings, Reddings Road, Moseley, Birmingham Tel: 0121 499 2149
Colours Red and black
Captain 1996-97 A Houston
Courage Leagues 1996-97 Div 2 8th   **Pilkington Cup 1996-97** Lost 14-24 to Wakefield
(6th round)

The Birmingham club will have looked enviously at their rivals along the motorway as Coventry showed just how to mix money and planning. Moseley and Coventry have had some great duels down the years, but Coventry seem to have the edge at the moment. There has been huge movement of personnel – players and officials – in recent times as Moseley try to find the elusive formula for success. They have a terrific catchment area and potentially great support, but sponsors and fans will want to see more resolution and co-ordination before they come flocking to the Reddings's gates. Perhaps the arrival of former Gloucester stalwart, Ian Smith, will have the same galvanising impact as Eves at Coventry.

League Record 1996-97

Date	Venue	Opponents	Result	Scorers
7 Sept	H	Wakefield	17-30	*T:* Houston *P:* Dossett 4
14 Sept	A	Waterloo	13-20	*T:* Johal *C:* Quick *P:* Quick 2
21 Sept	H	Nottingham	34-22	*T:* McKinnon 2, Birch, Harris, Wilkinson
				C: Dossett 3 *P:* Dossett
28 Sept	A	Blackheath	3-28	*P:* Dossett
5 Oct	H	Richmond	15-87	*T:* McKinnon, Poll *C:* Birch *P:* Birch
12 Oct	A	Rugby	22-29	*T:* Batey, Faiva, McKinnon *C:* Birch 2
				P: Birch
19 Oct	H	Newcastle	9-75	*P:* Quick 3
26 Oct	A	London Scottish	10-42	*T:* Wilkinson *C:* Le Bas *P:* Le Bas
3 Nov	A	Bedford	9-64	*P:* Le Bas 3
9 Nov	H	Coventry	19-35	*T:* Harris *C:* Le Bas *P:* Le Bas 3 *D:* Dossett
16 Nov	A	Rotherham	9-18	*P:* Le Bas 3
18 Jan	H	Blackheath	21-18	*T:* O'Mahony, Ridge *C:* Le Bas *P:* Le Bas 3
1 Feb	A	Nottingham	22-11	*T:* O'Mahony 3 *C:* Le Bas 2 *P:* Le Bas
8 Feb	A	Richmond	27-37	*T:* O'Mahony 2, Charron *C:* Le Bas 3
				P: Le Bas 2
22 Feb	H	Waterloo	17-13	*T:* O'Mahony *P:* Le Bas 4
8 Mar	H	Rugby	34-11	*T:* O'Mahony 2, Denhardt, Jones *C:* Le Bas
				P: Le Bas 4
22 Mar	A	Newcastle	19-88	*T:* Hall, Turner, pen try *C:* Stuart 2
29 Mar	A	Wakefield	42-13	*T:* O'Mahony 2, Le Bas, Martin, Ridge
				C: Le Bas 4 *P:* Le Bas 3
5 Apr	H	London Scottish	44-16	*T:* O'Mahony 2, Binns, Harris, Le Bas,
				Smith *C:* Le Bas 4 *P:* Le Bas 2
12 Apr	H	Bedford	40-34	*T:* Binns, Harris. Le Bas, O'Mahony, Turner
				C: Le Bas 3 *P:* Le Bas 3
19 Apr	A	Coventry	18-33	*T:* Binns, Cockle *C:* Le Bas *P:* Le Bas 2
26 Apr	H	Rotherham	48-17	*T:* Charron, Hall, Martin, Mitchell, O'Mahony,
				Rolland *C:* Le Bas 6 *P:* Le Bas 2

Newcastle

Year of formation 1877, reformed in 1995
Ground Kingston Park, Brunton Road, Kenton Bank Foot, Newcastle upon Tyne
Tel: 0191 214 0422
Colours Black and white
Captain 1996-97 D Ryan
Courage Leagues 1996-97 Div 2 2nd – *promoted*   Pilkington Cup 1996-97 Lost 8-18 to
Leicester (quarter-final)

They may not have been the most popular side in the land but their massive potential
is there for all to see. Money breeds envy and there were many sneers about the spirit
of the club being destroyed as Sir John Hall's chequebook brought about a complete
transformation of faces. No one though could deny the power of Newcastle's rugby.
They set an astonishing aggregate record of points, 1,255 points in 22 matches, one
which will surely never be beaten. Likewise their 156-5 victory over poor Rugby, the
biggest win not just in the Second Division history but also in senior club rugby
throughout the world. John Bentley's 24 tries set a new mark, eclipsing the 20 scored
by Northampton's Matt Allen the previous year. The boot and direction of Rob
Andrew, who passed 1,000 Courage League points, kept his side pushing remorse-
lessly forward. A surprise reversal at Bedford apart, Newcastle were rarely troubled.
Their success, and potential for the First Division, was reflected in their five-strong
Lions contingent – Stimpson, Tait, Bentley, Weir and Tony Underwood.

League Record 1996-97

Date	Venue	Opponents	Result	Scorers
7 Sept	H	Waterloo	30-13	*T:* Andrew, Armstrong, Popplewell, Wilkinson *C:* Andrew 2 *P:* Andrew 2
14 Sept	A	Nottingham	74-29	*T:* Armstrong 4, Andrew, Archer, Blyth, Childs, Nesdale, Underwood, Weir, Wilkinson *C:* Andrew 7
21 Sept	H	Blackheath	61-0	*T:* Armstrong 2, Bentley 2, Graham 2, Arnold, Frankland,Underwood, Weir *C:* Andrew 4 *P:* Andrew
28 Sept	A	Richmond	20-20	*T:* Armstrong, Underwood *C:* Andrew 2 *P:* Andrew 2
5 Oct	H	Rugby	156-5	*T:* Armstrong 3, Graham 3, Nesdale 3, Ryan 3, Bentley 2, Popplewell 2, Tetlow 2, Underwood 2, Bates, Blyth, Stimpson, Weir *C:* Andrew 18
12 Oct	A	Wakefield	47-17	*T:* Archer, Armstrong, Bentley, O'Neill, Popplewell, Ryan, Stimpson *C:* Andrew 6
19 Oct	A	Moseley	75-9	*T:* Bentley 3, Tetlow 2, Armstrong, Nesdale, Popplewell, Ryan, O'Neill, Underwood *C:* Stimpson 7, Andrew 3
26 Oct	H	Bedford	49-12	*T:* Archer, Armstrong, Bentley, Blyth, Stimpson, Tetlow, pen try *C:* Andrew 3,Stimpson *P:* Andrew 2
3 Nov	A	Coventry	18-19	*P:* Andrew 5, *D:* Andrew
16 Nov	A	London Scottish	28-12	*T:* Stimpson 3 *C:* Andrew 2 *P:* Andrew 3
8 Feb	A	Rugby	70-8	*T:* Bentley 3, Nesdale 2, Armstrong, Hetherington, Lam, Underwood, Vanzandvliet, Weir *C:* Andrew 6 *P:* Andrew
8 Mar	H	Wakefield	57-10	*T:* Bentley 4, Underwood 2, Andrew, Tait, Vanzandvliet *C:* Andrew 6
16 Mar	H	Nottingham	53-17	*T:* Bates 3, Archer 2, Armstrong, Lam, Ryan, Shaw *C:* Andrew 3, Stimpson
22 Mar	H	Moseley	88-19	*T:* Bentley 3, Tuigamala 3, Lam 2, Stimpson 2, Armstrong, Nesdale, Wilson, pen try *C:* Andrew 4, Stimpson 5

29 Mar	H	Richmond	37-17	*T:* Archer, Popplewell, Ryan, Weir *C:* Andrew 4 *P:* Andrew 3
5 Apr	A	Bedford	28-34	*T:* Graham, Lam, Tait *C:* Andrew 2 *P:* Andrew 3
12 Apr	H	Coventry	49-17	*T:* Nesdale 2, Andrew, Bentley, Tait, Childs, Stimpson, Tuigamala *C:* Andrew 3 *P:* Andrew
16 Apr	A	Blackheath	72-10	*T:* Ryan 3, Bentley 2, Stimpson 2, Tuigamala 2, Andrew, Lam, Nesdale *C:* Andrew 2, Stimpson 4
19 Apr	A	Rotherham	45-21	*T:* Andrew, Archer, Bates, Bentley, Lam, Tuigamala, pen try *C:* Andrew 5
26 Apr	H	London Scottish	71-20	*T:* Armstrong 2, Tuigamala 2, Arnold, Bentley, Childs, Graham, O'Neill, Stimpson, Walton *C:* Andrew 5, Stimpson 3
30 Apr	A	Waterloo	66-24	*T:* Blyth 2, Lam 2, Tuigamala 2, Stimpson, Vanzandvliet, Walton *C:* Andrew 7, Stimpson 2 *P:* O'Neill
4 May	H	Rotherham	61-13	*T:* Lam 5, Armstrong 2, Bentley, Tait, Childs, Stimpson *C:* Tuigamala, Andrew, Stimpson

Northampton

Year of formation 1880
Ground Franklins Gardens, Weedon Road, Northampton Tel: Northampton (01604) 751543
Colours Black, green and gold
Captain 1996-97 T A K Rodber
Courage Leagues 1996-97 Div 1 8th **Pilkington Cup 1996-97** Lost 9-22 to Sale (quarter-final)

How are we to evaluate Northampton's season? By the fact that they had the great honour of five players – Rodber, Townsend, Grayson, Beal and Dawson – selected for the British Lions? Or by the fact that they finished eighth in their first year back in the top flight and were never in contention for any of the major prizes. True they were the only British club to get through to the quarter-finals of the European Conference and had a mighty win at Toulon to their credit. But a team with so much obvious talent and coached by Ian McGeechan really ought to have shown a better return. Franklins Gardens is one of the more professionally-run clubs in the land, with a great support base and a benefactor, Keith Barwell, who is not the meddling type.

The absence from the engine room of the experienced Martin Bayfield through a long-term pelvis injury obviously blighted Northampton's campaign, and there were few new additions to the roster, Shem Tatupu from Rugby League and prop Mattie Stewart from Blackheath the most notable. Individually there is little to fault in the Saints line-up: Allen Clarke played for Ireland at hooker and centre Matt Allen made the England tour party to Argentina. Collectively, though, they simply did not fire, particularly away where only one game was won, at Orrell. The home form was good enough: Bath and Leicester were both beaten and Wasps given a real run for their money in the deciding game of the championship. Northampton were prudent in the transfer market last time around. Perhaps too prudent. Maybe it's time to stir things up.

League Record 1996-97

Date	Venue	Opponents	Result	Scorers
31 Aug	H	West Hartlepool	46-20	*T:* Bell 2, Beal, Dawson, Moir, pen try *C:* Grayson 5 *P:* Grayson 2
7 Sept	A	London Irish	21-34	*T:* Dods, Rodber, pen try *C:* Dods 3
14 Sept	H	Bristol	29-21	*T:* Beal, Bell, Grayson, Rodber *P:* Grayson 2 *D:* Grayson

21 Sept	H	Orrell	41-7	*T:* Bell 2, Dawson, Hunter, MacKinnon, Rodber, Thorneycroft *C:* Grayson 3
28 Sept	H	Harlequins	15-20	*T:* Beal, Bell *C:* Grayson *P:* Grayson
5 Oct	H	Sale	30-12	*T:* Beal, Clarke *C:* Grayson *P:* Grayson 4 *D:* Grayson 2
29 Oct	A	Saracens	23-24	*T:* Allen, Beal *C:* Grayson 2 *P:* Grayson 3
9 Nov	H	Bath	9-6	*P:* Grayson 2 *D:* Grayson
8 Dec	A	Leicester	9-23	*P:* Grayson 2 *D:* Townsend
28 Dec	A	Wasps	13-18	*T:* Chandler *C:* Grayson *P:* Grayson 2
11 Jan	H	Leicester	22-19	*T:* Townsend *C:* Grayson *P:* Grayson 5
19 Jan	A	Bath	14-52	*T:* MacNaughton *P:* Beal 2, Grayson
8 Feb	H	Saracens	17-10	*T:* Hunter *P:* Grayson 4
4 Mar	A	Gloucester	6-19	*P:* Dods 2
9 Mar	A	Sale	15-31	*P:* Townsend 5
29 Mar	A	Orrell	50-14	*T:* Seely 2, Bell, Cohen, Thorneycroft, Townsend, Wright *C:* Townsend 3 *P:* Townsend 3
5 Apr	A	Bristol	11-20	*T:* Hunter *P:* Townsend 2
12 Apr	H	London Irish	31-21	*T:* Clarke, Hepher, Townsend *C:* Hepher 2 *P:* Hepher 4
19 Apr	A	West Hartlepool	57-17	*T:* Allen 2, Cassell 2, Townsend 2, Beal, Merlin, Thorneycroft *C:* Hepher 6
26 Apr	H	Wasps	15-26	*P:* Hepher 5
30 Apr	A	Harlequins	16-36	*T:* Hepher *C:* Hepher *P:* Hepher 2 *D:* Hepher
3 May	H	Gloucester	25-27	*T:* pen try *C:* Hepher *P:* Hepher 6

Nottingham

Year of formation 1877
Ground Ireland Avenue, Beeston, Nottingham Tel: Nottingham (0115) 9254238
Colours White and green
Captain 1996-97 A Royer
Courage Leagues 1996-97 Div 2 12th – *relegated*   Pilkington Cup 1996-97 Lost 11-25 to London Scottish (5th round)

Nottingham had advertised for a millionaire in the classified ads the year before. By mid-1997 still no one had come knocking. The Midlands club had no hope of competing against the big boys. Even so they will be disappointed that they did not put up more of a fight against some of the lesser brethren. Club stalwart, Simon Hodgkinson, returned to see if he could kick-start those around into meaningful activity but to little avail. The side conceded an average of 37 points a match and won only two League games all season. London Scottish saw them off, 25-11, in their first outing in the Pilkington Cup. Unless the club can find an investor there is every likelihood that the slide will continue.

League Record 1996-97

Date	Venue	Opponents	Result	Scorers
7 Sept	A	Bedford	23-41	*T:* Brennan, Jackson, Tomlinson *C:* Carroll *P:* Carroll 2
14 Sept	H	Newcastle	29-74	*T:* Royer 2, Tomlinson 2 *C:* Carroll 3 *P:* Carroll
21 Sept	A	Moseley	22-34	*T:* Bygrave, Royer, Webster *C:* Carroll 2 *P:* Carroll
28 Sept	H	London Scottish	12-26	*P:* Carroll 3, Hodgkinson
5 Oct	A	Coventry	22-102	*T:* Beese, Bygrave, Dawson, Jones *C:* Craig
12 Oct	H	Rotherham	21-44	*T:* Atkinson, Freer *C:* Hodgkinson *P:* Hodgkinson 3

19 Oct	H	Blackheath	12-22	*P:* Hodgkinson 3, Tomlinson
26 Oct	A	Waterloo	20-19	*T:* Dawson, Hartley *C:* Tomlinson 2 *P:* Tomlinson 2
3 Nov	H	Wakefield	18-40	*T:* Rees, pen try *C:* Wills *P:* Wills 2
9 Nov	A	Rugby	12-20	*P:* Hartley 4
16 Nov	H	Richmond	5-70	*T:* Sussum
28 Dec	H	Bedford	13-36	*T:* Rees *C:* Carroll *P:* Carroll 2
18 Jan	A	London Scottish	10-33	*T:* Dawson *C:* Evans *P:* Evans
1 Feb	H	Moseley	11-22	*T:* Bygrave *P:* Evans 2
8 Feb	H	Coventry	0-29	
8 Mar	A	Rotherham	24-30	*T:* Beatham, McCarthy, Wilcox *C:* Evans 3 *P:* Evans
16 Mar	A	Newcastle	17-53	*T:* Claydon, Hall, Wilcox *C:* Evans
22 Mar	A	Blackheath	0-24	
5 Apr	H	Waterloo	13-33	*T:* Evans *C:* Evans *P:* Evans 2
12 Apr	A	Wakefield	16-31	*T:* Byrom, Royer *P:* Evans 2
19 Apr	H	Rugby	44-10	*T:* Hall 3, Brennan, Bygrave, Dawson *C:* Evans 4 *P:* Evans 2
26 Apr	A	Richmond	0-34	

Orrell

Year of formation 1927
Ground Edge Hall Road, Orrell, Lancashire Tel: Upholland (01695) 623193
Colours Black and amber
Captain 1996-97 D Lyon
Courage Leagues 1996-97 Div 1 12th – *relegated* Pilkington Cup 1996-97 Lost 0-57 to Sale (6th round)

Many tears were shed for this most proud, proletarian and resilient of northern clubs as it battled in vain to keep pace with the monied classes. The writing had been on the wall for a couple of seasons as the committee tried various ways of averting the inevitable. The occasional ground share with Wigan was scrapped when it found little favour with members. As others flashed the chequebook Orrell stuck steadfastly to their careful, thrifty ways. New director of coaching, former fly-half and Rugby League convert, Peter Williams, had little to play with. New Zealander Frano Botica was briefly his before Llanelli spirited him away, and while those who were left behind scrapped as best they could, they haemorrhaged points, conceding 56 points at home to both Bath and Harlequins. Away from home it was an even sorrier tale with Wasps running in 62 points, bettered by 'Quins who rattled up 89 points. The committee stuck to their guns, refusing to bankrupt the club for short-terms gain. 'We might have self-destructed if we'd spent money we hadn't got,' said Des Seabrook, former coach and Orrell president.

Orrell lost 12 of their first-team squad from the previous season and will do well to hang on to the likes of Jim Naylor and Peter Anglesea now. The success story of Orrell was an improbable tale, the small outfit hanging on to their First Division status for 10 years and only missing out on the League title in 1992 on points difference to Bath. It will be some time before we see that scenario repeated. Orrell finished bottom of the league.

League Record 1996-97

Date	Venue	Opponents	Result	Scorers
31 Aug	H	Bath	13-56	*T:* Heslop, Tuigamala *P:* Botica
7 Sept	A	Bristol	10-38	*T:* Anglesea *C:* Botica *P:* Botica
14 Sept	H	Leicester	12-29	*T:* Naylor, Saverimutto *C:* Botica
21 Sept	A	Northampton	7-41	*T:* Tuigamala *C:* Tuigamala

28 Sept	H	Wasps	27-44	*T:* Bennett, Heslop, Lyon, Naylor *C:* Strett 2 *P:* Strett
5 Oct	A	Harlequins	18-89	*T:* Anglesea, Cook *C:* Strett *P:* Strett 2
9 Nov	A	Sale	11-37	*T:* Nelson *P:* Hitchmough 2
16 Nov	H	Gloucester	3-49	*P:* Hitchmough
7 Dec	H	West Hartlepool	22-15	*T:* Cook *C:* McCarthy *P:* McCarthy 2 *D:* McCarthy 3
11 Jan	A	West Hartlepool	8-24	*T:* Naylor *P:* McCarthy
18 Jan	H	Sale	8-40	*T:* Worsley *P:* McCarthy
8 Feb	A	Gloucester	0-30	
22 Feb	H	London Irish	32-27	*T:* Naylor, Tuigamala *C:* McCarthy 2 *P:* McCarthy 6
4 Mar	A	Saracens	15-24	*T:* Higgs, Naylor *C:* McCarthy *P:* McCarthy
8 Mar	H	Harlequins	20-56	*T:* McCarthy, Taberner *C:* McCarthy 2 *P:* McCarthy 2
22 Mar	A	Wasps	5-62	*T:* Heslop
29 Mar	H	Northampton	14-50	*T:* Bennett *P:* McCarthy 2 *D:* McCarthy
5 Apr	A	Leicester	14-36	*T:* Cook, pen try *C:* McCarthy 2
12 Apr	H	Bristol	27-28	*T:* Hitchmough 2, Anglesea, Rees *C:* McCarthy 2 *P:* McCarthy
19 Apr	A	Bath	14-20	*T:* Hope, Lyon *C:* Hitchmough 2
26 Apr	H	Saracens	22-44	*T:* Anglesea, McCarthy, Turner *C:* McCarthy 2 *P:* McCarthy
3 May	A	London Irish	48-27	*T:* Bennett 2, Lyon 2, Hitchmough, Naylor *C:* McCarthy 6 *P:* McCarthy 2

Richmond

Year of formation 1861
Ground Richmond Athletic Ground, Kew Foot Road, Richmond, Surrey Tel: 0181 332 7112
Colours Old gold, red and black
Captain 1996-97 B B Clarke
Courage Leagues 1996-97 Div 2 *Winners – promoted* **Pilkington Cup 1996-97** Lost 30-34 to Sale (5th round)

Even those with money are rarely known to throw it away. So when Monaco-based Ashley Levett pumped in £2.5 million it was no benevolent gesture; Levett got his return. Richmond did not rest on assumptions. Even though they had pulled together a considerable squad – Ben Clarke, the Quinnell brothers, Adrian Davies, Andy Moore, Richard West, Simon Mason and, as an amateur, Brian Moore – they were never complacent. They played with style and vigour throughout the season. They let slip a morale-boosting position against Sale in the Cup when Brian Moore was sent off but, that apart, their season was one of great merit, on and off the field. The club worked hard to enhance facilities and to provide entertainment for all the family. The blaring music which greeted each score was excessive. On every other point, though, Richmond, were right on-key. They were deserved champions.

League Record 1996-97

Date	Venue	Opponents	Result	Scorers
7 Sept	A	Coventry	16-16	*T:* Boyd, Whitford *P:* Mason 2
14 Sept	H	Rotherham	64-38	*T:* S Quinnell 3, Mason 2, A Moore, B Moore, Davies, Fallon *C:* Mason 8 *P:* Mason
21 Sept	A	Bedford	44-17	*T:* Cottrell 2, A Moore, Davies, Whitford, Hutton *C:* Mason 4 *P:* Mason 2
28 Sept	H	Newcastle	20-20	*T:* S Quinnell, pen try *C:* Mason 2 *P:* Mason *D:* Davies

Richmond celebrate with the Courage League Division 2 trophy after their victory over Nottingham.

5 Oct	A	Moseley	87-15	*T:* Fallon 3, S Quinnell 3, C Quinnell 2, Bateman, Clarke, Cottrell, Davies, Hutton, Mason *C:* Mason 7 *P:* Mason
12 Oct	H	London Scottish	54-13	*T:* Fallon 2, Bateman 2, Davies, Mason, S Quinnell *C:* Mason 5 *P:* Mason 3
19 Oct	H	Rugby	64-8	*T:* Fallon 3, Bateman 2, Davies 2, Leach 2, Mason *C:* Mason 7
26 Oct	A	Blackheath	40-21	*T:* Clarke, Harvey, pen try *C:* Mason 2 *P:* Mason 6 *D:* Davies
3 Nov	H	Waterloo	64-13	*T:* S Quinnell 4,C Quinnell 3, Brown 2, Bateman *C:* Mason 7
9 Nov	A	Wakefield	23-7	*T:* Clarke, Fallon, S Quinnell *C:* Gregory *P:* Gregory 2
16 Nov	A	Nottingham	70-5	*T:* Brown 2, Bateman 2, Boyd, Fallon, C Quinnell, Mason, S Quinnell, Whitford *C:* Mason 7 *P:* Mason 2
28 Dec	H	Coventry	39-10	*T:* S Quinnell 2, Boyd, Brown, Clarke *C:* Mason 4 *P:* Mason 2
25 Jan	H	Bedford	34-33	*T:* Brown, Clarke, Cottrell, Rodgers, Vander *C:* Mason 3 *P:* Mason
8 Feb	H	Moseley	37-27	*T:* C Quinnell 2, Brown, Clarke, Mason, Vander *C:* Mason 2 *P:* Mason
22 Feb	A	Rotherham	28-6	*T:* Bateman, Brown, Fallon *C:* Mason 2 *P:* Mason 3
8 Mar	A	London Scottish	37-18	*T:* Brown, Fallon, C Quinnell, Mason, Cuthbert *C:* Mason 3 *P:* Mason 2
22 Mar	A	Rugby	72-31	*T:* S Quinnell 3, A Moore, Clarke, Cottrell, Deane, Fallon, Jones, Mason *C:* Mason 8 *P:* Mason *D:* A Moore

29 Mar	A	Newcastle	17-37	*T:* Fallon 2, Clarke *C:* Mason
5 Apr	H	Blackheath	29-24	*T:* Clarke, Cook, Crompton, Jones *P:* Mason 3
12 Apr	A	Waterloo	58-29	*T:* C Quinnell 2, A Moore, Bateman, Cottrell, Davies, Fallon, S Quinnell *C:* Mason 6 *P:* Mason 2
19 Apr	H	Wakefield	55-22	*T:* Fallon 3, Brown 2, Clarke, Mason, Codling, S Quinnell *C:* Mason 5
26 Apr	H	Nottingham	34-0	*T:* A Moore 2, Clarke, Brown, Davies *P:* Mason 3

Rotherham

Year of formation 1923
Ground Clifton Lane, Badsley Moor, Rotherham Tel: Rotherham (01709) 370763
Colours Maroon, sky blue, navy blue and white
Captain 1996-97
Courage Leagues 1996-97 Div 2 7th **Pilkington Cup 1996-97** Lost 23-42 to Harlequins
(6th round)

The club which had left scorch marks across the rest of the Leagues with their scintillating progress – six promotions in nine seasons – never quite managed to set the Second Division alight but still finished a commendable seventh. Their success has been based on solid values. They are a community club backed by sound management, and a nucleus of players who have been with them throughout their triumphant march. They had the smallest turnover of players in any of the top divisions, neither chasing star names with fool's gold nor dispensing unnecessarily with those who had served them so well. They only came in to the Second Division on the back of the major reorganisation of the Leagues the year before, when they were the last of the four sides promoted from the Third Division. That they held their own so capably, with ten victories in 22 matches, suggests that money is not the answer to all ills.

League Record 1996-97

Date	Venue	Opponents	Result	Scorers
7 Sept	A	Blackheath	5-44	*T:* Heaselgrave
14 Sept	A	Richmond	38-64	*T:* Easterby 2, Miller *C:* Inman *P:* Inman 7
21 Sept	H	Rugby	49-18	*T:* Binns 2, Dudley 2, Easterby, Miller, Buzza *C:* Inman 4 *P:* Inman 2
28 Sept	A	Wakefield	29-25	*T:* Burnhill, Mills, Heaselgrave *C:* Inman *P:* Inman 4
5 Oct	H	Waterloo	38-23	*T:* Binns, Burnhill, Easterby, Harper, Heaselgrave *C:* Inman 2 *P:*Inman 2 *D:* Heaselgrave
12 Oct	A	Nottingham	44-21	*T:* Burns, Burnhill, Buzza, Harper, Webster, pen try *C:* Inman 4 *P:* Inman 2
19 Oct	A	Bedford	30-44	*T:* Heaselgrave 2, Buzza, Wareham *C:* Inman 2 *P:* Inman 2
26 Oct	H	Coventry	11-42	*T:* Kearney *P:*Inman 2
3 Nov	H	London Scottish	28-18	*T:* Easterby, Heaselgrave *P:* Lax 6
16 Nov	H	Moseley	18-9	*T:* Bayston, Easterby *C:* Lax *P:* Lax 2
28 Dec	H	Blackheath	39-11	*T:* Webster 2, Easterby, Miller, Wareham *C:* Lax 4 *P:* Lax *D:* Binns
18 Jan	H	Wakefield	12-19	*P:* Lax 4
8 Feb	A	Waterloo	27-23	*T:* Easterby, Lax *C:* Lax *P:* Lax 4 *D:* Binns
22 Feb	H	Richmond	6-28	*P:* Lax 2
8 Mar	H	Nottingham	30-24	*T:* Easterby 2, Lax, Miller, pen try *C:* Lax *P:* Lax

145

15 Mar	A	Rugby	41-16	*T:* Easterby 2, Binns, Bramley, Bunting, Harper *C:* Ashworth 4 *P:* Ashworth
22 Mar	H	Bedford	11-32	*T:* Hill *P:* Ashworth, Binns
5 Apr	A	Coventry	15-21	*T:* Buzza, Miller *C:* Binns *P:* Binns
12 Apr	A	London Scottish	3-25	*P:* Moffatt
19 Apr	H	Newcastle	21-45	*T:* Heaselgrave 2 *C:* Moffatt *P:* Moffatt 3
26 Apr	A	Moseley	17-48	*T:* Easterby, Heaselgrave, Sinclair *C:* Ashworth
4 May	A	Newcastle	13-61	*T:* Lax, Moffatt *P:* Lax

Rugby

Year of formation 1873, reformed 1994
Ground Webb Ellis Road, Rugby Tel: Rugby (01788) 542433
Colours Orange, black and white
Captain 1996-97 D Bishop
Courage Leagues 1996-97 Div 2 11th – *relegated* Pilkington Cup 1996-97 Lost 8-84 to Wasps (5th round)

It was the season's most stunning scoreline, one which would have driven many others clubs, not to mention players, to turn their face to the wall and wish it were all over. But somehow Rugby managed to confront the world after their record 156-5 destruction by Newcastle. Admittedly it was only a minor recovery – Rugby did concede 1,060 points in their 22 matches – but the humour and spirit shown in the wake of the defeat indicates that there is a resilient core at the club. Now they will need all their reserves of energy to cope with relegation. The club had won promotion the year before and with a clutch of representative players on their books would have expected better.

League Record 1996-97

Date	Venue	Opponents	Result	Scorers
7 Sept	A	London Scottish	7-43	*T:* Broady *C:* Quantrill
14 Sept	H	Coventry	3-61	*P:* Cummins
21 Sept	A	Rotherham	18-49	*T:* Bale 2, Bishop *D:* Kennedy
29 Sept	H	Bedford	6-34	*P:* Quantrill 2
5 Oct	A	Newcastle	5-156	*T:* Pell
12 Oct	H	Moseley	29-22	*T:* Saunders 3, Smith *P:* Quantrill 3
19 Oct	A	Richmond	8-64	*T:* Bale *P:* Quantrill
26 Oct	H	Wakefield	17-22	*T:* Carter, Saunders, pen try *C:* Quantrill
3 Nov	A	Blackheath	33-24	*T:* Bale 3, Baker, Cummins *C:* Quantrill 4
9 Nov	H	Nottingham	20-12	*T:* Baker, Curll *C:* Quantrill 2 *P:* Quantrill 2
16 Nov	H	Waterloo	15-56	*T:* Gallagher, Oram *C:* Quantrill *P:* Quantrill
18 Jan	A	Bedford	6-57	*P:* Quantrill 2
8 Feb	H	Newcastle	8-70	*T:* Glover *P:* Quantrill
23 Feb	A	Coventry	10-24	*T:* Bale *C:* Quantrill *P:* Quantrill
8 Mar	A	Moseley	11-34	*T:* Harrison *P:* Quantrill 2
15 Mar	H	Rotherham	16-41	*T:* Barr *C:* Barr *P:* Barr 3
22 Mar	H	Richmond	31-72	*T:* Milner 2, Jones, Glover, N Smith *C:* Barr 2, Quantrill
29 Mar	H	London Scottish	16-45	*T:* Quantrill *C:* Barr *P:* Barr 3
5 Apr	A	Wakefield	12-53	*T:* Milner, Saunders *C:* Barr
12 Apr	H	Blackheath	24-32	*T:* Milner, Oram, Saunders *C:* Barr 3 *P:* Barr
19 Apr	A	Nottingham	10-44	*T:* Barr, Saunders
26 Apr	A	Waterloo	12-45	*T:* Barr, Saunders *C:* Barr

Sale

Year of formation 1861
Ground Heywood Road, Brooklands, Sale, Cheshire Tel: 0161 973 6348
Colours Blue and white
Captain 1996-97 J Mallinder
Courage Leagues 1996-97 Div 1 5th **Pilkington Cup 1996-97** Lost 3-9 to Leicester (final)

Perhaps we should put our handkerchiefs away when we mourn the loss of Orrell, buckling under the pressures of the big money league. Sale did not have any more resources to play with; yet they enjoyed their most memorable season ever. They came so close to European glory, missing out on the fourth qualifying place when Leicester somehow held them to a draw on the last Saturday. The disappointing Pilkington Cup final was a game too far for them. It did not show them at their best.

Many thought the departure of their talisman fly-half Paul Turner to Bedford would trigger a decline in the club's fortunes. Far from it. The legacy of Turner's enterprising, confident style of play was not wasted. Indeed it was built upon the arrival of John Mitchell from Waikato as well as that of fellow New Zealander, fly-half Simon Mannix.

Sale had many promises of backers but it was not until the season's end that one finally came into view. They had to make do with shrewd nurturing and spotting of talent. They put together a formidable combination with real presence in the pack through the likes of second rows Dave Baldwin and John Fowler, the latter cruelly and seriously injured just as his name was announced in the England party to tour Argentina. Baldwin was a late call-up to the tour, belated but heartily deserved recognition of his talents. Charlie Vyvyan is one of the most underrated No 8s in the country. A broken ankle sustained in the last League match kept him out of the Pinkington Cup final. Sale badly missed him. The half-back combination of veteran Dewi Morris, brought out of retirement, and Mannix was irresistible. Dual Welsh international, Adrian Hadley, also the Sale team manager, brought the best out of the youngsters around him: Tom Beim and David Rees on the wings and Jos Baxendell alongside in the centre. Captain Jim Mallinder at full-back fully merited his call-up to the England tour squad and was also close to making the Lions party.

League Record 1996-97

Date	Venue	Opponents	Result	Scorers
31 Aug	H	Wasps	31-33	*T:* Beim 2, O'Grady, Rees *C:* Stocks *P:* Stocks 3
7 Sept	A	Gloucester	16-12	*T:* Diamond *C:* Griffin *P:* Griffin 3
14 Sept	H	West Hartlepool	58-18	*T:* Baxendell 2, Morris 2, Warr 2, Vyvyan, Rees, Verbickas *C:* Verbickas 5 *P:* Verbickas
21 Sept	A	London Irish	25-19	*T:* Ryan, Stocks, Warr *C:* Stocks 2 *P:* Stocks, Verbickas
28 Sept	H	Bristol	31-33	*T:* A Morris, Mallinder, Ryan, pen try *C:* Stocks *P:* Stocks 3
5 Oct	A	Northampton	12-30	*T:* Mallinder, Ryan *C:* Verbickas
30 Oct	H	Harlequins	24-13	*T:* D Morris 2, Vyvyan *P:* Mannix 3
9 Nov	H	Orrell	37-11	*T:* O'Grady 2, Baldwin, Beim, Erskine *C:* Mannix 3 *P:* Mannix 2
8 Dec	A	Saracens	17-17	*T:* McCartney *P:* Mannix 4
18 Jan	A	Orrell	40-8	*T:* Mannix 2, D Morris 2, A Smith, Beim, Mallinder, O'Grady
8 Feb	A	Harlequins	31-30	*T:* Baldwin 2, Fowler, Vyvyan *C:* Hadley *P:* Hadley 2 *D:* Yates
4 Mar	A	Leicester	9-25	*P:* Mannix 3
9 Mar	H	Northampton	31-15	*T:* Yates, Mannix *P:* Mannix 7

147

Date	Venue	Opponents	Result	Scorers
22 Mar	A	Bristol	24-34	*T:* Yates, Mallinder *C:* Verbickas *P:* Verbickas 4
2 Apr	H	Bath	11-5	*T:* Beim *P:* Mannix 2
5 Apr	A	West Hartlepool	43-22	*T:* Beim 3, D Morris, Mannix, Mitchell, Rees *C:* Mannix 4
12 Apr	H	Gloucester	52-12	*T:* Beim 2, Mannix 2, Erskine, Fowler, Hadley, pen try *C:* Mannix 6
15 Apr	H	Saracens	33-23	*T:* Driver 2, Yates, Hadley *C:* Mannix 2 *P:* Mannix 3
20 Apr	A	Wasps	10-36	*T:* Beim *C:* Hadley *P:* Mannix
23 Apr	H	London Irish	41-25	*T:* Beim 2, Rees 2, Erskine, Mallinder *C:* Hadley 4 *P:* Hadley
26 Apr	A	Bath	7-84	*T:* Hewson *C:* Griffin
3 May	H	Leicester	20-20	*T:* Mannix, Winstanley *C:* Mannix 2 *P:* Mannix 2

Saracens

Year of formation 1876
Ground The Stadium, Southbury Road, Enfield, Middlesex Tel: 0181 292 0665
Colours Black with red star and crescent
Captain 1996-97 A Diprose
Courage Leagues 1996-97 Div 1 6th **Pilkington Cup 1996-97** Lost 21-28 to Harlequins (quarter-final)

It began so well with victory, 25-23, on the opening day over Leicester in front of a full house at their new home at Enfield FC, but tailed away into anti-climax as injuries and lack of cover in critical positions took their toll. Saracens finished well outside the honours, a massive disappointment to the fans, one of whom, Nigel Wray had shelled out £2m in November 1995 in a bid to project the cosy little North London club onto the big stage. His bold initiative as one of the first to pledge money to an uncertain future looked as if it might pay off handsomely as a galaxy of stars arrived at what had been the First Division's most homespun club. Michael Lynagh and Philippe Sella were first to arrive and were followed in a mid-season coup by perhaps the most sensational signing of all – former Springbok captain, Francois Pienaar. Overnight Saracens went from cottage industry to blue chip trading company. There were also a host of other signings as Saracens ensured that never again would they have to put up with other clubs poaching the talent they had carefully groomed. In recent years they had lost Ben Clarke to Bath, Jason Leonard to Harlequins and Dean Ryan to Wasps. Now the boot was on the other foot. Kyran Bracken (Bristol), Paul Wallace (Blackrock), Richard Wallace (Garryowen) and Paddy Johns, among others, all beat a path to Saracens. But a mid-season injury to Lynagh halted the momentum, and Saracens finished sixth, buoyed a little by a last-day 36-29 win over Bath.

Saracens are hellbent on improving their lot, and they certainly have grounds for optimism. Tony Diprose is an outstanding No 8 and Richard Hill richly deserved his call-up to the England openside. Francois Pienaar took over as player-coach towards the end of the season. During the summer it was announced that Saracens would move out of their Enfield base and link with Watford FC.

League Record 1996-97

Date	Venue	Opponents	Result	Scorers
31 Aug	H	Leicester	25-23	*T:* Bracken *C:* Lynagh *P:* Lynagh 5 *D:* Tunningley
8 Sept	A	Wasps	21-36	*T:* Hill, pen try *C:* Tunningley *P:* Lynagh 2, Tunningley

14 Sept	H	Gloucester	41-11	*T:* Copsey 2, Chesney, P Wallace, R Wallace *C:* Lee 5 *P:* Lee 2
21 Sept	A	West Hartlepool	16-25	*T:* Ebongalame, R Wallace *P:* Tunningley 2
28 Sept	A	London Irish	37-23	*T:* Ebongalame, Hill, Johns, R Wallace, Ravenscroft *C:* Tunningley 2, Lee *P:* Tunningley *D:* Tunningley
5 Oct	A	Bristol	21-11	*T:* Chesney 2, Lee *P:* Tunningley, Lee
29 Oct	H	Northampton	24-23	*T:* Ebongalame, Ravenscroft, Sella *P:* Lynagh 3
8 Dec	H	Sale	17-17	*T:* Oliver *P:* Lynagh 4
4 Jan	A	Bath	33-35	*T:* Clark, Diprose, R Wallace, Smith *C:* Lynagh 2 *P:* Lynagh 3
19 Jan	H	Harlequins	28-20	*T:* Copsey, Diprose, Sella *C:* Lynagh 2 *P:* Lynagh 2 *D:* Lynagh
8 Feb	A	Northampton	10-17	*T:* Sella *C:* Lynagh *P:* Lynagh
4 Mar	H	Orrell	24-15	*T:* Copsey, Diprose *C:* Lynagh *P:* Lynagh 4
9 Mar	H	Bristol	33-15	*T:* Clark, P Wallace, Sella, Singer *C:* Lee 2 *P:* Lee 3
30 Mar	H	West Hartlepool	51-8	*T:* Bracken, Diprose, Friel, P Wallace, Lee, Ravenscroft, Sella, Tunningley *C:* Lee 2, Lynagh 2 *P:* Lynagh
5 Apr	A	Gloucester	6-9	*P:* Lee, Tunningley
9 Apr	A	Harlequins	0-27	
12 Apr	H	Wasps	15-28	*T:* Botterman, Diprose *C:* Lee *P:* Lee
15 Apr	A	Sale	23-33	*T:* Botterman, R Wallace *C:* Lee 2 *P:* Lee 3
19 Apr	A	Leicester	18-22	*T:* Ebongalame, P Wallace, Pienaar *P:* Lynagh
26 Apr	A	Orrell	44-22	*T:* Johns, P Wallace, Pienaar, Singer, Hill, Sorrell, pen try *C:* Lee 3 *P:* Lee
30 Apr	H	London Irish	45-0	*T:* R Wallace 3, Tunningley 2, Olsen, Pienaar *C:* Lynagh 5
3 May	H	Bath	36-29	*T:* Pienaar, R Wallace, Singer, Tunningley *C:* Lynagh 2 *P:* Lynagh 4

Wakefield

Year of formation 1901
Ground Pinderfields Road, College Grove, Wakefield Tel: Wakefield (01924) 374801
Colours Black and gold
Captain 1996-97 S Croft
Courage Leagues 1996-97 Div 2 6th   **Pilkington Cup 1996-97** Lost 21-25 to Gloucester (quarter-final)

It was a mixed season for Wakefield statistically – 11 wins and 11 defeats – but one of hope nonetheless for the future. They could not compete with the big spenders, including neighbours Leeds, and so will have to be more content with their placing of sixth, level on points with the side above them, London Scottish. The true worth of the club was shown in the Cup where victories over Waterloo and Moseley took them into the quarter-finals. Along with Newcastle they were the only Second Division side to reach that stage. They then ran Gloucester all the way to the final whistle but finally lost 25-21. Dave Scully was once again a prominent figure at College Grove, his all-round excellence and spirit dutifully rewarded with a place in the England team at the World Cup Sevens in Hong Kong. The deep human resources of the club should ensure that they once again cope with the invasion of men waving chequebooks. This is a club with great heart.

League Record 1996-97

Date	Venue	Opponents	Result	Scorers
7 Sept	A	Moseley	30-17	*T:* Hendry, Scully, Thompson, White *C:* Jackson, Scully *P:* Jackson, Scully

14 Sept	H	London Scottish	27-30	*T:* Massey, Scully *C:* Jackson *P:* Jackson 5
21 Sept	A	Coventry	25-24	*T:* Garnett, Petyt, Rushworth *C:* Scully 2
				P: Scully 2
28 Sept	H	Rotherham	25-29	*T:* Massey, Petyt, Scully *C:* Scully 2
				P: Scully 2
5 Oct	A	Bedford	19-25	*T:* Lancaster, Scully *P:* Jackson 2 *D:* Jackson
12 Oct	H	Newcastle	17-47	*T:* Jackson, Manley *C:* Jackson 2 *P:* Jackson
19 Oct	H	Waterloo	45-12	*T:* Wynn 2, Garnett, Jones, Manley, pen tries 2
				C: Jackson 5
26 Oct	A	Rugby	22-17	*T:* Scully, Stewart, pen try *C:* Jackson 2
				P: Jackson
3 Nov	A	Nottingham	40-18	*T:* Jackson, Massey, Scully, Stewart, Wilson
				C: Jackson 3 *P:* Jackson 3
9 Nov	H	Richmond	7-23	*T:* Scully *C:* Jackson
16 Nov	A	Blackheath	17-13	*T:* McClarron *P:* Jackson 4
18 Jan	A	Rotherham	19-12	*T:* McClarron *C:* Jackson *P:* Jackson 4
8 Feb	H	Bedford	17-29	*T:* Thompson, pen try *C:* Jackson 2
				P: Jackson
8 Mar	A	Newcastle	10-57	*T:* Manley 2
22 Mar	A	Waterloo	11-16	*T:* Jackson *P:* Jackson 2
29 Mar	H	Moseley	13-42	*T:* Massey *C:* Jackson *P:* Jackson 2
31 Mar	A	London Scottish	3-34	*P:* Jackson
5 Apr	H	Rugby	53-12	*T:* Hendry 2, Massey 2, Croft, Garnett, Scully,
				Wilson *C:* Jackson 5 *P:* Jackson
12 Apr	H	Nottingham	31-16	*T:* Garnett, Scully, Shelford *C:* Jackson 2
				P: Jackson 4
19 Apr	A	Richmond	22-55	*T:* Jackson, Massey, White *C:* Jackson 2
				P: Jackson
26 Apr	H	Blackheath	14-11	*T:* Thompson, Wynn *C:* Jackson 2
3 May	H	Coventry	37-18	*T:* Hendry, Jackson, pen try, Manley,
				Maynard *C:* Jackson 3 *P:* Jackson 2

Wasps

Year of formation 1867
Grounds Repton Avenue, Sudbury, Middlesex Tel: 0181 902 4220;
Loftus Road, Shepherd's Bush
Colours Black with gold wasp on left breast
Captain 1996-97 L B N Dallaglio
Courage Leagues 1996-97 Div 1 *Winners*   Pilkington Cup 1996-97 Lost 17-21 to Saracens
(6th round)

The club that almost fell apart the year before truly found itself this time around. The departures of Rob Andrew, Dean Ryan and Steve Bates in the dramatic coup by Sir John Hall destabilised the club. Even though they rallied under the leadership of Lawrence Dallaglio, there was still serious concern as to whether they would be able to raise the capital to compete with the other monied London clubs. They were the last to get their finances in place, but the deal was worth the wait. Chris Wright of Chrysalis Records pumped in £3 million of his company's money. The deal also embraced a ground share with QPR, the other part of Wright's sporting portfolio. Wasps were impressive at Loftus Road where the bulk of the matches were played on Sundays. Harlequins lowered their colours, 17-19, in a game only matched for excitement by the 25-25 draw with Bath, a difficult conversion by Gareth Rees deep into injury time claiming a share of the spoils for Wasps.

Rees, the Canadian captain, was one of the rocks upon which Wasps built their season and secured only their second ever Championship. He willingly moved to full-back to allow the flowering talent of Alex King in at fly-half. Dallaglio's captaincy was an inspiration as was his play on the field. His colleagues in the back row, Chris Sheasby (arrived from Harlequins) and the unsung Buster White helped make for a formidable combination. The Wasps management team also deserve plaudits. When Va'aiga Tuigamala headed back to Rugby League after his four-month stint many thought Wasps would struggle, particularly as a long-term injury had sidelined Damien Hopley. Nigel Melville, the director of rugby, had already lined up a replacement, London Irish centre Rob Henderson. Kenny Logan was also an inspired late season signing. The backroom influence of coaches Roger Uttley and Rob Smith should also be applauded. The Scottish duo of Damian Cronin and Andy Reed also did a decent job for Wasps in shoring up the second row. Andy Gomarsall and Chris Sheasby won first caps during the season.

Wasps had a poor European campaign and failed to qualify for the knock-out stages. They lost at home to Cardiff and were hammered in Munster, although they then confounded the form book by shredding the reigning champions, Toulouse, 77-17. Wasps made an early exit in the Pilkington Cup, too, losing 21-17 to Saracens. At least they were free then to concentrate on the League. They most certainly did not waste the opportunity.

League Record 1996-97

Date	Venue	Opponents	Result	Scorers
31 Aug	A	Sale	33-31	T: Gomarsall 2, Sampson C: Rees 3 P: Rees 4
8 Sept	H	Saracens	36-21	T: Gomarsall, Mitchell, Rees P: Rees 6 D: King
14 Sept	A	Bath	40-36	T: Sheasby 2, Mitchell, Sampson C: Rees 4 P: Rees 3 D: King
22 Sept	H	Leicester	14-7	T: P Hopley P: Rees 3
28 Sept	A	Orrell	44-27	T: Roiser 2, Scrase 2, Sheasby, Tuigamala C: Rees 4 P: Rees 2
6 Oct	A	Gloucester	23-28	T: Gomarsall, Scrase C: Rees, King P: Rees 3
16 Nov	A	London Irish	22-20	T: Dallaglio, Roiser, Sampson C: Ufton 2 P: Ufton
7 Dec	H	Bristol	15-13	T: King, White C: Ufton P: King
28 Dec	H	Northampton	18-13	P: Rees 6
5 Jan	H	Harlequins	17-19	T: Cronin P: Rees 3 D: King
11 Jan	A	Bristol	41-18	T: Tuigamala 2, Greenstock, Reed, Roiser, Sheasby C: Rees 4 P: Rees
8 Feb	A	West Hartlepool	48-23	T: Gomarsall, Henderson, King, Mitchell, Sheasby, White, pen try C: Rees 5 P: Rees
23 Feb	H	West Hartlepool	36-12	T: Gregory, Reed, Rees, Sheasby, Ufton, pen try C: Rees 3
9 Mar	H	Gloucester	36-10	T: Greenstock, King, Roiser C: Rees 3 P: Rees 5
22 Mar	H	Orrell	62-5	T: Logan 5, Roiser 2, Greenstock, Scrivener C: Rees 6, King P: Rees
26 Mar	H	London Irish	31-18	T: Greenstock, pen tries 2 C: Rees 2 P: Rees 3 D: King
2 Apr	A	Leicester	12-18	P: Rees 4
6 Apr	H	Bath	25-25	T: King C: Rees P: Rees 6
12 Apr	A	Saracens	28-15	T: Logan 2, Sheasby C: Rees 2 P: Rees 3
20 Apr	H	Sale	36-10	T: Greenstock, Henderson, Logan, Roiser C: Rees 2 P: Rees 3 D: King
26 Apr	A	Northampton	26-15	T: Logan, Roiser C: Rees 2 P: Rees 4
3 May	A	Harlequins	42-22	T: Henderson 2, Logan 2, Green, Rees C: Rees 3 P: Rees 2

Waterloo

Year of formation 1882
Grounds St Anthony's Road, Blundellsands, Liverpool Tel: 0151 924 4552
Colours Green, red and white
Captain 1996-97 N Allott
Courage Leagues 1996-97 Div 2 9th   **Pilkington Cup 1996-97** Lost 17-22 to Wakefield
(5th round)

The going gets tougher. After an encouraging fifth place the year before Waterloo
might have hoped for better. They rarely managed to strike any sort of sustained
form, winning only eight matches in all. Now they know that they will have to recruit
aggressively if they are to get out of the lower half of the division, particularly as
there are some well-backed outfits heading their way from the lower divisions. The
dilemma is how to attract players to a club which has always been a model of good
management and self-sufficiency. Many of their own young stars have been targeted
by other clubs. Given that Sale have managed to pull themselves up against the odds
in recent years, there is no reason why Waterloo, a club with fine traditions, cannot
do so too.

League Record 1996-97

Date	Venue	Opponents	Result	Scorers
7 Sept	A	Newcastle	13-30	*T:* Blyth *C:* Handley *P:* Handley 2
14 Sept	H	Moseley	20-13	*T:* Beckett, White, Wright *C:* Handley *P:* Handley
21 Sept	A	London Scottish	30-42	*T:* D Thompson, White, Wright *C:* C Thompson 3 *P:* C Thompson 3
28 Sept	H	Coventry	17-36	*T:* Hayton, Hucker *C:* Handley 2 *P:* Handley
5 Oct	A	Rotherham	23-38	*T:* Coast, White *C:* C Thompson 2 *P:* C Thompson 3
12 Oct	H	Bedford	11-34	*T:* Blyth *P:* C Thompson *D:* Handley
19 Oct	A	Wakefield	12-45	*P:* C Thompson 4
26 Oct	H	Nottingham	19-20	*T:* Coast *C:* C Thompson *P:* C Thompson 4
3 Nov	A	Richmond	13-64	*T:* Blyth *C:* Emmett *P:* Emmett 2
9 Nov	H	Blackheath	16-10	*T:* Aitchison *C:* Handley *P:* Handley 3
16 Nov	A	Rugby	56-15	*T:* Coast 2, Stevenson 2, Aitchison, Blyth, Buckton, Handley *C:* Handley 5 *P:* Handley 2
18 Jan	A	Coventry	16-28	*T:* Blyth *C:* C Thompson *P:* C Thompson 3
8 Feb	H	Rotherham	23-27	*T:* Coast, Holt *C:* C Thompson 2 *P:* C Thompson 3
22 Feb	A	Moseley	13-17	*T:* Bruce *C:* C Thompson *P:* C Thompson 2
8 Mar	A	Bedford	6-38	*P:* Griffiths 2
22 Mar	H	Wakefield	16-11	*T:* Griffiths *C:* Griffiths *P:* Griffiths 3
5 Apr	A	Nottingham	33-13	*T:* Blyth, Handley, Pilecki, Woolf *C:* Griffiths 2 *P:* Griffiths 3
12 Apr	H	Richmond	29-58	*T:* Blyth, Morris, Wolfenden, pen try *C:* Griffiths 3 *P:* Griffiths
19 Apr	A	Blackheath	48-27	*T:* Wolfenden 2, Woolf 2, Bruce, Mullins *C:* Griffiths 6 *P:* Griffiths 2
26 Apr	H	Rugby	45-12	*T:* Mullins 2, Allott, Bruce, Buckton, Wood, Wright *C:* Griffiths 5
30 Apr	H	Newcastle	24-66	*T:* Buckton, Morris, Pilecki *P:* Griffiths 3
3 May	H	London Scottish	23-17	*T:* Wolfenden *P:* Griffiths 6

West Hartlepool

Year of formation 1881
Grounds Brierton Lane, Hartlepool Tel: Hartlepool (01429) 272640
Colours Red, white and green
Captain 1996-97 K Moseley
Courage Leagues 1996-97 Div 1 11th – *relegated* Pilkington Cup 1996-97 Lost 10-51 to Newcastle (5th round)

There was no reprieve this time around, no sympathetic ear in the committee rooms to listen to West's plea for clemency. The previous year West Hartlepool had been cast adrift at the bottom of the table, without a single point to show from their 18 matches. The last day decision to expand the First Division to 12 clubs allowed them a stay of execution. From the opening day it was obvious that they would do well to survive for another term. The club had had the smallest turnover of any in the previous year, less than £600,000.

There was a spirited attempt to raise the flag again with the appointment of former Welsh international, Mark Ring, as player-coach. Ring lured a few countrymen north with him, Kevin Moseley and Matthew Silva arriving at Brierton Lane. The one player to really attract the headlines was famous by name if not yet by deed. Liam Botham, son of the mighty Ian, made his debut during the year and went on to make the England U-21 squad as a centre. West were always up against it, however, lacking firepower up front and real finishing class behind. They did better than last time around, overcoming Bristol, 19-8, Orrell, 24-8, and, surprisingly, Saracens, 25-16, all at home.

The club parted company with Ring towards the end of the season and appointed former All Black, Mike Brewer to his post. Brewer had been assistant coach to the Irish team.

League Record 1996-97

Date	Venue	Opponents	Result	Scorers
31 Aug	A	Northampton	20-46	*T:* Ions, S John, Stabler *C:* Silva *P:* C John
7 Sept	H	Harlequins	21-41	*T:* S John 2 *C:* C John *P:* C John 3
14 Sept	A	Sale	18-58	*T:* S John, Silva *C:* C John *P:* C John 2
21 Sept	H	Saracens	25-16	*T:* C John, Morgan, Ring *C:* C John 2 *P:* C John 2
28 Sept	A	Bath	10-46	*T:* S John *C:* Silva *P:* C John
5 Oct	H	Leicester	19-30	*T:* Wood 2, S John *C:* C John 2
9 Nov	H	Gloucester	14-23	*T:* Wood *P:* C John 3
7 Dec	A	Orrell	15-22	*T:* Wood, Cordle *C:* C John *P:* Silva
28 Dec	A	London Irish	41-52	*T:* Ions, Morgan, Stabler, Connolly *C:* Stabler 3 *P:* Stabler 5
4 Jan	H	Bristol	19-8	*T:* Connolly *C:* Stabler *P:* Stabler 3, Silva
11 Jan	H	Orrell	24-8	*T:* Earnshaw 2, Botham, Harvey *C:* Stabler 2
18 Jan	A	Gloucester	10-37	*T:* C John *C:* Stabler *P:* Stabler
8 Feb	H	Wasps	23-48	*T:* C John, Botham, Peacock *C:* C John *P:* C John 2
23 Feb	A	Wasps	12-36	*T:* S John 2 *C:* C John
8 Mar	A	Leicester	3-48	*P:* C John
22 Mar	A	Harlequins	10-48	*T:* Earnshaw, S John
27 Mar	H	Bath	16-24	*T:* S John, Barnes *P:* C John 2
30 Mar	A	Saracens	8-51	*T:* Moseley *P:* C John
5 Apr	H	Sale	22-43	*T:* S John 2 *P:* C John 4
19 Apr	H	Northampton	17-57	*T:* Silva 2 *C:* C John 2 *P:* C John
26 Apr	H	London Irish	18-33	*T:* D Mitchell, S John *C:* C John *P:* C John 2
4 May	A	Bristol	17-20	*T:* Ions *P:* C John 3 *D:* C John

OASIS IN THE DESERT

THE 1996-97 SEASON IN SCOTLAND
Bill McMurtie

Scotland's overwhelming victory against Ireland by 38-10 at Murrayfield in March was an oasis in a desert of despairing results on the international field. In the twelve months under review the Scots won only two of the eight internationals they played – an edgy victory against Italy, and that refreshing glimpse of potential against Ireland.

That game was Scotland's biggest score and widest margin in 58 victories against Ireland, but it was not just the extent of the victory that was so pleasing. The Scots displayed a killer instinct that has been all too rare in British Isles rugby over the years. When the Irish were down the Scots did not leave them there; they buried them.

An interval score of 7-7 was neither a reflection of Ireland's first-half fervour nor a hint of what was to follow. Peter Walton's try, just as the hour approached, edged Scotland ahead to 17-10, but the storm was unleashed only in the final quarter of an hour as Doddie Weir, Gregor Townsend and Tony Stanger hammered in the coffin nails.

Perhaps the Scots had learned lessons from defeats in their two previous Five Nations Championship matches. Inside just five minutes of the second half in the opening match a Scottish lead of 16-10 was overturned into a 15-point deficit as Wales ran in three tries on their way to a 34-19 victory, their first Murrayfield win since 1985. Neil Jenkins ignited that Welsh fire with a try as well as converting all three, the other tries being scored by the opportunist Arwel Thomas and the ever-ready Ieuan Evans.

Worse was to follow two weeks later against England at Twickenham. Not only did Scotland concede an early penalty try – a decision by New Zealand referee Paddy O'Brien that was without foundation in law – but they were again struck by three quick-fire tries. However, the circumstances at Twickenham were different. Jenkins, Thomas and Evans had turned the Murrayfield match for Wales whereas England were coasting at 22-13 when Andy Gomarsall, Will Carling and Phil de Glanville struck the killer blows for a 41-13 victory.

A month later Scotland's performance against Ireland raised hopes of further redemption in Paris. However, France, with a Grand Slam in sight, were not to be denied. Even the defeated Scots had to marvel at the French fluency in a 47-20 victory. Christophe Lamaison kicked 24 of the French points, though his

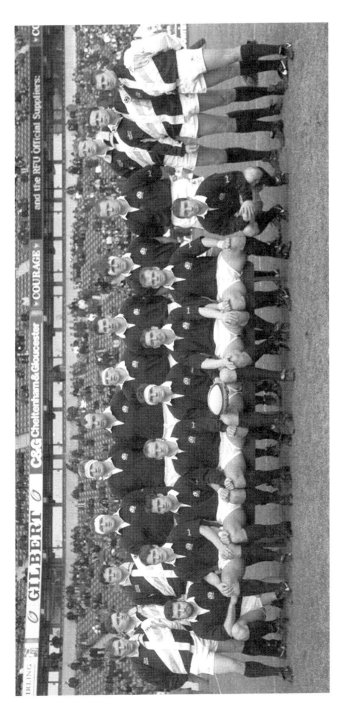

The Scotland team which lost to England at Twickenham. L-R, back row: G Armstrong (replacement), D I W Hilton (replacement), S J Brotherstone (replacement), P Walton, G W Weir, A I Reed, D G Ellis, D A Stark, T J Smith, M J Stewart, D S Munro (replacement), S Hastings (replacement), C M Chalmers (replacement); front row: B R S Eriksson, A G Stanger, K M Logan, G P J Townsend, R I Wainwright (capt), I R Smith, R J S Shepherd, B W Redpath.

personal success was soured by his citing and subsequent suspension because of a 'spear' tackle that concussed Craig Chalmers.

Few Scots stamped their marks on the championship, though Alan Tait was one exception. The former Kelso centre, the first Rugby League escapee to return to Scotland's XV, justified his recall with his performances against England, Ireland, and Wales, and his Newcastle colleague, Doddie Weir, did much to keep the Scots in contention in the line-out contests. However, the breakaway blend was not of the consistency so necessary for success, whatever the level, and that undoubtedly was a reason why one of that back-row number, Rob Wainwright, Scotland's captain, did not go on to take command of the Lions.

Scotland's year under review began in New Zealand with two Test defeats by the All Blacks – 62-31 in Dunedin, 36-12 in Auckland. It was an incidental that the Scots' score in the first Test was their highest in any match against New Zealand, and when international rugby resumed at Murrayfield in November the southern hemisphere again came out on top, Australia winning 29-19. Five weeks later, again at Murrayfield, Scotland beat Italy 29-22, but it was a win rather than a success; victory was secured only with Derek Stark's late try.

In sub-international rugby Scottish teams scored two memorable triumphs. Scotland A overwhelmed Emerging Wales by 56-11 at Goldenacre, Edinburgh, with three of their seven tries scored by the 19-year-old West of Scotland wing, James Craig, whose father, Jim, was part of Celtic's European Cup winning team in 1967. A week after the delights against Ireland at Murrayfield the young Scottish hopes for the future won their Under-19 encounter with England's by 26-18 at Balgray, Glasgow.

However, Scotland A won only two of their six matches – their other victory was against South Africa A by 32-19 at Hawick. The Under-21 Scots had a sole success in five matches – 41-15 against Italy at Inverleith, the old international ground in Edinburgh – and the Under-19 team could not follow up their success against England when they went to Buenos Aires for the FIRA junior tournament. They finished sixth, with wins against Portugal (56-3) and Italy (34-7) balanced by losses to Ireland (8-22) and South Africa (11-43).

Scottish rugby's entry into the Heineken Cup was no more successful. The Borders' 24-16 victory over Llanelli at Hawick was the only Scottish win in 12 matches, with Edinburgh and Caledonia failing to win a game, although the latter had a close game with Brive, the French club who went on to win the trophy. Glasgow, competing in the second-tier European Conference, achieved a runaway win at Newbridge to open their campaign but lost their four other matches.

Caledonia won the Inter-District title, beating Glasgow 20-14 in the decider. The change of name from North and Midlands brought immediate success, as it was the first time in the championship's 54 years that the title had gone across the Forth. Indeed, the bulk of the district trophies went that way as Caledonia took also the Under-21 and Under-19 championships and Midlands won the District Union and schools titles.

Melrose scored a clean sweep in club rugby, winning the Premier and Border Leagues and the Cup as well as their own sevens. Kelso, though, were the most successful in the abbreviated game, winning the Kings of the Sevens trophy by taking the prizes in the last four tournaments of the circuit – at Hawick, Jed-Forest, Langholm and Earlston.

SRU TENNENTS CHAMPIONSHIP REVIEW

Melrose swept all before them by winning every one of their 14 matches in retaining the SRU Tennents Premiership trophy, the sixth time in eight years that the Border club had taken the title. It was only the third time any club had gone through the First Division with a 100% record, Melrose matching Hawick's achievements in 1975-76 and 1983-84.

Only Watsonians ran Melrose close. The Myreside club lost only their two games against Melrose, and even in the first month of the season the race for the championship was developing into a 'two horse' contest. After three rounds of matches only Melrose and Hawick had maximum points. Melrose had already scored their first victory over Watsonians, albeit by only 27-26 in an exciting encounter at Myreside, with the defending champions notching four tries to two.

Melrose had set the pace with a 107-10 victory over Stirling County at the Greenyards on the opening day of the championship, with Scott Nichol scoring five of their 16 tries. Thereafter, even discounting that century, the champions averaged more than 36 points per match, and only three times were they held to winning margins in single figures – the two games against Watsonians and the home match against Boroughmuir, when the visitors scored three tries to one in a 19-23 defeat.

Hawick, after winning their first three matches, dropped away with six successive defeats. It was left to Currie to hang in closest to the two front-runners. After seven games their only loss was at Melrose, and the Malleny Park club finished third with five defeats – two each against the top pair and one away to Boroughmuir. Currie's successes included an overwhelming victory over Hawick by 61-10 at home, substantially the heaviest defeat the once perennial champions had suffered in the championship's 24 seasons.

Boroughmuir and Stirling County, the only clubs to interrupt Melrose's championship run in the past eight years, failed to set the heather on fire. Boroughmuir, champions in 1991, had a characteristic up-and-down season which opened with a 23-20 home defeat by Hawick and included only six wins whereas Stirling, winners of the title in 1995, suffered from the absence of established players in picking up only five League points, three of those from their two games against Boroughmuir. Reorganisation of the League saved both Stirling and Heriot's from relegation to the Second Division.

Edinburgh Academicals and West of Scotland secured promotion to the First Division, though the latter clinched their spot only with David Barrett's last-kick penalty goal for a 15-13 victory over Dundee High School FP in the second-place decider. Kirkcaldy and Gordonians took the respective titles in the Third and Fourth Divisions of the Premiership. Only Melrose of the competition's 11 division champions had a 100% record, but three clubs took National League titles with only one defeat apiece – Hutchesons'/Aloysians in the second, Annan in the third, and Garnock in the fifth.

SRU TENNENTS PREMIERSHIP

Division 1	P	W	D	L	F	A	Pts
Melrose	14	14	0	0	582	215	28
Watsonians	14	12	0	2	587	226	24
Currie	14	9	0	5	379	259	18
Boroughmuir	14	6	1	7	394	325	13
Hawick	14	5	0	9	268	397	10
Jed-Forest	14	4	0	10	217	509	8
Heriot's FP	14	3	0	11	224	416	6
Stirling County	14	2	1	11	220	524	5

Previous champions: Hawick 10 times, 1973-74 to 1977-78, 1981-82, 1983-84 to 1986-87; Gala 3 times, 1979-80, 1980-81, and 1982-83; Melrose 6 times, 1989-90, 1991-92 to 1993-94, 1995-96 & 1996-97; Kelso twice, 1987-88, 1988-89; Heriot's FP 1978-79; Boroughmuir 1990-91; Stirling County 1994-95

Division 2	P	W	D	L	F	A	Pts
Edinburgh Acads	14	11	0	3	388	187	22
West of Scotland	14	10	1	3	395	264	21
Dundee HS FP	14	10	1	3	334	205	21
GHK	14	8	1	5	337	265	17
Glasgow Acads	14	6	0	8	292	339	12
Kelso	14	5	0	9	308	431	10
Gala	14	2	1	11	314	392	5
Biggar	14	2	0	12	187	472	4

Division 3	P	W	D	L	F	A	Pts
Kirkcaldy	14	12	0	2	493	203	24
Kilmarnock	14	10	0	4	346	298	20
Preston Lodge FP	14	9	0	5	358	287	18
Peebles	14	8	0	6	305	304	16
Musselburgh	14	7	0	7	283	261	14
Selkirk	14	6	0	8	288	348	12
Glasgow Southern	14	2	0	12	249	335	4
Stewart's Melville FP	14	2	0	12	199	485	4

Division 4	P	W	D	L	F	A	Pts
Gordonians	14	12	0	2	296	205	24
Ayr	14	9	0	5	283	205	18
Hillhead/Jordanhill	14	8	1	5	388	222	17
Grangemouth	14	8	1	5	255	228	17
Glenrothes	14	6	1	7	247	211	13
Corstorphine	14	5	1	8	245	260	11
Langholm	14	3	0	11	206	305	6
Haddington	14	2	2	10	177	461	6

SRU TENNENTS NATIONAL LEAGUE

Division 1	P	W	D	L	F	A	Pts
Aberdeen GS FP	18	16	0	2	608	189	32
Stewartry	18	13	0	5	513	247	26
East Kilbride	18	10	2	6	466	330	22
Dunfermline	18	10	1	7	436	376	21
Duns	18	10	1	7	467	415	21
Trinity Acads	18	8	3	7	526	332	19
Edinburgh U	18	7	0	11	397	397	14
Portobello FP	18	6	1	11	222	464	13
Edinburgh Wands	18	4	2	12	220	414	10
Wigtownshire*	18	1	0	17	187	878	-1

Division 2	P	W	D	L	F	A	Pts
Hutchesons'/Aloysians	18	17	0	1	620	196	34
Berwick	18	15	0	3	743	199	30
Livingston	18	12	0	6	443	306	24
Dalziel	18	9	0	9	410	282	18

Royal High	18	9	0	9	316	332	18
Cambuslang	18	8	0	10	297	386	16
St Boswells	18	7	0	11	339	590	14
Allan Glen's	18	6	0	12	319	501	12
Dumfries*	18	4	1	13	231	542	7
Ardrossan Acads	18	2	1	15	176	560	5

Division 3	P	W	D	L	F	A	Pts
Annan	18	17	0	1	580	184	34
Howe of Fife	18	13	0	5	379	277	26
Linlithgow	17	11	1	5	413	245	23
Lismore	18	10	1	7	334	274	21
Morgan Acad FP	17	10	0	7	386	312	20
Perthshire	18	9	0	9	482	399	18
Cartha Queen's Pk	18	8	0	10	329	358	16
Alloa	18	4	0	14	194	585	8
Leith Academicals	17	3	0	14	243	468	6
Cumbernauld	17	2	0	15	181	419	4

Division 4	P	W	D	L	F	A	Pts
Ross High	18	15	1	2	644	157	31
Madras College FP	18	15	1	2	496	241	31
Highland	17	10	0	7	334	285	20
Clydebank	18	8	2	8	284	263	18
Penicuik	18	8	1	9	336	385	17
Aberdeenshire	18	8	0	10	359	325	16
Hillfoots	18	8	0	10	287	413	16
Paisley	18	6	1	11	210	335	13
North Berwick*	18	5	1	12	354	561	9
Waysiders/Drumpellier	17	2	1	14	173	512	5

Division 5	P	W	D	L	F	A	Pts
Garnock	18	17	0	1	738	130	34
Murrayfield	18	12	1	5	552	238	25
Lochaber	18	10	1	7	417	270	21
Falkirk	18	10	1	7	314	349	21
Lenzie	18	10	0	8	313	337	20
Dunbar	18	8	0	10	463	449	16
Greenock Wands	18	8	0	10	246	447	16
Aberdeen U*	18	6	0	12	353	494	10
Irvine*	18	5	1	12	245	625	9
Forrester FP	18	2	0	16	233	535	4

Division 6	P	W	D	L	F	A	Pts
Whitecraigs	16	13	0	3	379	162	26
Lasswade	16	13	0	3	354	166	26
Earlston	16	10	0	6	305	218	20
Moray	16	8	1	7	304	321	17
RAF Kinloss	16	6	1	9	232	244	13
Marr	16	6	0	10	205	283	12
Cumnock	16	6	0	10	206	289	12
St Andrews U	16	6	0	10	253	364	12
Inverleith	16	3	0	13	174	365	6

(Walkerburn were relegated to Division 7 for failing to fulfil fixtures. Their matches played were deducted from the Division 6 table.)

Division 7	P	W	D	L	F	A	Pts
Carnoustie HS FP	18	16	0	2	493	203	32
Helensburgh	18	15	1	2	537	124	31
Hamilton Acads	18	13	1	3	627	149	28
Panmure	18	9	1	8	378	272	19
RAF Lossiemouth*	18	10	0	8	481	257	18
Broughton FP	18	8	0	10	239	265	16
Dalkeith	18	5	0	13	230	483	10
Rosyth & District	18	5	0	13	189	486	10
Harris Acad FP*	18	5	0	13	193	652	8
Waid Acad FP*	18	2	0	16	206	682	2

(*Wigtownshire, Dumfries, North Berwick, Aberdeen University, Irvine, RAF Lossiemouth, Harris, and Waid each forfeited two championship points for failing to fulfil a fixture)

District League Champions
Edinburgh: Heriot-Watt University
Glasgow: Newton Stewart
Midlands: Strathmore
North: Orkney

Newton Stewart and Orkney won promotion to the National League's Seventh Division through a round-robin competition contested by the four District League champions.

BANK OF SCOTLAND BORDER LEAGUE

	P	W	D	L	F	A	B	Pts
Melrose	14	12	0	2	485	200	17	55
Gala	14	9	0	5	459	265	15	47
Jed-Forest	14	9	0	5	404	299	13	45
Hawick	14	7	0	7	361	270	9	37
Kelso	14	9	0	5	319	312	5	37
Peebles	14	4	0	10	260	497	1	23
Langholm	14	3	0	11	167	407	1	21
Selkirk	14	3	0	11	195	400	1	21

INTER-DISTRICT CHAMPIONSHIP

	P	W	D	L	F	A	Pts
Caledonia	3	2	1	0	77	53	5
Glasgow	3	2	0	1	73	57	4
Borders	3	1	1	1	65	71	3
Edinburgh	3	0	0	3	35	69	0

SCOTTISH INTER-DISTRICT CHAMPIONSHIP 1996-97

22 December, Murrayfield

Caledonia 26 (2G 4PG)   **Scottish Borders 26** (2G 4PG)
Caledonia: S A D Burns (Edinburgh Academicals); S Longstaff (Dundee HS FP), P R Rouse (Dundee HS FP), A K Carruthers (Kirkcaldy), J A Kerr (Watsonians); M McKenzie (Stirling County), P M S Simpson (Edinburgh Academicals); T J Smith (Watsonians), K D McKenzie (Stirling County), D J Herrington (Kirkcaldy), S J Campbell (Melrose), S D Grimes (Watsonians), D J McIvor (Glenrothes) *(capt)*, M Waite (Edinburgh Academicals), G N Flockhart (Stirling County)   *Replacements* D Officer (Currie) for Kerr, J J Manson (Stirling County) for Herrington
Scorers *Tries:* Herrington, Longstaff   *Conversions:* M McKenzie (2)   *Penalty Goals:* M McKenzie (4)
Scottish Borders: C W Turnbull (Hawick); M Changleng (Gala), A G Stanger (Hawick), S A Nichol (Melrose), G A Parker (Melrose); W S Welsh (Hawick), B W Redpath (Melrose) *(capt)*; N A McIlroy (Jed-Forest), S J Brotherstone (Melrose), S W Ferguson (Peebles), S A Aitken (Melrose), C D Hogg (Melrose), S Bennet (Kelso), R M Kirkpatrick (Boroughmuir), N J R Broughton (Melrose)
Replacements I Elliot (Hawick for Broughton, G J Aitchison (Kelso) for Stanger
Scorers *Tries:* Stanger, Welsh   *Conversions:* Parker (2)   *Penalty Goals:* Parker (4)
Referee R J Megson (Edinburgh Wanderers)

22 December, Murrayfield

Edinburgh 13 (1G 2PG)   **Glasgow 23** (1G 1PG 1DG 2T)
Edinburgh: D J Lee (Watsonians); H R Gilmour (Heriot's FP), S Hastings (Watsonians) *(capt)*, M P Craig (Currie), S D Reed (Boroughmuir); D W Hodge (Watsonians), D W Patterson (Heriot's FP); R B McNulty (Boroughmuir), D G Ellis (Currie), B D Stewart (Edinburgh Academicals), D G Burns (Boroughmuir), A Lucking (Currie), M W Ward (Currie), S J Reid (Boroughmuir), G F Dall (Heriot's FP)
Replacements A D G Binnie (Heriot's FP) for McNulty, M W Blair (Currie) for Lucking (temp)
Scorers *Try:* Patterson   *Conversion:* Hodge   *Penalty Goals:* Hodge (2)
Glasgow: K M Logan (Stirling County); D A Stark (Melrose), A J Bulloch (West of Scotland), A R Garry (Watsonians), G H Metcalfe (Glasgow Academicals); G C MacGregor (Glasgow Academicals), F H Stott (West of Scotland); G R McIlwham (GHK), G C Bulloch (West of Scotland) *(capt)*, G B Robertson (Stirling County), D S Munro (GHK), S Begley (Glasgow Academicals), F D Wallace (GHK), D R McLeish (West of Scotland), M I Wallace (GHK)   *Replacement* C M Sangster (Stirling County) for A J Bulloch
Scorers *Tries:* Logan, MacGregor, Stark   *Conversion:* Logan   *Penalty Goal:* MacGregor
Dropped Goal: MacGregor
Referee K W McCartney (Hawick)

29 December, Murrayfield

Glasgow 36 (4G 1PG 1T)   **Scottish Borders 24** (3PG 3T)
Glasgow: K M Logan (Stirling County); D A Stark (Melrose), C M Sangster (Stirling County), A R Garry (Watsonians), J M Craig (West of Scotland); G C MacGregor (Glasgow Academicals), F H Stott (West of Scotland); G R McIlwham (GHK), G C Bulloch (West of Scotland) *(capt)*, G B Robertson (Stirling County), D S Munro (GHK), M Norval (Stirling County), F D Wallace (GHK), D R McLeish (West of Scotland), M I Wallace (GHK)
Scorers *Tries:* Craig (2), Logan (2), McLeish   *Conversions:* MacGregor (4)   *Penalty Goal:* MacGregor
Scottish Borders: C W Turnbull (Hawick); M Changleng (Gala), A G Stanger (Hawick), S A Nichol (Melrose), G A Parker (Melrose); W S Welsh (Hawick), B W Redpath (Melrose) *(capt)*; N A McIlroy (Jed-Forest), J A Hay (Hawick), S W Ferguson (Peebles), S A Aitken (Melrose), I Elliot (Hawick), S Bennet (Kelso), C D Hogg (Melrose), R M Kirkpatrick (Boroughmuir)   *Replacements* G J Aitchison (Kelso) for Turnbull, K Davidson (Langholm) for Changleng
Scorers *Tries:* Bennet, Davidson, Nichol   *Penalty Goals:* Parker (3)
Referee J M Fleming (Boroughmuir)

29 December, Murrayfield

Caledonia 31 (2PG 5T)   **Edinburgh 13** (1G 2PG)
Caledonia: R J S Shepherd (Melrose); S Longstaff (Dundee HS FP), P R Rouse (Dundee HS FP), A K Carruthers (Kirkcaldy), J A Kerr (Watsonians); M McKenzie (Stirling County), P M S Simpson (Edinburgh Academicals); T J Smith (Watsonians), K D McKenzie (Stirling County), D J Herrington (Kirkcaldy), S J Campbell (Melrose), S D Grimes (Watsonians), D J McIvor (Glenrothes) *(capt)*, G N Flockhart (Stirling Counth), R I Wainwright (Watsonians)   *Replacements* B R Easson (Edinburgh Academicals) for M McKenzie, I A Fullarton (Dundee HS FP) for Flockhart
Scorers *Tries:* Carruthers, Longstaff, K D McKenzie, M McKenzie, Rouse   *Penalty Goals:* Shepherd (2)
Edinburgh: D J Lee (Watsonians); H R Gilmour (Heriot's FP), S Hastings (Watsonians) *(capt)*, M P Craig (Currie), S D Reed (Boroughmuir); D W Hodge (Watsonians), D W Patterson (Heriot's FP); B D Stewart (Edinburgh Academicals) and Currie, D G Ellis (Currie), S W Paul (Heriot's FP), D G Burns (Boroughmuir), A Lucking (Currie), C G Mather (Watsonians), S J Reid (Boroughmuir), G F Dall (Heriot's FP)
Replacements G Beveridge (Boroughmuir) for Patterson, A Donaldson (Currie) for Hastings

Scorers *Try:* Mather *Conversion:* Hodge *Penalty Goals:* Hodge (2)
Referee E Murray (Greenock Wanderers)

---

5 January, Murrayfield

Glasgow 14 (2G) **Caledonia 20** (1G 1PG 2T)
Glasgow: K M Logan (Stirling County); D A Stark (Melrose), C M Sangster (Stirling County), A R Garry (Watsonians), J M Craig (West of Scotland); G C MacGregor (Glasgow Academicals), F H Stott (West of Scotland); G R McIlwham (GHK), G C Bulloch (West of Scotland) (*capt*), G B Robertson (Stirling County), D S Munro (GHK), M Norval (Stirling County), F D Wallace (GHK), D R McLeish (West of Scotland), M I Wallace (GHK) *Replacements* G T Mackay (Glasgow Academicals) for McLeish, G H Metcalfe (Glasgow Academicals) for Garry, D Porte (Glasgow Academicals) for Bulloch (temp)
Scorers *Tries:* Craig, Stark *Conversions:* Logan (2)
Caledonia: S A D Burns (Edinburgh Academicals); S Longstaff (Dundee HS FP), P R Rouse (Dundee HS FP), A K Carruthers (Kirkcaldy), J A Kerr (Watsonians); M McKenzie (Stirling County), P M S Simpson (Edinburgh Academicals); T J Smith (Watsonians), K D McKenzie (Stirling County), D J Herrington (Kirkcaldy), S J Campbell (Melrose), S D Grimes (Watsonians), D J McIvor (Glenrothes) (*capt*), G N Flockhart (Stirling County), R I Wainwright (Watsonians) *Replacements* J J Manson (Stirling County) for Herrington
Scorers *Tries:* Longstaff (2), Kerr *Conversion:* M McKenzie *Penalty Goal:* M McKenzie
Referee I Ramage (Berwick)

---

5 January, Poynder Park, Kelso

Scottish Borders 15 (1G 1PG 1T) **Edinburgh 9** (3PG)
Scottish Borders: K Davidson (Langholm); M Moncrieff (Melrose), A G Stanger (Hawick) (*capt*), S A Nichol (Melrose), W S Welsh (Hawick), I T Fairley (Kelso); N A McIlroy (Jed-Forest), S J Brotherstone (Melrose), P H Wright (Melrose), R R Brown (Melrose), I Elliot (Hawick), S Bennet (Kelso), R M Kirkpatrick (Boroughmuir), K Armstrong (Jed-Forest) *Replacement* S A Aitken (Melrose) for Bennet
Scorers *Tries:* Kirkpatrick, Moncrieff *Conversion:* Parker *Penalty Goal:* Parker
Edinburgh: D J Lee (Watsonians); I C Glasgow (Heriot's FP), S Hastings (Watsonians) (*capt*), M P Craig (Currie), E J Bunney (Heriot's FP); D W Hodge (Watsonians), G Beveridge (Boroughmuir); B D Stewart (Edinburgh Academicals), D G Ellis (Currie), S W Paul (Heriot's FP), S Murray (Bedford), A Lucking (Currie), B W Ward (Currie), S J Reid (Boroughmuir), G F Dall (Heriot's FP)
Scorers *Penalty Goals:* Hodge (3)
Referee S W Piercy (England)

SRU TENNENTS CUP 1996-97

10 May 1997, Murrayfield
Melrose 31 (1G 3PG 3T) Boroughmuir 23 (1G 2PG 2T)

Melrose completed a Grand Slam by beating Boroughmuir 31-23 before a Murrayfield crowd of about 23,000 in the SRU Tennents Cup final, adding to the Premier and Border League trophies and their own sevens prize. Rowen Shepherd, Melrose's international full-back, contributed no fewer than 26 of Melrose's 31 points, including three tries.

For close on an hour Boroughmuir were in with a strong shout, as Melrose had to come from behind three times – 0-8, 8-13 at half-time, and 13-16. Shepherd, however, killed off the Edinburgh club with a scoring surge of 18 points, his second and third tries sandwiching a brace of penalty goals.

His opposite number, Campbell Aitken, drew first blood with a penalty goal, and Ally McLean soon added a try, the lively young wing finishing off from Stuart Reid's long touchline thrust. Shepherd struck back with a penalty goal and a try to draw Melrose

161

level, but strong Boroughmuir pressure before half-time paid off through two former international backs, Sean Lineen's long pass putting Douglas Wyllie over.

Only two minutes after the interval Bryan Redpath, the Melrose captain and international scrum-half, and Ross Brown opened the way for Mark Moncrieff to cross, and although Aitken restored 'Muir's lead yet again, with his second penalty goal, Shepherd put his team ahead for the first time with his second try, when he overlapped Derek Stark. The full-back's third try, from a five-metre scrum in front of the posts, finished off the 'Muir challenge, though McLean jinked in late on for his second.

Melrose: R J S Shepherd; D A Stark, S A Nichol, R N C Brown, M Moncrieff; C M Chalmers, B W Redpath (*capt*); M G Browne, S J Brotherstone, P H Wright, R R Brown, S A Aitken, M J Donnan, C D Hogg, N J R Broughton
Scorers *Tries:* Shepherd (3), Moncrieff *Conversion:* Shepherd *Penalty Goals:* Shepherd (3)
Boroughmuir: C K Aitken; N C Renton, D L Laird, S R P Lineen, A R McLean; D S Wyllie, G Beveridge; S K Paris, K R Allan, A K Penman, D G Burns, G J McCallum, A M Cadzow, S J Reid (*capt*), R M Kirkpatrick
Replacements S L Wands for Kirkpatrick, D G Cunningham for Allan
Scorers *Tries:* McLean (2), Wyllie *Conversion:* Aitken *Penalty Goals:* Aitken (2)
Referee E Murray (Greenock Wanderers)

A field of 128 clubs contested the second staging of the Scottish Cup, with minnows from the District Leagues competing for the first time. One of those small fry, Hawick Linden, remained until the last 16, when they were eliminated on a visit to Dundee High School FP.

When the 'big guns' from the Premier First Division entered the fray in the fourth round, two of them, Hawick and Currie, did not survive a match. Hawick, who had beaten Watsonians in the 1996 final, fell by 6-19 against Boroughmuir, the eventual finalists, whereas Currie went out to a 20-32 defeat by Second Division Gala. Melrose and Watsonians, champions and runners-up respectively in the League, each recorded a half-century in that round, as did two Third Division clubs, Kirkcaldy and Glasgow Southern.

Melrose beat their neighbours, St Boswells, by 70-10 and followed up with a fractionally higher score in disposing of another Border club, Kelso, by 71-37. Watsonians, too, had two successive half-centuries, beating Hawick Linden 60-3 and Gala 59-20, but they succumbed in the next round, losing to their Boroughmuir neighbours by 29-42. Melrose marched on with a 45-23 win on their visit to West of Scotland, and Kirkcaldy became the first Third Division club to reach the semi-finals when they won their home match against Dundee High School FP by 33-18.

Boroughmuir and Melrose qualified for the final in contrasting styles. 'Muir won through with a 45-0 win over Heriot's at Currie whereas Melrose were treated to stuffy opposition from Kirkcaldy before winning 36-9 at Galashiels. Not even the loss of their captain, Willie Anderson, sent off early in the match, could dampen Kirkcaldy's fire, and it was only in the final quarter that Melrose surged comfortably clear.

Hawick, following their fourth-round defeat, went on to qualify for the final of the second-tier Shield competition, but they were denied even a consolation for the loss of the Cup as they were overwhelmed in the second half by a rampant GHK, who won by 46-18 with Gerry Hawkes scoring three of the Glasgow club's six tries. Selkirk won the Bowl, beating Biggar 23-15 as compensation for losing in the final of the third-tier competition the previous season.

RESULTS

Third round
Ayr 23, Ross High 3; Berwick 14, Gordonians 6; Biggar 6, Gala 27; Corstorphine 41, Howe of Fife 22; Dundee HSFP 48, Hillhead/Jordanhill 13; Duns 20, Glasgow Academicals 37; Edinburgh University 33, East Kilbride 27; GHK 65, Helensburg 13; Glenrothes 19, Langholm 5; Grangemouth 12, Glasgow Southern 24; Haddington 26, Kilmarnock 49; Hamilton Academicals 21, Cartha Queen's Park 17; Hawick Trades 3, Garnock 0; Kelso 67, Livingston 3; Kirkcaldy 55, Dunfermline 3; Linlithgow 7, Hawick Linden 13; Lochaber 17, Musselburgh 43; Morgan Academy FP 15, West of Scotland 56; Peebles 27, Preston Lodge FP 6; Selkirk 14, Stewartry 15; St Boswells 20, Bute 9; Stewart's Melville FP 37, Aberdeenshire 6; Strathendrick 3, Edinburgh Academicals 69; Trinity Academicals 13, Aberdeen GSFP 16

Fourth round
Ayr 3, Kelso 9; Berwick 43, Corstorphine 0; Currie 20, Gala 32; Dundee HSFP 41, Glasgow Academicals 5; Edinburgh Academicals 17, Kilmarnock 32; Edinburgh University 14, Glenrothes 13; Glasgow

Southern 58, Aberdeen GSFP 17; Hawick 6, Boroughmuir 19; Hawick Linden 15, Stewart's Melville FP 9; Heriot's FP 24, Jed-Forest 11; Kirkcaldy 76, Hamilton Academicals 3; Peebles 32, Musselburgh 8; St Boswells 10, Melrose 70; Stirling County 31, Stewartry 7; West of Scotland 33, GHK 10.

Fifth round
Boroughmuir 71, Stirling County 9; Dundee HSFP 31, Hawick Linden 6; Edinburgh University 8, Kirkcaldy 48; Gala 20, Watsonians 59; Glasgow Southern 10, West of Scotland 15; Heriot's FP 37, Berwick 17; Melrose 71, Kelso 37; Peebles 22, Kilmarnock 10

Quarter-finals
Boroughmuir 42, Watsonians 29; Kirkcaldy 33, Dundee HSFP 18; Peebles 16, Heriot's FP 18; West of Scotland 23, Melrose 45

Semi-finals
Boroughmuir 45, Heriot's FP 0 (*at Malleny Park, Currie*); Kirkcaldy 9, Melrose 36 (*at Netherdale*)

SCOTLAND TO NEW ZEALAND 1996

THE TOURING PARTY

Manager J W Telfer   **Coach** J R Dixon   **Assistant Coach** D I Johnston
Captain R I Wainwright

FULL-BACKS

S D Lang (Heriot's FP)
R J S Shepherd (Melrose)

THREEQUARTERS

B R S Eriksson (London Scottish)
*I C Glasgow (Heriot's FP)
S Hastings (Watsonians)
I C Jardine (Stirling County)
C A Joiner (Melrose)
K M Logan (Stirling County)
A G Shiel (Melrose)
A G Stanger (Hawick)
D A Stark (Melrose)

HALF-BACKS

G Armstrong (Newcastle)
C M Chalmers (Melrose)
A D Nicol (Bath)
G P J Townsend (Northampton)

FORWARDS

N J R Broughton (Melrose)
S J Campbell (Dundee HSFP)
D F Cronin (Bourges)
D G Ellis (Currie)
D I W Hilton (Bath)
K D McKenzie (Stirling County)
S Murray (Edinburgh Academicals)
E W Peters (Bath)
B L Renwick (Hawick)
I R Smith (Gloucester)
T J Smith (Watsonians)
B D Stewart (Edinburgh Academicals)
P Walton (Newcastle)
R I Wainwright (Watsonians)
G W Weir (Newcastle)
P H Wright (Boroughmuir)

Replacement during tour

TOUR RECORD

All matches   Played 8   Won 4   Lost 4   Points for 266   Against 238
International matches   Played 2   Lost 2   Points for 43   Against 98

SCORING DETAILS

All matches						International matches					
For:	35T	20C	16PG	1DG	266 Pts	For:	5T	3C	3PG	1DG	43 Pts
Against:	30T	20C	15PG	1DG	238 Pts	Against:	14T	11C	2PG	0	98 Pts

MATCH DETAILS

1996	OPPONENTS	VENUE	RESULT
28 May	Wanganui	Wanganui	W 49-13
3 June	Northland	Whangerei	L 10-15
5 June	Waikato	Hamilton	L 35-39
8 June	Southland	Invercargill	W 31-21
11 June	South Island Divisional XV	Blenheim	W 63-21
15 June	NEW ZEALAND	Dunedin	L 31-62
18 June	Bay of Plenty	Rotorua	W 35-31
22 June	NEW ZEALAND	Auckland	L 12-36

MATCH 1   28 May, Cook's Gardens, Wanganui

Wanganui 13 (1PG 2T)   **Scotland 49** (4G 2PG 3T)
Wanganui: J K N Nahona; R A Gedye, J P Hamlin, G R J Lennox, A D Magicu;
E B T Hekenui, S B Brown; A M Bull, A K Edwards, V T Pomana,
G N Stantiali, M R Ward, A Renata, K P Whale (*capt*), J Gutsell
Replacement M B Collis for Gutsell (temp)
Scorers *Tries:* Gutsell, Renata   *Penalty Goal:* Nahona
Scotland: Lang; Joiner, Shiel, Jardine, Stark; Townsend (*capt*), Nicol; Hilton,
McKenzie, Stewart, Cronin, Murray, Walton, Peters, Broughton
Scorers *Tries:* Cronin, Joiner, Nicol, Peters, Stark (2), Walton
Conversions: Lang (4)   *Penalty Goals:* Lang (2)
Referee A G Riley (Waikato)

MATCH 2   31 May, Okara Park, Whangerei

Northland 15 (5PG)   **Scotland 10** (1G 1PG)
Northland: W B Johnston; N R Berryman, M R Going, B L Reid, H C Taylor;
D E Holwell, S L Moore; L Davies, D R Te Puni, I Fukofuka, N M Maxwell,
J P Pickering, G L Taylor, J W Campbell (*capt*), B R Waaka
Scorer *Penalty Goals:* Johnston (5)
Scotland: Shepherd; Stanger, Hastings, Eriksson, Logan; Chalmers, Armstrong;
T J Smith, Ellis, Wright, Campbell, Weir, Wainwright (*capt*), Renwick, I R Smith
Replacement Hilton for Wright
Scorers *Try:* Logan   *Conversion:* Shepherd   *Penalty Goal:* Shepherd
Referee G K Wahlstrom (Auckland)

MATCH 3   5 June, Rugby Park, Hamilton

Waikato 39 (4G 2PG 1T)   **Scotland 35** (3G 3PG 1T)
Waikato: B T Reihana; J W Walters, W S Warlow, M J A Cooper, W R Jennings;
I D Foster, R J Duggan; M J Driver, G J Smith, C M Stevenson, T Hemi,
S B Gordon (*capt*), D A C Coleman, D D Muir, D I Monkley
Replacement B K Meinung for Jennings, B M Foote for Monkley
Scorers *Tries:* Cooper, Monkley, Muir, Walters, Warlow   *Conversions:* Cooper (4)
Penalty Goals: Cooper (2)
Scotland: Shepherd; Joiner, Hastings, Jardine, Stark; Townsend, Nicol; Hilton,
McKenzie, Stewart, Cronin, Weir, Wainwright (*capt*), Peters, I R Smith
Replacements Logan for Stark, Walton for Cronin
Scorers *Tries:* Logan, Shepherd, Stark, Townsend   *Conversions:* Shepherd (3)
Penalty Goals: Shepherd (3)
Referee C J Hawke (South Canterbury)

MATCH 4   8 June, Homestead Rugby Stadium, Invercargill

Southland 21 (3G)   **Scotland 31** (2G 4PG 1T)
Southland: E J Crossan; P J Dynes, J D Heke, M B Seymour, H P Byars;
S D Culhane (*capt*), B J McCormack; S P Hayes, D J Heaps, R B Borland,
R L Newell, M Wilson, P W Henderson, S J Harvey, J P Winders
Replacements G M Dermody for McCormack (temp), D Batchelor for Hayes
(temp), B K Shepherd for Henderson (temp)
Scorers *Tries:* Byars, Wilson, pen try   *Conversions:* Culhane (3)
Scotland: Shepherd; Joiner, Hastings, Eriksson, Logan; Chalmers, Armstrong;
Hilton, McKenzie, Stewart, Weir, Campbell, Wainwright (*capt*), Renwick,
Broughton *Replacements* Lang for Joiner, Wright for Stewart (temp)
Scorers *Tries:* Logan, McKenzie, Wainwright   *Conversions:* Shepherd (2)
Penalty Goals: Shepherd (4)
Referee S Walsh (Wellington)

MATCH 5   11 June, Lansdowne Park, Blenheim

South Island Divisional XV 21 (1G 2PG 1DG 1T)   **Scotland 63** (5G 1PG 5T)
South Island Divisional XV: G I Dempster (South Canterbury); W Havilli
(Nelson Bays), J F Connelly (South Canterbury), S B Tarrant (South Canterbury),
G A Burgess (South Canterbury); L R MacDonald (Marlborough),
K G MacDowell (Marlborough); D C McCrea (Mid Canterbury), W J Fletcher
(Nelson Bays), G H Cameron (Mid Canterbury), A J Gillman (West Coast),
M J Kerr (Marlborough), J W Mawhinney (South Canterbury), R H Penney
(Marlborough) (*capt*), J T Taeiloa (North Otago) *Replacements* S J Todd (South
Canterbury) for Burgess, T J Stuart (Buller) for Taeiloa, T P Gresham (South
Canterbury) for Mawhinney, B G Johnson (Marlborough) for Fletcher
Scorers *Tries:* Connelly, MacDowell   *Conversion:* Dempster
Penalty Goals: Dempster (2)   *Dropped Goal:* MacDonald
Scotland: Lang; Stanger, Shiel, Eriksson, Logan; Chalmers (*capt*), Armstrong;
T J Smith, Ellis, Wright, Campbell, Murray, Walton, Peters, Broughton
Replacement Hastings for Shiel, Shepherd for Hastings
Scorers *Tries:* Armstrong, Broughton, Chalmers, Logan (2), Shepherd, Stanger (2),
Walton (2)   *Conversions:* Chalmers (5)   *Penalty Goal:* Chalmers
Referee P J Honiss (Canterbury)

MATCH 6   15 June, Carisbrook, Dunedin   1st Test
NEW ZEALAND 62 (7G 1PG 2T)   SCOTLAND 31 (2G 3PG 1DG 1T)

NEW ZEALAND: C M Cullen (Manawatu); J W Wilson (Otago), S J McLeod
(Waikato), F E Bunce (North Harbour), J T Lomu (Counties); A P Mehrtens
(Canterbury), J W Marshall (Canterbury); C W Dowd (Auckland),
S B T Fitzpatrick (Auckland) (*capt*), O M Brown (Auckland), I D Jones (North
Harbour), R M Brooke (Auckland), M N Jones (Auckland), Z V Brooke
(Auckland), J A Kronfeld (Otago) *Replacement* E J Rush (North Harbour) for
Lomu (67 mins)
Scorers *Tries:* Z V Brooke, Cullen (4), I D Jones, Lomu, Marshall, Mehrtens
Conversions: Mehrtens (7)   *Penalty Goal:* Mehrtens
SCOTLAND: Shepherd; Joiner, Jardine, Eriksson, Logan; Townsend, Armstrong,
Hilton, McKenzie, Wright, Weir, Cronin, Wainwright (*capt*), Peters, I R Smith
Scorers *Tries:* Joiner, Peters, Townsend   *Conversions:* Shepherd (2)
Penalty Goal: Shepherd (3)   *Dropped Goal:* Shepherd
Referee W J Erickson (Australia)

MATCH 7   18 June, Rotorua International Stadium

Bay of Plenty 31 (1G 3PG 3T)   **Scotland 35** (2G 2PG 3T)
Bay of Plenty: D A Kaui; G B Tamani, J R Spanhake, W Clarke, B W Daniel;
A J Miller, J J Tauiwi; S A Simpkins, J P R Edwards, P R Cook, G D Remnant,
M D Camp, P E Tupai, C R McMillan (*capt*), B D Sinkinson
Replacements D N Jones for Tupai, P C Thomas for Cook
Scorers *Tries:* Edwards, McMillan, Spanhake, Tamani   *Conversion:* Miller
Penalty Goals: Miller (3)
Scotland: Lang; Glasgow, Stanger, Eriksson, Stark; Chalmers (*capt*), Nicol;
T J Smith, Ellis, Stewart, Campbell, Murray, Walton, Renwick, Broughton
Replacement Hilton for Stewart
Scorers *Tries:* Nicol (2), Stark (3)   *Conversions:* Chalmers, Lang
Penalty Goals: Lang (2)
Referee P D O'Brien (Southland)

MATCH 9   22 June, Eden Park, Auckland   2nd Test
NEW ZEALAND 36 (4G 1PG 1T)   SCOTLAND 12 (1G 1T)

NEW ZEALAND: C M Cullen (Manawatu); J W Wilson (Otago), F E Bunce (North Harbour), W K Little (North Harbour), E J Rush (North Harbour); A P Mehrtens (Canterbury), J W Marshall (Canterbury); C W Dowd (Auckland), S B T Fitzpatrick (Auckland) (*capt*), O M Brown (Auckland), I D Jones (North Harbour), R M Brooke (Auckland), M N Jones (Ajckland), Z V Brooke (Auckland), J A Kronfeld (Otago) *Replacements* A R Cashmore (Auckland) for Wilson (63 mins), B P Larsen (North Harbour) for M N Jones (temp), M R Allen (Taranaki) for Dowd (temp)
Scorers *Tries:* M N Jones, Kronfeld (2), Z V Brooke, pen try
Conversions: Mehrtens (4) *Penalty Goal:* Mehrtens
SCOTLAND: Shepherd; Stanger, Hastings, Jardine, Logan; Townsend, Armstrong; Hilton, McKenzie, Stewart, Cronin, Weir, Wainwright (*capt*), Peters, I R Smith *Replacement* Stark for Jardine (25 mins)
Scorers *Tries:* Peters, Shepherd   *Conversion:* Shepherd
Referee W J Erickson (Australia)

SCOTTISH INTERNATIONAL PLAYERS
(up to 30 April 1997)

Note: Years given for Five Nations' matches are for second half of season; eg 1972 means season 1971-72. Years for all other matches refer to the actual year of the match. When a series has taken place, figures have been used to denote the particular matches in which players have featured. Thus 1981 *NZ* 1,2 indicates that a player appeared in the first and second Tests of the series. The abandoned game with Ireland at Belfast in 1885 is now included as a cap-match.

Abercrombie, C H (United Services) 1910 *I, E,* 1911 *F, W,* 1913 *F, W*
Abercrombie, J G (Edinburgh U) 1949 *F, W, I,* 1950 *F, W, I, E*
Agnew, W C C (Stewart's Coll FP) 1930 *W, I*
Ainslie, R (Edinburgh Inst FP) 1879 *I, E,* 1880 *I, E,* 1881 *E,* 1882 *I, E*
Ainslie, T (Edinburgh Inst FP) 1881 *E,* 1882 *I, E,* 1883 *W, I, E,* 1884 *W, I, E,* 1885 *W, I* 1,2
Aitchison, G R (Edinburgh Wands) 1883 *I*
Aitchison, T G (Gala) 1929 *W, I, E*
Aitken, A I (Edinburgh Inst FP) 1889 *I*
Aitken, G G (Oxford U) 1924 *W, I, E,* 1925 *F, W, I, E,* 1929 *F*
Aitken, J (Gala) 1977 *E, I, F,* 1981 *F, W, E, I, NZ* 1,2, *R, A,* 1982 *E, I, F, W,* 1983 *F, W, E, NZ,* 1984 *W, E, I, F, R*
Aitken, R (London Scottish) 1947 *W*
Allan, B (Glasgow Acads) 1881 *I*
Allan, J (Edinburgh Acads) 1990 *NZ* 1, 1991, *W, I, R,* [*J, I, WS, E, NZ*]
Allan, J L (Melrose) 1952 *F, W, I,* 1953 *W*
Allan, J L F (Cambridge U) 1957 *I, E*
Allan, J W (Melrose) 1927 *F,* 1928 *I,* 1929 *F, W, I, E,* 1930 *F, E,* 1931 *F, W, I, E,* 1932 *SA, W, I,* 1934 *I, E*
Allan, R C (Hutchesons' GSFP) 1969 *I*
Allardice, W D (Aberdeen GSFP) 1947 *A,* 1948 *F, W, I,* 1949 *F, W, I, E*
Allen, H W (Glasgow Acads) 1873 *E*
Anderson, A H (Glasgow Acads) 1894 *I*
Anderson, D G (London Scottish) 1889 *I,* 1890 *W, I, E,* 1891 *W, E,* 1892 *W, E*
Anderson, E (Stewart's Coll FP) 1947 *I, E*
Anderson, J W (W of Scotland) 1872 *E*
Anderson, T (Merchiston) 1882 *I*
Angus, A W (Watsonians) 1909 *W,* 1910 *F, W, E,* 1911 *W, I,* 1912 *F, W, I, E, SA,* 1913 *F, W,* 1914 *E,* 1920 *F, W, I, E*
Anton, P A (St Andrew's U) 1873 *E*
Armstrong, G (Jedforest, Newcastle) 1988 *A,* 1989 *W, E, I, F, Fj, R,* 1990 *I, F, W, E, NZ* 1,2, *Arg,* 1991 *F, W, E, I, R,* [*J, I, WS, E, NZ*], 1993 *I, F, W, E,* 1994 *E, I,* 1996 *NZ,* 1,2, *A,* 1997 *W*
Arneil, R J (Edinburgh Acads, Leicester and Northampton) 1968 *I, E, A,* 1969 *F, W, I, E, SA,* 1970 *F, W, I, E, A,* 1971 *F, W, I, E* (2[1C]), 1972 *F, W, E, NZ*
Arthur, A (Glasgow Acads) 1875 *E,* 1876 *E*
Arthur, J W (Glasgow Acads) 1871 *E,* 1872 *E*
Asher, A G G (Oxford U) 1882 *I,* 1884 *W, I, E,* 1885 *W,* 1886 *I, E*
Auld, W (W of Scotland) 1889 *W,* 1890 *W*
Auldjo, L J (Abertay) 1878 *E*

Bain, D McL (Oxford U) 1911 *E,* 1912 *F, W, E, SA,* 1913 *F, W, I, E,* 1914 *W, I*
Baird, G R T (Kelso) 1981 *A,* 1982 *E, I, F, W, A* 1,2, 1983 *I, F, W, E, NZ,* 1984 *W, E, I, F, A,* 1985 *I, W, E,* 1986 *F, W, E, I, R,* 1987 *E,* 1988 *I*
Balfour, A (Watsonians) 1896 *W, I, E,* 1897 *E*
Balfour, L M (Edinburgh Acads) 1872 *E*
Bannerman, E M (Edinburgh Acads) 1872 *E,* 1873 *E*
Bannerman, J M (Glasgow HSFP) 1921 *F, W, I, E,* 1922 *F, W, I, E,* 1923 *F, W, I, E,* 1924 *F, W, I, E,* 1925 *F, W, I, E,* 1926 *F, W, I, E,* 1927 *F, W, I, E, A,* 1928 *F, W, I, E,* 1929 *F, W, I, E*
Barnes, I (Hawick) 1972 *W,* 1974 *F* (R), 1975 *E* (R), *NZ,* 1977 *I, F, W*
Barrie, R W (Hawick) 1936 *E*
Bearne, K R F (Cambridge U, London Scottish) 1960 *F, W*
Beattie, J A (Hawick) 1929 *F, W,* 1930 *W,* 1931 *F, W, I, E,* 1932 *SA, W, I,* 1933 *W, E, I,* 1934 *I,* 1935 *W, I, E, NZ,* 1936 *W, I, E*

Beattie, J R (Glasgow Acads) 1980 *I, F, W, E,* 1981 *F, W, E, I,* 1983 *F, W, E, NZ,* 1984 *E* (R), *R, A,* 1985 *I,* 1986 *F, W, E, I, R,* 1987 *I, F, W, E*
Bedell-Sivright, D R (Cambridge U, Edinburgh U) 1900 *W,* 1901 *W, I, E,* 1902 *W, I, E,* 1903 *W, I, E,* 1905 *NZ,* 1906 *W, I, E, SA,* 1907 *W, I, E,* 1908 *W, I*
Bedell-Sivright, J V (Cambridge U) 1902 *W*
Begbie, T A (Edinburgh Wands) 1881 *I, E*
Bell, D L (Watsonians) 1975 *I, F, W, E*
Bell, J A (Clydesdale) 1901 *W, I, E,* 1902 *W, I, E*
Bell, L H I (Edinburgh Acads) 1900 *E,* 1904 *W, I*
Berkeley, W V (Oxford U) 1926 *F,* 1929 *F, W, I*
Berry, C W (Fettesian-Lorettonians) 1884 *I, E,* 1885 *W, I* 1, 1887 *I, W, E,* 1888 *W, I*
Bertram, D M (Watsonians) 1922 *F, W, I, E,* 1923 *F, W, I, E,* 1924 *W, I, E*
Biggar, A G (London Scottish) 1969 *SA,* 1970 *F, I, E, A,* 1971 *F, W, I, E* (2[1C]), 1972 *F, W*
Biggar, M A (London Scottish) 1975 *I, F, W, E,* 1976 *W, E, I,* 1977 *I, F, W,* 1978 *I, F, W, E, NZ,* 1979 *W, E, I, F, NZ,* 1980 *I, F, W, E*
Birkett, G A (Harlequins, London Scottish) 1975 *NZ*
Bishop, J M (Glasgow Acads) 1893 *I*
Bisset, A A (RIE Coll) 1904 *W*
Black, A W (Edinburgh U) 1947 *F, W,* 1948 *E,* 1950 *W, I, E*
Black, W P (Glasgow HSFP) 1948 *F, W, I, E,* 1951 *E*
Blackadder, W F (W of Scotland) 1938 *E*
Blaikie, C F (Heriot's FP) 1963 *I, E,* 1966 *E,* 1968 *A,* 1969 *F, W, I, E*
Blair, P C B (Cambridge U) 1912 *SA,* 1913 *F, W, I, E*
Bolton, W H (W of Scotland) 1876 *E*
Borthwick, J B (Stewart's Coll FP) 1938 *W, I*
Bos, F H ten (Oxford U, London Scottish) 1959 *E,* 1960 *F, W, SA,* 1961 *F, SA, W, I, E,* 1962 *F, W, I, E,* 1963 *F, W, I, E*
Boswell, J D (W of Scotland) 1889 *W, I,* 1890 *W, I, E,* 1891 *W, I, E,* 1892 *W, I, E,* 1893 *I, E,* 1894 *I, E*
Bowie, T C (Watsonians) 1913 *I, E,* 1914 *I, E*
Boyd, G M (Glasgow HSFP) 1926 *E*
Boyd, J L (United Services) 1912 *E, SA*
Boyle, A C W (London Scottish) 1963 *F, W, I*
Boyle, A H W (St Thomas's Hospital, London Scottish) 1966 *A,* 1967 *F, NZ,* 1968 *F, W, I*
Brash, J C (Cambridge U) 1961 *E*
Breakey, R W (Gosforth) 1978 *E*
Brewis, N T (Edinburgh Inst FP) 1876 *E,* 1878 *E,* 1879 *I, E,* 1880 *I, E*
Brewster, A K (Stewart's-Melville FP) 1977 *E,* 1980 *I, F,* 1986 *E, I, R*
Brown, A H (Heriot's FP) 1928 *E,* 1929 *F, W*
Brown, A R (Gala) 1971 *E* (2[1C]), 1972 *F, W, E*
Brown, C H C (Dunfermline) 1929 *E*
Brown, D I (Cambridge U) 1933 *W, E, I*
Brown, G L (W of Scotland) 1969 *SA,* 1970 *F, W* (R), *I, E, A,* 1971 *W, E* (2[1C]), 1972 *F, W, E, NZ,* 1973 *E* (R), *P,* 1974 *W, E, I, F,* 1975 *I, F, W, E, A,* 1976 *F, W, E, I*
Brown, J (Glasgow Acads) 1908 *W, I*
Brown, J B (Glasgow Acads) 1879 *I, E,* 1880 *I, E,* 1881 *I, E,* 1882 *I, E,* 1883 *W, I, E,* 1884 *W, I, E,* 1885 *I* 1,2, 1886 *W, I, E*
Brown, P C (W of Scotland, Gala) 1964 *F, NZ, W, I, E,* 1965 *I, E, SA,* 1966 *A,* 1969 *I, E,* 1970 *W, E,* 1971 *F, W, I, E* (2[1C]), 1972 *F, W, E, NZ,* 1973 *F, W, I, E, P*
Brown, T G (Heriot's FP) 1929 *W*
Brown, W D (Glasgow Acads) 1871 *E,* 1872 *E,* 1873 *E,* 1874 *E,* 1875 *E*
Brown, W S (Edinburgh Inst FP) 1880 *I, E,* 1882 *I, E,* 1883 *W, E*
Browning, A (Glasgow HSFP) 1920 *I,* 1922 *F, W, I, E,* 1923 *W, I, E*

Bruce, C R (Glasgow Acads) 1947 *F, W, I, E,* 1949 *F, W, I, E*
Bruce, N S (Blackheath, Army and London Scottish) 1958 *F, A, I, E,* 1959 *F, W, I, E,* 1960 *F, W, I, E, SA,* 1961 *F, SA, W, I, E,* 1962 *F, W, I, E,* 1963 *F, W, I, E,* 1964 *F, NZ, W, I, E*
Bruce, R M (Gordonians) 1947 *A,* 1948 *F, W, I*
Bruce-Lockhart, J H (London Scottish) 1913 *W,* 1920 *E*
Bruce-Lockhart, L (London Scottish) 1948 *E,* 1950 *F, W,* 1953 *I, E*
Bruce-Lockhart, R B (Cambridge U and London Scottish) 1937 *I,* 1939 *I, E*
Bryce, C C (Glasgow Acads) 1873 *E,* 1874 *E*
Bryce, R D H (W of Scotland) 1973 *I* (R)
Bryce, W E (Selkirk) 1922 *W, I, E,* 1923 *F, W, I, E,* 1924 *F, W, I, E*
Brydon, W R C (Heriot's FP) 1939 *W*
Buchanan, A (Royal HSFP) 1871 *E*
Buchanan, F G (Kelvinside Acads and Oxford U) 1910 *F,* 1911 *F, W*
Buchanan, J C R (Stewart's Coll FP) 1921 *W, I, E,* 1922 *W, I, E,* 1923 *F, W, I, E,* 1924 *F, W, I, E,* 1925 *F, I*
Buchanan-Smith, G A E (London Scottish, Heriot's FP) 1989 *Fj* (R), 1990 *Arg*
Bucher, A M (Edinburgh Acads) 1897 *E*
Budge, G M (Edinburgh Wands) 1950 *F, W, I, E*
Bullmore, H H (Edinburgh U) 1902 *I*
Burnell, A P (London Scottish) 1989 *E, I, F, Fj, R,* 1990 *I, F, W, E, Arg,* 1991 *F, W, E, I, R, [J, Z, I, WS, NZ],* 1992 *E, I, F, W,* 1993 *I, F, W, E, NZ,* 1994 *W, E, I, F, Arg* 1,2, SA, 1995 *[Iv, Tg* (R), *F* (R)], *WS*
Burnet, P J (London Scottish and Edinburgh Acads) 1960 *SA*
Burnet, W (Hawick) 1912 *E*
Burnet, W A (W of Scotland) 1934 *W,* 1935 *W, I, E, NZ,* 1936 *W, I, E*
Burnett, J N (Heriot's FP) 1980 *I, F, W, E*
Burrell, G (Gala) 1950 *F, W, I,* 1951 *SA*

Cairns, A G (Watsonians) 1903 *W, I, E,* 1904 *W, I, E,* 1905 *W, I, E,* 1906 *W, I, E*
Calder, F (Stewart's-Melville FP) 1986 *F, W, E, I, R,* 1987 *I, F, W, E, [F, Z, R, NZ],* 1988 *I, F, W, E,* 1989 *W, E, I, F, R,* 1990 *I, F, W, E, NZ* 1,2, 1991 *R, [J, I, WS, E, NZ]*
Calder, J H (Stewart's-Melville FP) 1981 *F, W, E, I, NZ* 1,2, R, A, 1982 *E, I, F, W, A* 1,2, 1983 *I, F, W, E, NZ,* 1984 *W, E, I, F, A,* 1985 *I, F, W*
Callander, G J (Kelso) 1984 *R,* 1988 *I, F, W, E, A*
Cameron, A (Glasgow HSFP) 1948 *W,* 1950 *I, E,* 1951 *F, W, I, E, SA,* 1953 *I, E,* 1955 *F, W, I, E,* 1956 *F, W, I*
Cameron, A D (Hillhead HSFP) 1951 *F,* 1954 *F, W*
Cameron, A W (Watsonians) 1887 *W,* 1893 *W,* 1894 *I*
Cameron, D (Glasgow HSFP) 1953 *I, E,* 1954 *F, NZ, I, E*
Cameron, N W (Glasgow U) 1952 *E,* 1953 *F, W*
Campbell, A J (Hawick) 1984 *I, F, R,* 1985 *I, F, W, E,* 1986 *F, W, E, I, R,* 1988 *F, W, A*
Campbell, G T (London Scottish) 1892 *W, I, E,* 1893 *I, E,* 1894 *W, I, E,* 1895 *W, I, E,* 1896 *W, I, E,* 1897 *I,* 1899 *I,* 1900 *E*
Campbell, H H (Cambridge U, London Scottish) 1947 *I, E,* 1948 *I, E*
Campbell, J A (W of Scotland) 1878 *E,* 1879 *I, E,* 1881 *I, E*
Campbell, J A (Cambridge U) 1900 *I*
Campbell, N M (London Scottish) 1956 *F, W*
Campbell, S J (Dundee HSFP) 1995 *C, I, F, W, E, R, [Iv, NZ* (R)], *WS* (t), 1996 *I, F, W, E*
Campbell-Lamerton, J R E (London Scottish) 1986 *F,* 1987 *[Z, R(R)]*
Campbell-Lamerton, M J (Halifax, Army, London Scottish) 1961 *F, SA, W, I,* 1962 *F, W, I, E,* 1963 *F, W, I, E,* 1964 *I, E,* 1965 *F, W, I, E, SA,* 1966 *F, W, I, E*
Carmichael, A B (W of Scotland) 1967 *I, NZ,* 1968 *F, W, I, E, A,* 1969 *F, W, I, E, SA,* 1970 *F, W, I, E, A,* 1971 *F, W, I, E* (2[1C]), 1972 *F, W, E, NZ,* 1973 *F, W, I, E, P,* 1974 *W, E, I, F,* 1975 *I, F, W, E, NZ, A,* 1976 *F, W, E, I,* 1977 *E, I* (R), *F, W,* 1978 *I*
Carmichael, J H (Watsonians) 1921 *F, W, I*
Carrick, J S (Glasgow Acads) 1876 *E,* 1877 *E*
Cassels, D Y (W of Scotland) 1880 *E,* 1881 *I,* 1882 *I, E,* 1883 *W, I, E*
Cathcart, C W (Edinburgh U) 1872 *E,* 1873 *E,* 1876 *E*
Cawkwell, G L (Oxford U) 1947 *F*
Chalmers, C M (Melrose) 1989 *W, E, I, F, Fj,* 1990 *I, F, W, E, NZ* 1,2, *Arg,* 1991 *F, W, E, I, R, [J, Z(R), I, WS, E,*

NZ], 1992 *E, I, F, W, A* 1,2, 1993 *I, F, W, E, NZ,* 1994 *W, SA,* 1995 *C, I, F, W, E, R, [Iv, Tg, F, NZ], WS,* 1996 *A, It,* 1997 *W, I, F*
Chalmers, T (Glasgow Acads) 1871 *E,* 1872 *E,* 1873 *E,* 1874 *E,* 1875 *E,* 1876 *E*
Chambers, H F T (Edinburgh U) 1888 *W, I,* 1889 *W, I*
Charters, R G (Hawick) 1955 *W, I, E*
Chisholm, D H (Melrose) 1964 *I, E,* 1965 *E, SA,* 1966 *F, I, E, A,* 1967 *F, W, NZ,* 1968 *F, W, I*
Chisholm, R W T (Melrose) 1955 *I, E,* 1956 *F, W, I, E,* 1958 *F, W, A, I,* 1960 *SA*
Church, W C (Glasgow Acads) 1906 *W*
Clark, R L (Edinburgh Wands, Royal Navy) 1972 *F, W, E, NZ,* 1973 *F, W, I, E, P*
Clauss, P R A (Oxford U) 1891 *W, I, E,* 1892 *W, E,* 1895 *I*
Clay, A T (Edinburgh Acads) 1886 *W, I, E,* 1887 *I, W, E,* 1888 *W*
Clunies-Ross, A (St Andrew's U) 1871 *E*
Coltman, S (Hawick) 1948 *I,* 1949 *F, W, I, E*
Colville, A G (Merchistonians, Blackheath) 1871 *E,* 1872 *E*
Connell, G C (Trinity Acads and London Scottish) 1968 *E, A,* 1969 *F, E,* 1970 *F*
Cooper, M McG (Oxford U) 1936 *W, I*
Corcoran, I (Gala) 1992 *A* 1(R)
Cordial, I F (Edinburgh Wands) 1952 *F, W, I, E*
Cotter, J L (Hillhead HSFP) 1934 *I, E*
Cottington, G S (Kelso) 1934 *I, E,* 1935 *W, I,* 1936 *E*
Coughtrie, S (Edinburgh Acads) 1959 *F, W, I, E,* 1962 *W, I, E,* 1963 *F, W, I, E*
Couper, J H (W of Scotland) 1896 *W, I,* 1899 *I*
Coutts, F H (Melrose, Army) 1947 *W, I, E*
Coutts, I D F (Old Alleynians) 1951 *F,* 1952 *E*
Cowan, R C (Selkirk) 1961 *F,* 1962 *F, W, I, E*
Cowie, W L K (Edinburgh Wands) 1953 *E*
Cownie, W B (Watsonians) 1893 *W, I, E,* 1894 *W, I, E,* 1895 *W, I, E*
Crabbie, G E (Edinburgh Acads) 1904 *W*
Crabbie, J E (Edinburgh Acads, Oxford U) 1900 *W,* 1902 *I,* 1903 *W, I,* 1904 *E,* 1905 *W*
Craig, J B (Heriot's FP) 1939 *W*
Cramb, R I (Harlequins) 1987 *[R(R)],* 1988 *I, F, A*
Cranston, A G (Hawick) 1976 *W, E, I,* 1977 *E, W,* 1978 *F* (R), *W, E, NZ,* 1981 *NZ* 1,2
Crawford, J A (Army, London Scottish) 1934 *I*
Crawford, W H (United Services, RN) 1938 *W, I, E,* 1939 *W, E*
Crichton-Miller, D (Gloucester) 1931 *W, I, E*
Crole, G B (Oxford U) 1920 *F, W, I, E*
Cronin, D F (Bath, London Scottish, Bourges, Wasps) 1988 *I, F, W, E, A,* 1989 *W, E, I, F, Fj, R,* 1990 *I, F, W, E, NZ* 1,2, 1991 *F, W, E, R, [Z],* 1992 *A* 2, 1993 *I, F, W, E, NZ,* 1995 *C, I, F, [Tg, F, NZ], WS,* 1996 *NZ* 1,2, A, It, 1997 *F* (R)
Cross, M (Merchistonians) 1875 *E,* 1876 *E,* 1877 *I, E,* 1878 *E,* 1879 *I, E,* 1880 *I, E*
Cross, W (Merchistonians) 1871 *E,* 1872 *E*
Cumming, R S (Aberdeen U) 1921 *F, W*
Cunningham, G (Oxford U) 1908 *W, I,* 1909 *W, E,* 1910 *F, I, E,* 1911 *E*
Cunningham, R F (Gala) 1978 *NZ,* 1979 *W, E*
Currie, L R (Dunfermline) 1947 *A,* 1948 *F, W, I,* 1949 *F, W, I, E*
Cuthbertson, W (Kilmarnock, Harlequins) 1980 *I,* 1981 *W, E, I, NZ* 1,2, R, A, 1982 *E, I, F, W, A* 1,2, 1983 *I, F, W, NZ,* 1984 *W, E, A*

Dalgleish, A (Gala) 1890 *W, E,* 1891 *W, I,* 1892 *W,* 1893 *W,* 1894 *W, I*
Dalgleish, K J (Edinburgh Wands, Cambridge U) 1951 *I, E,* 1953 *F, W*
Dallas, J D (Watsonians) 1903 *E*
Davidson, J A (London Scottish, Edinburgh Wands) 1959 *E,* 1960 *I, E*
Davidson, J N G (Edinburgh U) 1952 *F, W, I, E,* 1953 *F, W,* 1954 *F*
Davidson, J P (RIE Coll) 1873 *E,* 1874 *E*
Davidson, R S (Royal HSFP) 1893 *E*
Davies, D S (Hawick) 1922 *F, W, I, E,* 1923 *F, W, I, E,* 1924 *F, E,* 1925 *W, I, E,* 1926 *F, W, I, E,* 1927 *F, W, I*
Davies, J C (Glasgow Acads) 1947 *A,* 1948 *F, W,* 1949 *F, W, I,* 1950 *F, W, I, E,* 1951 *F, W, I, E, SA,* 1952 *F, W, I, E,* 1953 *E*

169

Deans, C T (Hawick) 1978 *F, W, E, NZ,* 1979 *W, E, I, F, NZ,* 1980 *I, F,* 1981 *F, W, E, I, NZ* 1,2, *R, A,* 1982 *E, I, F, W, A* 1,2, 1983 *I, F, W, E, NZ,* 1984 *W, E, I, F, A,* 1985 *I, F, W, E,* 1986 *F, W, E, I, R,* 1987 *I, F, W, E,* [*F, Z, R, NZ*]
Deans, D T (Hawick) 1968 *E*
Deas, D W (Heriot's FP) 1947 *F, W*
Dick, L G (Loughborough Colls, Jordanhill, Swansea) 1972 *W* (R), *E,* 1974 *W, E, I, F,* 1975 *I, F, W, E, NZ, A,* 1976 *F,* 1977 *E*
Dick, R C S (Cambridge U, Guy's Hospital) 1934 *W, I, E,* 1935 *W, I, E, NZ,* 1936 *W, I, E,* 1937 *W,* 1938 *W, I, E*
Dickson, G (Gala) 1978 *NZ,* 1979 *W, E, I, F, NZ,* 1980 *W,* 1981 *F,* 1982 *W* (R)
Dickson, M R (Edinburgh U) 1905 *I*
Dickson, W M (Blackheath, Oxford U) 1912 *F, W, E, SA,* 1913 *F, W, I*
Dobson, J (Glasgow Acads) 1911 *E,* 1912 *F, W, I, E, SA*
Dobson, J D (Glasgow Acads) 1910 *I*
Dobson, W G (Heriot's FP) 1922 *W, I, E*
Docherty, J T (Glasgow HSFP) 1955 *F, W,* 1956 *F, E,* 1958 *F, W, A, I, E*
Dods, F P (Edinburgh Acads) 1901 *I*
Dods, J H (Edinburgh Acads) 1895 *W, I, E,* 1896 *W, I, E,* 1897 *I, E*
Dods, M (Gala, Northampton) 1994 *(t), Arg* 1,2, 1995 *WS,* 1996 *I, F, W, E*
Dods, P W (Gala) 1983 *I, F, W, E, NZ,* 1984 *W, E, I, F, R, A,* 1985 *I, F, W, E,* 1989 *W, E, I, F,* 1991 *I* (R), *R,* [*Z, NZ* (R)]
Donald, D G (Oxford U) 1914 *W, I*
Donald, R L H (Glasgow HSFP) 1921 *W, I, E*
Donaldson, W P (Oxford U, W of Scotland) 1893 *I,* 1894 *I,* 1895 *E,* 1896 *I, E,* 1899 *I*
Don-Wauchope, A R (Fettesian-Lorettonians) 1881 *E,* 1882 *E,* 1883 *W,* 1884 *W, I, E,* 1885 *W, I* 1,2, 1886 *W, I, E,* 1888 *I*
Don-Wauchope, P H (Fettesian-Lorettonians) 1885 *I* 1,2, 1886 *W,* 1887 *I, W, E*
Dorward, A F (Cambridge U, Gala) 1950 *F,* 1951 *SA,* 1952 *W, I,* 1953 *F, W, E,* 1955 *F,* 1956 *I, E,* 1957 *F, W, I, E*
Dorward, T F (Gala) 1938 *W, I, E,* 1939 *I, E*
Douglas, G (Jedforest) 1921 *W*
Douglas, J (Stewart's Coll FP) 1961 *F, SA, W, I, E,* 1962 *F, W, I, E,* 1963 *F, W, I*
Douty, P S (London Scottish) 1927 *A,* 1928 *F, W*
Drew, D (Glasgow Acads) 1871 *E,* 1876 *E*
Druitt, W A H (London Scottish) 1936 *W, I, E*
Drummond, A H (Kelvinside Acads) 1938 *W, I*
Drummond, C W (Melrose) 1947 *F, W, I, E,* 1948 *F, I, E,* 1950 *F, W, I, E*
Drybrough, A S (Edinburgh Wands, Merchistonians) 1902 *I,* 1903 *I*
Dryden, R H (Watsonians) 1937 *E*
Drysdale, D (Heriot's FP) 1923 *F, W, I, E,* 1924 *F, W, I, E,* 1925 *F, W, I, E,* 1926 *F, W, I, E,* 1927 *F, W, I, E, A,* 1928 *F, W, I, E,* 1929 *F*
Duff, P L (Glasgow Acads) 1936 *W, I,* 1938 *W, I, E,* 1939 *W*
Duffy, H (Jedforest) 1955 *F*
Duke, A (Royal HSFP) 1888 *W, I,* 1889 *W, I,* 1890 *W, I*
Duncan, A W (Edinburgh U) 1901 *W, I, E,* 1902 *W, I, E*
Duncan, D D (Oxford U) 1920 *F, W, I, E*
Duncan, M D F (W of Scotland) 1986 *F, W, E, R,* 1987 *I, F, W, E,* [*F, Z, R, NZ*], 1988 *I, F, W, E, A,* 1989 *W*
Duncan, M M (Fettesian-Lorettonians) 1888 *W*
Dunlop, J W (W of Scotland) 1875 *E*
Dunlop, Q (W of Scotland) 1971 *E* (2[1C])
Dykes, A S (Glasgow Acads) 1932 *E*
Dykes, J C (Glasgow Acads) 1922 *F, E,* 1924 *I,* 1925 *F, W, I,* 1926 *F, W, I, E,* 1927 *F, W, I, E, A,* 1928 *F, I,* 1929 *F, W, I*
Dykes, J M (Clydesdale, Glasgow HSFP) 1898 *I, E,* 1899 *W, E,* 1900 *W, I,* 1901 *W, I, E,* 1902 *E*

Edwards, D B (Heriot's FP) 1960 *I, E, SA*
Edwards, N G B (Harlequins, Northampton) 1992 *E, I, F, W, A* 1, 1994 *W*
Elgie, M K (London Scottish) 1954 *NZ, I, E, W,* 1955 *F, W, I, E*
Elliot, C (Langholm) 1958 *E,* 1959 *F,* 1960 *F,* 1963 *E,* 1964 *F, NZ, W, I, E,* 1965 *F, W, I*
Elliot, M (Hawick) 1895 *W,* 1896 *E,* 1897 *I, E,* 1898 *I, E*
Elliot, T (Gala) 1905 *E*

Elliot, T (Gala) 1955 *W, I, E,* 1956 *F, W, I, E,* 1957 *F, W, I, E,* 1958 *W, A, I*
Elliot, T G (Langholm) 1968 *W, A,* 1969 *F, W,* 1970 *E*
Elliot, W I D (Edinburgh Acads) 1947 *F, W, E, A,* 1948 *F, W, I, E,* 1949 *F, W, I, E,* 1950 *F, W, I, E,* 1951 *F, W, I, E, SA,* 1952 *F, W, I, E,* 1954 *NZ, I, E, W*
Ellis, D G (Currie) 1997 *W, E, I, F*
Emslie, W D (Royal HSFP) 1930 *F,* 1932 *I*
Eriksson, B R S (London Scottish) 1996 *NZ* 1, A, 1997 *E*
Evans, H L (Edinburgh U) 1885 *I* 1,2
Ewart, E N (Glasgow Acads) 1879 *E,* 1880 *I, E*

Fahmy, Dr E C (Abertillery) 1920 *F, W, I, E*
Fasson, F H (London Scottish, Edinburgh Wands) 1900 *W,* 1901 *W, I,* 1902 *W, E*
Fell, A N (Edinburgh U) 1901 *W, I, E,* 1902 *W, E,* 1903 *W, E*
Ferguson, J H (Gala) 1928 *W*
Ferguson, W G (Royal HSFP) 1927 *A,* 1928 *F, W, I, E*
Fergusson, E A J (Oxford U) 1954 *F, NZ, I, E, W*
Finlay, A B (Edinburgh Acads) 1875 *E*
Finlay, J F (Edinburgh Acads) 1871 *E,* 1872 *E,* 1874 *E,* 1875 *E*
Finlay, N J (Edinburgh Acads) 1875 *E,* 1876 *E,* 1878 *E,* 1879 *I, E,* 1880 *I, E,* 1881 *I, E*
Finlay, R (Watsonians) 1948 *E*
Fisher, A T (Waterloo, Watsonians) 1947 *I, E*
Fisher, C D (Waterloo) 1975 *NZ, A,* 1976 *W, E, I*
Fisher, D (W of Scotland) 1893 *I*
Fisher, J P (Royal HSFP, London Scottish) 1963 *E,* 1964 *F, NZ, W, I, E,* 1965 *F, W, I, E, SA,* 1966 *F, W, I, E, A,* 1967 *F, W, I, E, NZ,* 1968 *F, W, I, E*
Fleming, C J N (Edinburgh Wands) 1896 *I, E,* 1897 *I*
Fleming, G R (Glasgow Acads) 1875 *E,* 1876 *E*
Fletcher, H N (Edinburgh U) 1904 *E,* 1905 *W*
Flett, A B (Edinburgh U) 1901 *W, I, E,* 1902 *W, I*
Forbes, J L (Watsonians) 1905 *W,* 1906 *I, E*
Ford, D St C (United Services, RN) 1930 *I, E,* 1931 *E,* 1932 *W, I*
Ford, J R (Gala) 1893 *I*
Forrest, J E (Glasgow Acads) 1932 *SA,* 1935 *E, NZ*
Forrest, J G S (Cambridge U) 1938 *W, I, E*
Forrest, W T (Hawick) 1903 *W, I, E,* 1904 *W, I, E,* 1905 *W, I*
Forsayth, H H (Oxford U) 1921 *F, W, I, E,* 1922 *W, I, E*
Forsyth, I W (Stewart's Coll FP) 1972 *NZ,* 1973 *F, W, I, E, P*
Forsyth, J (Edinburgh U) 1871 *E*
Foster, R A (Hawick) 1930 *W,* 1932 *SA, I, E*
Fox, J (Gala) 1952 *F, W, I, E*
Frame, J N M (Edinburgh U, Gala) 1967 *NZ,* 1968 *F, W, I, E,* 1969 *W, I, E, SA,* 1970 *F, W, I, E, A,* 1971 *F, W, I, E* (2[1C]), 1972 *F, W, E, I,* 1973 *P* (R)
France, C (Kelvinside Acads) 1903 *I*
Fraser, C F P (Glasgow U) 1888 *W,* 1889 *W*
Fraser, J W (Edinburgh Inst FP) 1881 *E*
Fraser, R (Cambridge U) 1911 *F, W, I, E*
French, J (Glasgow Acads) 1886 *W,* 1887 *I, W, E*
Frew, A (Edinburgh U) 1901 *W, I, E*
Frew, G M (Glasgow HSFP) 1906 *SA,* 1907 *W, I, E,* 1908 *W, I, E,* 1909 *W, I, E,* 1910 *F, W, I,* 1911 *I, E*
Friebe, J P (Glasgow HSFP) 1952 *E*
Fulton, A K (Edinburgh U, Dollar Acads) 1952 *F,* 1954 *F*
Fyfe, K C (Cambridge U, Sale, London Scottish) 1933 *W, E,* 1934 *E,* 1935 *W, I, E, NZ,* 1936 *W, E,* 1939 *I*

Gallie, G H (Edinburgh Acads) 1939 *W*
Gallie, R A (Glasgow Acads) 1920 *F, W, I, E,* 1921 *F, W, I, E*
Gammell, W B B (Edinburgh Wands) 1977 *I, F, W,* 1978 *W, E*
Geddes, I C (London Scottish) 1906 *SA,* 1907 *W, I, E,* 1908 *W, E*
Geddes, K I (London Scottish) 1947 *F, W, I, E*
Gedge, H T S (Oxford U, London Scottish, Edinburgh Wands) 1894 *W, I, E,* 1896 *E,* 1899 *W, E*
Gedge, P M S (Edinburgh Wands) 1933 *I*
Gemmill, R (Glasgow HSFP) 1950 *F, W, I, E,* 1951 *F, W, I*
Gibson, W R (Royal HSFP) 1891 *I, E,* 1892 *W, I, E,* 1893 *W, I, E,* 1894 *W, I, E,* 1895 *W, I, E*
Gilbert-Smith, D S (London Scottish) 1952 *E*
Gilchrist, J (Glasgow Acads) 1925 *F*

Gill, A D (Gala) 1973 *P*, 1974 *W, E, I, F*
Gillespie, J I (Edinburgh Acads) 1899 *E*, 1900 *W, E*, 1901 *W, I, E*, 1902 *W, I*, 1904 *I, E*
Gillies, A C (Watsonians) 1924 *W, I, E*, 1925 *F, W, E*, 1926 *F, W*, 1927 *F, W, I, E*
Gilray, C M (Oxford U, London Scottish) 1908 *E*, 1909 *W, E*, 1912 *I*
Glasgow, I C (Heriot's FP) 1997 *F* (R)
Glasgow, R J C (Dunfermline) 1962 *F, W, I, E*, 1963 *I, E*, 1964 *I, E*, 1965 *W, I*
Glen, W S (Edinburgh Wands) 1955 *W*
Gloag, L G (Cambridge U) 1949 *F, W, I, E*
Goodfellow, J (Langholm) 1928 *W, I, E*
Goodhue, F W J (London Scottish) 1890 *W, I, E*, 1891 *W, I, E*, 1892 *W, I, E*
Gordon, R (Edinburgh Wands) 1951 *W*, 1952 *F, W, I, E*, 1953 *W*
Gordon, R E (Royal Artillery) 1913 *F, W, I*
Gordon, R J (London Scottish) 1982 *A* 1,2
Gore, A C (London Scottish) 1882 *I*
Gossman, B M (W of Scotland) 1980 *W*, 1983 *F, W*
Gossman, J S (W of Scotland) 1980 *E* (R)
Gowans, J J (Cambridge U, London Scottish) 1893 *W*, 1894 *W, E*, 1895 *W, I, E*, 1896 *I, E*
Gowland, G C (London Scottish) 1908 *W*, 1909 *W, E*, 1910 *F, W, I, E*
Gracie, A L (Harlequins) 1921 *F, W, I, E*, 1922 *F, W, I, E*, 1923 *F, W, I, E*, 1924 *F*
Graham, I N (Edinburgh Acads) 1939 *I, E*
Graham, J (Kelso) 1926 *I, E*, 1927 *F, W, I, E, A*, 1928 *F, W, I, E*, 1930 *I, E*, 1932 *SA, W*
Graham, J H S (Edinburgh Acads) 1876 *E*, 1877 *I, E*, 1878 *E*, 1879 *I, E*, 1880 *I, E*, 1881 *I, E*
Grant, D (Hawick) 1965 *F, E, SA*, 1966 *F, W, I, E, A*, 1967 *F, W, I, E, NZ*, 1968 *F*
Grant, D M (East Midlands) 1911 *W, I*
Grant, M L (Harlequins) 1955 *F*, 1956 *F, W*, 1957 *F*
Grant, T O (Hawick) 1960 *I, E, SA*, 1964 *F, NZ, W*
Grant, W St C (Craigmount) 1873 *E*, 1874 *E*
Gray, C A (Nottingham) 1989 *W, E, I, F, Fj, R*, 1990 *I, F, W, E, NZ* 1,2, *Arg*, 1991 *W, E, I, [J, I, WS, E, NZ]*
Gray, D (W of Scotland) 1978 *E*, 1979 *I, F, NZ*, 1980 *I, F, W, E*, 1981 *F*
Gray, G L (Gala) 1935 *NZ*, 1937 *W, I, E*
Gray, T (Northampton, Heriot's FP) 1950 *E*, 1951 *F, E*
Greenlees, H D (Leicester) 1927 *A*, 1928 *F, W*, 1929 *I, E*, 1930 *E*
Greenlees, J R C (Cambridge U, Kelvinside Acads) 1900 *I*, 1902 *W, I, E*, 1903 *W, I, E*
Greenwood, J T (Dunfermline and Perthshire Acads) 1952 *F*, 1955 *F, W, I, E*, 1956 *F, W, I, E*, 1957 *F, W, E*, 1958 *F, W, A, I, E*, 1959 *F, W, I*
Greig, A (Glasgow HSFP) 1911 *I*
Greig, L L (Glasgow Acads, United Services) 1905 *NZ*, 1906 *SA*, 1907 *W*, 1908 *W, I*
Greig, R C (Glasgow Acads) 1893 *W*, 1897 *I*
Grieve, C F (Oxford U) 1935 *W*, 1936 *E*
Grieve, R M (Kelso) 1935 *W, I, E, NZ*, 1936 *W, I, E*
Gunn, A W (Royal HSFP) 1912 *F, W, I, SA*, 1913 *F*

Hamilton, A S (Headingley) 1914 *W*, 1920 *F*
Hamilton, H M (W of Scotland) 1874 *E*, 1875 *E*
Hannah, R S M (W of Scotland) 1971 *I*
Harrower, P R (London Scottish) 1885 *W*
Hart, J G M (London Scottish) 1951 *SA*
Hart, T M (Glasgow U) 1930 *W, I*
Hart, W (Melrose) 1960 *SA*
Harvey, L (Greenock Wands) 1899 *I*
Hastie, A J (Melrose) 1961 *W, I, E*, 1964 *I, E*, 1965 *E, SA*, 1966 *F, W, I, E, A*, 1967 *F, W, I, NZ*, 1968 *F, W*
Hastie, I R (Kelso) 1955 *F*, 1958 *F, E*, 1959 *F, W, I*
Hastie, J D H (Melrose) 1938 *W, I, E*
Hastings, A G (Cambridge U, Watsonians, London Scottish) 1986 *F, W, E, I, R*, 1987 *I, F, W, E, [F, Z, R, NZ]*, 1988 *I, F, W, E, A*, 1989 *Fj, R*, 1990 *I, F, W, E, NZ* 1,2, *Arg*, 1991 *F, W, E, I, [J, I, WS, E, NZ]*, 1992 *E, I, F, W, A* 1, 1993 *I, F, W, E, NZ*, 1994 *W, E, I, F, SA*, 1995 *C, I, F, W, E, R, [Iv, Tg, F, NZ]*
Hastings, S (Watsonians) 1986 *F, W, E, I, R*, 1987 *I, F, W, [R]*, 1988 *I, F, W, A*, 1989 *W, E, I, F, Fj, R*, 1990 *I, F, W, E, NZ* 1,2, *Arg*, 1991 *W, E, I, [J, Z, I, WS, E, NZ]*, 1992 *E, NZ* 1,2, *Arg*, 1993 *I, F, W, E, NZ*, 1994 *E, I, F, SA*, 1995 *W, E, R* (R), *[Tg, NZ]*, 1996 *I, F, W, E, NZ* 2, *It*, 1997 *W* (R)

Hay, B H (Boroughmuir) 1975 *NZ, A*, 1976 *F*, 1978 *I, F, W, E, NZ*, 1979 *W, E, I, F, NZ*, 1980 *I, F, W, E*, 1981 *F, W, E, I, NZ* 1,2
Hay, J A (Hawick) 1995 *WS*
Hay-Gordon, J R (Edinburgh Acads) 1875 *E*, 1877 *I, E*
Hegarty, C B (Hawick) 1978 *I, F, W, E*
Hegarty, J J (Hawick) 1951 *F*, 1953 *F, W, I, E*, 1955 *F*
Henderson, B C (Edinburgh Wands) 1963 *E*, 1964 *F, I, E*, 1965 *F, W, I, E*, 1966 *F, W, I, E*
Henderson, F W (London Scottish) 1900 *W, I*
Henderson, I C (Edinburgh Acads) 1939 *I, E*, 1947 *F, W, E, A*, 1948 *I, E*
Henderson, J H (Oxford U, Richmond) 1953 *F, W, I, E*, 1954 *F, NZ, I, E, W*
Henderson, J M (Edinburgh Acads) 1933 *W, E, I*
Henderson, J Y M (Watsonians) 1911 *E*
Henderson, M M (Dunfermline) 1937 *W, I, E*
Henderson, N F (London Scottish) 1892 *I*
Henderson, R G (Newcastle Northern) 1924 *I, E*
Hendrie, K G P (Heriot's FP) 1924 *F, W, I*
Hendry, T L (Clydesdale) 1893 *W, I, E*, 1895 *I*
Henriksen, E H (Royal HSFP) 1953 *I*
Hepburn, D P (Woodford) 1947 *A*, 1948 *F, W, I, E*, 1949 *F, W, I, E*
Heron, G (Glasgow Acads) 1874 *E*, 1875 *E*
Hill, C C P (St Andrew's U) 1912 *F, I*
Hilton, D I W (Bath) 1995 *C, I, F, W, E, R, [Tg, F, NZ], WS*, 1996 *I, F, W, E, NZ* 1,2, *A, It*, 1997 *W*
Hinshelwood, A J W (London Scottish) 1966 *F, W, I, E, A*, 1967 *F, W, I, E, NZ*, 1968 *F, W, I, E, A*, 1969 *F, W, I, SA*, 1970 *F, W*
Hodge D W (Watsonians) 1997 *F* (R)
Hodgson, C G (London Scottish) 1968 *I, E*
Hogg, C D (Melrose) 1992 *A* 1,2, 1993 *NZ* (R), 1994 *Arg* 1,2
Hogg, C G (Boroughmuir) 1978 *F* (R), *W* (R)
Holms, W F (RIE Coll) 1886 *W, E*, 1887 *I, E*, 1889 *W, I*
Horsburgh, G B (London Scottish) 1937 *W, I, E*, 1938 *W, I, E*, 1939 *W, I, E*
Howie, D D (Kirkcaldy) 1912 *F, W, I, E, SA*, 1913 *F, W*
Howie, R A (Kirkcaldy) 1924 *F, W, I, E*, 1925 *W, I, E*
Hoyer-Millar, G C (Oxford U) 1953 *I*
Huggan, J L (London Scottish) 1914 *E*
Hume, J (Royal HSFP) 1912 *F*, 1920 *F*, 1921 *F, W, I, E*, 1922 *F*
Hume, J W G (Oxford U, Edinburgh Wands) 1928 *I*, 1930 *F*
Hunter, F (Edinburgh U) 1882 *I*
Hunter, I G (Selkirk) 1984 *I* (R), 1985 *F* (R), *W, E*
Hunter, J M (Cambridge U) 1947 *F*
Hunter, M D (Glasgow High) 1974 *F*
Hunter, W J (Hawick) 1964 *F, NZ, W*, 1967 *F, W, I, E*
Hutchison, W R (Glasgow HSFP) 1911 *E*
Hutton, A H M (Dunfermline) 1932 *I*
Hutton, J E (Harlequins) 1930 *E*, 1931 *F*

Inglis, H M (Edinburgh Acads) 1951 *F, W, I, E, SA*, 1952 *W, I*
Inglis, J M (Selkirk) 1952 *E*
Inglis, W M (Cambridge U, Royal Engineers) 1937 *W, I, E*, 1938 *W, I, E*
Innes, J R S (Aberdeen GSFP) 1939 *W, I, E*, 1947 *A*, 1948 *F, W, I, E*
Ireland, J C H (Glasgow HSFP) 1925 *W, I, E*, 1926 *F, W, I, E*, 1927 *F, W, I, E*
Irvine, A R (Heriot's FP) 1972 *NZ*, 1973 *F, W, I, E, P*, 1974 *W, E, I*, 1975 *I, F, W, E, NZ, A*, 1976 *W, E, I*, 1977 *E, I, F, W*, 1978 *I, F, E, NZ*, 1979 *W, E, I, F, NZ*, 1980 *I, F, W, E*, 1981 *F, W, E, I, NZ* 1,2, *R, A*, 1982 *E, I, F, W, A* 1,2
Irvine, D R (Edinburgh Acads) 1878 *E*, 1879 *I, E*
Irvine, R W (Edinburgh Acads) 1871 *E*, 1872 *E*, 1873 *E*, 1874 *E*, 1875 *E*, 1876 *E*, 1877 *I, E*, 1878 *E*, 1879 *I, E*, 1880 *I, E*
Irvine T W (Edinburgh Acads) 1885 *I* 1,2, 1886 *W, I, E*, 1887 *I, W, E*, 1888 *W, I*, 1889 *I*

Jackson, K L T (Oxford U) 1933 *W, E, I*, 1934 *W*
Jackson, T G H (Army) 1947 *F, W, E, A*, 1948 *F, W, I, E*, 1949 *F, W, I, E*
Jackson, W D (Hawick) 1964 *I*, 1965 *E, SA*, 1968 *A*, 1969 *F, W, I, E*
Jamieson, J (W of Scotland) 1883 *W, I, E*, 1884 *W, I, E*, 1885 *W, I* 1,2

MacGregor, G (Cambridge U) 1890 *W, I, E,* 1891 *W, I, E,* 1893 *W, I, E,* 1894 *W, I, E,* 1896 *E*
MacGregor, I A A (Hillhead HSFP, Llanelli) 1955 *I, E, 1956 F, W, I, E,* 1957 *F, W, I*
MacGregor, J R (Edinburgh U) 1909 *I*
McGuinness, G M (W of Scotland) 1982 *A 1,2,* 1983 *I, 1985 I, F, W, E*
McHarg, A F (W of Scotland, London Scottish) 1968 *I, E, A,* 1969 *F, W, I, E,* 1971 *F, W, I, E* (2[1C]), 1972 *F, E, NZ,* 1973 *F, W, I, E, P,* 1974 *W, E, I,* 1975 *I, F, W, E, NZ, A,* 1976 *F, W, E, I,* 1977 *E, I, F, W,* 1978 *I, F, W, NZ, 1979 W, E*
McIndoe, F (Glasgow Acads) 1886 *W, I*
MacIntyre, I (Edinburgh Wands) 1890 *W, I, E,* 1891 *W, I, E*
McIvor, D J (Edinburgh Acads) 1992 *E, I, F, W,* 1993 *NZ,* 1994 *SA*
Mackay, E B (Glasgow Acads) 1920 *W,* 1922 *E*
McKeating, E (Heriot's FP) 1957 *F, W,* 1961 *SA, W, I, E*
McKendrick, J G (W of Scotland) 1889 *I*
Mackenzie, A D G (Selkirk) 1984 *A*
Mackenzie, C J G (United Services) 1921 *E*
Mackenzie, D D (Edinburgh U) 1947 *W, I, E,* 1948 *F, W, I*
Mackenzie, D K A (Edinburgh Wands) 1939 *I, E*
Mackenzie, J M (Edinburgh U) 1905 *NZ,* 1909 *W, I, E, 1910 W, I, E,* 1911 *W, I*
McKenzie, K D (Stirling County) 1994 *Arg 1,2,* 1995 *R, [Iv],* 1996 *I, F, W, E, NZ 1,2, A, It*
Mackenzie, R C (Glasgow Acads) 1877 *I, E,* 1881 *I, E*
Mackie, G Y (Highland) 1975 *A,* 1976 *F, W,* 1978 *F*
MacKinnon, A (London Scottish) 1898 *I, E,* 1899 *I, W, E,* 1900 *E*
Mackintosh, C E W C (London Scottish) 1924 *F*
Mackintosh, H S (Glasgow U, W of Scotland) 1929 *F, W, I, E,* 1930 *F, W, I, E,* 1931 *F, W, I, E,* 1932 *SA, W, I, E*
MacLachlan, L P (Oxford U, London Scottish) 1954 *NZ, I, E, W*
Maclagan, W E (Edinburgh Acads) 1878 *E,* 1879 *I, E, 1880 I, E,* 1881 *I, E,* 1882 *I, E,* 1883 *W, I, E,* 1884 *W, I, E, 1885 W, I* 1,2, 1887 *I, W, E,* 1888 *W, I,* 1890 *W, I, E*
McLaren, A (Durham County) 1931 *F*
McLaren, E (London Scottish, Royal HSFP) 1923 *F, W, I, E,* 1924 *F*
McLauchlan, J (Jordanhill) 1969 *E, SA,* 1970 *F, W,* 1971 *F, W, I, E* (2[1C]), 1972 *F, W, E, NZ,* 1973 *F, W, I, E, P, 1974 F, W, I, E,* 1975 *I, F, W, E, NZ, A,* 1976 *F, W, E, I, 1977 W,* 1978 *I, F, W, E, I, F, NZ*
McLean, D I (Royal HSFP) 1947 *I, E*
Maclennan, W D (Watsonians) 1947 *F, I*
MacLeod, D A (Glasgow U) 1886 *I, E*
MacLeod, G (Edinburgh Acads) 1878 *E,* 1882 *I*
McLeod, H F (Hawick) 1954 *F, NZ, I, E, W,* 1955 *F, W, I, E,* 1956 *F, W, I, E,* 1957 *F, W, I, E,* 1958 *F, W, A, I, E, 1959 F, W, I, E,* 1960 *F, W, I, E, SA,* 1961 *F, SA, W, I, E, 1962 F, W, I, E*
MacLeod, K G (Cambridge U) 1905 *NZ,* 1906 *W, I, E, SA,* 1907 *W, I, E,* 1908 *I, E*
MacLeod, L M (Cambridge U) 1904 *W, I, E,* 1905 *W, I, NZ*
Macleod, W M (Fettesian-Lorettonians, Edinburgh Wands) 1886 *W, I*
McMillan, K H D (Sale) 1953 *F, W, I, E*
MacMillan, R G (London Scottish) 1887 *W, I, E,* 1890 *W, I, E,* 1891 *W, I, E,* 1892 *W, I, E,* 1893 *W, E,* 1894 *W, I, E,* 1895 *W, I, E,* 1897 *I, E*
MacMyn, D J (Cambridge U, London Scottish) 1925 *F, W, I, E,* 1926 *F, W, I, E,* 1927 *E, A,* 1928 *F*
McNeil, A S B (Watsonians) 1935 *I*
McPartlin, J J (Harlequins, Oxford U) 1960 *F, W,* 1962 *F, W, I, E*
Macphail, J A R (Edinburgh Acads) 1949 *E,* 1951 *SA*
Macpherson, D G (London Hospital) 1910 *I, E*
Macpherson, G P S (Oxford U, Edinburgh Acads) 1922 *F, W, I, E,* 1924 *W, E,* 1925 *F, W, E,* 1927 *F, W, I, E,* 1928 *F, W, E, 1929 I, E,* 1930 *F, W, I, E,* 1931 *W, E,* 1932 *SA, E,* 1933 *I, E*
Macpherson, N C (Newport) 1920 *W, I, E,* 1921 *F, E, 1923 I, E*
McQueen, S B (Waterloo) 1923 *F, W, I, E*
Macrae, D J (St Andrew's U) 1937 *W, I, E,* 1938 *W, I, E, 1939 W, I, E*
Madsen, D F (Gosforth) 1974 *W, E, I, F,* 1975 *I, F, W, E, 1976 F,* 1977 *E, I, F, W,* 1978 *I, E*
Mair, N G R (Edinburgh U) 1951 *F, W, I, E*
Maitland, G (Edinburgh Inst FP) 1885 *W, I* 2

Maitland, R (Edinburgh Inst FP) 1881 *E,* 1882 *I, E, 1884 W,* 1885 *W*
Maitland, R P (Royal Artillery) 1872 *E*
Malcolm, A G (Glasgow U) 1888 *I*
Manson, J J (Dundee HSFP) 1995 *E* (R)
Marsh, J (Edinburgh Inst FP) 1889 *W, I*
Marshall, A (Edinburgh Acads) 1875 *E*
Marshall, G R (Selkirk) 1988 *A* (R), 1989 *Fj,* 1990 *Arg,* 1991 [*Z*]
Marshall, J C (London Scottish) 1954 *F, NZ, I, E, W*
Marshall, K W (Edinburgh Acads) 1934 *W, I, E,* 1935 *W, I, E,* 1936 *W,* 1937 *E*
Marshall, T R (Edinburgh Acads) 1871 *E,* 1872 *E,* 1873 *E,* 1874 *E*
Marshall, W (Edinburgh Acads) 1872 *E*
Martin, H (Edinburgh Acads, Oxford U) 1908 *W, I, E, 1909 W, E*
Masters, W H (Edinburgh Inst FP) 1879 *I,* 1880 *I, E*
Maxwell, F T (Royal Engineers) 1872 *E*
Maxwell, G H H P (Edinburgh Acads, RAF, London Scottish) 1913 *I, E,* 1914 *W, I, E,* 1920 *W, E,* 1921 *F, W, I, E,* 1922 *F, E*
Maxwell, J M (Langholm) 1957 *I*
Mein, J (Edinburgh Acads) 1871 *E,* 1872 *E,* 1873 *E, 1874 E,* 1875 *E*
Melville, C L (Army) 1937 *W, I, E*
Menzies, H F (W of Scotland) 1893 *W, I,* 1894 *W, E*
Methuen, A (London Scottish) 1889 *W, I*
Michie, E J S (Aberdeen U, Aberdeen GSFP) 1954 *F, NZ, I, E,* 1955 *W, I, E,* 1956 *F, W, I, E,* 1957 *F, W, I, E*
Millar, J N (W of Scotland) 1892 *W, I, E,* 1893 *W,* 1895 *I, E*
Millar, R K (London Scottish) 1924 *I*
Millican, J G (Edinburgh U) 1973 *W, I, E*
Milne, C J B (Fettesian-Lorettonians, W of Scotland) 1886 *W, I, E*
Milne, D F (Heriot's FP) 1991 [*J(R)*]
Milne, I G (Heriot's FP, Harlequins) 1979 *I, F, NZ,* 1980 *I, F,* 1981 *NZ 1,2, R, A,* 1982 *E, I, F, W, A 1,2,* 1983 *I, F, W, E, NZ,* 1984 *W, E, I, F, A,* 1985 *F, W, E,* 1986 *F, W, E, I, R,* 1987 *I, F, W, E, [F, Z, NZ],* 1988 *A,* 1989 *W,* 1990 *NZ 1,2*
Milne, K S (Heriot's FP) 1989 *W, E, I, F, Fj, R,* 1990 *I, F, W, E, NZ 2, Arg,* 1991 *F, W* (R), *E,* [*Z*], 1992 *E, I, F, W, A 1,* 1993 *I, F, W, E, NZ,* 1994 *W, E, I, F, SA,* 1995 *C, I, F, W, E, [Tg, F, NZ]*
Milne, W M (Glasgow Acads) 1904 *I, E,* 1905 *W, I*
Milroy, E (Watsonians) 1910 *W,* 1911 *E,* 1912 *W, I, E, SA,* 1913 *F, W, I, E,* 1914 *I, E*
Mitchell, G W E (Edinburgh Wands) 1967 *NZ,* 1968 *F, W*
Mitchell, J G (W of Scotland) 1885 *W, I* 1,2
Moncreiff, F J (Edinburgh Acads) 1871 *E,* 1872 *E,* 1873 *E*
Monteith, H G (Cambridge U, London Scottish) 1905 *E, 1906 W, I, E, SA,* 1907 *W, I,* 1908 *E*
Monypenny, D B (London Scottish) 1899 *I, W, E*
Moodie, A R (St Andrew's U) 1909 *E,* 1910 *F,* 1911 *F*
Moore, A (Edinburgh Acads) 1990 *NZ 2, Arg,* 1991 *F, W, E*
Morgan, D W (Stewart's-Melville FP) 1973 *W, I, E, P, 1974 I, F,* 1975 *I, F, W, E, NZ, A,* 1976 *F, W,* 1977 *I, F, W, 1978 I, F, W, E*
Morrison, I R (London Scottish) 1993 *I, F, W, E,* 1994 *W, SA,* 1995 *C, I, F, W, E, R, [Tg, F, NZ]*
Morrison, M C (Royal HSFP) 1896 *W, I, E,* 1897 *I, E, 1898 I, E,* 1899 *I, W, E,* 1900 *W, E,* 1901 *W, I, E,* 1902 *I, E,* 1903 *W, I,* 1904 *W, I, E*
Morrison, R H (Edinburgh U) 1886 *W, I, E*
Morrison, W H (Edinburgh Acads) 1900 *W*
Morton, D S (W of Scotland) 1887 *I, W, E,* 1888 *W, I, 1889 W, I,* 1890 *I, E*
Mowat, J G (Glasgow Acads) 1883 *W, E*
Muir, D E (Heriot's FP) 1950 *F, W, I, E,* 1952 *W, I, E*
Munnoch, N M (Watsonians) 1952 *F, W, I*
Munro, D S (Glasgow High Kelvinside) 1994 *W, E, I, F, Arg 1,2,* 1997 *W* (R)
Munro, P (Oxford U, London Scottish) 1905 *W, I, E, NZ, 1906 W, I, E, SA,* 1907 *I, E,* 1911 *F, W, I*
Munro, R (St Andrew's U) 1871 *E*
Munro, S (Ayr, W of Scotland) 1980 *I, F,* 1981 *F, W, E, I, NZ 1,2, R,* 1984 *W*
Munro, W H (Glasgow HSFP) 1947 *I, E*
Murdoch, W C W (Hillhead HSFP) 1935 *E, NZ,* 1936 *W, I,* 1939 *E,* 1948 *F, W, I, E*
Murray, G M (Glasgow Acads) 1921 *I,* 1926 *W*
Murray, H M (Glasgow U) 1936 *W, I*

Alan Tait drives on for Scotland against Ireland at Murrayfield.

Thom, J R (Watsonians) 1933 *W, E, I*
Thomson, A E (United Services) 1921 *F, W, E*
Thomson, A M (St Andrew's U) 1949 *I*
Thomson, B E (Oxford U) 1953 *F, W, I*
Thomson, I H M (Heriot's FP, Army) 1951 *W, I,* 1952 *F, W, I,* 1953 *I, E*
Thomson, J S (Glasgow Acads) 1871 *E*
Thomson, R H (London Scottish, PUC) 1960 *I, E, SA,* 1961 *F, SA, W, I, E,* 1963 *F, W, I, E,* 1964 *F, NZ, W*
Thomson, W H (W of Scotland) 1906 *SA*
Thomson, W J (W of Scotland) 1899 *W, E,* 1900 *W*
Timms, A B (Edinburgh U, Edinburgh Wands) 1896 *W, 1900 W, I,* 1901 *W, I, E,* 1902 *W, E,* 1903 *W, E,* 1904 *I, E,* 1905 *I, E*
Tod, H B (Gala) 1911 *F*
Tod, J (Watsonians) 1884 *W, I, E,* 1885 *W, I* 1,2, 1886 *W, I, E*
Todd, J K (Glasgow Acads) 1874 *E,* 1875 *E*
Tolmie, J M (Glasgow HSFP) 1922 *E*
Tomes, A J (Hawick) 1976 *E, I,* 1977 *E,* 1978 *I, F, W, E, NZ,* 1979 *W, E, I, F, NZ,* 1980 *F, W, E,* 1981 *F, W, E, I, NZ* 1,2, *R, A,* 1982 *E, I, F, W, A* 1,2, 1983 *I, F, W,* 1984 *W, E, I, F, R, A,* 1985 *W, E,* 1987 *I, F, E* (R), *[F, Z, R, NZ]*
Torrie, T J (Edinburgh Acads) 1877 *E*
Townsend, G P J (Gala, Northampton) 1993 *E* (R), 1994 *W, E, I, F, Arg* 1,2, 1995 *C, I, F, W, E, WS,* 1996 *I, F, W, E, NZ* 1,2, *A, It,* 1997 *W, E, I, F*
Tukalo, I (Selkirk) 1985 *I,* 1987 *I, F, W, E, [F, Z, R, NZ],* 1988 *F, W, E, A,* 1989 *W, E, I, F, Fj,* 1990 *I, F, W, E, NZ* 1, 1991 *I, R, [J, Z, I, WS, E, NZ],* 1992 *E, I, F, W, A* 1,2
Turk, A S (Langholm) 1971 *E* (R)
Turnbull, D J (Hawick) 1987 *[NZ],* 1988 *F, E,* 1990 *E* (R), 1991 *F, W, E, I, R, [Z],* 1993 *I, F, W, E,* 1994 *W*
Turnbull, F O (Kelso) 1951 *F, SA*
Turnbull, G O (W of Scotland) 1896 *I, E,* 1897 *I, E,* 1904 *W*
Turnbull, P (Edinburgh Acads) 1901 *W, I, E,* 1902 *W, I, E*
Turner, F H (Oxford U, Liverpool) 1911 *F, W, I, E,* 1912 *F, W, I, E, SA,* 1913 *F, W, I, E,* 1914 *I, E*
Turner, J W C (Gala) 1966 *W, A,* 1967 *F, W, I, E, NZ,* 1968 *F, W, I, E, A,* 1969 *F,* 1970 *E, A,* 1971 *F, W, I, E* (2[1C])

Usher, C M (United Services, Edinburgh Wands) 1912 *E,* 1913 *F, W, I, E,* 1914 *I, E,* 1920 *F, W, I, E,* 1921 *W, E,* 1922 *F, W, I, E*

Valentine, A R (RNAS, Anthorn) 1953 *F, W, I*
Valentine, D D (Hawick) 1947 *I, E*
Veitch, J P (Royal HSFP) 1882 *E,* 1883 *I,* 1884 *W, I, E,* 1885 *I* 1,2, 1886 *E*
Villar, C (Edinburgh Wands) 1876 *E,* 1877 *I, E*

Waddell, G H (London Scottish, Cambridge U) 1957 *E,* 1958 *F, W, A, I, E,* 1959 *F, W, I, E,* 1960 *I, E, SA,* 1961 *F,* 1962 *F, W, I, E*
Waddell, H (Glasgow Acads) 1924 *F, W, I, E,* 1925 *I, E,* 1926 *F, W, I, E,* 1927 *F, W, I, E,* 1930 *W*
Wade, A L (London Scottish) 1908 *E*
Wainwright, R I (Edinburgh Acads, West Hartlepool, Watsonians, Army) 1992 *I* (R), *F, A* 1,2, 1993 *NZ,* 1994 *W, E,* 1995 *C, I, F, W, E, R, [Iv, Tg, F, NZ], WS,* 1996 *I, F, W, E, NZ* 1,2, 1997 *W, E, I, F*
Walker, A (W of Scotland) 1881 *I,* 1882 *E,* 1883 *W, I, E*
Walker, A W (Cambridge U, Birkenhead Park) 1931 *F, W, I, E,* 1932 *I*
Walker, J G (W of Scotland) 1882 *E,* 1883 *W*
Walker, M (Oxford U) 1952 *F*
Wallace, A C (Oxford U) 1923 *F,* 1924 *F, W, E,* 1925 *F, W, I, E,* 1926 *F*
Wallace, W M (Cambridge U) 1913 *E,* 1914 *W, I, E*
Wallace, M I (Glasgow High Kelvinside) 1996 *A, It,* 1997 *W*
Walls, W A (Glasgow Acads) 1882 *E,* 1883 *W, I, E,* 1884 *W, I, E,* 1886 *W, I, E*
Walter, M W (London Scottish) 1906 *I, E, SA,* 1907 *W, I, 1908 W, I,* 1910 *I*
Walton, P (Northampton, Newcastle) 1994 *E, I, F, Arg* 1,2, 1995 *[Iv],* 1997 *W, E, I, F*
Warren, J R (Glasgow Acads) 1914 *I*
Warren, R C (Glasgow Acads) 1922 *W, I,* 1930 *W, I, E*
Waters, F H (Cambridge U, London Scottish) 1930 *F, W, I, E,* 1932 *SA, W, I*

Waters, J A (Selkirk) 1933 *W, E, I,* 1934 *W, I, E,* 1935 *W, I, E, NZ,* 1936 *W, I, E,* 1937 *W, I, E*
Waters, J B (Cambridge U) 1904 *I, E*
Watherston, J G (Edinburgh Wands) 1934 *I, E*
Watherston, W R A (London Scottish) 1963 *F, W, I*
Watson, D H (Glasgow Acads) 1876 *E,* 1877 *I, E*
Watson, W S (Boroughmuir) 1974 *W, E, I, F,* 1975 *NZ,* 1977 *I, F, W,* 1979 *I, F*
Watt, A G J (Glasgow High Kelvinside) 1991 *[Z],* 1993 *I, NZ,* 1994 *Arg* 2 (t & R)
Watt, A G M (Edinburgh Acads) 1947 *F, W, I, A,* 1948 *F, W*
Weatherstone, T G (Stewart's Coll FP) 1952 *E,* 1953 *I, E,* 1954 *F, NZ, I, E, W,* 1955 *F,* 1958 *W, A, I, E,* 1959 *W, I, E*
Weir, G W (Melrose, Newcastle) 1990 *Arg,* 1991 *R, [J, Z, I, WS, E, NZ],* 1992 *E, I, F, W, A* 1,2, 1993 *I, F, W, E, NZ,* 1994 *W* (R), *E, I, F, SA,* 1995 *F* (R), *W, E, R, [Iv, Tg, F, NZ], WS,* 1996 *I, F, W, E, NZ* 1,2, *A, It* (R), 1997 *W, E, I, F*
Welsh, R (Watsonians) 1895 *W, I, E,* 1896 *W*
Welsh, R B (Hawick) 1967 *I, E*
Welsh, W B (Hawick) 1927 *A,* 1928 *F, W, I,* 1929 *I, E,* 1930 *F, W, I, E,* 1931 *F, W, I, E,* 1932 *SA, W, I, E,* 1933 *W, E, I*
Welsh, W H (Edinburgh U) 1900 *I, E,* 1901 *W, I, E,* 1902 *W, I, E*
Wemyss, A (Gala, Edinburgh Wands) 1914 *W, I,* 1920 *F, E,* 1922 *F, W, I*
West, L (Edinburgh U, West Hartlepool) 1903 *W, I, E,* 1905 *I, E, NZ,* 1906 *W, I, E*
Weston, V G (Kelvinside Acads) 1936 *I, E*
White, D B (Gala, London Scottish) 1982 *F, W, A* 1,2, 1987 *W, E, [F, R, NZ],* 1988 *I, F, W, E, A,* 1989 *W, E, I, F, Fj, R,* 1990 *I, F, W, E, NZ* 1,2, 1991 *F, W, E, I, R, [J, Z, I, WS, E, NZ],* 1992 *E, I, F, W*
White, D M (Kelvinside Acads) 1963 *F, W, I, E*
White, T B (Edinburgh Acads) 1888 *W, I,* 1889 *W*
Whittington, T P (Merchistonians) 1873 *F*
Whitworth, R J E (London Scottish) 1936 *I*
Whyte, D J (Edinburgh Wands) 1965 *W, I, E, SA,* 1966 *F, W, I, E, A,* 1967 *F, W, I, E*
Will, J G (Cambridge U) 1912 *F, W, I, E,* 1914 *W, I, E*
Wilson, A W (Dunfermline) 1931 *F, I, E*
Wilson, G A (Oxford U) 1949 *F, W, E*
Wilson, G R (Royal HSFP) 1886 *E,* 1890 *W, I, E,* 1891 *I*
Wilson, J H (Watsonians) 1953 *I*
Wilson, J S (St Andrew's U) 1931 *F, W, I, E,* 1932 *E*
Wilson, J S (United Services, London Scottish) 1908 *I, 1909 W*
Wilson, R (London Scottish) 1976 *E, I,* 1977 *E, I, F,* 1978 *I, F,* 1981 *R,* 1983 *I*
Wilson, R L (Gala) 1951 *F, W, I, E, SA,* 1953 *F, W, E*
Wilson, R W (W of Scotland) 1873 *E,* 1874 *E*
Wilson, S (Oxford U, London Scottish) 1964 *F, NZ, W, I, E,* 1965 *W, I, E, SA,* 1966 *F, W, I, A,* 1967 *F, W, I, E, NZ,* 1968 *F, W, I, E*
Wood, A (Royal HSFP) 1873 *E,* 1874 *E,* 1875 *E*
Wood, G (Gala) 1931 *W, I,* 1932 *W, I, E*
Woodburn, J C (Kelvinside Acads) 1892 *I*
Woodrow, A N (Glasgow Acads) 1887 *I, W, E*
Wotherspoon, W (W of Scotland) 1891 *I,* 1892 *I,* 1893 *W, E,* 1894 *W, I, E*
Wright, F A (Edinburgh Acads) 1932 *E*
Wright, H B (Watsonians) 1894 *W*
Wright, K M (London Scottish) 1929 *F, W, I, E*
Wright, P H (Boroughmuir) 1992 *A* 1,2, 1993 *F, W, E,* 1994 *W,* 1995 *C, I, F, W, E, R, [Iv, Tg, F, NZ],* 1996 *W, E, NZ* 1
Wright, R W J (Edinburgh Wands) 1973 *F*
Wright, S T H (Stewart's Coll FP) 1949 *E*
Wright, T (Hawick) 1947 *A*
Wyllie, D S (Stewart's-Melville FP) 1984 *A,* 1985 *W* (R), *E,* 1987 *I, F, [F, Z, R, NZ],* 1989 *R,* 1991 *R, [J (R), Z],* 1993 *NZ* (R), 1994 *W* (R), *E, I, F*

Young, A H (Edinburgh Acads) 1874 *E*
Young, E T (Glasgow Acads) 1914 *E*
Young, R G (Watsonians) 1970 *W*
Young, T E B (Durham) 1911 *F*
Young, W B (Cambridge U, London Scottish) 1937 *W, I,* 1938 *W, I, E,* 1939 *W, I, E,* 1948 *E*

SCOTTISH INTERNATIONAL RECORDS (*up to 30 April 1997*)

MATCH RECORDS

MOST CONSECUTIVE TEST WINS

6 1925 F, W, I, E, 1926 F, W
6 1989 Fj, R, 1990 I, F, W, E

MOST CONSECUTIVE TESTS WITHOUT DEFEAT

P	W	D	Period
9	6*	3	1885–87
6	6	0	1925–26
6	6	0	1989–90
6	4	2	1877–80
6	5	1	1983–84

MOST POINTS IN A MATCH
by the team

Pts	Opp	Venue	Year
89	Iv	Rustenburg	1995
60	Z	Wellington	1987
55	R	Dunedin	1987
51	Z	Murrayfield	1991
49	A	Murrayfield	1990
49	R	Murrayfield	1995

by a player
44 by A G Hastings v Ivory Coast at Rustenburg — 1995
31 by A G Hastings v Tonga at Pretoria — 1995
27 by A G Hastings v Romania at Dunedin — 1987
21 by A G Hastings v England at Murrayfield — 1986
21 by A G Hastings v Romania at Bucharest — 1986

MOST TRIES IN A MATCH
by the team

T	Opp	Venue	Year
13	Iv	Rustenburg	1995
12	W	Raeburn Place	1887
11	Z	Wellington	1987
9	R	Dunedin	1987
9	Arg	Murrayfield	1990

by a player
5 by G C Lindsay v Wales at Raeburn Place — 1887
4 by W A Stewart v Ireland at Inverleith — 1913
4 by I S Smith v France at Inverleith — 1925
4 by I S Smith v Wales at Swansea — 1925
4 by A G Hastings v Ivory Coast at Rustenburg — 1995

MOST CONVERSIONS IN A MATCH
by the team

C	Opp	Venue	Year
9	Iv	Rustenburg	1995
8	Z	Wellington	1987
8	R	Dunedin	1987

by a player
9 by A G Hastings v Ivory Coast at Rustenburg — 1995
8 by A G Hastings v Zimbabwe at Wellington — 1987
8 by A G Hastings v Romania at Dunedin — 1987

MOST PENALTY GOALS IN A MATCH
by the team

P	Opp	Venue	Year
8	Tg	Pretoria	1995
6	F	Murrayfield	1986

by a player
8 by A G Hastings v Tonga at Pretoria — 1995
6 by A G Hastings v France at Murrayfield — 1986

MOST DROPPED GOALS IN A MATCH
by the team

D	Opp	Venue	Year
3	I	Murrayfield	1973
2	several instances		

by a player
2 by R C MacKenzie v Ireland at Belfast — 1877
2 by N J Finlay v Ireland at Glasgow — 1880
2 by B M Simmers v Wales at Murrayfield — 1965
2 by D W Morgan v Ireland at Murrayfield — 1973
2 by B M Gossman v France at Parc des Princes — 1983

2 by J Y Rutherford v New Zealand
at Murrayfield 1983
2 by J Y Rutherford v Wales at
Murrayfield 1985
2 by J Y Rutherford v Ireland at
Murrayfield 1987
2 by C M Chalmers v England at
Twickenham 1995

CAREER RECORDS

MOST CAPPED PLAYERS

Caps	Player	Career
65	S Hastings	1986–97
61	A G Hastings	1986–95
52	J M Renwick	1972–84
52	C T Deans	1978–87
52	C M Chalmers	1989–97
51	A R Irvine	1972–82
50	A B Carmichael	1967–78
48	A J Tomes	1976–87
47	R J Laidlaw	1980–88
45	A G Stanger	1989–97
45	G W Weir	1990–97

MOST CONSECUTIVE TESTS

Tests	Player	Span
49	A B Carmichael	1967–78
40	H F McLeod	1954–62
37	J M Bannerman	1921–29
35	A G Stanger	1989–94

MOST TESTS AS CAPTAIN

Tests	Captain	Span
25	D M B Sole	1989–92
20	A G Hastings	1993–95
19	J McLauchlan	1973–79
15	M C Morrison	1899–1904
15	A R Smith	1957–62
15	A R Irvine	1980–82

MOST TESTS IN INDIVIDUAL POSITIONS

Full-back	A G Hastings	61	1986–95
Wing	A G Stanger	42	1989–97
Centre	S Hastings	63	1986–97
Fly-half	C M Chalmers	51	1989–97
Scrum-half	R J Laidlaw	47	1980–88

Prop	A B Carmichael	50	1967–78
Hooker	C T Deans	52	1978–87
Lock	A J Tomes	48	1976–87
Flanker	J Jeffrey	40	1984–91
No 8	D B White	29	1982–92

MOST POINTS IN TESTS

Pts	Player	Tests	Career
667	A G Hastings	61	1986–95
273	A R Irvine	51	1972–82
210	P W Dods	23	1983–91
140	C M Chalmers	52	1989–97
96	A G Stanger	45	1989–97

MOST TRIES IN TESTS

Tries	Player	Tests	Career
24	I S Smith	32	1924–33
22	A G Stanger	45	1989–97
17	A G Hastings	61	1986–95
15	I Tukalo	37	1985–92
12	A R Smith	33	1955–62

MOST CONVERSIONS IN TESTS

Cons	Player	Tests	Career
86	A G Hastings	61	1986–95
26	P W Dods	23	1983–91
25	A R Irvine	51	1972–82
19	D Drysdale	26	1923–29
14	F H Turner	15	1911–14

MOST PENALTY GOALS IN TESTS

Pens	Player	Tests	Career
140	A G Hastings	61	1986–95
61	A R Irvine	51	1972–82
50	P W Dods	23	1983–91
24	C M Chalmers	52	1989–97
21	M Dods	8	1994–96

MOST DROPPED GOALS IN TESTS

Drops	Player	Tests	Career
12	J Y Rutherford	42	1979–87
9	C M Chalmers	52	1989–97
7	I R McGeechan	32	1972–79
6	D W Morgan	21	1973–78
5	H Waddell	15	1924–30

INTERNATIONAL CHAMPIONSHIP RECORDS

Record	Detail	Holder	Set
Most points in season	90	in four matches	1997
Most tries in season	17	in four matches	1925
Highest score	38	38–10 v Ireland	1997
Biggest win	28	31–3 v France	1912
	28	38–10 v Ireland	1997
Highest score conceded	47	20–47 v France	1997
Biggest defeat	27	20–47 v France	1997
Most appearances	42	J M Renwick	1972–83
Most points in matches	288	A G Hastings	1986–95
Most points in season	56	A G Hastings	1995
Most points in match	21	A G Hastings	v England, 1986
Most tries in matches	24	I S Smith	1924–33
Most tries in season	8	I S Smith	1925
Most tries in match	5	G C Lindsay	v Wales, 1887
Most cons in matches	20	A G Hastings	1986–95
Most cons in season	9	R J S Shepherd	1997
Most cons in match	5	F H Turner	v France, 1912
	5	J W Allan	v England, 1931
	5	R J S Shepherd	v Ireland, 1997
Most pens in matches	77	A G Hastings	1986–95
Most pens in season	14	A G Hastings	1986
Most pens in match	6	A G Hastings	v France, 1986
Most drops in matches	8	J Y Rutherford	1979–87
	8	C M Chalmers	1989–97
Most drops in season	3	J Y Rutherford	1987
Most drops in match	2	on several occasions	

MAJOR TOUR RECORDS

Record	Detail	Year	Place
Most individual points	69 by R J S Shepherd	1996	New Zealand
Most points in match	24 by D W Morgan	1975 v Wellington	Wellington (NZ)
	24 by A R Irvine	1981 v King Country	Taumarunui (NZ)
	24 by A R Irvine	1981 v Wairarapa/ Bush	Masterton (NZ)
Most tries in match	3 by A R Smith	1960 v E Transvaal	Springs (SA)
	3 by D A Stark	1996 v Bay of Plenty	Rotorua (NZ)

MISCELLANEOUS RECORDS

Record	Holder	Detail
Longest Test career	W C W Murdoch	14 seasons, 1934–35 to 1947–48
Youngest Test cap	N J Finlay	17 yrs 36 days in 1875*
Oldest Test cap	J McLauchlan	37 yrs 210 days in 1979

* C Reid, also 17 yrs 36 days on debut in 1881, was a day *older* than Finlay, having lived through an extra leap-year day.

SCOTLAND INTERNATIONAL CAREER RECORDS (*up to 30 April 1997*)

Player	Debut	Caps since last season	Caps	T	C	PG	DG	Pts
R J S Shepherd	1995 v WS	1996 *NZ* 1,2, *A*, *It*, 1997 *W*, *E*, *I*, *F*	13	1	12	15	1	77
C A Joiner	1994 v Arg	1996 *NZ* 1	17	3	0	0	0	15
D A Stark	1993 v I	1996 *NZ* 2 (R), *It* (R), 1997 ***W*** (R), *E*	8	2	0	0	0	10
K M Logan	1992 v A	1996 *NZ* 1,2, *A*, *It*, 1997 *W*, *E*, *I*, *F*	30	7	0	0	0	35
A G Stanger	1989 v Fj	1996 *NZ* 2, *A*, *It*, 1997 *W*, *E*, *I*, *F*	45	22	0	0	0	96
S Hastings	1986 v F	1996 *NZ* 2, *It*, 1997 *W*, *E* (R)	65	10	0	0	0	43
B R S Eriksson	1996 v NZ	1996 *NZ* 1, *A*, 1997 *E*	3	1	0	0	0	5
I C Jardine	1993 v NZ	1996 *NZ* 1,2	17	0	0	0	0	0
A V Tait	1987 v F	1997 *I*, *F*	10	7	0	0	0	31
I C Glasgow	1997 v F	1997 *F* (R)	1	0	0	0	0	0
M Dods	1994 v I		8	3	1	21	0	80
G P J Townsend	1993 v E	1996 *NZ* 1,2 *A*, *It*, 1997 *W*, *E*, *I*, *F*	25	4	0	0	3	29
C M Chalmers	1989 v W	1996 *A*, *It*, 1997 *W*, *I*, *F*	52	5	10	24	9	140
D W Hodge	1997 v F	1997 *F* (R)	1	0	0	0	0	0
A D Nicol	1992 v E		8	1	0	0	0	4
G Armstrong	1988 v A	1996 *NZ* 1,2 *A*, 1997 *W*	34	4	0	0	0	16
B W Redpath	1993 v NZ	1996 *A* (R), *It*, 1997 *E*, *I*, *F*	24	0	0	0	0	0
D G Ellis	1997 v W	1997 *W*, *E*, *I*, *F*	4	0	0	0	0	0
J A Hay	1995 v WS		1	0	0	0	0	0
K D McKenzie	1994 v Arg	1996 *NZ*, 1,2, *A*, *It*	12	1	0	0	0	5
T J Smith	1997 v E	1997 *E*, *I*, *F*	3	0	0	0	0	0
A G J Watt	1991 v Z		4	0	0	0	0	0
D I W Hilton	1995 v C	1996 *NZ* 1,2, *A*, *It*, 1997 *W*	19	1	0	0	0	5
M J Stewart	1996 v It	1996 *It*, 1997 *W*, *E*, *I*, *F*	5	0	0	0	0	0
B D Stewart	1996 v NZ	1996 *NZ* 2, *A*	2	0	0	0	0	0
P H Wright	1992 v A	1996 *NZ* 1	21	1	0	0	0	5
D F Cronin	1988 v I	1996 *NZ* 1,2, *A*, *It*, 1997 *F* (R)	41	4	0	0	0	18
G W Weir	1990 v Arg	1996 *NZ* 1,2, *A*, *It* (R), 1997 *W*, *E*, *I*, *F*	45	4	0	0	0	20
D S Munro	1994 v W	1997 *W* (R)	7	0	0	0	0	0
A I Reed	1993 v I	1996 *It*, 1997 *W*, *E*, *I*, *F*	15	0	0	0	0	0

S J Campbell	1995 v C		13	0	0	0	0	0
I R Smith	1992 v E	1996 *NZ* 1,2, *A, It*, 1997 *E, I, F*	23	0	0	0	0	0
R I Wainwright	1992 v I	1996 *NZ* 1,2, 1997 *W, E, I, F*	28	3	0	0	0	14
P Walton	1994 v E	1997 *W, E, I, F*	10	3	0	0	0	15
M I Wallace	1996 v A	1996 *A, It*, 1997 *W*	3	0	0	0	0	0
E W Peters	1995 v C	1996 *NZ* 1,2, *A, It*	17	5	0	0	0	25
S J Reid	1995 v WS		1	0	0	0	0	0

Eric Peters leads the Scottish defence against an attack spearheaded by Daniel Manu. Scotland-Australia, November 1996.

SCOTTISH CLUBS 1996-97

Biggar

Year of formation 1975
Ground Hartree Mill, Biggar   Tel: Biggar (01899) 221219
Colours Black jersey with red collar and cuffs
Captain 1996-97 L Graham
SRU Tennents Championship 1996-97 Div 2 8th **SRU Tennents Cup 1996-97** Lost 8-27
to Gala (third round)

Biggar had climbed to the Second Division of the national championship only 21
years after the formation of the club, but, frustrated by injuries, they did not enjoy
storybook success in 1996-97, though they contested the final of the SRU Bowl, the
third-tier knock-out competition. Successive victories against Gordonians, Lochaber, Linlithgow and Ross High took them through to that Murrayfield final, where
they lost to Selkirk by 15-23. In the Premiership, however, only late-season victories
against Gala and Glasgow Academicals saved Biggar from a League whitewash. If
relegation had not been in abeyance because of reorganisation of the League they
would have dropped back down, and in the SRU Tennents Cup they did not survive
their first tie, beaten 27-8 by Gala. Marty Hurring, Biggar's New Zealand stand-off,
was their most influential figure on the scoresheet in the first half of the season.
Lindsay Graham, who led Biggar from centre, also played a key role in trying to keep
the team on course, as did Ewan McAlpine in the pack.

League Record 1996-97

Date	Venue	Opponents	Results	
31 Aug	A	Edinburgh Acads	7-39	T: Hurring C: Hurring
7 Sep	H	Dundee HS FP	15-38	T: Abernethy, Graham C: Hurring
				P: Hurring
14 Sep	A	Glasgow Acads	11-56	T: A Cairns P: Hurring (2)
21 Sep	H	Kelso	17-30	T: Graham (2), R Young C: Hurring
28 Sep	H	West of Scotland	14-24	T: Hurring, E McAlpine C: Hurring (2)
5 Oct	A	Gala	36-40	T: Abernethy, Harrison (2), Hurring
				C: Hurring (2) P: Hurring (4)
16 Nov	H	GHK	12-32	T: Coughbrough, E McAlpine C: Hurring
11 Jan	A	Kelso	14-27	T: Campbell, Murray C: Hurring (2)
25 Jan	A	West of Scotland	3-46	P: Lavery
8 Feb	H	Gala	15-10	P: Hurring, Lavery (4)
15 Feb	A	GHK	7-29	T: Graham C: Lavery
22 Feb	H	Edinburgh Acads	3-50	P: Lavery
8 Mar	A	Dundee HS FP	6-38	P: Lavery (2)
29 Mar	H	Glasgow Acads	27-15	T: Armstrong, Cairns (2), E McAlpine
				C: Lavery (2) P: Lavery

Boroughmuir

Year of formation 1919 (Boroughmuir FP until 1974)
Ground Meggetland, Colinton Road, Edinburgh EH14 1AS   Tel: 0131-443 7571
Colours Blue and green quarters
Captain 1996-97 S J Reid
SRU Tennents Championship 1996-97 Div 1 4th **SRU Tennents Cup 1996-97** Lost to
Melrose 23-31 (final)

Boroughmuir had a thoroughly disappointing season in the League, but they came
good in the SRU Tennents Cup competition, reaching the final and giving Melrose a
close run before losing 23-31. They began their Cup campaign by removing the

holders, with a 19-6 victory at Hawick. A runaway victory followed against Stirling County by 71-9 at Meggetland, and then, avenging two League defeats, they won 42-29 at home against their Watsonian neighbours. A 45-0 drubbing disposed of Heriot's, and for close on an hour in the final Boroughmuir were in contention.

At the start of the season another victory against Heriot's, 38-8 at Goldenacre, with Neill Renton scoring four tries, was Boroughmuir's only win in their first five League matches. Not even successive victories against Jed-Forest, Hawick and Heriot's could settle Boroughmuir, and their enigmatic League season continued with consecutive defeats by Watsonians, Melrose and Stirling County. Boroughmuir lost to the champions by only 19-23 at the Greenyards, but they took only one point from their two games against Stirling, who finished at the foot of the table.

League Record 1996-97

Date	Venue	Opponents	Result	Scorers
31 Aug	H	Hawick	20-23	T: Finnie, Renton C: Aitken (2) P: Aitken (2)
7 Sep	A	Heriot's FP	38-8	T: Mardon, Renton (4) C: Aitken (2) P: Aitken (3)
14 Sep	A	Watsonians	14-44	T: Wyllie P: Aitken, Knight (2)
21 Sep	H	Melrose	25-47	T: Finnie (2), Lineen, S J Reid C: Aitken P: Aitken
28 Sep	A	Currie	10-17	T: Mardon C: Wyllie P: Mardon
5 Oct	H	Jed-Forest	76-0	T: Burns, Finnie (2), Jennings, Kirkpatrick (3), Laird, McLean (2), Renton, Wylie (2) C: Flockhart, Laird (3) P: Flockhart
16 Nov	A	Hawick	38-23	T: Burns, Flockhart, Laird, Lineen, McLean, Reekie C: Reekie (4)
23 Nov	H	Heriot's FP	27-19	T: Aitken, Cadzow, Renton P: Reekie (3) D: Reekie
30 Nov	A	Stirling County	26-26	T: Burns, Laird C: Reekie (2) P: Reekie (4)
7 Dec	H	Watsonians	31-35	T: Beveridge (2), Kirkpatrick, McLean C: Reekie P: Reekie (3)
11 Jan	A	Melrose	19-23	T: Kirkpatrick, Laird, S J Reid C: Reekie (2)
25 Jan	H	Stirling County	22-28	T: Kirkpatrick, Pemnan, pen try C: Reekie (2) P: Reekie
8 Feb	H	Currie	25-15	T: Allan, Beveridge, Burns, McLean C: Reekie P: Reekie
15 Feb	A	Jed-Forest	23-17	T: Aitken, McLean, Penman C: Reekie P: Aitken D: Reekie

Currie

Year of formation 1970
Ground Malleny Park, Balerno, Edinburgh EH14 5HA
Colours Amber and black
Captain 1996-97 C Boyd
SRU Tennents Championship 1996-97 Div 1 3rd **SRU Tennents Cup 1996-97** Lost 20-32 to Gala (fourth round)

Currie, third behind Melrose and Watsonians, enjoyed their most profitable League season. The club from Edinburgh's south-west fringe lost all four of their matches against the two clubs who finished ahead of them in the table, but their only other blemish was a 25-15 away defeat by Boroughmuir. Currie's most remarkable victory of their nine was by 61-10 at home against Hawick, the most substantial defeat those once dominant Borderers had suffered in League rugby. Ally Donaldson, the Edinburgh and Scotland A stand-off, was again Currie's most prolific scorer with 179 League points, including 21 against Hawick, and David Officer ran in nine Premiership tries. Currie, however, could not translate their League form into the

Cup as they stumbled to 32-20 defeat at home against Gala before falling 20-43 to the avenging Hawick in the Tennents Shield competition. Graham Ellis became the first player to be capped out of the Currie club when he took over from the injured Kevin McKenzie as Scotland's hooker for the match against Wales in January.

League Record 1996-97

Date	Venue	Opponents	Result	Scorers
31 Aug	H	Heriot's FP	45-5	T: McIntyre, Officer (2), Rogerson, Simpson, Thompson C: Donaldson (3) P: Donaldson (3)
7 Sep	A	Stirling County	36-21	T: Donaldson, Keen, Officer, Wilson C: Donaldson (2) P: Donaldson (4)
14 Sep	A	Melrose	19-35	T: Officer C: Donaldson P: Donaldson (4)
21 Sep	A	Jed-Forest	28-21	T: Blair, Lucking, Officer C: Donaldson (2) P: Donaldson (3)
28 Sep	H	Boroughmuir	17-10	T: Officer P: Donaldson (2) D: Donaldson (2)
5 Oct	A	Hawick	26-12	T: Blair, Watt, pen try C: Donaldson P: Donaldson (2) D: Officer
16 Nov	A	Heriot's FP	10-3	T: Donaldson C: Donaldson P: Donaldson
30 Nov	A	Watsonians	10-35	T: Forrester C: Donaldson P: Donaldson
11 Jan	H	Jed-Forest	37-3	T: Blair, Craig, Lucking, Mainwaring C: Donaldson (4) P: Donaldson (3)
25 Jan	H	Watsonians	3-37	P: Donaldson
8 Feb	A	Boroughmuir	15-25	T: Hamilton, Watt C: Donaldson P: Donaldson
15 Feb	H	Hawick	61-10	T: Blair, Donaldson, Forrester, McIntyre, Officer, Simpson, Ward, Wilson (2) C: Donaldson (8)
22 Feb	H	Stirling County	50-5	T: Donaldson, Glen, McIntyre, Officer (2), Thomson, Ward C: Donaldson (6) P: Donaldson
8 Mar	H	Melrose	22-37	T: Forrester, Mainwaring P: Donaldson (4)

Dundee High School FP

Year of formation 1880
Ground Mayfield, Arbroath Road, Dundee   Tel: Dundee (01382) 453517 (ground); 451045 (clubhouse)
Colours Blue and red
Captain 1996-97 D R Hamilton
SRU Tennents Championship 1996-97 Div 2 3rd **SRU Tennents Cup 1996-97** Lost 18-33 to Kirkcaldy (quarter-final)

Dundee High School FP's bid to step back up to the First Division was frustrated by a last-kick penalty goal by David Barrett for West of Scotland in the final match of their League programme. That score not only gave West a 15-13 victory but also allowed them to edge Dundee for second place behind Edinburgh Academicals on points difference. Until then, despite early-season defeats by the Academicals of both Glasgow and Edinburgh, Dundee had seemed strong contenders with seven successive victories on the run-up to their decisive visit to West. That sequence included a vital 12-10 victory at home against Edinburgh Academicals. Shaun Longstaff, Dundee's New Zealand wing, who played district rugby for Caledonia, was a significant contributor to Dundee's promotion challenge in scoring nine tries, and Paul Rouse, the Scotland A Player, was equally vital in a pivotal role at centre. Dundee progressed comfortably past Glasgow Academicals and Hawick Linden in the Tennents Cup before they met their Midlands rivals, Kirkcaldy, in rampant mood, inflicting a 33-18 defeat on the Tayside club in the quarter-final round.

League Record 1996-97

Date	Venue	Opponents	Result	Scorers
31 Aug	H	Glasgow Acads	16-25	*T:* Gray, Longstaff *P:* Hogg (2)
7 Sep	A	Biggar	38-15	*T:* Fullarton, Lamont (2), Longstaff, Rouse *C:* Pearson (2) *P:* Pearson (2) *D:* Rouse
14 Sep	H	West of Scotland	29-12	*T:* Hayter, Longstaff, Pearson, Sandford *C:* Pearson (3) *P:* Pearson
21 Sep	A	Gala	25-25	*T:* Gray, Longstaff, van der Esch *C:* Pearson (2) *P:* Pearson *D:* Rouse
28 Sep	H	GHK	35-11	*T:* Karatiana, Milne (2), Sandford (2) *C:* Pearson (2) *P:* Pearson (2)
5 Oct	A	Edinburgh Acads	10-23	*T:* Pearson *C:* Pearson *P:* Pearson
16 Nov	H	Kelso	35-27	*T:* Gray, Longstaff (2), Rouse *C:* Paterson (2), Pearson *P:* Patterson, Pearson (2)
23 Nov	A	Glasgow Acads	29-6	*T:* Longstaff, McWhirter, Scott *C:* Pearson *P:* Pearson (4)
11 Jan	H	Gala	24-3	*T:* Gray (2), Lamont, McWhirter *C:* Paterson (2)
25 Jan	A	GHK	12-10	*T:* Longstaff, McWhirter *C:* Paterson
8 Feb	H	Edinburgh Acads	12-10	*T:* Hayter, McWhirter *C:* Paterson
15 Feb	A	Kelso	18-17	*T:* Samson, Scott *C:* Paterson *P:* Patterson (2)
8 Mar	H	Biggar	38-6	*T:* Featherstone, Gray (2), Longstaff, Rouse *C:* Patterson (5) *P:* Patterson
29 Mar	A	West of Scotland	13-15	*T:* Lamont *C:* Patterson *P:* Patterson, Rouse

Edinburgh Academicals

Year of formation 1857
Ground Raeburn Place, Stockbridge, Edinburgh EH4 1HQ   Tel: 0131-332 1070
Colours Blue and white hoops
Captain 1996-97 R Hoole
SRU Tennents Championship 1996-97 Div 2 *Winners* **SRU Tennents Cup 1996-97** Lost 17-32 to Kilmarnock (fourth round)

Edinburgh Academicals won promotion by taking the Second Division title in a close finale, finishing only a point ahead of West of Scotland and Dundee High School FP. However, the capital club could not convert League success into the Tennents Cup as they stumbled to a home defeat by Third Division Kilmarnock. Academicals set markers by winning their first six League matches, four of them with scores of more than 30 points. However, successive defeats by Glasgow Academicals and West of Scotland in November opened up the title race. Another defeat followed at Dundee, and the Edinburgh club were not assured of promotion until they won their final League match away at Gala by 29-12. Early in the season Academicals lost two highly promising young forwards – Scott Murray, the lock who had been a bench replacement for Scotland the previous season, signed for Bedford, and Paddy Haslett dropped out with a neck injury. However, the influential Bryan Easson, son of the club's coach, Bob, switched back to Raeburn Place from Stirling. Easson notched 123 League points for Academicals, and with the 43 he recorded for Stirling, he was among the top half-dozen scorers in the Premiership.

League Record 1996-97

Date	Venue	Opponents	Result	Scorers
31 Aug	H	Biggar	39-7	*T:* Allan, Burns, Leighton, Osbourne, Simpson *C:* Simmers (4) *P:* Simmers (2)

7 Sep	A	West of Scotland	39-14	*T:* Baillie, Bull (2), Burns, S Murray, Simmers *C:* Simmers (3) *P:* Simmers
14 Sep	H	Gala	38-26	*T:* Bull (2), Burns, Hoole (2), Richardson *C:* Simmers (4)
21 Sep	A	GHK	14-10	*T:* Hoole *P:* Simmers (2) *D:* Kiddie
28 Sep	A	Kelso	34-16	*T:* Haslett, Kiddie, McVie, Stewart, Waite *C:* Simmers (3) *P:* Simmers
5 Oct	H	Dundee HS FP	23-10	*T:* Allan, C Murray, Simpson *C:* Simmers *P:* Kiddie, Simmers
16 Nov	A	Glasgow Acads	11-17	*T:* Kiddie *P:* Duncan (2)
30 Nov	H	West of Scotland	16-17	*T:* Hoole *C:* Easson *P:* Easson (3)
11 Jan	H	GHK	30-8	*T:* Waite, Burns *C:* Easson *P:* Easson (6)
25 Jan	H	Kelso	27-25	*T:* Bull (2) *C:* Easson *P:* Easson (4) *D:* Easson
8 Feb	A	Dundee HS FP	10-12	*T:* Waite *C:* Easson *P:* Easson
15 Feb	H	Glasgow Acads	18-10	*T:* Dick, Leighton *C:* Easson *P:* Easson (2)
22 Feb	A	Biggar	50-3	*T:* Duncan, Geldenhuys, Leighton, McVie, Osbourne, Simpson (2), Waite *C:* Easson (2) *P:* Easson (2)
8 Mar	A	Gala	39-12	*T:* Leighton, Macdonald, C Murray, Osbourne, Simmers *C:* Duncan, Easson (3) *P:* Duncan, Easson

Gala

Year of formation 1875
Ground Netherdale, Nether Road, Galashiels TD1 3HE   Tel: Galashiels (01896) 755145
Colours Maroon
Captain 1996-97 I Corcoran
SRU Tennents Championship 1996-97 Div 2 7th **SRU Tennents Cup 1996-97** Lost 20-59 to Watsonians (fifth round)

Gala's 69-15 home victory over Kelso brought back memories of happy days, as did their 32-20 away win over Currie in the fourth round of the SRU Tennents Cup. Both results, however, were totally out of character with the rest of Gala's season. The Netherdale club, Scottish champions three times in the past, almost slipped to what would have been their most lowly position in the 24-year-old championship – only the recasting of the competition saved them from relegation to the Third Division. Gala's losing sequence was interrupted only by a 25-25 draw with Dundee High School FP and victories against Biggar by 40-36 and Kelso – all at home. After the Cup win over Currie the Netherdale club were brought back down to earth in a 59-20 home defeat by Watsonians. Gala had high hopes of Thinus Pienaar, the South African who scored 20 points in the draw with Dundee and 51 in all the first four League matches, but injury forced him to go home. Thereafter, the Changeleng twins dominated Gala's scoresheets – David with 48 points, Malcolm with eight tries.

League Record 1996-97

Date	Venue	Opponents	Result	Scores
31 Aug	A	Kelso	16-30	*T:* Boland *C:* Pienaar *P:* Pienaar (3)
7 Sep	H	GHK	26-30	*T:* Dalgleish, C Patterson *C:* Pienaar (2) *P:* Pienaar (4)
14 Sep	A	Edinburgh Acads	26-38	*T:* M Changleng (2), Scott (2) *P:* Pienaar (2)
21 Sep	H	Dundee HS FP	25-25	*T:* Amos *C:* Pienaar *P:* Pienaar (6)
28 Sep	A	Glasgow Acads	26-32	*T:* Ballantyne, M Changleng (2), Laing *C:* C Patterson (3)
5 Oct	H	Biggar	40-36	*T:* Dalziel, M Changleng (2), Perrett, Weir *C:* C Patterson (3) *P:* Paterson (3)
16 Nov	A	West of Scotland	11-33	*T:* D Changleng *P:* D Changleng, C Paterson

23 Nov	H	Kelso	69-15	*T:* Boland, M Changleng (2), Corcoran, G Dalgleish (2), Johnston, Scott, Swan, Weir (2) *C:* D Changleng (7)
30 Nov	A	GHK	11-25	*T:* Boland *P:* C Paterson (2)
11 Jan	A	Dundee HS FP	3-24	*P:* D Changleng
25 Jan	H	Glasgow Acads	21-23	*P:* D Changleng (7)
8 Feb	A	Biggar	10-15	*T:* Weir *C:* C Paterson *P:* C Paterson
15 Feb	H	West of Scotland	18-27	*T:* Corcoran, G Dalgleish *C:* C Paterson *P:* Paterson (2)
8 Mar	A	Edinburgh Acads	12-39	*T:* Corcoran, C Dalgleish *C:* D Changleng

GHK

Year of formation 1982 (on amalgamation of Glasgow High RFC and Kelvinside Academicals)
Ground Old Anniesland, 637 Crow Road, Glasgow   Tel: 0141-959 1154
Colours Navy blue, green and white
Captain 1996-97 M I Wallace
SRU Tennents Championship 1996-97 Div 2 4th **SRU Tennents Cup 1996-97** Lost 10-33 to West of Scotland (fourth round)

GHK won the SRU Tennents Shield by beating Hawick 46-18 in the final at Murrayfield, and if Glasgow had had an internal championship the Old Anniesland club would have won it, as they were unbeaten in their four Premiership matches against the city's other clubs in the Second Division. The only blot on that record was the 29-25 draw with West of Scotland on the first day of the League season. Later in the season GHK had a resounding victory over West at Burnbrae, and they also achieved the double against their neighbours, Glasgow Academicals. However, GHK's promotion challenge floundered in home and away defeats against each of two other contenders, Dundee High School FP and Edinburgh Academicals. GHK were also less successful against West in the Cup, losing 10-33 at Burnbrae, though they went on to reach the final of the second-tier competition with victories against Jed-Forest and Aberdeen Grammar School FP. That win over Jed was typical of their season as they had to recover from a 3-27 deficit before winning 42-27. George Breckenridge, GHK's Glasgow full-back, recorded a century of League points (115), and Geoff Caldwell, the Scotland Under-21 wing, was among the Premiership's top try-scorers with nine. However, it was the other wing, Gerry Hawkes, who left his mark on the Shield final with three tries against Hawick.

League Record 1996-97

Date	Venue	Opponents	Result	Scorers
31 Aug	H	West of Scotland	29-29	*T:* Common, Minto, F D Wallace, M I Wallace *C:* Breckenridge (3) *P:* Breckenridge
7 Sep	A	Gala	30-26	*T:* Bassi, Breckenridge (2) *C:* Breckenridge (3) *P:* Breckenridge (3)
14 Sep	A	Kelso	18-31	*T:* Caldwell (2) *C:* Breckenridge *P:* Breckenridge (2)
21 Sep	H	Edinburgh Acads	10-14	*T:* M I Wallace *C:* Breckenridge *P:* Breckenridge
28 Sep	A	Dundee HS FP	11-35	*T:* Breckenrideg *P:* Breckenridge *D:* Breckenridge
5 Oct	H	Glasgow Acads	35-26	*T:* Breckenridge, Common, Logan, M I Wallace *C:* Breckenridge (2), MacLeod *P:* Breckenridge (2), MacLeod
16 Nov	A	Biggar	32-12	*T:* Caldwell (2), Kerr, Manning *C:* Manning (3) *P:* Manning *D:* Little
30 Nov	H	Gala	25-11	*T:* Caldwell, Common, M I Wallace *C:* Manning (2) *P:* Manning (2)
11 Jan	A	Edinburgh Acads	8-30	*T:* Hawkes *P:* Manning

25 Jan	H	Dundee HS FP	10-12	T: Kerr	C: Breckenridge	P: Breckenridge
8 Feb	A	Glasgow Acads	23-7	T: Hawkes, Little	C: Breckenridge (2)	
				P: Breckenridge (3)		
15 Feb	H	Biggar	29-7	T: Blackie, Hawkes, Little, Ness		
				C: Breckenridge (3)	P: Breckenridge	
22 Feb	A	West of Scotland	34-8	T: Caldwell, Hawkes, Little, Ness (2)		
				C: Breckenridge (3)	P: Breckenridge	
8 Mar	H	Kelso	45-17	T: Bassi, Caldwell, Common, Docherty,		
				Hawkes, Little	C: Breckenridge (6)	
				P: Breckenridge		

Glasgow Academicals

Year of formation 1867
Ground New Anniesland, Helensburgh Drive, Glasgow   Tel: 0141-959 1101
Colours Navy blue and white hoops
Captain 1996-97 S M Simmers
SRU Tennents Championship 1996-97 Div 2 5th **SRU Tennents Cup 1996-97** Lost 5-41
to Dundee HS FP (fourth round)

Glasgow Academicals experienced incredibly contrasting halves to their League season. At the halfway point they had won five of their seven matches and seemed on course for promotion to the First Division. They opened their League programme with a satisfying 25-16 away win against Dundee High, and their only defeats in that run were by two other Glasgow clubs, West of Scotland and GHK. However, in the second half of the season Academicals were a frustration to their New Zealand mentor, Kevin Greene, the former Waikato coach, as they won only one match, 23-21, against Gala at Netherdale. They were equally unsuccessful in knock-out competitions in the New Year, beaten 41-5 by Dundee on their return to Mayfield for a Tennents Cup tie and 22-15 at Glenrothes in the SRU Shield. Calum MacGregor, Academicals' 35-year-old district stand-off, had another successful season with the boot, scoring no fewer than 115 of his club's 292 League points.

League Record 1996-97

Date	Venue	Opponents	Result	Scorers
31 Aug	A	Dundee HS FP	25-16	T: Mackay, Metcalfe (2)
				C: C G MacGregor (2)
				P: C G MacGregor (2)
7 Sep	H	Kelso	27-16	T: C G MacGregor, Strawbridge (2)
				C: C G MacGregor (3)
				P: C G MacGregor (2)
14 Sep	H	Biggar	56-11	T: Begley (2), Doran, J Mason, Metcalfe (2),
				Simmers, Strawbridge C: C G MacGregor (5)
				P: C G MacGregor
21 Sep	A	West of Scotland	20-40	T: C G MacGregor, J Mason
				C: C G MacGregor (2)
				P: C G MacGregor (2)
28 Sep	H	Gala	32-26	T: Ablett, Hart, Metcalfe (2), Richmond
				C: C G MacGregor (2) P: MacGregor
5 Oct	A	GHK	26-35	T: Hart, C G MacGregor, Mackay, Strawbridge
				C: C G MacGregor (3)
16 Nov	H	Edinburgh Acads	17-11	T: Mackay P: C G MacGregor (3)
				D: C G MacGregor
23 Nov	H	Dundee HS FP	6-29	P: C G MacGregor (2)
30 Nov	A	Kelso	23-24	T: C G MacGregor, Mathewson
				C: C G MacGregor (2)
				P: C G MacGregor (2) D: C G MacGregor

189

25 Jan	A	Gala	23-21	T: Ablett, Mackay, Moore
				C: C G MacGregor P: C G MacGregor (2)
8 Feb	H	GHK	7-23	T: Mackay C: C G MacGregor
15 Feb	A	Edinburgh Acads	10-18	T: Pen try C: Hart P: C G MacGregor
8 Mar	H	West of Scotland	5-42	T: Boundy
29 Mar	A	Biggar	15-27	T: Bruce (2) C: Bruce P: Bruce

Hawick

Year of formation 1873
Ground Mansfield Park, Mansfield Road, Hawick, Roxburghshire
Tel: Hawick (01450) 737429
Colours Dark green
Captain 1996-97 B L Renwick
SRU Tennents Championship 1996-97 Div 1 5th **SRU Tennents Cup 1996-97** Lost 6-19 to Boroughmuir (fourth round)

Hawick, Scottish champions 10 times between 1974 and 1987, fell far short of their former glories in the League, and they also lost their hold of the SRU Tennents Cup through a 19-6 defeat by Boroughmuir in the fourth round. Hawick's League commitments started with a 23-20 away victory over Boroughmuir, a result that hinted at more success to follow, but wins over Jed-Forest and Stirling County were followed by six successive defeats, including two by the championship challengers, Watsonians. Victory over Heriot's provided Hawick with a temporary respite, but worse was to follow: the 61-10 defeat at Currie was the heaviest setback Hawick had suffered in the championship's 24 years. Injuries handicapped Hawick – Keith Suddon, the club's most effective try-scorer, missed the first couple of months of the season, and Scott Welsh's season was cut short after he had recorded 107 points in League matches. Elimination from the Cup diverted Hawick into the Shield competition, where they swept Stewart's Melville and St Boswells aside and avenged two League defeats by Currie before losing in the final against GHK by 18-46.

League Record 1996-97

Date	Venue	Opponents	Result	Scorers
31 Aug	A	Boroughmuir	23-20	T: Harris, Murray, Stanger C: Welsh P: Welsh (2)
7 Sep	H	Jed-Forest	33-21	T: Cottrill, McDonnell, Murray, Turnbull C: Welsh (2) P: Welsh (3)
14 Sep	A	Stirling County	12-3	P: Welsh (4)
21 Sep	H	Watsonians	15-25	P: Welsh (5)
28 Sep	A	Melrose	13-35	T: Turnbull C: Welsh P: Welsh (2)
5 Oct	H	Currie	12-26	P: Turnbull (4)
16 Nov	H	Boroughmuir	23-38	T: Cottrill, Murray C: Turnbull (2) P: Turnbull (3)
30 Nov	A	Heriot's FP	19-47	T: Suddon (2), Welsh C: Welsh (2)
11 Jan	A	Watsonians	15-47	T: Stanger, Suddon C: Welsh P: Welsh
25 Jan	H	Heriot's FP	27-12	T: Scott, Turnbull, Welsh C: Welsh (3) P: Welsh (2)
8 Feb	H	Melrose	8-22	T: Welsh P: Welsh
15 Feb	A	Currie	10-61	T: Suddon (2)
22 Feb	A	Jed-Forest	14-21	T: Sharp, Suddon C: Sharp, Wear
8 Mar	H	Stirling County	44-19	T: Huggan, Murray, Parkes, Reid, Stanger, Wear C: Sharp (4) P: Sharp (2)

Heriot's FP

Year of formation 1890
Ground Goldenacre, Bangholm Terrace, Edinburgh EH3 5QN   Tel: 0131-552 4097
(groundstaff) and 0131-552 5925 (clubhouse)
Colours Blue and white horizontal stripes
Captain 1996-97 I C Glasgow
SRU Tennents Championship 1996-97 Div 1 7th **SRU Tennents Cup 1996-97** Lost 0-45
to Boroughmuir (semi-final)

Heriot's endured a mundane League season, winning only three of their 14 Premiership matches, a record that would have relegated them to the Second Division but for reorganisation of the competition. Two of those victories were against Stirling County, the only club to finish behind Heriot's in the table, and the other win was an isolated high point, when they beat Hawick 47-19 at Goldenacre, the home team scoring six tries to three. Hugh Gilmour's two tries in that match was the only instance of a Heriot's player recording more than one in a League game. Heriot's had to rely heavily on young Gordon Ross, the Scotland Under-21 and Under-19 stand-off, who scored 107 of the club's 224 League points. Heriot's had a good run in the SRU Tennents Cup, beating Jed-Forest, Berwick and Peebles before succumbing to Boroughmuir by 0-45 in the semi-final on neutral Edinburgh territory at Currie.

League Record 1996-97

Date	Venue	Opponents	Result	Scorers
31 Aug	A	Currie	5-45	*T:* Bunney
7 Sep	H	Boroughmuir	8-38	*T:* Lawrie *P:* Smith
14 Sep	H	Jed-Forest	26-30	*T:* Lang, Proctor *C:* Ross (2) *P:* Ross (4)
21 Sep	H	Stirling County	22-9	*T:* Ross *C:* Ross *P:* Ross (5)
28 Sep	A	Watsonians	15-52	*T:* Ross, Smith *C:* Ross *P:* Ross
5 Oct	H	Melrose	18-62	*T:* Keenan, Proctor *C:* Ross *P:* Ross (2)
16 Nov	H	Currie	3-10	*P:* Ross
23 Nov	A	Boroughmuir	19-27	*T:* Lang, Walker *P:* Ross (3)
30 Nov	H	Hawick	47-19	*T:* A Dall, Elliot, H R Gilmour (2), O'Kane, Proctor *C:* Ross (4) *P:* Ross (3)
11 Jan	A	Stirling County	25-24	*T:* Boswell, Glasgow, Lawrie *C:* Ross (2) *D:* Lang, Ross
25 Jan	A	Hawick	12-27	*P:* Ross (3) *D:* Ross
8 Feb	H	Watsonians	8-38	*T:* Lang *P:* Ross
15 Feb	A	Melrose	0-18	
8 Mar	A	Jed-Forest	16-17	*T:* Lang *C:* Lang *P:* Lang (2) *D:* Fowler

Jed-Forest

Year of formation 1885
Ground Riverside Park, Jedburgh
Colours Royal blue
Captain 1996-97 K Armstrong
SRU Tennents Championship 1996-97 Div 1 6th **SRU Tennents Cup 1996-97** Lost 11-24
to Heriot's FP (fourth round)

Jed-Forest finished third to last in the First Division, winning only four matches – the home and away games against Heriot's and the Riverside Park contests with Stirling County and Hawick. Jed's 30-26 away win over Heriot's was a personal triumph for Gregor McKechnie, who scored 20 of his team's points to add to all 21 in the defeat at Hawick the previous week. When Jed beat Stirling at Riverside they had won two of their first six matches, but this was followed by three successive away defeats. It was only in their last two League matches that Jed clawed their way out of last place with home wins against Hawick and Heriot's. However, Jed's League

191

double over Heriot's was not extended into the Cup competition as the Borderers were eliminated in a 24-11 defeat at Goldenacre in the fourth round. That diverted Jed into the SRU Shield competition, where they beat Ayr 42-17 before allowing a 27-3 lead to be overturned in a 42-27 defeat by GHK in Glasgow.

League Record 1996-97

Date	Venue	Opponents	Result	Scorers
31 Aug	H	Watsonians	17-54	*T:* Campbell, Dunnet, Robertson *C:* Amos
7 Sep	A	Hawick	21-33	*P:* McKechnie (6) *D:* McKechnie
14 Sep	A	Heriot's FP	30-26	*T:* C K Brown, Campbell, McKechnie (2) *C:* McKechnie (2) *P:* McKechnie (2)
21 Sep	H	Currie	21-28	*T:* Amos, Forster *C:* Amos *P:* Amos, Gibson (2)
28 Sep	H	Stirling County	21-14	*T:* Dungait (2) *C:* Amos *P:* Amos (3)
5 Oct	A	Boroughmuir	0-76	
16 Nov	A	Watsonians	23-48	*T:* Amos, Forster, Hule *C:* Richards *P:* Richards (2)
30 Nov	A	Melrose	7-69	*T:* Hule *C:* Richards
11 Jan	A	Currie	3-37	*P:* McKechnie
25 Jan	H	Melrose	13-45	*T:* Elder *C:* Richards *P:* Richards (2)
8 Feb	A	Stirling County	6-26	*P:* Richards (2)
15 Feb	H	Boroughmuir	17-23	*T:* Amos *P:* Richards (4)
22 Feb	H	Hawick	21-14	*T:* Elder (2), Szkudro *P:* Richards (2)
8 Mar	H	Heriot's FP	17-16	*T:* C J Brown, Graham *C:* Richards (2) *P:* Richards

Kelso

Year of formation 1876
Ground Poynder Park, Bowmont Street, Kelso, Roxburghshire   Tel: Kelso (01573) 224300 and 223773
Colours Black and white
Captain 1996-97 I T Fairley
SRU Tennents Championship 1996-97 Div 2 6th **SRU Tennents Cup 1996-97** Lost 37-71 to Melrose (fifth round)

This year Kelso's successes were confined to the abbreviated game as they won the Kings of the Sevens Trophy on the Border circuit, with consecutive victories in the Hawick, Jed-Forest, Langholm and Earlston tournaments. Seven-a-side prowess is a proud tradition at the Kelso club, and it was a commendation of their perseverance that they could still focus on that aspect of their game after their 15-a-side performances had fallen below average. They won only five of their 14 Second Division League matches, and in the SRU Tennents Cup, following an uneasy 9-3 win at Ayr, they were swept aside by 71-37 at Melrose. It had looked much brighter when Kelso won three of their first four League matches, with home victories over Gala and GHK followed by success at Biggar. However, only two more wins followed, including the second leg of a League double over Biggar. Kelso also ran the championship-challenging Edinburgh Academicals close before losing by only 25-27.

League Record 1996-97

Date	Venue	Opponents	Result	Scorers
31 Aug	H	Gala	30-16	*T:* Fairley, Ross, Roxburgh *C:* Aitchison (3) *P:* Aitchison (3)
7 Sep	A	Glasgow Acads	16-27	*T:* Little, Utterson *P:* Aitchison (2)
14 Sep	H	GHK	31-18	*T:* Aitchison, Fairley, Hogarth, Tait *C:* Aitchison *P:* Aitchison (2) *D:* Utterson
21 Sep	A	Biggar	30-17	*T:* Fairley (2) *C:* Aitchison *P:* Aitchison (6)

28 Sep	H	Edinburgh Acads	16-34	*T:* Roxburgh *C:* Aitchison *P:* Aitchison (3)
5 Oct	H	West of Scotland	27-36	*T:* Jackson, Roxburgh (3) *C:* Baird (2) *P:* Utterson
16 Nov	A	Dundee HS FP	27-35	*T:* G Laing (2), Ross, Thomson, Walker *C:* Aitchison
23 Nov	A	Gala	15-69	*T:* Bennet, G Cowe *C:* Aitchison *P:* Jones
30 Nov	H	Glasgow Acads	24-23	*T:* Aitchison, Rowley *C:* Aitchison *P:* Aitchison (4)
11 Jan	H	Biggar	27-14	*T:* Ross (2), Roxburgh, Tait *C:* Tait (2) *P:* Tait
25 Jan	A	Edinburgh Acads	25-27	*T:* Hendry, Millar, Tait *C:* Jones (2) *P:* Jones (2)
8 Feb	A	West of Scotland	6-52	*P:* Tait (2)
15 Feb	H	Dundee HS FP	17-18	*T:* Millar *P:* Tait (4)
4 Mar	A	GHK	17-45	*T:* Aitchison, Bennet *C:* Aitchison (2) *P:* Aitchison

Melrose

Year of formation 1877
Ground The Greenyards, Melrose, Roxburghshire TD6 9SA
Tel: Melrose (01896 82) 2993 (office) and 2559 (clubrooms)
Colours Yellow and black hoops
Captain 1996-97 B W Redpath
SRU Tennents Championship 1996-97 Div 1 *Winners* **SRU Tennents Cup 1996-97** *Winners*
– beat Boroughmuir 31-23 (final)

A glorious season for Melrose ended with victory in the SRU Tennents Cup to add to the Premiership, Border League and their own sevens trophy. They cruised through the Premier League with a 100% record, matching Hawick's 1975-76 and 1983-84 achievement, and on only three occasions were they held to winning margins of single figures.

Melrose set their marker in the League by running up a century in beating Stirling County by 107-10 at the Greenyards on the opening Saturday. Scott Nichol, the former Selkirk centre, ran in five of the 16 tries in that rout, and he went on to top the Premiership's scoring list with 16. Gary Parker notched 171 League points before he went off to a place-kicking role in gridiron football. Melrose cruised past two Border clubs – St Boswells by 70-10 and Kelso by 71-37 – before they had to pull out the stops for a 45-23 victory on their visit to West of Scotland. A substantial 36-9 victory followed against Kirkcaldy in the semi-final at Galashiels, though Melrose were given a stiff contest despite the fact that their Third Division opponents were down to 14 men for much of the match. Melrose came from behind three times to beat Boroughmuir by 31-23 in the Cup final, with Rowen Shepherd scoring 26 points with three tries, a conversion and three penalty goals.

League Record 1996-97

Date	Venue	Opponents	Result	Scorers
31 Aug	H	Stirling County	107-10	*T:* Bain, Broughton (2), R R Brown (2), M G Browne, Chalmers, Nichol (5), B W Redpath, Shepherd, Stark (2) *C:* Parker (12) *P:* Parker
7 Sep	A	Watsonians	27-16	*T:* Aitken (2), Nichol (2) *C:* Parker (2) *P:* Parker
14 Sep	H	Currie	35-19	*T:* Brotherstone, Broughton, Nichol, Turnbull *C:* Parker (3) *P:* Parker (3)
21 Sep	A	Boroughmuir	47-25	*T:* Bain, Broughton, R R Brown, Chalmers, Nichol, C Redpath, Shepherd *C:* Parker (3) *P:* Parker (2)

28 Sep	H	Hawick	35-13	T: Atken, Bain, Parker, Stark C: Parker (3)
				P: Parker (3)
5 Oct	A	Heriot's FP	62-18	T: Aitken, Bain, Chalmers, Nichol (2), Parker,
				Shepherd, Stark (2), pen try C: Parker (6)
16 Nov	A	Stirling County	29-13	T: Chalmers, Moncrieff (2), Shepherd
				C: Parker (3) P: Parker
30 Nov	H	Jed-Forest	69-7	T: Aitken, Brotherstone, Moncrieff (2),
				Nichol (2), Parker, C Redpath, Stark (2), pen try
				C: Parker (7)
11 Jan	H	Boroughmuir	23-19	T: Moncrieff P: Parker (6)
25 Jan	A	Jed-Forest	45-13	T: Aitken, Broughton (2), Moncrieff, Nichol,
				Stark (2) C: Parker (3), Shepherd (2)
8 Feb	A	Hawick	22-8	T: B W Redpath, Shepherd (2) C: Parker (2)
				P: Parker
15 Feb	H	Heriot's FP	18-0	T: M G Browne, Nichol Wright P: Parker
22 Feb	H	Watsonians	26-22	T: Chalmers, Parker, Stark, Wright
				C: Parker (3)
8 Mar	A	Currie	37-22	T: Nichol, Purves, Shepherd, Stark
				C: Shepherd (4) P: Shepherd (2) D: Bain

Stirling County

Year of formation 1904
Ground Bridgehaugh, Causewayhead Road, Stirling   Tel: Stirling (01786) 474827
Colours Red, white and black
Captain 1996-97 I C Jardine
SRU Tennents Championship 1996-97 Div 1 8th **SRU Tennents Cup 1996-96** Lost 9-71
to Boroughmuir (fifth round)

Stirling County, successively champions and runners-up in the two previous years, had a miserable 1996-97 season. Not only did they finish at the foot of the First Division table with just two wins, they also suffered several humiliating defeats: the worst was losing 10-107 at Melrose on the opening day of the league season, and three times later they conceded a half century of points, twice against Watsonians. In the Cup County were swept aside in a 71-9 defeat by Boroughmuir.

In the absence of key figures the team floundered. Stewart Hamilton's retirement left a considerable gap in the second row, and Ian Jardine, the international centre who had been appointed captain, hardly played because of injury. His fellow cap, Kenny Logan, missed the early weeks of the season, and Mark McKenzie had an even longer absence. By the time he returned to League rugby his brother, Kevin, Scotland's hooker, had been sidelined by injury, and before the end of the season Logan had gone over the border. Mark McKenzie's value could be measured in his 68 points out of the 108 County scored in the League matches in which he played.

League Record 1996-97

Date	Venue	Opponents	Result	Scorers
31 Aug	A	Melrose	10-107	T: Cairney, Crawford
7 Sep	H	Currie	21-36	T: Flockhart, MacRobert C: Easson
				P: Easson (3)
14 Sep	H	Hawick	3-12	P: Easson
21 Sep	A	Heriot's FP	9-22	P: Easson (3)
28 Sep	A	Jed-Forest	14-21	T: Wylie P: Easson (3)
5 Oct	H	Watsonians	16-58	T: Pen try C: Easson P: Easson (3)
16 Nov	H	Melrose	13-29	T: D Dunsire C: Logan P: Logan (2)
30 Nov	H	Boroughmuir	26-26	T: MacPhail, pen try C: Logan (2)
				PG:Logan (3) D: Sangster
11 Jan	H	Heriot's FP	24-25	T: D Dunsire, Flockhart C: M McKenzie
				P: M McKenzie (3) D: M McKenzie

25 Jan	A	Boroughmuir	28-22	*T:* Logan (2), M McKenzie
				C: M McKenzie (2) *P:* M McKenzie (3)
8 Feb	H	Jed-Forest	26-6	*T:* C Dunsire, Logan *C:* M McKenzie (2)
				P: M McKenzie (4)
15 Feb	A	Watsonians	6-66	*P:* M McKenzie (2)
22 Feb	A	Currie	5-50	*T:* Imrie
8 Mar	A	Hawick	19-44	*T:* Wright *C:* M McKenzie
				P: M McKenzie (3) *D:* M McKenzie

Watsonians

Year of formation 1875
Ground Myreside, Myreside Road, Edinburgh EH10 5DB   Tel: 0131-447 5200
Colours Maroon and white hoops
Captain 1996-97 G McKelvey
SRU Tennents Championship 1996-97 Div 1 2nd **SRU Tennents Cup 1996-97** Lost 29-42 to Boroughmuir (quarter-final)

Although Watsonians finished second to Melrose in the Tennants Premiership, they fell short of expectation in the Cup, where they suffered a 42-29 defeat by their neighbours, Boroughmuir, in the quarter-final round. Watsonians' only League defeats were at the hands of Melrose, the eventual champions – both narrowly – by 27-26 at home and 26-22 at the Greenyards. In only one other match, when they won 25-15 at Hawick, did they fail to score more than 30 points. Duncan Hodge, Watsonians' stand-off who was capped as a replacement against France, was in prolific scoring form with 252 points, the only player to attain a double century in the Premiership. Two of the club's players were among the leading try-scorers – John Kerr, the Caledonia wing, had 14, second only to Scott Nichol (Melrose), and Derrick Lee, Edinburgh's full-back, scored nine before he departed to London Scottish. Watsonians opened the Border spring sevens circuit with a stylish win in the Gala tournament, and they scored comfortable Scottish Cup victories over Hawick Trades (60-3) and Gala (59-20) before succumbing to Boroughmuir.

League Record 1996-97

Date	Venue	Opponents	Result	Scorers
31 Aug	A	Jed-Forest	54-17	*T:* Grimes, Hodge, Kerr, MacDonald, Mayer (2), Stanaway *C:* Hodge (5) *P:* Hodge (3)
7 Sep	H	Melrose	26-27	*T:* Hastings, Hodge *C:* Hodge (2) *P:* Hodge (4)
14 Sep	H	Boroughmuir	44-14	*T:* Garry, Kerr (3), Lee *C:* Hodge (5) *P:* Hodge (3)
21 Sep	A	Hawick	25-15	*T:* MacDonald *C:* Hodge *P:* Hodge (5) *D:* Hodge
28 Sep	H	Heriot's FP	52-15	*T:* Henderson (2), Kerr (2), Lee (2), Mather, pen try *C:* Hodge (6)
5 Oct	A	Stirling County	58-12	*T:* Brown (2), Hastings, Kerr (2), MacDonald, Mather, Weston *C:* Hodge (3) *P:* Hodge (4)
16 Nov	H	Jed-Forest	48-23	*T:* Kerr (2), Lee (2), MacDonald, pen try *C:* Hodge (3) *P:* Hodge (4)
30 Nov	H	Currie	35-10	*T:* Brown, Hannah (2), MacDonald *C:* Hodge (3) *P:* Hodge (3)
7 Dec	A	Boroughmuir	35-31	*T:* Garry, Hannah, Hastings, pen try *C:* Hodge (3) *P:* Hodge (2) *D:* Hodge
11 Jan	H	Hawick	47-15	*T:* Brown, Burnett, Hannah, Henderson, Lee, Mayer *C:* Hodge (4) *P:* Hodge (2) *D:* Hodge
25 Jan	A	Currie	37-3	*T:* Kerr (2), Lee, Mather, Mayer *C:* Hodge (3) *P:* Hodge (2)

8 Feb	A	Heriot's FP	38-8	*T:* Brown, Hannah, Smith, Weston
				C: Hodge (3) *P:* Hodge (4)
15 Feb	H	Stirling County	66-6	*T:* Grimes, Hodge, Hannah, Hastings (2), Lee,
				Kerr (2), Mayer *C:* Hodge (6)
				P: Hodge (3)
22 Feb	A	Melrose	22-26	*T:* Lee *C:* Hodge *P:* Hodge (5)

West of Scotland

Year of formation 1865
Ground Burnbrae, Glasgow Road, Milngavie, Glasgow G62 6HX   Tel: 0141-956 3116
Colours Red and yellow hoops
Captain 1996-97 G C Bulloch
SRU Tennents Championship 1996-97 Div 2 2nd **SRU Tennents Cup 1996-97** Lost 23-45
to Melrose (quarter-final)

West kept their supporters on tenterhooks throughout the season before they came
through to win promotion to the First Division with the last kick of the final match.
Their prospects had looked far from bright after they had drawn 29-29 with GHK in
the opening League match and then lost two successive games. West, however, then
won eight League matches in a row before a 43-8 home defeat by GHK. The
subsequent 42-5 win against Glasgow Academicals meant that West had to beat
Dundee by at least two points at Burnbrae to gain promotion, and it was only a
last-minute penalty goal by David Barrett, his fifth of the game, which secured a
15-13 victory. Barrett, the 33-year-old former Glasgow full-back and stand-off,
surpassed 100 League points with that winning goal, and Richie Craig was only just
short of a century, his 94 including eight tries. The latter's young brother, James,
scored 13 League tries for West as well as making his mark with three in the Scotland
A team's 56-11 victory over Emerging Wales. West disposed of two city rivals, GHK
and Glasgow Southern, in the Tennents Cup and ran Melrose close in the first half of
the quarter-final at Burnbrae before the Borderers pulled away to a 45-23 win.

League Record 1996-97

Date	Venue	Opponents	Result	Scorers
31 Aug	A	GHK	29-29	*T:* J M Craig (3), Steel *C:* Barrett,
				R Craig (2) *P:* R Craig
7 Sep	H	Edinburgh Acads	14-39	*T:* M Craig, Shaw *C:* Barrett (2)
14 Sep	A	Dundee HS FP	12-29	*T:* Barrett, R Craig *C:* Barrett
21 Sep	H	Glasgow Acads	40-20	*T:* A J Bulloch, R Craig, Greenshields,
				McKechnie, Shaw *C:* R Craig (3)
				P: R Craig (3)
28 Sep	A	Biggar	24-14	*T:* G C Bulloch, J M Craig (2)
				P: R Craig (2), Barrett
30 Nov	A	Edinburgh Acads	17-16	*T:* Stott, Williamson *C:* Barrett (2)
				P: Barrett
25 Jan	H	Biggar	46-3	*T:* J M Craig (2), R Craig (2), Lonergan, Stott,
				Williamson (2) *C:* Barrett, R Craig (2)
8 Feb	H	Kelso	52-6	*T:* Barrett, Greenshields, Lonergan, McLeish,
				Stott (2), Williamson (2) *C:* Barrett (6)
15 Feb	A	Gala	27-18	*T:* A J Bulloch, J M Craig (2), Lonergan
				C: Barrett (2) *P:* Barrett
22 Feb	H	GHK	8-34	*T:* J M Craig *P:* Barrett
8 Mar	A	Glasgow Acads	42-5	*T:* Barrett, A J Bulloch, J M Craig, Lonergan
				C: Barrett (2) *P:* Barrett (6)
29 Mar	H	Dundee HS FP	15-13	*P:* Barrett (5)

A MAD HATTER'S TEA PARTY

THE 1996-97 SEASON IN IRELAND
Sean Diffley *Irish Independent*

Events at international level in Ireland last season could be said to resemble those at the Mad Hatter's Tea Party. Alice would have been as bemused as most Irish supporters by the sight of two coaches, one of whom is now contracted into the next century, 35 players selected for the seven games played, and three captains, Niall Hogan, Keith Wood and Jim Staples.

Apart from the bizarre element of yet another triumph in Cardiff, the only other constant was the survival through thick and thin of the manager and chief selector, Pat Whelan. Whelan presided over the humiliation against Western Samoa, the not unexpected reverse against Australia and the historic first by Italy, all of which took place in front of the Lansdowne Road faithful. These defeats led to the dismissal of the New Zealand coach, Murray Kidd, and the employment on a six-year contract of Brian Ashton. Another casualty was the traditional five-man selection committee, with the exception of Whelan who remains as the conduit of the IRFU Executive Committee. In future Ashton himself would have the main say in the selection process.

Ashton inherited a squad to which he was barely able to put names to all the faces, with inevitable consequences. But as the season rolled on and the points against column mounted horrendously – except in Cardiff, of course – Ashton stoutly maintained that the structure of Irish rugby was correct, that there was talent, and that, even if the playing population was relatively small, a brighter future lay ahead.

Of the 35 players who pulled on Irish shirts last season, only four started all seven matches: Jonathan Bell, Jeremy Davidson, David Corkery and Paul Wallace. Three outside-halves were tried (David Humphreys, Eric Elwood and Paul Burke), three full-backs (Jim Staples, Simon Mason and Conor O'Shea), three scrum-halves (Niall Hogan, Stephen McIvor and Brian O'Meara) and three hookers (Keith Wood, Allen Clarke and Ross Nesdale). In all, 18 backs and 17 forwards were used during the season.

Last season contracted Irish players were given £30,000 and a car, while English-based players received £800 for attending a training session and a £3,000 match fee. It is unlikely that such a lavish hand-out will be forthcoming for the 1997-98 season. The IRFU has declared its intention to concentrate on a tiered system, contracting around 100 players from promising youngsters and upwards, and offering inducements aimed at keeping the better

The Ireland team which beat Wales at Cardiff. L-R back row: D G Humphreys (replacement), G M Fulcher (replacement), S C McIvor (replacement), K P McQuilkin (replacement), J C Bell, D S Corkery, P S Johns, J W Davidson, E R P Miller, P Flavin (replacement), P S Wallace, N J Popplewell, R P Nesdale, S J Byrne (replacement); front row: D A Hickie, M J Field, E P Elwood, R M Deacy (President), J E Staples (capt), W D McBride, N A Hogan, D J Crotty.

players at home. An important lesson for the new professional era was learned last year, as many of those named in the original contracted squad never made the grade, and some didn't even reach the A team.

There is no doubt that the absence of so many leading players with English clubs did devalue the All Ireland League. The season was a protracted one, starting early, taking a long break, and never quite recapturing the excitement and enthusiasm of previous seasons. Not that this would have concerned Shannon, on their way to a third successive title, too much. Once again they underlined the unique competitive tradition of Limerick, and indeed of the province of Munster who took the Guinness Inter-Provincial Championship.

One remarkable feature of the All Ireland has been the progress of those junior clubs who have joined the Fourth Division after winning their junior provincial Leagues. Last season both Suttonians and Ballynahinch made successful AIL debuts, occupying the top two spots with some ease and earning their places in the Third Division for next season.

Next season's League will have a new sponsor at the helm, since the Insurance Corporation of Ireland are discontinuing their support. Although there appears to be no shortage of companies interested in taking ICI's place, one wonders if poor international returns and lacklustre All Irelands might, eventually, discourage new sponsors from becoming involved.

INSURANCE CORPORATION ALL-IRELAND LEAGUE 1996-97

Division 1	P	W	D	L	F	A	Pts
Shannon	13	12	0	1	362	193	24
Lansdowne	13	9	0	4	349	184	18
Terenure College	13	9	0	4	301	179	18
St Mary's College	13	8	1	4	305	279	17
Ballymena	13	8	0	5	258	247	16
Cork Constitution	13	7	1	6	299	252	14
Garryowen	13	7	0	6	287	283	14
Blackrock College	13	7	0	6	288	288	14
Young Munster	13	6	0	7	233	274	12
Dungannon	13	5	0	8	324	344	10
Old Crescent	13	4	0	9	239	281	8
Old Belvedere	13	4	0	9	193	287	8
Old Wesley	13	3	0	10	206	327	6
Instonians	13	1	0	12	182	408	2

Division 2	P	W	D	L	F	A	Pts
Clontarf	13	11	0	2	329	173	22
Dolphin	13	9	1	3	294	236	19
Bective Rangers	13	9	0	4	259	146	18
Skerries	13	9	0	4	225	193	18
DLS Palmerston	13	6	2	5	285	243	14
Monkstown	13	6	2	5	242	254	14
UC, Cork	13	7	0	6	251	273	14
Sunday's Well	13	6	1	6	300	292	13
Malone	13	6	0	7	261	256	12
Greystones	13	6	0	7	242	260	12
Wanderers	13	5	1	7	223	280	11
Derry	13	3	0	10	217	303	6
N.I.F.C.	13	2	1	10	183	324	5
Highfield	13	2	0	11	206	284	4

Division 3	P	W	D	L	F	A	Pts
Buccaneers	10	9	1	0	201	112	19
Galwegians	10	8	1	1	206	100	17
Bohemians	10	8	0	2	249	110	16
Portadown	10	7	0	3	337	135	14
UC, Dublin	10	6	1	3	162	179	13
Queen's University	10	5	0	5	166	157	10
Collegians	10	4	0	6	153	221	8
Galway Corinthians	10	3	1	6	150	164	7
Dublin University	10	2	0	8	172	298	4
Bangor	10	1	0	9	96	262	2
Waterpark	10	0	0	10	107	261	0

Division 4	P	W	D	L	F	A	Pts
Suttonians	9	9	0	0	359	102	18
Ballynahinch	9	8	0	1	295	96	16
Ards	9	7	0	2	202	117	14
Ballina	9	5	1	3	142	153	11

199

Richmond	9	5	0	4	156	127	10
Creggs	9	4	0	5	149	180	8
C.I.Y.M.S.	9	2	0	7	125	180	4
Sligo	9	2	0	7	62	176	4
Armagh*	9	1	1	7	87	308	3
UC, Galway	9	1	0	8	82	220	2

*Armagh in play-off following round-robin
with four provincial junior League champions

DIVISION ONE

Leading Scorers
166 pts A Thompson (Shannon) *(4T, 28C 30PG)*
129 pts R O'Gara (Cork Constitution) *(1T, 20C, 25PG, 3DG)*
118 pts E Elwood (Lansdowne) *(2T, 15C, 24PG, 2DG)*
113 pts A O'Halloran (Young Munster) *(10C, 25PG, 6DG)*
104 pts S Bond (Instonians) *(13C, 26PG)*
103 pts K Keane (Garryowen) *(2T, 12C, 22PG, 1DG)*
103 pts C Fitzpatrick (St Mary's) *(1T, 13C, 24PG)*
100 pts R McIlmoyle (Ballymena) *(1T, 7C, 24PG, 3DG)*

Leading Try Scorers
10 D Coleman (Terenure)
8 C Clarke (Terenure)
K Nowlan (St Mary's)
M Dillon (Lansdowne)
D O'Mahony (Lansdowne)
7 D Lyons (St Mary's)

Guinness Inter-Provincial Tournament 1996

21 September, Ravenhill, Belfast

Leinster 35 (3G 3PG 1T)   **Ulster 25** (2G 2PG 1T)
Leinster: P McKenna (Old Belvedere); D Coleman (Terenure College), M Ridge (Old Belvedere), K McQuilkin (Lansdowne), D Hickie (St Mary's College); R Governey (Lansdowne), N Hogan (Oxford University); H Hurley (Moseley), M McDermott (Lansdowne), A McKeen (Lansdowne), S Jameson (St Mary's College), G Duffy (Old Wesley), C Pim (Old Wesley), K Spicer (Oxford University), D Oswald (Blackrock College) *Replacements* S Rooney (Lansdowne) for Oswald, G Dempsey (Terenure College) for Coleman
Scorers *Tries:* McKenna (2), Jameson, Spicer *Conversions:* Governey (3) *Penalty Goals:* Governey (3)
Ulster: R Morrow (Queen's Univ); J Topping (Ballymena), M McCall (Dungannon), M Field (Malene), J Cunningham (Dublin Univ); S Laing (Portadown), S Bell (Dungannon); R Mackey (Malone), S Ritchie (Ballymena), C Boyd (Currie), C Simpson (Dungannon), G Longwell (Ballymena), S Duncan (Malone), S McKinty (Bangor), D McBride (Malone)
Scorers *Tries:* Topping, Ritchie, Duncan *Conversions:* Laing (2) *Penalty Goals:* Laing (2)
Referee L Mayne

21 September, Temple Hill, Cork

Munster 45 (4G 3PG 1DG 1T)   **Connacht 28** (2G 3PG 1T)
Munster: S McCahill (Sunday's Well); J Lacey (Sunday's Well), B Walsh (Cork Constitution), M Lynch (Young Munster), A Thompson (Shannon); A O'Halloran (Young Munster), C McIvor (Garryowen); I Murray (Cork Constitution), P Cunningham (Garryowen), N Healy (Shannon), M Galwey (Shannon), L Dineen (Old Crescent), A Foley (Shannon), B Cronin (Garryowen), E Halvey (Shannon).
Scorers *Tries:* Lacey (2), Foley, McCahill, Walsh *Conversions:* O'Halloran (4) *Penalty Goals:* O'Halloran (2) Thompson *Dropped Goals:* O'Halloran
Connacht: B Carey (Blackrock College); M Devine (Buccaneers), A Reddan (Lansdowne), N Barry (Clontarf), D Finnegan (Wanderers); E Elwood (Lansdowne), C McGuinness (St Mary's College); J Maher (Bective Rangers), W Mulcahy (Skerries), R Ward (Old Belvedere), G Heaslip (Galwegians), M O'Neill (Blackrock College), R Rogers (Blackrock College), B Gavin (Galwegians), K Delvin (St Mary's College) *Replacements* N Carolan (Corinthians) for Barry, D Reddan (Galwegians) for Carey
Scorers *Tries:* Reddan, Devine (2) *Conversions:* Elwood (2) *Penalty Goals:* Elwood (3)
Referee A Watson

September 28, Ravenhill, Belfast

Ulster 32 (1G 5PG 2T)   **Connacht 27** (1G 5PG 1T)
Ulster: R Morrow (Queen's Univ); J Topping (Ballymena), M McCall (Dungannon), M Field (Malone), J Cunningham (Dublin Univ); S Laing (Portadown), S Bell (Dungannon); R Mackey (Malone), S Ritchie (Ballymena), C Boyd (Currie), A Robinson (Ballymena), G Longwell (Ballymena), S Duncan (Malone), S McKinty (Bangor), D McBride (Malone)

Scorers *Tries:* Topping, Duncan, Laing *Conversions:* Laing *Penalty Goals:* Laing (5)
Connacht: B Carey (Blackrock College); M Devine (Buccaneers), A Reddan (Lansdowne), N Carolan (Corinthians), D Finnegan (Wanderers); E Elwood (Lansdowne), C McGuinness (St Mary's College); J Maher (Bective Rangers), W Mulcahy (Skerries), M Finlay (Wanderers), S Leahy (Lansdowne), G Heaslip (Galwegians), R Rogers (Blackrock College), B Gavin (Galwegians), K Devlin (St Mary's College) *Replacement* O Cobbe (Wanderers) for Finnegan
Scorers *Tries:* Elwood, Carey *Conversion:* Elwood *Penalty Goals:* Elwood (5)
Referee B Smith

September 28, Donnybrook, Dublin

Munster 45 (3G 7PG 1DG)   **Leinster 40** (3G 3PG 2T)
Munster: D Crotty (Garryowen); S McCahill (Sunday's Well), M Lynch (Young Munster), B Walsh (Cork Constitution), B Begley (Old Crescent); K Keane (Garryowen), S McIvor (Garryowen); I Murray (Cork Constitution), T Kingston (Dolphin), N Healy (Shannon), M Galwey (Shannon), L Dineen (Old Crescent), A Foley (Shannon), B Cronin (Garryowen), E Halvey (Shannon) *Replacement* A Thompson (Shannon) for Begley
Scorers *Tries:* Galwey (2), Halvey *Conversions:* Begley, Lynch (2) *Penalty Goals:* Begley (5), Lynch (2)
Dropped Goal: Keane
Leinster: P McKenna (Old Belvedere); D Coleman (Terenure College), M Ridge (Old Belvedere), K McQuilkin (Lansdowne), D Hickie (St Mary's College); R Governey (Lansdowne), A Rolland (Blackrock College); H Hurley (Moseley), M McDermott (Lansdowne), A McKeen (Lansdowne), S Jameson (St Mary's College), N Francis (Old Belvedere), C Pim (Old Wesley), K Spicer (Oxford Univ), S Rooney (Lansdowne) *Replacements* P Flavin (Blackrock College) for McKeen, G Dempsey (Terenure College) for Coleman
Scorers *Tries:* Coleman, Ridge, McQuilkin, Francis, Hickie *Conversions:* Governey (3)
Penalty Goals: Governey (3)
Referee G Hughes

5 October, Thomond Park, Limerick

Munster 27 (1G 3PG 2DG 1T)   **Ulster 24** (1G 4PG 1T)
Munster: D Crotty (Garryowen); S McCahill (Sunday's Well), B Walsh (Cork Constitution), M Lynch (Young Munster), B Begley (Old Crescent); K Keane (Garryowen), S McIvor (Garryowen); I Murray (Cork Constitution), T Kingston (Dolphin), N Healy (Shannon), M Galwey (Shannon), L Dineen (Old Crescent), A Foley (Shannon), B Cronin (Garryowen), E Halvey (Shannon) *Replacement* P McCarthy (Cork Constitution) for Healy
Scorers *Tries:* Dineen, Galwey *Conversion:* Begley *Penalty Goals:* Begley (3) *Dropped Goals:* McIvor, Keane
Ulster: R Morrow (Queen's Univ); J Topping (Ballymena), M McCall (Dungannon), S Coulter (Ballymena), J Cunningham (Dublin Univ); S Laing (Portadown), S Bell (Dungannon); R Mackey (Malone), S Ritchie (Ballymena), C Boyd (Currie), G Longwell (Ballymena), A Robinson (Ballymena), S Duncan (Malone), B McKinty (Bangor), D McBride (Malone)
Scorers *Tries:* Duncan, Coulter *Conversion:* Laing *Penalty Goals:* Laing (4)
Referee A Lewis

5 October, Sportsground, Galway

Connacht 22 (2T 4PG)   **Leinster 13** (1G 2PG)
Connacht: B Carey (Blackrock College); M Devine (Buccaneers), A Reddan (Lansdowne), N Carolan (Corinthians), M Kearin (Lansdowne); E Elwood (Lansdowne), C McGuinness (St Mary's College); J Maher (Bective Rangers), W Mulcahy (Skerries), M Finlay (Wanderers), G Heaslip (Galwegians), S Leahy (Lansdowne), R Rogers (Blackrock College), B Gavin (Galwegians), K Devlin (St Mary's College) *Replacement* M O'Neill (Blackrock College) for Leahy
Scorers *Tries:* Elwood, Leahy *Penalty Goals:* Elwood (4)
Leinster: P McKenna (Old Belvedere); P Gavin (Old Belvedere), K McQuilkin (Lansdowne), M Ridge (Old Belvedere), D O'Mahoney (Lansdowne); R Governey (Lansdowne), A Rolland (Blackrock College); P Flavin (Blackrock College), M McDermott (Lansdowne), A McKeen (Lansdowne), S Jameson (St Mary's College), N Francis (Old Belvedere), K Leahy (Wanderers), K Spicer (Oxford Univ), S Rooney (Lansdowne) *Replacements* S Byrne (Blackrock College) for McDermott, V Cunningham (Bective Rangers) for Ridge, G Duffy (Old Wesley) for Francis
Scorers *Try:* Francis *Conversion:* Governey *Penalty Goals:* Governey (2)
Referee G Crothers

FINAL TABLE

	P	W	D	L	F	A	Pts
Munster	3	3	0	0	117	92	6
Leinster	3	1	0	2	88	92	2
Ulster	3	1	0	2	81	89	2
Connacht	3	1	0	2	77	90	2

IRISH INTERNATIONAL PLAYERS
(*up to 30 April 1997*)

Note: Years given for Five Nations' matches are for second half of season; eg 1972 means season 1971-72. Years for all other matches refer to the actual year of the match. When a series has taken place, figures have been used to denote the particular matches in which players have featured. Thus 1981 *SA* 2 indicates that a player appeared in the second Test of the series. The abandoned game with Scotland at Belfast in 1885 is now included as a cap match.

NB – The second of Ireland's two matches against France in 1972 was a non-championship match.

Abraham, M (Bective Rangers) 1912 *E, S, W, SA*, 1914 *W*
Adams, C (Old Wesley), 1908 *E*, 1909 *E, F*, 1910 *F*, 1911 *E, S, W, F*, 1912 *S, W, SA*, 1913 *W, F*, 1914 *F, E, S*
Agar, R D (Malone) 1947 *F, E, S, W*, 1948 *F*, 1949 *S, W*, 1950 *F, E, W*
Agnew, P J (CIYMS) 1974 *F* (R), 1976 *A*
Ahearne, T (Queen's Coll, Cork) 1899 *E*
Aherne, L F P (Dolphin, Lansdowne) 1988 *E* 2, *WS, It*, 1989 *F, W, E, S, NZ*, 1990 *E, S, F, W* (R), 1992 *E, S, F, A*
Alexander, R (NIFC, Police Union) 1936 *E, S, W*, 1937 *E, S, W*, 1938 *E, S*, 1939 *E, S, W*
Allen, C E (Derry, Liverpool) 1900 *E, S, W*, 1901 *E, S, W*, 1903 *S, W*, 1904 *E, S, W*, 1905 *E, S, W, NZ*, 1906 *E, S, W, SA*, 1907 *S, W*
Allen, G G (Derry, Liverpool) 1896 *E, S, W*, 1897 *E, S*, 1898 *E, S*, 1899 *E, W*
Allen, T C (NIFC) 1885 *E, S* 1
Allen, W S (Wanderers) 1875 *E*
Allison, J B (Edinburgh U) 1899 *E, S*, 1900 *E, S, W*, 1901 *E, S, W*, 1902 *E, S, W*, 1903 *S*
Anderson, F E (Queen's U, Belfast, NIFC) 1953 *F, E, S, W*, 1954 *NZ, E, S, W*, 1955 *F, E, S, W*
Anderson, H J (Old Wesley) 1903 *E, S*, 1906 *E, S*
Anderson, W A (Dungannon) 1984 *A*, 1985 *S, F, W, E*, 1986 *F, S, R*, 1987 *E, S, F, W, [W, C, Tg, A]*, 1988 *S, F, W, E* 1,2, 1989 *F, W, E, NZ*, 1990 *E, S*
Andrews, G (NIFC) 1875 *E*, 1876 *E*
Andrews, H W (NIFC) 1888 *M*, 1889 *S, W*
Archer, A M (Dublin U, NIFC) 1879 *S*
Arigho, J E (Lansdowne) 1928 *F, E, W*, 1929 *F, E, S, W*, 1930 *F, E, S, W*, 1931 *F, E, S, W, SA*
Armstrong, W K (NIFC) 1960 *SA*, 1961 *E*
Arnott, D T (Lansdowne) 1876 *E*
Ash, W H (NIFC) 1875 *E*, 1876 *E*, 1877 *S*
Aston, H R (Dublin U) 1908 *E, W*
Atkins, A P (Bective Rangers) 1924 *F*
Atkinson, J M (NIFC) 1927 *F, A*
Atkinson, J R (Dublin U) 1882 *W, S*

Bagot, J C (Dublin U, Lansdowne) 1879 *S, E*, 1880 *E, S*, 1881 *S*
Bailey, A H (UC Dublin, Lansdowne) 1934 *W*, 1935 *E, S, W, NZ*, 1936 *E, S, W*, 1937 *E, S, W*, 1938 *E, S*
Bailey, N (Northampton) 1952 *E*
Bardon, M E (Bohemians) 1934 *E*
Barlow, M (Wanderers) 1875 *E*
Barnes, R J (Dublin U, Armagh) 1933 *W*
Barr, A (Methodist Coll, Belfast) 1898 *W*, 1899 *S*, 1901 *E, S*
Barry, N J (Garryowen) 1991 *Nm* 2 (R)
Beamish, C E St J (RAF, Leicester) 1933 *W, S*, 1934 *S, W*, 1935 *E, S, W, NZ*, 1936 *E, S, W*, 1938 *W*
Beamish, G R (RAF, Leicester) 1925 *E, S, W*, 1928 *F, E, S, W*, 1929 *F, E, S, W*, 1930 *F, S, W*, 1931 *F, E, S, W, SA*, 1932 *E, S, W*, 1933 *E, W, S*
Beatty, W J (NIFC, Richmond) 1910 *F*, 1912 *F, W*
Becker, V A (Lansdowne) 1974 *F, W*
Beckett, G G P (Dublin U) 1908 *E, S, W*
Bell, J C (Ballymena, Northampton) 1994 *A* 1,2, *US*, 1995 *S, It*, *[NZ, W, F]*, *Fj*, 1996 *US, S, F, W, E, WS, A*, 1997 *It, F, W, E, S*
Bell, R J (NIFC) 1875 *E*, 1876 *E*
Bell, W E (Belfast Collegians) 1953 *F, E, S, W*
Bennett, F (Belfast Collegians) 1913 *S*
Bent, G C (Dublin U) 1882 *W, E*
Berkery, P J (Lansdowne) 1954 *W*, 1955 *W*, 1956 *S, W*, 1957 *F, E, S, W*, 1958 *A, E, S*
Bermingham, J J C (Blackrock Coll) 1921 *E, S, W, F*

Blackham, J C (Queen's Coll, Cork) 1909 *S, W, F*, 1910 *E, S, W*
Blake-Knox, S E F (NIFC) 1976 *E, S*, 1977 *F* (R)
Blayney, J J (Wanderers) 1950 *S*
Bond, A T W (Derry) 1894 *S, W*
Bornemann, W W (Wanderers) 1960 *E, S, W, SA*
Bowen, D St J (Cork Const) 1977 *W, E, S*
Boyd, C A (Dublin U) 1900 *S*, 1901 *S, W*
Boyle, C V (Dublin U) 1935 *NZ*, 1936 *E, S, W*, 1937 *E, S, W*, 1938 *W*, 1939 *W*
Brabazon, H M (Dublin U) 1884 *E*, 1885 *S* 1, 1886 *E*
Bradley, M J (Dolphin) 1920 *W, F*, 1922 *E, S, W, F*, 1923 *E, S, W, F*, 1925 *F, S, W*, 1926 *F, E, S, W*, 1927 *F, W*
Bradley, M T (Cork Constitution) 1984 *A*, 1985 *S, F, W*, *E*, 1986 *F, W, E, S, R*, 1987 *E, S, F, W, [W, C, Tg, A]*, 1988 *S, F, W, E* 1, 1990 *W*, 1992 *NZ* 1,2, 1993 *S, F, W, E, R*, 1994 *F, W, E, S, A* 1,2, *US*, 1995 *S, F, [NZ]*
Bradshaw, G (Belfast Collegians) 1903 *W*
Bradshaw, R M (Wanderers) 1885 *E, S* 1,2
Brady, A M (UC Dublin, Malone) 1966 *S*, 1968 *E, S, W*
Brady, J A (Wanderers) 1976 *E, S*
Brady, J R (CIYMS) 1951 *S, W*, 1953 *F, E, S, W*, 1954 *W*, 1956 *W*, 1957 *F, E, S, W*
Bramwell, T (NIFC) 1928 *F*
Brand, T N (NIFC) 1924 *NZ*
Brennan, J I (CIYMS) 1957 *S, W*
Bresnihan, F P K (UC Dublin, Lansdowne, London Irish) 1966 *E, W*, 1967 *A* 1, *E, S, W, F*, 1968 *F, E, S, W, A*, 1969 *F, S, W*, 1970 *SA, F, E, S, W*, 1971 *F, E, S, W*
Brett, J T (Monkstown) 1914 *W*
Bristow, J R (NIFC) 1879 *E*
Brophy, N H (Blackrock Coll, UC Dublin, London Irish) 1957 *F, E*, 1959 *E, S, W, F*, 1960 *F, SA*, 1961 *S, W*, 1962 *E, S, W*, 1963 *E, W*, 1967 *E, S, W, F, A* 2
Brown, E L (Instonians) 1958 *F*
Brown, G S (Monkstown, United Services) 1912 *S, W, SA*
Brown, H (Windsor) 1877 *E*
Brown, T (Windsor) 1877 *E, S*
Brown, W H (Dublin U) 1899 *E*
Brown, W J (Malone) 1970 *SA, F, S, W*
Brown, W S (Dublin U) 1893 *S, W*, 1894 *E, S, W*
Browne, A W (Dublin U) 1951 *SA*
Browne, D (Blackrock Coll) 1920 *F*
Browne, H C (United Services and RN) 1929 *E, S, W*
Browne, W F (United Services and Army) 1925 *S, W*, 1926 *S, W*, 1927 *F, E, S, W, A*, 1928 *E, S*
Browning, D R (Wanderers) 1881 *E, S*
Bruce, S A M (NIFC) 1883 *E, S*, 1884 *E*
Brunker, A A (Lansdowne) 1895 *E, W*
Bryant, C H (Cardiff) 1920 *E, S*
Buchanan, A McM (Dublin U) 1926 *E, S, W*, 1927 *S, W, A*
Buchanan, J W B (Dublin U) 1882 *S*, 1884 *E, S*
Buckley, J H (Sunday's Well) 1973 *E, S*
Bulger, L Q (Lansdowne) 1896 *E, S, W*, 1897 *E, S*, 1898 *E, S, W*
Bulger, M J (Dublin U) 1888 *M*
Burges, J H (Rosslyn Park) 1950 *F, E*
Burgess, R B (Dublin U) 1912 *SA*
Burke, P A (Cork Constitution, Bristol) 1995 *E, S, W* (R), *It, [J], Fj*, 1996 *US* (R), *A*, 1997 *It, S* (R)
Burkitt, J C S (Queen's Coll, Cork) 1881 *E*
Burns, I J (Wanderers) 1980 *E* (R)
Butler, L G (Blackrock Coll) 1960 *W*
Butler, N (Bective Rangers) 1920 *E*
Byers, R M (NIFC) 1928 *S, W*, 1929 *E, S, W*
Byrne, E M J (Blackrock Coll) 1977 *S, F*, 1978 *F, W, E, NZ*
Byrne, N F (UC Dublin) 1962 *F*

Byrne, S J (UC Dublin, Lansdowne) 1953 *S, W,* 1955 *F*
Byron, W G (NIFC) 1896 *E, S, W,* 1897 *E, S,* 1898 *E, S,
W,* 1899 *E, S, W*

Caddell, E D (Dublin U, Wanderers) 1904 *S,* 1905 *E, S,
W, NZ,* 1906 *E, S, W, SA,* 1907 *E, S,* 1908 *S, W*
Cagney, S J (London Irish) 1925 *W,* 1926 *F, E, S, W,*
1927 *F,* 1928 *E, S, W,* 1929 *F, E, S, W*
Callan, C P (Lansdowne) 1947 *F, E, S, W,* 1948 *F, E, S,
W,* 1949 *F, E*
Cameron, E D (Bective Rangers) 1891 *S, W*
Campbell, C E (Old Wesley) 1970 *SA*
Campbell, E F (Monkstown) 1899 *S, W,* 1900 *E. W*
Campbell, S B B (Derry) 1911 *E, S, W, F,* 1912 *F, E, S,
W, SA,* 1913 *E, S, F*
Campbell, S O (Old Belvedere) 1976 *A,* 1979 *A 1,2,*
1980 *E, S, F, W,* 1981 *F, W, E, S, SA 1,* 1982 *W, E, S, F,*
1983 *S, F, W, E,* 1984 *F, W*
Canniffe, D M (Lansdowne) 1976 *W, E*
Cantrell, J L (UC Dublin, Blackrock Coll) 1976 *A, F, W,
E, S,* 1981 *S, SA 1,2, A*
Carey, R W (Dungannon) 1992 *NZ 1,2*
Carpendale, M J (Monkstown) 1886 *S,* 1887 *W,* 1888
W, S
Carr, N J (Ards) 1985 *S, F, W, E,* 1986 *W, E, S, R,* 1987
E, S, W
Carroll, C (Bective Rangers) 1930 *F*
Carroll, R (Lansdowne) 1947 *F,* 1950 *S, W*
Casement, B N (Dublin U) 1875 *E,* 1876 *E,* 1879 *E*
Casement, F (Dublin U) 1906 *E, S, W*
Casey, J C (Young Munster) 1930 *S,* 1932 *E*
Casey, P J (UC Dublin, Lansdowne) 1963 *F, E, S, W, NZ,*
1964 *E, S, W, F,* 1965 *F, E, S*
Chambers, J (Dublin U) 1886 *E, S,* 1887 *E, S, W*
Chambers, R R (Instonians) 1951 *F, E, S, W,* 1952 *F, W*
Clancy, T P J (Lansdowne) 1988 *W, E 1,2, WS, It,* 1989
F, W, E, S
Clarke, A T H (Northampton) 1995 *Fj (R),* 1996 *W, E,
WS,* 1997 *F (R)*
Clarke, C P (Terenure Coll) 1993 *F, W, E*
Clarke, D J (Dolphin) 1991 *W, Nm 1,2, [J, A],* 1992 *NZ
2(R)*
Clarke, J A B (Bective Rangers) 1922 *S, W, F,* 1923 *F,*
1924 *E, S, W*
Clegg, R J (Bangor) 1973 *F,* 1975 *E, S, F, W*
Clifford, J T (Young Munster) 1949 *F, E, S, W,* 1950 *F,
E, S, W,* 1951 *F, E, SA,* 1952 *F, S, W*
Clinch, A D (Dublin U, Wanderers) 1892 *S,* 1893 *W,*
1895 *E, S, W,* 1896 *E, S, W,* 1897 *E, S*
Clinch, J D (Wanderers, Dublin U) 1923 *W,* 1924 *F, E, S,
W, NZ,* 1925 *F, E, S,* 1926 *E, S, W,* 1927 *F,* 1928 *F, E, S,
W,* 1929 *F, E, S, W,* 1930 *F, E, S, W,* 1931 *F, E, S, W, SA*
Clohessy, P M (Young Munster) 1993 *F, W, E,* 1994 *F, W,
E, S, A 1,2, US,* 1995 *E, S, F, W,* 1996 *S, F*
Clune, J J (Blackrock Coll) 1912 *SA,* 1913 *W, F,* 1914 *F,
E, W*

Coffey, J J (Lansdowne) 1900 *E,* 1901 *W,* 1902 *E, S, W,*
1903 *E, S, W,* 1905 *E, S, W, NZ,* 1906 *E, S, W, SA,* 1907
E, 1908 *W,* 1910 *F*
Cogan, W St J (Queen's Coll, Cork) 1907 *E, S*
Collier, S R (Queen's Coll, Belfast) 1883 *S*
Collins, P C (Lansdowne, London Irish) 1987 *[C],* 1990
S (R)
Collis, W R F (KCH, Harlequins) 1924 *F, W, NZ,* 1925 *F,
E, S,* 1926 *F*
Collis, W S (Wanderers) 1884 *W*
Collopy, G (Bective Rangers) 1891 *S,* 1892 *S*
Collopy, R (Bective Rangers) 1923 *E, S, W, F,* 1924 *F, E,
S, W, NZ,* 1925 *F, E, S, W*
Collopy, W P (Bective Rangers) 1914 *F, E, S, W,* 1921 *E,
S, W, F,* 1922 *E, S, W, F,* 1923 *S, W, F,* 1924 *F, E, S, W*
Combe, A (NIFC) 1875 *E*
Condon, H C (London Irish) 1984 *S (R)*
Cook, H G (Lansdowne) 1884 *W*
Coote, P B (RAF, Leicester) 1933 *S*
Corcoran, J C (London Irish) 1947 *A,* 1948 *F*
Corken, T S (Belfast Collegians) 1937 *E, S, W*
Corkery, D S (Cork Constitution, Bristol) 1994 *A 1,2,
US,* 1995 *E, [NZ, J, W, F], Fj,* 1996 *US, S, F, W, E, WS, A,*
1997 *It, F, W, E, S*
Corley, H H (Dublin U, Wanderers) 1902 *E, S, W,* 1903
E, S, W, 1904 *E, S*
Cormac, H S T (Clontarf) 1921 *E, S, W*
Costello, P (Bective Rangers) 1960 *F*

Costello, R A (Garryowen) 1993 *S*
Costello, V C P (St Mary's Coll, London Irish) 1996 *US,
F, W, E. WS (R)*
Cotton, J (Wanderers) 1889 *W*
Coulter, H H (Queen's U, Belfast) 1920 *E, S, W*
Courtney, A W (UC Dublin) 1920 *S, W, F,* 1921 *E, S, W, F*
Cox, H L (Dublin U) 1875 *E,* 1876 *E,* 1877 *E, S*
Craig, R G (Queen's U, Belfast) 1938 *S, W*
Crawford, E C (Dublin U) 1885 *E, S 1*
Crawford, W E (Lansdowne) 1920 *E, S, W, F,* 1921 *E, S,
W, F,* 1922 *E, S,* 1923 *E, S, W, F,* 1924 *F, E, W, NZ,* 1925
F, E, S, W, 1926 *E, S, W,* 1927 *F, E, S, W*
Crean, T J (Wanderers) 1894 *E, S, W,* 1895 *E, S, W,*
1896 *E, S, W*
Crichton, R Y (Dublin U) 1920 *E, S, W, F,* 1921 *F,* 1922
E, 1923 *W, F,* 1924 *F, E, S, W, NZ,* 1925 *E, S*
Croker, E W D (Limerick) 1878 *E*
Cromey, G E (Queen's U, Belfast) 1937 *E, S, W,* 1938 *E,
S, W,* 1939 *E, S, W*
Cronin, B M (Lansdowne) 1995 *S,* 1997 *S*
Cronyn, A P (Dublin U, Lansdowne) 1875 *E,* 1876 *E,*
1880 *S*
Crossan, K D (Instonians) 1982 *S,* 1984 *F, W, E, S,* 1985
S, F, W, E, 1986 *E, S, R,* 1987 *E, S, F, W, [W, C, Tg. A],*
1988 *S, F, W, E 1, WS, It,* 1989 *W, S, NZ,* 1990 *E, S, F, W,
Arg,* 1991 *E, S, Nm 2 [Z, J, S],* 1992 *W*
Crotty, D J (Garryowen) 1996 *A,* 1997 *It, F, W*
Crowe, J F (UC Dublin) 1974 *NZ*
Crowe, L (Old Belvedere) 1950 *E, S, W*
Crowe, M P (Lansdowne) 1929 *W,* 1930 *E, S, W,* 1931 *F,
S, W, SA,* 1932 *S, W,* 1933 *W, S,* 1934 *E*
Crowe, P M (Blackrock Coll) 1935 *E,* 1938 *E*
Cullen, T J (UC Dublin) 1949 *F*
Cullen, W J (Monkstown and Manchester) 1920 *E*
Culliton, M G (Wanderers) 1959 *E, S, W, F,* 1960 *E, S,
W, F, SA,* 1961 *E, S, W, F,* 1962 *S, F,* 1964 *E, S, W, F*
Cummins, W E A (Queen's Coll, Cork) 1879 *S,* 1881 *E,*
1882 *E*
Cunningham, D McC (NIFC) 1923 *E, S, W,* 1925 *F, E, W*
Cunningham, M J (UC Cork) 1955 *F, E, S, W,* 1956 *F,
S, W*
Cunningham, V J G (St Mary's Coll) 1988 *E 2, It,* 1990
Arg (R), 1991 *Nm 1,2, [Z, J(R)],* 1992 *NZ 1,2, A,* 1993 *S,
F, W, E, R,* 1994 *F*
Cunningham, W A (Lansdowne) 1920 *W,* 1921 *E, S, W,
F,* 1922 *E,* 1923 *S, W*
Cuppaidge, J L (Dublin U) 1879 *E,* 1880 *E, S*
Currell, J (NIFC) 1877 *S*
Curtis, A B (Oxford U) 1950 *F, E, S*
Curtis, D M (London Irish) 1991 *W, E, S, Nm 1,2, [Z, J,
S, A],* 1992 *W, E, S (R), F*
Cuscaden, W A (Dublin U, Bray) 1876 *E*
Cussen, D J (Dublin U) 1921 *E, S, W, F,* 1922 *E,* 1923 *E,
S, W, F,* 1926 *F, E, S, W,* 1927 *F, E*

Daly, J C (London Irish) 1947 *F, E, S, W,* 1948 *E, S, W*
Daly, M J (Harlequins) 1938 *E*
Danaher, P P A (Lansdowne, Garryowen) 1988 *S, F, W,
WS, It,* 1989 *F, NZ (R),* 1990 *F,* 1992 *S, F, NZ 1, A,* 1993
S, F, W, E, R, 1994 *F, W, E, S, A 1,2, US,* 1995 *E, S, F, W*
Dargan, M J (Old Belvedere) 1952 *S, W*
Davidson, C T (NIFC) 1921 *F*
Davidson, I G (NIFC) 1899 *E,* 1900 *S, W,* 1901 *E, S, W,*
1902 *E, S, W*
Davidson, J C (Dungannon) 1969 *F, E, S, W,* 1973 *NZ,*
1976 *NZ*
Davidson, J W (Dungannon, London Irish) 1995 *Fj,*
1996 *S, F, W, E, WS, A,* 1997 *It, F, W, E, S*
Davies, F E (Lansdowne) 1892 *S, W,* 1893 *E, S, W*
Davis, J L (Monkstown) 1898 *E, S*
Davis, W J N (Edinburgh U, Bessbrook) 1890 *S, W, E,*
1891 *E, S, W,* 1892 *E, S,* 1895 *S*
Davison, W (Belfast Academy) 1887 *W*
Davy, E O'D (UC Dublin, Lansdowne) 1925 *W,* 1926 *F,
E, S, W,* 1927 *F, E, S, W,* 1928 *F, E, S, W,* 1929 *F, E, S,
W,* 1930 *F, E, S, W,* 1931 *F, E, S, W, SA,* 1932 *E, S, W,*
1933 *E, W, S,* 1934 *E*
Dawson, A R (Wanderers) 1958 *A, E, S, W, F,* 1959 *E, S,
W, F,* 1960 *F, SA,* 1961 *E, S, W, F, SA,* 1962 *S, F, W,* 1963
F, E, S, W, NZ, 1964 *E, S, F*
Dean, P M (St Mary's Coll) 1981 *SA 1,2, A,* 1982 *W, E,
S, F,* 1984 *A,* 1985 *S, F, W, E,* 1986 *F, W, R,* 1987 *E, S, F,
W, [W, A],* 1988 *S, F, W, E 1,2, WS, It,* 1989 *F, W, E, S*
Deane, E C (Monkstown) 1909 *E*

Jeremy Davidson wins the line-out for Ireland in their match with England at Lansdowne Road, Dublin.

Deering, M J (Bective Rangers) 1929 *W*
Deering, S J (Bective Rangers) 1935 *E, S, W, NZ,* 1936 *E, S, W,* 1937 *E, S*
Deering, S M (Garryowen, St Mary's Coll) 1974 *W,* 1976 *F, W, E, S,* 1977 *W, E,* 1978 *NZ*
de Lacy, H (Harlequins) 1948 *E, S*
Delany, M G (Bective Rangers) 1895 *W*
Dennison, S P (Garryowen) 1973 *F,* 1975 *E, S*
Dick, C J (Ballymena) 1961 *W, F, SA,* 1962 *W,* 1963 *F, E, S, W*
Dick, J S (Queen's U, Belfast) 1962 *E*
Dick, J S (Queen's U, Cork) 1887 *E, S, W*
Dickson, J A N (Dublin U) 1920 *E, W, F*
Doherty, A E (Old Wesley) 1974 *P* (R)
Doherty, W D (Guy's Hospital) 1920 *E, S, W,* 1921 *E, S, W, F*
Donaldson, J A (Belfast Collegians) 1958 *A, E, S, W*
Donovan, T M (Queen's Coll, Cork) 1889 *S*
Dooley, J F (Galwegians) 1959 *E, S, W*
Doran, B R W (Lansdowne) 1900 *S, W,* 1901 *E, S, W,* 1902 *E, S, W*
Doran, E F (Lansdowne) 1890 *S, W*
Doran, G P (Lansdowne) 1899 *S, W,* 1900 *E, S,* 1902 *S, W,* 1903 *W,* 1904 *E*
Douglas, A C (Instonians) 1923 *F,* 1924 *E, S,* 1927 *A,* 1928 *S*
Downing, A J (Dublin U) 1882 *W*
Dowse, J C A (Monkstown) 1914 *F, S, W*
Doyle, J A P (Greystones) 1984 *E, S*
Doyle, J T (Bective Rangers) 1935 *W*
Doyle, M G (Blackrock Coll, UC Dublin, Cambridge U, Edinburgh Wands) 1965 *F, E, S, W, SA,* 1966 *F, E, S, W,* 1967 *A* 1, *E, S, W, F, A* 2, 1968 *F, E, S, W, A*
Doyle, T J (Wanderers) 1968 *E, S, W*
Duggan, A T A (Lansdowne) 1963 *NZ,* 1964 *F,* 1966 *W,* 1967 *A* 1, *S, W, A* 2, 1968 *F, E, S, W,* 1969 *F, E, S, W,* 1970 *SA, F, E, S, W,* 1971 *F, E, S, W,* 1972 *F* 2
Duggan, W (UC Cork) 1920 *S, W*
Duggan, W P (Blackrock Coll) 1975 *E, S, F, W,* 1976 *A, F, W, S, NZ,* 1977 *W, E, S, F,* 1978 *S, F, W, E, NZ,* 1979 *E, S, A* 1,2, 1980 *E,* 1981 *F, W, E, S, SA* 1,2, *A,* 1982 *W, E, S,* 1983 *S, F, W, E,* 1984 *F, W, E, S*
Duncan, W R (Malone) 1984 *W, E*
Dunlea, F J (Lansdowne) 1989 *W, E, S*
Dunlop, R (Dublin U) 1889 *W,* 1890 *S, W, E,* 1891 *E, S, W,* 1892 *E, S,* 1893 *W,* 1894 *W*
Dunn, P E F (Bective Rangers) 1923 *S*
Dunn, T B (NIFC) 1935 *NZ*
Dunne, M J (Lansdowne) 1929 *F, E, S, W,* 1930 *F, E, S, W,* 1932 *E, S, W,* 1933 *E, W, S,* 1934 *E, S, W*
Dwyer, P J (UC Dublin) 1962 *W,* 1963 *F, NZ,* 1964 *S, W*

Edwards, H G (Dublin U) 1877 *E,* 1878 *E*
Edwards, R W (Malone) 1904 *W*
Edwards, T (Lansdowne) 1888 *M,* 1890 *S, W, E,* 1892 *W,* 1893 *E*
Edwards, W V (Malone) 1912 *F, E*
Egan, J D (Bective Rangers) 1922 *S*
Egan, J T (Cork Constitution) 1931 *F, E, SA*
Egan, M S (Garryowen) 1893 *E,* 1895 *S*
Ekin, W (Queen's Coll, Belfast) 1888 *W, S*
Elliott, W R J (Bangor) 1979 *S*
Elwood, E P (Lansdowne) 1993 *W, E, R,* 1994 *F, W, E, S, A* 1,2, 1995 *F, W, [NZ, W, F],* 1996 *US, S,* 1997 *F, W, E*
English, M A F (Lansdowne, Limerick Bohemians) 1958 *W, F,* 1959 *E, S, F,* 1960 *E, S,* 1961 *S, W, F,* 1962 *F, W,* 1963 *E, S, W, NZ*
Ennis, F N G (Wanderers) 1979 *A* 1 (R)
Ensor, A H (Wanderers) 1973 *W, F,* 1974 *F, W, E, S, P, NZ,* 1975 *E, S, F, W,* 1976 *A, F, W, E, NZ,* 1977 *E,* 1978 *S, F, W, E*
Entrican, J C (Queen's U, Belfast) 1931 *S*

Fagan, G L (Kingstown School) 1878 *E*
Fagan, W B C (Wanderers) 1956 *F, E, S*
Farrell, J L (Bective Rangers) 1926 *F, E, S, W,* 1927 *F, E, S, W, A,* 1928 *F, E, S, W,* 1929 *F, E, S, W,* 1930 *F, E, S, W,* 1931 *F, E, S, W, SA,* 1932 *E, S, W*
Feddis, N (Lansdowne) 1956 *E*
Feighery, C F P (Lansdowne) 1972 *F* 1, *E, F* 2
Feighery, T A O (St Mary's Coll) 1977 *W, E*
Ferris, H H (Queen's Coll, Belfast) 1901 *W*
Ferris, J H (Queen's Coll, Belfast) 1900 *E, S, W*

Field, M J (Malone) 1994 *E, S, A* 1 (R), 1995 *F* (R), *W* (t), *It* (R), *[NZ(t + R), J], Fj,* 1996 *F* (R), *W, E, A* (R), 1997 *F, W, E, S*
Finlay, J E (Queen's Coll, Belfast) 1913 *E, S, W,* 1920 *E, S, W*
Finlay, W (NIFC) 1876 *E,* 1877 *E, S,* 1878 *E,* 1879 *S, E,* 1880 *S,* 1882 *S*
Finn, M C (UC Cork, Cork Constitution) 1979 *E,* 1982 *W, E, S, F,* 1983 *S, F, W, E,* 1984 *E, S, A,* 1986 *F, W*
Finn, R G A (UC Dublin) 1977 *F*
Fitzgerald, C C (Glasgow U, Dungannon) 1902 *E,* 1903 *E, S*
Fitzgerald, C F (St Mary's Coll) 1979 *A* 1,2, 1980 *E, S, F, W,* 1982 *W, E, S, F,* 1983 *S, F, W, E,* 1984 *F, W, A,* 1985 *S, F, W, E,* 1986 *F, W, E, S*
Fitzgerald, D C (Lansdowne, De La Salle Palmerston) 1984 *E, S,* 1986 *W, E, S, R,* 1987 *E, S, F, W, [W, C, A],* 1988 *S, F, W, E* 1, 1989 *NZ* (R), 1990 *E, S, F, W, Arg,* 1991 *F, W, E, S, Nm* 1, *[J], A],* 1992 *W, S* (R)
Fitzgerald, J (Wanderers) 1884 *W*
Fitzgerald, J J (Young Munster) 1988 *S, F,* 1990 *S, F, W,* 1991 *F, W, E, S, [J],* 1994 *A* 1,2
Fitzgibbon, M J J (Shannon) 1992 *W, E, S, F, NZ* 1,2
Fitzpatrick, M P (Wanderers) 1978 *S,* 1980 *S, F, W,* 1981 *F, W, E, S, A,* 1985 *F* (R)
Flavin, P (Blackrock Coll) 1997 *F* (R), *S*
Fletcher, W W (Kingstown) 1882 *W, S,* 1883 *E*
Flood, R S (Dublin U) 1925 *W*
Flynn, M K (Wanderers) 1959 *F,* 1960 *F,* 1962 *E, S, F, W,* 1964 *E, S, W, F,* 1965 *F, E, S, W, SA,* 1966 *F, E, S,* 1972 *F* 1, *E, F* 2, 1973 *NZ*
Fogarty, T (Garryowen) 1891 *W*
Foley, A G (Shannon) 1995 *E, S, F, W, It, [J(t + R)],* 1996 *A,* 1997 *It, E* (R)
Foley, B O (Shannon) 1976 *F, E,* 1977 *W* (R), 1980 *F, W,* 1981 *F, E, S, SA* 1,2, *A*
Forbes, R E (Malone) 1907 *E*
Forrest, A J (Wanderers) 1880 *E, S,* 1881 *E, S,* 1882 *W, E,* 1883 *E,* 1885 *S* 2
Forrest, E G (Wanderers) 1888 *M,* 1889 *S, W,* 1890 *S, E,* 1891 *E,* 1893 *S,* 1894 *E, S, W,* 1895 *W,* 1897 *E, S*
Forrest, H (Wanderers) 1893 *S, W*
Fortune, J J (Clontarf) 1963 *NZ,* 1964 *E*
Foster, A R (Derry) 1910 *E, S, F,* 1911 *E, S, W, F,* 1912 *F, E, S, W,* 1914 *E, S, W,* 1921 *E, S, W*
Francis, N P J (Blackrock Coll, London Irish, Old Belvedere) 1987 *[Tg, A],* 1988 *WS, It,* 1989 *S,* 1990 *E, F, W,* 1991 *E, S, Nm* 1,2, *[Z, J, S, A],* 1992 *W, E, S,* 1993 *F, R,* 1994 *F, W, E, S, A* 1,2, *US,* 1995 *E, [NZ, J, W, F], Fj,* 1996 *US, S*
Franks, J G (Dublin U) 1898 *E, S, W*
Frazer, E F (Bective Rangers) 1891 *S,* 1892 *S*
Freer, A E (Lansdowne) 1901 *E, S, W*
Fulcher, G M (Cork Constitution, London Irish) 1994 *A* 2, *US,* 1995 *E* (R), *S, F, W, It, [NZ, W, F], Fj,* 1996 *US, S, F, W, E, A,* 1997 *It, W* (R)
Fulton, J (NIFC) 1895 *S, W,* 1896 *E,* 1897 *E,* 1898 *W,* 1899 *E,* 1900 *W,* 1901 *E,* 1902 *E, S, W,* 1903 *E, S, W,* 1904 *E, S*
Furlong, J N (UC Galway) 1992 *NZ* 1,2

Gaffikin, W (Windsor) 1875 *E*
Gage, J H (Queen's U, Belfast) 1926 *S, W,* 1927 *S, W*
Galbraith, E (Dublin U) 1875 *E*
Galbraith, H T (Belfast Acad) 1890 *W*
Galbraith, R (Dublin U) 1875 *E,* 1876 *E,* 1877 *E*
Galwey, M J (Shannon) 1991 *F, W, Nm* 2 (R), *[J],* 1992 *E, S, F, NZ* 1,2, *A,* 1993 *F, W, E, R,* 1994 *F, W, E, S, A* 1, *US* (R), 1995 *E,* 1996 *WS*
Ganly, J B (Monkstown) 1927 *F, E, S, W, A,* 1928 *F, E, S, W,* 1929 *F, S,* 1930 *F*
Gardiner, F (NIFC) 1900 *E, S,* 1901 *E, W,* 1902 *E, S, W,* 1903 *E, W,* 1904 *E, S, W,* 1906 *E, S, W,* 1907 *S, W,* 1908 *S, W,* 1909 *E, S, F*
Gardiner, J B (NIFC) 1923 *E, S, W, F,* 1924 *F, E, S, W, NZ,* 1925 *F, E, S*
Gardiner, S (Belfast Albion) 1893 *E, S*
Gardiner, W (NIFC) 1892 *E, S,* 1893 *E, S, W,* 1894 *E, S, W,* 1895 *E, S, W,* 1896 *E, S, W,* 1897 *E, S,* 1898 *W*
Garry, M G (Bective Rangers) 1909 *E, S, W, F,* 1911 *E, S, W*
Gaston, J T (Dublin U) 1954 *NZ, F, E, S, W,* 1955 *W* 1956 *F, E*
Gavin, T J (Moseley, London Irish) 1949 *F, E*

Johns, P S (Dublin U, Dungannon, Saracens) 1990 *Arg*, 1992 *NZ* 1,2, *A*, 1993 *S, F, W, E, R*, 1994 *F, W, E, S, A* 1,2, *US*, 1995 *E, S, W, It*, [*NZ, J, W, F*], *Fj*, 1996 *US, S, F, WS*, 1997 *It* (R), *F, W, E, S*
Johnston, J (Belfast Acad) 1881 *S*, 1882 *S*, 1884 *S*, 1885 *S* 1,2, 1886 *E*, 1887 *E, S, W*
Johnston, M (Dublin U) 1880 *E, S*, 1881 *E, S*, 1882 *E*, 1884 *E, S*, 1886 *E*
Johnston, R (Wanderers) 1893 *E, W*
Johnston, R W (Dublin U) 1890 *S, W, E*
Johnston, T J (Queen's Coll, Belfast) 1892 *E, S, W*, 1893 *E, S*, 1895 *E*
Johnstone, W E (Dublin U) 1884 *W*
Johnstone-Smyth, T R (Lansdowne) 1882 *E*

Kavanagh, J R (UC Dublin, Wanderers) 1953 *F, E, S, W*, 1954 *NZ, S, W*, 1955 *F, E*, 1956 *E, S, W*, 1957 *F, E, S, W*, 1958 *A, E, S, W*, 1959 *E, S, W, F*, 1960 *E, S, W, F, SA*, 1961 *E, S, W, F, SA*, 1962 *F*
Kavanagh, P J (UC Dublin, Wanderers) 1952 *E*, 1955 *W*
Keane, M I (Lansdowne) 1974 *F, W, E, S, P, NZ*, 1975 *E, S, F, W*, 1976 *A, F, W, E, S, NZ*, 1977 *W, E, S, F*, 1978 *S, F, W, E, NZ*, 1979 *F, W, E, S, A* 1,2, 1980 *E, S, F, W*, 1981 *F, W, E, S*, 1982 *W, E, S, F*, 1983 *S, F, W, E*, 1984 *F, W, E, S*
Kearney, R K (Wanderers) 1982 *F*, 1984 *A*, 1986 *F, W*
Keeffe, E (Sunday's Well) 1947 *F, E, S, W, A*, 1948 *F*
Kelly, H C (NIFC) 1877 *E, S*, 1878 *E*, 1879 *S*, 1880 *E, S*
Kelly, J C (UC Dublin) 1962 *F, W*, 1963 *F, E, S, W, NZ*, 1964 *E, S, W, F*
Kelly, S (Lansdowne) 1954 *S, W*, 1955 *S*, 1960 *W, F*
Kelly, W (Wanderers) 1884 *S*
Kennedy, A G (Belfast Collegians) 1956 *F*
Kennedy, A P (London Irish) 1986 *W, E*
Kennedy, F (Wanderers) 1880 *E*, 1881 *E*, 1882 *W*
Kennedy, F A (Wanderers) 1904 *E, W*
Kennedy, H (Bradford) 1938 *S, W*
Kennedy, J M (Wanderers) 1882 *W*, 1884 *W*
Kennedy, K W (Queen's U, Belfast, London Irish) 1965 *F, E, S, W, SA*, 1966 *F, E, W*, 1967 *A* 1, *E, S, W, F, A* 2, 1968 *F, A*, 1969 *F, E, S, W*, 1970 *SA, F, E, S, W*, 1971 *F, E, S, W*, 1972 *F* 1, *E, F* 2, 1973 *NZ, E, S, W, F*, 1974 *F, W, E, S, P, NZ*, 1975 *F, W*
Kennedy, T J (St Mary's Coll) 1978 *NZ*, 1979 *F, W, E* (R), *A* 1,2, 1980 *S, F, W*, 1981 *SA* 1,2, *A*
Kenny, P (Wanderers) 1992 *NZ* 2 (R)
Keogh, F S (Bective Rangers) 1964 *W, F*
Keon, J J (Limerick) 1879 *E*
Keyes, R P (Cork Constitution) 1986 *E*, 1991 [*Z, J, S, A*], 1992 *W, E, S*
Kidd, F W (Dublin U, Lansdowne) 1877 *E, S*, 1878 *E*
Kiely, M D (Lansdowne) 1962 *W*, 1963 *F, E, S, W*
Kiernan, M J (Dolphin, Lansdowne) 1982 *W* (R), *E, S, F*, 1983 *S, F, W, E*, 1984 *E, S, A*, 1985 *S, F, W, E*, 1986 *F, W, E, S, R*, 1987 *E, S, F, W*, [*W, C, A*], 1988 *S, F, W, E* 1,2, *WS*, 1989 *F, W, E, S*, 1990 *E, S, F*, *Arg*, 1991 *F*
Kiernan, T J (UC Cork, Cork Const) 1960 *E, S, W, F, SA*, 1961 *E, S, W, F, SA*, 1962 *E, W*, 1963 *F, S, W, NZ*, 1964 *E, S*, 1965 *F, E, S, W, SA*, 1966 *F, E, S, W*, 1967 *A* 1, *E, S, W, F, A* 2, 1968 *F, E, S, W, A*, 1969 *F, E, S, W*, 1970 *SA, F, E, S, W*, 1971 *F, E, S, W*, 1972 *F* 1, *E, F* 2, 1973 *NZ, E, S*
Killeen, G V (Garryowen) 1912 *E, S, W*, 1913 *E, S, W, F*, 1914 *E, S, W*
King, H (Dublin U) 1883 *E, S*
Kingston, T J (Dolphin) 1987 [*W, Tg, A*], 1988 *S, F, W, E* 1, 1990 *F, W*, 1991 [*J*], 1993 *W, E, R*, 1994 *F, W, E, S*, 1995 *F, W, It*, [*NZ, J* (R), *W, F*], *Fj*, 1996 *US, S, F*
Knox, J H (Dublin U, Lansdowne) 1904 *W*, 1905 *E, S, W, NZ*, 1906 *E, S, W*, 1907 *W*, 1908 *S*
Kyle, J W (Queen's U, Belfast, NIFC) 1947 *F, E, S, W, A*, 1948 *F, E, S, W*, 1949 *F, E, S, W*, 1950 *F, E, S, W*, 1951 *F, E, S, W, SA*, 1952 *F, S, W, E*, 1953 *F, E, S, W*, 1954 *NZ, F*, 1955 *F, E, W*, 1956 *F, E, S, W*, 1957 *F, E, S, W*, 1958 *A, E, S*

Lambert, N H (Lansdowne) 1934 *S, W*
Lamont, R A (Instonians) 1965 *F, E, SA*, 1966 *F, E, S, W*, 1970 *SA, F, E, S, W*
Landers, M F (Cork Const) 1904 *W*, 1905 *E, S, W, NZ*
Lane, D (UC Cork) 1934 *S, W*, 1935 *E, S*
Lane, M F (UC Cork) 1947 *W*, 1949 *F, E, S, W*, 1950 *F, E, S, W*, 1951 *F, E, S, W, SA*, 1952 *F, S*, 1953 *F, E*
Lane, P (Old Crescent) 1964 *W*
Langan, D J (Clontarf) 1934 *W*
Langbroek, J A (Blackrock Coll) 1987 [*Tg*]
Lavery, P (London Irish) 1974 *W*, 1976 *W*

Lawlor, P J (Clontarf) 1951 *S, SA*, 1952 *F, S, W, E*, 1953 *F*, 1954 *NZ, E, S*, 1956 *F, E*
Lawlor, P J (Bective Rangers) 1935 *E, S, W*, 1937 *E, S, W*
Lawlor, P J (Bective Rangers) 1990 *Arg*, 1992 *A*, 1993 *S*
Leahy, K T (Wanderers) 1992 *NZ* 1
Leahy, M W (UC Cork) 1964 *W*
Lee, S (NIFC) 1891 *E, S, W*, 1892 *E, S, W*, 1893 *E, S, W*, 1894 *E, S, W*, 1895 *E, W*, 1896 *E, S, W*, 1897 *E*, 1898 *E*
Le Fanu, V C (Cambridge U, Lansdowne) 1886 *E, S*, 1887 *E, W*, 1888 *S*, 1889 *W*, 1890 *E*, 1891 *E*, 1892 *E, S, W*
Lenihan, D G (UC Cork, Cork Const) 1981 *A*, 1982 *W, E, S, F*, 1983 *S, F, W, E*, 1984 *F, W, E, S*, 1985 *S, F, W, E*, 1986 *F, W, E, S, R*, 1987 *E, S, F, W*, [*W, C, Tg, A*], 1988 *S, F, W, E* 1,2, *WS, It*, 1989 *F, W, E, S, NZ*, 1990 *S, F, W, Arg*, 1991 *Nm* 2, [*Z, S, A*], 1992 *W*
L'Estrange, L P F (Dublin U) 1962 *E*
Levis, F H (Wanderers) 1884 *E*
Lightfoot, E J (Lansdowne) 1931 *F, E, S, W, SA*, 1932 *E, S, W*, 1933 *E, W, S*
Lindsay, H (Dublin U, Armagh) 1893 *E, S, W*, 1894 *E, S, W*, 1895 *E*, 1896 *E, S, W*, 1898 *E, S, W*
Little, T J (Bective Rangers) 1898 *W*, 1899 *S, W*, 1900 *S, W*, 1901 *E, S*
Lloyd, R A (Dublin U, Liverpool) 1910 *E, S*, 1911 *E, S, W, F*, 1912 *F, E, S, W, SA*, 1913 *E, S, W, F*, 1914 *F, E*, 1920 *E, F*
Lydon, C T J (Galwegians) 1956 *S*
Lyle, R K (Dublin U) 1910 *W, F*
Lyle, T R (Dublin U) 1885 *E, S* 1,2, 1886 *E*, 1887 *E, S*
Lynch, J F (St Mary's Coll) 1971 *F, E, S, W*, 1972 *F* 1, *E, F* 2, 1973 *NZ, E, S, W*, 1974 *F, W, E, S, P, NZ*
Lynch, L (Lansdowne) 1956 *S*
Lytle, J H (NIFC) 1894 *E, S, W*, 1895 *W*, 1896 *E, S, W*, 1897 *E, S, W*, 1898 *E, S*, 1899 *S*
Lytle, J N (NIFC) 1888 *M*, 1889 *W*, 1890 *E*, 1891 *E, S*, 1894 *E, S, W*
Lyttle, V J (Collegians, Bedford) 1938 *E*, 1939 *E, S*

McAleese, D R (Ballymena) 1992 *F*
McAllan, G H (Dungannon) 1896 *S, W*
Macauley, J (Limerick) 1887 *E, S*
McBride, W D (Malone) 1988 *W, E* 1, *WS, It*, 1989 *S*, 1990 *F, W, Arg*, 1993 *S, F, W, E, R*, 1994 *W, E, S, A* 1 (R), 1995 *S, F*, [*NZ, W, F*], *Fj* (R), 1996 *W, E, WS, A*, 1997 *It* (R), *F, W, E, S*
McBride, W J (Ballymena) 1962 *E, S, F, W*, 1963 *F, E, S, W, NZ*, 1964 *E, S, F*, 1965 *F, E, S, W, SA*, 1966 *F, E, S, W*, 1967 *A* 1, *E, S, W, F, A* 2, 1968 *F, E, S, W, A*, 1969 *F, E, S, W*, 1970 *SA, F, E, S, W*, 1971 *F, E, S, W*, 1972 *F* 1, *E, F* 2, 1973 *NZ, E, S, W, F*, 1974 *F, W, E, S, P, NZ*, 1975 *E, S, F, W*
McCahill, S A (Sunday's Well) 1995 *Fj* (t)
McCall, B W (London Irish) 1985 *F* (R), 1986 *E, S*
McCall, M C (Bangor, Dungannon) 1992 *NZ* 1 (R), 2, 1994 *W*, 1996 *E* (R), *A*, 1997 *It*
McCallan, B (Ballymena) 1960 *E, S*
McCarten, R J (London Irish) 1961 *E, W, F*
McCarthy, E A (Kingstown) 1882 *W*
McCarthy, J S (Dolphin) 1948 *F, E, S, W*, 1949 *F, E, S*, *W*, 1950 *W*, 1951 *F, E, S, W, SA*, 1952 *F, S, W, E*, 1953 *F, E, S*, 1954 *NZ, F, E, S, W*, 1955 *F, E*
McCarthy, P D (Cork Const) 1992 *NZ* 1,2, *A*, 1993 *S, R* (R)
MacCarthy, St G (Dublin U) 1882 *W*
McCarthy, T (Cork) 1898 *W*
McClelland, T A (Queen's U, Belfast) 1921 *E, S, W, F*, 1922 *E, W, F*, 1923 *E, S, W, F*, 1924 *F, E, S, W, NZ*
McClenahan, R O (Instonians) 1923 *E, S, W*
McClinton, A N (NIFC) 1910 *W, F*
McCombe, W McM (Dublin U, Bangor) 1968 *F*, 1975 *E, S, F, W*
McConnell, A A (Collegians) 1947 *A*, 1948 *F, E, S, W*, 1949 *F, E*
McConnell, G (Derry, Edinburgh U) 1912 *F, E*, 1913 *W, F*
McConnell, J W (Lansdowne) 1913 *S*
McCormac, F M (Wanderers) 1909 *W*, 1910 *W, F*
McCormick, W J (Wanderers) 1930 *E*
McCoull, H C (Belfast Albion) 1895 *E, S, W*, 1899 *E*
McCourt, D (Queen's U, Belfast) 1947 *A*
McCoy, J J (Dungannon, Bangor, Ballymena) 1984 *W, A*, 1985 *S, F, W, E*, 1986 *F*, 1987 [*Tg*], 1988 *E* 2, *WS, It*, 1989 *F, W, E, S, NZ*
McCracken, H (NIFC) 1954 *W*
McDermott, S J (London Irish) 1955 *S, W*

Macdonald, J A (Methodist Coll, Belfast) 1875 *E*, 1876 *E*, 1877 *S*, 1878 *E*, 1879 *S*, 1880 *E*, 1881 *S*, 1882 *E, S,* 1883 *E, S,* 1884 *E, S*
McDonald, J P (Malone) 1987 [*C*], 1990 *E* (R), *S, Arg*
McDonnell, A C (Dublin U) 1889 *W,* 1890 *S, W,* 1891 *E*
McDowell, J C (Instonians) 1924 *F, NZ*
McFarland, B A T (Derry) 1920 *S, W, F,* 1922 *W*
McGann, B J (Lansdowne) 1969 *F, E, S, W,* 1970 *SA, F, E, S, W,* 1971 *F, E, S, W,* 1972 *F* 1, *E, F* 2, 1973 *NZ, E, S, W,* 1976 *F, W, E, S, NZ*
McGowan, A N (Blackrock Coll) 1994 *US*
McGown, T M W (NIFC) 1899 *E, S,* 1901 *S*
McGrath, D G (UC Dublin, Cork Const) 1984 *S,* 1987 [*W, C, Tg, A*]
McGrath, N F (Oxford U, London Irish) 1934 *W*
McGrath, P J (UC Cork) 1965 *E, S, W, SA,* 1966 *F, E, S, W,* 1967 *A* 1, *A* 2
McGrath, R J M (Wanderers) 1977 *W, E, F* (R), 1981 *SA* 1,2, 1982 *W, E, S, F,* 1983 *S, F, W, E,* 1984 *F, W*
McGrath, T (Garryowen) 1956 *W,* 1958 *F,* 1960 *E, S, W, F,* 1961 *SA*
McGuire, E P (UC Galway) 1963 *E, S, W, NZ,* 1964 *E, S, W, F*
MacHale, S (Lansdowne) 1965 *F, E, S, W, SA,* 1966 *F, E, S, W,* 1967 *S, W, F*
McIldowie, G (Malone) 1906 *SA,* 1910 *E, S, W*
McIlrath, J A (Ballymena) 1976 *A, F, NZ,* 1977 *W, E*
McIlwaine, E H (NIFC) 1895 *S, W*
McIlwaine, E N (NIFC) 1875 *E,* 1876 *E*
McIlwaine, J E (NIFC) 1897 *E, S,* 1898 *E, S, W,* 1899 *E, W*
McIntosh, L M (Dublin U) 1884 *S*
MacIvor, C V (Dublin U) 1912 *F, E, S, W,* 1913 *E, S, F*
McIvor, S C (Garryowen) 1996 *A,* 1997 *It, S* (R)
McKay, J W (Queen's U, Belfast) 1947 *F, E, S, W, A,* 1948 *F, E, S, W,* 1949 *F, E, S, W,* 1950 *F, E, S, W,* 1951 *F, E, S, W,* 1952 *F*
McKee, W D (NIFC) 1947 *A,* 1948 *F, E, S, W,* 1949 *F, E, S, W,* 1950 *F, E,* 1951 *SA*
McKelvey, J M (Queen's U, Belfast) 1956 *F, E*
McKibbin, A R (Instonians, London Irish) 1977 *W, E, S,* 1978 *S, F, W, E, NZ,* 1979 *F, W, E, S,* 1980 *E, S*
McKibbin, C H (Instonians) 1976 *S* (R)
McKibbin, D (Instonians) 1950 *F, E, S, W,* 1951 *F, E, S, W*
McKibbin, H R (Queen's U, Belfast) 1938 *W,* 1939 *E, S, W*
McKinney, S A (Dungannon) 1972 *F* 1, *E, F* 2, 1973 *W, F,* 1974 *F, E, S, P, NZ,* 1975 *E, S,* 1976 *A, F, W, E, S, NZ,* 1977 *W, E,* 1978 *S* (R), *F, W, E*
McLaughlin, J H (Derry) 1887 *E, S,* 1888 *W, S*
McLean, R E (Dublin U) 1881 *S,* 1882 *W, E, S,* 1883 *E, S,* 1884 *E, S,* 1885 *E, S* 1
Maclear, B (Cork County, Monkstown) 1905 *E, S, W, NZ,* 1906 *E, S, W, SA,* 1907 *E, S, W*
McLennan, A C (Wanderers) 1977 *F,* 1978 *S, F, W, E, NZ,* 1979 *F, W, E, S,* 1980 *E, F,* 1981 *F, W, E, S, SA* 1,2
McLoughlin, F M (Northern) 1976 *A*
McLoughlin, G A J (Shannon) 1979 *F, W, E, S, A* 1,2, 1980 *E,* 1981 *SA* 1,2, 1982 *W, E, S, F,* 1983 *S, F, W, E,* 1984 *F*
McLoughlin, R J (UC Dublin, Blackrock Coll, Gosforth) 1962 *E, S, F,* 1963 *E, S, W, NZ,* 1964 *E, S,* 1965 *F, E, S, W, SA,* 1966 *F, E, S, W,* 1971 *F, E, S, W,* 1972 *F* 1, *E, F* 2, 1973 *NZ, E, S, W, F,* 1974 *F, W, E, S, P, NZ,* 1975 *E, S, F, W*
McMahon, L B (Blackrock Coll, UC Dublin) 1931 *E, SA,* 1933 *E,* 1934 *E,* 1936 *E, S, W,* 1937 *E, S, W,* 1938 *E, S*
McMaster, A W (Ballymena) 1972 *F* 1, *E, F* 2, 1973 *NZ, E, S, W, F,* 1974 *F, E, S, P,* 1975 *F, W,* 1976 *A, F, W, NZ*
McMordie, J (Queen's Coll, Belfast) 1886 *S*
McMorrow, A (Garryowen) 1951 *W*
McMullen, A R (Cork) 1881 *E, S*
McNamara, V (UC Cork) 1914 *E, S, W*
McNaughton, P P (Greystones) 1978 *S, F, W, E,* 1979 *F, W, E, S, A* 1,2, 1980 *E, S, F, W,* 1981 *F*
MacNeill, H P (Dublin U, Oxford U, Blackrock Coll, London Irish) 1981 *F, W, E, S, A,* 1982 *W, E, S, F,* 1983 *S, F, W, E,* 1984 *F, A,* 1985 *S, F, W, E,* 1986 *F, W, E, S, R,* 1987 *E, S, W,* [*W, C, Tg, A*], 1988 *S* (R), *E* 1,2
McQuilkin, K P (Bective Rangers, Lansdowne) 1996 *US, S, F,* 1997 *W* (t & R), *S*
MacSweeney, D A (Blackrock Coll) 1955 *S*
McVicker, H (Army, Richmond) 1927 *E, S, W, A,* 1928 *F*
McVicker, J (Collegians) 1924 *F, E, S, W, NZ,* 1925 *F, E, S, W,* 1926 *F, E, S, W,* 1927 *F, E, S, W, A,* 1928 *F, W,* 1930 *F*
McVicker, S (Queen's U, Belfast) 1922 *E, S, W, F*

Madden, M N (Sunday's Well) 1955 *E, S, W*
Magee, J T (Bective Rangers) 1895 *E, S*
Magee, A M (Louis) (Bective Rangers, London Irish) 1895 *E, S, W,* 1896 *E, S, W,* 1897 *E, S,* 1898 *E, S, W,* 1899 *E, S, W,* 1900 *E, S, W,* 1901 *E, S, W,* 1902 *E, S, W,* 1903 *E, S, W,* 1904 *W*
Maginiss, R M (Dublin U) 1875 *E,* 1876 *E*
Magrath, R M (Cork Constitution) 1909 *S*
Maguire, J F (Cork) 1884 *S*
Mahoney, J (Dolphin) 1923 *E*
Malcolmson, G L (RAF, NIFC) 1935 *NZ,* 1936 *E, S, W,* 1937 *E, S, W*
Malone, N G (Oxford U, Leicester) 1993 *S, F,* 1994 *US* (R)
Mannion, N P (Corinthians, Lansdowne, Wanderers) 1988 *WS, It,* 1989 *F, W, E, S, NZ,* 1990 *E, S, F, W, Arg,* 1991 *Nm* 1 (R), 2, [*J*], 1993 *S*
Marshall, B D E (Queen's U, Belfast) 1963 *E*
Mason, S J P (Orrell, Richmond) 1996 *E, WS*
Massey-Westropp, R H (Limerick, Monkstown) 1886 *E*
Matier, R N (NIFC) 1878 *E,* 1879 *S*
Matthews, P M (Ards, Wanderers) 1984 *A,* 1985 *S, F, W, E,* 1986 *R,* 1987 *E, S, F, W,* [*W, Tg, A*], 1988 *S, F, W, E* 1,2, *WS, It,* 1989 *F, W, E, S, NZ,* 1990 *E, S,* 1991 *F, W, E, S, Nm* 1 [*Z, S, A*], 1992 *W, E, S*
Mattsson, J (Wanderers) 1948 *E*
Mayne, R B (Queen's U, Belfast) 1937 *W,* 1938 *E, W,* 1939 *E, S, W*
Mayne, R H (Belfast Academy) 1888 *W, S*
Mayne, T (NIFC) 1921 *E, S, F*
Mays, K M A (UC Dublin) 1973 *NZ, E, S, W*
Meares, A W D (Dublin U) 1899 *S, W,* 1900 *E, W*
Megaw, J (Richmond, Instonians) 1934 *W,* 1938 *E*
Millar, A (Kingstown) 1880 *E, S,* 1883 *E*
Millar, H J (Monkstown) 1904 *W,* 1905 *E, S, W*
Millar, S (Ballymena) 1958 *F,* 1959 *E, S, W, F,* 1960 *E, S, W, F, SA,* 1961 *E, S, W, SA,* 1962 *E, S, F,* 1963 *F, E, S, W,* 1964 *F,* 1968 *F, E, S, W, A,* 1969 *F, E, S, W,* 1970 *SA, F, E, S, W*
Millar, W H J (Queen's U, Belfast) 1951 *E, S, W,* 1952 *S, W*
Miller, E R P (Leicester) 1997 *It, F, W, E*
Miller, F H (Wanderers) 1886 *S*
Milliken, R A (Bangor) 1973 *E, S, W, F,* 1974 *F, W, E, S, P, NZ,* 1975 *E, S, F, W*
Millin, T J (Dublin U) 1925 *W*
Minch, J B (Bective Rangers) 1912 *SA,* 1913 *E, S,* 1914 *E, S*
Moffat, J (Belfast Academy) 1888 *W, S, M,* 1889 *S,* 1890 *S, W,* 1891 *S*
Moffatt, J E (Old Wesley) 1904 *S,* 1905 *E, S, W*
Moffett, J W (Ballymena) 1961 *E, S*
Molloy, M G (UC Galway, London Irish) 1966 *F, E,* 1967 *A* 1, *E, S, W, F, A* 2, 1968 *F, E, S, W, A,* 1969 *F, E, S, W,* 1970 *F, S, W,* 1971 *F, E, S, W,* 1973 *F,* 1976 *A*
Moloney, J J (St Mary's Coll) 1972 *F* 1, *E, F* 2, 1973 *NZ, E, S, W, F,* 1974 *F, W, E, S, P, NZ,* 1975 *E, S, F, W,* 1976 *S,* 1978 *S, F, W, E,* 1979 *A* 1,2, 1980 *S, W*
Moloney, L A (Garryowen) 1976 *W* (R), *S,* 1978 *S* (R), *NZ*
Molony, J U (UC Dublin) 1950 *S*
Monteith, J D E (Queen's U, Belfast) 1947 *E, S, W*
Montgomery, A (NIFC) 1895 *S*
Montgomery, F P (Queen's U, Belfast) 1914 *E, S, W*
Montgomery, R (Cambridge U) 1887 *E, S, W,* 1891 *E,* 1892 *W*
Moore, C M (Dublin U) 1887 *S,* 1888 *W, S*
Moore, D F (Wanderers) 1883 *E, S,* 1884 *E, W*
Moore, F W (Wanderers) 1884 *W,* 1885 *E, S* 2, 1886 *S*
Moore, H (Windsor) 1876 *E,* 1877 *S*
Moore, H (Queen's, Belfast) 1910 *S,* 1911 *W, F,* 1912 *F, E, S, W, SA*
Moore, T A P (Highfield) 1967 *A* 2, 1973 *NZ, E, S, W, F,* 1974 *F, W, E, S, P, NZ*
Moore, W D (Queen's Coll, Belfast) 1878 *E*
Moran, F G (Clontarf) 1936 *E,* 1937 *E, S, W,* 1938 *S, W,* 1939 *E, S, W*
Morell, H B (Dublin U) 1881 *E, S,* 1882 *W, E*
Morgan, G J (Clontarf) 1934 *E, S, W,* 1935 *E, S, W, NZ,* 1936 *E, S, W,* 1937 *E, S, W,* 1938 *E, S, W,* 1939 *E, S, W*
Moriarty, C C H (Monkstown) 1899 *W*
Moroney, J C M (Garryowen) 1968 *W, A,* 1969 *F, E, S, W*
Moroney, R J M (Lansdowne) 1984 *F, W,* 1985 *F*
Moroney, T A (UC Dublin) 1964 *W,* 1967 *A* 1, *E*

Stevenson, T H (Belfast Acad) 1895 *E, W*, 1896 *E, S, W*, 1897 *E, S*
Stewart, A L (NIFC) 1913 *W, F*, 1914 *F*
Stewart, W J (Queen's U, Belfast, NIFC) 1922 *F*, 1924 *S*, 1928 *F, E, S, W*, 1929 *F, E, S, W*
Stoker, F W (Wanderers) 1888 *W, S*
Stoker, F O (Wanderers) 1886 *S*, 1888 *W, M*, 1889 *S*, 1891 *W*
Stokes, O S (Cork Bankers) 1882 *E*, 1884 *E*
Stokes, P (Garryowen) 1913 *E, S*, 1914 *F*, 1920 *E, S, W, F*, 1921 *E, S, F*, 1922 *W, F*
Stokes, R D (Queen's Coll, Cork) 1891 *S, W*
Strathdee, E (Queen's U, Belfast) 1947 *E, S, W, A*, 1948 *W, F*, 1949 *E, S, W*
Stuart, C P (Clontarf) 1912 *SA*
Stuart, I M B (Dublin U) 1924 *E, S*
Sugars, H S (Dublin U) 1905 *NZ*, 1906 *SA*, 1907 *S*
Sugden, M (Wanderers) 1925 *F, E, S, W*, 1926 *F, E, S, W*, 1927 *E, S, W, A*, 1928 *F, E, S, W*, 1929 *F, E, S, W*, 1930 *F, E, S, W*, 1931 *F, E, S, W*
Sullivan, D B (UC Dublin) 1922 *E, S, W, F*
Sweeney, J A (Blackrock Coll) 1907 *E, S, W*
Symes, G R (Monkstown) 1895 *E*
Synge, J S (Lansdowne) 1929 *S*

Taggart, T (Dublin U) 1887 *W*
Taylor, A S (Queen's Coll, Belfast) 1910 *E, S, W*, 1912 *F*
Taylor, D R (Queen's Coll, Belfast) 1903 *E*
Taylor, J (Belfast Collegians) 1914 *E, S, W*
Taylor, J W (NIFC) 1879 *S*, 1880 *E, S*, 1881 *S*, 1882 *E, S*, 1883 *E, S*
Tector, W R (Wanderers) 1955 *F, E, S*
Tedford, A (Malone) 1902 *E, S, W*, 1903 *E, S, W*, 1904 *E, S, W*, 1905 *E, S, W, NZ*, 1906 *E, S, W, SA*, 1907 *E, S, W*, 1908 *E, S, W*
Teehan, C (UC Cork) 1939 *E, S, W*
Thompson, C (Belfast Collegians) 1907 *E, S*, 1908 *E, S, W*, 1909 *E, S, W, F*, 1910 *E, S, W, F*
Thompson, J A (Queen's Coll, Belfast) 1885 *S* 1,2
Thompson, J K S (Dublin U) 1921 *W*, 1922 *E, S, F*, 1923 *E, S, W, F*
Thompson, R G (Lansdowne) 1882 *W*
Thompson, R H (Instonians) 1951 *SA*, 1952 *F*, 1954 *NZ, F, E, S, W*, 1955 *F, S, W*, 1956 *W*
Thornhill, T (Wanderers) 1892 *E, S, W*, 1893 *E*
Thrift, H (Dublin U) 1904 *W*, 1905 *E, S, W, NZ*, 1906 *E, W, SA*, 1907 *E, S, W*, 1908 *E, S, W*, 1909 *E, S, W, F*
Tierney, D (UC Cork) 1938 *S, W*, 1939 *E*
Tillie, C R (Dublin U) 1887 *E, S*, 1888 *W, S*
Todd, A W P (Dublin U) 1913 *W, F*, 1914 *F*
Topping, J A (Ballymena) 1996 *WS, A*, 1997 *It, F, E*
Torrens, J D (Bohemians) 1938 *W*, 1939 *E, S, W*
Tucker, C C (Shannon) 1979 *F, W*, 1980 *F* (R)
Tuke, B B (Bective Rangers) 1890 *E*, 1891 *E, S*, 1892 *E*, 1894 *E, S, W*, 1895 *E, S*
Turley, N (Blackrock Coll) 1962 *E*
Tweed, D A (Ballymena) 1995 *F, W, It, [J]*
Tydings, J J (Young Munster) 1968 *A*
Tyrrell, W (Queen's U, Belfast) 1910 *F*, 1913 *E, S, W, F*, 1914 *F, E, S, W*

Uprichard, R J H (Harlequins, RAF) 1950 *S, W*

Waide, S L (Oxford U, NIFC) 1932 *E, S, W*, 1933 *E, W*
Waites, J (Bective Rangers) 1886 *S*, 1888 *M*, 1889 *W*, 1890 *S, W, E*, 1891 *E*
Waldron, O C (Oxford U, London Irish) 1966 *S, W*, 1968 *A*
Walker, S (Instonians) 1934 *E, S*, 1935 *E, S, W, NZ*, 1936 *E, S, W*, 1937 *E, S, W*, 1938 *E, S, W*
Walkington, D B (NIFC) 1887 *E, W*, 1888 *W*, 1890 *W, E*, 1891 *E, S, W*

Walkington, R B (NIFC) 1875 *E*, 1876 *E*, 1877 *E, S*, 1878 *E*, 1879 *S*, 1880 *E, S*, 1882 *E, S*
Wall, H (Dolphin) 1965 *S, W*
Wallace, Jas (Wanderers) 1904 *E, S*
Wallace, Jos (Wanderers) 1903 *S, W*, 1904 *E, S, W*, 1905 *E, S, W, NZ*, 1906 *W*
Wallace, P S (Blackrock Coll, Saracens) 1995 *[J], Fj*, 1996 *US, W, E, WS, A*, 1997 *It, F, W, E, S*
Wallace, R M (Garryowen, Saracens) 1991 *Nm* 1 (R), 1992 *W, E, S, F, A*, 1993 *S, F, W, E, R*, 1994 *F, W, E, S*, 1995 *W, It, [NZ, J, W], Fj*, 1996 *US, S, F, WS*
Wallace, T H (Cardiff) 1920 *E, S, W*
Wallis, A K (Wanderers) 1892 *E, S, W*, 1893 *E, W*
Wallis, C O'N (Old Cranleighans, Wanderers) 1935 *NZ*
Wallis, T G (Wanderers) 1921 *F*, 1922 *E, S, W, F*
Wallis, W A (Wanderers) 1880 *S*, 1881 *E, S*, 1882 *W*, 1883 *S*
Walmsley, G (Bective Rangers) 1894 *E*
Walpole, A (Dublin U) 1888 *S, M*
Walsh, E J (Lansdowne) 1887 *E, S, W*, 1892 *E, S, W*, 1893 *E*
Walsh, H D (Dublin U) 1875 *E*, 1876 *E*
Walsh, J C (UC Cork, Sunday's Well) 1960 *S, SA*, 1961 *E, S, F, SA*, 1963 *E, S, W, NZ*, 1964 *E, S, W, F*, 1965 *F, S, W, SA*, 1966 *F, S, W*, 1967 *E, S, W, F, A* 2
Ward, A J P (Garryowen, St Mary's Coll, Greystones) 1978 *S, F, W, E, NZ*, 1979 *F, W, E, S*, 1981 *W, E, S, A*, 1983 *E* (R), 1984 *E, S*, 1986 *S*, 1987 *[C, Tg]*
Warren, J P (Kingstown) 1883 *E*
Warren, R G (Lansdowne) 1884 *W*, 1885 *E, S* 1,2, 1886 *E*, 1887 *E, S, W*, 1888 *W, S, M*, 1889 *S, W*, 1890 *S, W, E*
Watson, R (Wanderers) 1912 *SA*
Wells, H G (Bective Rangers) 1891 *S, W*, 1894 *E, S*
Westby, A J (Dublin U) 1876 *E*
Wheeler, G H (Queen's Coll, Belfast) 1884 *S*, 1885 *E*
Wheeler, J R (Queen's U, Belfast) 1922 *E, S, W, F*, 1924 *E*
Whelan, P C (Garryowen) 1975 *S*, 1976 *NZ*, 1977 *W, E, S, F*, 1978 *S, F, W, E, NZ*, 1979 *F, W, E, S*, 1981 *F, W, E*
White, M (Queen's Coll, Cork) 1906 *E, S, W, SA*, 1907 *E, W*
Whitestone, A M (Dublin U) 1877 *E*, 1879 *S, E*, 1880 *E*, 1883 *S*
Whittle, D (Bangor) 1988 *F*
Wilkinson, C R (Malone) 1993 *S*
Wilkinson, R W (Wanderers) 1947 *A*
Williamson, F W (Dolphin) 1930 *E, S, W*
Willis, W J (Lansdowne) 1879 *E*
Wilson, F (CIYMS) 1977 *W, E, S*
Wilson, H G (Glasgow U, Malone) 1905 *E, S, W, NZ*, 1906 *E, S, W, SA*, 1907 *E, S, W*, 1908 *E, S, W*, 1909 *E, S, W*, 1910 *W*
Wilson, W H (Bray) 1877 *E, S*
Withers, H H C (Army, Blackheath) 1931 *F, E, S, W, SA*
Wolfe, E J (Armagh) 1882 *E*
Wood, G H (Dublin U) 1913 *W*, 1914 *F*
Wood, B G M (Garryowen) 1954 *E, S*, 1956 *F, E, S, W*, 1957 *F, E, S, W*, 1958 *A, E, S, W, F*, 1959 *E, S, W, F*, 1960 *E, S, W, F, SA*, 1961 *E, S, W, F, SA*
Wood, K G M (Garryowen, Harlequins) 1994 *A* 1,2, *US*, 1995 *E, S, [J]*, 1996 *A*, 1997 *It, F*
Woods, D C (Bessbrook) 1888 *M*, 1889 *S*
Woods, N K P J (Blackrock Coll) 1994 *A* 1,2, 1995 *E, F*, 1996 *F, W, E*
Wright, R A (Monkstown) 1912 *S*

Yeates, R A (Dublin U) 1889 *S, W*
Young, G (UC Cork) 1913 *E*
Young, R M (Collegians) 1965 *F, E, S, W, SA*, 1966 *F, E, S, W*, 1967 *W, F*, 1968 *W, A*, 1969 *F, E, S, W*, 1970 *SA, F, E, S, W*, 1971 *F, E, S, W*

IRISH INTERNATIONAL RECORDS
(up to 30 April 1997)

MATCH RECORDS

MOST CONSECUTIVE TEST WINS

6 1968 *S, W, A*, 1969 *F, E, S*

MOST CONSECUTIVE TESTS WITHOUT DEFEAT

P	W	D	Period
7	6	1	1968–69
5	4	1	1972–73

MOST POINTS IN A MATCH
by the team

Pts	Opp	Venue	Year
60	R	Dublin	1986
55	Z	Dublin	1991
50	J	Bloemfontein	1995
49	WS	Dublin	1988
46	C	Dunedin	1987

by a player

24 by P A Burke v Italy at Dublin 1997
23 by R P Keyes v Zimbabwe at Dublin 1991
21 by S O Campbell v Scotland at Dublin 1982
21 by S O Campbell v England at Dublin 1983
20 by M J Kiernan v Romania at Dublin 1986
20 by E P Elwood v Romania at Dublin 1993
20 by S J P Mason v Western Samoa at Dublin 1996

MOST TRIES IN A MATCH
by the team

T	Opp	Venue	Year
10	R	Dublin	1986
8	WS	Dublin	1988
8	Z	Dublin	1991
7	J	Bloemfontein	1995

by a player

4 by B F Robinson v Zimbabwe at Dublin 1991
3 by R Montgomery v Wales at Birkenhead 1887
3 by J P Quinn v France at Cork 1913
3 by E O'D Davy v Scotland at Murrayfield 1930
3 by S J Byrne v Scotland at Murrayfield 1953
3 by K D Crossan v Romania at Dublin 1986
3 by B J Mullin v Tonga at Brisbane 1987

MOST CONVERSIONS IN A MATCH
by the team

C	Opp	Venue	Year
7	R	Dublin	1986
6	J	Bloemfontein	1995
5	C	Dunedin	1987

by a player

7 by M J Kiernan v Romania at Dublin 1986
6 by P A Burke v Japan at Bloemfontein 1995
5 by M J Kiernan v Canada at Dunedin 1987

MOST PENALTY GOALS IN A MATCH
by the team

P	Opp	Venue	Year
8	It	Dublin	1997
6	S	Dublin	1982
6	R	Dublin	1993
6	US	Atlanta	1996
6	WS	Dublin	1996

by a player

8 by P A Burke v Italy at Dublin 1997
6 by S O Campbell v Scotland at Dublin 1982
6 by EP Elwood v Romania at Dublin 1993
6 by S J P Mason v Western Samoa at Dublin 1996

MOST DROPPED GOALS IN A MATCH
by the team

D	Opp	Venue	Year
2	A	Dublin	1967
2	F	Dublin	1975
2	A	Sydney	1979
2	E	Dublin	1981
2	C	Dunedin	1987
2	E	Dublin	1993

by a player

2 by C M H Gibson v Australia at Dublin		1967
2 by W M McCombe v France at Dublin		1975
2 by S O Campbell v Australia at Sydney		1979
2 by E P Elwood v England at Dublin		1993

CAREER RECORDS

MOST CAPPED PLAYERS

Caps	Player	Career
69	C M H Gibson	1964–79
63	W J McBride	1962–75
61	J F Slattery	1970–84
58	P A Orr	1976–87
55	B J Mullin	1984–95
54	T J Kiernan	1960–73
52	D G Lenihan	1981–92
51	M I Keane	1974–84
46	J W Kyle	1947–58
45	K W Kennedy	1965–75

MOST CONSECUTIVE TESTS

Tests	Player	Span
52	W J McBride	1964–75
49	P A Orr	1976–86
43	D G Lenihan	1981–89
39	M I Keane	1974–81
37	G V Stephenson	1920–29

MOST TESTS AS CAPTAIN

Tests	Captain	Span
24	T J Kiernan	1963–73
19	C F Fitzgerald	1982–86
17	J F Slattery	1979–81
17	D G Lenihan	1986–90

MOST TESTS IN INDIVIDUAL POSITIONS

Full-back	T J Kiernan	54	1960–73
Wing	K D Crossan	41	1982–92
Centre	B J Mullin	55	1984–95
Fly-half	J W Kyle	46	1947–58
Scrum-half	M T Bradley	40	1984–95
Prop	P A Orr	58	1976–87
Hooker	K W Kennedy	45	1965–75
Lock	W J McBride	63	1962–75
Flanker	J F Slattery	61	1970–84
No 8	W P Duggan	39	1975–84

MOST POINTS IN TESTS

Pts	Player	Tests	Career
308	M J Kiernan	43	1982–91
217	S O Campbell	22	1976–84
167	E P Elwood	19	1993–97
158	T J Kiernan	54	1960–73
113	A J P Ward	19	1978–87

MOST TRIES IN TESTS

Tries	Player	Tests	Career
17	B J Mullin	55	1984–95
14	G V Stephenson	42	1920–30
12	K D Crossan	41	1982–92
11	A T A Duggan	25	1963–72
11	S P Geoghegan	37	1991–96

MOST CONVERSIONS IN TESTS

Cons	Player	Tests	Career
40	M J Kiernan	43	1982–91
26	T J Kiernan	54	1960–73
16	R A Lloyd	19	1910–20
15	S O Campbell	22	1976–84
13	G V Stephenson	42	1920–1930
13	E P Elwood	19	1993–97

MOST PENALTY GOALS IN TESTS

Pens	Player	Tests	Career
62	M J Kiernan	43	1982–91
54	S O Campbell	22	1976–84
45	E P Elwood	19	1993–97
31	T J Kiernan	54	1960–73
29	A J P Ward	19	1978–87

MOST DROPPED GOALS IN TESTS

Drops	Player	Tests	Career
7	R A Lloyd	19	1910–20
7	S O Campbell	22	1976–84
6	C M H Gibson	69	1964–79
6	B J McGann	25	1969–76
6	M J Kiernan	43	1982–91

INTERNATIONAL CHAMPIONSHIP RECORDS

Record	Detail		Set
Most points in seaon	71	in four matches	1983
Most tries in season	12	in four matches	1928 & 1953
Highest score	30	30–17 v Wales	1996
Biggest win	24	24–0 v France	1913
Highest score conceded	46	6–46 v England	1997
Biggest defeat	40	6–46 v England	1997
Most appearances	56	C M H Gibson	1964–79
Most points in matches	207	M J Kiernan	1982–91
Most points in season	52	S O Campbell	1983
Most points in match	21	S O Campbell	v Scotland, 1982
	21	S O Campbell	v England, 1983
Most tries in matches	14	G V Stephenson	1920–30
Most tries in season	5	J E Arigho	1928
Most tries in match	3	R Montgomery	v Wales, 1887
	3	J P Quinn	v France, 1913
	3	E O'D Davy	v Scotland, 1930
	3	S J Byrne	v Scotland, 1953
Most cons in matches	21	M J Kiernan	1982–91
Most cons in season	7	R A Lloyd	1913
Most cons in match	4	P F Murray	v Scotland, 1932
	4	R J Gregg	v Scotland, 1953
Most pens in matches	48	S O Campbell	1980–84
Most pens in season	14	S O Campbell	1983
	14	E P Elwood	1994
Most pens in match	6	S O Campbell	v Scotland, 1982
Most drops in matches	7	R A Lloyd	1910–20
Most drops in season	2	on several occasions	
Most drops in match	2	W M McCombe	v France, 1975
	2	E P Elwood	v England, 1993

MAJOR TOUR RECORDS

Record	Detail	Year	Place
Most individual points	60 by S O Campbell	1979	Australia
Most points in match	19 by A J P Ward	1979 v A C T	Canberra
	19 by S O Campbell	1979 v Australia	Brisbane
	19 by E P Elwood	1994 v W Australia	Perth
Most tries in match	3 by A T A Duggan	1967 v Victoria	Melbourne
	3 by J F Slattery	1981 v SA President's XV	East London (SA)
	3 by M J Kiernan	1981 v Gold Cup XV	Oudtshoorn (SA)
	3 by M J Field	1994 v W Australia	Perth

MISCELLANEOUS RECORDS

Record	Holder	Detail
Longest Test career	A J F O'Reilly	16 seasons, 1954–55 to 1969–70
	C M H Gibson	16 seasons, 1963–64 to 1979
Youngest Test cap	F S Hewitt	17 yrs 157 days in 1924
Oldest Test cap	C M H Gibson	36 yrs 195 days in 1979

IRELAND INTERNATIONAL CAREER RECORDS *(up to 30 April 1997)*

Player	Debut	Caps since last season	Caps	T	C	PG	DG	Pts
C M P O'Shea	1993 v R	1997 *It, F, S* (R)	16	0	1	3	1	14
S J P Mason	1996 v W	1996 *WS*	3	0	3	12	0	42
J E Staples	1991 v W	1996 *A*, 1997 *W, E, S*	26	5	2	0	0	25
D J Crotty	1996 v A	1996 *A*, 1997 *It, F, W*	4	0	0	0	0	0
R M Wallace	1991 v Nm	1996 *WS*	25	5	0	0	0	23
J A Topping	1996 v WS	1996 *WS, A*, 1997 *It, F, E*	5	0	0	0	0	0
S P Geoghegan	1991 v F		37	11	0	0	0	51
D A Hickie	1997 v W	1997 *W, E, S*	3	2	0	0	0	10
N K P J Woods	1994 v A		7	1	0	0	0	5
M C McCall	1992 v NZ	1996 *A*, 1997 *It*	6	0	0	0	0	0
J C Bell	1994 v A	1996 *WS, A*, 1997 *It, F, W, E, S*	21	3	0	0	0	15
R A J Henderson	1996 v WS	1996 *WS*	1	0	0	0	0	0
K P McQuilkin	1996 v US	1997 *F* (t & R), *S*	5	0	0	0	0	0
M J Field	1994 v E	1996 *A* (R), 1997 *F, W, E, S*	17	0	0	0	0	0
D G Humphreys	1996 v F	1996 *WS*, 1997 *E* (R), *S*	6	0	2	2	1	13
P A Burke	1995 v E	1996 *A* 1997 *It, S* (R)	10	0	11	26	1	103
E P Elwood	1993 v W	1997 *F, W, E*	19	0	13	45	2	167
N A Hogan	1995 v E	1996 *WS*, 1997 *F, W, E*	12	1	0	0	0	5
C Saverimutto	1995 v Fj		3	0	0	0	0	0
B T O'Meara	1997 v E	1997 *E* (R), *S*	2	0	0	0	0	0
S C McIvor	1996 v A	1996 *A*, 1997 *It, S* (R)	3	0	0	0	0	0
A T H Clarke	1995 v Fj	1996 *WS*, 1997 *F* (R)	5	0	0	0	0	0
R P Nesdale	1997 v W	1997 *W, E, S*	3	0	0	0	0	0
T J Kingston	1987 v W		29	2	0	0	0	8
K G M Wood	1994 v A	1996 *A*, 1997 *It, F*	9	0	0	0	0	0
H D Hurley	1995 v Fj	1996 *WS*	2	0	0	0	0	0
P Flavin	1997 v F	1997 *F* (R), *S*	2	0	0	0	0	0
N J Popplewell	1989 v NZ	1996 *A*, 1997 *It, F, W, E*	44	3	0	0	0	13
P S Wallace	1995 v J	1996 *WS, A*, 1997 *It, F, W, E, S*	12	2	0	0	0	10
G F Halpin	1990 v E		11	1	0	0	0	5
G M Fulcher	1994 v A	1996 *A*, 1997 *It, W* (R)	19	1	0	0	0	5
J W Davidson	1995 v Fj	1996 *WS, A*, 1997 *It, F, W, E, S*	12	0	0	0	0	0

P S Johns	1990 v Arg	1996 *WS*, 1997 *It* (R), *F, W, E, S*	34	2	0	0	0	10
M J Galwey	1991 v F	1996 *WS*	22	1	0	0	0	5
N P J Francis	1987 v Tg		36	4	0	0	0	19
E O Halvey	1995 v F		6	2	0	0	0	10
W D McBride	1988 v W	1996 *WS*, *A*, 1997 *It* (R), *F, W, E, S*	32	4	0	0	0	18
D S Corkery	1994 v A	1996 *WS*, *A*, 1997 *It*, *F, W, E, S*	21	3	0	0	0	15
V C P Costello	1996 v US	1996 *WS* (R)	5	0	0	0	0	0
A G Foley	1995 v E	1996 *A*, 1997 *It*, *E* (R)	9	1	0	0	0	5
B M Cronin	1995 v S	1997 *S*	2	0	0	0	0	0
E R P Miller	1997 v It	1997 *It*, *F, W, E*	4	1	0	0	0	5

David Corkery in action during Ireland's victory over Wales at Cardiff Arms Park.

IRISH CLUBS 1996-97

Ballymena

Year of formation 1922
Ground Eaton Park, Raceview Road, Ballymena   Tel: Ballymena 656746
Colours Black
Captain 1996-97 C Wallace
Insurance Corporation League Div 1 5th **First Trust Bank Ulster Senior Cup** *Winners –*
Beat Malone 20-13 (final)

The turning point in Ballymena's season came three days after their heavy defeat by
Dungannon in the second League game of the season, when new coach Neille Smith
took up his post. He led the side to eight League wins from eleven games, with the
defeats against Shannon, Cork Constitution and Blackrock all being close games. As
always the Ballymena strength lay in their pack, and their South African coach built
upon this, developing the rolling maul to such an extent that they were able to maul
from their own half to score against Garryowen. Dean McCartney, in the back row,
hooker Stephen Ritchie and prop Rab Irwin had fine seasons and both McCartney
and Ritchie were rewarded with selection for the Irish Development tour to New
Zealand. With two years left on coach Smith's contract, and young players such as
the versatile threequarter Sheldon Coulter in the squad, the future looks bright for
the Ulster Cup winners.

League Record 1996-97

Date	Venue	Opponents	Result	Scorers
7 Dec	H	Terenure College	15-22	*P:* McIlmoyles (3), McAleese *D:* McIlmoyle
14 Dec	A	Dungannon	6-35	*P:* McAleese (2)
21 Dec	H	Old Crescent	16-9	*T:* T McCartney *C:* McIlmoyle *P:* McAleese (2), McIlmoyle
11 Jan	A	Instonians	16-9	*T:* Ritchie, McKernan *P:* McIlmoyle (2)
25 Jan	H	Shannon	25-37	*T:* Beatty, D McCartney *P:* McIlmoyle (5)
8 Feb	A	Cork Constitution	18-33	*T:* Law, D McCartney *C:* Harron *P:* Harron (2)
22 Feb	H	St Mary's College	25-22	*T:* McBride, Ritchie, Beattie *C:* McIlmoyle (2) *P:* McAleese *D:* McIlmoyle
8 Mar	A	Lansdowne	10-9	*T:* Ritchie *C:* McIlmoyle *P:* McIlmoyle
15 Mar	A	Young Munster	19-6	*T:* McAleese, D McCartney *P:* McIlmoyle (3)
22 Mar	H	Garryowen	26-10	*T:* Topping, Wallace, McAleese *C:* McIlmoyle *P:* McIlmoyle (2) *D:* McIlmoyle
29 Mar	A	Old Wesley	47-22	*T:* McIlmoyle, McAleese, McCartney (2), Topping, Graham *C:* McIlmoyle (3), McAleese *P:* McIlmoyle (3)
5 Apr	H	Old Belvedere	12-3	*P:* McIlmoyle (3), McAleese
12 Apr	A	Blackrock College	23-30	*T:* Ritchie, McAleese, Rainey, Smyth *P:* McIlmoyle

Blackrock College

Year of formation 1882
Ground Stradbrook Road, Blackrock, Dublin   Tel: Dublin 2805967
Colours Royal blue and white hoops
Captain 1996-97 M Brewer
Insurance Corporation League Div 1 8th **Heineken Leinster Senior Cup** Lost 16-21 to
Bective Rangers (quarter-final)

Blackrock started the League season in the most promising fashion, gaining their first ever away League victory against Garryowen, with an emphatic six-one try count. This result was quickly put into perspective when it was followed by a single-point win over eventual relegation candidates Old Wesley. The side, coached and captained by Mike Brewer, who was also Brian Ashton's assistant with the Ireland side, contained many young promising backs such as Emmet Farrell, who won Ireland Under-21 honours during the season, Nicky Assaf, who had moved from Dungannon, and Aden Guinan, who many judged to be the most improved player in the side. The season finished on a high with an excellent victory to end Ballymena's six-match winning sequence, and victory in the final of the All Ireland Under-20's competition. The loss of Mike Brewer to West Hartlepool for next season may be a crucial factor in determining whether this young talented side can take the next step up to challenge for League honours.

League Record 1996-97

Date	Venue	Opponents	Result	Scorers
7 Dec	A	Garryowen	43-13	T: Carey (2), O'Brien (2), Farrell, Kennedy C: McGowan (5) P: McGowan
14 Dec	H	Old Wesley	12-11	P: McGowan (4)
21 Dec	A	Old Belvedere	10-12	T: Assaf, Farrell
11 Jan	H	Young Munster	32-21	T: Assaf, Kearns, Farrell, McGowan C: McGowan (3) P: McGowan (2)
25 Jan	H	Terenure College	8-22	T: O'Brien P: McGowan
8 Feb	A	Dungannon	14-13	T: Brewer, McGowan C: Lynagh (2)
22 Feb	H	Old Crescent	23-9	T: Lynagh, Roche C: Lynagh (2) P: Lynagh (3)
8 Mar	A	Instonians	22-19	T: Carey, Guinan, McGowan C: Lynagh (2) P: Lynagh
15 Mar	H	Shannon	15-21	T: Farrell, Assaf C: Lynagh P: Lynagh
22 Mar	A	Cork Constitution	21-39	T: Hunt, Lynagh, McGowan C: Lynagh (3)
29 Mar	H	St Mary's College	40-43	T: Johnson, Kennedy, Guinan, pen try C: Lynagh (4) P: Lynagh (3) D: Farrell
5 Apr	A	Lansdowne	18-42	T: Guinan, Assaf C: Lynagh P: Lynagh (2)
12 Apr	H	Ballymena	30-23	T: Guinan, Assaf, Brewer, McGowan C: Lynagh (2) P: Lynagh (2)

Cork Constitution

Year of formation 1892
Ground Temple Hill, Ballintemple, Cork   Tel: Cork 292563
Colours White
Captain 1996-97 N Murray
Insurance Corporation League Div 1 6th **Carling Munster Senior Cup** Lost 20-21 to Sunday's Well (2nd round)

The prospects of a successful season were not high when the club lost five internationals to English clubs in the close season, including Paul Burke, David Corkery and Gabriel Fulcher, but this gave the club the impetus to introduce several young players. These included the skilful outside-half Ronan O'Gara, who finished the season as the League's second highest points scorer with 129, and his half-back partner, new international Brian O'Meara. These young backs were greatly helped by the presence of the vastly experienced Kenny Murphy who played both full-back and wing during the season. The side were short of a few experienced forwards and despite the presence of McCarthy, Murray and Soden in the front row, the pack often failed to produce the quality of possession needed for the threequarters to show their adventurous best. The season finished on a disappointing note with an unexpected defeat in the Carling Munster Cup against Second Division Sunday's Well.

League Record 1996-97

Date	Venue	Opponents	Result	Scorers
7 Dec	H	Instonians	28-0	T: O'Gara, Walsh (2) C: O'Gara (2) P: O'Gara (2), O'Brien
14 Dec	A	Shannon	11-24	T: O'Rien P: O'Gara (2)
21 Dec	A	Young Munster	25-9	T: Horgan (2), J Murray C: O'Gara (2) P: O'Gara (2)
11 Jan	H	St Mary's College	23-23	T: K Murphy, N Murray, Horgan C: O'Gara P: O'Gara (2)
25 Jan	A	Lansdowne	6-30	P: O'Gara D: O'Gara
8 Feb	H	Ballymena	33-18	T: O'Brien (2), O'Callaghan C: O'Gara (3) P: O'Gara (3) D: O'Gara
22 Feb	A	Garryowen	16-28	T: K Murphy C: O'Gara P: O'Gara (2) D: O'Gara
8 Mar	H	Old Wesley	18-23	T: O'Brien (2) C: O'Gara P: O'Gara (2)
15 Mar	A	Old Belvedere	18-7	T: Twomey, J Murray C: O'Gara P: O'Gara (2)
22 Mar	H	Blackrock College	39-21	T: Canning, O'Callaghan, Horgan, J Murray, N Murray, K Murphy C: O'Gara (3) P: O'Gara
29 Mar	A	Terenure College	6-30	P: O'Gara (2)
5 Apr	H	Dungannon	47-24	T: Horgan (2), K Murphy (2), O'Brien, J Murray, Walsh C: O'Gara (3) P: O'Gara (2)
12 Apr	H	Old Crescent	29-15	T: Walsh (2), J Murray, K Murphy C: O'Gara (3) P: O'Gara

Dungannon

Year of formation 1873
Ground Stevenson Park, Dungannon   Tel: Dungannon 22387
Colours Blue and white hoops
Captain 1996-97 M Patton
Insurance Corporation League Div 1 10th **First Trust Bank Ulster Senior Cup** Lost
6-16 to Ballymena (semi-final)

In the close season Dungannon had lost two of their most influential forwards, Paddy Johns and Jeremy Davidson, to Bedford and London Irish respectively, and if this were not a big enough blow, Davidson was followed to London Irish by coach Willie Anderson just before the League campaign commenced. The side's game plan was built on new scrum-half Stephen Bell and outside-half Ashley Blair (last season's scrum-half) linking with international centre Mark McCall to create a fast open style. However, after McCall had suffered a severe thumb injury which prevented him from playing until the final League match of the season, the club were forced simply to consolidate their position in the top division. This was achieved by the end of March, when they saw off the challenge of Old Crescent and Instonians. Tight-head prop Gary Leslie was rewarded for a fine season with an Ireland A cap and young winger Roger Cowan gained much praise for his defence-splitting attacking runs. Coach David Haslett is to work as assistant to Brian Ashton next season, and is to be replaced by former club captain, and Irish schools coach, Keith Patton.

League Record 1996-97

Date	Venue	Opponents	Result	Scorers
7 Dec	A	Lansdowne	15-26	T: Bell, Leslie C: Blair P: Blair
14 Dec	H	Ballymena	35-6	T: Bell (2), Carey, Patterson C: Blair (3) P: Blair (2) D: Blair

21 Dec	A	Garryowen	31-53	*T:* Carey, Stephens, McDowell, Cowan
				C: Blair *P:* Blair (3)
11 Jan	H	Old Wesley	41-7	*T:* Sandford (2), Carey (2), Leslie, Hastings
				C: Blair (4) *P:* Blair
25 Jan	A	Old Belvedere	23-36	*T:* Leslie, Bell, Dunne *C:* Blair *P:* Blair
				D: Blair
8 Feb	H	Blackrock College	13-14	*T:* Cowan *C:* Blair *P:* Blair *D:* Bell
22 Feb	A	Terenure College	13-14	*T:* Cowan *C:* Blair *P:* Blair *D:* Bell
8 Mar	H	Young Munster	18-21	*T:* Carey, Patterson *C:* McGarry
				P: McGarry (2)
15 Mar	H	Old Crescent	26-21	*T:* Beggs, Patton *C:* McGarry (2)
				P: McGarry (4)
22 Mar	A	Instonians	25-10	*T:* Sandford, Bell, pen try *C:* McGarry (2)
				P: McGarry (2)
29 Mar	H	Shannon	12-34	*T:* Hastings, Leslie *C:* McGarry
5 Apr	A	Cork Constitution	24-47	*T:* Hutchinson, Blair *C:* McGarry
				P: McGarry (4)
12 Apr	H	St Mary's College	43-24	*T:* Callaghan, McCall, Patton, Curry
				C: McGarry (4) *P:* McGarry (5)

Garryowen

Year of formation 1884
Ground Dooradoyle, Limerick   Tel: Limerick 303099
Colours Light blue with white five pointed star
Captain 1996-97 P Hogan
Insurance Corporation League Div 1 7th **Carling Munster Senior Cup** *Winners* – beat
Young Munster 12-6 (final)

Although Garryowen were disappointing in the League, the club generally had one of their most successful seasons ever, with victory in the Munster Senior Cup augmented by trophies at second team, third team and Under-20 levels. In fact, some of the first team's most influential players had developed from the successful Under-20's side, including hooker Pat Humphries and flanker David Wallace, who was a member of the Irish Development squad in New Zealand. The single-point defeat by Shannon in February effectively finished Garryowen's League challenge; however, the club continued to play attractive rugby under coach Phil Danaher, who favored an open running game. This was especially evident in their successful Munster Cup campaign, which included a comprehensive victory over Shannon.

League Record 1996-97

Date	Venue	Opponents	Result	Scorers
7 Dec	H	Blackrock College	13-43	*T:* Crotty *C:* Everett *P:* Keane (2)
14 Dec	A	Terenure College	23-16	*T:* McIvor, Cronin, Linnane *C:* Everett
				P: Everett (2)
21 Dec	H	Dungannon	53-31	*T:* Clarke (2), Everett, O'Grady, Sheehan,
				Crotty, Costello *C:* Keane (3) *P:* Keane (4)
11 Jan	A	Old Crescent	24-22	*T:* Everett, Clarke *C:* Keane *P:* Keane (4)
25 Jan	H	Instonians	39-9	*T:* Clarke (2), Brooks, Larkin, O'Grady, Hogan,
				Leahy *C:* Keane (2)
8 Feb	A	Shannon	16-17	*T:* Leahy *C:* Keane *P:* Keane (3)
22 Feb	H	Cork Constitution	28-16	*T:* Wallace (2), Clarke *C:* Keane (2)
				P: Keane (3)
8 Mar	A	St Mary's College	27-35	*T:* Keane (2), O'Grady, Larkin *C:* Keane (2)
				P: Keane
15 Mar	H	Lansdowne	19-15	*T:* Everett, Ronan *P:* Keane (2) *D:* Everett
2 Mar	A	Ballymena	10-26	*T:* Leahy *C:* Keane *P:* Keane
29 Mar	A	Young Munster	11-8	*T:* Crotty *P:* Everett *D:* Everett

| 5 Apr | H | Old Wesley | 18-28 | *T:* McNamara (2), Humphreys | *P:* Keane |
| 12 Apr | A | Old Belvedere | 6-16 | *P:* Keane | *D:* Keane |

Instonians

Year of formation 1919
Ground Shane Park, Stockmans Lane, Belfast   Tel: Belfast 660629
Colours Purple, yellow and black
Captain 1996-97 A Adair
Insurance Corporation League Div 1 14th – *relegated*   **First Trust Bank Ulster Senior Cup** Lost 15-29 to Malone (1st round)

A disappointing season for this young side was not helped by the way in which they lost some winnable games, such as those against Blackrock and Young Munster, by only a few points. Indeed, the game against Young Munster summed up the frustration of their season, with a missed penalty in the last few minutes resulting in a one-point defeat. The season had got off to the worst possible start with a heavy defeat in Cork, and they lost five consecutive matches. Despite the team's overall poor season, there were several players whose individual contributions stood out. As always, Kevin McKee and Roger Wilson in the back row were magnificent and their efforts were supplemented by second rows Keith Parker and John Gardiner.

League Record 1996-97

Date	Venue	Opponents	Result	Scorers
7 Dec	A	Cork Constitution	0-28	
14 Dec	H	St Mary's College	11-22	*T:* Moffett *P:* Knox (2)
21 Dec	A	Lansdowne	10-47	*T:* Gray (2)
11 Jan	H	Ballymena	9-16	*P:* Bond (3)
25 Jan	A	Garryowen	9-39	*P:* Bond (3)
8 Feb	H	Old Wesley	29-15	*T:* Wilson (2), Moffett, Gray *P:* Bond (3)
22 Feb	A	Old Belvedere	26-36	*T:* Moffett (2), Gray *C:* Bond *P:* Bond (3)
8 Mar	H	Blackrock College	19-22	*T:* McNevison, McKee *P:* Bond (3)
15 Mar	A	Terenure College	11-63	*T:* Hill *P:* Bond (2)
22 Mar	H	Dungannon	10-25	*T:* Peak *C:* Bond *P:* Bond
29 Mar	A	Old Crescent	11-35	*T:* Hillman *P:* Bond (2)
5 Apr	H	Young Munster	21-22	*T:* McKee, Gray *C:* Bond *P:* Bond (3)
12 Apr	H	Shannon	16-38	*T:* Wilson *C:* Bond *P:* Bond (3)

Lansdowne

Year of formation 1872
Ground Lansdowne Road, Dublin   Tel: Dublin 6689300
Colours Red, yellow and black
Captain 1996-97 M McDermott
Insurance Corporation League Div 1 2nd   **Heineken Leinster Senior Cup** *Winners –* beat Bective Rangers 40-8 (final)

Lansdowne's challenge for the League was dealt a severe blow when they lost at home by a point against Ballymena in a game they could, and should, have won. The club had had high hopes of bringing the title to Dublin with the arrival of several new faces, including internationals Kurt McQuilkin and David O'Mahoney (the club's player of the season), and Marcus Dillon, who had returned from Dubai. With players of this calibre joining Eric Elwood and Richard Governey, it was inevitable that the club would favour an expansive game; an aim they successfully achieved with 41 tries scored in the League campaign. A long-term injury to Brian Glennon, who only played in the final two months of the League, coupled with provincial and international calls, meant the team were unable to field a settled full-strength side for much of the season. This was a determining factor in the crucial defeat by Ballymena, when five key players were unavailable. Governey, who played at both full-back and outside-half, won Irish Under-21 honours and, along with Dillon, was selected for the Irish Development tour of New Zealand, while club captain Mark Mcdermott was an A International.

League Record 1996-97

Date	Venue	Opponents	Results	Scorers
7 Dec	H	Dungannon	26-15	T: Kearin (2), Governey C: Elwood P: Elwood (2) D: Elwood
14 Dec	A	Old Crescent	29-3	T: Elwood, O'Mahony C: Elwood (2) P: Elwood (4) D: Elwood
21 Dec	H	Instonians	47-10	T: Kearin, Corrigan, McCoy, Elwood, McKean, McQuilkin C: Elwood (4) P: Elwood (3)
11 Jan	A	Shannon	17-26	T: Cooney P: Elwood (4)
25 Jan	H	Cork Constitution	30-6	T: Corrigan, O'Mahony, McCermott, pen try C: Elwood (2) P: Elwood (2)
8 Feb	A	St Mary's College	19-13	T: Dillon C: Elwood P: Elwood (4)
22 Feb	A	Young Munster	42-15	T: Dillon (3), McKeen, pen try C: Governey (4) P: Governey (3)
8 Mar	H	Ballymena	9-10	P: Governey (3)
15 Mar	A	Garryowen	15-19	T: Rooney, Glennon C: Fassbender P: Fassbender
22 Mar	H	Old Wesley	25-17	T: Dillon (2), McEntee, Bohan C: Gunne P: Gunne
29 Mar	A	Old Belvedere	32-6	T: O'Mahony (3), Becker, Rooney C: Elwood (2) P: Elwood
5 Apr	H	Blackrock College	42-18	T: Dillon (2), Governey, Becker, O'Mahony, Rooney C: Elwood (3) P: Elwood (2)
12 Apr	A	Terenure College	16-26	T: O'Mahony (2) P: Elwood (2)

Old Belvedere

Year of formation 1930
Ground Angelsea Road, Ballsbridge, Dublin   Tel: Dublin 6689748
Colours Black and white hoops
Captain 1996-97 S Tormey
Insurance Corporation League Div 1 12th   **Heineken Leinster Senior Cup** Lost 13-30 to Terenure College (2nd round)

Old Belvedere lost their way in the early part of the League season, leaving them in the position of having to win their final game against Garryowen to secure their First Division future. However, it could have been much easier for this young side, who had only three players over the age of 30. In seven of their games they led after an hour, but they were only able to win one of these matches. Kevin Spicer moved to London Irish towards the end of the season, but Neil Francis played a key role in moulding some good young players into a cohesive pack. With strong Under-19 and Under-20 sides, new coach Stephen Dodds (who led Suttonians to the Division Four title this year) will have a strong base to work from next season.

League Record 1996-97

Date	Venue	Opponents	Result	Scorers
7 Dec	A	Old Wesley	13-18	T: Colgan C: Murphy P: Philpott (2)
14 Dec	H	Young Munster	11-20	T: Bewley P: Murphy D: Murphy

21 Dec	H	Blackrock College	12-10	*T:* McKenna, Spicer *C:* McKenna
11 Jan	A	Terenure College	11-13	*T:* O'Beirne *P:* Murphy (2)
25 Jan	H	Dungannon	36-23	*T:* Tormey (2), Shanley, Bewley, McKenna
				C: Treacy (4) *P:* Treacy
8 Feb	A	Old Crescent	17-37	*T:* Spicer, Carswell *C:* Treacy (2) *P:* Treacy
22 Feb	H	Instonians	36-26	*T:* Ward (2), McDonnell, O'Beirne, Bewley
				C: Treacy (4) *P:* Treacy
8 Mar	A	Shannon	15-51	*T:* Francis, Johnston *C:* Treacy *P:* Treacy
15 Mar	H	Cork Constitution	7-18	*T:* Francis *C:* Murphy
22 Mar	A	St Mary's College	10-21	*T:* O'Beirne *C:* Treacy *P:* Treacy
29 Mar	H	Lansdowne	6-32	*P:* Treacy (2)
5 Apr	A	Ballymena	3-12	*P:* Treacy
12 Apr	H	Garryowen	16-6	*T:* Francis *C:* Treacy *P:* Treacy
				D: Treacy (2)

Old Crescent

Year of formation 1947
Ground Rosbrien, Limerick   Tel: Limerick 228083
Colours Navy, blue and white strips
Captain 1996-97 L Toland
Insurance Corporation League Div 1 11th   **Carling Munster Senior Cup** Lost 8-20 to Cork Constitution (1st round)

Old Crescent had high hopes of a successful campaign after winning the Division Two title the previous season, but found the transition to the top flight much more difficult than they had imagined. They initially adopted an open expansive style, but after four games they were at the bottom of the table without a win. At this point they altered their plans, kept the ball tight, and won three of their next four to guarantee that they kept their place in the top division. At the start of the season Len Dineen had returned to the club from Cork Constitution and, although plagued by injuries, his contribution was vital, with the club winning each of the four League games which he completed. The change of style also suited second row John Forde, who was the club's player of the year, while outside-half Stephen Tuohy was again the club's top scorer with 93 League points.

League Record 1996-97

Date	Venue	Opponents	Result	Scorers
7 Dec	A	St Mary's College	21-42	*T:* McDonagh, Forde, Bowles *P:* Begley (2)
14 Dec	H	Lansdowne	3-29	*P:* Begley
21 Dec	A	Ballymena	9-16	*P:* Tuohy (3)
11 Jan	H	Garryowen	22-24	*T:* Tuohy, Bowles, Dinneen *C:* Tuohy (2)
				P: Tuohy
25 Jan	A	Old Wesley	18-6	*P:* Tuohy (6)
8 Feb	H	Old Belvedere	37-17	*T:* Forde (2), O'Neill (2), Madigan
				C: Tuohy (3) *P:* Tuohy (2)
22 Feb	A	Blackrock College	9-13	*P:* Tuohy (3)
8 Mar	H	Terenure College	17-7	*T:* Walsh *P:* Tuohy (3) *D:* Tuohy
15 Mar	A	Dungannon	21-26	*T:* Bowles, Tuohy, O'Dwyer *P:* Tuohy (2)
22 Mar	H	Young Munster	17-23	*T:* Duggan, Forde *C:* Tuohy (2) *P:* Tuohy
29 Mar	H	Instonians	35-11	*T:* Bowles (2), Forde, O'Dwyer, Noonan
				C: Madigan (2) *P:* Tuohy, O'Neill
5 Apr	A	Shannon	15-28	*T:* Forde, Walsh, Bowles
12 Apr	A	Cork Constitution	15-29	*T:* Bowles, Madigan *C:* Halissey
				P: Halissey

Old Wesley

Year of formation 1891
Ground Donnybrook, Dublin
Colours White with blue and red band
Captain 1996-97 C Hoey
Insurance Corporation League Div 1 13th – *relegated*   **Heineken Leinster Senior Cup**
Lost 21-22 to Dublin University (2nd round)

The demands placed on the players by the All Ireland League were graphically illustrated by Old Wesley. During the season 23 of their 30 first-team squad suffered injuries which forced them to miss at least one League match. The worst-hit area was the front row, where experienced prop John Feehan and first and second choice hookers Matt Keane and John Quirke were all long-term casualties. Indeed, in the final match of the season the club were forced to field their third team prop as hooker. However, the team showed such strength of character despite these problems and early in the season were unlucky not to win against Terenure and, after missing a last-minute penalty, against Blackrock. Their penultimate match saw a fine victory against Garryowen in Limerick when, as they had done all season, John Kennefick at scrum-half and winger Rob Casey produced quality performances.

League Record 1996-97

Date	Venue	Opponents	Result	Scorers
7 Dec	H	Old Belvedere	18-13	*T:* Pim, Hoey *C:* Hawe *P:* Hawe, Farren
14 Dec	A	Blackrock College	11-12	*T:* Browne *P:* Hawe (2)
21 Dec	H	Terenure College	6-11	*P:* Hawe *D:* Hawe
11 Jan	A	Dungannon	7-41	*T:* Younger *C:* Hawe
25 Jan	H	Old Crescent	6-18	*P:* Hawe (2)
8 Feb	A	Instonians	15-29	*T:* Browne, Higginson, Kenefick
22 Feb	H	Shannon	12-38	*P:* Hawe (2) *D:* Hawe (2)
8 Mar	A	Cork Constitution	23-18	*T:* Kenefick, Love *C:* Hawe (2) *P:* Hawe *D:* Hawe, Moloney
15 Mar	H	St Mary's College	24-28	*T:* Moloney (2), Gill *C:* Hawe (3) *P:* Hawe
22 Mar	A	Lansdowne	17-25	*T:* Younger *P:* Mitchell (4)
29 Mar	H	Ballymena	22-47	*T:* Casey *C:* Mitchell *P:* Mitchell (5)
5 Apr	A	Garryowen	28-18	*T:* Casey, Younger, Kennefick, Duffy *C:* Mitchell *P:* Mitchell, Hawe
12 Apr	A	Young Munster	17-29	*T:* Casey *P:* Mitchell (2), Hawe (2)

St Mary's College

Year of formation 1900
Ground Templeville Road, Templeogue, Dublin   Tel: Dublin 4900440
Colours Royal Blue with five pointed white star
Captain 1996-97 B Keane
Insurance 1996-97 B Keane
Insurance Corporation League Div 1 4th   **Heineken Leinster Senior Cup** Lost 17-28
to Blackrock College (2nd round)

At the beginning of the season St Mary's would have been pleased at the prospect of finishing the League in the top four, but as the season progressed they became realistic title challengers, being the only side to beat Shannon and topping the table throughout January. However, in February they suffered narrow defeats against Lansdowne and Ballymena, both in games which Mary's could have won. Both Kevin Potts and Steve Jameson were, as always, vital in the pack, and their work was supplemented by the return of Victor Costello from London Irish mid-way through the season. The speed of Denis Hickie, who won his first international caps, was an advantage to a back line whose average age was only 22. Many of the side had progressed through the club's excellent junior teams. Next season, former players Steve Hennessy and Hugh McGuire will replace former Irish captain Ciaran Fitzgerald as coach.

League Record 1996-97

Date	Venue	Opponents	Result	Scorers
7 Dec	H	Old Crescent	42-21	T: Nowlan, Hickie, Lyons, McCormack C: Campion (2) P: Campion (6)
14 Dec	A	Instonians	22-11	T: Fitzgerald C: Campion P: Campion (5)
21 Dec	H	Shannon	13-11	T: Lyons C: Fitzpatrick P: Fitzpatrick, Campion
11 Jan	A	Cork Constitution	23-23	T: Hickie, pen try C: Fitzpatrick (2) P: Fitzpatrick (3)
25 Jan	A	Young Munster	19-11	T: Lyons C: Fitzpatrick P: Fitzpatrick (4)
8 Feb	H	Lansdowne	13-19	T: Hickie, Costello P: Fitzpatrick
22 Feb	H	Ballymena	22-25	T: Nowlan, Lyons, McIlreavey C: Fitzpatrick (2) P: Fitzpatrick
8 Mar	H	Garryowen	35-27	T: Lyons (2), Nowlan (2), McWeeney C: Fitzpatrick (2) P: Fitzpatrick (2)
15 Mar	A	Old Wesley	28-24	T: McWeeney (2), Gannon, Lyons C: Fitzpatrick P: Fitzpatrick (2)
22 Mar	H	Old Belvedere	21-10	T: McWeeney, Nowlan C: Fitzpatrick P: Fitzpatrick (3)
29 Mar	A	Blackrock College	43-40	T: Nowlan (3), Hickie (2), McWeeney C: Fitzpatrick (2) P: Fitzpatrick (3)
5 Apr	H	Terenure College	0-14	
12 Apr	A	Dungannon	24-43	T: Fitzpatrick, McWeeney C: Fitzpatrick P: Fitzpatrick (4)

Shannon

Year of formation 1884
Ground Thomond Park, Limerick   Tel: Limerick 452350
Colours Black and blue hoops
Captain 1996-97 C McDermott
Insurance Corporation League Div 1 *Winners*   **Carling Munster Senior Cup** Lost 18-28 to Garryowen (semi-final)

For the third year in a row Shannon dominated the All Ireland League, winning the title by six points. As always, their success was built on the strength and power of their forwards. Alan Quinlan, Eddie Halvey and Anthony Foley created a cohesive back-row unit and the experienced Mick Galwey was joined mid-way through the season by the young, extremely talented Rory Sheriff in the second row. The arrival of Sheriff forced John Hayes, who returned to the club from New Zealand this season, to move forward to prop, where he settled with great ease. This season also saw a move to creating more opportunities wide out and to this end Jim Galvin at outside-half and Alan McGrath in the centre played a crucial role. Alan Thompson was the League's top points scorer with 166, despite having his favourite boots stolen halfway through the season. Thompson and Galvin have now played throughout every match in the three successful League campaigns. Despite a loss to St Mary's just before Christmas, they bounced back in the New Year and led the League for the final two months. McGrath, Sheriff, Foley and Halvey were rewarded with places on the Irish Development tour to New Zealand.

League Record 1996-97

Date	Venue	Opponents	Result	Scorers
7 Dec	A	Young Munster	22-14	T: Galvin, Galwey, Halvey C: Thomspon (2) P: Thompson

14 Dec	H	Cork Constitution	24-11	*T:* Galvin, Galwey, Foley *P:* Thompson (3)
21 Dec	A	St Mary's College	11-13	*T:* O'Shea *P:* Thompson (2)
11 Jan	H	Lansdowne	26-17	*T:* Galwey, Halvey, Thompson *C:* Thompson *P:* Thompson (2) *D:* Murray
25 Jan	A	Ballymena	37-25	*T:* O'Shea, McGoey, Foley, Halvey, Quinlan *C:* Thompson (3) *P:* Thompson (2)
8 Feb	H	Garryowen	17-16	*T:* O'Shea *P:* Thompson (4)
22 Feb	A	Old Wesley	38-12	*T:* Thompson (2), Murray, Maher, Sheriff *C:* Thompson (5) *P:* Thompson
8 Mar	H	Old Belvedere	51-15	*T:* Russell (2), Halvey, Healy, Quinlan, Hayes *C:* Thompson (6) *P:* Thompson (3)
15 Mar	A	Blackrock College	21-15	*T:* Galwey, Maher *C:* Thompson *P:* Thompson (2) *D:* Galvin
22 Mar	H	Terenure College	15-12	*P:* Thompson (5)
29 Mar	A	Dungannon	34-12	*T:* McGrath, Quinlan, Foley, McDermott *C:* Thompson (4) *P:* Thompson (2)
5 Apr	H	Old Crescent	28-15	*T:* Thompson, McGrath (2), Healy *C:* Thompson *P:* Thompson (2)
12 Apr	A	Instonians	38-16	*T:* Thompson, Galwey (2), McGoey, Hayes *C:* Thompson (5) *P:* Thompson

Terenure College

Year of formation 1940
Ground Lakelands Park, Greenlea, Terenure, Dublin   Tel: Dublin 4907572
Colours Purple, black and white
Captain 1996-97 J Blayney
Insurance Corporation League Div 1 3rd **Heineken Leinster Senior Cup** Lost 30-32 to Lansdowne (quarter-final)

Terenure, who had finished third in the Second Division last season, had a magnificent season, finishing third in the top division and lost only to the four Limerick clubs. The open style employed by former Irish coach Gerry Murphy was well suited to this squad, which contained a small, mobile pack and some excellent threequarters. Winger David Coleman and full-back Ciaran Clarke were the League's two top try scorers with ten and eight respectively, and they formed a formidable back-three with Leinster young-player-of-the-season Girvan Dempsey. Dempsey also played full-back for Ireland Under-21's. The side were further bolstered by the return of Niall Hogan from Oxford after two League games. Although they ran Shannon close, their lack of forward power was exposed against Young Munster and they may need to introduce some larger, more dominant forwards if they are to build on this season's successes.

League Record 1996-97

Date	Venue	Opponents	Result	Scorers
7 Dec	A	Ballymena	22-15	*T:* Clarke (2), Coleman *C:* Walsh (2) *P:* Walsh
14 Dec	H	Garryowen	16-23	*T:* Coleman (2) *P:* Walsh (2)
21 Dec	A	Old Wesley	11-6	*T:* Clarke *P:* Walsh (2)
11 Jan	H	Old Belvedere	13-11	*T:* Clarke *C:* Walsh *P:* Walsh (2)
25 Jan	A	Blackrock College	22-8	*T:* Walsh, Hogan, Browne *C:* Walsh (2) *P:* Walsh
8 Feb	H	Young Munster	20-33	*T:* Hyland, Clarke, Hennebry *C:* Walsh *P:* Walsh
22 Feb	H	Dungannon	45-18	*T:* Clarke (2), Coleman (2), Smyth *C:* Walsh (4) *P:* Walsh (4)
8 Mar	A	Old Crescent	7-17	*T:* Smyth *C:* Walsh

15 Mar	H	Instonians	63-11	*T:* Coleman (4), DeGascum (3), Dempsey, Clarke, Hogan *C:* Dempsey (5) *P:* Dempsey
22 Mar	A	Shannon	12-15	*P:* Dempsey (4)
29 Mar	H	Cork Constitution	30-6	*T:* O'Malley (2), Dempsey (2) *C:* Hegarty (2) *P:* Hegarty (2)
5 Apr	A	St Mary's College	14-0	*T:* Coleman *P:* Hegarty (3)
12 Apr	H	Lansdowne	26-16	*T:* Smyth, Walsh, Kelly *C:* Hegarty *P:* Hegarty (2) *D:* Clarke

Young Munster

Year of formation 1895
Ground Tom Clifford Park, Greenfields, Limerick   Tel: Limerick 228433
Colours Black and amber hoops
Captain 1996-97 D Edwards
Insurance Corporation League Div 1 9th **Carling Munster Senior Cup** Lost 6-12 to Garryowen (final)

Young Munster suffered wretched home form all season, winning only one of their seven League games at Tom Clifford Park, and that on the final Saturday against relegated Old Wesley. As ever, outside-half Aidan O'Halloran was a vital part of their team, scoring 113 League points, and centre Mick Lynch also had a fine season, winning a place on the Irish Development tour to New Zealand. Dan Mooney, who had taken over the coaching duties from Tony Grant, had endeavoured to introduce a more expansive style, but it was the side's continuing forward power which ensured they were able to maintain their Division One status. The back row of Des Clohessy, Ger Earls and Declan Edwards played a key role, with Clohessy finishing as the side's top League try scorer. The disappointing season was compounded by defeat in the final of the Munster Cup final, their third defeat in the final in four seasons.

League Record 1996-97

Date	Venue	Opponents	Result	Scorers
7 Dec	H	Shannon	14-22	*T:* O'Meara *P:* A O'Halloran (2), Lynch
14 Dec	A	Old Belvedere	20-11	*T:* Edwards, O'Meara *C:* A O'Halloran (2) *P:* A O'Halloran (2)
21 Dec	H	Cork Constitution	9-25	*P:* A O'Halloran (3)
11 Jan	A	Blackrock College	21-32	*T:* Clohessy, Tobin *C:* A O'Halloran *D:* A O'Halloran (3)
25 Jan	H	St Mary's College	11-19	*T:* Tobin *P:* A O'Halloran (2)
8 Feb	A	Terenure College	33-20	*T:* McNamara, M Fitzgerald, Clohessy, Herlihy *C:* A O'Halloran (2) *P:* A O'Halloran (2) *D:* A O'Halloran
22 Feb	H	Lansdowne	15-42	*T:* Clohessy, Lynch *C:* A O'Halloran *P:* A O'Halloran
8 Mar	A	Dungannon	21-18	*T:* O'Meara, Lynch *C:* A O'Halloran *P:* A O'Halloran (2), Lynch
15 Mar	H	Ballymena	6-19	*P:* A O'Halloran (2)
22 Mar	A	Old Crescent	23-17	*T:* Clohessy, Lynch, Boland *C:* A O'Halloran *P:* A O'Halloran *D:* A O'Halloran
29 Mar	H	Garryowen	9-11	*P:* A O'Halloran (3)
5 Apr	A	Instonians	22-21	*T:* Carey, Earls, Edwards *C:* A O'Halloran (2) *P:* Lynch
12 Apr	H	Old Wesley	29-17	*T:* Clohessy *P:* A O'Halloran (5), Lynch (2) *D:* A O'Halloran

WRU SELL OFF HALLOWED TURF

THE 1996-97 SEASON IN WALES
John Billot *Western Mail*

Turmoil is an inadequate description of events in Wales. Pay for play has increasingly plunged clubs into huge financial commitments. With combined total debts of £700,000 at the end of the season, Stuart Gallacher, the Llanelli RFC chairman, warned, 'The future of the club is in the balance.' On the international field, Wales were seeking a team with the ability to enrich the imagination. Many thought that this discovery had been made following victory at Murrayfield, when Wales scored three tries in four fateful minutes, two from the fortunate bounce of the ball. But, by the end of the season, Terry Cobner, Wales's director of rugby, reflected sombrely, 'We were carried away by our victory in Scotland. We were not so good as we thought, but we were not so bad as some people said.'

The outside-half position proved to be a two-pipe problem for coach Kevin Bowring. He was convinced of the need for a master of the calculated risk and Arwel Thomas, Swansea's erratic genius, was chosen for the role. However, this necessitated Neil Jenkins ('I'm not a full back – there are two better ones in my club!') being shunted to the No 15 jersey.

Wales needed a coach who would restore confidence and the 'Silver Guru' appeared to have achieved this once he had curbed his back-row's obsession to drive from just about everywhere. 'We go from high euphoria to the depths of gloom,' he observed after that demeaning defeat by Ireland in Cardiff. 'Players must accept more responsibility.' He was getting his retaliation in first, with the two most difficult games still to come.

Undeniably, Bowring introduced a more dynamic and wider approach in Paris, but even with what was virtually their second string, France were still too strong. Finally, England exposed the shortcomings of players operating under extreme pressure. Visions of reality had been blurred by that opening match in Scotland; but England put it all into perspective in the last international match to be played at historic Arms Park. They dismantled Wales 34-13.

Few shared the view that much-loved Arms Park should be destroyed in the name of progress. There was a great sadness, and even resentment, among the many great players who had performed so heroically on the ground. On a desolate Sunday in April, the last rites were accorded at an auction on the pitch.

Giovanni Malacrino, a Cardiff restaurateur, purchased most of the hallowed turf for £4,500 as well as the horseshoe-shaped bar

The Wales team which lost to Ireland at Cardiff L-R, back row: L Mustoe (replacement), G R Jenkins (replacement), P John (replacement), D R James, L S Quinnell, M Rowley, G O Llewellyn, S M Williams, C L Charvis, G Thomas, J C Quinnell (replacement), J Davies (replacement), K P Jones (replacement); front row: I S Gibbs, D Young, C D Loader, I C Evans, J M Humphreys (capt), A C Thomas, N R Jenkins, R Howley.

from the WRU president's suite to grace his establishment. A woman paid £80 for four seats to send to her son in Singapore. A Gorseinon market trader became the owner of the leather padded elbow chair used by Princess Diana in the south stand and installed it for his customers to rest on. Now the race is on to complete the new ground, which could prove even more costly than the revised sum of £114m, in time for the 1999 Rugby World Cup final.

Another act of what many considered 'vandalism' was the reduction of the National League's First Division from 12 to eight clubs with effect from the start of the 1997-98 season. The implementation of this scheme, without giving a season's notice for clubs to prepare for it, drew widespread criticism. Some threatened legal action, but the WRU promised compensation packages and the move was sanctioned by 206 votes to 147 at a Special General Meeting in April.

Newport's director of rugby, Tom David, accused the WRU of rewarding spendthrift clubs, who had gained a place in the top eight by spending heavily on buying in players. 'The decision to cut the First Division is totally irresponsible,' he said. Darryl Jones, Neath's rugby supremo, considered that the reorganisation would hamper the development of young players rather than help it. 'I don't understand where Wales are going,' he complained. England's plundering of promising players was still of grave concern.

Vernon Pugh, chairman of the WRU committee, emphasised the essential need for the eight-club structure at the pinnacle of the pyramid: 'This will enable the WRU to plan more efficiently and manage the professional end of the game, fast-track the talent and retain the quality players in Wales. Almost everything necessary to obtain future success is in place. The requirement now is for skill, determination and expertise in its delivery.'

Yet there were misgivings that the traditional power base of the clubs was being eroded. Time will tell and, hopefully, these fears will prove unfounded.

FIRST TITLE FOR SMART PONTY

WRU NATIONAL LEAGUE 1996-97

Neil Jenkins has always insisted that Pontypridd do not have to rely exclusively on him to bring consistent success, and this claim was proved during the closing stages of the season when he was absent from the last eight games after breaking his left forearm in the Wales-England match. Crispin Cormack switched from full-back to wear the No 10 jersey and kick the goals; a mission he accomplished expertly, helping to fire Ponty to their first National League championship, which was clinched with a 52-24 victory at Bridgend with two games remaining.

It was a triumph Pontypridd had long sought and fulfilled a dream nurtured by their chief coach Dennis John. 'We always aim to entertain – our players as well as our supporters,' is his philosophy. The simplicity of this camouflages the enormous amount of planning he injects into shaping and tuning a superbly-balanced team. The goal kicking of Jenkins, the most famous kicker in Welsh rugby history, is a decisive factor and no one disputes his influence as a creative controller. Yet the aggressive tackling and uncannily perceptive support running has made the team the most potent force on the League scene.

The line-out method of Greg Prosser and Mark Rowley was more tyranny than domination, while the dynamic dimension that Dale McIntosh brought to all aspects from his back-row berth set an inspiring example. Paul John, son of the coach, is a quick-thinking scrum-half whose vision is extraordinary, whether plotting tries or scoring them. His audacity was seldom curbed. Kevin Morgan was voted the most promising player in Wales as an attacking full-back. Pontypridd were unbeaten at home in the League for a second successive season and lost only to Swansea and Llanelli.

Swansea challenged keenly for the title until they faltered in the last few games. An unthinkable defeat at Newbridge by 31-24 proved a crippling blow (only Caerphilly and Treorchy had lost there) and then a heavy defeat at Neath extinguished all hopes. Only Llanelli won at St Helen's, but Swansea failed repeatedly away to the top teams. However, their play always contained an exciting flavour with Arwel Thomas's dummies and darting runs varying from the sneaky to the outrageous.

Llanelli made a limping start with defeat in three of their first five games, and it was not until they bought in New Zealander Frano Botica that their fortunes revived. In the end they finished in third place, behind Swansea, with only Neath defeating them at Stradey.

Cardiff's start was calamitous. Three straight defeats was as many as they had suffered through the whole of the previous season, and a 27-all draw at Dunvant was a jolt to a team with so many international stars. Only Llanelli won at Cardiff, but fourth place in the League was considered to be an under-achievement.

There was no promotion for the Second Division in the restructuring to an eight-team Premier Division for 1997-98. The fourth team to join Caerphilly, Newbridge and Treorchy in relegation was not decided until the final day of the season, when Neath and Newport won to safeguard their places. Gallant Dunvant scored eight tries in winning at Treorchy, but it failed to save them from the drop. The WRU instituted a complicated bonus system that proved highly controversial. For example, Swansea defeated Caerphilly 52-38 but did not earn a bonus point whereas the losers did!

Pontypridd's Kevin Morgan on the attack for the Welsh champions against Benetton Treviso.

THE HEINEKEN LEAGUES
1996-97

Division 1	P	W	D	L	F	A	T	Bon	Pts
Pontypridd	22	20	0	2	944	334	124	22	62
Swansea	22	14	0	8	879	471	128	22	50
Llanelli	22	16	2	4	789	351	111	16	50
Cardiff	22	14	1	7	750	543	99	12	41
Bridgend	22	10	1	11	604	527	79	10	31
Newport	22	12	2	8	541	632	71	5	31
Ebbw Vale	22	12	2	8	431	552	50	4	30
Neath	22	10	0	12	524	603	74	9	29
Dunvant	22	10	2	10	524	601	69	5	27
Caerphilly	22	2	0	20	422	801	59	10	14
Treorchy	22	3	0	19	413	825	57	4	10
Newbridge	22	4	0	18	358	939	45	0	8

Division 2	P	W	D	L	F	A	T	Bon	Pts
Aberavon	22	16	1	5	703	288	107	20	53
Llandovery	22	16	0	6	722	309	109	20	52
Cross Keys	22	18	0	4	696	346	96	14	50
S W Police	22	12	1	9	555	514	82	8	33
Pontypool	22	11	2	9	535	402	71	9	33
UWIC	22	10	1	11	580	574	86	11	32
Abertillery	22	13	0	9	404	385	54	6	32
Bonymaen	22	11	1	10	474	473	65	8	31
Maesteg	22	9	0	13	476	517	53	7	25
Blackwood	22	7	0	15	358	588	44	3	17
Abercynon*	22	4	0	18	302	853	40	4	10
Ystradgynlais	22	2	0	20	305	861	36	2	6

Division 3	P	W	D	L	F	A	T	Bon	Pts
Rumney	22	17	1	4	741	317	114	17	52
Merthyr	22	15	1	6	592	333	85	14	45
Tondu	22	15	1	6	570	366	78	13	44
Pyle	22	11	1	10	618	408	87	15	38
Kenfig Hill	22	12	0	10	571	544	75	9	33
Tenby United	22	12	0	10	451	486	57	5	29
Llanharan	22	8	1	13	458	415	55	6	23
Mountain Ash	22	10	0	12	412	479	44	3	23
Tredegar	22	8	0	14	438	468	58	6	22
Narberth	22	9	2	11	352	585	40	2	22
Builth Wells	22	9	0	13	392	617	48	3	21
Penarth	22	2	1	19	291	868	39	2	7

Division 4	P	W	D	L	F	A	T	Bon	Pts
St Peters	22	16	1	5	671	336	95	14	47
Whitland	22	16	1	5	648	270	90	14	47
Oakdale	22	16	1	5	597	341	79	12	45
Carmarthen Quins	22	14	1	7	638	303	89	15	44
Kidwelly	22	13	1	8	542	410	88	13	40
Llantrisant	22	11	1	10	477	456	57	6	29
Glynneath	22	12	0	10	440	460	50	5	29
Glamorgan W	22	8	1	13	476	553	69	10	27
Rhymney	22	9	0	13	419	479	51	5	23
Blaina	22	9	0	13	377	570	50	4	22
Vardre	22	4	1	17	325	603	46	2	11
Tumble	22	0	0	22	284	1113	40	2	4

Division 5	P	W	D	L	F	A	T	Bon	Pts
Ystrad Rhondda	22	17	0	5	666	287	91	18	52
Felinfoel	22	17	1	4	695	297	94	11	46
Bedwas	22	14	0	8	582	426	85	11	39
Tonmawr	22	14	1	7	503	334	69	10	39
Resolven	22	13	0	9	543	484	79	8	34
Aberavon Quins	22	11	1	10	450	399	60	11	34
Abergavenny	22	11	0	11	401	394	56	10	32
Garndiffaith	22	10	1	11	449	472	62	6	27
Seven Sisters	22	8	0	14	362	488	54	9	25
Waunarlwydd	22	8	0	14	411	575	62	4	20
Cardiff HSOB	22	4	0	18	316	854	45	4	12
Pontypool Utd	22	2	2	18	323	691	46	5	11

2 points deducted for failing to field a side

WALKER'S WONDER-TRY TURNS IT

THE SWALEC CUP 1996-97
26 April, Cardiff Arms Park

Cardiff 33 (3G 4PG)   **Swansea 26** (3G 1T)

It seemed too much to expect a breathtaking final for the second successive year; but that was what 39,000 spectators witnessed at this last match at the original Cardiff Arms Park. Work on the ground had already begun with the destruction of the west stand, but if Cardiff, leading 33-14 midway through the second half, anticipated a similar job on Swansea, they were in for a surprise. The underdogs had a few painful bites left in them!

Cardiff needed this victory to rescue themselves from a disappointing season after spending vast amounts on assembling a highly talented team. They became Cup winners for a seventh time on their 10th appearance in the final. The man who turned the game for them was Nigel Walker, rejected by Wales on the grounds that he was not big enough. Just two minutes after the interval, with Swansea in front 14-9, Walker went to work when offered a cramped overlap and some 50 yards to cover. Garin Jenkins's desperate horizontal ankle-tap could not stop the speeding left wing, who swung inside Andy Booth and outside Matthew Back within a few paces. The master of the sinuous swerve accelerated away, recovered from a momentary unbalancing from Stuart Davies's despairing dive and was across for one of the most amazing and memorable solo tries in a Cup final. Surely no team could lose after such a magical moment?

Swansea had led through a penalty try when defenders took a scrum down and then another try when Mark Taylor was put across by smart Aled Williams, who converted both scores. Lee Jarvis had kicked three penalty goals for Cardiff, the third from near halfway. He then converted Walker's try and Cardiff pulled away with a try by Justin Thomas following another thrust by Leigh Davies, whose midfield aggression eclipsed Scott Gibbs and earned the Cardiff man the Lloyd Lewis Memorial Award as the game's outstanding player. Jarvis converted again, kicked a fourth penalty goal and added the points to a sparkling try by Mike Hall.

With stubborn refusal to be overawed, Swansea, who had dominated the first half, came again and Mark Taylor broke clear from a knot of players to surprise everyone with his second try. Then Steve Moore crashed over and Williams converted. Another such goal would have tied the scores and in that event Swansea would have won on the 'most tries' ruling, by five to three. A close run thing, indeed, especially as Swansea were without injured international stars Arwel Thomas, Colin Charvis and Christian Loader.

Cardiff: W J L Thomas; S D Hill, M R Hall, L B Davies, N Walker; L Jarvis, R Howley; A L P Lewis, J M Humphreys, L Mustoe, K Stewart, D Jones, H T Taylor (*capt*), O Williams, R G Jones *Replacements* J Davies for L Davies (temp, 23 mins), P Young for Humphreys (temp, 17 mins)
Scorers *Tries:* Walker, Thomas, Hall *Conversions:* Jarvis (3)
Penalty Goals: Jarvis (4)
Swansea: M Back; S J Davies, M Taylor, I S Gibbs, A R Harris; D A Williams, A Booth; I M Buckett, G R Jenkins (*capt*), S Evans, S Moore, P Arnold, A Reynolds, S Davies, R C Appleyard *Replacements* D Niblo for Reynolds (temp, 17 mins), K Colclough for Evans (81 mins).
Scorers *Tries:* Taylor (2), Moore, pen try *Conversions:* Williams (3)
Referee D R Davies (Llanbradach)

Cardiff's Leigh Davies tries to power through against Swansea in the SWALEC Cup final.

235

There was another sensational try for Cardiff in their semi-final victory by 36-26 against Llanelli at St Helen's. The scorer this time was Robert Howley. Unlike Walker in the final, he did not have to evade tacklers, but the scrum-half was required to go to a greater distance. In fact, he raced 80 yards along the pavilion side touchline after spotting a tiny unguarded loophole. It completed his team's sixth success in nine encounters with the Scarlets and was his third try of an enthralling match. Cardiff, with Derwyn Jones dominating the line-out until Llanelli brought on Vernon Cooper to win the short throw in the second half, established a commanding 28-9 lead by the interval. Llanelli recovered to claw their way back at 31-26 only for Howley to enact his phantom role and ghost Cardiff into the final.

Swansea's semi-final was far less dramatic, though there was tension enough when Aled Williams missed three reasonable penalty attempts in the opening half at Cardiff RFC ground and Swansea were in front only 7-0 after controlling virtually all the play. However, Aled Williams then made up for his kicking errors by scoring a startling interception try, helping his team to an eventual 26-15 victory. Ebbw Vale had reached their first semi-final for 20 years through a try by hooker Steve Jones during injury time to put out Bridgend 17-16 after the visitors led 16-3. It was white knuckle time for the Vale.

Swansea's visit to the Gnoll in the quarter-finals proved a voyage of discovery for them as the lead changed six times before a late try by Mark Taylor, who scored in every round, provided them with a safe passage by 32-24. Cardiff had no such problems against the all-amateur South Wales Police, winning by 57-30, though the visitors can claim to have scored more points than any team to have contested a Cup tie at the Cardiff ground. Leigh Davies, regaining peak form at just the right time, collected four of the nine home tries.

Cardiff had plundered an even bigger try tally in the seventh round, crossing 15 times for their record Cup score of 99-7 against Dinas Powys. Steve Ford winged away for five tries and, in the process, broke the career record of 185 tries by Bleddyn Williams, set 42 years earlier. Lee Jarvis, considered the next best goal-kicker in Wales after Neil Jenkins, supplied 29 points with a try and 12 conversions.

At this stage Swansea knocked out the Cup holders, Pontypridd, by a whisker at 20-19. Mark Taylor galloped 70 yards for an interception try that shocked a Ponty side looking to banish a bogey at St Helen's that has haunted them since their last success there in 1972.

For the first time Division One clubs were exempted until round six because of their involvement in the European competitions.

RESULTS

Third round

Abercarn 11, Cardigan 6; Aberdare 3, Pencoed 18; Abergavenny 32, Beddau 13; Bethesda 5, Tonyrefail 40; Birchgrove (Swansea) 29, Llangennech 13; Bridgend Sports Club 16, Trinant 9; Briton Ferry 24, Cwmavon 10; Carmarthen Ath 12, Senghenydd 6; Cwmbran 25, Cwmgwrach 22; Cwmllynfell 34, Bynea 11; Dinas Powys 23, Garndiffaith 12; Dolgellau 33, Risca 20; Felinfoel 51, Aberaeron 6; Glais 16, Croesyceiliog 14; Gorseinon 10, Pill Harriers 33; Morriston 17, Haverfordwest 8; Mumbles 15, Pontypool Utd 5; Nantyffyllon 9, Waunarlwydd 3; Neath Ath 13, Ammanford 21; Penygraig 10, Fairwater 8; Pontycymmer 20, Aberavon Quins 16; Banwen 9, Bridgend Ath 12; Resolven 27, Cardiff Harlequins 26; RTB (Ebbw Vale) 51, Llandeilo 10; Ruthin 18, Amman Utd 16; Seven Sisters 0, Taffs Well 26; St Joseph's OB 17, Newcastle Emlyn 22; Talywain 18, Brecon 7; Wrexham 9, Gilfach Goch 15; Ynysybwl 30, Hirwaun 38; Ystrad Rhondda 18, Tonmawr 5.

Fourth round

Abercarn 27, RTB (Ebbw Vale) 6; Abergavenny 14, Penarth 10; Builth Wells 15, Rumney 13; Briton Ferry 13, Whitland 21 (aet); Bridgend Sports 6, Narberth 9; Carmarthen Ath 47, Glamorgan Wanderers 5; Cwmllynfell 15, Bedwas 17; Dinas Powys 39, Merthyr 33; Felinfoel 34, Ystrad Rhondda 19; Gilfach Goch 30, St Peter's 8; Glais 15, Ammanford 28; Glynneath 36, Blaina 22; Llantrisant 21, Oakdale 19; Morriston 19, Carmarthen Quins 26; Mountain Ash 9, Kenfig Hill 8; Mumbles 21, Tredegar 24; Nantyffyllon 9, Tonyrefail 13; Newcastle Emlyn 48, Cwmbran 7; Pencoed 15, Llanharan 9; Penygraig 34, Bridgend Ath 8; Pill Harriers 10, Dolgellau 15; Pontycymmer 21, Tumble 12; Rhymney 23, Talywain 5; Ruthin 12, Birchgrove (Swansea) 27; Taffs Well 15, Resolven 35 (aet); Tenby Utd 10, Hirwaun 19; Tondu 9, Pyle 26; Vardre 18, Kidwelly 29.

Fifth round

Abercarn 22, Ystradgynlais 31; Bedwas 10, Abercynon 23; Blackwood 44, Hirwaun 10; Cross Keys 39, Tonyrefail 20; Felinfoel 34, Narberth 3; Kidwelly 16, Carmarthen Quins 22; Llandovery 22, Birchgrove 8; Llantrisant 10, Dinas Powys 27; Maesteg 22, Aberavon 39; Mountain Ash 5, Gilfach Goch 28; Newcastle Emlyn 29, Resolven 12; Pencoed 33, Glynneath 8; Penygraig 32, Tredegar 16; Pontycymmer 17, Abergavenny 10; Pontypool 12, Dolgellau 3; Pyle 11,

Carmarthen Ath 0; Rhymney 31, Ammanford 19; SW Police 13, Bonymaen 3; UWIC 6, Abertillery 11; Whitland 18, Builth Wells 0.

Sixth round

Aberavon 8, Ebbw Vale 32; Bridgend 26, Newbridge 20; Caerphilly 17, Llanelli 20; Cross Keys 13, Abertillery 13 (Abertillery through on tries 2-1); Dinas Powys 18, Pontycymmer 5; Felinfoel 10, Pontypridd 90; Llandovery 18, Pyle 16; Neath 57, Abercynon 6; Newcastle Emlyn 24, Gilfach Gooch 16; Newport 30, Cardiff 44; Penygraig 12, Carmarthen Quins 18; Pontypool 21, Pencoed 9; Rhymney 11, Treorchy 59; SW Police 39, Blackwood 7; Swansea 71, Dunvant 10; Whitland 18, Ystradgynlais 8.

Seventh round

Abertillery 10, Llanelli 27; Cardiff 99, Dinas Powys 7; Carmarthen Quins 19, Neath 44; Llandovery 19, SW Police 29; Newcastle Emlyn 0, Ebbw Vale 43; Pontypool 26, Whitland 24; Swansea 20, Pontypridd 19; Treorchy 13, Bridgend 22.

Quarter-final

Cardiff 57, SW Police 30; Ebbw Vale 17, Bridgend 16; Llanelli 59, Pontypool 17; Neath 24, Swansea 32.

Semi-finals

Swansea 26, Ebbw Vale 15 (*at Cardiff RFC*); Cardiff 36, Llanelli 26 (*at St Helen's*)

Final (at Cardiff Arms Park)

Cardiff 33, Swansea 26

Previous finals

(all at Cardiff Arms Park)

1972	Neath 15 Llanelli 9	
1973	Llanelli 30 Cardiff 7	
1974	Llanelli 12 Aberavon 10	
1975	Llanelli 15 Aberavon 6	
1976	Llanelli 16 Swansea 4	
1977	Newport 16 Cardiff 15	
1978	Swansea 13 Newport 9	
1979	Bridgend 18 Pontypridd 12	
1980	Bridgend 15 Swansea 9	
1981	Cardiff 14 Bridgend 6	
1982*	Cardiff 12 Bridgend 12	
1983	Pontypool 18 Swansea 6	
1984	Cardiff 24 Neath 19	
1985	Llanelli 15 Cardiff 14	
1986	Cardiff 28 Newport 21	
1987	Cardiff 16 Swansea 15	
1988	Llanelli 28 Neath 13	
1989	Neath 14 Llanelli 13	
1990	Neath 16 Bridgend 10	
1991	Llanelli 24 Pontypool 9	
1992	Llanelli 16 Swansea 7	
1993	Llanelli 21 Neath 18	
1994	Cardiff 15 Llanelli 8	
1995	Swansea 17 Pontypridd 12	
1996	Pontypridd 29 Neath 22	

* *Winners on 'most tries' rule*

WALES TO AUSTRALIA 1996

THE TOURING PARTY

Manager T J Cobner **Coaches** K W Bowring, A Lewis
Captain J M Humphreys

FULL-BACK
C Cormack (Pontypridd)

THREEQUARTERS
I C Evans (Llanelli)
W T Proctor (Llanelli)
S D Hill (Cardiff)
G Thomas (Bridgend)
L B Davies (Neath)
N G Davies (Llanelli)
D James (Bridgend)
J Funnell (Neath)

HALF-BACKS
N R Jenkins (Pontypridd)
A C Thomas (Bristol)
R Howley (Bridgend)
A P Moore (Cardiff)

FORWARDS
C D Loader (Swansea)

A L P Lewis (Cardiff)
J D Davies (Neath)
L Mustoe (Cardiff)
J M Humphreys (Cardiff)
G R Jenkins (Swansea)
G O Llewellyn (Neath)
D Jones (Cardiff)
P Arnold (Swansea)
S Ford (Bridgend)
M J Voyle (Newport)
E W Lewis (Cardiff)
A Gibbs (Newbridge)
R G Jones (Llanelli)
K P Jones (Ebbw Vale)
H T Taylor (Cardiff)
S Williams (Neath)
*B Williams (Neath)

Replacement during tour

TOUR RECORD

All matches Played 8 Won 3 Lost 5 Points for 272 Against 277
International matches Played 2 Lost 2 Points for 28 Against 98

SCORING DETAILS

All matches					International matches				
For:	39T	22C	11PG	272 Pts	For:	3T	2C	3PG	28 Pts
Against:	36T	23C	17PG	277 Pts	Against:	13T	9C	5PG	98 Pts

MATCH DETAILS

1996	OPPONENTS	VENUE	RESULT
29 May	Western Australia	Perth	W 62-20
2 June	Australian Capital Territory	Canberra	L 30-69
5 June	New South Wales	Sydney	L 20-27
8 June	AUSTRALIA	Brisbane	L 25-56
12 June	Australia B	Brisbane	L 41-51
15 June	NSW Country	Moree	W 49-3
18 June	Victoria	Melbourne	W 42-9
22 June	AUSTRALIA	Sydney	L 3-42

MATCH 1 29 May, Perth

Western Australia 20 (2G 2PG) **Wales XV 62** (6G 4T)
Western Australia: J Shirkey; D Dunbar, M Skiffington, C Schaumkel, B Hart;
C McMullen, A McDonald (*capt*); D Gleghorn, J O'Callaghan, M Meredith;
K Angus, T Thomas; M Porter, G Howard, M Brain *Replacements* S Apaapa for
Hart (40 mins), G Thomas for Angus (75 mins)

Scorers *Tries:* T Thomas, Schaumkel   *Conversions:* Schaumkel (2)
Penalty Goals: Schaumkel (2)
Wales XV: Cormack; Hill, G Thomas, Funnell, James; N Jenkins, Moore;
A Lewis, G Jenkins, Mustoe; Arnold, D Jones; E Lewis, Taylor (*capt*), K Jones
Replacements N Davies for Hill (54 mins), Voyle for E Lewis (64 mins)
Scorers *Tries:* G Thomas (5), Hill (2), Moore, James, K Jones
Conversions: Jenkins (6)
Referee P Marshall (ARU)

MATCH 2   2 June, Canberra

Australian Capital Territory 69 (8G 1PG 2T)   **Wales XV 30** (2G 2PG 2T)
Australian Capital Territory: S Larkham; M Hardy, A Magro, P Howard, J Roff;
D Knox, G Gregan; P Noriega, M Caputo, E McKenzie; J Langford, D Giffin;
I Fenukitau, B Robinson (*capt*), O Finegan *Replacements* G Didier for McKenzie
(70 mins), P Brown for Gregan (74 mins), T Tavalea for Caputo (75 mins)
Scorers *Tries:* Roff (4), Howard, Larkham, Gregan, Finegan, Hardy,
Robinson   *Conversions:* Knox (8)   *Penalty Goal:* Knox
Wales XV: Cormack; Hill, L Davies, Funnell, G Thomas; N Jenkins, Howley;
Loader, Humphreys (*capt*), J Davies; Llewellyn, D Jones; Gibbs, S Williams,
Taylor *Replacement* James for L Davies (67 mins)
Scorers *Tries:* Howley (2), Williams, Hill   *Conversions:* Jenkins (2)
Penalty Goals: Jenkins (2)
Referee W Erickson (ARU)

MATCH 3   5 June, Sydney Football Stadium, Sydney

New South Wales 27 (1G 5PG 1T)   **Wales XV 20** (2G 2PG)
New South Wales: T Kelaher; G Bond, J Madz, R Tombs, M Miller; P Wallace,
A Ekert; A Heath, M Bell, A Blades; W Waugh, J Welborn; W Ofahengaue,
T Gavin (*capt*), D Williams *Replacements* A Apps for Kelaher (13 mins), S Domoni
for Williams (74 mins)
Scorers *Tries:* Bond, Ekert   *Conversion:* Wallace   *Penalty Goals:* Wallace (5)
Wales XV: Cormack; Evans, G Thomas, N Davies, James; A Thomas, Moore;
A Lewis, B Williams, Mustoe; Voyle, Llewellyn (*capt*); E Lewis, S Williams,
G Jones *Replacements* K Jones for G Jones (62 mins), Gibbs for E Lewis (70 mins),
Loader for A Lewis (76 mins)
Scorers *Tries:* Davies, Evans *Conversions:* A Thomas (2) *Penalty Goals:* A Thomas (2)
Referee B Leask (ARU)

MATCH 4   8 June, Ballymore Oval, Brisbane   1st Test
AUSTRALIA 56 (6G 3PG 1T)   WALES 25 (2G 2PG 1T)

AUSTRALIA: M Burke (NSW); D I Campese (NSW), J W Roff (ACT),
T J Horan (Queensland), A R Murdoch (NSW); P W Howard (ACT),
G M Gregan (ACT); R L L Harry (NSW), M Caputo (ACT), E J A McKenzie
(ACT); G J Morgan (Queensland), J A Eales (Queensland) (*capt*); O Finegan
(ACT), D T Manu (NSW), D J Wilson (Queensland) *Replacement* M C Brial
(NSW) for Manu (60 mins)
Scorers *Tries:* Roff, Caputo, Wilson, Manu, Howard, Murdoch,
Morgan   *Conversions:* Burke (6)   *Penalty Goals:* Burke (3)
WALES: Proctor; Evans, L Davies, N Davies, G Thomas; N Jenkins, Howley;
Loader, Humphreys (*capt*), J Davies; Llewellyn, D Jones; Taylor, S Williams,
G Jones *Replacements* Mustoe for J Davies (69 mins), Voyle for G Jones (temp 9-20
mins) and Voyle for Jones (temp 43-45 mins)
Scorers *Tries:* Proctor, Taylor, Llewellyn   *Conversions:* Jenkins (2)
Penalty Goals: Jenkins (2)
Referee G K Wahlstrom (New Zealand)

MATCH 5   12 June, Ballymore Oval, Brisbane

Australia B 51 (3G 6T)   **Wales XV 41** (4G 1PG 2T)
Australia B: S Larkham (ACT); M Hardy (ACT), D Herbert (Queensland),
R Tombs (NSW), R Constable (Queensland); S Bowen (NSW), S Payne (NSW);
D Crowley (Queensland), M Foley (Queensland), A Heath (NSW); D Giffin
(ACT), J Welborn (NSW); B Robinson (ACT), T Gavin (NSW) (*capt*), M Brial
(NSW) *Replacement* A Blades (NSW) for Crowley (64 mins)
Scorers *Tries:* Herbert (3), Larkham (2), Payne, Brial, Hardy, Gavin
Conversions: Bowen (2), Payne
Wales XV: Proctor; Hill, G Thomas, N Davies (*capt*), James; A Thomas, Moore;
A Lewis, B Williams, Mustoe; Arnold, D Jones; Gibbs, E Lewis, K Jones
Replacements Taylor for E Lewis (53 mins), J Davies for A Lewis (68 mins)
Scorers *Tries:* Proctor, James, G Thomas, Moore, Gibbs, A Thomas
Conversions: A Thomas (4)   *Penalty Goal:* A Thomas
Referee S Dickinson (ARU)

MATCH 6   15 June, Weebollabolla Oval, Moree

NSW Country 3 (1PG)   **Wales XV 49** (4G 2PG 3T)
NSW Country: N Lavelle; S Rutledge, D West, A Harding, M Dowling; C Doyle,
S Merrick; D Phelps, D Koertz, W Petty; M Harber, G McQueen; B Klasson,
A McCalman, P Fox
Scorer *Penalty Goal:* Lavelle
Wales XV: Cormack; Evans, G Thomas, N Davies, Hill; N Jenkins, Moore;
Loader, B Williams, J Davies; Voyle, Llewellyn (*capt*); Gibbs, S Williams, Taylor
Replacements James for Thomas (55 mins), Ford for Voyle (61 mins), K Jones for
Taylor (71 mins), A Lewis for S Williams (75 mins)
Scorers *Tries:* Cormack (2), Evans, S Williams, J Davies, Hill, N Davies
Conversions: Jenkins (4)   *Penalty Goals:* Jenkins (2)
Referee B Fienberg (ARU)

MATCH 7   18 June, Olympic Park, Melbourne

Victoria 9 (3PG)   **Wales XV 42** (2G 1PG 5T)
Victoria: S Chrilia; P Ioane, M Nasalio, L Strauss, M Bell; A Hendry, L Daley;
A Charles, D Thompson, S Iakovidis; A Scott, B Parsons; C Frater (*capt*),
P Holstead, J Walshe *Replacements* R Bird for Chrilia (42 mins), P McLean for
Walshe (62 mins)
Scorer *Penalty Goals:* Hendry (3)
Wales XV: Cormack; Proctor, James, Funnell, Hill; A Thomas, Moore (*capt*);
A Lewis, B Williams, J Davies; Ford, Arnold; Gibbs, Voyle, K Jones
Replacement D Jones for Arnold (32 mins)
Scorers *Tries:* Cormack (3), Moore, Proctor, Voyle, Gibbs   *Conversions:* Thomas (2)
Penalty Goal: Thomas
Referee M Keogh (ARU)

MATCH 8   22 June, Sydney Football Stadium, Sydney 2nd Test
AUSTRALIA 42 (3G 2PG 3T)   WALES 3 (1PG)

AUSTRALIA: M Burke (NSW); D I Campese (NSW), J W Roff (ACT),
T J Horan (Queensland), B N Tune (Queensland); P W Howard (ACT),
S J Payne (NSW); R L L Harry (NSW), M Caputo (ACT), E J A McKenzie
(ACT); G J Morgan (Queensland), J A Eales (Queensland) (*capt*); O Finegan
(ACT), M C Brial (NSW), D J Wilson (Queensland) *Replacements* D Crowley for
McKenzie (9 mins), M Foley for Caputo (45 mins), S Larkham (ACT) for Burke
(60 mins), D Manu (NSW) for Foley (70 mins)
Scorers *Tries:* Finegan, Burke, Roff, Foley, Morgan, Horan

Conversions: Burke (2), Eales *Penalty Goals:* Burke (2)
WALES: Proctor; Evans, G Thomas, N Davies, Hill; N Jenkins, Howley; Loader, Humphreys (*capt*), Mustoe; Llewellyn, D Jones; Gibbs, Taylor, S Williams
Replacements A Lewis for Loader (temporary 18 to 31 mins), James for N Davies (77 mins)
Scorer *Penalty Goal:* Jenkins
Referee C J Hawke (New Zealand)

UNITED STATES TO WALES 1997

THE TOURING PARTY
Head Coach J Clark   **Team Manager** M DeJong   **Captain** D Lyle

FULL-BACKS
C **Morrow** (Gentlemen of Aspen)
M **Williams** (Gentlemen of Aspen)

THREEQUARTERS
V **Anitoni** (San Mateo Yankees)
C **Curtis** (US Combined Services)
B **Hightower** (Gentlemen of Aspen)
M **Scharrenberg** (Reading, England)
E **Schram** (OMBAC, San Diego)
K **Shuman** (Pennsylvania State University)
B **Wikeepa** (Seattle)

HALF-BACKS
M **Alexander** (Denver Barbarians)
I **Stevens** (Belmont Shore)
A **Bachelet** (Reading, England)
B **Howard** (Life College, Georgia)

FORWARDS
B **LeClerc** (Gentlemen of Aspen)
R **Lehner** (Blackheath, England)
C **Lippert** (OMBAC & Rugby, England)
S **O'Boyle** (Golden Gate, San Francisco)
S **Allen** (Rugby, England)
T **Billups** (Blackheath, England)
L **Gross** (Harlequins, England)
A **Parker** (Gentlemen of Aspen)
R **Randell** (United, Salt Lake City)
C **Vogl** (Bridgend, Wales)
D **Hodges** (OMBAC, San Diego)
D **Lyle** (Bath, England)
P **Vogel** (Chicago Lions)
J **Walker** (Gentlemen of Aspen)
J **Wilkerson** (Belmont Shore)
R **Lumkong** (Pontypridd, Wales)
R **Tardits** (Life College, Georgia)

TOUR DETAILS
All matches: Played 3   Won 1   Lost 2   Points for 44   Against 86
International matches: Played 1   Lost 1   Points for 14   Against 34

SCORING DETAILS

All matches					International matches				
For:	5T	2C	5PG	44 Pts	For:	1T	0C	3PG	14 Pts
Against:	12T	7C	4PG	86 Pts	Against:	4T	4C	2PG	34 Pts

MATCH DETAILS

1997	Opponents	Venue	Result
1 Jan	Emerging Wales	Cardiff	cancelled
4 Jan	Neath	Cardiff	L 15-39
7 Jan	Pontypridd	Cardiff	W 15-13
11 Jan	WALES	Cardiff	L 14-34

MATCH 1   1 January, National Stadium, Cardiff

Emerging Wales v USA – match cancelled (frozen pitch)

MATCH 2   4 January, National Stadium, Cardiff

Neath 39 (3G 1PG 3T)   **USA 15** (1G 1PG 1T)
Neath: A Flowers; C Higgs, G Evans, J Funnell, J Young; P Williams, P Horgan;
L Gerrard, B Williams, D Morris; M Glover, N Watkins; A Kembury, S Williams
(*capt*), I Boobyer *Replacements:* M Thomas for B Williams (44 mins), D Hawkins
for Horgan (56 mins), R Jones for Kembury (56 mins), G Newman for Boobyer
(64 mins), K Allen for Morris (76 mins)
Scorers *Tries:* Higgs, Horgan, B Williams, S Williams, Allen, Evans
Conversions: P Williams (3)   *Penalty Goal:* P Williams
USA: Morrow; Anitoni, Wikeepa, Scharrenberg, Hightower; Alexander, Bachelet;
Lippert, Billups, LeClerc; Gross, Parker; Lyle (*capt*), Lumkong, Tardits
Replacements R Lehner for Lippert (33 mins), J Wilkerson for Tardits (64 mins)
Scorers *Tries:* Bachelet, Scharrenberg   *Conversion:* Alexander
Penalty Goal: Alexander
Referee J Bacigalupo (Scotland)

MATCH 3   7 January, Cardiff Arms Park, Cardiff

Pontypridd 13 (1PG 2T)   **United States XV 15** (1G 1PG 1T)
Pontypridd: K Morgan; G Wyatt, J Lewis (*capt*), S Enoch, J Lee; J Strange,
M de Maid; N Eynon, J Evans, C Martin; G Prosser, P Owen; M Lloyd,
M Edwards, R Collins *Replacements* A Metcalfe for Edwards (32 mins), P Thomas
for Collins (74 mins), C Cormack for Lewis (78 mins)
Scorers *Tries:* Owen, Wyatt   *Penalty Goal:* Strange
United States XV: Morrow; Curtis, Schram, Williams (*capt*), Hightower; Stevens,
Howard; Lippert, Allen, O'Boyle; Gross, Vogl; Walker, Randell, Wilkerson
Replacements Tardits for Schram (66 mins), Hodges for Randell (78 mins)
Scorers *Tries:* Curtis, Tardits   *Conversion:* Williams   *Penalty Goal:* Williams
Referre S Piercey (England)

MATCH 4   11 January, Cardiff Arms Park, Cardiff Test Match
WALES 34 (4G 2PG)   **UNITED STATES 14** (3PG 1T)

WALES: W J L Thomas (Cardiff); I C Evans (Llanelli), A G Bateman
(Richmond), I S Gibbs (Swansea) (*capt*), G Thomas (Bridgend); A C Thomas
(Swansea), R Howley (Cardiff); C D Loader (Swansea), G R Jenkins (Swansea),
D Young (Cardiff); G O Llewellyn (Harlequins), M Rowley (Pontypridd);
S M Williams (Neath), L S Quinnell (Richmond), C Charvis (Swansea)
Replacements J Davies (Cardiff) for Gibbs (temporary 67 to 71 mins), J C Quinnell
(Richmond) for Rowley (71 mins), R G Jones (Cardiff) for Charvis (74 mins),
P John (Pontypridd) for Howley (76 mins)
Scorers *Tries:* Evans (2), Gibbs, pen try   *Conversions:* A Thomas (4)
Penalty Goals: A Thomas (2)
UNITED STATES: Williams; Anitoni, Tardits, Scharrenberg, Hightower;
Alexander, Bachelet; Lehner, Billups, LeClerc; Vogl, Parker; Lyle (*capt*), Lumkong,
Wilkerson *Replacement* Morrow for Williams (60 mins)
Scorers *Try:* Bachelet   *Penalty Goals:* Alexander (3)
Referee L Mayne (Ireland)

WELSH INTERNATIONAL PLAYERS
(up to 30 April 1997)

Note: Years given for Five Nations' matches are for second half of season; eg 1972 means season 1971-72. Years for all other matches refer to the actual year of the match. When a series has taken place, figures have been used to denote the particular matches in which players have featured. Thus 1969 *NZ 2* indicates that a player appeared in the second Test of the series.

Ackerman, R A (Newport, London Welsh) 1980 *NZ,* 1981 *E, S, A,* 1982 *I, F, E, S,* 1983 *S, I, F, R,* 1984 *S, I, F, E, A,* 1985 *S, I, F, E, Fj*
Alexander, E P (Llandovery Coll, Cambridge U) 1885 *S,* 1886 *E, S,* 1887 *E, I*
Alexander, W H (Llwynypia) 1898 *I, E,* 1899 *E, S, I,* 1901 *S, I*
Allen, A G (Newbridge) 1990 *F, E, I*
Allen, C P (Oxford U, Beaumaris) 1884 *E, S*
Andrews, F (Pontypool) 1912 *SA,* 1913 *E, S, I*
Andrews, F G (Swansea) 1884 *E, S*
Andrews, G E (Newport) 1926 *E, S,* 1927 *E, F, I*
Anthony, L (Neath) 1948 *E, S, F*
Arnold, P (Swansea) 1990 *Nm* 1, 2, *Bb,* 1991 *E, S, I, F* 1, *A,* [*Arg, A*], 1993 *F* (R), *Z* 2, 1994 *Sp, Fj,* 1995 *SA,* 1996 *Bb* (R)
Arnold, W R (Swansea) 1903 *S*
Arthur, C S (Cardiff) 1888 *I, M,* 1891 *E*
Arthur, T (Neath) 1927 *S, F, I,* 1929 *E, S, F, I,* 1930 *E, S, I, F,* 1931 *E, S, F, I, SA,* 1933 *E, S*
Ashton, C (Aberavon) 1959 *E, S, I,* 1960 *E, S, I,* 1962 *I*
Attewell, S L (Newport) 1921 *E, S, F*

Back, M J (Bridgend) 1995 *F* (R), *E* (R), *S, I*
Badger, O (Llanelli) 1895 *E, S, I,* 1896 *E*
Baker, A (Neath) 1921 *I,* 1923 *E, S, F, I*
Baker, A M (Newport) 1909 *S, F,* 1910 *S*
Bancroft, J (Swansea) 1909 *E, S, F, I,* 1910 *F, E, S, I,* 1911 *E, F, I,* 1912 *E, S, I,* 1913 *I,* 1914 *E, S, F*
Bancroft, W J (Swansea) 1890 *S, E, I,* 1891 *E, S, I,* 1892 *E, S, I,* 1893 *E, S, I,* 1894 *E, S, I,* 1895 *E, S, I,* 1896 *E, S, I,* 1897 *E,* 1898 *I, E,* 1899 *E, S, I,* 1900 *E, S, I,* 1901 *E, S, I*
Barlow, T M (Cardiff) 1884 *I*
Barrell, R J (Cardiff) 1929 *S, F, I,* 1933 *I*
Bartlett, J D (Llanelli) 1927 *S,* 1928 *E, S*
Bassett, A (Cardiff) 1934 *I,* 1935 *E, S, I,* 1938 *E, S*
Bassett, J A (Penarth) 1929 *E, S, F, I,* 1930 *E, S, I,* 1931 *E, S, F, I, SA,* 1932 *E, S, I*
Bateman, A G (Neath, Richmond) 1990 *S, I, Nm* 1,2, 1996 *SA,* 1997 *US, S, F, E*
Bayliss, G (Pontypool) 1933 *S*
Bebb, D I E (Carmarthen TC, Swansea) 1959 *E, S, I, F,* 1960 *E, S, I, F, SA,* 1961 *E, S, I, F,* 1962 *E, S, F, I,* 1963 *E, F, NZ,* 1964 *E, S, F, SA,* 1965 *E, S, I, F,* 1966 *F, A,* 1967 *S, I, F, E*
Beckingham, G (Cardiff) 1953 *E, S,* 1958 *F*
Bennett, A M (Cardiff) 1995 [*NZ*] *SA, Fj*
Bennett, I (Aberavon) 1937 *I*
Bennett, P (Cardiff Harlequins) 1891 *E, S,* 1892 *S, I*
Bennett, P (Llanelli) 1969 *F* (R), 1970 *SA, S, F,* 1972 *S* (R), *NZ,* 1973 *S, I, F, A,* 1974 *S, I, F, E,* 1975 *S* (R), *I,* 1976 *E, S, I, F,* 1977 *I, F, E, S,* 1978 *E, S, I, F*
Bergiers, R T E (Cardiff Coll of Ed, Llanelli) 1972 *E, S, F, NZ,* 1973 *E, S, I, F, A,* 1974 *E,* 1975 *I*
Bevan, G W (Llanelli) 1947 *E*
Bevan, J A (Cambridge U) 1881 *E*
Bevan, J C (Cardiff, Cardiff Coll of Ed) 1971 *E, S, I, F,* 1972 *E, S, F, NZ,* 1973 *E, S*
Bevan, J D (Aberavon) 1975 *F, E, S, A*
Bevan, S (Swansea) 1904 *I*
Beynon, B (Swansea) 1920 *E, S*
Beynon, G E (Swansea) 1925 *F, I*
Bidgood, R A (Newport) 1992 *S,* 1993 *Z* 1,2, *Nm, J* (R)
Biggs, N W (Cardiff) 1888 *M,* 1889 *I,* 1892 *I,* 1893 *E, S, I,* 1894 *E, I*
Biggs, S H (Cardiff) 1895 *E, S,* 1896 *S,* 1897 *E,* 1898 *I, E,* 1899 *S, I,* 1900 *I*
Birch, J (Neath) 1911 *S, F*
Birt, F W (Newport) 1911 *E, S,* 1912 *E, S, I, F, SA,* 1913 *E*
Bishop, D J (Pontypool) 1984 *A*
Bishop, E H (Swansea) 1889 *S*

Blackmore, J H (Abertillery) 1909 *E*
Blackmore, S W (Cardiff) 1987 *I,* [*Tg* (R), *C, A*]
Blake, J (Cardiff) 1899 *E, S, I,* 1900 *E, S, I,* 1901 *E, S, I*
Blakemore, R E (Newport) 1947 *E*
Bland, A F (Cardiff) 1887 *E, S, I,* 1888 *S, I, M,* 1890 *S, E, I*
Blyth, L (Swansea) 1951 *SA,* 1952 *E, S*
Blyth, W R (Swansea) 1974 *E,* 1975 *S* (R), 1980 *F, E, S, I*
Boobyer, N (Llanelli) 1993 *Z* 1 (R), 2, *Nm,* 1994 *Fj, Tg*
Boon, R W (Cardiff) 1930 *S, F,* 1931 *E, S, F, I, SA,* 1932 *E, S, I,* 1933 *E, I*
Booth, J (Pontymister) 1898 *I*
Boots, J G (Newport) 1898 *I, E,* 1899 *I,* 1900 *E, S, I,* 1901 *E, S, I,* 1902 *E, S, I,* 1903 *E, S, I,* 1904 *E*
Boucher, A W (Newport) 1892 *E, S, I,* 1893 *E, S, I,* 1894 *E,* 1895 *E, S, I,* 1896 *E, I,* 1897 *E*
Bowcott, H M (Cardiff, Cambridge U) 1929 *S, F, I,* 1930 *E,* 1931 *E, S,* 1933 *E, I*
Bowdler, F A (Cross Keys) 1927 *A,* 1928 *E, S, I, F,* 1929 *E, S, F, I,* 1930 *E,* 1931 *SA,* 1932 *E, S, I,* 1933 *I*
Bowen, B (S Wales Police, Swansea) 1983 *R,* 1984 *S, I, F, E,* 1985 *Fj,* 1986 *E, S, I, F, Fj, Tg, WS,* 1987 [*C, E, NZ*], *US,* 1988 *E, S, I, F, WS,* 1989 *S, I*
Bowen, C A (Llanelli) 1896 *E, S, I,* 1897 *E*
Bowen, D H (Llanelli) 1883 *E,* 1886 *E, S,* 1887 *E*
Bowen, G E (Swansea) 1887 *S, I,* 1888 *S, I*
Bowen, W (Swansea) 1921 *S, F,* 1922 *E, S, I, F*
Bowen, Wm A (Swansea) 1886 *E, S,* 1887 *E, S, I,* 1888 *M,* 1889 *S, I,* 1890 *S, E, I,* 1891 *E, S*
Brace, D O (Llanelli, Oxford U) 1956 *E, S, I, F,* 1957 *E,* 1960 *S, I, F,* 1961 *I*
Braddock, K J (Newbridge) 1966 *A,* 1967 *S, I*
Bradshaw, K (Bridgend) 1964 *E, S, I, F, SA,* 1966 *E, S, I, F*
Brewer, T J (Newport) 1950 *E,* 1955 *E, S*
Brice, A B (Aberavon) 1899 *E, S, I,* 1900 *E, S, I,* 1901 *E, S, I,* 1902 *E, S, I,* 1903 *E, S, I,* 1904 *E, S, I*
Bridges, C J (Neath) 1990 *Nm* 1,2, *Bb,* 1991 *E* (R), *I, F* 1, *A*
Bridie, R H (Newport) 1882 *I*
Britton, G R (Newport) 1961 *S*
Broughton, A S (Treorchy) 1927 *A,* 1929 *S*
Brown, A (Newport) 1921 *I*
Brown, J (Cardiff) 1925 *I*
Brown, J A (Cardiff) 1907 *E, S, I,* 1908 *E, S, F,* 1909 *E*
Brown, M (Pontypool) 1983 *R,* 1986 *E, S, Fj* (R), *Tg, WS*
Bryant, D J (Bridgend) 1988 *NZ* 1,2, *WS, R,* 1989 *S, I, F, E*
Buchanan, A (Llanelli) 1987 [*Tg, E, NZ, A*], 1988 *I*
Buckett, I M (Swansea) 1994 *Tg*
Burcher, D H (Newport) 1977 *I, F, E, S*
Burgess, R C (Ebbw Vale) 1977 *I, F, E, S,* 1981 *I, F,* 1982 *F, E, S*
Burnett, R (Newport) 1953 *E*
Burns, J (Cardiff) 1927 *F, I*
Bush, P F (Cardiff) 1905 *NZ,* 1906 *E, SA,* 1907 *I,* 1908 *E, S,* 1910 *S, I*
Butler, E T (Pontypool) 1980 *F, E, S, I, NZ* (R), 1982 *S,* 1983 *E, S, I, F, R,* 1984 *S, I, F, E, A*

Cale, W R (Newbridge, Pontypool) 1949 *E, S, I,* 1950 *E, S, I, F*
Carter, A J (Newport) 1991 *E, S*
Cattell, A (Llanelli) 1883 *E, S*
Challinor, C (Neath) 1939 *E*
Charvis, C L (Swansea) 1996 *A* 3(R), *SA,* 1997 *US, S, I, F*
Clapp, T J S (Newport) 1882 *I,* 1883 *E, S,* 1884 *E, S, I,* 1885 *E, S,* 1886 *S,* 1887 *E, S, I,* 1888 *S, I*
Clare, J (Cardiff) 1883 *E*
Clark, S S (Neath) 1882 *I,* 1887 *I*
Cleaver, W B (Cardiff) 1947 *E, S, F, I, A,* 1948 *E, S, F, I,* 1949 *I,* 1950 *E, S, I, F*

Clegg, B G (Swansea) 1979 *F*
Clement, A (Swansea) 1987 *US* (R), 1988 *E, NZ* 1, *WS* (R), *R*, 1989 *NZ*, 1990 *S* (R), *I* (R), *Nm* 1,2, 1991 *S* (R), *A* (R), *F* 2, [*WS, A*], 1992 *I, F, E, S*, 1993 *I* (R), *F, J, C*, 1994 *S, I, F, Sp, C* (R), *Tg, WS, It, SA*, 1995 *F, E*, [*J, NZ, I*]
Clement, W H (Llanelli) 1937 *E, S, I*, 1938 *E, S, I*
Cobner, T J (Pontypool) 1974 *S, I, F, E*, 1975 *F, E, S, I, A*, 1976 *E, S*, 1977 *F, E, S*, 1978 *E, S, I, F, A* 1
Coldrick, A P (Newport) 1911 *E, S, I*, 1912 *E, S, F*
Coleman, E (Newport) 1949 *E, S, I*
Coles, F C (Pontypool) 1960 *S, I, F*
Collins, J (Aberavon) 1958 *A, E, S, F*, 1959 *E, S, I, F*, 1960 *E*, 1961 *F*
Collins, R G (S Wales Police, Cardiff, Pontypridd) 1987 *E* (R), *I*, [*I, E, NZ*], *US*, 1988 *E, S, I, F, R*, 1990 *E, S, I*, 1991 *A, F* 2, [*WS*], 1994 *C, Fj, Tg, WS, It, SA*, 1995 *F, E, S, I*
Collins, T (Mountain Ash) 1923 *I*
Conway-Rees, J (Llanelli) 1892 *S*, 1893 *E*, 1894 *E*
Cook, T (Cardiff) 1949 *S, I*
Cope, W (Cardiff, Blackheath) 1896 *S*
Copsey, A H (Llanelli) 1992 *I, F, E, S, A*, 1993 *E, S, I, J, C*, 1994 *E* (R), *Pt, Sp* (R), *Fj, Tg, WS* (R)
Cornish, F H (Cardiff) 1897 *E*, 1898 *I, E*, 1899 *I*
Cornish, R A (Cardiff) 1923 *E, S*, 1924 *E*, 1925 *E, S, F*, 1926 *E, S, I, F*
Coslett, K (Aberavon) 1962 *E, S, F*
Cowey, B T V (Welch Regt, Newport) 1934 *E, S, I*, 1935 *E*
Cresswell, B (Newport) 1960 *E, S, I, F*
Cummins, W (Treorchy) 1922 *E, S, I, F*
Cunningham, L J (Aberavon) 1960 *E, S, I, F*, 1962 *E, S, F, I*, 1963 *NZ*, 1964 *E, S, I, F, SA*

Dacey, M (Swansea) 1983 *E, S, I, F, R*, 1984 *S, I, F, E, A*, 1986 *Fj, Tg, WS*, 1987 *F* (R), [*Tg*]
Daniel, D J (Llanelli) 1891 *S*, 1894 *E, S, I*, 1898 *I, E*, 1899 *E, I*
Daniel, L T D (Newport) 1970 *S*
Daniels, P C T (Cardiff) 1981 *A*, 1982 *I*
Darbishire, G (Bangor) 1881 *E*
Dauncey, F H (Newport) 1896 *E, S, I*
Davey, C (Swansea) 1930 *F*, 1931 *E, S, F, I, SA*, 1932 *E, S, I*, 1933 *E, S*, 1934 *E, S, I*, 1935 *E, S, I, NZ*, 1936 *S*, 1937 *E, I*, 1938 *E, I*
David, R J (Cardiff) 1907 *I*
David, T P (Llanelli, Pontypridd) 1973 *F, A*, 1976 *I, F*
Davidge, G D (Newport) 1959 *F*, 1960 *S, I, F, SA*, 1961 *E, S, I*, 1962 *F*
Davies, A (Cambridge U, Neath, Cardiff) 1990 *Bb* (R), 1991 *A*, 1993 *Z* 1,2, *J, C*, 1994 *Fj*, 1995 [*J, I*]
Davies, A C (London Welsh) 1889 *I*
Davies, A E (Llanelli) 1984 *A*
Davies, B (Llanelli) 1895 *E*, 1896 *E*
Davies, C (Cardiff) 1947 *S, F, I, A*, 1948 *E, S, F, I*, 1949 *F*, 1950 *E, S, I, F*, 1951 *E, S, I*
Davies, C H A (Llanelli, Cardiff) 1957 *I*, 1958 *A, E, S, I*, 1960 *SA*, 1961 *F*
Davies, C L (Cardiff) 1956 *E, S, I*
Davies, C R (Bedford, RAF) 1934 *E*
Davies, D (Bridgend) 1921 *I*, 1925 *I*
Davies, D B (Llanelli) 1907 *E*
Davies, D B (Llanelli) 1962 *I*, 1963 *E, S*
Davies, D G (Cardiff) 1923 *E, S*
Davies, D H (Neath) 1904 *S*
Davies, D H (Aberavon) 1924 *E*
Davies, D I (Swansea) 1939 *E*
Davies, D J (Neath) 1962 *I*
Davies, D M (Somerset Police) 1950 *E, S, I, F*, 1951 *E, S, I, F, SA*, 1952 *E, S, I, F*, 1953 *I, F, NZ*, 1954 *E*
Davies, E (Aberavon) 1947 *A*, 1948 *I*
Davies, E (Maesteg) 1919 *NZA*
Davies, E G (Cardiff) 1912 *E, F*
Davies, E G (Cardiff) 1928 *F*, 1929 *E*, 1930 *S*
Davies, G (Swansea) 1900 *E, S, I*, 1901 *E, S, I*, 1905 *E, S, I*
Davies, G (Cambridge U, Pontypridd) 1947 *S, A*, 1948 *E, S, F, I*, 1949 *E, S, F, I*, 1951 *E, S*
Davies, G (Llanelli) 1921 *F, I*, 1925 *F*
Davies, H (Swansea) 1898 *I, E*, 1901 *S, I*
Davies, H (Swansea, Llanelli) 1939 *S, I*, 1947 *E, S, F, I*
Davies, H (Neath) 1912 *E, S*
Davies, H (Bridgend) 1984 *S, I, F, E*
Davies, H J (Cambridge U, Aberavon) 1959 *E, S*

Davies, H J (Newport) 1924 *S*
Davies, I T (Llanelli) 1914 *S, F, I*
Davies, J (Neath, Llanelli, Cardiff) 1985 *E, Fj*, 1986 *E, S, I, F, Fj, Tg, WS*, 1987 *F, E, S, I*, [*I, Tg* (R), *C, E, NZ, A*], 1988 *E, S, I, F, NZ* 1,2, *WS, R*, 1996 *NZ* A 3, 1997 *US* (t), *S* (R), *F* (R), *E*
Davies, Rev J A (Swansea) 1913 *S, F, I*, 1914 *E, S, F, I*
Davies, J D (Neath) 1991 *I, F* 1, 1993 *F* (R), *Z* 2, *J, C*, 1994 *S, I, F, E, Pt, Sp, C, WS, R, It, SA*, 1995 *F, E*, [*J, NZ, I*] *SA*, 1996 *It, E, S, I, F* 1, *A* 1, *Bb, F* 2, *It*
Davies, J H (Aberavon) 1923 *I*
Davies, J (Swansea) 1939 *S, I*
Davies, L (Bridgend) 1966 *E, S, I*
Davies, L B (Neath, Cardiff) 1996 *It, E, S, I, F* 1, *A* 1, *Bb, F* 2, *It* (R)
Davies, L M (Llanelli) 1954 *F, S*, 1955 *I*
Davies, M (Swansea) 1981 *A*, 1982 *I*, 1985 *Fj*
Davies, M J (Blackheath) 1939 *S, I*
Davies, N G (London Welsh) 1955 *E*
Davies, N G (Llanelli) 1988 *NZ* 2, *WS*, 1989 *S, I*, 1993 *F*, 1994 *S, I, E, Pt, Sp, C, Fj, Tg* (R), *WS, R, It*, 1995 *E, S, I, Fj*, 1996 *E, S, I, F* 1, *A* 1,2, *Bb, F* 2, 1997 *E*
Davies, P T (Llanelli) 1985 *E, Fj*, 1986 *E, S, I, F, Fj, Tg, WS*, 1987 *F, E, I*, [*Tg, C, NZ*], 1988 *WS, R*, 1989 *S, I, F, E, NZ*, 1990 *F, E, S*, 1991 *I, F* 1, *A, F* 2, [*WS, Arg, A*], 1993 *F, Z* 1, *Nm*, 1994 *S, I, F, E, C, Fj* (R), *WS, R, It*, 1995 *F, I*
Davies, R H (Oxford U, London Welsh) 1957 *S, I, F*, 1958 *A*, 1962 *E, S*
Davies, S (Treherbert) 1923 *I*
Davies, S (Swansea) 1992 *I, F, E, S, A*, 1993 *E, S, I, Z* 1 (R), 2, *Nm, J*, 1995 *F*, [*J, I*]
Davies, T G R (Cardiff, London Welsh) 1966 *A*, 1967 *S, I, F, E*, 1968 *E, S*, 1969 *S, I, F, NZ* 1,2, *A*, 1971 *E, S, I, F*, 1972 *E, S, F, NZ*, 1973 *E, S, I, F, A*, 1974 *S, F, E*, 1975 *F, E, S, I*, 1976 *E, S, I, F*, 1977 *I, F, E, S*, 1978 *E, S*
Davies, T J (Devonport Services, Swansea, Llanelli) 1953 *E, S, I, F*, 1957 *E, S, I, F*, 1958 *A, E, S, F*, 1959 *E, S, I, F*, 1960 *E, SA*, 1961 *E, S, F*
Davies, T M (London Welsh, Swansea) 1969 *S, I, F, E, NZ* 1,2, *A*, 1970 *SA, S, E, I, F*, 1971 *E, S, I, F*, 1972 *E, S, F, NZ*, 1973 *E, S, I, F, A*, 1974 *S, I, F, E*, 1975 *F, E, S, I, A*, 1976 *E, S, I, F*
Davies, W (Cardiff) 1896 *S*
Davies, W (Swansea) 1931 *SA*, 1932 *E, S, I*
Davies, W A (Aberavon) 1912 *S, I*
Davies, W G (Cardiff) 1978 *A* 1,2, *NZ*, 1979 *S, I, F, E*, 1980 *F, E, S, NZ*, 1981 *E, S, A*, 1982 *I, F, E, S*, 1985 *S, I, F*
Davies, W T H (Swansea) 1936 *I*, 1937 *E, I*, 1939 *E, S, I*
Davis, C E (Newbridge) 1978 *A* 2, 1981 *E, S*
Davis, M (Newport) 1991 *A*
Davis, W E N (Cardiff) 1939 *E, S, I*
Dawes, S J (London Welsh) 1964 *I, F, SA*, 1965 *E, S, I, F*, 1966 *A*, 1968 *I, F*, 1969 *E, NZ* 2, *A*, 1970 *SA, S, E, I, F*, 1971 *E, S, I, F*
Day, H C (Newport) 1930 *S, I, F*, 1931 *E, S*
Day, H T (Newport) 1892 *I*, 1893 *E, S*, 1894 *S, I*
Day, T B (Swansea) 1931 *E, S, F, I, SA*, 1932 *E, S, I*, 1934 *S, I*, 1935 *E, S, I*
Deacon, J T (Swansea) 1891 *I*, 1892 *E, S, I*
Delahay, W J (Bridgend) 1922 *E, S, I, F*, 1923 *E, S, F, I*, 1924 *NZ*, 1925 *E, S, F, I*, 1926 *E, S, I, F*, 1927 *S*
Delaney, L (Llanelli) 1989 *I, F, E*, 1990 *E*, 1991 *F* 2, [*WS, Arg, A*], 1992 *I, F, E*
Devereux, D (Neath) 1958 *A, E, S*
Devereux, J A (S Glamorgan Inst, Bridgend) 1986 *E, S, I, F, Fj, Tg, WS*, 1987 *F, E, S, I*, [*I, C, E, NZ, A*], 1988 *NZ* 1,2, *R*, 1989 *S, I*
Diplock, R (Bridgend) 1988 *R*
Dobson, G (Cardiff) 1900 *S*
Dobson, T (Cardiff) 1898 *I, E*, 1899 *E, S*
Donovan, A J (Swansea) 1978 *A* 2, 1981 *I* (R), *A*, 1982 *E, S*
Donovan, R (S Wales Police) 1983 *F* (R)
Douglas, M H J (Llanelli) 1984 *S, I, F*
Douglas, W M (Cardiff) 1886 *E, S*, 1887 *E, S*
Dowell, W H (Newport) 1907 *E, S, I*, 1908 *E, S, F, I*
Dyke, J C M (Penarth) 1906 *SA*
Dyke, L M (Penarth, Cardiff) 1910 *I*, 1911 *S, F, I*

Edmunds, D A (Neath) 1990 *I* (R), *Bb*
Edwards, A B (London Welsh, Army) 1955 *E, S*
Edwards, B O (Newport) 1951 *I*
Edwards, D (Glynneath) 1921 *E*

Edwards, G O (Cardiff, Cardiff Coll of Ed) 1967 *F, E, NZ,* 1968 *E, S, I, F,* 1969 *S, I, F, E, NZ* 1,2, *A,* 1970 *SA, S, E, I, F,* 1971 *E, S, I, F,* 1972 *E, S, F, NZ,* 1973 *E, S, I, F, A,* 1974 *S, I, F, E,* 1975 *F, E, S, I, A,* 1976 *E, S, I, F,* 1977 *I, F, E, S,* 1978 *E, S, I, F*
Eidman, I H (Cardiff) 1983 *S, R,* 1984 *I, F, E, A,* 1985 *S, I, Fj,* 1986 *E, S, I, F*
Elliott, J E (Cardiff) 1894 *I,* 1898 *I, E*
Elsey, W J (Cardiff) 1895 *E*
Emyr, Arthur (Swansea) 1989 *E, NZ,* 1990 *F, E, S, I, Nm* 1,2, 1991 *F* 1,2, *[WS, Arg, A]*
Evans, A (Pontypool) 1924 *E, I, F*
Evans, B (Swansea) 1933 *S*
Evans, B (Llanelli) 1933 *E, S,* 1936 *E, S, I,* 1937 *E*
Evans, B S (Llanelli) 1920 *E,* 1922 *E, S, I, F*
Evans, C (Pontypool) 1960 *E*
Evans, D (Penygraig) 1896 *S, I,* 1897 *E,* 1898 *E*
Evans, D B (Swansea) 1926 *E*
Evans, D D (Cheshire, Cardiff U) 1934 *E*
Evans, D P (Llanelli) 1960 *SA*
Evans, D W (Cardiff) 1889 *S, I,* 1890 *E, I,* 1891 *E*
Evans, D W (Oxford U, Cardiff, Treorchy) 1989 *F, E, NZ,* 1990 *F, E, S, I, Bb,* 1991 *A* (R), *F* 2 (R), *[A* (R)], 1995 *[J* (R)]
Evans, E (Llanelli) 1937 *E,* 1939 *S, I*
Evans, F (Llanelli) 1921 *S*
Evans, G (Cardiff) 1947 *E, S, F, I, A,* 1948 *E, S, F, I,* 1949 *E, S, I*
Evans, G (Maesteg) 1981 *S* (R), *I, F, A,* 1982 *I, F, E, S,* 1983 *F, R*
Evans, G L (Newport) 1977 *F* (R), 1978 *F, A* 2 (R)
Evans, I (London Welsh) 1934 *S, I*
Evans, I (Swansea) 1922 *E, S, I, F*
Evans, I C (Llanelli) 1987 *F, E, S, I, [I, C, E, NZ, A],* 1988 *E, S, I, F, NZ* 1,2, 1989 *I, F, E,* 1991 *E, S, I, F* 1, *A, F* 2, *[WS, Arg, A],* 1992 *I, F, E, S, A,* 1993 *E, S, I, F, J, C,* 1994 *S, I, E, Pt, Sp, C, Fj, Tg, WS, R,* 1995 *E, S, I, [J, NZ, I], SA, Fj,* 1996 *It, E, S, I, F* 1, *A* 1,2, *Bb, F* 2, *A* 3, *SA,* 1997 *US, S, I, F*
Evans, I L (Llanelli) 1991 *F* 2 (R)
Evans, J (Llanelli) 1896 *S, I,* 1897 *E*
Evans, J (Blaina) 1904 *E*
Evans, J (Pontypool) 1907 *E, S, I*
Evans, J D (Cardiff) 1958 *I, F*
Evans, J E (Llanelli) 1924 *S*
Evans, J R (Newport) 1934 *E*
Evans, O J (Cardiff) 1887 *E, S,* 1888 *S, I*
Evans, P D (Llanelli) 1951 *E, F*
Evans, R (Cardiff) 1889 *S*
Evans, R (Bridgend) 1963 *S, I, F*
Evans, R L (Llanelli) 1993 *E, S, I, F,* 1994 *S, I, F, E, Pt, Sp, C, Fj, WS, R, It, SA,* 1995 *F, [NZ, I* (R)]
Evans, R T (Newport) 1947 *F, I,* 1950 *E, S, I, F,* 1951 *E, S, I, F*
Evans, S (Swansea, Neath) 1985 *F, E,* 1986 *Fj, Tg, WS,* 1987 *F, E, [I, Tg]*
Evans, T (Swansea) 1924 *I*
Evans, T G (London Welsh) 1970 *SA, S, E, I,* 1972 *E, S, F*
Evans, T H (Llanelli) 1906 *I,* 1907 *E, S, I,* 1908 *I, A,* 1909 *E, S, F, I,* 1910 *F, E, S, I,* 1911 *E, S, F, I*
Evans, T P (Swansea) 1975 *F, E, S, I, A,* 1976 *E, S, I, F,* 1977 *I*
Evans, V (Neath) 1954 *I, F, S*
Evans, W (Llanelli) 1958 *A*
Evans, W F (Rhymney) 1882 *I,* 1883 *S*
Evans, W G (Brynmawr) 1911 *I*
Evans, W H (Llwynypia) 1914 *E, S, F, I*
Evans, W J (Pontypool) 1947 *S*
Evans, W R (Bridgend) 1958 *A, E, S, I, F,* 1960 *SA,* 1961 *E, S, I, F,* 1962 *E, S, I*
Everson, W A (Newport) 1926 *S*

Faulkner, A G (Pontypool) 1975 *F, E, S, I, A,* 1976 *E, S, I, F,* 1978 *E, S, I, F, A* 1,2, *NZ,* 1979 *S, I, F*
Faull, J (Swansea) 1957 *I, F,* 1958 *A, E, S, I, F,* 1959 *E, S, I,* 1960 *E, F*
Fauvel, T J (Aberavon) 1988 *NZ* 1 (R)
Fear, A G (Newport) 1934 *S, I,* 1935 *S, I*
Fender, N H (Cardiff) 1930 *I, F,* 1931 *E, S, F, I*
Fenwick, S P (Bridgend) 1975 *F, E, S, A,* 1976 *E, S, I, F,* 1977 *I, F, E, S,* 1978 *E, S, I, F, A* 1,2, *NZ,* 1979 *S, I, F, E,* 1980 *F, E, S, I, NZ,* 1981 *E, S*
Finch, E (Llanelli) 1924 *F, NZ,* 1925 *F, I,* 1926 *F,* 1927 *A,* 1928 *I*

Finlayson, A A J (Cardiff) 1974 *I, F, E*
Fitzgerald, D (Cardiff) 1894 *S, I*
Ford, F J V (Welch Regt, Newport) 1939 *E*
Ford, I (Newport) 1959 *E, S*
Ford, S P (Cardiff) 1990 *I, Nm* 1,2, *Bb,* 1991 *E, S, I, A*
Forward, A (Pontypool, Mon Police) 1951 *S, SA,* 1952 *E, S, I, F*
Fowler, I J (Llanelli) 1919 *NZA*
Francis, D G (Llanelli) 1919 *NZA,* 1924 *S*
Francis, P (Maesteg) 1987 *S*

Gabe, R T (Cardiff, Llanelli) 1901 *I,* 1902 *E, S, I,* 1903 *E, S, I,* 1904 *E, S, I,* 1905 *E, S, I, NZ,* 1906 *E, I, SA,* 1907 *E, S, I,* 1908 *E, S, F, I*
Gale, N R (Swansea, Llanelli) 1960 *I,* 1963 *E, S, I, NZ,* 1964 *E, S, I, F, SA,* 1965 *E, S, I, F,* 1966 *E, S, I, F, A,* 1967 *E, NZ,* 1968 *E,* 1969 *NZ* 1 (R), 2, *A*
Gallacher, I S (Llanelli) 1970 *F*
Garrett, R M (Penarth) 1888 *M,* 1889 *S,* 1890 *S, E, I,* 1891 *S, I,* 1892 *E*
Geen, W P (Oxford U, Newport) 1912 *SA,* 1913 *E, I*
George, E E (Pontypridd, Cardiff) 1895 *S, I,* 1896 *E*
George, G M (Newport) 1991 *E, S*
Gething, G I (Neath) 1913 *F*
Gibbs, A (Newbridge) 1995 *I, SA,* 1996 *A* 2
Gibbs, I S (Neath, Swansea) 1991 *E, S, I, F* 1, *A, F* 2, *[WS, Arg, A],* 1992 *I, F, E, S, A,* 1993 *E, S, I, F, J, C,* 1996 *It, A* 3, *SA,* 1997 *US, S, I, F*
Gibbs, R A (Cardiff) 1906 *S, I,* 1907 *E, S,* 1908 *E, S, F, I,* 1910 *F, E, S, I,* 1911 *E, S, F, I*
Giles, R (Aberavon) 1983 *R,* 1985 *Fj* (R), 1987 *[C]*
Girling, B E (Cardiff) 1881 *E*
Goldsworthy, S J (Swansea) 1884 *I,* 1885 *E, S*
Gore, J H (Blaina) 1924 *I, F, NZ,* 1925 *E*
Gore, W (Newbridge) 1947 *S, F, I*
Gould, A J (Newport) 1885 *E, S,* 1886 *E, S,* 1887 *E, S, I,* 1888 *S,* 1889 *I,* 1890 *S, E, I,* 1892 *E, S, I,* 1893 *E, S, I,* 1894 *E, S,* 1895 *E, S, I,* 1896 *E, S, I,* 1897 *E*
Gould, G H (Newport) 1892 *I,* 1893 *S, I*
Gould, R (Newport) 1882 *I,* 1883 *E, S,* 1884 *E, S, I,* 1885 *E, S,* 1886 *E,* 1887 *E, S*
Graham, T C (Newport) 1890 *I,* 1891 *S, I,* 1892 *E, S,* 1893 *E, S, I,* 1894 *E, S,* 1895 *E, S*
Gravell, R W R (Llanelli) 1975 *F, E, S, I, A,* 1976 *E, S, I, F,* 1978 *E, S, I, F, A* 1,2, *NZ,* 1979 *S, I,* 1981 *I, F,* 1982 *F, E, S*
Gray, A J (London Welsh) 1968 *E, S*
Greenslade, D (Newport) 1962 *S*
Greville, H G (Llanelli) 1947 *A*
Griffin, Dr J (Edinburgh U) 1883 *S*
Griffiths, C (Llanelli) 1979 *E* (R)
Griffiths, D (Llanelli) 1888 *M,* 1889 *I*
Griffiths, G (Llanelli) 1889 *I*
Griffiths, G M (Cardiff) 1953 *E, S, I, F, NZ,* 1954 *I, F, S,* 1955 *I, F,* 1957 *E, S*
Griffiths, J L (Llanelli) 1988 *NZ* 2, 1989 *S*
Griffiths, M (Bridgend, Cardiff) 1988 *WS, R,* 1989 *S, I, F, E, NZ,* 1990 *F, E, Nm* 1,2, *Bb,* 1991 *I, F* 1,2, *[WS, Arg, A],* 1992 *I, F, E, S, A,* 1993 *Z* 1,2, *Nm, J, C,* 1995 *F* (R), *E, S, I, [J, I]*
Griffiths, V M (Newport) 1924 *S, I, F*
Gronow, B (Bridgend) 1910 *F, E, S, I*
Gwilliam, J A (Cambridge U, Newport) 1947 *A,* 1948 *I, 1949 E, S, F,* 1950 *E, S, I, F,* 1951 *E, S, I, SA,* 1952 *E, S, I, F,* 1953 *E, I, F, NZ,* 1954 *E*
Gwynn, D (Swansea) 1883 *E,* 1887 *S,* 1890 *E, I,* 1891 *E, S*
Gwynn, W H (Swansea) 1884 *E, S, I,* 1885 *E, S*

Hadley, A M (Cardiff) 1983 *R,* 1984 *S, I, F, E,* 1985 *F, E, Fj,* 1986 *E, S, I, F, Fj, Tg,* 1987 *S* (R), *I, [I, Tg, C, E, NZ, A], US,* 1988 *E, S, I, F*
Hall, I (Aberavon) 1967 *NZ,* 1970 *SA, S, E,* 1971 *S,* 1974 *S, I, F*
Hall, M R (Cambridge U, Bridgend, Cardiff) 1988 *NZ* 1 (R), 2, 1989 *S, I, F, E, NZ,* 1990 *F, E, S,* 1991 *A, F* 2, *[WS, Arg, A],* 1992 *I, F, E, S, A,* 1993 *E, S, I,* 1994 *S, I, F, E, Pt, Sp, C, Tg, R, It, SA,* 1995 *F, S, I, [J, NZ, I]*
Hall, W H (Bridgend) 1988 *WS*
Hancock, F E (Cardiff) 1884 *I,* 1885 *E, S,* 1886 *S*
Hannan, J (Newport) 1888 *M,* 1889 *S, I,* 1890 *S, E, I,* 1891 *E,* 1892 *E, S, I,* 1893 *E, S, I,* 1894 *E, S, I,* 1895 *E, S, I*
Harding, A F (London Welsh) 1902 *E, S, I,* 1903 *E, S, I,* 1904 *E, S, I,* 1905 *E, S, I, NZ,* 1906 *E, S, I, SA,* 1907 *I,* 1908 *E, S*

Ieuan Evans beats Rowen Shepherd and Kenny Logan to score the fourth Welsh try in their 34-19 victory over Scotland at Murrayfield.

Jenkin, A M (Swansea) 1895 *I*, 1896 *E*
Jenkins, A (Llanelli) 1920 *E, S, F, I*, 1921 *S, F*, 1922 *F*, 1923 *E, S, F, I*, 1924 *NZ*, 1928 *S, I*
Jenkins, D M (Treorchy) 1926 *E, S, I, F*
Jenkins, D R (Swansea) 1927 *A*, 1929 *E*
Jenkins, E (Newport) 1910 *S, I*
Jenkins, E M (Aberavon) 1927 *S, F, I, A*, 1928 *E, S, I, F*, 1929 *F*, 1930 *E, S, I, F*, 1931 *E, S, F, I, SA*, 1932 *E, S, I*
Jenkins, G R (Pontypool, Swansea) 1991 *F* 2, [*WS* (R), *Arg, A*], 1992 *I, F, E, S, A*, 1993 *C*, 1994 *S, I, F, E, Pt, Sp, C, Tg, WS, R, It, SA*, 1995 *F, E, S, I*, [*J*], *SA* (R), *Fj* (t), 1996 *E* (R), 1997 *US*
Jenkins, J C (London Welsh) 1906 *SA*
Jenkins, J L (Aberavon) 1923 *S, F*
Jenkins, L H (Mon TC, Newport) 1954 *I*, 1956 *E, S, I, F*
Jenkins, N R (Pontypridd) 1991 *E, S, I, F* 1, 1992 *I, F, E, S*, 1993 *E, S, I, F, Z* 1,2, *Nm, J, C*, 1994 *S, I, F, E, Pt, Sp, C, Tg, WS, R, It, SA*, 1995 *F, E, S, I*, [*J, NZ, I*], *SA, Fj*, 1996 *F* 1, *A* 1,2, *Bb, F* 2, *It, A* 3(R), *SA*, 1997 *US*, *S* (R)
Jenkins, V G J (Oxford U, Bridgend, London Welsh) 1933 *E, I*, 1934 *S, I*, 1935 *E, S, NZ*, 1936 *E, S, I*, 1937 *E*, 1938 *E, S*, 1939 *E*
Jenkins, W (Cardiff) 1912 *I, F*, 1913 *S, I*
John, B (Llanelli, Cardiff) 1966 *A*, 1967 *S, NZ*, 1968 *E, S, I, F*, 1969 *S, I, F, E, NZ* 1,2, *A*, 1970 *SA, S, E, I*, 1971 *E, S, I, F*, 1972 *E, S, F*
John, D A (Llanelli) 1925 *I*, 1928 *E, S, I*
John, D E (Llanelli) 1923 *F, I*, 1928 *E, S, I*
John, E R (Neath) 1950 *E, S, I, F*, 1951 *E, S, I, F, SA*, 1952 *E, S, I, F*, 1953 *E, S, I, F, NZ*, 1954 *E, F*
John G (St Luke's Coll, Exeter) 1954 *E, F*
John, J H (Swansea) 1926 *E, S, I, F*, 1927 *E, S, F, I*
John, P (Pontypridd) 1994 *Tg*, 1996 *Bb* (t), 1997 *US* (R)
John, S C (Llanelli) 1995 *S, I*, 1997 *E* (R)
Johnson, T A (Cardiff) 1921 *E, F, I*, 1923 *E, S, F*, 1924 *E, S, NZ*, 1925 *E, S, F*
Johnson, W D (Swansea) 1953 *E*
Jones, A H (Cardiff) 1933 *E, S*
Jones, B (Abertillery) 1914 *E, S, F, I*
Jones, Bert (Llanelli) 1934 *S, I*
Jones, Bob (Llwynypia) 1901 *I*
Jones, B J (Newport) 1960 *I, F*
Jones, B Lewis (Devonport Services, Llanelli) 1950 *E, S, I, F*, 1951 *E, S, SA*, 1952 *E, I, F*
Jones, C W (Cambridge U, Cardiff) 1934 *E, S, I*, 1935 *E, S, I, NZ*, 1936 *E, S, I*, 1938 *E, S, I*
Jones, C W (Bridgend) 1920 *E, S, F*
Jones, D (Neath) 1927 *A*
Jones, D (Aberavon) 1897 *E*
Jones, D (Swansea) 1947 *E, F, I*, 1949 *E, S, I, F*
Jones, D (Treherbert) 1902 *E, S, I*, 1903 *E, S, I*, 1905 *E, S, I, NZ*, 1906 *E, S, NZ*
Jones, D (Newport) 1926 *E, S, I, F*, 1927 *E*
Jones, D (Llanelli) 1948 *E*
Jones, D (Cardiff) 1994 *SA*, 1995 *F, E, S*, [*J, NZ, I*], *SA, Fj*, 1996 *It, E, S, I, F* 1, *A* 1,2, *Bb, It, A* 3
Jones, D K (Llanelli, Cardiff) 1962 *E, S, F, I*, 1963 *E, F, NZ*, 1964 *E, S, SA*, 1966 *E, S, I, F*
Jones, D P (Pontypool) 1907 *I*
Jones, E H (Neath) 1929 *E, S*
Jones, E L (Llanelli) 1930 *F*, 1933 *E, S, I*, 1935 *E*
Jones, Elvet L (Llanelli) 1939 *S*
Jones, G (Ebbw Vale) 1963 *S, I, F*
Jones, G (Llanelli) 1988 *NZ* 2, 1989 *F, E, NZ*, 1990 *F*
Jones, G G (Cardiff) 1930 *S*, 1933 *I*
Jones, G H (Bridgend) 1995 *SA*
Jones, H (Penygraig) 1902 *S, I*
Jones, H (Neath) 1904 *I*
Jones, H (Swansea) 1930 *I, F*
Jones, Iorwerth (Llanelli) 1927 *A*, 1928 *E, S, I, F*
Jones, I C (London Welsh) 1968 *I*
Jones, Ivor E (Llanelli) 1924 *E, S*, 1927 *S, F, I, A*, 1928 *E, S, I, F*, 1929 *E, S, F, I*, 1930 *E, S*
Jones, J (Aberavon) 1901 *E*
Jones, J (Swansea) 1924 *F*
Jones, Jim (Aberavon) 1919 *NZA*, 1920 *E, S*, 1921 *S, F, I*
Jones, J A (Cardiff) 1883 *S*
Jones, J P (Tuan) (Pontypool) 1913 *S*
Jones, J P (Pontypool) 1908 *A*, 1909 *E, S, F, I*, 1910 *F, E*, 1912 *E, F*, 1913 *F, I*, 1920 *F, I*, 1921 *E*
Jones, K D (Cardiff) 1960 *SA*, 1961 *E, S, I*, 1962 *E, F*, 1963 *E, S, I, NZ*
Jones, K J (Newport) 1947 *E, S, F, I, A*, 1948 *E, S, F, I*, 1949 *E, S, I, F*, 1950 *E, S, I, F*, 1951 *E, S, I, F, SA*, 1952

E, S, I, F, 1953 *E, S, I, F, NZ*, 1954 *E, I, F, S*, 1955 *E, S, I, F*, 1956 *E, S, I, F*, 1957 *S*
Jones, K P (Ebbw Vale) 1996 *Bb, F* 2, *It, A* 3, 1997 *I* (R), *E*
Jones, K W J (Oxford U, London Welsh) 1934 *E*
Jones, M A (Neath) 1987 *S*, 1988 *NZ* 2 (R), 1989 *S, I, F, E, NZ*, 1990 *F, E, S, I, Nm* 1,2, *Bb*
Jones, P (Newport) 1912 *SA*, 1913 *E, S, F*, 1914 *E, S, F, I*
Jones, P B (Newport) 1921 *S*
Jones, R (Swansea) 1901 *I*, 1902 *E*, 1904 *E, S, I*, 1905 *E*, 1908 *F, I, A*, 1909 *E, S, F, I*, 1910 *F, E*
Jones, R (London Welsh) 1929 *E*
Jones, R (Northampton) 1926 *E, S, F*
Jones, R (Swansea) 1927 *A*, 1928 *F*
Jones, R B (Cambridge U) 1933 *E, S*
Jones, R E (Coventry) 1967 *F, E*, 1968 *S, I, F*
Jones, R G (Llanelli, Cardiff) 1996 *It, E, S, I, F* 1, *A* 1, 1997 *US* (R), *S* (R)
Jones, R L (Llanelli) 1993 *Z* 1,2, *Nm, J, C*
Jones, R N (Swansea) 1986 *E, S, I, F, Fj, Tg, WS*, 1987 *F, E, S, I, [I, Tg, E, NZ, A], US*, 1988 *E, S, I, F, NZ* 1, *WS, R*, 1989 *I, F, E, NZ*, 1990 *F, E, S, I*, 1991 *E, S, F* 2, [*WS, Arg, A*], 1992 *I, F, E, S, A*, 1993 *E, S, I*, 1994 *I* (R), *Pt*, 1995 *F, E, S, I*, [*NZ, I*]
Jones, S T (Pontypool) 1983 *S, I, F, R*, 1984 *S*, 1988 *E, S, F, NZ* 1,2
Jones, Tom (Newport) 1922 *E, S, I, F*, 1924 *E, S*
Jones, T B (Newport) 1882 *I*, 1883 *E, S*, 1884 *S*, 1885 *E, S*
Jones, W (Cardiff) 1898 *I, E*
Jones, W (Mountain Ash) 1905 *I*
Jones, W I (Llanelli, Cambridge U) 1925 *E, S, F, I*
Jones, W J (Llanelli) 1924 *I*
Jones, W K (Cardiff) 1967 *NZ*, 1968 *E, S, I, F*
Jones-Davies, T E (London Welsh) 1930 *E, I*, 1931 *E, S*
Jordan, H M (Newport) 1885 *E, S*, 1889 *S*
Joseph, W (Swansea) 1902 *E, S, I*, 1903 *E, S, I*, 1904 *E, S*, 1905 *E, S, I, NZ*, 1906 *E, S, I, SA*
Jowett, W F (Swansea) 1903 *E*
Judd, S (Cardiff) 1953 *E, S, I, F, NZ*, 1954 *E, F, S*, 1955 *E, S*
Judson, J H (Llanelli) 1883 *E, S*

Kedzlie, Q D (Cardiff) 1888 *S, I*
Keen, L (Aberavon) 1980 *F, E, S, I*
Knight, P (Pontypridd) 1990 *Nm* 1,2, *Bb* (R), 1991 *E, S*
Knill, F M D (Cardiff) 1976 *F* (R)

Lamerton, A E H (Llanelli) 1993 *F, Z* 1,2, *Nm, J*
Lane, S M (Cardiff) 1978 *A* 1 (R), 2, 1979 *I* (R), 1980 *S, I*
Lang, J (Llanelli) 1931 *F, I*, 1934 *S, I*, 1935 *E, S, I, NZ*, 1936 *E, S, I*, 1937 *E*
Lawrence, S (Bridgend) 1925 *S, I*, 1926 *S, I, F*, 1927 *E*
Law, V J (Newport) 1939 *I*
Legge, W S G (Newport) 1937 *I*, 1938 *I*
Leleu, J (London Welsh, Swansea) 1959 *E, S*, 1960 *F, SA*
Lemon, A (Neath) 1929 *I*, 1930 *S, I, F*, 1931 *E, S, F, I, SA*, 1932 *E, S, I*, 1933 *I*
Lewis, A J L (Ebbw Vale) 1970 *F*, 1971 *E, I, F*, 1972 *E, S, F*, 1973 *E, S, I, F*
Lewis, A L P (Cardiff) 1996 *It, E, S, I, A* 2(t)
Lewis, A R (Abertillery) 1966 *E, S, I, F, A*, 1967 *I*
Lewis, B R (Swansea, Cambridge U) 1912 *I*, 1913 *I*
Lewis, C P (Llandovery Coll) 1882 *I*, 1883 *E, S*, 1884 *E, S*
Lewis, D H (Cardiff) 1886 *E, S*
Lewis, E J (Llandovery) 1881 *E*
Lewis, E W (Llanelli, Cardiff) 1991 *I, F* 1, *A, F* 2, [*WS, Arg, A*], 1992 *I, F, S, A*, 1993 *E, S, F, Z* 1,2, *Nm, J, C*, 1994 *S, I, F, E, Pt, Sp, WS, R, It, SA*, 1995 *E, S, I*, [*J*], 1996 *It, E, S, I, F1*
Lewis, G W (Richmond) 1960 *E, S*
Lewis, H (Swansea) 1913 *S, F, I*, 1914 *E*
Lewis, J G (Llanelli) 1887 *I*
Lewis, J M C (Cardiff, Cambridge U) 1912 *E*, 1913 *S, F, I*, 1914 *E, S, F, I*, 1921 *I*, 1923 *E, S*
Lewis, J R (S Glam Inst, Cardiff) 1981 *E, S, I, F*, 1982 *F, E, S*
Lewis, M (Treorchy) 1913 *F*
Lewis, P I (Llanelli) 1984 *A*, 1985 *S, I, F, E*, 1986 *E, S, I*
Lewis, T W (Cardiff) 1926 *E*, 1927 *E, S*
Lewis, W (Llanelli) 1925 *F*
Lewis, W H (London Welsh, Cambridge U) 1926 *I*, 1927 *E, F, I, A*, 1928 *F*
Llewelyn, D B (Newport, Llanelli) 1970 *SA, S, E, I, F*, 1971 *E, S, I, F*, 1972 *E, S, F, NZ*

The Welsh place-kicker Neil Jenkins in action against France at Parc des Princes.

Llewellyn, G D (Neath) 1990 *Nm* 1,2, *Bb*, 1991 *E, S, I, F* 1, *A, F* 2
Llewellyn, G O (Neath, Harlequins) 1989 *NZ*, 1990 *E, S, I*, 1991 *E, S, A* (R), 1992 *I, F, E, S, A*, 1993 *E, S, I, F, Z* 1,2, *Nm, J, C*, 1994 *S, I, F, E, Pt, Sp, C, Tg, WS, R, It, SA*, 1995 *F, E, S, I,* [*J, NZ, I*], 1996 *It, E, S, I, F* 1, *A* 1,2, *Bb, F* 2, *It, A* 3, *SA*, 1997 *US, S, I, F, E*
Llewellyn, P D (Swansea) 1973 *I, F, A*, 1974 *S, E*
Llewellyn, W (Llwynypia) 1899 *E, S, I*, 1900 *E, S, I*, 1901 *E, S, I*, 1902 *E, S, I*, 1903 *I*, 1904 *E, S, I*, 1905 *E, S, I, NZ*
Lloyd, D J (Bridgend) 1966 *E, S, I, F, A*, 1967 *S, I, F, E*, 1968 *S, I, F*, 1969 *S, I, F, E, NZ* 1, *A*, 1970 *F*, 1972 *E, S, F*, 1973 *E, S*
Lloyd, E (Llanelli) 1895 *S*
Lloyd, G L (Newport) 1896 *I*, 1899 *S, I*, 1900 *E, S*, 1901 *E, S*, 1902 *S, I*, 1903 *E, S, I*
Lloyd, P (Llanelli) 1890 *S. E*, 1891 *E, I*
Lloyd, R A (Pontypool) 1913 *S, F, I*, 1914 *E, S, F, I*
Lloyd, T (Maesteg) 1953 *I, F*
Lloyd, T C (Neath) 1909 *F*, 1913 *F, I*, 1914 *E, S, F, I*
Loader, C D (Swansea) 1995 *SA, Fj*, 1996 *F* 1, *A* 1,2, *Bb, F* 2, *It, A* 3, *SA*, 1997 *US, S, I, F, E*
Lockwood, T W (Newport) 1887 *E, S, I*
Long, E C (Swansea) 1936 *E, S, I*, 1937 *E, S*, 1939 *S, I*
Lyne, H S (Newport) 1883 *S*, 1884 *E, S, I*, 1885 *E*

McBryde, R C (Swansea, Llanelli) 1994 *Fj, SA* (t)
McCall, B E W (Welch Regt, Newport) 1936 *E, S, I*
McCarley, A (Neath) 1938 *E, S, I*
McCutcheon, W M (Swansea) 1891 *S*, 1892 *E, S*, 1893 *E, S, I*, 1894 *E*
McIntosh, D L M (Pontypridd) 1996 *SA*, 1997 *E* (R)
Maddock, H T (London Welsh) 1906 *E, S, I*, 1907 *E, S*, 1910 *F*
Maddocks, K (Neath) 1957 *E*
Main, D R (London Welsh) 1959 *E, S, I, F*
Mainwaring, H J (Swansea) 1961 *F*
Mainwaring, W T (Aberavon) 1967 *S, I, F, E, NZ*, 1968 *E*
Major, W C (Maesteg) 1949 *F*, 1950 *S*
Male, B O (Cardiff) 1921 *F*, 1923 *S*, 1924 *S, I*, 1927 *E, S, F, I*, 1928 *S, I, F*
Manfield, L (Mountain Ash, Cardiff) 1939 *S, I*, 1947 *A*, 1948 *E, S, F, I*
Mann, B B (Cardiff) 1881 *E*
Mantle, J T (Loughborough Colls, Newport) 1964 *E, SA*
Margrave, F L (Llanelli) 1884 *E, S*
Marsden-Jones, D (Cardiff) 1921 *E*, 1924 *NZ*
Martin, A J (Aberavon) 1973 *A*, 1974 *S, I*, 1975 *F, E, S, I, A*, 1976 *E, S, I, F*, 1977 *I, F, E, S*, 1978 *E, S, I, F, A* 1,2, *NZ*, 1979 *S, I, F, E*, 1980 *F, E, S, I, NZ*, 1981 *I, F*
Martin, W J (Newport) 1912 *I, F*, 1919 *NZA*
Mason, J (Pontypridd) 1988 *NZ* 2 (R)
Mathews, Rev A A (Lampeter) 1886 *S*
Mathias, R (Llanelli) 1970 *F*
Matthews, C (Bridgend) 1939 *I*
Matthews, J (Cardiff), 1947 *E, A*, 1948 *E, S, F*, 1949 *E, S, I, F*, 1950 *E, S, I, F*, 1951 *E, S, I, F*
May, P S (Llanelli) 1988 *E, S, I, F, NZ* 1,2, 1991 [*WS*]
Meek, N N (Pontypool) 1993 *E, S, I*
Meredith, A (Devonport Services) 1949 *E, S, I*
Meredith, B V (St Luke's Coll, London Welsh, Newport) 1954 *I, F, S*, 1955 *E, S, I, F*, 1956 *E, S, I, F*, 1957 *E, S, I, F*, 1958 *A, E, S, I*, 1959 *E, S, I, F*, 1960 *E, S, F, SA*, 1961 *E, S, I*, 1962 *E, S, F, I*
Meredith, C C (Neath) 1953 *S, NZ*, 1954 *E, I, F, S*, 1955 *E, S, I, F*, 1956 *E, I*, 1957 *E, S*
Meredith, J (Swansea) 1888 *S, I*, 1890 *S, E*
Merry, A E (Pill Harriers) 1912 *I, F*
Michael, G (Swansea) 1923 *E, S, F*
Michaelson, R C B (Aberavon, Cambridge U) 1963 *E*
Miller, F (Mountain Ash) 1896 *I*, 1900 *E, S, I*, 1901 *E, S, I*
Mills, F M (Swansea, Cardiff) 1892 *E, S, I*, 1893 *E, S, I*, 1894 *E, S, I*, 1895 *E, S, I*, 1896 *E*
Moon, R H StJ B (Llanelli) 1993 *F, Z* 1,2, *Nm, J, C*, 1994 *S, I, F, E, Sp, C, Fj, WS, R, It, SA*, 1995 *F, E* (R)
Moore, A P (Cardiff) 1995 [*J*], *SA, Fj*, 1996 *It*
Moore, A P (Swansea) 1995 *SA* (R), *Fj*
Moore, W J (Bridgend) 1933 *I*
Morgan, C H (Llanelli) 1957 *I, F*
Morgan, C I (Cardiff) 1951 *I, F, SA*, 1952 *E, S, I*, 1953 *S, I, F, NZ*, 1954 *I, S*, 1955 *E, S, I, F*, 1956 *E, S, I, F*, 1957 *E, S, I, F*, 1958 *E, S, I, F*

Morgan, D (Swansea) 1885 *S*, 1886 *E, S*, 1887 *E, S, I*, 1889 *I*
Morgan, D (Llanelli) 1895 *I*, 1896 *E*
Morgan, D R R (Llanelli) 1962 *E, S, F, I*, 1963 *E, S, I, F, NZ*
Morgan, E (Llanelli) 1920 *I*, 1921 *E, S, F*
Morgan, Edgar (Swansea) 1914 *E, S, F, I*
Morgan, E T (London Welsh) 1902 *E, S, I*, 1903 *I*, 1904 *E, S, I*, 1905 *E, S, I, NZ*, 1906 *E, S, I, SA*, 1908 *F*
Morgan, F L (Llanelli) 1938 *E, S, I*, 1939 *E*
Morgan, H J (Abertillery) 1958 *E, S, I, F*, 1959 *I, F*, 1960 *E, I*, 1961 *E, S, I, F*, 1962 *E, S, F, I*, 1963 *S, I, F*, 1965 *E, S, I, F*, 1966 *E, S, I, F, A*
Morgan, H P (Newport) 1956 *E, S, I, F*
Morgan, I (Swansea) 1908 *A*, 1909 *E, S, F, I*, 1910 *F, E, S, I*, 1911 *E, F, I*, 1912 *S*
Morgan, J L (Llanelli) 1912 *SA*, 1913 *E*
Morgan, M E (Swansea) 1938 *E, S, I*, 1939 *E*
Morgan, N (Newport) 1960 *S, I, F*
Morgan, P E J (Aberavon) 1961 *E, S, F*
Morgan, P J (Llanelli) 1980 *S* (R), *I, NZ* (R), 1981 *I*
Morgan, R (Newport) 1984 *S*
Morgan, T (Llanelli) 1889 *I*
Morgan, W G (Cambridge U) 1927 *F, I*, 1929 *E, S, F, I*, 1930 *I, F*
Morgan, W L (Cardiff) 1910 *S*
Moriarty, R D (Swansea) 1981 *A*, 1982 *I, F, E, S*, 1983 *E*, 1984 *S, I, F, E*, 1985 *S, I, F*, 1986 *Fj, Tg, WS*, 1987 [*I, Tg, C* (R), *E, NZ, A*]
Moriarty, W P (Swansea) 1986 *I, F, Fj, Tg, WS*, 1987 *F, E, S, I,* [*I, Tg, C, E, NZ, A*]*, US*, 1988 *E, S, I, F, NZ* 1
Morley, J C (Newport) 1929 *E, S, F, I*, 1930 *E, I*, 1931 *E, S, F, I, SA*, 1932 *E, S, I*
Morris, G L (Swansea) 1882 *I*, 1883 *E, S*, 1884 *E, S*
Morris, H T (Cardiff) 1951 *F*, 1955 *I, F*
Morris, J I T (Swansea) 1924 *E, S*
Morris, M S (S Wales Police, Neath) 1985 *S, I, F*, 1990 *I, Nm* 1,2, *Bb*, 1991 *I, F* 1, [*WS* (R)], 1992 *E*
Morris, R R (Swansea, Bristol) 1933 *S*, 1937 *S*
Morris, S (Cross Keys) 1920 *E, S, F, I*, 1922 *E, S, I, F*, 1923 *E, S, F, I*, 1924 *E, S, F, NZ*, 1925 *E, S, F*
Morris, W (Abertillery) 1919 *NZA*, 1920 *F*, 1921 *I*
Morris, W (Llanelli) 1896 *S, I*, 1897 *E*
Morris, W D (Neath) 1967 *F, E*, 1968 *E, S, I, F*, 1969 *S, I, F, E, NZ* 1,2, *A*, 1970 *SA, S, I, F*, 1971 *E, S, I, F*, 1972 *E, S, F, NZ*, 1973 *E, S, I, A*, 1974 *S, I, F, E*
Morris, W J (Newport) 1965 *S*, 1966 *F*
Morris, W J (Pontypool) 1963 *S, I*
Moseley, K (Pontypool, Newport) 1988 *NZ* 2, *R*, 1989 *S, I*, 1990 *F*, 1991 *F* 2, [*WS, Arg, A*]
Murphy, C D (Cross Keys) 1935 *E, S, I*
Mustoe, L (Cardiff) 1995 *Fj*, 1996 *A* 1(R),2

Nash, D (Ebbw Vale) 1960 *SA*, 1961 *E, S, I, F*, 1962 *F*
Newman, C H (Newport) 1881 *E*, 1882 *I*, 1883 *E, S*, 1884 *E, S*, 1885 *E, S*, 1886 *E*, 1887 *E*
Nicholas, D L (Llanelli) 1981 *E, S, I, F*
Nicholas, T J (Cardiff) 1919 *NZA*
Nicholl, C B (Cambridge U, Llanelli) 1891 *I*, 1892 *E, S, I*, 1893 *E, S, I*, 1894 *E, S*, 1895 *E, S, I*, 1896 *E, S, I*
Nicholl, D W (Llanelli) 1894 *I*
Nicholls, E G (Cardiff) 1896 *S, I*, 1897 *E*, 1898 *I, E*, 1899 *E, S, I*, 1900 *S, I*, 1901 *E, S, I*, 1902 *E, S, I*, 1903 *I*, 1904 *E*, 1905 *I, NZ*, 1906 *E, S, I, SA*
Nicholls, F E (Cardiff Harlequins) 1892 *I*
Nicholls, H (Cardiff) 1958 *I*
Nicholls, S H (Cardiff) 1888 *M*, 1889 *S, I*, 1891 *S*
Norris, C H (Cardiff) 1963 *F*, 1966 *F*
Norster, R L (Cardiff) 1982 *S*, 1983 *E, S, I, F*, 1984 *S, I, F, E, A*, 1985 *S, I, F, E, Fj*, 1986 *Fj, Tg, WS*, 1987 *F, E, S, I,* [*I, C, E*]*, US*, 1988 *E, S, I, F, NZ* 1, *WS*, 1989 *F, E*
Norton, W B (Cardiff) 1882 *I*, 1883 *E, S*, 1884 *E, S, I*

O'Connor, A (Aberavon) 1960 *SA*, 1961 *E, S*, 1962 *F, I*
O'Connor, R (Aberavon) 1957 *E*
O'Neill, W (Cardiff) 1904 *S, I*, 1905 *E, S, I*, 1907 *E, I*, 1908 *E, S, F, I*
O'Shea, J P (Cardiff) 1967 *S, I*, 1968 *S, I, F*
Oliver, G (Pontypool) 1920 *E, S, F, I*
Osborne, W T (Mountain Ash) 1902 *E, S, I*, 1903 *E, S, I*
Ould, W J (Cardiff) 1924 *E, S*
Owen, A (Swansea) 1924 *E*
Owen, G D (Newport) 1955 *I, F*, 1956 *E, S, I, F*
Owen, R M (Swansea) 1901 *I*, 1902 *E, S, I*, 1903 *E, S, I,*

1904 *E, S, I,* 1905 *E, S, I, NZ,* 1906 *E, S, I, SA,* 1907 *E, S,* 1908 *F, I, A,* 1909 *E, S, F, I,* 1910 *F, E,* 1911 *E, S, F, I,* 1912 *E, S*

Packer, H (Newport) 1891 *E,* 1895 *S, I,* 1896 *E, S, I,* 1897 *E*
Palmer, F (Swansea) 1922 *E, S, I*
Parfitt, F C (Newport) 1893 *E, S, I,* 1894 *E, S, I,* 1895 *S,* 1896 *S, I*
Parfitt, S A (Swansea) 1990 *Nm* 1 (R), *Bb*
Parker, D S (Swansea) 1924 *I, F, NZ,* 1925 *E, S, F, I,* 1929 *F, I,* 1930 *E*
Parker, T (Swansea) 1919 *NZA,* 1920 *E, S, I,* 1921 *E, S, F, I,* 1922 *E, S, I, F,* 1923 *E, S, F*
Parker, W (Swansea) 1899 *E, S*
Parsons, G W (Newport) 1947 *E*
Pascoe, D (Bridgend) 1923 *F, I*
Pask, A E I (Abertillery) 1961 *F,* 1962 *E, S, F, I,* 1963 *E, S, I, F, NZ,* 1964 *E, S, I, F, SA,* 1965 *E, S, I, F,* 1966 *E, S, I, F, A,* 1967 *S, I*
Payne, G W (Army, Pontypridd) 1960 *E, S, I*
Payne, H (Swansea) 1935 *NZ*
Peacock, H (Newport) 1929 *S, F, I,* 1930 *S, I, F*
Peake, E (Chepstow) 1881 *E*
Pearce, G P (Bridgend) 1981 *I, F,* 1982 *I* (R)
Pearson, T W (Cardiff, Newport) 1891 *E, I,* 1892 *E, S,* 1894 *S, I,* 1895 *E, S, I,* 1897 *E,* 1898 *I, E,* 1903 *E*
Pegge, E V (Neath) 1891 *E*
Perego, M A (Llanelli) 1990 *S,* 1993 *F, Z* 1, *Nm* (R), 1994 *S, I, F, E, Sp*
Perkins, S J (Pontypool) 1983 *S, I, F, R,* 1984 *S, I, F, E, A,* 1985 *S, I, F, E, Fj,* 1986 *E, S, I, F*
Perrett, F L (Neath) 1912 *SA,* 1913 *E, S, F, I*
Perrins, V C (Newport) 1970 *SA, S*
Perry, W (Neath) 1911 *E*
Phillips, A J (Cardiff) 1979 *E,* 1980 *F, E, S, I, NZ,* 1981 *E, S, I, F, A,* 1982 *I, F, E, S,* 1987 *[C, E, A]*
Phillips, B (Aberavon) 1925 *E, S, F, I,* 1926 *E*
Phillips, D H (Swansea) 1952 *F*
Phillips, H P (Newport) 1892 *E,* 1893 *E, S, I,* 1894 *E, S*
Phillips, H T (Newport) 1927 *E, S, F, I, A,* 1928 *E, S, I, F*
Phillips, K H (Neath) 1987 *F, [I, Tg, NZ],* US, 1988 *E, NZ* 1, 1989 *NZ,* 1990 *F, E, S, I, Nm* 1,2, *Bb,* 1991 *E, S, I, F* 1, *A*
Phillips, L A (Newport) 1900 *E, S, I,* 1901 *S*
Phillips, R (Neath) 1987 *US,* 1988 *E, S, I, F, NZ* 1,2, *WS,* 1989 *S, I*
Phillips, W D (Cardiff) 1881 *E,* 1882 *I,* 1884 *E, S, I*
Pickering, D F (Llanelli) 1983 *E, S, I, F, R,* 1984 *S, I, F, E, A,* 1985 *S, I, F, E, Fj,* 1986 *E, S, I, F, Fj,* 1987 *F, E, S*
Plummer, R C S (Newport) 1912 *S, I, F, SA,* 1913 *E*
Pook, T (Newport) 1895 *S*
Powell, G (Ebbw Vale) 1957 *I, F*
Powell, J (Cardiff) 1906 *I*
Powell, J (Cardiff) 1923 *I*
Powell, R W (Newport) 1888 *S, I*
Powell, W C (London Welsh) 1926 *S, I, F,* 1927 *E, F, I,* 1928 *S, I, F,* 1929 *E, S, I, F,* 1930 *S, I, F,* 1931 *E, S, F, I, SA,* 1932 *E, S, I,* 1935 *E, S, I*
Powell, W J (Cardiff) 1920 *E, S, F, I*
Price, B (Newport) 1961 *I, F,* 1962 *E, S,* 1963 *E, S, F, NZ,* 1964 *E, S, I, F, SA,* 1965 *E, S, I, F,* 1966 *E, S, I, F, A,* 1967 *S, I, F, E,* 1969 *S, I, F, NZ* 1,2, *A*
Price, G (Pontypool) 1975 *F, E, S, I, A,* 1976 *E, S, I, F,* 1977 *I, F, E, S,* 1978 *E, S, I, F, A* 1,2, *NZ,* 1979 *S, I, F, E,* 1980 *F, E, S, I, NZ,* 1981 *E, S, I, F, A,* 1982 *I, F, E, S,* 1983 *E, I, F*
Price, M J (Pontypool, RAF) 1959 *E, S, I, F,* 1960 *E, S, I, F,* 1962 *E*
Price, R E (Weston-s-Mare) 1939 *S, I*
Price, T G (Llanelli) 1965 *E, S, I, F,* 1966 *E, A,* 1967 *S, F*
Priday, A J (Cardiff) 1958 *I,* 1961 *I*
Pritchard, C (Pontypool) 1928 *E, S, I, F,* 1929 *E, S, F, I*
Pritchard, C C (Newport, Pontypool) 1904 *S, I,* 1905 *NZ,* 1906 *E, S*
Pritchard, C M (Newport) 1904 *I,* 1905 *E, S, NZ,* 1906 *E, S, I, SA,* 1907 *E, S, I,* 1908 *E,* 1910 *F, E, A* 1,2, *Bb, F* 2, *It, A* 3, 1997 *E* (R)
Prosser, D R (Neath) 1934 *S, I*
Prosser, G (Neath) 1934 *E, S, I,* 1935 *NZ*
Prosser, G (Pontypridd) 1995 *[NZ]*

Prosser, J (Cardiff) 1921 *I*
Prosser, T R (Pontypool) 1956 *S, F,* 1957 *E, S, I, F,* 1958 *A, E, S, I, F,* 1959 *E, S, I, F,* 1960 *E, S, I, F, SA,* 1961 *I, F*
Prothero, G J (Bridgend) 1964 *S, I, F,* 1965 *E, S, I, F,* 1966 *E, S, I, F*
Pryce-Jenkins, T J (London Welsh) 1888 *S, I*
Pugh, C (Maesteg) 1924 *E, S, I, F, NZ,* 1925 *E, S*
Pugh, J D (Neath) 1987 *US,* 1988 *S* (R), 1990 *S*
Pugh, P (Neath) 1989 *NZ*
Pugsley, J (Cardiff) 1910 *E, S, I,* 1911 *E, S, F, I*
Pullman, J J (Neath) 1910 *F*
Purdon, F T (Newport) 1881 *E,* 1882 *I,* 1883 *E, S*

Quinnell, D L (Llanelli) 1972 *F* (R), *NZ,* 1973 *E, S, A,* 1974 *S, F,* 1975 *E* (R), 1977 *I* (R), *F, E, S,* 1978 *E, S, I, F, A* 1, *NZ,* 1979 *S, I, F, E,* 1980 *NZ*
Quinnell, J C (Llanelli, Richmond) 1995 *Fj,* 1996 *A* 3(R), 1997 *US* (R), *I* (R), *E* (R)
Quinnell, L S (Llanelli, Richmond) 1993 *C,* 1994 *S, I, F, E, Pt, Sp, C, WS,* 1997 *US, S, I, F, E*

Radford, W J (Newport) 1923 *I*
Ralph, A R (Newport) 1931 *F, I, SA,* 1932 *E, S, I*
Ramsey, S H (Treorchy) 1896 *E,* 1904 *E*
Randell, R (Aberavon) 1924 *I, F*
Raybould, W H (London Welsh, Cambridge U, Newport) 1967 *S, I, F, E, NZ,* 1968 *I, F,* 1970 *SA, E, I, F* (R)
Rayer, M A (Cardiff) 1991 *[WS* (R), *Arg, A* (R)*],* 1992 *E* (R), *A,* 1993 *E, S, I, Z* 1, *Nm, J* (R), 1994 *S* (R), *I* (R), *E, Pt, C, Fj, WS, R, It*
Rees, Aaron (Maesteg) 1919 *NZA*
Rees, Alan (Maesteg) 1962 *E, S, F*
Rees, A M (London Welsh) 1934 *E,* 1935 *E, S, I,* 1936 *E, S, I,* 1937 *E, S, I,* 1938 *E, S*
Rees, B I (London Welsh) 1967 *S, I, F*
Rees, C F W (London Welsh) 1974 *I,* 1975 *A,* 1978 *NZ,* 1981 *F, A,* 1982 *I, F, E, S,* 1983 *E, S, I, F*
Rees, D (Swansea) 1968 *S, I, F*
Rees, Dan (Swansea) 1900 *E,* 1903 *E, S,* 1905 *E, S*
Rees, E B (Swansea) 1919 *NZA*
Rees, H (Cardiff) 1937 *S, I,* 1938 *E, S, I*
Rees, H E (Neath) 1979 *S, I, F, E,* 1980 *F, E, S, I, NZ,* 1983 *E, S, I, F*
Rees, J (Swansea) 1920 *E, S, F, I,* 1921 *E, S, I,* 1922 *E,* 1923 *E, F, I,* 1924 *E*
Rees, J I (Swansea) 1934 *E, S, I,* 1935 *S, NZ,* 1936 *E, S, I,* 1937 *E, S, I,* 1938 *E, S, I*
Rees, L M (Cardiff) 1933 *I*
Rees, P (Llanelli) 1947 *F, I*
Rees, P M (Newport) 1961 *E, S, I,* 1964 *I*
Rees, T (Newport) 1935 *S, I, NZ,* 1936 *E, S, I,* 1937 *E, S*
Rees, T A (Llandovery) 1881 *E*
Rees, T E (London Welsh) 1926 *I, F,* 1927 *A,* 1928 *E*
Rees-Jones, G R (Oxford U, London Welsh) 1934 *E, S,* 1935 *I, NZ,* 1936 *E*
Reeves, F (Cross Keys) 1920 *F, I,* 1921 *E*
Reynolds, A (Swansea) 1990 *Nm* 1,2 (R), 1992 *A* (R)
Rhapps, J (Penygraig) 1897 *E*
Rice-Evans, W (Swansea) 1890 *S,* 1891 *E, S*
Richards, B (Swansea) 1960 *F*
Richards, C (Pontypool) 1922 *E, S, I, F,* 1924 *I*
Richards, D S (Swansea) 1979 *F, E,* 1980 *F, E, S, I, NZ,* 1981 *E, S, I, F,* 1982 *I, F,* 1983 *E, S, I, R* (R)
Richards, E G (Cardiff) 1927 *S*
Richards, E S (Swansea) 1885 *E,* 1887 *S*
Richards, H D (Neath) 1986 *Tg* (R), 1987 *[Tg, E* (R), *NZ]*
Richards, I (Cardiff) 1925 *E, S, F*
Richards, K H L (Bridgend) 1960 *SA,* 1961 *E, S, I, F*
Richards, M C R (Cardiff) 1968 *I, F,* 1969 *S, I, F, E, NZ* 1,2, *A*
Richards, R (Aberavon) 1913 *S, F, I*
Richards, R (Cross Keys) 1956 *F*
Richards, T (Maesteg) 1923 *I*
Richardson, S J (Aberavon) 1978 *A* 2 (R), 1979 *E*
Rickards, A R (Cardiff) 1924 *F*
Ring, J (Aberavon) 1921 *E*
Ring, M G (Cardiff, Pontypool) 1983 *E,* 1984 *A,* 1985 *S, I, F,* 1987 *F, [I, Tg, A],* US, 1988 *E, S, I, F, NZ* 1,2, 1989 *NZ,* 1990 *F, E, S, I, Nm* 1,2, *Bb,* 1991 *E, S, I, F* 1,2, *[WS, Arg, A]*
Ringer, P (Ebbw Vale, Llanelli) 1978 *NZ,* 1979 *S, I, F, E,* 1980 *F, E, NZ*

250

Roberts, C (Neath) 1958 *I, F*
Roberts, D E A (London Welsh) 1930 *E*
Roberts, E (Llanelli) 1886 *E*, 1887 *I*
Roberts, E J (Llanelli) 1888 *S, I*, 1889 *I*
Roberts, G J (Cardiff) 1985 *F* (R), *E*, 1987 [*I, Tg, C, E, A*]
Roberts, H M (Cardiff) 1960 *SA*, 1961 *E, S, I, F*, 1962 *S, F*, 1963 *I*
Roberts, J (Cardiff) 1927 *E, S, F, I, A*, 1928 *E, S, I, F*, 1929 *E, S, F, I*
Roberts, M G (London Welsh) 1971 *E, S, I, F*, 1973 *I, F*, 1975 *S*, 1979 *E*
Roberts, T (Newport, Risca) 1921 *S, F, I*, 1922 *E, S, I, F*, 1923 *E, S*
Roberts, W (Cardiff) 1929 *E*
Robins, J D (Birkenhead Park) 1950 *E, S, I, F*, 1951 *E, S, I, F*, 1953 *E, I, F*
Robins, R J (Pontypridd) 1953 *S*, 1954 *F, S*, 1955 *E, S, I, F*, 1956 *E, F*, 1957 *E, S, I, F*
Robinson, I R (Cardiff) 1974 *F, E*
Rocyn-Jones, D N (Cambridge U) 1925 *I*
Roderick, W B (Llanelli) 1884 *I*
Rosser, M A (Penarth) 1924 *S, F*
Rowland, E M (Lampeter) 1885 *E*
Rowlands, C F (Aberavon) 1926 *I*
Rowlands, D C T (Pontypool) 1963 *E, S, I, F, NZ*, 1964 *E, S, I, F, SA*, 1965 *E, S, I, F*
Rowlands, G (RAF, Cardiff) 1953 *NZ*, 1954 *E, F*, 1956 *F*
Rowlands, K A (Cardiff) 1962 *F, I*, 1963 *I*, 1965 *I, F*
Rowles, G R (Penarth) 1892 *E*
Rowley, M (Pontypridd) 1996 *SA*, 1997 *US, S, I, F*
Roy, W S (Cardiff) 1995 [*J* (R)]
Russell, S (London Welsh) 1987 *US*

Samuel, D (Swansea) 1891 *I*, 1893 *I*
Samuel, F (Mountain Ash) 1922 *S, I, F*
Samuel, J (Swansea) 1891 *I*
Scourfield, T (Torquay) 1930 *F*
Scrine, G F (Swansea) 1899 *E, S*, 1901 *I*
Shanklin, J L (London Welsh) 1970 *F*, 1972 *NZ*, 1973 *I, F*
Shaw, G (Neath) 1972 *NZ*, 1973 *E, S, I, F, A*, 1974 *S, I, F, E*, 1977 *I, F*
Shaw, T W (Newbridge) 1983 *R*
Shea, J (Newport) 1919 *NZA*, 1920 *E, S*, 1921 *E*
Shell, R C (Aberavon) 1973 *A* (R)
Simpson, H J (Cardiff) 1884 *S, I*
Skrimshire, R T (Newport) 1899 *E, S, I*
Skym, A (Llanelli) 1928 *E, S, I, F*, 1930 *E, S, I, F*, 1931 *E, S, F, I, SA*, 1932 *E, S, I*, 1933 *E, S, I*, 1935 *E*
Smith, J S (Cardiff) 1884 *E, I*, 1885 *E*
Sparks, B (Neath) 1954 *I*, 1955 *E, F*, 1956 *E, S, I*, 1957 *S*
Spiller, W J (Cardiff) 1910 *S, I*, 1911 *E, S, F, I*, 1912 *E, F, SA*, 1913 *E*
Squire, J (Newport, Pontypool) 1977 *I, F*, 1978 *E, S, I, F, A* 1, *NZ*, 1979 *S, I, F, E*, 1980 *F, E, S, I, NZ*, 1981 *E, S, I, F, A*, 1982 *I, F, E*, 1983 *E, S, I, F*
Stadden, W J W (Cardiff) 1884 *I*, 1886 *E, S*, 1887 *I*, 1888 *S, M*, 1890 *S, E*
Stephens, C J (Llanelli) 1992 *I, F, E, A*
Stephens, G (Neath) 1912 *E, S, I, F, SA*, 1913 *E, S, F, I*, 1919 *NZA*
Stephens, I (Bridgend) 1981 *E, S, I, F, A*, 1982 *I, F, E, S*, 1984 *I, F, E, A*
Stephens, Rev J G (Llanelli) 1922 *E, S, I, F*
Stephens, J R G (Neath) 1947 *E, S, F, I*, 1948 *I*, 1949 *S, I, F*, 1951 *F, SA*, 1952 *E, S, I, F*, 1953 *E, S, I, F, NZ*, 1954 *E, I*, 1955 *E, S, I, F*, 1956 *S, I, F*, 1957 *E, S, I, F*
Stock, A (Newport) 1924 *F, NZ*, 1926 *E, S*
Stone, P (Llanelli) 1949 *F*
Strand-Jones, J (Llanelli) 1902 *E, S, I*, 1903 *E, S*
Summers, R H B (Haverfordwest) 1881 *E*
Sutton, R (Pontypool, S Wales Police) 1982 *F, E*, 1987 *F, E, S, I*, [*C, NZ* (R), *A*]
Sweet-Escott, R B (Cardiff) 1891 *S*, 1894 *I*, 1895 *I*

Tamplin, W E (Cardiff) 1947 *S, F, I, A*, 1948 *E, S, F*
Tanner, H (Swansea, Cardiff) 1935 *NZ*, 1936 *E, S, I*, 1937 *E, S, I*, 1938 *E, S, I*, 1939 *E, S, I*, 1947 *E, S, F, I*, 1948 *E, S, F, I*, 1949 *E, S, I, F*
Tarr, D J (Swansea, Royal Navy) 1935 *NZ*
Taylor, A R (Cross Keys) 1937 *I*, 1938 *I*, 1939 *E*
Taylor, C G (Ruabon) 1884 *E, S, I*, 1885 *E, S*, 1886 *E, S*, 1887 *E, I*
Taylor, H T (Cardiff) 1994 *Pt, C, Fj, Tg, WS* (R), *R, It,*

SA, 1995 *E, S,* [*J, NZ, I*], *SA, Fj*, 1996 *It, E, S, I, F* 1, *A* 1,2, *It, A* 3
Taylor, J (London Welsh) 1967 *S, I, F, E, NZ*, 1968 *I, F*, 1969 *S, I, F, E, NZ* 1, *A*, 1970 *F*, 1971 *E, S, I, F*, 1972 *E, S, F, NZ*, 1973 *E, S, I, F*
Taylor, M (Pontypool, Swansea) 1994 *SA*, 1995 *F, E, SA* (R)
Thomas, A (Newport) 1963 *NZ*, 1964 *E*
Thomas, A C (Bristol, Swansea) 1996 *It, E, S, I, F* 2(R), *SA*, 1997 *US, S, I, F*
Thomas, A G (Swansea, Cardiff) 1952 *E, S, I, F*, 1953 *S, I, F*, 1954 *E, I, F*, 1955 *S, I, F*
Thomas, Bob (Swansea) 1900 *E, S, I*, 1901 *E*
Thomas, Brian (Neath, Cambridge U) 1963 *E, S, I, F, NZ*, 1964 *I, F, SA*, 1965 *E, I*, 1966 *E, S, I*, 1967 *NZ*, 1969 *S, I, F, E, NZ* 1,2
Thomas, C (Bridgend) 1925 *E, S*
Thomas, C J (Newport) 1888 *I, M*, 1889 *S, I*, 1890 *S, E, I*, 1891 *E, I*
Thomas, D (Aberavon) 1961 *I*
Thomas, D (Llanelli) 1954 *I*
Thomas, Dick (Mountain Ash) 1906 *SA*, 1908 *F, I*, 1909 *S*
Thomas, D J (Swansea) 1904 *E*, 1908 *A*, 1910 *E, S, I*, 1911 *E, S, F, I*, 1912 *E*
Thomas, D J (Swansea) 1930 *S, I*, 1932 *E, S, I*, 1933 *E, S*, 1934 *E*, 1935 *E, S, I*
Thomas, D L (Neath) 1937 *E*
Thomas, E (Newport) 1904 *S, I*, 1909 *S, F, I*, 1910 *F*
Thomas, G (Llanelli) 1923 *E, S, F, I*
Thomas, G (Newport) 1888 *M*, 1890 *I*, 1891 *S*
Thomas, G (Bridgend) 1995 [*J, NZ, I*], *SA, Fj*, 1996 *F* 1, *A* 1,2, *Bb, F* 2, *It, A* 3, 1997 *US, S, I, F, E*
Thomas, H (Llanelli) 1912 *F*
Thomas, H (Neath) 1936 *E, S, I*, 1937 *E, S, I*
Thomas, H W (Swansea) 1912 *SA*, 1913 *E*
Thomas, I (Bryncethin) 1924 *E*
Thomas, L C (Cardiff) 1885 *E, S*
Thomas, M C (Newport, Devonport Services) 1949 *F*, 1950 *E, S, I, F*, 1951 *E, S, I, F, SA*, 1952 *E, S, I, F*, 1953 *E*, 1956 *E, S, I, F*, 1957 *E, S*, 1958 *E, S, I, F*, 1959 *I, F*
Thomas, M G (St Bart's Hospital) 1919 *NZA*, 1921 *S, F, I*, 1923 *F*, 1924 *E*
Thomas, N (Bath) 1996 *SA* (R)
Thomas, R (Pontypool) 1909 *F, I*, 1911 *S, F*, 1912 *E, S, SA*, 1913 *E*
Thomas, R C C (Swansea) 1949 *F*, 1952 *I, F*, 1953 *S, I, F, NZ*, 1954 *E, I, F, S*, 1955 *S, I*, 1956 *E, S, I*, 1957 *E*, 1958 *A, E, S, I, F*, 1959 *E, S, I, F*
Thomas, R L (London Welsh) 1889 *S, I*, 1890 *I*, 1891 *E, S, I*, 1892 *E*
Thomas, S (Llanelli) 1890 *S, E*, 1891 *I*
Thomas, W D (Llanelli) 1966 *A*, 1968 *S, I, F*, 1969 *E, NZ* 2, *A*, 1970 *SA, S, E, I, F*, 1971 *E, S, I, F*, 1972 *E, S, F, NZ*, 1973 *E, S, I, F*, 1974 *E*
Thomas, W G (Llanelli, Waterloo, Swansea) 1927 *E, S, F, I*, 1929 *E, S, I, SA*, 1932 *E, S, I*, 1933 *E, S*
Thomas, W H (Llandovery Coll, Cambridge U) 1885 *S*, 1886 *E, S*, 1887 *E, S*, 1888 *S, I*, 1890 *E, I*, 1891 *S, I*
Thomas, W J (Cardiff) 1961 *F*, 1963 *F*
Thomas, W J L (Llanelli, Cardiff) 1995 *SA, Fj*, 1996 *It, E, S, I, F* 1, 1996 *Bb* (R), 1997 *US*
Thomas, W L (Newport) 1894 *S*, 1895 *E, I*
Thomas, W T (Abertillery) 1930 *E*
Thompson, J F (Cross Keys) 1923 *E*
Thorburn, P H (Neath) 1985 *F, E, Fj*, 1986 *E, S, I, F*, 1987 *F*, [*I, Tg, C, E, NZ, A*], *US*, 1988 *S, F, NZ* (R), 1989 *S, I, F, E, NZ*, 1990 *F, E, S, I, Nm* 1,2, *Bb*, 1991 *E, S, I, F* 1, *A*
Titley, M H (Bridgend, Swansea) 1983 *R*, 1984 *S, I, F, E, A*, 1985 *S, I, Fj*, 1986 *F, Fj, Tg, WS*, 1990 *F, E*
Towers, W H (Swansea) 1887 *I*, 1888 *M*
Travers, G (Pill Harriers) 1903 *E, S, I*, 1905 *E, S, I, NZ*, 1906 *E, S, I, SA*, 1907 *E, S, I*, 1908 *E, S, F, I, A*, 1909 *E, S, I*, 1911 *S, F, I*
Travers, W H (Newport) 1937 *S, I*, 1938 *E, S, I*, 1939 *E, S, I*, 1949 *E, S, I, F*
Treharne, E (Pontypridd) 1881 *E*, 1883 *E*
Trew, W J (Swansea) 1900 *E, S, I*, 1901 *E, S*, 1903 *S*, 1905 *S*, 1906 *S*, 1907 *E, S*, 1908 *E, S, F, I, A*, 1909 *E, S, F, I*, 1910 *F, E, S*, 1911 *E, S, F, I*, 1912 *S*, 1913 *S, F*
Trott, R F (Cardiff) 1948 *E, S, F, I*, 1949 *E, S, I, F*
Truman, W H (Llanelli) 1934 *E*, 1935 *E*
Trump, L C (Newport) 1912 *E, S, I, F*

Turnbull, B R (Cardiff) 1925 *I*, 1927 *E, S*, 1928 *E, F*, 1930 *S*
Turnbull, M J L (Cardiff) 1933 *E, I*
Turner, P (Newbridge) 1989 *I* (R), *F, E*

Uzzell, H (Newport) 1912 *E, S, I, F*, 1913 *S, F, I*, 1914 *E, S, F, I*, 1920 *E, S, F, I*
Uzzell, J R (Newport) 1963 *NZ*, 1965 *E, S, I, F*

Vickery, W E (Aberavon) 1938 *E, S, I*, 1939 *E*
Vile, T H (Newport) 1908 *E, S*, 1910 *I*, 1912 *I, F, SA*, 1913 *E*, 1921 *S*
Vincent, H C (Bangor) 1882 *I*
Voyle, M J (Newport, Llanelli) 1996 *A* 1(t), *F* 2, 1997 *E*

Wakeford, J D M (S Wales Police) 1988 *WS, R*
Waldron, R (Neath) 1965 *E, S, I, F*
Walker, N (Cardiff) 1993 *I, F, J*, 1994 *S, F, E, Pt, Sp*, 1995 *F, E*
Waller, P D (Newport) 1908 *A*, 1909 *E, S, F, I*, 1910 *F*
Walters, N (Llanelli) 1902 *E*
Wanbon, R (Aberavon) 1968 *E*
Ward, W S (Cross Keys) 1934 *S, I*
Warlow, J (Llanelli) 1962 *I*
Waters, D R (Newport) 1986 *E, S, I, F*
Waters, K (Newbridge) 1991 [*WS*]
Watkins, D (Newport) 1963 *E, S, I, F, NZ*, 1964 *E, S, I, F, SA*, 1965 *E, S, I, F*, 1966 *E, S, I, F*, 1967 *I, F, E*
Watkins, E (Neath) 1924 *E, S, I*
Watkins, E (Blaina) 1926 *S, I, F*
Watkins, E (Cardiff) 1935 *NZ*, 1937 *S, I*, 1938 *E, S, I*, 1939 *E, S*
Watkins, H (Llanelli) 1904 *S, I*, 1905 *E, S, I*, 1906 *E*
Watkins, I J (Ebbw Vale) 1988 *E* (R), *S, I, F, NZ* 2, *R*, 1989 *S, I, F, E*
Watkins, L (Oxford U, Llandaff) 1881 *E*
Watkins, M J (Newport) 1984 *I, F, E, A*
Watkins, S J (Newport, Cardiff) 1964 *S, I, F*, 1965 *E, S, I, F*, 1966 *E, S, I, F, A*, 1967 *S, I, F, E, NZ*, 1968 *E, S*, 1969 *S, I, F, E, NZ* 1, 1970 *E, I*
Watkins, W R (Newport) 1959 *F*
Watts, D (Maesteg) 1914 *E, S, F, I*
Watts, J (Llanelli) 1907 *E, S, I*, 1908 *E, S, F, I, A*, 1909 *S, F, I*
Watts, W (Llanelli) 1914 *E*
Watts, W H (Newport) 1892 *E, S, I*, 1893 *E, S, I*, 1894 *E, S, I*, 1895 *E, I*, 1896 *E*
Weaver, D (Swansea) 1964 *E*
Webb, J (Abertillery) 1907 *S*, 1908 *E, S, F, I, A*, 1909 *E, S, F, I*, 1910 *F, E, S, I*, 1911 *E, S, F, I*, 1912 *E, S*
Webb, J E (Newport) 1888 *M*, 1889 *S*
Webbe, G M C (Bridgend) 1986 *Tg* (R), *WS*, 1987 *F, E, S*, [*Tg*], *US*, 1988 *F* (R), *NZ* 1, *R*
Webster, R E (Swansea) 1987 [*A*], 1990 *Bb*, 1991 [*Arg, A*], 1992 *I, F, E, S, A*, 1993 *E, S, I, F*
Wells, G T (Cardiff) 1955 *E, S*, 1957 *I, F*, 1958 *A, E, S*
Westacott, D (Cardiff) 1906 *I*
Wetter, H (Newport) 1912 *SA*, 1913 *E*
Wetter, J J (Newport) 1914 *S, F, I*, 1920 *E, S, F, I*, 1921 *E*, 1924 *I, NZ*
Wheel, G A D (Swansea) 1974 *I, E* (R), 1975 *F, E, I, A*, 1976 *E, S, I, F*, 1977 *I, E, S*, 1978 *E, S, I, F, A* 1,2, *NZ*, 1979 *S, I*, 1980 *F, E, S, I*, 1981 *E, S, I, F, A*, 1982 *I*
Wheeler, P J (Aberavon) 1967 *NZ*, 1968 *E*
Whitefoot, J (Cardiff) 1984 *A* (R), 1985 *S, I, F, E, Fj*, 1986 *E, S, I, F, Fj, Tg, WS*, 1987 *F, E, S, I*, [*I, C*]
Whitfield, J (Newport) 1919 *NZA*, 1920 *E, S, F, I*, 1921 *E*, 1922 *E, S, I, F*, 1924 *S, I*
Whitson, G K (Newport) 1956 *F*, 1960 *S, I*
Wilkins, G (Bridgend) 1994 *Tg*
Williams, A (Bridgend, Swansea) 1990 *Nm* 2 (R), 1995 *Fj* (R)
Williams, B (Llanelli) 1920 *S, F, I*
Williams, B (Neath) 1996 *F* 2
Williams, B L (Cardiff) 1947 *E, S, F, I, A*, 1948 *E, S, F, I*, 1949 *E, S, I*, 1951 *I, SA*, 1952 *S, I, F, NZ*, 1954 *S*, 1955 *E*
Williams, B R (Neath) 1990 *S, I, Bb*, 1991 *E, S*
Williams, C (Llanelli) 1924 *NZ*, 1925 *E*
Williams, C (Aberavon, Swansea) 1977 *E, S*, 1980 *F, E, S, I, NZ*, 1983 *E*
Williams, C D (Cardiff, Neath) 1955 *F*, 1956 *F*
Williams, D (Ebbw Vale) 1963 *E, S, I, F*, 1964 *E, S, I, F, SA*, 1965 *E, S, I, F*, 1966 *E, S, I, A*, 1967 *F, E, NZ*, 1968

E, 1969 *S, I, F, E, NZ* 1,2, *A*, 1970 *SA, S, E, I*, 1971 *E, S, I, F*
Williams, D B (Newport, Swansea) 1978 *A* 1, 1981 *E, S*
Williams, E (Neath) 1924 *NZ*, 1925 *F*
Williams, E (Aberavon) 1925 *E, S*
Williams, F L (Cardiff) 1929 *S, F, I*, 1930 *E, S, I, F*, 1931 *F, I, SA*, 1932 *E, S, I*, 1933 *I*
Williams, G (Aberavon) 1936 *E, S, I*
Williams, G (London Welsh) 1950 *I, F*, 1951 *E, S, I, F, SA*, 1952 *E, S, I, F*, 1953 *NZ*, 1954 *E*
Williams, G (Bridgend) 1981 *I, F*, 1982 *E* (R), *S*
Williams, G P (Bridgend) 1980 *NZ*, 1981 *E, S, A*, 1982 *I*
Williams, J (Blaina) 1920 *E, S, F, I*, 1921 *S, F, I*
Williams, J F (London Welsh) 1905 *I, NZ*, 1906 *S, SA*
Williams, J J (Llanelli) 1973 *F* (R), *A*, 1974 *S, I, F, E*, 1975 *F, E, S, I, A*, 1976 *E, S, I, F*, 1977 *I, F, E, S*, 1978 *E, S, I, F, A* 1,2, *NZ*, 1979 *S, I, F, E*
Williams, J L (Cardiff) 1906 *SA*, 1907 *E, S, I*, 1908 *E, S, I, A*, 1909 *E, S, F, I*, 1910 *I*, 1911 *E, S, F, I*
Williams, J P R (London Welsh, Bridgend) 1969 *S, I, F, E, NZ* 1,2, *A*, 1970 *SA, S, E, I, F*, 1971 *E, S, I, F*, 1972 *E, S, F, NZ*, 1973 *E, S, I, F, A, NZ*, 1974 *S, I, F*, 1975 *F, E, S, I, A*, 1976 *E, S, I, F*, 1977 *I, F, E, S*, 1978 *E, S, I, F, A* 1,2, *NZ*, 1979 *S, I, F, E*, 1980 *NZ*, 1981 *E, S*
Williams, L (Llanelli, Cardiff) 1947 *E, S, F, I, A*, 1948 *I*, 1949 *E*
Williams, L H (Cardiff) 1957 *S, I, F*, 1958 *E, S, I, F*, 1959 *E, S, I*, 1961 *F*, 1962 *E, S*
Williams, M (Newport) 1923 *F*
Williams, M E (Pontypridd) 1996 *Bb*, *F* 2, *It* (t)
Williams, O (Bridgend) 1990 *Nm* 2
Williams, O (Llanelli) 1947 *E, S, A*, 1948 *E, S, F, I*
Williams, R (Llanelli) 1954 *S*, 1957 *F*, 1958 *A*
Williams, R D G (Newport) 1881 *E*
Williams, R F (Cardiff) 1912 *SA*, 1913 *E, S*, 1914 *I*
Williams, R H (Llanelli) 1954 *I, F, S*, 1955 *S, I, F*, 1956 *E, S, I*, 1957 *E, S, I, F*, 1958 *A, E, S, I, F*, 1959 *E, S, I, F*, 1960 *E*
Williams, S (Llanelli) 1947 *E, S, F, I*, 1948 *E, S, F*
Williams, S A (Aberavon) 1939 *E, S, I*
Williams, S M (Neath) 1994 *Tg*, 1996 *E* (t), *A* 1,2, *Bb, F* 2, *It, A* 3, *SA*, 1997 *US, S, I, F, E*
Williams, T (Pontypridd) 1882 *I*
Williams, T (Swansea) 1888 *S, I*
Williams, T (Swansea) 1912 *I*, 1913 *F*, 1914 *E, S, F, I*
Williams, Tudor (Swansea) 1921 *F*
Williams, T G (Cross Keys) 1935 *S, I, NZ*, 1936 *E, S, I*, 1937 *S, I*
Williams, W A (Crumlin) 1927 *E, S, F, I*
Williams, W A (Newport) 1952 *I, F*, 1953 *E*
Williams, W E O (Cardiff) 1887 *S, I*, 1889 *S*, 1890 *S, E*
Williams, W H (Pontymister) 1900 *E, S, I*, 1901 *E*
Williams, W O G (Swansea, Devonport Services) 1951 *F, SA*, 1952 *E, S, I, F*, 1953 *E, S, I, F, NZ*, 1954 *E, I, F, S*, 1955 *E, S, I, F*, 1956 *E, S, I*
Williams, W P J (Neath) 1974 *I, F*
Williams-Jones, H (S Wales Police, Llanelli) 1989 *S* (R), 1990 *F* (R), *I*, 1991 *A*, 1992 *S, A*, 1993 *E, S, I, F, E, Z* 1, *Nm*, 1994 *Fj, Tg, WS* (R), *It* (t), 1995 *E* (R)
Willis, W R (Cardiff) 1950 *E, S, F*, 1951 *E, S, I, F, SA*, 1952 *E, S*, 1953 *S, I*, 1954 *E, I, F, S*, 1955 *E, S, I, F*
Wiltshire, M L (Aberavon) 1967 *NZ*, 1968 *E, S, F*
Windsor, R W (Pontypool) 1973 *A*, 1974 *S, I, F, E*, 1975 *F, E, S, I, A*, 1976 *E, S, I, F*, 1977 *I, F, E, S*, 1978 *E, S, I, F, A* 1,2, *NZ*, 1979 *S, I, F*
Winfield, H B (Cardiff) 1903 *I*, 1904 *E, S, I*, 1905 *NZ*, 1906 *E, S, I*, 1907 *S, I*, 1908 *E, S, F, I, A*
Winmill, S (Cross Keys) 1921 *E, S, F, I*
Wintle, M E (Llanelli) 1996 *It*
Wintle, R V (London Welsh) 1988 *WS* (R)
Wooller, W (Sale, Cambridge U, Cardiff) 1933 *E, S, I*, 1935 *E, S, I, NZ*, 1936 *E, S, I*, 1937 *E, S, I*, 1938 *S, I*, 1939 *E, S, I*
Wyatt, M A (Swansea) 1983 *E, S, I, F*, 1984 *A*, 1985 *S, I*, 1987 *E, S, I*

Young, D (Swansea, Cardiff) 1987 [*E, NZ*], *US*, 1988 *E, S, I, F, NZ* 1,2, *WS, R*, 1989 *S, NZ*, 1990 *F*, 1996 *A* 3, *SA*, 1997 *US, S, I, F, E*
Young, G A (Cardiff) 1886 *E, S*
Young, J (Harrogate, RAF, London Welsh) 1968 *S, I, F*, 1969 *S, I, F, E, NZ* 1, 1970 *E, I, F*, 1971 *E, S, I, F*, 1972 *E, S, F, NZ*, 1973 *E, S, I, F*

WELSH INTERNATIONAL RECORDS
(*up to 30 April 1997*)

MATCH RECORDS

MOST CONSECUTIVE TEST WINS

11 1907 *I*, 1908 *E, S, F, I, A*, 1909 *E, S, F, I*, 1910 *F*
8 1970 *F*, 1971 *E, S, I, F*, 1972 *E, S, F*

MOST CONSECUTIVE TESTS WITHOUT DEFEAT

P	W	D	Period
11	11	0	1907–10
8	8	0	1970–72

MOST POINTS IN A MATCH
by the team

Pts	Opp	Venue	Year
102	Pt	Lisbon	1994
57	J	Bloemfontein	1995
55	J	Cardiff	1993
54	Sp	Madrid	1994
49	F	Cardiff	1910

by a player
24 by N R Jenkins v Canada at Cardiff — 1993
24 by N R Jenkins v Italy at Cardiff — 1994
22 by N R Jenkins v Portugal at Lisbon — 1994
22 by N R Jenkins v Japan at Bloemfontein — 1995
21 by P H Thorburn v Barbarians at Cardiff — 1990
20 by N Walker v Portugal at Lisbon — 1994

MOST TRIES IN A MATCH
by the team

T	Opp	Venue	Year
16	Pt	Lisbon	1994
11	F	Paris	1909
10	F	Swansea	1910
9	F	Cardiff	1908
9	J	Cardiff	1993

by a player
4 by W Llewellyn v England at Swansea — 1899
4 by R A Gibbs v France at Cardiff — 1908
4 by M C R Richards v England at Cardiff — 1969
4 by I C Evans v Canada at Invercargill — 1987
4 by N Walker v Portugal at Lisbon — 1994

MOST CONVERSIONS IN A MATCH
by the team

C	Opp	Venue	Year
11	Pt	Lisbon	1994
8	F	Swansea	1910
7	F	Paris	1909

by a player
11 by N R Jenkins v Portugal at Lisbon — 1994
8 by J Bancroft v France at Swansea — 1910
6 by J Bancroft v France at Paris — 1909

MOST PENALTY GOALS IN A MATCH
by the team

P	Opp	Venue	Year
8	C	Cardiff	1993
7	It	Cardiff	1994
6	F	Cardiff	1982
6	Tg	Nuku'alofa	1994

by a player
8 by N R Jenkins v Canada at Cardiff — 1993
7 by N R Jenkins v Italy at Cardiff — 1994
6 by G Evans v France at Cardiff — 1982
6 by N R Jenkins v Tonga at Nuku'alofa — 1994

MOST DROPPED GOALS IN A MATCH
by the team

D	Opp	Venue	Year
2	S	Swansea	1912
2	S	Cardiff	1914
2	E	Swansea	1920
2	S	Swansea	1921
2	F	Paris	1930
2	E	Cardiff	1971
2	F	Cardiff	1978

2	E	Twickenham	1984
2	I	Wellington	1987
2	S	Cardiff	1988

by a player

2 by J Shea v England at Swansea 1920
2 by A Jenkins v Scotland at
Swansea 1921
2 by B John v England at Cardiff 1971
2 by M Dacey v England at
Twickenham 1984
2 by J Davies v Ireland at
Wellington 1987
2 by J Davies v Scotland at Cardiff 1988

CAREER RECORDS

MOST CAPPED PLAYERS

Caps	Player	Career
71	I C Evans	1987–97
57	G O Llewellyn	1989–97
55	J P R Williams	1969–81
54	R N Jones	1986–95
53	G O Edwards	1967–78
50	N R Jenkins	1991–97
46	T G R Davies	1966–78
46	P T Davies	1985–95
44	K J Jones	1947–57
42	M R Hall	1988–95

MOST CONSECUTIVE TESTS

Tests	Player	Span
53	G O Edwards	1967–78
43	K J Jones	1947–56
39	G Price	1975–83
38	T M Davies	1969–76
33	W J Bancroft	1890–1901

MOST TESTS AS CAPTAIN

Tests	Captain	Span
28	I C Evans	1991–95
18	A J Gould	1889–97
17	J M Humphreys	1995–97
14	D C T Rowlands	1963–65
14	W J Trew	1907–13

MOST TESTS IN INDIVIDUAL POSITIONS

Full-back J P R Williams		54	1969–81
Wing I C Evans		71	1987–97

Centre M R Hall	32	1988–95
Fly-half N R Jenkins	35	1991–96
Scrum-half G O Edwards	53	1967–78
R N Jones	53	1986–95
Prop G Price	41	1975–83
Hooker B V Meredith	34	1954–62
Lock G O Llewellyn	56	1989–97
Flanker W D Morris	32	1967–74
No 8 T M Davies	38	1969–76

MOST POINTS IN TESTS

Pts	Player	Tests	Career
534	N R Jenkins	50	1991–97
304	P H Thorburn	37	1985–91
166	P Bennett	29	1969–78
157	I C Evans	71	1987–97
152	S P Fenwick	30	1975–81

MOST TRIES IN TESTS

Tries	Player	Tests	Career
33	I C Evans	71	1987–97
20	G O Edwards	53	1967–78
20	T G R Davies	46	1966–78
17	R A Gibbs	16	1906–11
17	J L Williams	17	1906–11
17	K J Jones	44	1947–57

MOST CONVERSIONS IN TESTS

Cons	Player	Tests	Career
65	N R Jenkins	50	1991–97
43	P H Thorburn	37	1985–91
38	J Bancroft	18	1909–14
20	W J Bancroft	33	1890–1901
18	P Bennett	29	1969–78

MOST PENALTY GOALS IN TESTS

Pens	Player	Tests	Career
122	N R Jenkins	50	1991–97
70	P H Thorburn	37	1985–91
36	P Bennett	29	1969–78
35	S P Fenwick	30	1975–81
22	G Evans	10	1981–83

MOST DROPPED GOALS IN TESTS

Drops	Player	Tests	Career
13	J Davies	32	1985–97
8	B John	25	1966–72
7	W G Davies	21	1978–85

INTERNATIONAL CHAMPIONSHIP RECORDS

Record	Detail		Set
Most points in season	102	in four matches	1976
Most tries in season	21	in four matches	1910
Highest score	49	49–14 v France	1910
Biggest win	35	49–14 v France	1910
Highest score conceded	36	3–36 v France	1991
Biggest defeat	33	3–36 v France	1991
Most appearances	45	G O Edwards	1967–78
Most points in matches	191	N R Jenkins	1991–97
Most points in season	52	P H Thorburn	1986
Most points in match	19	J Bancroft	v France, 1910
	19	K S Jarrett	v England, 1967
	19	P Bennett	v Ireland, 1976
	19	N R Jenkins	v Scotland, 1997
Most tries in matches	18	G O Edwards	1967–78
Most tries in season	6	M C R Richards	1969
Most tries in match	4	W Llewellyn	v England, 1899
	4	M C R Richards	v England, 1969
Most cons in matches	32	J Bancroft	1909–1914
Most cons in season	9	J Bancroft	1910
	9	J A Bassett	1931
Most cons in match	8	J Bancroft	v France, 1910
Most pens in matches	48	N R Jenkins	1991–97
Most pens in season	16	P H Thorburn	1986
Most pens in match	6	G Evans	v France, 1982
Most drops in matches	8	J Davies	1985–97
Most drops in season	4	J Davies	1988
Most drops in match	2	J Shea	v England, 1920
	2	A Jenkins	v Scotland, 1921
	2	B John	v England, 1971
	2	M Dacey	v England, 1984
	2	J Davies	v Scotland, 1988

MAJOR TOUR RECORDS

Record	Detail	Year	Place
Most individual points	89 by N R Jenkins	1993	Africa
Most points in match	28 by M A Rayer	1990 v N Region	Namibia
Most tries in match	5 by G Thomas	1996 v W Australia	Perth

MISCELLANEOUS RECORDS

Record	Holder	Detail
Longest Test career	W J Trew	14 seasons, 1899–1900 to 1912–13
	T H Vile	14 seasons, 1907–08 to 1920–21
	H Tanner	14 seasons, 1935–36 to 1948–49
Youngest Test cap	N Biggs	18 yrs 49 days in 1888
Oldest Test cap	T H Vile	38 yrs 152 days in 1921

WALES INTERNATIONAL CAREER RECORDS (*up to 30 April 1997*)

Player	Debut	Caps since last season	Caps	T	C	PG	DG	Pts
W J L Thomas	1995 v SA	1996 *Bb* (R), 1997 *US*	9	1	0	0	0	5
W T Proctor	1992 v A	1996 *A* 1,2, *Bb, F, It, A* 3, 1997 *E* (R)	29	5	0	0	0	25
I C Evans	1987 v F	1996 *A* 1, 2 *Bb, F, A* 3, *SA*, 1997 *US, S, I, F*	71	33	0	0	0	157
S D Hill	1993 v Z	1996 *A* 2, *F* (R), *It*, 1997 *E*	12	2	0	0	0	10
D R James	1996 v A	1996 *A* 2 (R), *It, A* 3, *SA*, 1997 *I*	5	1	0	0	0	5
G Thomas	1995 v J	1996 *A* 1,2, *Bb, F, It, A* 3, 1997 *US, S, I, F, E*	17	8	0	0	0	40
N G Davies	1988 v NZ	1996 *A* 1,2, *Bb, F*, 1997 *E*	29	5	0	0	0	23
A G Bateman	1990 v S	1996 *SA*, 1997 *US, S, F, E*	9	1	0	0	0	5
L B Davies	1996 v It	1996 *A* 1, *Bb, F, It* (R)	9	0	0	0	0	0
I S Gibbs	1991 v E	1996 *It, A* 3, *SA*, 1997 *US, S, I, F*	27	3	0	0	0	15
J Davies	1985 v E	1996 *A* 3, 1997 *US* (t), *S* (R), *F* (R), *E*	32	5	2	6	13	81
N R Jenkins	1991 v E	1996 *A* 1,2, *Bb, F, It, A* 3 (R), *SA*, 1997 *S, I, F, E*	50	6	65	122	3	534
A C Thomas	1996 v It	1996 *F* (R), *SA*, 1997 *US, S, I, F*	10	2	9	11	0	61
Paul John	1994 v Tg	1996 *Bb* (t), 1997 *US* (R)	3	0	0	0	0	0
R Howley	1996 v E	1996 *A* 1,2, *Bb, F, It, A* 3, *SA*, 1997 *US, S, I, F, E*	16	5	0	0	0	25
A P Moore	1995 v J		4	2	0	0	0	10
G R Jenkins	1991 v F	1997 *US*	31	1	0	0	0	5
J M Humphreys	1995 v NZ	1996 *A* 1, 2, *Bb, It, A* 3, *SA*, 1997 *S, I, F, E*	19	2	0	0	0	10
B Williams	1996 v F	1996 *F*	1	1	0	0	0	5
C D Loader	1995 v SA	1996 *A* 1,2, *Bb, F, It, A* 3, *SA*, 1997 *US, S, I, F, E*	15	0	0	0	0	0
S C John	1995 v S	1997 *E* (R)	3	0	0	0	0	0
A L P Lewis	1996 v It	1996 *A* 2 (t)	5	0	0	0	0	0
D Young	1987 v E	1996 *A* 3, *SA*, 1997 *US, S, I, F, E*	21	1	0	0	0	4
L Mustoe	1995 v Fj	1996 *A* 1 (R),2	3	0	0	0	0	0
J D Davies	1991 v I	1996 *A* 1, *Bb, F, It*	32	1	0	0	0	5
P Arnold	1990 v Nm	1996 *Bb* (R)	16	2	0	0	0	8

Name	Debut	Seasons						
D Jones	1994 v SA	1996 *A* 1,2, *Bb, It, A* 3	19	0	0	0	0	0
G O Llewellyn	1989 v NZ	1996 *A* 1,2, *Bb, F, It, A* 3, *SA*, 1997 *US, S, I, F, E*	57	5	0	0	0	24
M Rowley	1996 v SA	1996 *SA*, 1997 *US, S, I, F*	5	0	0	0	0	0
M J Voyle	1996 v A	1996 *A* 1 (t), *F*, 1997 *E*	3	0	0	0	0	0
N Thomas	1996 v SA	1996 *SA* (R)	1	0	0	0	0	0
K P Jones	1996 v Bb	1996 *Bb, F, It, A* 3, 1997 *I* (R), *E*	6	0	0	0	0	0
M E Williams	1996 v Bb	1996 *Bb, F, It* (t)	3	0	0	0	0	0
H T Taylor	1994 v Pt	1996 *A* 1,2, *It, A* 3	24	5	0	0	0	25
R G Jones	1996 v It	1996 *A* 1, 1997 *US* (R), *S* (R)	8	0	0	0	0	0
A Gibbs	1995 v I	1996 *A* 2	3	0	0	0	0	0
J C Quinnell	1995 v Fj	1996 *A* 3 (R), 1997 *US* (R), *S* (R), *I* (R), *E* (R)	6	0	0	0	0	0
C L Charvis	1996 v A	1996 *A* 3 (R), *SA*, 1997 *US, S, I, F*	6	0	0	0	0	0
R E Webster	1987 v A		13	1	0	0	0	4
E W Lewis	1991 v I		41	3	0	0	0	15
S M Williams	1994 v Tg	1996 *A* 1,2, *Bb, F, It, A* 3, *SA*, 1997 *US, S, I, F, E*	14	0	0	0	0	0
D L M McIntosh	1996 v SA	1996 *SA*, 1997 *E* (R)	2	0	0	0	0	0
L S Quinnell	1993 v C	1997 *US, S, I, F, E*	14	5	0	0	0	25

WELSH CLUBS 1996-97

Bridgend

Year of formation 1878
Ground Brewery Field, Tondu Road, Bridgend, Mid Glamorgan Tel: Bridgend (01656) 652707 and 659032
Colours Blue and white hoops
Captain 1996-97 I Greenslade
WRU Leagues 1996-97 Div 1 5th   **SWALEC Cup 1996-97** Lost 16-17 to Ebbw Vale (quarter-final)

After an encouraging start had brought five victories from six matches, Bridgend's League season tailed away with seven defeats in their last nine games. Cup hopes evaporated at Ebbw Vale in the eighth round, though by a whisker at 17-16. However, there was some satisfaction at the Brewery Field when, four days after Cardiff had won the Cup, Bridgend defeated their great rivals 17-0. It was the first occasion for seven-and-a-half years that Cardiff had failed to score in any match, and took on added significance because Bridgend's captain, Robert Howley, had joined Cardiff.

Cliff Vogl, a USA Eagle, proved a rousing forward and John Graf, captain of Canada, was a scrum-half recruit, but six players were released as a cost-cutting measure. Matthew Lewis returned on transfer from Wasps. Matthew Back was 'sacked' for failing to turn up for the European Conference game at Narbonne, Glen Webbe retired and backs' coach Gerald Williams, the former Wales scrum-half, stood down. Kevin Ellis, who had left Bridgend in 1990 for a Rugby League career, returned as player/coach to work with chief coach John Phelps. Adrian Durston was top scorer with 128 League points and Gareth Thomas obtained 18 tries.

League Record 1996-97

Date	Venue	Opponents	Result	Scorers
31 Aug	H	Llanelli	13-9	*T:* G Thomas *C:* L Griffiths *P:* L Griffiths 2
3 Sep	A	Treorchy	11-8	*T:* P Jones *P:* A Durston 2
7 Sep	H	Ebbw Vale	16-18	*T:* D James *C:* L Griffiths *P:* L Griffiths 3
14 Sep	A	Newbridge	64-29	*T:* G Thomas 4, D James 2, A Durston, C Michaluk, P Jones *C:* L Griffiths 8 *D:* G Thomas
18 Sep	H	Dunvant	80-0	*T:* G Thomas 2, P Jones 2, G Wilkins 2, A Durston, J Forster, D James, C Michaluk, W Morris, C Stephens *C:* L Griffiths 7 *P:* L Griffiths 2
21 Sep	H	Neath	59-13	*T:* G Wilkins 2, A Durston, J Forster, G Thomas, I Jones, D James, W Morris *C:* M Back 3, A Durston 2 *P:* M Back, A Durston, G Thomas
28 Sep	A	Cardiff	25-33	*T:* A Williams, L Griffiths *P:* L Griffiths 5
9 Nov	H	Newport	32-32	*T:* G Thomas 2, M Lewis 2 *C:* M Lewis 3 *P:* M Lewis 2
16 Nov	A	Caerphilly	29-7	*T:* D James 2, W Morris *C:* L Griffiths *P:* L Griffiths 3 *D:* M Lewis
7 Dec	A	Pontypridd	9-53	*P:* M Lewis 3
28 Dec	H	Treorchy	26-21	*T:* G Thomas 2, J Graf *C:* A Durston *P:* A Durston 2, M Lewis
8 Feb	H	Newbridge	45-14	*T:* C Vogl 2, R Boobyer 2, pen try, G Thomas, P Jones *C:* M Lewis 2 *P:* M Lewis 2
8 Mar	A	Neath	22-30	*T:* P Jones, A Durston, M Lewis *C:* M Lewis 2 *P:* M Lewis

2 Apr	H	Swansea	18-25	*T:* A Durston, D James *C:* M Lewis
				P: M Lewis 2
5 Apr	A	Newport	26-31	*T:* D James, C Bradshaw, C Stephens, C Vogl
				C: M Lewis 3
16 Apr	A	Llanelli	17-31	*T:* A Williams 2 *C:* M Lewis 2 *P:* M Lewis
19 Apr	H	Caerphilly	49-15	*T:* J Forster 2, C Bradshaw, P Jones, G Thomas,
				K Walker, L Davies, S Greenway, K Ellis
				C: G Thomas, A Durston
25 Apr	A	Dunvant	0-15	
30 Apr	H	Cardiff	17-0	*T:* K Walker *P:* A Durston 2, M Lewis
				D: L Davies
3 May	H	Pontypridd	24-52	*T:* G Thomas, C Michaluk, A Williams
				C: A Durston 3 *P:* A Durston
7 May	A	Ebbw Vale	5-27	*T:* S Greenway
10 May	A	Swansea	17-64	*T:* L Davies, C Ferris, A Williams
				C: A Durston

Caerphilly

Year of formation 1886
Ground Virginia Park, Pontygwindy Road, Caerphilly Tel: Caerphilly (01222) 882573
Colours Green and white hoops
Captain 1996-97 D Phillips
WRU Leagues 1996-97 Div 1 10th – *relegated*   **SWALEC Cup 1996-97** Lost 17-20 to
Llanelli (6th round)

Promoted for the first time, Caerphilly played attractive, open rugby with a light but
mobile pack. However, heavier forwards wore them down and there were only two
League successes during the season: a sensational 14-9 victory over Llanelli at
Virginia Park in September, and then an impressive home display to rout Newbridge
by 50-7. David Phillips, an astute captain with his wide experience and his cool,
controlling influence at outside-half, was an invaluable factor in numerous determined performances. A number of matches were lost by narrow margins: 39-32 at
Neath, 28-25 against Ebbw Vale, and to score 38 points in an astonishing tussle at
Swansea was remarkable indeed before losing by 52-38.

Brett Davey was recruited at full-back to make a notable contribution while a
busy back row, which featured Dai Duly, Chris Brown and Phil Agar, never relaxed
in defence or attack. Davey was top scorer with 117 points; and Agar contributed
seven tries. Disappointingly, Caerphilly were the only Division One team not to be
included in the new European Conference. They opened a 1,000 seat stand costing
£170,000 in March.

League Record 1996-97

Date	Venue	Opponents	Result	Scorers
31 Aug	A	Newport	10-29	*T:* D Phillips, D Starr
3 Sep	H	Dunvant	24-35	*T:* D Phillips, D Starr, R Hammond, S Price
				C: B Davey 2
7 Sep	H	Swansea	3-57	*P:* B Davey
14 Sep	A	Pontypridd	25-38	*T:* R Bilton, W Evans, J Payne, J Lougher
				C: P Phillips *P:* P Phillips
18 Sep	H	Llanelli	14-9	*T:* W Evans *P:* P Phillips 3
21 Sep	A	Treorchy	16-31	*T:* R Hammond *C:* P Phillips
				P: P Phillips 3
28 Sep	H	Ebbw Vale	25-28	*T:* A Owen, B Davey, P Agar *C:* P Phillips 2
				P: P Phillips 2
9 Nov	A	Newbridge	16-29	*T:* R Hammond 2 *P:* P Phillips 2
16 Nov	H	Bridgend	7-29	*T:* pen try *C:* B Davey

30 Nov	A	Neath	32-39	T: R Bidgood, L Griffiths, S Jenkins, S Law C: D Phillips 3 P: D Phillips 2
7 Dec	H	Cardiff	20-34	T: I Phillips, D Starr, pen try C: D Phillips D: D Phillips
8 Feb	H	Pontypridd	8-68	T: R Bidgood P: P Phillips
22 Feb	H	Newport	26-32	T: P Agar 2, B Davey, P Phillips C: B Davey 3
1 Mar	A	Llanelli	12-47	T: P Agar, R Hammond C: B Davey
8 Mar	H	Treorchy	15-32	T: P Agar, W Gray, I Jones
23 Mar	A	Ebbw Vale	9-25	P: P Phillips 2, D Phillips
5 Apr	H	Newbridge	50-7	T: D Starr 2, R Bidgood 2, P Agar, D Duly, B Davey, C Brown C: B Davey 5
12 Apr	A	Dunvant	17-42	T: D Phillips, J Lougher C: B Davey 2 P: B Davey
19 Apr	A	Bridgend	15-49	T: D Starr, D Duly C: B Davey P: B Davey
29 Apr	A	Swansea	38-52	T: A Tucker 2, R Bidgood, S Jenkins, A Owen, P Phillips C: B Davey 4
3 May	A	Cardiff	21-69	T: T Carless, P Agar, A Owen C: B Davey 3
10 May	H	Neath	19-20	T: D Phillips, A Owen, B Davey C: B Davey 2

Cardiff

Year of formation 1876
Ground Cardiff Arms Park, Westgate Street, Cardiff CF1 1JA Tel: Cardiff (01222) 383546
Colours Cambridge blue and black
Captain 1996-97 H T Taylor
WRU Leagues 1996-97 Div 1 4th   **SWALEC Cup 1996-97** Winners – beat Swansea 33-26 (final)

Cardiff should have achieved more success than just the SWALEC Cup after signing such luminaries as Robert Howley, Leigh Davies, Justin Thomas, David Young, Gwyn Jones and the phenomenal Lee Jarvis. Ultimately they had to settle for fourth place in the League and a semi-final spot in the European Cup. However, two notable records were broken: first Steve Ford passed Bleddyn Williams's career try record of 185, set 42 years earlier, while scoring five tries in the Cup tie against Dinas Powys, which brought Cardiff their record Cup tally of 99-7; then Jarvis scored 408 points to top the club record in a season of 383 by former Wales fly-half Gareth Davies, now the club's chief executive. Jonathan Davies scored 185 points; while Steve Ford's haul was 19 tries in all matches followed by Jarvis (16) Mike Hall (15) and Robert Howley (14).

A disastrous start to the League programme saw defeats in the opening three games to Swansea, Pontypridd and Llanelli. Then came the club's heaviest ever home defeat: 24-53 by Harlequins in October. The defeat by Agen 64-14 at Leicester in August in the European Conference competition was the worst of all-time. Alex Evans returned from Australia to resume as coaching supremo late in the season, and Cardiff became a limited company in February.

League Record 1996-97

Date	Venue	Opponents	Result	Scorers
31 Aug	A	Swansea	23-49	T: S Hill 2, R Howley C: J Davies P: J Davies, L Jarvis
4 Sep	A	Pontypridd	14-24	T: M Hall, R Howley C: L Jarvis 2
7 Sep	H	Llanelli	12-30	P: L Jarvis 4
14 Sep	A	Treorchy	23-22	T: P Booth, H Taylor, pen try C: J Davies P: J Davies 2
18 Sep	H	Ebbw Vale	75-17	T: S Ford 3, S Hill 3, M Hall 2, L Mustoe, P Booth, J Ringer C: J Davies 10

21 Sep	A	Newbridge	64-11	*T:* E Lewis 2, J Davies, S Ford, M Hall, R Howley, G Jones, J Ringer, J Thomas, N Walker *C:* J Davies 7
28 Sep	H	Bridgend	33-25	*T:* J Thomas 2, S Ford, J Davies, M Hall *C:* J Davies *P:* J Davies 2
9 Nov	A	Neath	27-26	*T:* S Hill 2, J Thomas *C:* L Jarvis 3 *P:* L Jarvis 2
7 Dec	A	Caerphilly	34-20	*T:* G Jones, S Hill, J Davies, L Davies, pen try *C:* J Davies 3 *P:* J Davies
28 Dec	H	Pontypridd	23-37	*T:* J Davies, J Thomas *C:* J Davies 2 *P:* J Davies 3
8 Feb	H	Treorchy	60-22	*T:* S Hill 2, J Davies 2, L Jarvis, J Hewlett, L Mustoe, J Ringer, pen try *C:* L Jarvis 6 *P:* L Jarvis
26 Feb	A	Llanelli	26-48	*T:* L Jarvis 2, S Ford, R Howley *C:* L Jarvis 3
1 Mar	A	Ebbw Vale	38-35	*T:* M Hall, L Davies *C:* L Jarvis 2 *P:* L Jarvis 7 *D:* L Jarvis
8 Mar	H	Newbridge	45-20	*T:* M Hall 2, S Ford 2, L Davies, L Jarvis, J Ringer *C:* L Jarvis 4, G Jones
29 Mar	A	Dunvant	27-27	*T:* L Davies, N Walker *C:* J Davies *P:* L Jarvis 5
31 Mar	H	Newport	26-13	*T:* S Ford, L Jarvis, N Walker *C:* L Jarvis *P:* L Jarvis 2 *D:* Jarvis
5 Apr	H	Neath	46-17	*T:* S Hill 2, J Ringer, S Ford, N Walker *C:* L Jarvis 3 *P:* L Jarvis 5
19 Apr	H	Dunvant	43-19	*T:* N Walker 2, P Booth 2, G Jones, R Howley, J Wakeford *C:* J Davies 2, J Hewlett 2
30 Apr	A	Bridgend	0-17	
3 May	H	Caerphilly	69-21	*T:* L Jarvis 3, M Hall 2, H Taylor 2, L Davies, N Walker, J Humphreys, J Ringer *C:* L Jarvis 6, N Walker
7 May	H	Swansea	31-20	*T:* P Booth, J Humphreys, L Jarvis, pen try *C:* L Jarvis 4 *P:* L Jarvis
10 May	A	Newport	11-23	*T:* O Williams *P:* L Jarvis 2

Dunvant

Year of formation 1888
Ground Broadacre, Killay, Swansea SA2 7RU Tel: Swansea (01792) 207291
Colours Red and green hoops
Captain 1996-97 Dean Evans
WRU Leagues 1996-97 Div 1 9th – *relegated*   **SWALEC Cup 1996-97** Lost 10-71 to Swansea (6th round)

Dunvant had returned to Division One as champions of Division Two, but were relegated again after a gallant season. 'The WRU decision to reduce the top division to eight teams and the cock-eyed bonus system robbed us,' lamented captain Dean Evans. Dunvant began promisingly, winning their first four League games, including a surprise home victory by 26-18 against Swansea. Neath were defeated twice, including a 43-26 margin at the Gnoll, while there was considerable merit in a 17-17 result at Ebbw Vale. Then Cardiff were denied in an amazing draw at Broadacre. Narrow defeats were suffered at home from visitors Llanelli, Treorchy and Newport; and it was an anxious struggle for Llanelli to win 29-24 at Stradey.

Five players were released in February to fund the recruitment of Fijian internationals Joeli Veitayaki, the 21st prop and former captain of Fiji, and Emori Katalau, both of whom made a major impact. Richard Greenwood was an outstanding back row and Mark Thomas a fine goal-kicker. He top scored with 209 points, while Ceri Davies scored 12 tries.

League Record 1996-97

Date	Venue	Opponents	Result	Scorers
31 Aug	H	Ebbw Vale	21-10	*T:* M David, S Jenkins, S Dixon *P:* D Morgan, Dean Evans
3 Sep	A	Caerphilly	35-24	*T:* M Harris 2, G Evans, M Thomas, S Wake *C:* M Thomas 5
7 Sep	A	Newbridge	36-24	*T:* D Chick, Dean Evans, G Evans, M Davies, J Williams *C:* J Williams 4 *P:* J Williams
14 Sep	H	Swansea	26-18	*T:* J Dodd, S Wake *C:* M Thomas 2 *P:* M Thomas 4
18 Sep	A	Bridgend	0-80	
21 Sep	H	Pontypridd	10-25	*T:* M Davies *C:* M Thomas *P:* M Thomas
28 Sep	A	Neath	43-26	*T:* C Thomas, S Wake, P Thorburn, S Dixon, pen try *C:* M Thomas 3 *P:* M Thomas 4
9 Nov	H	Llanelli	24-25	*T:* Dean Evans, W Lloyd *C:* M McCarthy *P:* M McCarthy 2 *D:* M McCarthy 2
30 Nov	H	Treorchy	19-25	*T:* J Dodd *C:* M Thomas *P:* M Thomas 3 *D:* M McCarthy
7 Dec	A	Newport	22-45	*T:* C Thomas 2, M Thomas, Dean Evans, *C:* D Morgan
8 Feb	A	Swansea	12-38	*T:* E Katalau, C Davies *C:* D Morgan
22 Feb	H	Newbridge	37-17	*T:* C Davies, Deiniol Evans, M Davies, S Wake, M Harris *C:* M Thomas 3 *P:* M Thomas 2
8 Mar	A	Pontypridd	6-48	*P:* M Thomas 2
15 Mar	A	Ebbw Vale	17-17	*T:* C Davies, N Davies *C:* M Thomas 2 *P:* M Thomas
22 Mar	H	Neath	34-22	*T:* C Davies, M Davies, S Wake, N Spender, R Greenwood *C:* M Thomas 3 *D:* M Thomas
29 Mar	H	Cardiff	27-27	*T:* N Spender 2, C Davies, J Veitayaki *C:* M Thomas 2 *D:* S Wake
5 Apr	A	Llanelli	24-29	*T:* M Thomas, N Spender, S Wake, A Killa *C:* M Thomas 2
12 Apr	H	Caerphilly	42-17	*T:* C Davies 2, S Wake, M Harris, J Veitayaki, M Thomas *C:* M Thomas 3 *P:* M Thomas 2
19 Apr	A	Cardiff	19-43	*T:* E Harris, N Spender, M Harris *C:* M Thomas, S Morgan
25 Apr	H	Bridgend	15-0	*T:* M Davies, N Spender *C:* M Thomas *P:* M Thomas
3 May	H	Newport	9-14	*P:* M Thomas 3
10 May	A	Treorchy	46-27	*T:* A Killa 2, M Davies, L Williams, R Llewellyn, W Lloyd, C Davies, S Wake *C:* M Thomas 2, S Wake

Ebbw Vale

Year of formation 1880
Ground Eugene Cross Park, Ebbw Vale, Gwent Tel: Ebbw Vale (01495) 302995
Colours Red, white and green
Captain 1996-97 K P Jones
WRU Leagues 1996-97 Div 1 7th   **SWALEC Cup 1996-97** Lost 15-26 to Swansea (semi-final)

For the first time in 20 years Ebbw Vale reached the semi-final of the Cup, and they also retained their place in the top division after a confident start, in which they won five of their first seven games. Kingsley Jones was an inspiring leader and Mark Jones, the former Wales and Neath No 8, settled in quickly as a powerful member of an energetic pack when he joined from Rugby League club, Warrington. Byron Hayward was often a match-winner at outside-half with his dropped goals and opportunist tries. He top-scored with 297 points, including 14 tries. David Llewellyn partnered him shrewdly, while Mike Boys was a canny centre. Jonah Lomu, the New Zealand wing, played for Ebbw in a charity match in December.

Mark Jones made history when he took the WRU to the High Court after he was banned for four weeks for fighting with Swansea prop Stuart Evans, winning the right for a personal hearing by the WRU.

League Record 1996-97

Date	Venue	Opponents	Result	Scorers
31 Aug	A	Dunvant	10-21	*T:* D Llewellyn *C:* B Hayward *P:* B Hayward
3 Sep	H	Newbridge	22-7	*T:* B Hayward 2, S Marshall *C:* B Hayward 2 *P:* B Hayward
7 Sep	A	Bridgend	18-16	*T:* I Jeffreys, J Williams *C:* B Hayward *P:* B Hayward 2
14 Sep	H	Neath	21-15	*T:* I Jeffreys, S Marshall *C:* B Hayward *P:* B Hayward 3
18 Sep	A	Cardiff	17-75	*T:* B Hayward, S Marshall, C Price *C:* B Hayward
22 Sep	H	Newport	24-23	*T:* I Jeffreys, B Hayward *C:* B Hayward *P:* B Hayward 4
28 Sep	A	Caerphilly	28-25	*T:* K Jones, D Llewellyn, C Price *C:* B Hayward 2 *P:* B Hayward 3
9 Nov	H	Swansea	13-9	*T:* B Hayward *C:* B Hayward *P:* B Hayward *D:* B Hayward
16 Nov	A	Pontypridd	26-50	*T:* B Hayward, pen try *C:* B Hayward 2 *P:* B Hayward 4
7 Dec	A	Treorchy	17-13	*T:* M Jones, I Jeffreys *C:* B Hayward 2 *P:* B Hayward
8 Feb	A	Neath	16-15	*T:* J Hawker *C:* B Hayward *P:* B Hayward 3
1 Mar	H	Cardiff	35-38	*T:* pen tries 2, L Lewis, P Pook *C:* B Hayward 3 *P:* B Hayward 3
8 Mar	A	Newport	6-13	*P:* B Hayward 2
15 Mar	H	Dunvant	17-17	*T:* J Hawker, B Hayward *C:* B Hayward 2 *P:* B Hayward
23 Mar	H	Caerphilly	25-9	*T:* B Hayward 2, K Jones, S Jones *C:* B Hayward *P:* B Hayward
2 Apr	H	Llanelli	16-16	*T:* C Billen *C:* B Hayward *P:* B Hayward 2 *D:* B Hayward
5 Apr	A	Swansea	12-59	*T:* S Marshall, G Spence *C:* G Spence
15 Apr	A	Newbridge	22-14	*T:* B Hayward, I Jeffreys, P Pook *C:* B Hayward 2 *P:* B Hayward
19 Apr	H	Pontypridd	7-47	*T:* S Marshall *C:* B Hayward
4 May	H	Treorchy	39-12	*T:* A Harries 2, J Hawker, D Bell, B Hayward, D Llewellyn *C:* B Hayward 3 *D:* B Hayward
7 May	H	Bridgend	27-5	*T:* A Harries, B Hayward, S Marshall, B Watkins *C:* B Hayward 2 *P:* B Hayward
10 May	A	Llanelli	13-53	*T:* G Bisp *C:* B Hayward *P:* B Hayward *D:* B Hayward

Llanelli

Year of formation 1872
Ground Stradey Park, Llanelli, Dyfed SA15 4BT
Tel: Llanelli (01554) 774060 and 0891 660221
Colours Scarlet and white
Captain 1996-97 I C Evans
WRU Leagues 1996-97 Div 1 3rd   **SWALEC Cup 1996-97** Lost 26-36 to Cardiff (semi-final)

263

Llanelli's fortunes took a turn for the better with the enlistment of Frano Botica to solve a fly-half problem and kick vital goals. The arrival of the former NZ Test star revitalised the entire team after they had experienced a stuttering start to the League programme. Neath had broken the Stradey ground record in the first match and there were narrow defeats at Bridgend and Caerphilly. Key players had been lost, among them Gwyn Jones and Justin Thomas to Cardiff; former captain Phil Davies to Leeds; Craig Quinnell to Richmond and smart No 2 scrum-half Huw Harries to Harlequins. Mike Voyle joined from Newport. Ieuan Evans was appointed captain with Garan Evans a dangerous attacker on the other wing, Rupert Moon ruled the scrum-half spot with customary audacity.

The Scarlets twice defeated Cardiff in the League, but lost to them by 36-26 in the semi-final stage of the Cup. This defeat was the only reverse they suffered after their 35-36 loss to Sale on December 13. Llanelli set a Division One record score by winning 97-10 against Newbridge and defeated Western Samoa by 23-15. Overall Botica contributed 260 points and Garan Evans 17 tries.

League Record 1996-97

Date	Venue	Opponents	Result	Scorers
31 Aug	A	Bridgend	9-13	*P:* S Jones 3
4 Sep	H	Neath	20-25	*T:* M Perego, M Voyle, P Morris *C:* M McCarthy *P:* M McCarthy
7 Sep	A	Cardiff	30-12	*T:* H Jenkins 2, G Evans, W Proctor, N Boobyer *C:* S Jones *P:* I Evans
14 Sep	H	Newport	55-5	*T:* I Jones 2, R Moon, N Davies, C Wyatt, P Morris, S John, I Evans, G Evans *C:* S Jones 5
18 Sep	A	Caerphilly	9-14	*P:* S Jones 3
21 Sep	H	Swansea	30-17	*T:* I Evans 2, W Proctor *P:* I Evans 5
28 Sep	A	Pontypridd	6-29	*P:* T Davies 2
9 Nov	A	Dunvant	25-24	*T:* R Moon *C:* F Botica *P:* F Botica 5 *D:* F Botica
7 Dec	H	Newbridge	97-10	*T:* I Evans 4, A Gibbs 3, N Boobyer 2, G Evans 2, H Williams-Jones 2, I Jones, N Davies *C:* F Botica 11
8 Feb	A	Newport	18-18	*T:* R Moon, Richards *C:* F Botica *P:* F Botica 2
26 Feb	H	Cardiff	48-26	*T:* R Moon 2, P Morris, W Proctor, M Wintle, pen try *C:* F Botica 6 *P:* F Botica 2
1 Mar	H	Caerphilly	47-12	*T:* N Boobyer 2, W Proctor 2, S Ford, F Botica, A Gibbs, M Wintle, P Morris *C:* F Botica
8 Mar	A	Swansea	42-12	*T:* N Boobyer 2, G Evans, M Wintle, A Gibbs, W Proctor *C:* F Botica 6
25 Mar	H	Treorchy	87-5	*T:* G Evans 4, C Wyatt 3, S Ford 2, I Evans, M Wintle, R McBryde, M Voyle *C:* F Botica 10, C Warlow
29 Mar	H	Pontypridd	31-16	*T:* I Boobyer, M Wintle, C Warlow, R Moon *C:* C Warlow 4 *P:* C Warlow
2 Apr	A	Ebbw Vale	16-16	*T:* R McBryde *C:* C Warlow *P:* C Warlow 2 *D:* N Boobyer
5 Apr	H	Dunvant	29-24	*T:* R Jones, C Warlow, W Proctor, S Gale, P Morris *C:* C Warlow 2
16 Apr	H	Bridgend	31-17	*T:* N Boobyer, R Moon, C Warlow, C Wyatt *C:* C Warlow 4 *P:* C Warlow
19 Apr	A	Treorchy	55-25	*T:* W Proctor 3, H Jenkins 2, C Warlow 2, S Jones, pen try *C:* C Warlow 4, N Boobyer
30 Apr	A	Newbridge	38-15	*T:* F Botica 3, C Warlow, A Gibbs, C Wyatt *C:* C Warlow 4

7 May	A	Neath	13-3	*T:* N Davies *C:* F Botica *P:* F Botica *D:* C Warlow
10 May	H	Ebbw Vale	53-13	*T:* G Evans 2, A Gibbs 2, J Hyatt 2, W Proctor, I Jones, S Ford *C:* F Botica 4

Neath

Year of formation 1871
Ground The Gnoll, Gnoll Park Road, Neath, West Glamorgan Tel: Neath (01639) 636547
Colours All black with white Maltese cross
Captain 1996-97 J D Davies
WRU Leagues 1996-97 Div 1 8th   **SWALEC Cup 1996-97** Lost 24-32 to Swansea
(quarter-final)

Relegation fears dogged John Davies's team right to the last match as they spent an anxious time rebuilding after losing their international locks, brothers Gareth and Glyn Llewellyn, to Harlequins and centre Leigh Davies to Cardiff. The financial situation also proved worrying, but was somewhat reduced when they released hooker Barry Williams on £100,000 transfer fee to Richmond at the end of the season. There were some behind-the-scenes problems, too, which resulted in Lyn Jones leaving the coaching staff after a personality clash with director of rugby Darryl Jones. Richard Jones was recruited to the coaching squad.

On the field there were some heavy defeats, notably the worst in the club's history by 72-12 at Pontypridd. Ponty also inflicted a 60-19 defeat at the National Stadium on September 1 in a special fixture in which Neath, as League champions of the previous season, met Cup-holders Pontypridd. For the first time Neath finished lower than fourth in the League. Darren Case scored 101 points; Chris Higgs 11 tries.

League Record 1996-97

Date	Venue	Opponents	Result	Scorers
4 Sep	A	Llanelli	25-20	*T:* C Bridges, H Woodland, G Taylor *C:* C Bridges 2 *P:* C Bridges 2
7 Sep	H	Treorchy	46-19	*T:* G Evans 2, B Grabham 2, C Higgs, I Boobyer, G Taylor *C:* S Williams *P:* D Morris 2, C Bridges
14 Sep	A	Ebbw Vale	15-21	*T:* G Taylor, Richard Jones *C:* M Williams *P:* M Williams
18 Sep	H	Newbridge	65-10	*T:* C Higgs 2, P Williams 2, B Williams, I Boobyer, B Grabham, P Horgan, M Williams, H Woodland *C:* M Williams 6 *P:* M Williams
21 Sep	A	Bridgend	13-59	*T:* B Williams, C Higgs *P:* D Case
28 Sep	H	Dunvant	26-43	*T:* G Evans 2, S Gardiner, M Thomas *C:* D Morris 3
9 Nov	H	Cardiff	26-27	*T:* I Boobyer, B Grabham, S Williams *C:* G Davies *P:* G Davies 3
16 Nov	A	Newport	13-18	*T:* L Gerrard, J Davies *P:* G Davies
23 Nov	A	Treorchy	15-10	*T:* B Williams, H Woodland *C:* P Williams *D:* P Williams
30 Nov	H	Caerphilly	39-32	*T:* Robin Jones, J Davies, P Williams, M Thomas, J Funnell, pen try *C:* P Williams 3 *P:* P Williams
7 Dec	A	Swansea	10-49	*T:* P Williams *C:* P Williams *P:* P Williams
8 Feb	H	Ebbw Vale	15-16	*T:* J Davies, S Williams *C:* P Williams *P:* P Williams
1 Mar	A	Newbridge	29-16	*T:* D Morris, D Hawkins, C Higgs, J Davies, S Williams *C:* D Case 2

8 Mar	H	Bridgend	30-22	T: I Boobyer, B Grabham, G Evans
				C: D Case 3 P: D Case 3
22 Mar	A	Dunvant	22-34	T: B Williams, D Hawkins, P Williams
				C: D Case 2 P: D Case
31 Mar	H	Pontypridd	3-29	P: D Case
5 Apr	A	Cardiff	17-46	T: C Bridges, S Williams C: D Case 2
				P: D Case
19 Apr	H	Newport	38-8	T: P Williams 2, Richie Jones, C Higgs,
				D Morris, G Evans C: D Case 3, G Evans
25 Apr	A	Pontypridd	12-72	T: D Case, pen try C: D Case
3 May	H	Swansea	42-20	T: I Boobyer 3, D Case, S Williams,
				B Grabham C: G Evans 3 P: D Case 2
7 May	H	Llanelli	3-13	P: P Williams
10 May	A	Caerphilly	20-19	T: G Evans, J Davies C: D Case 2
				P: D Case 2

Newbridge

Year of formation 1888
Ground The Welfare Ground, Bridge Street, Newbridge, Gwent Tel: Newbridge (01495)
243247
Colours Blue and black hoops
Captain 1996-97 L Phillips
WRU Leagues 1996-97 Div 1 12th – *relegated*   **SWALEC Cup 1996-97** Lost 20-26 to
Bridgend (6th round)

With just four League victories, Newbridge finished bottom of the First Division
and lost their place among the elite for the first time. The entire coaching staff had
resigned at the end of September, by which time they had just a win over Treorchy
to show from eight games, including three defeats by scores in excess of 60 points. It
was an anxious season for new captain and hooker Leighton Phillips, whose only real
moment of satisfaction came in April with an unexpected 31-24 success against
Swansea. Among the players who sought pastures new were Andrew Gibbs, Phil
Withers, Iwan Jones, Gareth Taylor, Paul Pook, Matthew Silva, Richard Smith and
the storming David Dunn, who returned to New Zealand. Lack of scoring power
was always evident and Newbridge were the only First Division team to fail to
register a bonus point. Jason Williams scored 186 points; Damian Cooper nine tries.

League Record 1996-97

Date	Venue	Opponents	Result	Scorers
31 Aug	A	Treorchy	23-17	T: P Kawulok, J Powell C: J Williams 2
				P: J Williams 3
3 Sep	A	Ebbw Vale	7-22	T: L Phillips C: J Williams
7 Sep	H	Dunvant	24-36	T: K Williams, M Yendle C: J Williams
				P: J Williams 4
14 Sep	H	Bridgend	29-64	T: D Rees, J Derrick, A Gwilym, J Powell
				C: J Williams 3 P: J Williams
18 Sep	A	Neath	10-65	T: L Phillips C: J Williams P: J Williams
21 Sep	H	Cardiff	11-64	T: D Meredith P: J Williams 2
28 Sep	A	Newport	10-44	T: D Meredith, S Jenkins
9 Nov	H	Caerphilly	29-16	T: I Perryment, R Clarke, R Smith, D Cooper
				C: J Williams 3 P: J Williams
16 Nov	A	Swansea	5-67	T: D Meredith
23 Nov	H	Pontypridd	0-47	
7 Dec	A	Llanelli	10-97	T: L Phillips, J Derrick
8 Feb	A	Bridgend	14-45	T: D Cooper, J Powell C: J Williams 2
22 Feb	A	Dunvant	17-37	T: L Phillips, pen try C: J Williams 2
				P: J Williams

1 Mar	H	Neath	16-29	*T:* J Williams, D Cooper *P:* J Williams 2
8 Mar	A	Cardiff	20-45	*T:* M Cox 2, D Cooper *C:* J Williams *P:* J Williams
22 Mar	H	Treorchy	25-20	*T:* D Cooper 2, M Rossiter *C:* J Williams 2 *P:* J Williams 2
29 Mar	H	Newport	26-42	*T:* R Clarke, D Cooper *C:* J Williams 2 *P:* J Williams 4
5 Apr	A	Caerphilly	7-50	*T:* pen try *C:* J Williams
15 Apr	H	Ebbw Vale	14-22	*T:* I Perryment *P:* K Williams 3
19 Apr	H	Swansea	31-24	*T:* J Derrick, J Williams, A Gwilym, R Williams, L Phillips *C:* J Williams 3
30 Apr	H	Llanelli	15-38	*T:* D Cooper, J Powell *C:* J Williams *P:* J Williams
10 May	A	Pontypridd	15-48	*T:* A Gwilym, I Perryment *C:* J Williams *P:* J Williams

Newport

Year of formation 1874
Ground Rodney Parade, Newport, Gwent Tel: Newport (01633) 258193 or 267410
Colours Black and amber
Captain 1996-97 R Goodey
WRU Leagues 1996-97 Div 1 6th   **SWALEC Cup 1996-97** Lost 30-44 to Cardiff (6th round)

Newport were one of the most frugal clubs with regard to buying players and they almost found themselves relegated as a result. Had they known before the season started that the WRU were going to prune the First Division to eight teams, they would no doubt have spent more money strengthening the team. As it was they enlisted the services of Pierre Villepreux in late September to advise on tactics and coaching, but it was always a season of struggle and they could not defeat any of the top four League teams, while the Barbarians routed them 86-33.

Newport lost Gareth Rees, their star Canadian kicker, to Wasps and others who were lured away or released included Mike Voyle, Kevin Moseley, Jason Hewlett, Mark Yendle, Richard Rees, Adam Palfrey, Robert Saddler, Duncan Hughes and Alun Carter. Shaun Connor proved a valuable fly half-recruit until he broke an ankle in the Japan Sevens, while others brought in to play valuable parts included Nicky Lloyd, Vince Davies, James Alvis and Gareth Taylor. Connor provided 256 points; and Czech international No 8 Jan Machacek scored 12 tries.

League Record 1996-97

Date	Venue	Opponents	Result	Scorers
31 Aug	H	Caerphilly	29-10	*T:* N Lloyd 2, M Workman, S Connor *C:* S Connor 3 *P:* S Connor
3 Sep	A	Swansea	18-82	*T:* N Lloyd, I Harvey *C:* S Connor *P:* S Connor 2
7 Sep	H	Pontypridd	32-54	*T:* S Connor, M Cox, D Gray, N Lloyd, S Reed *C:* S Connor 2 *P:* S Connor
14 Sep	A	Llanelli	5-55	*T:* M Llewellyn
18 Sep	H	Treorchy	34-29	*T:* M Llewellyn, pen try, J Colderley, D Hurford *C:* S Connor 4 *P:* S Connors 2
22 Sep	A	Ebbw Vale	23-24	*T:* S Davies, J Colderley, J Machacek *C:* S Connor *P:* S Connor *D:* S Connor
28 Sep	H	Newbridge	44-10	*T:* G Curtis 2, T Barnes, S Davies, J Colderley, J Alvis, S Webley *C:* S Connor 3 *P:* S Connor
9 Nov	A	Bridgend	32-32	*T:* C Smith 2, G Taylor, M Llewellyn *C:* S Connor 2, A Lawson *P:* S Connor 2

16 Nov	H	Neath	18-13	*T:* S Connor, M Llewellyn *C:* S Connor
				P: S Connor 2
7 Dec	H	Dunvant	45-22	*T:* S Connor 2, J Lowry 2, J Colderley,
				J Machacek, R Snow *C:* S Connor 5
28 Dec	H	Swansea	17-42	*T:* I Jones J Machacek *C:* S Connor 2
				P: S Connor
8 Feb	H	Llanelli	18-18	*P:* S Connor 6
22 Feb	A	Caerphilly	32-26	*T:* S Connor 2, S Davies, N Lloyd, S Cronk
				C: S Connor 2 *P:* S Connor
8 Mar	H	Ebbw Vale	13-6	*T:* V Davies, J Machacek *P:* S Connor
29 Mar	A	Newbridge	42-26	*T:* S Connor, S Duggan, S Davies, S Taylor,
				J Machacek *C:* S Connor 4 *P:* S Connor 3
31 Mar	A	Cardiff	13-26	*T:* J Colderley *C:* S Connor *P:* S Connor 2
5 Apr	H	Bridgend	31-26	*T:* G Taylor, N Lloyd, I Gough, pen try,
				J Machacek *C:* S Connor 3
19 Apr	A	Neath	8-38	*T:* G Smith *P:* G Curtis
26 Apr	A	Treorchy	30-19	*T:* I Jones 2, G Taylor, J Lowry *C:* J Lowry 2
				P: J Lowry 2
3 May	A	Dunvant	14-9	*T:* N Lloyd *P:* J Lowry 3
7 May	A	Pontypridd	20-54	*T:* J Colderley, I Gough, J Machacek
				C: D Burn *P:* D Burn
10 May	H	Cardiff	23-11	*T:* J Machacek 2, N Lloyd, D Burn
				P: S Davies

Pontypridd

Year of formation 1876
Ground Sardis Road Ground, Pwllgwaun, Pontypridd
Tel: Pontypridd (01443) 405006 and 407170
Colours Black and white hoops
Captain 1996-97 N R Jenkins
WRU Leagues 1996-97 Div 1 *Winners*   **SWALEC Cup 1996-97** Lost 19-20 to Swansea (7th round)

A first National League title was the highlight of another momentous season for Pontypridd under new captain Neil Jenkins, though a broken arm against England meant he missed the last two months of the season. Although they lost Lee Jarvis, Nigel Bezani, Nicky Lloyd, James Alvis and Richie Collins, coach Dennis John still enjoyed the luxury of a superb squad. Neil Jenkins, of course, was top scorer with 370 points in 20 games, while Crispin Cormack deputised admirably for him at outside-half and scored 224 points in 27 appearances. Wing David Manley crossed for 19 tries in 22 games, and Phil Ford, on the other wing, also crossed for some exciting tries as Ponty garnered 330 points in their last six games at an average of 55 points per match. Ponty went out of the Cup 20-19 at Swansea, where they have not won for 25 years, but were unbeaten at home in the League.

League Record 1996-97

Date	Venue	Opponents	Result	Scorers
4 Sep	H	Cardiff	24-14	*T:* M Lloyd, G Prosser *C:* N Jenkins
				P: N Jenkins 4
7 Sep	A	Newport	54-32	*T:* S Enoch 2, M de Maid, J Evans, N Eynon,
				J Lewis *C:* N Jenkins 6 *P:* N Jenkins 3
				D: N Jenkins
14 Sep	H	Caerphilly	38-25	*T:* D Manley 2, P Owen, K Morgan, pen try,
				M Spiller *C:* N Jenkins 4
17 Sep	A	Swansea	19-33	*T:* K Morgan *C:* N Jenkins *P:* N Jenkins 4
21 Sep	A	Dunvant	25-10	*T:* C Cormack, M Lloyd, O Robbins, P Ford
				C: C Cormack *P:* C Cormack

28 Sep	H	Llanelli	29-6	T: M Williams, D Manley, D McIntosh C: N Jenkins P: N Jenkins 4
9 Nov	A	Treorchy	46-15	T: D Manley 2, N Jenkins, Paul John, S Lewis C: N Jenkins 3 P: N Jenkins 5
16 Nov	H	Ebbw Vale	50-26	T: N Eynon 2, J Lewis, M Williams, J Lee C: N Jenkins 5 P: N Jenkins 5
23 Nov	A	Newbridge	47-0	T: R Collins 2, G Lewis 2, C Cormack, M Rowley, M Spiller C: N Jenkins 6
7 Dec	H	Bridgend	53-9	T: G Lewis, J Lewis, G Prosser, S Lewis, M Lloyd C: N Jenkins 5 P: N Jenkins 6
28 Dec	A	Cardiff	37-23	T: J Lewis, D Manley, Paul John, pen try C: N Jenkins 4 P: N Jenkins 3
8 Feb	A	Caerphilly	68-8	T: N Jenkins 2, D Manley 2, N Eynon, J Lewis, M Williams, K Morgan, Paul John C: N Jenkins 7 P: N Jenkins 3
2 Mar	H	Swansea	31-7	T: G Lewis, P Ford, N Jenkins C: N Jenkins 2 P: N Jenkins 4
8 Mar	H	Dunvant	48-6	T: P Ford 2, J Evans, C Cormack, pen try, N Jenkins, G Prosser C: N Jenkins 5 P: N Jenkins
29 Mar	A	Llanelli	16-31	T: S Lewis C: C Cormack P: C Cormack 3
31 Mar	A	Neath	29-3	T: S Lewis 2, Paul John, G Lewis, G Wyatt C: C Cormack 2
5 Apr	H	Treorchy	57-8	T: J Evans 2, Paul John 2, S Lewis, M Williams, C Cormack, J Lewis, K Morgan C: C Cormack 6
19 Apr	A	Ebbw Vale	47-7	T: M Lloyd 2, Paul John, J Lewis, M Spiller, P Ford, D Manley C: C Cormack 3 P: C Cormack 2
25 Apr	H	Neath	72-12	T: P Ford 3, C Cormack 2, D Manley 2, J Lewis, M Rowley, G Wyatt, pen try C: C Cormack 7 P: C Cormack
3 May	A	Bridgend	52-24	T: K Morgan 2, J Lewis 2, D Manley, M Williams, M Lloyd, P Ford C: C Cormack 6
7 May	H	Newport	54-20	T: G Wyatt 2, C Cormack, M de Maid, J Lewis, G Lewis, M Lloyd, M Spiller C: C Cormack 7
10 May	H	Newbridge	48-15	T: M Lloyd 3, C Cormack, G Wyatt, J Lewis, P Ford, J Evans C: C Cormack 4

Swansea

Year of formation 1873
Ground St Helen's Ground, Bryn Road, Swansea, West Glamorgan SA2 0AR Tel: Swansea (01792) 466593
Colours All white
Captain 1996-97 G R Jenkins
WRU Leagues 1996-97 Div 1 2nd   **SWALEC Cup 1996-97** Lost 26-33 to Cardiff (final)

At one stage Swansea were chasing the glamorous double of League champions and Cup winners. In the event, neither materialised: they reached the Cup final for the eighth time, but lost to Cardiff, and Pontypridd's amazing consistency meant that Swansea finished runners-up in the League. Overall, however, it was a promising season for a side undergoing transformation. Garin Jenkins had been appointed captain and Scott Gibbs was recruited back from St Helens Rugby League club in a deal worth some £200,000. Arwel Thomas was obtained from Bristol, Stuart Evans and Paul Moriarty from Rugby League, and other valuable newcomers were Matthew Back, Danzi Niblo, Adam Palfrey, Robbie Jones and Luc Evans. On the debit side scrum-half Robert Jones departed to Bristol and eight players were released from contract in January because of cash-flow difficulties. It was the last of six seasons for Mike Ruddock, their influential director of rugby, who left to take up the same post in Ireland with Leinster. Arwel Thomas scored 279 points; Simon Davies and Mark Taylor each crossed for 18 tries.

League Record 1996-97

Date	Venue	Opponents	Result	Scorers
31 Aug	H	Cardiff	49-23	*T:* Stuart Davies 3, M Taylor, D Weatherley, pen try *C:* A Thomas 5 *P:* A Thomas *D:* A Thomas, A Booth
3 Sep	H	Newport	82-18	*T:* A Palfrey 2, Simon Davies 2, M Taylor 2, A Thomas 2, Stuart Davies, A Booth, C Charvis, D Weatherley *C:* A Thomas 6, A Williams 2 *P:* A Thomas 2
7 Sep	A	Caerphilly	57-3	*T:* A Booth 2, R Appleyard, H Bevan, Simon Davies, Stuart Davies, S Gibbs, S Moore, A Williams *C:* A Williams 6
14 Sep	A	Dunvant	18-26	*T:* Stuart Davies, L Evans *C:* A Thomas *P:* A Thomas 2
17 Sep	H	Pontypridd	33-19	*T:* P Arnold, M Taylor, R Boobyer, L Evans *C:* A Thomas 2 *P:* A Thomas 2 *D:* A Thomas
21 Sep	A	Llanelli	17-30	*T:* A Thomas 2 *C:* A Thomas 2 *P:* A Thomas
28 Sep	H	Treorchy	85-21	*T:* C Charvis 2, Simon Davies 2, A Thomas 2, S Gibbs, P Arnold, L Davies, A Harris, C McDonald, Stuart Davies, M Taylor *C:* A Thomas 9, L Davies
9 Nov	A	Ebbw Vale	9-13	*P:* A Thomas 3
16 Nov	H	Newbridge	67-5	*T:* A Booth 2, A Palfrey 2, A Harris, C Charvis, C Loader, P Moriarty, M Taylor, A Thomas *C:* A Thomas 7 *P:* A Thomas
7 Dec	H	Neath	49-10	*T:* A Booth 3, Simon Davies 2, M Taylor C Anthony *C:* A Thomas 3, A Williams *P:* A Thomas 2
28 Dec	A	Newport	42-17	*T:* A Booth 2, C Loader 2, C Charvis, A Harris, G Jenkins, S Moore *C:* A Thomas
8 Feb	H	Dunvant	38-12	*T:* C Charvis 3, L Evans, A Thomas, D Thomas *C:* A Thomas 4
2 Mar	A	Pontypridd	7-31	*T:* C Charvis *C:* A Harris
8 Mar	H	Llanelli	12-42	*T:* S Gibbs, A Harris *C:* A Harris
2 Apr	A	Bridgend	25-18	*T:* Simon Davies, A Booth, S Moore *C:* A Williams 2 *P:* A Williams 2
5 Apr	H	Ebbw Vale	59-12	*T:* L Davies 4, D Thomas, S Moore, M Taylor, pen try, W Leach *C:* A Williams 7
16 Apr	A	Treorchy	50-12	*T:* A Harris 3, S Gibbs 2, A Booth, Stuart Davies, M Taylor *C:* A Williams 5
19 Apr	A	Newbridge	24-31	*T:* R Appleyard 2, A Harris, D Niblo *C:* A Williams, A Thomas
29 Apr	H	Caerphilly	52-38	*T:* A Harris 3, S Gibbs 2, P Arnold, L Evans, P Moriarty *C:* A Williams 6
3 May	A	Neath	20-42	*T:* S Gibbs, M Taylor *C:* L Davies 2 *P:* A Williams 2
7 May	A	Cardiff	20-31	*T:* L Davies, S Moore *C:* L Davies 2 *P:* L Davies 2
10 May	H	Bridgend	64-17	*T:* H Thomas 3, L Davies 2, A Booth, A Reynolds, P Moriarty, I Buckett, Robbie Jones *C:* L Davies 7

Treorchy

Year of formation 1886
Ground The Oval, Treorchy, Rhondda Tel: Treorchy (01443) 434671
Colours Black and white hoops
Captain 1996-97 G Owen
WRU Leagues 1996-97 Div 1 11th – *relegated*   **SWALEC Cup 1996-97** Lost 13-22 to
Bridgend (7th round)

Treorchy were always candidates for relegation after winning just one of their first
nine League matches. However, captain Gavin Owen inspired his Zebras to
numerous moments of defiance. Cardiff were worried until they snatched a 23-22
verdict at The Oval, and Newport, Neath, Ebbw Vale and Bridgend all experienced
difficulty in winning tight games. Although Treorchy secured the services of their
former breakaway forward Lyn Jones as player/coach, once he left Neath, and
recruited former Wigan and Great Britain Rugby League full-back, 35-year-old
Steve Hampson, in March, they only achieved three League successes. Carl
Hammans again proved an outstanding scrum half. David Evans scored 127 points;
Scott Eggar and Robert Morgan each scored nine tries.

League Record 1996-97

Date	Venue	Opponents	Result	Scorers
31 Aug	H	Newbridge	17-23	*T:* K Jones, P Jones *C:* D Evans 2
				P: D Evans
3 Sep	H	Bridgend	8-11	*T:* D Lloyd *P:* D Evans
7 Sep	A	Neath	19-46	*T:* D Grant, A Thomas *P:* D Lloyd 3
14 Sep	H	Cardiff	22-23	*T:* A Thomas, R Wintle, D Owen
				C: W Booth 2 *P:* W Booth
18 Sep	A	Newport	29-34	*T:* R Morgan 2, K Ellis, J Riggs, P Jones
				C: W Booth 2
21 Sep	H	Caerphilly	31-16	*T:* C Hammans 3, A Thomas, S Eggar
				C: D Lloyd 3
28 Sep	A	Swansea	21-85	*T:* D Lloyd, pen try, J Cicero *C:* D Lloyd 3
9 Nov	H	Pontypridd	15-46	*T:* A Thomas, C Hammans *C:* W Booth
				P: W Booth
23 Nov	H	Neath	10-15	*T:* S Davies *C:* D Evans *P:* D Evans
30 Nov	A	Dunvant	25-19	*T:* K Ellis, R Wintle, R Phillips *C:* D Evans 2
				P: D Evans 2
7 Dec	H	Ebbw Vale	13-17	*T:* R Morgan *C:* D Evans *P:* D Evans 2
28 Dec	A	Bridgend	21-26	*T:* D Lloyd, C Hammans *C:* D Lloyd
				P: D Lloyd 3
8 Feb	A	Cardiff	22-60	*T:* P Jones, R Wintle, S Eggar *C:* D Evans 2
				P: D Evans
8 Mar	A	Caerphilly	32-15	*T:* D Evans 2, R Wintle, P Jones *C:* D Evans 3
				P: D Evans 2
22 Mar	A	Newbridge	20-25	*T:* R Morgan, G Owen *C:* D Evans, D Lloyd
				P: D Evans 2
25 Mar	A	Llanelli	5-87	*T:* S Evans
5 Apr	A	Pontypridd	8-57	*T:* S Eggar *P:* D Evans
16 Apr	H	Swansea	12-50	*T:* S Eggar, S Hampson *C:* S Eggar
19 Apr	H	Llanelli	25-55	*T:* A Lewis, L Gilbey, K Orrell, R Wintle
				C: K Matthews *P:* S Eggar
26 Apr	H	Newport	19-30	*T:* R Pask, P Jones, C Hammans *C:* W Booth 2
4 May	A	Ebbw Vale	12-39	*T:* S Eggar, C Hammans *C:* W Booth
10 May	H	Dunvant	27-46	*T:* P Jones 2, S Eggar, J Rigg, R Wintle
				C: S Eggar

A FIFTH GRAND SLAM

THE 1996-97 SEASON IN FRANCE
Bob Donahue *International Tribune*

Call it a roller-coaster season for France, with happy highs and dismal lows. There was that incredible comeback at Twickenham, and then the Grand Slam decider against Scotland in a delirious Parc des Princes – followed by defeat at the hands of Italy. Before all that, there had been Brive's romp against Leicester in the Heineken final, but only after Wasps had demolished Toulouse.

Wasps must have been surprised at the end of the season when Toulouse won the French club final. The early-season disgrace in England had hardened the club's resolve. Meanwhile, adding to everyone's puzzlement, mighty Brive were knocked out of the club championship's final phase by modest Colomiers.

Was professionalism somehow to blame for the season's ups and downs? Some observers thought they saw unusual swings in senior players' motivation. There was certainly a good deal of confusion as players and officials adjusted to the new era. And what about the high number of injuries?

Injuries were much of the reason why France used 48 players in its 11 Tests: against Argentina twice, Wales, South Africa twice, Ireland, Wales again, England, Scotland, Italy and Romania. Of the 15 men selected for the first Test in Argentina in June, only six were in the starting XV against Scotland in March.

In those 11 Tests, France employed three captains, five goal kickers, ten half-back combinations and 13 front-row combinations. Twenty-eight Frenchmen played in the Five Nations. Finally, four uncapped newcomers were in the squad that flew out for the post-season tour in Australia.

Only Jean-Luc Sadourny (full-back) and Fabien Pelous (No 8 or lock) started every Test, although Abdelatif Benazzi (No 6 or 8, and captain from the first South Africa Test onwards) and big Olivier Merle (lock) started ten of them. But the season was memorable for its new faces, as coach Jean-Claude Skrela cast about for the right men to master his 'system of play' in time for the 1999 World Cup.

For example, there was Olivier Magne of Dax, who impressed against England a few months after ranking 25th in *Mid Olympique*'s annual summer review of the country's flankers. Laurent Leflamand of Bourgoin-Jallieu was not named in the weekly's roster of 15 best wings, Marc Dal Maso of Agen ranked eighth among hookers, and Christophe Lamaison of Brive eighth among centres.

Fourteen Five Nations tries were a French record. (But England totalled 15.) So were 11 penalty goals. (England kicked 15.) You

The France team which beat Scotland to win the Grand Slam in Paris. L-R, back row: J-L Jordana (replacement), D Casadei, F Tournaire, M Dal Maso, R Castel (replacement), O Magne, H Miorin, F Pelous, O Merle; front row: M de Rougemont (replacement), U Mola (replacement), G Accoceberry, D Aucagne, L Leflamand, S Glas, A Benazzi (capt), C Lamaison, D Venditti, J-L Sadourny, P Bondouy (replacement); absent: P Carbonneau (replacement).

could argue that the total rugby sought by Skrela and his illustrious new assistant, Pierre Villepreux, was taking shape. With Jo Maso as manager, three Barbarians were now running the French show.

Few in France have thought harder about the game than Villepreux and Skrela. Clubs were supposed to be following the national squad's style. Yet when things got serious in the spring, the club quarter-finals, semi-finals and final (seven matches in all) yielded 53 penalty goals and only 14 tries.

The national idea, in any case, was running rugby with a minimum of kicks to touch; instant switching from aggressive defence to ambitious counterattack; and astute support play, with backs and forwards interchanging positions as required. This 'system' demanded intelligence, and also the drilled teamwork that enables random groups of players, or dispersed players, to react in unison to sudden change. France were meant to play their own game, at pace, and keep on playing it come what may.

Skrela and his men had studied videos of recent Super-12 matches, especially those involving Auckland. The coach was impatient to discover whether his team could live with Australia in the two tour Tests in June.

FRENCH CLUB CHAMPIONSHIP FINAL
31 May, Parc des Princes
Toulouse 12 (3PG 1DG) **Bourgoin-Jallieu 6** (2PG)

L'Equipe called this the most boring club final in memory. Still, a fourth consecutive championship for Toulouse was an enormous achievement, all the more so since their season had begun so badly. Christophe Deylaud was man of the match; he tackled, kicked his goals and waited for the adversary to make mistakes. Bourgoin were worthy finalists, but, as Marc Cécillon admitted after the match, their inexperience (in their first club final) cost them the match.

This was the last final at the Parc des Princes, just as the Scotland match had been the last Five Nations event there.

Toulouse: S Ougier; M Marfaing, N Martin, T Castaignède, D Berty; C Deylaud (*capt*), J Cazalbou; C Califano, P Soula, J-L Jordana, H Miorin, F Belot, D Lacroix, S Dispagne, R Sonnes *Replacements* O Carbonneau for Martin (80 mins); P Lasserre for Jordana (67 mins)
Scorers *Penalty Goals:* Deylaud (3) *Dropped Goal:* Deylaud
Bourgoin-Jallieu: N Geany; L Leflamand, S Glas, A Péclier, L Saunier; G Cassagne, D Mazille; P Vessiller, J-P Sanchez, D Morgan, M Cécillon (*capt*), J Daudé, A Chazalet, P Raschi, M Malafosse *Replacements* P Fernandez for Glas (17 mins); J Frier for Raschi (72 mins); F Nibelle for Daudé (59 mins); L Gomez for Morgan (51 mins)
Scorer *Penalty Goals:* Geany (2)
Referee D Gillet (Périgord-Agenais)

FRANCE TO ARGENTINA 1996

THE TOURING PARTY
Manager J Dunyach   **Coaches** J-C Skrela M Godemet   **Captain** P Saint-Andre

FULL-BACK
J-L Sadourny (Colomiers)

THREEQUARTERS
E Ntamack (Toulouse)
R Dourthe (Dax)
Y Delaigue (Toulon)
S Glas (Bourgoin)
D Venditti (Bourgoin)
P Bernat-Salles (Begles-Bordeaux)
G Bouic (Agen)
D Berty (Toulouse)
P Saint-Andre (Montferrand)
*M Marfaing (Narbonne)

HALF-BACKS
A Penaud (Brive)
T Castaignede (Toulouse)
P Carbonneau (Toulouse)
G Accoceberry (Begles-Bordeaux)

FORWARDS
C Soulette (Beziers)
C Califano (Toulouse)
F Tournaire (Narbonne)
M de Rougemont (Toulon)
H Guiraud (Nimes)
J-L Jordana (Pau)
O Merle (Montferrand)
O Roumat (Dax)
H Miorin (Toulouse)
L Bonventre (Brive)
F Pelous (Dax)
A Benazzi (Agen)
T Labrousse (Brive)
P Benetton (Agen)
M Lievremont (Perpignan)
C Moni (Nice)
*J-P Versailles (Montferrand)
*T Lievremont (Argeles)

Replacement during tour

TOUR RECORD
All matches   Played 6   Won 5   Lost 1   Points for 187   Against 100
International matches   Played 2   Won 2   Points for 68   Against 42

SCORING DETAILS

All matches					International matches				
For:	24T	14C	13PG	187 Pts	For:	9T	4C	5PG	68 Pts
Against:	7T	4C	19PG	100 Pts	Against:	4T	2C	6PG	42 Pts

MATCH DETAILS

1996	OPPONENTS	VENUE	RESULT
10 June	Cordoba	Cordoba	W 22-19
15 June	Buenos Aires	Buenos Aires	L 26-29
18 June	Tucuman	Tucuman	W 20-10
22 June	ARGENTINA	Buenos Aires	W 34-27
25 June	San Juan	San Juan	W 51-0
29 June	ARGENTINA	Buenos Aires	W 34-15

MATCH 1   10 June, Cordoba

Cordoba 19 (1G 4PG)   **France XV 22** (2G 1PG 1T)
Cordoba: Scorers *Try:* Barrea   *Conversion:* Luna   *Penalty Goals:* Luna (4)
France XV: Scorers *Tries:* Bernat-Salles, Delaigue, Guiraud   *Conversions:*
Dourthe (2)   *Penalty Goal:* Dourthe

MATCH 2 15 June, San Isidro Stadium, Buenos Aires

Buenos Aires 29 (8PG 1T) **France XV 26** (2G 4PG)
Buenos Aires: Scorers *Try:* Sporleder *Penalty Goals:* Cilley (8)
France XV: Scorers *Tries:* Califano, Castaignede *Conversions:* Castaignede (2)
Penalty Goals: Castaignede (4)

MATCH 3 18 June, Tucuman

Tucuman 10 (1G 1PG) **France XV 20** (2G 2PG)
Tucuman: Scorers *Try:* Macone *Conversion:* Aguirre *Penalty Goal:* Aguirre
France XV: Scorers *Tries:* Tournaire, Sadourny *Conversions:* Dourthe (2)
Penalty Goals: Dourthe (2)

MATCH 4   22 June, Ferrocarril Oeste Stadium,
Buenos Aires   1st Test
ARGENTINA 27 (2G 1PG 2T)   FRANCE 34 (3G 1PG 2T)

ARGENTINA: L Criscuolo (Alumni); M Pfister (Tucuman), F Garcia (Alumni),
F del Castillo (Jockey Club, Rosario), F Soler (Tala RC); J-L Cilley (San Isidro
Club), A Pichot (CA San Isidro), R D Grau (Liceo), C Promanzio (Duendes),
M Reggiardo (Castres, France); P Sporleder (Curupayti) *(capt)*, J Simes (Tala
RC); R Martin (San Isidro Club), P Bouza (Duendes), P J Camerlinckx (Regatas
Bella Vista) *Replacements* J Legora (Tablada) for del Castillo (52 mins),
N Fernandez-Miranda (Hindu) for Pichot (temp)
Scorers *Tries:* Garcia (2), pen try, Soler *Conversions:* Cilley (2) *Penalty Goal:* Cil-
ley
FRANCE: Sadourny; Ntamack, Dourthe, Castaignede, Saint-Andre *(capt)*;
Penaud, Accoceberry; Califano, De Rougemont, Tournaire; Merle, Roumat;
Benazzi, Pelous, Benetton *Replacements* M Livremont for Benazzi (70 mins),
Jordana for Tournaire (temp)
Scorers *Tries:* Dourthe, Castaignede, Ntamack (2), Saint-Andre
Conversions: Dourthe (3) *Penalty Goal:* Dourthe
Referee G Simmonds (Wales)

MATCH 5 25 June, San Juan

San Juan 0 **France XV 51** (4G 1PG 4T)
France XV: Scorers *Tries:* Berty (3), Glas, Bernat-Salles (2), Marfaing,
Jordana *Conversions:* Delaigue, Castaignede (3) *Penalty Goal:* Castaignede

MATCH 6   29 June, Ferrocarril Oeste Stadium,
Buenos Aires   2nd Test
ARGENTINA 15 (5PG)   FRANCE 34 (1G 4PG 3T)

ARGENTINA: L Criscuolo (Alumni); D-L Albanese (San Isidro Club), F Garcia
(Alumni), J Legora (Tablada), F Soler (Tala RC); J-L Cilley (San Isidro Club),
A Pichot (CA San Isidro); R D Grau (Liceo), C Promanzio (Duendes), M Reggiardo
(Castres, France); P Sporleder (Curupayti) *(capt)*, J Simes (Tala RC); R Martin
(San Isidro Club), P Bouza (Duendes), P J Camerlinckx (Regatas Bella Vista)
Scorer *Penalty Goals:* Cilley (5)
FRANCE: Sadourny; Ntamack, Dourthe, Castaignede, Saint-Andre *(capt)*; Penaud,
Carbonneau; Califano, de Rougemont, Jordana; Merle, Roumat; Benazzi, Pelous,
Benetton *Replacements* Glas for Penaud (74 mins), Tournaire for Califano (84 mins)
Scorers *Tries:* Pelous, Saint-Andre, Ntamack, Benetton *Conversion:* Castaignede
Penalty Goals: Dourthe, Castaignede (3)
Referee C Thomas (Wales)

FRENCH INTERNATIONAL PLAYERS
(up to 30 April 1997)

Note: Years given for Five Nations matches are for second half of season, eg 1972 refers to season 1971-72. Years for all other matches refer to the actual year of the match. When a series has taken place, or more than one match has been played against a country in the same year, figures have been used to denote the particular matches in which players have featured. Thus 1967 *SA* 2,4 indicates that a player appeared in the second and fourth Tests of the 1967 series against South Africa. This list includes only those players who have appeared in FFR International Matches '*donnant droit au titre d'international*'.

Abadie, A (Pau) 1964 *I*
Abadie, A (Graulhet) 1965 *R*, 1967 *SA* 1, 3, 4, *NZ*, 1968 *S, I*
Abadie, L (Tarbes) 1963 *R*
Accoceberry, G (Bègles) 1994 *NZ* 1,2, *C* 2, 1995 *W, E, S, I, R* 1, [*Iv, S*], *It*, 1996 *I, W* 1, *R, Arg* 1, *W* 2(R), *SA* 2, 1997 *S, It*
Aguerre, R (Biarritz O) 1979 *S*
Aguilar, D (Pau) 1937 *G*
Aguirre, J-M (Bagnères) 1971 *A* 2, 1972 *S*, 1973 *W, I, J, R*, 1974 *I, W, Arg* 2, *R, SA* 1, 1976 *W* (R), *E, US, A* 2, *R*, 1977 *W, E, S, I, Arg* 1,2, *NZ* 1,2, *R*, 1978 *E, S, I, W, R*, 1979 *I, W, E, S, NZ* 1,2, *R*, 1980 *W, I*
Ainciart, E (Bayonne) 1933 *G*, 1934 *G*, 1935 *G*, 1937 *G, It*, 1938 *G* 1
Albaladejo, P (Dax) 1954 *E, It*, 1960 *W, I, It, R*, 1961 *S, SA, E, W, I, NZ* 1,2, *A*, 1962 *S, E, W, I*, 1963 *S, I, E, W, It*, 1964 *S, NZ, W, It, I, SA, Fj*
Alvarez, A-J (Tyrosse) 1945 *B2*, 1946 *B, I, K, W*, 1947 *S, I, W, E*, 1948 *I, A, S, W, E*, 1949 *I, E, W*, 1951 *S, E, W*
Amand, H (SF) 1906 *NZ*
Ambert, A (Toulouse) 1930 *S, I, E, G, W*
Amestoy, J-B (Mont-de-Marsan) 1964 *NZ, E*
André, G (RCF) 1913 *SA, E, W, I*, 1914 *I, W, E*
Andrieu, M (Nîmes) 1986 *Arg* 2, *NZ* 1, *R* 2, *NZ* 2, 1987 [*R, Z*], 1988 *E, S, I, W, Arg* 1,2,3,4, *R*, 1989 *I, W, E, S, NZ* 2, *B, A* 2, 1990 *W, E, I* (R)
Anduran, J (SCUF) 1910 *W*
Araou, R (Narbonne) 1924 *E*
Arcalis, R (Brive) 1950 *S, I*, 1951 *I, E, W*
Arino, M (Agen) 1962 *R*
Aristouy, P (Pau) 1948 *S*, 1949 *Arg* 2, 1950 *S, I, E, W*
Arlettaz, P (Perpignan) 1995 *R* 2
Armary, L (Lourdes) 1987 [*R*], *R*, 1988 *S, I, W, Arg* 3,4, *R*, 1989 *W, S, A* 1,2, 1990 *W, E, S, I, A* 1,2,3, *NZ* 1, 1991 *W* 2, 1992 *S, I, R, Arg* 1,2, *SA* 1, 2, *Arg*, 1993 *E, S, I, W, SA* 1,2, *R* 2, *A* 1, 1994 *I, W, NZ* 1 (t), 2 (t), 1995 *I, R* 1 [*Tg, I, SA*]
Arnal, J-M (RCF) 1914 *I, W*
Arnaudet, M (Lourdes) 1964 *I*, 1967 *It, W*
Arotca, R (Bayonne) 1938 *R*
Arrieta, J (SF) 1953 *E, W*
Arthapignet, P (see Harislur-Arthapignet)
Astre, R (Béziers) 1971 *R*, 1972 *I* 1, 1973 *E* (R), 1975 *E, S, I, SA* 1,2, *Arg* 2, 1976 *A* 2, *R*
Aucagne, D (Pau) 1997 *W* (R), *S, It*
Augé, J (Dax) 1929 *S, W*
Augras-Fabre, L (Agen) 1931 *I, S, W*
Averous, J-L (La Voulte) 1975 *S, I, SA* 1,2, 1976 *I, W, E, US, A* 2, *R*, 1977 *W, E, S, I, Arg* 1, *R*, 1978 *E, S, I*, 1979 *NZ* 1,2, 1980 *S, I* 1981 *A* 2
Azam, O (Montferrand) 1995 *R* 2, *Arg* (R)
Azarete, J-L (Dax, St Jean-de-Luz) 1969 *W, R*, 1970 *S, I, W, R*, 1971 *S, I, E, SA* 1,2, *A* 1, 1972 *E, W, I* 2, *A* 1, *R*, 1973 *NZ, W, I, R*, 1974 *I, R, SA* 1,2, 1975 *W*

Bader, E (Primevères) 1926 *M*, 1927 *I, S*
Badin, C (Chalon) 1973 *W, I*, 1975 *Arg* 1
Baillette, M (Perpignan) 1925 *I, NZ, S*, 1926 *W, M*, 1927 *I, W, G* 2, 1929 *G*, 1930 *S, I, E, G*, 1931 *I, S, E*. 1932 *G*
Baladie, G (Agen) 1945 *B* 1,2, *W*, 1946 *B, I, K*
Ballarin, J (Tarbes) 1924 *E*, 1925 *NZ, S*
Baquey, J (Toulouse) 1921 *I*
Barbazanges, A (Roanne) 1932 *G*, 1933 *G*
Barrau, M (Beaumont, Toulouse) 1971 *S, E, W*, 1972 *E, W, A* 1,2, 1973 *S, NZ, E, I, J, R*, 1974 *I, S*
Barrère, P (Toulon) 1929 *G*, 1931 *W*
Barrière, R (Béziers) 1960 *R*
Barthe, E (SBUC) 1925 *W, E*

Barthe, J (Lourdes) 1954 *Arg* 1,2, 1955 *S*, 1956 *I, W, It, E, Cz*, 1957 *S, I, E, W, R* 1,2, 1958 *S, E, A, W, It, I, SA* 1,2, 1959 *S, E, It, W*
Basauri, R (Albi) 1954 *Arg* 1
Bascou, P (Bayonne) 1914 *E*
Basquet, G (Agen) 1945 *W*, 1946 *B, I, K, W*, 1947 *S, I, W, E*, 1948 *I, A, S, W, E*, 1949 *S, I, E, W, Arg* 1, 1950 *S, I, E, W*, 1951 *S, I, E, W*, 1952 *S, I, SA, W, E, It*
Bastiat, J-P (Dax) 1969 *R*, 1970 *S, I, W*, 1971 *S, I, SA* 2, 1972 *S, A* 1, 1973 *E*, 1974 *Arg* 1,2, *SA* 2, 1975 *W, Arg* 1,2, *R*, 1976 *S, I, W, E, A* 1,2, *R*, 1977 *W, E, S, I*, 1978 *E, S, I, W*
Baudry, N (Montferrand) 1949 *S, I, W, Arg* 1,2
Baulon, R (Vienne, Bayonne) 1954 *S, NZ, W, E, It*, 1955 *I, E, W, It*, 1956 *S, I, E, W, It, E, Cz*, 1957 *S, I, It*
Baux, J-P (Lannemezan) 1968 *NZ* 1,2, *SA* 1,2
Bavozet, J (Lyon) 1911 *S, E, W*
Bayard, J (Toulouse) 1923 *S, W, E*, 1924 *W, R, US*
Bayardon, J (Chalon) 1964 *S, NZ, E*
Beaurin-Gressier, C (SF) 1907 *E*, 1908 *E*
Bégu, J (Dax) 1982 *Arg* 2 (R), 1984 *E, S*
Béguerie, C (Agen) 1979 *NZ* 1
Beguet, L (RCF) 1922 *I*, 1923 *S, W, E, I*, 1924 *S, I, E, R, US*
Behoteguy, A (Bayonne, Cognac) 1923 *E*, 1924 *S, I, E, W, R, US*, 1926 *E*, 1927 *E, G* 1,2, 1928 *A, I, E, G, W*, 1929 *S, W, E*
Behoteguy, H (RCF, Cognac) 1923 *W*, 1928 *A, I, E, G, W*
Belascain, C (Bayonne) 1977 *R*, 1978 *E, S, I, W, R*, 1979 *I, W, E, S*, 1982 *W, E, S, I*, 1983 *E, S, I, W*
Belletante, G (Nantes) 1951 *I, E, W*
Benazzi, A (Agen) 1990 *A* 1,2,3, *NZ* 1,2, 1991 *E, US* 1 (R), 2, [*R, Fj, C*], 1992 *SA* 1 (R), 2, *Arg*, 1993 *E, S, I, W, A* 1,2, 1994 *I, W, E, S, C, NZ* 1,2, *C* 2, 1995 *W, E, S, I*, [*Tg, Iv, S, SA, E*], *NZ* 1, 1996 *E, S, I, W* 1, *Arg* 1,2, *W* 2, *SA* 1, 1997 *I, W, E, S*
Bénésis, R (Narbonne) 1969 *W, R*, 1970 *S, I, W, E, R*, 1971 *S, I, E, W, A* 2, *R*, 1972 *S, I* 1, *E, W, I* 2, *A* 1, *R*, 1973 *NZ, E, W, I, R*, 1974 *I, W, E, S*
Benetière, J (Roanne) 1954 *It, Arg* 1
Benetton, P (Agen) 1989 *B*, 1990 *NZ* 2, 1991 *US* 2, 1992 *Arg* 1,2 (R), *SA* 1 (R), 2, *Arg*, 1993 *E, S, I, W, SA* 1,2, *R* 2, *A* 1,2, 1994 *I, W, E, S, C* 1, *NZ* 1,2, *C* 2, 1995 *W, E, S, I*, [*Tg, Iv* (R), *S*], *It, R* 2 (R), *Arg, NZ* 1, 1996 *Arg* 1,2, *W* 2, *SA* 1,2, 1997 *I, It*
Benezech, L (RCF) 1994 *E, S, C* 1, *NZ* 1,2, *C* 2, 1995 *W, E*, [*Iv, S, E*], *R* 2, *Arg, NZ* 1, 2
Berbizier, P (Lourdes, Agen) 1981 *S, I, W, E, NZ* 1,2, 1982 *I, W*, 1983 *S, I*, 1984 *S* (R), *NZ* 1,2, 1985 *Arg* 1,2, 1986 *S, I, W, E, R* 1, *Arg* 1, *A, NZ* 1, *R* 2, *NZ* 2,3, 1987 *W, E, S, I*, [*S, R, Fj, A, NZ*], *R*, 1988 *E, S, I, W, Arg* 1,2, 1989 *I, W, E, S, NZ* 1,2, *B, A* 1, 1990 *W, E*, 1991 *S, I, W, I, R*
Berejnoi, J-C (Tulle) 1963 *R*, 1964 *S, W, It, I, SA, Fj, R*, 1965 *S, I, E, W, It, R*, 1966 *S, I, E, W, It, R*, 1967 *S, A, E, It, W, I, R*
Berges, B (Toulouse) 1926 *I*
Berges-Cau, R (Lourdes) 1976 *E* (R)
Bergese, F (Bayonne) 1936 *G* 2, 1937 *G, It*, 1938 *G* 1, *R, G* 2
Bergougnan, Y (Toulouse) 1945 *B* 1, *W*, 1946 *B, I, K, W*, 1947 *S, I, W, E*, 1948 *S, W, E*, 1949 *S, E, Arg* 1,2
Bernard, R (Bergerac) 1951 *S, I, E, W*
Bernat-Salles, P (Pau, Bègles-Bordeaux) 1992 *Arg*, 1993 *R* 1, *SA* 1,2, *R* 2, *A* 1,2, 1994 *I*, 1995 *E, S*, 1996 *E* (R)
Bernon, J (Lourdes) 1922 *I*, 1923 *S*
Bérot, J-L (Toulouse) 1968 *NZ* 3, *A*, 1969 *S, I*, 1970 *E, R*, 1971 *S, I, E, W, SA* 1,2, *A* 1,2, *R*, 1972 *S, I* 1, *E, W, A* 1, 1974 *I*

277

Bérot, P (Agen) 1986 *R* 2, *NZ* 2, 3, 1987 *W, E, S, I, R,* 1988 *E, S, I, Arg* 1, 2, 3, 4, *R,* 1989 *S, NZ* 1, 2
Bertrand, P (Bourg) 1951 *I, E, W,* 1953 *S, I, E, W, It*
Bertranne, R (Bagnères) 1971 *E, W, SA* 2, *A* 1,2, 1972 *S, I* 1, 1973 *NZ, E, J, R,* 1974 *I, W, E, S, Arg* 1,2, *R, SA* 1, 1975 *W, E, S, I, SA* 1,2, *Arg* 1,2, *R,* 1976 *S, I, W, E, US, A* 1,2, *R,* 1977 *W, E, S, I, Arg* 1,2, *NZ* 1,2, *R,* 1978 *E, S, I, W, R,* 1979 *I, W, E, S, R,* 1980 *W, E, S, I, SA, R,* 1981 *S, I, W, E, R, NZ* 1,2
Berty, D (Toulouse) 1990 *NZ* 2, 1992 *R* (R), 1993 *R* 2, 1995 *NZ* 1 (R), 1996 *W* 2(R), *SA* 1
Besset, E (Grenoble) 1924 *S*
Besset, L (SCUF) 1914 *W, E*
Besson, M (CASG) 1924 *I,* 1925 *I, E,* 1926 *S, W,* 1927 *I*
Besson, P (Brive) 1963 *S, I, E,* 1965 *R,* 1968 *SA* 1
Betsen, S (Biarritz) 1997 *It* (R)
Bianchi, J (Toulouse) 1986 *Arg* 1
Bichindaritz, J (Biarritz O) 1954 *It, Arg* 1,2
Bidart, L (La Rochelle) 1953 *W*
Biemouret, P (Agen) 1969 *E, W,* 1970 *I, W, E,* 1971 *W, SA* 1,2, *A* 1, 1972 *E, W, I* 2, *A* 2, *R,* 1973 *S, NZ, E, W, I*
Biénès, R (Cognac) 1950 *S, I, E, W,* 1951 *S, I, E, W,* 1952 *S, I, SA, W, E, It,* 1953 *S, I, E,* 1954 *S, I, NZ, W, E, Arg* 1,2, 1956 *S, I, W, E*
Bigot, C (Quillan) 1930 *S, E,* 1931 *I, S*
Bilbao, L (St Jean-de-Luz) 1978 *I,* 1979 *I*
Billac, E (Bayonne) 1920 *S, E, W, I, US,* 1921 *S, W,* 1922 *W,* 1923 *E*
Billière, M (Toulouse) 1968 *NZ* 3
Bioussa, A (Toulouse) 1924 *W, US,* 1925 *I, NZ, S, E,* 1926 *S, I, E,* 1928 *E, G, W,* 1929 *I, S, W, E,* 1930 *S, I, E, G, W*
Bioussa, C (Toulouse) 1913 *W, I,* 1914 *I*
Biraben, M (Dax) 1920 *W, I, US,* 1921 *S, W, E, I,* 1922 *S, E, I*
Blain, A (Carcassonne) 1934 *G*
Blanco, S (Biarritz O) 1980 *SA, R,* 1981 *S, W, E, A* 1,2, *R, NZ* 1,2, 1982 *W, E, S, I, R, Arg* 1,2, 1983 *E, S, I, W,* 1984 *I, W, E, S, NZ* 1,2, *R,* 1985 *E, S, I, W, Arg* 1,2, 1986 *S, I, W, E, R* 1, *Arg* 2, *A, NZ* 1, *R* 2, *NZ* 2,3, 1987 *W, E, S, I, [S, R, Fj, A, NZ], R,* 1988 *E, S, I, W, Arg* 1,2,3,4, *R,* 1989 *I, W, E, S, NZ* 1,2, *B, A* 1, 1990 *E, S, I, R, A* 1,2,3, *NZ* 1,2, 1991 *S, I, W* 1, *E, R, US* 1,2, *W* 2, [*R, Fj, C, E*]
Blond, J (SF) 1935 *G,* 1936 *G* 2, 1937 *G,* 1938 *G* 1, *R, G* 2
Blond, X (RCF) 1990 *A* 3, 1991 *S, I, W* 1, *E,* 1994 *NZ* 2 (R)
Boffelli, V (Aurillac) 1971 *A* 2, *R,* 1972 *S, I* 1, 1973 *J, R,* 1974 *I, W, E, S, Arg* 1,2, *R, SA* 1,2, 1975 *W, S, I*
Bonal, J-M (Toulouse) 1968 *E, W, Cz, NZ* 2,3, *SA* 1,2, *R,* 1969 *S, I, E, R,* 1970 *W, E*
Bonamy, R (SB) 1928 *A, I*
Bondouy, P (Narbonne) 1997 *S* (R), *It*
Boniface, A (Mont-de-Marsan) 1954 *I, NZ, W, E, It, Arg* 1,2, 1955 *S, I,* 1956 *S, I, W, It, Cz,* 1957 *S, I, W, E* 2, 1958 *S, E,* 1959 *E,* 1961 *NZ* 1,3, *A, R,* 1962 *E, W, I, It, R,* 1963 *S, I, E, W, It, R,* 1964 *S, NZ, E, W, It,* 1965 *W, It, R,* 1966 *S, I, E, W*
Boniface, G (Mont-de-Marsan) 1960 *W, I, It, R, Arg* 1,2,3, 1961 *S, SA, E, W, It, I, NZ* 1,2,3, *R,* 1962 *R,* 1963 *S, I, E, W, It, R,* 1964 *S, I, E, W, It, R,* 1966 *S, I, E, W*
Bonnes, E (Narbonne) 1924 *W, R, US*
Bonneval, E (Toulouse) 1984 *NZ* 2 (R), 1985 *W, Arg* 1, 1986 *W, E, R* 1, *Arg* 1,2, *A, R* 2, *NZ* 2,3, 1987 *W, E, S, I, [Z],* 1988 *E*
Bonnus, F (Toulon) 1950 *S, I, E, W*
Bonnus, M (Toulon) 1937 *It,* 1938 *G* 1, *R, G* 2, 1940 *B*
Bontemps, D (La Rochelle) 1968 *SA* 2
Borchard, G (RCF) 1908 *E,* 1909 *E, W, I,* 1911 *I*
Borde, F (RCF) 1920 *I, US,* 1921 *S, W, E,* 1922 *S, W,* 1923 *S, I,* 1924 *E,* 1925 *I,* 1926 *E*
Bordenave, L (Toulon) 1948 *A, S, W, E,* 1949 *S*
Boubée, J (Tarbes) 1921 *S, E, I,* 1922 *E, W,* 1923 *E, I,* 1925 *NZ, S*
Boudreaux, R (SCUF) 1910 *W, S*
Bouet, D (Dax) 1989 *NZ* 1,2, *B, A* 2, 1990 *A* 3
Bouguyon, G (Grenoble) 1961 *SA, E, W, It, I, NZ* 1,2,3, *A*
Bouic, G (Agen) 1996 *SA* 1
Boujet, C (Grenoble) 1968 *NZ* 2, *A* (R), *SA* 1
Bouquet, J (Bourgoin, Vienne) 1954 *S,* 1955 *E,* 1956 *S, I, W, It, E, Cz,* 1957 *S, E, W, R* 2, 1958 *S, E,* 1959 *S, It, W, I,* 1960 *S, E, W, I, R,* 1961 *S, SA, E, W, It, I, R,* 1962 *S, E, W, I*
Bourdeu, J R (Lourdes) 1952 *S, I, SA, W, E, It,* 1953 *S, I, E*

Bourgarel, R (Toulouse) 1969 *R,* 1970 *S, I, E, R,* 1971 *W, SA* 1,2, 1973 *S*
Bourguignon, G (Narbonne) 1988 *Arg* 3, 1989 *I, E, B, A* 1, 1990 *R*
Bousquet, A (Béziers) 1921 *E, I,* 1924 *R*
Bousquet, R (Albi) 1926 *M,* 1927 *I, S, W, E, G* 1, 1929 *W, E,* 1930 *W*
Boyau, M (SBUC) 1912 *I, S, W, E,* 1913 *W, I*
Boyer, P (Toulon) 1935 *G*
Branca, G (SF) 1928 *S,* 1929 *I, S*
Branlat, A (RCF) 1906 *NZ, E,* 1908 *W*
Brejassou, R (Tarbes) 1952 *S, I, SA, W, E,* 1953 *W, E,* 1954 *S, I, NZ,* 1955 *S, I, E, W, It*
Brethes, R (St Sever) 1960 *Arg* 2
Bringeon, A (Biarritz O) 1925 *W*
Brouzet, O (Grenoble) 1994 *S, NZ* 2 (R), 1995 *E, S, I, R* 1, *[Tg, Iv, E* (t)], *It, Arg* (R), 1996 *W* 1(R)
Brun, G (Vienne) 1950 *E, W,* 1951 *S, E, W,* 1952 *S, I, SA, W, E, It,* 1953 *S, I, E,* 1954 *S, I, NZ, W, E, Arg* 1,2, 1956 *S, I, W*
Bruneau, M (SBUC) 1910 *W, E,* 1913 *SA, E*
Brunet, Y (Perpignan) 1975 *SA* 1, 1977 *Arg* 1
Buchet, E (Nice) 1980 *R,* 1982 *E, R* (R), *Arg* 1,2
Buisson, H (see Empereur-Buisson)
Buonomo, Y (Béziers) 1971 *A* 2, *R,* 1972 *I* 1
Burgun, M (RCF) 1909 *I,* 1910 *W, S, I,* 1911 *S, E,* 1912 *I, S,* 1913 *S, E,* 1914 *E*
Bustaffa, D (Carcassonne) 1977 *Arg* 1,2, *NZ* 1,2, 1978 *W, R,* 1980 *W, E, S, SA, R*
Buzy, C-E (Lourdes) 1946 *K, W,* 1947 *S, I, W, E,* 1948 *I, A, S, W, E,* 1949 *S, I, E, W, Arg* 1,2

Cabanier, J-M (Montauban) 1963 *R,* 1964 *S, Fj,* 1965 *S, I, W, It, R,* 1966 *S, I, E, W, It, R,* 1967 *S, A, E, It, W, I, SA* 1,3, *NZ, R,* 1968 *S, I*
Cabannes, L (RCF) 1990 *NZ* 2 (R), 1991 *S, I, W* 1, *E, US* 2, *W* 2, [*R, Fj, C, E*], 1992 *W, E, S, I, Arg* 1,2, 1993 *E, S, I, W, R* 1, *SA* 1,2, 1994 *E, S, C* 1, *NZ* 1,2, 1995 *W, E, S, R* 1, [*Tg* (R), *Iv, S, I, SA, E*], 1996 *E, S, I, W* 1
Cabrol, H (Béziers) 1972 *A* 1 (R), 2, 1973 *J,* 1974 *SA* 2
Cadenat, J (SCUF) 1910 *S, E,* 1911 *W, I,* 1912 *W, E,* 1913 *I*
Cadieu, J-M (Toulouse) 1991 *R, US* 1, [*R, Fj, C, E*], 1992 *W, I, R, Arg* 1,2, *SA* 1
Cahuc, F (St Girons) 1922 *S*
Califano, C (Toulouse) 1994 *NZ* 1,2, *C* 2, 1995 *W, E, S, I, [Iv, S, I, SA, E], It, Arg, NZ* 1, 2, 1996 *E, S, I, W* 1, *R, Arg* 1,2, *SA* 1,2, 1997 *I, W, E*
Cals, R (RCF) 1938 *G* 1
Calvo, G (Lourdes) 1961 *NZ* 1,3
Camberabero, D (La Voulte, Béziers) 1982 *R, Arg* 1,2, 1983 *E, W,* 1987 [*R* (R), *Z, Fj* (R), *A, NZ*], 1988 *I,* 1989 *B, A* 1, 1990 *W, S, I, R, A* 1,2,3, *NZ* 1,2, 1991 *S, I, W* 1, *E, R, US* 1,2, *W* 2, [*R, Fj, C*], 1993 *E, S, I*
Camberabero, G (La Voulte) 1961 *NZ* 3, 1962 *R,* 1964 *R,* 1967 *A, E, It, W, I, SA* 1,3,4, 1968 *S, E, W*
Camberabero, L (La Voulte) 1964 *R,* 1965 *S, I,* 1966 *E, W,* 1967 *A, E, It, W, I,* 1968 *S, E, W*
Cambré, T (Oloron) 1920 *E, W, I, US*
Camel, A (Toulouse) 1928 *S, A, I, E, G, W,* 1929 *W, E, G,* 1930 *S, I, E, G, W,* 1935 *G*
Camel, M (Toulouse) 1929 *S, W, E*
Camicas, F (Tarbes) 1927 *G* 2, 1928 *S, I, E, G, W,* 1929 *I, S, W, E*
Camo, E (Villeneuve) 1931 *I, S, W, E, G,* 1932 *G*
Campaes, A (Lourdes) 1965 *W,* 1967 *NZ,* 1968 *S, I, E, W, Cz, NZ* 1,2, *A, R,* 1969 *S, W,* 1972 *R,* 1973 *NZ*
Campan, O (Agen) 1993 *SA* 1 (R), 2 (R), *R* 2 (R), 1996 *I, W* 1, *R*
Cantoni, J (Béziers) 1970 *W, R,* 1971 *S, I, E, W, SA* 1,2, *A* 1, *R,* 1972 *S, I* 1, 1973 *S, NZ, W, I,* 1975 *W* (R)
Capdouze, J (Pau) 1964 *SA, Fj, R,* 1965 *S, I, E*
Capendeguy, J-M (Bègles) 1967 *NZ, R*
Capitani, P (Toulon) 1954 *Arg* 1,2
Capmau, J-L (Toulouse) 1914 *E*
Carabignac, G (Agen) 1951 *S, I,* 1952 *SA, W, E,* 1953 *S, I*
Carbonne, J (Perpignan) 1927 *W*
Carbonneau, P (Toulouse, Brive) 1995 *R* 2, *Arg, NZ* 1, 2, 1996 *E, S, R* (R), *Arg* 2, *W* 2, *SA* 1, 1997 *I* (R), *W, E, S* (R)
Carminati, A (Béziers, Brive) 1986 *R* 2, *NZ* 2, 1987 [*R, Z*], 1988 *I, W, Arg* 1,2, 1989 *I, W, S, NZ* 1 (R), 2, *A* 2, 1990 *S,* 1995 *It, R* 2, *Arg, NZ* 1, 2
Caron, L (Lyon O, Castres) 1947 *E,* 1948 *I, A, W, E,* 1949 *S, I, E, W, Arg* 1

Carpentier, M (Lourdes) 1980 *E, SA, R*, 1981 *S, I, A* 1, 1982 *E, S*

Carrère, C (Toulon) 1966 *R*, 1967 *S, A, E, W, I, SA* 1,3,4, *NZ, R*, 1968 *S, I, E, W, Cz, NZ* 3, *A, R*, 1969 *S, I*, 1970 *S, I, W, E*, 1971 *E, W*

Carrère, J (Vichy, Toulon) 1956 *S*, 1957 *E, W, R* 2, 1958 *S, SA* 1,2, 1959 *I*

Carrère, R (Mont-de-Marsan) 1953 *E, It*

Casadei, D (Brive) 1997 *S*

Casaux, L (Tarbes) 1959 *I, It*, 1962 *S*

Cassagne, P (Pau) 1957 *It*

Cassayet-Armagnac, A (Tarbes, Narbonne) 1920 *S, E, W, US*, 1921 *W, E, I*, 1922 *S, E, W*, 1923 *S, W, E, I*, 1924 *S, E, W, R, US*, 1925 *I, NZ, S, W*, 1926 *S, I, E, W, M*, 1927 *I, S, W*

Cassiède, M (Dax) 1961 *NZ* 3, *A, R*

Castaignède, T (Toulouse) 1995 *R* 2, *Arg, NZ* 1, 2, 1996 *E, S, I, W* 1, *Arg* 1,2, 1997 *S*

Castel, R (Toulouse, Béziers) 1996 *I, W* 1, *W* 2, *SA* 1(R),2, 1997 *I* (R), *W, E* (R), *S* (R)

Castets, J (Toulon) 1923 *W, E, I*

Caujolle, J (Tarbes) 1909 *E*, 1913 *SA, E*, 1914 *W, E*

Caunègre, R (SB) 1938 *R, G* 2

Caussade, A (Lourdes) 1978 *R*, 1979 *I, W, E, NZ* 1,2, *R*, 1980 *W, E, S*, 1981 *S* (R), *I*

Caussarieu, G (Pau) 1929 *I*

Cayrefourcq, E (Tarbes) 1921 *E*

Cazals, P (Mont-de-Marsan) 1961 *NZ* 1, *A, R*

Cazenave, A (Pau) 1927 *E, G* 1, 1928 *S, A, G*

Cazenave, F (RCF) 1950 *E*, 1952 *S*, 1954 *I, NZ, W, E*

Cecillon, M (Bourgoin) 1988 *I, W, Arg* 2,3,4, *R*, 1989 *I, E, NZ* 1,2, *A* 1, 1991 *S, I, E* (R), *R, US* 1, *W* 2, *[E]*, 1992 *W, E, S, I, R, Arg* 1,2, *SA* 1,2, 1993 *E, S, I, W, R* 1,2, *R* 2, *A* 1,2, 1994 *I, W, NZ* 1 (R), 1995 *I, R* 1, *[Tg, S* (R), *I, SA]*

Celaya, M (Biarritz O, SBUC) 1953 *E, W, It*, 1954 *I, E, It, Arg* 1,2, 1955 *S, I, E, W, It*, 1956 *S, I, W, It, E, Cz* 1957 *S, I, E, W, R* 2, 1958 *S, E, A, W, It*, 1959 *S, E, S, 1960 S, E, W, I, R, Arg* 1,2,3, 1961 *S, SA, E, W, It, I, NZ* 1,2,3, *A, R*

Celhay, M (Bayonne) 1935 *G*, 1936 *G* 1, 1937 *G, It*, 1938 *G* 1, 1940 *B*

Cessieux, N (Lyon) 1906 *NZ*

Cester, E (TOEC, Valence) 1966 *S, I, E*, 1967 *W*, 1968 *S, I, E, W, Cz, NZ* 1,3, *A, SA* 1,2, *R*, 1969 *S, I, E, W*, 1970 *S, I, W, E*, 1971 *A* 1, 1972 *R*, 1973 *S, NZ, W, I, J, R*, 1974 *I, W, E, S*

Chaban-Delmas, J (CASG) 1945 *B* 2

Chabowski, H (Nice, Bourgoin) 1985 *Arg* 2, 1986 *R* 2, *NZ* 2, 1989 *B* (R)

Chadebech, P (Brive) 1982 *R, Arg* 1,2, 1986 *S, I*

Champ, E (Toulon) 1985 *Arg* 1,2, 1986 *I, W, E, R* 1, *Arg* 1,2, *A, NZ* 1, *R* 2, *NZ* 2,3, 1987 *W, E, S, I, [S, R, Fj, A, NZ]*, *R*, 1988 *E, S, Arg* 1,3,4, *R*, 1989 *W, S, A* 1, 1990 *W, E, NZ* 1, 1991 *R, US* 1, *[R, Fj, C, E]*

Chapuy, L (SF) 1926 *S*

Charpentier, G (SF) 1911 *E*, 1912 *W, E*

Charton, P (Montferrand) 1940 *B*

Charvet, D (Toulouse) 1986 *W, E, R* 1, *Arg* 1, *A, NZ* 1,3, 1987 *W, E, S, I, [S, R, Z, Fj, A, NZ]*, *R*, 1989 *E* (R), 1990 *W, E*, 1991 *S, I*

Chassagne, J (Montferrand) 1938 *G* 1

Chatau, A (Bayonne) 1913 *SA*

Chaud, E (Toulon) 1932 *G*, 1934 *G*, 1935 *G*

Chenevay, C (Grenoble) 1968 *SA* 1

Chevallier, B (Montferrand) 1952 *S, I, SA, W, E, It*, 1953 *E, W, It*, 1954 *S, I, NZ, W, Arg* 1, 1955 *S, I, E, W, It*, 1956 *S, I, W, It, E, Cz*, 1957 *S*

Chiberry, J (Chambéry) 1955 *It*

Chilo, A (RCF) 1920 *S, W*, 1925 *I, NZ*

Cholley, G (Castres) 1975 *E, S, I, SA* 1,2, *Arg* 1,2, *R*, 1976 *S, I, W, E, A* 1,2, *R*, 1977 *W, E, S, I, Arg* 1,2, *NZ* 1,2, *R*, 1978 *E, S, I, W, R*, 1979 *I, S*

Choy, J (Narbonne) 1930 *S, I, E, G, W*, 1931 *I*, 1933 *G*, 1934 *G*, 1935 *G*, 1936 *G* 2

Cigagna, A (Toulouse) 1995 *[E]*

Cimarosti, J (Castres) 1976 *US* (R)

Clady, A (Lezignan) 1929 *G*, 1931 *I, S, E, G*

Clarac, H (St Girons) 1938 *G* 1

Claudel, R (Lyon) 1932 *G*, 1934 *G*

Clauzel, F (Béziers) 1924 *E, W*, 1925 *W*

Clavé, J (Agen) 1936 *G* 2, 1938 *R, G* 2

Claverie, H (Lourdes) 1954 *NZ, W*

Clément, G (RCF) 1931 *W*

Clément, J (RCF) 1921 *S, W, E*, 1922 *S, E, W, I*, 1923 *S, W, I*

Clemente, M (Oloron) 1978 *R*, 1980 *S, I*

Cluchague, L (Biarritz O) 1924 *S*, 1925 *E*

Coderc, J (Chalon) 1932 *G*, 1933 *G*, 1934 *G*, 1935 *G*, 1936 *G* 1

Codorniou, D (Narbonne) 1979 *NZ* 1,2, *R*, 1980 *W, E, S, I*, 1981 *S, W, E, A* 2, 1983 *E, S, I, W, A* 1,2, *R*, 1984 *I, W, E, S, NZ* 1,2, *R*, 1985 *E, S, I, W, Arg* 1,2

Coeurveille, C (Agen) 1992 *Arg* 1 (R), 2

Cognet, L (Montferrand) 1932 *G*, 1936 *G* 1,2, 1937 *G, It*

Colombier, J (St Junien) 1952 *SA, W, E*

Colomine, G (Narbonne) 1979 *NZ* 1

Combe, J (SF) 1910 *S, E, I*, 1911 *S*

Combes, G (Fumel) 1945 *B* 2

Communeau, M (SF) 1906 *NZ, E*, 1907 *E*, 1908 *E, W*, 1909 *E, W, I*, 1910 *S, E, I*, 1911 *S, E, I*, 1912 *I, S, W, E*, 1913 *SA, E, W*

Condom, J (Boucau, Biarritz O) 1982 *R*, 1983 *E, S, I, W, A* 1,2, *R*, 1984 *I, W, E, S, NZ* 1,2, *R*, 1985 *E, S, I, W, Arg* 1,2, 1986 *S, I, W, E, R* 1, *Arg* 1,2, *NZ* 1, *R* 2, *NZ* 2,3, 1987 *W, E, S, I, [S, R, Z, A, NZ]*, *R*, 1988 *E, S, W, Arg* 1,2,3,4, *R*, 1989 *I, W, E, S, NZ* 1,2, *A* 1, 1990 *I, R, A* 2,3 (R)

Conilh de Beyssac, J-J (SBUC) 1912 *I, S*, 1914 *I, W, E*

Constant, G (Perpignan) 1920 *W*

Coscolla, G (Béziers) 1921 *S, W*

Costantino, J (Montferrand) 1973 *R*

Costes, A (Montferrand) 1994 *C* 2, 1995 *R* 1, *[Iv]*, 1997 *It*

Costes, F (Montferrand) 1979 *E, S, NZ* 1,2, *R*, 1980 *W, I*

Couffignal, H (Colomiers) 1993 *R* 1

Coulon, E (Grenoble) 1928 *S*

Courtiols, M (Bègles) 1991 *R, US* 1, *W* 2

Crabos, R (RCF) 1920 *S, E, W, I, US*, 1921 *S, W, E, I*, 1922 *S, E, W, I*, 1923 *S, I*, 1924 *S, I*

Crampagne, J (Bègles) 1967 *SA* 4

Crancee, R (Lourdes) 1960 *Arg* 3, 1961 *S*

Crauste, M (RCF, Lourdes) 1957 *R* 1,2, 1958 *S, E, A, W, It, I*, 1959 *E, It, W, I*, 1960 *S, E, W, I, R, Arg* 1,3, 1961 *S, SA, E, W, It, I, NZ* 1,2,3, *A, R*, 1962 *S, E, W, I, It, R*, 1963 *S, I, E, W, It, R, NZ, S, A, W, I, SA, Fj, R*, 1965 *S, I, E, W, It, R*, 1966 *S, I, E, W, It*

Cremaschi, M (Lourdes) 1980 *R*, 1981 *R, NZ* 1,2, 1982 *W, S*, 1983 *A* 1,2, *R*

Crenca, J-J (Agen) 1996 *SA* 2(R)

Crichton, W H (Le Havre) 1906 *NZ, E*

Cristina, J (Montferrand) 1979 *R*

Cussac, P (Biarritz O) 1934 *G*

Cutzach, A (Quillan) 1929 *G*

Daguerre, F (Biarritz O) 1936 *G* 1

Daguerre, J (CASG) 1933 *G*

Dal Maso, M (Mont-de-Marsan, Agen) 1988 *R* (R), 1990 *NZ* 2, 1996 *SA* 1(R),2, 1997 *I, W, E, S, It*

Danion, J (Toulon) 1924 *I*

Danos, P (Toulon, Béziers) 1954 *Arg* 1,2, 1957 *R* 2, 1958 *S, E, W, It, I, SA* 1,2, 1959 *S, E, It, W, I*, 1960 *S, E*

Darbos, P (Dax) 1969 *R*

Darracq, R (Dax) 1957 *It*

Darrieussecq, A (Biarritz O) 1973 *E*

Darrieussecq, J (Mont-de-Marsan) 1953 *It*

Darrouy, C (Mont-de-Marsan) 1957 *I, E, W, R* 1, 1959 *E*, 1961 *R*, 1963 *S, I, E, W, It*, 1964 *NZ, E, W, It, I, SA, Fj, R*, 1965 *S, I, E, It, R*, 1966 *S, I, E, W, It, R*, 1967 *S, A, E, It, W, I, SA* 1, *R*

Daudignon, G (SF) 1928 *S*

Dauga, B (Mont-de-Marsan) 1964 *S, NZ, E, W, It, I, SA, Fj, R*, 1965 *S, I, E, W, It, R*, 1966 *S, I, E, W, It, R*, 1967 *S, A, E, It, W, I, SA* 1,2,3,4, *NZ, R*, 1968 *S, I, NZ* 1,2,3, *A, SA* 1,2, *R*, 1969 *S, I, E, R*, 1970 *S, I, W, E, R*, 1971 *S, I, E, W, SA* 1,2, *A* 1,2, 1972 *I* 1, *W*

Dauger, J (Bayonne) 1945 *B* 1,2, 1953 *S*

Daulouede, P (Tyrosse) 1937 *G, It*, 1938 *G* 1, 1940 *B*

Decamps, P (RCF) 1911 *S*

Dedet, J (SF) 1910 *S, E*, 1911 *W, I*, 1912 *S*, 1913 *E, I*

Dedeyn, P (RCF) 1906 *NZ*

Dedieu, P (Béziers) 1963 *E, It*, 1964 *W, It, I, SA, Fj, R*, 1965 *S, I, E, W*

De Gregorio, J (Grenoble) 1960 *S, E, W, I, It, R, Arg* 1,2, 1961 *S, SA, E, W, It, I*, 1962 *S, E, W*, 1963 *S, W, It*, 1964 *NZ, E*

Dehez, J-L (Agen) 1967 *SA* 2, 1969 *R*

De Jouvencel, E (SF) 1909 *W, I*

De Laborderie, M (RCF) 1921 *I*, 1922 *I*, 1925 *W, E*

Delage, C (Agen) 1983 *S, I*

De Malherbe, H (CASG) 1932 *G*, 1933 *G*
De Malmann, R (RCF) 1908 *E, W*, 1909 *E, W, I*, 1910 *E, I*
De Muizon, J J (SF) 1910 *I*
Delaigue, G (Toulon) 1973 *J, R*
Delaigue, Y (Toulon) 1994 *S, NZ* 2 (R), *C* 2, 1995 *I, R* 1, [*Tg, Iv*], *It, R* 2 (R), 1997 *It*
Delque, A (Toulouse) 1937 *It*, 1938 *G* 1, *R, G* 2
De Rougemont, M (Toulon) 1995 *E* (t), *R* 1 (t), [*Iv*], *NZ* 1, 2, 1996 *I* (R), *Arg* 1,2, *W* 2, *SA* 1, 1997 *E* (R), *S* (R), *It*
Descamps, P (SB) 1927 *G* 2
Desclaux, F (RCF) 1949 *Arg* 1,2, 1953 *It*
Desclaux, J (Perpignan) 1934 *G*, 1935 *G*, 1936 *G* 1,2, 1937 *G, It*, 1938 *G* 1, *R, G* 2, 1945 *B* 1
Deslandes, C (RCF) 1990 *A* 1, *NZ* 2, 1991 *W* 1, 1992 *R, Arg* 1,2
Desnoyer, L (Brive) 1974 *R*
Destarac, L (Tarbes) 1926 *S, I, E, W, M*, 1927 *W, E, G* 1,2
Desvouges, R (SF) 1914 *W*
Detrez, P-E (Nîmes) 1983 *A* 2 (R), 1986 *Arg* 1 (R), 2, *A* (R), *NZ*1
Devergie, T (Nîmes) 1988 *R*, 1989 *NZ* 1,2, *B, A* 2, 1990 *W, E, S, I, R, A* 1,2,3, 1991 *US* 2, *W* 2, 1992 *R* (R), *Arg* 2 (R)
Deygas, M (Vienne) 1937 *It*
Deylaud, C (Toulouse) 1992 *R, Arg* 1,2, *SA* 1, 1994 *C* 1, *NZ* 1,2, 1995 *W, E, S*, [*Iv* (R), *S, I, SA*], *It, Arg*
Dintrans, P (Tarbes) 1979 *NZ* 1,2, *R*, 1980 *E, S, I, SA, R*, 1981 *S, I, W, E, A* 1,2, *R, NZ* 1,2, 1982 *W, E, S, I, R, Arg* 1,2, 1983 *E, W, A* 1,2, *R*, 1984 *I, W, E, S, R*, 1985 *E, S, I, W, Arg* 1,2, 1987 [*R*], 1988 *Arg* 1,2,3, 1989 *W, E, S*, 1990 *R*
Dispagne, S (Toulouse) 1996 *I* (R), *W* 1
Dizabo, P (Tyrosse) 1948 *A, S, E*, 1949 *S, I, E, W, Arg* 2, 1950 *S, I*, 1960 *Arg* 1,2,3
Domec, A (Carcassonne) 1929 *W*
Domec, H (Lourdes) 1953 *W, It*, 1954 *S, I, NZ, W, E, It*, 1955 *S, I, E, W*, 1956 *I, W, It*, 1958 *E, A, W, It, I*
Domenech, A (Vichy, Brive) 1954 *W, E, It*, 1955 *S, I, E, W*, 1956 *S, I, W, It, E, Cz*, 1957 *S, I, E, W, It, R* 1,2, 1958 *S, E, It*, 1959 *I*, 1960 *S, E, W, I, It, R, Arg* 1,2,3, 1961 *S, SA, E, W, It, I, NZ* 1,2,3, *A, R*, 1962 *S, E, W, I, It, R*, 1963 *W, It*
Domercq, J (Bayonne) 1912 *I, S*
Dorot, J (RCF) 1935 *G*
Dospital, P (Bayonne) 1977 *R*, 1980 *I*, 1981 *S, I, W, E*, 1982 *I, R, Arg* 1,2, 1983 *E, S, I, W*, 1984 *E, S, NZ* 1,2, *R*, 1985 *E, S, I, W, Arg* 1
Dourthe, C (Dax) 1966 *R*, 1967 *S, A, E, W, I, SA* 1,2,3, *NZ*, 1968 *W, NZ* 3, *SA* 1,2, 1969 *W*, 1971 *SA* 2 (R), *R*, 1972 *I* 1,2, *A* 1,2, *R*, 1973 *S, NZ, E*, 1974 *I, Arg* 1,2, *SA* 1,2, 1975 *W, E, S*
Dourthe, R (Dax) 1995 *R* 2, *Arg, NZ* 1, 2, 1996 *E, R*, 1996 *Arg* 1,2, *W* 2, *SA* 1,2, 1997 *W*
Doussau, E (Angoulême) 1938 *R*
Droitecourt, M (Montferrand) 1972 *R*, 1973 *NZ* (R), *E*, 1974 *E, S, Arg* 1, *SA* 2, 1975 *SA* 1,2, *Arg* 1,2, *R*, 1976 *S, I, W, A* 1, 1977 *Arg* 2
Dubertrand, A (Montferrand) 1971 *A* 2, *R*, 1972 *I* 2, 1974 *I, W, E, S, A* 2, 1975 *Arg* 1,2, *R*, 1976 *S, US*
Dubois, D (Bègles) 1971 *S*
Dubroca, D (Agen) 1979 *NZ* 2, 1981 *NZ* 2 (R), 1982 *E, S*, 1984 *W, E, S*, 1985 *Arg* 2, 1986 *S, I, W, E, R* 1, *Arg* 2, *A, NZ* 1, *R* 2, *NZ* 2,3, 1987 *W, E, S, I*, [*S, Z, Fj, A, NZ*], *R*, 1988 *E, S, I, W*
Duché, A (Limoges) 1929 *G*
Duclos, A (Lourdes) 1931 *S*
Ducousso, J (Tarbes) 1925 *S, W, E*
Dufau, G (RCF) 1948 *I, A*, 1949 *I, W*, 1950 *S, E, W*, 1951 *S, I, E, W*, 1952 *SA, W*, 1953 *S, I, E, W*, 1954 *S, I, NZ, W, E, It*, 1955 *S, I, E, W, It*, 1956 *S, I, W, It*, 1957 *S, I, E, W, It, R* 1
Dufau, J (Biarritz) 1912 *I, S, W, E*
Duffaut, Y (Agen) 1954 *Arg* 1,2
Duffour, R (Tarbes) 1911 *W*
Dufourcq, J (SBUC) 1906 *NZ, E*, 1907 *E*, 1908 *W*
Duhard, Y (Bagnères) 1980 *E*
Duhau, J (SF) 1928 *I*,1930 *I, G*, 1931 *I, S, W*, 1933 *G*
Dulaurens, C (Toulouse) 1926 *I*, 1928 *S*, 1929 *W*
Duluc, A (Béziers) 1934 *G*
Du Manoir, Y le P (RCF) 1925 *I, NZ, S, W, E*, 1926 *S*, 1927 *I, S*
Dupont, C (Lourdes) 1923 *S, W, I*, 1924 *S, I, W, R, US*, 1925 *S*, 1927 *E, G* 1,2, 1928 *A, G, W*, 1929 *I*
Dupont, J-L (Agen) 1983 *S*

Dupont, L (RCF) 1934 *G*, 1935 *G*, 1936 *G* 1,2, 1938 *R, G* 2
Dupouy, A (SB) 1924 *W, R*
Duprat, B (Bayonne) 1966 *E, W, It, R*, 1967 *S, A, E, SA* 2,3, 1968 *S, I*, 1972 *E, W, I* 2, *A* 1
Dupré, P (RCF) 1909 *W*
Dupuy, J (Tarbes) 1956 *S, I, W, It, E, Cz*, 1957 *S, I, E, W, It, R* 2, 1958 *S, E, SA* 1,2, 1959 *S, E, It, W, I*, 1960 *W, I, It, Arg* 1,3, 1961 *S, SA, E, NZ* 2, *R*, 1962 *S, E, W, I, It*, 1963 *W, It, R*, 1964 *S*
Du Souich, C J (see Judas du Souich)
Dutin, B (Mont-de-Marsan) 1968 *NZ* 2, *A, SA* 2, *R*
Dutour, F X (Toulouse) 1911 *E, I*, 1912 *S, W, E*, 1913 *S*
Dutrain, H (Toulouse) 1945 *W*, 1946 *B, I*, 1947 *E*, 1949 *I, E, W, Arg* 1
Dutrey, J (Lourdes) 1940 *B*
Duval, R (SF) 1908 *E, W*, 1909 *E*, 1911 *E, W, I*

Echavé, L (Agen) 1961 *S*
Elissalde, E (Bayonne) 1936 *G* 2, 1940 *B*
Elissalde, J-P (La Rochelle) 1980 *SA, R*, 1981 *A* 1,2, *R*
Empereur-Buisson, H (Béziers) 1931 *E, G*
Erbani, D (Agen) 1981 *A* 1,2, *NZ* 1,2, 1982 *Arg* 1,2, 1983 *S* (R), *I, W, A* 1,2, *R*, 1984 *W, E, R*, 1985 *E, W* (R), *Arg* 2, 1986 *S, I, W, E* 1, *Arg* 2, *NZ* 1,2 (R), 3, 1987 *W, E, S, I*, [*S, R, Fj, A, NZ*], 1988 *E, S*, 1989 *I* (R), *W, E, S, NZ* 1, *A*, 2, 1990 *W, E*
Escaffre, P (Narbonne) 1933 *G*, 1934 *G*
Escommier, M (Montelimar) 1955 *It*
Esponda, J-M (RCF) 1967 *SA* 1,2,3, *R*, 1968 *NZ* 1,2, *SA* 2, *R*, 1969 *S, I* (R), *E*
Estève, A (Béziers) 1971 *SA* 1, 1972 *I* 1, *E, W, I* 2, *A* 2, *R*, 1973 *S, NZ, E, I*, 1974 *I, W, E, S, R, SA* 1,2, 1975 *W, E*
Estève, P (Narbonne, Lavelanet) 1982 *R, Arg* 1,2, 1983 *E, S, I, W, A* 1, 1984 *I, W, E, S, NZ* 1,2, *R*, 1985 *E, S, I, W*, 1986 *S, I*, 1987 [*S, Z*]
Etcheberry, J (Rochefort, Cognac) 1923 *W, I*, 1924 *S, I, E, W, R, US*, 1926 *S, I, E, M*, 1927 *I, S, W, G* 2
Etchenique, J-M (Biarritz O) 1974 *R, SA* 1, 1975 *E, Arg* 2
Etchepare, A (Bayonne) 1922 *I*
Etcheverry, M (Pau) 1971 *S, I*
Eutrope, A (SCUF) 1913 *I*

Fabre, E (Toulouse) 1937 *It*, 1938 *G* 1,2
Fabre, J (Toulouse) 1963 *S, I, E, W, It*, 1964 *S, NZ, E*
Fabre, L (Lezignan) 1930 *G*
Fabre, M (Béziers) 1981 *A* 1, *R, NZ* 1,2, 1982 *I, R*
Failliot, P (RCF) 1911 *S, W, I*, 1912 *I, S, E*, 1913 *E, W*
Fargues, G (Dax) 1923 *I*
Fauré, F (Tarbes) 1914 *I, W, E*
Fauvel, J-P (Tulle) 1980 *R*
Favre, M (Lyon) 1913 *E, W*
Ferrand, L (Chalon) 1940 *B*
Ferrien, R (Tarbes) 1950 *S, I, E, W*
Finat, R (CASG) 1932 *G*, 1933 *G*
Fite, R (Brive) 1963 *W, It*
Forestier, J (SCUF) 1912 *W*
Forgues, F (Bayonne) 1911 *S, E, W*, 1912 *I, W, E*, 1913 *S, SA, W*, 1914 *I, E*
Fort, J (Agen) 1967 *It, W, I, SA* 1,2,3,4
Fourcade, G (BEC) 1909 *E, W*
Foures, H (Toulouse) 1951 *S, I, E, W*
Fournet, F (Montferrand) 1950 *W*
Fouroux, J (La Voulte) 1972 *I* 2, *R*, 1974 *W, E, Arg* 1,2, *R, SA* 1,2, 1975 *W, Arg* 1, *R*, 1976 *S, I, W, E, US, A* 1, 1977 *W, E, S, I, Arg* 1,2
Francquenelle, A (Vaugirard) 1911 *S*, 1913 *W, I*
Furcade, R (Perpignan) 1952 *S*

Gabernet, S (Toulouse) 1980 *E, S*, 1981 *S, I, W, E, A* 1,2, *R, NZ* 1,2, 1982 *I*, 1983 *A* 2, *R*
Gachassin, J (Lourdes) 1961 *S, I*, 1963 *R*, 1964 *S, NZ, E, W, It, I, SA, Fj, R*, 1965 *S, I, E, W, It, R*, 1966 *S, I, E, W*, 1967 *S, A, It, W, I, SA* 1, 1968 *S, I, E, W, Cz*, 1969 *S*
Galau, H (Toulouse) 1924 *S, I, E, W, US*
Galia, J (Quillan) 1927 *E, G* 1,2, 1928 *S, A, I, E, W*, 1929 *I, E, G*, 1930 *S, I, E, G, W*, 1931 *S, W, E, G*
Gallart, P (Béziers) 1990 *R, A* 1,2 (R), 3, 1992 *S, I, R, Arg* 1,2, *Arg*, 1994 *I, W, E*, 1995 *I* (t), *R* 1, [*Tg*]
Gallion, J (Toulon) 1978 *E, S, I, W*, 1979 *I, W, E, S, NZ* 2, *R*, 1980 *W, E, S, I*, 1983 *A* 1,2, *R*, 1984 *I, W, E, S, R*, 1985 *E, S, I, W*, 1986 *Arg* 2

Galthié, F (Colomiers) 1991 *R, US* 1, [*R, Fj, C, E*], 1992 *W, E, S, R, Arg*, 1994 *I, W, E*, 1995 [*SA, E*], 1996 *W* 1(R), 1997 *I*
Galy, J (Perpignan) 1953 *W*
Garuet-Lempirou, J-P (Lourdes) 1983 *A* 1,2, *R*, 1984 *I, NZ* 1,2, *R*, 1985 *E, S, I, W, Arg* 1, 1986 *S, I, W, E, R* 1, *Arg* 1, *NZ* 1, *R* 2, *NZ* 2,3, 1987 *W, E, S, I*, [*S, R, Fj, A, NZ*], 1988 *E, S, Arg* 1,2, *R*, 1989 *E* (R), *S, NZ* 1,2, 1990 *W, E*
Gasc, J (Graulhet) 1977 *NZ* 2
Gasparotto, G (Montferrand) 1976 *A* 2, *R*
Gauby, G (Perpignan) 1956 *Cz*
Gaudermen, P (RCF) 1906 *E*
Gayraud, W (Toulouse) 1920 *I*
Geneste, R (BEC) 1945 *B* 1, 1949 *Arg* 2
Genet, J-P (RCF) 1992 *S, I, R*
Gensane, R (Béziers) 1962 *S, E, W, I, It, R*, 1963 *S*
Gerald, G (RCF) 1927 *E, G* 2, 1928 *S*, 1929 *I, S, W, E, G*, 1930 *S, I, E, G, W*, 1931 *I, S, E, G*
Gerintes, G (CASG) 1924 *R*, 1925 *I*, 1926 *W*
Geschwind, P (RCF) 1936 *G* 1,2
Giacardy, M (SBUC) 1907 *E*
Gimbert, P (Bègles) 1991 *R, US* 1, 1992 *W, E*
Glas, S (Bourgoin) 1996 *S* (t), *I* (R), *W* 1, *R, Arg* 2(R), *W* 2, *SA* 1,2, 1997 *I, W, E, S*
Gommes, J (RCF) 1909 *I*
Gonnet, C-A (Albi) 1921 *E, I*, 1922 *E, W*, 1924 *S, E*, 1926 *S, I, E, W, M*, 1927 *I, S, W, E, G* 1
Gonzalez, J-M (Bayonne) 1992 *Arg* 1,2, *SA* 1,2, *Arg*, 1993 *R* 1, *SA* 1,2, *R* 2, *A* 1,2, 1994 *I, W, E, S, C* 1, *NZ* 1,2, *C* 2, 1995 *W, E, S, I, R* 1, [*Tg, S, I, SA, E*], *It, Arg*, 1996 *E, S, I, W* 1
Got, R (Perpignan) 1920 *I, US*, 1921 *S, W*, 1922 *S, E, W, I*, 1924 *I, E, W, R, US*
Gourdon, J-F (RCF, Bagnères) 1974 *S, Arg* 1, 2, *R, SA* 1, 2, 1975 *W, E, S, I, R*, 1976 *S, I, W, E*, 1978 *E, S*, 1979 *W, E, S, R*, 1980 *I*
Gourragne, J-F (Béziers) 1990 *NZ* 2, 1991 *W* 1
Goyard, A (Lyon U) 1936 *G* 1,2, 1937 *G, It*, 1938 *G* 1, *R, G* 2
Graciet, R (SBUC) 1926 *I, W*, 1927 *S, G* 1, 1929 *E*, 1930 *W*
Graou, S (Auch, Colomiers) 1992 *Arg* (R), 1993 *SA* 1,2, *R* 2, *A* 2 (R), 1995 *R* 2, *Arg* (t), *NZ* 2 (R)
Gratton, J (Agen) 1984 *NZ* 2, *R*, 1985 *E, S, I, W, Arg* 1,2, 1986 *S, NZ* 1
Graule, V (Arl Perpignan) 1926 *I, E, W*, 1927 *S, W*, 1931 *G*
Greffe, M (Grenoble) 1968 *W, Cz, NZ* 1,2, *SA* 1
Griffard, J (Lyon U) 1932 *G*, 1933 *G*, 1934 *G*
Gruarin, A (Toulon) 1964 *W, It, I, SA, Fj, R*, 1965 *S, I, E, W, It*, 1966 *S, I, E, W, It, R*, 1967 *S, A, E, It, W, I, NZ*, 1968 *S, I*
Guelorget, P (RCF) 1931 *E, G*
Guichemerre, A (Dax) 1920 *E*, 1921 *E, I*, 1923 *S*
Guilbert, A (Toulon) 1975 *E, S, I, W, SA* 1,2, 1976 *A* 1, 1977 *Arg* 1,2, *NZ* 1,2, *R*, 1979 *I, W, E*
Guillemin, P (RCF) 1908 *E, W*, 1909 *E, I*, 1910 *W, S, E, I*, 1911 *S, E, W*
Guilleux, P (Agen) 1952 *SA, It*
Guiral, M (Agen) 1931 *G*, 1932 *G*, 1933 *G*
Guiraud, H (Nîmes) 1996 *R*

Haget, A (PUC) 1953 *E*, 1954 *I, NZ, E, Arg* 2, 1955 *E, W, It*, 1957 *I, E, It, R* 1, 1958 *It, SA* 2
Haget, F (Agen, Biarritz O) 1974 *Arg* 1,2, 1975 *SA* 2, *Arg* 1,2, *R*, 1976 *S*, 1978 *S, I, W, R*, 1979 *I, W, E, S, NZ* 1,2, *R*, 1980 *W, S, I*, 1984 *S, NZ* 1,2, *R*, 1985 *E, S, I*, 1986 *S, I, W, E, R* 1, *Arg* 1, *A, NZ* 1, 1987 *S, I*, [*R, Fj*]
Haget, H (CASG) 1928 *S*, 1930 *G*
Halet, R (Strasbourg) 1925 *NZ, S, W*
Harislur-Arthapignet, P (Tarbes) 1988 *Arg* 4 (R)
Harize, D (Cahors, Toulouse) 1975 *SA* 1,2, 1976 *A* 1,2, *R*, 1977 *W, E, S, I*
Hauc, J (Toulon) 1928 *E, G*, 1929 *I, S, G*
Hauser, M (Lourdes) 1969 *E*
Hedembaigt, M (Bayonne) 1913 *S, SA*, 1914 *W*
Hericé, D (Bègles) 1950 *I*
Herrero, A (Toulon) 1963 *R*, 1964 *NZ, E, W, It, I, SA, Fj, R*, 1965 *S, I, E, W*, 1966 *W, It, R*, 1967 *S, A, E, It, I, R*
Herrero, B (Nice) 1983 *I*, 1986 *Arg* 1
Heyer, F (Montferrand) 1990 *A* 2
Hiquet, J-C (Agen) 1964 *E*
Hoche, M (PUC) 1957 *I, E, W, It, R* 1
Hondagné-Monge, M (Tarbes) 1988 *Arg* 2 (R)

Hontas, P (Biarritz) 1990 *S, I, R*, 1991 *R*, 1992 *Arg*, 1993 *E, S, I, W*
Hortoland, J-P (Béziers) 1971 *A* 2
Houblain, H (SCUF) 1909 *E*, 1910 *W*
Houdet, R (SF) 1927 *S, W, G* 1, 1928 *G, W*, 1929 *I, S, E*, 1930 *S, E*
Hourdebaigt, A (SBUC) 1909 *I*, 1910 *W, S, E, I*
Hubert, A (ASF) 1906 *E*, 1907 *E*, 1908 *E, W*, 1909 *E, W, I*
Hueber, A (Lourdes, Toulon) 1990 *A* 3, *NZ* 1, 1991 *US* 2, 1992 *I, Arg* 1,2, *SA* 1,2, 1993 *E, S, I, W, R* 1, *SA* 1,2, *R* 2, *A* 1,2, 1995 [*Tg, S* (R), *I*]
Hutin, R (CASG) 1927 *I, S, W*
Hyardet, A (Castres) 1995 *It, Arg* (R)

Ibanez, R (Dax) 1996 *W* 1(R), 1997 *It* (R)
Icard, J (SF) 1909 *E, W*
Iguiniz, E (Bayonne) 1914 *E*
Ihingoué, D (BEC) 1912 *I, S*
Imbernon, J-F (Perpignan) 1976 *I, W, E, US, A* 1, 1977 *W, E, S, I, Arg* 1,2, *NZ* 1,2, 1978 *E, R*, 1979 *I*, 1981 *S, I, W, E*, 1982 *I*, 1983 *I, W*
Iraçabal, J (Bayonne) 1968 *NZ* 1,2, *SA* 1, 1969 *S, I, W, R*, 1970 *S, I, W, E, R*, 1971 *W, SA* 1,2, *A* 1, 1972 *E, W, I* 2, *A* 2, *R*, 1973 *S, NZ, E, W, I*, 1974 *I, W, E, S, Arg* 1,2, *SA* 2 (R)
Isaac, H (RCF) 1907 *E*, 1908 *E*
Ithurra, E (Biarritz O) 1936 *G* 1,2, 1937 *G*

Janeczek, T (Tarbes) 1982 *Arg* 1,2, 1990 *R*
Janik, K (Toulouse) 1987 *R*
Jarasse, A (Brive) 1945 *B* 1
Jardel, J (SB) 1928 *I, E*
Jaureguy, A (RCF, Toulouse, SF) 1920 *S, E, W, I, US*, 1922 *S, W*, 1923 *S, W, E, I*, 1924 *S, W, R, US*, 1925 *I, NZ*, 1926 *S, E, W, M*, 1927 *I, E*, 1928 *S, A, E, G, W*, 1929 *I, S, E*
Jaureguy, P (Toulouse) 1913 *S, SA, W, I*
Jeangrand, M-H (Tarbes) 1921 *I*
Jeanjean, P (Toulon) 1948 *I*
Jérôme, G (SF) 1906 *NZ, E*
Joinel, J-L (Brive) 1977 *NZ* 1, 1978 *R*, 1979 *I, W, E, S, NZ* 1,2, *R*, 1980 *W, E, S, I, SA*, 1981 *S, I, W, E, R, NZ* 1,2, 1982 *E, S, I, R*, 1983 *E, S, I, W, A* 1,2, *R*, 1984 *I, W, E, S*, *NZ* 1,2, 1985 *S, I, W, Arg* 1, 1986 *S, I, W, E, R* 1, *Arg* 1,2, *A*, 1987 [*Z*]
Jol, M (Biarritz O) 1947 *S, I, W, E*, 1949 *S, I, E, W, Arg* 1,2
Jordana, J-L (Pau, Toulouse) 1996 *R* (R), *Arg* 1(t),2, *W* 2, 1997 *I* (t), *W, S* (R)
Judas du Souich, C (SCUF) 1911 *W, I*
Juillet, C (Montferrand) 1995 *R* 2, *Arg*
Junquas, L (Tyrosse) 1945 *B* 1,2, *W*, 1946 *B, I, K, W*, 1947 *S, I, W, E*, 1948 *S, W*

Kaczorowski, D (Le Creusot) 1974 *I* (R)
Kaempf, A (St Jean-de-Luz) 1946 *B*

Labadie, P (Bayonne) 1952 *S, I, SA, W, E, It*, 1953 *S, I, It*, 1954 *S, I, NZ, W, E, Arg* 2, 1955 *S, I, E, W*, 1956 *I*, 1957 *I*
Labarthete, R (Pau) 1952 *S*
Labazuy, A (Lourdes) 1952 *I*, 1954 *S, W*, 1956 *E*, 1958 *A, W, I*, 1959 *S, E, It, W*
Laborde, C (RCF) 1962 *It, R*, 1963 *R*, 1964 *SA*, 1965 *E*
Labrousse, T (Brive) 1996 *R, SA* 1
Lacans, P (Béziers) 1980 *SA*, 1981 *W, E, A* 2, *R*, 1982 *W*
Lacassagne, H (SBUC) 1906 *NZ*, 1907 *E*
Lacaussade, R (Bègles) 1948 *A, S*
Lacaze, C (Lourdes, Angoulême) 1961 *NZ* 2,3, *A, R*, 1962 *E, W, I, It*, 1963 *W, R*, 1964 *S, NZ, E*, 1965 *It, R*, 1966 *S, I, E, W, It, R*, 1967 *S, E, SA* 1,2,3,4, *R*, 1968 *S, E, W, Cz, NZ* 1, 1969 *E*
Lacaze, H (Périgueux) 1928 *I, G, W*, 1929 *I, W*
Lacaze, P (Lourdes) 1958 *SA* 1,2, 1959 *S, E, It, W, I*
Lacazedieu, C (Dax) 1923 *W, I*, 1928 *A, I*, 1929 *S*
Lacombe, B (Agen) 1989 *B*, 1990 *A* 2
Lacome, M (Pau) 1960 *Arg* 2
Lacoste, R (Tarbes) 1914 *I, W, E*
Lacrampe, F (Béziers) 1949 *Arg* 2
Lacroix, P (Mont-de-Marsan, Agen) 1958 *A*, 1960 *W, I, It, R, Arg* 1,2,3, 1961 *S, SA, E, W, I, NZ* 1,2,3, *A, R*, 1962 *S, E, W, I, R*, 1963 *S, I, E*
Lacroix, T (Dax) 1989 *A* 1 (R), 2, 1991 *W* 1 (R), 2 (R), [*R, C* (R), *E*], 1992 *SA* 2, 1993 *E, S, I, W, SA* 1,2, *R* 2, *A* 1,2, 1994 *I, W, E, S, C* 1, *NZ* 1,2, *C* 2, 1995 *W, E, S, R* 1 [*Tg, Iv, S, I, SA, E*], 1996 *E, S, I*

281

Revillon, J (RCF) 1926 *I, E*, 1927 *S*
Ribère, E (Perpignan, Quillan) 1924 *I*, 1925, *I, NZ, S*,
1926 *S, I, W, M*, 1927 *I, S, W, E, G* 1,2, 1928 *S, A, I, E, G,*
W, 1929 *I, E, G*, 1930 *S, I, E, W*, 1931 *I, S, W, E, G*, 1932
G, 1933 *G*
Rives, J-P (Toulouse, RCF) 1975 *E, S, I, Arg* 1,2, *R*,
1976 *S, I, W, E, US, A* 1,2, *R*, 1977 *W, E, S, I, Arg* 1,2, *R*,
1978 *E, S, I, W, R*, 1979 *I, W, E, S, NZ* 1,2, *R*, 1980 *W, E,*
S, I, SA, 1981 *S, I, W, E, A* 2, 1982 *W, E, S, I, R*, 1983 *E,*
S, I, W, A 1,2, *R*, 1984 *I, W, E, S*
Rochon, A (Montferrand) 1936 *G* 1
Rodrigo, M (Mauléon) 1931 *I, W*
Rodriguez, L (Mont-de-Marsan, Montferrand, Dax)
1981 *A* 1,2, *R, NZ* 1,2, 1982 *W, E, S, I, R*, 1983 *E, S*, 1984
I, NZ 1,2, *R*, 1985 *E, S, I, W*, 1986 *Arg* 1, *A, R* 2, *NZ* 2,3,
1987 *W, E, S, I*, [*S, Z, Fj, A, NZ*]*. R*, 1988 *E, S, I, W. Arg*
1,2,3,4, *R*, 1989 *I, E, S, NZ* 1,2, *B, A* 1, 1990 *W, E, S, I,*
NZ 1
Rogé, L (Béziers) 1952 *It*, 1953 *E, W, It*, 1954 *S, Arg* 1,2,
1955 *S, I*, 1956 *W, It, E*, 1957 *S*, 1960 *S, E*
Rollet, J (Bayonne) 1960 *Arg* 3, 1961 *NZ* 3, *A*, 1962 *It*,
1963 *I*
Romero, H (Montauban) 1962 *S, E, W, I, It, R*, 1963 *E*
Romeu, J-P (Montferrand) 1972 *R*, 1973 *S, NZ, E, W, I,*
R, 1974 *W, E, S, Arg* 1,2, *R, SA* 1,2 (R), 1975 *W, SA* 2,
Arg 1,2, *R*, 1976 *S, I, W, E, US*, 1977 *W, E, S, I, Arg* 1,2,
NZ 1,2, *R*
Roques, A (Cahors) 1958 *A, W, It, I, SA* 1,2, 1959 *S, E,*
W, I, 1960 *S, E, W, I, Arg* 1,2,3, 1961 *S, SA, E, W, It, I*,
1962 *S, E, W, I, It*, 1963 *S*
Roques, J-C (Brive) 1966 *S, I, It, R*
Rossignol, J-C (Brive) 1972 *A* 2
Rouan, J (Narbonne) 1953 *S, I*
Roucaries, G (Perpignan) 1956 *S*
Rouffia, L (Narbonne) 1945 *B* 2, *W*, 1946 *W*, 1948 *I*
Rougerie, J (Montferrand) 1973 *J*
Rougé-Thomas, P (Toulouse) 1989 *NZ* 1,2
Roujas, F (Tarbes) 1910 *I*
Roumat, O (Dax) 1989 *NZ* 2 (R), *B*, 1990 *W, E, S, I, R, A*
1,2,3, *NZ* 1,2, 1991 *S, I, W* 1, *E, R, US* 1, *W* 2, [*R, Fj, C,*
E], 1992 *W* (R), *E* (R), *S, I, SA* 1,2, *Arg*. 1993 *E, S, I, W*
R 1, *SA* 1,2, *R* 2, *A* 1,2, 1994 *I, W, E, C* 1, *NZ* 1,2, *C* 2,
1995 *W, E, S*, [*Iv, S, I, SA, E*], 1996 *E, S, I, W* 1, *Arg* 1,2
Rousie, M (Villeneuve) 1931 *S, G*, 1932 *G*, 1933 *G*
Rousset, G (Béziers) 1975 *SA* 1, 1976 *US*
Ruiz, A (Tarbes) 1968 *SA* 2, *R*
Rupert, J-J (Tyrosse) 1963 *R*, 1964 *S, Fj*, 1965 *E, W, It*,
1966 *S, I, E, W, It*, 1967 *It, R*, 1968 *S*

Sadourny, J-L (Colomiers) 1991 *W* 2 (R), [*C* (R)], 1992
E (R), *S, I, Arg* 1 (R), 2, *SA* 1,2, 1993 *R* 1, *SA* 1,2, *R* 2, *A*
1,2, 1994 *I, W, E, S, C* 1, *NZ* 1,2, *C* 2, 1995 *W, E, S, I, R*
1, [*Tg, S, I, SA, E*], *It, R* 2, *Arg, NZ* 1, 2, 1996 *E, S, I, W* 1,
Arg 1,2, *W* 2, *SA* 1,2, 1997 *I, W, E, S, It*
Sagot, P (SF) 1906 *NZ*, 1908 *E*, 1909 *W*
Sahuc, A (Métro) 1945 *B* 1,2
Sahuc, F (Toulouse) 1936 *G* 2
Saint-André, P (Montferrand) 1990 *R, A* 3, *NZ* 1,2, 1991
I (R), *W* 1, *E, US*, *W* 2, [*R, Fj, C, E*], 1992 *W, E, S, I,*
R, Arg 1,2, *SA* 1,2, 1993 *E, S, I, W, SA* 1,2, *A* 1,2, 1994 *I,*
W, E, S, C 1, *NZ* 1,2, *C* 2, 1995 *W, E, S, I, R* 1, [*Tg, Iv, S,*
I, SA, E], *It, R* 2, *Arg, NZ* 1, 2, 1996 *E, S, I, W* 1, *R, Arg*
1,2, *W* 2, 1997 *It*
Saisset, O (Béziers) 1971 *R*, 1972 *S, I* 1, *A* 1,2, 1973 *S,*
NZ, E, W, I, J, R, 1974 *I, Arg* 2, *SA* 1,2, 1975 *W*
Salas, P (Narbonne) 1979 *NZ* 1,2, *R*, 1980 *W, E*, 1981 *A*
1, 1982 *Arg* 2
Salinié, R (Perpignan) 1923 *E*
Sallefranque, M (Dax) 1981 *A* 2, 1982 *W, E, S*
Salut, J (TOEC) 1966 *R*, 1967 *S*, 1968 *I, E, Cz, NZ* 1,
1969 *I*
Samatan, R (Agen) 1930 *S, I, E, G, W*, 1931 *I, S, W, E, G*
Sanac, A (Perpignan) 1952 *It*, 1953 *S, I*, 1954 *E*, 1956
Cz, 1957 *S, I, E, W, It*
Sangalli, F (Narbonne) 1975 *I, SA* 1,2, 1976 *S, A* 1,2, *R*,
1977 *W, E, S, I, Arg* 1,2, *NZ* 1,2
Sanz, H (Narbonne) 1988 *Arg* 3,4, *R*, 1989 *A* 2, 1990 *S,*
I, R, A 1,2, *NZ* 2, 1991 *W* 2
Sappa, M (Nice) 1973 *J, R*, 1977 *R*
Sarrade, P (Pau) 1929 *I*
Saux, J-P (Pau) 1960 *W, It, Arg* 1,2, 1961 *SA, E, W, It, I,*
NZ 1,2,3, *A*, 1962 *S, E, W, I, It*, 1963 *S, I, E, It*
Savitsky, M (La Voulte) 1969 *R*
Savy, M (Montferrand) 1931 *I, S, W, E*, 1936 *G* 1

Sayrou, J (Perpignan) 1926 *W, M*, 1928 *E, G, W*, 1929 *S,*
W, E, G
Scohy, R (BEC) 1931 *S, W, E, G*
Sébedio, J (Tarbes) 1913 *S, E*, 1914 *I*, 1920 *S, I, US*,
1922 *S, E*, 1923 *S*
Seguier, N (Béziers) 1973 *J, R*
Seigne, L (Agen, Merignac) 1989 *B, A* 1, 1990 *NZ* 1,
1993 *E, S, I, W, R* 1, *A* 1,2, 1994 *S, C* 1, 1995 *E* (R), *S*
Sella, P (Agen) 1982 *R, Arg* 1,2, 1983 *E, S, I, W, A* 1,2, *R*,
1984 *I, W, E, S, NZ* 1,2, *R*, 1985 *E, S, I, W, Arg* 1,2, 1986
S, I, W, E, R 1, *Arg* 1,2, *A, NZ* 1, *R* 2, *NZ* 2,3, 1987 *W, E,*
S, I, [*S, R, Z* (R), *Fj, A, NZ*], 1988 *E, S, I, W, Arg* 1,2,3,4,
R, 1989 *I, W, E, S, NZ* 1,2, *B, A* 1,2, 1990 *W, E, S, I, A*
1,2,3, 1991 *W* 1, *E, R, US* 1,2, *W* 2, [*Fj, C, E*], 1992 *W, E,*
S, I, Arg, 1993 *E, S, I, W, R* 1, *SA* 1,2, *R* 2, *A* 1,2, 1994 *I,*
W, E, S, C 1, *NZ* 1,2, *C* 2, 1995 *W, E, S, I*, [*Tg, S, I, SA, E*]
Semmartin, J (SCUF) 1913 *W, I*
Senal, G (Béziers) 1974 *Arg* 1,2, *R, SA* 1,2, 1975 *W*
Sentilles, J (Tarbes) 1912 *W, E*, 1913 *S, SA*
Serin, L (Béziers) 1928 *E*, 1929 *W, E, G*, 1930 *S, I, E, G,*
W, 1931 *I, W, E*
Serre, P (Perpignan) 1920 *S, E*
Serrière, P (RCF) 1986 *A*, 1987 *R*, 1988 *E*
Servole, L (Toulon) 1931 *I, S, W, E, G*, 1934 *G*, 1935 *G*
Sicart, N (Perpignan) 1922 *I*
Sillières, J (Tarbes) 1968 *R*, 1970 *S, I*, 1971 *S, I, E*, 1972
E, W
Siman, M (Montferrand) 1948 *E*, 1949 *S*, 1950 *S, I, E, W*
Simon, S (Bègles) 1991 *R, US* 1
Simonpaoli, R (SF) 1911 *I*, 1912 *I, S*
Sitjar, M (Agen) 1964 *W, It, I, R*, 1965 *It, R*, 1967 *A, E,*
It, W, I, SA 1,2
Skrela, J-C (Toulouse) 1971 *SA* 1,2, *A* 2, 1972 *I* 1 (R), *E,*
W, I 2, *A* 1, 1973 *W, J, R*, 1974 *W, E, S, Arg* 1, *R*, 1975 *W*
(R), *E, S, I, SA* 1,2, *Arg* 1,2, *R*, 1976 *S, I, W, E, US, A* 1,2,
R, 1977 *W, E, S, I, Arg* 1,2, *NZ* 1,2, *R*, 1978 *E, S, I, W*
Soler, M (Quillan) 1929 *G*
Soro, R (Lourdes, Romans) 1945 *B* 1,2, *W*, 1946 *B, I, K*,
1947 *S, I, W, E*, 1948 *I, A, S, W, E*, 1949 *S, I, E, W, Arg*
1,2
Sorondo, L-M (Montauban) 1946 *K*, 1947 *S, I, W, E,*
1948 *I*
Soulié, E (CASG) 1920 *E, I, US*, 1921 *S, E, I*, 1922 *E, W, I*
Sourgens, J (Bègles) 1926 *M*
Spanghero, C (Narbonne) 1971 *E, W, SA* 1,2, *A* 1,2, *R*,
1972 *S, E, W, I* 2, *A* 1,2, 1974 *I, W, E, S, R, SA* 1, 1975 *E,*
S, I
Spanghero, W (Narbonne) 1964 *SA, Fj, R*, 1965 *S, I, E,*
W, It, R, 1966 *S, I, E, W, It, R*, 1967 *S, A, E, SA* 1,2,3,4,
NZ, 1968 *S, I, E, W, NZ* 1,2,3, *A, SA* 1, *R*, 1969 *S, I, W*,
1970 *R*, 1971 *E, W, SA* 1, 1972 *E* 2, *A* 1,2, *R*, 1973 *S,*
NZ, E, W, I
Stener, G (PUC) 1956 *S, I, E*, 1958 *SA* 1,2
Struxiano, P (Toulouse) 1913 *W, I*, 1920 *S, E, W, I, US*
Sutra, G (Narbonne) 1967 *SA* 2, 1969 *W*, 1970 *S, I*
Swierczinski, C (Bègles) 1969 *E*, 1977 *Arg* 2

Tachdjian, M (RCF) 1991 *S, I, E*
Taffary, M (RCF) 1975 *W, E, S*
Taillantou, J (Pau) 1930 *I, G, W*
Tarricq, P (Lourdes) 1958 *A, W, It, I*
Tavernier, H (Toulouse) 1913 *I*
Techoueyres, W (SBUC) 1994 *E, S*, 1995 [*Iv*]
Terreau, M-M (Bourg) 1945 *W*, 1946 *B, I, K, W*, 1947 *S,*
I, W, E, 1948 *I, A, W, E*, 1949 *S, Arg* 1,2, 1951 *S*
Theuriet, A (SCUF) 1909 *E, W*, 1910 *S, W*, 1911 *W*, 1913 *E*
Thevenot, M (SCUF) 1910 *W, E, I*
Thierry, R (RCF) 1920 *S, E, W, US*
Thiers, P (Montferrand) 1936 *G* 1,2, 1937 *G, It*, 1938 *G*
1,2, 1940 *B*, 1945 *B*, 1,2
Tignol, P (Toulouse) 1953 *S, I*
Tilh, H (Nantes) 1912 *W, E*, 1913 *S, SA, E, W*
Tolot, J-L (Agen) 1987 [*Z*]
Tordo, J-F (Nice) 1991 *US* 1 (R), 1992 *W, E, S, I, R, Arg*
1,2, *SA* 1, *Arg*, 1993 *E, S, I, W, R* 1
Torreilles, S (Perpignan) 1956 *S*
Tournaire, F (Narbonne) 1995 *It*, 1996 *I, W* 1, *R, Arg*
1,2(R), *W* 2, *SA* 1,2, 1997 *I, E, S, It*
Tourte, R (St Girons) 1940 *B*
Trillo, J (Bègles) 1967 *SA* 3,4, *NZ, R*, 1968 *S, I, NZ*
1,2,3, *A*, 1969 *I, E, W, R*, 1970 *E, R*, 1971 *S, I, SA* 1,2, *A*
1,2, 1972 *S, A* 1,2, *R*, 1973 *S, E*
Triviaux, R (Cognac) 1931 *E, G*
Tucco-Chala, M (PUC) 1940 *B*

Ugartemendia, J-L (St Jean-de-Luz) 1975 *S, I*

Vaills, G (Perpignan) 1928 *A*, 1929 *G*
Vallot, C (SCUF) 1912 *S*
Van Heerden, A (Tarbes) 1992 *E, S*
Vannier, M (RCF, Chalon) 1953 *W*, 1954 *S, I, Arg* 1,2, 1955 *S, I, E, W, It*, 1956 *S, I, W, It, E*, 1957 *S, I, E, W, It, R* 1,2, 1958 *S, E, A, W, It, I*, 1960 *S, E, W, I, It, R, Arg* 1,3, 1961 *SA, E, W, It, I, NZ* 1, *A*
Vaquer, F (Perpignan) 1921 *S, W*, 1922 *W*
Vaquerin, A (Béziers) 1971 *R*, 1972 *S, I* 1, *A* 1, 1973 *S*, 1974 *W, E, S, Arg* 1,2, *R, SA* 1,2, 1975 *W, E, S, I*, 1976 *US, A* 1 (R), 2, *R*, 1977 *Arg* 2, 1979 *W, E*, 1980 *S, I*
Vareilles, C (SF) 1907 *E*, 1908 *E, W*, 1910 *S, E*
Varenne, F (RCF) 1952 *S*
Varvier, T (RCF) 1906 *E*, 1909 *E, W*, 1911 *E, W*, 1912 *I*
Vassal, G (Carcassonne) 1938 *R, G* 2
Vaysse, J (Albi) 1924 *US*, 1926 *M*
Vellat, E (Grenoble) 1927 *I, E, G* 1,2, 1928 *A*
Venditti, D (Bourgoin, Brive) 1996 *R, SA* 1(R),2, 1997 *I, W, E, S*
Vergé, L (Bègles) 1993 *R* 1 (R)
Verger, A (SF) 1927 *W, E, G* 1, 1928 *I, E, G, W*
Verges, S-A (SF) 1906 *NZ, E*, 1907 *E*

Viard, G (Narbonne) 1969 *W*, 1970 *S, R*, 1971 *S, I*
Viars, S (Brive) 1992 *W, E, I, R, Arg* 1,2, *SA* 1,2 (R), *Arg,* 1993 *R* 1, 1994 *C* 1 (R), *NZ* 1 (t), 1995 *E* (R), [*Iv*]
Vigerie, M (Agen) 1931 *W*
Vigier, R (Montferrand) 1956 *S, W, It, E, Cz*, 1957 *S, E, W, It, R* 1,2, 1958 *S, E, A, W, It, I, SA* 1,2, 1959 *S, E, It, W, I*
Vigneau, A (Bayonne) 1935 *G*
Vignes, C (RCF) 1957 *R* 1,2, 1958 *S, E*
Vila, E (Tarbes) 1926 *M*
Vilagra, J (Vienne) 1945 *B* 2
Villepreux, P (Toulouse) 1967 *It, I, SA* 2, *NZ*, 1968 *I, Cz, NZ* 1,2,3, *A*, 1969 *S, I, E, W, R*, 1970 *S, I, W, E, R*, 1971 *S, I, E, W, A* 1,2, *R*, 1972 *I* 1, *E, W, I* 2, *A* 1,2
Viviès, B (Agen) 1978 *E, S, I, W*, 1980 *SA, R*, 1981 *S, A* 1, 1983 *A* 1 (R)
Volot, M (SF) 1945 *W*, 1946 *B, I, K, W*

Weller, S (Grenoble) 1989 *A* 1,2, 1990 *A* 1, *NZ* 1
Wolf, J-P (Béziers) 1980 *SA, R*, 1981 *A* 2, 1982 *E*

Yachvili, M (Tulle, Brive) 1968 *E, W, Cz, NZ* 3, *A, R*, 1969 *S, I, R*, 1971 *E, SA* 1,2 *A* 1, 1972 *R*, 1975 *SA* 2

Zago, F (Montauban) 1963 *I, E*

Despite the attentions of Ireland's Jonathan Bell, David Vendetti scores the third try for France in their 32-15 victory at Lansdowne Road.

FRENCH INTERNATIONAL RECORDS
(up to 30 April 1997)

MATCH RECORDS

MOST CONSECUTIVE TEST WINS

10 1931 *E, G*, 1932 *G*, 1933 *G*, 1934 *G*, 1935 *G*, 1936 *G* 1,2, 1937 *G, It*
7 1954 *E, It, Arg* 1,2, 1955 *S, I, E*
7 1991 *R, US* 1,2, *W* 2, *R, Fj, C*

MOST CONSECUTIVE TESTS WITHOUT DEFEAT

P	W	D	Period
10	10	0	1931–38
10	8	2	1958–59
10	9	1	1986–87

MOST POINTS IN A MATCH
by the team

Pts	Opp	Venue	Year
70	Z	Auckland	1987
64	R	Aurillac	1996
60	It	Toulon	1967
59	R	Paris	1924
55	R	Wellington	1987

by a player

30 by D Camberabero v Zimbabwe at Auckland	1987
27 by G Camberabero v Italy at Toulon	1967
26 by T Lacroix v Ireland at Durban	1995
25 by J-P Romeu v United States at Chicago	1976
25 by P Berot v Romania at Agen	1987
25 by T Lacroix v Tonga at Pretoria	1995

MOST TRIES IN A MATCH
by the team

T	Opp	Venue	Year
13	R	Paris	1924
13	Z	Auckland	1987
11	It	Toulon	1967
10	R	Aurillac	1996

by a player

4 by A Jauréguy v Romania at Paris	1924
4 by M Celhay v Italy at Paris	1937

MOST CONVERSIONS IN A MATCH
by the team

C	Opp	Venue	Year
9	It	Toulon	1967
9	Z	Auckland	1987
8	R	Wellington	1987

by a player

9 by G Camberabero v Italy at Toulon	1967
9 by D Camberabero v Zimbabwe at Auckland	1987
8 by G Laporte v Romania at Wellington	1987

MOST PENALTY GOALS IN A MATCH
by the team

P	Opp	Venue	Year
8	I	Durban	1995
6	Arg	Buenos Aires	1977
6	S	Paris	1997

by a player

8 by T Lacroix v Ireland at Durban	1995
6 by J-M Aguirre v Argentina at Buenos Aires	1977
6 by C Lamaison v Scotland at Paris	1997

MOST DROPPED GOALS IN A MATCH
by the team

D	Opp	Venue	Year
3	I	Paris	1960
3	E	Twickenham	1985
3	NZ	Christchurch	1986
3	A	Sydney	1990
3	S	Paris	1991
3	NZ	Christchurch	1994

by a player

3 by P Albaladejo v Ireland at Paris	1960
3 by J-P Lescarboura v England at Twickenham	1985
3 by J-P Lescarboura v New Zealand at Christchurch	1986
3 by D Camerabero v Australia at Sydney	1990

CAREER RECORDS

MOST CAPPED PLAYERS

Caps	Player	Career
111	P Sella	1982–95
93	S Blanco	1980–91
69	R Bertranne	1971–81
64	P Saint-André	1990–97
63	M Crauste	1957–66
63	B Dauga	1964–72
61	J Condom	1982–90
61	O Roumat	1989–96
59	J-P Rives	1975–84

MOST CONSECUTIVE TESTS

Tests	Player	Span
46	R Bertranne	1973–79
45	P Sella	1982–87
44	M Crauste	1960–66
35	B Dauga	1964–68

MOST TESTS AS CAPTAIN

Tests	Captain	Span
34	J-P Rives	1978–84
29	P Saint-André	1994–96
25	D Dubroca	1986–88
24	G Basquet	1948–52
22	M Crauste	1961–66

MOST TESTS IN INDIVIDUAL POSITIONS

Full-back	S Blanco	81	1980–91
Wing	P Saint-André	62	1990–97
Centre	P Sella	104	1982–95
Fly-half	J-P Romeu	33	1972–77
Scrum-half	P Berbizier	56	1981–91
Prop	R Paparemborde	55	1975–83
Hooker	P Dintrans	50	1979–90
Lock	J Condom	61	1982–90
Flanker	J-P Rives	59	1975–84
No 8	G Basquet	33	1945–52

MOST POINTS IN TESTS

Pts	Player	Tests	Career
357	T Lacroix	38	1989–96
354	D Camberabero	36	1982–93
265	J-P Romeu	34	1972–77
233	S Blanco	93	1980–91
200	J-P Lescarboura	28	1982–90

MOST TRIES IN TESTS

Tries	Player	Tests	Career
38	S Blanco	93	1980–91
31	P Saint-André	64	1990–97
30	P Sella	111	1982–95
23	C Darrouy	40	1957–67
20	P Lagisquet	46	1983–91

MOST CONVERSIONS IN TESTS

Cons	Player	Tests	Career
48	D Camberabero	36	1982–93
45	M Vannier	43	1953–61
30	T Lacroix	38	1989–96
29	P Villepreux	34	1967–72
27	J-P Romeu	34	1972–77

MOST PENALTY GOALS IN TESTS

Pens	Player	Tests	Career
87	T Lacroix	38	1989–96
59	D Camberabero	36	1982–93
56	J-P Romeu	34	1972–77
33	P Villepreux	34	1967–72
33	P Bérot	19	1986–89

MOST DROPPED GOALS IN TESTS

Drops	Player	Tests	Career
15	J-P Lescarboura	28	1982–90
12	P Albaladejo	30	1954–64
11	G Camberabero	14	1961–68
11	D Camberabero	36	1982–93
9	J-P Romeu	34	1972–77

INTERNATIONAL CHAMPIONSHIP RECORDS

Record	Detail		Set
Most points in season	129	in four matches	1997
Most tries in season	14	in four matches	1997
Highest score	47	47–20 v Scotland	1997
Biggest win	35	45–10 v Ireland	1996
Highest score conceded	49	14–49 v Wales	1910
Biggest defeat	37	0–37 v England	1911
Most appearances	50	P Sella	1983–95
Most points in matches	113	D Camberabero	1983–93
Most points in season	54	J-P Lescarboura	1984
Most points in match	24	S Viars	v Ireland, 1992
	24	C Lamaison	v Scotalnd, 1997
Most tries in matches	14	S Blanco	1981–91
	14	P Sella	1983–95
Most tries in season	5	P Estève	1983
	5	E Bonneval	1987
Most tries in match	3	M Crauste	v England, 1962
	3	C Darrouy	v Ireland, 1963
	3	E Bonneval	v Scotland, 1987
	3	D Venditti	v Ireland, 1997
Most cons in matches	18	P Villepreux	1967–72
Most cons in season	7	P Villepreux	1972
Most cons in match	5	P Villepreux	v England, 1972
	5	S Viars	v Ireland, 1992
	5	T Castaignède	v Ireland, 1996
Most pens in matches	22	T Lacroix	1991–96
Most pens in season	10	J-P Lescarboura	1984
Most pens in match	6	C Lamaison	v Scotland, 1997
Most drops in matches	9	J-P Lescarboura	1982–88
Most drops in season	5	G Camberabero	1967
Most drops in match	3	P Albaladejo	v Ireland, 1960
	3	J-P Lescarboura	v England, 1985

MAJOR TOUR RECORDS

Record	Detail	Year	Place
Most individual points	112 by S Viars	1992	Argentina
Most points in match	28 by P Lagisquet	1988 v Paraguayan XV	Ascunción (Paraguay)
Most tries in match	7 by P Lagisquet	1988 v Paraguayan XV	Ascunción (Paraguay)

MISCELLANEOUS RECORDS

Record	Holder	Detail
Longest Test career	F Haget	14 seasons, 1974 to 1987
Youngest Test cap	C Dourthe	18 yrs 7 days in 1966
Oldest Test cap	A Roques	37 yrs 329 days in 1963

FRANCE INTERNATIONAL CAREER RECORDS (*up to 30 April 1997*)

Player	Debut	Caps since last season	Caps	T	C	PG	DG	Pts
J-L Sadourny	1991 v W	1996 *Arg* 1,2, *W, SA* 1,2, 1997 *I, W, E, S, It*	52	11	0	0	3	63
P Bernat-Salles	1992 v Arg		11	6	0	0	0	30
P Saint-André	1990 v R	1996 *Arg* 1,2, *W*, 1997 *It*	64	31	0	0	0	146
E Ntamack	1994 v W	1996 *Arg* 1,2, *W*, 1997 *I*	27	17	1	1	0	90
D Berty	1990 v NZ	1996 *W* (R), *SA* 1	6	0	0	0	0	0
D Venditti	1996 v R	1996 *SA* 1 (R), 2, 1997 *I, W, E, S*	7	4	0	0	0	20
S Ougier	1992 v R	1997 *It*	4	0	2	0	0	4
S Glas	1996 v S	1996 *Arg* 2 (R), *W, SA* 1,2, 1997 *I, W, E, S*	12	4	0	0	0	20
R Dourthe	1995 v R	1996 *Arg* 1,2, *W, SA* 1,2, 1997 *W*	12	2	15	14	0	82
T Castaignède	1995 v R	1996 *Arg* 1,2, 1997 *I*	11	4	17	10	2	90
O Campan	1993 v SA		6	1	0	0	0	5
Y Delaigue	1994 v S	1997 *It*	10	2	0	0	2	16
M Marfaing	1992 v R		2	0	0	0	0	0
G Bouic	1996 v SA	1996 *SA* 1	1	0	0	0	0	0
P Bondouy	1997 v S	1997 *S* (R), *It*	2	2	0	0	0	10
U Mola	1997 v S	1997 *S* (R)	1	0	0	0	0	0
L Leflamand	1996 v SA	1996 *SA* 2, 1997 *W, E, S*	4	4	0	0	0	20
T Lacroix	1989 v A		38	6	30	87	2	357
L Mazas	1992 v Arg	1996 *SA* 1	2	0	0	0	0	0
C Lamaison	1996 v SA	1996 *SA* 1 (R),2, 1997 *W, E, S*	5	1	5	8	1	42
A Penaud	1992 v W	1996 *Arg* 1,2, *W*, 1997 *I, E*	28	7	0	0	5	47
D Aucagne	1997 v W	1997 *W* (R), *S, It*	3	0	4	3	0	17
P Carbonneau	1995 v R	1996 *Arg* 2, *W, SA* 1, 1997 *I* (R), *W, E, S* (R)	14	2	0	0	0	10
G Accoceberry	1994 v NZ	1996 *Arg* 1, *W* (R), *SA* 2, 1997 *S, It*	19	2	0	0	0	10
F Galthié	1991 v R	1997 *I*	18	3	0	0	0	14
M Dal Maso	1988 v R	1996 *SA* 1 (R),2, 1997 *I, W, E, S, It*	9	0	0	0	0	0
R Ibanez	1996 v W	1997 *It* (R)	2	0	0	0	0	0
M de Rougemont	1995 v E	1996 *Arg* 1,2, *W, SA* 1, 1997 *E* (R), *S* (R), *It*	13	0	0	0	0	0
H Guiraud	1996 v R		1	0	0	0	0	0

F Tournaire	1995 v It	1996 *Arg* 1,2 (R), *W, SA* 1,2, 1997 *I, E, S, It*	13	1	0	0	0	5
D Casadei	1997 v S	1997 *S*	1	0	0	0	0	0
J-J Crenca	1996 v SA	1996 *SA* 2 (R)	1	0	0	0	0	0
J-L Jordana	1996 v R	1996 *Arg* 1 (t),2, *W*, 1997 *I* (t), *W, S* (R)	7	0	0	0	0	0
C Califano	1994 v NZ	1996 *Arg* 1,2, *SA* 1,2, 1997 *I, W, E*	28	3	0	0	0	15
C Soulette	None		0	0	0	0	0	0
O Roumat	1989 v NZ	1996 *Arg* 1,2	61	5	0	0	0	0
F Pelous	1995 v R	1996 *Arg* 1,2, *W, SA* 1,2, 1997 *I, W, E, S, It*	18	2	0	0	0	10
H Miorin	1996 v R	1996 *SA* 1, 1997 *I, W, E, S, It*	7	0	0	0	0	0
O Merle	1993 v SA	1996 *Arg* 1,2, *W, SA* 2, 1997 *I, W, E, S, It*	38	3	0	0	0	15
O Brouzet	1994 v S		12	0	0	0	0	0
C Moni	1996 v R		1	1	0	0	0	5
T Lievremont	1996 v W	1996 *W* (R)	1	0	0	0	0	0
S Betsen	1997 v It	1997 *It* (R)	1	0	0	0	0	0
A Costes	1994 v C	1997 *It*	4	1	0	0	0	5
R Castel	1996 v I	1996 *W, SA* 1 (R),2, 1997 *I* (R), *W, E*(R), *S* (R)	9	2	0	0	0	10
P Benetton	1989 v BL	1996 *Arg* 1,2, *W, SA* 1,2, 1997 *I, It*	44	7	0	0	0	34
O Magne	1997 v W	1997 *W* (R), *E, S*	3	1	0	0	0	5
M Lievremont	1995 v It	1996 *Arg* 1 (R), *SA* 2 (R)	7	1	0	0	0	5
T Labrousse	1996 v R	1996 *SA* 1	2	2	0	0	0	10
A Benazzi	1990 v A	1996 *Arg* 1,2, *W, SA* 1,2, 1997 *I, W, E, S*	53	5	0	0	0	25
S Dispagne	1996 v I		2	0	0	0	0	0

TIME FOR CHANGE

THE 1996-97 SEASON IN ITALY

There can no longer be any doubt about it. Italy must be given a target date by which they will be admitted to the Five Nations Championship. They have proven beyond all reasonable doubt, as our learned friends would say, that they merit a place. They have either beaten or performed creditably against all the other leading European nations over the past few seasons.

Of course the administrators were right to be cautious initially. If Italy had been a one-season or one-generation wonder then it would have harmed both their own rugby as well as the tournament itself to have admitted them unconditionally. But Italy have shown that their development programme is serious. What they need now is support and incentive.

The Five Nations committee were concerned also that Italy would not be able to fill their stadiums. There is a simple answer to that: if they become part of a recognised formal competitive structure then the stadiums will soon be full to capacity. Spectators, or the new fan, needs the lure of a league table, a genuine competition. Friendly matches do not fill stadiums in the British Isles or France either.

So the Five Nations must state quite categorically that, at the very latest, if Italy reproduce their form and results from now until the 1999 World Cup then they will be admitted to the championship in 2000. It would be no bad thing if it were to happen even sooner.

ITALIAN CLUB CHAMPIONSHIP FINAL
7 June, Stadio Bentegodi, Verona
Benetton Treviso 34 (1G 9PG) Milan 29 (2G 5PG)

Lance Sherrell – how South Africa could have done with him in their series with the Lions – was the man of the match in the final. The fly-half who toured New Zealand with the 1994 Springboks kicked ten goals and was the tactical controller who brought victory for Treviso. Milan were the fancied side going into the final. They had lost only once during the season and headed the round-robin part of the tournament.

In truth, the match was a disappointing affair for the neutrals among the 7,000 crowd. For the finalists' partisan supporters, however, there was plenty of nervous excitement in a tight match that boiled down to a duel between the championship's deadliest kickers.

At the end it was the left boot of the South African that carried the day. He landed five first-half penalties to keep Treviso in touch at 15-16 at the interval, the former Waikato captain Richard Turner having scored Milan's first try. Then Treviso went out to 31-19 before an exchange of penalties and a penalty try awarded to Milan completed the scoring.

Benetton Treviso: M Dotto; M Perziano, F Mazzariol, T Visentin, L Manteri; L Sherrell, I Francescato; G Grespan, A Moscardi, A Castellani, A Gritti, C Signori, A Sgorlon, J Gardner, L Bot *Replacements* P-F Donati for Manteri (46 mins); M Dal Sie for Grespan (48 mins); S Rigo for Bot (56 mins); D Scaglia for Gritti (68 mins); N De Meneghi for Castellani (temp)
Scorers *Try:* Manteri *Conversion:* Sherrell *Penalty Goals:* Sherrell (9)
Amatori Milan: F Williams; P Scanziani, A Stoica, M Tommasi, Marc Cuttitta; D Dominguez, F Gomez; Mass Cuttitta, A Marengoni, F Properzi Curti, G Croci, P-P Pedroni, D Beretta, R Turner, O Arancio *Replacements* T Cicciò for Beretta (41 mins); C Orlandi for Marengoni (41 mins)
Scorers *Tries:* Turner, pen try *Conversions:* Dominguez (2)
Penalty Goals: Dominguez (5)
Referee A Lombardi (Naples)

ITALY INTERNATIONAL CAREER RECORDS *(up to 30 April 1997)*

Player	Debut	Caps since last season	Caps	T	C	PG	DG	Pts
J A Pertile	1994 v R	1996 *W* (R), *A, E, S,* 1997 *I, F*	8	0	0	0	0	0
P Donati	None		0	0	0	0	0	0
C Pilat	None		0	0	0	0	0	0
S Babbo	1996 v Pt		1	2	0	0	0	10
L Manteri	1996 v W	1996 *W, A, E, S* (R)	4	0	0	0	0	0
F Mazzariol	1995 v F	1997 *F* (R)	6	1	0	0	0	5
N Mazzucato	1995 v SA	1996 *S,* 1997 *I* (R)	4	1	0	0	0	5
M Platania	1994 v F		4	2	0	0	0	10
M Ravazzolo	1993 v Cr	1996, *W, A*	19	3	0	0	0	15
F Roselli	1995 v F		3	1	0	0	0	5
P Vaccari	1991 v Nm	1996 *W, E, S,* 1997 *I, F*	41	15	0	0	0	72
Marc Cuttitta	1987 v Pt	1996 *S,* 1997 *I, F*	44	24	0	0	0	105
S Bordon	1990 v R	1996 *W, A, E,* 1997 *I, F*	29	1	0	0	0	5
G Filizzola	1993 v Pt		12	5	16	5	0	72
I Francescato	1990 v F	1996 *W, A, E, S,* 1997 *F*	34	13	0	0	0	62
M Piovene	1995 v NZ		1	0	0	0	0	0
T Visentin	1996 v W		1	0	0	0	0	0
A Stoica	1997 v I	1997 *I*	1	0	0	0	0	0
A Scanavacca	None		0	0	0	0	0	0
D Dominguez	1991 v F	1996 *W, A, E, S,* 1997 *I, F*	35	5	64	95	6	456
M Bonomi	1988 v F		34	6	5	13	5	93
G L Guidi	1996 v Pt	1996 *E* (t), 1997 *F* (t)	3	0	0	0	0	0

A Troncon	1994 v Sp	1996 *W, A, E, S*, 1997 *I, F*	26	5	0	0	0	25
G P De Carli	1996 v W		1	0	0	0	0	0
A Moscardi	1993 v Pt	1996 *S* (R)	3	1	0	0	0	5
C Orlandi	1992 v S	1996 *W, A, E, S*, 1997 *I, F*	33	4	0	0	0	20
A Castellani	1994 v Cz	1996 *W* (R), *S*	5	1	0	0	0	5
Mass Cuttitta	1990 v Po	1996 *W, E, S*, 1997 *I, F*	53	6	0	0	0	29
M Dal Sie	1993 v Pt	1996 *A*	7	0	0	0	0	0
F Properzi-Curti	1990 v Po	1996 *W, A, E*, 1997 *I, F*	38	3	0	0	0	15
P-P Pedroni	1989 v Z	1996 *W*	25	2	0	0	0	10
A Giacon	None		0	0	0	0	0	0
D Scaglia	1994 v R	1996 *W, A*	5	0	0	0	0	0
W Cristofoletto	1992 v R	1996, *A, E, S*, 1997 *I, F*	10	0	0	0	0	0
A Barattin	1996 v A	1996 *A* (R), *E* (R)	2	0	0	0	0	0
G Croci	1990 v Sp	1996 *S*, 1997 *I, F*	17	3	0	0	0	13
M David	None		0	0	0	0	0	0
J M Gardner	1992 v R	1997 *I, F*	16	3	0	0	0	15
R Piovan	1996 v Pt		1	0	0	0	0	0
R Rampazzo	1996 v W	1996 *W* (R)	1	0	0	0	0	0
A Sgorlon	1993 v Pt	1996 *W, A, E* (R), *S*, 1997 *I, F*	26	0	0	0	0	0
M Giovanelli	1989 v Z	1996 *A, E, S*, 1997 *F*	37	3	0	0	0	14
O Arancio	1993 v Ru	1996 *W, A, E, S*, 1997 *I*	24	2	0	0	0	10
C Checchinato	1990 v Sp	1996 *W, E*, 1997 *I* (R)	33	8	0	0	0	40
F Spazzolini	None		0	0	0	0	0	0
C Covi	1988 v F	1996 *E*	19	1	0	0	0	4

The Italy team against England at Twickenham. L-R, back row: A Barattin (replacement), A Castellani (replacement), G-L Guidi (replacement), M Cuttitta, F Properzi Curti, C Orlandi, C Checchinato, W Cristofoletto, O Arancio, C Covi, A Scanavacca (replacement), N Mazzucato (replacement), A Sgorlon (replacement); front row: J A Pertile, S Bordon, A Troncon, I Francescato, M Giovanelli (capt), D Dominguez, P Vaccari, L Manteri.

AN EVENTFUL YEAR

THE 1996 SEASON IN SOUTH AFRICA
Dan Retief

With 13 internationals crammed into the last six months of the year, on top of the inaugural Super-12 and a double round of the Currie Cup, there was never any doubt South Africa's season was going to be an eventful one. But not even a best-selling writer of fiction could have come up with a plot as packed full of incident as the year which eventually unfolded.

It was the start of a great new southern hemisphere rivalry as leading provinces did battle in the Super 12, while the Springboks, the Wallabies and the All Blacks matched wits and brawn in the first of what is to be an annual home-and-away Tri-Nations series.

The revised laws were enthusiastically embraced in a celebration of running rugby and spectacular tries but, not surprisingly, the first tremors of controversy were provided by SARFU's despotic ruler Louis Luyt.

After what had appeared to be promising start he summarily dismissed his English-born and personally appointed chief executive Edward Griffiths. Griffiths was generally credited with having transformed South Africa's dubious reputation, but Luyt saw fit to simply fire off a fax from his office at Ellis Park to Griffiths at Newlands informing him that his services were no longer required.

No explanation was provided – before, at the time, or since – and in due course Luyt's son-in-law and the man who had been SARFU's chief organiser of the World Cup, Rian Oberholzer, was recalled from his posting as chief executive of SANZAR's Sydney office and installed in the SARFU's top non-elected job.

But if Griffiths' dismissal caused a stir, worse was to follow – the axeing of Francois Pienaar, the captain who had held up the World Cup and was the handsome embodiment of the new image of South African rugby.

Pienaar's dismissal came after a traumatic few months in which victorious World Cup coach Kitch Christie became ill and was forced to relinquish his position to his appointed understudy, Andre Markgraaff, while the Springboks and their fans began to experience the misery of defeat after an unprecedented run of 15 straight Test victories.

Over a succession of trying Saturdays an outstanding All Black team, one which will one day be ranked as one of the best of all time, righted a historical wrong by becoming the first New Zealand team to win a series in South Africa; thus avenging the 4-0 drubbing of 1949 and in the process registering an unheard of four successive victories over the men in green and gold.

Captained by Sean Fitzpatrick and coached by John Hart, the All Blacks set a precedent for modern touring by arriving with a party of 36 players to ensure the fitness and vitality of their Test team.

Against this the Springboks suffered a savage run of injuries – among them Pienaar – and bumbled through more controversy. First James Small was banned for having slipped out of the team's hotel to spend a late night in a nightclub and then Os du Randt was reinstated after apparently having been concussed.

The upshot was that in his first eight Tests Markgraaff was forced to use 30 players and on no occasion was he able to field an unchanged team.

A face-saving 32-22 victory in the final Test at Ellis Park meant the historic record between the Springboks and the All Blacks had been squared up at 22 victories apiece with three matches drawn, thus setting the scene for ever more intense and passionate chapters in the chronicles of these two great rivals.

But while the All Blacks basked in the glory of their tickertape Auckland welcome, South Africa's tired players charged straight into the climax of the Currie Cup competition.

Super-12 finalists Natal were clearly the team of the year but their march to their fourth final in the 1980's was overshadowed when, shortly after Natal had seen off Griquas in the quarter-finals, Andre Markgraaff announced a team to tour Argentina, France and Wales which did not include Francois Pienaar. Such was the public outrage that in the ensuing week Markgraaff would receive death threats, and newspaper and radio polls showed overwhelming support for the deposed captain.

Pienaar was galvanised to lead heroically from the front as his Transvaal team upset Northern Transvaal at home in one semi-final, but the following week he failed to re-kindle the inspiration as Natal, thanks to two masterful tries from Andre Joubert, retained the golden trophy to provide sweet revenge for their popular coach Ian McIntosh; himself a victim of Luyt's predilection for wilful dismissals.

Gary Teichmann picked up the reins of what might have been a disillusioned and fatigued touring team and returned home with a 100% Test record as well as the achievement of having become the first touring side to win a series in France during the 1990's.

Defeat might have provoked a clamour for Pienaar's reinstatement but the former captain had already made up his mind. While the Boks were preparing for their date with France at the Parc des Princes, Pienaar, soon to be followed by the World Cup dropped goal hero Joel Stransky, announced that a good offer (coupled to a favourable exchange rate of nearly £8 to the Rand) had persuaded him to throw in his lot with Saracens.

And so ended South African rugby's first professional year. Passionate, intense, exciting and controversial.

CURRIE CUP

Section A	P	W	D	L	F	A	Pts
Natal	12	12	0	0	673	212	24
Transvaal	12	9	1	2	458	252	19
South-Eastern Transvaal	12	6	2	4	292	363	14
Boland	12	6	0	6	250	308	12
Eastern Province	12	3	1	8	245	341	7
Border	12	2	2	8	244	422	6
Western Transvaal	12	1	0	11	268	530	2

Section B	P	W	D	L	F	A	Pts
Northern Transvaal	12	11	0	1	707	207	22
Free State	12	9	1	2	558	280	19
Western Province	12	8	0	4	537	249	16
Griquas	12	7	1	4	437	322	15
Eastern Transvaal	12	3	0	9	281	552	6
Northern Free State	12	3	0	9	243	529	6
South-Western Districts	12	0	0	12	216	840	0

Quarter-finals
Northern Transvaal 55, Boland 23; Free State 21, South Eastern Transvaal 3; Transvaal 56, Western Province 22; Natal 51, Griqualand West 3

Semi-finals
Natal 35, Free State 20; Northern Transvaal 21, Transvaal 31

Final
Played at Ellis Park
Natal 33 (3G 4PG)   **Transvaal 15** (5PG)
Natal *Tries:* J Thomson, A Joubert (2)   *Conversions:* H Honiball (3)
Penalty Goals: H Honiball (4)
Transvaal *Penalty Goals:* G Lawless (5)

BANKFIN NITE SERIES FINAL: Free State 46, Border 34
SUPER 12 SERIES FINAL: Auckland 45, Natal 21

SOUTH AFRICA TO ARGENTINA, FRANCE AND WALES 1996

THE TOURING PARTY
Manager/Coach A T Markgraaf   **Assistant Manager** J J de Beer
Assistant Coaches N V H Mallett H M Reece-Edwards   **Captain** G Teichmann

FULL-BACKS
R G Bennett (Border)
A J Joubert (Natal)
B J Paulse (Western Province)

THREEQUARTERS
J Olivier (Northern Transvaal)
H P le Roux (Transvaal)
J T Small (Natal)
J Swart (Western Province)
J W Gillingham (Transvaal)
J C Mulder (Transvaal)
A H Snyman (Northern Transvaal)
J Thomson (Natal)
D van Schalkwyk (Northern Transvaal)
D J Muir (Natal)

HALF-BACKS
H W Honiball (Natal)
P F Smith (Griqualand West)
K B Putt (Natal)
J H van der Westhuizen (Northern Transvaal)
J Viljoen (Western Province)

FORWARDS
A C Garvey (Natal)
M H Hurter (Northern Transvaal)
G L Pagel (Western Province)
D Theron (Griqualand West)
A van der Linde (Western Province)
J Dalton (Transvaal)
C le C Rossouw (Transvaal)
H Tromp (Northern Transvaal)
M G Andrews (Natal)
K Otto (Northern Transvaal)
J J Strydom (Transvaal)
J J Wiese (Transvaal)
W Fyvie (Natal)
R J Kruger (Northern Transvaal)
L T Oosthuysen (Griqualand West)
F J van Heerden (Western Province)
A G Venter (Orange Free State)
S Bekker (Northern Transvaal)
G Teichmann (Natal)
***J Erasmus** (Free State)
***A E Drotské** (Free State)

Replacements during tour

TOUR RECORD
All matches   Played 10   Won 8   Lost 2   Points for 367   Against 205
International matches   Played 5   Won 5   Points for 162   Against 80

SCORING DETAILS

All matches					International matches				
For:	53T	30C	14PG	367 Pts	For:	21T	12C	11PG	162 Pts
Against:	19T	13C	28PG	205 Pts	Against:	5T	2C	17PG	80 Pts

MATCH DETAILS

1996	OPPONENTS	VENUE	RESULT
5 Nov	Rosario	Rosario	W 45-36
9 Nov	ARGENTINA	Buenos Aires	W 46-15
12 Nov	Mendoza	Mendoza	W 89-19
16 Nov	ARGENTINA	Buenos Aires	W 44-21
23 Nov	French Barbarians	Brive	L 22-30
26 Nov	South East Selection	Lyon	W 36-20
30 Nov	FRANCE	Bordeaux	W 22-12
3 Dec	French Universities	Lille	L 13-20
7 Dec	FRANCE	Paris	W 13-12
15 Dec	WALES	Cardiff	W 37-20

MATCH 1 5 November, Rosario

Rosario 36 (4G 1PG 1T)   **South Africa XV 45** (5G 2T)
Rosario: E Jurado; L Dippe, D Flook, M Molina, G Acuna; L Bouza, R Crexell;
C Promanzio, D Silvetti, H Cespedes; N Bossicovich, R Perez; G Garcia, P Bouza,
J Oviedo
Scorers *Tries:* Perez, Crexell, Acuna, Flook, Promanzio   *Conversions:* Crexell (4)
Penalty Goal: Crexell
South Africa XV: Bennett; Snyman, Muir, Gillingham, Swart; Smith, Putt; van
der Linde, Tromp, Hurter; Otto, Strydom; van Heerden, Bekker, Fyvie (*capt*)
Replacement Viljoen for Putt (40 mins)
Scorers *Tries:* van der Linde, Muir (2), Bekker, Snyman, Fyvie, Swart
Conversions: Smith (5)
Referee G Morandin (Italy)

**MATCH 2   9 November, Ferro Carril Oeste Stadium,
Buenos Aires**   **1st Test**

ARGENTINA 15 (1G 1PG 1T)   **SOUTH AFRICA 46** (4G 1PG 3T)

ARGENTINA: F Soler (Tala RC); O Bartolucci (Rosario Alteico), G Camardon
(Alumni), L Arbizu (Belgrono AC) (*capt*), T Solari (Hindu); J L Cilley (San Isidro
Club), N Fernandez-Miranda (Hindu); R D Grau (Liceo), F Mendez (Mendoza
RC), O Hasan Jalil (Natacion y Gimnasia); P Sporleder (Curupayti), G Llanes (La
Plata RC); R Martin (San Isidro Club), P J Camerlinckx (Regatas Bella Vista),
R Perez (Duendes RC) *Replacement* C Barrea (Cordoba Athletic) for
Fernandez-Miranda (temp 4-8 mins), E Simone (Liceo Naval) for Camardon (45
mins)
Scorers *Tries:* Camardon, Martin   *Conversion:* Cilley   *Penalty Goal:* Cilley
SOUTH AFRICA: Joubert; Small, Mulder, le Roux, Olivier; Honiball, van der
Westhuizen; Theron, Dalton, Garvey; Wiese, Andrews; Kruger, Teichmann (*capt*),
Venter *Replacements* van der Linde for Theron (65 mins), van Heerden for Wiese
(75 mins)
Scorers *Tries:* Venter, Andrews, le Roux, pen try, Joubert, Small, van der
Westhuizen   *Conversions:* Honiball (3), Joubert   *Penalty Goal:* Honiball
Referee J M Fleming (Scotland)

MATCH 3   12 November, Independiente Rivadavia Stadium, Mendoza

Mendoza 19 (2G 1T)   **South Africa XV 89** (7G 8T)
Mendoza: A Castro; C Villaneuva, F Serpa, C Filizola, G Diaz; L Speroni,
M Diaz; R Grau, F Bertolini, F Mendez; P Lambert, M Ruiz; G Nasazzi,
J Chiapetta, G C Llano *Replacement* C Bertona for Mendez (60 mins)
Scorers *Tries:* G Diaz (2), Caernoud   *Conversions:* Speroni (2)
South Africa XV: Bennett; Snyman, Thomson, Muir, Paulse; Smith, Putt; Pagel,
Rossouw, Hurter; van Heerden, Otto; Oosthuysen, Bekker, Fyvie *Replacements*
Tromp for Rossouw (16 mins), Viljoen for Putt (60 mins), Strydom for Otto (62
mins), van der Linde for Bekker (66 mins), Gillingham for Muir (75 mins), Muir
for Oosthuysen (77 mins)
Scorers *Tries:* Putt (2), Paulse (4), Tromp, Smith, Oosthuysen, Bekker (2),
Bennett (2), Thomson, Snyman   *Conversions:* Smith (7)
Referee J Dumé (France)

MATCH 4   16 November, Ferro Carril Oeste Stadium, Buenos Aires
ARGENTINA 21 (1G 3PG 1T)   SOUTH AFRICA 44 (4G 2PG 2T)

ARGENTINA: E Jurado (Jockey Club, Rosario); D L Albanese (San Isidro Club), E Simone (Liceo Naval), L Arbizu (Belgrano) (*capt*), F Soler (Tala RC); J L Cilley (San Isidro Club), N Fernandez-Miranda (Hindu); R D Grau (Liceo), F Mendez (Mendoza RC), O Hasan Jalil (Natacion y Gimnasia); P Sporleder (Curupayti), G Llanes (La Plata RC); R Martin (San Isidro Club), P J Camerlinckx (Regatas Bella Vista), R Perez (Duendes) *Replacements* G Quesada (Hindu) for Cilley (50 mins), M Scelzo (Banco Hipotecano) for Hasan Jalil (72 mins), C Viel (Newman) for Sporleder (75 mins)
Scorers *Tries:* Martin, Fernandez-Miranda   *Conversion:* Cilley
Penalty Goals: Cilley (2), Quesada
SOUTH AFRICA: Joubert; Small, Mulder, le Roux, Olivier; Honiball, van der Westhuizen; Theron, Dalton, Garvey; Wiese, Andrews; Kruger, Teichmann (*capt*), Venter *Replacements* Snyman for Small (57 mins), Tromp for Dalton (70 mins), van der Linde for Theron (70 mins), van Heerden for Andrews (74 mins), Fyvie for Teichmann (75 mins)
Scorers *Tries:* Mulder, Kruger (2), Venter, Olivier, le Roux
Conversions: Honiball (3), Joubert   *Penalty Goals:* Honiball (2)
Referee E Murray (Scotland)

MATCH 5   23 November, Municipal Stadium, Brive

French Barbarians 30 (3G 3PG)   **South Africa XV 22** (1G 3T)
French Barbarians: S Viars (Brive); F Corrihons (Grenoble), P Sella (Saracens), G Bouic (Agen), D Venditti (Brive); L Mazas (Biarritz), F Galthie (Colomiers); P Triep-Capdeville (Pau), M Dal Maso (Agen), M Reggiardo (Castres); G Ross (Brive), M Cecillon (Bourgoin); M Lievremont (Perpignan) (*capt*), T Labrousse (Brive), J Kronfeld (Otago) *Replacements* M Marfaing (Toulouse) for Corrihons (29 mins), D Arrieta (Grenoble) for Venditti (60 mins), J-M Gonzalez (Bayonne) for Dal Maso (60 mins), M James (Perpignan) for Ross (69 mins), R Crespy (Brive) for Reggiardo (72 mins), G Kacala (Brive) for Cecillon (73 mins)
Scorers *Tries:* Dal Maso, Venditti, Mazas   *Conversions:* Viars (3)
Penalty Goals: Viars (3)
South Africa XV: Bennett; Snyman, Thomson, Muir, Gillingham; Smith, Putt; Pagel, Tromp, Hurter; Strydom, van Heerden; Fyvie (*capt*), Erasmus, Oosthuysen *Replacements* van der Linde for Pagel (58 mins), Dalton for Strydom (60 mins), Otto for Strydom (62 mins)
Scorers *Tries:* Oosthuysen (2), Fyvie, Bennett   *Conversion:* Smith
Referee P Thomas (Provence)

MATCH 6   26 November, Stade Gerland, Lyon

South East Selection 20 (2G 2PG)   **South Africa XV 36** (4G 1PG 1T)
South East Selection: N Nadau (Montferrand); L Leflamand (Bourgoin), C Lamaison (Brive), E Artiguste (Castres), C Dominici (Toulon); B Bellot (Perpignan), A Hueber (Toulon) (*capt*); L Toussaint (Castres), F Grange (Bourgoin), R Crespy (Brive); G Orsoni (Grenoble), J Daude (Bourgoin); O Magne (Dax), P Raschi (Bourgoin), A Chazalet (Bourgoin) *Replacements* F Landreau (Grenoble) for Grange (40 mins), C Moni (Toulon) for Magne (57 mins), C Soulette (Beziers) for Toussaint (59 mins), P Bondouy (Narbonne) for Nadau (65 mins)

Scorers *Tries:* Leflamand, Artiguste   *Conversions:* Bellot (2)
Penalty Goals: Bellot (2)
South Africa XV: Swart; Gillingham, Thomson, Muir, Paulse; Smith, Putt; van
der Linde, Tromp, Hurter; Strydom, Otto; Fyvie (*capt*), Erasmus, Oosthuysen
Replacement Snyman for Paulse (75 mins)
Scorers *Tries:* Hurter, Strydom, Swart, Otto, Paulse   *Conversions:* Smith (4)
Penalty Goal: Smith
Referee C Giacomel (Italy)

MATCH 7   30 November, Parc Lescure, Bordeaux   1st Test
FRANCE 12 (4PG)   SOUTH AFRICA 22 (4PG 2T)

FRANCE: J-L Sadourny (Colomiers); R Dourthe (Dax), S Glas (Bourgoin),
G Bouic (Agen), D Berty (Toulouse); L Mazas (Biarritz), P Carbonneau (Brive);
C Califano (Toulouse), M de Rougemont (Toulon), F Tournaire (Narbonne);
H Miorin (Toulouse), F Pelous (Dax); A Benazzi (Agen) (*capt*), T Labrousse
(Brive), P Benetton (Agen) *Replacements* D Venditti (Brive) for Berty (48 mins),
R Castel (Beziers) for Labrousse (58 mins), C Lamaison (Brive) for Bouic (70
mins), M Dal Maso (Agen) for de Rougemont (72 mins)
Scorer *Penalty Goals:* Dourthe (4)
SOUTH AFRICA: Joubert; Small, Mulder, le Roux, Olivier; Honiball, van der
Westhuizen; Theron, Dalton, Garvey; Wiese, Andrews; Kruger, Teichmann (*capt*),
Venter *Replacement* van der Linde for Theron (70 mins), Tromp for Dalton (77
mins)
Scorers *Tries:* Small, Joubert   *Penalty Goals:* Honiball (4)
Referee B W Stirling (Ireland)

MATCH 8   3 December, Stade du Nord, Lille

French Universities 20 (5PG 1T)   **South Africa XV 13** (1G 2PG)
French Universities: N Brusque (Pau); F Tauzin (Begles-Bordeaux),
F Ribeyrolles (Montferrand), L Lafforgue (Begles-Bordeaux), J-M Souvergie
(Pau); D Aucagne (Pau), G Sudre (Agen); O Azam (Montferrand), R Ibanez
(Dax) (*capt*), O Sourgens (Begles-Bordeaux); T Cleda (Pau), C Gaston (Castres);
S Betsen (Biarritz), C Dongieu (Bayonne), A Costes (Montferrand)
Replacements W Rebeyrotte (Dax) for Azam (53 mins), Y Lemeur
(Begles-Bordeaux) for Gaston (64 mins)
Scorers *Try:* Souvergie   *Penalty Goals:* Aucagne (5)
South Africa XV: Bennett; Paulse, Thomson, Muir, Swart; Smith, Viljoen; Pagel,
Drotske, Hurter; van Heerden, Otto; Fyvie (*capt*), Erasmus, Oosthuysen
Replacements Putt for Viljoen (40 mins), Gillingham for Paulse (49 mins), van der
Linde for Pagel (64 mins)
Scorers *Try:* Gillingham   *Conversion:* Smith   *Penalty Goals:* Smith (2)
Referee P de Luca (Argentina)

MATCH 9   7 December, Parc des Princes, Paris   2nd Test
FRANCE 12 (4PG)   SOUTH AFRICA 13 (1G 2PG)

FRANCE: J-L Sadourny (Colomiers); L Leflamand (Bourgoin), R Dourthe
(Dax), S Glas (Bourgoin), D Venditti (Brive); C Lamaison (Brive), G Accoceberry
(Begles-Bordeaux); C Califano (Toulouse), M Dal Maso (Agen), F Tournaire
(Narbonne); O Merle (Montferrand), F Pelous (Dax); P Benetton (Agen),
A Benazzi (Agen) (*capt*), R Castel (Beziers) *Replacements* M Lievremont
(Perpignan) for Benetton (68 mins), J-J Crenca (Agen) for Tournaire (73 mins)

Scorer *Penalty Goals:* Dourthe (4)
SOUTH AFRICA: Joubert; Small, Mulder, le Roux, Olivier; Honiball, van der Westhuizen; Theron, Dalton, Garvey; Wiese, Andrews; Kruger, Teichmann *(capt)*, Venter
Scorers *Try:* Dalton *Conversion:* Honiball *Penalty Goals:* Honiball (2)
Referee W D Bevan (Wales)

MATCH 10 15 December, Cardiff Arms Park, Cardiff
Test Match

WALES 20 (5PG 1T) SOUTH AFRICA 37 (3G 2PG 2T)

WALES: N R Jenkins (Pontypridd); I C Evans (Llanelli), I S Gibbs (Swansea), A G Bateman (Richmond), D R James (Bridgend); A C Thomas (Swansea), R Howley (Cardiff); C D Loader (Swansea), J M Humphreys (Cardiff) *(capt)*, D Young (Cardiff); G O Llewellyn (Harlequins), M Rowley (Pontypridd); D L M McIntosh (Pontypridd), S M Williams (Neath), C L Charvis (Swansea)
Replacement N Thomas (Bath) for McIntosh (68 mins)
Scorers *Try:* A C Thomas *Penalty Goals:* Jenkins (5)
SOUTH AFRICA: Joubert; Small, Mulder, le Roux, Olivier; Honiball, van der Westhuizen; Theron, Dalton, Garvey; Wiese, Andrews; Kruger, Teichmann *(capt)*, Venter *Replacements* van der Linde for Theron (23 mins), Strydom for Andrews (42 mins), Snyman for Olivier (75 mins)
Scorers *Tries:* van der Westhuizen (3), Joubert, Olivier *Conversions:* Honiball (2), Joubert *Penalty Goals:* Honiball (2)
Referee S J D Lander (England)

SOUTH AFRICAN INTERNATIONAL PLAYERS
(up to 30 April 1997)

Ackermann, D S P (WP) 1955 *BI* 2,3,4, 1956 *A* 1,2, *NZ* 1,3, 1958 *F* 2

Ackermann, J N (NT) 1996 *Fj, A* 1, *NZ* 1, *A* 2

Albertyn, P K (SWD) 1924 *BI* 1,2,3,4

Alexander, F A (GW) 1891 *BI* 1,2

Allan, J (N) 1993 *A* 1 (R), *Arg* 1,2 (R), 1994 *E* 1,2, *NZ* 1,2,3, 1996 *Fj, A* 1, *NZ* 1, *A* 2, *NZ* 2

Allen, P B (EP) 1960 *S*

Allport, P H (WP) 1910 *BI* 2,3

Anderson, J W (WP) 1903 *BI* 3

Anderson, J H (WP) 1896 *BI* 1,3,4

Andrew, J B (Tvl) 1896 *BI* 2

Andrews, K S (WP) 1992 *E*, 1993 *F* 1,2, *A* 1 (R), 2,3, *Arg* 1 (R), 2, 1994 *NZ* 3

Andrews, M G (N) 1994 *E* 2, *NZ* 1,2,3, *Arg* 1,2, *S, W,* 1995 *WS,* [*A, WS, F, NZ*], *W, It, E,* 1996 *Fj, A* 1, *NZ* 1, *A* 2, *NZ* 2,3,4,5, *Arg* 1,2, *F* 1, 2, *W*

Antelme, M J G (Tvl) 1960 *NZ* 1,2,3,4, 1961 *F*

Apsey, J T (WP) 1933 *A* 4,5, 1938 *BI* 2

Ashley, S (WP) 1903 *BI* 2

Aston, F T D (Tvl) 1896 *BI* 1,2,3,4

Atherton, S (N) 1993 *Arg* 1,2, 1994 *E* 1,2, *NZ* 1,2,3, 1996 *NZ* 2

Aucamp, J (WT) 1924 *BI* 1,2

Baard, A P (WP) 1960 *I*

Babrow, L (WP) 1937 *A* 1,2, *NZ* 1,2,3

Badenhorst, C (OFS) 1994 *Arg* 2, 1995 *WS* (R)

Barnard, A S (EP) 1984 *S Am* 1,2, 1986 *Cv* 1,2

Barnard, J H (Tvl) 1965 *S, A* 1,2, *NZ* 3,4

Barnard, R W (Tvl) 1970 *NZ* 2 (R)

Barnard, W H M (NT) 1949 *NZ* 4, 1951 *W*

Barry, J (WP) 1903 *BI* 1,2,3

Bartmann, W J (Tvl, N) 1986 *Cv* 1,2,3,4, 1992 *NZ, A, F,* 1,2

Bastard, W E (N) 1937 *A* 1, *NZ* 1,2,3, 1938 *BI* 1,3

Bates, J A (WT) 1969 *E*, 1970 *NZ* 1,2, 1972 *E*

Bayvel, P C R (Tvl) 1974 *BI* 2,4, *F* 1,2, 1975 *F* 1,2, 1976 *NZ* 1,2,3,4

Beck, J J (WP) 1981 *NZ* 2 (R), 3 (R), *US*

Bedford, T P (N) 1963 *A* 1,2,3,4, 1964 *W, F,* 1965 *I, A* 1,2, 1968 *BI* 1,2,3,4, *F* 1,2, 1969 *A* 1,2,3,4, *S, E,* 1970 *I, W,* 1971 *F* 1,2

Bekker, H J (WP) 1981 *NZ* 1,3

Bekker, H P J (NT) 1952 *E, F,* 1953 *A* 1,2,3,4, 1955 *BI* 2,3,4, 1956 *A* 1,2, *NZ* 1,2,3,4

Bekker, M J (NT) 1960 *S*

Bekker, R P (NT) 1953 *A* 3,4

Bergh, W F (SWD) 1931 *W, I,* 1932 *E, S,* 1933 *A* 1,2,3,4,5, 1937 *A* 1,2, *NZ* 1,2,3, 1938 *BI* 1,2,3

Bestbier, A (OFS) 1974 *F* 2 (R)

Bester, J J N (WP) 1924 *BI* 2,4

Bester, J L A (WP) 1938 *BI* 2,3

Beswick, A M (Bor) 1896 *BI* 2,3,4

Bezuidenhoudt, C E (NT) 1962 *BI* 2,3,4

Bezuidenhoudt, N S E (NT) 1972 *E*, 1974 *BI* 2,3,4, *F* 1,2, 1975 *F* 1,2, 1977 *Wld*

Bierman, J N (Tvl) 1931 *I*

Bisset, W M (WP) 1891 *BI* 1,3

Blair, R (WP) 1977 *Wld*

Bosch, G R (Tvl) 1974 *BI* 2, *F* 1,2, 1975 *F* 1,2, 1976 *NZ* 1,2,3,4

Bosman, N J S (Tvl) 1924 *BI* 2,3,4

Botha, D S (NT) 1981 *NZ* 1

Botha, H E (NT) 1980 *S Am* 1,2, *BI* 1,2,3,4, *S Am* 3,4, *F,* 1981 *I* 1,2, *NZ* 1,2,3, *US,* 1982 *S Am* 1,2, 1986 *Cv* 1,2,3,4, 1989 *Wld* 1,2, 1992 *NZ, A, F* 1,2, *E*

Botha, J A (Tvl) 1903 *BI* 3

Botha, J P F (NT) 1962 *BI* 2,3,4

Botha, P H (Tvl) 1965 *A* 1,2

Boyes, H C (GW) 1891 *BI* 1,2

Brand, G H (WP) 1928 *NZ* 2,3, 1931 *W, I,* 1932 *E, S,* 1933 *A* 1,2,3,4,5, 1937 *A* 1,2, *NZ* 2,3, 1938 *BI* 1

Bredenkamp, M J (GW) 1896 *BI* 1,3

Breedt, J C (Tvl) 1986 *Cv* 1,2,3,4, 1989 *Wld* 1,2, 1992 *NZ, A*

Brewis, J D (NT) 1949 *NZ* 1,2,3,4, 1951 *S, I, W,* 1952 *E, F,* 1953 *A* 1

Briers, T P D (WP) 1955 *BI* 1,2,3,4, 1956 *NZ* 2,3,4

Brink D J (WP) 1906 *S, W, E*

Brink, R (WP) 1995 [*R, C*]

Brooks, D (Bor) 1906 *S*

Brown, C B (WP) 1903 *BI* 1,2,3

Brynard, G S (WP) 1965 *A* 1, *NZ* 1,2,3,4, 1968 *BI* 3,4

Buchler, J U (Tvl) 1951 *S, I, W,* 1952 *E, F,* 1953 *A* 1,2,3,4, 1956 *A* 2

Burdett, A F (WP) 1906 *S, I*

Burger, J M (WP) 1989 *Wld* 1,2

Burger, M B (NT) 1980 *BI* 2 (R), *S Am* 2, 1981 *US* (R)

Burger, S W P (WP) 1984 *E* 1,2, 1986 *Cv* 1,2,3,4

Burger, W A G (Bor) 1906 *S, I, W,* 1910 *BI* 2

Carelse, G (EP) 1964 *W, F,* 1965 *I, S,* 1967 *F* 1,2,3, 1968 *F* 1,2, 1969 *A* 1,2,3,4, *S*

Carlson, R A (WP) 1972 *E*

Carolin, H W (WP) 1903 *BI* 3, 1906 *S, I*

Castens, H H (WP) 1891 *BI* 3

Chignell, T W (WP) 1891 *BI* 3

Cilliers, G D (OFS) 1963 *A* 1,3,4

Cilliers, N V (WP) 1996 *NZ* 3 (t)

Claassen, J T (WT) 1955 *BI* 1,2,3,4, 1956 *A* 1,2, *NZ* 1,2,3,4, 1958 *F* 1,2, 1960 *S, NZ* 1,2,3, *W, I,* 1961 *E, S, F, I, A* 1,2, 1962 *BI* 1,2,3,4

Claassen, W (N) 1981 *I* 1,2, *NZ* 2,3, *US,* 1982 *S Am* 1,2

Clark, W H G (Tvl) 1933 *A* 3

Clarkson, W A (N) 1921 *NZ* 1,2, 1924 *BI* 1

Cloete, H A (WP) 1896 *BI* 4

Cockrell, C H (WP) 1969 *S,* 1970 *I, W*

Cockrell, R J (WP) 1974 *F* 1,2, 1975 *F* 1,2, 1976 *NZ* 1,2, 1977 *Wld,* 1981 *NZ* 1,2 (R), 3, *US*

Coetzee, J H H (WP) 1974 *BI* 1, 1975 *F* 2 (R), 1976 *NZ* 1,2,3,4

Cope, D K (Tvl) 1896 *BI* 2

Cotty, W (GW) 1896 *BI* 3

Crampton, G (GW) 1903 *BI* 2

Craven, D H (WP) 1931 *W, I,* 1932 *S,* 1933 *A* 1,2,3,4,5, 1937 *A* 1,2, *NZ* 1,2,3, 1938 *BI* 1,2,3,

Cronje, P A (Tvl) 1971 *F* 1,2, *A* 1,2,3, 1974 *BI* 3,4

Crosby, J H (Tvl) 1896 *BI* 2

Crosby, N J (Tvl) 1910 *BI* 1,3

Currie, C (GW) 1903 *BI* 2

D'Alton, G (WP) 1933 *A* 1

Dalton, J (Tvl) 1994 *Arg* 1 (R), 1995 [*A, C*], *W, It, E,* 1996 *NZ* 4 (R), 5, *Arg* 1,2, *F* 1,2, *W*

Daneel, G M (WP) 1928 *NZ* 1,2,3,4, 1931 *W, I,* 1932 *E, S*

Daneel, H J (WP) 1906 *S, I, W, E*

Davison, P M (EP) 1910 *BI* 1

De Bruyn, J (OFS) 1974 *BI* 3

De Jongh, H P K (WP) 1928 *NZ* 3

De Klerk, I J (Tvl) 1969 *E,* 1970 *I, W*

De Klerk, K B H (Tvl) 1974 *BI* 1,2,3 (R), 1975 *F* 1,2, 1976 *NZ* 2 (R), 3,4, 1980 *S Am* 1,2, *BI* 2, 1981 *I* 1,2

De Kock, A N (GW) 1891 *BI* 2

De Kock, J S (WP) 1921 *NZ* 3, 1924 *BI* 3

Delport, W H (EP) 1951 *S, I, W,* 1952 *E, F,* 1953 *A* 1,2,3,4

De Melker, S C (GW) 1903 *BI* 2, 1906 *E*

Devenish, C E (GW) 1896 *BI* 2

Devenish, G St L (Tvl) 1896 *BI* 2

Devenish, M J (Tvl) 1891 *BI* 1

De Villiers, D I (Tvl) 1910 *BI* 1,2,3

De Villiers, D J (WP, Bol) 1962 *BI* 2,3, 1965 *I, NZ* 1,3,4, 1967 *F* 1,2,3,4, 1968 *BI* 1,2,3,4, *F* 1,2, 1969 *A* 1,4, *E,* 1970 *I, W, NZ* 1,2,3,4

De Villiers, H A (WP) 1906 *S, W, E*

De Villiers, H O (WP) 1967 *F* 1,2,3,4, 1968 *F* 1,2, 1969 *A* 1,2,3,4, *S, E,* 1970 *I, W*

De Villiers, P du P (WP) 1928 *NZ* 1,3,4, 1932 *E,* 1933 *A* 4, 1937 *A* 1,2, *NZ* 1

Devine, D (Tvl) 1924 *BI* 3, 1928 *NZ* 2

De Vos, D J J (WP) 1965 *S*, 1969 *A* 3, *S*
De Waal, A N (WP) 1967 *F* 1,2,3,4
De Waal, P J (WP) 1896 *BI* 4
De Wet, A E (WP) 1969 *A* 3,4, *E*
De Wet, P J (WP) 1938 *BI* 1,2,3
Dinkelmann, E E (NT) 1951 *S, I*, 1952 *E, F*, 1953 *A* 1,2
Dirksen, C W (NT) 1963 *A* 4, 1964 *W*, 1965 *I, S*, 1967 *F* 1,2,3,4, 1968 *BI* 1,2
Dobbin, F J (GW) 1903 *BI* 1,2, 1906 *S, W, E*, 1910 *BI* 1, 1912 *S, I, W*
Dobie, J A R (Tvl) 1928 *NZ* 2
Dormehl, P J (WP) 1896 *BI* 3,4
Douglass, F W (EP) 1896 *BI* 1
Drotské, A E (OFS) 1993 *Arg* 2, 1995 [*WS* (R)], 1996 *A* 1 (R)
Dryburgh, R G (WP) 1955 *BI* 2,3,4, 1956 *A* 2, *NZ* 1,4, 1960 *NZ* 1,2
Duff, B R (WP) 1891 *BI* 1,2,3
Duffy, B A (Bor) 1928 *NZ* 1
Du Plessis, C J (WP) 1982 *S Am* 1,2, 1984 *E* 1,2, *S Am* 1,2, 1986 *Cv* 1,2,3,4, 1989 *Wld* 1,2
Du Plessis, D C (NT) 1977 *Wld*, 1980 *S Am* 2
Du Plessis, F (Tvl) 1949 *NZ* 1,2,3
Du Plessis, M (WP) 1971 *A* 1,2,3, 1974 *BI* 1,2, *F* 1,2, 1975 *F* 1,2, 1976 *NZ* 1,2,3,4, 1977 *Wld*, 1980 *S Am* 1,2, *BI* 1,2,3,4, *S Am* 4, *F*
Du Plessis, M J (WP) 1984 *S Am* 1,2, 1986 *Cv* 1,2,3,4, 1989 *Wld* 1,2
Du Plessis, N J (WT) 1921 *NZ* 2,3, 1924 *BI* 1,2,3
Du Plessis, P G (NT) 1972 *E*
Du Plessis, T D (NT) 1980 *S Am* 1,2
Du Plessis, W (WP) 1980 *S Am* 1,2, *BI* 1,2,3,4, *S Am* 3,4, *F*, 1981 *NZ* 1,2,3, 1982 *S Am* 1,2
Du Plooy, A J J (EP) 1955 *BI* 1
Du Preez, F C H (NT) 1961 *E, S, A* 1,2, 1962 *BI* 1,2,3,4, 1963 *A* 1, 1964 *W, F*, 1965 *A* 1,2, *NZ* 1,2,3,4, 1967 *F* 4, 1968 *BI* 1,2,3,4, *F* 1,2, 1969 *A* 1,2, *S*, 1970 *I, W, NZ* 1,2,3,4, 1971 *F* 1,2, *A* 1,2,3
Du Preez, J G H (WP) 1956 *NZ* 1
Du Preez, R J (N) 1992 *NZ, A*, 1993 *F* 1,2, *A* 1,2,3
Du Rand, J A (R, NT) 1949 *NZ* 2,3, 1951 *S, I, W*, 1952 *E, F*, 1953 *A* 1,2,3,4, 1955 *BI* 1,2,3,4, 1956 *A* 1,2, *NZ* 1,2,3,4
Du Randt, J P (OFS) 1994 *Arg* 1,2, *S, W*, 1995 *WS*, [*A, WS, F, NZ*], 1996 *Fj, A* 1, *NZ* 1, *A* 2, *NZ* 2,3,4
Du Toit, A F (WP) 1928 *NZ* 3,4
Du Toit, B A (Tvl) 1938 *BI* 1,2,3
Du Toit, P A (NT) 1949 *NZ* 2,3,4, 1951 *S, I, W*, 1952 *E, F*
Du Toit, P G (WP) 1981 *NZ* 1, 1982 *S Am* 1,2, 1984 *E* 1,2
Du Toit, P S (WP) 1958 *F* 1,2, 1960 *NZ* 1,2,3,4, *W, I*, 1961 *E, S, F, I, A* 1,2
Duvenhage, F P (GW) 1949 *NZ* 1,3

Edwards, P (NT) 1980 *S Am* 1,2
Ellis, J H (SWA) 1965 *NZ* 1,2,3,4, 1967 *F* 1,2,3,4, 1968 *BI* 1,2,3,4, *F* 1,2, 1969 *A* 1,2,3,4, *S*, 1970 *I, W, NZ* 1,2,3,4, 1971 *F* 1,2, *A* 1,2,3, 1972 *E*, 1974 *BI* 1,2,3,4, *F* 1,2, 1976 *NZ* 1
Ellis, M C (Tvl) 1921 *NZ* 2,3, 1924 *BI* 1,2,3
Engelbrecht, J P (WP) 1960 *S, W, I*, 1961 *E, S, F, A* 1,2, 1962 *BI* 2,3,4, 1963 *A* 2,3, 1964 *W, F*, 1965 *I, S, A* 1,2, *NZ* 1,2,3,4, 1967 *F* 1,2,3,4, 1968 *BI* 1,2, *F* 1,2, 1969 *A* 1,2
Erasmus, F S (NT, EP) 1986 *Cv* 3,4, 1989 *Wld* 2
Etlinger, T E (WP) 1896 *BI* 4

Ferreira, C (OFS) 1986 *Cv* 1,2
Ferreira, P S (WP) 1984 *S Am* 1,2
Ferris, H H (Tvl) 1903 *BI* 3
Forbes, H H (Tvl) 1896 *BI* 2
Fourie, C (EP) 1974 *F* 1,2, 1975 *F* 1,2
Fourie, T T (SET) 1974 *BI* 3
Fourie, W L (SWA) 1958 *F* 1,2
Francis, J A J (Tvl) 1912 *S, I, W*, 1913 *E, F*
Frederickson, C A (Tvl) 1974 *BI* 2, 1980 *S Am* 1,2
Frew, A (Tvl) 1903 *BI* 1
Froneman, D C (OFS) 1977 *Wld*
Froneman, I L (Bor) 1933 *A* 1
Fuls, H T (Tvl, EP) 1992 *NZ* (R), 1993 *F* 1,2, *A* 1,2,3, *Arg* 1,2
Fry, S P (WP) 1951 *S, I, W*, 1952 *E, F*, 1953 *A* 1,2,3,4, 1955 *BI* 1,2,3,4

Fyvie, W (N) 1996 *NZ* 4 (t & R), 5 (R), *Arg* 2 (R)

Gage, J H (OFS) 1933 *A* 1
Gainsford, J L (WP) 1960 *S, NZ* 1,2,3,4, *W, I*, 1961 *E, S, F, A* 1,2, 1962 *BI* 1,2,3,4, 1963 *A* 1,2,3,4, 1964 *W, F*, 1965 *I, S, A* 1,2, *NZ* 1,2,3,4, 1967 *F* 1,2,3
Garvey, A C (N) 1996 *Arg* 1,2, *F* 1,2, *W*
Geel, P J (OFS) 1949 *NZ* 3
Geere, V (Tvl) 1933 *A* 1,2,3,4,5
Geffin, A O (Tvl) 1949 *NZ* 1,2,3,4, 1951 *S, I, W*
Geldenhuys, A (EP) 1992 *NZ, A, F* 1,2
Geldenhuys, S B (NT) 1981 *NZ* 2,3, *US*, 1982 *S Am* 1,2, 1989 *Wld* 1,2
Gentles, T A (WP) 1955 *BI* 1,2,4, 1956 *NZ* 2,3, 1958 *F* 2
Geraghty, E M (Bor) 1949 *NZ* 4
Gerber, D M (EP, WP) 1980 *S Am* 3,4, *F*, 1981 *I* 1,2, *NZ* 1,2,3, *US*, 1982 *S Am* 1,2, 1984 *E* 1,2, *S Am* 1,2, 1986 *Cv* 1,2,3,4, 1992 *NZ, A, F* 1,2, *E*
Gerber, M C (EP) 1958 *F* 1,2, 1960 *S*
Gericke, F W (Tvl) 1960 *S*
Germishuys, J S (OFS, Tvl) 1974 *BI* 2, 1976 *NZ* 1,2,3,4, 1977 *Wld*, 1980 *S Am* 1,2, *BI* 1,2,3,4, *S Am* 3,4, *F*, 1981 *I* 1,2, *NZ* 2,3, *US*
Gibbs, B (GW) 1903 *BI* 2
Goosen, C P (OFS) 1965 *NZ* 2
Gorton, H C (Tvl) 1896 *BI* 1
Gould, R L (N) 1968 *BI* 1,2,3,4
Gray, B G (WP) 1931 *W*, 1932 *E, S*, 1933 *A* 5
Greenwood, C M (WP) 1961 *I*
Greyling, P J F (OFS) 1967 *F* 1,2,3,4, 1968 *BI* 1, *F* 1,2, 1969 *A* 1,2,3,4, *S, E*, 1970 *I, W, NZ* 1,2,3,4, 1971 *F* 1,2, *A* 1,2,3, 1972 *E*
Grobler, C J (OFS) 1974 *BI* 4, 1975 *F* 1,2
Guthrie, F H (WP) 1891 *BI* 1,3, 1896 *BI* 1

Hahn, C H L (Tvl) 1910 *BI* 1,2,3
Hamilton, F (EP) 1891 *BI* 1
Harris, T A (Tvl) 1937 *NZ* 2,3, 1938 *BI* 1,2,3
Hartley, A J (WP) 1891 *BI* 3
Hattingh, H (NT) 1992 *A* (R), *F* 2 (R), *E*, 1994 *Arg* 1,2
Hattingh, L B (OFS) 1933 *A* 2
Heatlie, B H (WP) 1891 *BI* 2,3, 1896 *BI* 1,4, 1903 *BI* 1,3
Hendriks, P (Tvl) 1992 *NZ, A*, 1994 *S, W*, 1995 [*A, R, C*], 1996 *A* 1, *NZ* 1, *A* 2, *NZ* 2,3,4,5
Hepburn, T B (WP) 1896 *BI* 4
Heunis, J W (NT) 1981 *NZ* 3 (R), *US*, 1982 *S Am* 1,2, 1984 *E* 1,2, *S Am* 1,2, 1986 *Cv* 1,2,3,4, 1989 *Wld* 1,2
Hill, R A (R) 1960 *W, I*, 1961 *I, A* 1,2, 1962 *BI* 4, 1963 *A* 3
Hills, W G (NT) 1992 *F* 1,2, *E*, 1993 *F* 1,2, *A* 1
Hirsch, J G (EP) 1906 *I*, 1910 *BI* 1
Hobson, T E C (WP) 1903 *BI* 3
Hoffman, R S (Bol) 1953 *A* 3
Holton, D N (EP) 1960 *S*
Honiball, H W (N) 1993 *A* 3 (R), *Arg* 2, 1995 *WS* (R), 1996 *Fj, A* 1, *NZ* 5, *Arg* 1,2, *F* 1,2, *W*
Hopwood, D J (WP) 1960 *S, NZ* 3,4, *W*, 1961 *E, S, F, I, A* 1,2, 1962 *BI* 1,2,3,4, 1963 *A* 1,2,4, 1964 *W, F*, 1965 *S, NZ* 3,4
Howe, B F (Bor) 1956 *NZ* 1,4
Howe-Browne, N R F G (WP) 1910 *BI* 1,2,3
Hugo, D P (WP) 1989 *Wld* 1,2
Hurter, M H (NT) 1995 [*R, C*], *W*, 1996 *Fj, A* 1, *NZ* 1,2,3,4,5

Immelman, J H (WP) 1913 *F*

Jackson, D C (WP) 1906 *I, W, E*
Jackson, J S (WP) 1903 *BI* 2
Jansen, E (OFS) 1981 *NZ* 1
Jansen, J S (OFS) 1970 *NZ* 1,2,3,4, 1971 *F* 1,2, *A* 1,2,3, 1972 *E*
Jennings, C B (Bor) 1937 *NZ* 1
Johnson, G K (Tvl) 1993 *Arg* 2, 1994 *NZ* 3, *Arg* 1, 1995 *WS*, [*R, C, WS*]
Johnstone, P G A (WP) 1951 *S, I, W*, 1952 *E, F*, 1956 *A* 1, *NZ* 1,2,4
Jones, C H (Tvl) 1903 *BI* 1,2
Jones, P S T (WP) 1896 *BI* 1,3,4
Jordaan, R P (NT) 1949 *NZ* 1,2,3,4
Joubert, A J (OFS, N) 1989 *Wld* 1 (R), 1993 *A* 3, *Arg* 1, 1994 *E* 1,2, *NZ* 1,2 (R), 3, *Arg* 2, *S, W*, 1995 [*A, C, WS, F, NZ*], *W, It, E*, 1996 *Fj, A* 1, *NZ* 1,3,4,5, *Arg* 1,2, *F* 1,2, *W*
Joubert, S J (WP) 1906 *I, W, E*

Oelofse, J S A (Tvl) 1953 *A* 1,2,3,4
Oliver, J F (Tvl) 1928 *NZ* 3,4
Olivier, E (WP) 1967 *F* 1,2,3,4, 1968 *BI* 1,2,3,4, *F* 1,2, 1969 *A* 1,2,3,4, *S, E*
Olivier, J (NT) 1992 *F* 1,2, *E*, 1993 *F* 1,2 *A* 1,2,3, *Arg* 1, 1995 *W, It* (R), *E*, 1996 *Arg* 1,2, *F* 1,2, *W*
Olver, E (EP) 1896 *BI* 1
Oosthuizen, J J (WP) 1974 *BI* 1, *F* 1,2, 1975 *F* 1,2, 1976 *NZ* 1,2,3,4
Oosthuizen, O W (NT, Tvl) 1981 *I* 1 (R), 2, *NZ* 2,3, *US*, 1982 *S Am* 1,2, 1984 *E* 1,2
Osler, B L (WP) 1924 *BI* 1,2,3,4, 1928 *NZ* 1,2,3,4, 1931 *W, I*, 1932 *E, S*, 1933 *A* 1,2,3,4,5
Osler, S G (WP) 1928 *NZ* 1
Otto, K (NT) 1995 [*R, C* (R), *WS* (R)]
Oxlee, K (N) 1960 *NZ* 1,2,3,4, *W, I*, 1961 *S, A* 1,2, 1962 *BI* 1,2,3,4, 1963 *A* 1,2,4, 1964 *W*, 1965 *NZ* 1,2

Pagel, G L (WP) 1995 [*A* (R), *R, C, NZ* (R)], 1996 *NZ* 5 (R)
Parker, W H (EP) 1965 *A* 1,2
Partridge, J E C (Tvl) 1903 *BI* 1
Payn, C (N) 1924 *BI* 1,2
Pelser, H J M (Tvl) 1958 *F* 1, 1960 *NZ* 1,2,3,4, *W, I*, 1961 *F, I, A* 1,2
Pfaff, B D (WP) 1956 *A* 1
Pickard, J A J (WP) 1953 *A* 3,4, 1956 *NZ* 2, 1958 *F* 2
Pienaar, J F (Tvl) 1993 *F* 1,2, *A* 1,2,3, *Arg* 1,2, 1994 *E* 1,2, *NZ* 2,3, *Arg* 1,2, *S, W*, 1995 *WS*, [*A, C, WS, F, NZ*], *W, It, E*, 1996 *Fj, A* 1, *NZ* 1, *A* 2, *NZ* 2
Pienaar, Z M J (OFS) 1980 *S Am* 2 (R), *BI* 1,2,3,4, *S Am* 3,4, *F*, 1981 *I* 1,2, *NZ* 1,2,3
Pitzer, G (NT) 1967 *F* 1,2,3,4, 1968 *BI* 1,2,3,4, *F* 1,2, 1969 *A* 3,4
Pope, C F (WP) 1974 *BI* 1,2,3,4, 1975 *F* 1,2, 1976 *NZ* 2,3,4
Potgieter, H J (OFS) 1928 *NZ* 1,2
Potgieter, H L (OFS) 1977 *Wld*
Powell, A W (GW) 1896 *BI* 3
Powell, J M (GW) 1891 *BI* 2, 1896 *BI* 3, 1903 *BI* 1,2
Prentis, R B (Tvl) 1980 *S Am* 1,2, *BI* 1,2,3,4, *S Am* 3,4, *F*, 1981 *I* 1,2
Pretorius, N F (Tvl) 1928 *NZ* 1,2,3,4
Prinsloo, J (Tvl) 1958 *F* 1,2
Prinsloo, J (NT) 1963 *A* 3
Prinsloo, J P (Tvl) 1928 *NZ* 1
Putter, D J (WT) 1963 *A* 1,2,4

Raaff, J W E (GW) 1903 *BI* 1,2, 1906 *S, W, E*, 1910 *BI* 1
Ras, W J de Wet (OFS) 1976 *NZ* 1 (R), 1980 *S Am* 2 (R)
Reece-Edwards, H (N) 1992 *F* 1,2, 1993 *A* 2
Reid, A (WP) 1903 *BI* 3
Reid, B C (Bor) 1933 *A* 4
Reinach, J (OFS) 1986 *Cv* 1,2,3,4
Rens, I J (Tvl) 1953 *A* 3,4
Retief, D F (NT) 1955 *BI* 1,2,4, 1956 *A* 1,2, *NZ* 1,2,3,4
Reyneke, H J (WP) 1910 *BI* 3
Richards, A R (WP) 1891 *BI* 1,2,3
Richter, A (NT) 1992 *F* 1,2, *E*, 1994 *E* 2, *NZ* 1,2,3, 1995 [*R, C, WS* (R)]
Riley, N M (ET) 1963 *A* 3
Riordan, C A (Tvl) 1910 *BI* 1,2
Robertson, I W (R) 1974 *F* 1,2, 1976 *NZ* 1,2,4
Rodgers, P H (NT, Tvl) 1989 *Wld* 1,2, 1992 *NZ, F* 1,2
Rogers, C D (Tvl) 1984 *E* 1,2, *S Am* 1,2
Roos, G D (WP) 1910 *BI* 2,3
Roos, P J (WP) 1903 *BI* 3, 1906 *I, W, E*
Rosenberg, W (Tvl) 1955 *BI* 2,3,4, 1956 *NZ* 3, 1958 *F* 1
Rossouw, C L C (Tvl) 1995 *WS*, [*R, WS, F, NZ*]
Rossouw, D H (WP) 1953 *A* 3, 4
Rousseau, W P (WP) 1928 *NZ* 3,4
Roux, F du T (WP) 1960 *W*, 1961 *A* 1,2, 1962 *BI* 1,2,3,4, 1963 *A* 2, 1965 *A* 1,2, *NZ* 1,2,3,4, 1968 *BI* 3,4, *F* 1,2 1969 *A* 1,2,3,4, 1970 *I, NZ* 1,2,3,4
Roux, J P (Tvl) 1994 *E* 2, *NZ* 1,2,3, *Arg* 1, 1995 [*R, C, F* (R)], 1996 *A* 1 (R), *NZ* 1, *A* 2, *NZ* 3
Roux, O A (NT) 1969 *S, E*, 1970 *I, W*, 1972 *E*, 1974 *BI* 3,4

Samuels, T A (GW) 1896 *BI* 2,3,4
Sauermann, J T (Tvl) 1971 *F* 1,2, *A* 1, 1972 *E*, 1974 *BI* 1
Schlebusch, J J J (OFS) 1974 *BI* 3,4, 1975 *F* 2
Schmidt, L U (NT) 1958 *F* 2, 1962 *BI* 2

Schmidt, U L (NT, Tvl) 1986 *Cv* 1,2,3,4, 1989 *Wld* 1,2, 1992 *NZ, A*, 1993 *F* 1,2, *A* 1,2,3, 1994 *Arg* 1,2, *S, W*
Schoeman, J (WP) 1963 *A* 3,4, 1965 *I, S, A* 1, *NZ* 1,2
Scholtz, C P (WP, Tvl) 1994 *Arg* 1, 1995 [*R, C, WS*]
Scholtz, H H (WP) 1921 *NZ* 1,2
Schutte, P J W (Tvl) 1994 *S, W*
Scott, P A (Tvl) 1896 *BI* 1,2,3,4
Sendin, W D (GW) 1921 *NZ* 2
Serfontein, D J (WP) 1980 *BI* 1,2,3,4, *S Am* 3,4, *F*, 1981 *I* 1,2, *NZ* 1,2,3, *US*, 1982 *S Am* 1,2, 1984 *E* 1,2, *S Am* 1,2
Shand, R (GW) 1891 *BI* 2,3
Sheriff, A R (Tvl) 1938 *BI* 1,2,3
Shum, E H (Tvl) 1913 *E*
Sinclair, D J (Tvl) 1955 *BI* 1,2,3,4
Sinclair, J H (Tvl) 1903 *BI* 1
Skene, A L (WP) 1958 *F* 2
Slater, J T (EP) 1924 *BI* 3,4, 1928 *NZ* 1
Smal, G P (WP) 1986 *Cv* 1,2,3,4, 1989 *Wld* 1,2
Small, J T (Tvl, N) 1992 *NZ, A, F* 1,2, *E*, 1993 *F* 1,2, *A* 1,2,3, *Arg* 1,2, 1994 *E* 1,2, *NZ* 1,2,3 (t), *Arg* 1, 1995 *WS*, [*A, R, F, NZ*], *W, It, E* (R), 1996 *Fj, A* 1, *NZ* 1, *A* 2, *NZ* 2, *Arg* 1,2, *F* 1,2
Smit, F C (WP) 1992 *E*
Smith, C M (OFS) 1963 *A* 3,4, 1964 *W, F*, 1965 *A* 1,2, *NZ* 2
Smith, C W (GW) 1891 *BI* 2, 1896 *BI* 2,3
Smith, D (GW) 1891 *BI* 2
Smith D J (Z-R) 1980 *BI* 1,2,3,4
Smith, G A C (EP) 1938 *BI* 3
Smollan, F C (Tvl) 1933 *A* 3,4,5
Snedden, R C D (GW) 1891 *BI* 2
Snyman, A H (NT) 1996 *NZ* 3,4, *Arg* 2 (R), *W* (R)
Snyman, D S L (WP) 1972 *E*, 1974 *BI* 1,2 (R), *F* 1,2, 1975 *F* 1,2, 1976 *NZ* 2,3, 1977 *Wld*
Snyman, J C P (OFS) 1974 *BI* 2,3,4
Sonnekus, G H H (OFS) 1974 *BI* 3, 1984 *E* 1,2
Spies, J J (NT) 1970 *NZ* 1,2,3,4
Stander, J C J (OFS) 1974 *BI* 4 (R), 1976 *NZ* 1,2,3,4
Stapelberg, W P (NT) 1974 *F* 1,2
Starke, J J (WP) 1956 *NZ* 4
Starke, K T (WP) 1924 *BI* 1,2,3,4
Steenekamp, J G A (Tvl) 1958 *F* 1
Stegmann, A C (WP) 1906 *S, I*
Stegmann, J A (Tvl) 1912 *S, I, W*, 1913 *E, F*
Stewart, D A (WP) 1960 *S*, 1961 *E, S, F, I*, 1963 *A* 1,3,4, 1964 *W, F*, 1965 *I*
Stofberg, M T S (OFS, NT, WP) 1976 *NZ* 2,3, 1977 *Wld*, 1980 *S Am* 1,2, *BI* 1,2,3,4, *S Am* 3,4, *F*, 1981 *I* 1,2, *NZ* 1,2, *US*, 1982 *S Am* 1,2, 1984 *E* 1,2
Strachan, L C (Tvl) 1932 *E, S*, 1937 *A* 1,2, *NZ* 1,2,3, 1938 *BI* 1,2,3
Stransky, J (N, WP) 1993 *A* 1,2,3, *Arg* 1, 1994 *Arg* 1,2, 1995 *WS*, [*A, R* (t), *C, F, NZ*], *W, It, E*, 1996 *Fj* (R), *NZ* 1, *A* 2, *NZ* 2,3,4,5 (R)
Straeuli, R A W (Tvl) 1994 *NZ* 1, *Arg* 1,2, *S, W*, 1995 *WS*, [*A, WS, NZ* (R)], *E* (R)
Strauss, C P (WP) 1992 *F* 1,2, *E*, 1993 *F* 1,2, *A* 1,2,3, *Arg* 1,2, 1994 *E* 1, *NZ* 1,2, *Arg* 1,2
Strauss, J A (WP) 1984 *S Am* 1,2
Strauss, J H P (Tvl) 1976 *NZ* 3,4, 1980 *S Am* 1
Strauss, S S F (GW) 1921 *NZ* 3
Strydom, C F (OFS) 1955 *BI* 3, 1956 *A* 1,2, *NZ* 1,4, 1958 *F* 1,
Strydom, J J (Tvl) 1993 *F* 2, *A* 1,2,3, *Arg* 1,2, 1994 *E* 1, 1995 [*A, C, F, NZ*], 1996 *A* 2 (R), *NZ* 2 (R). 3,4, *W* (R)
Strydom, L J (NT) 1949 *NZ* 1,2
Styger, J J (OFS) 1992 *NZ* (R), *A. F* 1,2, *E*, 1993 *F* 2 (R), *A* 3 (R)
Suter, M R (N) 1965 *I. S*
Swart, J (WP) 1996 *Fj, NZ* 1 (R), *A* 2, *NZ* 2,3,4,5
Swart, J J N (SWA) 1955 *BI* 1
Swart, I S (Tvl) 1993 *A* 1,2,3, *Arg* 1, 1994 *E* 1,2, *NZ* 1,3, *Arg* 2 (R), 1995 *WS*, [*A, WS, F, NZ*], *W*, 1996 *A* 2

Taberer, W S (GW) 1896 *BI* 2
Taylor, O B (N) 1962 *BI* 1
Teichmann, G H (N) 1995 *W*, 1996 *Fj, A* 1, *NZ* 1, *A* 2, *NZ* 2,3,4,5, *Arg* 1,2, *F* 1,2, *W*
Theron, D F (GW) 1996 *A* 2 (R), *NZ* 2 (R), 5, *Arg* 1,2, *F* 1,2, *W*
Theunissen, D J (GW) 1896 *BI* 3
Thompson, G (WP) 1912 *S, I, W*
Tindall, J C (WP) 1924 *BI* 1, 1928 *NZ* 1,2,3,4

Tobias, E G (SARF, Bol) 1981 *I* 1,2, 1984 *E* 1,2, *S Am* 1,2
Tod, N S (N) 1928 *NZ* 2
Townsend, W H (N) 1921 *NZ* 1
Trenery, W E (GW) 1891 *BI* 2
Tromp, H (NT) 1996 *NZ*3,4, *Arg* 2 (R), *F* 1 (R)
Truter, D R (WP) 1924 *BI* 2,4
Truter, J T (N) 1963 *A* 1, 1964 *F*, 1965 *A* 2
Turner, F G (EP) 1933 *A* 1,2,3, 1937 *A* 1,2, *NZ* 1,2,3, 1938 *BI* 1,2,3
Twigge, R J (NT) 1960 *S*

Ulyate, C A (Tvl) 1955 *BI* 1,2,3,4, 1956 *NZ* 1,2,3
Uys, P de W (NT) 1960 *W*, 1961 *E, S, I, A* 1,2, 1962 *BI* 1,4, 1963 *A* 1,2, 1969 *A* 1 (R), 2

Van Aswegen, H J (WP) 1981 *NZ* 1, 1982 *S Am* 2 (R)
Van Broekhuizen, H D (WP) 1896 *BI* 4
Van Buuren, M C (Tvl) 1891 *BI* 1
Van de Vyver, D F (WP) 1937 *A* 2
Van den Berg, D S (N) 1975 *F* 1,2, 1976 *NZ* 1,2
Van den Berg, M A (WP) 1937 *A* 1, *NZ* 1,2,3
Van den Bergh, E (EP) 1994 *Arg* 2 (t & R)
Van der Linde, A (WP) 1995 *It, E*, 1996 *Arg* 1 (R), 2 (R), *F* 1 (R), *W* (R)
Van der Merwe, A J (Bol) 1955 *BI* 2,3,4, 1956 *A* 1,2, *NZ* 1,2,3,4, 1958 *F* 1, 1960 *S, NZ* 2
Van der Merwe, A V (WP) 1931 *W*
Van der Merwe, B S (NT) 1949 *NZ* 1
Van der Merwe, H S (NT) 1960 *NZ* 4, 1963 *A* 2,3,4, 1964 *F*
Van der Merwe, J P (WP) 1970 *W*
Van der Merwe, P R (SWD, WT, GW) 1981 *NZ* 2,3, *US*, 1986 *Cv* 1,2, 1989 *Wld* 1
Vanderplank, B E (N) 1924 *BI* 3,4
Van der Schyff, J H (GW) 1949 *NZ* 1,2,3,4, 1955 *BI* 1
Van der Watt, A E (WP) 1969 *S* (R), *E*, 1970 *I*
Van der Westhuizen, J C (WP) 1928 *NZ* 2,3,4, 1931 *I*
Van der Westhuizen, J H (WP) 1931 *I*, 1932 *E, S*
Van der Westhuizen, J H (NT) 1993 *Arg* 1,2, 1994 *E* 1,2 (R), *Arg* 2, *S, W*, 1995 *WS*, [*A, C* (R), *WS, F, NZ*], *W, It, E*, 1996 *Fj, A* 1,2 (R), *NZ* 2,3 (R), 4,5, *Arg* 1,2, *F* 1,2, *W*
Van Druten, N J V (Tvl) 1924 *BI* 1,2,3,4, 1928 *NZ* 1,2,3,4
Van Heerden, A J (Tvl) 1921 *NZ* 1,3
Van Heerden, F J (WP) 1994 *E* 1,2 (R), *NZ* 3, 1995 *It, E*, 1996 *NZ* 5 (R), *Arg* 1 (R), 2 (R)
Van Heerden, J L (NT, Tvl) 1974 *BI* 3,4, *F* 1,2, 1975 *F* 1,2, 1976 *NZ* 1,2,3,4, 1977 *Wld*, 1980 *BI* 1,3,4, *S Am* 3,4, *F*
Van Jaarsveld, C J (Tvl) 1949 *NZ* 1
Van Jaarsveldt, D C (R) 1960 *S*
Van Niekerk, J A (WP) 1928 *NZ* 4
Van Reenen, G L (WP) 1937 *A* 2, *NZ* 1
Van Renen, C G (WP) 1891 *BI* 3, 1896 *BI* 1,4
Van Renen, W (WP) 1903 *BI* 1,3
Van Rensburg, J T J (Tvl) 1992 *NZ, A, E*, 1993 *F* 1,2, *A* 1, 1994 *NZ* 2
Van Rooyen, G W (Tvl) 1921 *NZ* 2,3
Van Ryneveld, R C B (WP) 1910 *BI* 2,3
Van Schalkwyk, D (NT) 1996 *Fj* (R), *NZ* 3,4,5
Van Schoor, R A M (R) 1949 *NZ* 2,3,4, 1951 *S, I, W*, 1952 *E, F*, 1953 *A* 1,2,3,4
Van Vollenhoven, K T (NT) 1955 *BI* 1,2,3,4, 1956 *A* 1,2, *NZ* 3
Van Vuuren, T F (EP) 1912 *S, I, W*, 1913 *E, F*

Van Wyk, C J (Tvl) 1951 *S, I, W*, 1952 *E, F*, 1953 *A* 1,2,3,4, 1955 *BI* 1
Van Wyk, J F B (NT) 1970 *NZ* 1,2,3,4, 1971 *F* 1,2, *A* 1,2,3, 1972 *E*, 1974 *BI* 1,3,4, 1976 *NZ* 3,4
Van Wyk, S P (WP) 1928 *NZ* 1,2
Van Zyl, B P (WP) 1961 *I*
Van Zyl, C G P (OFS) 1965 *NZ* 1,2,3,4
Van Zyl, G H (WP) 1958 *F* 1, 1960 *S, NZ* 1,2,3,4, *W, I*, 1961 *E, S, F, I, A* 1,2, 1962 *BI* 1,3,4
Van Zyl, H J (Tvl) 1960 *NZ* 1,2,3,4, *I*, 1961 *E, S, I, A* 1,2
Van Zyl, P J (Bol) 1961 *I*
Veldsman, P E (WP) 1977 *Wld*
Venter, A G (OFS) 1996 *NZ* 3,4,5, *Arg* 1,2, *F* 1,2, *W*
Venter, B (OFS) 1994 *E* 1,2, *NZ* 1,2,3, *Arg* 1,2, 1995 [*R, C, WS* (R), *NZ* (R)], 1996 *A* 1, *NZ* 1, *A* 2
Venter, F D (Tvl) 1931 *W*, 1932 *S*, 1933 *A* 3
Versfeld, C (WP) 1891 *BI* 3
Versfeld, M (WP) 1891 *BI* 1,2,3
Vigne, J T (Tvl) 1891 *BI* 1,2,3
Viljoen, J F (GW) 1971 *F* 1,2, *A* 1,2,3, 1972 *E*
Viljoen, J T (N) 1971 *A* 1,2,3
Villet, J V (WP) 1984 *E* 1,2
Visagie, P J (GW) 1967 *F* 1,2,3,4, 1968 *BI* 1,2,3,4, *F* 1,2, 1969 *A* 1,2,3,4, *S, E*, 1970 *NZ* 1,2,3,4, 1971 *F* 1,2, *A* 1,2,3
Visagie, R G (OFS, N) 1984 *E* 1,2, *S Am* 1,2, 1993 *F* 1
Visser, J de V (WP) 1981 *NZ* 2, *US*
Visser, M (WP) 1995 *WS* (R)
Visser, P J (Tvl) 1933 *A* 2
Viviers, S S (OFS) 1956 *A* 1,2, *NZ* 2,3,4
Vogel, M L (OFS) 1974 *BI* 2 (R)

Wagenaar, C (NT) 1977 *Wld*
Wahl, J J (WP) 1949 *NZ* 1
Walker, A P (N) 1921 *NZ* 1,3, 1924 *BI* 1,2,3,4
Walker, H N (OFS) 1953 *A* 3, 1956 *A* 2, *NZ* 1,4
Walker, H W (Tvl) 1910 *BI* 1,2,3
Walton, D C (N) 1964 *F*, 1965 *I, S, NZ* 3,4, 1969 *A* 1,2, *E*
Waring, F W (WP) 1931 *I*, 1932 *E*, 1933 *A* 1,2,3,4,5
Wegner, N (WP) 1993 *F* 2, *A* 1,2,3
Wessels, J J (WP) 1896 *BI* 1,2,3
Whipp, P J M (WP) 1974 *BI* 1,2, 1975 *F* 1, 1976 *NZ* 1,3,4, 1980 *S Am* 1,2
White, J (Bor) 1931 *W*, 1933 *A* 1,2,3,4,5, 1937 *A* 1,2, *NZ* 1,2
Wiese, J J (Tvl) 1993 *F* 1, 1995 *WS*, [*R, C, WS, F, NZ*], *W, It, E*, 1996 *NZ* 3 (R), 4 (R), 5, *Arg* 1,2, *F* 1,2, *W*
Williams, A E (GW) 1910 *BI* 1
Williams, A P (WP) 1984 *E* 1,2
Williams, C M (WP) 1993 *Arg* 2, 1994 *E* 1,2, *NZ* 1,2,3, *Arg* 1,2, *S, W*, 1995 *WS*, [*WS, F, NZ*], *It, E*
Williams, D O (WP) 1937 *A* 1,2, *NZ* 1,2,3, 1938 *BI* 1,2,3
Williams, J G (NT) 1971 *F* 1,2, *A* 1,2,3, 1972 *E*, 1974 *BI* 1,2,4, *F* 1,2, 1976 *NZ* 1,2
Wilson, L G (WP) 1960 *NZ* 3,4, *W, I*, 1961 *E, F, I, A* 1,2, 1962 *BI* 1,2,3,4, 1963 *A* 1,2,3,4, 1964 *W, F*, 1965 *I, S, A* 1,2, *NZ* 1,2,3,4
Wolmarans, B J (OFS) 1977 *Wld*
Wright, G D (EP, Tvl) 1986 *Cv* 3,4, 1989 *Wld* 1,2, 1992 *F* 1,2, *E*
Wyness, M R K (WP) 1962 *BI* 1,2,3,4, 1963 *A* 2

Zeller, W C (N) 1921 *NZ* 2,3
Zimerman, M (WP) 1931 *W, I*, 1932 *E, S*

SOUTH AFRICAN INTERNATIONAL RECORDS (*up to 30 April 1997*)

MATCH RECORDS

MOST CONSECUTIVE TEST WINS

15 1994 *Arg* 1,2, *S, W* 1995 *WS, A, R, C, WS, F, NZ, W, It, E* 1996 *Fj*
10 1949 *NZ* 1,2,3,4, 1951 *S, I, W*, 1952 *E, F*, 1953 *A* 1

MOST CONSECUTIVE TESTS WITHOUT DEFEAT

P	W	D	Period
16	15	1	1994–96
15	12	3	1960–63
11	9	2	1967–69

MOST POINTS IN A MATCH
by the team

Pts	Opp	Venue	Year
60	WS	Johannesburg	1995
52	Arg	Buenos Aires	1993
50	SAm	Pretoria	1982
46	Arg	Johannesburg	1994
46	Arg	Buenos Aires	1996

by a player

28 by G K Johnson v Western Samoa at Johannesburg — 1995
25 by J T Stransky v Australia at Bloemfontein — 1996
22 by G R Bosch v France at Pretoria — 1975
22 by G K Johnson v Argentina at Buenos Aires — 1993
22 by J T Stransky v Argentina at Port Elizabeth — 1994
22 by J T Stransky v Australia at Cape Town — 1995

MOST TRIES IN A MATCH
by the team

T	Opp	Venue	Year
10	I	Dublin	1912
9	F	Bordeaux	1913
9	S	Murrayfield	1951
9	WS	Johannesburg	1995

by a player

4 by C M Williams v Western Samoa at Johannesburg — 1995
3 by E E McHardy v Ireland at Dublin — 1912

3 by J A Stegmann v Ireland at Dublin — 1912
3 by K T van Vollenhoven v British Isles at Cape Town — 1955
3 by H J van Zyl v Australia at Johannesburg — 1961
3 by R H Mordt v New Zealand at Auckland — 1981
3 by R H Mordt v United States at New York — 1981
3 by D M Gerber v South America at Pretoria — 1982
3 by D M Gerber v England at Johannesburg — 1984
3 by G K Johnson v Western Samoa at Johannesburg — 1995
3 by J H van der Westhuizen v Wales at Cardiff — 1996

MOST CONVERSIONS IN A MATCH
by the team

C	Opp	Venue	Year
7	S	Murrayfield	1951
6	SAm	Pretoria	1982
6	WS	Johannesburg	1995
5	BI	Bloemfontein	1962

by a player

7 by A Geffin v Scotland at Murrayfield — 1951
6 by H E Botha v South America at Pretoria — 1982
5 by K Oxlee v British Isles at Bloemfontein — 1962
5 by G K Johnson v Western Samoa at Johannesburg — 1995

MOST PENALTY GOALS IN A MATCH
by the team

P	Opp	Venue	Year
7	F	Pretoria	1975
6	A	Bloemfontein	1996
5	several instances		

by a player

6 by G R Bosch v France at Pretoria — 1975
6 by J T Stransky v Australia at Bloemfontein — 1996
5 by A Geffin v New Zealand at Cape Town — 1949

5 by R Blair v World XV at
Pretoria   1977
5 by H E Botha v New Zealand at
Wellington   1981
5 by J W Heunis v England at Port
Elizabeth   1984
5 by H E Botha v New Zealand
Cavaliers at Johannesburg   1986
5 by J T J van Rensburg v France at
Durban   1993
5 by A J Joubert v England at
Pretoria   1994

MOST DROPPED GOALS IN A MATCH
by the team

D	Opp	Venue	Year
3	SAm	Durban	1980
3	I	Durban	1981

by a player

3 by H E Botha v South America at
Durban   1980
3 by H E Botha v Ireland at
Durban   1981
2 by B L Osler v New Zealand at
Durban   1928
2 by H E Botha v New Zealand
Cavaliers at Cape Town   1986
2 by J T Stransky v New Zealand
at Johannesburg   1995

CAREER RECORDS

MOST CAPPED PLAYERS

Caps	Player	Career
38	F C H du Preez	1961–71
38	J H Ellis	1965–76
36	J T Small	1992–96
35	J F K Marais	1963–74
33	J P Engelbrecht	1960–69
33	J L Gainsford	1960–67
30	A J Joubert	1989–96
29	J F Pienaar	1993–96
29	M G Andrews	1983–96

MOST CONSECUTIVE TESTS

Tests	Player	Span
25	S H Nomis	1967–72
23	J L Gainsford	1961–67
23	J F K Marais	1968–71
22	L G Wilson	1961–65
20	P J F Greyling	1968–72

MOST TESTS AS CAPTAIN

Tests	Captain	Span
29	J F Pienaar	1993–96
22	D J de Villiers	1965–70
15	M du Plessis	1975–80
11	J F K Marais	1971–74
10	A S Malan	1960–65

MOST TESTS IN INDIVIDUAL POSITIONS

Full-back	A J Joubert	30	1989–96
Wing	J T Small	33*	1992–96
	J P Engelbrecht	33	1960–69
Centre	J L Gainsford	33	1960–67
Fly-half	H E Botha	28	1980–92
Scrum-half	J H van der Westhuizen	26	1993–96
Prop	J F K Marais	35	1963–74
Hooker	G F Malan	18	1958–65
Lock	F C H du Preez	31	1961–71
Flanker	J H Ellis	38	1965–76
No 8	D J Hopwood	22	1960–65

* excludes an appearance as a temporary
replacement

MOST POINTS IN TESTS

Pts	Player	Tests	Career
312	H E Botha	28	1980–92
240	J T Stransky	22	1993–96
130	P J Visagie	25	1967–71
112	A J Joubert	30	1989–96
89	G R Bosch	9	1974–76

MOST TRIES IN TESTS

Tries	Player	Tests	Career
19	D M Gerber	24	1980–92
13	C M Williams	16	1993–95
13	J T Small	36	1992–96
13	J H van der Westhuizen	28	1993–96
12	J S Germishuys	20	1974–81
12	R H Mordt	18	1980–84

MOST CONVERSIONS IN TESTS

Cons	Player	Tests	Career
50	H E Botha	28	1980–92
30	J T Stransky	22	1993–96
20	P J Visagie	25	1967–71
14	K Oxlee	19	1960–65
14	G K Johnson	7	1993–95

MOST PENALTY GOALS IN TESTS

Pens	Player	Tests	Career
50	H E Botha	28	1980–92
47	J T Stransky	22	1993–96
23	G R Bosch	9	1974–76
19	P J Visagie	25	1967–71
17	A J Joubert	30	1989–96
17	H W Honiball	11	1993–96

MOST DROPPED GOALS IN TESTS

Drops	Player	Tests	Career
18	H E Botha	28	1980–92
5	J D Brewis	10	1949–53
5	P J Visagie	25	1967–71
4	B L Osler	17	1924–33

TRI-NATIONS RECORDS

Record	Detail	Holder	Set
Most points in matches	39	J T Stransky	1996
Most points in season	39	J T Stransky	1996
Most points in match	25	J T Stransky	v Australia (h) 1996
Most tries in matches	1	several players	1996
Most tries in season	1	several players	1996
Most tries in match	1	several players	1996
Most cons in matches	2	J T Stransky	1996
Most cons in season	2	J T Stransky	1996
Most cons in match	1	three instances	1996
Most pens in matches	10	J T Stransky	1996
Most pens in season	10	J T Stransky	1996
Most pens in match	6	J T Stransky	v Australia (h) 1996

SERIES RECORDS

Record	Holder	Detail
Most tries	E E McHardy	6 in Europe 1912–12
Most points	H E Botha	69 v Cavaliers, 1986

MAJOR TOUR RECORDS

Record	Detail	Year	Place
Most team points	753	1937	A & NZ
Most team tries	161	1937	A & NZ
Most individual points	190 by G H Brand	1937	A & NZ
Most individual tries	22 by J A Loubser	1906–07	Europe
Most points in match	38 by A J Joubert	1994 v Swansea	Swansea
Most tries in match	6 by R G Dryburgh	1956 v Queensland	Brisbane

MISCELLANEOUS RECORDS

Record	Holder	Detail
Longest Test Career	J M Powell/B H Heatlie/D M Gerber/ H E Botha	13 seasons, 1891–1903/ 1891–1903/1980–1992/ 1980–1992

SOUTH AFRICA INTERNATIONAL CAREER RECORDS *(up to 30 April 1997)*

Player	Debut	Caps since last season	Caps	T	C	PG	DG	Pts
A J Joubert	1989 v Wld	1996 *Fj, A* 1, *NZ* 1,3,4,5, *Arg* 1, 2, *F* 1, 2, *W*	30	9	8	17	0	112
G K Johnson	1993 v Arg		7	5	14	11	0	86
J Olivier	1992 v F	1996 *Arg* 1,2 *F* 1,2, *W*	17	3	0	0	0	15
J T Small	1992 v NZ	1996 *Fj, A* 1, *NZ* 1, *A* 2, *NZ* 2, *Arg* 1, 2, *F* 1, 2, *W*	36	13	0	0	0	65
C M Williams	1993 v Arg		16	13	0	0	0	65
P Hendriks	1992 v NZ	1996 *A* 1, *NZ* 1, *A* 2, *NZ* 2,3,4,5	14	2	0	0	0	10
J Swart	1996 v Fj	1996 *Fj, NZ* 1 (R), *A* 2, *NZ* 2,3,4,5	7	0	0	0	0	0
D van Schalkwyk	1996 v Fj	1996 *Fj* (R), *NZ* 4,5	4	2	0	0	0	10
A H Snyman	1996 v NZ	1996 *NZ* 3,4 *Arg* 2 (R), *W* (R)	4	0	0	0	0	0
H P le Roux	1993 v F	1996 *Fj, NZ* 2, *Arg* 1,2 *F* 1,2 *W*	27	4	1	4	0	34
B Venter	1994 v E	1996 *A* 1, *NZ* 1, *A* 2	14	1	0	0	0	5
J C Mulder	1994 v NZ	1996 *Fj, A* 1, *NZ* 1, *A* 2, *NZ* 2,5, *Arg* 1,2, *F* 1,2 *W*	23	6	0	0	0	30
H W Honiball	1993 v A	1996 *Fj, A* 1, *NZ* 5, *Arg* 1,2, *F* 1,2, *W*	11	0	13	17	0	77
N V Cilliers	1996 v NZ	1996 *NZ* 3 (R)	1	0	0	0	0	0
J T Stransky	1993 v A	1996 *Fj* (R), *NZ* 1, *A* 2, *NZ* 2,3,4,5 (R)	22	6	30	47	3	240
J P Roux	1994 v E	1996 *A* 1 (R), *NZ* 1, *A* 2, *NZ* 3	12	2	0	0	0	10
J H van der Westhuizen	1993 v Arg	1996 *Fj, A* 1,2 (R), *NZ* 2,3 (R),4,5, *Arg* 1,2, *F* 1,2, *W*	28	13	0	0	0	65
J Allan	1993 v A	1996 *Fj, A* 1, *NZ* 1, *A* 2, *NZ* 2	13	0	0	0	0	0
J Dalton	1994 v Arg	1996 *NZ* 4 (R),5, *Arg* 1,2, *F* 1,2, *W*	13	0	0	0	0	0
H Tromp	1996 v NZ	1996 *NZ* 3,4, *Arg* 2 (R), *F* 1 (R)	4	0	0	0	0	0
G L Pagel	1995 v A	1996 *NZ* 5 (R)	5	0	0	0	0	0
J P du Randt	1994 v Arg	1996 *Fj, A* 1, *NZ* 1, *A* 2, *NZ* 2,3,4	16	0	0	0	0	0

A van der Linde	1995 v It	1996 *Arg* 1 (R),2 (R), *F* 1 (R), *W* (R)	6	0	0	0	0	0
A C Garvey	1996 v Arg	1996 *Arg* 1,2, *F* 1,2, *W*	5	0	0	0	0	0
M H Hurter	1995 v R	1996 *Fj, A* 1, *NZ* 1,2,3,4,5	10	0	0	0	0	0
I S Swart	1993 v A	1996 *A* 2	16	0	0	0	0	0
D F Theron	1996 v A	1996 *A* 2 (R), *NZ* 2 (R),5, *Arg* 1,2, *F* 1,2, *W*	8	0	0	0	0	0
J Ackermann	1996 v Fj	1996 *Fj, A* 1, *NZ* 1, *A* 2	4	0	0	0	0	0
M G Andrews	1994 v E	1996 *Fj, A* 1, *NZ* 1, *A* 2, *NZ* 2,3,4,5, *Arg* 1,2, *F* 1,2, *W*	29	5	0	0	0	25
J J Wiese	1993 v F	1996 *NZ* 3 (R),4 (R),5, *Arg* 1,2, *F* 1,2, *W*	18	1	0	0	0	5
F J van Heerden	1994 v E	1996 *NZ* 5 (R), *Arg* 1 (R),2 (R)	8	0	0	0	0	0
J J Strydom	1993 v F	1996 *A* 2 (R), *NZ* 2 (R),3,4, *W* (R)	16	1	0	0	0	5
S Atherton	1993 v Arg	1996 *NZ* 2	8	0	0	0	0	0
J F Pienaar	1993 v F	1996 *Fj, A* 1, *NZ* 1, *A* 2, *NZ* 2	29	3	0	0	0	15
R J Kruger	1993 v Arg	1996 *Fj, A* 1, *NZ* 1, *A* 2, *NZ* 2,3,4,5, *Arg* 1,2, *F* 1,2, *W*	26	4	0	0	0	20
A E Drotske	1993 v Arg	1996 *A* 1 (R)	3	0	0	0	0	0
W Fyvie	1996 v NZ	1996 *NZ* 4 (t&R),5 (R), *Arg* 2 (R)	3	0	0	0	0	0
A G Venter	1996 v NZ	1996 *NZ* 3,4,5, *Arg* 1,2, *F* 1,2, *W*	8	2	0	0	0	10
G H Teichmann	1995 v W	1996 *Fj, A* 1, *NZ* 1, *A* 2, *NZ* 2,3,4,5, *Arg* 1,2, *F* 1,2, *W*	14	1	0	0	0	5

UNEVEN GROUND YIELDS FINEST VINTAGE

The 1996 Season in New Zealand
Donald Cameron *New Zealand Herald*

Only the brave or foolish would have proclaimed last February that New Zealand rugby was about to have a year of the finest vintage. In the previous 12 months the amateur NZRFU had battled to cope with the rampant rise of professionalism in the uncomfortable knowledge that the newly freed players had only barely been persuaded not to chase the butterflies of world-championship rugby.

The 1996 season saw composite New Zealand provincial teams making an experimental entry into a strong Super-12 competition. A three-way home-and-away Test series would be followed by a hectic tour of South Africa when four Tests (the last of the Tri-series, then a three-Test rubber) would be played on four consecutive Saturdays. The NZRFU was still adjusting to the earthy leadership of Richie Guy, whose Waipu farm is a world away from the power base of Wellington. The All Blacks also had a new coach, John Hart, spurned by the NZRFU for so long that people worried he might have lost the magic touch he had found with Auckland in the last half of the 1980's. At the same time, officials looked at sagging profits and wondered whether the national championship and Ranfurly Shield would wither away in the heat of professionalism.

Seven months later, the victorious All Blacks were given a tickertape welcome along Auckland's Queen Street. The Prime Minister, Jim Bolger, headed a long list of politicians who paid tribute to the triumphant national side (there was an election just around the corner, after all) even if he was reduced to borrowing a newspaper tag; calling the 1996 All Blacks the 'Incomparables' to accompany the 'Originals' of 1905 and the 'Invincibles' of 1924-25. But incomparable they, and New Zealand rugby, were in 1996. The Super-12 competition drew amazing local support, and Auckland went on to record some spectacular wins in the final stages.

The All Blacks dipped their toes into the Test-match water with a comfortable floodlit 51-10 win over Western Samoa, which served to introduce the latest wunderkind, Christian Cullen, to international rugby – and instant fame. Cullen, and the polished play Hart was developing, were too much for Scotland, who were beaten 62-31 in the First Test at Carisbrook, and by 36-12 at Eden Park.

In the mud and rain of Athletic Park, on its last legs as a Test-match venue, praise be, the All Blacks slaughtered the Wallabies 43-6, but they reverted to the tight-fisted, penalty-ridden habits of the past in the 15-11 win over South Africa at Christchurch. In

Brisbane the All Blacks were outplayed for three-quarters of the game, but two late tries got them out of jail by 32-25. Then it was on to South Africa. New Zealand finished off the Tri-series with a decisive 29-18 win, and started their new three-Test campaign with a heart-stopping recovery to 23-19. The All Black machine was beginning to wind down, but they had still kept enough powder dry to hold out for a last-gasp 33-26 victory to become the first New Zealand team to take a series in South Africa. It mattered not that the Springboks stormed back to win the last match by 32-22, for the whole of New Zealand was already hanging out the flags. Ten Test matches, nine wins, one loss – the All Blacks may never achieve such dominating glory again, for no one will ever again devise such a tough, indeed, almost impossible programme.

Domestic rugby, too, had its spectacular flourishes. Bay of Plenty broke hearts by losing a Ranfurly Shield challenge 29-30 to an Auckland side which needed a converted try in the last minute to win. Taranaki then set the country alight by taking the Shield from Auckland, and holding it against North Harbour. Waikato joined the parade, beating Taranaki and dousing North Harbour's second challenge. Auckland, back to All Black power, dismissed Waikato 27-7, and handed North Harbour their third shield defeat, 69-27.

So the season ended as it had started, with the Ranfurly Shield safely in Auckland's locker. But what glory there had been in *annus mirabilis* for New Zealand rugby.

NATIONAL CHAMPIONSHIP

Division 1	P	W	D	L	F	A	Pts
Auckland	8	6	0	2	314	162	33
Counties	8	6	0	2	241	180	28
Canterbury	8	5	0	3	240	193	26
Otago	8	5	0	3	249	224	22
Wellington	8	4	0	4	205	223	20
Waikato	8	4	0	4	165	168	19
Taranaki	8	4	0	4	205	273	19
North Harbour	8	2	0	6	166	212	13
King Country	8	0	0	8	151	301	0

Semi-finals: Auckland 59, Otago 18; Counties 46, Canterbury 33
Final: Auckland 46, Counties 15

Division 2	P	W	D	L	F	A	Pts
Southland	8	7	0	1	313	212	34
Northland	8	6	0	2	306	132	29
Manawatu	8	6	0	2	240	171	29
Hawke's Bay	8	4	0	4	229	160	23
Bay of Plenty	8	4	0	4	260	243	19
Nelson Bays	8	3	1	4	183	207	19
S Canterbury	8	3	0	5	205	276	15
Thames Valley	8	2	1	6	132	256	12
Wairarapa-Bush	8	0	0	8	186	396	4

Semi-finals: Northland 31, Manawatu 16; Southland 23, Hawke's Bay 11

Final: Southland 12, Northland 6

Division 3	P	W	D	L	F	A	Pts
Marlborough	8	8	0	0	330	120	37
Wanganui	8	7	0	1	190	103	31
Buller	8	5	0	3	148	135	23
Mid-Canterbury	8	4	0	4	166	205	21
Horowhenua	8	4	0	4	174	200	19
North Otago	8	3	0	5	162	206	18
Poverty Bay	8	3	0	5	193	171	16
West Coast	8	2	0	6	121	202	10
East Coast	8	0	0	8	131	272	3

Semi-finals: Wanganui 22, Buller 15; Marlborough 34, Mid-Canterbury 22
Final: Wanganui 22, Marlborough 17

RANFURLY SHIELD

Auckland 88, Poverty Bay 20 (Gisborne); Auckland 30, Bay of Plenty 29 (Auckland); Taranaki 42, Auckland 39 (Auckland); Taranaki 13, North Harbour 11 (New Plymouth); Waikato 40, Taranaki 19 (New Plymouth); Waikato 17, North Harbour 14 (Hamilton); Auckland 27, Waikato 7 (Hamilton); Auckland 69, North Harbour (Auckland)

WESTERN SAMOA TO NEW ZEALAND 1996

THE TOURING PARTY

Manager T Simi **Coach** B G Williams **Assistant Coach** T Salesa
Captain P Lam

FULL-BACKS

V **Patu** (Vaiala)
T **Fa'amasino** (Toshiba, Japan)

THREEQUARTERS

B **Lima** (Auckland, NZ)
A **Telea** (Wellington, NZ)
T **Vaega** (Te Atatu & Southland, NZ)
G **Leaupepe** (Counties & Taranaki, NZ)
K **Tuigamala** (Scopa)
T **Fanolua** (Auckland B, NZ)
*V **Fa'aofo** (Counties & Otago, NZ)
*M **Fatialofa** (Wellington, NZ)

HALF-BACKS

F **Tanoai** (Marist St Joseph's)
T **Samania** (Taranaki, NZ)
J **Filemu** (Wellington, NZ)
T **Nu'uali'itia** (Auckland, NZ)

FORWARDS

T **Leiasamaivao** (Wellington, NZ)
O **Matauiau** (Moataa)
B **Reidy** (Marist St Patrick's & Wellington, NZ)
G **Latu** (Vaimoso)
P **Fatialofa** (Counties, NZ)
L **Falaniko** (Marist St Joseph's)
P **Leavasa** (Hawkes Bay, NZ)
L **Tone** (Vaimoso)
S **Vaifale** (Hawke's Bay, NZ & Mitsubishi, Japan)
S **Kaleta** (Mitsubishi, Japan)
M **Kolomatangi** (Waitemata)
S **Tiatia** (Taranaki, NZ)
P R **Lam** (North Harbour & Canterbury, NZ)
S **Smith** (North Harbour, NZ)
*S **Ta'ala** (Wellington, NZ)
*R **Ale** (Marist St Joseph's)

Replacement during tour

TOUR RECORD

All matches Played 7 Won 4 Lost 3 Points for 162 Against 206
International match Played 1 Lost 1 Points for 10 Against 51

SCORING DETAILS

All matches				International match			
For:	21T 12C 11PG		162 Pts	For:	1T 1C 1PG		10 Pts
Against:	26T 14C 14PG 2DG		206 Pts	Against:	7T 5C 1PG 1DG		51 Pts

MATCH DETAILS

1996	OPPONENTS	VENUE	RESULT
26 May	Wellington	Wellington	L 30-52
29 May	Counties	Pukekohe	W 31-19
1 June	Taranaki	New Plymouth	W 26-18
3 June	Wairarapa-Bush	Masterton	W 23-18
7 June	NEW ZEALAND	Napier	L 10-51
11 June	King Country	Taupo	W 27-20
14 June	NZ Maoris	Auckland	L 15-28

MATCH 1 26 May, Wellington

Wellington 52 (5G 4PG 1T) **Western Samoa XV 30** (2G 2PG 2T)
Wellington: Scorers *Tries:* Cavubati (2), Rolleston (2), Byers, Feaunati *Conversions:* Preston (5) *Penalty Goals:* Preston (4)

Western Samoa XV: Scorers *Tries:* Patu, Telea, Lima, Fanolua
Conversions: Samania (2) *Penalty Goals:* Samania (2)

MATCH 2   29 May, Pukekohe Stadium

Counties 19 (3PG 2T)   **Western Samoa XV 31** (3G 2T)
Counties: Scorers *Tries:* Alatini, Brain *Penalty Goals:* Lowe (3)
Western Samoa XV: Scorers *Tries:* Lima (2), Filemu, Fa'amasino, pen try
Conversions: Tanaoi (3)

MATCH 3   1 June, Rugby Park, New Plymouth

Taranaki 18 (1G 2PG, 1T)   **Western Samoa XV 26** (3G 1T)
Taranaki: Scorers *Tries:* Whiting, Patterson *Conversion:* Lilley
Penalty Goals: Lilley (2)
Western Samoa XV: Scorers *Tries:* Samania, Lima, Filemu, Lam
Conversions: Tanoai (3)

MATCH 4   3 June, Memorial Park, Masterton

Wairarapa-Bush 18 (1PG 3T)   **Western Samoa XV 23** (1G 2PG 2T)
Wairarapa-Bush: Scorers *Tries:* Beales (2), Sullivan *Penalty Goal:* Carroll
Western Samoa XV: Scorers *Tries:* M Fatialofa, Fanoloa, Lam *Conversion:*
Tanoai *Penalty Goals:* Tanoai (2)

MATCH 5   7 June, McLean Park, Napier   Test Match
NEW ZEALAND 51 (5G 1PG 1DG 2T)   WESTERN SAMOA 10 (1G 1PG)

NEW ZEALAND: C M Cullen (Manawatu); J W Wilson (Otago), F E Bunce
(North Harbour), S J McLeod (Waikato), J T Lomu (Counties); A P Mehrtens
(Canterbury), J W Marshall (Canterbury); C W Dowd (Auckland),
S B T Fitzpatrick (Auckland) (*capt*), O M Brown (Auckland); I D Jones (North
Harbour), R M Brooke (Auckland); M N Jones (Auckland), Z V Brooke
(Auckland), J A Kronfeld (Otago)
Scorers *Tries:* Cullen (3), Wilson, McLeod, Marshall, Brown
Conversions: Mehrtens (5) *Penalty Goal:* Mehrtens *Dropped Goal:* Mehrtens
WESTERN SAMOA: Fa'amasino; Lima, Vaega, Leaupepe, Telea; Filemu,
Nu'uali'itia; Reidy, Leiasamaivao, P Fatialofa, Leavasa, Falaniko, Kaleta, Lam
(*capt*), Vaifale *Replacements* Samania for Fa'amasino (50 mins), Fanolua for Vaega
(55 mins)
Scorers *Try:* Telea *Conversion:* Fa'amasino *Penalty Goal:* Fa'amasino
Referee T Henning (South Africa)

MATCH 6   11 June, Owen Delaney Park, Taupo

King Country 20 (2G 1PG 1DG)   **Western Samoa XV 27** (1G 5PG 1T)
King Country: Scorers *Tries:* Graham, Anglesey *Conversions:* Blank (2)
Penalty Goal: Blank *Dropped Goal:* Blank
Western Samoa XV: Scorers *Tries:* Ale, Ta'ala *Conversion:* Samania
Penalty Goals: Samania (4), Tanoai

MATCH 7   14 June, Ericsson Stadium, Auckland

New Zealand Maoris 28 (1G 2PG 3T)   **Western Samoa XV 15** (1G 1PG 1T)
NZ Maoris: Scorers Brain (2), M Going, Brown *Conversion:* Brown
Penalty Goals: Brown (2)
Western Samoa XV: Scorers *Tries:* Telea, Filemu *Conversion:* Samania
Penalty Goal: Samania

NEW ZEALAND TO SOUTH AFRICA 1996

THE TOURING PARTY

Manager M Banks   **Coach** J Hart   **Assistant Coaches** R Cooper G Hunter
Captain S B T Fitzpatrick

FULL-BACKS

M J A Cooper (Waikato)
C M Cullen (Manawatu)

THREEQUARTERS

J T Lomu (Counties)
G M Osborne (North Harbour)
E J Rush (North Harbour)
J W Wilson (Otago)
F E Bunce (North Harbour)
A Ieremia (Wellington)
W K Little (North Harbour)
J T F Matson (Canterbury
S J McLeod (Waikato)

HALF-BACKS

S D Culhane (Southland)
A P Mehrtens (Canterbury)
C J Spencer (Auckland)
J W Marshall (Canterbury)
J P Preston (Wellington)
O F J Tonu'u (Auckland)

FORWARDS

M R Allen (Taranaki)
C K Barrell (Canterbury)
O M Brown (Auckland)
P H Coffin (King Country)
C W Dowd (Auckland)
S B T Fitzpatrick (Auckland)
N J Hewitt (Southland)
A D Oliver (Otago)
R M Brooke (Auckland)
I D Jones (North Harbour)
B P Larsen (North Harbour)
G L Taylor (Northland)
T J Blackadder (Canterbury)
A Blowers (Auckland)
C S Davis (Manawatu)
M N Jones (Auckland)
J A Kronfeld (Otago)
Z V Brooke (Auckland)
T Randell (Otago)

TOUR RECORD

All matches   Played 7   Won 5   Drawn 1   Lost 1   Points for 190   Against 139
International matches   Played 3   Won 2   Lost 1   Points for 78   Against 77

SCORING DETAILS

All matches
For: 24T 14C 13PG 1DG   190 Pts
Against: 14T 9C 17PG   139 Pts

International matches
For: 9T 6C 6PG 1DG   78 Pts
Against: 7T 3C 12PG   77 Pts

MATCH DETAILS

DATE	OPPONENTS	VENUE	RESULT
6 Aug	Boland Invitation XV	Worcester	W 32-21
13 Aug	Eastern Province	Port Elizabeth	W 31-23
17 Aug	SOUTH AFRICA	Durban	W 23-19
20 Aug	Western Transvaal	Potchefstroom	W 31-0
24 Aug	SOUTH AFRICA	Pretoria	W 33-26
27 Aug	Griqualand West	Kimberley	D 18-18
31 Aug	SOUTH AFRICA	Johannesburg	L 22-32

MATCH 1   6 August, Esselenpark, Worcester

Boland Invitation XV 21 (3G)   **New Zealand XV 32** (3G 2PG 1T)
Boland Invitation XV: M Goosen; F Horn, M Moolman, M Bayly (*capt*),
B Paulse; P O'Neil, P Roux; P Marais, D Santon, C Visagie; J Trytsman,
J Swanepoel; J Coetzee, R Nelson, H de Kock *Replacements* M Hendriks for Paulse
(57 mins), V Wium for Coetzee (63 mins)
Scorers *Tries:* Moolman, Paulse, O'Neil   *Conversions:* Horn (3)

New Zealand XV: Cooper; Osborne, McLeod, Ieremia, Rush; Culhane, Tonu'u; Allen, Hewitt, Barrell; Larsen, Taylor; Blackadder, Randell (*capt*), Blowers
Replacement Davis for Larsen (67 mins)
Scorers *Tries:* McLeod, Tonu'u, Blowers, Larsen   *Conversions:* Culhane (3)
Penalty Goals: Culhane (2)
Referee C Spannenberg (Western Province)

MATCH 2   13 August, Boet Erasmus Stadium, Port Elizabeth

Eastern Province 23 (2G 3PG)   **New Zealand XV 31** (1G 3PG 3T)
Eastern Province: B Kruger; D Marshall, R Potgieter, R Fourie, H Pedro; R van Jaarsveld, C Alcock; M van der Merwe, J Kirsten, W Meyer; E van der Bergh, C du Plessis; F Tiema, A Vos (*capt*), M Wood *Replacement* A Fourie for van Jaarsveld (48 mins)
Scorers *Tries:* R Fourie, Kirsten   *Conversions:* Kruger (2)
Penalty Goals: Kruger (3)
New Zealand XV: Cooper; Rush, Matson, McLeod, Lomu; Spencer, Preston; Allen, Oliver, Coffin; Larsen, Taylor; Blackadder, Randell (*capt*), Blowers
Scorers *Tries:* Cooper (2), Lomu, Preston   *Conversion:* Preston
Penalty Goals: Preston (2), Cooper
Referee S Neethling (Boland)

MATCH 3   17 August, King's Park, Durban   1st Test
SOUTH AFRICA 19 (1G 4PG)   NEW ZEALAND 23 (1G 2PG 2T)

SOUTH AFRICA: A J Joubert (Natal); J Swart (Western Province), A H Snyman (Northern Transvaal), D van Schalkwyk (Northern Transvaal), P Hendriks (Transvaal); J T Stransky (Western Province), J P Roux (Transvaal); J P du Randt (Free State), H Tromp (Northern Transvaal), M H Hurter (Northern Transvaal); M G Andrews (Natal), J J Strydom (Transvaal); R J Kruger (Northern Transvaal), G H Teichmann (Natal) (*capt*), A G Venter (Free State) *Replacements* N V Cilliers (Western Province) for Stransky (temp 1-7 mins), J H van der Westhuizen for Roux (75 mins), J J Wiese for Strydom (75 mins)
Scorers *Try:* van Schalkwyk   *Conversion:* Stransky   *Penalty Goals:* Stransky (4)
NEW ZEALAND: Cullen; Wilson, Bunce, Little, Osborne; Culhane, Marshall; Dowd, Fitzpatrick (*capt*), Brown; I Jones, R Brooke; M Jones, Z Brooke, Kronfeld
Scorers *Tries:* Cullen, Wilson, Z Brooke   *Conversion:* Culhane
Penalty Goals: Culhane (2)
Referee P Thomas (France)

MATCH 4   20 August, Olen Park, Potchefstroom

Western Transvaal 0   New Zealand XV 31 (3G 2T)
Western Transvaal: D Basson; W Lourens, F Heymans, T Lincoln, C Bensch; A J de Jager, E Hare (*capt*); A Coetzer, L Boshoff, R Peddar; L Swart, G Laufs; R Ferreira, K Tromp, J Beukes *Replacements* T Hendriks for Peddar (40 mins), H van der Merwe for Coezter (40 mins), R Mitchell for Boshoff (52 mins), D P Swart for Basson (66 mins)
New Zealand XV: Cooper; Rush, Matson, Ieremia, Lomu; Spencer, Tonu'u; Allen, Hewitt, Coffin; Larsen, Taylor; Davis, Randell (*capt*), Blowers
Replacements Oliver for Hewitt (64 mins), Blackadder for Blowers (66 mins)
Scorers *Tries:* Cooper, Rush, Iremia, Spencer, Tonu'u   *Conversions:* Cooper (3)
Referee A Watson (Eastern Transvaal)

MATCH 5   24 August, Loftus Versfeld, Pretoria   2nd Test
SOUTH AFRICA 26 (1G 3PG 2T)   NEW ZEALAND 33 (3G 3PG 1DG)

SOUTH AFRICA: A J Joubert (Natal); J Swart (Western Province), A H Snyman (Northern Transvaal), D van Schalkwyk (Northern Transvaal), P Hendriks (Transvaal); J T Stransky (Western Province), J H van der Westhuizen (Northern Transvaal); J P du Randt (Free State), H Tromp (Northern Transvaal), M H Hurter (Northern Transvaal); M G Andrews (Natal), J J Strydom (Transvaal); R J Kruger (Northern Transvaal), G Teichmann (Natal) (*capt*), A G Venter (Free State) *Replacements* J J Wiese (Transvaal) for Strydom (27 mins), J Dalton (Transvaal) for Tromp (65 mins), W Fyvie (Natal) for Teichmann (72 mins) **Scorers** *Tries:* van der Westhuizen, Kruger, Strydom   *Conversion:* Stransky *Penalty Goals:* Stransky (3)
NEW ZEALAND: Cullen; Wilson, Bunce, Little, Osborne; Culhane, Marshall; Dowd, Fitzpatrick (*capt*), Brown; I Jones, R Brooke; M Jones, Z Brooke, Kronfeld *Replacements* Preston for Culhane (63 mins), Blowers for Kronfeld (72 mins), Larsen for I Jones (72 mins)
Scorers *Tries:* Wilson (2), Z Brooke   *Conversions:* Culhane (3) *Penalty Goals:* Preston (2), Culhane   *Dropped Goal:* Z Brooke
Referee D Méné (France)

MATCH 6   **27 August, Hoffepark, Kimberley**

Griqualand West 18 (1G 2PG 1T)   **New Zealand XV 18** (1G 2PG 1T)
Griqualand West: B Wessels; L van der Wath, A Vermeulen, T de Jager, I Horn; F Smith, A Pretorius; D W Venter, A Bester (*capt*), P Bester; M Cloete, A Cloete; T Oosthuizen, P Smit, G Watts *Replacements* L Venter for de Jager (49 mins), S Engelbrecht for Smit (40 mins), D Bosman for Engelbrecht (75 mins)
Scorers *Tries:* van der Wath, A Cloete   *Conversion:* Wessels *Penalty Goals:* Wessels (2)
New Zealand XV: Cooper; Rush, McLeod, Ieremia, Lomu; Preston, Tonu'u; Allen, Hewitt, Barrell; Larsen, Taylor; Blackadder, Randell (*capt*), Blowers *Replacements* Osborne for Lomu (40 mins), Coffin for Barrell (65 mins)
Scorers *Tries:* McLeod, Osborne   *Conversion:* Preston   *Penalty Goals:* Preston (2)
Referee T Henning (Northern Transvaal)

MATCH 7   31 August, Ellis Park, Johannesburg   3rd Test
SOUTH AFRICA 32 (1G 5PG 2T)   NEW ZEALAND 22 (2G 1PG 1T)

SOUTH AFRICA: A J Joubert (Natal); J Swart (Western Province), J C Mulder (Transvaal), D van Schalkwyk (Northern Transvaal), P Hendriks (Transvaal); H W Honiball (Natal), J H van der Westhuizen (Northern Transvaal); D Theron (Griquland West), J Dalton (Transvaal), M H Hurter (Northern Transvaal); M G Andrews (Natal), J J Wiese (Transvaal); R J Kruger (Northern Transvaal), G Teichmann (Natal) (*capt*), A G Venter (Free State) *Replacements* F J van Heerden (Western Province) for Andrews (39 mins), J T Stransky (Western Province) for Mulder (47 mins), G L Pagel (Western Province) for Theron (66 mins), W Fyvie (Natal) for Venter (74 mins)
Scorers *Tries:* van der Westhuizen (2), Joubert   *Conversion:* Honiball *Penalty Goals:* Joubert (3), Honiball (2)
NEW ZEALAND: Cullen; Wilson, Bunce, Little, Osborne; Mehrtens, Marshall; Dowd, Fitzpatrick (*capt*), Brown; I Jones, R Brooke; M Jones, Z Brooke, Kronfeld *Replacements* Taylor for M Jones (52 mins), Ieremia for Cullen (69 mins)
Scorers *Tries:* Little, Marshall, Fitzpatrick   *Conversions:* Mehrtens (2) *Penalty Goal:* Mehrtens
Referee W D Bevan (Wales)

NEW ZEALAND BARBARIANS TO ENGLAND 1996

THE TOURING PARTY

Manager M Banks   **Coach** J Hart   **Assistant Coach** P Sloane
Captain S B T Fitzpatrick

FULL-BACK

C M Cullen (Manawatu)

THREEQUARTERS

G M Osborne (North Harbour)
A Ieremia (Wellington)
M Ranby (Manawatu)
L Stensness (Auckland)

HALF-BACKS

C J Spencer (Auckland)
A P Mehrtens (Canterbury)
J W Marshall (Canterbury)
M Robinson (North Harbour)

FORWARDS

S B T Fitzpatrick (Auckland)
A D Oliver (Otago)
M R Allen (Taranaki)
M Collins (Waikato)
O M Brown (Auckland)
R M Brooke (Auckland)
I D Jones (North Harbour)
G L Taylor (Northland)
D G Mika (Auckland)
A Blowers (Auckland)
M N Jones (Auckland)
T Randell (Otago)
C S Davis (Manawatu)

MATCH 1   24 November, McAlpine Stadium, Huddersfield

North Division 0   NZ Barbarians 86 (8G 6T)
North Division: P Massey (Wakefield); R Thompson (Wakefield), J Harper (Rotherham), D Lyon (Orrell), G Anderton (Wakefield); S Binns (Rotherham), D Scully (Wakefield) (*capt*); M Worsley (Orrell), T Garnett (Wakefield), S Turner (Orrell); P Rees (Orrell), P Stewart (Wakefield); P Manley (Wakefield), J Dudley (Rotherham), P Anglesea (Orrell) *Replacements* A Ludiman (Harrogate) for Stewart (57 mins), R Latham (Wakefield) for Worsley (62 mins), C Lee (West Hartlepool) for Harper (67 mins), S Burnhill (Rotherham) for Anderton (69 mins)
NZ Barbarians: Cullen; Osborne, Ieremia, Stensness, Lomu; Spencer, Marshall; Allen, Fitzpatrick (*capt*), Brown; Taylor, R Brooke; Mika, Randell, Blowers *Replacements* Vidiri for Osborne (41 mins), Mehrtens for Cullen (44 mins), I Jones for Taylor (66 mins), Robinson for Ieremia (68 mins)
Scorers *Tries:* Randell, Brown, Blowers (3), Mika, Cullen (2), Vidiri (3), Spencer, Brooke, Robinson   *Conversions:* Spencer (7), Mehrtens
Referee P Adams (Wales)

MATCH 2   30 November, Twickenham

ENGLAND XV 19 (3PG 2T)   **NZ BARBARIANS 34** (1G 4PG 3T)
ENGLAND XV: T R G Stimpson (Newcastle); J M Sleightholme (Bath), W D C Carling (Harlequins), P R de Glanville (Bath) (*capt*), A A Adebayo (Bath); M J Catt (Bath), A C T Gomarsall (Wasps); G C Rowntree (Leicester), M P Regan (Bristol), J Leonard (Harlequins); M O Johnson (Leicester), S D Shaw (Bristol); T A K Rodber (Northampton), C M A Sheasby (Wasps), L B N Dallaglio (Wasps)
Scorers *Tries:* Sleightholme, Stimpson   *Penalty Goals:* Catt (3)
NEW ZEALAND BARBARIANS: Cullen; Vidiri, Ieremia, Stensness, Lomu; Mehrtens, J Marshall; Allen, Fitzpatrick (*capt*), Brown; I Jones, R Brooke; Jones, Randell, Blowers *Replacements* Mika (Auckland) for Randell (56 mins), Spencer for Mehrtens (60 mins), Osborne for Vidiri (80 mins)
Scorers *Tries:* Brooke, Blowers, Spencer, Vidiri   *Conversion:* Spencer
Penalty Goals: Mehrtens (2), Spencer (2)
Referee C Thomas (Wales)

NEW ZEALAND INTERNATIONAL PLAYERS
(up to 30 April 1997)

Abbott, H L (Taranaki) 1906 F
Aitken, G G (Wellington) 1921 SA 1,2
Allen, F R (Auckland) 1946 A 1,2, 1947 A 1,2, 1949 SA 1,2
Allen, M R (Taranaki) 1993 WS (t), 1996 S 2 (t)
Allen, N H (Counties) 1980 A 3, W
Alley, G T (Canterbury) 1928 SA 1,2,3
Anderson, A (Canterbury) 1983 S, E, 1984 A 1,2,3, 1987 [F]
Anderson, B L (Wairarapa-Bush) 1986 A 1
Archer, W R (Otago, Southland) 1955 A 1,2, 1956 SA 1,3
Argus, W G (Canterbury) 1946 A 1,2, 1947 A 1,2
Arnold, D A (Canterbury) 1963 I, W, 1964 E, F
Arnold, K D (Waikato) 1947 A 1,2
Ashby, D L (Southland) 1958 A 2
Asher, A A (Auckland) 1903 A
Ashworth, B G (Auckland) 1978 A 1,2
Ashworth, J C (Canterbury, Hawke's Bay) 1978 A 1,2,3, 1980 A 1,2,3, 1981 SA 1,2,3, 1982 A 1,2, 1983 BI 1,2,3,4, A, 1984 F 1,2, A 1,2,3, 1985 E 1,2, A
Atkinson, H (West Coast) 1913 A 1
Avery, H E (Wellington) 1910 A 1,2,3

Bachop, G T M (Canterbury) 1989 W, I, 1990 S 1,2, A 1,2,3, F 1,2, 1991 Arg 1,2, A 1,2, [E, US, C, A, S], 1992 Wld 1, 1994 SA 1,2,3, A, 1995 C, [I, W, S, E, SA], A 1,2
Bachop, S J (Otago) 1994 F 2, SA 1,2,3, A
Badeley, C E O (Auckland) 1921 SA 1,2
Baird, J A S (Otago) 1913 A 2
Ball, N (Wellington) 1931 A, 1932 A 2,3, 1935 W, 1936 E
Barrett, J (Auckland) 1913 A 2,3
Barry, E F (Wellington) 1934 A 2
Barry, L J (North Harbour) 1995 F 2
Batty, G B (Wellington, Bay of Plenty) 1972 W, S, 1973 E 1, I, F, E 2, 1974 A 1,3, I, 1975 S, 1976 SA 1,2,3,4, 1977 BI 1
Batty, W (Auckland) 1930 BI 1,3,4, 1931 A
Beatty, G E (Taranaki) 1950 BI 1
Bell, R H (Otago) 1951 A 3, 1952 A 1,2
Bellis, E A (Wanganui) 1921 SA 1,2,3
Bennet, R (Otago) 1905 A
Berghan, T (Otago) 1938 A 1,2,3
Berry, M J (Wairarapa-Bush) 1986 A 3 (R)
Bevan, V D (Wellington) 1949 A 1,2, 1950 BI 1,2,3,4
Birtwistle, W M (Canterbury) 1965 SA 1,2,3,4, 1967 E, W, S
Black, J E (Canterbury) 1977 F 1, 1979 A, 1980 A 3
Black, N W (Auckland) 1949 SA 3
Black, R S (Otago) 1914 A 1
Blake, A W (Wairarapa) 1949 A 1
Blowers, A F (Auckland) 1996 SA 2 (R), 4 (R)
Boggs, E G (Auckland) 1946 A 2, 1949 SA 1
Bond, J G (Canterbury) 1949 A 2
Booth, E E (Otago) 1906 F, 1907 A 1,3
Boroevich, K G (Wellington) 1986 F 1, A 1, F 3 (R)
Botica, F M (North Harbour) 1986 F 1, A 1,2,3, F 2,3, 1989 Arg 1 (R)
Bowden, N J G (Taranaki) 1952 A 2
Bowers, R G (Wellington) 1954 I, F
Bowman, A W (Hawke's Bay) 1938 A 1,2,3
Braid, G J (Bay of Plenty) 1983 S, E
Bremner, S G (Auckland, Canterbury) 1952 A 2, 1956 SA 2
Brewer, M R (Otago, Canterbury) 1986 F 1, A 1,2,3, F 2,3, 1988 A 1, 1989 A, W, I, 1990 S 1,2, A 1,2,3, 1992 I 2, A 1, 1994 F 1,2, SA 1,2,3, A, 1995 C, [I, W, E, SA], A 1,2
Briscoe, K C (Taranaki) 1959 BI 2, 1960 SA 1,2,3,4, 1963 I, W, 1964 E, S
Brooke, R M (Auckland) 1992 I 2, A 1,2,3, SA, 1993 BI 1,2,3, A, WS, 1994 SA 2,3, 1995 C, [J, S, E, SA], A 1,2, It, F 1,2, 1996 WS, S 1, 2, A 1, SA 1, A 2, SA 2,3,4,5

Brooke, Z V (Auckland) 1987 [Arg], 1989 Arg 2 (R), 1990 A 1,2,3, F 1 (R), 1991 Arg 2, A 1,2, [E, It, C, A, S], 1992 A 2,3, SA, 1993 BI 1,2,3 (R), WS (R), S, E, 1994 F 2, SA 1,2,3, A, 1995 [J, S, E, SA], A 1,2, It, F 1,2, 1996 WS, S 1,2 A 1, SA 1, A 2, SA 2,3,4,5
Brooke-Cowden, M (Auckland) 1986 F 1, A 1, 1987 [W]
Brown, C (Taranaki) 1913 A 2,3
Brown, O M (Auckland) 1992 I 2, A 1,2,3, SA, 1993 BI 1,2,3, A, S, E, 1994 F 1,2, SA 1,2,3, A, 1995 C, [I, W, S, E, SA], A 1,2, It, F 1,2, 1996 WS, S 1,2, A 1, SA 1, A 2, SA 2,3,4,5
Brown, R H (Taranaki) 1955 A 3, 1956 SA 1,2,3,4, 1957 A 1,2, 1958 A 1,2,3, 1959 BI 1,3, 1961 F 1,2,3, 1962 A 1
Brownlie, C J (Hawke's Bay) 1924 W, 1925 E, F
Brownlie, M J (Hawke's Bay) 1924 I, W, 1925 E, F, 1928 SA 1,2,3,4
Bruce, J A (Auckland) 1914 A 1,2
Bruce, O D (Canterbury) 1976 SA 1,2,4, 1977 BI 2,3,4, F 1,2, 1978 A 1,2, I, W, E, S
Bryers, R F (King Country) 1949 A 1
Budd, T A (Southland) 1946 A 2, 1949 A 2
Bullock-Douglas, G A H (Wanganui) 1932 A 1,2,3, 1934 A 1,2
Bunce, F E (North Harbour) 1992 Wld 1,2,3, I 1,2, A 1,2,3, SA, 1993 BI 1,2,3, A, WS, S, E, 1994 F 1,2, SA 1,2,3, A, 1995 C, [I, W, S, E, SA], A 1,2, It, F 1,2, 1996 WS, S 1,2, A1, SA 1, A 2, SA 2,3,4,5
Burgess, G A J (Auckland) 1981 SA 2
Burgess, G F (Southland) 1905 A
Burgess, R E (Manawatu) 1971 BI 1,2,3, 1972 A 3, W, 1973 I, F
Burke, P S (Taranaki) 1955 A 1, 1957 A 1,2
Burns, P J (Canterbury) 1908 AW 2, 1910 A 1,2,3, 1913 A 3
Bush, R G (Otago) 1931 A
Bush, W K (Canterbury) 1974 A 1,2, 1975 S, 1976 I, SA, 2,4, 1977 BI 2,3,4 (R), 1978 I, W, 1979 A
Buxton, J B (Canterbury) 1955 A 3, 1956 SA 1

Cain, M J (Taranaki) 1913 US, 1914 A 1,2,3
Callesen, J A (Manawatu) 1974 A 1,2,3, 1975 S
Cameron, D (Taranaki) 1908 AW 1,2,3
Cameron, L M (Manawatu) 1980 A 3, 1981 SA 1 (R), 2,3, R
Carleton, S R (Canterbury) 1928 SA 1,2,3, 1929 A 1,2,3
Carrington, K R (Auckland) 1971 BI 1,3,4
Carter, M P (Auckland) 1991 A 2, [It, A]
Casey, S T (Otago) 1905 S, I, E, W, 1907 A 1,2,3, 1908 AW 1
Cashmore, A R (Auckland) 1996 S2 (R)
Catley, E H (Waikato) 1946 A 1, 1947 A 1,2, 1949 SA 1,2,3,4
Caughey, T H C (Auckland) 1932 A 1,3, 1934 A 1,2, 1935 S, I, 1936 E, A 1, 1937 SA 3
Caulton, R W (Wellington) 1959 BI 2,3,4, 1960 SA 1,4, 1961 F 2, 1963 E 1,2, I, W, 1964 E, S, F, A 1,2,3
Cherrington, N P (North Auckland) 1950 BI 1
Christian, D L (Auckland) 1949 SA 4
Clamp, M (Wellington) 1984 A 2,3
Clark, D W (Otago) 1964 A 1,2
Clark, W H (Wellington) 1953 W, 1954 I, E, S, 1955 A 1,2, 1956 SA 3,4
Clarke, A H (Auckland) 1958 A 3, 1959 BI 4, 1960 SA 1
Clarke, D B (Waikato) 1956 SA 3,4, 1957 A 1,2, 1958 A 1,3, 1959 BI 1,2,3,4, 1960 SA 1,2,3,4, 1961 F 1,2,3, 1962 A 1,2,3,4,5, 1963 E 1,2, I, W, 1964 E, S, F, A 2,3
Clarke, E (Auckland) 1992 Wld 2,3, I 1,2, 1993 BI 1,2, S (R), E
Clarke, I J (Waikato) 1953 W, 1955 A 1,2,3, 1956 SA 1,2,3,4, 1957 A 1,2, 1958 A 1,3, 1959 BI 1,2, 1960 SA 2,4, 1961 F 1,2,3, 1962 A 1,2,3, 1963 E 1,2
Clarke, R L (Taranaki) 1932 A 2,3
Cobden, D G (Canterbury) 1937 SA 1
Cockerill, M S (Taranaki) 1951 A 1,2,3

Cockroft, E A P (South Canterbury) 1913 *A* 3, 1914 *A* 2,3

Codlin, B W (Counties) 1980 *A* 1,2,3

Collins, A H (Taranaki) 1932 *A* 2,3, 1934 *A* 1

Collins, J L (Poverty Bay) 1964 *A* 1, 1965 *SA* 1,4

Colman, J T H (Taranaki) 1907 *A* 1,2, 1908 *AW* 1,3

Connor, D M (Auckland) 1961 *F* 1,2,3, 1962 *A* 1,2,3,4,5, 1963 *E* 1,2, 1964 *A* 2,3

Conway, R J (Otago, Bay of Plenty) 1959 *BI* 2,3,4, 1960 *SA* 1,3,4, 1965 *SA* 1,2,3,4

Cooke, A E (Auckland, Wellington) 1924 *I, W*, 1925 *E, F*, 1930 *BI* 1,2,3,4

Cooke, R J (Canterbury) 1903 *A*

Cooksley, M S B (Counties, Waikato) 1992 *Wld* 1, 1993 *BI* 2,3 (R), *A*, 1994 *F* 1,2, *SA* 1,2, *A*

Cooper, G J L (Auckland, Otago) 1986 *F* 1, *A* 1,2, 1992 *Wld* 1,2,3, *I* 1

Cooper, M J A (Waikato) 1992 *I* 2, *SA* (R), 1993 *BI* 1 (R), 3 (t), *WS* (t), *S*, 1994 *F* 1,2

Corner, M M N (Auckland) 1930 *BI* 2,3,4, 1931 *A*, 1934 *A* 1, 1936 *E*

Cossey, R R (Counties) 1958 *A* 1

Cottrell, A I (Canterbury) 1929 *A* 1,2,3, 1930 *BI* 1,2,3,4, 1931 *A*, 1932 *A* 1,2,3

Cottrell, W D (Canterbury) 1968 *A* 1,2, *F* 2,3, 1970 *SA* 1, 1971 *BI* 1,2,3,4

Couch, M B R (Wairarapa) 1947 *A* 1, 1949 *A* 1,2

Coughlan, T D (South Canterbury) 1958 *A* 1

Creighton, J N (Canterbury) 1962 *A* 4

Crichton, S (Wellington) 1983 *S, E*

Cross, T (Canterbury) 1904 *BI*, 1905 *A*

Crowley, K J (Taranaki) 1985 *E* 1,2, *A, Arg* 1,2, 1986 *A* 3, *F* 2,3, 1987 [*Arg*], 1990 *S* 1,2, *A* 1,2,3, *F* 1,2, 1991 *Arg* 1,2, [*A*]

Crowley, P J B (Auckland) 1949 *SA* 3,4, 1950 *BI* 1,2,3,4

Culhane, S D (Southland) 1995 [*J*], *It, F* 1,2, 1996 *SA* 3,4

Cullen C M (Manawatu) 1996 *WS, S* 1,2, *A* 1, *SA* 1, *A* 2, *SA* 2,3,4,5

Cummings, W (Canterbury) 1913 *A* 2,3

Cundy, R T (Wairarapa) 1929 *A* 2 (R)

Cunningham, G R (Auckland) 1979 *A, S, E*, 1980 *A* 1,2

Cunningham, W (Auckland) 1905 *S, I*, 1906 *F*, 1907 *A* 1,2,3, 1908 *AW* 1,2,3

Cupples, L F (Bay of Plenty) 1924 *I, W*

Currie, C J (Canterbury) 1978 *I, W*

Cuthill, J E (Otago) 1913 *A* 1, *US*

Dalley, W C (Canterbury) 1924 *I*, 1928 *SA* 1,2,3,4

Dalton, A G (Counties) 1977 *F* 2, 1978 *A* 1,2,3, *I, W, E, S*, 1979 *F* 1,2, *S*, 1981 *S* 1,2, *SA* 1,2,3, *R, F* 1,2, 1982 *A* 1,2,3, 1983 *BI* 1,2,3,4, *A*, 1984 *F* 1,2, *A* 1,2,3, 1985 *E* 1,2, *A*

Dalton, D (Hawke's Bay) 1935 *I, W*, 1936 *A* 1,2, 1937 *SA* 1,2,3, 1938 *A* 1,2

Dalton, R A (Wellington) 1947 *A* 1,2

Dalzell, G N (Canterbury) 1953 *W*, 1954 *I, E, S, F*

Davie, M G (Canterbury) 1983 *E* (R)

Davies, W A (Auckland, Otago) 1960 *SA* 4, 1962 *A* 4,5, 1955 *A* 2, 1958 *A* 1,2,3

Davis, K (Auckland) 1952 *A* 2, 1953 *W*, 1954 *I, E, S, F*, 1955 *A* 2, 1958 *A* 1,2,3

Davis, L J (Canterbury) 1976 *I*, 1977 *BI* 3,4

Davis, W L (Hawke's Bay) 1967 *A, E, W, F, S*, 1968 *A* 1,2, *F* 1, 1969 *W* 1,2, 1970 *SA* 2

Deans, I B (Canterbury) 1988 *W* 1,2, *A* 1,2,3, 1989 *F* 1,2, *Arg* 1,2, *A*

Deans, R G (Canterbury) 1905 *S, I, E, W*, 1908 *AW* 3

Deans, R M (Canterbury) 1983 *S, E*, 1984 *A* 1 (R), 2,3

Delamore, G W (Wellington) 1949 *SA* 4

Dewar, H (Taranaki) 1913 *A* 1, *US*

Diack, E S (Otago) 1959 *BI* 2

Dick, J (Auckland) 1937 *SA* 1,2, 1938 *A* 3

Dick, M J (Auckland) 1963 *I, W*, 1964 *E, S, F*, 1965 *SA* 3, 1966 *BI* 4, 1967 *A, E, W, F*, 1969 *W* 1,2, 1970 *SA* 1,4

Dixon, M J (Canterbury) 1954 *I, E, S, F*, 1956 *SA* 1,2,3,4, 1957 *A* 1,2

Dobson, R L (Auckland) 1949 *A* 1

Dodd, E H (Wellington) 1905 *A*

Donald, A J (Wanganui) 1983 *S, E*, 1984 *F* 1,2, *A* 1,2,3

Donald, J G (Wairarapa) 1921 *SA* 1,2

Donald, Q (Wairarapa) 1924 *I, W*, 1925 *E, F*

Donaldson, M W (Manawatu) 1977 *F* 1,2, 1978 *A* 1,2,3, *I, E, S*, 1979 *F* 1,2, *A, S* (R), 1981 *SA* 3 (R)

Dougan, J P (Wellington) 1972 *A* 1, 1973 *E* 2

Dowd, C W (Auckland) 1993 *BI* 1,2,3, *A, WS, S, E*, 1994 *SA* 1 (R), 1995 *C*, [*I, W, J, E, SA*], *A* 1,2, *It, F* 1,2, 1996 *WS, S* 1,2, *A* 1, *SA* 1, *A* 2, *SA* 2,3,4,5

Dowd, G W (North Harbour) 1992 *I* 1 (R)

Downing, A J (Auckland) 1913 *A* 1, *US*, 1914 *A* 1,2,3

Drake, J A (Auckland) 1986 *F* 2,3, 1987 [*Fj, Arg, S, W, F*], *A*

Duff, R H (Canterbury) 1951 *A* 1,2,3, 1952 *A* 1,2, 1955 *A* 2,3, 1956 *SA* 1,2,3,4

Duncan, J (Otago) 1903 *A*

Duncan, M G (Hawke's Bay) 1971 *BI* 3 (R), 4

Duncan, W D (Otago) 1921 *SA* 1,2,3

Dunn, E J (North Auckland) 1979 *S*, 1981 *S* 1

Dunn, I T W (North Auckland) 1983 *BI* 1,4, *A*

Dunn, J M (Auckland) 1946 *A* 1

Earl, A T (Canterbury) 1986 *F* 1, *A* 1, *F* 3 (R), 1987 [*Arg*], 1989 *W, I*, 1991 *Arg* 1 (R), 2, *A* 1, [*E* (R), *US, S*], 1992 *A* 2,3 (R)

Eastgate, B P (Canterbury) 1952 *A* 1,2, 1954 *S*

Elliott, K G (Wellington) 1946 *A* 1,2

Ellis, M C G (Otago) 1993 *S, E*, 1995 *C*, [*I* (R), *W, J, S, SA* (R)]

Elsom, A E G (Canterbury) 1952 *A* 1,2, 1953 *W*, 1955 *A* 1,2,3

Elvidge, R R (Otago) 1946 *A* 1,2, 1949 *SA* 1,2,3,4, 1950 *BI* 1,2,3

Erceg, C P (Auckland) 1951 *A* 1,2,3, 1952 *A* 1

Evans, D A (Hawke's Bay) 1910 *A* 2

Eveleigh, K A (Manawatu) 1976 *SA* 2,4, 1977 *BI* 1,2

Fanning, A H N (Canterbury) 1913 *A* 3

Fanning, B J (Canterbury) 1903 *A*, 1904 *BI*

Farrell, C P (Auckland) 1977 *BI* 1,2

Fawcett, C L (Auckland) 1976 *SA* 2,3

Fea, W R (Otago) 1921 *SA* 3

Finlay, B E L (Manawatu) 1959 *BI* 1

Finlay, J (Manawatu) 1946 *A* 1

Finlayson, I (North Auckland) 1928 *SA* 1,2,3,4, 1930 *BI* 1,2

Fitzgerald, J T (Wellington) 1952 *A* 1

Fitzpatrick, B B J (Wellington) 1953 *W*, 1954 *I, F*

Fitzpatrick, S B T (Auckland) 1986 *F* 1, *A* 1, *F* 2,3, 1987 [*It, Fj, Arg, S, W, F*], *A*, 1988 *W* 1,2, *A* 1,2,3, 1989 *F* 1,2, *Arg* 1,2, *A, W, I*, 1990 *S* 1,2, *A* 1,2,3, *F* 1,2, 1991 *Arg* 1,2, *A* 1,2, [*E, US, It, C, A, S*], 1992 *Wld* 1,2,3, *I* 1,2, *A* 1,2,3, *SA*, 1993 *BI* 1,2,3, *A, WS, S, E*, 1994 *F* 1,2, *SA* 1,2,3, *A*, 1995 *C*, [*I, W, S, E, SA*], *A* 1,2, *It, F* 1,2, 1996 *WS, S* 1,2, *A* 1, *SA* 1, *A* 2, *SA* 2,3,4,5

Fleming, J K (Wellington) 1979 *S, E*, 1980 *A* 1,2,3

Fletcher, C J C (North Auckland) 1921 *SA* 3

Fogarty, R (Taranaki) 1921 *A* 1,3

Ford, B R (Marlborough) 1977 *BI* 3,4, 1978 *I*, 1979 *E*

Forster, S T (Otago) 1993 *S, E*, 1994 *F* 1,2, 1995 *It, F* 1

Fox, G J (Auckland) 1985 *Arg* 1, 1987 [*It, Fj, Arg, S, W, F*], *A*, 1988 *W* 1,2, *A* 1,2,3, 1989 *F* 1,2, *Arg* 1,2, *A, W, I*, 1990 *S* 1,2, *A* 1,2,3, *F* 1,2, 1991 *Arg* 1,2, *A* 1,2, [*E, It, C, A*], 1992 *Wld* 1,2 (R), *A* 1,2,3, *SA*, 1993 *BI* 1,2,3, *A, WS*

Francis, A R H (Auckland) 1905 *A*, 1907 *A* 1,2,3, 1908 *AW* 1,2,3, 1910 *A* 1,2,3

Francis, W C (Wellington) 1913 *A* 2,3, 1914 *A* 1,2,3

Fraser, B G (Wellington) 1979 *S, E*, 1980 *A* 3, *W*, 1981 *S* 1,2, *SA* 1,2,3, *R, F* 1,2, 1982 *A* 1,2,3, 1983 *BI* 1,2,3,4, *A, S, E*, 1984 *A* 1

Frazer, H F (Hawke's Bay) 1946 *A* 1,2, 1947 *A* 1,2, 1949 *SA* 2

Fryer, F C (Canterbury) 1907 *A* 1,2,3, 1908 *AW* 2

Fuller, W B (Canterbury) 1910 *A* 1,2

Furlong, B D M (Hawke's Bay) 1970 *SA* 4

Gallagher, J A (Wellington) 1987 [*It, Fj, S, W, F*], *A*, 1988 *W* 1,2, *A* 1,2,3, 1989 *F* 1,2, *Arg* 1,2, *A, W, I*

Gallaher, D (Auckland) 1903 *A*, 1904 *BI*, 1905 *S, E, W*, 1906 *F*

Gard, P C (North Otago) 1971 *BI* 4

Gardiner, A J (Taranaki) 1974 *A* 3

Geddes, J H (Southland) 1929 *A* 1

Geddes, W McK (Auckland) 1913 *A* 2

Gemmell, B McL (Auckland) 1974 *A* 1,2

George, V L (Southland) 1938 *A* 1,2,3

Gilbert, G D M (West Coast) 1935 *S, I, W*, 1936 *E*

Gillespie, C T (Wellington) 1913 *A* 2

Gillespie, W D (Otago) 1958 *A* 3

The New Zealander Christian Cullen is caught by Jeff Roff during the New Zealand-Australia international at Athletic Park, Wellington.

Gillett, G A (Canterbury, Auckland) 1905 *S, I, E, W,* 1907 *A* 2,3, 1908 *AW* 1,3
Gillies, C C (Otago) 1936 *A* 2
Gilray, C M (Otago) 1905 *A*
Glasgow, F T (Taranaki, Southland) 1905 *S, I, E, W,* 1906 *F,* 1908 *AW* 3
Glenn, W S (Taranaki) 1904 *BI,* 1906 *F*
Goddard, M P (South Canterbury) 1946 *A* 2, 1947 *A* 1,2, 1949 *SA* 3,4
Going, S M (North Auckland) 1967 *A, F,* 1968 *F* 3, 1969 *W* 1,2, 1970 *SA* 1 (R), 4, 1971 *BI* 1,2,3,4, 1972 *A* 1,2,3, *W, S,* 1973 *E* 1, *I, F, E* 2, 1974 *I,* 1975 *S,* 1976 *I* (R), *SA* 1,2,3,4, 1977 *BI* 1,2
Gordon, S B (Waikato) 1993 *S, E*
Graham, D J (Canterbury) 1958 *A* 1,2, 1960 *SA* 2,3, 1961 *F* 1,2,3, 1962 *A* 1,2,3,4,5, 1963 *E* 1,2, *I, W,* 1964 *E, S, F, A* 1,2,3
Graham, J B (Otago) 1913 *US,* 1914 *A* 1,3

Graham, W G (Otago) 1979 *F* 1 (R)
Grant, L A (South Canterbury) 1947 *A* 1,2, 1949 *SA* 1,2
Gray, G D (Canterbury) 1908 *AW* 2, 1913 *A* 1, *US*
Gray, K F (Wellington) 1963 *I, W,* 1964 *E, S, F, A* 1,2,3, 1965 *SA* 1,2,3,4, 1966 *BI* 1,2,3,4, 1967 *W, F, S,* 1968 *A* 1, *F* 2,3, 1969 *W* 1,2
Gray, W N (Bay of Plenty) 1955 *A* 2,3, 1956 *SA* 1,2,3,4
Green, C I (Canterbury) 1983 *S* (R), *E,* 1984 *A* 1,2,3, 1985 *E* 1,2, *A, Arg* 1,2, 1986 *A* 2,3, *F* 2,3, 1987 [*It, Fj, S, W, F*], *A*
Grenside, B A (Hawke's Bay) 1928 *SA* 1,2,3,4, 1929 *A* 2,3
Griffiths, J L (Wellington) 1934 *A* 2, 1935 *S, I, W,* 1936 *A* 1,2, 1938 *A* 3
Guy, R A (North Auckland) 1971 *BI* 1,2,3,4

Haden, A M (Auckland) 1977 *BI* 1,2,3,4, *F* 1,2, 1978 *A* 1,2,3, *I, W, E, S,* 1979 *F* 1,2, *A, S, E,* 1980 *A* 1,2,3, *W,*

1981 *S* 2, *SA* 1,2,3, *R, F* 1,2, 1982 *A* 1,2,3, 1983 *BI* 1,2,3,4, *A*, 1984 *F* 1,2, 1985 *Arg* 1,2
Hadley, S (Auckland) 1928 *SA* 1,2,3,4
Hadley, W E (Auckland) 1934 *A* 1,2, 1935 *S, I, W*, 1936 *E, A* 1,2
Haig, J S (Otago) 1946 *A* 1,2
Haig, L S (Otago) 1950 *BI* 2,3,4, 1951 *A* 1,2,3, 1953 *W*, 1954 *E, S*
Hales, D A (Canterbury) 1972 *A* 1,2,3, *W*
Hamilton, D C (Southland) 1908 *AW* 2
Hammond, I A (Marlborough) 1952 *A* 2
Harper, E T (Canterbury) 1904 *BI*, 1906 *F*
Harris, P C (Manawatu) 1976 *SA* 3
Hart, A H (Taranaki) 1924 *I*
Hart, G F (Canterbury) 1930 *BI* 1,2,3,4, 1931 *A*, 1934 *A* 1, 1935 *S, I, W*, 1936 *A* 1,2
Harvey, B A (Wairarapa-Bush) 1986 *F* 1
Harvey, I H (Wairarapa) 1928 *SA* 4
Harvey, L R (Otago) 1949 *SA* 1,2,3,4, 1950 *BI* 1,2,3,4
Harvey, P (Canterbury) 1904 *BI*
Hasell, E W (Canterbury) 1913 *A* 2,3
Hayward, H O (Auckland) 1908 *AW* 3
Hazlett, E J (Southland) 1966 *BI* 1,2,3,4, 1967 *A, E*
Hazlett, W E (Southland) 1928 *SA* 1,2,3,4, 1930 *BI* 1,2,3,4
Heeps, T R (Wellington) 1962 *A* 1,2,3,4,5
Heke, W R (North Auckland) 1929 *A* 1,2,3
Hemi, R C (Waikato) 1953 *W*, 1954 *I, E, S, F*, 1955 *A* 1,2,3, 1956 *SA* 1,3,4, 1957 *A* 1,2, 1959 *BI* 1,3,4
Henderson, P (Wanganui) 1949 *SA* 1,2,3,4, 1950 *BI* 2,3,4
Henderson, P W (Otago) 1991 *Arg* 1, [*C*], 1992 *Wld* 1,2,3, *I* 1, 1995 [*J*]
Herewini, M A (Auckland) 1962 *A* 5, 1963 *I*, 1964 *S, F*, 1965 *SA* 4, 1966 *BI* 1,2,3,4, 1967 *A*
Hewett, J A (Auckland) 1991 [*It*]
Hewitt, N J (Southland) 1995 [*I* (t), *J*], 1996 *A* 1 (R)
Hewson, A R (Wellington) 1981 *S* 1,2, *SA* 1,2,3, *R, F* 1,2, 1982 *A* 1,2,3, 1983 *BI* 1,2,3,4, *A*, 1984 *F* 1,2, *A* 1
Higginson, G (Canterbury, Hawke's Bay) 1980 *W*, 1981 *S* 1, *SA* 1, 1982 *A* 1,2, 1983 *A*
Hill, S F (Canterbury) 1955 *A* 3, 1956 *SA* 1,3,4, 1957 *A* 1,2, 1958 *A* 3, 1959 *BI* 1,2,3,4
Hines, G R (Waikato) 1980 *A* 3
Hobbs, M J B (Canterbury) 1983 *BI* 1,2,3,4, *A, S, E*, 1984 *F* 1,2, *A* 1,2,3, 1985 *E* 1,2, *A, Arg* 1,2, 1986 *A* 2,3, *F* 2,3
Holder, E C (Buller) 1934 *A* 2
Hook, L S (Auckland) 1929 *A* 1,2,3
Hooper, J A (Canterbury) 1937 *SA* 1,2,3
Hopkinson, A E (Canterbury) 1967 *S*, 1968 *A* 2, *F* 1,2,3, 1969 *W* 2, 1970 *SA* 1,2,3
Hore, J (Otago) 1930 *BI* 2,3,4, 1932 *A* 1,2,3, 1934 *A* 1,2, 1935 *S*, 1936 *E*
Horsley, R H (Wellington) 1960 *SA* 2,3,4
Hotop, J (Canterbury) 1952 *A* 1,2, 1955 *A* 3
Howarth, S P (Auckland) 1994 *SA* 1,2,3, *A*
Hughes, A M (Auckland) 1949 *A* 1,2, 1950 *BI* 1,2,3,4
Hughes, E (Southland, Wellington) 1907 *A* 1,2,3, 1908 *AW* 1, 1921 *SA* 1,2
Hunter, B A (Otago) 1971 *BI* 1,2,3
Hunter, J (Taranaki) 1905 *S, I, E, W*, 1906 *F*, 1907 *A* 1,2,3, 1908 *AW* 1,2,3
Hurst, I A (Canterbury) 1973 *I, F, E* 2, 1974 *A* 1,2

Ieremia, A I (Wellington) 1994 *SA* 1,2,3, 1995 [*J*], 1996 *SA* 2 (R), 5 (R)
Ifwersen, K D (Auckland) 1921 *SA* 3
Innes, C R (Auckland) 1989 *W, I*, 1990 *A* 1,2,3, *F* 1,2, 1991 *Arg* 1,2, *A* 1,2, [*E, US, It, C, A, S*]
Innes, G D (Canterbury) 1932 *A* 2
Irvine, I B (North Auckland) 1952 *A* 1
Irvine, J G (Otago) 1914 *A* 1,2,3
Irvine, W R (Hawke's Bay, Wairarapa) 1924 *I, W*, 1925 *E, F*, 1930 *BI* 1
Irwin, M W (Otago) 1955 *A* 1,2, 1956 *SA* 1, 1958 *A* 2, 1959 *BI* 3,4, 1960 *SA* 1

Jackson, E S (Hawke's Bay) 1936 *A* 1,2, 1937 *SA* 1,2,3, 1938 *A* 3
Jaffray, J L (Otago, South Canterbury) 1972 *A* 2, 1975 *S*, 1976 *I, SA* 1, 1977 *BI* 2, 1979 *F* 1,2
Jarden, R A (Wellington) 1951 *A* 1,2, 1952 *A* 1,2, 1953 *W*, 1954 *I, E, S, F*, 1955 *A* 1,2,3, 1956 *SA* 1,2,3,4

Jefferd, A C R (East Coast) 1981 *S* 1,2, *SA* 1
Jessep, E M (Wellington) 1931 *A*, 1932 *A* 1
Johnson, L M (Wellington) 1928 *SA* 1,2,3,4
Johnston, W (Otago) 1907 *A* 1,2,3
Johnstone, B R (Auckland) 1976 *SA* 2, 1977 *BI* 1,2, *F* 1,2, 1978 *I, W, E, S*, 1979 *F* 1,2, *S, E*
Johnstone, P (Otago) 1949 *SA* 2,4, 1950 *BI* 1,2,3,4, 1951 *A* 1,2,3
Jones, I D (North Auckland, North Harbour) 1990 *S* 1,2, *A* 1,2,3, *F* 1,2, 1991 *Arg* 1,2, *A* 1,2, [*E, US, It, C, A, S*], 1992 *Wld* 1,2,3, *I* 1,2, *A* 1,2,3, *SA*, 1993 *BI* 1,2 (R), 3, *WS, S, E*, 1994 *F* 1,2, *SA* 1,3, *A*, 1995 *C*, [*I, W, S, A, SA*], *A* 1,2, *It, F* 1,2, 1996 *WS, S* 1,2, *A* 1, *SA* 1, *A* 2, *SA* 2,3,4,5
Jones, M G (North Auckland) 1973 *E* 2
Jones, M N (Auckland) 1987 [*It, Fj, S, F*], *A*, 1988 *W* 1,2, *A* 2,3, 1989 *F* 1,2, *Arg* 1,2, 1990 *F* 1,2, 1991 *Arg* 1,2, *A* 1,2, [*E, US, S*], 1992 *Wld* 1,3, *I* 2, *A* 1,3, *SA*, 1993 *BI* 1,2,3, *A, WS*, 1994 *SA* 3 (R), *A*, 1995 *A* 1 (R), 2, *It, F* 1,2, 1996 *WS, S* 1,2, *A* 1, *SA* 1, *A* 2, *SA* 2,3,4,5
Jones, P F H (North Auckland) 1954 *E, S*, 1955 *A* 1,2, 1956 *SA* 3,4, 1958 *A* 1,2,3, 1959 *BI* 1, 1960 *SA* 1
Joseph, H T (Canterbury) 1971 *BI* 2,3
Joseph, J W (Otago) 1992 *Wld* 2,3 (R), *I* 1, *A* 1 (R), 3, *SA*, 1993 *BI* 1,2,3, *A, WS, S, E*, 1994 *SA* 2 (t), 1995 *C*, [*I, W, J* (R)], *S, SA* (R)]

Karam, J F (Wellington, Horowhenua) 1972 *W, S*, 1973 *E* 1, *I, F*, 1974 *A* 1,2,3, *I*, 1975 *S*
Katene, T (Wellington) 1955 *A* 2
Kearney, J C (Otago) 1947 *A* 2, 1949 *SA* 1,2,3
Kelly, J W (Auckland) 1949 *A* 1,2
Kember, G F (Wellington) 1970 *SA* 4
Ketels, R C (Counties) 1980 *W*, 1981 *S* 1,2, *R, F* 1
Kiernan, H A D (Auckland) 1903 *A*
Kilby, F D (Wellington) 1932 *A* 1,2,3, 1934 *A* 2
Killeen, B A (Auckland) 1936 *A* 1
King, R R (West Coast) 1934 *A* 2, 1935 *S, I, W*, 1936 *E, A* 1,2, 1937 *SA* 1,2,3, 1938 *A* 1,2,3
Kingstone, C N (Taranaki) 1921 *SA* 1,2,3
Kirk, D E (Auckland) 1985 *E* 1,2, *A, Arg* 1, 1986 *F* 1, *A* 1,2,3, *F* 2,3, 1987 [*It, Fj, Arg, S, W, F*], *A*
Kirkpatrick, I A (Canterbury, Poverty Bay) 1967 *F*, 1968 *A* 1 (R), 2, *F* 1,2,3, 1969 *W* 1,2, 1970 *SA* 1,2,3,4, 1971 *BI* 1,2,3,4, 1972 *A* 1,2,3, *W, S*, 1973 *E* 1, *I, F, E* 2, 1974 *A* 1,2,3, *I* 1975 *S*, 1976 *SA* 1,2,3,4, 1977 *BI* 1,2,3,4
Kirton, E W (Otago) 1967 *E, W, F, S*, 1968 *A* 1,2, *F* 1,2,3, 1969 *W* 1,2, 1970 *SA* 2,3
Kirwan, J J (Auckland) 1984 *F* 1,2, 1985 *E* 1,2, *A, Arg* 1,2, 1986 *F* 1, *A* 1,2,3, *F* 2,3, 1987 [*It, Fj, Arg, S, W, F*], *A*, 1988 *W* 1,2, *A* 1,2,3, 1989 *F* 1,2, *Arg* 1,2, *A*, 1990 *S* 1,2, *A* 1,2,3, *F* 1,2, 1991 *Arg* 2, *A* 1,2, [*E, It, C, A, S*], 1992 *Wld* 1,2 (R), 3, *I* 1,2, *A* 1,2,3, *SA*, 1993 *BI* 2,3, *A, WS*, 1994 *F* 1,2, *SA* 1
Kivell, A L (Taranaki) 1929 *A* 2,3
Knight, A (Auckland) 1934 *A* 1
Knight, G A (Manawatu) 1977 *F* 1,2, 1978 *A* 1,2,3, *E, S*, 1979 *F* 1,2, *A*, 1980 *A* 1,2,3, *W*, 1981 *S* 1,2, *SA* 1,3, 1982 *A* 1,2,3, 1983 *BI* 1,2,3,4, *A*, 1984 *F* 1,2, *A* 1,2,3, 1985 *E* 1,2, *A*, 1986 *A* 2,3
Knight, L G (Poverty Bay) 1977 *BI* 1,2,3,4, *F* 1,2
Koteka, T T (Waikato) 1981 *F* 2, 1982 *A* 3
Kreft, A J (Otago) 1968 *A* 2
Kronfeld, J A (Otago) 1995 *C*, [*I, W, S, E, SA*], *A* 1,2 (R) 1996 *WS, S* 1,2, *A* 1, *SA* 1, *A* 2, *SA* 2,3,4,5

Laidlaw, C R (Otago, Canterbury) 1964 *F, A* 1, 1965 *SA* 1,2,3,4, 1966 *BI* 1,2,3,4, 1967 *E, W, S*, 1968 *A* 1,2, *F* 1,2, 1970 *SA* 1,2,3
Laidlaw, K F (Southland) 1960 *SA* 2,3,4
Lambert, K K (Manawatu) 1972 *S* (R), 1973 *E* 1, *I, F, E* 2, 1974 *I*, 1976 *SA* 1,3,4, 1977 *BI* 1,4
Lambourn, A (Wellington) 1934 *A* 1,2, 1935 *S, I, W*, 1936 *E*, 1937 *SA* 1,2,3, 1938 *A* 3
Larsen, B P (North Harbour) 1992 *Wld* 2,3, *I* 1, 1994 *F* 1,2, *SA* 1,2,3, *A* (t), 1995 [*I, W, J, E(R)*], *It, F* 1, 1996 *S* 2 (t), *SA* 4 (R)
Le Lievre, J M (Canterbury) 1962 *A* 4
Lendrum, R N (Counties) 1973 *E* 2
Leslie, A R (Wellington) 1974 *A* 1,2,3, *I*, 1975 *S*, 1976 *I, SA* 1,2,3,4
Leys, E T (Wellington) 1929 *A* 3
Lilburne, H T (Canterbury, Wellington) 1928 *SA* 3,4, 1929 *A* 1,2,3, 1930 *BI* 1,4, 1931 *A*, 1932 *A* 1, 1934 *A* 2

F, 1929 *A* 1, 1930 *BI* 1,2,3,4
Nesbit, S R (Auckland) 1960 *SA* 2,3
Newton, F (Canterbury) 1905 *E, W*, 1906 *F*
Nicholls, H E (Wellington) 1921 *SA* 1
Nicholls, M F (Wellington) 1921 *SA* 1,2,3, 1924 *I, W*, 1925 *E, F*, 1928 *SA* 4, 1930 *BI* 2,3
Nicholson, G W (Auckland) 1903 *A*, 1904 *BI*, 1907 *A* 2,3
Norton, R W (Canterbury) 1971 *BI* 1,2,3,4, 1972 *A* 1,2,3, *W, S*, 1973 *E* 1, *I, F, E* 2, 1974 *A* 1,2,3, *I*, 1975 *S*, 1976 *I, SA* 1,2,3,4, 1977 *BI* 1,2,3,4

O'Brien, J G (Auckland) 1914 *A* 1
O'Callaghan, M W (Manawatu) 1968 *F* 1,2,3
O'Callaghan, T R (Wellington) 1949 *A* 2
O'Donnell, D H (Wellington) 1949 *A* 2
Old, G H (Manawatu) 1981 *SA* 3, *R* (R), 1982 *A* 1 (R)
O'Leary, M J (Auckland) 1910 *A* 1,3, 1913 *A* 2,3
Oliver, C J (Canterbury) 1929 *A* 1,2, 1934 *A* 1, 1935 *S, I, W*, 1936 *E*
Oliver, D J (Wellington) 1930 *BI* 1,2
Oliver, D O (Otago) 1954 *I, F*
Oliver, F J (Southland, Otago, Manawatu) 1976 *SA* 4, 1977 *BI* 1,2,3,4, *F* 1,2, 1978 *A* 1,2,3, *I, W, E, S*, 1979 *F* 1,2, 1981 *SA* 2
Orr, R W (Otago) 1949 *A* 1
Osborne, G M (North Harbour) 1995 *C*, [*I, W, J, E, SA*], *A* 1,2, *F* 1 (R), 2, 1996 *SA* 2,3,4,5
Osborne, W M (Wanganui) 1975 *S*, 1976 *SA* 2 (R), 4 (R), 1977 *BI* 1,2,3,4, *F* 1 (R), 2, 1978 *I, W, E, S*, 1980 *W*, 1982 *A* 1,3
O'Sullivan, J M (Taranaki) 1905 *S, I, E, W*, 1907 *A* 3
O'Sullivan, T P A (Taranaki) 1960 *SA* 1, 1961 *F* 1, 1962 *A* 1,2

Page, J R (Wellington) 1931 *A*, 1932 *A* 1,2,3, 1934 *A* 1,2
Palmer, B P (Auckland) 1929 *A* 2, 1932 *A* 2,3
Parker, J H (Canterbury) 1924 *I, W*, 1925 *E*
Parkhill, A A (Otago) 1937 *SA* 1,2,3, 1938 *A* 1,2,3
Parkinson, R M (Poverty Bay) 1972 *A* 1,2,3, *W, S*, 1973 *E* 1,2
Paterson, A M (Otago) 1908 *AW* 2,3, 1910 *A* 1,2,3
Paton, H (Otago) 1910 *A* 1,3
Pene, A R B (Otago) 1992 *Wld* 1 (R), 2,3, *I* 1,2, *A* 1,2 (R), 1993 *BI* 3, *A, WS, S, E*, 1994 *F* 1,2 (R), *SA* 1 (R)
Phillips, W J (King Country) 1937 *SA* 2, 1938 *A* 1,2
Philpott, S (Canterbury) 1991 [*It* (R), *S* (R)]
Pickering, E A R (Waikato) 1958 *A* 2, 1959 *BI* 1,4
Pierce, M J (Wellington) 1985 *E* 1,2, *A, Arg* 1, 1986 *A* 2,3, *F* 2,3, 1987 [*It, Arg, S, W, F*], *A*, 1988 *W* 1,2, *A* 1,2,3, 1989 *F* 1,2, *Arg* 1,2, *A, W, I*
Pokere, S T (Southland, Auckland) 1981 *SA* 3, 1982 *A* 1,2,3, 1983 *BI* 1,2,3,4, *A, S, E*, 1984 *F* 1,2, *A* 2,3, 1985 *E* 1,2, *A*
Pollock, H R (Wellington) 1932 *A* 1,2,3, 1936 *A* 1,2
Porter, C G (Wellington) 1925 *F*, 1929 *A* 2,3, 1930 *BI* 1,2,3,4
Preston, J P (Canterbury, Wellington) 1991 [*US, S*], 1992 *SA* (R), 1993 *BI* 2,3, *A, WS*, 1996 *SA* 4 (R)
Procter, A C (Otago) 1932 *A* 1
Purdue, C A (Southland) 1905 *A*
Purdue, E (Southland) 1905 *A*
Purdue, G B (Southland) 1931 *A*, 1932 *A* 1,2,3
Purvis, G H (Waikato) 1991 [*US*], 1993 *WS*
Purvis, N A (Otago) 1976 *I*

Quaid, C E (Otago) 1938 *A* 1,2

Rangi, R E (Auckland) 1964 *A* 2,3, 1965 *SA* 1,2,3,4, 1966 *BI* 1,2,3,4
Rankin, J G (Canterbury) 1936 *A* 1,2, 1937 *SA* 2
Reedy, W J (Wellington) 1908 *AW* 2,3
Reid, A R (Waikato) 1952 *A* 1, 1956 *SA* 3,4, 1957 *A* 1,2
Reid, H R (Bay of Plenty) 1980 *A* 1,2, *W*, 1983 *S, E*, 1985 *Arg* 1,2, 1986 *A* 2,3
Reid, K H (Wairarapa) 1929 *A* 1,3
Reid, S T (Hawke's Bay) 1935 *S, I, W*, 1936 *E, A* 1,2, 1937 *SA* 1,2,3
Reside, W B (Wairarapa) 1929 *A* 1
Rhind, P K (Canterbury) 1946 *A* 1,2
Richardson, J (Otago, Southland) 1921 *SA* 1,2,3, 1924 *I, W*, 1925 *E, F*
Rickit, H (Waikato) 1981 *S* 1,2
Ridland, A J (Southland) 1910 *A* 1,2,3

Roberts, E J (Wellington) 1914 *A* 1,2,3, 1921 *SA* 2,3
Roberts, F (Wellington) 1905 *S, I, E, W*, 1907 *A* 1,2,3, 1908 *AW* 1,3, 1910 *A* 1,2,3
Roberts, R W (Taranaki) 1913 *A* 1, *US*, 1914 *A* 1,2,3
Robertson, B J (Counties) 1972 *A* 1,3, *S*, 1973 *E* 1, *I, F*, 1974 *A* 1,2,3, *I*, 1976 *I, SA* 1,2,3,4, 1977 *BI* 1,3,4, *F* 1,2, 1978 *A* 1,2,3, *W, E, S*, 1979 *F* 1,2, *A*, 1980 *A* 2,3, *W*, 1981 *S* 1,2
Robertson, D J (Otago) 1974 *A* 1,2,3, *I*, 1975 *S*, 1976 *I, SA* 1,3,4, 1977 *BI* 1
Robilliard, A C C (Canterbury) 1928 *SA* 1,2,3,4
Robinson, C E (Southland) 1951 *A* 1,2,3, 1952 *A* 1,2
Rollerson, D L (Manawatu) 1980 *W*, 1981 *S* 2, *SA* 1,2,3, *R, F* 1 (R), 2
Roper, R A (Taranaki) 1949 *A* 2, 1950 *BI* 1,2,3,4
Rowley, H C B (Wanganui) 1949 *A* 2
Rush, E J (North Harbour) 1995 [*W* (R), *J*], *It, F* 1,2, 1996 *S* 1 (R), 2, *A* 1 (t), *SA* 1 (R)
Rutledge, L M (Southland) 1978 *A* 1,2,3, *I, W, E, S*, 1979 *F* 1,2, *A*, 1980 *A* 1,2,3
Ryan, J (Wellington) 1910 *A* 2, 1914 *A* 1,2,3

Sadler, B S (Wellington) 1935 *S, I, W*, 1936 *A* 1,2
Salmon, J L B (Wellington) 1981 *R, F* 1,2 (R)
Savage, L T (Canterbury) 1949 *SA* 1,2,4
Saxton, C K (South Canterbury) 1938 *A* 1,2,3
Schuler, K J (Manawatu, North Harbour) 1990 *A* 2 (R), 1992 *A* 2, 1995 [*I* (R), *J*]
Schuster, N J (Wellington) 1988 *A* 1,2,3, 1989 *F* 1,2, *Arg* 1,2, *A, W, I*
Scott, R W H (Auckland) 1946 *A* 1,2, 1947 *A* 1,2, 1949 *SA* 1,2,3,4, 1950 *BI* 1,2,3,4, 1953 *W*, 1954 *I, E, S, F*
Scown, A I (Taranaki) 1972 *A* 1,2,3, *W* (R), *S*
Scrimshaw, G (Canterbury) 1928 *SA* 1
Seear, G A (Otago) 1977 *F* 1,2, 1978 *A* 1,2,3, *I, W, E, S*, 1979 *F* 1,2, *A*
Seeling, C E (Auckland) 1904 *BI*, 1905 *S, I, E, W*, 1906 *F*, 1907 *A* 1,2, 1908 *AW* 1,2,3
Sellars, G M V (Auckland) 1913 *A* 1, *US*
Shaw, M W (Manawatu, Hawke's Bay) 1980 *A* 1,2,3 (R), *W*, 1981 *S* 1,2, *SA* 1,2, *R, F* 1,2, 1982 *A* 1,2,3, 1983 *BI* 1,2,3,4, *A, S, E*, 1984 *F* 1,2, *A* 1, 1985 *E* 1,2, *A, Arg* 1,2, 1986 *A* 3
Shelford, F N K (Bay of Plenty) 1981 *SA* 3, *R*, 1984 *A* 2,3
Shelford, W T (North Harbour) 1986 *F* 2,3, 1987 [*It, Fj, S, W, F*], *A*, 1988 *W* 1,2, *A* 1,2,3, 1989 *F* 1,2, *Arg* 1,2, *A, W, I*, 1990 *S* 1,2
Siddells, S K (Wellington) 1921 *SA* 3
Simon, H J (Otago) 1937 *SA* 1,2,3
Simpson, J G (Auckland) 1947 *A* 1,2, 1949 *SA* 1,2,3,4, 1950 *BI* 1,2,3
Simpson, V L J (Canterbury) 1985 *Arg* 1,2
Sims, G S (Otago) 1972 *A* 2
Skeen, J R (Auckland) 1952 *A* 2
Skinner, K L (Otago, Counties) 1949 *SA* 1,2,3,4, 1950 *BI* 1,2,3,4, 1951 *A* 1,2,3, 1952 *A* 1,2, 1953 *W*, 1954 *I, E, S, F*, 1956 *SA* 3,4
Skudder, G R (Waikato) 1969 *W* 2
Sloane, P H (North Auckland) 1979 *E*
Smith, A E (Taranaki) 1969 *W* 1,2, 1970 *SA* 1
Smith, B W (Waikato) 1984 *F* 1,2, *A* 1
Smith, G W (Auckland) 1905 *S, I*
Smith, I S T (Otago, North Otago) 1964 *A* 1,2,3, 1965 *SA* 1,2,4, 1966 *BI* 1,2,3
Smith, J B (North Auckland) 1946 *A* 1, 1947 *A* 2, 1949 *A* 1,2
Smith, R M (Canterbury) 1955 *A* 1
Smith, W E (Nelson) 1905 *A*
Smith, W R (Canterbury) 1980 *A* 1, 1982 *A* 1,2,3, 1983 *BI* 2,3, *S, E*, 1984 *F* 1,2, *A* 1,2,3, 1985 *E* 1,2, *A, Arg* 2
Snow, E M (Nelson) 1929 *A* 1,2,3
Solomon, F (Auckland) 1931 *A*, 1932 *A* 2,3
Sonntag, W T C (Otago) 1929 *A* 1,2,3
Speight, M W (Waikato) 1986 *A* 1
Spencer, J C (Wellington) 1905 *A*, 1907 *A* 1 (R)
Spiers, J E (Counties) 1979 *S, E*, 1981 *R, F* 1,2
Spillane, A P (South Canterbury) 1913 *A* 2,3
Stanley, J T (Auckland) 1986 *F* 1, *A* 1,2,3, *F* 2,3, 1987 [*It, Fj, Arg, S, W, F*], *A*, 1988 *W* 1,2, *A* 1,2,3, 1989 *F* 1,2, *Arg* 1,2, *A, W, I*, 1990 *S* 1,2
Stead, J W (Southland) 1904 *BI*, 1905 *S, I, E*, 1906 *F*, 1908 *AW* 1,3

Steel, A G (Canterbury) 1966 *BI* 1,2,3,4, 1967 *A, F, S,* 1968 *A* 1,2
Steel, J (West Coast) 1921 *SA* 1,2,3, 1924 *W,* 1925 *E, F*
Steele, L B (Wellington) 1951 *A* 1,2,3
Steere, E R G (Hawke's Bay) 1930 *BI* 1,2,3,4, 1931 *A,* 1932 *A* 1
Stensness, L (Auckland) 1993 *BI* 3, *A, WS*
Stephens, O G (Wellington) 1968 *F* 3
Stevens, I N (Wellington) 1972 *S,* 1973 *E* 1, 1974 *A* 3
Stewart, A J (Canterbury, South Canterbury) 1963 *E* 1,2, *I, W,* 1964 *E, S, F, A* 3
Stewart, J D (Auckland) 1913 *A* 2,3
Stewart, K W (Southland) 1973 *E* 2, 1974 *A* 1,2,3, *I,* 1975 *S,* 1976 *I, SA* 1,3, 1979 *S, E,* 1981 *SA* 1,2
Stewart, R T (South Canterbury, Canterbury) 1928 *SA* 1,2,3,4, 1930 *BI* 2
Stohr, L B (Taranaki) 1910 *A* 1,2,3
Stone, A M (Waikato, Bay of Plenty) 1981 *F* 1,2, 1983 *BI* 3 (R), 1984 *A* 3, 1986 *F* 1, *A* 1,3, *F* 2,3
Storey, P W (South Canterbury) 1921 *SA* 1,2
Strachan, A D (Auckland, North Harbour) 1992 *Wld* 2,3, *I* 1,2, *A* 1,2,3, *SA,* 1993 *BI* 1, 1995 [*J, SA* (t)]
Strahan, S C (Manawatu) 1967 *A, E, W, F, S,* 1968 *A* 1,2, *F* 1,2,3, 1970 *SA* 1,2,3, 1972 *A* 1,2,3, 1973 *E* 2
Strang, W A (South Canterbury) 1928 *SA* 1,2, 1930 *BI* 3,4, 1931 *A*
Stringfellow, J C (Wairarapa) 1929 *A* 1 (R), 3
Stuart, K C (Canterbury) 1955 *A* 1
Stuart, R C (Canterbury) 1949 *A* 1,2, 1953 *W,* 1954 *I, E, S, F*
Stuart, R L (Hawke's Bay) 1977 *F* 1 (R)
Sullivan, J L (Taranaki) 1937 *SA* 1,2,3, 1938 *A* 1,2,3
Sutherland, A R (Marlborough) 1970 *SA* 2,4, 1971 *BI* 1, 1972 *A* 1,2,3, *W,* 1973 *E* 1, *I, F*
Svenson, K S (Wellington) 1924 *I, W,* 1925 *E, F*
Swain, J P (Hawke's Bay) 1928 *SA* 1,2,3,4

Tanner, J M (Auckland) 1950 *BI* 4, 1951 *A* 1,2,3, 1953 *W*
Tanner, K J (Canterbury) 1974 *A* 1,2,3, *I,* 1975 *S,* 1976 *I, SA* 1
Taylor, G L (Northland) 1996 *SA* 5 (R)
Taylor, H M (Canterbury) 1913 *A* 1, *US,* 1914 *A* 1,2,3
Taylor, J M (Otago) 1937 *SA* 1,2,3, 1938 *A* 1,2,3
Taylor, M B (Waikato) 1979 *F* 1,2, *A, S, E,* 1980 *A* 1,2
Taylor, N M (Bay of Plenty, Hawke's Bay) 1977 *BI* 2, 4 (R), *F* 1,2, 1978 *A* 1,2,3, *I,* 1982 *A* 2
Taylor, R (Taranaki) 1913 *A* 2,3
Taylor, W T (Canterbury) 1983 *BI* 1,2,3,4, *A, S,* 1984 *F* 1,2, *A* 1,2, 1985 *E* 1,2, *A, Arg* 1,2, 1986 *A* 2, 1987 [*It, Fj, S, W, F*], *A,* 1988 *W* 1,2
Tetzlaff, P L (Auckland) 1947 *A* 1,2
Thimbleby, N W (Hawke's Bay) 1970 *SA* 3
Thomas, B T (Auckland, Wellington) 1962 *A* 5, 1964 *A* 1,2,3
Thomson, H D (Wellington) 1908 *AW* 1
Thorne, G S (Auckland) 1968 *A* 1,2, *F* 1,2,3, 1969 *W* 1, 1970 *SA* 1,2,3,4
Thornton, N H (Auckland) 1947 *A* 1,2, 1949 *SA* 1
Tilyard, J T (Wellington) 1913 *A* 3
Timu, J K R (Otago) 1991 *Arg* 1, *A* 1,2, [*E, US, C, A*], 1992 *Wld* 2, *I* 2, *A* 1,2,3, *SA,* 1993 *BI* 1,2,3, *A, WS, S, E,* 1994 *F* 1,2, *SA* 1,2,3, *A*
Tindill, E W T (Wellington) 1936 *E*
Townsend, L J (Otago) 1955 *A* 1,3
Tremain, K R (Canterbury, Hawke's Bay) 1959 *BI* 2,3,4, 1960 *SA* 1,2,3,4, 1961 *F* 2,3 1962 *A* 1,2,3, 1963 *E* 1,2, *I, W,* 1964 *E, F, A* 1,2,3, 1965 *SA* 1,2,3,4, 1966 *BI* 1,2,3,4, 1967 *A, E, W, S,* 1968 *A* 1, *F* 1,2,3
Trevathan, D (Otago) 1937 *SA* 1,2,3
Tuck, J M (Waikato) 1929 *A* 1,2,3
Tuigamala, V L (Auckland) 1991 [*US, It, C, S*], 1992 *Wld* 1,2,3, *I* 1, *A* 1,2,3, *SA,* 1993 *BI* 1,2,3, *A, WS, S, E*
Turner, R S (North Harbour) 1992 *Wld* 1,2 (R)
Turtill, H S (Canterbury) 1905 *A*
Twigden, T M (Auckland) 1980 *A* 2,3
Tyler, G A (Auckland) 1903 *A,* 1904 *BI,* 1905 *S, I, E, W,* 1906 *F*

Udy, D K (Wairarapa) 1903 *A*
Urbahn, R J (Taranaki) 1959 *BI* 1,3,4
Urlich, R A (Auckland) 1970 *SA* 3,4
Uttley, I N (Wellington) 1963 *E* 1,2

Vincent, P B (Canterbury) 1956 *SA* 1,2
Vodanovich, I M H (Wellington) 1955 *A* 1,2,3

Wallace, W J (Wellington) 1903 *A,* 1904 *BI,* 1905 *S, I, E, W,* 1906 *F,* 1907 *A* 1,2,3, 1908 *AW* 2
Walsh, P T (Counties) 1955 *A* 1,2,3, 1956 *SA* 1,2,4, 1957 *A* 1,2, 1958 *A* 1,2,3, 1959 *BI* 1, 1963 *E* 2
Ward, R H (Southland) 1936 *A* 2, 1937 *SA* 1,3
Waterman, A C (North Auckland) 1929 *A* 1,2
Watkins, E L (Wellington) 1905 *A*
Watt, B A (Canterbury) 1962 *A* 1,4, 1963 *E* 1,2, *W,* 1964 *E, S, A* 1
Watt, J M (Otago) 1936 *A* 1,2
Watt, J R (Wellington) 1958 *A* 2, 1960 *SA* 1,2,3,4, 1961 *F* 1,3, 1962 *A* 1,2
Watts, M G (Taranaki) 1979 *F* 1,2, 1980 *A* 1,2,3 (R)
Webb, D S (North Auckland) 1959 *BI* 2
Wells, J (Wellington) 1936 *A* 1,2
West, A H (Taranaki) 1921 *SA* 2,3
Whetton, A J (Auckland) 1984 *A* 1 (R), 3 (R), 1985 *A* (R), *Arg* 1 (R), 1986 *A* 2, 1987 [*It, Fj, Arg, S, W, F*], *A,* 1988 *W* 1,2, *A* 1,2,3, 1989 *F* 1,2, *Arg* 1,2, *A,* 1990 *S* 1,2, *A* 1,2,3, *F* 1,2, 1991 *Arg* 1, [*E, US, It, C, A*]
Whetton, G W (Auckland) 1981 *SA* 3, *R, F* 1,2, 1982 *A* 3, 1983 *BI* 1,2,3,4, 1984 *F* 1,2, *A* 1,2,3, 1985 *E* 1,2, *A, Arg* 2, 1986 *A* 2,3, *F* 2,3, 1987 [*It, Fj, Arg, S, W, F*], *A,* 1988 *W* 1,2, *A* 1,2,3, 1989 *F* 1,2, *Arg* 1,2, *A, W, I,* 1990 *S* 1,2, *A* 1,2,3, *F* 1,2, 1991 *Arg* 1,2, *A* 1,2, [*E, US, It, C, A, S*]
Whineray, W J (Canterbury, Waikato, Auckland) 1957 *A* 1,2, 1958 *A* 1,2,3, 1959 *BI* 1,2,3,4, 1960 *SA* 1,2,3,4, 1961 *F* 1,2,3, 1962 *A* 1,2,3,4,5, 1963 *E* 1,2, *I, W,* 1964 *E, S, F,* 1965 *SA* 1,2,3,4
White, A (Southland) 1921 *SA* 1, 1924 *I,* 1925 *E, F*
White, H L (Auckland) 1954 *I, E, F,* 1955 *A* 3
White, R A (Poverty Bay) 1949 *A* 1,2, 1950 *BI* 1,2,3,4, 1951 *A* 1,2,3, 1952 *A* 1,2, 1953 *W,* 1954 *I, E, S, F,* 1955 *A* 1,2,3, 1956 *SA* 1,2,3,4
White, R M (Wellington) 1946 *A* 1,2, 1947 *A* 1,2
Whiting, G J (King Country) 1972 *A* 1,2, *S,* 1973 *E* 1, *I, F*
Whiting, P J (Auckland) 1971 *BI* 1,2,4, 1972 *A* 1,2,3, *W, S,* 1973 *E* 1, *I, F,* 1974 *A* 1,2,3, *I,* 1976 *I, SA* 1,2,3,4
Williams, B G (Auckland) 1970 *SA* 1,2,3,4, 1971 *BI* 1,2,4, 1972 *A* 1,2,3, *W, S,* 1973 *E* 1, *I, F, E* 2, 1974 *A* 1,2,3, *I,* 1975 *S,* 1976 *I, SA* 1,2,3,4, 1977 *BI* 1,2,3,4, *F* 1, 1978 *A* 1,2,3, *I* (R), *W, E, S*
Williams, G C (Wellington) 1967 *E, W, F, S,* 1968 *A* 2
Williams, P (Otago) 1913 *A* 1
Williment, M (Wellington) 1964 *A* 1, 1965 *SA* 1,2,3, 1966 *BI* 1,2,3,4, 1967 *A*
Willocks, C (Otago) 1946 *A* 1,2, 1949 *SA* 1,3,4
Wilson, B W (Otago) 1977 *BI* 3,4, 1978 *A* 1,2,3, 1979 *F* 1,2, *A*
Wilson, D D (Canterbury) 1954 *E, S*
Wilson, H W (Otago) 1949 *A* 1, 1950 *BI* 4, 1951 *A* 1,2,3
Wilson, J W (Otago) 1993 *S, E,* 1994 *A,* 1995 *C,* [*I, J, S, E, SA*], 1994 *A* 1,2, *It, F* 1, 1996 *WS, S* 1,2, *A* 1, *A* 2, *SA* 2,3,4,5
Wilson, N A (Wellington) 1908 *AW* 1,2, 1910 *A* 1,2,3, 1913 *A* 2,3, 1914 *A* 1,2,3
Wilson, N L (Otago) 1951 *A* 1,2,3
Wilson, R G (Canterbury) 1979 *S, E*
Wilson, S S (Wellington) 1977 *F* 1,2, 1978 *A* 1,2,3, *I, W, E, S,* 1979 *F* 1,2, *A, S, E,* 1980 *A* 1, *W,* 1981 *S* 1,2, *SA* 1,2,3, *R, F* 1,2, 1982 *A* 1,2,3, 1983 *BI* 1,2,3,4, *A, S, E*
Wolfe, T N (Wellington, Taranaki) 1961 *F* 1,2,3, 1962 *A* 2,3, 1963 *E* 1
Wood, M E (Canterbury, Auckland) 1903 *A,* 1904 *BI*
Woodman, F A (North Auckland) 1981 *SA* 1,2, *F* 2
Wrigley, E (Wairarapa) 1905 *A*
Wright, T J (Auckland) 1986 *F* 1, *A* 1, 1987 [*Arg*], 1988 *W* 1,2, *A* 1,2,3, 1989 *F* 1,2, *Arg* 1,2, *A, W, I,* 1990 *S* 1,2, *A* 1,2,3, *F* 1,2, 1991 *Arg* 1,2, *A* 1,2, [*E, US, It, S*]
Wylie, J T (Auckland) 1913 *A* 1, *US*
Wyllie, A J (Canterbury) 1970 *SA* 2,3, 1971 *BI* 2,3,4, 1972 *W, S,* 1973 *E* 1, *I, F, E* 2

Yates, V M (North Auckland) 1961 *F* 1,2,3
Young, D (Canterbury) 1956 *SA* 2, 1958 *A* 1,2,3, 1960 *SA* 1,2,3,4, 1961 *F* 1,2,3, 1962 *A* 1,2,3,5, 1963 *E* 1,2, *I, W,* 1964 *E, S, F*

NEW ZEALAND INTERNATIONAL RECORDS (*up to 30 April 1997*)

MATCH RECORDS

MOST CONSECUTIVE TEST WINS

17   1965 *SA* 4, 1966 *BI* 1,2,3,4, 1967 *A,E,W,F,S*, 1968 *A* 1,2, *F* 1,2,3, 1969 *W* 1,2

12   1988 *A* 3, 1989 *F* 1,2, *Arg* 1,2, *A,W,I*, 1990 *S* 1,2, *A* 1,2

MOST CONSECUTIVE TESTS WITHOUT DEFEAT

P	W	D	Period
23	22	1	1987–90
17	15	2	1961–64
17	17	0	1965–69

MOST POINTS IN A MATCH
by the team

Pts	Opp	Venue	Year
145	J	Bloemfontein	1995
74	Fj	Christchurch	1987
73	C	Auckland	1995
70	It	Auckland	1987
70	It	Bologna	1995

by a player
45 by S D Culhane v Japan at Bloemfontein   1995
30 by M C G Ellis v Japan at Bloemfontein   1995
28 by A P Mehrtens v Canada at Auckland   1995
26 by A R Hewson v Australia at Auckland   1982
26 G J Fox v Fiji at Christchurch   1987

MOST TRIES IN A MATCH
by the team

T	Opp	Venue	Year
21	J	Bloemfontein	1995
13	US	Berkeley	1913
12	It	Auckland	1987
12	Fj	Christchurch	1987
11	I	Wellington	1992

by a player
6 by M C G Ellis v Japan at Bloemfontein   1995
4 by D McGregor v England at Crystal Palace   1905

4 by C I Green v Fiji at Christchurch   1987
4 by J A Gallagher v Fiji at Christchurch   1987
4 by J J Kirwan v Wales at Christchurch   1988
4 by J T Lomu v England at Cape Town   1995
4 by C M Cullen v Scotland at Dunedin   1996

MOST CONVERSIONS IN A MATCH
by the team

C	Opp	Venue	Year
20	J	Bloemfontein	1995
10	Fj	Christchurch	1987
8	It	Auckland	1987
8	W	Auckland	1988

by a player
20 by S D Culhane v Japan at Bloemfontein   1995
10 by G J Fox v Fiji at Christchurch 1987
8 by G J Fox v Italy at Auckland   1987
8 by G J Fox v Wales at Auckland   1988

MOST PENALTY GOALS IN A MATCH
by the team

P	Opp	Venue	Year
7	WS	Auckland	1993
6	BI	Dunedin	1959
6	E	Christchurch	1985
6	Arg	Wellington	1987
6	S	Christchurch	1987
6	F	Paris	1990
6	SA	Auckland	1994
6	A	Brisbane	1996

by a player
7 by G J Fox v Western Samoa at Auckland   1993
6 by D B Clarke v British Isles at Dunedin   1959
6 by K J Crowley v England at Christchurch   1985
6 by G J Fox v Argentina at Wellington   1987
6 by G J Fox v Scotland at Christchurch   1987
6 by G J Fox v France at Paris   1990
6 by S P Howarth v South Africa at Auckland   1994

6 by A P Mehrtens v Australia at
Brisbane   1996

MOST DROPPED GOALS IN A MATCH
by the team

D	Opp	Venue	Year
3	F	Christchurch	1986

by a player

2 by O D Bruce v Ireland at
  Dublin   1978
2 by F M Botica v France at
  Christchurch   1986
2 by A P Mehrtens v Australia at
  Auckland   1995

CAREER RECORDS

MOST CAPPED PLAYERS

Caps	Player	Career
83	S B T Fitzpatrick	1986–96
63	J J Kirwan	1984–94
58	G W Whetton	1981–91
58	I D Jones	1990–96
55	C E Meads	1957–71
50	M N Jones	1987–96
49	R W Loe	1987–95
47	Z V Brooke	1987–96
46	S C McDowell	1985–92
46	G J Fox	1985–93

MOST CONSECUTIVE TESTS

Tests	Player	Span
63	S B T Fitzpatrick	1986–95
40	G W Whetton	1986–91
38	I A Kirkpatrick	1968–77
38	S C McDowell	1987–92
34	M G Mexted	1979–85

MOST TESTS AS CAPTAIN

Tests	Captain	Span
43	S B T Fitzpatrick	1992–96
30	W J Whineray	1958–65
19	G N K Mourie	1977–82
18	B J Lochore	1966–70
17	A G Dalton	1981–85

MOST TESTS IN INDIVIDUAL POSITIONS

Full-back D B Clarke		31	1956–64
Wing J J Kirwan		63	1984–94
Centre W K Little		40	1990–96
Fly-half G J Fox		46	1985–93
Scrum-half G T M Bachop	31	1989–95
Prop R W Loe		48*	1987–95
Hooker S B T Fitzpatrick		83	1986–96
Lock G W Whetton		58	1981–91
Flanker M N Jones		48	1987–96
No 8 Z V Brooke		41	1987–96

* Excludes an appearance as a temporary replacement

MOST POINTS IN TESTS

Pts	Player	Tests	Career
645	G J Fox	46	1985–93
274	A P Mehrtens	16	1995–96
207	D B Clarke	31	1956–64
201	A R Hewson	19	1981–84
143	J J Kirwan	63	1984–94

MOST TRIES IN TESTS

Tries	Player	Tests	Career
35	J J Kirwan	63	1984–94
19	S S Wilson	34	1977–83
19	T J Wright	30	1986–91
17	F E Bunce	43	1992–96
16	I A Kirkpatrick	39	1967–77

MOST CONVERSIONS IN TESTS

Cons	Player	Tests	Career
118	G J Fox	46	1985–93
49	A P Mehrtens	16	1995–96
33	D B Clarke	31	1956–64
32	S D Culhane	6	1995–96
23	W F McCormick	16	1965–71

MOST PENALTY GOALS IN TESTS

Pens	Player	Tests	Career
128	G J Fox	46	1985–93
46	A P Mehrtens	16	1995–96
43	A R Hewson	19	1981–84
38	D B Clarke	31	1956–64
24	W F McCormick	16	1965–71

MOST DROPPED GOALS IN TESTS

Drops	Player	Tests	Career
7	G J Fox	46	1985–93
6	A P Mehrtens	16	1995–96
5	D B Clarke	31	1956–64
5	M A Herewini	10	1962–67
5	O D Bruce	14	1976–78

TRI-NATIONS RECORDS

Record	Detail	Holder	Set
Most points in matches	69	A P Mehrtens	1996
Most points in season	69	A P Mehrtens	1996
Most points in match	22	A P Mehrtens	v Australia (a) 1996
Most tries in matches	2	J W Marshall	1996
Most tries in season	2	J W Marshall	1996
Most tries in match	1	several players	1996
Most cons in matches	6	A P Mehrtens	1996
Most cons in season	6	A P Mehrtens	1996
Most cons in match	2	A P Mehrtens	three times, 1996
Most pens in matches	19	A P Mehrtens	1996
Most pens in season	19	A P Mehrtens	1996
Most pens in match	6	A P Mehrtens	v Australia (a) 1996

SERIES RECORDS

Record	Holder	Detail
Most tries	J J Kirwan	6 v Wales 1988
Most points	A R Hewson	46 v British Isles 1983

MAJOR TOUR RECORDS

Record	Detail	Year	Place
Most team points	976	1905–06	Europe & N Am
Most team tries	243	1905–06	Europe & N Am
Most individual points	246 by W J Wallace	1905–06	Europe & N Am
Most individual tries	44 by J Hunter	1905–06	Europe & N Am
Most points in match	43 by R M Deans	1984 v Australia	Adelaide
Most tries in match	8 by T R Heeps	1962 v N NSW	Quirindi

MISCELLANEOUS RECORDS

Record	Holder	Detail
Longest Test career	E Hughes/C E Meads	15 seasons, 1907–21/1957–71
Youngest Test cap	J T Lomu	19 yrs 45 days in 1994
Oldest Test cap	E Hughes	40 yrs 123 days in 1921

NEW ZEALAND INTERNATIONAL CAREER RECORDS (*up to 30 April 1997*)

Player	Debut	Caps since last season	Caps	T	C	PG	DG	Pts
C M Cullen	1996 v WS	1996 *WS, S* 1,2, *A* 1, *SA* 1, *A* 2, *SA* 2,3,4,5,	10	9	0	0	0	45
G M Osborne	1995 v C	1996 *SA* 2,3,4,5	14	7	0	0	0	35
A R Cashmore	1996 v S	1996 *S* 2 (R)	1	0	0	0	0	0
J Vidiri	None		0	0	0	0	0	0
J W Wilson	1993 v S	1996 *WS, S* 1,2, *A* 1, *SA* 1, *A* 2, *SA* 2,3,4,5	23	14	1	3	0	81
J T Lomu	1994 v F	1996 *WS, S* 1, *A* 1, *SA* 1, *A* 2	17	14	0	0	0	70

E J Rush	1995 v W	1996 *S*1 (R),2, *A* 1 (t), *SA* 1 (R)	9	5	0	0	0	25
F E Bunce	1992 v Wd	1996 *WS, S* 1,2, *A* 1, *SA* 1, *A* 2, *SA* 2,3,4,5	43	17	0	0	0	81
A I Ieremia	1994 v SA	1996 *SA* 2 (R),5 (R)	6	1	0	0	0	5
S J McLeod	1996 v WS	1996 *WS, S* 1	2	1	0	0	0	5
W K Little	1990 v S	1996 *S* 2, *A* 1, *SA* 1, *A* 2, *SA* 2,3,4,5	44	8	0	0	0	39
M Ranby	None		0	0	0	0	0	0
L Stensness	1993 v BI		3	1	0	0	0	5
C J Spencer	None		0	0	0	0	0	0
A P Mehrtens	1995 v C	1996 *WS, S* 1,2, *A* 1, *SA* 1, *A* 2, *SA* 2,5	16	4	49	46	6	274
S D Culhane	1995 v J	1996 *SA* 3,4	6	1	32	15	0	114
J P Preston	1991 v US	1996 *SA* 4 (R)	8	1	4	7	0	34
J W Marshall	1995 v F	1996 *WS, S* 1, 2, *A* 1, *SA* 1, *A* 2, *SA* 2,3,4,5	11	5	0	0	0	25
S T Forster	1993 v S		6	0	0	0	0	0
M Robinson	None		0	0	0	0	0	0
S B T Fitzpatrick	1986 v F	1996 *WS, S* 1,2, *A* 1, *SA* 1, *A* 2, *SA* 2,3,4,5	83	11	0	0	0	50
N J Hewitt	1995 v I	1996 *A* 1 (R)	3	0	0	0	0	0
A D Oliver	None		0	0	0	0	0	0
M R Allen	1993 v WS	1996 *S* 2 (t)	2	0	0	0	0	0
M Collins	None		0	0	0	0	0	0
C W Dowd	1993 v BI	1996 *WS, S* 1,2, *A* 1, *SA* 1, *A* 2, *SA* 2,3,4,5	29	2	0	0	0	10
O M Brown	1992 v I	1996 *WS, S* 1,2, *A* 1, *SA* 1, *A* 2, *SA* 2,3,4,5	38	2	0	0	0	10
I D Jones	1990 v S	1996 *WS, S* 1,2, *A* 1, *SA* 1, *A* 2, *SA* 2,3,4,5	58	6	0	0	0	27
R M Brooke	1992 v I	1996 *WS, S* 1,2, *A* 1, *SA* 1, *A* 2, *SA* 2,3,4,5	32	2	0	0	0	10
B P Larsen	1992 v Wd	1996 *S* 2 (t), *SA* 4 (R)	17	1	0	0	0	4
A F Blowers	1996 v SA	1996 *SA* 2 (R),4 (R)	2	0	0	0	0	0
M N Jones	1987 v It	1996 *WS, S* 1,2, *A* 1, *SA* 1, *NZ* 2, *SA* 2,3,4,5	50	12	0	0	0	51
J A Kronfeld	1995 v C	1996 *WS, S* 1,2, *A* 1, *SA* 1, *A* 2, *SA* 2,3,4,5	18	5	0	0	0	25
G L Taylor	1996 v SA	1996 *SA* 5 (R)	1	0	0	0	0	0
T Randell	None		0	0	0	0	0	0
Z V Brooke	1987 v Arg	1996 *WS, S* 1,2, *A* 1, *SA* 1, *A* 2, *SA* 2,3,4,5	47	15	0	0	2	76
D G Mika	None		0	0	0	0	0	0

CAMPESE REACHES HIS CENTURY

THE 1996 SEASON IN AUSTRALIA
Peter Jenkins

It was a season of money, mayhem and mixed results as Australia embraced professionalism in all its guises. Internationally, there was the introduction of the Super-12 provincial championship, the round-robin involving sides from Australia, New Zealand and South Africa, and the Tri-Nations series with the same three countries taking part. And on the domestic front, there was a week by week explosion of top-level matches. The game's profile mushroomed, the crowds flocked in as never before. As Rugby League fought court battles, Rugby Union fought for and won a new-found popularity.

It was also the year David Campese, Brit-basher and wing maestro, reached the milestone of 100 Test appearances in his last international season, the first Australian and only the second player worldwide to manage the feat (after French centre Philippe Sella).

It was coincidental, but strangely fitting, that he reached his century in the northern Italian town of Padua. Tony Campese, his father, was born just 20 minutes from the Plebiscito Stadium where Campo, in front of 8,000 fans, added another entry to a bulging portfolio.

In a season of change, there was also a new skipper in lock John Eales, taking over from the retired Michael Lynagh and the injured Phil Kearns, and a new coach in Greg Smith.

Now in his forties, Smith has already been coaching for 23 seasons. A schoolteacher in Sydney, he had first guided Randwick Boys High, a team frequently foiled by a trio of brothers from nearby Matraville called Ella. He then coached the Eastern Suburbs Colts, moved up to grade, and carried the club out of the Sydney Second Division and into successive grand finals. After three seasons with NSW he then took over the big one, replacing Bob Dwyer.

Smith finished the season with eight wins from 11 Tests, an unbeaten tour of Europe – the first Wallaby coach to return home from Britain with an unblemished record – and a record win earlier in the season over Canada.

These are impressive statistics yet, midway through the European tour, Smith was a man under pressure. If he had lost any of the Test matches to Italy, Scotland, Ireland or Wales, there was every chance that his two-year contract would have been terminated at its midpoint.

There was criticism of the Wallabies style of play, while there had also been major concerns raised by a record loss to New Zealand in Wellington, in the first of the Tri-Nations matches in July.

It was for Smith, and for the Wallabies, a turbulent season with the peaks and troughs eventually settling, by season end, into a consistent victory pattern, if not necessarily pleasing to the eye.

Smith's idea was to play the game at pace, to ruck like the Kiwis, and to move the ball wide in the traditional Australian style, but only when the forwards had made their progress. In practice, there were times the Australians resembled a Rugby League team, crashing it up one off the ruck, taking it three or four phases, then giving the backs their chance.

The international season, following on from the enormous success of the Super-12 series, had opened in June, with Australia beating Wales twice and, at the end of the month, crushing Canada.

There were new caps aplenty – Owen Finegan in the back row, Marco Caputo and Mark Bell at hooker with Phil Kearns out for the season injured and Michael Foley also hurt, props Richard Harry and Andrew Heath, winger Ben Tune, half-back Sam Payne, and utility back Steve Larkham.

There was also fiddling with the fly-half role as Scott Bowen and Pat Howard were given their chances. Smith remained unconvinced, and at the end of the year was still not satisfied after calling up another option, David Knox. This position remains a major trouble spot for the Wallabies.

The Tri-Nations series followed a week later, and the All Blacks ran in six tries to nil. A hostile press descended, but the Wallabies regrouped and a week later brought off a victory over world champions South Africa in Sydney.

A fortnight later it was New Zealand again, and this time the Wallabies blew an early lead to go down by six points. They could have won – but did not – their last encounter a week later against South Africa in Bloemfontein.

After a break of seven weeks, the Wallabies were in Europe, disposing of Italy and moving on to Britain, where the Australians went back to mauling. Smith said this was to keep the ball away from pilfering and fringing back-rowers. The result was far from the pacey, run them off their feet approach he had wanted to employ. But the coach, by nature of his team's unbeaten run through Europe, avoided any challenge to his position. Success brooks no argument.

The Wallabies also had a string of injuries, including Eales, who was replaced by Tim Horan as skipper against Wales. Campese, after being dropped for the internationals against Scotland and Ireland, returned to make his final Test appearance against the Welsh.

Smith would later claim the different styles of the three Super-12 provinces, Queensland, NSW and ACT, had made his task as national coach difficult, in terms of the battle to mould players to his own on-field beliefs. But the Super-12 had provided enormous benefits.

The ACT Brumbies were a patchwork side with local stars such as Joe Roff and George Gregan joined by off-cuts from NSW and Queensland, players unable to win regular first team spots in their home states. However, the Brumbies, coached by former Australian selector Rod MacQueen, upset Queensland, Auckland and Natal and, at one stage, looked likely to qualify for the semi-finals. They missed in the end by one point to Natal.

NSW had a miserable season in Super-12, finishing seventh, two places below the Brumbies, after five wins from 11 games. Queensland topped the table with nine victories, but were soundly beaten in a semi-final at Ballymore by Natal. The South Africans lost a week later, in the final, to Auckland.

The Super-12 also brought a new points-scoring system, with teams awarded four for a win, two for a draw, one for losing by less than seven and one for scoring four tries or more. The scoring incentives inflated scores, but the entertainment factor was mirrored in record crowds for provincial matches in all three countries.

While Queensland won the first inter-state match 15-13 against NSW, a game incorporated into the Super-12, the Waratahs reversed the result in June, before the internationals kicked off. NSW won 29-25 in Sydney.

On the Australian club scene, GPS were the surprising premiers in Brisbane, downing hotshots Souths 12-6 in a tryless decider. In Sydney, Randwick won their eighth title in 10 years, beating Warringah 28-6 in the grand final.

CANADA TO AUSTRALIA 1996

THE TOURING PARTY

Manager D Whidden   **Coach** P Parfrey   **Assistant Coach** D Docherty
Captain J Graf

FULL-BACKS

S **Stewart** (UBC Old Boys)
A **Armstrong** (Ottowa Irish)
K **Kawaguchi** (Burnaby Lake, BC)

THREEQUARTERS

D **Clarke** (Swilers, Nfd)
B **Ebl** (Vancouver Kats)
S **Gray** (Vancouver Kats)
D **Lougheed** (Balmy Beach, Ont)
W **Stanley** (University of BC)
T **Woods** (James Bay, BC)
*R **Toews** (Meraloma)

HALF-BACKS

J **Graf** (UBC Old Boys)
B **Ross** (James Bay, BC)
R **Card** (Oak Bay Castaways, BC)

FORWARDS

M **Cardinal** (James Bay, BC)
S **Hendry** (Balmy Beach, Ont)
D **Penney** (Swilers, Nfd)
R **Bice** (Vancouver Rowing Club)
N **Clappinson** (Ottowa Irish)
R **Snow** (Swilers, Nfd)
A **Charron** (Ottowa Irish)
I **Gordon** (James Bay)
J **Hutchinson** (UBC Old Boys)
C **Whittaker** (James Bay, BC)
G **Mosgrove** (Ottowa Irish)
K **Whitley** (Calgary Irish)
M **James** (Burnaby Lake, BC)
P **Murphy** (Crusaders, Ont)
J **Tomlinson** (Balmy Beach, Ont)

Replacement during tour

TOUR RECORD

All matches   Played 5   Won 2   Lost 3   Points for 72   Against 160
International match   Played 1   Lost 1   Points for 9   Against 74

SCORING DETAILS

All matches					International match				
For:	7T	5C	9PG	72 Pts	For:			3PG	9 Pts
Against:	21T	14C	9PG	160 Pts	Against:	10T	9C	2PG	74 Pts

MATCH DETAILS

1996	OPPONENTS	VENUE	RESULT
15 June	Queensland B	Rockhampton	L 6-23
19 June	New South Wales	Newcastle	L 19-44
22 June	South Australia	Adelaide	W 19-13
25 June	Australian Universities	Sydney	W 19-6
29 June	AUSTRALIA	Brisbane	L 9-74

MATCH 1   15 June, Rockhampton

Queensland B: 23 (1G 2PG 2T)   **Canada XV 6** (2PG)
Queensland B: Scorers *Tries:* Constable, R Johnstone, B Johnstone
Conversion: Flatley   *Penalty Goals:* Flatley, Pini
Canada XV: Scorer *Penalty Goals:* Graf (2)

MATCH 2   19 June, Newcastle

New South Wales 44 (3G 1PG 4T)   **Canada XV 19** (2G 1T)
New South Wales: Scorers *Tries:* Murdoch (3), Ekert, Madz, Dixon, pen try
Conversions: Wallace (3)   *Penalty Goal:* Wallace
Canada XV: Scorers *Tries:* Charron, Lougheed, Ross   *Conversions:* Ross (2)

MATCH 3   22 June, Adelaide

South Australia 13 (1G 2PG)   **Canada XV 19** (1G 4PG)
South Australia: Scorers *Try:* Walsh   *Conversion:* Williamson
Penalty Goals: Williamson (2)
Canada XV: Scorers *Try:* Graf   *Conversion:* Ross   *Penalty Goals:* Ross (4)

MATCH 4   25 June, Sydney

Australian Universities 6 (2PG)   **Canada XV 19** (2G 1T)
Australian Universities: Scorer *Penalty Goals:* Madz (2)
Canada XV: Scorers *Tries:* Ebl, Stanley, pen try   *Conversions:* Ross (2)

MATCH 5   29 June, Ballymore Oval, Brisbane   Test Match
AUSTRALIA 74 (9G 2PG 1T)   **CANADA 9** (3PG)

AUSTRALIA: M Burke (NSW); D I Campese (NSW), D J Herbert
(Queensland), T J Horan (Queensland), B N Tune (Queensland); S Bowen,
S J Payne (NSW); D J Crowley (Queensland), M Bell (NSW), A Heath (NSW);
G Morgan (Queensland), J A Eales (Queensland) (*capt*); O Finegan (ACT),
M C Brial (NSW), D J Wilson (Queensland) *Replacement* G M Gregan (ACT) for
Payne (temp 44-52 mins)
Scorers *Tries:* Burke (3), Wilson (2), Campese, Horan, Payne, Herbert, Tune
Conversions: Burke (9)   *Penalty Goals:* Burke (2)
CANADA: Stewart; Lougheed, Gray, Clarke, Stanley; Ross, Graf (*capt*); Snow,
Cardinal, Bice; James, Whittaker; Gordon, Charron, Hutchinson
Replacement Tomlinson for Charron and Hutchinson (temp); Card for Graf (26
mins); Penney for Bice (60 mins); Toews for Lougheed (70 mins)
Scorer *Penalty Goals:* Ross (3)
Referee A Watson (South Africa)

AUSTRALIA TO EUROPE 1996

THE TOURING PARTY

Manager P R A Falk **Coach** G Smith **Assistant Coaches** J L P Howard, L F Walker **Captain** J A Eales

FULL-BACK

M Burke (Eastwood & NSW)

THREEQUARTERS

D I Campese (Randwick & NSW)
B Tune (GPS & Queensland)
J W Roff (Canberra Kookaburras & ACT)
D J Herbert (GPS & Queensland)
T J Horan (Souths & Queensland)
P W Howard (Queensland University & ACT)
J S Little (Souths & Queensland)
R C Tombs (Northern Suburbs & NSW)
S Larkham (Canberra Kookaburras & ACT)
*A R Murdoch (Gordon & NSW)
*A Magro (Randwick & ACT)

HALF-BACKS

D J Knox (Randwick & ACT)
T M Wallace (Gordon & NSW)
G M Gregan (Randwick & ACT)
S J Payne (Eastern Suburbs & NSW)

FORWARDS

R L L Harry (Sydney University & NSW)
C Blades (Gordon & NSW)
A T Blades (Gordon & NSW)
A Heath (Eastern Suburbs & NSW)
M Caputo (Canberra Kookaburras & ACT)
M A Foley (Souths & Queensland)
D Giffin (Sunnybank, Brisbane & ACT)
W W Waugh (Randwick & NW)
J A Eales (Brothers & Queensland)
B J Robinson (Souths & ACT)
G Morgan (Souths & Queensland)
J Welborn (Eastern Suburbs & NSW)
D J Wilson (Easts & Queensland)
D T Manu (Eastwood & NSW)
*T B Gavin (Eastern Suburbs & NSW)
T Kefu (Souths & Queensland)
M C Brial (Eastern Suburbs & NSW)
M Connors (Souths & Queensland)
*D J Crowley (Souths & Queensland)
*J Langford (Gordon ACT)
*O Finegan (Randwick & ACT)
*D A Williams (ARU trainer)
Replacements during tour

TOUR RECORD

All matches   Played 12   Won 12   Points for 453   Against 212
International matches   Played 4   Won 4   Points for 119   Against 68

SCORING DETAILS

All matches				International matches			
For:	55T 41C 32PG		453 Pts	For:	10T 9C 17PG		119 Pts
Against:	14T 8C 39PG 3DG		212 Pts	Against:	5T 2C 12PG 1DG		68 Pts

MATCH DETAILS

1996	OPPONENTS	VENUE	RESULT
19 Oct	Italy A	Catania	W 55-19
23 Oct	ITALY	Padova	W 40-18
30 Oct	Scotland A	Netherdale	W 47-20
2 Nov	Glasgow-Edinburgh	Anniesland	W 37-19
5 Nov	Scottish Districts	Perth	W 25-9
9 Nov	SCOTLAND	Murrayfield	W 29-19
13 Nov	Connacht	Galway	W 37-20
16 Nov	Ulster	Belfast	W 39-26

23 Nov	IRELAND	Dublin	W 22-12
26 Nov	Munster	Limerick	W 55-19
1 Dec	WALES	Cardiff	W 28-19
7 Dec	Barbarians	Twickenham	W 39-12

MATCH 1   19 October, Catania, Sicily

Italy A 19 (1G 4PG)   **Australia XV 55** (6G 1PG 2T)
Italy A: J Pertile; F Roselli, F Scipioni, P Donati, N Mazzucato; F Mazzariol,
G Guidi (*capt*); G de Carli, A Moscardi, A Castellani; M David, S Racca;
F Spazzolini, A Barattin, T Ravasini *Replacements* C Pilat for Mazzucato (50 mins),
V Golfetti for Mazzariol (78 mins), G Gumiero for Pertile (79 mins)
Scorers *Try:* Roselli   *Conversion:* Mazzariol   *Penalty Goals:* Mazzariol (4)
Australia XV: Larkham; Tune, Little, Tombs, Roff; Wallace, Payne; C Blades,
Caputo, A Blades; Giffin, Morgan; Kefu, Connors, Robinson *Replacement* Welborn
for Giffin (52 mins)
Scorers *Tries:* Payne, Tombs, Roff, Little, Connors, Kefu, Robinson,
Larkham   *Conversions:* Wallace (6)   *Penalty Goals:* Wallace
Referee P Thomas (France)

MATCH 2   23 October, Stadio Plebiscito, Padova   Test Match
ITALY 18 (1G 1PG 1DG 1T)   AUSTRALIA 40 (4G 4PG)

ITALY: J Pertile; M Ravazzolo, S Bordon, I Francescato, L Manteri;
D Dominguez, A Troncon; M Dal Sie, C Orlandi, F Properzi; W Cristofoletto,
D Scaglia; M Giovanelli (*capt*), O Arancio, A Sgorlon *Replacement* A Barattin for
Cristofoletto (71 mins)
Scorers *Tries:* Bordon, Dominguez   *Conversion:* Dominguez
Penalty Goal: Dominguez   *Dropped Goal:* Dominguez
AUSTRALIA: Burke; Campese, Herbert, Howard, Horan; Knox, Gregan; Harry,
Foley, Heath; Welborn, Eales (*capt*); Manu, Brial, Wilson *Replacements* Robinson
for Brial (45 mins), Little for Knox (47 mins)
Scorers *Tries:* Wilson (2), Foley, Horan   *Conversions:* Burke (4)
Penalty Goals: Burke (4)
Referee E Sorenson (USA)

MATCH 3   30 October, Netherdale

Scotland A 20 (4PG 1DG 1T)   **Australia XV 47** (5G 4PG)
Scotland A: S Lang (Heriot's FP); A Stanger (Hawick), M Craig (Nottingham),
R Eriksson (London Scottish), J Kerr (Watsonians); D Hodge (Watsonians),
G Burns (Watsonians); T Smith (Watsonians), G Ellis (Currie), S Ferguson
(Peebles); S Munro (Glasgow High/Kelvinside), S Murray (Bedford); P Walton
(Newcastle), C Hogg (Melrose) (*capt*), M Wallace (Glasgow High/Kelvinside)
Replacement A Watt (Glasgow High/Kelvinside) for Munro (60 mins)
Scorers *Try:* Smith   *Penalty Goals:* Hodge (4)   *Dropped Goal:* Hodge
Australia XV: Burke; Horan, Herbert, Little, Roff; Howard, Payne; A Blades,
Foley, Heath; Giffin, Eales (*capt*); Kefu, Brial, Wilson *Replacements* Tombs for
Little (19 mins), Connors for Brial (25 mins)
Scorers *Tries:* Horan (2), Burke, Payne, Connors   *Conversions:* Burke (5)
Penalty Goals: Burke (4)
Referee J Pearson (England)

MATCH 4   2 November, Old Anniesland, Glasgow

Glasgow-Edinburgh 19 (1G 4PG)   **Australia XV 37** (3G 2PG 2T)
Glasgow-Edinburgh: D Lee (Watsonians); D Stark (Melrose), S Hastings
(Watsonians) (*capt*), A Garry (Watsonians), K Logan (Stirling County);
A Donaldson (Currie), G Beveridge (Boroughmuir); A Watt (Currie), G Bulloch
(West of Scotland), B Stewart (Edinburgh Academicals); P Jennings
(Boroughmuir), A Lucking (Currie); D Clark (Currie), S Reid (Boroughmuir),
D McLeish (West of Scotland)
Scorers *Try:* Logan   *Conversion:* Donaldson   *Penalty Goals:* Donaldson (4)
Australia XV: Roff; Campese, Herbert, Howard, Tune; Knox, Gregan; Harry,
Foley, A Blades; Waugh, Welborn; Manu, Connors, Wilson (*capt*)
Replacements Kefu for Connors (66 mins), Caputo for Manu (77 mins)
Scorers *Tries:* Connors, Knox, Campese, Manu, Wilson   *Conversions:* Knox (3)
Penalty Goals: Knox (2)
Referee A Watson (Ireland)

MATCH 5   5 November, McDiarmid Park, Perth

Scottish Districts 9 (3PG)   **Australia XV 25** (2G 2PG 1T)
Scottish Districts: G Fraser (London Irish); D Officer (Currie), P Rouse (Dundee
HSFP), I Wynn (Wakefield), G Parker (Melrose); J Steele (London Scottish),
D Patterson (Heriot's FP); W Anderson (Kircaldy), M Scott (Orrell), M Stewart
(Northampton); D Burns (Boroughmuir), I Elliott (Hawick); D McIvor (Glenrothes)
(*capt*), M Waite (Edinburgh Academicals), B Pountney (Northampton)
Scorer *Penalty Goals:* Parker (3)
Australia XV: Larkham; Tune, Magro, Tombs (*capt*), Roff; Wallace, Gregan;
C Blades, Caputo, Heath; Welborn, Gavin; Williams, Kefu, Finegan
Scorers *Tries:* Williams, Magro, Roff   *Conversions:* Wallace (2)
Penalty Goals: Wallace (2)
Referee T Rowlands (Wales)

MATCH 6   9 November, Murrayfield   Test Match
SCOTLAND 19 (3PG 2T)   AUSTRALIA 29 (2G 5PG)

SCOTLAND: R J S Shepherd (Melrose); A G Stanger (Hawick),
G P J Townsend (Northampton) (*capt*), B R S Eriksson (London Scottish),
K M Logan (Stirling County); C M Chalmers (Melrose), G Armstrong
(Newcastle); D I W Hilton (Bath), K D McKenzie (Stirling County), B D Stewart
(Edinburgh Academicals); D F Cronin (Wasps), G W Weir (Newcastle);
M I Wallace (Glasgow H/Kelvinside), E W Peters (Bath), I R Smith (Gloucester)
Replacement B W Redpath (Melrose) for Armstrong (76 mins)
Scorers *Tries:* Logan, Stanger   *Penalty Goals:* Shepherd (3)
AUSTRALIA: Burke; Horan, Herbert, Howard, Roff; Knox, Payne; Harry, Foley,
A Blades; Waugh, Eales (*capt*); Finegan, Manu, Wilson *Replacement* Robinson for
Finegan (65 mins)
Scorers *Tries:* Waugh, Herbert   *Conversions:* Burke (2)   *Penalty Goals:* Burke (5)
Referee P Thomas (France)

MATCH 7   13 November, The Sports Ground, Galway

Connacht 20 (5PG 1T)   **Australia XV 37** (3G 2PG 2T)
Connacht: B Carey; M Kearin, A Reddan, N Barry, N Carolan; E Elwood,
C McGuinness; J Maher, W Mulcahy, M Finlay; G Heaslip, S Leahy; H Taylor,
B Gavin, R Rogers *Replacements* M Reilly for Taylor (53 mins), R Ward for Maher

(63 mins), M Murphy for Barry (77 mins)
Scorers *Try:* Leahy   *Penalty Goals:* Elwood (5)
Australia XV: Wallace; Tune, Murdoch, Tombs, Campese; Larkham, Gregan;
C Blades, Caputo, Heath; Giffin, Gavin; Kefu, Finegan, Robinson
Scorers *Tries:* Gregan (2), Gavin, Finegan, Murdoch   *Conversions:* Wallace (3)
Penalty Goals: Wallace (2)
Referee S Piercy (England)

MATCH 8   16 November, Ravenhill, Belfast

Ulster 26 (2G 4PG)   **Australia XV 39** (4G 2PG 1T)
Ulster: R Morrow; J Topping, M Field, M McCall, J Cunningham; S Laing,
A Matchett; R Mackey, S Ritchie, G Leslie; S Duncan, G Longwell; S McKinty,
P Johns, D McBride *(capt)*
Scorers *Tries:* Topping, pen try   *Conversions:* Laing (2)   *Penalty Goals:* Laing (4)
Australia XV: Burke; Campese, Herbert, Horan, Roff; Knox, Gregan; Harry,
Foley, A Blades; Brial, Waugh; Eales *(capt)*, Manu, Wilson *Replacement* Robinson
for Waugh (35 mins)
Scorers *Tries:* Roff (2), Eales, Campese, pen try   *Conversions:* Burke (4)
Penalty Goals: Burke, Knox
Referee K McCartney (Scotland) Sub: C Muir (28 mins)

MATCH 9   23 November, Lansdowne Road, Dublin Test Match
IRELAND 12 (4PG)   AUSTRALIA 22 (1G 5PG)

IRELAND: J E Staples (Harlequins); J A Topping (Ballymena), J C Bell
(Northampton), M C McCall (Dungannon), D J Crotty (Garryowen); P A Burke
(Bristol), S C McIvor (Garryowen); N J Popplewell (Newcastle), K G M Wood
(Harlequins) *(capt)*, P S Wallace (Saracens); G M Fulcher (London Irish),
J W Davidson (London Irish); D S Corkery (Bristol), A G Foley (Shannon),
W D McBride (Malone) *Replacement* M J Field (Malone) for Staples (13 mins)
Scorer *Penalty Goals:* Burke (4)
AUSTRALIA: Burke; Little, Herbert, Horan, Roff; Knox, Gregan; Crowley,
Foley, A Blades; Waugh, Eales *(capt)*; Manu, Brial, Wilson *Replacement* Robinson
for Eales (65 mins)
Scorers *Try:* Knox   *Conversion:* Burke   *Penalty Goals:* Burke (5)
Referee B Campsall (England)

MATCH 10   26 November, Thomond Park, Limerick

Munster 19 (1G 3PG 1DG)   **Australia XV 55** (5G 4T)
Munster: P Murray; R Wallace, B Walsh, S McCahill, D Crotty; K Keane,
S McIvor; J Fitzgerald, T Kingston, N Healy; M Galwey, D Kirby; A Foley,
B Cronin, D Corkery *Replacements* P Clohessy for Healy (40 mins), L Dinneen for
Kirby (50 mins), M Lynch for Walsh (65 mins)
Scorers *Try:* Keane   *Conversion:* Keane   *Penalty Goals:* Keane (3)
Dropped Goal: Murray
Australia XV: Larkham; Campese, Little, Tombs, Tune; Howard, Payne;
C Blades, Caputo, Heath; Gavin, Giffin; Kefu, Finegan, Robinson
Replacements Wallace for Larkham (72 mins), Murdoch for Little (72 mins)
Scorers *Tries:* Campese (2), Murdoch (2), Finegan, Kefu, Little, Payne,
Tune   *Conversions:* Larkham (5)
Referee D Davies (Wales)

MATCH 11 1 December, Cardiff Arms Park, Cardiff Test Match
WALES 19 (1G 4PG) AUSTRALIA 28 (2G 3PG 1T)

WALES: W T Proctor (Llanelli); I C Evans (Llanelli), G Thomas (Bridgend),
I S Gibbs (Swansea), D R James (Bridgend); J Davies (Cardiff), R Howley
(Cardiff); C D Loader (Swansea), J M Humphreys (Cardiff) *(capt)*, D Young
(Cardiff); G O Llewellyn (Harlequins), D Jones (Cardiff); H T Taylor (Cardiff),
S M Williams (Neath), K P Jones (Ebbw Vale) *Replacements* C L Charvis
(Swansea) for Taylor (16 mins); N R Jenkins (Pontypridd) for Proctor (49 mins),
J C Quinnell (Richmond) for D Jones (70 mins)
Scorers *Try:* Thomas *Conversion:* Davies *Penalty Goal:* Davies (4)
AUSTRALIA: Burke; Campese, Little, Horan *(capt)*, Roff; Howard, Gregan;
Crowley, Foley, A Blades; Gavin, Giffin; Finegan, Brial, Wilson
Scorers *Tries:* Burke, Brial, pen try *Conversions:* Burke (2)
Penalty Goals: Burke (3)
Referee D I Ramage (Scotland)

MATCH 12 7 December, Twickenham

Barbarians 12 (1G 1T) **Australia XV 39** (4G 2PG 1T)
Barbarians: T R G Stimpson (Newcastle); N K Walker (Cardiff), A G Bateman
(Richmond), G P J Townsend (Northampton), T Underwood (Newcastle);
C R Andrew (Newcastle) *(capt)*, R Howley (Cardiff); N J Popplewell (Newcastle),
N J Hewitt (Southland, NZ), D J Garforth (Leicester); I D Jones (North Harbour,
NZ), J C Quinnell (Richmond); D McIntosh (Pontypridd), L S Quinnell
(Richmond), N A Back (Leicester) *Replacements* J T Stransky (Western Province, SA)
for Stimpson (22 mins), A P Moore (Richmond) for Howley (58 mins), M Allen
(Northampton) for Townsend, G W Weir (Newcastle) for C Quinnell (79 mins)
Scorers *Tries:* Bateman, C Quinnell *Conversion:* Andrew
Australia: Burke; Campese, Herbert, Horan *(capt)*, Roff; Howard, Payne;
Crowley, Caputo, A Blades; Giffin, Gavin; Finegan, Brial, Wilson
Replacements: Robinson for Brial (23 mins), Foley for Caputo (26 mins), Tombs
for Howard (72 mins), Heath for Blades (76 mins), Larkham for Burke (78 mins)
Scorers *Tries:* Burke (2), Roff, Campese, Horan *Conversions:* Burke (4)
Penalty Goals: Burke (2)
Referee E Morrison (England)

AUSTRALIAN INTERNATIONAL PLAYERS
(up to 30 April 1997)

N.B. In the summer of 1986, the ARU retrospectively granted full Australian Test status to the five international matches played by the 1927-28 touring team to Europe. In 1988 Test status was extended to all those who played overseas in the 1920s.

Abrahams, A M F (NSW) 1967 NZ, 1968 NZ 1, 1969 W
Adams, N J (NSW) 1955 NZ 1
Adamson, R W (NSW) 1912 US
Allan, T (NSW) 1946 NZ 1, M, NZ 2, 1947 NZ 2, S, I, W, 1948 E, F, 1949 M 1,2,3, NZ 1,2
Anlezark, E A (NSW) 1905 NZ
Armstrong, A R (NSW) 1923 NZ 1,2
Austin, L R (NSW) 1963 E

Baker, R L (NSW) 1904 BI 1,2
Baker, W H (NSW) 1914 NZ 1,2,3
Ballesty, J P (NSW) 1968 NZ 1,2, F, I, S, 1969 W, SA 2,3,4,
Bannon, D P (NSW) 1946 M
Bardsley, E J (NSW) 1928 NZ 1,3, M (R)
Barker, H S (NSW) 1952 Fj 1,2, NZ 1,2, 1953 SA 4, 1954 Fj 1,2
Barnett, J T (NSW) 1907 NZ 1,2,3, 1908 W, 1909 E
Barry, M J (Q) 1971 SA 3
Barton, R F D (NSW) 1899 BI 3
Batch, P G (Q) 1975 S, W, 1976 E, Fj 1,2,3, F 1,2, 1978 W 1,2, NZ 1,2,3, 1979 Arg 2
Batterham, R P (NSW) 1967 NZ, 1970 S
Battishall, B R (NSW) 1973 E
Baxter, A J (NSW) 1949 M 1,2,3, NZ 1,2, 1951 NZ 1,2, 1952 NZ 1,2
Baxter, T J (Q) 1958 NZ 3
Beith, B McN (NSW) 1914 NZ 3
Bell, K R (Q) 1968 S
Bell, M D NSW) 1996 C
Bennett, W G (Q) 1931 M, 1933 SA 1,2,3,
Bermingham, J V (Q) 1934 NZ 1,2, 1937 SA 1
Berne, J E (NSW) 1975 S
Besomo, K S (NSW) 1979 I 2
Betts, T N (Q) 1951 NZ 2,3, 1954 Fj 2
Biilmann, R R (NSW) 1933 SA 1,2,3,4
Birt, R (Q) 1914 NZ 2
Black, J W (NSW) 1985 C 1,2, NZ, Fj 1
Blackwood, J G (NSW) 1923 NZ 1,2,3, 1925 NZ, 1927 I, W, S, 1928 E, F
Blades, A T (NSW) 1996 S, I, W 3
Blair, M R (NSW) 1928 F, 1931 M, NZ
Bland, G V (NSW) 1928 NZ 3, M, 1932 NZ 1,2,3, 1933 SA 1,2,4,5
Blomley, J (NSW) 1949 M 1,2,3, NZ 1,2, 1950 BI 1,2
Boland, S B (Q) 1899 BI 3,4, 1903 NZ
Bond, J H (NSW) 1921 NZ
Bonis, E T (Q) 1929 NZ 1,2,3, 1930 BI, 1931 M, NZ, 1932 NZ 1,2,3, 1933 SA 1,2,3,4,5, 1934 NZ 1,2, 1936 NZ 1,2, M, 1937 SA 1, 1938 NZ 1
Bosler, J M (NSW) 1953 SA 1
Bouffler, R G (NSW) 1899 BI 3
Bourke, T K (Q) 1947 NZ 2
Bowen, S (NSW) 1993 SA 1,2,3, 1995 [R], NZ 1,2, 1996 C, NZ 1, SA 2
Bowers, A J A (NSW) 1923 NZ 3, 1925 NZ, 1927 I
Boyce, E S (NSW) 1962 NZ 1,2, 1964 NZ 1,2,3, 1965 SA 1,2, 1966 W, S, 1967 E, I 1, F, I 2
Boyce, J S (NSW) 1962 NZ 3,4,5, 1963 E. SA 1,2,3,4, 1964 NZ 1,3, 1965 SA 1,2
Boyd, A (NSW) 1899 BI 3
Boyd, A F McC (Q) 1958 M 1
Brass, J E (NSW) 1966 BI 2, W, S, 1967 E, I 1, F, I 2, NZ, 1968 NZ 1, F, I, S
Breckenridge, J W (NSW) 1927 I, W, S, 1928 E, F, 1929 NZ 1,2,3, 1930 BI
Brial, M C (NSW) 1993 F 1 (R), 2, 1996 W 1 (R), 2, C, NZ 1, SA 1, NZ 2, SA 2, It, I, W 3

Bridle, O L (V) 1931 M, 1932 NZ 1,2,3, 1933 SA 3,4,5, 1934 NZ 1,2, 1936 NZ 1,2, M
Broad, E G (Q) 1949 M 1
Brockhoff, J D (NSW) 1949 M 2,3, NZ 1,2, 1950 BI 1,2, 1951 NZ 2,3
Brown, B R (Q) 1972 NZ 1,3
Brown, J V (NSW) 1956 SA 1,2, 1957 NZ 1,2, 1958 W, I, E, S, F
Brown, R C (NSW) 1975 E 1,2
Brown, S W (NSW) 1953 SA 2,3,4
Bryant, H (NSW) 1925 NZ
Buchan, A J (NSW) 1946 NZ 1,2, 1947 NZ 1,2, S, I, W, 1948 E, F, 1949 M 3
Bull, D (NSW) 1928 M
Buntine, H (NSW) 1923 NZ 1 (R)
Burdon, A (NSW) 1903 NZ, 1904 BI 1,2, 1905 NZ
Burge, A B (NSW) 1907 NZ 3, 1908 W
Burge, P H (NSW) 1907 NZ 1,2,3
Burge, R (NSW) 1928 NZ 1,2,3 (R), M (R)
Burke, B T (NSW) 1988 S (R)
Burke, C T (NSW) 1946 NZ 2, 1947 NZ 1,2, S, I, W, 1948 E, F, 1949 M 2,3, NZ 1,2, 1950 BI 1,2, 1951 NZ 1,2,3, 1953 SA 2,3,4, 1954 Fj 1, 1955 NZ 1,2,3, 1956 SA 1,2,
Burke, M (NSW) 1993 SA 3 (R), F 1, 1994 I 1,2, It 1,2, 1995 [C, R, E], NZ 1,2, 1996 W 1,2, C, NZ 1, SA 1, NZ 2, SA 2, It, S, I, W 3
Burke, M P (NSW) 1984 E [R], 1985 C 1,2, NZ, Fj 1,2, 1986 It (R), F, Arg 1,2, NZ 1,2,3, 1987 SK, [US, J, I, F, W], NZ, Arg 1,2
Burnet, D R (NSW) 1972 F 1,2, NZ 1,2,3, Fj
Butler, O F (NSW) 1969 SA 1,2, 1970 S, 1971 SA 2,3, F 1,2

Calcraft, W J (NSW) 1985 C 1, 1986 It, Arg 2
Caldwell, B C (NSW) 1928 NZ 3
Cameron, A S (NSW) 1951 NZ 1,2,3, 1952 Fj 1,2, NZ 1,2, 1953 SA 1,2,3,4, 1954 Fj 1,2, 1955 NZ 1,2,3, 1956 SA 1,2, 1957 NZ 1, 1958 I
Campbell, J D (NSW) 1910 NZ 1,2,3
Campbell, W A (Q) 1984 Fj, 1986 It, F, Arg 1,2, NZ 1,2,3, 1987 SK, [E, US, J (R), I, F], NZ, 1988 E, 1989 BI 1,2,3, NZ, 1990 NZ 2,3
Campese, D I (ACT, NSW) 1982 NZ 1,2,3, 1983 US, Arg 1,2, NZ, It, F 1,2, 1984 Fj, NZ 1,2,3, E, I, W, S, 1985 Fj 1,2, 1986 It, F, Arg 1,2, NZ 1,2,3, 1987 [E, US, J, I, F, W], NZ, 1988 E 1,2, NZ 1,2,3, E, S, It, 1989 BI 1,2,3, NZ, F 1,2, 1990 F 2,3, US, NZ 1,2,3, 1991 W, E, NZ 1,2, [Arg, WS, W, I, NZ, E], 1992 S 1,2, NZ 1,2,3, SA, I, W, 1993 Tg, NZ, SA 1,2,3, F 1,2, 1994 I 1,2, It 1,2, WS, NZ, 1995 Arg 1,2, [SA, C, E], NZ 2 (R), 1996 W 1,2, C, NZ 1, SA 1, NZ 2, SA 2, It, W3
Canniffe, W D (Q) 1907 NZ 2
Caputo, M E (ACT) 1996 W 1,2
Carberry, C M (NSW, Q) 1973 Tg 2, E, 1976 I, US, Fj 1,2,3, 1981 F 1,2, I, W, S, 1982 E
Cardy, A M (NSW) 1966 BI 1,2, W, S, 1967 E, I 1, F, 1968 NZ 1,2
Carew, P J (Q) 1899 BI 1,2,3,4
Carmichael, P (Q) 1904 BI 2, 1907 NZ 1, 1908 W, 1909 E
Carozza, P V (Q) 1990 F 1,2,3, NZ 2,3, 1992 S 1,2, NZ 1,2,3, SA, I, W, 1993 Tg, NZ
Carpenter, M G (V) 1938 NZ 1,2,
Carr, E T A (NSW) 1913 NZ 1,2,3, 1914 NZ 1,2,3
Carr, E W (NSW) 1921 NZ 1, F, It, W3
Carroll, D B (NSW) 1908 W, 1912 US
Carroll, J C (NSW) 1953 SA 1

341

David Campese walks off the pitch after his final international appearance, against Wales at Cardiff Arms Park in December 1996.

Currie, E W (Q) 1899 *BI* 2
Cutler, S A G (NSW) 1982 *NZ* 2 (R), 1984 *NZ* 1,2,3, *E, I, W, S*, 1985 *C* 1,2, *NZ, Fj* 1,2, 1986 *It, F, NZ* 1,2,3, 1987 *SK*, [*E, J, I, F, W*], *NZ, Arg* 1,2, 1988 *E* 1,2, *NZ* 1,2,3, *E, S, It*, 1989 *BI* 1,2,3, *NZ*, 1991 [*WS*]

Daly, A J (NSW) 1989 *NZ, F* 1,2, 1990 *F* 1,2,3, *US, NZ* 1,2,3, 1991 *W, E, NZ* 1,2, [*Arg, W, I, NZ, E*], 1992 *S* 1,2, *NZ* 1,2,3, *SA*, 1993 *Tg, NZ, SA* 1,2,3, *C, F* 1,2, 1994 *I* 1,2, *It* 1,2, *WS, NZ*, 1995 [*C, R*]
D'Arcy, A M (Q) 1980 *Fj, NZ* 3, 1981 *F* 1,2, *I, W, S*, 1982 *E, S* 1,2
Darveniza, P (NSW) 1969 *W, SA* 2,3,4
Davidson, R A L (NSW) 1952 *Fj* 1,2, *NZ* 1,2, 1953 *SA* 1, 1957 *NZ* 1,2, 1958 *W, I, E, S, F, M* 1
Davis, C C (NSW) 1949 *NZ* 1, 1951 *NZ* 1,2,3
Davis, E H (V) 1947 *S, W*, 1949 *M* 1,2
Davis, G V (NSW) 1963 *E, SA* 1,2,3,4, 1964 *NZ* 1,2,3, 1965 *SA* 1, 1966 *BI* 1,2, *W, S*, 1967 *E, I* 1, *F, I* 2, *NZ*, 1968 *NZ* 1,2, *F, I, S*, 1969 *W, SA* 1,2,3,4, 1970 *S*, 1971 *SA* 1,2,3, *F* 1,2, 1972 *F* 1,2, *NZ* 1,2,3
Davis, G W G (NSW) 1955 *NZ* 2,3
Davis, R A (NSW) 1974 *NZ* 1,2,3
Davis, T S R (NSW) 1921 *NZ*, 1923 *NZ* 1,2,3
Davis, W (NSW) 1899 *BI* 1,3,4
Dawson, W L (NSW) 1946 *NZ* 1,2
Diett, L J (NSW) 1959 *BI* 1,2
Dix, W (NSW) 1907 *NZ* 1,2,3, 1909 *E*
Dixon, E J (Q) 1904 *BI* 3
Donald, K J (Q) 1957 *NZ* 1, 1958 *W, I, E, S, M* 2,3, 1959 *BI* 1,2
Dore, E (Q) 1904 *BI* 1
Dore, M J (Q) 1905 *NZ*
Dorr, R W (V) 1936 *M*, 1937 *SA* 1
Douglas, J A (V) 1962 *NZ* 3,4,5
Dowse, J H (NSW) 1961 *Fj* 1,2, *SA* 1,2
Dunbar, A R (NSW) 1910 *NZ* 1,2,3, 1912 *US*
Dunlop, E E (V) 1932 *NZ* 3, 1934 *NZ* 1
Dunn, P K (NSW) 1958 *NZ* 1,2,3, 1959 *BI* 1,2
Dunn, V A (NSW) 1921 *NZ*
Dunworth, D A (Q) 1971 *F* 1,2, 1972 *F* 1,2, 1976 *Fj* 2
Dwyer, L J (NSW) 1910 *NZ* 1,2,3, 1912 *US*, 1913 *NZ* 3, 1914 *NZ* 1,2,3

Eales, J A (Q) 1991 *W, E, NZ* 1,2, [*Arg, WS, W, I, NZ, E*], 1992 *S* 1,2, *NZ* 1,2,3, *SA, I*, 1994 *I* 1,2, *It* 1,2, *WS, NZ*, 1995 *Arg* 1,2, [*SA, C, R, E*], 1996 *W* 1,2, *C, NZ* 1, *SA* 1, *NZ* 2, *SA* 2, *It, S, I*
Eastes, C C (NSW) 1946 *NZ* 1,2, 1947 *NZ* 1,2, 1949 *M* 1,2
Egerton, R H (NSW) 1991 *W, E, NZ* 1,2, [*Arg, W, I, NZ, E*]
Ella, G A (NSW) 1982 *NZ* 1,2, 1983 *F* 1,2, 1988 *E* 2, *NZ* 1
Ella, G J (NSW) 1982 *S* 1, 1983 *It*, 1985 *C* 2 (R), *Fj* 2
Ella, M G (NSW) 1980 *NZ* 1,2,3, 1981 *F* 2, *S*, 1982 *E, S* 1, *NZ* 1,2,3, 1983 *US, Arg* 1,2, *NZ, It, F* 1,2, 1984 *Fj, NZ* 1,2,3, *E, I, W, S*
Ellem, M A (NSW) 1976 *Fj* 3 (R)
Elliott, F M (NSW) 1957 *NZ* 1
Elliott, R E (NSW) 1921 *NZ*, 1923 *NZ* 1,2,3
Ellis, C S (NSW) 1899 *BI* 1,2,3,4
Ellis, K J (NSW) 1958 *NZ* 1,2,3, 1959 *BI* 1,2
Ellwood, B J (NSW) 1958 *NZ* 1,2,3, 1961 *Fj* 2,3, *SA* 1, *F*, 1962 *NZ* 1,2,3,4,5, 1963 *SA* 1,2,3,4, 1964 *NZ* 3, 1965 *SA* 1,2, 1966 *BI* 1
Emanuel, D M (NSW) 1957 *NZ* 2, 1958 *W, I, E, S, F, M* 1,2,3
Emery, N A (NSW) 1947 *NZ* 2, *S, I, W*, 1948 *E, F*, 1949 *M* 2,3, *NZ* 1,2
Erasmus, D J (NSW) 1923 *NZ* 1,2
Erby, A B (NSW) 1923 *NZ* 2,3
Evans, L J (Q) 1903 *NZ*, 1904 *BI* 1,3
Evans, W T (Q) 1899 *BI* 1,2

Fahey, E J (NSW) 1912 *US*, 1913 *NZ* 1,2, 1914 *NZ* 3
Fairfax, R L (NSW) 1971 *F* 1,2, 1972 *F* 1,2, *NZ* 1, *Fj*, 1973 *W, E*
Farmer, E H (Q) 1910 *NZ* 1
Farr-Jones, N C (NSW) 1984 *E, I, W, S*, 1985 *C* 1,2, *NZ, Fj* 1,2, 1986 *It, F, Arg* 1,2, *NZ* 1,2,3, 1988 *E* 1,2, *NZ* 1,2,3, *E, S, It*, 1989 *BI* 1,2,3, *NZ, F* 1,2, 1990 *F* 1,2,3, *US, NZ* 1,2,3, 1991 *W, E,*

NZ 1,2, [*Arg, WS, I, NZ, E*], 1992 *S* 1,2, *NZ* 1,2,3, *SA*, 1993 *NZ, SA* 1,2,3
Fay, G (NSW) 1971 *SA* 2, 1972 *NZ* 1,2,3, 1973 *Tg* 1,2, *W, E*, 1974 *NZ* 1,2,3, 1975 *E* 1,2, *J* 1, *S, W*, 1976 *I, US*, 1978 *W* 1,2, *NZ* 1,2,3, 1979 *I* 1
Fenwicke, P T (NSW) 1957 *NZ* 1, 1958 *W, I, E*, 1959 *BI* 1,2
Ferguson, R T (NSW) 1923 *NZ* 3
Fihelly, J A (Q) 1907 *NZ* 2
Finegan, O (ACT) 1996 *W* 1,2, *C, NZ* 1, *SA* 1 (t), *S, W* 3
Finlay, A N (NSW) 1927 *I, W, S*, 1928 *E, F*, 1929 *NZ* 1,2,3, 1930 *BI*
Finley, F G (NSW) 1904 *BI* 3
Finnane, S C (NSW) 1975 *E* 1, *J* 1,2, 1976 *E*, 1978 *W* 1,2
FitzSimons, P (NSW) 1989 *F* 1,2, 1990 *F* 1,2,3, *US, NZ* 1
Flanagan, P (Q) 1907 *NZ* 1,2
Flett, J A (NSW) 1990 *US, NZ* 2,3, 1991 [*WS*]
Flynn, J P (Q) 1914 *NZ* 1,2
Fogarty, J R (Q) 1949 *M* 2,3
Foley, M A (Q) 1995 [*C* (R), *R*], 1996 *W* 2(R), *NZ* 1, *SA* 1, *NZ* 2, *SA* 2, *It, S, I, W* 3
Forbes, C F (Q) 1953 *SA* 2,3,4, 1954 *Fj* 1, 1956 *SA* 1,2
Ford, B (Q) 1957 *NZ* 2
Ford, E E (NSW) 1927 *I, W, S*, 1928 *E, F*, 1929 *NZ* 1,3
Ford, J A (NSW) 1925 *NZ*, 1927 *I, W, S*, 1928 *E*, 1929 *NZ* 1,2,3, 1930 *BI*
Forman, T R (NSW) 1968 *I, S*, 1969 *W, SA* 1,2,3,4
Fox, C L (NSW) 1921 *NZ*, 1928 *F*
Fox, O G (NSW) 1958 *F*
Francis, E (Q) 1914 *NZ* 1,2
Frawley, D (Q, NSW) 1986 *Arg* 2 (R), 1987 *Arg* 1,2, 1988 *E* 1,2, *NZ* 1,2,3, *S, It*
Freedman, J E (NSW) 1962 *NZ* 3,4,5, 1963 *SA* 1
Freeman, E (NSW) 1946 *NZ* 1 (R), *M*
Freney, M E (Q) 1972 *NZ* 1,2,3, 1973 *Tg* 1, *W, E* (R)
Furness, D C (NSW) 1946 *M*
Futter, F C (NSW) 1904 *BI* 3

Gardner, J M (Q) 1987 *Arg* 2, 1988 *E* 1, *NZ* 1, *E*
Gardner, W C (NSW) 1950 *BI* 1
Garner, R L (NSW) 1949 *NZ* 1,2
Gavin, K A (NSW) 1909 *E*
Gavin, T B (NSW) 1988 *NZ* 2,3, *S, It* (R), 1989 *NZ* (R), *F* 1,2, 1990 *F* 1,2,3, *US, NZ* 1,2,3, 1991 *W, E, NZ* 1, 1992 *S* 1,2, *SA, I, W*, 1993 *Tg, NZ, SA* 1,2,3, *C, F* 1,2, 1994 *I* 1,2, *It* 1,2, *WS, NZ*, 1995 *Arg* 1,2, [*SA, C, R, E*], *NZ* 1,2, 1996 *NZ* 2 (R), *SA* 2, *W* 3
Gelling, A M (NSW) 1972 *NZ* 1, *Fj*
George, H W (NSW) 1910 *NZ* 1,2,3, 1912 *US*, 1913 *NZ* 1,3, 1914 *NZ* 1,3
George, W G (NSW) 1923 *NZ* 1,2, 1928 *NZ* 1,2,3, *M*
Gibbons, E de C (NSW) 1936 *NZ* 1,2, *M*
Gibbs, P R (V) 1966 *S*
Giffin, D (ACT) 1996 *W* 3
Gilbert, H (NSW) 1910 *NZ* 1,2,3
Girvan, B (ACT) 1988 *E*
Gordon, G C (NSW) 1929 *NZ* 1
Gordon, K M (NSW) 1950 *BI* 1,2
Gould, R G (Q) 1980 *NZ* 1,2,3, 1981 *I, W, S*, 1982 *S* 2, *NZ* 1,2,3, 1983 *US, Arg* 1, *F* 1,2, 1984 *NZ* 1,2,3, *E, I, W, S*, 1985 *NZ*, 1986 *It*, 1987 *SK*, [*E*]
Gourley, S R (NSW) 1988 *S, It*, 1989 *BI* 1,2,3
Graham, C S (Q) 1899 *BI* 2
Graham, R (NSW) 1973 *Tg* 1,2, *W, E*, 1974 *NZ* 2,3, 1975 *E* 2, *J* 1,2, *S, W*, 1976 *I, US, Fj* 1,2,3, *F* 1,2
Gralton, A S I (Q) 1899 *BI* 1,4, 1903 *NZ*
Grant, J C (NSW) 1988 *E* 1, *NZ* 2,3, *E*
Graves, R H (NSW) 1907 *NZ* 1 (R)
Greatorex, E N (NSW) 1923 *NZ* 3, 1928 *E, F*
Gregan, G M (ACT) 1994 *It* 1,2, *WS, NZ*, 1995 *Arg* 1,2, [*SA, C* (R), *R, E*], 1996 *W* 1, *C* (t), *SA* 1, *NZ* 2, *SA* 2, *It, I, W* 3
Gregory, S C (Q) 1968 *NZ* 3, *F, I, S*, 1969 *SA* 1,3, 1971 *SA* 1,3, 1972 *F* 1,2, 1973 *Tg* 1,2, *W, E*
Grey, G O (NSW) 1972 *F* 2 (R), *NZ* 1,2,3, *Fj* (R)
Griffin, T S (NSW) 1907 *NZ* 1,3, 1908 *W*, 1910 *NZ* 1,2, 1912 *US*
Grigg, P C (Q) 1980 *NZ* 3, 1982 *S* 2, *NZ* 1,2,3, 1983 *Arg* 2, *NZ*, 1984 *Fj, W, S*, 1985 *C* 1,2, *NZ, Fj* 1,2, 1986 *Arg* 1,2, *NZ* 1,2, 1987 *SK*, [*E, J, I, F, W*]
Grimmond, D N (NSW) 1964 *NZ* 2
Gudsell, K E (NSW) 1951 *NZ* 1,2,3

1,2, 1961 *SA* 1,2, *F*, 1962 *NZ* 2,3,4,5, 1965 *SA* 1,2, 1966 *W, S*, 1967 *E, I* 1, *F, I* 2
L'Estrange, R D (Q) 1971 *F* 1,2, 1972 *NZ* 1,2,3, 1973 *Tg* 1,2, *W, E*, 1974 *NZ* 1,2,3, 1975 *S, W*, 1976 *I, US*
Lewis, L S (Q) 1934 *NZ* 1,2, 1936 *NZ* 2, 1938 *NZ* 1
Lidbury, S (NSW) 1987 *Arg* 1, 1988 *E* 2
Lillicrap, C P (Q) 1985 *Fj* 2, 1987 [*US, I, F, W*], 1989 *BI* 1, 1991 [*WS*]
Lindsay, R T G (Q) 1932 *NZ* 3
Lisle, R J (NSW) 1961 *Fj* 1,2,3, *SA* 1
Little, J S (Q) 1989 *F* 1,2, 1990 *F* 1,2,3, *US*, 1991 *W, E, NZ* 1,2, [*Arg, W, I, NZ, E*], 1992 *NZ* 1,2,3, *SA, I, W*, 1993 *Tg, NZ, SA* 1,2,3, *C, F* 1,2, 1994 *WS, NZ*, 1995 *Arg* 1,2, [*SA, C, E*], *NZ* 1,2, 1996 *It* (R), *I, W* 3
Livermore, A E (Q) 1946 *NZ* 1, *M*
Loane, M E (Q) 1973 *Tg* 1,2, 1974 *NZ* 1, 1975 *E* 1,2, *J* 1, 1976 *E, I, Fj* 1,2,3, *F* 1,2, 1978 *W* 1,2, 1979 *I* 1,2, *NZ, Arg* 1,2, 1981 *F* 1,2, *I, W, S*, 1982 *E, S* 1,2
Logan, D L (NSW) 1958 *M* 1
Loudon, D B (NSW) 1921 *NZ*
Loudon, R B (NSW) 1923 *NZ* 1 (R), 2,3, 1928 *NZ* 1,2,3, *M*, 1929 *NZ* 2, 1933 *SA* 2,3,4,5, 1934 *NZ* 2
Love, E W (NSW) 1932 *NZ* 1,2,3
Lowth, D R (NSW) 1958 *NZ* 1
Lucas, B C (Q) 1905 *NZ*
Lucas, P W (NSW) 1982 *NZ* 1,2,3
Lutge, D (NSW) 1903 *NZ*, 1904 *BI* 1,2,3
Lynagh, M P (Q) 1984 *Fj, E, I, W, S*, 1985 *C* 1,2, *NZ*, 1986 *It, F, Arg* 1,2, *NZ* 1,2,3, 1987 [*E, US, J, I, F, W*], *Arg* 1,2, 1988 *E* 1,2, *NZ* 1,3 (R), *E, S, It*, 1989 *BI* 1,2,3, *NZ, F* 1,2, 1990 *F* 1,2,3, *US, NZ* 1,2,3, 1991 *W, E, NZ* 1,2, [*Arg, WS, W, I, NZ, E*], 1992 *S* 1,2, *NZ* 1,2,3, *SA, I*, 1993 *Tg, C, F* 1,2, 1994 *I* 1,2, *It* 1, 1995 *Arg* 1,2, [*SA, C, E*]

McArthur, M (NSW) 1909 *E*
McBain, M I (Q) 1983 *It, F* 1, 1985 *Fj* 2, 1986 *It* (R), 1987 [*J*], 1988 *E* 2 (R), 1989 *BI* 1 (R)
MacBride, J W T (NSW) 1946 *NZ* 1, *M, NZ* 2, 1947 *NZ* 1,2, *S, I, W*, 1948 *E, F*
McCabe, A J M (NSW) 1909 *E*
McCall, R J (Q) 1989 *F* 1,2, 1990 *F* 1,2,3, *US, NZ* 1,2,3, 1991 *W, E, NZ* 1,2, [*Arg, W, I, NZ, E*], 1992 *S* 1,2, *NZ* 1,2,3, *SA, I, W*, 1993 *Tg, NZ, SA* 1,2,3, *C, F* 1,2, 1994 *It* 2, 1995 *Arg* 1,2, [*SA, R, E*]
McCarthy, F J C (Q) 1950 *BI* 1
McCowan, R H (Q) 1899 *BI* 1,2,4
McCue, P A (NSW) 1907 *NZ* 1,3, 1908 *W*, 1909 *E*
McDermott, L C (Q) 1962 *NZ* 1,2
McDonald, B S (NSW) 1969 *SA* 4, 1970 *S*
McDonald, J C (Q) 1938 *NZ* 2,3
Macdougall, D G (NSW) 1961 *Fj* 1, *SA* 1
Macdougall, S G (NSW, ACT) 1971 *SA* 3, 1973 *E*, 1974 *NZ* 1,2,3, 1975 *E* 1,2, 1976 *E*
McGhie, G H (Q) 1929 *NZ* 2,3, 1930 *BI*
McGill, A N (NSW) 1968 *NZ* 1,2, *F*, 1969 *W, SA* 1,2,3,4, 1970 *S*, 1971 *SA* 1,2,3, *F* 1,2, 1972 *F* 1,2, *NZ* 1,2,3, 1973 *Tg* 1,2
McIntyre, A J (Q) 1982 *NZ* 1,2,3, 1983 *F* 1,2, 1984 *Fj, NZ* 1,2,3, *E, I, W, S*, 1985 *C* 1,2, *NZ, Fj* 1,2, 1986 *It, F, Arg* 1,2, 1987 [*E, US, I, F, W*], *NZ, Arg* 2, 1988 *E* 1,2, *NZ* 1,2,3, *E, S, It*, 1989 *NZ*
McKenzie, E J A (NSW, ACT) 1990 *F* 1,2,3, *US, NZ* 1,2,3, 1991 *W, E, NZ* 1,2, [*Arg, W, I, NZ, E*], 1992 *S* 1,2, *NZ* 1,2,3, *SA, I, W*, 1993 *Tg, NZ, SA* 1,2,3, *C, F* 1,2, 1994 *I* 1,2, *It* 1, 2, *WS, NZ*, 1995 *Arg* 1,2, [*SA, C* (R), *R, E*], 2, 1996 *W* 1,2
McKid, W A (NSW) 1976 *E, Fj* 1, 1978 *NZ* 2,3, 1979 *I* 1,2
McKinnon, A (Q) 1904 *BI* 2
McKivat, C H (NSW) 1907 *NZ* 1,3, 1908 *W*, 1909 *E*
McLaughlin, R E M (NSW) 1936 *NZ* 1,2
McLean, A D (Q) 1933 *SA* 1,2,3,4,5, 1934 *NZ* 1,2, 1936 *NZ* 1,2, *M*
McLean, J D (Q) 1904 *BI* 2,3, 1905 *NZ*
McLean, J J (Q) 1971 *SA* 2,3, *F* 1,2, 1972 *F* 1,2, *NZ* 1,2,3, *Fj*, 1973 *W, E*, 1974 *NZ* 1
McLean, P E (Q) 1974 *NZ* 1,2,3, 1975 *J* 1,2, *S, W*, 1976 *E, I, Fj* 1,2,3, *F* 1,2, 1978 *NZ* 2, 1979 *I* 1,2, *NZ, Arg* 1,2, 1980 *Fj*, 1981 *F* 1,2, *I, W, S*, 1982 *E, S* 2
McLean, P W (Q) 1978 *NZ* 1,2,3, 1979 *I* 1,2, *NZ, Arg* 1,2, 1980 *Fj* (R), *NZ* 3, 1981 *I, W, S*, 1982 *E, S* 1,2
McLean, R A (NSW) 1971 *SA* 1,2,3, *F* 1,2
McLean, W M (Q) 1946 *NZ* 1, *M, NZ* 2, 1947 *NZ* 1,2
McMahon, M J (Q) 1913 *NZ* 1

McMaster, R E (Q) 1946 *NZ* 1, *M, NZ* 2, 1947 *NZ* 1,2, *I, W*
MacMillan, D I (Q) 1950 *BI* 1,2
McMullen, K V (NSW) 1962 *NZ* 3,5, 1963 *E, SA* 1
McShane, J M S (NSW) 1937 *SA* 1,2
Mackney, W A R (NSW) 1933 *SA* 1,5, 1934 *NZ* 1,2
Magrath, E (NSW) 1961 *Fj* 1, *SA* 2, *F*
Maguire, D J (Q) 1989 *BI* 1,2,3
Malcolm, S J (NSW) 1927 *S*, 1928 *E, F, NZ* 1,2, *M*, 1929 *NZ* 1,2,3, 1930 *BI*, 1931 *NZ*, 1932 *NZ* 1,2,3, 1933 *SA* 4,5, 1934 *NZ* 1,2
Malone, J H (NSW) 1936 *NZ* 1,2, *M*, 1937 *SA* 2
Malouf, B P (NSW) 1982 *NZ* 1
Mandible, E F (NSW) 1907 *NZ* 2,3, 1908 *W*
Manning, J (NSW) 1904 *BI* 2
Manning, R C S (Q) 1967 *NZ*
Mansfield, B W (NSW) 1975 *J* 2
Manu, D T (NSW) 1995 [*R* (t)], *NZ* 1,2, 1996 *W* 1,2 (R), *SA* 1, *NZ* 2, *It, S, I*
Marks, H (NSW) 1899 *BI* 1,2
Marks, R J P (Q) 1962 *NZ* 4,5, 1963 *E, SA* 2,3,4, 1964 *NZ* 1,2,3, 1965 *SA* 1,2, 1966 *W, S*, 1967 *E, I* 1, *F, I* 2
Marrott, W J (NSW) 1923 *NZ* 1,2
Marshall, J S (NSW) 1949 *M* 1
Martin, G J (Q) 1989 *BI* 1,2,3, *NZ, F* 1,2, 1990 *F* 1,3 (R), *NZ* 1
Martin, M C (NSW) 1980 *Fj, NZ* 1,2, 1981 *F* 1,2, *W* (R)
Massey-Westropp, M (NSW) 1914 *NZ* 3
Mathers, M J (NSW) 1980 *Fj, NZ* 2 (R)
Maund, J W (NSW) 1903 *NZ*
Meadows, J E C (V, Q) 1974 *NZ* 1, 1975 *S, W*, 1976 *I, US, Fj* 1,3, *F* 1,2, 1978 *NZ* 1,2,3, 1979 *I* 1,2, 1981 *I, S*, 1982 *E, NZ* 2,3, 1983 *US, Arg* 2, *NZ*
Meadows, R W (NSW) 1958 *M* 1,2,3, *NZ* 1,2,3
Meagher, F W (NSW) 1923 *NZ* 3, 1925 *NZ*, 1927 *I, W*
Meibusch, J H (Q) 1904 *BI* 3
Meibusch, L S (Q) 1912 *US*
Melrose, T C (NSW) 1978 *NZ* 3, 1979 *I* 1,2, *NZ, Arg* 1,2
Merrick, S (NSW) 1995 *NZ* 1,2
Messenger, H H (NSW) 1907 *NZ* 2,3
Middleton, S A (NSW) 1909 *E*, 1910 *NZ* 1,2,3
Miller, A R (NSW) 1952 *Fj* 1,2, *NZ* 1,2, 1953 *SA* 1,2,3,4, 1954 *Fj* 1,2, 1955 *NZ* 1,2,3, 1956 *SA* 1, 1957 *NZ* 1,2, 1958 *W, E, S, F, M* 1,2,3, 1959 *BI* 1,2, 1961 *Fj* 1,2,3, *SA* 2, *F*, 1962 *NZ* 1,2, 1966 *BI* 1,2, *W, S*, 1967 *I* 1, *F, I* 2
Miller, J M (NSW) 1962 *NZ* 1, 1963 *E, SA* 1, 1966 *W, S*, 1967 *E*
Miller, J S (Q) 1986 *NZ* 2,3, 1987 *SK*, [*US, I, F*], *NZ, Arg* 1,2, 1988 *E* 1,2, *NZ* 2,3, *E, S, It*, 1989 *BI* 1,2,3, *NZ*, 1990 *F* 1,3, 1991 *W*, [*WS, W, I*]
Miller, S W J (NSW) 1899 *BI* 3
Mingey, N (NSW) 1923 *NZ* 1,2
Monaghan, L E (NSW) 1973 *E*, 1974 *NZ* 1,2,3, 1975 *E* 1,2, *S, W*, 1976 *E, I, US, F* 1, 1978 *W* 1,2, *NZ* 1, 1979 *I* 1,2
Monti, C I A (Q) 1938 *NZ* 2
Moon, B J (Q) 1978 *NZ* 2,3, 1979 *I* 1,2, *NZ, Arg* 1,2, 1980 *Fj, NZ* 1,2,3, 1981 *F* 1,2, *I, W, S*, 1982 *E, S* 1,2, 1983 *US, NZ, Arg, It, F* 1,2, 1984 *Fj, NZ* 1,2,3, *E*, 1986 *It, F, Arg* 1,2
Mooney, T P (Q) 1954 *Fj* 1,2
Moran, H M (NSW) 1908 *W*
Morgan, G (Q) 1992 *NZ* 1 (R), 3 (R), *W*, 1993 *Tg, NZ, SA* 1,2,3, *C, F* 1,2, 1994 *I* 1,2, *It* 1, *WS, NZ*, 1996 *W* 1,2, *C, NZ* 1, *SA* 1, *NZ* 2
Morrissey, C V (NSW) 1925 *NZ*
Morrissey, W (NSW) 1914 *NZ* 2
Morton, A R (NSW) 1957 *NZ* 1,2, 1958 *F, M* 1,2,3, *NZ* 1,2,3, 1959 *BI* 1,2
Mossop, R P (NSW) 1949 *NZ* 1,2, 1950 *BI* 1,2, 1951 *NZ* 1
Moutray, I E (NSW) 1963 *SA* 2
Munsie, A (NSW) 1928 *NZ* 2
Murdoch, A R (NSW) 1993 *F* 1, 1996 *W* 1
Murphy, P J (Q) 1910 *NZ* 1,2,3, 1913 *NZ* 1,2,3, 1914 *NZ* 1,2,3
Murphy, W (Q) 1912 *US*

Nasser, B P (Q) 1989 *F* 1,2, 1990 *F* 1,2,3, *US, NZ* 2, 1991 [*WS*]
Nicholson, F C (Q) 1904 *BI* 3
Nicholson, F V (Q) 1903 *NZ*, 1904 *BI* 1
Niuqila, A S (NSW) 1988 *S, It*, 1989 *BI* 1
Nothling, O E (NSW) 1921 *NZ*, 1923 *NZ* 1,2,3

WS, NZ, 1995 *Arg* 1,2, [*SA, R, E*], *NZ* 1,2
Smith, F B (NSW) 1905 *NZ*, 1907 *NZ* 1,2,3
Smith, L M (NSW) 1905 *NZ*
Smith, N C (NSW) 1923 *NZ* 1
Smith, P V (NSW) 1967 *NZ*, 1968 *NZ* 1,2, *F, I, S*, 1969 *W, SA* 1
Smith, R A (NSW) 1971 *SA* 1,2, 1972 *F* 1,2, *NZ* 1,2 (R), 3, *Fj*, 1975 *E* 1,2, *J* 1,2, *S, W*, 1976 *E, I, US, Fj* 1,2,3, *F* 1,2
Smith, T S (NSW) 1921 *NZ*, 1925 *NZ*
Snell, H W (NSW) 1928 *NZ* 3
Solomon, H J (NSW) 1949 *M* 3, *NZ* 2, 1950 *BI* 1,2, 1951 *NZ* 1,2, 1952 *Fj* 1,2, *NZ* 1,2, 1953 *SA* 1,2,3, 1955 *NZ* 1
Spragg, S A (NSW) 1899 *BI* 1,2,3,4
Stanley, R G (NSW) 1921 *NZ*, 1923 *NZ* 1,2,3
Stapleton, E T (NSW) 1951 *NZ* 1,2,3, 1952 *Fj* 1,2, *NZ* 1,2, 1953 *SA* 1,2,3,4, 1954 *Fj* 1, 1955 *NZ* 1,2,3, 1958 *NZ* 1
Steggall, J C (Q) 1931 *M, NZ*, 1932 *NZ* 1,2,3, 1933 *SA* 1,2,3,4,5
Stegman, T R (NSW) 1973 *Tg* 1,2
Stephens, O G (NSW) 1973 *Tg* 1,2, *W*, 1974 *NZ* 2,3
Stewart, A A (NSW) 1979 *NZ, Arg* 1,2
Stone, A H (NSW) 1937 *SA* 2, 1938 *NZ* 2,3
Stone, C G (NSW) 1938 *NZ* 1
Stone, J M (NSW) 1946 *M, NZ* 2
Storey, G P (NSW) 1927 *I, W, S*, 1928 *E, F*, 1929 *NZ* 3 (R), 1930 *BI*
Storey, K P (NSW) 1936 *NZ* 2
Storey, N J D (NSW) 1962 *NZ* 1
Strachan, D J (NSW) 1955 *NZ* 2,3
Street, N O (NSW) 1899 *BI* 2
Streeter, S F (NSW) 1978 *NZ* 1
Stuart, R (NSW) 1910 *NZ* 2,3
Stumbles, B D (NSW) 1972 *NZ* 1 (R), 2,3, *Fj*
Sturtridge, G S (V) 1929 *NZ* 2, 1932 *NZ* 1,2,3, 1933 *SA* 1,2,3,4,5
Sullivan, P D (NSW) 1971 *SA* 1,2,3, *F* 1,2, 1972 *F* 1,2, *NZ* 1,2, *Fj*, 1973 *Tg* 1,2, *W*
Summons, A J (NSW) 1958 *W, I, E, S, M* 2, *NZ* 1,2,3, 1959 *BI* 1,2
Suttor, D C (NSW) 1913 *NZ* 1,2,3
Swannell, B I (NSW) 1905 *NZ*
Sweeney, T L (Q) 1953 *SA* 1

Taafe, B S (NSW) 1969 *SA* 1, 1972 *F* 1,2
Tabua, I (Q) 1993 *SA* 2,3, *C, F* 1, 1994 *I* 1,2, *It* 1,2, 1995 [*C, R*]
Tancred, A J (NSW) 1927 *I, W, S*
Tancred, J L (NSW) 1928 *F*
Tanner, W H (Q) 1899 *BI* 1,2
Tasker, W G (NSW) 1913 *NZ* 1,2,3, 1914 *NZ* 1,2,3
Tate, M J (NSW) 1951 *NZ* 3, 1952 *Fj* 1,2, *NZ* 1,2, 1953 *SA* 1, 1954 *Fj* 1,2
Taylor, D A (Q) 1968 *NZ* 1,2, *F, I, S*
Taylor, H C (NSW) 1923 *NZ* 1,2,3
Taylor, J I (NSW) 1971 *SA* 1, 1972 *F* 1,2, *Fj*
Teitzel, R G (Q) 1966 *W, S*, 1967 *E, I* 1, *F, I* 2, *NZ*
Thompson, C E (NSW) 1923 *NZ* 1
Thompson, E G (Q) 1929 *NZ* 1,2,3, 1930 *BI*
Thompson, F (NSW) 1913 *NZ* 1,2,3, 1914 *NZ* 1,2,3
Thompson, J (Q) 1914 *NZ* 1
Thompson, P D (Q) 1950 *BI* 1
Thompson, R J (WA) 1971 *SA* 3, *F* 2 (R), 1972 *Fj*
Thorn, A M (NSW) 1921 *NZ*
Thorn, E J (NSW) 1923 *NZ* 1,2,3
Thornett, J E (NSW) 1955 *NZ* 1,2,3, 1956 *SA* 1,2, 1958 *W, I, S, F, M* 2,3, *NZ* 2,3, 1959 *BI* 1,2, 1961 *Fj* 2,3, *SA* 1,2, *F*, 1962 *NZ* 2,3,4,5, 1963 *E, SA* 1,2,3,4, 1964 *NZ* 1,2,3, 1965 *SA* 1,2, 1966 *BI* 1,2, 1967 *F*
Thornett, R N (NSW) 1961 *Fj* 1,2,3, *SA* 1,2, *F*, 1962 *NZ* 1,2,3,4,5
Thorpe, A C (NSW) 1929 *NZ* 1 (R)
Timbury, F R V (Q) 1910 *NZ* 1,2,
Tindall, E N (NSW) 1973 *Tg* 2
Toby, A E (NSW) 1925 *NZ*
Tolhurst, H A (NSW) 1931 *M, NZ*
Tombs, R C (NSW) 1992 *S* 1,2, 1994 *I* 2, *It* 1, 1996 *NZ* 2
Tonkin, A E J (NSW) 1947 *S, I, W*, 1948 *E, F*, 1950 *BI* 2
Tooth, R M (NSW) 1951 *NZ* 1,2,3, 1954 *Fj* 1,2, 1955 *NZ* 1,2,3, 1957 *NZ* 1,2
Towers, C H T (NSW) 1927 *I*, 1928 *E, F, NZ* 1,2,3, *M*, 1929 *NZ* 1,3, 1930 *BI*, 1931 *M, NZ*, 1934 *NZ* 1,2, 1937 *SA* 1,2

Trivett, R K (Q) 1966 *BI* 1,2
Tune, B N (Q) 1996 *W* 2, *C, NZ* 1, *SA* 1, *NZ* 2, *SA* 2
Turnbull, A (V) 1961 *Fj* 3
Turnbull, R V (NSW) 1968 *I*
Tuynman, S N (NSW) 1983 *F* 1,2, 1984 *E, I, W, S*, 1985 *C* 1,2, *NZ, Fj* 1,2, 1986 *It, F, Arg* 1,2, *NZ* 1,2,3, 1987 *SK*, [*E, US, J, I, W*], *NZ, Arg* 1 (R), 2, 1988 *E, It*, 1989 *BI* 1,2,3, *NZ*, 1990 *NZ* 1
Tweedale, E (NSW) 1946 *NZ* 1,2, 1947 *NZ* 2, *S, I*, 1948 *E, F*, 1949 *M* 1,2,3

Vaughan, D (NSW) 1983 *US, Arg* 1, *It, F* 1,2
Vaughan, G N (V) 1958 *E, S, F, M* 1,2,3
Verge, A (NSW) 1904 *BI* 1,2

Walden, R J (NSW) 1934 *NZ* 2, 1936 *NZ* 1,2, *M*
Walker, A K (NSW) 1947 *NZ* 1, 1948 *E, F*, 1950 *BI* 1,2
Walker, A S B (NSW) 1912 *US*, 1921 *NZ*
Walker, L F (NSW) 1988 *NZ* 2,3, *S, It*, 1989 *BI* 1,2,3, *NZ*
Walker, L R (NSW) 1982 *NZ* 2,3
Wallace, A C (NSW) 1921 *NZ*, 1927 *I, W, S*, 1928 *E, F*
Wallace, T M (NSW) 1994 *It* 1 (R), 2
Wallach, C (NSW) 1913 *NZ* 1,3, 1914 *NZ* 1,2,3
Walsh, J J (NSW) 1953 *SA* 1,2,3,4
Walsh, P B (NSW) 1904 *BI* 1,2,3
Walsham, K P (NSW) 1962 *NZ* 3, 1963 *E*
Ward, P G (NSW) 1899 *BI* 1,2,3,4
Ward, T (Q) 1899 *BI* 2
Watson, G W (Q) 1907 *NZ* 1
Watson, W T (NSW) 1912 *US*, 1913 *NZ* 1,2,3, 1914 *NZ* 1
Waugh, W W (NSW) 1993 *SA* 1, 1995 [*C*], *NZ* 1,2, 1996 *S, I*
Weatherstone, L J (ACT) 1975 *E* 1,2, *J* 1,2, *S* (R), 1976 *E, I*
Webb, W (NSW) 1899 *BI* 3,4
Welborn J (NSW) 1996 *SA* 2, *It*
Wells, B G (NSW) 1958 *M* 1
Westfield, R E (NSW) 1928 *NZ* 1,2,3, *M*, 1929 *NZ* 2,3
White, C J B (NSW) 1899 *BI* 1, 1903 *NZ*, 1904 *BI* 1
White, J M (NSW) 1904 *BI* 3
White, J P L (NSW) 1958 *NZ* 1,2,3, 1961 *Fj* 1,2,3, *SA* 1,2, *F*, 1962 *NZ* 1,2,3,4,5, 1963 *E, SA* 1,2,3,4, 1964 *NZ* 1,2,3, 1965 *SA* 1,2
White, M C (Q) 1931 *M, NZ* 1932 *NZ* 1,2, 1933 *SA* 1,2,3,4,5
White, S W (NSW) 1956 *SA* 1,2, 1958 *I, E, S, M* 2,3
White, W G S (Q) 1933 *SA* 1,2,3,4,5, 1934 *NZ* 1,2, 1936 *NZ* 1,2, *M*
White, W J (NSW) 1928 *NZ* 1, *M*, 1932 *NZ* 1
Wickham, S M (NSW) 1903 *NZ*, 1904 *BI* 1,2,3, 1905 *NZ*
Williams, D (Q) 1913 *NZ* 3, 1914 *NZ* 1,2,3
Williams, I M (NSW) 1987 *Arg* 1,2, 1988 *E* 1,2, *NZ* 1,2,3, 1989 *BI* 2,3, *NZ, F* 1,2, 1990 *F* 1,2,3, *US, NZ* 1
Williams, J L (NSW) 1963 *SA* 1,3,4
Williams, S A (NSW) 1980 *Fj, NZ* 1,2, 1981 *F* 1,2, 1982 *E, NZ* 1,2,3, 1983 *US, Arg* 1 (R), 2, *NZ, It, F* 1,2, 1984 *NZ* 1,2,3, *E, I, W, S*, 1985 *C* 1,2, *NZ, Fj* 1,2
Wilson, B J (NSW) 1949 *NZ* 1,2
Wilson, C R (Q) 1957 *NZ* 1, 1958 *NZ* 1,2,3
Wilson, D J (Q) 1992 *S* 1,2, *NZ* 1,2,3, *SA, I, W*, 1993 *Tg, NZ, SA* 1,2,3, *C, F* 1,2, 1994 *I* 1,2, *It* 1,2, *WS, NZ*, 1995 *Arg* 1,2, [*SA, R, E*], 1996 *W* 1,2, *C, NZ* 1, *SA* 1, *NZ* 2, *SA* 2, *It, S, I, W* 3
Wilson, V W (Q) 1937 *SA* 1,2, 1938 *NZ* 1,2,3
Windon, C J (NSW) 1946 *NZ* 1,2, 1947 *NZ* 1, *S, I, W*, 1948 *E, F*, 1949 *M* 1,2,3, *NZ* 1,2, 1951 *NZ* 1,2,3, 1952 *Fj* 1,2, *NZ* 1,2
Windon, K S (NSW) 1937 *SA* 1,2, 1946 *M*
Windsor, J C (Q) 1947 *NZ* 2
Winning, K C (Q) 1951 *NZ* 1
Wogan, L W (NSW) 1913 *NZ* 1,2,3, 1914 *NZ* 1,2,3, 1921 *NZ*
Wood, F (NSW) 1907 *NZ* 1,2,3, 1910 *NZ* 1,2,3, 1913 *NZ* 1,2,3, 1914 *NZ* 1,2,3
Wood, R N (Q) 1972 *Fj*
Woods, H F (NSW) 1925 *NZ*, 1927 *I, W, S*, 1928 *E*
Wright, K J (NSW) 1975 *E* 1,2, *J* 1, 1976 *US, F* 1,2, 1978 *NZ* 1,2,3

Yanz, K (NSW) 1958 *F*

AUSTRALIAN INTERNATIONAL RECORDS (*up to 30 April 1997*)

MATCH RECORDS

MOST CONSECUTIVE TEST WINS

10 1991 *Arg, WS, W, I, NZ, E,* 1992 *S* 1,2, *NZ* 1,2
9 1993 *F* 2, 1994 *I* 1,2, *It* 1,2, *WS, NZ,* 1995 *Arg* 1,2

MOST CONSECUTIVE TESTS WITHOUT DEFEAT

P	W	D	Period
10	10	0	1991–92
9	9	0	1993–95
7	7	0	1985–86

MOST POINTS IN A MATCH
by the team

Pts	Opp	Venue	Year
74	C	Brisbane	1996
73	WS	Sydney	1994
67	US	Brisbane	1990
65	SK	Brisbane	1987
63	W	Brisbane	1991

by a player
39 by M Burke v Canada at Brisbane 1996
28 by M P Lynagh v Argentina at Brisbane 1995
24 by M P Lynagh v United States at Brisbane 1990
24 by M P Lynagh v France at Brisbane 1990
23 several instances

MOST TRIES IN A MATCH
by the team

T	Opp	Venue	Year
13	SK	Brisbane	1987
12	US	Brisbane	1990
12	W	Brisbane	1991
11	WS	Sydney	1994
10	C	Brisbane	1996

by a player
4 by G Cornelsen v New Zealand at Auckland 1978
4 by D I Campese v United States at Sydney 1983
3 by A D McLean v New Zealand Maoris at Palmerston N 1936

3 by J R Ryan v Japan at Brisbane 1975
3 by M P Burke v Canada at Brisbane 1985
3 by M P Burke v South Korea at Brisbane 1987
3 by D I Campese v Italy at Rome 1988
3 by A S Nuiqila v Italy at Rome 1988
3 by D I Campese v Canada at Calgary 1993
3 by M Burke v Canada at Brisbane 1996

MOST CONVERSIONS IN A MATCH
by the team

C	Opp	Venue	Year
9	C	Brisbane	1996
8	It	Rome	1988
8	US	Brisbane	1990
7	C	Sydney	1985

by a player
9 by M Burke v Canada at Brisbane 1996
8 by M P Lynagh v Italy at Rome 1988
8 by M P Lynagh v United States at Brisbane 1990
7 by M P Lynagh v Canada at Sydney 1985

MOST PENALTY GOALS IN A MATCH
by the team

P	Opp	Venue	Year
6	NZ	Sydney	1984
6	F	Sydney	1986
6	E	Brisbane	1988
5	several instances		

by a player
6 by M P Lynagh v France at Sydney 1986
6 by M P Lynagh v England at Brisbane 1988
5 several instances

MOST DROPPED GOALS IN A MATCH
by the team

D	Opp	Venue	Year
3	E	Twickenham	1967
3	I	Dublin	1984
3	Fj	Brisbane	1985

by a player

3 by P F Hawthorne v England at
    Twickenham   1967
2 by M G Ella v Ireland at Dublin 1984
2 by D J Knox v Fiji at Brisbane   1985

CAREER RECORDS

MOST CAPPED PLAYERS

Caps	Player	Career
101	D I Campese	1982–96
72	M P Lynagh	1984–95
63	N C Farr Jones	1984–93
59	S P Poidevin	1980–91
49	P N Kearns	1989–95
47	T B Gavin	1988–96
47	T J Horan	1989–96
47	E J A McKenzie	1990–96
42	P G Johnson	1959–71

MOST CONSECUTIVE TESTS

Tests	Player	Span
46	P N Kearns	1989–95
42	D I Campese	1990–95
37	P G Johnson	1959–68
34	M P Lynagh	1988–92

MOST TESTS AS CAPTAIN

Tests	Captain	Span
36	N C Farr Jones	1988–92
19	A G Slack	1984–87
16	J E Thornett	1962–67
16	G V Davis	1969–72
15	A A Shaw	1978–81
15	M P Lynagh	1988–95

MOST TESTS IN INDIVIDUAL POSITIONS

Full-back	R G Gould	25	1980–87
Wing	D I Campese	85	1982–96
Centre	T J Horan	45	1989–96
Fly-half	M P Lynagh	64	1984–95
Scrum-half	N C Farr Jones	62	1984–93
Prop	E J A McKenzie	47	1990–96
Hooker	P N Kearns	49	1989–95

Lock	S A G Cutler	40	1982–91
	R J McCall	40	1989–95
Flanker	S P Poidevin	59	1980–91
No 8	T B Gavin	43	1988–96

MOST POINTS IN TESTS

Pts	Player	Tests	Career
911	M P Lynagh	72	1984–95
315	D I Campese	101	1982–96
260	P E McLean	30	1974–82
224	M Burke	22	1993–96
114	M C Roebuck	23	1991–93

MOST TRIES IN TESTS

Tries	Player	Tests	Career
64	D I Campese	101	1982–96
20	T J Horan	47	1989–96
17	M P Lynagh	72	1984–95
15	M P Burke	23	1984–87
14	B J Moon	35	1978–86

MOST CONVERSIONS IN TESTS

Cons	Player	Tests	Career
140	M P Lynagh	72	1984–95
31	M Burke	22	1993–96
27	P E McLean	30	1974–82
14	R G Gould	25	1980–87

MOST PENALTY GOALS IN TESTS

Pens	Player	Tests	Career
177	M P Lynagh	72	1984–95
62	P E McLean	30	1974–82
39	M Burke	22	1993–96
23	M C Roebuck	23	1991–93
16	A N McGill	21	1968–73

MOST DROPPED GOALS IN TESTS

Drops	Player	Tests	Career
9	P F Hawthorne	21	1962–67
9	M P Lynagh	72	1984–95
8	M G Ella	25	1980–84
4	P E McLean	30	1974–82

TRI-NATIONS RECORDS

Record	Detail	Holder	Set
Most points in matches	40	M Burke	1996
Most points in season	40	M Burke	1996
Most points in match	20	M Burke	v N Zealand (h) 1996
Most tries in matches	1	several players	1996
Most tries in season	1	several players	1996
Most tries in match	1	several players	1996
Most cons in matches	1	M Burke & J A Eales	1996
Most cons in season	1	M Burke & J A Eales	1996
Most cons in match	1	M Burke	v S Africa (h) 1996
		J A Eales	v S Africa (a) 1996
Most pens in matches	11	M Burke	1996
Most pens in season	11	M Burke	1996
Most pens in match	5	M Burke	v N Zealand (h) 1996

SERIES RECORDS

Record	Holder	Detail
Most tries	D I Campese	6 in Europe 1988
Most points	M Burke	74 in Europe 1996

MAJOR TOUR RECORDS

Record	Detail	Year	Place
Most team points	500	1947–48	Europe
Most team tries	115	1947–48	Europe
Most individual points	154 by P E McLean	1975–76	Britain & Ireland
Most individual tries	23 by C J Russell	1908–09	Britain
Most points in match	26 by A J Leeds	1986 v Buller (NZ)	Westport
Most tries in match	6 by J S Boyce	1962 v Wairarapa (NZ)	Masterton

MISCELLANEOUS RECORDS

Record	Holder	Detail
Longest Test Career	G M Cooke/A R Miller	16 seasons, 1932–1947–48/1952–67
Youngest Test Cap	B W Ford	18 yrs 90 days in 1957
Oldest Test Cap	A R Miller	38 yrs 113 days in 1967

AUSTRALIAN INTERNATIONAL CAREER RECORDS (*up to 30 April 1997*)

Player	Debut	Caps since last season	Caps	T	C	PG	DG	Pts
M Burke	1993 v SA	1996 *W* 1,2, *C*, *NZ* 1, *SA* 1, *NZ* 2, *SA* 2, *It*, *S*, *I*, *W* 3	22	9	31	39	0	224
D I Campese	1982 v NZ	1996 *W* 1,2, *C*, *NZ* 1, *SA* 1, *NZ* 2, *SA* 2, *It*, *W* 3	101	64	8	7	2	315
S Larkham	1996 v W	1996 *W* 2 (R)	1	0	0	0	0	0
A R Murdoch	1993 v F	1996 *W* 1	2	1	0	0	0	5
J W Roff	1995 v C	1996 *W* 1,2, *NZ* 1, *SA* 1, *NZ* 2, *SA* 2 (R), *S*, *I*, *W* 3	13	6	1	2	0	38
B N Tune	1996 v W	1996 *W* 2, *C*, *NZ* 1, *SA* 1, *NZ* 2, *SA* 2	6	2	0	0	0	10
A Magro	None		0	0	0	0	0	0
J S Little	1989 v F	1996 *It* (R), *I*, *W* 3	41	10	0	0	0	47
D J Herbert	1994 v I	1996 *C*, *SA* 2, *It*, *S*, *I*	13	4	0	0	0	20
T J Horan	1989 v NZ	1996 *W* 1,2, *C*, *NZ* 1, *SA* 1, *It*, *S*, *I*, *W* 3	47	20	0	0	0	90
R C Tombs	1992 v S	1996 *NZ* 2	5	0	0	0	0	0
S Bowen	1993 v SA	1996 *C*, *NZ* 1, *SA* 2	9	0	0	0	0	0
P W Howard	1993 v NZ	1996 *W* 1,2, *SA* 1, *NZ* 2, *SA* 2, *It*, *S*, *W* 3	13	2	0	0	0	10
D J Knox	1985 v Fj	1996 *It*, *S*, *I*	8	1	12	10	2	65
T M Wallace	1994 v It		2	0	1	6	0	20
G M Gregan	1994 v It	1996 *W* 1, *C* (t), *SA* 1, *NZ* 2, *SA* 2, *It*, *I*, *W* 3	18	2	0	0	0	10
S J Payne	1996 v W	1996 *W* 2, *C*, *NZ* 1, *S*	4	1	0	0	0	5
M A Foley	1995 v C	1996 *W* 2 (R), *NZ* 1, *SA* 1, *NZ* 2, *SA* 2, *It*, *S*, *I*, *W* 3	11	3	0	0	0	15
M E Caputo	1996 v W	1996 *W* 1,2	2	1	0	0	0	5
M D Bell	1996 v C	1996 *C*	1	0	0	0	0	0
E J A McKenzie	1990 v F	1996 *W* 1,2	47	2	0	0	0	9
A Heath	1996 v C	1996 *C*, *SA* 1, *NZ* 2, *SA* 2, *It*	5	0	0	0	0	0
R L L Harry	1996 v W	1996 *W* 1,2, *NZ* 1, *SA* 1 (t), *NZ* 2, *It*, *S*	7	0	0	0	0	0
D J Crowley	1989 v BI	1996 *W* 2 (R), *C*, *NZ* 1, *SA* 1,2, *I*, *W* 3	19	0	0	0	0	0
A T Blades	1996 v S	1996 *S*, *I*, *W* 3	3	0	0	0	0	0
C Blades	None		0	0	0	0	0	0
J Welborn	1996 v SA	1996 *SA* 2, *It*	2	0	0	0	0	0
G J Morgan	1992 v NZ	1996 *W* 1,2, *C*, *NZ* 1, *SA* 1, *NZ* 2	22	3	0	0	0	15

D Giffin	1996 v W	1996 *W* 3	1	0	0	0	0	0
J A Eales	1991 v W	1996 *W* 1,2, *C*, *NZ* 1, *SA* 1, *NZ* 2, *SA* 2, *It*, *S*, *I*	41	2	6	3	0	30
W W Waugh	1993 v SA	1996 *S*, *I*	6	1	0	0	0	5
D J Wilson	1992 v S	1996 *W* 1,2, *C*, *NZ* 1, *SA* 1, *NZ* 2, *SA* 2, *It*, *S*, *I*, *W* 3	38	9	0	0	0	45
B J Robinson	1996 v It	1996 *It* (R), *S* (R), *I* (R)	3	0	0	0	0	0
D T Manu	1995 v R	1996 *W* 1,2 (R), *SA* 1, *NZ* 2, *It*, *S*, *I*	10	1	0	0	0	5
O Finegan	1996 v W	1996 *W* 1,2, *C*, *NZ* 1, *SA* 1 (t), *S*, *W* 3	7	1	0	0	0	5
T Kefu	None		0	0	0	0	0	0
M C Brial	1993 v F	1996 *W* 1 (R), 2, *C*, *NZ* 1, *SA* 1, *NZ* 2, *SA* 2, *It*, *I*, *W* 3	12	1	0	0	0	5
M Connors	None		0	0	0	0	0	0
T B Gavin	1988 v NZ	1996 *NZ* 2 (R), *SA* 2, *W* 3	47	9	0	0	0	40

Australia's Matthew Burke prepares to take a conversion during his team's 28-19 victory over Wales at Cardiff Arms Park.

INTERNATIONAL MATCH APPEARANCES FOR BRITISH ISLES TEAMS
(up to 30 April 1997)

From 1910 onwards, when British Isles teams first became officially representative of the four Home Unions. (*Uncapped when first selected to play in a Test match for the British Isles.)

Aarvold, C D (Cambridge U, Blackheath and England) 1930 *NZ* 1,2,3,4, *A*
Ackerman, R A (London Welsh and Wales) 1983 *NZ* 1,4 (R)
Ackford, P J (Harlequins and England) 1989 *A* 1,2,3
Alexander, R (NIFC and Ireland) 1938 *SA* 1,2,3
Andrew, C R (Wasps and England) 1989 *A* 2,3, 1993 *NZ* 1,2,3
Arneil, R J (Edinburgh Acads and Scotland) 1968 *SA* 1,2,3,4
Ashcroft, A (Waterloo and England) 1959 *A* 1, *NZ* 2

Bainbridge, S J (Gosforth and England) 1983 *NZ* 3,4
Baird, G R T (Kelso and Scotland) 1983 *NZ* 1,2,3,4
Baker, A M (Newport and Wales) 1910 *SA* 3
Baker, D G S (Old Merchant Taylors' and England) 1955 *SA* 3,4
Bassett, J (Penarth and Wales) 1930 *NZ* 1,2,3,4, *A*
Bayfield, M C (Northampton and England) 1993 *NZ* 1,2,3
Beamish, G R (Leicester, RAF and Ireland) 1930 *NZ* 1,2,3,4, *A*
Beattie, J R (Glasgow Acads and Scotland) 1983 *NZ* 2 (R)
Beaumont, W B (Fylde and England) 1977 *NZ* 2,3,4, 1980 *SA* 1,2,3,4
Bebb, D I E (Swansea and Wales) 1962 *SA* 2,3, 1966 *A* 1,2, *NZ* 1,2,3,4
Bennett, P (Llanelli and Wales) 1974 *SA* 1,2,3,4, 1977 *NZ* 1,2,3,4
Bevan, J C (Cardiff Coll of Ed, Cardiff and Wales) 1971 *NZ* 1
Black, A W (Edinburgh U and Scotland) 1950 *NZ* 1,2
Black, B H (Oxford U, Blackheath and England) 1930 *NZ* 1,2,3,4, *A*
Blakiston, A F (Northampton and England) 1924 *SA* 1,2,3,4
Bowcott, H M (Cambridge U, Cardiff and Wales) 1930 *NZ* 1,2,3,4, *A*
Boyle, C V (Dublin U and Ireland) 1938 *SA* 2,3
Brand, T N (NIFC and *Ireland) 1924 *SA* 1,2
Bresnihan, F P K (UC Dublin and Ireland) 1968 *SA* 1,2,4
Brophy, N H (UC Dublin and Ireland) 1962 *SA* 1,4
Brown, G L (W of Scotland and Scotland) 1971 *NZ* 3,4, 1974 *SA* 1,2,3, 1977 *NZ* 2,3,4
Budge, G M (Edinburgh Wands and Scotland) 1950 *NZ* 4
Burcher, D H (Newport and Wales) 1977 *NZ* 3
Burnell, A P (London Scottish and Scotland) 1993 *NZ* 1
Butterfield, J (Northampton and England) 1955 *SA* 1, 2,3,4

Calder, F (Stewart's-Melville FP and Scotland) 1989 *A* 1,2,3
Calder, J H (Stewart's-Melville FP and Scotland) 1983 *NZ* 3
Cameron, A (Glasgow HSFP and Scotland) 1955 *SA* 2 (R), 3,4, 1983 *NZ* 1,2,3,4
Campbell, S O (Old Belvedere and Ireland) 1980 *SA* 2 (R), 3,4, 1983 *NZ* 1,2,3,4
Campbell-Lamerton, M J (Halifax, Army and Scotland) 1962 *SA* 1,2,3,4, 1966 *A* 1,2, *NZ* 1,3
Carleton, J (Orrell and England) 1980 *SA* 1,2,4, 1983 *NZ* 2,3,4
Carling, W D C (Harlequins and England) 1993 *NZ* 1
Chalmers, C M (Melrose and Scotland) 1989 *A* 1
Clarke, B B (Bath and England) 1993 *NZ* 1,2,3

Cleaver, W B (Cardiff and Wales) 1950 *NZ* 1,2,3
Clifford, T (Young Munster and Ireland) 1950 *NZ* 1,2,3, *A* 1,2
Cobner, T J (Pontypool and Wales) 1977 *NZ* 1,2,3
Colclough, M J (Angoulême and England) 1980 *SA* 1,2,3,4, 1983 *NZ* 1,2,3,4
Connell, G C (Trinity Acads and Scotland) 1968 *SA* 4
Cotton, F E (Loughborough Colls, Coventry and England) 1974 *SA* 1,2,3,4, 1977 *NZ* 2,3,4
Coulman, M J (Moseley and England) 1968 *SA* 3
Cove-Smith, R (Old Merchant Taylors' and England) 1924 *SA* 1,2,3,4
Cowan, R C (Selkirk and Scotland) 1962 *SA* 4
Cromey, G E (Queen's U, Belfast and Ireland) 1938 *SA* 3
Cunningham, W A (Lansdowne and Ireland) 1924 *SA* 3

Dancer, G T (Bedford) 1938 *SA* 1,2,3
Davies, C (Cardiff and Wales) 1950 *NZ* 4
Davies, D M (Somerset Police and Wales) 1950 *NZ* 3,4, *A* 1
Davies, D S (Hawick and Scotland) 1924 *SA* 1,2,3,4
Davies, H J (Newport and Wales) 1924 *SA* 2
Davies, T G R (Cardiff, London Welsh and Wales) 1968 *SA* 3, 1971 *NZ* 1,2,3,4
Davies, T J (Llanelli and Wales) 1959 *NZ* 2,4
Davies, T M (London Welsh, Swansea and Wales) 1971 *NZ* 1,2,3,4, 1974 *SA* 1,2,3,4
Davies, W G (Cardiff and Wales) 1980 *SA* 2
Davies, W P C (Harlequins and England) 1955 *SA* 1,2,3
Dawes, S J (London Welsh and Wales) 1971 *NZ* 1,2,3,4
Dawson, A R (Wanderers and Ireland) 1959 *A* 1,2, *NZ* 1,2,3,4
Dixon, P J (Harlequins and England) 1971 *NZ* 1,2,4
Dodge, P W (Leicester and England) 1980 *SA* 3,4
Dooley, W A (Preston Grasshoppers and England) 1989 *A* 2,3
Doyle, M G (Blackrock Coll and Ireland) 1968 *SA* 1
Drysdale, D (Heriot's FP and Scotland) 1924 *SA* 1,2,3,4
Duckham, D J (Coventry and England) 1971 *NZ* 2,3,4
Duggan, W P (Blackrock Coll and Ireland) 1977 *NZ* 1,2,3,4
Duff, P L (Glasgow Acads and Scotland) 1938 *SA* 2,3

Edwards, G O (Cardiff and Wales) 1968 *SA* 1,2, 1971 *NZ* 1,2,3,4, 1974 *SA* 1,2,3,4
Evans, G (Maesteg and Wales) 1983 *NZ* 3,4
Evans, G L (Newport and Wales) 1977 *NZ* 2,3,4
Evans, I C (Llanelli and Wales) 1989 *A* 1,2,3, 1993 *NZ* 1,2,3
Evans, R T (Newport and Wales) 1950 *NZ* 1,2,3,4, *A* 1,2
Evans, T P (Swansea and Wales) 1977 *NZ* 1
Evans, W R (Cardiff and Wales) 1959 *A* 2, *NZ* 1,2,3

Farrell, J L (Bective Rangers and Ireland) 1930 *NZ* 1,2,3,4, *A*
Faull, J (Swansea and Wales) 1959 *A* 1, *NZ* 1,3,4
Fenwick, S P (Bridgend and Wales) 1977 *NZ* 1,2,3,4
Fitzgerald, C F (St Mary's Coll and Ireland) 1983 *NZ* 1,2,3,4
Foster, A R (Queen's U, Belfast and Ireland) 1910 *SA* 1,2

Gibbs, I S (Swansea and Wales) 1993 *NZ* 2,3
Gibson, C M H (Cambridge U, NIFC and Ireland) 1966 *NZ* 2,3,4, 1968 *SA* 1 (R), 2,3,4, 1971 *NZ* 1,2,3,4
Giles, J L (Coventry and England) 1938 *SA* 1,3

353

Orr, P A (Old Wesley and Ireland) 1977 *NZ* 1
O'Shea, J P (Cardiff and Wales) 1968 *SA* 1

Parker, D (Swansea and Wales) 1930 *NZ* 1,2,3,4, *A*
Pask, A E I (Abertillery and Wales) 1962 *SA* 1,2,3, 1966 *A* 1,2, *NZ* 1,3,4
Patterson, C S (Instonians and Ireland) 1980 *SA* 1,2,3
Patterson, W M (Sale and *England) 1959 *NZ* 2
Paxton, I A M (Selkirk and Scotland) 1983 *NZ* 1,2,3,4
Pedlow, A C (CIYMS and Ireland) 1955 *SA* 1,4
Pillman, C H (Blackheath and England) 1910 *SA* 2,3
Piper, O J S (Cork Const and Ireland) 1910 *SA* 1
Poole, H (Cardiff) 1930 *NZ* 3
Popplewell, N J (Greystones and Ireland) 1993 *NZ* 1,2,3
Preece, I (Coventry and England) 1950 *NZ* 1
Prentice, F D (Leicester and England) 1930 *NZ* 2, *A*
Price, B (Newport and Wales) 1966 *A* 1,2, *NZ* 1,4
Price, G (Pontypool and Wales) 1977 *NZ* 1,2,3,4, 1980 *SA* 1,2,3,4, 1983 *NZ* 1,2,3,4
Price, M J (Pontypool and Wales) 1959 *A* 1,2, *NZ* 1,2,3
Prosser, T R (Pontypool and Wales) 1959 *NZ* 4
Pullin, J V (Bristol and England) 1968 *SA* 2,3,4, 1971 *NZ* 1,2,3,4

Quinnell, D L (Llanelli and *Wales) 1971 *NZ* 3, 1977 *NZ* 2,3, 1980 *SA* 1,2

Ralston, C W (Richmond and England) 1974 *SA* 4
Reed, A I (Bath and Scotland) 1993 *NZ* 1
Rees, H E (Neath and *Wales) 1977 *NZ* 4
Reeve, J S R (Harlequins and England) 1930 *NZ* 1,3,4, *A*
Reid, T E (Garryowen and Ireland) 1955 *SA* 2,3
Renwick, J M (Hawick and Scotland) 1980 *SA* 1
Rew, H (Blackheath, Army and England) 1930 *NZ* 1,2,3,4
Reynolds, F J (Old Cranleighans and England) 1938 *SA* 1,2
Richards, D (Leicester and England) 1989 *A* 1,2,3, 1993 *NZ* 1,2,3
Richards, D S (Swansea and Wales) 1980 *SA* 1
Richards, M C R (Cardiff and Wales) 1968 *SA* 1,3,4
Richards, T J (Bristol and Australia) 1910 *SA* 1,2
Rimmer, G (Waterloo and England) 1950 *NZ* 3
Ringland, T M (Ballymena and Ireland) 1983 *NZ* 1
Risman, A B W (Loughborough Colls and England) 1959 *A* 1,2, *NZ* 1,4
Robbie, J C (Greystones and Ireland) 1980 *SA* 4
Robins, J D (Birkenhead Park and Wales) 1950 *NZ* 1,2,3, *A* 1,2
Robins, R J (Pontypridd and Wales) 1955 *SA* 1,2,3,4
Rogers, D P (Bedford and England) 1962 *SA* 1,4
Rowlands, K A (Cardiff and Wales) 1962 *SA* 1,2,4
Rutherford, D (Gloucester and England) 1966 *A* 1
Rutherford, J Y (Selkirk and Scotland) 1983 *NZ* 3

Savage, K F (Northampton and England) 1968 *SA* 1,2,3,4
Scotland, K J F (Cambridge U, Heriot's FP and Scotland) 1959 *A* 1,2, *NZ* 1,3,4
Sharp, R A W (Oxford U, Redruth and England) 1962 *SA* 3,4
Slattery, J F (Blackrock Coll and Ireland) 1974 *SA* 1,2,3,4
Slemen, M A C (Liverpool and England) 1980 *SA* 1
Smith, A R (Edinburgh Wands, London Scottish and Scotland) 1962 *SA* 1,2,3
Smith, D F (Richmond and England) 1910 *SA* 1,2,3
Smith, D W C (London Scottish and Scotland) 1950 *A* 1
Smith, G K (Kelso and Scotland) 1959 *A* 1,2, *NZ* 1,4
Smith, I S (Oxford U, London Scottish and Scotland) 1924 *SA* 1,2
Smyth, T (Malone, Newport and Ireland) 1910 *SA* 2,3
Sole, D M B (Edinburgh Acads and Scotland) 1989 *A* 1,2,3
Spong, R S (Old Millhillians and England) 1930 *NZ* 1,2,3,4, *A*
Spoors, J A (Bristol) 1910 *SA* 1,2,3
Squire, J (Newport, Pontypool and Wales) 1977 *NZ* 4, 1980 *SA* 1,2,3,4, 1983 *NZ* 1
Squires, P J (Harrogate and England) 1977 *NZ* 1
Stagg, P K (Oxford U, Sale and Scotland) 1968 *SA* 1,3,4
Steele, W C C (Bedford, RAF and Scotland) 1974 *SA* 1,2
Stephens, I (Bridgend and Wales) 1983 *NZ* 1
Stephens, J R G (Neath and Wales) 1950 *A* 1,2

Stevenson, R C (St Andrew's U and Scotland) 1910 *SA* 1,2,3

Tanner, H (Swansea and Wales) 1938 *SA* 2
Taylor, A R (Cross Keys and Wales) 1938 *SA* 1,2
Taylor, J (London Welsh and Wales) 1971 *NZ* 1,2,3,4
Taylor, R B (Northampton and England) 1968 *SA* 1,2,3,4
Teague, M C (Gloucester, Moseley and England) 1989 *A* 2,3, 1993 *NZ* 2 (t)
Telfer, J W (Melrose and Scotland) 1966 *A* 1,2, *NZ* 1,2,4, 1968 *SA* 2,3,4
Thomas, M C (Devonport Services, Newport and Wales) 1950 *NZ* 2,3, *A* 1, 1959 *NZ* 2
Thomas, R C C (Swansea and Wales) 1955 *SA* 3,4
Thomas, W D (Llanelli and *Wales) 1966 *NZ* 2,3, 1968 *SA* 3 (R), 4, 1971 *NZ* 1,2,4 (R)
Thompson, R H (Instonians, London Irish and Ireland) 1955 *SA* 1,2,4
Travers, W H (Newport and Wales) 1938 *SA* 2,3
Tucker, C C (Shannon and Ireland) 1980 *SA* 3,4
Turner, J W C (Gala and Scotland) 1968 *SA* 1,2,3,4

Underwood, R (RAF, Leicester and England) 1989 *A* 1,2,3, 1993 *NZ* 1,2,3
Unwin, E J (Rosslyn Park, Army and England) 1938 *SA* 1,2
Uttley, R M (Gosforth and England) 1974 *SA* 1,2,3,4

Voyce, A T (Gloucester and England) 1924 *SA* 3,4

Waddell, G H (Cambridge U, London Scottish and Scotland) 1962 *SA* 1,2
Waddell, H (Glasgow Acads and Scotland) 1924 *SA* 1,2,4
Walker, S (Instonians and Ireland) 1938 *SA* 1,2,3
Wallace, W (Percy Park) 1924 *SA* 1
Waller, P D (Newport and Wales) 1910 *SA* 1,2,3
Ward, A J P (Garryowen and Ireland) 1980 *SA* 1
Waters, J A (Selkirk and Scotland) 1938 *SA* 3
Watkins, D (Newport and Wales) 1966 *A* 1,2, *NZ* 1,2,3,4
Watkins, S J (Newport and Wales) 1966 *A* 1,2, *NZ* 3
Webb, J (Abertillery and Wales) 1910 *SA* 1,2,3
Welsh, W B (Hawick and Scotland) 1930 *NZ* 4
Weston, M P (Richmond, Durham City and England) 1962 *SA* 1,2,3,4, 1966 *A* 1,2
Wheeler, P J (Leicester and England) 1977 *NZ* 2,3,4, 1980 *SA* 1,2,3,4
White, D B (London Scottish and Scotland) 1989 *A* 1
Whitley, H (Northern and *England) 1924 *SA* 1,3,4
Willcox, J G (Oxford U, Harlequins and England) 1962 *SA* 1,2,4
Williams, B L (Cardiff and Wales) 1950 *NZ* 2,3,4, *A* 1,2
Williams, C (Swansea and Wales) 1980 *SA* 1,2,3,4
Williams, D (Ebbw Vale and Wales) 1966 *A* 1,2, *NZ* 1,2,4
Williams, D B (Cardiff and *Wales) 1977 *NZ* 1,2,3
Williams, J J (Llanelli and Wales) 1974 *SA* 1,2,3,4, 1977 *NZ* 1,2,3,4
Williams, J P R (London Welsh and Wales) 1971 *NZ* 1,2,3,4, 1974 *SA* 1,2,3,4
Williams, R H (Llanelli and Wales) 1955 *SA* 1,2,3,4, 1959 *A* 1,2, *NZ* 1,2,3,4
Williams, S H (Newport and *England) 1910 *SA* 1,2,3
Williams, W O G (Swansea and Wales) 1955 *SA* 1,2,3,4
Willis, W R (Cardiff and Wales) 1950 *NZ* 4, 4, 1,2
Wilson, S (London Scottish and Scotland) 1966 *A* 2, *NZ* 1,2,3,4
Windsor, R W (Pontypool and Wales) 1974 *SA* 1,2,3,4, 1977 *NZ* 1
Winterbottom, P J (Headingley, Harlequins and England) 1983 *NZ* 1,2,3,4, 1993 *NZ*, 1,2,3
Wood, B G M (Garryowen and Ireland) 1959 *NZ* 1,3
Wood, K B (Leicester) 1910 *SA* 1,3
Woodward, C R (Leicester and England) 1980 *SA* 2,3

Young, A T (Cambridge U, Blackheath and England) 1924 *NZ* 2
Young, D (Cardiff and Wales) 1989 *A* 1,2,3
Young, J (Harrogate, RAF and Wales) 1968 *SA* 1
Young, J R C (Oxford U, Harlequins and England) 1959 *NZ* 2
Young, R M (Queen's U, Belfast, Collegians and Ireland) 1966 *A* 1,2, *NZ* 1, 1968 *SA* 3

RESULTS OF BRITISH ISLES MATCHES
(up to 30 April 1997)

From 1910 onwards – the tour to South Africa in that year was the first fully representative one in which the four Home Unions co-operated.

BRITISH ISLES v SOUTH AFRICA
Played 30   British Isles won 8, South Africa won 18, Drawn 4
Highest scores: British Isles 28–9 in 1974, South Africa 34–14 in 1962
Biggest wins: British Isles 28–9 in 1974, South Africa 34–14 in 1962

1910 *1* Johannesburg **South Africa** 14–10
　　 2 Port Elizabeth **British Isles** 8–3
　　 3 Cape Town **South Africa** 21–5
　　 South Africa won series 2-1
1924 *1* Durban **South Africa** 7–3
　　 2 Johannesburg **South Africa** 17–0
　　 3 Port Elizabeth **Drawn** 3–3
　　 4 Cape Town **South Africa** 16–9
　　 South Africa won series 3-0, with 1 draw
1938 *1* Johannesburg **South Africa** 26–12
　　 2 Port Elizabeth **South Africa** 19–3
　　 3 Cape Town **British Isles** 21–16
　　 South Africa won series 2-1
1955 *1* Johannesburg **British Isles** 23–22
　　 2 Cape Town **South Africa** 25–9
　　 3 Pretoria **British Isles** 9–6
　　 4 Port Elizabeth **South Africa** 22–8
　　 Series drawn 2-2
1962 *1* Johannesburg **Drawn** 3–3

2 Durban **South Africa** 3–0
3 Cape Town **South Africa** 8–3
4 Bloemfontein **South Africa** 34–14
South Africa won series 3-0, with 1 draw
1968 *1* Pretoria **South Africa** 25–20
　　 2 Port Elizabeth **Drawn** 6–6
　　 3 Cape Town **South Africa** 11–6
　　 4 Johannesburg **South Africa** 19–6
　　 South Africa won series 3-0, with 1 draw
1974 *1* Cape Town **British Isles** 12–3
　　 2 Pretoria **British Isles** 28–9
　　 3 Port Elizabeth **British Isles** 26–9
　　 4 Johannesburg **Drawn** 13–13
　　 British Isles won series 3-0, with 1 draw
1980 *1* Cape Town **South Africa** 26–22
　　 2 Bloemfontein **South Africa** 26–19
　　 3 Port Elizabeth **South Africa** 12–10
　　 4 Pretoria **British Isles** 17–13
　　 South Africa won series 3-1

BRITISH ISLES v NEW ZEALAND
Played 31   British Isles won 6, New Zealand won 23, Drawn 2
Highest scores: British Isles 20–7 in 1993, New Zealand 38–6 in 1983
Biggest wins: British Isles 20–7 in 1993, New Zealand 38–6 in 1983

1930 *1* Dunedin **British Isles** 6–3
　　 2 Christchurch **New Zealand** 13–10
　　 3 Auckland **New Zealand** 15–10
　　 4 Wellington **New Zealand** 22–8
　　 New Zealand won series 3-1
1950 *1* Dunedin **Drawn** 9–9
　　 2 Christchurch **New Zealand** 8–0
　　 3 Wellington **New Zealand** 6–3
　　 4 Auckland **New Zealand** 11–8
　　 New Zealand won series 3-0, with 1 draw
1959 *1* Dunedin **New Zealand** 18–17
　　 2 Wellington **New Zealand** 11–8
　　 3 Christchurch **New Zealand** 22–8
　　 4 Auckland **British Isles** 9–6
　　 New Zealand won series 3-1
1966 *1* Dunedin **New Zealand** 20–3
　　 2 Wellington **New Zealand** 16–12
　　 3 Christchurch **New Zealand** 19–6
　　 4 Auckland **New Zealand** 24–11
　　 New Zealand won series 4-0

1971 *1* Dunedin **British Isles** 9–3
　　 2 Christchurch **New Zealand** 22–12
　　 3 Wellington **British Isles** 13–3
　　 4 Auckland **Drawn** 14–14
　　 British Isles won series 2-1, with 1 draw
1977 *1* Wellington **New Zealand** 16–12
　　 2 Christchurch **British Isles** 13–9
　　 3 Dunedin **New Zealand** 19–7
　　 4 Auckland **New Zealand** 10–9
　　 New Zealand won series 3-1
1983 *1* Christchurch **New Zealand** 16–12
　　 2 Wellington **New Zealand** 9–0
　　 3 Dunedin **New Zealand** 15–8
　　 4 Auckland **New Zealand** 38–6
　　 New Zealand won series 4-0
1993 *1* Christchurch **New Zealand** 20–18
　　 2 Wellington **British Isles** 20–7
　　 3 Auckland **New Zealand** 30–13
　　 New Zealand won series 2-1

BRITISH ISLES v AUSTRALIA
Played 10   British Isles won 8, Australia won 2, Drawn 0
Highest scores: British Isles 31–0 in 1966, Australia 30–12 in 1989
Biggest wins: British Isles 31–0 in 1966, Australia 30–12 in 1989

1930 Sydney **Australia** 6–5
1950 *1* Brisbane **British Isles** 19–6
    2 Sydney **British Isles** 24–3
    British Isles won series 2-0
1959 *1* Brisbane **British Isles** 17–6
    2 Sydney **British Isles** 24–3
    British Isles won series 2-0

1966 *1* Sydney **British Isles** 11–8
    2 Brisbane **British Isles** 31–0
    British Isles won series 2-0
1989 *1* Sydney **Australia** 30–12
    2 Brisbane **British Isles** 19–12
    3 Sydney **British Isles** 19–18
    British Isles won series 2-1

BRITISH ISLES INTERNATIONAL RECORDS
(up to 30 April 1997)

From 1910 onwards – the tour to South Africa in that year was the first fully representative one in which the four Home Unions co-operated.

MATCH RECORDS

MOST CONSECUTIVE TEST WINS

3 1950 *A* 1,2, 1955 *SA* 1
3 1974 *SA* 1,2,3

MOST CONSECUTIVE TESTS WITHOUT DEFEAT

P	W	D	Period
6	4	2	1971–74

MOST POINTS IN A MATCH
by the team

Pts	Opp	Venue	Year
31	A	Brisbane	1966
28	SA	Pretoria	1974
26	SA	Port Elizabeth	1974
24	A	Sydney	1950
24	A	Sydney	1959

by a player
18 by A J P Ward v South Africa at Cape Town — 1980
18 by A G Hastings v New Zealand at Christchurch — 1993
17 by T J Kiernan v South Africa at Pretoria — 1968
16 by B L Jones v Australia at Brisbane — 1950
15 by A G Hastings v Australia at Sydney — 1989

MOST TRIES IN A MATCH
by the team

T	Opp	Venue	Year
5	A	Sydney	1950
5	SA	Johannesburg	1955
5	A	Sydney	1959
5	A	Brisbane	1966
5	SA	Pretoria	1974

by a player
2 by C D Aarvold v New Zealand at Christchurch — 1930
2 by J E Nelson v Australia at Sydney — 1950
2 by M J Price v Australia at Sydney — 1959
2 by M J Price v New Zealand at Dunedin — 1959
2 by D K Jones v Australia at Brisbane — 1966
2 by T G R Davies v New Zealand at Christchurch — 1971
2 by J J Williams v South Africa at Pretoria — 1974
2 by J J Williams v South Africa at Port Elizabeth — 1974

MOST CONVERSIONS IN A MATCH
by the team

C	Opp	Venue	Year
5	A	Brisbane	1966
4	SA	Johannesburg	1955
3	A	Sydney	1950
3	A	Sydney	1959

by a player

5 by S Wilson v Australia at
  Brisbane   1966
4 by A Cameron v South Africa at
  Johannesburg   1955
2 several instances

MOST PENALTY GOALS IN A MATCH

by the team

P	Opp	Venue	Year
6	NZ	Christchurch	1993
5	SA	Pretoria	1968
5	SA	Cape Town	1980
5	A	Sydney	1989

by a player

6 by A G Hastings v New Zealand
  at Christchurch   1993
5 by T J Kiernan v South Africa
  at Pretoria   1968
5 by A J P Ward v South Africa at
  Cape Town   1980
5 by A G Hastings v Australia at
  Sydney   1989

MOST DROPPED GOALS IN A MATCH

by the team

D	Opp	Venue	Year
2	SA	Port Elizabeth	1974

by a player

2 by P Bennett v South Africa at
  Port Elizabeth   1974

CAREER RECORDS

MOST CAPPED PLAYERS

Caps	Player	Career
17	W J McBride	1962–74
13	R E G Jeeps	1955–62
12	C M H Gibson	1966–71
12	G Price	1977–83
10	A J F O'Reilly	1955–59
10	R H Williams	1955–59
10	G O Edwards	1968–74

MOST CONSECUTIVE TESTS

Tests	Player	Span
15	W J McBride	1966–74
12	C M H Gibson	1966–71
12	G Price	1977–83

MOST TESTS AS CAPTAIN

Tests	Captain	Span
6	A R Dawson	1959
4	R Cove-Smith	1924
4	M J Campbell-Lamerton	1966
4	T J Kiernan	1968
4	S J Dawes	1971
4	W J McBride	1974
4	P Bennett	1977
4	W B Beaumont	1980
4	C F Fitzgerald	1983

MOST TESTS IN INDIVIDUAL POSITIONS

Full-back J P R Williams	8	1971–74
Wing A J F O'Reilly	9	1955–59
Centre C M H Gibson	8	1966–71
Fly-half P Bennett	8	1974–77
Scrum-half R E G Jeeps	13	1955–62
Prop G Price	12	1977–83
Hooker B V Meredith	8	1955–62
Lock W J McBride	17	1962–74
Flanker N A A Murphy	8	1959–66
No 8 T M Davies	8	1971–74

MOST POINTS IN TESTS

Pts	Player	Tests	Career
66	A G Hastings	6	1989–93
44	P Bennett	8	1974–77
35	T J Kiernan	5	1962–68
30	S Wilson	5	1966
30	B John	5	1968–71

MOST TRIES IN TESTS

Tries	Player	Tests	Career
6	A J F O'Reilly	10	1955–59
5	J J Williams	7	1974–77
4	M J Price	5	1959

MOST CONVERSIONS IN TESTS

Cons	Player	Tests	Career
6	S Wilson	5	1966
4	B L Jones	3	1950
4	A Cameron	2	1955

MOST PENALTY GOALS IN TESTS

Pens	Player	Tests	Career
20	A G Hastings	6	1989–93
11	T J Kiernan	5	1962–68
10	P Bennett	8	1974–77
7	S O Campbell	7	1980–83

MOST DROPPED GOALS IN TESTS

Drops	Player	Tests	Career
2	D Watkins	6	1966
2	B John	5	1968–71
2	P Bennett	8	1974–77
2	C R Andrew	5	1989–93

SERIES RECORDS

Record	Holder	Detail
Most team points		79 in S Africa 1974
Most team tries		10 in S Africa 1955 & 1974
Most points by player	A G Hastings	38 in N Zealand 1993
Most tries by player	J J Williams	4 in S Africa 1974

MAJOR TOUR RECORDS

Record	Detail	Year	Place
Most team points	842	1959	A, NZ & C
Most team tries	165	1959	A, NZ & C
Most individual points	188 by B John	1971	A & NZ
Most individual tries	22 by A J F O'Reilly	1959	A, NZ & C
Most points in match	37 by A G B Old	1974 v SW Districts	Mossel Bay, SA
Most tries in match	6 by D J Duckham	1971 v W Coast/Buller	Greymouth, NZ
	6 by J J Williams	1974 v SW Districts	Mossel Bay, SA

MISCELLANEOUS RECORDS

Record	Holder	Detail
Longest Test career	W J McBride	13 seasons, 1962–74
Youngest Test cap	A J F O'Reilly	19 yrs 91 days in 1955
Oldest Test cap	W J McBride	34 yrs 51 days in 1974

RESULTS OF INTERNATIONAL MATCHES *(up to 30 April 1997)*

Cap matches only.
Years for Five Nations matches are for the second half of the season: eg 1972 means season 1971-72. Years for matches against touring teams from the Southern Hemisphere refer to the actual year of the match.

Points-scoring was first introduced in 1886, when an International Board was formed by Scotland, Ireland and Wales. Points values varied between countries until 1890, when England agreed to join the Board, and uniform values were adopted.

Northern Hemisphere seasons	Try	Conversion	Penalty goal	Dropped goal	Goal from mark
1890-91	1	2	2	3	3
1891-92 to 1892-93	2	3	3	4	4
1893-94 to 1904-05	3	2	3	4	4
1905-06 to 1947-48	3	2	3	4	3
1948-49 to 1970-71	3	2	3	3	3
1971-72 to 1991-92	4	2	3	3	3*
1992-93 onwards	5	2	3	3	–

*The goal from mark ceased to exist when the free-kick clause was introduced, 1977-78.
WC indicates a fixture played during the Rugby World Cup finals. LC indicates a fixture played in the Latin Cup. TN indicates a fixture played in the Tri-Nations.

ENGLAND v SCOTLAND
Played 114   England won 58, Scotland won 39, Drawn 17
Highest scores England 41-13 in 1997, Scotland 33-6 in 1986
Biggest wins England 41-13 in 1997, Scotland 33-6 in 1986

1871 Raeburn Place (Edinburgh) **Scotland** 1G 1T to 1T
1872 The Oval (London) **England** 1G 1DG 2T to 1DG
1873 Glasgow **Drawn** no score
1874 The Oval **England** 1DG to 1T
1875 Raeburn Place **Drawn** no score
1876 The Oval **England** 1G 1T to 0
1877 Raeburn Place **Scotland** 1 DG to 0
1878 The Oval **Drawn** no score
1879 Raeburn Place **Drawn** Scotland 1DG England 1G
1880 Manchester **England** 2G 3T to 1G
1881 Raeburn Place **Drawn** Scotland 1G 1T England 1DG 1T
1882 Manchester **Scotland** 2T to 0
1883 Raeburn Place **England** 2T to 1T
1884 Blackheath (London) **England** 1G to 1T
1885 No Match
1886 Raeburn Place **Drawn** no score
1887 Manchester **Drawn** 1T each
1888 No Match
1889 No Match
1890 Raeburn Place **England** 1G 1T to 0
1891 Richmond (London) **Scotland** 9-3
1892 Raeburn Place **England** 5-0
1893 Leeds **Scotland** 8-0
1894 Raeburn Place **Scotland** 6-0
1895 Richmond **Scotland** 6-3
1896 Glasgow **Scotland** 11-0
1897 Manchester **England** 12-3

1898 Powderhall (Edinburgh) **Drawn** 3-3
1899 Blackheath **Scotland** 5-0
1900 Inverleith (Edinburgh) **Drawn** 0-0
1901 Blackheath **Scotland** 18-3
1902 Inverleith **England** 6-3
1903 Richmond **Scotland** 10-6
1904 Inverleith **Scotland** 6-3
1905 Richmond **Scotland** 8-0
1906 Inverleith **England** 9-3
1907 Blackheath **Scotland** 8-3
1908 Inverleith **Scotland** 16-10
1909 Richmond **Scotland** 18-8
1910 Inverleith **England** 14-5
1911 Twickenham **England** 13-8
1912 Inverleith **Scotland** 8-3
1913 Twickenham **England** 3-0
1914 Inverleith **England** 16-15
1920 Twickenham **England** 13-4
1921 Inverleith **England** 18-0
1922 Twickenham **England** 11-5
1923 Inverleith **England** 8-6
1924 Twickenham **England** 19-0
1925 Murrayfield **Scotland** 14-11
1926 Twickenham **Scotland** 17-9
1927 Murrayfield **Scotland** 21-13
1928 Twickenham **England** 6-0
1929 Murrayfield **Scotland** 12-6
1930 Twickenham **Drawn** 0-0
1931 Murrayfield **Scotland** 28-19
1932 Twickenham **England** 16-3
1933 Murrayfield **Scotland** 3-0

1934 Twickenham **England** 6-3
1935 Murrayfield **Scotland** 10-7
1936 Twickenham **England** 9-8
1937 Murrayfield **England** 6-3
1938 Twickenham **Scotland** 21-16
1939 Murrayfield **England** 9-6
1947 Twickenham **England** 24-5
1948 Murrayfield **Scotland** 6-3
1949 Twickenham **England** 19-3
1950 Murrayfield **Scotland** 13-11
1951 Twickenham **England** 5-3
1952 Murrayfield **England** 19-3
1953 Twickenham **England** 26-8
1954 Murrayfield **England** 13-3
1955 Twickenham **England** 9-6
1956 Murrayfield **England** 11-6
1957 Twickenham **England** 16-3
1958 Murrayfield **Drawn** 3-3
1959 Twickenham **Drawn** 3-3
1960 Murrayfield **England** 21-12
1961 Twickenham **England** 6-0
1962 Murrayfield **Drawn** 3-3
1963 Twickenham **England** 10-8
1964 Murrayfield **Scotland** 15-6
1965 Twickenham **Drawn** 3-3
1966 Murrayfield **Scotland** 6-3
1967 Twickenham **England** 27-14
1968 Murrayfield **England** 8-6
1969 Twickenham **England** 8-3
1970 Murrayfield **Scotland** 14-5

1971 Twickenham **Scotland** 16-15
1971 Murrayfield **Scotland** 26-6
Special centenary match – non-championship
1972 Murrayfield **Scotland** 23-9
1973 Twickenham **England** 20-13
1974 Murrayfield **Scotland** 16-14
1975 Twickenham **England** 7-6
1976 Murrayfield **Scotland** 22-12
1977 Twickenham **England** 26-6
1978 Murrayfield **England** 15-0
1979 Twickenham **Drawn** 7-7
1980 Murrayfield **England** 30-18
1981 Twickenham **England** 23-17
1982 Murrayfield **Drawn** 9-9
1983 Twickenham **Scotland** 22-12
1984 Murrayfield **Scotland** 18-6
1985 Twickenham **England** 10-7
1986 Murrayfield **Scotland** 33-6
1987 Twickenham **England** 21-12
1988 Murrayfield **England** 9-6
1989 Twickenham **Drawn** 12-12
1990 Murrayfield **Scotland** 13-7
1991 Twickenham **England** 21-12
1991 Murrayfield *WC* **England** 9-6
1992 Murrayfield **England** 25-7
1993 Twickenham **England** 26-12
1994 Murrayfield **England** 15-14
1995 Twickenham **England** 24-12
1996 Murrayfield **England** 18-9
1997 Twickenham **England** 41-13

ENGLAND v IRELAND

Played 110   England won 64, Ireland won 38, Drawn 8
Highest scores England 46-6 in 1997, Ireland 26-21 in 1974
Biggest wins England 46-6 in 1997, Ireland 22-0 in 1947

1875 The Oval (London) **England** 1G 1DG
   1T to 0
1876 Dublin **England** 1G 1T to 0
1877 The Oval **England** 2G 2T to 0
1878 Dublin **England** 2G 1T to 0
1879 The Oval **England** 2G 1DG 2T to 0
1880 Dublin **England** 1G 1T to 1T
1881 Manchester **England** 2G 2T to 0
1882 Dublin **Drawn** 2T each
1883 Manchester **England** 1G 3T to 1T
1884 Dublin **England** 1G to 0
1885 Manchester **England** 2T to 1T
1886 Dublin **England** 1T to 0
1887 Dublin **Ireland** 2G to 0
1888 No Match
1889 No Match
1890 Blackheath (London) **England** 3T to 0
1891 Dublin **England** 9-0
1892 Manchester **England** 7-0
1893 Dublin **England** 4-0
1894 Blackheath **Ireland** 7-5
1895 Dublin **England** 6-3
1896 Leeds **Ireland** 10-4
1897 Dublin **Ireland** 13-9
1898 Richmond (London) **Ireland** 9-6
1899 Dublin **Ireland** 6-0

1900 Richmond **England** 15-4
1901 Dublin **Ireland** 10-6
1902 Leicester **England** 6-3
1903 Dublin **Ireland** 6-0
1904 Blackheath **England** 19-0
1905 Cork **Ireland** 17-3
1906 Leicester **Ireland** 16-6
1907 Dublin **Ireland** 17-9
1908 Richmond **England** 13-3
1909 Dublin **England** 11-5
1910 Twickenham **Drawn** 0-0
1911 Dublin **Ireland** 3-0
1912 Twickenham **England** 15-0
1913 Dublin **England** 15-4
1914 Twickenham **England** 17-12
1920 Dublin **England** 14-11
1921 Twickenham **England** 15-0
1922 Dublin **England** 12-3
1923 Leicester **England** 23-5
1924 Belfast **England** 14-3
1925 Twickenham **Drawn** 6-6
1926 Dublin **Ireland** 19-15
1927 Twickenham **England** 8-6
1928 Dublin **England** 7-6
1929 Twickenham **Ireland** 6-5
1930 Dublin **Ireland** 4-3

361

1931 Twickenham **Ireland** 6-5
1932 Dublin **England** 11-8
1933 Twickenham **England** 17-6
1934 Dublin **England** 13-3
1935 Twickenham **England** 14-3
1936 Dublin **Ireland** 6-3
1937 Twickenham **England** 9-8
1938 Dublin **England** 36-14
1939 Twickenham **Ireland** 5-0
1947 Dublin **Ireland** 22-0
1948 Twickenham **Ireland** 11-10
1949 Dublin **Ireland** 14-5
1950 Twickenham **England** 3-0
1951 Dublin **Ireland** 3-0
1952 Twickenham **England** 3-0
1953 Dublin **Drawn** 9-9
1954 Twickenham **England** 14-3
1955 Dublin **Drawn** 6-6
1956 Twickenham **England** 20-0
1957 Dublin **England** 6-0
1958 Twickenham **England** 6-0
1959 Dublin **England** 3-0
1960 Twickenham **England** 8-5
1961 Dublin **Ireland** 11-8
1962 Twickenham **England** 16-0
1963 Dublin **Drawn** 0-0
1964 Twickenham **Ireland** 18-5
1965 Dublin **Ireland** 5-0
1966 Twickenham **Drawn** 6-6
1967 Dublin **England** 8-3
1968 Twickenham **Drawn** 9-9

1969 Dublin **Ireland** 17-15
1970 Twickenham **England** 9-3
1971 Dublin **England** 9-6
1972 Twickenham **Ireland** 16-12
1973 Dublin **Ireland** 18-9
1974 Twickenham **Ireland** 26-21
1975 Dublin **Ireland** 12-9
1976 Twickenham **Ireland** 13-12
1977 Dublin **England** 4-0
1978 Twickenham **England** 15-9
1979 Dublin **Ireland** 12-7
1980 Twickenham **England** 24-9
1981 Dublin **England** 10-6
1982 Twickenham **Ireland** 16-15
1983 Dublin **Ireland** 25-15
1984 Twickenham **England** 12-9
1985 Dublin **Ireland** 13-10
1986 Twickenham **England** 25-20
1987 Dublin **Ireland** 17-0
1988 Twickenham **England** 35-3
1988 Dublin **England** 21-10
Non-championship match
1989 Dublin **England** 16-3
1990 Twickenham **England** 23-0
1991 Dublin **England** 16-7
1992 Twickenham **England** 38-9
1993 Dublin **Ireland** 17-3
1994 Twickenham **Ireland** 13-12
1995 Dublin **England** 20-8
1996 Twickenham **England** 28-15
1997 Dublin **England** 46-6

ENGLAND v WALES
Played 103   England won 43, Wales won 48, Drawn 12
Highestscores England 34-6 in 1990 & 34-13 in 1997, Wales 34-21 in 1967
Biggest wins England 34-6 in 1990, Wales 25-0 in 1905

1881 Blackheath (London) **England** 7G
     1DG 6T to 0
1882 No Match
1883 Swansea **England** 2G 4T to 0
1884 Leeds **England** 1G 2T to 1G
1885 Swansea **England** 1G 4T to 1G 1T
1886 Blackheath **England** 1GM 2T to 1G
1887 Llanelli **Drawn** no score
1888 No Match
1889 No Match
1890 Dewsbury **Wales** 1T to 0
1891 Newport **England** 7-3
1892 Blackheath **England** 17-0
1893 Cardiff **Wales** 12-11
1894 Birkenhead **England** 24-3
1895 Swansea **England** 14-6
1896 Blackheath **England** 25-0
1897 Newport **Wales** 11-0
1898 Blackheath **England** 14-7
1899 Swansea **Wales** 26-3
1900 Gloucester **Wales** 13-3
1901 Cardiff **Wales** 13-0
1902 Blackheath **Wales** 9-8
1903 Swansea **Wales** 21-5
1904 Leicester **Drawn** 14-14

1905 Cardiff **Wales** 25-0
1906 Richmond (London) **Wales** 16-3
1907 Swansea **Wales** 22-0
1908 Bristol **Wales** 28-18
1909 Cardiff **Wales** 8-0
1910 Twickenham **England** 11-6
1911 Swansea **Wales** 15-11
1912 Twickenham **England** 8-0
1913 Cardiff **England** 12-0
1914 Twickenham **England** 10-9
1920 Swansea **Wales** 19-5
1921 Twickenham **England** 18-3
1922 Cardiff **Wales** 28-6
1923 Twickenham **England** 7-3
1924 Swansea **England** 17-9
1925 Twickenham **England** 12-6
1926 Cardiff **Drawn** 3-3
1927 Twickenham **England** 11-9
1928 Swansea **England** 10-8
1929 Twickenham **England** 8-3
1930 Cardiff **England** 11-3
1931 Twickenham **Drawn** 11-11
1932 Swansea **Wales** 12-5
1933 Twickenham **Wales** 7-3
1934 Cardiff **England** 9-0

1935 Twickenham **Drawn** 3-3
1936 Swansea **Drawn** 0-0
1937 Twickenham **England** 4-3
1938 Cardiff **Wales** 14-8
1939 Twickenham **England** 3-0
1947 Cardiff **England** 9-6
1948 Twickenham **Drawn** 3-3
1949 Cardiff **Wales** 9-3
1950 Twickenham **Wales** 11-5
1951 Swansea **Wales** 23-5
1952 Twickenham **Wales** 8-6
1953 Cardiff **England** 8-3
1954 Twickenham **England** 9-6
1955 Cardiff **Wales** 3-0
1956 Twickenham **Wales** 8-3
1957 Cardiff **England** 3-0
1958 Twickenham **Drawn** 3-3
1959 Cardiff **Wales** 5-0
1960 Twickenham **England** 14-6
1961 Cardiff **Wales** 6-3
1962 Twickenham **Drawn** 0-0
1963 Cardiff **England** 13-6
1964 Twickenham **Drawn** 6-6
1965 Cardiff **Wales** 14-3
1966 Twickenham **Wales** 11-6
1967 Cardiff **Wales** 34-21
1968 Twickenham **Drawn** 11-11
1969 Cardiff **Wales** 30-9
1970 Twickenham **Wales** 17-13

1971 Cardiff **Wales** 22-6
1972 Twickenham **Wales** 12-3
1973 Cardiff **Wales** 25-9
1974 Twickenham **England** 16-12
1975 Cardiff **Wales** 20-4
1976 Twickenham **Wales** 21-9
1977 Cardiff **Wales** 14-9
1978 Twickenham **Wales** 9-6
1979 Cardiff **Wales** 27-3
1980 Twickenham **England** 9-8
1981 Cardiff **Wales** 21-19
1982 Twickenham **England** 17-7
1983 Cardiff **Drawn** 13-13
1984 Twickenham **Wales** 24-15
1985 Cardiff **Wales** 24-15
1986 Twickenham **England** 21-18
1987 Cardiff **Wales** 19-12
1987 Brisbane *WC* **Wales** 16-3
1988 Twickenham **Wales** 11-3
1989 Cardiff **Wales** 12-9
1990 Twickenham **England** 34-6
1991 Cardiff **England** 25-6
1992 Twickenham **England** 24-0
1993 Cardiff **Wales** 10-9
1994 Twickenham **England** 15-8
1995 Cardiff **England** 23-9
1996 Twickenham **England** 21-15
1997 Cardiff **England** 34-13

ENGLAND v FRANCE

Played 74   England won 40, France won 27, Drawn 7
Highest scores England 41-13 in 1907, France 37-12 in 1972
Biggest wins England 37-0 in 1911, France 37-12 in 1972

1906 Paris **England** 35-8
1907 Richmond (London) **England** 41-13
1908 Paris **England** 19-0
1909 Leicester **England** 22-0
1910 Paris **England** 11-3
1911 Twickenham **England** 37-0
1912 Paris **England** 18-8
1913 Twickenham **England** 20-0
1914 Paris **England** 39-13
1920 Twickenham **England** 8-3
1921 Paris **England** 10-6
1922 Twickenham **Drawn** 11-11
1923 Paris **England** 12-3
1924 Twickenham **England** 19-7
1925 Paris **England** 13-11
1926 Twickenham **England** 11-0
1927 Paris **France** 3-0
1928 Twickenham **England** 18-8
1929 Paris **England** 16-6
1930 Twickenham **England** 11-5
1931 Paris **France** 14-13
1947 Twickenham **England** 6-3
1948 Paris **France** 15-0
1949 Twickenham **England** 8-3
1950 Paris **France** 6-3
1951 Twickenham **France** 11-3
1952 Paris **England** 6-3

1953 Twickenham **England** 11-0
1954 Paris **France** 11-3
1955 Twickenham **France** 16-9
1956 Paris **France** 14-9
1957 Twickenham **England** 9-5
1958 Paris **England** 14-0
1959 Twickenham **Drawn** 3-3
1960 Paris **Drawn** 3-3
1961 Twickenham **Drawn** 5-5
1962 Paris **France** 13-0
1963 Twickenham **England** 6-5
1964 Paris **England** 6-3
1965 Twickenham **England** 9-6
1966 Paris **France** 13-0
1967 Twickenham **France** 16-12
1968 Paris **France** 14-9
1969 Twickenham **England** 22-8
1970 Paris **France** 35-13
1971 Twickenham **Drawn** 14-14
1972 Paris **France** 37-12
1973 Twickenham **England** 14-6
1974 Paris **Drawn** 12-12
1975 Twickenham **France** 27-20
1976 Paris **France** 30-9
1977 Twickenham **France** 4-3
1978 Paris **France** 15-6
1979 Twickenham **England** 7-6

1980 Paris **England** 17-13
1981 Twickenham **France** 16-12
1982 Paris **England** 27-15
1983 Twickenham **France** 19-15
1984 Paris **France** 32-18
1985 Twickenham **Drawn** 9-9
1986 Paris **France** 29-10
1987 Twickenham **France** 19-15
1988 Paris **France** 10-9
1989 Twickenham **England** 11-0

1990 Paris **England** 26-7
1991 Twickenham **England** 21-19
1991 Paris *WC* **England** 19-10
1992 Paris **England** 31-13
1993 Twickenham **England** 16-15
1994 Paris **England** 18-14
1995 Twickenham **England** 31-10
1995 Pretoria *WC* **France** 19-9
1996 Paris **France** 15-12
1997 Twickenham **France** 23-20

ENGLAND v NEW ZEALAND
Played 18   England won 4, New Zealand won 14, Drawn 0
Highest scores England 29-45 in 1995, New Zealand 45-29 in 1995
Biggest wins England 13-0 in 1936, New Zealand 42-15 in 1985

1905 Crystal Palace (London) **New Zealand** 15-0
1925 Twickenham **New Zealand** 17-11
1936 Twickenham **England** 13-0
1954 Twickenham **New Zealand** 5-0
1963 *1* Auckland **New Zealand** 21-11
    2 Christchurch **New Zealand** 9-6
    New Zealand won series 2-0
1964 Twickenham **New Zealand** 14-0
1967 Twickenham **New Zealand** 23-11
1973 Twickenham **New Zealand** 9-0

1973 Auckland **England** 16-10
1978 Twickenham **New Zealand** 16-6
1979 Twickenham **New Zealand** 10-9
1983 Twickenham **England** 15-9
1985 *1* Christchurch **New Zealand** 18-13
    2 Wellington **New Zealand** 42-15
    New Zealand won series 2-0
1991 Twickenham *WC* **New Zealand** 18-12
1993 Twickenham **England** 15-9
1995 Cape Town *WC* **New Zealand** 45-29

ENGLAND v SOUTH AFRICA
Played 13   England won 4, South Africa won 8, Drawn 1
Highest scores England 33-16 in 1992, South Africa 35-9 in 1984
Bigegst wins England 33-16 in 1992 & 32-15 in 1994, South Africa 35-9 in 1984

1906 Crystal Palace (London) **Drawn** 3-3
1913 Twickenham **South Africa** 9-3
1932 Twickenham **South Africa** 7-0
1952 Twickenham **South Africa** 8-3
1961 Twickenham **South Africa** 5-0
1969 Twickenham **England** 11-8
1972 Johannesburg **England** 18-9
1984 *1* Port Elizabeth **South Africa** 33-15

    2 Johannesburg **South Africa** 35-9
    South Africa won series 2-0
1992 Twickenham **England** 33-16
1994 *1* Pretoria **England** 32-15
    2 Cape Town **South Africa** 27-9
    Series drawn 1-1
1995 Twickenham **South Africa** 24-14

ENGLAND v AUSTRALIA
Played 19   England won 7, Australia won 12, Drawn 0
Highest scores England 28-19 in 1988, Australia 40-15 in 1991
Biggest wins England 20-3 in 1973 & 23-6 in 1976, Australia 40-15 in 1991

1909 Blackheath (London) **Australia** 9-3
1928 Twickenham **England** 18-11
1948 Twickenham **Australia** 11-0
1958 Twickenham **England** 9-6
1963 Sydney **Australia** 18-9
1967 Twickenham **Australia** 23-11
1973 Twickenham **England** 20-3
1975 *1* Sydney **Australia** 16-9
    2 Brisbane **Australia** 30-21
    Australia won series 2-0
1976 Twickenham **England** 23-6

1982 Twickenham **England** 15-11
1984 Twickenham **Australia** 19-3
1987 Sydney *WC* **Australia** 19-6
1988 *1* Brisbane **Australia** 22-16
    2 Sydney **Australia** 28-8
    Australia won series 2-0
1988 Twickenham **England** 28-19
1991 Sydney **Australia** 40-15
1991 Twickenham *WC* **Australia** 12-6
1995 Cape Town *WC* **England** 25-22

ENGLAND v NEW ZEALAND NATIVES
Played 1   England won 1
Highest score England 7-0 in 1889, NZ Natives 0-7 in 1889
Biggest win England 7-0 in 1889, NZ Natives no win

1889 Blackheath **England** 1G 4T to 0

ENGLAND v RFU PRESIDENT'S XV
Played 1   President's XV won 1
Highest score England 11-28 in 1971, RFU President's XV 28-11 in 1971
Biggest win RFU President's XV 28-11 in 1971

1971 Twickenham **President's XV** 28-11

ENGLAND v ARGENTINA
Played 7   England won 5, Argentina won 1, Drawn 1
Highest scores England 51-0 in 1990, Argentina 19-19 in 1981
Biggest wins England 51-0 in 1990, Argentina 15-13 in 1990

1981 *1* Buenos Aires **Drawn** 19-19
  2 Buenos Aires **England** 12-6
  England won series 1-0 with 1 draw
1990 *1* Buenos Aires **England** 25-12
  2 Buenos Aires **Argentina** 15-13

Series drawn 1-1
1990 Twickenham **England** 51-0
1995 Durban *WC* **England** 24-18
1996 Twickenham **England** 20-18

ENGLAND v ROMANIA
Played 3   England won 3
Highest scores England 58-3 in 1989, Romania 15-22 in 1985
Biggest win England 58-3 in 1989, Romania no win

1985 Twickenham **England** 22-15
1989 Bucharest **England** 58-3

1994 Twickenham **England** 54-3

ENGLAND v JAPAN
Played 1   England won 1
Highest score England 60-7 in 1987, Japan 7-60 in 1987
Biggest win England 60-7 in 1987, Japan no win

1987 Sydney *WC* **England** 60-7

ENGLAND v UNITED STATES
Played 2   England won 2
Highest scores England 37-9 in 1991, United States 9-37 in 1991
Biggest win England 37-9 in 1991, United States no win

1987 Sydney *WC* **England** 34-6

1991 Twickenham *WC* **England** 37-9

ENGLAND v FIJI
Played 3   England won 3
Highest scores England 58-23 in 1989, Fiji 23-58 in 1989
Biggest win England 58-23 in 1989, Fiji no win

1988 Suva **England** 25-12
1989 Twickenham **England** 58-23

1991 Suva **England** 28-12

ENGLAND v ITALY
Played 3 England won 3
Highest scores England 54-21 in 1996, Italy 21-54 in 1996
Biggest win England 54-21 in 1996, Italy no win

1991 Twickenham *WC* **England** 36-6   1996 Twickenham **England** 54-21
1995 Durban *WC* **England** 27-20

ENGLAND v CANADA
Played 2 England won 2
Highest scores England 60-19 in 1994, Canada 19-60 in 1994
Biggest win England 60-19 in 1994, Canada no win

1992 Wembley **England** 26-13   1994 Twickenham **England** 60-19

ENGLAND v WESTERN SAMOA
Played 2 England won 2
Highest scores England 44-22 in 1995, Western Samoa 22-44 in 1995
Biggest win England 44-22 in 1995, Western Samoa no win

1995 Durban *WC* **England** 44-22   1995 Twickenham **England** 27-9

SCOTLAND v IRELAND
Played 109 Scotland won 58, Ireland won 45, Drawn 5, Abandoned 1
Highest scores Scotland 38-10 in 1997, Ireland 26-8 in 1953
Biggest wins Scotland 38-10 in 1997, Ireland 21-0 in 1950

1877 Belfast **Scotland** 4G 2DG 2T to 0	1906 Dublin **Scotland** 13-6
1878 No Match	1907 Inverleith **Scotland** 15-3
1879 Belfast **Scotland** 1G 1DG 1T to 0	1908 Dublin **Ireland** 16-11
1880 Glasgow **Scotland** 1G 2DG 2T to 0	1909 Inverleith **Scotland** 9-3
1881 Belfast **Ireland** 1DG to 1T	1910 Belfast **Scotland** 14-0
1882 Glasgow **Scotland** 2T to 0	1911 Inverleith **Ireland** 16-10
1883 Belfast **Scotland** 1G 1T to 0	1912 Dublin **Ireland** 10-8
1884 Raeburn Place (Edinburgh) **Scotland** 2G 2T to 1T	1913 Inverleith **Scotland** 29-14
	1914 Dublin **Ireland** 6-0
1885 Belfast **Abandoned** Ireland 0 Scotland 1T	1920 Inverleith **Scotland** 19-0
	1921 Dublin **Ireland** 9-8
1885 Raeburn Place **Scotland** 1G 2T to 0	1922 Inverleith **Scotland** 6-3
1886 Raeburn Place **Scotland** 3G 1DG 2T to 0	1923 Dublin **Scotland** 13-3
	1924 Inverleith **Scotland** 13-8
1887 Belfast **Scotland** 1G 1GM 2T to 0	1925 Dublin **Scotland** 14-8
1888 Raeburn Place **Scotland** 1G to 0	1926 Murrayfield **Ireland** 3-0
1889 Belfast **Scotland** 1DG to 0	1927 Dublin **Ireland** 6-0
1890 Raeburn Place **Scotland** 1DG 1T to 0	1928 Murrayfield **Ireland** 13-5
1891 Belfast **Scotland** 14-0	1929 Dublin **Scotland** 16-7
1892 Raeburn Place **Scotland** 2-0	1930 Murrayfield **Ireland** 14-11
1893 Belfast **Drawn** 0-0	1931 Dublin **Ireland** 8-5
1894 Dublin **Ireland** 5-0	1932 Murrayfield **Ireland** 20-8
1895 Raeburn Place **Scotland** 6-0	1933 Dublin **Scotland** 8-6
1896 Dublin **Drawn** 0-0	1934 Murrayfield **Scotland** 16-9
1897 Powderhall (Edinburgh) **Scotland** 8-3	1935 Dublin **Ireland** 12-5
1898 Belfast **Scotland** 8-0	1936 Murrayfield **Ireland** 10-4
1899 Inverleith (Edinburgh) **Ireland** 9-3	1937 Dublin **Ireland** 11-4
1900 Dublin **Drawn** 0-0	1938 Murrayfield **Scotland** 23-14
1901 Inverleith **Scotland** 9-5	1939 Dublin **Ireland** 12-3
1902 Belfast **Ireland** 5-0	1947 Murrayfield **Ireland** 3-0
1903 Inverleith **Scotland** 3-0	1948 Dublin **Ireland** 6-0
1904 Dublin **Scotland** 19-3	1949 Murrayfield **Ireland** 13-3
1905 Inverleith **Ireland** 11-5	1950 Dublin **Ireland** 21-0

1951 Murrayfield **Ireland** 6-5
1952 Dublin **Ireland** 12-8
1953 Murrayfield **Ireland** 26-8
1954 Belfast **Ireland** 6-0
1955 Murrayfield **Scotland** 12-3
1956 Dublin **Ireland** 14-10
1957 Murrayfield **Ireland** 5-3
1958 Dublin **Ireland** 12-6
1959 Murrayfield **Ireland** 8-3
1960 Dublin **Scotland** 6-5
1961 Murrayfield **Scotland** 16-8
1962 Dublin **Scotland** 20-6
1963 Murrayfield **Scotland** 3-0
1964 Dublin **Scotland** 6-3
1965 Murrayfield **Ireland** 16-6
1966 Dublin **Scotland** 11-3
1967 Murrayfield **Ireland** 5-3
1968 Dublin **Ireland** 14-6
1969 Murrayfield **Ireland** 16-0
1970 Dublin **Ireland** 16-11
1971 Murrayfield **Ireland** 17-5
1972 No Match
1973 Murrayfield **Scotland** 19-14
1974 Dublin **Ireland** 9-6

1975 Murrayfield **Scotland** 20-13
1976 Dublin **Scotland** 15-6
1977 Murrayfield **Scotland** 21-18
1978 Dublin **Ireland** 12-9
1979 Murrayfield **Drawn** 11-11
1980 Dublin **Ireland** 22-15
1981 Murrayfield **Scotland** 10-9
1982 Dublin **Ireland** 21-12
1983 Murrayfield **Ireland** 15-13
1984 Dublin **Scotland** 32-9
1985 Murrayfield **Ireland** 18-15
1986 Dublin **Scotland** 10-9
1987 Murrayfield **Scotland** 16-12
1988 Dublin **Ireland** 22-18
1989 Murrayfield **Scotland** 37-21
1990 Dublin **Scotland** 13-10
1991 Murrayfield **Scotland** 28-25
1991 Murrayfield *WC* **Scotland** 24-15
1992 Dublin **Scotland** 18-10
1993 Murrayfield **Scotland** 15-3
1994 Dublin **Drawn** 6-6
1995 Murrayfield **Scotland** 26-13
1996 Dublin **Scotland** 16-10
1997 Murrayfield **Scotland** 38-10

SCOTLAND v WALES
Played 101   Scotland won 44, Wales won 55, Drawn 2
Highest scores Scotland 35-10 in 1924, Wales 35-12 in 1972
Biggest wins Scotland 35-10 in 1924, Wales 35-12 in 1972 & 29-6 in 1994

1883 Raeburn Place (Edinburgh) **Scotland**
    3G to 1G
1884 Newport **Scotland** 1DG 1T to 0
1885 Glasgow **Drawn** no score
1886 Cardiff **Scotland** 2G 8T to 0
1887 Raeburn Place **Scotland** 4G 8T to 0
1888 Newport **Wales** 1T to 0
1889 Raeburn Place **Scotland** 2T to 0
1890 Cardiff **Scotland** 1G 2T to 1T
1891 Raeburn Place **Scotland** 15-0
1892 Swansea **Scotland** 7-2
1893 Raeburn Place **Wales** 9-0
1894 Newport **Wales** 7-0
1895 Raeburn Place **Scotland** 5-4
1896 Cardiff **Wales** 6-0
1897 No Match
1898 No Match
1899 Inverleith (Edinburgh) **Scotland** 21-10
1900 Swansea **Wales** 12-3
1901 Inverleith **Scotland** 18-8
1902 Cardiff **Wales** 14-5
1903 Inverleith **Scotland** 6-0
1904 Swansea **Wales** 21-3
1905 Inverleith **Wales** 6-3
1906 Cardiff **Wales** 9-3
1907 Inverleith **Scotland** 6-3
1908 Swansea **Wales** 6-5
1909 Inverleith **Wales** 5-3
1910 Cardiff **Wales** 14-0
1911 Inverleith **Wales** 32-10
1912 Swansea **Wales** 21-6
1913 Inverleith **Wales** 8-0

1914 Cardiff **Wales** 24-5
1920 Inverleith **Scotland** 9-5
1921 Swansea **Scotland** 14-8
1922 Inverleith **Drawn** 9-9
1923 Cardiff **Scotland** 11-8
1924 Inverleith **Scotland** 35-10
1925 Swansea **Scotland** 24-14
1926 Murrayfield **Scotland** 8-5
1927 Cardiff **Scotland** 5-0
1928 Murrayfield **Wales** 13-0
1929 Swansea **Wales** 14-7
1930 Murrayfield **Scotland** 12-9
1931 Cardiff **Wales** 13-8
1932 Murrayfield **Wales** 6-0
1933 Swansea **Scotland** 11-3
1934 Murrayfield **Wales** 13-6
1935 Cardiff **Wales** 10-6
1936 Murrayfield **Wales** 13-3
1937 Swansea **Scotland** 13-6
1938 Murrayfield **Scotland** 8-6
1939 Cardiff **Wales** 11-3
1947 Murrayfield **Wales** 22-8
1948 Cardiff **Wales** 14-0
1949 Murrayfield **Scotland** 6-5
1950 Swansea **Wales** 12-0
1951 Murrayfield **Scotland** 19-0
1952 Cardiff **Wales** 11-0
1953 Murrayfield **Wales** 12-0
1954 Swansea **Wales** 15-3
1955 Murrayfield **Scotland** 14-8
1956 Cardiff **Wales** 9-3
1957 Murrayfield **Scotland** 9-6

1958 Cardiff **Wales** 8-3	1978 Cardiff **Wales** 22-14
1959 Murrayfield **Scotland** 6-5	1979 Murrayfield **Wales** 19-13
1960 Cardiff **Wales** 8-0	1980 Cardiff **Wales** 17-6
1961 Murrayfield **Scotland** 3-0	1981 Murrayfield **Scotland** 15-6
1962 Cardiff **Scotland** 8-3	1982 Cardiff **Scotland** 34-18
1963 Murrayfield **Wales** 6-0	1983 Murrayfield **Wales** 19-15
1964 Cardiff **Wales** 11-3	1984 Cardiff **Scotland** 15-9
1965 Murrayfield **Wales** 14-12	1985 Murrayfield **Wales** 25-21
1966 Cardiff **Wales** 8-3	1986 Cardiff **Wales** 22-15
1967 Murrayfield **Scotland** 11-5	1987 Murrayfield **Scotland** 21-15
1968 Cardiff **Wales** 5-0	1988 Cardiff **Wales** 25-20
1969 Murrayfield **Wales** 17-3	1989 Murrayfield **Scotland** 23-7
1970 Cardiff **Wales** 18-9	1990 Cardiff **Scotland** 13-9
1971 Murrayfield **Wales** 19-18	1991 Murrayfield **Scotland** 32-12
1972 Cardiff **Wales** 35-12	1992 Cardiff **Wales** 15-12
1973 Murrayfield **Scotland** 10-9	1993 Murrayfield **Scotland** 20-0
1974 Cardiff **Wales** 6-0	1994 Cardiff **Wales** 29-6
1975 Murrayfield **Scotland** 12-10	1995 Murrayfield **Scotland** 26-13
1976 Cardiff **Wales** 28-6	1996 Cardiff **Scotland** 16-14
1977 Murrayfield **Wales** 18-9	1997 Murrayfield **Wales** 34-19

SCOTLAND v FRANCE

Played 69   Scotland won 32, France won 34, Drawn 3
Highest scores Scotland 31-3 in 1912, France 47-20 in 1997
Biggest wins Scotland 31-3 in 1912, France 47-20 in 1997

1910 Inverleith (Edinburgh) **Scotland** 27-0	1965 Paris **France** 16-8
1911 Paris **France** 16-15	1966 Murrayfield **Drawn** 3-3
1912 Inverleith **Scotland** 31-3	1967 Paris **Scotland** 9-8
1913 Paris **Scotland** 21-3	1968 Murrayfield **France** 8-6
1914 No Match	1969 Paris **Scotland** 6-3
1920 Paris **Scotland** 5-0	1970 Murrayfield **France** 11-9
1921 Inverleith **France** 3-0	1971 Paris **France** 13-8
1922 Paris **Drawn** 3-3	1972 Murrayfield **Scotland** 20-9
1923 Inverleith **Scotland** 16-3	1973 Paris **France** 16-13
1924 Paris **France** 12-10	1974 Murrayfield **Scotland** 19-6
1925 Inverleith **Scotland** 25-4	1975 Paris **France** 10-9
1926 Paris **Scotland** 20-6	1976 Murrayfield **France** 13-6
1927 Murrayfield **Scotland** 23-6	1977 Paris **France** 23-3
1928 Paris **Scotland** 15-6	1978 Murrayfield **France** 19-16
1929 Murrayfield **Scotland** 6-3	1979 Paris **France** 21-17
1930 Paris **France** 7-3	1980 Murrayfield **Scotland** 22-14
1931 Murrayfield **Scotland** 6-4	1981 Paris **France** 16-9
1947 Paris **France** 8-3	1982 Murrayfield **Scotland** 16-7
1948 Murrayfield **Scotland** 9-8	1983 Paris **France** 19-15
1949 Paris **Scotland** 8-0	1984 Murrayfield **Scotland** 21-12
1950 Murrayfield **Scotland** 8-5	1985 Paris **France** 11-3
1951 Paris **France** 14-12	1986 Murrayfield **Scotland** 18-17
1952 Murrayfield **France** 13-11	1987 Paris **France** 28-22
1953 Paris **France** 11-5	1987 Christchurch *WC* **Drawn** 20-20
1954 Murrayfield **France** 3-0	1988 Murrayfield **Scotland** 23-12
1955 Paris **France** 15-0	1989 Paris **France** 19-3
1956 Murrayfield **Scotland** 12-0	1990 Murrayfield **Scotland** 21-0
1957 Paris **Scotland** 6-0	1991 Paris **France** 15-9
1958 Murrayfield **Scotland** 11-9	1992 Murrayfield **Scotland** 10-6
1959 Paris **France** 9-0	1993 Paris **France** 11-3
1960 Murrayfield **France** 13-11	1994 Murrayfield **France** 20-12
1961 Paris **France** 11-0	1995 Paris **Scotland** 23-21
1962 Murrayfield **France** 11-3	1995 Pretoria *WC* **France** 22-19
1963 Paris **Scotland** 11-6	1996 Murrayfield **Scotland** 19-14
1964 Murrayfield **Scotland** 10-0	1997 Paris **France** 47-20

SCOTLAND v NEW ZEALAND
Played 20   Scotland won 0, New Zealand won 18, Drawn 2
Highest scores Scotland 31-62 in 1996, New Zealand 62-31 in 1996
Biggest wins Scotland no win, New Zealand 51-15 in 1993

1905 Inverleith (Edinburgh) **New Zealand** 12-7
1935 Murrayfield **New Zealand** 18-8
1954 Murrayfield **New Zealand** 3-0
1964 Murrayfield **Drawn** 0-0
1967 Murrayfield **New Zealand** 14-3
1972 Murrayfield **New Zealand** 14-9
1975 Auckland **New Zealand** 24-0
1978 Murrayfield **New Zealand** 18-9
1979 Murrayfield **New Zealand** 20-6
1981 *1* Dunedin **New Zealand** 11-4
    2 Auckland **New Zealand** 40-15

New Zealand won series 2-0
1983 Murrayfield **Drawn** 25-25
1987 Christchurch *WC* **New Zealand** 30-3
1990 *1* Dunedin **New Zealand** 31-16
    2 Auckland **New Zealand** 21-18
New Zealand won series 2-0
1991 Cardiff *WC* **New Zealand** 13-6
1993 Murrayfield **New Zealand** 51-15
1995 Pretoria *WC* **New Zealand** 48-30
1996 *1* Dunedin **New Zealand** 62-31
    2 Auckland **New Zealand** 36-12
New Zealand won series 2-0

SCOTLAND v SOUTH AFRICA
Played 9   Scotland won 3, South Africa won 6, Drawn 0
Highest scores Scotland 10-18 in 1960 & 10-34 in 1994, South Africa 44-0 in 1951
Biggest wins Scotland 6-0 in 1906, South Africa 44-0 in 1951

1906 Glasgow **Scotland** 6-0
1912 Inverleith **South Africa** 16-0
1932 Murrayfield **South Africa** 6-3
1951 Murrayfield **South Africa** 44-0
1960 Port Elizabeth **South Africa** 18-10

1961 Murrayfield **South Africa** 12-5
1965 Murrayfield **Scotland** 8-5
1969 Murrayfield **Scotland** 6-3
1994 Murrayfield **South Africa** 34-10

SCOTLAND v AUSTRALIA
Played 15   Scotland won 7, Australia won 8, Drawn 0
Highest scores Scotland 24-15 in 1981, Australia 37-12 in 1984 & 37-13 in 1992
Biggest wins Scotland 24-15 in 1981, Australia 37-12 in 1984

1927 Murrayfield **Scotland** 10-8
1947 Murrayfield **Australia** 16-7
1958 Murrayfield **Scotland** 12-8
1966 Murrayfield **Scotland** 11-5
1968 Murrayfield **Scotland** 9-3
1970 Sydney **Australia** 23-3
1975 Murrayfield **Scotland** 10-3
1981 Murrayfield **Scotland** 24-15
1982 *1* Brisbane **Scotland** 12-7

    2 Sydney **Australia** 33-9
Series drawn 1-1
1984 Murrayfield **Australia** 37-12
1988 Murrayfield **Australia** 32-13
1992 *1* Sydney **Australia** 27-12
    2 Brisbane **Australia** 37-13
Australia won series 2-0
1996 Murrayfield **Australia** 29-19

SCOTLAND v SRU PRESIDENT'S XV
Played 1   Scotland won 1
Highest scores Scotland 27-16 in 1972, SRU President's XV 16-27 in 1973
Biggest win Scotland 27-16 in 1973, SRU President's XV no win

1973 Murrayfield **Scotland** 27-16

SCOTLAND v ROMANIA
Played 7   Scotland won 5, Romania won 2, Drawn 0
Highest scores Scotland 55-28 in 1987, Romania 28-55 in 1987 & 28-22 in 1984
Biggest wins Scotland 49-16 in 1995, Romania 28-22 in 1984 & 18-12 in 1991

1981 Murrayfield **Scotland** 12-6
1984 Bucharest **Romania** 28-22
1986 Bucharest **Scotland** 33-18
1987 Dunedin *WC* **Scotland** 55-28

1989 Murrayfield **Scotland** 32-0
1991 Bucharest **Romania** 18-12
1995 Murrayfield **Scotland** 49-16

SCOTLAND v ZIMBABWE
Played 2   Scotland won 2
Highest scores Scotland 60-21 in 1987, Zimbabwe 21-60 in 1987
Biggest win Scotland 60-21 in 1987 & 51-12 in 1991, Zimbabwe no win

1987 Wellington *WC* **Scotland** 60-21   1991 Murrayfield *WC* **Scotland** 51-12

SCOTLAND v FIJI
Played 1   Scotland won 1
Highest scores Scotland 38-17 in 1989, Fiji 17-38 in 1989
Biggest win Scotland 38-17 in 1989, Fiji no win

1989 Murrayfield **Scotland** 38-17

SCOTLAND v ARGENTINA
Played 3   Scotland won 1, Argentina won 2, Drawn 0
Highest scores Scotland 49-3 in 1990, Argentina 19-17 in 1994
Biggest wins Scotland 49-3 in 1990, Argentina 19-17 in 1994

1990 Murrayfield **Scotland** 49-3   *2* Buenos Aires **Argentina** 19-17
1994 *1* Buenos Aires **Argentina** 16-15   *Argentina won series 2-0*

SCOTLAND v JAPAN
Played 1   Scotland won 1
Highest scores Scotland 47-9 in 1991, Japan 9-47 in 1991
Biggest win Scotland 47-9 in 1991, Japan no win

1991 Murrayfield *WC* **Scotland** 47-9

SCOTLAND v WESTERN SAMOA
Played 2   Scotland won 1, Drawn 1
Highest scores Scotland 28-6 in 1991, Western Samoa 15-15 in 1995
Biggest win Scotland 28-6 in 1991, Western Samoa no win

1991 Murrayfield *WC* **Scotland** 28-6   1995 Murrayfield **Drawn** 15-15

SCOTLAND v CANADA
Played 1   Scotland won 1
Highest scores Scotland 22-6 in 1995, Canada 6-22 in 1995
Biggest win Scotland 22-6 in 1995, Canada no win

1995 Murrayfield **Scotland** 22-6

SCOTLAND v IVORY COAST
Played 1   Scotland won 1
Highest scores Scotland 89-0 in 1995, Ivory Coast 0-89 in 1995
Biggest win Scotland 89-0 in 1995, Ivory Coast no win

1995 Rustenburg *WC* **Scotland** 89-0

SCOTLAND v TONGA
Played 1   Scotland won 1
Highest scores Scotland 41-5 in 1995, Tonga 5-41 in 1995
Biggest win Scotland 41-5 in 1995, Tonga no win

1995 Pretoria *WC* **Scotland** 41-5

SCOTLAND v ITALY

Played 1   Scotland won 1
Highest scores Scotland 29-22 in 1996, Italy 22-29 in 1996
Biggest win Scotland 29-22 in 1996, Italy no win

1996 Murrayfield **Scotland** 29-22

IRELAND v WALES

Played 101   Ireland won 37, Wales won 58, Drawn 6
Highest scores Ireland 30-17 in 1996, Wales 34-9 in 1976
Biggest wins Ireland 19-3 in 1925, Wales 29-0 in 1907

1882 Dublin **Wales** 2G 2T to 0
1883 No Match
1884 Cardiff **Wales** 1DG 2T to 0
1885 No Match
1886 No Match
1887 Birkenhead **Wales** 1DG 1T to 3T
1888 Dublin **Ireland** 1G 1DG 1T to 0
1889 Swansea **Ireland** 2T to 0
1890 Dublin **Drawn** 1G each
1891 Llanelli **Wales** 6-4
1892 Dublin **Ireland** 9-0
1893 Llanelli **Wales** 2-0
1894 Belfast **Ireland** 3-0
1895 Cardiff **Wales** 5-3
1896 Dublin **Ireland** 8-4
1897 No Match
1898 Limerick **Wales** 11-3
1899 Cardiff **Ireland** 3-0
1900 Belfast **Wales** 3-0
1901 Swansea **Wales** 10-9
1902 Dublin **Wales** 15-0
1903 Cardiff **Wales** 18-0
1904 Belfast **Ireland** 14-12
1905 Swansea **Wales** 10-3
1906 Belfast **Ireland** 11-6
1907 Cardiff **Wales** 29-0
1908 Belfast **Wales** 11-5
1909 Swansea **Wales** 18-5
1910 Dublin **Wales** 19-3
1911 Cardiff **Wales** 16-0
1912 Belfast **Ireland** 12-5
1913 Swansea **Wales** 16-13
1914 Belfast **Wales** 11-3
1920 Cardiff **Wales** 28-4
1921 Belfast **Wales** 6-0
1922 Swansea **Wales** 11-5
1923 Dublin **Ireland** 5-4
1924 Cardiff **Ireland** 13-10
1925 Belfast **Ireland** 19-3
1926 Swansea **Wales** 11-8
1927 Dublin **Ireland** 19-9
1928 Cardiff **Ireland** 13-10
1929 Belfast **Drawn** 5-5
1930 Swansea **Wales** 12-7
1931 Belfast **Wales** 15-3
1932 Cardiff **Ireland** 12-10
1933 Belfast **Ireland** 10-5
1934 Swansea **Wales** 13-0
1935 Belfast **Ireland** 9-3
1936 Cardiff **Wales** 3-0

1937 Belfast **Ireland** 5-3
1938 Swansea **Wales** 11-5
1939 Belfast **Wales** 7-0
1947 Swansea **Wales** 6-0
1948 Belfast **Ireland** 6-3
1949 Swansea **Ireland** 5-0
1950 Belfast **Wales** 6-3
1951 Cardiff **Drawn** 3-3
1952 Dublin **Wales** 14-3
1953 Swansea **Wales** 5-3
1954 Dublin **Wales** 12-9
1955 Cardiff **Wales** 21-3
1956 Dublin **Ireland** 11-3
1957 Cardiff **Wales** 6-5
1958 Dublin **Wales** 9-6
1959 Cardiff **Wales** 8-6
1960 Dublin **Wales** 10-9
1961 Cardiff **Wales** 9-0
1962 Dublin **Drawn** 3-3
1963 Cardiff **Ireland** 14-6
1964 Dublin **Wales** 15-6
1965 Cardiff **Wales** 14-8
1966 Dublin **Ireland** 9-6
1967 Cardiff **Ireland** 3-0
1968 Dublin **Ireland** 9-6
1969 Cardiff **Wales** 24-11
1970 Dublin **Ireland** 14-0
1971 Cardiff **Wales** 23-9
1972 No Match
1973 Cardiff **Wales** 16-12
1974 Dublin **Drawn** 9-9
1975 Cardiff **Wales** 32-4
1976 Dublin **Wales** 34-9
1977 Cardiff **Wales** 25-9
1978 Dublin **Wales** 20-16
1979 Cardiff **Wales** 24-21
1980 Dublin **Ireland** 21-7
1981 Cardiff **Wales** 9-8
1982 Dublin **Ireland** 20-12
1983 Cardiff **Wales** 23-9
1984 Dublin **Wales** 18-9
1985 Cardiff **Ireland** 21-9
1986 Dublin **Wales** 19-12
1987 Cardiff **Ireland** 15-11
1987 Wellington *WC* **Wales** 13-6
1988 Dublin **Wales** 12-9
1989 Cardiff **Ireland** 19-13
1990 Dublin **Ireland** 14-8
1991 Cardiff **Drawn** 21-21
1992 Dublin **Wales** 16-15

1993 Cardiff **Ireland** 19-14
1994 Dublin **Wales** 17-15
1995 Cardiff **Ireland** 16-12

1995 Johannesburg *WC* **Ireland** 24-23
1996 Dublin **Ireland** 30-17
1997 Cardiff **Ireland** 26-25

IRELAND v FRANCE

Played 71   Ireland won 25, France won 41, Drawn 5
Highest scores Ireland 25-5 in 1911 & 25-6 in 1975, France 45-10 in 1996
Biggest wins Ireland 24-0 in 1913, France 45-10 in 1996

1909 Dublin **Ireland** 19-8
1910 Paris **Ireland** 8-3
1911 Cork **Ireland** 25-5
1912 Paris **Ireland** 11-6
1913 Cork **Ireland** 24-0
1914 Paris **Ireland** 8-6
1920 Dublin **France** 15-7
1921 Paris **France** 20-10
1922 Dublin **Ireland** 8-3
1923 Paris **France** 14-8
1924 Dublin **Ireland** 6-0
1925 Paris **Ireland** 9-3
1926 Belfast **Ireland** 11-0
1927 Paris **Ireland** 8-3
1928 Belfast **Ireland** 12-8
1929 Paris **Ireland** 6-0
1930 Belfast **France** 5-0
1931 Paris **France** 3-0
1947 Dublin **France** 12-8
1948 Paris **Ireland** 13-6
1949 Dublin **France** 16-9
1950 Paris **Drawn** 3-3
1951 Dublin **Ireland** 9-8
1952 Paris **Ireland** 11-8
1953 Belfast **Ireland** 16-3
1954 Paris **France** 8-0
1955 Dublin **France** 5-3
1956 Paris **France** 14-8
1957 Dublin **Ireland** 11-6
1958 Paris **France** 11-6
1959 Dublin **Ireland** 9-5
1960 Paris **France** 23-6
1961 Dublin **France** 15-3
1962 Paris **France** 11-0
1963 Dublin **France** 24-5
1964 Paris **France** 27-6

1965 Dublin **Drawn** 3-3
1966 Paris **France** 11-6
1967 Dublin **France** 11-6
1968 Paris **France** 16-6
1969 Dublin **Ireland** 17-9
1970 Paris **France** 8-0
1971 Dublin **Drawn** 9-9
1972 Paris **Ireland** 14-9
1972 Dublin **Ireland** 24-14
Non-championship match
1973 Dublin **Ireland** 6-4
1974 Paris **France** 9-6
1975 Dublin **Ireland** 25-6
1976 Paris **France** 26-3
1977 Dublin **France** 15-6
1978 Paris **France** 10-9
1979 Dublin **Drawn** 9-9
1980 Paris **France** 19-18
1981 Dublin **France** 19-13
1982 Paris **France** 22-9
1983 Dublin **Ireland** 22-16
1984 Paris **France** 25-12
1985 Dublin **Drawn** 15-15
1986 Paris **France** 29-9
1987 Dublin **France** 19-13
1988 Paris **France** 25-6
1989 Dublin **France** 26-21
1990 Paris **France** 31-12
1991 Dublin **France** 21-13
1992 Paris **France** 44-12
1993 Dublin **France** 21-6
1994 Paris **France** 35-15
1995 Dublin **France** 25-7
1995 Durban *WC* **France** 36-12
1996 Paris **France** 45-10
1997 Dublin **France** 32-15

IRELAND v NEW ZEALAND

Played 13   Ireland won 0, New Zealand won 12, Drawn 1
Highest scores Ireland 21-24 in 1992, New Zealand 59-6 in 1992
Biggest win Ireland no win, New Zealand 59-6 in 1992

1905 Dublin **New Zealand** 15-0
1924 Dublin **New Zealand** 6-0
1935 Dublin **New Zealand** 17-9
1954 Dublin **New Zealand** 14-3
1963 Dublin **New Zealand** 6-5
1973 Dublin **Drawn** 10-10
1974 Dublin **New Zealand** 15-6

1976 Wellington **New Zealand** 11-3
1978 Dublin **New Zealand** 10-6
1989 Dublin **New Zealand** 23-6
1992 *1* Dunedin **New Zealand** 24-21
2 Wellington **New Zealand** 59-6
New Zealand won series 2-0
1995 Johannesburg *WC* **New Zealand** 43-19

IRELAND v SOUTH AFRICA

Played 10   Ireland won 1, South Africa won 8, Drawn 1
Highest scores Ireland 15-23 in 1981, South Africa 38-0 in 1912
Biggest wins Ireland 9-6 in 1965, South Africa 38-0 in 1912

1906 Belfast **South Africa** 15-12
1912 Dublin **South Africa** 38-0
1931 Dublin **South Africa** 8-3
1951 Dublin **South Africa** 17-5
1960 Dublin **South Africa** 8-3
1961 Cape Town **South Africa** 24-8

1965 Dublin **Ireland** 9-6
1970 Dublin **Drawn** 8-8
1981 *1* Cape Town **South Africa** 23-15
    2 Durban **South Africa** 12-10
    South Africa won series 2-0

IRELAND v AUSTRALIA

Played 17   Ireland won 6, Australia won 11, Drawn 0
Highest scores Ireland 27-12 in 1979, Australia 42-17 in 1992
Biggest wins Ireland 27-12 in 1979, Australia 42-17 in 1992

1927 Dublin **Australia** 5-3
1947 Dublin **Australia** 16-3
1958 Dublin **Ireland** 9-6
1967 Dublin **Ireland** 15-8
1967 Sydney **Ireland** 11-5
1968 Dublin **Ireland** 10-3
1976 Dublin **Australia** 20-10
1979 *1* Brisbane **Ireland** 27-12
    2 Sydney **Ireland** 9-3
    Ireland won series 2-0

1981 Dublin **Australia** 16-12
1984 Dublin **Australia** 16-9
1987 Sydney *WC* **Australia** 33-15
1991 Dublin *WC* **Australia** 19-18
1992 Dublin **Australia** 42-17
1994 *1* Brisbane **Australia** 33-13
    2 Sydney **Australia** 32-18
    Australia won series 2-0
1996 Dublin **Australia** 22-12

IRELAND v NEW ZEALAND NATIVES

Played 1   New Zealand Natives won 1
Highest scores Ireland 4-13 in 1888, Zew Zealand Natives 13-4 in 1888
Biggest win Ireland no win, New Zealand Natives 13-4 in 1888

1888 Dublin **New Zealand Natives** 4G 1T to 1G 1T

IRELAND v IRU PRESIDENT'S XV

Played 1   Drawn 1
Highest scores Ireland 18-18 in 1974, IRFU President's XV 18-18 in 1974

1974 Dublin **Drawn** 18-18

IRELAND v ROMANIA

Played 2   Ireland won 2
Highest scores Ireland 60-0 in 1986, Romania 3-25 in 1993
Biggest win Ireland 60-0 in 1986, Romania no win

1986 Dublin **Ireland** 60-0

1993 Dublin **Ireland** 25-3

IRELAND v CANADA

Played 1   Ireland won 1
Highest scores Ireland 46-19 in 1987, Canada 19-46 in 1987
Biggest win Ireland 46-19 in 1987, Canada no win

1987 Dunedin *WC* **Ireland** 46-19

IRELAND v TONGA

Played 1   Ireland won 1
Highest scores Ireland 32-9 in 1987, Tonga 9-32 in 1987
Biggest win Ireland 32-9 in 1987, Tonga no win

1987 Brisbane *WC* **Ireland** 32-9

IRELAND v WESTERN SAMOA

Played 2   Ireland won 1, Western Samoa won 1, Drawn 0
Highest scores Ireland 49-22 in 1988, Western Samoa 40-25 in 1996
Biggest wins Ireland 49-22 in 1988, Western Samoa 40-25 in 1996

1988 Dublin **Ireland** 49-22   1996 Dublin **Western Samoa** 40-25

IRELAND v ITALY

Played 3   Ireland won 1, Italy won 2, Drawn 0
Highest scores Ireland 31-15 in 1988, Italy 37-29 in 1997
Biggest wins Ireland 31-15 in 1988, Italy 22-12 in 1995

1988 Dublin **Ireland** 31-15   1997 Dublin **Italy** 37-29
1995 Treviso **Italy** 22-12

IRELAND v ARGENTINA

Played 1   Ireland won 1
Highest scores Ireland 20-18 in 1990, Argentina 18-20 in 1990
Biggest win Ireland 20-18 in 1990, Argentina no win

1990 Dublin **Ireland** 20-18

IRELAND v NAMIBIA

Played 2   Namibia won 2
Highest scores Ireland 15-26 in 1991, Namibia 26-15 in 1991
Biggest win Ireland no win, Namibia 26-15 in 1991

1991 *1* Windhoek **Namibia** 15-6   *2* Windhoek **Namibia** 26-15
                                              Namibia won series 2-0

IRELAND v ZIMBABWE

Played 1   Ireland won 1
Highest scores Ireland 55-11 in 1991, Zimbabwe 11-55 in 1991
Biggest win Ireland 55-11 in 1991, Zimbabwe no win

1991 Dublin *WC* **Ireland** 55-11

IRELAND v JAPAN

Played 2   Ireland won 2
Highest scores Ireland 50-28 in 1995, Japan 28-50 in 1995
Biggest win Ireland 50-28 in 1995, Japan no win

1991 Dublin *WC* **Ireland** 32-16   1995 Bloemfontein *WC* **Ireland** 50-28

IRELAND v UNITED STATES

Played 2   Ireland won 2
Highest scores Ireland 26-15 in 1994, United States 18-25 in 1996
Biggest win Ireland 26-15 in 1994, United States no win

1994 Dublin **Ireland** 26-15   1996 Atlanta **Ireland** 25-18

IRELAND v FIJI
Played 1   Ireland won 1
Highest scores Ireland 44-8 in 1995, Fiji 8-44 in 1995
Biggest win Ireland 44-8 in 1995, Fiji no win

1995 Dublin **Ireland** 44-8

WALES v FRANCE
Played 72   Wales won 38, France won 31, Drawn 3
Highest scores Wales 49-14 in 1910, France 40-33 in 1996
Biggest wins Wales 47-5 in 1909, France 36-3 in 1991

1908 Cardiff **Wales** 36-4	1965 Paris **France** 22-13
1909 Paris **Wales** 47-5	1966 Cardiff **Wales** 9-8
1910 Swansea **Wales** 49-14	1967 Paris **France** 20-14
1911 Paris **Wales** 15-0	1968 Cardiff **France** 14-9
1912 Newport **Wales** 14-8	1969 Paris **Drawn** 8-8
1913 Paris **Wales** 11-8	1970 Cardiff **Wales** 11-6
1914 Swansea **Wales** 31-0	1971 Paris **Wales** 9-5
1920 Paris **Wales** 6-5	1972 Cardiff **Wales** 20-6
1921 Cardiff **Wales** 12-4	1973 Paris **France** 12-3
1922 Paris **Wales** 11-3	1974 Cardiff **Drawn** 16-16
1923 Swansea **Wales** 16-8	1975 Paris **Wales** 25-10
1924 Paris **Wales** 10-6	1976 Cardiff **Wales** 19-13
1925 Cardiff **Wales** 11-5	1977 Paris **France** 16-9
1926 Paris **Wales** 7-5	1978 Cardiff **Wales** 16-7
1927 Swansea **Wales** 25-7	1979 Paris **France** 14-13
1928 Paris **France** 8-3	1980 Cardiff **Wales** 18-9
1929 Cardiff **Wales** 8-3	1981 Paris **France** 19-15
1930 Paris **Wales** 11-0	1982 Cardiff **Wales** 22-12
1931 Swansea **Wales** 35-3	1983 Paris **France** 16-9
1947 Paris **Wales** 3-0	1984 Cardiff **France** 21-16
1948 Swansea **France** 11-3	1985 Paris **France** 14-3
1949 Paris **France** 5-3	1986 Cardiff **France** 23-15
1950 Cardiff **Wales** 21-0	1987 Paris **France** 16-9
1951 Paris **France** 8-3	1988 Cardiff **France** 10-9
1952 Swansea **Wales** 9-5	1989 Paris **France** 31-12
1953 Paris **Wales** 6-3	1990 Cardiff **France** 29-19
1954 Cardiff **Wales** 19-13	1991 Paris **France** 36-3
1955 Paris **Wales** 16-11	1991 Cardiff **France** 22-9
1956 Cardiff **Wales** 5-3	*Non-championship match*
1957 Paris **Wales** 19-13	1992 Cardiff **France** 12-9
1958 Cardiff **France** 16-6	1993 Paris **France** 26-10
1959 Paris **France** 11-3	1994 Cardiff **Wales** 24-15
1960 Cardiff **France** 16-8	1995 Paris **France** 21-9
1961 Paris **France** 8-6	1996 Cardiff **Wales** 16-15
1962 Cardiff **Wales** 3-0	1996 Cardiff **France** 40-33
1963 Paris **France** 5-3	*Non-championship match*
1964 Cardiff **Drawn** 11-11	1997 Paris **France** 27-22

WALES v NEW ZEALAND
Played 16   Wales won 3, New Zealand won 13, Drawn 0
Highest scores Wales 16-19 in 1972, New Zealand 54-9 in 1988
Biggest wins Wales 13-8 in 1953, New Zealand 52-3 in 1988

1905 Cardiff **Wales** 3-0	1953 Cardiff **Wales** 13-8
1924 Swansea **New Zealand** 19-0	1963 Cardiff **New Zealand** 6-0
1935 Cardiff **Wales** 13-12	1967 Cardiff **New Zealand** 13-6

1969 *1* Christchurch **New Zealand** 19-0
    2 Auckland **New Zealand** 33-12
    New Zealand won series 2-0
1972 Cardiff **New Zealand** 19-16
1978 Cardiff **New Zealand** 13-12
1980 Cardiff **New Zealand** 23-3

1987 Brisbane *WC* **New Zealand** 49-6
1988 *1* Christchurch **New Zealand** 52-3
    2 Auckland **New Zealand** 54-9
    New Zealand won series 2-0
1989 Cardiff **New Zealand** 34-9
1995 Johannesburg *WC* **New Zealand** 34-9

WALES v SOUTH AFRICA
Played 10   Wales won 0, South Africa won 9, Drawn 1
Highest scores Wales 20-37 in 1996, South Africa 37-20 in 1996
Biggest win Wales no win, South Africa 40-11 in 1995

1906 Swansea **South Africa** 11-0
1912 Cardiff **South Africa** 3-0
1931 Swansea **South Africa** 8-3
1951 Cardiff **South Africa** 6-3
1960 Cardiff **South Africa** 3-0

1964 Durban **South Africa** 24-3
1970 Cardiff **Drawn** 6-6
1994 Cardiff **South Africa** 20-12
1995 Johannesburg **South Africa** 40-11
1996 Cardiff **South Africa** 37-20

WALES v AUSTRALIA
Played 19   Wales won 8, Australia won 11, Drawn 0
Highest scores Wales 28-3 in 1975, Australia 63-6 in 1991
Biggest wins Wales 28-3 in 1975, Australia 63-6 in 1991

1908 Cardiff **Wales** 9-6
1927 Cardiff **Australia** 18-8
1947 Cardiff **Wales** 6-0
1958 Cardiff **Wales** 9-3
1966 Cardiff **Australia** 14-11
1969 Sydney **Wales** 19-16
1973 Cardiff **Wales** 24-0
1975 Cardiff **Wales** 28-3
1978 *1* Brisbane **Australia** 18-8
    2 Sydney **Australia** 19-17
    Australia won series 2-0

1981 Cardiff **Wales** 18-13
1984 Cardiff **Australia** 28-9
1987 Rotorua *WC* **Wales** 22-21
1991 Brisbane **Australia** 63-6
1991 Cardiff *WC* **Australia** 38-3
1992 Cardiff **Australia** 23-6
1996 *1* Brisbane **Australia** 56-25
    2 Sydney **Australia** 42-3
    Australia won series 2-0
1996 Cardiff **Australia** 28-19

WALES v NEW ZEALAND NATIVES
Played 1   Wales won 1
Highest scores Wales 5-0 in 1888, New Zealand Natives 0-5 in 1888
Biggest win Wales 5-0 in 1888, New Zealand Natives no win

1888 Swansea **Wales** 1G 2T to 0

WALES v NEW ZEALAND ARMY
Played 1   New Zealand Army won 1
Highest scores Wales 3-6 in 1919, New Zealand Army 6-3 in 1919
Biggest win Wales no win, New Zealand Army 6-3 in 1919

1919 Swansea **New Zealand Army** 6-3

WALES v ROMANIA
Played 3   Wales won 1, Romania won 2
Highest scores Wales 16-9 in 1994, Romania 24-6 in 1983
Biggest wins Wales 16-9 in 1994, Romania 24-6 in 1983

1983 Bucharest **Romania** 24-6
1988 Cardiff **Romania** 15-9

1994 Bucharest **Wales** 16-9

WALES v FIJI
Played 4   Wales won 4
Highest scores Wales 40-3 in 1985, Fiji 15-22 in 1986 & 15-19 in 1995
Biggest win Wales 40-3 in 1985, Fiji no win

1985 Cardiff **Wales** 40-3	1994 Suva **Wales** 23-8
1986 Suva **Wales** 22-15	1995 Cardiff **Wales** 19-15

WALES v TONGA
Played 3   Wales won 3
Highest scores Wales 29-16 in 1987, Tonga 16-29 in 1987
Biggest win Wales 29-16 in 1987, Tonga no win

1986 Nuku'Alofa **Wales** 15-7	1994 Nuku'Alofa **Wales** 18-9
1987 Palmerston North *WC* **Wales** 29-16	

WALES v WESTERN SAMOA
Played 4   Wales won 2, Western Samoa won 2, Drawn 0
Highest scores Wales 32-14 in 1986, Western Samoa 34-9 in 1994
Biggest wins Wales 28-6 in 1988, Western Samoa 34-9 in 1994

1986 Apia **Wales** 32-14	1991 Cardiff *WC* **Western Samoa** 16-13
1988 Cardiff **Wales** 28-6	1994 Moamoa **Western Samoa** 34-9

WALES v CANADA
Played 3   Wales won 2, Canada won 1, Drawn 0
Highest scores Wales 40-9 in 1987, Canada 26-24 in 1993
Biggest wins Wales 40-9 in 1987, Canada 26-24 in 1993

1987 Invercargill *WC* **Wales** 40-9	1994 Toronto **Wales** 33-15
1993 Cardiff **Canada** 26-24	

WALES v UNITED STATES
Played 2   Wales won 2
Highest scores Wales 46-0 in 1987, United States 14-34 in 1997
Biggest win Wales 46-0 in 1987, United States no win

1987 Cardiff **Wales** 46-0	1997 Cardiff **Wales** 34-14

WALES v NAMIBIA
Played 3   Wales won 3
Highest scores Wales 38-23 in 1993, Namibia 30-34 in 1990
Biggest win Wales 38-23 in 1993, Namibia no win

1990 *1* Windhoek **Wales** 18-9	*Wales won series 2-0*
2 Windhoek **Wales** 34-30	1993 Windhoek **Wales** 38-23

WALES v BARBARIANS
Played 2   Wales won 1, Barbarians won 1
Highest scores Wales 31-10 in 1996, Barbarians 31-24 in 1990
Biggest wins Wales 31-10 in 1996, Barbarians 31-24 in 1990

1990 Cardiff **Barbarians** 31-24	1996 Cardiff **Wales** 31-10

Arwell Thomas (Wales) is tackled but has Scott Gibbs and Colin Charvis in support. Wales-USA, Cardiff 1997.

WALES v ARGENTINA
Played 1   Wales won 1
Highest scores Wales 16-7 in 1991, Argentina 7-16 in 1991
Biggest win Wales 16-7 in 1991, Argentina no win

1991 Cardiff *WC* **Wales** 16-7

WALES v ZIMBABWE
Played 2   Wales won 2
Highest scores Wales 42-13 in 1993, Zimbabwe 14-35 in 1993
Biggest win Wales 42-13 in 1993, Zimbabwe no win

1993 *1* Bulawayo **Wales** 35-14   *2* Harare **Wales** 42-13
                                         Wales won series 2-0

WALES v JAPAN
Played 2   Wales won 2
Highest scores Wales 57-10 in 1995, Japan 10-57 in 1995
Biggest win Wales 55-5 in 1993, Japan no win

1993 Cardiff **Wales** 55-5   1995 Bloemfontein *WC* **Wales** 57-10

WALES v PORTUGAL
Played 1   Wales won 1
Highest scores Wales 102-11 in 1994, Portugal 11-102 in 1994
Biggest win Wales 102-11 in 1994, Portugal no win

1994 Lisbon **Wales** 102-11

WALES v SPAIN
Played 1   Wales won 1
Highest scores Wales 54-0 in 1994, Spain 0-54 in 1994
Bigegst win Wales 54-0 in 1994, Spain no win

1994 Madrid **Wales** 54-0

WALES v ITALY
Played 3   Wales won 3
Highest scores Wales 31-26 in 1996 & 31-22 in 1996, Italy 26-31 in 1996
Biggest win Wales 29-19 in 1994, Italy no win

1994 Cardiff **Wales** 29-19

1996 Cardiff **Wales** 31-26
1996 Rome **Wales** 31-22

FRANCE v NEW ZEALAND
Played 32   France won 8, New Zealand won 24, Drawn 0
Highest scores France 24-19 in 1979, New Zealand 38-8 in 1906
Biggest wins France 22-8 in 1994, New Zealand 38-8 in 1906

1906 Paris **New Zealand** 38-8
1925 Toulouse **New Zealand** 30-6
1954 Paris **France** 3-0
1961 *1* Auckland **New Zealand** 13-6
    2 Wellington **New Zealand** 5-3
    3 Christchurch **New Zealand** 32-3
    New Zealand won series 3-0
1964 Paris **New Zealand** 12-3
1967 Paris **New Zealand** 21-15
1968 *1* Christchurch **New Zealand** 12-9
    2 Wellington **New Zealand** 9-3
    3 Auckland **New Zealand** 19-12
    New Zealand won series 3-0
1973 Paris **France** 13-6
1977 *1* Toulouse **France** 18-13
    2 Paris **New Zealand** 15-3
    Series drawn 1-1
1979 *1* Christchurch **New Zealand** 23-9
    2 Auckland **France** 24-19
    Series drawn 1-1
1981 *1* Toulouse **New Zealand** 13-9
    2 Paris **New Zealand** 18-6

1984 *1* Christchurch **New Zealand** 10-9
    2 Auckland **New Zealand** 31-18
    New Zealand won series 2-0
1986 Christchurch **New Zealand** 18-9
1986 *1* Toulouse **New Zealand** 19-7
    2 Nantes **France** 16-3
    Series drawn 1-1
1987 Auckland *WC* **New Zealand** 29-9
1989 *1* Christchurch **New Zealand** 25-17
    2 Auckland **New Zealand** 34-20
    New Zealand won series 2-0
1990 *1* Nantes **New Zealand** 24-3
    2 Paris **New Zealand** 30-12
    New Zealand won series 2-0
1994 *1* Christchurch **France** 22-8
    2 Auckland **France** 23-20
    France won series 2-0
1995 *1* Toulouse **France** 22-15
    2 Paris **New Zealand** 37-12
    Series drawn 1-1

FRANCE v SOUTH AFRICA
Played 26   France won 5, South Africa won 16, Drawn 5
Highest scores France 29-16 in 1992, South Africa 38-5 in 1913 & 38-25 in 1975
Biggest wins France 29-16 in 1992, South Africa 38-5 in 1913

1913 Bordeaux **South Africa** 38-5
1952 Paris **South Africa** 25-3
1958 *1* Cape Town **Drawn** 3-3
    2 Johannesburg **France** 9-5
    France won series 1-0, with 1 draw
1961 Paris **Drawn** 0-0
1964 Springs (SA) **France** 8-6
1967 *1* Durban **South Africa** 26-3
    2 Bloemfontein **South Africa** 16-3
    3 Johannesburg **France** 19-14
    4 Cape Town **Drawn** 6-6
    South Africa won series 2-1, with 1 draw
1968 *1* Bordeaux **South Africa** 12-9
    2 Paris **South Africa** 16-11
    South Africa won series 2-0
1971 *1* Bloemfontein **South Africa** 22-9
    2 Durban **Drawn** 8-8
    South Africa won series 1-0, with 1 draw

1974 *1* Toulouse **South Africa** 13-4
    2 Paris **South Africa** 10-8
    South Africa won series 2-0
1975 *1* Bloemfontein **South Africa** 38-25
    2 Pretoria **South Africa** 33-18
    South Africa won series 2-0
1980 Pretoria **South Africa** 37-15
1992 *1* Lyons **South Africa** 20-15
    2 Paris **France** 29-16
    Series drawn 1-1
1993 *1* Durban **Drawn** 20-20
    2 Johannesburg **France** 18-17
    France won series 1-0, with 1 draw
1995 Durban *WC* **South Africa** 19-15
1996 *1* Bordeaux **South Africa** 22-12
    2 Paris **South Africa** 13-12
    South Africa won series 2-0

FRANCE v AUSTRALIA

Played 25   France won 13, Australia won 10, Drawn 2
Highest scores France 34-6 in 1976, Australia 48-31 in 1990
Biggest wins France 34-6 in 1976, Australia 24-3 in 1993

1928 Paris **Australia** 11-8
1948 Paris **France** 13-6
1958 Paris **France** 19-0
1961 Sydney **France** 15-8
1967 Paris **France** 20-14
1968 Sydney **Australia** 11-10
1971 *1* Toulouse **Australia** 13-11
    2 Paris **France** 18-9
    Series drawn 1-1
1972 *1* Sydney **Drawn** 14-14
    2 Brisbane **France** 16-15
    France won series 1-0, with 1 draw
1976 *1* Bordeaux **France** 18-15
    2 Paris **France** 34-6
    France won series 2-0
1981 *1* Brisbane **Australia** 17-15
    2 Sydney **Australia** 24-14

Australia won series 2-0
1983 *1* Clermont-Ferrand **Drawn** 15-15
    2 Paris **France** 15-6
    France won series 1-0, with 1 draw
1986 Sydney **Australia** 27-14
1987 Sydney *WC* **France** 30-24
1989 *1* Strasbourg **Australia** 32-15
    2 Lille **France** 25-19
    Series drawn 1-1
1990 *1* Sydney **Australia** 21-9
    2 Brisbane **Australia** 48-31
    3 Sydney **France** 28-19
    Australia won series 2-1
1993 *1* Bordeaux **France** 16-13
    2 Paris **Australia** 24-3
    Series drawn 1-1

FRANCE v UNITED STATES

Played 5   France won 4, United States won 1, Drawn 0
Highest scores France 41-9 in 1991, United States 17-3 in 1924
Biggest wins France 41-9 in 1991, United States 17-3 in 1924

1920 Paris **France** 14-5
1924 Paris **United States** 17-3
1976 Chicago **France** 33-14
1991 *1* Denver **France** 41-9

    2 Colorado Springs **France** 10-3*
    **Abandoned after 43 mins*
    France won series 2-0

FRANCE v ROMANIA

Played 43   France won 33, Romania won 8, Drawn 2
Highest scores France 64-12 in 1996, Romania 21-33 in 1991
Biggest wins France 59-3 in 1924, Romania 15-0 in 1980

1924 Paris **France** 59-3
1938 Bucharest **France** 11-8
1957 Bucharest **France** 18-15
1957 Bordeaux **France** 39-0
1960 Bucharest **Romania** 11-5
1961 Bayonne **Drawn** 5-5
1962 Bucharest **Romania** 3-0
1963 Toulouse **Drawn** 6-6
1964 Bucharest **France** 9-6
1965 Lyons **France** 8-3
1966 Bucharest **France** 9-3
1967 Nantes **France** 11-3
1968 Bucharest **Romania** 15-14
1969 Tarbes **France** 14-9
1970 Bucharest **France** 14-3
1971 Béziers **France** 31-12
1972 Constanza **France** 15-6
1973 Valence **France** 7-6
1974 Bucharest **Romania** 15-10
1975 Bordeaux **France** 36-12
1976 Bucharest **Romania** 15-12
1977 Clermont-Ferrand **France** 9-6

1978 Bucharest **France** 9-6
1979 Montauban **France** 30-12
1980 Bucharest **Romania** 15-0
1981 Narbonne **France** 17-9
1982 Bucharest **Romania** 13-9
1983 Toulouse **France** 26-15
1984 Bucharest **France** 18-3
1986 Lille **France** 25-13
1986 Bucharest **France** 20-3
1987 Wellington *WC* **France** 55-12
1987 Agen **France** 49-3
1988 Bucharest **France** 16-12
1990 Auch **Romania** 12-6
1991 Bucharest **France** 33-21
1991 Béziers *WC* **France** 30-3
1992 Le Havre **France** 25-6
1993 Bucharest **France** 37-20
1993 Brive **France** 51-0
1995 Bucharest **France** 24-15
1995 Tucumán *LC* **France** 52-8
1996 Aurillac **France** 64-12

FRANCE v NEW ZEALAND MAORIS
Played 1   New Zealand Maoris won 1
Highest scores France 3-12 in 1926, New Zealand Maoris 12-3 in 1926
Biggest win France no win, New Zealand Maoris 12-3 in 1926

1926 Paris **New Zealand Maoris** 12-3

FRANCE v GERMANY
Played 15   France won 13, Germany won 2, Drawn 0
Highest scores France 38-17 in 1933, Germany 17-16 in 1927 & 17-38 in 1933
Biggest wins France 34-0 in 1931, Germany 3-0 in 1938

1927 Paris **France** 30-5	1934 Hanover **France** 13-9
1927 Frankfurt **Germany** 17-16	1935 Paris **France** 18-3
1928 Hanover **France** 14-3	1936 *1* Berlin **France** 19-14
1929 Paris **France** 24-0	2 Hanover **France** 6-3
1930 Berlin **France** 31-0	*France won series 2-0*
1931 Paris **France** 34-0	1937 Paris **France** 27-6
1932 Frankfurt **France** 20-4	1938 Frankfurt **Germany** 3-0
1933 Paris **France** 38-17	1938 Bucharest **France** 8-5

FRANCE v ITALY
Played 19   France won 18, Italy won 1, Drawn 0
Highest scores France 60-13 in 1967, Italy 40-32 in 1997
Biggest wins France 60-13 in 1967, Italy 40-32 in 1997

1937 Paris **France** 43-5	1961 Chambéry **France** 17-0
1952 Milan **France** 17-8	1962 Brescia **France** 6-3
1953 Lyons **France** 22-8	1963 Grenoble **France** 14-12
1954 Rome **France** 39-12	1964 Parma **France** 12-3
1955 Grenoble **France** 24-0	1965 Pau **France** 21-0
1956 Padua **France** 16-3	1966 Naples **France** 21-0
1957 Agen **France** 38-6	1967 Toulon **France** 60-13
1958 Naples **France** 11-3	1995 Buenos Aires *LC* **France** 34-22
1959 Nantes **France** 22-0	1997 Grenoble **Italy** 40-32
1960 Treviso **France** 26-0	

FRANCE v BRITISH XVs
Played 5   France won 2, British XVs won 3, Drawn 0
Highest scores France 27-29 in 1989, British XV 36-3 in 1940
Biggest wins France 21-9 in 1945, British XV 36-3 in 1940

1940 Paris **British XV** 36-3	1946 Paris **France** 10-0
1945 Paris **France** 21-9	1989 Paris **British XV** 29-27
1945 Richmond **British XV** 27-6	

FRANCE v NEW ZEALAND ARMY
Played 1   New Zealand Army won 1
Highest scores France 9-14 in 1946, New Zealand Army 14-9 in 1946
Biggest win France no win, New Zealand Army 14-9 in 1946

1946 Paris **New Zealand Army** 14-9

FRANCE v ARGENTINA
Played 29   France won 24, Argentina won 4, Drawn 1
Highest scores France 47-12 in 1995, Argentina 27-31 in 1974 & 27-34 in 1996
Biggest wins France 47-12 in 1995, Argentina 18-6 in 1988

1949 *1* Buenos Aires **France** 5-0	1954 *1* Buenos Aires **France** 22-8
2 Buenos Aires **France** 12-3	2 Buenos Aires **France** 30-3
France won series 2-0	*France won series 2-0*

1960 *1* Buenos Aires **France** 37-3
    2 Buenos Aires **France** 12-3
    3 Buenos Aires **France** 29-6
    France won series 3-0
1974 *1* Buenos Aires **France** 20-15
    2 Buenos Aires **France** 31-27
    France won series 2-0
1975 *1* Lyons **France** 29-6
    2 Paris **France** 36-21
    France won series 2-0
1977 *1* Buenos Aires **France** 26-3
    2 Buenos Aires **Drawn** 18-18
    France won series 1-0, with 1 draw
1982 *1* Toulouse **France** 25-12
    2 Paris **France** 13-6
    France won series 2-0
1985 *1* Buenos Aires **Argentina** 24-16
    2 Buenos Aires **France** 23-15

Series drawn 1-1
1986 *1* Buenos Aires **Argentina** 15-13
    2 Buenos Aires **France** 22-9
    Series drawn 1-1
1988 *1* Buenos Aires **France** 18-15
    2 Buenos Aires **Argentina** 18-6
    Series drawn 1-1
1988 *1* Nantes **France** 29-9
    2 Lille **France** 28-18
    France won series 2-0
1992 *1* Buenos Aires **France** 27-12
    2 Buenos Aires **France** 33-9
    France won series 2-0
1992 Nantes **Argentina** 24-20
1995 Buenos Aires *LC* **France** 47-12
1996 *1* Buenos Aires **France** 34-27
    2 Buenos Aires **France** 34-15
    France won series 2-0

FRANCE v CZECHOSLOVAKIA
Played 2   France won 2
Highest scores France 28-3 in 1956, Czechoslovakia 6-19 in 1968
Biggest win France 28-3 in 1956, Czechoslovakia no win

1956 Toulouse **France** 28-3   1968 Prague **France** 19-6

FRANCE v FIJI
Played 3   France won 3
Highest scores France 33-9 in 1991, Fiji 16-31 in 1987
Biggest win France 33-9 in 1991, Fiji no win

1964 Paris **France** 21-3   1991 Grenoble *WC* **France** 33-9
1987 Auckland *WC* **France** 31-16

FRANCE v JAPAN
Played 1   France won 1
Highest scores France 30-18 in 1973, Japan 18-30 in 1973
Biggest win France 30-18 in 1973, Japan no win

1973 Bordeaux **France** 30-18

FRANCE v ZIMBABWE
Played 1   France won 1
Highest scores France 70-12 in 1987, Zimbabwe 12-70 in 1987
Biggest win France 70-12 in 1987, Zimbabwe no win

1987 Auckland *WC* **France** 70-12

FRANCE v CANADA
Played 3   France won 2, Canada won 1, Drawn 0
Highest scores France 28-9 in 1994, Canada 18-16 in 1994
Biggest wins France 28-9 in 1994, Canada 18-16 in 1994

1991 Agen *WC* **France** 19-13   1994 Besançon **France** 28-9
1994 Nepean **Canada** 18-16

FRANCE v TONGA
Played 1   France won 1
Highest scores France 38-10 in 1995, Tonga 10-38 in 1995
Biggest win France 38-10 in 1995, Tonga no win

1995 Pretoria *WC* **France** 38-10

FRANCE v IVORY COAST
Played 1   France won 1
Highest scores France 54-18 in 1995, Ivory Coast 18-54 in 1995
Biggest win France 54-18 in 1995, Ivory Coast no win

1995 Rustenburg *WC* **France** 54-18

NEW ZEALAND v SOUTH AFRICA
Played 47   New Zealand won 22, South Africa won 22, Drawn 3
Highest scores New Zealand 33-26 in 1996, South Africa 32-22 in 1996
Biggest wins New Zealand 20-3 in 1965, South Africa 17-0 in 1928

1921 *1* Dunedin **New Zealand** 13-5
     2 Auckland **South Africa** 9-5
     3 Wellington **Drawn** 0-0
     Series drawn 1-1, with 1 draw
1928 *1* Durban **South Africa** 17-0
     2 Johannesburg **New Zealand** 7-6
     3 Port Elizabeth **South Africa** 11-6
     4 Cape Town **New Zealand** 13-5
     Series drawn 2-2
1937 *1* Wellington **New Zealand** 13-7
     2 Christchurch **South Africa** 13-6
     3 Auckland **South Africa** 17-6
     South Africa won series 2-1
1949 *1* Cape Town **South Africa** 15-11
     2 Johannesburg **South Africa** 12-6
     3 Durban **South Africa** 9-3
     4 Port Elizabeth **South Africa** 11-8
     South Africa won series 4-0
1956 *1* Dunedin **New Zealand** 10-6
     2 Wellington **South Africa** 8-3
     3 Christchurch **New Zealand** 17-10
     4 Auckland **New Zealand** 11-5
     New Zealand won series 3-1
1960 *1* Johannesburg **South Africa** 13-0
     2 Cape Town **New Zealand** 11-3
     3 Bloemfontein **Drawn** 11-11
     4 Port Elizabeth **South Africa** 8-3
     South Africa won series 2-1, with 1 draw
1965 *1* Wellington **New Zealand** 6-3
     2 Dunedin **New Zealand** 13-0

3 Christchurch **South Africa** 19-16
4 Auckland **New Zealand** 20-3
New Zealand won series 3-1
1970 *1* Pretoria **South Africa** 17-6
     2 Cape Town **New Zealand** 9-8
     3 Port Elizabeth **South Africa** 14-3
     4 Johannesburg **South Africa** 20-17
     South Africa won series 3-1
1976 *1* Durban **South Africa** 16-7
     2 Bloemfontein **New Zealand** 15-9
     3 Cape Town **South Africa** 15-10
     4 Johannesburg **South Africa** 15-14
     South Africa won series 3-1
1981 *1* Christchurch **New Zealand** 14-9
     2 Wellington **South Africa** 24-12
     3 Auckland **New Zealand** 25-22
     New Zealand won series 2-1
1992 Johannesburg **New Zealand** 27-24
1994 *1* Dunedin **New Zealand** 22-14
     2 Wellington **New Zealand** 13-9
     3 Auckland **Drawn** 18-18
     New Zealand won series 2-0, with 1 draw
1995 Johannesburg *WC* **South Africa** 15-12
     (*aet*)
1996 Christchurch *TN* **New Zealand** 15-11
1996 Cape Town *TN* **New Zealand** 29-18
1996 *1* Durban **New Zealand** 23-19
     2 Pretoria **New Zealand** 33-26
     3 Johannesburg **South Africa** 32-22
     New Zealand won series 2-1

NEW ZEALAND v AUSTRALIA
Played 102   New Zealand won 70, Australia won 27, Drawn 5
Highest scores New Zealand 43-6 in 1996, Australia 30-16 in 1978
Biggest wins New Zealand 43-6 in 1996, Australia 26-10 in 1980

1903 Sydney **New Zealand** 22-3
1905 Dunedin **New Zealand** 14-3
1907 *1* Sydney **New Zealand** 26-6
     2 Brisbane **New Zealand** 14-5
     3 Sydney **Drawn** 5-5

New Zealand won series 2-0, with 1 draw
1910 *1* Sydney **New Zealand** 6-0
     2 Sydney **Australia** 11-0
     3 Sydney **New Zealand** 28-13
     New Zealand won series 2-1

1913 *1* Wellington **New Zealand** 30-5
    2 Dunedin **New Zealand** 25-13
    3 Christchurch **Australia** 16-5
    New Zealand won series 2-1
1914 *1* Sydney **New Zealand** 5-0
    2 Brisbane **New Zealand** 17-0
    3 Sydney **New Zealand** 22-7
    New Zealand won series 3-0
1929 *1* Sydney **Australia** 9-8
    2 Brisbane **Australia** 17-9
    3 Sydney **Australia** 15-13
    Australia won series 3-0
1931 Auckland **New Zealand** 20-13
1932 *1* Sydney **Australia** 22-17
    2 Brisbane **New Zealand** 21-3
    3 Sydney **New Zealand** 21-13
    New Zealand won series 2-1
1934 *1* Sydney **Australia** 25-11
    2 Sydney **Drawn** 3-3
    Australia won series 1-0, with 1 draw
1936 *1* Wellington **New Zealand** 11-6
    2 Dunedin **New Zealand** 38-13
    New Zealand won series 2-0
1938 *1* Sydney **New Zealand** 24-9
    2 Brisbane **New Zealand** 20-14
    3 Sydney **New Zealand** 14-6
    New Zealand won series 3-0
1946 *1* Dunedin **New Zealand** 31-8
    2 Sydney **New Zealand** 14-10
    New Zealand won series 2-0
1947 *1* Brisbane **New Zealand** 13-5
    2 Sydney **New Zealand** 27-14
    New Zealand won series 2-0
1949 *1* Wellington **Australia** 11-6
    2 Auckland **Australia** 16-9
    Australia won series 2-0
1951 *1* Sydney **New Zealand** 8-0
    2 Sydney **New Zealand** 17-11
    3 Brisbane **New Zealand** 16-6
    New Zealand won series 3-0
1952 *1* Christchurch **Australia** 14-9
    2 Wellington **New Zealand** 15-8
    Series drawn 1-1
1955 *1* Wellington **New Zealand** 16-8
    2 Dunedin **New Zealand** 8-0
    3 Auckland **Australia** 8-3
    New Zealand won series 2-1
1957 *1* Sydney **New Zealand** 25-11
    2 Brisbane **New Zealand** 22-9
    New Zealand won series 2-0
1958 *1* Wellington **New Zealand** 25-3
    2 Christchurch **Australia** 6-3
    3 Auckland **New Zealand** 17-8
    New Zealand won series 2-1
1962 *1* Brisbane **New Zealand** 20-6
    2 Sydney **New Zealand** 14-5
    New Zealand won series 2-0
1962 *1* Wellington **Drawn** 9-9
    2 Dunedin **New Zealand** 3-0
    3 Auckland **New Zealand** 16-8
    New Zealand won series 2-0, with1 draw
1964 *1* Dunedin **New Zealand** 14-9

    2 Christchurch **New Zealand** 18-3
    3 Wellington **Australia** 20-5
    New Zealand won series 2-1
1967 Wellington **New Zealand** 29-9
1968 *1* Sydney **New Zealand** 27-11
    2 Brisbane **New Zealand** 19-18
    New Zealand won series 2-0
1972 *1* Wellington **New Zealand** 29-6
    2 Christchurch **New Zealand** 30-17
    3 Auckland **New Zealand** 38-3
    New Zealand won series 3-0
1974 *1* Sydney **New Zealand** 11-6
    2 Brisbane **Drawn** 16-16
    3 Sydney **New Zealand** 16-6
    New Zealand won series 2-0, with 1 draw
1978 *1* Wellington **New Zealand** 13-12
    2 Christchurch **New Zealand** 22-6
    3 Auckland **Australia** 30-16
    New Zealand won series 2-1
1979 Sydney **Australia** 12-6
1980 *1* Sydney **Australia** 13-9
    2 Brisbane **New Zealand** 12-9
    3 Sydney **Australia** 26-10
    Australia won series 2-1
1982 *1* Christchurch **New Zealand** 23-16
    2 Wellington **Australia** 19-16
    3 Auckland **New Zealand** 33-18
    New Zealand won series 2-1
1983 Sydney **New Zealand** 18-8
1984 *1* Sydney **Australia** 16-9
    2 Brisbane **New Zealand** 19-15
    3 Sydney **New Zealand** 25-24
    New Zealand won series 2-1
1985 Auckland **New Zealand** 10-9
1986 *1* Wellington **Australia** 13-12
    2 Dunedin **New Zealand** 13-12
    3 Auckland **Australia** 22-9
    Australia won series 2-1
1987 Sydney **New Zealand** 30-16
1988 *1* Sydney **New Zealand** 32-7
    2 Brisbane **Drawn** 19-19
    3 Sydney **New Zealand** 30-9
    New Zealand won series 2-0, with 1 draw
1989 Auckland **New Zealand** 24-12
1990 *1* Christchurch **New Zealand** 21-6
    2 Auckland **New Zealand** 27-17
    3 Wellington **Australia** 21-9
    New Zealand won series 2-1
1991 *1* Sydney **Australia** 21-12
    2 Auckland **New Zealand** 6-3
1991 Dublin *WC* **Australia** 16-6
1992 *1* Sydney **Australia** 16-15
    2 Brisbane **Australia** 19-17
    3 Sydney **New Zealand** 26-23
    Australia won series 2-1
1993 Dunedin **New Zealand** 25-10
1994 Sydney **Australia** 20-16
1995 Auckland **New Zealand** 28-16
1995 Sydney **New Zealand** 34-23
1996 Wellington *TN* **New Zealand** 43-6
1996 Brisbane *TN* **New Zealand** 32-25

NEW ZEALAND v UNITED STATES
Played 2   New Zealand won 2
Highest scores New Zealand 51-3 in 1913, United States 6-46 in 1991
Biggest win New Zealand 51-3 in 1913, United States no win

1913 Berkeley **New Zealand** 51-3   1991 Gloucester *WC* **New Zealand** 46-6

NEW ZEALAND v ROMANIA
Played 1   New Zealand won 1
Highest score New Zealand 14-6 in 1981, Romania 6-14 in 1981
Biggest win New Zealand 14-6 in 1981, Romania no win

1981 Bucharest **New Zealand** 14-6

NEW ZEALAND v ARGENTINA
Played 7   New Zealand won 6, Drawn 1
Highest scores New Zealand 60-9 in 1989, Argentina 21-21 in 1985
Biggest win New Zealand 60-9 in 1989, Argentina no win

1985 *1* Buenos Aires **New Zealand** 33-20   *2* Wellington **New Zealand** 49-12
2 Buenos Aires **Drawn** 21-21   *New Zealand won series 2-0*
New Zealand won series 1-0, with 1 draw   1991 *1* Buenos Aires **New Zealand** 28-14
1987 Wellington *WC* **New Zealand** 46-15   *2* Buenos Aires **New Zealand** 36-6
1989 *1* Dunedin **New Zealand** 60-9   *New Zealand won series 2-0*

NEW ZEALAND v ITALY
Played 3   New Zealand won 3
Highest scores New Zealand 70-6 in 1987 & 70-6 in 1995, Italy 21-31 in 1991
Biggest win New Zealand 70-6 in 1987 & 70-6 in 1995, Italy no win

1987 Auckland *WC* **New Zealand** 70-6   1995 Bologna **New Zealand** 70-6
1991 Leicester *WC* **New Zealand** 31-21

NEW ZEALAND v FIJI
Played 1   New Zealand won 1
Highest scores New Zealand 74-13 in 1987, Fiji 13-74 in 1987
Biggest win New Zealand 74-13 in 1987, Fiji no win

1987 Christchurch *WC* **New Zealand** 74-13

NEW ZEALAND v CANADA
Played 2   New Zealand won 2
Highest scores New Zealand 73-7 in 1995, Canada 13-29 in 1991
Biggest win New Zealand 73-7 in 1995, Canada no win

1991 Lille *WC* **New Zealand** 29-13   1995 Auckland **New Zealand** 73-7

NEW ZEALAND v WORLD XVs
Played 3   New Zealand won 2, World XV won 1, Drawn 0
Highest scores New Zealand 54-26 in 1992, World XV 28-14 in 1992
Biggest wins New Zealand 54-26 in 1992, World XV 28-14 in 1992

1992 *1* Christchurch **World XV** 28-14   *3* Auckland **New Zealand** 26-15
2 Wellington **New Zealand** 54-26   *New Zealand won series 2-1*

385

NEW ZEALAND v WESTERN SAMOA
Played 2   New Zealand won 2
Highest scores New Zealand 51-10 in 1996, Western Samoa 13-35 in 1993
Biggest win New Zealand 51-10 in 1996, Western Samoa no win

1993 Auckland **New Zealand** 35-13	1996 Napier **New Zealand** 51-10

NEW ZEALAND v JAPAN
Played 1   New Zealand won 1
Highest scores New Zealand 145-17 in 1995, Japan 17-145 in 1995
Biggest win New Zealand 145-17 in 1995, Japan no win

1995 Bloemfontein *WC* **New Zealand** 145-17

SOUTH AFRICA v AUSTRALIA
Played 35   South Africa won 24, Australia won 11, Drawn 0
Highest scores South Africa 30-11 in 1989, Australia 28-20 in 1993
Biggest wins South Africa 28-3 in 1961, Australia 26-3 in 1992

1933 *1* Cape Town **South Africa** 17-3
 2 Durban **Australia** 21-6
 3 Johannesburg **South Africa** 12-3
 4 Port Elizabeth **South Africa** 11-0
 5 Bloemfontein **Australia** 15-4
 South Africa won series 3-2
1937 *1* Sydney **South Africa** 9-5
 2 Sydney **South Africa** 26-17
 South Africa won series 2-0
1953 *1* Johannesburg **South Africa** 25-3
 2 Cape Town **Australia** 18-14
 3 Durban **South Africa** 18-8
 4 Port Elizabeth **South Africa** 22-9
 South Africa won series 3-1
1956 *1* Sydney **South Africa** 9-0
 2 Brisbane **South Africa** 9-0
 South Africa won series 2-0
1961 *1* Johannesburg **South Africa** 28-3
 2 Port Elizabeth **South Africa** 23-11
 South Africa won series 2-0
1963 *1* Pretoria **South Africa** 14-3
 2 Cape Town **Australia** 9-5
 3 Johannesburg **Australia** 11-9

 4 Port Elizabeth **South Africa** 22-6
 Series drawn 2-2
1965 *1* Sydney **Australia** 18-11
 2 Brisbane **Australia** 12-8
 Australia won series 2-0
1969 *1* Johannesburg **South Africa** 30-11
 2 Durban **South Africa** 16-9
 3 Cape Town **South Africa** 11-3
 4 Bloemfontein **South Africa** 19-8
 South Africa won series 4-0
1971 *1* Sydney **South Africa** 19-11
 2 Brisbane **South Africa** 14-6
 3 Sydney **South Africa** 18-6
 South Africa won series 3-0
1992 Cape Town **Australia** 26-3
1993 *1* Sydney **South Africa** 19-12
 2 Brisbane **Australia** 28-20
 3 Sydney **Australia** 19-12
 Australia won series 2-1
1995 Cape Town *WC* **South Africa** 27-18
1996 Sydney *TN* **Australia** 21-16
1996 Bloemfontein *TN* **South Africa** 25-19

SOUTH AFRICA v WORLD XVs
Played 3   South Africa won 3
Highest scores South Africa 45-24 in 1977, World XV 24-45 in 1977
Biggest win South Africa 45-24 in 1977, World XV no win

1977 Pretoria **South Africa** 45-24	2 Johannesburg **South Africa** 22-16
1989 *1* Cape Town **South Africa** 20-19	*South Africa won series 2-0*

SOUTH AFRICA v SOUTH AMERICA
Played 8   South Africa won 7, South America won 1, Drawn 0
Highest scores South Africa 50-18 in 1982, South America 21-12 in 1982
Biggest wins South Africa 50-18 in 1982, South America 21-12 in 1982

1980 *1* Johannesburg **South Africa** 24-9	1980 *1* Montevideo **South Africa** 22-13
2 Durban **South Africa** 18-9	*2* Santiago **South Africa** 30-16
South Africa won series 2-0	*South Africa won series 2-0*

1982 *1* Pretoria **South Africa** 50-18
　　 2 Bloemfontein **South America** 21-12
　　 Series drawn 1-1

1984 *1* Pretoria **South Africa** 32-15
　　 2 Cape Town **South Africa** 22-13
　　 South Africa won series 2-0

SOUTH AFRICA v UNITED STATES
Played 1　South Africa won 1
Highest scores South Africa 38-7 in 1981, United States 7-38 in 1981
Biggest win South Africa 38-7 in 1981, United States no win

1981 Glenville **South Africa** 38-7

SOUTH AFRICA v NEW ZEALAND CAVALIERS
Played 4　South Africa won 3, New Zealand Cavaliers won 1, Drawn 0
Highest scores South Africa 33-18 in 1986, New Zealand Cavaliers 19-18 in 1986
Biggest wins South Africa 33-18 in 1986, New Zealand Cavaliers 19-18 in 1986

1986 *1* Cape Town **South Africa** 21-15
　　 2 Durban **New Zealand Cavaliers**
　　　 19-18

　　 3 Pretoria **South Africa** 33-18
　　 4 Johannesburg **South Africa** 24-10
　　 South Africa won series 3-1

SOUTH AFRICA v ARGENTINA
Played 6　South Africa won 6
Highest scores South Africa 52-23 in 1993, Argentina 26-29 in 1993 & 26-46 in 1994
Biggest wins South Africa 46-15 in 1996, Argentina no win

1993 *1* Buenos Aires **South Africa** 29-26
　　 2 Buenos Aires **South Africa** 52-23
　　 South Africa won series 2-0
1994 *1* Port Elizabeth **South Africa** 42-22
　　 2 Johannesburg **South Africa** 46-26

　　 South Africa won series 2-0
1996 *1* Buenos Aires **South Africa** 46-15
　　 2 Buenos Aires **South Africa** 44-21
　　 South Africa win series 2-0

SOUTH AFRICA v WESTERN SAMOA
Played 2　South Africa won 2
Highest scores South Africa 60-8 in 1995, Western Samoa 14-42 in 1995
Biggest win South Africa 60-8 in 1995, Western Samoa no win

1995 Johannesburg **South Africa** 60-8

1995 Johannesburg *WC* **South Africa** 42-14

SOUTH AFRICA v ROMANIA
Played 1　South Africa won 1
Highest score South Africa 21-8 in 1995, Romania 8-21 in 1995
Biggest win South Africa 21-8 in 1995, Romania no win

1995 Cape Town *WC* **South Africa** 21-8

SOUTH AFRICA v CANADA
Played 1　South Africa won 1
Highest scores South Africa 20-0 in 1995, Canada 0-20 in 1995
Biggest win South Africa 20-0 in 1995, Canada no win

1995 Port Elizabeth *WC* **South Africa** 20-0

SOUTH AFRICA v ITALY
Played 1　South Africa won 1
Highest scores South Africa 40-21 in 1995, Italy 21-40 in 1995
Biggest win South Africa 40-21 in 1995, Italy no win

1995 Rome **South Africa** 40-21

SOUTH AFRICA v FIJI
Played 1   South Africa won 1
Highest scores South Africa 43-18 in 1996, Fiji 18-43 in 1996
Biggest win South Africa 43-18 in 1996, Fiji no win

1996 Pretoria **South Africa** 43-18

AUSTRALIA v UNITED STATES
Played 5   Australia won 5
Highest scores Australia 67-9 in 1990, United States 12-24 in 1976 & 12-47 in 1987
Biggest win Australia 67-9 in 1990, United States no win

1912 Berkeley **Australia** 12-8	1987 Brisbane *WC* **Australia** 47-12
1976 Los Angeles **Australia** 24-12	1990 Brisbane **Australia** 67-9
1983 Sydney **Australia** 49-3	

AUSTRALIA v NEW ZEALAND MAORIS
Played 10   Australia won 4, New Zealand Maoris won 4, Drawn 2
Highest scores Australia 31-6 in 1936, New Zealand Maoris 20-0 in 1946
Biggest wins Australia 31-6 in 1936, New Zealand Maoris 20-0 in 1946

1928 Wellington **New Zealand Maoris** 9-8	*3* Sydney **Australia** 18-3
1931 Palmerston North **Australia** 14-3	*Series drawn 1-1, with 1 draw*
1936 Palmerston North **Australia** 31-6	1958 *1* Brisbane **Australia** 15-14
1946 Hamilton **New Zealand Maoris** 20-0	*2* Sydney **Drawn** 3-3
1949 *1* Sydney **New Zealand Maoris** 12-3	*3* Melbourne **New Zealand Maoris** 13-6
2 Brisbane **Drawn** 8-8	*Series drawn 1-1, with 1 draw*

AUSTRALIA v FIJI
Played 15   Australia won 12, Fiji won 2, Drawn 1
Highest scores Australia 52-28 in 1985, Fiji 28-52 in 1985
Biggest wins Australia 52-28 in 1985, Fiji 17-15 in 1952 & 18-16 in 1954

1952 *1* Sydney **Australia** 15-9	1972 Suva **Australia** 21-19
2 Sydney **Fiji** 17-15	1976 *1* Sydney **Australia** 22-6
Series drawn 1-1	*2* Brisbane **Australia** 21-9
1954 *1* Brisbane **Australia** 22-19	*3* Sydney **Australia** 27-17
2 Sydney **Fiji** 18-16	*Australia won series 3-0*
Series drawn 1-1	1980 Suva **Australia** 22-9
1961 *1* Brisbane **Australia** 24-6	1984 Suva **Australia** 16-3
2 Sydney **Australia** 20-14	1985 *1* Brisbane **Australia** 52-28
3 Melbourne **Drawn** 3-3	*2* Sydney **Australia** 31-9
Australia won series 2-0, with 1 draw	*Australia won series 2-0*

AUSTRALIA v TONGA
Played 3   Australia won 2, Tonga won 1, Drawn 0
Highest scores Australia 52-14 in 1993, Tonga 16-11 in 1973
Biggest wins Australia 52-14 in 1993, Tonga 16-11 in 1973

1973 *1* Sydney **Australia** 30-12	*2* Brisbane **Tonga** 16-11
	Series drawn 1-1
	1993 Brisbane **Australia** 52-14

AUSTRALIA v JAPAN
Played 3   Australia won 3
Highest scores Australia 50-25 in 1975, Japan 25-50 in 1973
Biggest win Australia 50-25 in 1975, Japan no win

1975 *1* Sydney **Australia** 37-7	1987 Sydney *WC* **Australia** 42-23
2 Brisbane **Australia** 50-25	
Australia won series 2-0	

AUSTRALIA v ARGENTINA

Played 11   Australia won 7, Argentina won 3, Drawn 1
Highest scores Australia 53-7 in 1995, Argentina 27-19 in 1987
Biggest wins Australia 53-7 in 1995, Argentina 18-3 in 1983

1979 *1* Buenos Aires **Argentina** 24-13
    2 Buenos Aires **Australia** 17-12
    Series drawn 1-1
1983 *1* Brisbane **Argentina** 18-3
    2 Sydney **Australia** 29-13
    Series drawn 1-1
1986 *1* Brisbane **Australia** 39-19
    2 Sydney **Australia** 26-0
    Australia won series 2-0

1987 *1* Buenos Aires **Drawn** 19-19
    2 Buenos Aires **Argentina** 27-19
    Argentina won series 1-0, with 1 draw
1991 Llanelli *WC* **Australia** 32-19
1995 *1* Brisbane **Australia** 53-7
    2 Sydney **Australia** 30-13
    Australia won series 2-0

AUSTRALIA v WESTERN SAMOA

Played 2   Australia won 2
Highest scores Australia 73-3 in 1994, Western Samoa 3-9 in 1991 & 3-73 in 1994
Biggest win Australia 73-3 in 1994, Western Samoa no win

1991 Pontypool *WC* **Australia** 9-3

1994 Sydney **Australia** 73-3

AUSTRALIA v ITALY

Played 6   Australia won 6
Highest scores Australia 55-6 in 1988, Italy 20-23 in 1994
Biggest win Australia 55-6 in 1988, Italy no win

1983 Rovigo **Australia** 29-7
1986 Brisbane **Australia** 39-18
1988 Rome **Australia** 55-6
1994 *1* Brisbane **Australia** 23-20

    2 Melbourne **Australia** 20-7
    Australia won series 2-0
1996 Padua **Australia** 40-18

AUSTRALIA v CANADA

Played 5   Australia won 5
Highest scores Australia 74-9 in 1996, Canada 16-43 in 1993
Biggest win Australia 74-9 in 1996, Canada no win

1985 *1* Sydney **Australia** 59-3
    2 Brisbane **Australia** 43-15
    Australia won series 2-0

1993 Calgary **Australia** 43-16
1995 Port Elizabeth *WC* **Australia** 27-11
1996 Brisbane **Australia** 74-9

AUSTRALIA v KOREA

Played 1   Australia won 1
Highest scores Australia 65-18 in 1987, Korea 18-65 in 1987
Biggest win Australia 65-18 in 1987, Korea no win

1987 Brisbane **Australia** 65-18

AUSTRALIA v ROMANIA

Played 1   Australia won 1
highest scores Australia 42-3 in 1995, Romania 3-42 in 1995
Biggest win Australia 42-3 in 1995, Romania no win

1995 Stellenbosch *WC* **Australia** 42-3

INTERNATIONAL HONOURS

WORLD CUP WINNERS
New Zealand once: 1987
Australia once: 1991
South Africa once: 1995

GRAND SLAM WINNERS
England 11 times: 1913, 1914, 1921, 1923, 1924, 1928, 1957, 1980, 1991, 1992, 1995.
Wales 8 times: 1908, 1909, 1911, 1950, 1952, 1971, 1976, 1978. **France** 5 times: 1968, 1977, 1981, 1987, 1997. **Scotland** 3 times; 1925, 1984, 1990. **Ireland** once: 1948.

TRIPLE CROWN WINNERS
England 20 times: 1883, 1884, 1892, 1913, 1914, 1921, 1923, 1924, 1928, 1934, 1937, 1954, 1957, 1960, 1980, 1991, 1992, 1995, 1996, 1997. **Wales** 17 times: 1893, 1900, 1902, 1905, 1908, 1909, 1911, 1950, 1952, 1965, 1969, 1971, 1976, 1977, 1978, 1979, 1988. **Scotland** 10 times: 1891, 1895, 1901, 1903, 1907, 1925, 1933, 1938, 1984, 1990. **Ireland** 6 times: 1894, 1895, 1901, 1903, 1907, 1925, 1933, 1938, 1984, 1990. **Ireland** 6 times: 1894, 1899, 1948, 1949, 1982, 1985.

INTERNATIONAL CHAMPIONSHIP WINNERS

Year	Winner	Year	Winner	Year	Winner	Year	Winner
1883	England	1912 {	England / Ireland	1947 {	Wales / England	1972*	—
1884	England	1913	England	1948	Ireland	1973	Quintuple tie
1885*	—	1914	England	1949	Ireland	1974	Ireland
1886 {	England / Scotland	1920 {	England / Scotland / Wales	1950	Wales	1975	Wales
1887	Scotland	1921	England	1951	Ireland	1976	Wales
1888*	—	1922	Wales	1952	Wales	1977	France
1889*	—	1923	England	1953	England	1978	Wales
1890 {	England / Scotland	1924	England	1954 {	England / France / Wales	1979	Wales
1891	Scotland	1925	Scotland	1955 {	France / Wales	1980	England
1892	England	1926 {	Scotland / Ireland	1956	Wales	1981	France
1893	Wales	1927 {	Scotland / Ireland	1957	England	1982	Ireland
1894	Ireland	1928	England	1958	England	1983 {	France / Ireland
1895	Scotland	1929	Scotland	1959	France	1984	Scotland
1896	Ireland	1930	England	1960 {	France / England	1985	Ireland
1897*	—	1931	Wales	1961	France	1986 {	France / Scotland
1898*	—	1932 {	England / Wales / Ireland	1962	France	1987	France
1899	Ireland	1933	Scotland	1963	England	1988 {	Wales / France
1900	Wales	1934	England	1964 {	Scotland / Wales	1989	France
1901	Scotland	1935	Ireland	1965	Wales	1990	Scotland
1902	Wales	1936	Wales	1966	Wales	1991	England
1903	Scotland	1937	England	1967	France	1992	England
1904	Scotland	1938	Scotland	1968	France	1993	France
1905	Wales	1939 {	England / Wales / Ireland	1969	Wales	1994**	Wales
1906 {	Ireland / Wales			1970 {	France / Wales	1995	England
1907	Scotland			1971	Wales	1996**	England
1908	Wales					1997	France
1909	Wales						
1910	England						
1911	Wales						

*Matches not completed, for various reasons
** Indicates winners of the Five Nations Trophy (introduced 1993) on points difference

Wales and England have won the title outright 22 times each; Scotland 13 times; France 11 and Ireland 10.

LATIN CUP WINNERS
France once: 1995

TRI-NATIONS WINNERS
New Zealand once: 1996.

INTERNATIONAL REFEREES 1996-97

Leading Referees

Up to 30 April 1997, in major international matches. These include all matches for which senior members of the International Board have awarded caps, and also all matches played in the World Cup final stages.

12 or more internationals

W D Bevan	Wales	32	F Palmade	France	17
J M Fleming	Scotland	27	S R Hilditch	Ireland	17
C Norling	Wales	25	B S Cumberlege	England	16
D J Bishop	New Zealand	24	O E Doyle	Ireland	16
K D Kelleher	Ireland	23	D I H Burnett	Ireland	15
D G Walters	Wales	23	C H Gadney	England	15
M Joseph	Wales	22	I David	Wales	14
R C Williams	Ireland	21	Dr I R Vanderfield	Australia	14
K V J Fitzgerald	Australia	21	R G Byres	Australia	13
F A Howard	England	20	J P Murphy	New Zealand	13
A M Hosie	Scotland	19	N R Sanson	Scotland	13
Capt M J Dowling	Ireland	18	K H Lawrence	New Zealand	13
A E Freethy	Wales	18	R F Johnson	England	12
R C Quittenton	England	18	T D Schofield	Wales	12
J R West	Ireland	18	T H Vile	Wales	12
J B Anderson	Scotland	18	W Williams	England	12
R Hourquet	France	18	A R MacNeill	Australia	12
E F Morrison	England	18	B W Stirling	Ireland	12
D P D'Arcy	Ireland	17			

Major international match appearances 1996-97

Matches controlled between 1 May 1996 and 30 April 1997

1996
NZ v WS   **W T S Henning** (South Africa)
A v W   **G K Wahlstrom** (New Zealand)
NZ v S (2) **W J Erickson** (Australia)
A v W   **C J Hawke** (New Zealand)
Arg v F   **G Simmonds** (Wales)
A v C   ***A Watson** (South Africa)
Arg v F   **C Thomas** (Wales)
SA v Fj   **J Meuwesen** (Namibia)
NZ v A   **E F Morrison** (England)
A v SA   **A J Spreadbury** (England)
NZ v SA   **R J Megson** (Scotland)
A v NZ   **J M Fleming** (Scotland)
SA v A   **B W Stirling** (Ireland)
SA v NZ   **D T M McHugh** (Ireland)
SA v NZ   **P Thomas** (France)
SA v NZ   **D Méné** (France)
W v Bb   **J M Fleming** (Scotland)
SA v NZ   **W D Bevan** (Wales)
W v F   **G Gadjovich** (Canada)
It v W   ***C Spannenberg** (South Africa)
It v A   ***E Sorensen** (United States)

S v A   **P Thomas** (France)
Arg v SA   **J M Fleming** (Scotland)
I v WS   ***S Borsani** (Argentina)
Arg v SA   **E Murray** (Scotland)
E v It   ***P Deluca** (Argentina)
I v A   **B Campsall** (England)
F v SA   **B W Stirling** (Ireland)
W v A   ***D I Ramage** (Scotland)
F v SA   **W D Bevan** (Wales)
E v Arg   **W T S Henning** (South Africa)
S v It   ***D Gillet** (France)
W v SA   **S Lander** (England)
1997
I v It   ***R G Davies** (Wales)
W v US   ***L Mayne** (Ireland)
S v W   ***H A Smith** (Ireland)
I v F   **A Watson** (South Africa)
W v I   **W J Erickson** (Australia)
E v S   **P D O'Brien** (New Zealand)
F v W   **P Marshall** (Australia)
I v E   **C J Hawke** (New Zealand)
E v F   **J M Fleming** (Scotland)

S v I	**G Simmonds** (Wales)	F v S	**E F Morrison** (England)
W v E	**J Dumé** (France)	F v It	**D T M McHugh** (Ireland)

*Denotes debut in a major international

Referees dismissing players in a major international

A E Freethy	E v NZ	1925	**F A Howard**	Nm v W	1990
K D Kelleher	S v NZ	1967	**A J Spreadbury**	A v F	1990
R T Burnett	A v E	1975	**C Norling**	A v F	1990
W M Cooney	A v Fj	1976	**C J Hawke**	E v Arg	1991
N R Sanson (2)	W v I	1977	**E F Morrison**	R v F	1991
D I H Burnett	E v W	1980	**J M Fleming** (2)	Arg v WS	1991*
C Norling	F v I	1984	**S R Hilditch** (2)	F v E	1992
K V J Fitzgerald	NZ v W	1987*	**D J Bishop**	NZ v Wld	1992
F A Howard	A v W	1987*	**E F Morrison**	A v SA	1993
K V J Fitzgerald	Fj v E	1988	**I Rogers** (2)	C v F	1994
O E Doyle	Arg v F	1988	**D Méné**	W v E	1995
B W Stirling (2)	E v Fj	1989	**S Lander**	F v Tg	1995*
F A Howard	W v F	1990	**D T M McHugh** (3)	SA v C	1995*
F A Howard	S v F	1990	**J Dumé**	SA v W	1995

*World Cup matches

WORLD INTERNATIONAL RECORDS

Both match and career records are for official cap matches played by senior members of the International Board, up to 30 April 1997. Figures include Test performances for the Lions (shown in brackets).

MATCH RECORDS

MOST CONSECUTIVE TEST WINS

17 by N Zealand 1965 *SA* 4, 1966 *BI* 1,2,3,4, 1967 *A, E, W, F, S,* 1968 *A* 1,2, *F* 1,2,3, 1969 *W* 1,2

15 by S Africa 1994 *Arg* 1,2,*S*,*W* 1995 *WS, A, R, C, WS, F, NZ, W, It, E,* 1996 *Fj*

MOST CONSECUTIVE TESTS WITHOUT DEFEAT

P	W	D	Period
23 by NZ	22	1	1987–90
17 by NZ	15	2	1961–64
17 by NZ	17	0	1965–69

MOST POINTS IN A MATCH
by the team

Pts	Opps	Venue	Year
145 by NZ	J	Bloemfontein	1995
102 by W	Pt	Lisbon	1994
89 by S	Iv	Rustenburg	1995
74 by NZ	Fj	Christchurch	1987
74 by A	C	Brisbane	1996

by a player
45 by S D Culhane, New Zealand v Japan at Bloemfontein — 1995
44 by A G Hastings, Scotland v Ivory Coast at Rustenburg — 1995
39 by M Burke, Australia v Canada at Brisbane — 1996
31 by A G Hastings, Scotland v Tonga at Pretoria — 1995
30 by D Camberabero, France v Zimbabwe at Auckland — 1987
30 by C R Andrew, England v Canada at Twickenham — 1994
30 by M C G Ellis, New Zealand v Japan at Bloemfontein — 1995

MOST TRIES IN A MATCH
by the team

Tries	Opps	Venue	Year
21 by NZ	J	Bloemfontein	1995
16 by W	Pt	Lisbon	1994
13 by E	W	Blackheath	1881
13 by NZ	US	Berkeley	1913
13 by F	R	Paris	1924
13 by A	SK	Brisbane	1987
13 by F	Z	Auckland	1987
13 by S	Iv	Rustenburg	1995

by a player
6 by M C G Ellis, New Zealand v Japan at Bloemfontein — 1995
5 by G C Lindsay, Scotland v Wales at Raeburn Place — 1887
5 by D Lambert, England v France at Richmond — 1907
5 by R Underwood, England v Fiji at Twickenham — 1989

MOST CONVERSIONS IN A MATCH
by the team

Cons	Opps	Venue	Year
20 by NZ	J	Bloemfontein	1995
11 by W	Pt	Lisbon	1994
10 by NZ	Fj	Christchurch	1987
9 by F	It	Toulon	1967
9 by F	Z	Auckland	1987
9 by S	Iv	Rustenburg	1995
9 by A	C	Brisbane	1996

by a player
20 by S D Culhane, New Zealand v Japan at Bloemfontein — 1995
11 by N R Jenkins, Wales v Portugal at Lisbon — 1994
10 by G J Fox, New Zealand v Fiji at Christchurch — 1987
9 by G Camberabero, France v Italy at Toulon — 1967
9 by D Camberabero, France v Zimbabwe at Auckland — 1987
9 by A G Hastings, Scotland v Ivory Coast at Rustenburg — 1995
9 by M Burke, Australia v Canada at Brisbane — 1996

MOST PENALTY GOALS IN A MATCH
by the team

Penalties	Opps	Venue	Year
8 by W	C	Cardiff	1993
8 by S	Tg	Pretoria	1995
8 by F	I	Durban	1995
8 by I	It	Dublin	1997

by a player

8 by N R Jenkins, Wales v Canada at Cardiff		1993
8 by A G Hastings, Scotland v Tonga at Pretoria		1995
8 by T Lacroix, France v Ireland at Durban		1995
8 by P A Burke, Ireland v Italy at Dublin		1997

MOST DROPPED GOALS IN A MATCH

by the team

Drops	Opps	Venue	Year
3 by F	I	Paris	1960
3 by A	E	Twickenham	1967
3 by S	I	Murrayfield	1973
3 by SA	SAm	Durban	1980
3 by SA	I	Durban	1981
3 by A	I	Dublin	1984
3 by F	E	Twickenham	1985
3 by A	Fj	Brisbane	1985

3 by F	NZ	Christchurch	1986
3 by NZ	F	Christchurch	1986
3 by F	A	Sydney	1990
3 by F	S	Paris	1991
3 by F	NZ	Christchurch	1994

by a player

3 by P Albaladejo, France v Ireland at Paris	1960
3 by P F Hawthorne, Australia v England at Twickenham	1967
3 by H E Botha, South Africa v S America at Durban	1980
3 by H E Botha, South Africa v Ireland at Durban	1981
3 by J-P Lescarboura, France v England at Twickenham	1985
3 by J-P Lescarboura, France v New Zealand at Christchurch	1986
3 by D Camberabero, France v Australia at Sydney	1990

CAREER RECORDS

MOST CAPPED PLAYERS

Caps	Player	Career
111	P Sella (France)	1982–95
101	D I Campese (Australia)	1982–96
93	S Blanco (France)	1980–91
91 (6)	R Underwood (England/Lions)	1984–96
83	S B T Fitzpatrick (New Zealand)	1986–96
81(12)	C M H Gibson (Ireland/Lions)	1964–79
80(17)	W J McBride (Ireland/Lions)	1962–75
77 (6)	I C Evans (Wales/Lions)	1987–97
76 (5)	C R Andrew (England/Lions)	1985–97
73 (1)	W D C Carling (England/Lions)	1988–97
72	M P Lynagh (Australia)	1984–95

MOST CONSECUTIVE TESTS

Tests	Player	Span
63	S B T Fitzpatrick (New Zealand)	1986–95
53	G O Edwards (Wales)	1967–78
52	W J McBride (Ireland)	1964–75
49	A B Carmichael (Scotland)	1967–78
49	P A Orr (Ireland)	1976–86

MOST TESTS AS CAPTAIN

Tests	Captain	Span
59	W D C Carling (England)	1988–96
43	S B T Fitzpatrick (New Zealand)	1992–96
36	N C Farr-Jones (Australia)	1988–92
34	J-P Rives (France)	1978–84
30	W J Whineray (New Zealand)	1958–65

| 29 | J F Pienaar (South Africa) | 1993–96 |
| 29 | P Saint-André (France) | 1994–96 |

MOST TESTS IN INDIVIDUAL POSITIONS

Full-back S Blanco (France)	81		1980–91
Wing R Underwood (England/Lions)	91	(6)	1984–96
Centre P Sella (France)	104		1982–95
Fly-half C R Andrew (England/Lions)	75	(5)	1985–97
Scrum-half G O Edwards (Wales/Lions)	63	(10)	1967–78
Prop P A Orr (Ireland/Lions)	59	(1)	1976–87
Hooker S B T Fitzpatrick (New Zealand)	83		1986–96
Lock W J McBride (Ireland/Lions)	80	(17)	1962–75
Flanker J F Slattery (Ireland/Lions)	65	(4)	1970–84
P J Winterbottom (England/Lions)	65	(7)	1982–93
No 8 D Richards (England/Lions)	53*	(6)	1986–96

* *excludes an appearance as a temporary replacement*

MOST POINTS IN TESTS

Points	Player	Tests	Career
911	M P Lynagh (Australia)	72	1984–95
733(66)	A G Hastings (Scotland/Lions)	67(6)	1986–95
645	G J Fox (New Zealand)	46	1985–93
534	N R Jenkins (Wales)	50	1991–97
407(11)	C R Andrew (England/Lions)	76(5)	1985–97

MOST TRIES IN TESTS

Tries	Player	Tests	Career
64	D I Campese (Australia)	101	1982–96
50(1)	R Underwood (England/Lions)	91(6)	1984–96
38	S Blanco (France)	93	1980–91
35	J J Kirwan (N Zealand)	63	1984–94
34(1)	I C Evans (Wales/Lions)	77(6)	1987–97

MOST CONVERSIONS IN TESTS

Cons	Player	Tests	Career
140	M P Lynagh (Australia)	72	1984–95
118	G J Fox (N Zealand)	46	1985–93
87(1)	A G Hastings (Scotland/Lions)	67(6)	1986–95
65	N R Jenkins (Wales)	50	1991–97
50	H E Botha (S Africa)	28	1980–92

MOST PENALTY GOALS IN TESTS

Penalties	Player	Tests	Career
177	M P Lynagh (Australia)	72	1984–95
160(20)	A G Hastings (Scotland/Lions)	67(6)	1986–95
128	G J Fox (N Zealand)	46	1985–93
122	N R Jenkins (Wales)	50	1991–97
87 (1)	C R Andrew (England/Lions)	76(5)	1985–97
87	T Lacroix (France)	38	1989–96

MOST DROPPED GOALS IN TESTS

Drops	Player	Tests	Career
23(2)	C R Andrew (England/Lions)	76(5)	1985–97
18	H E Botha (S Africa)	28	1980–92
15	J-P Lescarboura (France)	28	1982–90
13	J Davies (Wales)	32	1985–97
12	P Albaladejo (France)	30	1954–64
12(0)	J Y Rutherford (Scotland/Lions)	43(1)	1979–87

INTERNATIONAL CHAMPIONSHIP RECORDS

Record	Detail		Set
Most points in season	141 by England	in four matches	1997
Most tries in season	21 by Wales	in four matches	1910
Highest Score	49 by Wales	49-14 v France	1910
Biggest win	40 by England	46-6 v Ireland	1997
Most appearances	56 for Ireland	C M H Gibson	1964–79
Most points in matches	288 for Scotland	A G Hastings	1986–95
Most points in season	67 for England	J M Webb	1992
Most points in match	24 for France	S Viars	v Ireland, 1992
	24 for England	C R Andrew	v Scotland, 1995
	24 for France	C Lamaison	v Scotland, 1997
Most tries in matches	24 for Scotland	I S Smith	1924–1933
Most tries in season	8 for England	C N Lowe	1914
	8 for Scotland	I S Smith	1925
Tries in all four games	For England	H C Catcheside	1924
	For Scotland	A C Wallace	1925
	For France	P Estève	1983
	For France	P Sella	1986
Most tries in match	5 for Scotland	G C Lindsay	v Wales, 1887
Most cons in matches	32 for Wales	J Bancroft	1909–14
Most cons in season	11 for England	J M Webb	1992
Most cons in match	8 for Wales	J Bancroft	v France, 1910
Most pens in matches	77 for Scotland	A G Hastings	1986–95
Most pens in season	18 for England	S D Hodgkinson	1991
Most pens in match	7 for England	S D Hodgkinson	v Wales, 1991
	7 for England	C R Andrew	v Scotland, 1995
Most drops in matches	9 for France	J-P Lescarboura	1982–88
	9 for England	C R Andrew	1985–97
Most drops in season	5 for France	G Camberabero	1967
Drops in all four games	For France	J-P Lescarboura	1984
Most drops in match	3 for France	P Albaladejo	v Ireland, 1960
	3 for France	J-P Lescarboura	v England, 1985

PARTNERSHIP RECORDS

Position	Holders	Detail	Span
Centre threequarters	W D C Carling & J C Guscott	45 (1) for England/ Lions	1989–96
Half-backs	M P Lynagh & N C Farr-Jones	47 for Australia	1985–92
Front row	A J Daly, P N Kearns & E J A McKenzie	37 for Australia	1990–95
Second row	I D Jones & R M Brooke	29 for N Zealand	1992–96
Back row	J Matheu, G Basquet & J Prat	22 for France	1945–51

OTHER MAJOR TEST RECORDS

Record	Holder	Detail
Fastest to 100 points	A P Mehrtens	in his 5th Test for N Zealand
	S D Culhane	in his 5th Test for N Zealand
Fastest to ten tries	M C G Ellis	in his 6th Test for N Zealand

MAJOR TOUR RECORDS

Record	Detail	Year	Place
Most team points	976 by NZ	1905–06	Europe & NAm
Most team tries	243 by NZ	1905–06	Europe & NAm
Biggest win	117-6 by NZ	1974 v S Australia	Adelaide
Most individual points	246 by W J Wallace	1905–06 for NZ	Europe & NAm
Most individual tries	44 by J Hunter	1905–06 for NZ	Europe & NAm
Most points in match	43 by R M Deans	1984 v S Australia for NZ	Adelaide
Most tries in match	8 by T R Heeps	1962 v Northern NSW for NZ	Quirindi

OTHER INTERNATIONAL MATCH RECORDS

Up to 30 April 1997. These are included for comparison and cover performances since 1971 by teams and players in Test matches for nations which are not senior members of the International Board.

Most points in a match
By a team
164 Hong Kong v Singapore 1994 Kuala Lumpar
By a player
50 A Billington Hong Kong v Singapore 1994

Most tries in a match
By a team
26 Hong Kong v Singapore 1994 Kuala Lumpar
By a player
10 A Billington Hong Kong v Singapore 1994

Most conversions in a match
By a team
17 Hong Kong v Singapore 1994 Kuala Lumpar

By a player
17 J McKee Hong Kong v Singapore 1994

Most penalty goals in a match
By a team
8 Canada v Scotland 1991 St John
8 Italy v Romania 1994 Catania
8 Argentina v Canada 1995 Buenos Aires
By a player
8 M A Wyatt Canada v Scotland 1991 St John
8 D Dominguez Italy v Romania 1994 Catania
8 S E Meson Argentina v Canada 1995 Buenos Aires

Most dropped goals in a match
By a team
3 Argentina v SA Gazelles 1971 Pretoria
3 Argentina v Australia 1979 Buenos Aires

3 Argentina v New Zealand 1985 Buenos
   Aires
By a player
3 T A Harris-Smith Argentina v SA
   Gazelles 1971
3 H Porta Argentina v Australia 1979
3 H Porta Argentina v New Zealand
   1985

Most points in matches
530 H Porta (Argentina/S America)
483 S Bettarello (Italy)
456 D Dominguez (Italy)

Most tries in matches
24 Marcello Cuttitta (Italy)

Most conversions in matches
64 D Dominguez (Italy)

54 H Porta (Argentina/S America)
46 S Bettarello (Italy)

Most penalty goals in matches
109 H Porta (Argentina/S America)
104 S Bettarello (Italy)
 95 D Dominguez (Italy)

Most dropped goals in matches
25 H Porta (Argentina/S America)
17 S Bettarello (Italy)

Most matches as captain
43 H Porta (Argentina/S America)

Biggest win on a major tour
128-0 W Samoa v Marlborough
   (New Zealand) 1993 Blenheim

France's Christian Lamaison, who equalled the Five Nations record of 24 points scored in a match against Scotland.

BAA-BAAS ENJOY CONTINENTAL FLAVOUR IN BUSY SEASON

THE BARBARIANS 1996-97
Geoff Windsor-Lewis

Matches against Scotland, Wales and Australia and virtually a full Italian XV kept the Baa-Baas very much to the fore throughout the first full professional season. A very full year was rounded off by a return to the Middlesex Sevens, to win the tournament in great style, participation in the Air France Sevens in Paris, and a tour to Italy.

The Baa-Baas were honoured to be invited by the Scottish Rugby Union to play Scotland in aid of the Dunblane Charity and thereby pay their respects to the Dunblane community. In a seesaw game in which 15 tries and 93 points were scored, with the lead changing hands 11 times, the Barbarians edged home with a late try from Irish lock forward Paddy Johns to maintain their unbeaten record against Scotland. The visitors, drawn from eight different countries, lived up to their adventurous traditions and always had the edge over a Scottish team that found it difficult to adapt to the pace and flow of the game.

The last appearance of the Baa-Baas at the old Cardiff Arms Park was against a Wales team anxious to make early preparations for the season. After only three minutes Wales had scored a soft opening try by Nigel Davies but, prompted by Augustine Pichot and Arron Pene, the visitors soon reacted. Pene ploughed over from close range and then the visitors gave scope to their new French full-back David Arrieta who excited the crowd with some vintage long-range assaults. Several times throughout the game it seemed that the Baa-Baas would score after some exciting moves, but Wales tackled superbly and the Barbarian runner always seemed one pass away from the goal-line.

The visit to Newport produced a handsome victory for the Baa-Baas in a winning score of 86-33. Richmond wing Mike Hutton scored four tries in a game which the Baa-Baas dominated and produced some scintillating attacking rugby.

With a near capacity crowd of 70,000 and a Barbarian side including 13 internationals, the Baa-Baas gave the touring Australians some anxious moment before the visitors took the upper hand and established a comfortable lead. Matthew Burke was in particularly fine form for the tourists and scored two tries. The Barbarians tried to play expansive rugby and ran the ball continuously in an effort to break down the Australian defence, but the visitors were too secure, and turned over possession left the Barbarian defence vulnerable.

The traditional Christmas fixture with Leicester was postponed to February due to Leicester's involvement in the Heineken European Cup semi-final. On a cold wet evening over 11,000 spectators watched a surprisingly good match in which the Barbarians side included 10 internationals from five different countries. A score line of 28-22 reflected the Baa-Baa dominance of a fine match.

The Mobbs Memorial match at Northampton gave the Baa-Baas a clear victory against East Midlands by 72-38. Eight internationals graced the field for the visitors and the 12 Barbarians tries resulted in sponsors Scottish Amicable donating £3,600 to English youth rugby. The Amicable have now donated a total of £90,300 to youth rugby in the four Home Unions and the Barbarians are extremely grateful for their involvement with the club.

After an absence of 63 years the Baa-Baas returned to the final stages to the Middlesex Sevens in May, and maintained their unbeaten record in the event. Captained by Dave Scully, steadied by Derek Eves and Adam Roxburgh and ignited by four Fijians, the Barbarians provided the tournament with a boost and produced some of the best rugby of the whole tournament. Marika Vunibaka was in devastating form and he and his Fijian colleagues emphasised how adept they are in the seven-a-side game.

In June the Baa-Baas took part in the Air France Sevens and just lost to France in the quarter-final stages of the tournament. Again captained by Dave Scully his team were just unable to keep the upper hand and, in spite of the Fijian presence, France deserved their win. The tournament was dominated by the full Fijian team who are so effective at this form of rugby.

The Baa-Baas then set off for a short tour of Italy to conclude their season, playing matches against Lupi in Rome and Zebre in Brescia, two invitation teams very much on similar lines to the Barbarian club. After losing to Lupi in a difficult game by 37-5, the Baa-Baas were determined to take on a Zebre XV which included 12 current Italian internationals, supplemented by Xavier Blond, the French wing forward. The match demonstrated many of the best aspects of the game and was hard fought throughout, with the Italian team emerging as eventual 48-38 winners.

Throughout the season the Baa-Baas have continued to spread the base of their activities. The club intends to adapt and flourish in a modern professional world and, whilst there will inevitably be changes, the club is determined to re-adjust and retain the principles from which it originated.

RESULTS 1996-97 (up to 30 April 1997)

Played 6   Won 4   Lost 2   Drawn 0   Points for 266 (23G 21T)   **Points Against 208** (22G 3PG 9T)

1996

17 Aug	**Beat Scotland** at Murrayfield. (The Dunblane International) 48 (4G 4T) to 45 (5G 2T)
24 Aug	**Lost to Wales** at Cardiff Arms Park 10 (2T) to 31 (3G 2T)
8 Oct	**Beat Newport** at Rodney Parade 86 (8G 6T) to 33 (4G 1T)
7 Dec	**Lost to Australia** at Twickenham 12 (1G 1T) to 39 (4G 1T 2PG)

1997

25 Feb	**Beat Leicester** at Welford Road 38 (4G 2T) to 22 (2G 1T 1PG)
5 Mar	**Beat East Midlands** at Franklins Gardens 72 (6G 6T) to 38 (4G 2T)

PLAYERS 1996-97 (up to 30 April 1997)

Abbreviations: *S* – Scotland; *W* – Wales; *N* – Newport; *A* – Australia; *L* – Leicester; *EM* – East Midlands; (R) – Replacement; *-New Barbarian

Full-backs: A G Hastings (Watsonians & Scotland) *S*; *D Arrieta (Biarritz) *W*; *C Cormack (Pontypridd) *N*; *T Stimpson (Newcastle & England) *A*; M A Rayer (Bedford & Wales) *L*; *N Grecian (Newbury) *EM*; *D Hodge (Watsonians) *S*(R); *J. Stransky (Western Province & South Africa) *A*(R).

Wings: *A Bose (Mana) *S*, *W*; T Underwood (Newcastle & England) *S*, *A*; N K Walker (Cardiff & Wales) *W*, *A*; *D Tiueti (Bristol) *N*; *M Hutton (Richmond) *N*; *P Vaccari (Calvisano & Italy) *L*; *D James (Bridgend & Wales) *L*; *B Johnson (Newbury) *EM*; *P Hopley (Wasps) *EM*; I C Glasgow (Heriots) *S*(R).

Centres: *Y Motoki (Kobe Steel & Japan) *S*; *A McCormick (Toshiba & Japan) *S*; S Glas (Bourgoin-Jailleu & France) *W*; *R Dourthe (Dax & France) *W*; *F Waters (Bristol) *N*; *T Whitford (Richmond) *N*; *A Bateman (Richmond & Wales) *A*; G Townsend (Northampton & Scotland) *A*; * L Arbizu (Belgrano & Argentina) *L*, *EM*; *R Henderson (Wasps & Ireland) *L*; *R Robinson (Coventry) *EM*; R Liley (Leicester) *EM*(R); *M Allen (Northampton) *A*(R).

Fly-halves: P W Howard (Queensland & Australia) *S*, *W*; *S J Mannix (Wellington & New Zealand) *N*; C R Andrew (Newcastle & England) *A*; D Dominguez (Milan & Italy) *L*; *A Boyd (Richmond) *EM*; R H Q B Moon (Walsall) *N*(R).

Scrum-halves: A Pichot (C A San Isidro & Argentina) *S*, *W*; *A Moore (Richmond & Wales) *N*, *A*(R); R Howley (Cardiff & Wales) *A*: * A Troncon (Treviso & Italy) *L*; *D Scully (Wakefield) *EM*

Forwards: G Rowntree (Leicester & England) *S*; R Cockerill (Leicester) *S*; D Garforth (Leicester) *S*; P Johns (Saracens & Ireland) *S*; *R J McCall (Queensland & Australia) *S*, *W*; *M Gasuna (Mana) *S*, *W*; *A R B Pene (Kaneka & New Zealand) *S*, W; I Morrison (London Scottish & Scotland) *S*; K Milne (Heriots F P & Scotland) *S*(R); D McIvor (Glenrothes & scotland0 *S*(R); A G J Watt (Currie & Scotland) *W*; J A Hay (Hawick & Scotland) *W*; *R Snow (Newfoundland Dogs & Canada) *W*; D Sims (Gloucester) *W*; D S Corkery (Bristol & Ireland) *W*; R G Collins (Pontypridd & Wales) *W*(R); R Hardwick (Coventry) *N*; *N McCarthy (Bath) *N*; J A Probyn (Bedford & England) *N*, *L*; *V Cooper (Llanelli) *N*; *D Grewcock (Coventry) *N*, *L*; P Walton (Newcastle & Scotland) *N*; *J Mitchell (Sale) *N*; D Eves (Coventry) *N*, *EM*; M S Linnett (Worcester & Engand) *N*(R), *EM*; *J Evans (Pontypridd) *N*(R); N Popplewell (Newcastle & Ireland) *A*; *N Hewitt (Southlands & New Zealand) *A*; J C Quinnell (Richmond & Wales) *A*; I D Jones (North Harbour & New Zealand) *A*; *D McInosh (Pontypridd) *A*; L S Quinnell (Richmond & Wales) *A*; N A Back (Leicester & England) *A*; G W Weir (Newcastle & Scotland) *A*(R); K Colclough (Swansea) *L*; *F Mendez (Bath & Argentina) *L*; *P S Sportleder (Curupanti & Argentina) *L*, *EM*; *R Martin (San Isidro & Argentina) *L*, *EM*; *M Richardson (Aspatria) *L*; *M White (Wasps) *L*; *M Cuttitta (Milan & Italy) *EM*; *F Freshwater (Leicester) *EM*; *R Brown (Melrose) *EM*; J Gardner (Bennetton Treviso & Italy) *EM*; A Sharp (Coventry & Scotland) *EM*(R)

TRAGIC LOSS FOR DARK BLUES

THE VARSITY MATCH 1996 (*for the Bowring Bowl*)

10 December 1996, Twickenham
Cambridge University 23 (2G 2PG 1DG)
Oxford University 7 (1G)

The drowning of sorrows in the Oxford camp on a bleak December evening had little to do with the emphatic defeat suffered earlier that day at the hands of their great rivals in the 115th Varsity Match. This time the tears were for real: many of the Oxford players broke down and wept in the dressing room as the burden they had borne following the death six weeks earlier of their Australian centre, Ian Tucker, finally took its toll.

Tucker's death, on 27 October, from head injuries sustained in a tackle during a match against Saracens the previous day, had had a profound effect on his team-mates. As a mark of respect the Oxford side took the field without the No 12 shirt, although Tucker had actually been wearing No 13 in the fateful game. His replacement in the Varsity team, fellow Australian Trevor Walsh, explained the reasoning: 'Tucks played most of his rugby at No 12. We decided to miss that out rather than 13, because in years to come people might think we've just done it for superstitious reasons. Personally, the whole thing affected me very deeply.' The Oxford team had all had counselling in the wake of the tragedy, and several players questioned whether they would ever play again. In the end they pulled together under the leadership of South African Quentin de Bruyn.

There was a deeply disturbing moment in the Varsity Match when it appeared that tragedy was about to repeat itself. De Bruyn took a heavy knock early on and thereafter looked very groggy indeed. When he suffered another blow to the head 14 minutes into the second half he was stretchered off. One of the loudest cheers of the day from the 72,000 strong crowd was prompted by the announcement that De Bruyn was sitting up in good shape in the dressing room.

After an injury-plagued term, Cambridge, the favourites, managed to field eight Blues against just three from Oxford. The Dark Blues had a hard time of it all afternoon. Their opponents dominated the match: Cambridge had the whip hand in the forwards and more authority at half-back, and Oxford had no one to match the finishing skills of Light Blue centre Matthew Singer. Singer, slim, sprightly and resourceful, scored both his side's tries and also popped over a dropped goal. Oxford battled away in the loose, where the back row and Ireland scrum-half Niall Hogan tackled ferociously, but it was very much a rearguard action.

The overall quality of play never rose above the mediocre. The afternoon began well enough for Oxford when Walsh charged down Ashforth's kick in the third minute and steamed in from 50 metres. Averis converted. Surridge knocked over the first of his two penalty goals for Cambridge three minutes later. As ever there was plenty of industry and craft, but there were far too many errors from both sides. Gradually the Cambridge pack got on top. Richard Bramley, the captain, gave a typically rousing performance in the second row which was put to best use by the dynamic punch offered by his back row of Hyde, Griffiths and Earnshaw.

Just before half-time, Singer began to etch his name in the history books with his first contribution to the scoresheet. He cut inside De Bruyn and rounded Maher for the first of his tries. On the stroke of the half-time whistle, he dropped a left-footed goal.

The second half was dominated by Cambridge, although the scores did not come until late. Surridge kicked his second goal in the 77th minute before Singer's *pièce de résistance* saw him beat four defenders en route to the tryline.

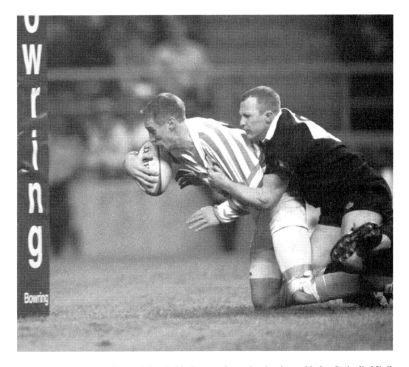

Matthew Singer scores his and Cambridge's second try, despite the tackle by Oxford's Niall Hogan, in the 1996 Varsity match.

Cambridge University: P A Surridge (St Kentigern Coll, Auckland & Hughes Hall); N J Walne (Caerleon CS & St Catharine's), M J Singer (Wycliffe Coll & Homerton), N J Hill (St Ignatius, Sydney & St Edmund's), R Phillips (Ysgol Gyfun, Llanhari & Homerton); R W Ashforth (Bradford GS & Peterhouse), B C I Ryan (Wimbledon Coll & Homerton); G M Reynolds (Cheshunt School & Homerton), T D Murphy (St Joseph's, Brisbane & St Edmund's), N J Holgate (Armthorpe CS & Robinson); R A Bramley (Queen Elizabeth GS, Wakefield & St Edmund's) (*capt*), A M Craig (Taurarigo Coll, NZ & Hughes Hall), M J Hyde (St Ignatius, Sydney & St Edmund's), R D Earnshaw (Yarm & St John's), J P Griffiths (Crossley Heath, Halifax & St Edmund's)
Scorers *Tries:* Singer (2) *Conversions:* Surridge (2) *Penalty Goals:* Surridge (2) *Dropped Goal:* Singer
Oxford University: R A O Maher (St Ignatius, Sydney & University); C J Smart (Sherborne & Trinity), Q A de Bruyn (Diocesan Coll, Cape Town & Keble) (*capt*), T A Walsh (St Joseph's, Brisbane & Keble), R F J Browne (St Michael's, Dublin & University); J M M Averis (Bristol Cathedral School & St Cross), N A Hogan (Terenure Coll, Dublin & Merton); J H F Bothwell (Marlborough & Merton), N C Hockley (KES Birmingham & Worcester), D N Penney (Mount Pearl HS, Newfoundland & Wolfson); T S Eisenhauer (St Ignatius, Sydney & St Anne's), K M J Spicer (Clongowes Wood Coll, Dublin & St Anne's); M G P S Orsler (King's School, Canterbury & Christ Church), J P Kindon (Millfield & Queen's), C A P McCarthy (St Mary's Coll, Dublin & Templeton) *Replacement* T P P Jensen (St Edmund's, Canberra & St Anne's) for De Bruyn (54 mins)
Scorers *Try:* Walsh *Conversion:* Averis
Referee J J M Pearson (Durham Society)

10 December 1996, Stoop Memorial Ground

Oxford University Under-21s 22 (1G 5PG)   **Cambridge University Under-21s 13** (1G 2PG)
Oxford University Under-21s: M Knowles (Worcester); N Booth (Worcester), T Stringer (Keble), G Lewis (St Anne's), J Parker (St Hugh's); S Ure (Keble), G MacLeod (Worcester); M Wilding (Corpus Christi), M Pace (Worcester), N Sharp (Brasenose), D Thomas (University), J Finnegan (Jesus), S Showell (St Anne's), P Prichard-Jones (St Edmund Hall) (*capt*), S Mathiason (Keble)
Scorers *Try:* MacLeod *Conversion:* Ure *Penalty Goals:* Ure (5)
Cambridge University Under-21s: A Janisch (Trinity); A Whittaker (Magdalene), J Flood (Peterhouse), F Jarvis (Christ's), M Garfield (Fitzwilliam); W House (Trinity), N Thwaites (Jesus); J Stacey (Trinity), J Gilbert (St Catharine's), E Debenham (Gonville & Caius), T Quick (Magdalene), A Howard (Emanuel), A Brown (Downing) (*capt*), A Foote (Christ's), C Bond (Trinity)
Scorers *Try:* Janisch *Conversion:* Garfield *Penalty Goals:* Garfield (2)
Referee T Henning (South Africa)

5 December, Grange Road, Cambridge

Cambridge University LX Club 35 (3G 3PG 1T)   **Oxford University Greyhounds 22** (2G 1PG 1T)
Cambridge University LX Club: S Jones (Homerton); M Garfield (Fitzwilliam), A Green (St John's), I Higgins (Emanuel), S Lippiat (Corpus Christi); O Jones (St John's), R Elliot (St Edmunds); H Thomas (St Edmunds), G Edwards (St Catharine's), P Godfrey (St John's), N Corbyn (St Catharine's), C Courtenay (St John's), M Cripps (Hughes Hall), M Fyvie (Wolfson), J Cocks (St Edmund's) (*capt*) *Replacement* J Hurst (Homerton) for Jones (10 mins)
Scorers *Tries:* Pen try, Lippiat, S Jones, Elliot *Conversions:* Garfield (3) *Penalty Goals:* Garfield (3)
Oxford University Greyhounds: G Williams (Keble); N Booth (Worcester), M Dumbel (Brasenose), J Riondet (Mansfield), J Bursell (New); T Jenson (St Anne's), C Jones (University); D Grant (Worcester), P Davies (St Edmund Hall), B Parsons (Keble), Rory Elliott (Oriel) (*capt*), A Roberts (New College), C Lavin (St Edmund Hall), F Whitefield (Balliol), D Carson (Linacre)
Scorers *Tries:* Grant, C Jones, Booth *Conversions:* Jenson (2) *Penalty Goal:* Jenson
Referee S Kent (Liverpool)

VARSITY MATCH RESULTS

115 Matches played   Oxford 48 wins   Cambridge 54 wins   13 Draws

*Match played at Oxford 1871-72; Cambridge 1872-73; The Oval 1873-74 to 1879-80; Blackheath 1880-81 to 1886-87; Queen's Club 1887-88 to 1920-21; then Twickenham. *At this date no match could be won unless a goal was scored. †Penalty try.*

Season	Winner	Score
1871-72	Oxford	1G 1T to 0
1872-73	Cambridge	1G 2T to 0
1873-74	Drawn	1T each
1874-75*	Drawn	Oxford 2T to 0
1875-76	Oxford	1T to 0
1876-77	Cambridge	1G 2T to 0
1877-78	Oxford	2T to 0
1878-79	Drawn	No score
1879-80	Cambridge	1G 1DG to 1DG
1880-81	Drawn	1T each
1881-82	Oxford	2G 1T to 1G
1882-83	Oxford	1T to 0
1883-84	Oxford	3G 4T to 1G
1884-85	Oxford	3G 1T to 1T
1885-86	Cambridge	2T to 0
1886-87	Cambridge	3T to 0
1887-88	Cambridge	1DG 2T to 0
1888-89	Cambridge	1G 2T to 0
1889-90	Oxford	1G 1T to 0
1890-91	Drawn	1G each
1891-92	Cambridge	2T to 0
1892-93	Drawn	No score
1893-94	Oxford	1T to 0
1894-95	Drawn	1G each
1895-96	Cambridge	1G to 0
1896-97	Oxford	1G 1DG to 1G 1T
1897-98	Oxford	2T to 0
1898-99	Cambridge	1G 2T to 0
1899-1900	Cambridge	2G 4T to 0
1900-01	Oxford	2G to 1G 1T
1901-02	Oxford	1G 1T to 0
1902-03	Drawn	1G 1T each
1903-04	Oxford	3G 1T to 2G 1T
1904-05	Cambridge	3G to 2G
1905-06	Cambridge	3G (15) to 2G 1T (13)
1906-07	Oxford	4T (12) to 1G 1T (8)
1907-08	Oxford	1G 4T (17) to 0
1908-09	Drawn	1G (5) each
1909-10	Oxford	4G 5T (35) to 1T (3)
1910-11	Oxford	4G 1T (23) to 3G 1T (18)
1911-12	Oxford	2G 3T (19) to 0
1912-13	Cambridge	2G (10) to 1T (3)
1913-14	Cambridge	1DG 3T (13) to 1T (3)
1914-18	*No matches*	
1919-20	Cambridge	1PG 1DG (7) to 1G (5)
1920-21	Oxford	1G 4T (17) to 1G 3T (14)
1921-22	Oxford	1G 2T (11) to 1G (5)
1922-23	Cambridge	3G 2T (21) to 1G 1T (8)
1923-24	Oxford	3G 2T (21) to 1G 1PG 2T (14)
1924-25	Oxford	1G 2T (11) to 2T (6)
1925-26	Cambridge	3G 6T (33) to 1T (3)
1926-27	Cambridge	3G 5T (30) to 1G (5)
1927-28	Cambridge	2G 2PG 2T (22) to 1G 3T (14)
1928-29	Cambridge	1G 3T (14) to 1PG 1DG 1T (10)
1929-30	Oxford	1G 1DG (9) to 0
1930-31	Drawn	Oxford 1PG (3) Cambridge 1T (3)
1931-32	Oxford	1DG 2T (10) to 1T (3)
1932-33	Oxford	1G 1T (8) to 1T (3)
1933-34	Oxford	1G (5) to 1T (3)
1934-35	Cambridge	2G 1PG 1DG 4T (29) to 1DG (4)
1935-36	Drawn	No score
1936-37	Cambridge	2T (6) to 1G (5)
1937-38	Oxford	1G 4T (17) to 1DG (4)
1938-39	Cambridge	1G 1PG (8) to 2PG (6)
1939-45	*War-time series*	
1945-46	Cambridge	1G 2T (11) to 1G 1PG (8)
1946-47	Oxford	1G 1DG 2T (15) to 1G (5)
1947-48	Cambridge	2PG (6) to 0
1948-49	Oxford	1G 2DG 2T (14) to 1G 1PG (8)
1949-50	Oxford	1T (3) to 0
1950-51	Oxford	1G 1PG (8) to 0
1951-52	Oxford	2G 1T (13) to 0
1952-53	Cambridge	1PG 1T (6) to 1G (5)
1953-54	Drawn	Oxford 1PG 1T (6) Cambridge 2PG (6)
1954-55	Cambridge	1PG (3) to 0
1955-56	Oxford	1PG 2T (9) to 1G (5)
1956-57	Cambridge	1G 1PG 1DG 1T (14) to 2PG 1T (9)
1957-58	Oxford	1T (3) to 0
1958-59	Cambridge	1G 1PG 3T (17) to 1PG 1T (6)
1959-60	Oxford	3PG (9) to 1PG (3)
1960-61	Cambridge	2G 1T (13) to 0
1961-62	Cambridge	1DG 2T (9) to 1DG (3)
1962-63	Cambridge	1G 1PG 1DG 1T (14) to 1G 1PG 1DG (11)
1963-64	Cambridge	2G 1PG 2T (19) to 1G 1PG 1DG (11)
1964-65	Oxford	2G 1PG 2T (19) to 1PG 1GM (6)
1965-66	Drawn	1G (5) each
1966-67	Oxford	1G 1T (8) to 1DG 1T (6)
1967-68	Cambridge	1T 1PG (6) to 0
1968-69	Cambridge	1T 1PG 1DG (9) to 2T (6)
1969-70	Oxford	3PG (9) to 2PG (6)
1970-71	Oxford	1G 1DG 2T (14) to 1PG (3)
1971-72	Oxford	3PG 3T (21) to 1PG (3)
1972-73	Cambridge	1G 1PG 1DG 1T (16) to 2PG (6)
1973-74	Cambridge	1PG 1DG 2T (14) to 1G 2PG (12)
1974-75	Cambridge	1G 2PG 1T (16) to 5PG (15)
1975-76	Cambridge	2G 5PG 1DG 1T (34) to 3PG 1DG (12)
1976-77	Cambridge	1G 3PG (15) to 0
1977-78	Oxford	4PG 1T (16) to 2PG 1T (10)
1978-79	Cambridge	2G 3PG 1T (25) to 1PG 1T (7)
1979-80	Oxford	2PG 1DG (9) to 1PG (3)
1980-81	Cambridge	3PG 1T (13) to 3PG (9)
1981-82	Cambridge	3PG (9) to 2PG (6)
1982-83	Cambridge	3PG 1DG 2T (20) to 1G 1PG 1T (13)
1983-84	Cambridge	4PG 2T (20) to 3PG (9)
1984-85	Cambridge	4G (32) to 2PG (6)
1985-86	Oxford	1PG 1T (7) to 2PG (6)
1986-87	Oxford	3PG 2DG (15) to 1PG 1DG 1T (10)
1987-88	Cambridge	1DG 3T (15) to 2PG 1T (10)
1988-89	Oxford	2G 1DG 3T (27) to 1DG 1T (7)
1989-90	Cambridge	2G 2PG 1T (22) to 1G 1PG 1T (13)
1990-91	Oxford	2G 2PG 1DG (21) to 1G 2PG (12)
1991-92	Cambridge	2PG 1DG 2T (17) to 1DG 2T (11)
1992-93	Cambridge	1G 2PG 2DG (26) to 1PG 1DG 1T (11)
1993-94	Oxford	3PG 2DG 1T (20) to 1DG 1T (8)
1994-95	Cambridge	1G 1PG 2DG 2T (26) to 1G 2PG 1DG 1T (21)
1995-96	Cambridge	1G† 3PG 1T (21) to 1G 3PG 1DG (19)
1996-97	Cambridge	2G 2PG 1DG (23) to 1G (7)

A FITTING CLIMAX

CIS COUNTY CHAMPIONSHIP

19 April 1997, Twickenham
Cumbria 21 (1G 3PG 1T) **Somerset 13** (1PG 2T)

This was a fitting climax to the long career of Cumbria's captain, Mark Richardson. The Aspatria No 8, in his 67th appearance for the county, a record, took them to their first title since 1924 and only their second in the 108-year history of the competition.

Cumbria deserved their win and provided plenty of entertainment for the meagre crowd of 8,000. Their backs showed great resolve in defence, and possessed a sharper cutting edge.

Somerset opened the scoring when Nick Edmonds landed an early penalty, but a couple of goals from Scott and an Andrew Bell try from a tapped penalty put Cumbria ahead as half-time approached. The Somerset line-out was dominant throughout, and was the source of tries either side of the interval.

First, Chris Rees took advantage of a wayward Cumbrian throw to score at the corner. Then, from an attacking line-out at the start of the second half, Martin Rackham made a lovely two-handed catch to set up a drive from which Jason King scored. Five minutes later his opposite number Stephen Milnes finished off the move of the match with the try that proved to be the match breaker.

Cumbria: G Cook (Aspatria); D Warwick (Waterloo), P Burns (Furness), M Lynch (Wigton), S Davidson (Aspatria); M Scott (Aspatria), P Thompson (Wigton); S Irving (Aspatria), M Armstrong (Wigton), J McCune (Aspatria), A Bell (Wigton), B Atkinson (Egremont), S Milnes (Aspatria), M Richardson (Aspatria) (*capt*), S Cusack (Aspatria) *Replacements* J Cartmell (Wigton) for S Cusack (25 mins); D Johnston (Wigton for McCune (67 mins); P Cusack (Cockermouth) for Cook (70 mins); P Hancock (Aspatria) for Atkinson (72 mins)
Scorers *Tries:* Bell, Milnes *Conversion:* Scott *Penalty Goals:* Scott (3)
Somerset: M Westcott (Keynsham); D Underwood (Weston-super-Mare), D Fox (Keynsham), A Webber (Bridgwater & Albion), P Blackett (Keynsham); N Edmonds (Bridgwater & Albion), L Hirons (Keynsham); J Barnes (Bridgwater & Albion), C Rees (Bridgwater & Albion), A Harris (Bridgwater & Albion), M Rackham (Bridgwater & Albion), M Curry (Exeter), J King (Hornets), S Withey (Keynsham), M Venner (Weston-super-Mare) (*capt*)
Replacements S Bennett (Keynsham) for Fox (40 mins); B Thirlwall (Bridgwater & Albion) for Venner (40 mins); N Lloyd (Clifton) for Hirons (75 mins)
Scorers *Tries:* Rees, King *Penalty Goal:* Edmonds
Referee B Campsall (Yorkshire)

Lancashire and Gloucestershire have won the title 16 times each, Yorkshire 12, Warwickshire 10, Middlesex 8, Durham 8 (twice jointly), Devon 7 (once jointly), Kent 3 times, Hampshire, East Midlands, Cheshire, Northumberland, Cumbria (formerly Cumberland) and Cornwall twice each, Surrey twice (once jointly), and Midlands, Somerset, Leicestershire, Staffordshire and North Midlands once each.

BIG GUNS FLATTEN WASPS

SANYO CUP

24 May 1997, Twickenham
Sanyo World XV 52 (6G 2T) **Wasps 31** (4G 1PG)

The second Sanyo World Challenge – a match that pits the English League champions against a World XV – brought down the curtain on another English domestic season. Yet with the Lions in South Africa and England touring Argentina, the club champions were stripped of half-a-dozen or so of their leading players, devaluing the fixture. In future, perhaps a better time for this welcome match would be as a curtain-raiser to the season in August.

For all that, a crowd of 25,000 enjoyed seeing the likes of David Campese and Philippe Sella strutting their stuff, possibly for the last time at Twickenham. The big guns of the Invitation XV were always going to be too good for Wasps and, as expected, won comfortably against a makeshift side.

Two Fijians, Waisale Serevi and the lesser-known uncapped wing Marika Vunibaka, were the stars of the World show, scoring five tries. Bob Dwyer, the World XV's coach, was so impressed by the pair that he signed them both on three-year contracts for Leicester.

Gareth Rees, the Wasps captain, jetted in from Hong Kong where earlier in the day he had played for Canada, and set up a try for Kenny Logan, kicked the goals that made the scores 17-all at the break, and did everything possible to keep Wasps in the match.

Wasps: J Ufton; S Roiser, L Scrase, M Hall, K Logan; G Rees (*capt*), M Wood; W Green, S Mitchell, A Black, D Cronin, A Reed, M Greenwood, P Scrivener, M White *Replacements* K Dunn for Green (40 mins); A James for Scrase (45 mins); R Kinsey for Reed (51 mins); M Griffiths for Mitchell (61 mins); J Worsley for Cronin (61 mins); M Skinner for Ufton (67 mins); D Cronin for James (71 mins)
Scorers *Tries:* Logan (2), Roiser, White *Conversions:* Rees (4) *Penalty Goal:* Rees
Sanyo World XV: S Viars (France); D I Campese (Australia), P Sella (France) (*capt*), L Arbizu (Argentina), E J Rush (New Zealand); W Serevi (Fiji), G T M Bachop (New Zealand); D F Theron (South Africa), J Dalton (South Africa), I S Swart (South Africa), J J Strydom (South Africa), O Roumat (France), V Ofahengaue (Australia), J W Joseph (New Zealand), J F Pienaar (South Africa) *Replacements* F J van Heerden (South Africa) for Strydom (26 mins); B W Redpath (Scotland) for Bachop (41 mins); J-M Gonzalez (France) for Dalton (41 mins); Y Yoshida (Japan) for Campese (41 mins); M Vunibaka (Fiji) for Rush (41 mins); N J Popplewell (Ireland) for Swart (54 mins); E J Rush (New Zealand) for Pienaar (62 mins); J J Strydom (South Africa) for Roumat (67 mins)
Scorers *Tries:* Serevi (3), Vunibaka (2), Campese, Ofahengaue, Sella
Conversions: Viars (6)
Referee D Méné (France)
Previous Result 1996 Leicester 31, Sanyo World XV 40

BAA-BAAS SCOOP JACKPOT

MIDDLESEX SEVENS

17 May 1997, Twickenham
Barbarians 57 (6G 3T) Saracens 5 (1T)

For the first time, the organisers of this annual event offered prize money to the winning side. It was the Barbarians, arguably the last of the true-blue amateurs in a sea of professionalism, who scooped the £50,000 jackpot. Sadly, only 19,000 spectators – a sharp contrast to the 60,000-odd who turned out to see Wigan win in 1996 – witnessed the guest side play some of the most sparkling sevens ever seen at Twickenham.

The club had last entered the Middlesex event in 1934 when they won with an all-international seven drawn from the Home Unions. The class of '97 was more cosmopolitan and included four Fijians, one of whom – Marika Vunibaka – had been one of the successes of their World Cup-winning squad in March. At Twickenham, he again showed his class at the shortened game, collecting ten tries including three hat-tricks in the tournament.

RESULTS
Sixth round: London Scottish 17, Wasps 12; Richmond 24, Sale 17; Blackheath 33, Leicester 28; Barbarians 34, Orrell 0; South American Barbarians 38, Guildford & Godalming 5; Harlequins 26, Oxford University 14; Saracens 29, Bath 5; Italy 19, Bristol 12
Seventh round: London Scottish 38, Richmond 7; Barbarians 42, Blackheath 7; South American Barbarians 33, Harlequins 14; Saracens 29, Italy 14
Semi-finals: Barbarians 27, London Scottish 7; Saracens 19, South American Barbarians 14 (aet)
Final: Barbarians 57, Saracens 5

Teams in the final
Barbarians: L Koroi, I Maraiwai, M Vunibaka, D Scully (*capt*); A Roxburgh, D Eves, J Tuikabe *Replacements* O Williams for Roxburgh; A Hepher for Maraiwai; B Johnson for Vunibaka
Scorers *Tries:* Vunibaka (3), Tuikabe (2), Eves, Maraiwai, Roxburgh, Johnson *Conversions:* Scully (5), Hepher
Saracens: M Ebongalame, K Sorrell, S Ravenscroft, P Friel; G Clark (*capt*), K Chesney, B Sternham *Replacements* H van Niekerk for Ebongalame; C Davis for Sorrell; S Gregory for Chesney
Scorers *Try:* van Niekerk
Referee R C Rees (London Society)

Harlequins have won the title 13 times, Richmond 9 (including one by their second VII), London Welsh 8, London Scottish 7, St Mary's Hospital and Loughborough Colleges 5 each, Rosslyn Park and Wasps 4 each, Barbarians, Blackheath and St Luke's College (now Exeter University) twice, Sale, Met Police, Cardiff, Cambridge University, Notts (now Nottingham), Heriot's FP, Stewart's-Melville FP, Western Samoa, Bath, Leicester and Wigan once each.

ARMY TAKE BOWL

WILLIS CORROON INTER-SERVICES TOURNAMENT
1997

With the Services announcing that for the first time points difference would determine the title should a tie occur, the Inter-Services tournament was not decided until the final whistle of the final match. In the event the calculators were not required, for the RAF and the Royal Navy could only draw on the last afternoon of the competition. The soldiers therefore, led once again from hooker by Julian Brammer, took the Willis Corroon Bowl for the first time since 1990.

There were 21,000 present – the best crowd since 1948 – to see the Army beat the Navy in the opening match. Scotland's Rob Wainwright and Mattie Stewart strengthened the winner's forwards against a very experienced Navy pack. Against the RAF, however, the Army had to put their celebrations on hold after surrendering a 25-10 interval advantage. The flying Rory Underwood crossed for a try as the RAF established a 35-28 lead in the second half, before replacement John Murley scored a late try for the Army with virtually his first touch of the ball and Howard Graham converted to tie the match.

The RAF needed a victory margin of three or more points in their last match to win the championship. But the Navy's pack brought the airmen down to earth in the forward exchanges and only a late try by Underwood (equalling the Inter-Services appearance record) and conversion by Steve Lazenby levelled the scores for the RAF's second draw of the series.

RESULTS

12 April, Twickenham Army 18, Royal Navy 16
16 April, Twickenham Army 35, Royal Air Force 35
23 April, Twickenham Royal Navy 24, Royal Air Force 24

FINAL TABLE

	P	W	D	L	F	A	Pts
Army	2	1	1	0	53	51	3
RAF	2	0	2	0	59	59	2
Navy	2	0	1	1	40	42	1

The Army have won the tournament 29 times, The Royal Navy 17 times and the Royal Air Force 14 times. The Army and the Royal Air Force have shared it on 2 occassions and there have been 10 triple ties.

A GREAT DAY OUT

NPI JUNIOR & INTERMEDIATE CUPS 1996-97

In 1996-97, there was a new sponsor and a new competition for the
clubs who form the backbone of the English game. Previously, the
Junior Clubs Knock-out final for the Pilkington Shield had been
staged as a curtain-raiser to the RFU Cup final. With increasing
demand for tickets for the main event, however, it was felt more
appropriate to give the supporters of the successful smaller clubs a
day out of their own.

The move was a great success. More than 10,000 spectators from
four clubs turned out at Twickenham to see the finals of two
competitions sponsored by NPI. Harpenden took the Junior Cup
and Thanet Wanderers were the first winners of the Intermediate
Cup – a new competition designed to bridge the gap for clubs that
fail to qualify for either the senior or junior cups.

3 May 1997, Twickenham
Harpenden 34 (4G 2PG)   **Crewe Nantwich 31** (2G 3PG 1DG 1T) –
after extra time

Harpenden: T Baxter; A Phillips, S Smith, D Talbot, N Sinfield; D Ford,
R Humphrey; D Craddock, D Collier, D Alpert, D Foster, D Horsley, T Stanford,
D Phillips (*capt*), A McPherson *Replacements* A Kiff for Alpert (32 mins);
I Hamilton for A Phillips (80 mins); J Cartmell for Ford (90 mins); P Butler for
Sinfield (97 mins)
Scorers *Tries:* Baxter (2), Talbot, Smith   *Conversions:* Ford (4)
Penalty Goals: Ford (2)
Crewe & Nantwich: S Wall; P Harrison, J Nicholls, A Manicom, M Pemberton;
C Widdowson, S MacKeen; A Pemberton, N Tilley, S Taylor, G Davies, R Harper
(*capt*), J Charlesworth, A McGarrigle, S Hayter *Replacements* M Morgan for
McGarrigle (40 mins); R Thomas for Manicom (54 mins); L Gray for Harrison
(68 mins); J Forster for MacKeen (79 mins)
Scorers *Tries:* McGarrigle, Morgan, Nicholls   *Conversions:* Wall (2)
Penalty Goals: Wall (3)   *Dropped Goal:* Nicholls
Referee S Savage (North Midlands)

3 May 1997, Twickenham
Thanet Wanderers 21 (1G 3PG 1T) **Doncaster 13** (1G 2PG)

Thanet Wanderers: G Redmond; E Stokes, P Macaulay, M Coyne, M Meyer;
G Harper, J Ward; B Guild, C Smith, T Carlier (*capt*), P Hughes, G Hingley,
T Michael, D Langley, C Marson *Replacements* M Pond for Stokes (40 mins);
S Harris for Michael (61 mins)
Scorers *Tries:* Coyne, Meyer   *Conversion:* Redmond   *Penalty Goals:* Redmond (3)
Doncaster: J Ellis; D E Fairclough, D S Fairclough (*capt*), S Manson,
R Harrison; P Matthews, A Pascoe; D Bosworth, N Waddington, C Yemm,
M Bailey, K Westgarth, R Senior, M Longworth, D Senior *Replacement* D Clarke
for Westgarth (46 mins)
Scorers *Try:* Ellis   *Conversion:* D S Fairclough   *Penalty Goals:* D S Fairclough (2)

GRASS ROOTS INVESTMENT REQUIRED

STUDENT RUGBY 1996-97
Harry Townsend

The 1996 Student World Cup was a travesty for English student rugby. 27 of the original 37 man 'long squad' withdrew for various reasons; and although the additional fifteen players selected at short notice benefited immensely from the experience, England were one of only four countries that failed to make the quarter-finals. In contrast, winners France took the competition so seriously that they withdrew six players from their senior squad to tour Argentina.

If there is another Student World Cup, these problems must be addressed. 1997 Lions Shaw, Dallaglio, Hill, Healey and Stimpson withdrew; so did England tourists Gomarsall, King, Allan and Greenstock. But the re-jigged squad included current (new) England tourists Yates, Grewcock, Catling and Rees; whilst Winters, Kay, Shaw and Zaltzman made the Under-21 tour to Australia. All were thrust forward at short notice, demonstrating that student rugby is an immense reservoir of talent: more than 10,000 players who need to be kept within the game.

Two very significant steps have been taken this season. First, the first four RUSLOs (Rugby Union Student Liaison Officers) are in post. Recently retired and with vast rugby experience these officers, such as former international referee Mike Titcombe, receive little more than their expenses as each works with three or four IHEs in their area to assist with the organisation of playing, coaching, refereeing and administration: helping student clubs to get their act together. They cover 14 IHEs in total: if money was available, the remaining 116 IHEs could be similarly covered.

Second, we must remember that present students are the club stalwarts of the future; the stars will be well looked after. So more enjoyable and competitive rugby within the peer group is needed: and this season, after the completion of the leagues in the first term, teams qualified for one of three knock-out competitions. The Championship, Shield and Plate each catered for 32 teams, so that there was meaningful competition through the second term.

Representative matches: England Students 14, France Students 25 (Grange Road, Cambridge); Wales Students 20, England Students 46 (Pontypridd); Scottish Universities 12, Welsh Universities 67 (Peffermill); English Universities 39, Scottish Universities 13 (Rosslyn Park); Welsh Universities 11, Irish Universities 19 (Cardiff Institute); Irish Universities 38, English Universities 14

(Trinity College, Dublin); Scottish Universities 5, Irish Universities 27 (Peffermill); Welsh Universities 28, English Universities 17 (Cardiff Institute); England Students Under-21s 27, Irish Exiles Under-21s 17 (Newbury); England Students Under-21s 48, Combined Services Under-21s 16 (Twickenham); Scottish Universities Under-19s 24, Edinburgh Under-20s Development XV 27 (Meggetland)

BRITISH UNIVERSITIES SPORTS ASSOCIATION CHAMPIONSHIP 1996-97
Sponsored by Halifax

19 March, Twickenham
Brunel University College 9 (3PG)   **Loughborough 8** (1PG 1T)

Brunel University College, who had taken the title two years before under the name of West London Institute, returned to Twickenham to meet 25-times champions Loughborough, whose cupboard had been bare since the 'universitisation' of more than 70 IHEs four years ago.

Loughborough, who had lost 6-3 in a penalty shoot-out to Cardiff Institute the previous year, returned with the mature influence of former England B cap Alan Buzza in the centre.

Buzza had scored every point, including a last-minute try and conversion, in their quarter-final victory over dark horses Trinity College Carmarthen. Success against Cardiff Institute 26-23 in the semi-final, a reversal of the 1996 final result, owed a similar debt to the kicking of Stuart Moffatt.

Brunel UC had reached the final without problems, winning their five League matches 287-32 and then defeating West of England, UMDS, Birmingham (League victors over Loughborough) and dark horses Wolverhampton 41-3 in the other semi-final with England Students scrum-half Ben Harvey scoring 31 points.

'Home' team Brunel UC, living on the doorstep in Isleworth, played to a dour and uncompromising pattern of hard tackling, line-out dominance through England Student locks Gillies and Zaltzman, and driving rucks and mauls. Current student Alex King must have been itching to take part.

Loughborough, the more expansive side, were deprived of a late first-half try when England Under-21 wing Nick Miller brushed the corner flag as he dived over; but their more adventurous approach was rewarded when Moffatt, a rugby and cricket scholarship freshman, scored the only try of the match mid-way through the second half, when he sliced through from halfway to add to his penalty success and take the lead.

However, Harvey secured the title for Brunel UC with his third successful penalty five minutes from time.

Brunel University College: D Dunlop; P Perry, M Deane, P Davies, R Francis; R Ballard, B Harvey; S Turner, S Rodgers, I Peel, D Zaltzman, C Gillies, D Muckalt (*capt*), P Volley, C Palmer *Replacements* D Alexopolous for Turner (25 mins), C Tytherleigh for Rodgers (40 mins), P Morgan for Perry (57 mins)
Scorer *Penalty Goals:* Harvey (3)
Loughborough University: S Moffatt; N Miller, S Brocklehurst, A Buzza, N Malone, N Osman (*capt*), A Dart; R Tarrant, R Protherough, E Webb, W Fuller, R White, J Beardshaw, R Winters, G Webster *Replacement* S Beaufoy for Tarrant (50 mins)
Scorer *Penalty Goal:* Moffatt *Try:* Moffatt
Referee A Rowden (Berkshire)

Second XV final: Cardiff Institute 21, Durham 12
Third XV final: Manchester 24, Durham 12

BUSA CHAMPIONSHIPS
Sponsored by Halifax
Knock-out rounds
1st play-off round: Edinburgh 15, Hull 5; Harper Adams 7, Wolverhampton 27; Nene 10, Chichester 22; Bath 24, UW Swansea 34; Chester 3, Birmingham 55; Northumbria 46, Heriot Watt 12; UMDS 16, Luton 15; Brunel UC 48, West of England 10; Newcastle 36, Manchester 13; Nottingham 39, St Mary's Hosp 13; Cardiff Inst 111, Reading 0; Exeter 103, Canterbury/Christchurch 0; Durham 35, Liverpool 5; Loughborough 96, UCL 0; Bristol 17, Trinith 27; Kent 3, St Mary's UC 43
2nd play-off round: Edinburgh 6, Wolverhampton 26; Chichester 10, UW Swansea 25; Birmingham 23, Northumbria 8; Brunel UC w/o UMDS; Newcastle 26, Nottingham 10; Cardiff Inst 99, Exeter 5; Durham 10, Loughborough 24; Trinity 9, St Mary's UC 5
Quarter-finals: Wolverhampton 19, UW Swansea 13; Birmingham 0, Brunel UC 30; Newcastle 16, Cardiff Inst 55; Loughborough 19, Trinith 17
Semi-finals: Brunel UC 41, Wolverhampton 3; Cardiff Inst 23, Loughborough 26
Final: Brunel UC 9, Loughborough 8
Loughborough have won the title 25 times, Durham 8, Liverpool and Swansea 7, Bristol 5, Cardiff and Manchester 4, Bangor, Brunel University College (West London Institute) and UWIST 2, Aberystwyth, Birmingham, Leeds, Newcastle, Northumbria and Cardiff Institute once each.

BUSA SHIELD
Final: Cardiff Medics 19, Leeds 11

BUSA PLATE
Final: Teeside 17, Plymouth 18

ENGLISH UNIVERSITIES INTER-DIVISIONAL TOURNAMENT
11 December 1996, Nottingham RFC
Final: North 27, South West 15

BUSA SEVEN-A-SIDE TOURNAMENT
20 April 1997, Bristol University
Semi-finals: Bristol 43, Glamorgan 7; Exeter 7, Brunel UC 26
Final: Brunel UC 37, Bristol 12

SCOTTISH UNIVERSITIES SEVEN-A-SIDE TOURNAMENT
7 May 1997, Glasgow University
5/6 place play-off: Strathclyde 45, Abertay 17
3/4 place play off: Heriot Watt 29, St Andrews 24
Final: Dundee 19, Glasgow 17

ENGLAND'S CLEAN SWEEP

SCHOOLS RUGBY 1996-97
Brendan Gallagher *Daily Telegraph*

England 18 Group claimed their third junior Grand Slam in four years under the coaching of Geoff Wappett but left it late in their final game against Wales, an injury-time dropped goal from fly-half John Wilkinson finally bringing home the spoils. It was a fine effort from England who fielded an unusually young team; and after the rigours of a summer tour of Australia. With so many capped players to select from, they threaten to be truly formidable opposition this season.

Domestically Colston's Collegiate again dominated the scene in England, winning a third consecutive *Daily Mail* Under-18 Cup by defeating a spirited Kirkham GS 23-12 at Twickenham. John Fisher, Purley, won the prestigious Open title at the Shell Rosslyn Park National Schools Sevens, beating Durham 28-24 in an entertaining final. RGS High Wycombe successfully defended their Under-15 title by defeating Wellington 29-13. In Scotland, Gala Academy defeated hot favourites Dundee HS 8-7 to win the Bank of Scotland Cup at Meggetland and in Ireland Belfast Royal Academy overcame Royal Belfast Academical Institution 12-0 in the Ulster Schools Cup final at Ravenhill. Favourites Cowbridge CS edged home 8-6 against Brynteg CS to win the Welsh Schools Cup at Cardiff Arms Park.

MATCH DETAILS

21 December 1996, Foix

FRANCE 42   SCOTLAND 8
SCOTLAND *Try:* Ruthven   *Penalty Goal:* Thomson

4 January 1997, Murrayfield

SCOTLAND 15   WALES 17
SCOTLAND *Tries:* Kennedy, Cockburn   *Conversion:* Ruthven
Penalty Goal: Ruthven
WALES *Tries:* Cooper (2), Higgins   *Conversion:* Bowen

14 February 1997, Nimes

FRANCE 23   WALES 15
FRANCE *Tries:* Fabardil, Genin   *Pens:* Gelez (2), Skrela   *Conversions:* Gelez (2)
WALES *Tries:* Chiffi, Landry   *Conversion:* Bowen   *Penalty Goal:* Bowen

21 March 1997, Twickenham

ENGLAND 20   FRANCE 10
Tries: Brading, Best   *Conversions:* Wilkinson (2)   *Penalty Goals:* Wilkinson (2)

22 March 1997, Murrayfield

SCOTLAND 15   JAPAN 43
SCOTLAND *Tries:* Milne (2), Ruthven

29 March 1997, Lansdowne Road

IRELAND 9   ENGLAND 16
ENGLAND *Tries:* Best, Brading   *Penalty Goals:* Wilkinson
IRELAND *Penalty Goals:* McCombe (3)

5 April 1997, Maesteg

WALES 25   IRELAND 27
WALES *Tries:* Rogers (2), Rees, Williams   *Conversion:* Bowen   *Penalty Goal:* Bowen
IRELAND *Tries:* Brady, McCarey, Hughes   *Penalty Goals:* O'Driscoll (4)

9 April 1996, Preston Grasshoppers

ENGLAND 55   SCOTLAND 18
ENGLAND *Tries:* Roques (2), Tindall (2), Sheridan, Mears, Wilkinson,
Dawson   *Conversions:* Roques (6)   *Penalty Goal:* Wilkinson
SCOTLAND *Tries:* Carnochan, Ruthven   *Conversion:* Ruthven
Penalty Goals: Ruthven (2)
Referee: Mr P Swayne (Ireland)

12 April 1997, Ayr

SCOTLAND 11   IRELAND 48
SCOTLAND *Try:* Kennedy   *Penalty Goal:* Lind   *Dropped Goal:* Adamson
IRELAND *Tries:* Hughes (2), Lloyd, O'Callaghan, Hanlon, Dowling, O'Driscoll
Conversions: O'Driscoll (5)   *Penalty Goal:* O'Driscoll

12 April 1997, Narberth

WALES 17   ENGLAND 18
WALES *Tries:* Rogers, Cooper, R Williams   *Conversion:* Bowen
ENGLAND *Tries:* Tindall (2)   *Conversion:* Wilkinson   *Penalty Goal:*
Wilkinson   *Dropped Goal:* Wilkinson

ENGLAND

Full-back: I Balshaw (Stonyhurst) *F, I, S*; L Best (Durham) *W*
Threequarters: L Best (Durham) *F, I, S*; P Greenaway (Colston's) *S* (R), *W*;
T Southall (Poynton HS) *F, S*; M Tindall (QEGS Wakefield) *F* (R), *I, S, W*, S Brading
(Bedford) *F, I, S, W*; T May (Tonbridge) *F, I, W*; S Amor (Hampton) *W* (R)
Half-backs: J Wilkinson (Lord Wandsworth) *F, I, S, W*; D Smaje (RGS High
Wycombe) *F*; J Grindal (King Henry VIII, Coventry) *I, S, W*
Forwards: D Flatman (Dulwich College) *F, I, S, W*; A Hubbleday (King Edward VII,
Five Ways) *F*; L Mears (Colston's Collegiate) *I, S, W*; J Dawson (Dulwich College) *F, I,
S, W*; R Siveter (Colston's Collegiate) *S* (R); A Sheridan (Dulwich College) *F, I, S, W*;

S Borthwick (Hutton GS) *F, I, S, W*; A Roques (Sevenoaks) *F, I, S*; McCarrick
(Sevenoaks) *F, I, S, W*; A Beattie (Hampton) *F, I, S, W*; A Sanderson (Kirkham GS) *I*;
D Giles (Kirkham GS) *S* (R); S Williams (Colston's Collegiate *W* (R)
S Roques captained against France, Ireland and Scotland; J Wilkinson captained against Wales.

SCOTLAND

Full-back: B Ruthven (Earlston HS) *F, I* (R); P Cumming (Kelvinside Academy)
W, J, E, I
Threequarters: C Phillip (Edinburgh Academy) *F, W*; C Milne (Dundee HS) *F, W, J,
E, I*; C Carnochan (Dollar Academy) *F, W, J, E, I*; R Cooke (Glenalmond) *J, E, I*;
C Begg (Dollar Academy) *I* (R); P Hudson (Dollar Academy) *W, J, E*, I; B Aitchison
(Galashiels Academy) *J* (S), *E* (R); P Cumming (Kelvinside) *F*
Half-backs: J Thomson (Edinburgh Academy) *F*; D Adamson (Dollar Academy) *I*,
B Ruthven (Earlston HS) *W, J, E*; S Shiel (Earlston HS) *F* (R), *W*; S Grant (Heriot's) *F,
J, E, I*
Forwards: M Welch (Dunfermline HS) *F, W, J, E, I*, S McCready (Earlston HS) *W* (R);
W Mitchell (Earlston HS) *F, W, J, E*; A McLean (Heriot's) *E* (R), *I*; D MacNeill (Dollar
Academy) *I* (R); I Mackay (Morrison's Academy) *F*; B Douglas (Heriot's) *F* (S), *W, J,
E, I*; A Russell (Merchiston Castle) *F, W, J, E, I*; A Kennedy (Dundee HS) *F, W, J, E, I*;
J Gay (Dundee HS) *J, E*; T Parratt (Dundee HS) *F, W* (R), *J, E, I*; D Ingleby (Loretto)
W; P Cockburn (Galashiels Academy) *F, W, J, E, I*; D MacFadyen (Edinburgh Academy)
F (S), *W, J* (R); G Lind (Stewart's Melville) *F, E* (R), *I*; D Matheson (Strathallan) *I* (R)
*T Parratt captained the team against France, Japan, England and Ireland; B Ruthven
captained against Wales.*

IRELAND

Full-back: C Dowling (St Michael's College) *E, S, W*
Threequarters: D Wilmott (Coleraine AI) *E, W, S*; S Moore (Belvedere College) *E, W,
S*; B O'Driscoll (Blackrock College) *E, W, S*; P Magee (Royal School Dungannon) *S* (R);
D McCombe (Royal Belfast AI) *E*; S Conway (Crescent College) *W, S*; B McCracken
(Campbell College) *S* (R)
Half-backs: A Dunne (Belvedere College) *E, W, S*; C Scally (Blackrock College) *E*;
B Quigley (Clongowes College) *E* (R), *W, S*; N Wilson (Campbell College) *S* (R)
Forwards: N Brady (Royal School Dungannon) *E W, S*; D Blaney (Terenure College)
E, W, S; P Hanlon (CBC Cork) *E, W, S*; S McCullough (Clongowes Wood) *W* (R);
A O'Brien (Terenure College) *S* (R); D O'Callaghan (CBE Cork) *E, W, S*; P Callanan
(Clongowes College) *E* (R), *W*; G Lloyd (St Mary's College) *E, W* (R), *S*; N Coughlan
(Blackrock College) *E, W, S*; A Holmes (Royal School Dungannon) *E, W, S*; C McCarey
(Royal Belfast Academy) *E, W, S*
S Moore captained Ireland in all three games.

WALES

Full-back: C Rees (Llandovery College) *I, E*; C Morgan (Hawthorn) *S, F*
Threequarters: D Rogers (Ysgol Strade) *I, F, E*; R Williams (Cowbridge CS) *I, S, F, E*;
J Evans (Gowerton CS) *I, F, E*; C Landry (Pontypool College) *I, S, F, E*; I Higgins
(Whitchurch) *S*, D Price (Cross Keys) *S*
Half-backs: G Bowen (Neath College) *I, S, F, E*; G Cooper (Pencoed CS) *I, S, F, E*; A
Jenkins (Neath College) *E* (R)
Forwards: L Rees (Tregib) *S*; E Rees (Cowbridge CS) *I, F, E*, G Williams (Brynteg
CS) *I, S, F, E*; M Troake (Barry Boys) *I, S, F, E*; D Evans (Neath College) *I* (R); C
Hawkins (Gowerton CS) *I, E*; G Powell (Lllandovery College) *I, E*; S Carnell (Pontypool
College) *S*; A Jones (Olchfa CS) *I, F, E*; S Morgan (Neath College) *I, S, F, E*; A Chiffi
(Greenhill CS) *I, S, F, E*; C Hughes (Amman Valley CS) *I, S, E*; P Williams (Olchfa
CS) *I, S, F*; M Prosser (Olchfa CS) *F*; N Howard (Cowbridge) *E*; P Wheeler (Pencoed)
E (R)
*C Hughes was captain against Ireland and Scotland; G Williams captained against England
and France.*

KEEP YOUTH RUGBY IN THE PUBLIC EYE

COLTS AND YOUTH RUGBY 1996-97
Harry Townsend

One usually searches in vain for news of youth rugby: even international matches scarcely make the results columns, or merit television space. Even in rugby magazines, we can be excused for thinking that rugby is confined to the few elite teams that provoke the headlines. Yet youth is the lifeblood of the game; and money pumped into the development and publicising of junior rugby in the constituent bodies, and the recruitment and training of more YDOs, coaches and referees, is the fuel that drives the sports pages of the national press. The RFU is considering increased investment at this level; I applaud it, but it must come quickly.

Ireland, Wales and Scotland considered it money well spent to take 26-man squads to Argentina for the FIRA Youth Tournament. Wales, runners-up in 1996, clinched third place by beating debutants Ireland; Argentina retained the championship by beating France; while Scotland fell to South Africa at the final hurdle. More than 20 countries took part.

The Youth Team of the Year was unquestionably Pontypridd. Winning all 25 matches (1073-139) they defeated Bridgend 33-24 in the Welsh Youth Cup final at Cardiff Arms Park and beat Treherbert 39-3 to win the Rhondda and East Glamorgan District Cup. Matthew Rowlands scored 38 tries in 17 matches; seven players were capped. Other contenders included Cheltenham and Coventry, who are investing heavily in Youth rugby.

The following players took part in Youth/Colts international matches. Countries played against are shown after the name.
Abbreviations: *A* – Argentina, *C* – Canada, *E* – England, *F* – France, *I* – Ireland, *It* – Italy, *J* – Japan High Schools, *P* – Portugal, *Ru* – Russia, *S* – Scotland, *SA* – South Africa, *Sp* – Spain, *W* – Wales, *WS* – Welsh Schools, (R) – Replacement.

ENGLAND
Colts
Full-backs: R Hartley (Newcastle Falcons) *S, W, F*; R Jackson (Bedford) *W, F*
Threequarters: B Cohen (Northampton) *S, W, F*; S Brocklehurst (Loughborough U) *S*; J Pritchard (Bath) *S, W, F*; L Lloyd (Leicester Tigers) *S*; P Greaves (Northampton) *W, F*; G Samuels (Bath) *F* (R)
Half-backs: J Brown (Coventry) *S, W, F*; P Richards (London Irish) *S, W, F*; R Pellow (Bath) *S* (R)
Forwards: S Trethewey (Devonport Services) *S, W, F*; A Long (Bath) *S, W, F*; E Webb (Loughborough U) *S*; J Winterbottom (Wasps) *S, W, F*; T Butler (Leicester Tigers) *S, W, F*; L Moody (Leicester Tigers) *S, W, F*; P Ogilvie (Saracens) *S, W, F*; P Seymour (Harrogate) *S* (R), *W, F*; R Beattie (Newcastle Falcons) *S* (R), *W* (R); A Kershaw (London Irish) *F* (R)
Long was captain in all three matches.

IRELAND
Under-18s
Full-back: A Morrissey (Highfield) *W, S*
Threequarters: R O'Donovan (Cobb) *W, S*; A Considine (Ennis) *W, S*; S Horgan (Drogheda) *W, S*; M Cronin (Cobb) *S* (R); D Caughey (Malone) *S* (R); A Bell (Malone) *W, S*
Half-backs: M McHugh (Drogheda) *W, S*; S Cahill (Portadown) *W, S*; D Dalton (Youthall) *S* (R)
Forwards: N Foxe (Kilkenny) *W* (R), *S*; M Mulhaire (Thurles) *W, S* (R); P Whately (Dundalk) *W*; G Pusco (Barnhall) *W, S*; D Marmion (Dundalk) *W, S*; D Broughall (Cill Dara) *W, S*; J P Walsh (Westport) *W*; E Daly (Naas) *W, S*; S Maddigan (Shannon) *W, S* (R); D Murray (Cork Con.) *W* (R), *S*; D Quinn (Drogheda) *W* (R), *S*; D O'Kane (Portadown) *S*; D Madden (Old Christians) *S* (R); A Bohane (Highfield) *S* (R)
McHugh was captain in both matches.

FIRA Tournament
Full-backs: T Keating (Blackrock College) *P, S*; G McCullough (RBAI) *P, A, W*
Threequarters: D Nolan (Greystones) *P, W*; R Wallace (Dublin U) *P, W*; M Price (Blackrock College) *P, S, A*; K Hartigan (Garryowen) *P* (R), *S, A, W*; J Davis (Dungannon) *S, A, W*; D Quinlan (Blackrock College) *S, A*
Half-backs: B Cunningham (Dublin U) *P, W*; I Knox (Instonians) *P, S, A*; G Murphy (Naas) *P* (R), *S, A*; K Becker (St Michael's College) *W*
Forwards: S Keane (Sunday's Well) *P, A*; H Byrne (Tullow) *P, W*; E Scullion (Ballymena) *P, A*; R Casey (Blackrock College) *P, S, A*; B Dineth (Cistercian College, Roscrea) *P, A, W*; S Kennedy (London Irish) *P, S, A*; J Hogan (Lansdowne) *P, W*; R Neville (Old Crescent) *P, W*; L Cullen (Blackrock College) *P* (R), *S, A, W*; S Best (Newcastle) *P* (R), *S, W*; M Haslett (Belfast Royal Academy) *S, W*; S Elkinson (Terenure College) *S, A*; M O'Driscoll (UCD) *S, A, W*; R Hussey (Lansdowne) *S*
Cunningham was captain against Portugal; Cullen against Scotland, Argentina and Wales.

SCOTLAND
Under-18s
Full-backs: T Purves (Henley) *Sp, J, I, W*; K Davidson (Langholm), *I, W*; G McIntyre (Heriot's FP) *I* (R), *W*
Threequarters: D Donaldson *W* (R); C Brown (East Fell) *Sp*; A Raistrick (Watsonians) *J*; A Gibbon (Cartha Queen's Park) *Sp, J, I, W*; S McAllister (Stirling County) *Sp, J, I, W*; I McInroy (Garnock) *Sp, J, I, W*
Half-backs: C Duck (Stewartry) *Sp, J, I*; F Kennedy (Stirling County) *Sp, J, I*; R Laing (Stewart's Melville FP) *I* (R), *W*
Forwards: D Gillan (Gala) *Sp, J*; A Jacobsen (Preston Lodge FP) *J, I, W*; A Milne (Leicester) *W*; J Henderson (Jed Thistle) *Sp, J, I*; S Linden (Moray), *W*; R Mathieson (Colston) *Sp*; K Dickinson (Dunfermline/Rosyth) *J* (R), *I, W*; D Sumner (Preston Lodge) *Sp, J, W*; R Tod (Langholm) *Sp* (R), *J* (R), *I*; A Ness (Aberdeen U) *Sp, J, I, W*; D Landels (Hawick Wanderers) *Sp, J*; R Forbes (Millfield) *Sp, J, I, W*; A Stevenson (Hawick PSA) *I*; S Taylor (Stirling County) *I* (R), *W*; W Morgan (Gordonians) *SP, J, I*; C Capaldi (Stewart's Melville FP) *W*
Henderson was captain against Spain, Japan High Schools and Ireland; Ness against Wales.

Under-19s
The following team played against England:
Full-back: K Davidson (Langholm)
Threequarters: J Philip (London Scottish); M Di Rollo (Watsonians); A Dickson (Selkirk); S Walker (Heriot's FP)
Half-backs: G Ross (Heriot's FP), C Black (Edinburgh Acad.)

Forwards: c Smith (Berwick); A Mitchell (Mackie Academy FP); G Hoyle
(Aberdeen GSFP); J White (Watsonians); J Patton (Blackheath); T Stephens
(Stewart's Melville); S Pearman (Gloucester); S Taylor (Stirling County)
White was captain.

FIRA Tournament
Full-backs: J Davidson (Grangemouth) *P*; I McKerrow (Edinburgh Acad.) *P, I, It,
SA*
Threequarters: H Boyd (Boroughmuir) *P, I, It, SA*; A Dickson (Selkirk) *I*;
M Di Rollo (Watsonians) *P, It, SA*; R Haddow (Harrogate) *P* (R); C Murray
(Hawick) *P, It, SA*; J Philip (London Scottish) *I, It*
Half-backs: C Paterson (Gala) *P, I, It* (R), *SA*; G Ross (Heriot's FP) *P* (R), *I, It,
SA*; C Black (Edinburgh Acad.) *I, SA* (R); R Chrystie (Hawick Linden) *P, It, SA*
Forwards: C Buchanan (Watsonians) *P*; G Hoyle (Aberdeen GSFP) *I, It, SA*;
A Milne (Macclesfield) *P*; C Smith (Berwick) *I, It, SA*; S Linden (Gordonstoun) *P,
SA* (R); A Mitchell (Mackie Acad. FP) *I, It, SA*; J White (Watsonians) *P, I, It, SA*;
T Boyd (Glasgow Southern) *P, I, SA* (R); J Patton (Blackheath) *P* (R), *It, SA*;
C Capaldi (Stewart's Melville) *P, It, SA*; S Pearman (Gloucester) *I*; G Howieson
(Glasgow Southern) *P, I*; T Stephens (Stewart's Melville) *P, It, SA*; S Taylor
(Stirling County) *I, It, SA*
White was captain in all four matches.

WALES
Under-18s
Full-back: H Rees (Pencoed) *WS, I, S*
Threequarters: L Faulkener (Newport), *WS, I*; P Davies (Pontyberem) *WS, I, S*;
M J Watkins (Pontllanfraith) *WS, I, S*; M Jones (Builth Wells) *WS, I, S*; E Davies
(Carmarthen Quins) *I* (R), *S*; J Bowd (Abertillery) *S* (R); D Davies (Llanelli) *S*
(R)
Half-backs: R Davies (London Welsh) *WS, I, S*; T Richards (Dunvant) *WS, I, S*
(R); E Lewsay (Harlequins) *S*
Forwards: R Mills (Rhyader) *WS, I, S*; D Evans (Llanelli Wanderers) *WS, I* (R);
D Jones (Llanelli Wanderers) *WS, I, S*; R Bowen (Abertillery) *WS, I, S*; M Morgan
(Cardigan) *WS, I, S*; J Stenner (Cornelly/Kenfig Hill) *WS, I, S* (R); R Lewis
(Mumbles) *WS, I, S*; N Bonner-Evans (Llanelli Wanderers) *WS, S*; D Parker
(Newport) *WS* (R), *S* (R); D Bowles (Llanelli Wanderers) *WS* (R), *I*(R);
D Simons (Rumney) *I, S*; R Jones (Nantymoel) *I, S*; O Brace (Tenby) *I* (R); K
Tamplin (Crynant) *I* (R)
Watkins was captain against Welsh Schools and Ireland; Bonner-Evans against Scotland.

Under-19s
Full-backs: D Jones (Bridgend) *C*; M Williams (Cardiff) *E*
Threequarters: G Thomas (Llanelli) *C, F, E*; D Hawkins (Neath) *C, F, E*; S Ward
(Bath) *C, E*; M Giraud (London Welsh) *C*; S Winn (Bridgend) *F*; J Young (Neath)
F; S Greenaway (Bridgend) *E*
Half-backs: S Jones (Llanelli) *C, F, E* (R); M Kehoe (Briegend) *C*; S Daniel
(Waunarlwydd) *C* (R), *E* (R); T Price (Pontypridd) *F, E*; I Davies (Yetradgynlais)
F; M Harris (Waunarlwydd) *E*
Forwards: D Williams (Llandovery) *C, F, E*; C O'Donoghue (Rumney) *C*;
R Booth (Llanelli) *C, E*; R Edwards (Llanelli/UWIC) *C, F, E*; D Jones (Bath) *C, F*;
I McQueen (Pontypridd) *C*; R Francis (Swansea) *C, E* (R); G Bennett (Llanelli) *C,
E*; S Jones (Pontypridd) *C* (R), *F*; D Jones (Newport) *F*; G Lucas (Bridgend) *F, E*;
P Morgan (Bath) *F, E*; N Bonner-Evans (Llanelli Wanderers) *F, E*; M Davies
(Pontypridd) *E*; G Groves (Pontypridd) *E* (R)
Hawkins was captain against England and France; Kehoe against Canada.

FIRA Group and Tournament

Full-backs: G Curtis (Newport) *P, It, Ru, F*; D Jones (Bridgend) *SA, I*
Threequarters: S Greenaway (Bridgend) *P, It, Ru, SA, F, I*; J Fofana (Cardiff) *P, It, Ru, F*; D Hawkins (Neath) *P, It, Ru, SA, F, I*; M Bowen (Tumble) *P* (R), *Ru, SA* (R), *F* (R); M J Watkins (Pontllanfraith) *Ru* (R), *SA, F*; J Young (Neath) *It, SA, F, I*; C Moore (Llandaff) *P*
Half-backs: R Davies (London Welsh) *P, It, Ru, SA, F, I*; M Harris (Waunarlwydd) *It, Ru, SA, F*; T Richards (Dunvant) *P, F* (R), *I*
Forwards: R Booth (Swansea) *P, It, Ru, SA, F, I*; M Davies (Pontypridd) *P, It, Ru, SA, F, I* (R); J Scott (Crumlin) *P, It, Ru, SA, F* (R), *I*; L Robbins (Swansea) *It, Ru, F, I* (R); D Morris-Falconer (London Welsh) *It, Ru, SA*; C Lucas (Bridgend) *P, It, Ru, SA, F*; P Morgan (Bath) *P, It, Ru, SA, F, I*; N Bonner-Evans (Llanelli Wanderers) *P, It, Ru, SA, F, I*; I McQueen (Pontypridd) *P, Ru* (R), *SA* (R), *I*; D Jones (Llanelli Wanderers) *Ru* (R), *SA* (R), *I* (R); A Jones (Ystradgynlais) *Ru* (R), *I*; J Williams (Dunvant) *P* (R), *Ru* (R), *F* (R); S Mason (Cardiff) *Ru* (R), *F*; G Bennett (Llanelli) *P, Ru* (R), *SA, F, I*; R Bowen (Abertillery) *SA* (R), *F* (R), *I*; D Sweet (Pontypridd) *P* (R)
Hawkins was captain in all six matches.

MATCH DETAILS 1996-97

2 November 1996, Cardiff Arms Park

WALES U19 YOUTH 21   CANADA YOUTH 8
WALES *Tries:* G Thomas, D Williams   *Conversion:* Daniel
Penalty Goals: S Jones, S Davies, Daniel
CANADA *Try:* Prouse   *Penalty Goal:* Rogers
Referee S Buggy (Ireland)

29 December 1996, Bridgend

WALES FIRA GROUP YOUTH 67   PORTUGAL JUNIORS 12
WALES *Tries:* Greenaway (3), Lucas (2), Bennett, McQueen, Fofana, J Williams, Bowen   *Conversions:* Curtis (4)   *Penalty Goals:* Curtis (3)
PORTUGAL *Tries:* Lamas, Costa   *Conversion:* Malbeiro
Referee J Steele (Scotland)

5 February 1997, Neath

WALES U18 YOUTH 14   WELSH SCHOOLS 18 GROUP 8
WALES *Try:* Richards   *Penalty Goals:* R Davies (3)
WELSH SCHOOLS *Try:* Rogers   *Penalty Goal:* G Bowen
Referee D Bevan (Wales)

22 February 1997, Treviso

ITALY JUNIORS 10   WALES FIRA GROUP YOUTH 34
WALES *Tries:* Hawkins, Fofana, Bonner-Evans, Young   *Conversions:* Curtis (3)
Penalty Goals: Curtis

6 March 1997, Narberth

WALES U19 YOUTH 13   FRANCE JUNIORS 19
WALES *Try:* Young   *Conversion:* S Jones   *Penalty Goals:* S Jones (2)
FRANCE *Try:* Bidabe   *Conversion:* Teurlet   *Penalty Goals:* Teurlet (4)
Referee J Yuille (Scotland)

8 March 1997, Vittoria

SPAIN U18 YOUTH 20   SCOTLAND U18 YOUTH 10
SCOTLAND *Tries:* Purves, Henderson

8 March 1997, Kelvinside Academy, Balgray

SCOTLAND U19 YOUTH 26   ENGLAND COLTS 18
SCOTLAND *Tries:* Black, Dickson, Walker   *Conversion:* Ross
Penalty Goals: Rose (3)
ENGLAND *Tries:* Pritchard, Lloyd   *Conversion:* Brown   *Penalty Goals:* Brown (2)
Referee T Redmond (Ireland)

9 March 1997, Old Belvedere, Dublin

IRELAND U18 YOUTH 11   WALES U18 YOUTH 10
IRELAND *Try:* Bell   *Penalty Goals:* McHugh (2)
WALES *Tries:* M Jones, H Rees
Referee J Bacigalupo (Scotland)

16 March 1997, Myreside

SCOTLAND U18 YOUTH 29   JAPAN HIGH SCHOOLS 41
SCOTLAND *Tries:* Gibbon (2), McInroy (2), Forbes   *Conversions:* Duck (2)

5 April 1997, Stirling

SCOTLAND U18 YOUTH 5   IRELAND U18 YOUTH 22
SCOTLAND *Try:* McIntyre
IRELAND *Tries:* Morrissey, Bell, Cahill   *Conversions:* McHugh (2)
Penalty Goal: McHugh
Referee J Betaille (France)

12 April 1997, Iffley Road, Oxford University

ENGLAND COLTS 41   WALES U19 YOUTH 26
ENGLAND *Tries:* Moody (2), Jackson, Hartley, Richards, Long
Conversions: Brown (4)   *Penalty Goal:* Brown
WALES *Tries:* Harris, Thomas, Bonner-Evans, Pen try   *Conversions:* Price (2),
Daniel
Referee M Whyte (Ireland)

19 April 1997, Pontypridd

WALES U18 YOUTH 23   SCOTLAND U18 YOUTH 5
WALES *Tries:* D Jones, E Davies, Bonner-Evans   *Conversion:* R Davies
Penalty Goals: R Davies (2)
SCOTLAND *Try:* Taylor
Referee D Tyndall (Ireland)

19 April 1997, Le Puy

FRANCE YOUTH 22   ENGLAND COLTS 18(5PG 1DG)
ENGLAND *Penalty Goals:* Brown (5)   *Dropped Goal:* Brown

FIRA YOUTH TOURNAMENT, ARGENTINA

22 March 1997, San Andre Stadium

SCOTLAND 56   PORTUGAL 3
SCOTLAND *Tries:* Murray (2), Chrystie (2), Davidson, Capaldi, Ross
Conversions: Paterson (6)   *Penalties:* Paterson (3)

22 March 1997, San Luis, La Plata

WALES 46   RUSSIA 0
WALES *Tries:* Greenaway (2), R Davies (2), Lucas, Fofana, M Bowen, Williams
Conversions: Curtis (3)

24 March 1997, San Martin

IRELAND 39   PORTUGAL 20
IRELAND *Tries:* Price, Casey, Murphy, Nolan   *Conversions:* Murphy, Keating
Penalty Goals: Murphy (3), Keating (2)

26 March 1997, Cardinal Newman

SCOTLAND 8   IRELAND 22
SCOTLAND *Try:* McKerrow   *Penalty Goal:* Ross
IRELAND *Tries:* Cullen, Murphy, Hartigan   *Conversions:* Murphy (2)
Penalty Goal: Murphy

26 March 1997, Los Tilos, La Plata

WALES 16   SOUTH AFRICA 16
WALES *Try:* Harris   *Conversion:* R Davies   *Penalty Goals:* R Davies (3)

28 March 1997, San Cinaro

SCOTLAND 34   ITALY 3
SCOTLAND *Tries:* H Boyd, Di Rollo, Mitchell   *Conversions:* Ross (2)
Penalty Goals: Ross (5)

28 March 1997, Buenos Aires CRC

IRELAND 0   ARGENTINA 42

28 March 1997, La Plata

WALES 12   FRANCE 40
WALES *Tries:* Booth, Curtis   *Conversion:* R Davies
FRANCE *Tries:* Robic, Guffroy, Kuzbik   *Conversions:* Teurlet (2)
Penalty Goals: Teurlet (6)   *Dropped Goal:* Teurlet

30 March 1997, Buenos Aires

SCOTLAND 11   SOUTH AFRICA 43
SCOTLAND *Try:* T Boyd   *Penalty Goals:* Ross (2)

30 March 1997, Buenos Aires CRC

3rd/4th Place Play-off
WALES 30   IRELAND 17
WALES *Tries:* Greenaway, Morgan, Hawkins, D Jones   *Conversions:* R Davies (2)
Penalty Goals: R Davies (2)
IRELAND *Tries:* Cullen, Wallace   *Conversions:* Cunningham (2)
Penalty Goal: Cunningham

TOUGH WORLD CUP DEFENCE IN PROSPECT

WOMEN'S RUGBY
Vickie Sheriff

England had a tough but successful season in the run-up to the 1988 World Cup. The 1996-97 season was always planned to be one of regrouping and experimenting with new players and combinations prior to their world title defence next May. England's Home Nations title was secured for the second year, with the other Home Nations showing significant improvement on last year's performances. The benefits of an organised tournament with regular international fixtures are clearly showing.

Significantly, 1997 saw England wave goodbye to their impressive six-year-long unbeaten record. Previously only beaten once, by the USA in the final of the inaugural World Cup in 1991, they suffered a sore 17-15 defeat at the hands of France in February. France went to Northampton with a point to prove: women's rugby on the continent is fast-developing and England should no longer rest on its laurels or its reputation. A fierce contest with a nail-biting finish saw England unable to catch France's two-point lead. The first warning shots of a tough World Cup tournament ahead had been fired. Captain Gill Burns later said that the defeat was in some ways a relief because the burden of such a glowing reputation had been lifted from the squad.

A few months later, a revitalised England squad took the European Championships by storm. The loss to France was avenged with a 15-10 defeat on French home soil before England beat Scotland 24-8 in the final to emerge as European Champions. Success at home and on the continent has given the squad a confidence boost prior to the summer break. But continental success is cold-comfort when the real competition comes from the other side of the world.

Shock waves from the Canada Cup, where New Zealand trounced the 1994 World Cup finalists USA 83-0, are still reverberating around the globe. The England squad, sponsored by the RFUW, will be touring New Zealand in August in their first tour south of the equator, a crucial stage in England's World Cup preparations.

1997 HOME NATIONS CHAMPIONSHIP RESULTS
12 January: Scotland 10, Wales 0 (Boroughmuir)
26 January: England 23, Scotland 3 (Blackheath)
26 January: Wales 32, Ireland 5 (Bridgend)
9 February: Ireland 0, England 32 (Garryowen)
23 February: Scotland 28, Ireland 3 (Boroughmuir)
9 March: Wales 14, England 22 (Llanelli)

OTHER INTERNATIONAL MATCHES
12 October: England 17, Spain 15 (Headingley) *23 February:* England 15, France 17 (Northampton)

FIRA WOMEN'S RUGBY EUROPEAN CUP, NICE 1–7 April
(England's pool results)
Round 1: England 40, Holland 3; Scotland 31, Italy 7; Ireland 0, Spain 27
Round 2: England 15, France 10; Scotland 11, Spain 10
Final: England 24, Scotland 8

The RFUW has restructured the English Leagues for the 1997-98 season. The old six-league structure is being replaced with a super-eight level league system. The old Divisions One and Two will now become Premier Divisions One and Two with Divisions Three and below now being dubbed the National Challenge League. This new structure will create more competition for the middle-division teams while providing capacity for the stream of new teams entering the system.

Richmond took the English Division One title with an impressive 100 per cent record but were robbed of the Bread for Life National Cup by the defenders Saracens. A penalty goal in the final moments was enough to give Saracens the lead, taking the final score to 13-10. Wasps, keen to make an impression this season, crashed out of the Cup in the semi-final but made up for their losses by winning the National Sevens held at Marlow. They beat the title-holders, Richmond, 12-0 in the final.

In Wales, Cardiff Harlequins took Blaneau Gwent to a crushing 56-7 defeat in their National Cup at Ystradgynlais RFC. 'Quins went on to defend their Division One title with Swansea Uplands in runners-up position. The Welsh National Sevens competition held at Aberystwyth RFC was won by Swansea Uplands who beat their hosts 17-5 in the final.

Scotland's Keyline Cup was won this year by title defenders Edinburgh Wanderers. They beat Second Division Aberdeenshire 'Quins 39-0 to retain the Cup. Despite their Cup loss, 'Quins aim to disrupt the domination of Scottish club rugby by the Wanderers and Edinburgh Academicals when they join the ranks of Division One next season. The First Division was won by Edinburgh Academicals who also sealed victory in the Scottish Sevens competition. Accies beat fellow Edinburgh rivals, Wanderers, in the final.

RFUW National Division 1

	P	W	L	D	F	A	Pts
Richmond	14	13	0	1	305	51	27
Saracens	14	11	2	1	334	78	23
Wasps	14	10	3	1	385	134	21
Waterloo	14	6	7	1	203	198	13
Leeds	14	6	7	1	213	194	13
O Leams	14	4	10	0	207	447	8
Clifton	14	2	11	1	114	295	5
Blackheath	14	1	13	0	49	332	2

RFUW National Division 2

	P	W	L	D	F	A	Pts
Crawley	14	13	1	0	483	70	26
St Albans	14	10	3	1	301	54	21
Alton	14	7	6	1	170	183	15
Cheltenham	14	6	8	0	157	207	12
Richmond 2	14	5	8	1	178	151	11
Sale	14	4	10	0	98	274	8
Novocastrians	14	7	7	0	147	185	14
Eton Manor	14	0	14	0	42	390	0

OBITUARY 1996-97 (*up to 1 May 1997*)

Vincent David BEVAN (Wellington) was New Zealand's scrum-half in 1949 and 1950, when he was ever-present in the series against Karl Mullen's Lions. Bevan, a squat player noted for the length and accuracy of his pass, died in Wellington on 26 May.

John BURGESS CBE (Broughton Park), who died on New Year's Day, was a vigorous Lancastrian flanker who became a respected coach and was president of the Rugby Football Union in 1987-88. In 1972, he prepared the North-Western Counties XV that defeated the Sixth All Blacks, and as national coach in 1974-75 did an effective job raising the morale of the England side.

Ronald George BUSH (Auckland, Otago), a co-founder of the New Zealand Barbarians, made his niche in the game's history by becoming the first player to land four penalties in an international. His goals gave New Zealand a 20-13 win at Auckland against the 1931 Wallabies in his sole Test for the All Blacks. He died on 10 May in Auckland.

Gordon Stanley COTTINGTON (Kelso, Headingley), who died in Leeds in June, was Scotland's hooker five times between 1934 and 1936. Work commitments took him to Leeds in 1936 where he regularly turned out with internationalists from England, Wales and Ireland for Headingley during the club's heyday. He later turned professional with Castleford RL.

Manuera Ben Riwai COUCH (Wairarapa) toured Australia as a five-eighth with the 1947 All Blacks, winning his Test cap at Brisbane. As a Maori he was ineligible for the 1949 tour to South Africa but played in the home series against the Wallabies of that year. Later he was a distinguished Member of the New Zealand Parliament. Died 3 June in Masterton.

Carwyn DAVIES (Llanelli), the Welsh wing who won four caps in 1988-89, died tragically at Llangadog on 10 February. At Llanelli he was a powerful runner who harvested many tries, including a club record of 45 in 1987-88. Later he was the prime mover behind the foundation of the Llangadog club.

Sedley DAVIES (Maesteg) featured as a veteran in the second row of the unbeaten Maesteg side of 1947-48. Though deprived by War of full international honours, he was still good enough to play in the Welsh XV for the 1945-46 'Victory' series of matches that celebrated peace. Scored a try in Wales's win against France at Swansea. His death was reported in June 1996.

Eugene O'Donnell DAVY (UC Dublin, Lansdowne) was the midfield general of the Irish sides between the Wars. His long career as a centre/fly-half between 1925 and 1934 brought him 34 caps and he captained Ireland in 1933. His most remarkable feat in internationals was against Scotland at Murrayfield in 1930 when he scored a try hat-trick in a ten-minute purple patch before half-time. He died in Dublin on 11 November.

Pieter Stephanus du TOIT (Western Province, Boland) was the brave, imperturbable tight-head prop in 14 Springbok Tests between 1958 and 1961. Piet was only 20 when selected to make the 1956 tour of Australia and New Zealand, where he played 15 games. Quiet and unobtrusive, he retired young in 1962 to concentrate on running the family farm. Had completed a half-marathon only a fortnight before his sudden death in Hermanus on 26 February.

Victor Leslie GEORGE (Southland), who died at Wanaka on 10 August 1996, was the cornerstone of the 1938 All Black scrum in Australia. His robust play in the loose and excellent technique in the tight made him the automatic choice for the three Tests of the series. But for the War, he would almost certainly have made the 1940 All Black team that was scheduled to tour South Africa.

Alan GIBSON, the erudite writer and broadcaster whose wide-ranging interests included rugby football, died in Taunton on 10 April.

Colin Cuthbert GILLIES (Otago, North Otago) was unlucky to find himself in contention for All Black honours at the same time as several other first-rate New Zealand five-eighths. His only

Test was at Dunedin in 1936 when he sparked a side which rattled up a then record 38-13 victory. He died on 2 July in Timaru.

John Wood GODDARD (South Canterbury), the reserve full-back to Bob Scott on the 1949 All Black tour of South Africa, died in Timaru on 22 October. Post-war he was a regular New Zealand trialist, but never appeared in a Test. His younger brother Maurice (five caps) also played for the 1949 All Blacks in South Africa.

James Scott HAIG (Otago) played one season of Test rugby for New Zealand against Australia in 1946 before hopping codes to become a noted League half-back who won 21 caps for the Kiwis between 1947 and 1953. Like his elder brother, All Black Laurie Haig, he was a Scot by birth. Died in Dunedin on 28 October.

Cyril Butler HOLMES (Manchester) was the last Englishman to hold the Commonwealth 100 yards and 200 yards titles simultaneously, winning Golds at the 1938 Empire Games in Australia. He became a dual international in 1947, scoring a try on debut against Scotland in the first of three Rugby Union caps as a wing. His death was reported in early August.

Herbert Percy JACOB (Oxford University, Blackheath), who died aged 93 at Myaree, Western Australia, on July 8, was the senior England international player. He played as a wing and centre in Wavell Wakefield's Grand Slam XV of 1924, scoring four tries including a hat-trick at Twickenham against the French. Although he returned for only one more cap, six years later, he spent his entire international career on the winning side.

Winston JONES, the Welsh referee who controlled four major internationals, including the 1984 Grand Slam decider between Scotland and France, died in a dressing room while attending the Amsterdam Sevens on 18 May.

Basil John KENYON (Border) only played once for South Africa, yet is regarded as one of the country's greatest-ever skippers. He came to prominence when he led Border to a draw and a win against the 1949 All Blacks, and captained his country in the winning Fourth Test of that year's series. The automatic choice as leader of the Fourth Springboks to Europe, his career was brought to a premature end by a serious injury sustained in the third match of that tour, against Pontypool/Newbridge Combined. Later a national selector. He was 79 at the time of his death.

Eric Charles LACEY (Leicester) was a lock who played 175 games for the Tigers between 1947 and 1959 and was in the East Midlands XV that went down 3-0 to the Fourth Springboks at Leicester in 1951. He later served Leicester as a loyal administrator and was president of the club from 1979 to 1981. His death was reported in July.

François LOMBARD (Narbonne), who played for France as a scrum-half in 1934 and as a flanker in 1937, died in Brive in September. He was 91. He captained Narbonne to the French Championship title in 1936.

William Albert LUNN (Otago), who died in Alexandra on 22 December, was a hard-as-nails flanker whose two New Zealand Test caps were won against the 1949 Australians.

Franswa Pierre MARAIS (Border, Boland, S W Districts) won five caps for South Africa as a place-kicking wing between 1949 and 1953, when the Springboks were unofficial world champions. Buks Marais died in Cape Town on 12 December.

William Malcolm McLEAN (Queensland), a versatile second-row or loose forward who was the son, brother and father of Test players, captained Australia in four of his five Test appearances, 1946-47. He was, moreover, captain of the Third Wallabies to Britain, Europe and North America in 1947-48, but his playing part on that tour was cut short owing to a broken leg. He died at Sanctuary Cove on 9 December.

Bruce Edward McLEOD (Counties, Hawke's Bay) was an uncompromising forward whose run in the New Zealand pack coincided with the All Blacks' record run of straight Test victories in the mid to late 1960's. Altogether he won 24 caps between 1964 and 1970, having no equal as a mobile, quick-striking hooker. He died at Foxton Beach on 18 May.

Johann Karl OCHSE (Western Province), known to everybody as Chum, was the Springbok wing with the baggy shorts whose try against Wales in 1951 decided a match billed as for the championship of world rugby. He scored a try in every match he played in Wales with the 1951-52 tourists and altogether played in seven Tests for South Africa. Died at Paarl on 13 July.

Terence Patrick Anthony O'SULLIVAN (Taranaki), New Zealand's centre/second five eighth in 16 matches (including four Tests) between 1960 and 1962, died hiking on Mount Ruapehu on 25 April.

Elwyn PRICE, who died on 11 October, was for 34 years a big influence on young rugby players as a coach at St Brendan's College. He was also involved with Bristol Colts and Colston's Collegiate.

Thomas Eymard REID (Garryowen), one of the great characters of Irish rugby in the 1950's, died in Canada in October. He played 13 times for his country as a forward between 1953 and 1957. In 1955, he formed the second row with Rhys Williams of the Lions pack which secured a share of the rubber against Springboks. The genial Irishman joked that he was never in his life as fit as when he took part in that tour.

Jacobus REINACH (Orange Free State) was killed in a car crash near Kroonstad on 21 January, aged 35. He had played on the wing in the four Springbok Tests against the New Zealand Cavaliers in 1986 and since 1984 had held the South African 400m record.

Frank Jeffrey REYNOLDS (Old Cranleighans), a creative fly-half who played three times for England out of Old Cranleighans – one of the last players capped direct from an Old Boys club – died at Somerset West on 1 August. Only 21 on his England debut in 1937, he spearheaded a back division which won the Calcutta Cup, Triple Crown and International Championship. He went to South Africa with Sam Walker's Lions of 1938, making a good impression in the early matches before injury curtailed his tour appearances. In 1951, he emigrated to South Africa where he was in the hotel business.

Patrick Keith RHIND (Canterbury, Wellington) would have played for New Zealand on the 1940 tour to South Africa but for the outbreak of the War. When first-class rugby resumed in 1945, he was the anchorman of the famous Forces side, known as the Kiwis, that toured Britain and France. His only two Tests for the All Blacks were as prop against the 1946 Wallabies. Died in Christchurch on 10 September.

Dr Alexander William ROSS (New South Wales), was the outstanding Australian full-back between the Wars. An attacking player at a time when the position was regarded solely as a last line of defence, he starred as a member of the famous 1927-28 Australian side that toured Britain and France, and went on to lead the first Wallabies to visit South Africa, in 1933. He died on 30 August in Sydney where at 90 he was still practising medicine.

Willem Petrus ROUSSEAU (Western Province) was at centre for the Springboks in the final two Tests of the drawn 1928 series with New Zealand. A year later he played in the Varsity match for a winning Oxford side which included six South Africans. Willie died in Hermanus on 28 December at the age of 90.

René SALINIÉ (Perpignan) played in the centre for France against England in Paris in 1923. He was 99 and France's senior international player at the time of his death in Nice in December.

Henning SNYMAN, who died of cancer in Windhoek on 10 July, was Namibia's Mr Rugby, having become coach-president of the Union after enjoying a distinguished playing career as a centre and fly-half.

John Brinley George THOMAS MBE, whose name became synonymous with Welsh rugby during his 36-year stint as correspondent to the Cardiff *Western Mail*, died on 11 April. All told, he produced more than 30 books on the game and contributed countless articles to newspapers, magazines and match programmes worldwide. More than a mere chronicler of the game, Bryn campaigned vigorously for the introduction of neutral referees in overseas Tests and, like his friend and colleague, Vivian Jenkins, delighted in the introductions of the differential penalty and four-point try.

Richard Charles Clement THOMAS (Cambridge University, Swansea), the combative Welsh flanker whose cross-kick paved the way for Wales's famous win against the 1953 All Blacks, died at Swansea on 5 September. As a player Clem won 26 caps between 1949 and 1959, and played a lead role (after recovering from appendicitis) in the Lions' historic tied series with South Africa in 1955. After leading Wales nine times in 1958 and 1959, he retired to take up a successful career in rugby journalism. He was an equally combative critic mainly as rugby correspondent of the *Observer*, and wrote several thoughtful books on the game including the definitive history of the British Lions.

Clem Thomas, Cambridge University, Swansea and the British Lions, and much respected writer on the game, who died on 5 September 1996.

Ian TUCKER (Oxford University). The death of Ian Tucker on 27 October cast a shadow over the season generally and on Oxford rugby in particular. He was a former Australia Under-19 cap and was expected to win his Oxford Blue as a centre. Playing against Saracens he was injured in a tackle near the end of the match. He rejoined the game but collapsed a minute later and died in a London hospital the next day.

Edmond VELLAT (Grenoble), who died in Grenoble on 3 June eight months short of his 100th birthday, won five caps as France's right wing in the late 1920's. He will always have a prominent position in the annals of French rugby, for in 1927 it was his first-half try which gave France victory (3-0) over England for the first time.

Wilfred WOOLLER (Cambridge University, Cardiff, Sale) was a giant of Welsh sport for more than three decades. Beginning in the 1930s as a long-striding Rugby Union threequarter, he enjoyed arguably his finest hour for Wales in the 13-12 victory against New Zealand in 1935, setting up two of the tries. Then, after winning 18 Rugby Union caps, he returned from a Japanese prisoner of war camp and subsequently led Glamorgan to their maiden County Championship title at cricket in 1948. He represented the county until 1962, became a Test selector, and was a cricket commentator and rugby writer whose views on sport were always forthright and often controversial. Died on 10 March at Llandough.

FIXTURES 1997-98

Venues and fixtures are subject to alteration. We should like to thank all those who have assisted in the compilation of this list, particularly those at the various headquarters of the Home Unions. The identities of six of the eight Welsh clubs competing in the European Championships were unknown at the time of going to press.

Saturday, 16 August

NEW ZEALAND v AUSTRALIA
(Dunedin)
IRFU Provincial Championship
Connacht v Munster
Leinster v Ulster

WRU Leagues
Premier Division
Cardiff v Pontypridd
Ebbw Vale v Swansea
Llanelli v Neath
Newport v Bridgend
First Division
Aberavon v Dunvant
Abertillery v Treorchy
Bonymaen v Llandovery
Caerphilly v Rumney
Cross Keys v Blackwood
Maesteg v S Wales Police
Merthyr v Pontypool
UWIC v Newbridge

Saturday, 23 August

SOUTH AFRICA v AUSTRALIA
(Johannesburg)
IRFU Provincial Championship
Connacht v Ulster
Munster v Leinster

RFU Allied Dunbar Leagues
Division 1
Bath v Newcastle
Gloucester v Bristol
Northampton v Harlequins
Richmond v London Irish
Sale v Saracens
Wasps v Leicester

WRU Leagues
Premier Division
Bridgend v Llanelli
Neath v Cardiff
Pontypridd v Ebbw Vale
Swansea v Newport

First Division
Abertillery v Maesteg
Blackwood v Caerphilly
Dunvant v UWIC
Llandovery v Cross Keys
Newbridge v Merthyr
Pontypool v Bonymaen
Rumney v S Wales Police
Treorchy v Aberavon

Saturday, 30 August

WALES v ROMANIA (Wrexham FC)
IRFU Provincial Championship
Leinster v Connacht
Ulster v Munster

RFU Allied Dunbar Leagues
Division 1
Bristol v Wasps
Harlequins v Bath
Leicester v Gloucester
London Irish v Sale
Newcastle v Northampton
Saracens v Richmond
Division 2
Bedford v Rotherham
Coventry v Moseley
London Scottish v Fylde
Orrell v Blackheath
Wakefield v Exeter
West Hartlepool v Waterloo

RFU National League
Division 1
Leeds v Harrogate
Liverpool St Helens v Worcester
Lydney v Rugby
Newbury v Reading
Otley v Nottingham
Rosslyn Park v Morley
Wharfedale v London Welsh

SRU League Trophy
Group A
Currie v Musselburgh
Gala v Glasgow Hawks

Hawick v Melrose
Heriot's FP v Kirkcaldy
Preston Lodge FP v Edinburgh Acads
Group B
Dundee HSFP v Biggar
Peebles v Boroughmuir
Stirling County v Kelso
Watsonians v Jed-Forest
West of Scotland v Kilmarnock

Saturday, 6 September
Heineken Championships
European Cup
Bourgoin v Wales 4
Brive v Borders
Caledonia v Wales 3
Harlequins v Munster
Leicester v Milan
Leinster v Toulouse
Pontypridd v Bath
Swansea v Wasps
Treviso v Pau
Ulster v Glasgow
European Conference
Bristol v La Rochelle
Colomiers v Richmond
Connacht v Northampton
Dax v Romanian XV
Gloucester v Padova
Grenoble v Wales 1
London Irish v Stade Francais
Montferrand v Sale
Narbonne v Saracens
Newcastle v Biarritz
Nice v Begles-Bordeaux
Perpignan v Edinburgh
Toulon v Beziers
Wales 2 v Montpelier
Wales 3 v Agen
Wales 4 v Castres

RFU Allied Dunbar Leagues
Division 2
Coventry v Exeter
Fylde v Bedford
London Scottish v Blackheath
Moseley v Rotherham
Waterloo v Wakefield
West Hartlepool v Orrell

RFU National League
Division 1
Harrogate v London Welsh
Liverpool St Helens v Leeds
Morley v Wharfedale
Nottingham v Rosslyn Park
Reading v Otley
Rugby v Newbury
Worcester v Lydney

SRU League Trophy
Group A
Edinburgh Acads v Musselburgh
Gala v Hawick
Glasgow Hawks v Currie
Kirkcaldy v Melrose
Preston Lodge FP v Heriot's FP
Group B
Boroughmuir v Watsonians
Jed-Forest v Kelso
Kilmarnock v Biggar
Stirling County v Peebles
West of Scotland v Dundee HSFP

WRU Leagues
First Division
Aberavon v Abertillery
Bonymaen v Newbridge
Cross Keys v Pontypool
Caerphilly v Llandovery
Maesteg v Rumney
Merthyr v Dunvant
S Wales Police v Blackwood
UWIC v Treorchy

WRU SWALEC Cup: *Preliminary round*

Saturday, 13 September
Heineken Championships
European Cup
Bath v Borders
Brive v Pontypridd
Caledonia v Treviso
Glasgow v Wasps
Harlequins v Bourgoin
Leinster v Leicester
Milan v Toulouse
Pau v Wales 3
Swansea v Ulster
Wales 4 v Munster

European Conference
Beziers v Padova
Colomiers v Grenoble
Dax v London Irish
Edinburgh v Biarritz
Gloucester v Toulon
La Rochelle v Agen
Montferrand v Wales 2
Montpelier v Sale
Newcastle v Perpignan
Nice v Connacht
Northampton v Begles-Bordeaux
Saracens v Castres
Stade Francais v Romanian XV
Wales 1 v Richmond
Wales 3 v Bristol
Wales 4 v Narbonne

RFU Allied Dunbar Leagues
Division 2
Blackheath v Wakefield
Exeter v Bedford
Fylde v Coventry
Moseley v West Hartlepool
Rotherham v Orrell
Waterloo v London Scottish

RFU National League
Division 1
Harrogate v Morley
London Welsh v Leeds
Lydney v Liverpool St Helens
Newbury v Worcester
Otley v Rugby
Rosslyn Park v Reading
Wharfedale v Nottingham

RFU Cup: *1st round*

SRU League Trophy
Group A
Currie v Preston Lodge FP
Hawick v Kirkcaldy
Heriot's FP v Edinburgh Acads
Melrose v Glasgow Hawks
Musselburgh v Gala
Group B
Biggar v Boroughmuir
Kelso v Dundee HSFP
Kilmarnock v Jed-Forest
Peebles v Watsonians
Stirling County v West of Scotland

SRU Cup: *1st round*

WRU Leagues
First Division
Aberavon v Maesteg
Abertillery v UWIC
Blackwood v Rumney
Dunvant v Bonymaen
Llandovery v S Wales Police
Newbridge v Cross Keys
Pontypool v Caerphilly
Treorchy v Merthyr

Saturday, 20 September
Heineken Championships
European Cup
Bath v Brive
Borders v Pontypridd
Glasgow v Swansea
Milan v Leinster
Munster v Bourgoin
Pau v Caledonia
Toulouse v Leicester
Wales 3 v Treviso
Wales 4 v Harlequins
Wasps v Ulster
European Conference
Agen v Bristol
Begles-Bordeaux v Connacht
Beziers v Gloucester
Biarritz v Perpignan
Castres v Narbonne
Edinburgh v Newcastle
La Rochelle v Wales 3
Montpelier v Montferrand
Northampton v Nice
Padova v Toulon
Richmond v Grenoble
Romanian XV v London Irish
Sale v Wales 2
Saracens v Wales 4
Stade Francais v Dax
Wales 1 v Colomiers

RFU Allied Dunbar Leagues
Division 2
Bedford v London Scottish
Blackheath v Fylde
Exeter v Waterloo
Orrell v Moseley
Rotherham v West Hartlepool
Wakefield v Coventry

RFU National League
Division 1
Liverpool St Helens v Newbury
Lydney v Leeds
Morley v London Welsh
Nottingham v Harrogate
Reading v Wharfedale
Rugby v Rosslyn Park
Worcester v Otley

SRU League Trophy
Group A
Edinburgh Acads v Currie
Gala v Heriot's FP
Glasgow Hawks v Kirkcaldy
Hawick v Musselburgh
Melrose v Preston Lodge FP
Group B
Boroughmuir v Stirling County
Dundee HSFP v Jed-Forest
Kelso v Biggar
Watsonians v Kilmarnock
West of Scotland v Peebles

WRU Leagues
First Division
Bonymaen v Treorchy
Caerphilly v Newbridge
Cross Keys v Dunvant
Maesteg v Blackwood
Merthyr v Abertillery
Rumney v Llandovery
S Wales Police v Pontypool
UWIC v Aberavon

Saturday, 27 September
Heineken Championships
European Cup
Borders v Bath
Bourgoin v Harlequins
Leicester v Leinster
Munster v Wales 4
Pontypridd v Brive
Toulouse v Milan
Treviso v Caledonia
Ulster v Swansea
Wales 3 v Pau
Wasps v Glasgow
European Conference
Agen v La Rochelle
Begles-Bordeaux v Northampton
Biarritz v Edinburgh
Bristol v Wales 3

Castres v Saracens
Connacht v Nice
Grenoble v Colomiers
London Irish v Dax
Narbonne v Wales 4
Padova v Beziers
Perpignan v Newcastle
Richmond v Wales 1
Romanian XV v Stade Francais
Sale v Montpelier
Toulon v Gloucester
Wales 2 v Montferrand

RFU Allied Dunbar Leagues
Division 2
Coventry v Bedford
Fylde v Rotherham
London Scottish v Orrell
Moseley v Exeter
Waterloo v Blackheath
West Hartlepool v Wakefield

RFU National League
Division 1
Harrogate v Reading
Leeds v Morley
London Welsh v Nottingham
Newbury v Lydney
Otley v Liverpool St Helens
Rosslyn Park v Worcester
Wharfedale v Rugby

SRU League Trophy
Group A
Hawick v Glasgow Hawks
Heriot's FP v Currie
Kirkcaldy v Edinburgh Acads
Musselburgh v Melrose
Preston Lodge FP v Gala
Group B
Biggar v Watsonians
Dundee HSFP v Boroughmuir
Jed-Forest v Stirling County
Peebles v Kilmarnock
West of Scotland v Kelso

WRU SWALEC Cup: *1st round*

WRU Leagues
First Division
Aberavon v Merthyr
Abertillery v Bonymaen
Dunvant v Caerphilly

Llandovery v Blackwood
Pontypool v Rumney
S Wales Police v Newbridge
Treorchy v Cross Keys
UWIC v Maesteg

Saturday, 4 October
Heineken Championships
European Cup
Bourgoin v Munster
Brive v Bath
Caledonia v Pau
Harlequins v Wales 4
Leicester v Toulouse
Leinster v Milan
Pontypridd v Borders
Swansea v Glasgow
Treviso v Wales 3
Ulster v Wasps
European Conference
Bristol v Agen
Colomiers v Wales 1
Connacht v Begles-Bordeaux
Dax v Stade Francais
Gloucester v Beziers
Grenoble v Richmond
London Irish v Romanian XV
Montferrand v Montpelier
Narbonne v Castres
Newcastle v Edinburgh
Nice v Northampton
Perpignan v Biarritz
Toulon v Padova
Wales 2 v Sale
Wales 3 v La Rochelle
Wales 4 v Saracens

RFU Allied Dunbar Leagues
Division 2
Bedford v Waterloo
Blackheath v Coventry
Exeter v West Hartlepool
Orrell v Fylde
Rotherham v London Scottish
Wakefield v Moseley

RFU Cup: *2nd round*

SRU League Trophy
Group A
Currie v Hawick
Edinburgh Acads v Glasgow Hawks
Gala v Melrose

Kirkcaldy v Preston Lodge FP
Musselburgh v Heriot's FP
Group B
Boroughmuir v Jed-Forest
Kilmarnock v Kelso
Peebles v Biggar
Stirling County v Dundee HSFP
Watsonians v West of Scotland

WRU Leagues
First Division
Blackwood v Pontypool
Bonymaen v Aberavon
Caerphilly v Treorchy
Cross Keys v Abertillery
Llandovery v Maesteg
Merthyr v UWIC
Rumney v Newbridge
S Wales Police v Dunvant

Saturday, 11 October
Heineken Championships
European Cup
Bath v Pontypridd
Borders v Brive
Glasgow v Ulster
Milan v Leicester
Munster v Harlequins
Pau v Treviso
Toulouse v Leinster
Wales 3 v Caledonia
Wales 4 v Bourgoin
Wasps v Swansea
European Conference
Agen v Wales 3
Begles-Bordeaux v Nice
Beziers v Toulon
Biarritz v Newcastle
Castres v Wales 4
Edinburgh v Perpignan
La Rochelle v Bristol
Montpelier v Wales 2
Northampton v Connacht
Padova v Gloucester
Richmond v Colomiers
Romanian XV v Dax
Sale v Montferrand
Saracens v Narbonne
Stade Francais v London Irish
Wales 1 v Grenoble

RFU Allied Dunbar Leagues
Division 2
Coventry v Rotherham
Fylde v Exeter
London Scottish v Wakefield
Moseley v Bedford
Waterloo v Orrell
West Hartlepool v Blackheath

RFU National League
Division 1
Liverpool St Helens v Rosslyn Park
Lydney v Otley
Newbury v Leeds
Nottingham v Morley
Reading v London Welsh
Rugby v Harrogate
Worcester v Wharfedale

SRU League Trophy
Group A
Currie v Gala
Glasgow Hawks v Preston Lodge FP
Hawick v Heriot's FP
Melrose v Edinburgh Acads
Musselburgh v Kirkcaldy
Group B
Boroughmuir v Kilmarnock
Dundee HSFP v Watsonians
Jed-Forest v West of Scotland
Kelso v Peebles
Stirling County v Biggar

SRU Cup: *2nd round*

WRU Leagues
First Division
Aberavon v Cross Keys
Abertillery v Caerphilly
Dunvant v Rumney
Maesteg v Merthyr
Newbridge v Blackwood
Pontypool v Llandovery
Treorchy v S Wales Police
UWIC v Bonymaen

Saturday, 18 October
FRANCE v ITALY (Auch)
ARGENTINA v ROMANIA (Auch)

RFU Allied Dunbar Leagues
Division 1
Bath v Bristol
Gloucester v London Irish
Northampton v Leicester
Richmond v Harlequins
Sale v Newcastle
Wasps v Saracens
Division 2
Bedford v West Hartlepool
Blackheath v Moseley
Exeter v London Scottish
Orrell v Coventry
Rotherham v Waterloo
Wakefield v Fylde

RFU National League
Division 1
Harrogate v Worcester
Leeds v Nottingham
London Welsh v Rugby
Morley v Reading
Otley v Newbury
Rosslyn Park v Lydney
Wharfedale v Liverpool St Helens

SRU League Trophy
Group A
Gala v Edinburgh Acads
Glasgow Hawks v Musselburgh
Heriot's FP v Melrose
Kirkcaldy v Currie
Preston Lodge FP v Hawick
Group B
Biggar v Jed-Forest
Kelso v Watsonians
Kilmarnock v Stirling County
Peebles v Dundee HSFP
West of Scotland v Boroughmuir

WRU SWALEC Cup: *2nd round*

WRU Leagues
First Division
Blackwood v Dunvant
Bonymaen v Merthyr
Caerphilly v Aberavon
Cross Keys v UWIC
Llandovery v Newbridge
Pontypool v Maesteg
Rumney v Treorchy
S Wales Police v Abertillery

Sunday, 19 October

SRU Districts Championship
Glasgow v Edinburgh
Scottish Borders v Caledonia

Wednesday, 22 October

FRANCE v ROMANIA (Lourdes)
ITALY v ARGENTINA (Lourdes)

Saturday, 25 October

RFU Allied Dunbar Leagues
Division 1
Bristol v Northampton
Harlequins v Sale
Leicester v Bath
London Irish v Wasps
Newcastle v Richmond
Saracens v Gloucester
Division 2
Coventry v Wakefield
Fylde v Blackheath
London Scottish v Bedford
Moseley v Orrell
Waterloo v Exeter
West Hartlepool v Rotherham

RFU National League
Division 1
Liverpool St Helens v Harrogate
Lydney v Wharfedale
Newbury v Rosslyn Park
Otley v Leeds
Reading v Nottingham
Rugby v Morley
Worcester v London Welsh

SRU League Trophy
Group A
Edinburgh Acads v Hawick
Heriot's FP v Glasgow Hawks
Kirkcaldy v Gala
Melrose v Currie
Musselburgh v Preston Lodge FP
Group B
Biggar v West of Scotland
Boroughmuir v Kelso
Dundee HSFP v Kilmarnock
Jed-Forest v Peebles
Watsonians v Stirling County

WRU Leagues
Premier Division
Cardiff v Ebbw Vale
Llanelli v Swansea
Neath v Bridgend
Newport v Pontypridd
First Division
Aberavon v S Wales Police
Abertillery v Rumney
Dunvant v Llandovery
Maesteg v Bonymaen
Merthyr v Cross Keys
Newbridge v Pontypool
Treorchy v Blackwood
UWIC v Caerphilly

Sunday, 26 October

FRANCE v ARGENTINA (Tarbes)
ITALY v ROMANIA (Tarbes)
SRU Districts Championship
Edinburgh v Caledonia
Scottish Borders v Glasgow

Saturday, 1 November

ARGENTINA v AUSTRALIA
(Buenos Aires)
Heineken Championships
Quarter-final play-offs

RFU Cup: *3rd round*

WRU Leagues
Premier Division
Bridgend v Cardiff
Ebbw Vale v Newport
Pontypridd v Llanelli
Swansea v Neath
First Division
Blackwood v Abertillery
Caerphilly v Merthyr
Cross Keys v Bonymaen
Llandovery v Treorchy
Newbridge v Maesteg
Pontypool v Dunvant
Rumney v Aberavon
S Wales Police v UWIC

Saturday, 8 November

ARGENTINA v AUSTRALIA
(Buenos Aires)
ITALY v SOUTH AFRICA

Heineken Championships *Quarter-finals*

RFU Allied Dunbar Leagues
Division 1
Bath v London Irish
Gloucester v Harlequins
Northampton v Saracens
Richmond v Leicester
Sale v Bristol
Wasps v Newcastle
Division 2
Bedford v Coventry
Blackheath v Waterloo
Exeter v Moseley
Orrell v London Scottish
Rotherham v Fylde
Wakefield v West Hartlepool

RFU National League
Division 1
Harrogate v Lydney
Leeds v Reading
London Welsh v Liverpool St Helens
Morley v Worcester
Nottingham v Rugby
Rosslyn Park v Otley
Wharfedale v Newbury

WRU Leagues
First Division
Aberavon v Blackwood
Abertillery v Llandovery
Bonymaen v Caerphilly
Dunvant v Newbridge
Maesteg v Cross Keys
Merthyr v S Wales Police
Treorchy v Pontypool
UWIC v Rumney

Sunday, 9 November
SRU Cup: *3rd round*

Tuesday, 11 November
Ireland Development XV v New Zealanders (Belfast)

Saturday, 15 November
ENGLAND v AUSTRALIA
(Twickenham)
IRELAND v CANADA (Dublin)
FRANCE v SOUTH AFRICA

RFU National League
Division 1
Liverpool St Helens v Morley
Lydney v London Welsh
Newbury v Harrogate
Otley v Wharfedale
Rosslyn Park v Leeds
Rugby v Reading
Worcester v Nottingham

SRU Tennents Premiership
Division 1
Hawick v Currie
Heriot's FP v Stirling County
Melrose v Boroughmuir
Watsonians v Edinburgh Acads
West of Scotland v Jed-Forest
Division 2
Dundee HSFP v Kelso
Kilmarnock v Musselburgh
Kirkcaldy v Glasgow Hawks
Peebles v Gala
Preston Lodge FP v Biggar
Division 3
Ayr v Stewartry
Gordonians v Stewart's Melville FP
Grangemouth v Aberdeen GSFP
Hillhead-Jordanhill v Glenrothes
Selkirk v Glasgow Southern

Sunday, 16 November
WALES v NEW ZEALAND
(Wembley)

Wednesday, 19 November
IRFU All Ireland Leagues
Division 1
Lansdowne v Old Belvedere

Saturday, 22 November
ENGLAND v NEW ZEALAND
(Old Trafford)
SCOTLAND v AUSTRALIA
(Murrayfield)
FRANCE v SOUTH AFRICA (Parc des Princes)
RFU National League
Division 1
Harrogate v Otley
Leeds v Rugby
London Welsh v Newbury
Morley v Lydney

Nottingham v Liverpool St Helens
Reading v Worcester
Wharfedale v Rosslyn Park

IRFU All Ireland Leagues
Division 1
Ballymena v Dolphin
Clontarf v Old Crescent
Cork Constitution v Terenure Coll
Garryowen v Young Munster
Shannon v Dungannon
St Mary's Coll v Blackrock Coll

WRU SWALEC Cup: *3rd round*

WRU Leagues
First Division
Aberavon v Llandovery
Abertillery v Pontypool
Bonymaen v S Wales Police
Cross Keys v Caerphilly
Maesteg v Dunvant
Merthyr v Rumney
Treorchy v Newbridge
UWIC v Blackwood

Tuesday, 25 November
WALES v TONGA (Llanelli)

Saturday, 29 November
ENGLAND v SOUTH AFRICA
(Twickenham)
IRELAND v NEW ZEALAND
(Dublin)

RFU County Championship
Southern Group
Cornwall v Sussex
Devon v Middlesex
Dorset & Wilts v Gloucestershire
Hampshire v Kent
Hertfordshire v Berkshire
Oxfordshire v Somerset
Surrey v Buckinghamshire
North & Midlands Group
Cumbria v Notts, Lincs &
  Derbyshire
Leicestershire v Cheshire
North Midlands v Lancashire
Northumberland v Staffordshire
Warwickshire v Durham
Yorkshire v East Midlands

SRU Tennents Premiership
Division 1
Boroughmuir v Heriot's FP
Currie v West of Scotland
Edinburgh Acads v Melrose
Jed-Forest v Watsonians
Stirling County v Hawick
Division 2
Biggar v Kilmarnock
Gala v Kirkcaldy
Glasgow Hawks v Dundee HSFP
Kelso v Preston Lodge FP
Musselburgh v Peebles
Division 3
Aberdeen GSFP v Stewartry
Ayr v Selkirk
Glenrothes v Gordonians
Glasgow Southern v
  Hillhead-Jordanhill
Stewart's Melville FP v Grangemouth

WRU Leagues
First Division
Blackwood v Merthyr
Caerphilly v Maesteg
Dunvant v Treorchy
Llandovery v UWIC
Newbridge v Abertillery
Pontypool v Aberavon
Rumney v Bonymaen
S Wales Police v Cross Keys

Saturday, 6 December
ENGLAND v NEW ZEALAND
(Twickenham)
SCOTLAND v SOUTH AFRICA
(Murrayfield)

RFU County Championship
Southern Group
Devon v Oxfordshire
Dorset & Wilts v Hertfordshire
Gloucestershire v Berkshire
Hampshire v Surrey
Kent v Buckinghamshire
Middlesex v Somerset
Sussex v Eastern Counties
North & Midlands Group
Cheshire v Lancashire
Cumbria v Warwickshire
East Midlands v Staffordshire
Leicestershire v North Midlands

Notts, Lincs & Derbyshire v Durham
Yorkshire v Northumberland

IRFU All Ireland Leagues
Division 1
Blackrock Coll v Lansdowne
Dolphin v Garryowen
Dungannon v Cork Constitution
Old Belvedere v Ballymena
Old Crescent v Shannon
Terenure Coll v St Mary's Coll
Young Munster v Clontarf

WRU Leagues
Premier Division
Bridgend v Swansea
Llanelli v Ebbw Vale
Neath v Pontypridd
Newport v Cardiff
First Division
Aberavon v Newbridge
Abertillery v Dunvant
Bonymaen v Blackwood
Caerphilly v S Wales Police
Cross Keys v Rumney
Maesteg v Treorchy
Merthyr v Llandovery
UWIC v Pontypool

Sunday, 7 December
SRU Cup: *4th round*

Tuesday, 9 December
Oxford University v Cambridge University (Twickenham)

Saturday, 13 December
RFU County Championship
Southern Group
Berkshire v Dorset & Wilts
Buckinghamshire v Hampshire
Eastern Counties v Cornwall
Hertfordshire v Gloucestershire
Oxfordshire v Middlesex
Somerset v Devon
Surrey v Kent
North & Midlands Group
Durham v Cumbria
Lancashire v Leicestershire
North Midlands v Cheshire
Northumberland v East Midlands

Staffordshire v Yorkshire
Warwickshire v Notts, Lincs & Derbyshire

RFU Allied Dunbar Leagues
Division 1
Bristol v Richmond
Harlequins v Wasps
Leicester v Sale
London Irish v Northampton
Newcastle v Gloucester
Saracens v Bath
Division 2
Coventry v Blackheath
Fylde v Orrell
London Scottish v Rotherham
Moseley v Wakefield
Waterloo v Bedford
West Hartlepool v Exeter

SRU Tennents Premiership
Division 1
Edinburgh Acads v Jed-Forest
Hawick v Boroughmuir
Melrose v Heriot's FP
Watsonians v Currie
West of Scotland v Stirling County
Division 2
Biggar v Kelso
Dundee HSFP v Gala
Kilmarnock v Peebles
Kirkcaldy v Musselburgh
Preston Lodge FP v Glasgow Hawks
Division 3
Glenrothes v Stewart's Melville FP
Gordonians v Glasgow Southern
Hillhead-Jordanhill v Ayr
Selkirk v Aberdeen GSFP
Stewartry v Grangemouth

IRFU All Ireland Leagues
Division 1
Ballymena v Blackrock Coll
Dolphin v Young Munster
Garryowen v Old Belvedere
Old Crescent v Cork Constitution
Shannon v Clontarf
St Mary's Coll v Dungannon

WRU Leagues
Premier Division
Cardiff v Swansea
Ebbw Vale v Neath

Newport v Llanelli
Pontypridd v Bridgend
First Division
Blackwood v Cross Keys
Dunvant v Aberavon
Llandovery v Bonymaen
Newbridge v UWIC
Pontypool v Merthyr
Rumney v Caerphilly
S Wales Police v Maesteg
Treorchy v Abertillery

Sunday, 14 December
IRFU All Ireland Leagues
Division 1
Lansdowne v Terenure Coll

Saturday, 20 December
ITALY v IRELAND
Heineken Championship *Semi-finals*

RFU Allied Dunbar Leagues
Division 1
Bath v Gloucester
Leicester v Harlequins
London Irish v Bristol
Newcastle v Saracens
Richmond v Northampton
Wasps v Sale
Division 2
Bedford v Moseley
Blackheath v West Hartlepool
Exeter v Fylde
Orrell v Waterloo
Rotherham v Coventry
Wakefield v London Scottish

RFU National League
Division 1
Liverpool St Helens v Reading
London Welsh v Otley
Lydney v Nottingham
Newbury v Morley
Rosslyn Park v Harrogate
Wharfedale v Leeds
Worcester v Rugby

SRU Tennents Premiership
Division 1
Boroughmuir v West of Scotland
Currie v Edinburgh Acads
Heriot's FP v Hawick

Jed-Forest v Melrose
Stirling County v Watsonians
Division 2
Gala v Preston Lodge FP
Glasgow Hawks v Biggar
Kelso v Kilmarnock
Musselburgh v Dundee HSFP
Peebles v Kirkcaldy
Division 3
Ayr v Gordonians
Glasgow Southern v Stewart's Melville
    FP
Grangemouth v Glenrothes
Hillhead-Jordanhill v Aberdeen GSFP
Stewartry v Selkirk

WRU SWALEC Cup: *4th round*

Saturday, 27 December
RFU Allied Dunbar Leagues
Division 1
Bristol v Newcastle
Gloucester v Richmond
Harlequins v London Irish
Northampton v Wasps
Sale v Bath
Saracens v Leicester

RFU National League
Division 1
Harrogate v Wharfedale
Leeds v Worcester
London Welsh v Rosslyn Park
Morley v Otley
Nottingham v Newbury
Reading v Lydney
Rugby v Liverpool St Helens

SRU Tennents Premiership
Division 1
Edinburgh Acads v Stirling Co
Jed-Forest v Currie
Melrose v Hawick
Watsonians v Boroughmuir
West of Scotland v Heriot's FP
Division 2
Biggar v Gala
Dundee HSFP v Peebles
Kelso v Glasgow Hawks
Kilmarnock v Kirkcaldy
Preston Lodge FP v Musselburgh

Division 3
Aberdeen GSFP v Glenrothes
Glasgow Southern v Ayr
Gordonians v Selkirk
Grangemouth v Hillhead-Jordanhill
Stewart's Melville FP v Stewartry

WRU Leagues
Premier Division
Bridgend v Ebbw Vale
Llanelli v Cardiff
Neath v Newport
Swansea v Pontypridd
First Division
Aberavon v Treorchy
Bonymaen v Pontypool
Caerphilly v Blackwood
Cross Keys v Llandovery
Maesteg v Abertillery
Merthyr v Newbridge
S Wales Police v Rumney
UWIC v Dunvant

Tuesday, 30 December
RFU Allied Dunbar Leagues
Division 1
Bath v Northampton
Harlequins v Bristol
Leicester v Newcastle
London Irish v Saracens
Sale v Gloucester
Wasps v Richmond

Saturday, 3 January
RFU Cup: *4th round*

RFU National League
Division 1
Liverpool St Helens v Nottingham
Lydney v Morley
Newbury v London Welsh
Otley v Harrogate
Rosslyn Park v Wharfedale
Rugby v Leeds
Worcester v Reading

IRFU All Ireland Leagues
Division 1
Blackrock Coll v Garryowen
Clontarf v Cork Constitution
Dungannon v Lansdowne
Old Belvedere v Dolphin

Old Crescent v St Mary's Coll
Shannon v Young Munster
Terenure Coll v Ballymena

WRU Leagues
Premier Division
Bridgend v Newport
Neath v Llanelli
Pontypridd v Cardiff
Swansea v Ebbw Vale
First Division
Abertillery v Aberavon
Blackwood v S Wales Police
Dunvant v Merthyr
Llandovery v Caerphilly
Newbridge v Bonymaen
Pontypool v Cross Keys
Rumney v Maesteg
Treorchy v UWIC

Sunday, 4 January
SRU Districts Championship
Caledonia v Glasgow
Edinburgh v Scottish Borders

Saturday, 10 January
RFU Allied Dunbar Leagues
Division 1
Bristol v Leicester
Gloucester v Wasps
Newcastle v London Irish
Northampton v Sale
Richmond v Bath
Saracens v Harlequins
Division 2
Coventry v Orrell
Fylde v Wakefield
London Scottish v Exeter
Moseley v Blackheath
Waterloo v Rotherham
West Hartlepool v Bedford

RFU National League
Division 1
Harrogate v Newbury
Leeds v Rosslyn Park
London Welsh v Lydney
Morley v Liverpool St Helens
Nottingham v Worcester
Reading v Rugby
Wharfedale v Otley

SRU Tennents Premiership
Division 1
Boroughmuir v Edinburgh Acads
Currie v Melrose
Hawick v West of Scotland
Heriot's FP v Watsonians
Stirling County v Jed-Forest
Division 2
Gala v Kelso
Glasgow Hawks v Kilmarnock
Kirkcaldy v Dundee HSFP
Musselburgh v Biggar
Peebles v Preston Lodge FP
Division 3
Glasgow Southern v Grangemouth
Glenrothes v Ayr
Selkirk v Hillhead-Jordanhill
Stewartry v Gordonians
Stewart's Melville FP v Aberdeen
    GSFP

IRFU All Ireland Leagues
Division 1
Ballymena v Dungannon
Cork Constitution v Shannon
Dolphin v Blackrock Coll
Garryowen v Terenure Coll
Lansdowne v Old Crescent
St Mary's Coll v Clontarf
Young Munster v Old Belvedere

WRU Leagues
First Division
Bonymaen v Dunvant
Caerphilly v Pontypool
Cross Keys v Newbridge
Maesteg v Aberavon
Merthyr v Treorchy
Rumney v Blackwood
S Wales Police v Llandovery
UWIC v Abertillery

Saturday, 17 January
RFU Allied Dunbar Leagues
Division 1
Bristol v Gloucester
Harlequins v Northampton
Leicester v Wasps
London Irish v Richmond
Newcastle v Bath
Saracens v Sale

Division 2
Bedford v Fylde
Blackheath v London Scottish
Exeter v Coventry
Orrell v West Hartlepool
Rotherham v Moseley
Wakefield v Waterloo

RFU National League
Division 1
Liverpool St Helens v London Welsh
Lydney v Harrogate
Newbury v Wharfedale
Otley v Rosslyn Park
Reading v Leeds
Rugby v Nottingham
Worcester v Morley

SRU Tennents Premiership
Division 1
Currie v Stirling County
Edinburgh Acads v Heriot's FP
Jed-Forest v Boroughmuir
Melrose v West of Scotland
Watsonians v Hawick
Division 2
Biggar v Peebles
Glasgow Hawks v Gala
Kelso v Musselburgh
Kilmarnock v Dundee HSFP
Preston Lodge FP v Kirkcaldy
Division 3
Aberdeen GSFP v Gordonians
Ayr v Stewart's Melville FP
Glasgow Southern v Glenrothes
Hillhead-Jordanhill v Stewartry
Selkirk v Grangemouth

IRFU All Ireland Leagues
Division 1
Blackrock Coll v Old Belvedere
Clontarf v Lansdowne
Cork Constitution v Young Munster
Dungannon v Garryowen
Old Crescent v Ballymena
Shannon v St Mary's Coll
Terenure Coll v Dolphin

WRU Leagues
First Division
Aberavon v UWIC
Abertillery v Merthyr
Blackwood v Maesteg

Dunvant v Cross Keys
Llandovery v Rumney
Newbridge v Caerphilly
Pontypool v S Wales Police
Treorchy v Bonymaen

Saturday, 24 January
ITALY v SCOTLAND
Italy A v Scotland A
Italy U-21 v Scotland U-21
RFU Cup: *5th round*

RFU National League
Division 1
Harrogate v Liverpool St Helens
Leeds v Otley
London Welsh v Worcester
Morley v Rugby
Nottingham v Reading
Rosslyn Park v Newbury
Wharfedale v Lydney

IRFU All Ireland Leagues
Division 1
Ballymena v Clontarf
Dolphin v Dungannon
Garryowen v Old Crescent
Lansdowne v Shannon
Old Belvedere v Terenure Coll
St Mary's Coll v Cork Constitution
Young Munster v Blackrock Coll

WRU SWALEC Cup: *5th round*

Saturday, 31 January
Heineken European
Championships: *Finals*
RFU Allied Dunbar Leagues
Division 1
Bath v Harlequins
Gloucester v Leicester
Northampton v Newcastle
Richmond v Saracens
Sale v London Irish
Wasps v Bristol
Division 2
Bedford v Orrell
Coventry v West Hartlepool
Exeter v Blackheath
Fylde v Waterloo
Moseley v London Scottish
Rotherham v Wakefield

RFU National League
Division 1
Liverpool St Helens v Wharfedale
Lydney v Rosslyn Park
Newbury v Otley
Nottingham v Leeds
Reading v Morley
Rugby v London Welsh
Worcester v Harrogate

SRU Tennents Premiership
Division 1
Boroughmuir v Currie
Hawick v Edinburgh Acads
Heriot's FP v Jed-Forest
Melrose v Stirling County
West of Scotland v Watsonians
Division 2
Dundee HSFP v Preston Lodge FP
Kilmarnock v Gala
Kirkcaldy v Biggar
Musselburgh v Glasgow Hawks
Peebles v Kelso
Division 3
Aberdeen GSFP v Glasgow Southern
Gordonians v Hillhead-Jordanhill
Grangemouth v Ayr
Selkirk v Stewart's Melville FP
Stewartry v Glenrothes

IRFU All Ireland Leagues
Division 1
Clontarf v Garryowen
Cork Constitution v Lansdowne
Dungannon v Old Belvedere
Old Crescent v Dolphin
Shannon v Ballymena
St Mary's Coll v Young Munster
Terenure Coll v Blackrock Coll

WRU Leagues
Premier Division
Cardiff v Neath
Ebbw Vale v Pontypridd
Llanelli v Bridgend
Newport v Swansea
First Division
Blackwood v Llandovery
Bonymaen v Abertillery
Caerphilly v Dunvant
Cross Keys v Treorchy
Maesteg v UWIC
Merthyr v Aberavon

Newbridge v S Wales Police
Rumney v Pontypool

Saturday, 7 February
IRELAND v SCOTLAND (Dublin)
FRANCE v ENGLAND (Paris)
WALES v ITALY (Cardiff)
Ireland A v Scotland A
Ireland U-21 v Scotland U-21
RFU National League
Division 1
Harrogate v Rugby
Leeds v Newbury
London Welsh v Reading
Morley v Nottingham
Otley v Lydney
Rosslyn Park v Liverpool St Helens
Wharfedale v Worcester

Wednesday, 11 February
IRFU All Ireland Leagues
Division 1
Lansdowne v St Mary's Coll

Saturday, 14 February
RFU Allied Dunbar Leagues
Division 1
Bristol v Saracens
Gloucester v Northampton
Leicester v London Irish
Newcastle v Harlequins
Richmond v Sale
Wasps v Bath
Division 2
Blackheath v Rotherham
London Scottish v Coventry
Orrell v Exeter
Wakefield v Bedford
Waterloo v Moseley
West Hartlepool v Fylde

RFU National League
Division 1
Liverpool St Helens v Otley
Lydney v Newbury
Morley v Leeds
Nottingham v London Welsh
Reading v Harrogate
Rugby v Wharfedale
Worcester v Rosslyn Park

SRU Tennents Premiership
Division 1
Currie v Heriot's FP
Edinburgh Acads v West of Scotland
Jed-Forest v Hawick
Stirling County v Boroughmuir
Watsonians v Melrose
Division 2
Biggar v Dundee HSFP
Gala v Musselburgh
Glasgow Hawks v Peebles
Kelso v Kirkcaldy
Preston Lodge FP v Kilmarnock
Division 3
Ayr v Aberdeen GSFP
Glenrothes v Selkirk
Gordonians v Grangemouth
Stewartry v Glasgow Southern
Stewart's Melville FP v
  Hillhead-Jordanhill

IRFU All Ireland Leagues
Division 1
Ballymena v Cork Constitution
Blackrock Coll v Dungannon
Dolphin v Clontarf
Garryowen v Shannon
Old Belvedere v Old Crescent
Young Munster v Terenure Coll

WRU Leagues
Premier Division
Bridgend v Neath
Ebbw Vale v Cardiff
Pontypridd v Newport
Swansea v Llanelli
First Division
Aberavon v Bonymaen
Abertillery v Cross Keys
Dunvant v S Wales Police
Maesteg v Llandovery
Newbridge v Rumney
Pontypool v Blackwood
Treorchy v Caerphiilly
UWIC v Merthyr

Saturday, 21 February
ENGLAND v WALES (Twickenham)
SCOTLAND v FRANCE
  (Murrayfield)
Scotland A v France A
Scotland U-21 v France U-21

443

RFU National League
Division 1
Harrogate v Nottingham
Leeds v Lydney
London Welsh v Morley
Newbury v Liverpool St Helens
Otley v Worcester
Rosslyn Park v Rugby
Wharfedale v Reading

IRFU All Ireland Leagues
Division 1
Clontarf v Old Belvedere
Cork Constitution v Garryowen
Dungannon v Terenure Coll
Lansdowne v Young Munster
Old Crescent v Blackrock Coll
Shannon v Dolphin
St Mary's Coll v Ballymena

Saturday, 28 February
RFU Cup: *Quarter-finals*

RFU County Championship:
Quarter-finals

SRU Cup: *5th round*

IRFU All Ireland Leagues
Division 1
Ballymena v Lansdowne
Blackrock Coll v Clontarf
Dolphin v Cork Constitution
Garryowen v St Mary's Coll
Old Belvedere v Shannon
Terenure Coll v Old Crescent
Young Munster v Dungannon

WRU SWALEC Cup: *6th round*

Saturday, 7 March
WALES v SCOTLAND (Wembley)
FRANCE v IRELAND (Paris)
Wales A v Scotland A
Wales U-21 v Scotland U-21
RFU Allied Dunbar Leagues
Division 1
Bristol v Bath
Harlequins v Richmond
Leicester v Northampton
London Irish v Gloucester
Newcastle v Sale

Saracens v Wasps
Division 2
Bedford v Blackheath
Coventry v Waterloo
Exeter v Rotherham
Fylde v Moseley
London Scottish v West Hartlepool
Wakefield v Orrell

RFU National League
Division 1
Leeds v London Welsh
Liverpool St Helens v Lydney
Morley v Harrogate
Nottingham v Wharfedale
Reading v Rosslyn Park
Rugby v Otley
Worcester v Newbury

Saturday, 14 March
RFU Allied Dunbar Leagues
Division 1
Bath v Leicester
Gloucester v Saracens
Northampton v Bristol
Richmond v Newcastle
Sale v Harlequins
Wasps v London Irish
Division 2
Bedford v Wakefield
Coventry v London Scottish
Exeter v Orrell
Fylde v West Hartlepool
Moseley v Waterloo
Rotherham v Blackheath

RFU National League
Division 1
Leeds v Liverpool St Helens
London Welsh v Harrogate
Lydney v Worcester
Newbury v Rugby
Otley v Reading
Rosslyn Park v Nottingham
Wharfedale v Morley

WRU Leagues
First Division
Blackwood v Newbridge
Bonymaen v UWIC
Caerphilly v Abertillery
Cross Keys v Aberavon
Llandovery v Pontypool

Merthyr v Maesteg
Rumney v Dunvant
S Wales Police v Treorchy

Saturday, 21 March
IRELAND v WALES (Dublin)
RFU National League
Division 1
Harrogate v Leeds
London Welsh v Wharfedale
Morley v Rosslyn Park
Nottingham v Otley
Reading v Newbury
Rugby v Lydney
Worcester v Liverpool St Helens

Sunday, 22 March
SCOTLAND v ENGLAND
(Murrayfield)
Scotland A v England A
Scotland U-21 v England U-21

Wednesday, 25 March
BUSA Cup Final (Twickenham)

Saturday, 28 March
RFU County Championship:
Semi-finals
RFU Allied Dunbar Leagues
Division 1
Bristol v Sale
Harlequins v Gloucester
Leicester v Richmond
London Irish v Bath
Newcastle v Wasps
Saracens v Northampton
Division 2
Blackheath v Exeter
London Scottish v Moseley
Orrell v Bedford
Wakefield v Rotherham
Waterloo v Fylde
West Hartlepool v Coventry

RFU Cup: *Semi-finals*

IRFU All Ireland Leagues
Division 1
Ballymena v Young Munster
Clontarf v Terenure Coll
Cork Constitution v Old Belvedere
Lansdowne v Garryowen

Old Crescent v Dungannon
Shannon v Blackrock Coll
St Mary's Coll v Dolphin

WRU Leagues
First Division
Aberavon v Caerphilly
Abertillery v S Wales Police
Dunvant v Blackwood
Maesteg v Pontypool
Merthyr v Bonymaen
Newbridge v Llandovery
Treorchy v Rumney
UWIC v Cross Keys

Saturday, 4 April
ENGLAND v IRELAND
(Twickenham)
SRU Cup: *Quarter-finals*

Sunday, 5 April
WALES v FRANCE (Wembley)

Saturday, 11 April
RFU Allied Dunbar Leagues
Division 1
Bath v Saracens
Gloucester v Newcastle
Northampton v London Irish
Richmond v Bristol
Sale v Leicester
Wasps v Harlequins
Division 2
Blackheath v Orrell
Exeter v Wakefield
Fylde v London Scottish
Moseley v Coventry
Rotherham v Bedford
Waterloo v West Hartlepool

RFU National League
Division 1
Liverpool St Helens v Rugby
Lydney v Reading
Newbury v Nottingham
Otley v Morley
Rosslyn Park v London Welsh
Wharfedale v Harrogate
Worcester v Leeds

Melrose Sevens
IRFU All Ireland Leagues

445

Division 1
Blackrock Coll v Cork Constitution
Dolphin v Lansdowne
Dungannon v Clontarf
Garryowen v Ballymena
Old Belvedere v St Mary's Coll
Terenure Coll v Shannon
Young Munster v Old Crescent

WRU SWALEC Cup: *Quarter-finals*

WRU Leagues
First Division
Blackwood v Treorchy
Bonymaen v Maesteg
Caerphilly v UWIC
Cross Keys v Merthyr
Llandovery v Dunvant
Pontypool v Newbridge
Rumney v Abertillery
S Wales Police v Aberavon

Saturday, 18 April
RFU County Championship: *Final*
  (Twickenham)
SRU Cup: *Semi-finals*

RFU Allied Dunbar Leagues
Division 1
Bristol v London Irish
Gloucester v Bath
Harlequins v Leicester
Northampton v Richmond
Sale v Wasps
Saracens v Newcastle
Division 2
Bedford v Exeter
Coventry v Fylde
London Scottish v Waterloo
Orrell v Rotherham
Wakefield v Blackheath
West Hartlepool v Moseley

WRU Leagues
Premier Division
Cardiff v Bridgend
Llanelli v Pontypridd
Neath v Swansea
Newport v Ebbw Vale
First Division
Aberavon v Rumney
Abertillery v Blackwood
Bonymaen v Cross Keys

Dunvant v Pontypool
Maesteg v Newbridge
Merthyr v Caerphilly
Treorchy v Llandovery
UWIC v S Wales Police

Saturday, 25 April
Army v Royal Navy (Twickenham)
RFU Allied Dunbar Leagues
Division 1
Bath v Sale
Leicester v Saracens
London Irish v Harlequins
Newcastle v Bristol
Richmond v Gloucester
Wasps v Northampton
Division 2
Blackheath v Bedford
Moseley v Fylde
Orrell v Wakefield
Rotherham v Exeter
Waterloo v Coventry
West Hartlepool v London Scottish

RFU National League
Division 1
Harrogate v Rosslyn Park
Leeds v Wharfedale
Morley v Newbury
Nottingham v Lydney
Otley v London Welsh
Reading v Liverpool St Helens
Rugby v Worcester

WRU SWALEC Cup: *Semi-finals*

WRU Leagues
First Division
Blackwood v Aberavon
Caerphilly v Bonymaen
Cross Keys v Maesteg
Llandovery v Abertillery
Newbridge v Dunvant
Pontypool v Treorchy
Rumney v UWIC
S Wales Police v Merthyr

Saturday, 2 May

RFU Allied Dunbar Leagues
Division 1
Bristol v Harlequins
Gloucester v Sale
Newcastle v Leicester
Northampton v Bath
Richmond v Wasps
Saracens v London Irish

WRU Leagues
Premier Division
Cardiff v Newport
Ebbw Vale v Llanelli
Pontypridd v Neath
Swansea v Bridgend
First Division
Blackwood v UWIC
Caerphilly v Cross Keys
Dunvant v Maesteg
Llandovery v Aberavon
Newbridge v Treorchy
Pontypool v Abertillery
Rumney v Merthyr
S Wales Police v Bonymaen

RFU Junior & Intermediate Cup:
Finals (Twickenham)

Wednesday, 6 May

Royal Navy v Royal Air Force
 (Twickenham)

Saturday, 9 May

RFU CUP FINAL (Twickenham)
SRU CUP FINAL (Murrayfield)
WRU SWALEC CUP FINAL

WRU Leagues
Premier Division
Bridgend v Pontypridd
Llanelli v Newport
Neath v Ebbw Vale
Swansea v Cardiff
First Division
Aberavon v Pontypool
Abertillery v Newbridge
Bonymaen v Rumney
Cross Keys v S Wales Police
Maesteg v Caerphilly

Merthyr v Blackwood
Treorchy v Dunvant
UWIC v Llandovery

Sunday, 10 May

RFU Allied Dunbar Leagues
Division 1
Bath v Richmond
Harlequins v Saracens
Leicester v Bristol
London Irish v Newcastle
Sale v Northampton
Wasps v Gloucester

Wednesday, 13 May

Army v Royal Air Force
 (Twickenham)

Saturday, 16 May

RFU Allied Dunbar Leagues
Division 1
Bath v Wasps
Harlequins v Newcastle
London Irish v Leicester
Northampton v Gloucester
Sale v Richmond
Saracens v Bristol

Middlesex Sevens (Twickenham)

WRU Leagues
Premier Division
Cardiff v Llanelli
Ebbw Vale v Bridgend
Newport v Neath
Pontypridd v Swansea
First Division
Blackwood v Bonymaen
Dunvant v Abertillery
Llandovery v Merthyr
Newbridge v Aberavon
Pontypool v UWIC
Rumney v Cross Keys
S Wales Police v Caerphilly
Treorchy v Maesteg

Saturday, 23 May

Sanyo World Challenge
 (Twickenham) – *provisional*

MAJOR FIXTURES 1997-98

August 1997
16 NEW ZEALAND v AUSTRALIA (Dunedin)
23 SOUTH AFRICA v AUSTRALIA (Johannesburg)
30 WALES v ROMANIA (Wrexham FC)

October
18 FRANCE v ITALY (Auch)
ARGENTINA v ROMANIA (Auch)
22 FRANCE v ROMANIA (Lourdes)
ITALY v ARGENTINA (Lourdes)
26 FRANCE v ARGENTINA (Tarbes)
ITALY v ROMANIA (Tarbes)

November
1 ARGENTINA v AUSTRALIA (Buenos Aires)
8 ARGENTINA v AUSTRALIA (Buenos Aires)
ITALY v SOUTH AFRICA
15 ENGLAND v AUSTRALIA (Twickenham)
IRELAND v CANADA (Dublin)
FRANCE v SOUTH AFRICA
16 WALES v NEW ZEALAND (Wembley)
22 ENGLAND v NEW ZEALAND (Old Trafford)
SCOTLAND v AUSTRALIA (Murrayfield)
FRANCE v SOUTH AFRICA
25 WALES v TONGA (Llanelli)
29 ENGLAND v SOUTH AFRICA (Twickenham)
IRELAND v NEW ZEALAND (Dublin)

December
6 ENGLAND v NEW ZEALAND (Twickenham)

SCOTLAND v SOUTH AFRICA (Murrayfield)
9 Oxford University v Cambridge University (Twickenham)
20 ITALY v IRELAND

January 1998
24 ITALY v SCOTLAND
Italy A v Scotland A
31 Heineken European Championships: *Finals*

February
7 IRELAND v SCOTLAND (Dublin)
FRANCE v ENGLAND (Paris)
WALES v ITALY (Cardiff)
Ireland A v Scotland A
21 ENGLAND v WALES (Twickenham)
SCOTLAND v FRANCE (Murrayfield)
Scotland A v France A

March
7 WALES v SCOTLAND (Wembley)
FRANCE v IRELAND (Paris)
Wales A v Scotland A
21 IRELAND v WALES (Dublin)
22 SCOTLAND v ENGLAND (Murrayfield)
Scotland A v England A
25 BUSA Cup Final (Twickenham)

April
4 ENGLAND v IRELAND (Twickenham)
5 WALES v FRANCE (Wembley)
18 RFU County Championship: *Final* (Twickenham)

May
9 RFU CUP FINAL (Twickenham)
SRU CUP FINAL (Murrayfield)
WRU SWALEC CUP FINAL
23 Sanyo World Challenge (Twickenham) – *provisional*